To my husband, John, and the relationship that has survived six editions of this book, and to our daughter Paige and granddaughter Isabella, who keep me in touch with the real world of young adults and children

Brief Contents

Contents

Chapter 9
Children with Social, Emotional, and Behavioral Disorders . . . 205

Chapter 10
Children with Attention-Deficit/Hyperactivity Disorder . 235

PART III
Resources and Practice for Inclusive Early Childhood Education

The landscape of early childhood is changing, and with it, the fields of early childhood education and early childhood special education. The early childhood years have long been recognized as an important time of physical growth and development. Now they are also viewed as a prime time for cognitive and emotional development. Brain research confirms that the plasticity of the brain holds the potential for risk and resilience. For children with special needs the early years are critical, and the educators who work with these children must be competent, dedicated, and passionate because they truly make a difference in the lives of children. Early childhood education has the potential to minimize developmental delay, thus reducing the need for special education when children are older.

This book provides essential information about all children including children with a variety of special needs and their families, as well as information about the disabilities themselves and ways to plan for children in inclusive settings. This text is written as a resource for students and developing professionals. It has something for now and something to come back to later. It is written for the educational system of the twenty-first century in which future teachers need to be prepared to have a child with cerebral palsy and several English language learners included in their class one year, and the next year a child with attention-deficit/hyperactivity disorder as well as some children who are gifted and talented. Educators have to be prepared to respond with interventions for children who are not learning in the general educational curriculum and to help in the diagnostic process of children who may need specialized instruction or special education. They have to be prepared to do all of this while they teach and enjoy all the children in their class. There are entire books written on specific disabilities and curricula that have greater depth in each area than this book does. However, this book offers prospective educators a foundation to work from in which to include children with special needs while they make themselves experts on the particular children in their classroom.

This book covers many different special needs, but it does not stop there. It takes that information and helps educators apply it to children by providing guidelines and information on planning, adapting, and individualizing curriculum and for reflecting on their practice. It helps students move from identifying the annual goals for a child to embedding those goals in the regular classroom routine. It is set up to provide information and then to ask, "So what?" by connecting research, development, and practice. As a textbook, it may seem lengthy, but it is designed to carry preservice teachers through their first years of teaching as a reference and a resource.

Organization

●●●
Part I: Early Childhood
Development and Intervention

This part is designed to frame the field of inclusive early childhood education.

Chapter 1 introduces the field of early childhood education and early childhood special education, as well as the legal and educational basis for intervention, with an emphasis on inclusion. Chapter 2 focuses on the child in the context of his family, looking at the impact of the child on the family and the family on the child, the changing American family, families and their culture and ways of working with families in culturally competent ways. Chapter 3 covers assessment and evaluation and entitlement decisions. Chapter 4 looks at curriculum and goals and standards; how the general curriculum is influenced by state and professional standards; and how curriculum and standards are incorporated into an inclusive learning environment. Chapter 5 examines the process of individualized planning for individualized education programs and individualized family service plans. Chapter 6 focuses on prenatal development, particularly early brain development and many of the underlying causes of disabilities, both genetic and environmental.

●●●
Part II: Inclusive Early
Childhood Education

Part II has 13 chapters. Chapter 7 begins by looking at infants and toddlers, including those who are at risk for disabilities and developmental delays. The remaining chapters each focus on a particular disabilities or at-risk conditions. Chapter 8 focuses on children with specific learning disabilities and includes information on response to instruction and response to intervention. Chapter 9 provides information on social, emotional, and behavioral disorders, including attachment disorders. Chapter 10 focuses on attention-deficit/hyperactivity disorders. Chapter 11 is on communication disorders, including both speech and language disorders. Chapter 12 discusses children who are English language learners, with information on children in immigrant families and some of their particular challenges. Chapter 13 covers children with autism spectrum disorders. Chapters 14 focuses on children who have intellectual delays and disabilities, whereas Chapter 15 looks at children who are gifted and talented. Chapter 16 describes children with a variety of special health care needs. The last three chapters focus on sensory impairments: Chapter 17 on children with orthopedic and neurological impairments, Chapter 18 on hearing impairments, and Chapter 19 on visual impairments.

These chapters take a functional approach to understanding ability or disability, the potential for impacting the child's behavior, and guidelines for adapting the learning environment. Disability-specific information is woven into the fabric of general development while acknowledging that children with disabilities have some needs that are different from their peers. Accommodations that are necessary to allow *some* children to participate are also designed to expand the learning and creative opportunities of *all* children in the class. Disabilities are viewed as part of a continuum of children's abilities.

Chapters in Part II follow a pattern that begins with a vignette and helps students move beyond looking at the vignette as an interesting story, to reflect on its significance. All chapters contain information about abilities and disabilities, including the definitions, prevalence rates, and probable causes of specific conditions. The chapters detail various characteristics of the disabilities, as well as developmental information pertinent to early identification, and provide guidelines for including these children in the classroom, as well as curriculum adaptations. Each chapter concludes with a summary and additional educational resources for further investigation.

Part III: Resources and Practice for Inclusive Early Childhood Education

Part III contains six Resource chapters focusing on information and activities to support social awareness, English language arts, discovery, wellness, and the creative arts. The final chapter in this part addresses activities for infants and toddlers. Continuations of these chapters on the book companion website (www.cengagebrain.com) provide additional information and resources. Each chapter contains activities that focus on a particular curriculum area and include information on ways to accommodate a variety of learners and suggestions for integrating activities into the general curriculum. The activities are arranged by the goals and standards they meet. English language arts and mathematics use the Common Core State Standards. Other areas use goals and standards from professional organizations. The goals are most useful for preschool children, and the standards, for school-age children. The chapter on infants and toddlers uses both early learning guidelines and age to organize the activities All six chapters have more activities and Educational Resources on line at www.cengagebrain.com.

The final section of the book includes a Children's Bibliography that topically annotates books for children that relate to cultural and family diversity, and understanding of special needs or related areas such as fears, loss, or family disruption. Age ranges are given for each book. The Children's Bibliography online includes additional books and educational resources. The book has two glossaries, one that defines the words used in the text, the other for acronyms. The book concludes with the references and a combined author and subject index.

Features

The book has a variety of features that are designed to make inclusive early childhood education come alive to preservice teachers and also to help them translate research to practice. Each chapter starts with a vignette that is designed to set the tone for a chapter or provide a perspective for viewing the field. Other features that appear in every chapter include the following.

In the Field

This feature helps the text come alive with real stories from real families, and dilemmas and solutions that real educators teaching real children have faced and coped with. Although these have been edited, each was written or told by practicing educators, parents, administrators, or children. They offer developing educators real world scenarios, ethical and moral dilemmas upon which to reflect, and the opportunity to imagine these issues before they are faced with them.

Reflective Practice

The goal of Reflective Practice sections is to educate reflective practitioners who learn from their own practice and the practice of others. They are designed to make the book more interactive and help preservice teachers think about themselves as decision makers and the implications of decisions. It helps teachers go beyond what was written to look at the implications of information in the context of their own teaching and what is happening in the field.

Implications for Educators

This section is designed to help students apply the information they are learning in the context of their own practice. Educators move from looking at a description of a particular special need to looking at the implications of having a child with that particular disability in their classroom.

The Evidence Base

Increasingly, educators are using research to decide how to teach children. Research-based practice is best practice. However, learning how to evaluate and use this evidence in the classroom is challenging. Research does not always reach firm conclusions, and the results are sometimes in conflict. This section presents research and research synopses as a way of educating preservice teachers about the evidence base that forms the foundation of their teaching practice.

Guidelines

Each chapter in Part II has a disability or ability focus and a section on guidelines that help students think about the general principles they will use to adapt their teaching style and techniques to include children with a particular special need.

Curriculum Adaptations

Whereas guidelines focus on children, curriculum adaptations focus on each curriculum area and discuss how a particular area can be used to strengthen a child's skills, or how to adapt or modify a particular area. This helps students apply the information they are learning in order to think more inclusively, and understand that most children can be included with good planning and adaptations.

Educational Resources

The text provides annotated educational resources, primarily Internet-based, to help educators themselves and to support parents in extending their learning about particular disabilities, issues, and the supports that are available. Students acquire a lifelong skill by updating and extending their knowledge and going beyond the information provided in the text.

TeachSource Videos

Relevant video clips are included in each chapter to help preservice teachers see early childhood education in action and to hear experts discuss some of the major issues in the field.

Developmentally Appropriate Practice (DAP)

DAP The entire text was written based on the principles of developmentally appropriate practices. However, some content relates very specifically to DAP. These areas are highlighted with the DAP icon.

Standards

STANDARDS States and professional groups have developed standards about what children should know and be able to do at different age/grade levels. These are highlighted with the standards icon.

Activities

The text has over 300 activities to enhance students' knowledge of what and how to plan for inclusive classrooms. Of these activities, 180 are in the text and an additional 120 activities are on the book companion website. Some of the activities are designed to hone skills for children who need experiences in particular areas; these are based on the general education curriculum and are designed to help all children meet state goals and standards. Other activities are designed to increase young children's awareness of what it might be like to have a particular ability or disability.

Ancillaries

Book Companion Website

A book companion website at www.cengagebrain.com includes resources for both students and instructors.

RESOURCES FOR STUDENTS AND INSTRUCTORS

Parts I and II. Some resources are designed as an expansion of the textbook and are available for both students and instructors. These resources are arranged in the same order as the chapters in the book and are titled that way.

- Expanded and additional Educational Resources—This section includes the Educational Resources in the text and additional ones that have been added. All were current at the time of publication. Having them on the web with live links allows easy access to the information.

- Reflections—These questions are designed to help preservice teachers think about the profession and some of the challenges they might face in teaching children with particular disabilities and special needs in inclusive classrooms. The goal is to make students reflective practioners with the support and insight of instructors.

Part III. The Resource chapters have been expanded in an effort to support the new Common Core State Standards and professional standards. As the standards are more detailed than goals, more activities are required to show how to meet them even for one grade level, and these can be found on the web. The Children's Bibliography, greatly expanded, also has an online component that includes about 200 additional annotated

books arranged by topic. More specifically, the online supports for Part III include the following:

- Resource Chapter 1w Online   Social Awareness Activities: Social Competence and Social Studies
- Resource Chapter 2w Online   English Language Arts Activities: Speaking and Listening, Reading, Writing, and Language
- Resource Chapter 3w Online   Discovery Activities: Mathematics, Science, and Technology
- Resource Chapter 4w Online   Wellness Activities: Health and Safety, Physical Education, and Sensory Motor Integration
- Resource Chapter 5w Online   Creative Arts Activities: Visual Arts, Music, Movement and Dance, and Dramatic Play and Theater
- Resource Chapter 6w Online   Infant and Toddler Activities: Young Infants, Mobile Infants, and Toddlers
- Children's Bibliography Online

RESOURCES FOR INSTRUCTORS

Designed specifically for instructors, the instructors' area offers access to password-protected resources. The following information is included for each chapter in Parts I and II:

- Electronic instructors manual that includes
  - A variety of suggested teaching strategies including many that employ problem-based learning
  - Potential assignments
- Annotated audiovisual materials that support each chapter, as well as sources where these can be obtained if your college or university does not currently have them
- A recommended reading section that shares some of the most important and relevant sources that the author used
- A test bank for each chapter that contains multiple choice and true/false questions as well as essay questions with scoring rubrics all different from student tutorial quizzes
- PowerPoint Slides for each chapter

RESOURCES FOR STUDENTS

Student resources include a variety of study tools and useful resources to help student understand and extend their knowledge base.

- Key Term Flashcards—These are the terms most important in understanding each chapter. They also include the acronyms used in a particular chapter.
- Tutorial quizzes—These include sample multiple choice and true/false questions for each chapter, none the same as those in the Instructor's Manual.

Summary of Overall General Changes from the Fifth Edition

This book is the sixth edition of *Inclusive Early Childhood Education: Development, Resources, and Practice*. The first edition was published in 1983, the second in 1993, the third in 1999, the fourth in 2005, and the fifth in 2010. The major changes in the texts are reflections of changes in our knowledge base, the population identified as having special needs, the legislation that underlies early childhood education, and best practice in the field. The general changes include the following:

- Updated information has been added on disabilities and abilities and their etiologies.
- Updated information on cultural diversity and family types has been added.
- There is a greater emphasis on culture, ethnicity, and language throughout the book.
- The book has been reorganized (both within and between chapters) to make the text flow better and to eliminate duplication.
- Professional content standards and the Common Core State Standards have been included, and activities have been linked to these standards.
- All the activities in the Resources chapters are indexed to both standards and goals, and 60 new activities have been written to meet the standards.
- The glossary has been updated, and approximately 60 new key terms have been added.
- Video clips have been added to illustrate the text.
- Developmentally appropriate practices have been updated and clearly identified with the DAP icon.
- An index of acronyms has been added.
- The reflections at the end of each chapter have been moved to the Student and Instructor areas of the book companion website.

Summary of Specific Changes

Part I: Early Childhood Development and Intervention

Chapter 1, *Including All Children in a Dynamic Educational System*, is updated, the writing streamlined, and information has been added about developmentally appropriate practice and DEC recommended practices.

Chapter 2, *Partnering with Families and Honoring Their Diversity*, includes more information on family systems theory and the grief cycle. Where possible, the category Asian has been separated from that of Native Hawaiian and Other Pacific Islanders; and census data has been updated. Chapter 2 includes more and updated information on diversity in families, including biracial children and their families, grandparents as parents, cohabiting families, families with different structural configurations and those who face special challenges, as well as immigrant and migrant families.

Chapter 3, *Assessment and Evaluation*, has more information on early intervening services, response to instruction and response to intervention, and the assessment of English language learners.

Chapter 4, *Curriculum and Standards in Inclusive Settings* has major changes. Some areas have been combined and refocused; the geography, history, and civics standards have been eliminated, and the social studies standards expanded. The

Common Core State Standards in Mathematics and English Language Arts have been added, as well as the standards for dance and theater. The goals for many activities have been revised. The standards themselves and the activities that support them are indexed before the first Resource chapter. The goals are also in a separate index there.

Chapter 5, *Individualized Planning*, is updated, with examples taken from the Common Core State Standards.

Chapter 6, *Prenatal Development: Typical and Atypical*, is renamed and refocused to include the essentials that students need to understand the prenatal causes of specific disabilities and chronic illnesses. Early brain development was moved to this chapter.

Part II: Inclusive Early Childhood Education

All chapters in Part II are updated to reflect what has been learned since the fifth edition. The curriculum adaptations demonstrate new professional standards and the Common Core State Standards.

Chapter 7, *Infants and Toddlers At Risk*, includes more information on early learning guidelines and their use.

Chapter 8, *Children with Specific Learning Disabilities*, is reorganized, and aspects of the law that were quoted are now paraphrased. The information on Recognition and Response, response to intervention, and reading with children is expanded, with additional information provided.

Chapter 9, *Children with Social, Emotional, and Behavioral Disorders*, has additional information on bullying, and the text is reorganized and updated.

Chapter 10, *Children with Attention-Deficit/Hyperactivity Disorder*, has had a major reorganization, with more In the Field sections added.

Chapter 11, *Children with Communication Disorders*, provides additional information on specific language impairments, and aphasia, and speech and sound disorders have been added.

Chapter 12, *Children Who Are English Language Learners*, focuses on the increasing number of children whose families speak a language other than English at home. It includes information on the achievement gap, school readiness, comprehensive school reform, and the dilemma of how best to teach these children. More information on undocumented immigrants and the effects of deportation on children is included.

Chapter 13, *Children with Autism Spectrum Disorders (ASD)*, provides more information on the research that looks into the causes of autism and why the number of children with autism is increasing. The APA diagnostic criteria for autistic disorder has been added, and more information on early identification and Asperger's syndrome is provided.

Chapter 14, *Children with Intellectual Delays and Disabilities*, provides more information on how to work with children who come from families who do not provide stimulating environments and what early intervention can do to help. The title has been changed from "Children with Intellectual Disabilities and Developmental Delays" because the term *developmental delay* is used in different ways in the literature.

Chapter 15, *Children Who Are Gifted and Talented*, has had a major revision, including the definitions of the types of giftedness children might display. The standards for gifted education developed by the National Association for Gifted Children have been added.

Chapter 16, *Children with Special Health Care Needs*, is updated and has undergone some internal reorganization. Information on asthma, bleeding disorders, hepatitis, overweight and obesity, and sickle cell disease has been expanded.

Chapter 17, *Children with Orthopedic and Neurological Impairments*, is streamlined and updated with additional information on traumatic brain injury.

Chapter 18, *Children with Hearing Impairments*, is updated and more information is provided about assessing hearing impairments, assistive listening devices, and assistive technology.

Chapter 19, *Children with Visual Impairments*, is updated, and additional information on cortical visual impairments added.

● ● ●
Part III: Resources and Practice for Inclusive Early Childhood Education

Part III includes information for Using the Resources and Guidelines for Adapting Activities for Children with Special Needs. The goals and standards and the activities that support these are indexed separately and are located directly before Resource Chapter 1. These are the standards that children are expected to have met by the end of kindergarten. Infant and toddler activities are listed by early learning guidelines and by age.

There are 30 activities in the book for each Resource Chapter, and the remainder are on the web. Some of the web activities are devised so that the template for the materials to be used can be downloaded.

Resource Chapter 1, *Social Awareness Activities: Social Competence and Social Studies*, combines self-esteem and inclusion into social competence, and activities have been added to social studies to meet the standards. The chapter was renamed to reflect these changes.

Resource Chapter 2, *English Language Arts: Speaking and Listening, Reading, Writing, and Language* has had a major reorganization and revision, with a new title (the old title was "Language and Literacy Activities: Speaking, Listening, Reading, and Writing") and new activities written to support the Common Core State Standards in English Language Arts and Literacy in History/Social Studies, Science, and Technical Subjects. Approximately 30 activities were added or had major revisions to meet these standards. Full citations were added for children's books that are cited and, where possible, lexile levels have been added. Additionally, standards for English language arts appear throughout the activities, as they are designed to support other subject matter areas. The chapter was reorganized to combine speaking and listening, and a section on language was added.

Resource Chapter 3, *Discovery Activities: Mathematics, Science, and Technology* is revised and expanded to reflect the standards in these three areas, particularly the Common Core State Standards in Mathematics. Approximately 30 new activities have been added or had major revisions.

Resource Chapter 4, *Wellness Activities: Health and Safety, Physical Education, and Sensory Motor Integration,* has activities designed to meet the health and physical education standards. Activities were added to health and safety and physical education. The title was revised to reflect these changes.

Resource Chapter 5, *Creative Arts Activities: Visual Arts, Music, Movement and Dance, and Dramatic Play and Theater* has new and revised activities to meet the visual arts, music, dance, and theater standards. The old title was "Creative Arts Activities: Visual Arts, Music, Creative Movement, and Dramatic Play."

Resource Chapter 6, *Infant and Toddler Activities: Young Infants, Mobile Infants, and Toddlers*, has been reorganized to meet the most commonly used early learning guidelines. The activities are divided by these guidelines as well as by age.

The Children's Bibliography is updated and expanded, and the older books have been placed on the book companion website.

Using the Text

The text is designed to be used flexibly to fit professor and student needs. Although complementary, each part of the book is independent, as are the chapters. Course sequences, the availability of practicum settings, different service delivery systems, and instructor preference may influence the order in which the chapters are read.

The activities and resource materials provided in the book are just that, resources for current and future use. As such, they will be useful in both preservice and in-service education and with all educators and specialists in early childhood education and early childhood special education, and they can be shared with families. They can be referred to, used, and modified throughout one's career. Above all, this text is meant to be used. Five years from now, I hope this book is highlighted, dog-eared, and has handwritten comments in the very small margins, noting where you have updated information that has changed and which activities have succeeded, as well as revisions for those that flopped.

Acknowledgments

No author writes a text without academic and emotional support. I particularly want to thank my husband, John, who helped with the early copyediting of the book. He is in a different academic field, and I learned that if he couldn't understand it, it needed to be revised. I also want to thank my daughter, Paige, who was truly there for me through the long haul, and her daughter, Isabella, who keeps me in touch with the realities of growing up and the challenges the educational system faces.

The University of Delaware Laboratory Preschool and the Early Learning Center, directed by Peg Bradley, was an invaluable resource, especially its master teachers, Nancy Edwards, Tara Sutton, Laura Morris, Katie Pollock, and the support staff. In addition, Tara Sutton wrote some of the activities for the resource chapters. These teachers are inspirational as well as flexible and supportive.

I am grateful for the resources of the University of Delaware library and the reference librarians who are a source of knowledge and wisdom, particularly Rebecca Knight who continues to teach me more about tracking down references than I ever wanted to know.

Practicing teachers taking graduate courses played a particularly important part in the revisions of the text. They contributed to the In the Field sections and also shared their knowledge and practical suggestions. Teachers include Tina Albanese, Cara Cuccuini-Harmon, Michelle Eichinger, Mary Gerni, Faye Gillespie, Lisa Hunt, Jennifer Janowski, Kristin Jones, Verna Milner, Melissa Neeson, Katherine Ossolinski, Emily Pettyjohn, Jessica Phillips, and Kimberly Wagner. Linda Maxwell, one of the teachers, was a marvelous source for information and practical suggestions on autism and Asperger's syndrome. Joanne Gischner and Sharon Lyons continue to help me stay based in the real world of teachers and what they do on a day-to-day basis.

The graduate students in Individual and Family Studies served as a constant support and played an important role in making this book possible. Kim Madey helped with the Power-Points. Elizabeth Chambers wrote several In the Field sections and some of the examination questions, as well as the rubrics to grade the essays. Wei Qiu provided computer expertise and wrote vignettes in addition to increasing my cultural awareness. Working with her also increased my knowledge of online resources and how to use them effectively.

Friends play an exceedingly important role in the process. Gretchen and Glenn Taylor, Ron and Donna Coffin, Peggy and David Beers, and Bill and Sharon Crist provided support and encouragement when the going was tough. I particularly want to thank Gretchen, who can make almost everything work and do so with a sense of humor.

My deepest gratitude goes to my husband, John, whose unwavering emotional, moral, and practical support has helped bring this book to fruition. Our youngest daughter, Paige, was three years old when the first edition of this book was published. For this edition, she wrote some In the Fields and tried to help me keep my writing style current and in tune with technology. And although she has asked me on numerous occasions not to write any more books, she is now a journalist herself with a preschool-age daughter. Our two older children both live in California. Jamie is a speech-language pathologist with two children, Miles and Maya, and Michael works at the University of California Medical Center in San Francisco and also has two children, Natalie and Russell. Perhaps families influence their children in more ways than we think.

I would also like to extend my thanks to professional colleagues in the field Elizabeth Watters, Cuyahoga Community College; Clayton Ryan, Fisher College; Janice Hofschulte, Inver Hills Community College; Evia Davis, Langston University; Jennifer Jones, Oklahoma State University; Doug Carothers, Florida Gulf Coast University; Marissa Happ, Waubonsee Community College; Sandra Todaro, Bossier Parish Community College; Jennifer Kilgo, University of Alabama at Birmingham; Evia Davis, Langston University; Kari Chiasson, University of North Dakota, for their very helpful reviews and comments.

The production of a book such as this one is a long and complicated process. I want to acknowledge the support of Mark Kerr, who had faith that a sixth edition of this book was a valuable contribution to the literature in the field. I am pleased to have the opportunity to work with Caitlin Cox again. She supported many innovative ideas to make the book shorter without losing important aspects of the resources and truly made the book come together. Joshua Taylor was a great person to work with on the Resources for Instructors; and Elizabeth Momb, on the Resources for Students. Lynn Lustberg helped me wade through the many behind-the-scenes aspects of publishing a book with patience and humor, and Jill Pellarin is a copyeditor without equal.

Finally, I owe a great deal to children—my own children and their children, their peers, and the children and grandchildren of friends whom I have observed, as well as the children I taught, who in reality taught me—not so much the easy ones, but the ones who challenged me.

Inclusive Early Childhood Education

DEVELOPMENT, RESOURCES, AND PRACTICE

Early Childhood Development and Intervention

Part I provides information about early childhood education, early childhood special education, and the experiences and laws that serve as the foundation for individualized planning. It also looks at the importance of family-centered planning and partnering with families, and provides information on assessment, evaluation, and the issues involved in accurately measuring what children know.

Part I also discusses curriculum and the national standards set by professional organizations for fields such as science, technology, and music, as well as the Common Core State Standards in mathematics and the English language arts. It concludes with a chapter on prenatal development, including the development of the brain.

1 Including All Children in a Dynamic Educational System

After a struggle, we persuaded the reluctant principal and staff to let our son Don attend a traditional first-grade class for part of the day—about two hours every afternoon. The rest of the day he remained in a segregated classroom shared by other students with orthopedic disabilities—primarily those who used wheelchairs and were for the most part nonverbal. We believed inclusion was important for Don, but also for the "typical" children—we felt acceptance of differences should start early in life and we wanted to act on our beliefs—but we were weary from the fight. Don was finally allowed to attend the class; however, no other child with a disability was invited even though other children were more "able" than he.

Don loved the inclusive class. At age 7, he was still learning to drive a power wheelchair, and the paraeducator said that he tried to drive by the segregated classroom to get to the inclusive setting. We knew it was working for our son.

One day when I came early to pick up Don, I saw a line of first-graders waiting to enter the cafeteria. A few of Don's classmates in the segregated classroom silently rolled by the line of chattering children. As Don and I neared these kids, I prepared myself for the usual stares or pointing fingers. Instead, I heard, "Look, there's Don!" "Hi Don." "See you tomorrow, Don." Those warm greetings meant more to me than any straight-A report card. Don smiled and so did I—through happy tears. I felt there might be hope for inclusion.

Don attends a "typical school" now. He's just one of the gang—the kids in the school have accepted his presence as normal and he has many friends. However, one of the staff tells me that Don still gets those stares from one group of kids. They have a program at Don's school where gifted kids come once a week for enrichment. These kids have never had the opportunity of knowing a fellow classmate who uses a wheelchair. So, they still stare. Will they ever get to know Don from the inside out or only the outside in? It's their loss, our loss, and society's loss. Inclusion really works.

"Early childhood inclusion embodies the values, policies, and practices that support the right of every infant and young child and his or her family, regardless of ability, to participate in a broad range of activities and contexts as full members of families, communities, and society." (Division of Early Childhood (DEC) and the National Association for the Education of Young Children (NAEYC), 2009a, p. 2)

Historical Roots

To understand the challenges early childhood educators face today, we must look at how the field has changed and grown over time, as well as how related fields have contributed to our understanding of inclusive education. Although the history of inclusive education is relatively short, there is a long, interesting history of beliefs and decisions about children with disabilities and how they should be educated.

In the mid-1800s, little was known about disabilities or their causes. Disabilities were frequently blamed on "sinful living." People thought you could inherit lifestyle characteristics from your parents as well as genetic information (height, sex, etc.). It was commonly assumed that all disabilities were passed down through generations and that the only way to stop society from being overwhelmed by people with disabilities was to **sterilize** adults to stop reproduction (Berkson, 1993), a practice begun in the United States in the early 1900s and continued in some states until about 1980.

Mild disabilities were not identified until the turn of the century, when the work of Alfred Binet (1857–1911) identified disabilities that impacted school performance (Berkson, 1993). He showed that the scores of children classified as mentally retarded were similar to those of younger "normal" children.

Although there have always been children with disabilities, there have not always been educational services to address their needs. The originators of special education were young, ambitious European physicians. Some credit the French physician Jean Marc Gaspard Itard (1775–1838) as the founder of special education, based on the principles that he used to educate Victor. Victor, a boy of about 12, had been found wandering alone in the forest of Aveyron, France. and was considered a "wild boy" or hopeless idiot. Itard did not cure Victor, but he made significant changes in Victor's behavior by using a set of principles including individualized instruction, stimulation, sequenced learning tasks, a structured environment, immediate reward for correct performance, and focus on functional skills. He believed that all children could learn and therefore should be educated (Safford & Safford, 1996).

Itard's protégé, Edouard Seguin (1812–1880), also a pioneer in the field and one of the first early interventionists (Meisels & Shonkoff, 2000), gave children detailed assessments and developed specific sensory motor activities to improve their deficits. He believed in the importance of the early years of development (Safford & Safford, 1996). Maria Montessori (1870–1951) studied Seguin's methods and adapted them. She insisted that intellectual disabilities were an educational problem, not a medical one. Alexander and Mabel Bell supported her methods in the United States (Winzer, 1993).

Elizabeth Farrell, a teacher in New York City, attempted to modify educational practices to address the needs of children and youth with disabilities. She believed that although all children can learn, some needed different educational experiences. In 1922, Farrell and special educators from the United States and Canada founded the Council for Exceptional Children (CEC), which still exists today. They had a vision for serving children whose needs were not met within the regular educational system.

Within the public school system, the first special education schools and classes were established in the early 1900s for children who were identified as "educable mentally retarded." Most of these programs were in separate schools: some private, some public. Specialists taught children with sensory impairments in residential schools. These children went to school as early as age 3 and came home only for weekends, holidays, or the summer, unless the family lived nearby (Gearheart, Mullen, & Gearheart, 1993).

During the late 1920s, classes for children with physical impairments were added to the public school system. As other disabilities were recognized in the 1950s, it became clearer that these children needed *different* educational approaches. Special education as a field has focused on "difference" and what is exceptional rather than what is the same.

Special education traditionally focused on school-age children. It was further broken down into separate subfields such as mental retardation, learning disabilities, behavioral disorders, sensory impairments, and so on. These subfields focused on specially designed instruction to meet the unique and unusual needs of a particular group of children (Salvia & Ysseldyke, 2007). The special education

curriculum centered on teaching children with disabilities specific adaptive skills, with teachers providing instruction one-on-one or in small groups.

Immediately after World War II, several factors, both ideological and legal, led to a movement to normalize the lives of persons with disabilities. These factors came together in the social activism of the 1960s.

Moving Toward Normalization

Normalization is an approach that ensures that children requiring special services are not separated from experiences of normal life; that is, educational, social, and recreational environments are as close as possible to what they would be if children were developing typically. These are called natural settings or **natural environments**.

Schools not only impart academic information, they also impart social values. To the extent that children were segregated from regular schools and classrooms, whether because of physical impairment or skin color, they were seen as deficient. Beginning in the 1950s, the courts defended education as the *right* of every child regardless of race or disability.

Societal attitudes slowly began to change in the 1960s, and the first definition of developmental disabilities was written then. Early childhood educators had a growing interest in the concept of early developmental programming. Head Start was signed into law by President Johnson as part of the "War on Poverty." It began as an eight-week summer program to help low-income children catch up with their higher-income peers. It publicly acknowledged the nation's concern about the needs of children from low-income homes, the value of early childhood education, and the concept that education begins before public school age.

Head Start was viewed as compensatory education; that is, it acknowledged the possibility that educational programs could make up for inadequate early life experiences. Head Start was community based and concerned with not only education but also nutrition and health. Parents were involved as planners, teachers, and decision makers. Education was offered to children who were "disadvantaged." Parents of children with disabilities began to ask whether their children too could profit from early education, a request that reflected their belief in normalization for their children.

A very different influence was also changing social attitudes, creating a demand for a solution. In the 1960s and 1970s, the cost of education had outstripped the funds available to pay for it. Constructing and maintaining separate buildings to provide programs for those with disabilities multiplied costs to parents and taxpayers. Eliminating separate institutions and special schools would bring tremendous savings. Further savings would be possible if, through early identification and appropriate curricula, children with disabilities could attend regular classes and become contributing members of society.

People began to believe that people with disabilities were being deprived of their constitutional and human rights. In 1967, state institutions housed almost 200,000 persons with significant disabilities. Many of these restrictive settings provided only minimal food, clothing, and shelter (U.S. Department of Education, 2007a).

The interest in normalization emerged concurrently with the increasingly high costs of institutional care and the growing awareness of abuse and neglect in large institutions, as exposed in public scandals. Programs were, and continue to be, designed to reduce the rates and duration of seclusion and restraint in particular, practices that resulted in death and posttraumatic stress disorders (Jovanovic & Johnsen, 2006). Increasingly, the human rights of people with disabilities became an issue.

IN THE FIELD

In the late 1940s, Allan's parents left him on the steps of an institution for persons with mental retardation. By age 35, he had become blind and was frequently observed sitting in a corner of the room, slapping his heavily callused face as he rocked back and forth, humming to himself.

In the late 1970s, Allan was assessed properly for the first time. To the dismay of his examiners, they discovered he was of average intelligence; further review of his records revealed that by observing fellow residents of the institution, he had learned self-injurious behavior that caused his total loss of vision. Although the institution then began a special program to teach Allan to be more independent, a major portion of his life and his vision was lost because of a lack of appropriate assessments and effective interventions (U.S. Department of Education, 2007).

REFLECTIVE PRACTICE | Unfortunately, Allan's history was repeated in the life experiences of tens of thousands of people with disabilities. What does Allan's story teach you about segregated education? How does Allan's story help you understand why inclusion makes a difference?

Although parents viewed special education more positively than institutionalization, many still felt that there were problems with the system. They felt powerless in the face of school administrators who refused to allow some children with disabilities to attend public schools. Some progress was made by advocacy groups such as the Children's Defense Fund that made their position clear about the almost 2 million children who were not served by the public school system.

> [I]f a child is not white, or is white but not middle class, does not speak English, is poor, needs special help with seeing, hearing, walking, reading, learning, adjusting, growing up, is pregnant or married at age 15, is not smart enough or is too smart, then, in many places, school officials decide school is not the place for that child. In sum, out of school children share a common characteristic of differentness by virtue of race, income, physical, mental, or emotional "handicap," or age. They are, for the most part, out of school not by choice, but because they have been excluded (Children's Defense Fund, 1975, p. 4).

Legislative Basis for Integration

Integrating children with disabilities has followed two paths—one in the area of civil rights, the other in education.

It also has three distinct eras. However, before going into these, a brief review of how laws are made and interpreted is provided.

A law passed by Congress is referred to as a Public Law (P.L.), followed by two numbers. The first refers to the Congress that passed the law; the 94th Congress passed P.L. 94-142. The second number refers to the law's sequential position in the laws that particular Congress passed, in this case the 142nd law. Federal laws are often changed or amended. P.L. 94-142 was amended in 2004. Professionals in the field know the names or numbers of significant laws. When a law is passed, its meaning may not be clear. Within 18 months of passing the law, **regulations** often are developed to make the its meaning clearer. These are detailed in the Code of Federal Regulation (CFR). Individual states may go beyond what is required in the regulations; however, all states must meet the minimum requirements of the federal law.

● ● ●
Special Education: 1950–1970

Segregation on the basis of race and disability are inextricably intertwined. The 1954 case of *Brown v. Board of Education of Topeka, Kansas*, which focused on the civil rights of black Americans, had little to do with disabilities but much to do with segregation in education. Separate education was declared not equal, whether based on race or disability:

> *Separate educational facilities are inherently unequal. This inherent inequality stems from the stigma created by purposeful segregation which generates a feeling of inferiority that may affect their hearts and minds in a way unlikely ever to be undone. (Brown v. Board of Education, 1954)*

Tinker v. Des Moines Independent Community School District (1969) furthered civil rights for students. The court ruling was interesting: It declared that children are *persons* under the Constitution of the United States, they have civil rights independent of their parents, and they do not lose these civil rights when they attend school. This case set the stage for cases that used the violation of the First (right to free speech) and Fourteenth (right to **due process**) Amendments as grounds for bringing suit.

As parents of children with disabilities became increasingly dissatisfied, they sought legal remedies to make the educational system more responsive to their children's needs. Encouraged by an increasingly receptive public and strengthened by better organization and cooperation between themselves and professional groups, parents began to press their cause in court and in Congress.

The Handicapped Children's Early Education Program (HCEEP) of 1968, P. L. 90-538, was passed with a **mandate** to set up model demonstration projects. This officially acknowledged that the early childhood years were important and that educators did not know what systems or techniques would work effectively with young children with disabilities. This legislation was designed to find programs and methods that could be replicated throughout the country.

Special Education: 1970–1985

The Economic Opportunities Amendments of 1972, P.L. 92-424, mandated that 10 percent of Head Start's enrollment must be children with disabilities. The move to educate *all* children without discrimination was also supported by the Rehabilitation Act of 1973. **Section 504** of that act focused on nondiscrimination in programs or activities receiving federal funding, including public schools. Its definitions are far broader than those in educational laws. It defined a person with a **disability** as "Any person who (i) has a physical or mental impairment which substantially limits one or more of such person's major life activities, (ii) has a record of such an impairment, or (iii) is regarded as having such an impairment." (Major life activities include self-care, performing manual tasks, seeing, hearing, speaking, breathing, learning, and walking.) The regulations governing Section 504 stipulate:

> *No otherwise qualified handicapped individual … shall, solely by reason of his (or her) handicap, be excluded from the participation in, be denied the benefits of, or be subject to discrimination under any program or activity receiving federal financial assistance. (C.F.R. 104; P.L. 93-112)*

The **Family Educational Rights and Privacy Act of 1974, P.L. 93-380**, often called the Buckley Amendment, gives parents of students younger than age 18 and students 18 and older the right to examine records kept in the student's personal file and to have these explained. If found to be misleading or inaccurate, parents or students can request the records be amended by the school system. Written permission from parents is required for records to be released unless it is to other school officials (such as when students transfer).

The **Education for All Handicapped Children Act of 1975 (EHA), P.L. 94-142**, is the first in a series of laws focusing on the rights of children with disabilities to a **free appropriate public education (FAPE)**. **Education of the Handicapped Acts (EHA)** refers to the series of laws and amendments that require schools to meet the needs of students with disabilities. Legislation in this area has increasingly mandated states to provide educational services for younger children. Failure to comply can result in the loss of federal funding in other programs. Legislation has also supported the concept of **least restrictive environment (LRE)**, meaning that children should be educated in the same setting (or as close to the same setting as possible) in which they would have been educated if they did not have a disability.

Understanding the relationship between Section 504 of the Rehabilitation Act of 1973 and P. L. 94-142, the Education of All Handicapped Children Act of 1975 (EHA), is important. Section 504 also covers all children who are eligible for services under P.L. 94-142. However, Section 504 includes disabilities that may not interfere with learning. For example, a child who has asthma may not have a learning problem; however, he may need accommodations in physical education. Likewise, a child who tests HIV positive may have no symptoms that interfere with learning, but she may need accommodations to stay in school. Section 504 includes such children and requires that accommodations be made for them. If at some point their disability does interfere with their ability to learn, they will also be covered under P.L. 94-142.

IN THE FIELD

Mary Lee was born with **spina bifida**. Her parents use intermittent **catheterization** to empty her bladder because she cannot control it. As a 5-year-old, this was the only accommodation she needed to stay in school all day (Section 504). However, during second grade she was identified as having a learning disability. She now receives services under P.L. 94-142.

REFLECTIVE PRACTICE | Professionals in the field use shorthand to refer to the Rehabilitation Act of 1973 (Section 504) and the Education of All Handicapped Children Act of 1975 (P.L. 94-142). They might say, "She is covered under 504, but not 94-142." They will expect that you know what this means and that she needs some accommodations to be included in the class, but that her disability does not affect her ability to learn. Reflect on what this means for you as a professional in the field.

The passage of P.L. 94-142 in 1975 had a tremendous effect on the education of school-age children with disabilities but much less effect on the education of younger children with disabilities. Although children ages 3 to 5 *could* be included, that was not part of the original mandate. Educators had their hands full and little energy was left over for younger children.

Special Education: 1985 and Beyond

By the mid-1980s, the evidence supporting the efficacy of early intervention for children through age 5 was there, but there were no state-level systems of services. The need for greater interagency coordination was apparent, as was the push to serve all eligible young children (Hebbeler, Smith, & Black, 1991).

When the EHA was reauthorized in 1986, Education of the Handicapped Act Amendments of 1986 (P.L. 99-457), it lowered the age of eligibility for mandated services to 36 months, increased funding for preschool children (Part B), and established the Infants and Toddlers Program for children from birth to 3 (Part H). The Infants and Toddlers Program was **discretionary**; states could decide whether to participate and were allowed to develop their own definitions of "developmentally delayed," and each state could decide whether it would serve infants and toddlers "at risk."

The federal government also acknowledged the importance of technology when it passed the **Technology-Related Assistance for Individuals with Disabilities Act in 1988 (P.L. 100-407)**, commonly known as the Tech Act. This act was designed to explore the potential of technology to meet the needs of people with disabilities, including young children and the elderly. Increasingly, the field has become dependent on assistive devices to enable children with disabilities to function in regular settings.

In 1990, the Education for All Handicapped Children Act (EHA) was reauthorized and renamed the **Individuals with Disabilities Education Act of 1990**, and the abbreviation EHA was changed to IDEA. Like other laws, the Handicapped Children's Early Education Program (HCEEP) was renamed the Early Education Program for Children with Disabilities (EEPCD) in 1990.

The **Americans with Disabilities Act (ADA) of 1990** extended civil rights protection and nondiscrimination requirements of Section 504 to *all* settings, not just those that receive federal funds. This opened all early care and education settings and private schools to children with disabilities and also provided for the inclusion of children and adults with disabilities in the community.

The reauthorization of the Individuals with Disabilities Acts Amendments in 1997 (P.L. 105-17), referred to as the 1997 amendments, brought major modifications for children in the areas of behavioral intervention, transition, and assessment. An **Individualized Education Program (IEP)** had to be designed for each child, and classroom implementation strategies developed. The 1997 amendments also strengthened the role of parents in the educational process and made the federal government's position on "least restrictive environment" clearer. The reauthorization emphasized placing young children with disabilities in natural environments, such as their own homes, early care and education settings, and regular public school classrooms.

The **No Child Left Behind Act (NCLB) (P.L. 107-110)**, signed on January 8, 2002, is a federal law affecting education from kindergarten through high school. It is built on four principles: expanded local control and flexibility; doing what works based on scientific research; accountability for results; and more options for parents. The main goal of NCLB is to help all students reach proficiency in English language arts/reading and mathematics and to close the achievement gap between white middle-class children and black and Hispanic children and children whose families have few resources. Some of the tenants of NCBL impacted the reauthorization of the IDEA.

The IDEA was reauthorized again on December 3, 2004: the **Individuals with Disabilities Education Improvement Act Amendments of 2004 (P.L. 108-446)**. The final regulations were published in the Federal Register on August 14, 2006. Between when the law was passed and when the regulations were set, more than 5,500 individuals and/or organizations submitted comments on how the law should be interpreted (Walsh, 2006). This reauthorization eliminated the need to use benchmarks or objectives in the Individualized Education Program (IEP) for many school-age children. Following in the footsteps of No Child Left Behind, teachers are required to be "highly qualified" in the subject areas they are teaching. As special education teachers frequently teach multiple core subjects, many saw this as a particular challenge. However, new special education teachers now must have an academic major, advanced degree, or pass a competency exam in each subject area they teach (Mandlawitz, 2007). The underlying concept of another provision, **universal design**, is that products and services should be designed to be used with the widest possible range of functional capacities (Mandlawitz, 2007).

A major philosophical change in the 2004 amendments is a move into the prevention of disabilities. **Early intervening services (EIS)** allow school districts to spend 15 percent of the federal money they receive for children in kindergarten through grade 12, with a special emphasis on children in kindergarten through grade 3 who have not been identified as having special education needs, but who do need additional academic and behavioral interventions to succeed in the general curriculum (IDEA, 2004). EIS are about identifying children who are struggling in areas such as math and reading, and intervening to provide support quickly. Using EIS is also a way of focusing on **disproportion**, which looks at the relationship between the racial and ethnic backgrounds of the children in the school and those who are identified for special education services. Concern arises when children from some racial or ethnic groups are overrepresented in the special education population. EIS is designed

Changes in the laws have resulted in changes in all children's education.
© Cengage Learning 2012

to support these children early and prevent their identification as children needing special education services.

Another aspect of Early Intervening Services, **Response to Intervention (RTI)**, applies to children who have learning difficulties and do not perform at age/grade level. RTI focuses on the quality of the research used to support education and how to implement this evidenced-based research in the classroom.

THE EVIDENCE BASE

Evidence is an elusive quality, yet it is designed to be the basis for making decisions about how children learn. *The Center for Evidence-Based Practice: Young Children with Challenging Behavior* identified six different types of evidence that are used in decision making:

> **Type 1.** *Empirical evidence (qualitative or quantitative research)* published in **peer-reviewed journals** that have found positive outcomes for children or reviews of empirical evidence from peer-reviewed journals that cite the original studies.
>
> **Type 2.** *Evaluation reports* done by an outside source that provides data analysis that shows positive outcomes for children.
>
> **Type 3.** *Evaluation reports* analyzed by the system or program developer that provides evidence of positive outcomes for children.
>
> **Type 4.** *Survey or descriptive research* published in peer-reviewed journals that summarize impressions of outcomes.

The center further identifies two types of consensus documents:

> **Type 5.** *Multi-authored consensus documents* that indicate evidence for the use of some practice, but data to support the practice is not provided.
>
> Type 6. Descriptions of system features that are designed to provide positive outcomes, but evaluation data are not provided.

Source: Smith & Fox, 2003

Detailed information about the IDEA and its requirements and implications is given in Chapter 5. Table 1–1 provides a chronological summary of laws that relate to educating children with disabilities.

Legislation and Litigation

The relationship between legislation (laws and regulations) and litigation (law suits) is important. Litigation outcomes provide the impetus for new laws or clarify and determine the limits or interpretation of existing laws. *Pennsylvania Association of Retarded Children v. Commonwealth of Pennsylvania* (1971), a class action suit on behalf of the parents of 13 children, argued that the denial of a free public education for children with mental retardation was a violation of the Fourteenth Amendment of the U.S. Constitution, the right to due process. Education for *some* had to be education for *all*. In a settlement approved by the court, Pennsylvania agreed to provide education to all school-age children with mental retardation living in the state (including those in state institutions) within one year. A parallel decision, *Peter Mills v. Board of Education of the District of Columbia* (1972), added the stipulation that lack of funds was not an acceptable reason for excluding children.

Some court decisions concerned children who had been misplaced by the system. In *Diana v. State Board of Education of Monterey County, CA* (1970), the court ruled that children must be tested in their primary language. Previously, children whose primary language was not English had been tested in English and sometimes declared mentally retarded. This type of litigation provided the impetus for the passage of P.L. 94-142 in 1975.

Once P.L. 94-142 was passed, the outcomes of further litigation determined the minimum level of services required by law. The *Board of Education of the Hendrick Hudson Central School District v. Rowley* (1982) provides guidelines on what a "free appropriate public education" means. Amy Rowley was a child with a hearing impairment whose parents thought she would do better if she had an interpreter. They were probably right. However, Amy Rowley was functioning at the same level as her peers. The Supreme Court ruled against Rowley. Their interpretation was that the EHA was not intended to require any particular level of, or intensity of, educational services. Maximizing a child's potential was too high a standard, but providing only services available to children without disabilities was too low a standard. The EHA requires the provision of a "basic floor of opportunity" consisting of "access to specialized instruction and related services individually designed to provide educational benefit to the handicapped child." If the child is educated in the regular classroom, the program should be "reasonably calculated to enable the child to achieve passing marks and advance from grade to grade."

Additionally, it defined a free, appropriate public education as "personalized instruction with sufficient support services to permit a child to benefit educationally from instruction (at the public's expense) that meets the state's educational standards and approximate grade levels used in the state's regular education system and conforms to the IEP."

Inclusion of children with acquired immune deficiency syndrome (AIDS) in schools has been controversial. In *School Board of Nassau County, Florida v. Arline* (1987), the Supreme Court ruled that persons with infectious diseases, including AIDS, are covered under Section 504 of the Rehabilitation Act. The IDEA covers special educational services for children when they are needed.

Determination of the law's meaning is an ongoing process. The laws have required that increasingly younger children with disabilities be educated, even starting at birth. Special education starts at school age. Whereas early childhood education focused on young children without disabilities, early childhood special education was the solution for those with disabilities.

Inclusive Early Childhood Education

Deriving some of its characteristics from **special educa-tion**, and others from **early childhood education**, **early childhood special education** goes beyond applying special education techniques to younger children. It is a unique blend that has emerged into a field of its own. It includes aspects of family relations and family therapy, the creative arts, branches of psychology and sociology, and knowledge gained from compensatory education approaches. The field continues to change and expand in response to emerging evidence and information and the result of innovative techniques.

DAP Early childhood education concentrates on the development and education of children from birth through age 8. It is concerned with practice, research, and theory in the field and includes areas such as parenting, child care, curriculum, administration, discipline, and age-based topics focusing on infants, toddlers, preschool, and early elemen-tary school children. The field has a strong child development

TABLE 1–1   PUBLIC LAWS AFFECTING INCLUSIVE EARLY CHILDHOOD EDUCATION

Year	Public Law	Title and Significance
1968	90-538	*Handicapped Children's Early Education Assistance Act (HCEEP)* established model demonstration projects to develop programs to serve young children with disabilities. It was renamed the *Early Education Program for Children with Disabilities (EEPCD)* in 1990.
1972	92-424	*Economic Opportunities Amendments of 1972* mandated that 10 percent of the children in Head Start have disabilities.
1973	93-112	*Rehabilitation Act of 1973*, Section 504, mandated equal opportunities for children with disabilities in settings that receive *federal* funds.
1975	94-142	*Education for All Handicapped Children Act of 1975 (EHA)* mandated a free appropriate public education in the least restrictive environment for children and youth (5-21) with disabilities.
1983	98-199	*Education of the Handicapped Act Amendments of 1983 (EHA)* supported the development of model demonstration programs for preschool special education, early intervention, and transition.
1986	99-457	*Education of the Handicapped Act Amendments of 1986 (EHA)* established Part B mandating services for children 3 to 5 years. It also established Part H (changed to Part C in 1997) an entitlement program for infants and toddlers, birth to 3.
1988	100-407	*Technology-Related Assistance for Individuals with Disabilities Act of 1988 (Tech Act)* provided funding and incentives to increase the level of technology-related devices and services for individuals with disabilities.
1990	101-336	*Americans with Disabilities Act of 1990 (ADA)* extended civil rights protection to people with disabilities in all settings. Required that schools, employers, and government agencies provide reasonable accommodations to allow individuals with disabilities to participate fully.
1990	101-476	*Individuals with Disabilities Education Act of 1990 (IDEA)* renamed the EHA and made language changes by replacing the term *handicapped* with *disability* and used "people first language." It included services to children with autism, traumatic brain injury, serious emotional disturbances, and attention deficit disorder, as well as transition and assistive technology services.
1991	102-119	*Individuals with Disabilities Education Act Amendments of 1991* replaced the terms *language and speech* with *communication*, *psychosocial* with *social* or *emotional*, and *self-help skills* with *adaptive development*. *Case management services* are referred to as *service coordination*. Another important change is that "to the maximum extent appropriate," children are to be in natural environments, including the home, and community settings in which children without disabilities participate.
1997	105-17	*Individuals with Disabilities Education Act Amendments of 1997 (IDEA)* included use of the Developmental Delay eligibility category, at the discretion of states, for children through age 9; funding formulas were changed to include population and poverty data. Part C (formerly Part H), infant and toddlers, allowed young children who are not eligible for services to be monitored over time. Mediation processes were established; discipline procedures were clarified and there were also changes in the IEP, assessment procedures, and an emphasis that children with disabilities should be part of the regular curriculum and assessment procedures.
2001	107-110	*No Child Left Behind Act of 2001* increased accountability, provided choices for parents, gave greater flexibility to states and schools, and emphasized reading and math. It was designed to close the **achievement gap**.
2004	108-446	*Individuals with Disabilities Education Improvement Act Amendments of 2004* eliminated benchmarks or objectives in IEPs and tied annual goals to state standards. Teachers had to be highly qualified. It emphasized universal design, literacy and language skills, and intervention in natural environments for infants and toddlers. It added requirements related to early intervening services, disproportion, and response to intervention.
2008	110-325	*Americans with Disabilities Act Amendments Act of 2008 (ADAAA)* continued and expanded civil rights protection to children and adults with disabilities.

base, although it adheres to no single philosophy of educating children. It is committed to the principle that the years from birth through age 8 are critical years for development and that good programs are imperative during those years. There remains some debate as to whether the generally accepted, high-quality characteristics of early childhood programs for children without disabilities are equally appropriate and effective for children with disabilities.

> ▶❚❚ Educational Philosophies in the Classroom
>
> Watch the TeachSource Video Case "Lauren and Beth: Serving Students with Special Needs in an Inclusive Learning Environment," in which the girls' mothers and teachers describe the effect of their participation in an inclusive class. The video can be found in the Early Childhood Education Media Library under Special Education available at www.cengagebrain.com.

Early childhood special education emerged because neither special education nor early childhood education practitioners, while working separately, were able to effectively impact the lives of young children with disabilities and their families. Professionals from both groups found they were more effective when they blended their expertise and used a family-centered approach.

Change in the field of inclusive early childhood education is a result of interwoven social and legal factors. Much of the change has come as a result of research and the evidence it provided. We now recognize the importance of individualizing our teaching. This has facilitated the provision of attention to individual needs that is essential when working with children with disabilities. Early brain research focused on the potential for early intervention and the negative implications of "let's wait and see" (National Research Council and Institute of Medicine, 2000).

The importance of early life experiences has been established, as has the interactive influence of genetics and environment on the development of the human brain. The centrality of early relationships has also been acknowledged, especially with their potential for developing resilience or risk in children. The role of emotion, in all its complexity, has been increasingly explored and validated, especially as it relates to motivation and aggression. The ability to increase positive child outcomes through planned intervention has been established (National Research Council and Institute of Medicine, 2000).

Most educational research has focused on how (and what) to *teach* rather than how children *learn*. Swiss psychologist Jean Piaget (whose work was published in English in the early 1950s) focused his research on how children learn. Piaget (1970) argued that the teacher's role is to set up an environment that a child can actively explore. Classroom activities, which are part of the environment, should incorporate both familiar and new aspects. Lev Vygotsky, a Russian researcher whose works were translated into English in the 1980s, focused on social interactions and language as the foundation for cognitive development. When examining the adult–child relationship, he looked at the range of tasks that children could not accomplish alone but could do with the help of competent adults or peers. He called this the **zone of proximal development (ZPD)** (Vygotsky, 1934/1987). This concept has been very useful in teaching young children with disabilities. Techniques or strategies that adults use to allow children to accomplish increasingly difficult tasks are called **scaffolding**. From the work of Piaget and Vygotsky, scholars concluded that to learn, a child must actively interact with the environment and that the activities in the environment must be individualized to match and then expand the child's experience.

The work of Albert Bandura (1992) and others focused on how children learn by **modeling** other children. Segregating children at an early age meant that children with disabilities had only peers with disabilities available as models. Thus segregation effectively resulted in teaching children to become disabled. With teacher support and exposure, children with disabilities can learn to model and play with typically developing peers. All children can gain experience in interacting with a wide range of people.

Piaget's and Vygotsky's work helped make inclusion possible by changing our philosophy and methodology of education. Bandura's work helped make inclusion imperative by demonstrating that segregation deprived children with disabilities (and those without) of a full education and a full life.

Much of the controversy between early childhood education and early childhood special education focuses around the interpretation of **developmentally appropriate practices**. In response to this controversy, the National Association for the Education of Young Children (NAEYC) published guidelines specifying what is meant by developmentally appropriate practice (Copple & Bredekamp, 2009) and operationalized this for curriculum and assessment for children with and without disabilities. The Division for Exceptional Children also put forth the DEC recommended practices for early intervention and early childhood special education (Sandall, Hemmeter, et al., 2005).

DAP Developmentally appropriate practice has three distinct areas: age appropriateness, individual appropriateness, and social and cultural appropriateness. Age appropriateness focuses on the relationship between the materials and methods used and the age group that is being served. This is particularly an issue when development is either much faster or slower than average. If a second grader reads at an eighth-grade level, much of the available eighth-grade literature may be inappropriate for him. Likewise, if a second grader has the mental age of 3, many of the materials 3-year-olds use are inappropriate. The concept of universal design addresses this issue. The second aspect of developmentally appropriate practice requires that the environment, materials, and interactions with adults be consistent with the ability and needs of each child (Copple & Bredekamp, 2009). It focuses on providing options for children rather than expecting all children to do the same thing at the same time. In early childhood education, this has

Individualized planning takes into account a child's interests and needs, supports adaptive skills, and is responsive to family background and values.
© Cengage Learning 2012

frequently been interpreted as responding to a child's interests; in early childhood special education, it is viewed as responding to a child's needs. Individualized planning should take into account both children's interests and their needs. It is not an either/or situation. The third factor, social and cultural appropriateness, relates to educating children in a way that is respectful of and responsive to their family background and values, as well as community and societal values.

The DEC recommended practices focus on five direct services strands: (1) assessment, (2) child-focused practices, (3) family-based practices, (4) interdisciplinary models, and (5) technology applications. They identified a sixth strand, cultural/linguistic sensitivity, but found that it was a fundamental value that crossed all categories. They also identified two indirect supports: (1) policies, procedures, and systems change; and (2) personnel preparation (Sandall & Smith, 2005). These strands are based on the science of early childhood development and the knowledge and experience of researchers and other stakeholders (Sandall, Hemmeter, et al., 2005).

Early childhood special educators need a wide range of teaching strategies to provide education and early intervention. These strategies are individualized to facilitate learning. Partnership between families and early childhood special educators is family centered, and families play an active role in the decision-making process. Including children with disabilities in early childhood programs broadens expectations for educators' skills and assumes children will require varied care and learning environments.

DEC sets forth its beliefs and values, beginning with using mutual respect and appreciation as the basis for building relationships with children and families. It supports high-quality, comprehensive, coordinated, and family-centered services and supports, based on the research that shows that early intervention (EI) and early childhood special education

(ECSE) can make positive long-term differences in the quality of life for children and their families. They endorse the rights of all children to participate actively and meaningfully within their families and communities and support the principles of normalization and least restrictive environments. However, it is not enough that children are in these environments; a child's learning needs must be identified and matched with effective intervention strategies and supports. Like NAEYC, DEC sees children with disabilities as children first, and they are committed to using the guidelines and standards such as those recommended by NAEYC and Head Start that help provide quality programming for all children (Sandall, McLean, et al., 2005).

Labels and Labeling

Given concerns about the power of language, leaders in the field are questioning the use of labels and the need for labeling. They argue that the challenge for both research and implementation is delivering effective, comprehensive services for all children based on their individual educational needs rather than their labeled disability.

To alleviate the problem of mislabeling children, the IDEA allows the use of the category **developmental delay** for children from birth through age 9. This category previously had been available only for younger children. The term *developmentally delayed* solves some of the problems related to mislabeling. The developmentally delayed label is replaced by a more specific one (e.g., intellectual disability) as the child gets older and the disability can be more clearly identified, or is dropped altogether if the delay responds to intervention. However, if it is clear that a young child has a visual impairment, it serves no purpose to call the child developmentally delayed, as the more specific label may open an expanded array of service for young children "at risk" for developmental delays.

• • •
People First Language

Terminology in the field of disabilities is changing. Some changes are dramatic, others more subtle. However, the intent of all of the changes is to focus on people first and disabilities second. The terms **handicap** and disability are not synonymous. A handicap "is the cumulative result of the barriers imposed by society which come between a person and the environment of an activity which the person wants to do" (Blaska, 1993, p. 28). An inaccessible building is a handicap for a child using a wheelchair, just as reaching the top of a high bookshelf is a handicap for a short person. A *disability* is a general term referring to a condition or functional limitation that interferes with major life activities such as walking, hearing, or learning. The term *handicapped* has been replaced by the term *disability* when the reference is to a person. This change is reflected in the names of the laws passed. The Education of the Handicapped Acts (EHA) were renamed the Individuals with Disabilities Education Acts (IDEA) in 1990. The word *handicapped* is still used in citing laws or environmental barriers, but not in reference to people.

New terminology uses **people first language**. Think about how you might introduce yourself. Who are you? How would you describe yourself? The description you give will vary with the situation, making some aspects of you more relevant than others. An individual's disability is an aspect of that person. If not relevant, reference to the disability should be omitted. When used, the term *disability* should not be placed in a preceding adjectival phrase, nor should people and conditions be confused. Also avoid grouping individuals into categories such as "the disabled" (Blaska, 1993).

Say:	Do Not Say:
babies addicted to crack	crack babies
child with a disability	disabled child
child who has cerebral palsy	child who is cerebral palsied
child who is gifted	gifted child

When comparing children with disabilities and children without disabilities, do just that. If one refers to children without disabilities as normal children, the obvious implication is that children with disabilities are abnormal. Use terms such as **normal development**, **typically developing**, or **children without disabilities**. Be aware of the terms you use and be sure that they convey an accurate description of the child. Be wary of professionals and people whose language does not reflect a people first philosophy. If their language is out of date, their knowledge may be as well.

Some words used in the past to describe persons with disabilities have negative connotations and have created images of people who are to be pitied and who are not able. These words have been replaced with less value-laden terms, for example:

Say:	Do Not Say:
has epilepsy	is *afflicted* by epilepsy
has muscular dystrophy	*suffers* from muscular dystrophy
has AIDS	is a *victim* of AIDS
uses a wheelchair	is *confined* to a wheelchair
has Down syndrome	is *mongoloid*
is nonverbal	is *dumb* or *mute*
has a physical disability	is *crippled* or an *invalid*

Remember, it is not only what you say, but also how you say it. Even appropriate language can be used in a demeaning way.

The term *special* has also come under scrutiny. We all like to feel special sometimes such as on our birthday, we enjoy special events such as concerts, and we may even have particular clothing that makes us feel special. However, we don't want to be special all of the time. Sometimes we want to be just like everyone else, part of the group. The question then becomes, Should there be special education?

Using people first language requires us to use more words to describe an individual. Some people find this cumbersome, some unnecessary. Words shape attitudes. They are a reflection of the timeliness and accuracy of your knowledge.

Including All Children

All children are unique, yet they have much in common. Like adults, they all have strengths as well as limitations, and specialized needs some of the time. One child may have a cast on his broken leg, whereas another may forget her toilet training when her baby sister is born, and another may show her anger during her parents' divorce process. Needs change during crucial periods in children's lives just as with adults.

DAP So, if *all* children are part of regular settings and *all* children participate in the general curriculum, then *all* educators need to know techniques to care for and educate *all* children. One of the most powerful crossovers in inclusive education is that *all* educators are sharing the knowledge that *all* children are unique, that instruction needs to be individualized. Developmentally appropriate practices are important for *all* children, and what happens in classrooms is about *children*, as well as math, reading, and science.

When children have diverse needs, whether temporary or permanent, there is a danger of considering only how different those needs make them: Educators may lose sight of how much they resemble other children. They may forget these children have the same basic educational and personal needs as their classmates. They need friends, they need to develop a positive self-concept, and they need to see themselves as making a positive contribution to their class and society. The *whole* child must be planned for, not just the parts that are different. A child with a physical impairment needs to learn how to transfer and to use a wheel chair. However, she also needs to make friends and be included in the everyday activities of the classroom.

> ▶❚ Educational Philosophies in the Classroom
>
> Watch the TeachSource Video Case "Including Students with Physical Disabilities: Best Practices," in which you'll see how an elementary school teacher, in collaboration with her paraeducator, provides an optimal educational experience for a student with spina bifida. The video can be found in the Early Childhood Education Media Library under Special Education available at www.cengagebrain.com.

Educational settings may be new and possibly frightening. A child who is seen as different has an added fear—fear of rejection by adults or peers. Some children may have had few experiences away from the family and may associate school with painful experiences in a hospital or doctor's office. Parents may have had negative experiences with the school system. More than others, children with disabilities may need reassurance and may take time to develop a trusting relationship with teachers and peers. It is your responsibility to make the child feel safe and included in her classroom.

Educators can help children understand individual differences by developing an awareness of the diversity among all children as well as their commonalities. As an understanding of themselves and others grows, children can learn strategies for interacting with all of their peers—a valuable lifelong skill.

IN THE FIELD

I walked into my son's second-grade graduation ceremony brimming with pride. Surrounded by camera-wielding families, and children dressed in Sunday best, I sat looking forward to the performance. I walked out of that ceremony angry, sad, and disheartened—not at my son, but at the system that put him in the corner. All I kept thinking was, Why am I here? Why is my little boy here? What is the point of this mockery?

My agonizing frustration is that my son can learn. He has an intelligence demonstrated to us all the time, especially in front of the glow of a computer screen, the great educational equalizer, and with his rapier, albeit diabolical, wit. We sent our son to school to learn math skills, the wonders of science, and lessons from our past; we sent our son to learn about distant lands, the joy of a good book, and to learn the "pow" that comes from putting your ideas on paper.

I am not unrealistic; I see my son's weaknesses. I just want them to acknowledge his strengths, to build upon them, to teach him to use these strengths to compensate for his weaknesses. As parents of a child with special needs, we are in a constant state of angst and confrontation, eternally fighting to get services readily given to regular education children. We should not have to attend school with our son, sitting next to him with a copy of the Americans with Disabilities Act clenched tightly in one hand and the phone number of a good civil rights attorney in the other. I would love to be just another mom, one from whom the school administration doesn't flee upon seeing me in the hall.

Where do we go from here? I don't know. Up to this point, my husband thought we should leave him in the inclusive classroom with his peers. I think we have firmly established that it is now a moot point. According to my other son, they even moved him to another section of the cafeteria away from the kids in his grade, so even lunchtime encounters are history.

His needs in the classroom are as basic as any medical needs. An education is about dignity and independence, and having a reason to get up in the morning. Without the proper educational foundation, attaining these goals becomes impossible. Our best hope to cure the plague of negativity that keeps my son from developing his full potential, aside from teaching him at home, is that somewhere he will meet that special, rare teacher who will look beyond the minimum legal requirements and go the extra mile to assure that all children under her care are given the chance to learn. As I walked across the street to my car, tears flowing, I wondered if I would ever meet a teacher who would give him that chance.

REFLECTIVE PRACTICE | Are you that teacher? You can make a difference in children's lives. Not just the children for whom education is easy, but also the children who require something more. You can inspire, support, and grow with the children you teach. You can identify with the families of these children. You can empathize with their frustrations. You can be an advocate for those who do not have the skills themselves, and help families find the knowledge and resources they need to meet their children's needs. You can give children a chance. Compare this mother and child's experience with the one at the beginning of the chapter. How can you account for these differences? How can you make that difference?

Imagine how it might feel to be left out, excluded, from the typical activities of everyday life. Now, ask yourself, have you ever been excluded? Chosen last? Had to watch while others participated in something you could not do? How

did it feel? If this were an isolated event, it probably did not impact your self-concept; however, depending on the extent that you were excluded or even made fun of and laughed at, you may have felt isolated, lonely, and uncared for. Inclusion is more than physical proximity; it requires all participants to change their values—to include everyone.

The scope of inclusion is broader than just traditional school settings and includes all early care and education settings such as preschools, child care centers, and family child care homes. It expects children with disabilities to take swimming lessons at the local Y, to have friends in their neighborhood, and to attend religious services with their family if they choose to do so. Inclusion creates a challenge for many adults and volunteers. It requires them to expand and modify their roles to make reasonable accommodations to include increasingly diverse children, including those with developmental delays and disabilities.

In the education of young children, the concept of inclusion requires a **paradigm** shift, "a fundamental change in the way we think about differences among people, in the way we choose to organize schools for education, and how we view the purpose of that education" (Developmental Disabilities Task Force, n.d., p. 7). The hope is for an educational system in which there is no longer *special education* and *regular education*, just *education*. Inclusion is more than physically placing children in regular classroom environments originally designed for children without disabilities. Inclusion changes the care and education of *all* children (DEC, CEC, NAEYC, & Association of Teacher Educators [ATE], 1995)

IN THE FIELD

We have been friends with Matthew for a whole school year. We call him Matt. He likes school because he loves people. ... Matt has trouble understanding everything people say to him, so he uses lots of picture signs and some sign language. That's just the way he was born. We help him by taking turns being his buddy. When we are his buddies, Matt likes us to hold his hand firmly. He feels real sure we know what we are doing if we hang on that way. Many times he will thank us with a big hug. It's nice to be appreciated. (Zeph, Gilmeer, Brewer-Allen, & Moulton, 1992, p. 31)

Including children with diverse abilities can improve education for all—academically, as well as socially and emotionally. Designing services around children, rather than fitting children into existing services, is the goal of inclusion. When children with diverse abilities are included in a classroom setting, an intervention team will support the child and teacher. This team is composed of the child's parents, the teachers (regular and special education), and any specialists who work with the child. The needs and abilities of all of the children in the classroom must be considered when incorporating an individualized program for any child. This level of planning may require a level of teamwork that is new to some teachers, as well as a different array of services.

For inclusion to be done well, there must be support services for teachers, parents, and children. When children with disabilities were channeled off into special schools, the role of specialized services in the regular school was primarily diagnostic. As soon as a child was identified as having a disability, the child was moved; the task of the regular school support services was finished. Inclusion has expanded the roles of these specialists. School psychologists no longer just give tests, but also may do group or family counseling. Speech-language pathologists and occupational and physical therapists now work in early care and education settings and young children's homes. Social workers, adaptive physical education teachers, and home-school liaisons may all be part of a school setting. Although some of these specialists have been around for a long time, their previous practice of pulling children out of classes has changed. Now they perform some or all of their work within the classroom and often consult with the teacher to develop a classroom program for a child that complements the individual or small-group therapy that the specialist is carrying out.

Although the field of early childhood education as a whole supports the idea of inclusion, there is disagreement about *who* should be included. Most agree that children with mild to moderate disabilities should be included in regular classes. Some believe that *all* children, including children with profound disabilities, should be included.

The 1997 and 2004 amendments to the IDEA clarify the legal position on the inclusion of children with disabilities into regular neighborhood activities, schools, and classrooms. These children should be there. They should participate in the regular education curriculum and in the assessment procedures with necessary accommodations provided. When this cannot happen, there must be a rationale justifying why not. This legislation supports inclusion, but does not require full inclusion.

IN THE FIELD

As a special educator working in the public school system for 11 years, I have embraced inclusive models as best practice. However, I do wonder if full inclusion gives the needed level of support and appropriate curriculum to children with disabilities. In the past, I have worked as a resource room teacher, helping children learn the skills they need in the subjects in which they struggle. I feel this has given children the support they need to survive in the world.

However, it does seem important to have more inclusion in our school. I know that the research supports this. Our school has decided to use inclusion as much as possible in the coming year. Unfortunately, our district does not have the money to hire the special educators or paraeducators (paras) needed to make full inclusion successful.

The administrators decided to place children with learning and intellectual disabilities evenly throughout our four classrooms. One of these classrooms will be mine, the other classroom teachers only have a regular education background. None of the classrooms will have paras. Unfortunately, I will not be able to help instruct in their classrooms, as I will be teaching on my own. I will be in charge of writing Individualized Education Programs (IEPs) for children I do not teach; helping the other teachers accommodate students in their rooms, and helping teachers learn to keep data for each child's IEP. All of the teachers, including me, are worried about making this work.

I am not sure this is going to give children the level of support they need. In my classroom alone, I will have children with intellectual disabilities and those who are gifted and talented. This is hard enough in itself, without another staff member in my classroom. How am I going to help children in other classrooms? It seems that each day I will be pulled in a hundred different directions. How can I work with the administrators to come up with a better plan without giving them the idea that I am lazy or not willing to make a change? Would the old resource room program be better? I want children to get as much from school as they can.

Inclusion

One problem with inclusion is that there is not a single definition. According to DEC and NAEYC (2009)

> *The desired results of inclusive experiences for children with and without disabilities and their families include a sense of belonging and membership, positive social relationships and friendships, and development and learning to reach their full potential (p.2).*

The entire position paper can be accessed online at PositionStatement_Inclusion_Joint_updated-May2009-1.pdf.

Early supporters of inclusion were disenchanted with special education and its lack of accountability. They were also concerned that children who graduated from special education were not finding employment. There is consensus, however, that children who have been labeled and segregated from their peers are often stigmatized and have low self-esteem. In **pull-out programs**, children are taken out of the regular class and placed in a resource room to do concentrated work on subjects in which the child was performing below grade-level expectation. However, the underlying assumptions behind pull-out programs are questionable and inherently unequal. They focus almost exclusively on the child's weakest academic area. The special educators who teach these classes rarely observed the children they taught in regular education settings, thus they did not have a complete picture of the child's academic day—which includes areas of strength as well as social interactions with peers. While the child is out of the regular classroom, the other children are learning information this child will miss and will then fall behind in other areas as well. This particularistic

Inclusion is based on the underlying concept of equality for all.
© Cengage Learning 2012

approach rarely encourages the transfer and generalization of learning. It also requires children with disabilities to adjust to more transitions than their peers. The transition process itself identifies children who must learn in a segregated environment. Some feel this is an infringement on their civil rights (Yatvin, 1995).

Children were often identified for special educational services because they "failed" regular education. Children who struggled, but do not fail badly enough to be labeled, did not receive individualized services and may be falling between the cracks. The 2004 amendments to the IDEA are designed to identify and support these children through early intervening services like response to intervention.

THE EVIDENCE BASE

The National Professional Development Center on Inclusion summarized information about inclusion in early childhood education and provided nine synthesis points:

1. Inclusion takes many different forms; a single definition of inclusion does not exist.
2. Progress has been achieved in efforts to ensure access to inclusive programs, particularly for prekindergarten children (ages 3–5). However, in the United States, universal access to inclusive programs for all children with disabilities is far from a reality.
3. Children with disabilities in inclusive programs generally do at least as well as children in specialized programs. Inclusion can benefit children with and without disabilities, particularly with respect to their social development.
4. A variety of factors such as policies, resources, and beliefs influence the acceptance and implementation of inclusion.
5. Specialized instruction is an important component of inclusion and a factor affecting child outcomes.
6. Collaboration among parents, teachers, and specialists is a cornerstone of high-quality inclusion.
7. Families of children with disabilities generally view inclusion favorably.
8. Limited research suggests that the quality of early childhood programs that enroll young children with disabilities is as good as, or slightly better than, the quality of programs that do not enroll these children; however, most studies have focused on general program quality as opposed to the quality of inclusion for individual children with disabilities and their families.
9. Some evidence suggests that early childhood professionals may not be adequately prepared to serve young children with disabilities enrolled in inclusive programs.

Source: National Professional Development Center on Inclusion, 2007

REFLECTIVE PRACTICE | A research synthesis provides a systematic review of research studies related to a particular topic. It looks not only at the conclusions, but how these conclusions were researched and how confident we can feel about using these conclusions. Does inclusion work? There are so many levels of inclusion that research leading to a definitive answer is difficult. Also, it is a relatively new practice, thus there is little research to either support or refute its long-term effects. There are also concerns about what the objectives of inclusion are. How do we decide whether it has been successful? Reread the synthesis points. How do they inform what you know about inclusion? How will they influence your practice?

• • •
Concerns about Inclusion

There are a variety of concerns about inclusion that relate to the impact of children with disabilities on the social and learning environment in the class as well as on the education of children with and without disabilities. The inclusion of children with profound disabilities raises questions. Children with severe behavior disorders may hit or bite without warning or behave in extremely violent and aggressive ways that put other children in the class at risk. They may also display self-stimulatory or self-injurious behaviors that put them at risk and are highly disruptive in a group. The concern about children who are profoundly intellectually impaired relates to what they will gain from the academic aspect of the class and will miss in learning basic skills. They learn best when tasks are broken down into very small steps and repeated many times. This teaching style is rarely used in regular classrooms.

Another group where concern arises is children who are medically fragile. Their medical problems can be restrictive and life threatening. Although few question the social desirability of including these children in a regular classroom, the risk of infection needs to be evaluated. An additional concern is that a child's medical condition may worsen because of exposure to the other children; this may be related to either disease or injury.

Some professionals and families feel that children with certain disabilities learn better in segregated classrooms. They may oppose inclusive settings for such children. For example, children with hearing impairments may be in segregated classrooms or schools to learn sign language and auditory discrimination skills.

Finding satisfactory and realistic resolutions is difficult in strained economic times. The dilemmas mentioned are real and difficult to resolve. IDEA 2004 expects all children to begin their education in regular educational settings with the necessary support services. When these supports have been exhausted, children might move into more restricted settings.

The real crux of the inclusion issue is its implications for the system as a whole. If one believes in full inclusion, then one supports a paradigm shift to one educational system for all. If one believes that decisions should be made on a case-by-case basis, there will be separate systems with resources divided among them. Underlying support of equality for all is crucial to the success of inclusion. Whether "full" inclusion happens remains to be seen. The cumulative effect of legislation and litigation clearly supports moving toward greater inclusion.

REFLECTIVE PRACTICE | If families are truly part of the decision-making process for their children, how do we respond to families who do not want their children in an inclusive setting? Families may feel that a segregated classroom is safer and easier for them to cope with, and for the family this *is* the "least restrictive environment." What about families of children *without* disabilities who oppose the inclusion of children with disabilities in the class? Don't they have a legitimate right to oppose the inclusion of children they believe to be potentially harmful, disruptive, or overly demanding of the teacher's time? Or should only the families of children with disabilities be included in the decision making? These are tough questions with no easy answers. All families want what is best for their children. What do you think?

Barriers to Inclusion

Barriers to inclusion come in many forms; physical, ideological, institutional, financial, and conceptual are just a few of the notable ones. Physical barriers are perhaps the easiest to identify and correct. If a child in a wheelchair cannot use the stairs to get to the next floor, a ramp can be built or an elevator added or classrooms rearranged. To change ideological, institutional, and conceptual barriers, we must look at our society, the system, and within ourselves.

LACK OF AWARENESS

Awareness of issues related to inclusion does not just lie with the families of children with disabilities but with all of the stakeholders in the educational system: families of all children, early childhood educators, early childhood special educators, administrators, paraeducators, legislators, and business and community leaders. Support staff such as bus drivers, secretaries, and cafeteria workers need to be aware of inclusion and its purpose. Many stakeholders are not aware of legal requirements of the IDEA and the ADA to include children with disabilities in typical settings, or of the research that served as the foundation for these laws.

Positive attitudes are at the core of successful inclusion. This does not mean that a child with muscular dystrophy will necessarily play the same sports as a child without this disability, but rather the issue is, How can we include a child with muscular dystrophy in a manner that the child is physically and mentally capable of? Can the rules of the game be modified? Can the child be a coach or a scorekeeper? Disabilities are real; the intent is not to ignore the disability, but to meet the child's need to be included with accommodations for the disability.

Successful programs have a shared vision that all children belong and all children can learn and have the opportunity to reach their potential. There is a sense of community that helps each child develop in her own way, with a sense of self-worth, pride in each child's accomplishments, and mutual respect (CEC, 1994).

LACK OF PROFESSIONAL PREPARATION

Untrained staff and lack of consultative support is one of the main barriers to inclusion. Some teachers feel that they are not prepared to teach children with disabilities because they do not have enough knowledge about specific disabilities to accommodate these children's learning challenges. They are genuinely concerned that they might do something that will hurt the child. Families too wonder if all educators are prepared to care for and educate their child. Educators with a background in special education may feel that they do not have the management skills to teach larger groups

of children and lack child development knowledge. Many teachers feel they need trained paraeducators in the classroom to make inclusion work, and in difficult economic times this may not happen. Inclusion has forced educators to consider new and different ways of teaching children.

Teacher skills are an essential part of strategies for inclusion. Often, models include extensive initial training before inclusion, but research has shown that training should be ongoing and provide technical assistance to solve problems as they arise. Strategies to change teacher attitudes are both long and short term. The preservice training of students in higher education has to be evaluated against the skills needed for inclusive education. The Division for Early Childhood has a set of recommended practices for personnel preparation for early intervention and early childhood special education. The recommended practices look at the *process*, whereas the standards look at the *content* that is needed to provide services to young children (Miller & Stayton, 2005). The goal is to get institutions of higher education that train teachers to adopt these standards in their teacher preparation programs.

IN THE FIELD

I am a single father of a son with severe cerebral palsy and traumatic brain injury, which occurred during the birthing process. My wife passed away shortly after Neil was born, and I have had to make decisions about Neil's life on my own.

Neil is now getting ready to enter kindergarten in a school that practices inclusion. I am concerned about his educational and health needs. I was told that this classroom would have a regular education teacher, a special education teacher, and a paraeducator. Even with all this help, I worry that they do not have the expertise needed to change him, give his medication, and feed him through his stomach tube. Neil has seizures occasionally that require proper care.

Will a classroom that includes many children without special needs help him learn the basics? Neil is functioning at three years below his age. Will he be given the proper help to catch up? I don't want Neil to simply be seated in a corner and not be made part of the group. Who should I contact about my concerns? Are my worries even valid? Sometimes I feel I just don't know how I can ensure that Neil receives the best education he can get.

EDUCATIONAL ASSESSMENT

When children with disabilities are included in regular classrooms, they are taught the same education curriculum as their peers. If *all* children are in regular classrooms, then *all* children should be part of the state assessment system and meet the state standards. If children with disabilities are not part of the assessment procedures, there is no way to monitor their progress (CEC, 1996b). As standards are raised, it poses a dilemma. States must provide testing accommodations for some students with disabilities based on their Individualized Education Program. Some students with disabilities may not graduate (or take longer to graduate) from high school because they cannot meet the standards; others may drop out. However, to the extent that all children are included, more effort will be needed to ensure that they meet the standards. This might provide the incentive for creative and innovative teaching.

ADULT–CHILD RATIOS AND CLASS SIZE

Low adult–child ratios and larger class size are significant barriers to inclusion. Many educators want fewer children per adult so they have the opportunity to individualize programming and respond to each child's needs. Including children with disabilities increases the time educators need to spend in collaboration, planning, and carrying out plans.

IN THE FIELD

Rena has spina bifida. Her family wants her to attend and participate in the same education setting as her older brother. Her physician supports this decision. Two early childhood educators were trained by a public health nurse to catheterize Rena. This allows her to attend the full-day program. Rena has large and fine motor challenges. A physical therapist demonstrated lifting techniques and positioning to all the educators at the setting as well as the support staff and volunteers. This permits Rena to move safely from her wheelchair to chairs at activity tables that have special straps designed for her. She can also join in floor activities with appropriate supports (pillow rolls). Rena's interest in drawing, painting, and gluing are facilitated by the adapted crayons and brushes recommended by the occupational therapist. The itinerant early childhood special education consultant follows up on the recommendations from the nurse, physical therapist, and the occupational therapist in his twice-weekly visit to the center. During the visit, the consultant assists the two early childhood educators who have Rena in their group to plan and implement an IEP for Rena. He also provides suggestions and support to the volunteers who work with Rena (Deiner, Hardacre, & Dyck, 1999).

REFLECTIVE PRACTICE | Have you thought about the adults who might be in your classroom? How do you include and adapt to them as well as collaborate with them to educate young children? How do you see their role and yours in general? What do you think will happen when they are in the classroom? How do you plan to ensure the education of all the children while they are there?

IMPLICATIONS FOR EDUCATORS

Early childhood educators may have paraeducators or volunteers to help a child, and related services professionals in their class. This means these educators must not only have the techniques to teach all the children, including those with disabilities, but also need the skills to manage other adults. This is a typical "add-on" type of problem, except that not only the children, but the adults too, are being added on.

An inclusive model makes assumptions about the skills that teachers have and need. It may be that a different teaching model is preferable to having many paraeducators. In one co-teaching model, there are two trained teachers—one an early childhood educator, the other an early childhood special educator. These educators are always there and are expected to be able to teach all of the children in the same room at the same time. They may divide up their work differently during the course of the day. At one point, one educator may take the lead, whereas the other educator floats and troubleshoots. At another point, they may divide the content to be taught and teach small groups different information while others work independently.

They may parallel teach by dividing the children in the classroom in half so the groups are smaller. Or they may team teach as each teacher takes turns leading a discussion or modeling appropriate behavior in some area. Regardless of the model, time needs to be allocated for collaboration and for learning to use various teaching models.

LACK OF COMMUNICATION, COLLABORATION, AND RESPECT

We probably all feel that we do our jobs better than others without our training and orientation. Specialists may become territorial about what will happen to "their" children when these children are included in a classroom along with children without disabilities. Specialists chose a specialty because they felt an affinity for children with disabilities, and they fear that others may not share those feelings.

They believe that it takes a team of specialists to meet the needs of young children with disabilities and fear that the team will not be in place for them. Some of these fears are well founded.

The development of mutual trust and respect is one of the core components to inclusion. Strategies for success involve ongoing discussions and the willingness to share expertise with each other as well as working as teams. Communication among professionals is often difficult. When young children have disabilities, the need to communicate may be even greater and more difficult because there are many different individuals and institutions involved. The situations for these children may be tremendously complex, who may attend an early care and education setting, then go to an inclusive preschool program for part of the day, and finally return to the child care setting until their parents finish work. Often they have related services such as physical or speech and language therapy on a regular basis; they may have medical needs that require both regular and specialized medical care; they need regular assessment and evaluation; and so on.

The various professionals need to talk to and respect each other to communicate necessary information in a way that all can understand. Professionals must also be able to communicate respectfully and informatively with families. Successful communication frequently depends on the attitudes of professionals toward inclusion. The attitudes of children too play a very important role in making inclusive settings successful. Collaboration requires that staff, children, and their families support each other. Differences cannot be ignored, but must be respected, acknowledged, and even seen as cause for creative solutions.

LACK OF SUPPORTS

Strategies for achieving quality education include consideration of the supports that are necessary to make inclusion successful and communicating the value of these supports to both administrators and families. Lack of supports can take many forms. At times supports are not available because there is no common vision of what inclusion means and requires. Funding and budget cuts may limit money to hire support staff such as paraeducators or to make facilities accessible. Lack of teaching materials or training to support inclusion, limited or no preparation or collaboration time with team members, too many nonteaching assignments (lunch duty, hall duty, etc.), large classes, and no co-planning time can all contribute to lack of support. Community supports may be unavailable due to physical location or the limited number of available professionals.

Overcoming lack of supports is an administrative responsibility. The administration has to improve leadership and motivate and monitor commitment to the vision of inclusion, as well as provide a vision that all the stakeholders can believe in (CEC, 1996a). The vision is only the beginning; there must also be a commitment to follow through on the vision.

Inclusion is not the only item on the American education agenda. It exists in a context where competing concerns are voiced about other topics such as literacy, math, and the achievement gap. Consensus must be developed to reach *all* the goals on the agenda.

Culturally Diverse Children in Special Education

The cultural composition of the United States is becoming increasingly diverse. Those who teach young children will see this diversity earlier than it is reflected in the overall population statistics.

Culturally diverse children are overrepresented in special education. This presents a challenge to educators. Overidentification of specific racial/ethnic children may make teachers and other professionals reluctant to identify these

Culturally diverse children are overrepresented in special education.
© Cengage Learning 2012

children as needing individualized programming. Moving toward an inclusive educational system that meets the needs of children through early intervening services and response to intervention may better meet children's needs without the need for labeling and special education.

The federal government must be responsive to the growing needs of an increasingly diverse society. These challenges are detailed in Chapter 2.

Service Delivery Systems

Service delivery systems, individually or together, provide for the care and education of children with disabilities. Service delivery systems can be distinguished by their location, level of inclusion, focus (child or family), and whether the system is formal or informal. Children increasingly are being served by a combination of service delivery systems. Depending on the child's specific disability, medical condition, family needs, location of the community (especially rural versus urban), and availability of services and funding, a wide range of service delivery systems is possible.

Like the field itself, service delivery systems are struggling to find answers to questions such as these:

- Should all service delivery systems be inclusive?
- Should service delivery systems be designed to meet the needs of the child or the whole family?
- What level of participation/cooperation is expected between families and service delivery systems?
- How much input should families have in the decision-making process?
- How actively should service delivery systems pursue parent education programs?
- How is the role of advocacy divided between parents and service delivery systems?
- How much will adequate service delivery cost and who should pay?

Changing demographics are forcing service delivery systems to evaluate their policies in relation to their target population. Interagency collaboration is required to ensure quality programming for children. If parents or guardians work, whether single or married, home-based services may not be a feasible option unless educators are willing to work when families are available.

To meet the needs of the whole family, families may develop complicated "packages" based on child care, **early intervention**, education, therapy, and health services. Children with disabilities who attend school programs often need care before and after school as well as during the summer. This need extends past the time when other children can be left at home independently.

Theoretical differences influence the goals and supports that the delivery systems provide for children and their families. Viewing families as dynamic parts of a larger social system has brought about a change in how service is delivered. Empowering families to make choices in the best interests of both their child and family has affected delivery systems and the thoughts and actions of professionals in the field of early childhood (Sandall, Hemmeter, et al, 2005). Although service delivery systems vary, these systems move from the most to the least restrictive.

Hospital-Based Care and Intervention

Most hospitals are designed for high-volume, short-term acute care. Their top priority is to preserve life. The focus is primarily on medical rather than social needs. When an infant is born prematurely or critically ill, he is placed in a **neonatal intensive care unit (NICU)** (not all hospitals have these units) staffed by **neonatologists** and **neonatal nurses**. Infants may remain in a NICU for only a day or two for observation, or up to a year or more for some of the most fragile infants. When infants are medically stable, they move to an intermediate unit. Early intervention usually begins when the child exits intensive care. Some infants who remain in the NICU for extended times receive early intervention services there.

Some children have medical condition that require hospitalization (uncontrolled **seizures**, **technology dependence**, leukemia, etc.). The length of the child's stay and the seriousness of the illness will determine to a great extent how much contact a child will have with early interventionists/educators. Larger hospitals have **child life staff** and educators that provide stimulation and intervention to young children while they are in the hospital and work with children to prepare them for medical procedures.

Residential Care

A residential care program involves a treatment facility where children with chronic and serious medical problems live in order to receive intervention/educational services. Residential programs are being phased out for all children, but particularly very young children. Some children who are profoundly involved and whose families cannot care for them live in nursing homes or state institutions and receive care and education there.

Home-Based Early Intervention

Home-based service delivery systems usually use a consultation model that involves an **early interventionist (pediatric nurse, child development specialist**, and/or early childhood special educator) visiting the family in their home on a regularly scheduled basis. This type of service delivery is frequently used for infants and medically vulnerable young children.

The **consultant's** responsibilities to the family and child include sharing information with the family about available resources and services, answering parents' questions about the child's disability, and modeling and demonstrating activities and techniques for working with the child. The consultant may serve as a liaison between the medical and educational communities (Burns, 2004).

Success for this type of system depends on families understanding and following through on the intervention. Most consultants work a daytime schedule; frequently, the

mother, if not working, is the only one at home and then has the responsibility of carrying out the prescribed early intervention as well as interpreting for others what the consultant said. Increasingly, both parents are in the workforce, and this type of delivery system may only work for a short period. Unless a home-based program is flexible enough to schedule evening and weekend appointments, it would only be available for families who have a parent or guardian at home during the day.

Center-Based Early Intervention

Center-based early intervention service delivery systems may be situated in hospitals, schools, early care and education settings, and public or private agencies. A center-based program often has a team of specialists. Some programs are designed for children with a specific disability, such as hearing impairment, whereas others serve children with a variety of disabilities. These programs usually have specialized materials and equipment. Many of these programs are half-day, so they may represent only part of the service delivery system if the child needs full-time care.

The staff of early intervention centers is usually well trained in early childhood special education, and therapists not only make active contributions to the child's educational program but may provide needed therapy in the setting as well. The staff also does assessments. Families often feel more comfortable leaving young children in a setting with specialists. For a variety of reasons, including both philosophical and monetarial, these center-based services are likely to be segregated programs.

Public School Programs

Public schools play a major part in the service delivery system for children age 3 and older. When public schools serve children below the kindergarten level, they are faced with a dilemma. They receive funds to educate children *with* disabilities beginning at age 3, but not for those *without* disabilities. They are also required to educate these children in the least restrictive environment. If they are to create inclusive environments, they must have the families of children without disabilities pay for these public school services or they must integrate the children with disabilities into programs outside of the traditional public school. Some programs integrate children with disabilities into early care and education settings such as child care, Head Start, and preschools for all or some portion of the day. Beginning with the 1997 reauthorization of the IDEA, children without disabilities may profit from services designed for children with disabilities. However, it is unlikely that public schools can afford programs for 3- and 4-year-olds just for the purpose of inclusion.

Early Care and Education

Early care and education for children with disabilities is used in one of two ways by service delivery systems: child care before and/or after early intervention or as a primary site for the delivery of early intervention services. In the latter case, related services may be provided in the early care and education setting or elsewhere.

Programs that use child care as a **primary intervention site** typically use consultation models. The early childhood special education consultant and other professionals train the educator to function as an early childhood interventionist with the support of consultants who visit the site on a regular basis to answer questions and model behavior. Consultants also provide a variety of technical assistance services ranging from specialized equipment and a selection of toys, to telephone consultation.

The ADA (1990) requires that children with disabilities must be accepted, as any other child would be. Centers can deny admission on a case-by-case basis if the setting can show that accepting a specific child would "fundamentally alter" the services they provide or constitute an "undue burden." Otherwise, the expectation is that programs will make reasonable accommodations to include children with disabilities. A reasonable accommodation might involve adding balls with bells or other sounds inside for children with visual impairments, a specialized swing for a child with physical impairments, or not permitting class pets if a child has a chronic allergy.

An overarching issue is whether the amount and quality of individual attention provided in early care and education is enough to meet the needs of children with disabilities. This is actually part of the much broader issue addressing quality of early care and education for all young children, particularly infants.

HEAD START

Head Start began in the summer of 1965 as a comprehensive service system designed to deliver health, education, and social services to children and families who met low-income eligibility criteria. Since its inception, Head Start has had a strong commitment to family involvement and inclusion. In 1993, Head Start provided enrollment opportunities for children with disabilities as well as screening and referral services. The range of comprehensive services (medical, dental, and nutritional services) is designed to serve children with identified disabilities as well as those at risk (Meisels & Shonkoff, 2000). Head Start often uses a consultation model to provide technical assistance for children with disabilities.

Head Start programs are required to coordinate their efforts and responsibilities with the local school district. Collaboration with the public schools provides an inclusive setting for children with disabilities who do not meet Head Start income guidelines (up to 10 percent of children do not have to be from low-income families), and the school district often provides consultative services to the program.

Head Start programs are moving from half-day programs into programs with **wrap-around child care**. Head Start is increasing its commitment to *family* involvement and *family* (not just child) outcomes. Family outcomes relate to family literacy, adult education, substance abuse, and health (Office of Head Start, 2007).

EARLY HEAD START

Similar to Head Start programs for 3- and 4-year-olds, **Early Head Start** is designed for children from birth to age 3. It began in 1995, following the reauthorization of the Head Start Act. Early Head Start is a comprehensive year-round program designed to promote health; positive relationships with children, families, and staff; active family involvement; and the inclusion of children with special needs (Administration for Children and Families, 2006a). Early Head Start, however, has some of the same problems that other early care and education settings have relative to funding, low teacher salaries, and related concerns about program quality.

Formal and Informal Social Networks

Social networks are made up of people who are outside the home but engage in activities or supports (material and/or emotional) for the family. Research on social support for families of children with disabilities suggests that the presence of effective social supports can assist families in coping with stress and can enhance the well-being of these families. However, although families who have children with disabilities may benefit greatly from the existence of social support networks, they are also less likely to have them available than are families of children without disabilities (Seligman & Darling, 2007).

Social support networks can be formal or informal. Formal networks are generally made up of professionals involved with service agencies. Informal social networks are made up of friends, neighbors, and extended family members. Most families utilize informal social networks. There is concern that families with children with disabilities often lack these informal networks and rely on the support of professionals (Seligman & Darling, 2007). Perhaps one role of professionals is to help families develop and rely on an informal support network rather than a formal one.

Support networks offer three major types of support: (1) providing material goods and services when needed; (2) providing emotional support by communicating the person's value and worth to them; and (3) providing information about and referrals to other, perhaps more formal, support systems. In general, social networks work best when they are reciprocal in nature (although in some extreme situations the process of having to "pay back" support can itself add stress).

Social support empowers families to strengthen and add to their already existing networks. One relatively easy way for families to increase the size of their support network is to meet families of other children in their child's setting. Supporting families in building their own social support network is a lifetime skill that will continue to serve them.

Educational Philosophies in the Classroom

Watch the TeachSource Video Case "Teaching as a Profession: Collaboration with Colleagues," in which you'll see how elementary grade-level teachers work together to strengthen their math reporting system and how they present their recommendations at a faculty meeting. The video can be found in the Early Childhood Education Media Library under Introduction to ECE available at www.cengagebrain.com.

SUMMARY

- Education for children with disabilities has a history that has involved exclusion and segregation.
- Changing social, legal, and educational philosophies led to inclusion and individualized programming for children with disabilities.
- All children are entitled to a free, appropriate, public education in the least restrictive environment.
- Families are decision makers whose priorities, values, and needs must be reflected in the educational process.
- Including children with disabilities changes the role of the educator and makes it more complex.
- Some service delivery systems are home based, others are center based, and some use a combination; however, coordinating the total range of services is a challenge.
- The needs of the whole family are considered when planning and coordinating services for children.

EDUCATIONAL RESOURCES

Council for Exceptional Children (CEC) is a professional organization that has divisions for all major disability areas and is committed to advancing the quality of education for all children. Their web page contains links to other resources. They have student chapters. (888) 232-7733; FAX (703) 620-2521; www.cec.sped.org

Division for Early Childhood (DEC) is a division of CEC that focuses on young children with disabilities. It has state divisions and holds international conferences as well as publishing a newsletter and journal. www.dec-sped.org

Inclusion Press provides links to books, workshops, online training tools, and many other resources. It is a great site for families and educators. www.inclusion.com

National Association for the Education of Young Children (NAEYC) offers professional development opportunities to early childhood educators and publishes the journal *Young Children*. Its publications focus on including children with disabilities in early care and education settings, and it is a tremendous resource for educators and families. (202) 232-8777 (800) 424-2460 FAX (202) 328-1846; www.naeyc.org

National Information Center for Children and Youth with Disabilities (NICHCY) provides resource sheets for parents, educators, or students looking for information about different disabilities. *Basics for Parents* is a publication that examines aspects of special education processes. *News Digest* focuses on current information. (800) 695-0285; (202) 884-8200; FAX (202) 884-8441; www.nichcy.org

Office of the Americans with Disabilities Act enforces Titles II and III of the ADA. It also provides publications, technical assistance, and consultation on the ADA. (800) 514-0301 TDD (800) 514-0383; www.usdoj.gov

Office of Special Education Programs is dedicated to improving outcomes for children with disabilities, from birth through age 21, by providing leadership and financial support to states and local districts. It reports annually on the implementation of the IDEA. www.ed.gov/about/offices/list/osers/index.html?src=mr

For additional educational resources, visit the book companion website for this text at www.cengagebrain.com.

Partnering with Families and Honoring Their Diversity

I feel like a 25-year-old trapped in a 55-year-old body since gaining legal custody of our grandchildren—Jessica, 3, Jeff, 5, and John, 8. It was bad when their mother left and our son had the children alone. We always knew he had a drinking problem, but we didn't want to admit he was an alcoholic and addicted to drugs. He is now in treatment for his addictive behaviors. We hope someday he will be reunited with his children on a permanent basis and that his wife will change her self-destructive patterns and form a bond with her children. Until then, I guess the children are here to stay. After a year, we are learning more about the children, ourselves, and how to cope with each other.

All the children experienced anxiety at first. Although they knew us as their grandparents, we had seen little of them because they lived 3,000 miles away. All of a sudden, we were thrust on each other. The two younger children adjusted more easily; John had more difficulty. He had fitful sleep, broken by nightmares, and he couldn't focus on his schoolwork. He seemed to get along well with his peers. He was very confused about why he and his brother and sister were separated from their parents. Probably because of the unstructured and chaotic life he was used to, he found the structure of our home both comforting and distressing. Because of the children's circumstances and the fact that our son has a learning disability, shortly after taking custody of the children we requested that they be evaluated. I lived with my son's frustration before we knew he had a learning disability. We didn't find out until he was in high school. I will not let that happen to these children.

John was evaluated first as he was the only one in the public school system. Early in the school year, he had trouble staying focused on his work. He seemed to be in his own little world. He was frustrated with school and completed few assignments, struggling each night with his schoolwork. The evaluation results confirmed that he did not have a learning disability. However, they did indicate that he was abnormally impulsive and distractible. We then took him to our family physician, who diagnosed him as having attention deficit hyperactivity disorder (ADHD) and recommended that we give him Ritalin. It helped a great deal. (I know others have had problems, but it worked for him.) He turned into a learning sponge, and his difficult behaviors turned around. I'm really glad that he didn't have a learning disability like his father. I don't think I could bear the pain and humiliation again. Now that things are settling down a little, I'm beginning to worry about the medication. He is starting to lose weight, and I wonder about the long-term side effects.

© Cengage Learning 2012

Jeff was identified as "at risk" for learning disabilities and is enrolled in a public preschool where he receives speech and language therapy. Jessica, the youngest and only girl, seems hesitant and very withdrawn. She is considered at risk because of her lack of speech. She has severe articulation problems and is extremely difficult to understand when she does talk.

The children, even after a year, still have emotional problems. They frequently have nightmares and openly worry when I leave to go to the store. They need constant reassurance that we will not leave them. We need support as well.

Our lives have changed. I had to quit my job to stay home with the children. I have tried to organize the household to provide a safe and structured environment, but it is hard at times. It takes a lot of energy to provide the children with good nutrition, love, and a stable environment. At times, I wonder if we are doing the right thing. Although the children appear resilient, some of their behaviors worry me. Their previous life was anything but normal, so it must be difficult for them to accept this new way of life. ✲

REFLECTIVE PRACTICE | Children are part of families and their families impact their lives. Few parents or grandparents expect that their children will have disabilities. Families who have children with disabilities face not only the ordinary tasks of family life but must also confront issues that are idiosyncratic to the disability, its severity, and the demands of the family system. Reflect on this family's needs and what community resources might help this family with the challenges they face.

Family-Centered Practice

A family-centered approach is the best way to deliver services to *all* young children and their families. However, defining family-centered practice is elusive. One commonality in using the term is agreement on the centrality of the family. Although children's teachers, therapists, and environments change, the family unit is the constant in the child's life (Sandall, Smith, & McLean, 2005). Families have unique knowledge of their child and his environment, their values, and the consequences of their choices—past and future. The family is ultimately responsible for the child's growth and development.

The family-centered model is based on collaboration and open communication, requires mutual respect and equality in relationships between parents and professionals, is designed to meet the unique needs of a particular child and her family, honors the diversity of families, and recognizes that the family is not defined by the child's disability. Despite the support for family-centered services, many services, especially those in education, are child-centered. They don't focus on the broader context of children's lives. When the child is the sole focus, the importance of the family—its diversity, and its strengths and challenges—may be lost.

> ▶❚❚ TeachSource Video Case
>
> **Maddie: Positive Collaboration between School Professionals and Parents to Serve a Student with a Physical Disability**
>
> Watch the TeachSource Video Case *Maddie: Positive Collaboration between School Professionals and Parents to Serve a Student with a Physical Disability*, in which you'll hear about her experiences in the classroom and how parents have partnered with educational professionals. The video can be found in the Early Childhood Education Media Library under Special Education, available at www.cengagebrain.com.

Viewing Families as a System

A systems perspective provides a framework for looking at families and the intersection of families and other systems such as early care and education, public schools, and social services. One principle underlying family systems theory is that no individual can be understood without looking at how he fits into the family. It is not enough to know about a particular child and his disability; you must also learn how that child interacts with his parents and siblings and their shared history (Smith et al., 2009).

Another family systems principle is that families have to have rules governing structure or stability and rules for change. Structural rules organize a family's day-to-day functioning, affecting decisions about who gets up first, who drops the children off at child care, and so on. Without these rules, every day would involve constant decision making, resulting in chaos. So rules support family stability, but they are also required for change, to support family flexibility and adaptability (Lambie, 2000). All families must find a healthy balance between rules for stability and rules for change.

Rules for change may dominate the family system when a child with a disability is added. Existing rules may have to be adapted at several different levels.

- **Level I** involves changing or adapting existing rules or ways of doing things, or rearranging responsibilities, to accommodate the child with disabilities (Galvin, Bylund, & Brommel, 2007). It may mean that Dad now does the shopping instead of Mom or that a cleaning service is hired to keep the house clean. Most families try to deal with stress at this level. If these strategies do not work, then there are changes in the **metarules**—rules about the rules—so that new rules can be created to address the situation (Galvin, Bylund, & Brommel, 2007).

- **Level II** changes are major and fundamentally change the family system. At this level, families have to change not only the rules but also how rules are made and who makes them. If a child has a disability, rules about what is "fair" may change. The child herself may set rules such as which activities she feels safe participating in. New traditions may be developed and old ones let go. The family holiday gathering that used to be at Grandma's house may have to be moved because the house is no longer accessible to all family members.

- **Level III** strategies require changes in the basic assumptions about life and a reordering of value structures to address need (Galvin, Bylund, & Brommel, 2007). For instance, Dad may give up his job to care for his daughter if the family decides they will live on less money, because the health and well-being of their child requires that someone be home to care for her. The family may decide to move to an urban area where there are move services available for their child, thus giving up the secluded farm that had been in the family for generations. When one member of a family is not willing to consider changes at this level, the family is at risk of separation.

A third principle is that families interact with other systems and networks such as friends, extended family, early care and education settings, schools, and communities (Lambie, 2000). Although families do need time alone, they also are part of formal and informal support networks. If families isolate children with disabilities and segregate them from the ongoing social fabric of life, they place them further at risk.

To understand how a particular family system works, you must know something about the family's resources, interaction patterns, how members carry out family functions, and where the family is in its life cycle.

Families are diverse, living in geographically different areas and differing in economic and educational resources. As well, the personal characteristics and styles of family members influence how a family operates. A family's cultural and ideological background also influences how the family perceives diverse abilities and how it reacts to them.

Families come in different sizes and forms. The varying number of parents (including stepparents) and children (including step- and half-siblings), relationships with extended family, and the presence of live-in family members who may or may not be related by blood influence the family. Larger families potentially have more people to help with care and other chores and to absorb parent's expectations, but they may face economic hardship. Two-parent families have the potential for a supportive partner. Single-parent families may have no other adults in the household and/or fewer financial resources, or they may live in multigenerational families with a great support system. To work effectively with families, you have to find out each particular family's worldview.

Different disabilities make different demands on the family system. One must also look at the match between the family's lifestyle and the child's disability. A child with cerebral palsy might require more accommodations if born to a family of backpacking hikers and boaters than if born to a family who spent time watching television and listening to music.

The severity of the child's disability is an important variable. The more severe the disability, the more difficult it may be for the family to care for the child. Families may actually try to avoid becoming attached to a child with a severe disability for fear the child will die. Typically, young children with severe disabilities require more caregiving for a greater length of time. They also need a wide range of services involving many specialists, necessitating more appointments, more waiting, and more bills. However, one cannot necessarily assume that the more severe the disability, the greater the impact on the family. Children with more severe disabilities are more easily planned for and controlled, whereas children with milder disabilities are less predictable, especially over the long term. Regardless of the severity of the disability it is imperative that we look at our interactions and requests of the family in the context of the family system.

IN THE FIELD

Although I tried to sound reasonable on the phone, this new demand appalled me. I rehearsed angry, self-justifying speeches in my head. Jody, I thought, is blind, has cerebral palsy, and his development is delayed. We do his physical therapy daily and work with him on sounds and communication. We feed him each meal on our laps, bottle him, change him, bathe him, dry him, put him in a brace to sleep, launder his dirty bed linens daily, and go through a variety of routines designed to minimize his disabilities and enhance his joys and his development—all this in addition to trying to care for and enjoy our other young children and making time for each other and our careers. Now you tell me that I should spend 15 minutes every day on something that Jody will hate, an activity that will not help him walk or even defecate, but one that is aimed at the

health of his gums. This activity is not for a finite time, but forever. It is not guaranteed to help. But "it can't hurt." Well, it's too much. Where is that 15 minutes going to come from? What am I suppose to give up? Taking the kids to the park? Reading a bedtime story to my eldest? Washing the breakfast dishes? Sorting the laundry? Grading students' papers? Sleeping? Because there is no time in my life that hasn't been spoken for, and for every 15-minute activity that is added, one has to be taken away (adapted from Featherstone, 1980, pp. 77–78).

Children must be understood in the context of their families. We, as professionals, must think about family members as individuals as well as part of the family system. They must have the personal space to develop their uniqueness yet at the same time function together as a unit. The family unit tries to find a balance between separateness and connectedness, and between stability and change. A child with a disability may change this balance.

Over time, families develop typical patterns of interacting with each other that influence the closeness or distance of family members. These patterns, called boundaries in family systems theory, are clear and semipermeable in well-functioning families, whereas in less functional families they are rigid or blurred (Lambie, 2000). Families have both external and internal boundaries. External boundaries distinguish the family from other systems, whereas internal boundaries help define the relationships and interactions within the family (Galvin, Bylund, & Brommel, 2007). In families with clear and permeable boundaries, there is movement back and forth. In such families, it is easy to see the differences between the role of an early interventionist who comes into the home to help develop an individualized program for a young child with Down syndrome and the role of his mother. Although both are attentive, the mother is clearly the ultimate decision maker who decides how the early interventionist's suggestions will fit into family life and how the priorities should be set based on family values and beliefs. The interventionist provides specific activities to support developmental goals, but the family determines the goals. The interaction pattern is a warm egalitarian one between two experts: the expert on the child and the expert on early intervention. Together they develop a plan.

In dysfunctional families, boundaries may be obstacles to solutions. At one extreme, the family boundaries can be rigid and characterized by emotional distance and lack of sensitivity. Collaboration is difficult and communication may be limited. Appointments may be missed or canceled. Subtle suggestions may go unheeded. Family members may handle problems alone and become independent and autonomous at a very early age. Goals and priorities for more disengaged families may revolve around behaviors that support independence such as adaptive skills, working independently, and self-monitoring behaviors. The interventionist may have to stress the importance of intervention to get the attention and follow-through of the family. Although it may be tempting to judge or blame **disengaged families**, it is unwise and far more useful to explore the family's history with the early interventions system and other systems. A family's disengagement may be an indication of **burnout**.

Families must pace themselves, and there may be times when they need to slow the pace of intervention to regroup their personal resources.

At the opposite end of the continuum are families where boundaries are blurred and there is excessive closeness among members. **Enmeshed families** tend to be overprotective and supportive of reciprocal dependency. An early interventionist in this system may be invited to become almost part of the family. She may be invited to significant events such as birthdays and made to feel very much at home. Family goals and priorities may revolve around social involvement and interaction rather than adaptive achievement.

Interventionists must look at boundaries and not confuse intimacy with enmeshment. Likewise, they must be clear about the personal boundaries they set around themselves as professionals and how these mesh with the family systems they work with.

Like most complex systems, families are divided into subsystems. Boundaries define who is part of the subsystem and who is not. Although families have many subsystems, the ones we are primarily concerned with are the marital, or spousal, subsystem; the parental, or executive, subsystem; the sibling subsystem; and the extra familial subsystem.

Marital Subsystem

The husband and wife, couple, or partners constitute the marital subsystem. The ability of the marital subsystem to establish a clear boundary allows them to grow and develop as a couple as well as fulfilling other roles. The primary tasks of the marital system involve providing for the functional needs of the family and for the emotional and sexual needs of the individual partners (Lambie, 2002).

Parental Subsystem

In nuclear families, the same people who constitute the marital subsystem are also the parental subsystem. In remarried families, the parental subsystem may include stepparents as well as biological parents. The parental subsystem focuses on the interactions between parents and children.

The focus is on nurturing, teaching, and managing children's behavior. In some families, partners, grandparents, or aunts and uncles will be part of this subsystem. The diagnosis of a disability makes parenting roles more complicated, as the child's developmental course may be uncertain. Issues relating to developing independence and discipline also tax parental decision making.

Sibling Subsystem

The tasks of the sibling subsystem involve the socialization and development of the children. Although the longest and most enduring relationship in the family, sibling interactions seem to develop an ebb and flow of their own (Seligman & Darling, 2007). At a young age, children learn to share and take turn with their siblings. As they get older, siblings may rely on each other for advice and support or may drift apart.

Extrafamilial Subsystems

In addition to subsystems within the family, the family itself must interact with other systems and subsystems. Extrafamilial subsystems include extended family, friends, early intervention services, child care, school systems, and so on, which are a source of social and emotional support that can provide a variety of resources for the family. The extended family plays an important role in many families, frequently providing support for each other in a variety of ways such as babysitting, and emotional, or financial support.

Family Systems and the Family Life Cycle

Like the American family itself, the life cycle of the family changes as it responds to its members' entrances and exits. Looking at the family from a life-cycle perspective allows us to focus on some of the **stages** and transitions that most affect children with disabilities. The family systems perspective allows us to focus on the roles and relationships among family members and the family rules, boundaries, subsystems, and communication patterns within stages and transitions.

The family life-cycle perspective conceptualizes families as a system or unit of interacting individuals moving through time. The family experiences some periods of relative stability (stages) and other periods of change (transitions between stages). Some changes are relatively predictable; other changes such as discovering a child has a disability or an untimely death cannot be predicted. The family life cycle is one way of organizing information about the family.

Regardless of variations, this model focuses on the negotiation of underlying processes of family expansion, contraction, and the realignment of relationships to support the entry, exit, and development of family members in a functional way (Carter & McGoldrick, 1999). Another value of the family life-cycle approach is that it shows the different tasks family systems must accomplish at different times; how difficult it is to meet the needs of all the family members; and how patterns change based on the developmental needs of the family as family members interact with a changing society.

Some think of the family life cycle as a kind of dance. There are times when families are very close and other times when families open up to give their members more freedom or personal space. Childbirth is one of the coming-together times. Adolescence is an opening-up time.

The number of stages in the family life cycle varies with different scholars, different cultural and ethnic groups, and different families. The progression from one stage to the next is marked by change. Some change can be taken care of through flexibility or adaptation (Level I change). However, as the family moves through the life cycle, some changes require the family to approach things in new and different ways. The way they are currently doing things no longer works, regardless of how flexible the family is or how well they adapt (Level II or III change).

The family life cycle focuses on the addition of family members that changes young adults into parents, and parents become grandparents.
© Cengage Learning 2012

The traditional family life cycle focuses on **normative** changes. Because one focus of this text is on **nonnormative** events related to having a child with a disability it includes variations, such as discovering the child has a disability.

● ● ●

Families with Infants and Young Children

This stage of the family life cycle is characterized by adding a dependent member to the family. Becoming parents requires appending the role of parent to the role of partner. The adult moves up a generation and performs the task of caregiving for the young child.

TRANSITION TO PARENTHOOD

All family life-cycle transitions bring some accompanying stress, and the transition to parenthood is no exception. Becoming parents causes adults to clarify and reconsider the values and the decisions they made in young adulthood. The reality of the infant may be different from the expectation. A mother who initially planned to take a six-week leave from work and then place the infant in child care may decide that she does not want to leave her infant in the care of others. However, if she must go back to work, her situation becomes

stressful. Likewise, a mother who quits her job to be with the infant full-time may decide that full-time child care is not as fulfilling as she thought, and so she wants to return to work. As with all joint decisions, the partner may not have changed his thinking or may have changed in different directions.

The ability of the family to anticipate and respond to the ever-changing demands of an infant or young child is a central feature in this transition. For example, when a child with a disability is born, the family may have to modify previously workable rules to accommodate this new member. Families who have difficulty renegotiating rules may experience stress as they try to cope with the challenges they face. When the child's demands are ambiguous or if the family cannot meet the child's needs, families may become stressed. The challenge for the family is to synchronize the child's needs with the rhythm and pattern of the family (Newman, 2000). The family must also constantly adapt to the child's changing development. "First steps" bring joy but also require new vigilance, monitoring, and household adaptations. High demand for flexibility and change may result in parental role strain and stress.

DISCOVERING THE DISABILITY AT BIRTH

Parents are rarely told about their infant's condition in the delivery room, but they often get clues: hushed voices, questions not answered, and an overall air of concern. Newborns with disabilities often spend their first days, weeks, or even months in a neonatal intensive care unit (NICU) (Seligman & Darling, 2007). The monitors, tubes, and atmosphere make forming attachments challenging.

Reactions to having a child with a disability are highly individualistic and depend on the severity of the child's condition, supports available to the family, the family's culture, and other personal factors. One of the particular challenges in adjusting to the addition of a family member with disabilities relates to attachment. When medically fragile children hover between life and death, attachment is difficult. Others may find it difficult to respond to a child who is very different from the one they expected. The establishment of trust and attachment is important for later development. Parents may have to address painful issues of stigma and embarrassment. Sometimes parents themselves disagree about the appropriate path to take.

GRIEF CYCLE

Parents experience a variety of reactions when they learn their child has a disability. Many professionals see a "grief cycle" in which parents move through stages on their way to acceptance of the child. The exact stages, sequences, and the time spent in each stage are individualistic.

Most parents report feeling a sense of shock. Initially, they feel emotionally numb and may even show physical signs of shock. Shock often turns to denial; parents may deny the disability or the severity of it. For children who look "normal," this denial is easier and a way of buying time to adjust. It is psychologically highly adaptive; it cushions the blow and allows time for parents to gather their resources. Once reality is acknowledged, life will change.

Denial may be replaced by anxiety. Most adults feel anxious when facing an unknown situation. However, anxiety provides energy that may mobilize parents to find out what the diagnosis means, talk with other parents, and seek new information. As parents learn more, their reactions may move into fear, guilt, depression, and/or anger. Parents may feel angry with doctors, professionals, and even the infant himself. They may feel anger for the struggles that lie ahead for the child and for them. They want to know *why* and *how* it happened. For many families, these answers are unknown. To the extent that parents cannot find out why it happened, they cannot prevent it from happening again. If they plan to have more children, they know the risk is there.

Grieving may continue off and on throughout a child's life. This episodic process becomes especially strong at normal transition times such as birthdays, school entry, and at traditional times when families join for reunions. Seeing how easy certain things are for other children and how difficult they are for their child can bring back the tears or the anger. Even explaining the child's disability may activate the cycle for some parents. Rather than endure this, the family may reduce its social life and withdraw from all except medical associations within the community. There is disagreement about whether the goal of family acceptance is realistic. Perhaps a more realistic goal is for families to adjust to the reality of the disability in their own unique ways (Marshak & Prezant, 2007). One parent stated that you never reach "acceptance." You love your child, but you never quite accept the disability.

IN THE FIELD

We went to the hospital early one January morning to birth our third son. He was born quickly and uneventfully. However, there was an unusual quiet in the room after his birth. They didn't give him to me, but said something about cleaning him up and some other things I didn't grasp. They came back relatively soon and told us before we had time to make the first call announcing the birth that they thought our son had Down syndrome. I couldn't believe it. I was only 29 years old. How could this happen to us? The prenatal testing hadn't picked this up. They told us they needed to do additional testing to be sure. But they were sure. We talked before we made the calls to announce the birth of our son. We decided not to tell anyone about Dillon's probable diagnosis, reasoning that if people got to know him first, the disability would not influence their relationship.

IN THE FIELD

Our daughter Chelsea was born with a cleft palate. We were distressed and really wanted some support. We called my parents, as they were staying at our home with our oldest daughter. We told them about Chelsea's cleft palate and that although it would require several surgeries, she would be fine. My mother fainted and my father said to tell them before we brought Chelsea home so they could leave. They said they would come to see her in two years when she was "fixed." They live about a thousand miles away. In the two years after Chelsea's birth, they visited several times. They always stayed in a motel and had us drop Donna, Chelsea's older sister, off. I seethed with anger. On the one hand, I thought it was unfair of us to stop Donna from seeing her grandparents, but on the other hand I was resentful and hurt that my parents couldn't be there for Chelsea and me. It truly changed our relationship.

REFLECTIVE PRACTICE | Reflect on the experiences these two families had as they welcomed their newborns into their family. Think about how different disabilities and decisions affect the welcoming process and about how you might respond to a friend who gave birth to an infant with a disability. Would you visit and take presents or would you avoid the situation?

LATER DISCOVERY OF THE DISABILITY

For children whose disability is not identified at birth, a diagnosis is often made during early childhood. Initially, family members believe they have a typically developing infant. One parent may think something is wrong but is not sure. There is a sense of foreboding that is sometimes worse than knowing for sure that the child has a specific condition. Mothers are typically the first to sense difficulties, if the physician did not identify these at birth. Physicians and friends may attribute mothers' concerns to lack of experience or anxiety. Getting confirmation is often a long process, sometimes taking months or years. Sometimes, learning the child does have a disability is a relief; for example, parents may be relieved to find their child has a learning disability when their fear was an intellectual disability (Seligman & Darling, 2007).

Parents want an accurate diagnosis that helps them plan for a life with their child. Professionals vary in how they respond to parents' quest for this knowledge. Some focus on a worst-case scenario; others may try to be optimistic; and others are unwilling to make any prognosis without additional information. Parents have to decide whom and what to believe out of what they are told, consider what they know about their own child, and evaluate what they have learned on their own.

Parents adjust routines to include the care of all family members. The care for a child with a disability may be medically complicated and demanding. In the midst of day-to-day survival, personal fatigue, and self-doubt, many families identify positive contributions that the child and the disability bring to the family system. They become aware of individual and family strengths and value this opportunity for growth.

Parents make decisions about early intervention; specifically, what the most appropriate interventions are, given what is available; what is most useful to them; how much they can afford to pay; and what they see as the long- and short-term benefits. Parents are part of a team whose function is to develop the infant or toddler's Individualized Family Service Plan (IFSP). They decide on the role they want to take with the team and in what ways they want to participate, and they educate themselves about the disability and the service delivery systems.

The status of service delivery systems changes when a child reaches 36 months. Some children who were eligible for services from birth to age 3 may no longer meet eligibility criteria. However, for other children, where services were **discretionary** and may have to be paid for, they are now **mandated** and free. As services become more formalized, children often move from a home- or home/center-based approach to a center- or school-based system. This is a transition for children, parents, and service providers.

Siblings and extended family also have to cope with issues related to parental time and energy. Siblings of children with disabilities have many of the same feelings that parents do. They are proud of each accomplishment their sibling makes. At the same time, they may wonder why all this has happened to them and may be sad or angry about it. There may be times when they are embarrassed by their sibling. They may feel jealous of the extra attention she receives and yet feel guilty for having those feelings. All of these feelings are normal and expected. Although there will continue to be times when they are frustrated with their sibling (as with *any* brother or sister), most children learn to accept and love their sibling.

Siblings of children with disabilities have additional needs. They need information. They want to know what's going on. Parents, in an effort to "protect" them, often don't tell them very much. Limited or poor information adds to their confusion (Turnbull et al., 2006). If their brother or sister wears a hearing aid, they need to know why, how it works, and what it does to aid hearing.

Siblings need specific information about whether the disability is transmittable, how to talk to their friends about it, how to relate effectively to their sibling, and what family expectations are for their future role with their sibling with a disability. Despite what siblings are told, many have a private version of their sibling's disability and may feel that they are the cause of it (Seligman & Darling, 2007). Someone must learn about this private version and help siblings gain more accurate information about the causes of disabilities.

All children need time to develop friendships with peers. They also need private time with parents. If there are two parents in the family, each parent needs to spend some time alone with each child. Overburdening siblings with care responsibility can result in anger and resentment rather than acceptance. A child's sense of obligation for a sibling with disabilities can be a major concern and may require professional counseling. For the most part, siblings do not expect the situation to be "fixed"; they do, however, need a safe time and place to express their feelings and to be accepted (Seligman & Darling, 2007).

IN THE FIELD

My name is Kelly and I am 15 years old. My sister, Mara, is 6 and I really love her. Mara has a seizure disorder that really messes up her life and mine. I am glad that her seizures don't happen all the time. However, the thing that really bothers me is that Mara always has a seizure when something important is happening to me. I don't mind helping Mara, but sometimes she ruins everything.

One time, I was having a slumber party at my house when Mara began to have a seizure. She had to be taken to the hospital and then all my friends had to leave. Another time Mara had a seizure on my birthday and the whole family ended up spending the day in the hospital with her. Some birthday! We don't take family vacations any more because Mara might have a seizure.

I know I sound spoiled and mean, but she seems to get all the attention. Sometimes I am tired of being the big sister. I care about my sister and I want her to be well. It just seems like everything revolves around her. What about me?

Siblings may need specific support in developing their own identity. They may need the opportunity to talk with other siblings of children with disabilities. If one is available, they may want to be a part of a support group. Parents often think that siblings are coping much better than the siblings see themselves coping. Parents need to be aware of these possible differences in perception. Siblings need to be asked directly about their perceptions. Their parents cannot speak for them (Seligman & Darling, 2007).

IMPLICATIONS FOR EDUCATORS

Family members' feelings must be acknowledged as legitimate responses to difficult situations and should not be viewed as maladaptive. Parents who are in denial for long periods must be supported in gathering resources rather than confronted with their continuing inability to face up to the situation. Professionals must learn to cope with parents' anger, whether or not it is directed at them, and should provide families with a safety zone where feelings can be expressed. This is crucial as their informal support may be small. You may have siblings of children with disabilities in your class as well as children with disabilities. Find out what they have been told, what their questions are, and be a good, safe listener for them. Extended family and friends may stay away because they feel uncomfortable or don't know what to say, do, or ask. As children reach milestones such as school entry or changing service delivery systems, professionals should expect that there will be some grief associated with these marker events. This is not denial; it is grief.

●●●
Families with School-Age Children

Most children with disabilities enter school with some experience in early care and education settings. However, the transition to school is still a marker event. Depending upon the area, there may be a variety of placement options. Parents, as part of the Individualized Educational Program (IEP) team, learn about these options and decide which one is the best for their child and family.

If children enter a public school, parents must learn to work with the school and the bureaucracies inherent in that system. As children become part of a school system, families often become more active members of the community in which they live. They must locate community resources to arrange for after-school care, if needed, and decide on their child's extracurricular activities. These may entail extra expenses associated with their child's disability, such as tutoring or additional therapy.

IN THE FIELD

Please don't judge me. You may only have partial information. When my son was in elementary school, I volunteered to help the school nurse. During a major project, she needed to call me at home frequently, for input. Well . . . she would call at 10:00 or 11:00 A.M. and wake me up. She joked about my leisurely lifestyle. She later confided that she felt I was lazy. What she didn't know was that my autistic son rarely slept through the night. He would be up at all hours of the night (coming into my room at 2 A.M. to ask where his jeans were!).

Parents are adjusting emotionally to the educational implications for their child, both in the present and for the long term. Many parents worry about how their child will be treated by peers, whether he will make friends and be included as part of the group. Siblings need to be supported in finding the appropriate words and concepts to share with their friends. There may be continuing concerns related to jealousy and the limited time or money available for leisure and recreation (Seligman & Darling, 2007).

IMPLICATIONS FOR EDUCATORS

Educators must remember that even though families have been living with their children for about 5 years, they may cycle into a stage of denial as they approach a marker event such as entering kindergarten. For some families, elementary school will just be an extension of preschool services, whereas others will see it as a major hurdle. For most parents, school and performance at school create a new perspective on, and understanding of, their child's disability. This may be a difficult time for parents as they cope with these new understandings.

Parents may be wary of you, the teacher, and wonder whether you have the skill and ability to educate their child, particularly if you teach in an inclusive classroom and parents have come from a more segregated setting. Parents need your assurance that their child will be safe and that you will support their child's academic and social growth.

It is not unusual to discover that what parents and educators want for children is different. Educators need to think through these differences before approaching parents. It is imperative that families decide what is important to them and the areas in which they want to focus; early childhood professionals must frame parents' focus in a developmentally appropriate way (Turnbull et al., 2005).

• • •
Families with Adolescents

As children move into adolescence, families must evaluate and establish qualitatively different boundaries than they used when children were younger. Adolescents need freedom with guidance. They want to be like their peers, thus parental authority is often challenged. Adolescence is more complex when families have children with disabilities.

For parents in this stage of the family life cycle, the tasks involve adjusting emotionally to the possible chronic nature of the disability, the permanence of the disability, and the possible permanence of the adolescent's dependency (Lambie, 2000).

Parents must arrange for leisure activities that are age appropriate and within the adolescent's ability range. This is also a time when parents begin planning for career and vocational development and/or postsecondary education. By this time, siblings have a better understanding of the disability and its long-term implications. For many siblings, life goals and career choices may be affected by having a sibling with a disability. Many go into fields such as teaching and social work (Seligman & Darling, 2007).

IMPLICATIONS FOR EDUCATORS

Families with adolescents are beyond the age range that early childhood educators teach. However, it is important to keep in mind that children do grow up and, as we look at behaviors and skills, we need to keep this long-term view in mind. The behavior that is cute in a young child could place an older child at risk. Our role is to prepare all children for the life they will lead when they leave school. When children have disabilities, we should talk with parents about their expectations for their children, and plan for children to acquire the skills they will need. The transition from school to work is one of the most difficult ones families will face.

Each stage of the family life cycle brings with it a unique set of decisions that have to be made. As the age of majority is reached, individuals and families have a new set of decisions thrust upon them. Decisions made by early childhood special educators and children's families have implications for their quality of life in later years. Viewing the family from the family life-cycle systems perspective highlights some of the tasks families must perform at various stages, how these tasks change over time, and how a child with disabilities affects these tasks.

Tasks, obligations, and expectations vary with **sociohistorical time** as feelings about educating children with disabilities and the role of the family change. It is not possible to educate young children without taking into account what is happening in the world. What we know about disabilities and what is considered "best practice" changes. Today, best practice emphasizes natural environments, honors children's ethnic/cultural background, and is family centered.

Partnering with Families and Honoring Their Culture

The United States is a multiracial, multicultural, and multilingual society. This has to be acknowledged before effective strategies for interacting with diverse families can evolve. When trying to understand diversity, it is easy to overgeneralize and oversimplify differences. Not all members of an ethnic group are alike in the way they embrace their culture's lifestyle and values (Lambie, 2000). This section is not designed to be an exhaustive view of these cultures, but is intended to raise your awareness of the importance of recognizing cultural and ethnic differences and how they influence your work with families and their children. All parents have goals and expectations for their children. However, differences in parental goals and expectations arise because of varying cultural and societal expectations. We as educators need to be mindful of these differences as we interact with families and educate their children.

Their cultural background influences families' views. What we think, how we act, the language we speak, and even what we eat are part of our wider cultural context. Looking at cultural diversity is a balance between appreciating our common humanity and validating the differences among us.

• • •
Working with Families in a Cultural Context

Language, rituals, rules, and beliefs are not developed in a vacuum, but are part of the cultural heritage handed down to people through the family. Culture is a way of life, a blueprint for living. It is both learned and internalized by being part of a particular culture (Berger, 2004). All children come to educational settings with a cultural background and must be understood within this context.

Although the overall percentage of children in the United States population is decreasing, the proportion of children from non–European American populations is increasing. Knowledge of culture has to be both generalized and individualized. To be culturally sensitive, you as a prospective teacher must accomplish several tasks:

1. Conduct a cultural self-assessment. Take a close look at your culture and how it has shaped your values and beliefs, because you view children and their families through this lens. Become aware of the biases you hold. An awareness of your culture and its values increases the probability of becoming a culturally sensitive person who can validate the differences among people and appreciate their commonality (Lynch, 2004a; McGoldrick, 1993).

2. Learn about the communities in which families live. Gather and analyze **ethnographic** information about the cultural community. Meet families in their space. Recognize and understand the dynamics of difference. Culture contributes to obvious and subtle differences in individuals and communities. Obvious differences include such things as the language spoken, amount of eye contact, and body language used, whereas more subtle aspects of culture may influence the amount of self-disclosure someone is comfortable with. Avoid stereotyping (Lynch, 2004b).

3. Determine the degree to which the family operates **transculturally**. Child-rearing practices are designed to socialize children into their family and culture. Daily caregiving routines reflect a family's fundamental, deeply felt values and beliefs. Because children absorb their culture as part of the caregiving process, early care and education is important to parents. Child-rearing practices may provide a key to understanding socialization practices in different cultural contexts. If early care and education reflects only the values of the dominant culture, parents may be concerned about the practices used. Children may be deprived of a part of their culture, or they may experience inexplicable discontinuity between home and the educational setting. Examine each family's orientation to specific child-rearing issues while acknowledging and valuing diversity. There are cultural differences and these differences play a role in what families believe about children with disabilities and how they should be reared (Lynch, 2004b).

• • •
Acquiring Cultural Knowledge

Learning about different cultures is an ongoing process. Many books describe different ethnic groups, with some focusing on practices that relate to early childhood and children with disabilities (Lynch & Hanson, 2004). These serve as the foundation for building knowledge about individual families. See Table 2–1 for more specific information.

The next step with cultural knowledge is using the information and insights acquired to adapt educational practices to meet the needs of children and their families. This may challenge you to expand your definition of family to include grandparents and various significant others in conferences. Focus on the strengths that a particular cultural background brings to children with disabilities, and work with the strengths and priorities that families have set.

TABLE 2-1   ACQUIRING CULTURAL KNOWLEDGE

- *Reason for immigration.* What was the family seeking or leaving behind? Were they fleeing from political persecution, poverty, or war? Were they brought against their will as slaves?

- *Length of time since immigration.* How many generations has the family been in the United States?

- *Place of residence.* Does the family live in an ethnic neighborhood?

- *Order of migration.* Did the family come as a unit or did one member come first and others join later?

- *Socioeconomic status.* What is the socioeconomic status of the family and what are their attitudes toward education and upward mobility?

- *Religiosity.* What are the family's religious and political ties?

- *Language.* What languages do family members speak and what are their levels of comfort and fluency in different languages?

- *Intermarriage.* To what extent do family members have connections to other ethnic groups and how frequently have intermarriages occurred?

- *Attitudes.* What are the family members' attitudes toward their ethnic identity and its values?

Source: McGoldrick, 1993.

Answer the same cultural knowledge questions about yourself. Talk with family members if you are not sure about some of the answers.

IMPLICATIONS FOR EDUCATORS

Think about your personal background, your beliefs, and what this means in the classroom. If a child with a disability comes from a family who is poor and/or who speaks English haltingly, or the parents have little formal education, does that influence your expectations for their child? How will you support difference, not deficit; look for strength, not weakness? Many have had the strength to survive situations we cannot even imagine. How will you see families as a resource and not a liability?

Cultural Diversity in the United States

The cultural composition of the United States is becoming increasingly diverse. The projection for 2025 shows that 33 percent of the population will be from diverse racial/ethnic backgrounds and by 2050 they will compose 36 percent (U.S. Census Bureau, 2008a). The United States has approximately 311 million people (U.S. Census Bureau, 2011). There are six main groups of racial/ethnic families in the United States: white (non-Hispanic), Hispanic, black or African American, Asian, Native Hawaiian and Other Pacific Islander, and American Indian and Alaska Natives. People from other races and those who identify as having two or more races constitute 9 percent of the population (U.S. Census Bureau, 2010a) (see Table 2–2). In many ways, these groups are more similar than dissimilar to the dominant family forms that exist in the larger U.S. society. Children receive their basic identity and status within the family context. Some parents subscribe to the basic achievement and mobility values that exist within the larger society; others do not. A major concern is that children from minority cultures are disproportionately identified as having disabilities (IDEA, 2004).

TABLE 2-2   PROJECTED RATES OF POPULATION CHANGE IN THE UNITED STATES FROM NATURAL INCREASE AND MIGRATION: 2010–2050

Percent of Total Population	2010			2030			2050		
	Natural Increase	Migration		Natural Increase	Migration		Natural Increase	Migration	
White alone, not Hispanic	1.3 +	3.6 =	4.9	−1.1 +	3.7 =	2.6	−2.9 +	3.9 =	1.0
Hispanic (of any race)	17.7 +	13.5 =	31.2	14.8 +	9.8 =	24.6	8.7 +	7.7 =	16.4
Black alone	8.0 +	3.2 =	11.2	5.4 +	3.3 =	8.7	3.6 +	3.6 =	7.2
Asian alone	7.5 +	21.3 =	28.8	3.9 +	17.7 =	21.6	1.4 +	15.4 =	16.8
Two or more races	29.4 +	3.0 =	32.4	24.8 +	9.8 =	34.6	21.1 +	7.7 =	28.8

Source: U.S. Census Bureau, 2008a.

Demographers attribute the rising percentage of minority children to higher birth rates among nonwhite, non-Anglo women; increased immigration; and more women of childbearing age in the nonwhite groups. Early childhood special educators must develop cross-cultural competence, so they can better educate these diverse groups of children (Lynch, 2004a). To confirm these trends, see Table 2–3 for figures on the population younger than age 18 and the **median** ages.

There are elements of **individualism** and **collectivism** in all cultures. The dominant United States culture, and its schools, are extremely individualistic. Individualism emphases personal success and values such thing as hard work, intelligence, and "standing out." Collectivism focuses on successful relations with others, group values, and "fitting in" (Trumbull et al., 2001). To the extent that the family culture and the school culture vary on these dimensions, teachers will have to bridge the cultures.

The following brief sketches provide some demographic information that is relevant to your teaching. The resources at the end of the chapter and the references at the back of the book can help you locate additional information. It is useful to start with a common understanding of terminology. A **racial** group is a socially defined group distinguished by selected, inherited physical characteristics. African Americans and American Indians are racial designations according to census data. An **ethnic** group is distinguished by a sense of peoplehood or "consciousness of kind" based on a common national origin, religion, or language. Hispanic is an ethnic designation. Hispanics can be of any race. When race and ethnicity are separated most Hispanics (91%) chose white as their racial designation (U.S. Census Bureau, 2008a). If a racial or ethnic group is subordinate to the majority in terms of power and prestige (not necessarily in terms of number of members), members occupy a **minority** status as well (Eshleman, 2000).

• • • Latino Families

Latino families constitute the largest ethnic minority in the United States (Humes, Jones, & Ramirez, 2011). Hispanics, or Latinos, are people of Mexican, Puerto Rican, South or Central American, or other Spanish culture or origin regardless of race. Latinos include people from all countries in Latin America as well as parts of the Caribbean that have Latin-based languages. (*Note*: The words *Latino* and *Hispanic* are used interchangeably in this text.) They do not share a common racial background. The population is young, diverse, dynamic, and growing rapidly. They are a community of first-, second-, and third-generation immigrants, many of whom have uprooted their families and left their homes and relatives for economic, political, professional, ideological, and educational reasons (Carrasquillo, Lantigua, & Shea, 2000).

TABLE 2-3   ANNUAL ESTIMATES OF THE POPULATION BY AGE AND ETHNIC/RACIAL CHARACTERISTICS FOR THE UNITED STATES: JULY 1, 2009

Race	Younger Than Age 18	Percent	Older Than Age 18	Percent	Median Age
White	41,225,410	(20%)	158,625,830	(80%)	41
Hispanic	16,750,075	(35%)	31,669,674	(65%)	27
Black	11,280,366	(28%)	28,360,249	(72%)	31
Asian	3,307,272	(24%)	10,706,682	(76%)	35
American Indian/ Alaska Native	951,329	(30%)	2,199,955	(70%)	30
Native Hawaiian/ Pacific Islander	172,985	(30%)	405,368	(70%)	30

Source: U. S. Census Bureau, Population Estimates, 2009b.

Others are descendants of the native Mexicans who lived in the southwest before it became part of the United States. See Table 2–4 for additional information about Latinos and their families.

The number of Latino families with young children is increasing. The way their family embraces their culture will influence the food they eat, the values they have, and the languages they speak.

In the past, minority families were strongly encouraged to **assimilate** to be accepted. Assimilation required adopting U.S. customs and language as a way of being accepted and ignoring or not identifying with one's home culture. **Acculturation** is different; it signifies the adoption of the values of the host country but does not demand that cultural values be dropped. Typically, this means learning English and accepting and promoting American ideals (Halgunseth, 2004). The third option is **biculturalism. Bicultural adaptation** incorporates aspects of the home culture with the mainstream culture. Rather than replacing the home culture (existing cultural values and behaviors), mainstream values and information are added to it. Bicultural people can function in both the home culture and the majority culture (Halgunseth, 2004). Families and settings can support bicultural adaptation by teaching children about their ethnic identity and about the special experiences they may encounter because of their ethnic background. This approach is related to higher self-esteem and proactive styles of coping with discrimination (Halgunseth, 2004).

Most Hispanic families have high family cohesion and flexibility. Family is important to them and they frequently have supportive kin networks. Many families have a strong ethnic identity and, despite the stereotypes, most have egalitarian decision making.

Like African American families, they face many challenges. A primary challenge is increasing their level of

Children grow up in families and the culture of the family influences the language they speak and the foods they eat.
Penny Low Deiner

education and overcoming economic discrimination to gain financial resources. Less than half of the foreign-born Latino population comes with a high school diploma (Hernandez, 2006).

Many children from Latino families do not do well in U.S. schools. Home values may support relationships and interdependence (collectivism), whereas the school culture values independence (individualism), achievement, and self-expression (Trumbull et al., 2001). Over 20 percent of U.S. children between the ages of birth and 8 are Hispanic. Although many are from immigrant homes, about 90 percent

TABLE 2-4 STATISTICS AND DEMOGRAPHICS ABOUT LATINOS AND THEIR FAMILIES

- Latinos constitute the largest ethnic minority in the United States, with an estimated population of 51 million in 2010 (Humes, Jones, & Ramirez, 2011), 16 percent of the U.S. population (U.S. Census Bureau, 2010a).

- Between 2000 and 2010, the Hispanic growth rate increased by 43 percent while the non-Hispanic population increased by 5 percent (U.S. Census Bureau, 2010a).

- Over half of the growth in the total U.S. population between 2000 and 2010 was due to an increase in the Hispanic population (Humes et al., 2011).

- The median income of Latino families was $38,039 in 2009, whereas for all U.S. families it was $49,777 (U.S. Census Bureau, 2010b). Puerto Ricans (all of whom are U.S. citizens) have the lowest median family income, with 45 percent living below the poverty line in 2009 (U.S. Census Bureau, 2008–2009).

- Sixty-five percent of Hispanic children under age 6, 4.2 million children, lived in low-income families in 2009, with 35 percent living in poor families (Chau, Thampi, & Wright, 2010).

- With a median age of 27 compared to whites median of 41, the Latino population is the youngest. They also have the highest percentage of any ethnic/racial group of their population younger than age 18 (35%) (U.S. Census Bureau, 2009b).

- Sixty percent of Latinos living in the United States were born here and 40 percent were foreign born (U.S. Census Bureau, 2010a).

- More Latinos (32%) were without health insurance coverage in 2009 than any other racial/ethnic group (U.S. Census Bureau, 2010b).

- Most (68%) Hispanic children live in two-parent families, with 28 percent living in single-parent families. When no parents were present, 43 percent of Hispanic children lived with grandparents (Kreider, 2008).

- Approximately 20 percent of the people in the United States speak a language other than English at home. Of this 20 percent, about 12 percent speak Spanish or Spanish Creole, and about half of these speakers speak English less than "very well" (U.S. Census Bureau, 2009a).

of the children are U.S. citizens. Hispanic children are five times *more* likely to have a mother who did not graduate from high school and three times *less* likely to have a mother who is a college graduate then white children (Hernandez, 2006). Hispanic children, particularly those from disadvantaged circumstances, lag behind non-Hispanic whites on measures of school readiness and school achievement. High-quality early childhood programs and the use of both Spanish and English in these programs contribute to greater school readiness for these children (National Task Force on Early Childhood Education for Hispanics, 2007).

The extended family plays an important role in Latino families. Siblings, cousins, and other relatives provide a support network to families with young children. The overall attitude toward children is one of acceptance, putting less pressure on them to achieve milestones early. One marries to have children and children validate a marriage (Zuniga, 2004). Latinos tend to be nurturing and permissive in early childhood. Because of family values, mothers are expected to stay home and raise children, so young Latino children are less likely to be in early care and education settings. When this is not possible, extended family frequently takes over the care of young children. Some families may see sending young children to an early care and education setting as a sign of deteriorating family values. They may need home-based intervention with a bilingual/bicultural intervention-ist. Once trust is established, they may also feel comfortable in a home/center-based service delivery system.

Latino parenting styles foster interdependence and relational learning, whereas European American parents emphasize independence and self-initiated learning. Children with disabilities may receive special treatment from their families (Zuniga, 2004). They may come to school with fewer **adaptive skills**. The major strategy that Latino parents use in teaching is modeling. If there are older siblings, they may serve as models for teaching younger children (Halgunseth, 2004). If a Latino parent was teaching a 5-year-old to set the table, she would demonstrate how to do it and where the different utensils, cups, and plates go. A European American parent would use inquiry: "Where do you think the plate goes?" Then, if the child placed the plate in the right spot, the parent would be likely to say, "Great, you did that all by yourself." Because of their view of modeling as a way of teaching, Hispanics may talk less to their children, so young Latino children may not hear as much language as others.

Maintaining harmonious relationships is important to most Latino parents. They support the development of interpersonal skills in their children. They want others to enjoy their children and find them pleasant. Negative emotions such as aggression, anger, and arguing are often distressing. They also monitor body language and facial expressions more than European American parents. Being well educated includes not only the traditional three R's, but also a sense of inner importance that includes tranquility, obedience, and courtesy. Some of these skills may make them more passive and dependent upon adult authority (Halgunseth, 2004).

IN THE FIELD

I spent about four months in Costa Rica, doing research and working with families who had young children with disabilities. Because I was in Latin America, I was more conscious of issues relating to culture, but it was still hard to figure out how to get some of the services I thought a child needed. I would talk with the families about what they could do for their young children, but they often did not follow through. Many mothers felt that it was a wiser use of their time to spend a half hour in church on their knees praying for their child than to use that time working with the child or going to occupational therapy. I just did not understand it.

There are many distinctive differences among Hispanic populations. Only a few of these will be highlighted, but the differences are so great that it is important to know what specific group you are learning about and what aspects of the culture the people you are working with embrace.

MEXICAN AMERICAN FAMILIES

People of Mexican heritage made up 60 percent of the Latino population in the United States in 2006 (U.S. Census Bureau, 2010a). Over 1 million Mexican Americans are descendants of the native Mexicans who lived in the southwest and became U.S. citizens in 1848, when Arizona, California, Colorado, Nevada, New Mexico, and parts of Oklahoma, Texas, Utah, and Wyoming became U.S. territory. There was also large-scale migration from Mexico in the early 1900s, caused by the chaos of the Mexican Revolution and the demand for labor on cotton farms and railroads in California. The devaluation of the Mexican peso in 1994 contributed to migration. Mexicans make up over half (57%; over 5 million people) of undocumented immigrants in the United States (Passel, Capps, & Fix, 2004).

High fertility rates and strong family ties typify the Mexican American culture. Mexican Americans often live near nuclear and extended family members and share interests and concerns about the welfare of the family system. The needs of the family may supersede the needs of individual family members. The theme of family honor and unity is strong throughout Mexican American society irrespective of social class or geographic location.

Godparents play an important role in Mexican American families. Traditionally, expectant parents select a patrón, a married couple, or an extended family member to be the child's sponsor. This is considered both an honor and an obligation. The baptism ceremony establishes a social bond and godparents are thought of as being co-parents. The relationship is expected to last a lifetime, although this tradition is less strong than it has been in the past (Halgunseth, 2004).

In the past, Mexican Americans adhered to the traditional ideal of manliness (*machismo*), equated with authority, strength, sexual virility, and prowess. The male was the patriarch who made important decisions, as well as the provider and protector for his family. Today, decision making is becoming more egalitarian. In general, however, Mexican American males still exert power over their wives, and the women still do the majority of child care and household tasks. Mexican American families have a high fertility rate and have an average of 3.2 children (National Center for Health Statistics [NCHS], 2000). Fathers show a definite interest in their children and their behavior. Given the size of the family, along with minimal skills and low levels of income, it is often difficult for Mexican American families to live above the poverty line. Low levels of parental education confound this. About 66 percent of fathers and 64 percent of mothers did not graduate from high school, and about 40 percent completed only 8 years of formal education (Hernandez, 2006).

PUERTO RICAN FAMILIES

Puerto Rican families are the second-largest Latino subgroup, comprising 9 percent of the Latino population in 2006 (U.S. Census Bureau, 2010a). All Puerto Ricans are U.S. citizens. In the continental United States, families are heavily concentrated in eastern cities, especially New York City. Many have low-paying full-time jobs, part-time jobs, or sometimes no job at all. Males came to work in manufacturing jobs that required little education and few skills. However, in today's economy there are few such jobs.

More than other Hispanic groups, Puerto Ricans form families without marriage and have a high proportion (60%) of female-headed households. This poses challenges to these families. See Table 2–5 for ways of working with children with disabilities in Latino families.

IMPLICATIONS FOR EDUCATORS

Latino children may come to school with good language skills in both languages or with only rudimentary knowledge of English or Spanish. Communicating with Latino families who have limited English proficiency (LEP) may be challenging. Some families that speak Spanish may not read it. If the parents speak little or no English, try to have bilingual/bicultural support for parent–teacher conferences, and translate forms that are to be

sent home. However, translating forms may not solve the problem; Spanish has many dialects, just as English does. Additionally, there are some words families may not know in their home language that they have learned in English. Think about the IFSP or the IEP, whose concepts are based in U.S. law. Understanding the words does not convey the underlying concept, so a word-for-word translation does not suffice. Learn about families' cultures to enrich the curriculum, but also look at the values of individualism and collectivism and how you might use this understanding to bridge cultures.

Think about how you feel about immigration and immigrants—both legal and illegal—and how this might impact your practice. Also think about what you know about different Hispanic cultures and how you can include what you know in working with families and curriculum planning. Use the Resources at the end of this chapter and the section in the children's bibliography on *Latino Families and Children* to enhance cultural interactions with the children you teach.

This is just an overview for you to begin to think about children at risk and those with disabilities and how families are both similar and different. You cannot assume that because a family's members came from Latin America they will all have the values and beliefs discussed. Work with families to determine what they want for themselves and their children.

African American Families

African Americans have a rich heritage with a strong sense of family, community, and culture. Blacks or African Americans are people who have their origins in any of the black racial groups of Africa (Humes et al., 2011). (The terms *black* and *African American* are used interchangeably in this text.) Because of their unique historical and social experiences, many African Americans have lifestyles and values that differ considerably from those of the white majority. The development of their domestic units took many different paths (Tucker,

TABLE 2-5 IMPLICATIONS FOR WORKING WITH LATINO FAMILIES AND THEIR CHILDREN

- Discover the language skills, cultural characteristics, and values that affect children's learning and cognitive development.
- Evaluate your experience with culturally diverse people, especially those who speak English as a second language and those who have immigrated illegally.
- Assess your style of interacting with others, especially with regard to how you think about time. If you stress time pressure during your interactions and insist that decisions must be made *now*, families may interpret this as a lack of respect or concern.
- Learn to pronounce the children's names as the family does. Do not Americanize names unless the family requests that you do so. Talk to the children.
- Appreciate the opportunity you have been given to broaden your global knowledge and to look at your culture from another perspective. Learn some of the language the family uses, and appreciate the challenge they face learning English. Honor and value children's home language.
- Find out from families what they want for their children. Some families want children to be respectful, polite, and loving and are less concerned

- about independent thinking and problem-solving skills than are most European Americans.
- Have a culturally rich classroom that includes many artifacts and activities from children's home cultures and teaches the value of respecting others and their differences.
- Find out what families believe about the cause of their child's disability. They may believe it is a result of evil in the environment, a curse, a punishing God, or something else (and the child may be wearing an amulet to ward off the evil).
- Include someone who is Latina and bilingual on an IFSP/IEP team.
- Do not assume that families who speak Spanish and/or English can also read it. They may have learned words in English, particularly in relation to their child, that they have never seen or heard in Spanish.
- Learn more about the Latino culture in general, as well as the specific country/culture from which the families come. Attend Latin American community celebrations and watch films from and about Latin America. Identify community resources that are responsive to and supportive of Latinos in general and specific nationalities in particular.

Source: Halgunseth, 2004; Zuniga, 2004; Carrasquillo et al., 2000.

Subramanian, & James, 2004). See Table 2–6 for additional information.

The migration of African Americans from rural to urban areas has followed the general population trend. More than half of African Americans live in the South, and with the exception of California, there are fewer African Americans in the West. African American families, like white families, fit no one stereotypical view. Most do well and thrive, with increasing numbers completing their education and entering the work force (Willis, 2004). Strengths such as strong family ties, flexibility in family roles, and caring parenting give some families and their young children with disabilities a strong support network. Most African American families have a strong work motivation as well as a strong religious orientation. The African American family is an absorbing, adaptive, flexible, and amazingly resilient mechanism for the socialization of its children and survival in society (Tucker et al., 2004).

African American families face challenges based on the history of racism and discrimination in the United States. Major disparities still exist between blacks and whites. A persistent problem is that of black females finding partners. Because black males experience higher rates of unemployment and underemployment, it is difficult to attain a family income level that allows them to provide adequately for their families. When families (regardless of ethnicity) are constantly worrying about financial problems, they have less time and energy to devote to their children. Early childhood education can make a difference for some of these children.

REFLECTIVE PRACTICE | High-quality early childhood education works and it lasts; yet 95 percent of public investment in education occurs for children ages 5 and older. How would you convince people of the importance of investing in high-quality early care and education? What would you say about the social and economic gains? The prevention of crime and special education? The benefits for families and African American children at risk?

Although African American families are primarily nuclear families, they often have a strong social support network. Such a support system is important to families who have children with disabilities, particularly as 54 percent of black children live in single-parent families, with 38 percent living in two-parent families. When no parent is present, 61 percent of African American children live with grandparents (Kreider, 2008). Relatives, particularly grandmothers, form a significant part of the social support network. The importance of religion in family life at all social levels is another difference between African American and white populations. The religious community provides a social life for African American families as well as giving emotional support.

Within African American families, the typical adult pattern is egalitarian relationships where roles are flexible and tasks are often interchanged. Parents are often more authoritarian than in white families and encourage independence and self-sufficiency earlier. Many African American women value childbearing and child rearing as a validation of their womanhood. Education is valued for upward mobility. Most women work either out of necessity or out of desire to enhance family income. Some African Americans are asking for their differences as well as their similarities to be acknowledged and encouraged.

IMPLICATIONS FOR EDUCATORS

Like Latino families, some African American families embrace the values and lifestyles described, whereas others do not. Learn from the families you work with what is important to them. Knowing a person's culture does not mean you can predict his or her behavior (Gonzalez-Mena, 2005). Use the resources at the end of the chapter and the section in the children's bibliography on *African American Families and Children* to enrich your classroom with literature about African American families and their culture. Develop a plan for learning more about African American families and their children. Reflect on your own comfort in working with African American children.

THE EVIDENCE BASE

A 40-year follow-up study identified differences in African American children who attended a high-quality preschool and those who did not. From 1962 through 1967, at ages 3 and 4, 123 African Americans born in poverty and at risk for failing in school were divided into two groups. The Perry Group received high-quality preschool education based on the High/Scope model, whereas the control group received no preschool program. Of the 123 people, 97 percent were located and interviewed at age 40. See Figure 2–1.

TABLE 2-6   STATISTICS AND DEMOGRAPHICS ABOUT AFRICAN AMERICANS AND THEIR FAMILIES

- African Americans are the second largest distinct racial/ethnic group in the United States, numbering about 40 million; 13 percent of the U.S. population (U.S. Census Bureau, 2010a).
- Between 2000 and 2010, the African American growth rate increased by 12 percent (U.S. Census Bureau, 2010a).
- The median income for black American families was $32,584 in 2009 (U.S. Census Bureau, 2010b).
- Blacks have a median age of 31 compared to whites, whose median age is 41 (U.S. Census Bureau, 2010a).
- Of the black population, 28 percent is younger than 18 years, as compared to 20 percent of whites and 35 percent of Latinos (U.S. Census Bureau, 2009b).

- Sixty-seven percent of black children lived in single-parent households in 2009 (Annie E. Casey Foundation, 2010).
- Sixty-six percent of black children under age 6, 2.3 million, lived in low-income families in 2009, with 41 percent living in poor families (Chau, Thampi, & Wright, 2010).
- The poverty rate for blacks was 26 percent in 2009 (DeNavas-Walt, Proctor, Smith, U.S. Census Bureau, 2010).
- Sixty-two percent of black children lived in families with secure parental employment in 2005 (Federal Interagency Forum on Child and Family Statistics, 2007).
- Twenty-one percent of African Americans were without health insurance coverage in 2009 (U.S. Census Bureau, 2010b).

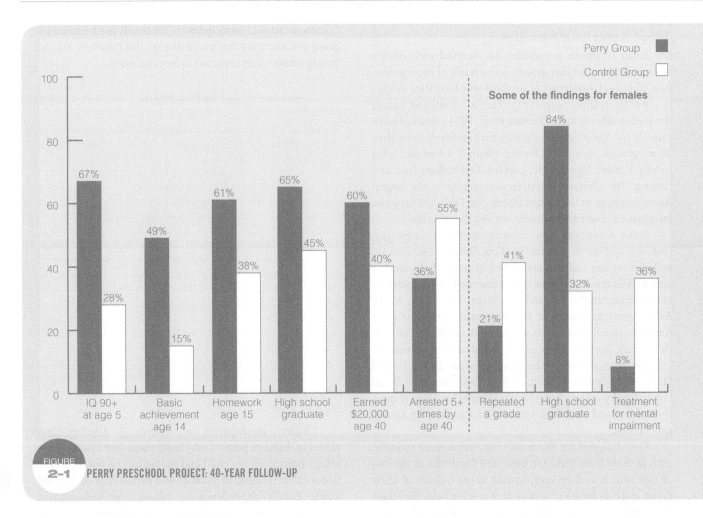

FIGURE 2-1 PERRY PRESCHOOL PROJECT: 40-YEAR FOLLOW-UP

Overall, the study documents a return to society of more than $16 for every tax dollar invested in quality early care and education. "These findings can be expected of any Head Start, state preschool, or child care program similar to the program High/Scope coordinated and then studied. Our teachers were well qualified; they served no more than eight children from low-income families at a time; they visited these families as part of the program to discuss their child's development; and the classes operated daily for children 3 and 4 years old," said Larry Schweinhart, High/Scope president (Perry Study, 2004; Perry Preschool Study, 2005).

As you learn more about African American culture, incorporate this knowledge into your teaching. Examine your teaching materials. Do you have stories about African American children and representative dolls available? When you discuss families, do you include a wide range of family configurations, including multigenerational families, those who have others living with them, single-parent families, and those with working mothers? Use the information in Table 2–7 to work with African American families.

TABLE 2-7 IMPLICATIONS FOR WORKING WITH AFRICAN AMERICAN FAMILIES WHO HAVE CHILDREN WITH DISABILITIES

- Value the strengths of kinship bonds and include extended family members.
- Work with the family's informal support network (friends, neighbors, church) whenever possible.
- Begin by addressing people formally (Ms. Waples) until the person asks you to change the form of address.
- Learn about the family's beliefs and situation relative to health and medical care, and make suggestions that are congruent with their beliefs.

- Learn about resources in the African American community.
- Evaluate assessment results with an awareness of potential bias in the assessment itself and the assessment process.
- Honor the home language of the family and child while emphasizing the importance of Standard English.
- Avoid stereotyping.
- Include African American specialists on IFSP/IEP teams.
- Learn more about African American culture by talking and reading about it.

Source: Tucker et al., 2004; Willis, 2004.

• • •
Asian American Families

The Asian American population has doubled each decade since 1970. Most of this growth is the result of immigration (see Table 2–2). Asian people are those who have their origins in any of the original people of the Far East, Southeast Asia or the Indian subcontinent (Humes et al., 2011). Asian Americans are not a homogeneous group; they represent more than 28 subgroups, including Chinese, Filipino, Japanese, Asian Indian, Korean, Vietnamese, Laotian, Cambodian, Thai, and Hmong. The Chinese American community is the largest Asian subgroup in the United States. See Table 2–8 for more information about Asian Americans and their families.

Asian Americans have different ancestors, languages, customs, and recency of immigration. The Chinese, Korean, and Vietnamese cultures are rooted in some of the world's oldest civilizations and have been influenced by the doctrines of Confucianism, Taoism, and Buddhism (Chan & Lee, 2004). Asian Americans marry at the same rate as the European American population (82%), and there is a high level of family stability. They are better educated and have higher median incomes than all other ethnic/racial groups in the United States (U.S. Census Bureau, 2007). Their strengths lie in family loyalty and a strong family orientation. They respect their elders and have high levels of mutual support among generations.

One challenge for those who have come more recently, such as those from Vietnam, Laos, and Cambodia, is the loss of ties with kin. They may distrust those outside of their group and may have a stigma against seeking help. They have high expectations for themselves and very high academic expectations for their children, with a strong emphasis on self-control (Ishii-Kuntz, 2004).

Overall, Asian Americans value family highly and tend to solve problems within the family settings. Family needs and interdependence often have precedence over individual needs and independence. Family ties are close, divorce rates are low, and there are fewer female-headed households. As a culture they avoid open confrontation and are unlikely to challenge educators, even if they disagree with them.

Communication is often indirect. The family is a harmonious group and anything that might disrupt this harmony, such as strong emotions, is expected to be suppressed.

IN THE FIELD

I had a difficult labor with our youngest son. I was in my 40s and the pregnancy was unexpected. I thought I was having menopause early and didn't seek medical care until I was about four and a half months pregnant. When Yong was born, the doctor pulled my husband aside and talked to him. When I asked him about it, he said it was nothing. I was exhausted and was just pleased to see our third son. When we left the hospital, I thought everything was fine. As I cared for Yong, I thought he was different from the other two boys, but then I decided that maybe I was just remembering wrong. He seemed floppy and less alert than they had been. I began to get concerned and talked to our pediatrician, who was also Chinese. He told me not to worry.

My mother-in-law lives two houses away, and finally she voiced some of my concerns when Yong was about 2. I also talked to my husband. He told me that the doctor had told him Yong had Down syndrome, and he had asked both the doctor and the pediatrician not to tell me. In my culture, my mother-in-law would have blamed me for the disability. It would have been my fault—something I had done. My husband did not want to have that friction in his family. He told me that now my mother-in-law wouldn't blame me because she had learned to love Yong. Although I appreciated his caring, it took me a long time to get over his deception. I changed doctors. I think about what I could have done for Yong earlier to help him and me.

Children are expected to conform. To develop these values in children, parents may teach them that disobedience brings ridicule on the child and shame on the family. Traditional cultural values of patience and persistence are handed down. Family dependency is valued over independent achievement, and cooperation over competition. Over time, some of the traditional cultural norms fade, such as speaking the native language, patriarchal authority, and traditional role expectations for wives and children. By the second or third generation, children tend to accept English as their dominant language, adopt the dress codes and musical preferences of their peers, and pick up dating and sexual patterns that are at odds with traditional and parental values. They often intermarry with members of other ethnic groups (Chan & Lee, 2004).

TABLE
2-8   STATISTICS AND DEMOGRAPHICS ABOUT ASIAN AMERICANS AND THEIR FAMILIES

- 15 million Asians live in the United States and made up approximately 5 percent of the U.S. population in 2010 (Humes et al., 2011).

- Between 2000 and 2010, the Asian population increased by 43 percent (Humes et al., 2011).

- The Asian population has a median age of 35 compared to whites, who have a median age of 41 (U.S. Census Bureau, 2009b).

- Twenty-three percent of their population is younger than 18 years as compared to 24 percent for whites and 34 percent for Latinos (U.S. Census Bureau, 2007).

- The median family income was $65,469 in 2009 (U.S. Census Bureau, 2010b).

- Seventeen percent of Asian families did not have health insurance in 2009 (U.S. Census Bureau, 2010b).

- Thirty-one percent of Asian children are under age 6, half a million, lived in low-income families in 2009 with 15 percent living in poor families (Chau et al., 2010).

- The poverty rate for Asian Americans was 13 percent in 2009 (DeNavas-Walt et al., 2010).

Asian American families often do well economically but still struggle with keeping traditions and deciding on the languages they want their children to speak at home and at school.
Penny Low Deiner

Parents generally show educators respect and expect their children to do the same and not to question what they say. Children may need to learn the skill of asking adults questions without challenging adults' authority and may also need support in learning skills for getting along with peers. They may need your help in learning to express themselves in ways that do not conflict with family values. As you work this out, consult with the parents for their ideas, and use parents as a resource for expanding your knowledge of the Asian cultures.

See Table 2–9 for ways of working with Asian American families and their children.

IMPLICATIONS FOR EDUCATORS

Considering your own knowledge about Asian American culture, think about how it would influence how you would talk to a family about a child with aggressive acting-out behaviors. If you were concerned about a child's developmental level and academic achievement, think about how you would approach the family and what you would show them to support your concerns. Use the Resources at the end of the chapter and the section in the children's bibliography about *Asian and Pacific Islander Families and Children*, and share this with the children you teach. Also use these stories to increase your knowledge base. Learn about differences as well as similarities in Asian cultures, and talk with parents about the aspects of the culture that are important to them.

NATIVE HAWAIIAN AND OTHER PACIFIC ISLANDER FAMILIES

Native Hawaiian and Other Pacific Islanders are people who have their origins in any of the original people from Hawaii, Guam, Samoa, or other Pacific Islands (Humes et al., 2011). This category does not represent an ethnic group. For more information see Table 2–10.

TABLE 2-9 IMPLICATIONS FOR WORKING WITH ASIAN FAMILIES AND THEIR CHILDREN

- To facilitate learning and be more relevant, materials and programming have to take the child's culture into account. Be aware, however, of the differences among Asian Americans. Japanese and Chinese people have both similar and different values. Even among members of one group, there is great variation. Learn about the particular families you interact with to decide which information applies.

- When greeting (or saying goodbye) to family members, begin with the oldest family member, and typically greet male members first. Use the appropriate title with either the last name (Chinese and Korean) or the person's first name (Cambodian, Laotian, and Vietnamese). Many women retain their own family name when they marry. It is appropriate to address such a woman as Mrs. Onn (Miss Onn becomes Mrs. Onn when she marries Mr. Kim, not Mrs. Kim).

- Initiate interactions slowly and cautiously. Ask general, not personal questions, but do not ask about U.S. foreign policy, the internal politics of their country of origin, or religion. Expect to be asked personal questions; this shows interest and concern.

- In general, avoid initiating physical contact, particularly between men and women. This includes shaking hands or hugging another person unless he or she initiates it.

- Keep your language and voice reserved and polite. Control your emotions and avoid direct confrontation. Do not show anger or criticize the family.

- Focus your attention on the family as a whole rather than only on the child.

- Consider the degree to which the family embraces traditional values and beliefs, particularly as they relate to spirituality and healing.

- Assess the English proficiency of the family and modify your language to accommodate their level. Speak more slowly for families who are not as proficient. Do not correct their English. Do not assume that people who speak with an accent are not proficient.

- Become aware of your nonverbal communication. Avoid sustained eye contact and winking or batting your eyes. Do not touch a child on the head, wave your arms, beckon, or point your index finger. These are considered to be signs of contempt.

- Learn the body language that is associated with negative and affirmative responses. Some families will say yes to you, even if they disagree with your suggestions. Learn when yes means no.

- When sitting in a chair, keep both feet on the floor and your hands visible.

- If the family does not wear shoes in the house, remove your shoes before entering. Expect to be offered food or drinks and enjoy the hospitality. Do not compliment or praise a particular household object; the family may feel compelled to give it to you.

- Families may offer you gifts. This frequently poses a dilemma as many agencies do not want you to accept these. If you do accept a gift, take it in both hands, express your gratitude, and do not open it in the presence of the giver.

- Include bilingual and bicultural professionals on IFSP and IEP teams.

Source: Chan & Lee, 2004; Santos & Chan, 2004; Mokuau & Tauili'ili, 2004.

TABLE 2-10 STATISTICS AND DEMOGRAPHICS ABOUT NATIVE HAWAIIAN AND OTHER PACIFIC ISLANDERS AND THEIR FAMILIES

- Native Hawaiian and Other Pacific Islanders numbered half a million, or 0.2 percent of the U.S. population, in 2010 (Humes et al., 2011).
- Between 2000 and 2010, the Native Hawaiian and Other Pacific Islanders growth rate increased by 35 percent (U.S. Census Bureau, 2010a).
- Over half (56%) of the Native Hawaiian and Other Pacific Islanders reported having more than one race in the 2010 census (Humes et al., 2011).

Native Hawaiians are the largest Pacific Islander group, with a total of 58 percent of the population (Paisano, 1993). A Native Hawaiian, as defined by Congress, "is any individual who is a descendent of the aboriginal people who, prior to 1778, occupied and exercised sovereignty in the area that now constitutes the state of Hawaii" (P. L. 103–150). Native Hawaiians define themselves by their relationship to each other, their ancestors, and their land (Office of Hawaiian Affairs, 2002). People are expected to be contributing members of the community and to use their talents to benefit the entire *ohana* (literally, "family"). Sharing is central to their culture, and they value collectivism over individualism. *Ohana*, the family, encompasses those who are related by blood and others who share *aloha* (love and compassion) (Office of Hawaiian Affairs, 2002).

Family is important for all children. Native Hawaiian families have great strengths but are overrepresented among the poor, and relationships are less stable than in other groups. Compared to the population of the state as a whole, Native Hawaiian mothers have lower rates of early prenatal care but fewer low-birth-weight babies (4% compared to 7%). Their average family size of 4 is larger than the state's average of 3. They have a higher percentage of children (67% compared to 50%) who receive free or reduced-cost lunch. And, as you might expect, they see their grandparents 4 times per week compared to the state average of 3 (Center on the Family, n.d.).

Samoa and Guam contain the largest number of other Pacific Islanders, with Samoans at 17 percent and Guamanians at 14 percent. In the continental United States, most Pacific Islanders live in California (Paisano, 1993). Approximately a fourth of Pacific Islanders speak a language other than English at home.

The word *family* in many Pacific languages can be used for many various kin groups: a nuclear family, members of a household, extended family, all the residents on a single block of land, and so on. These members share most of their food (Kick, 2001). In traditional families, there was a clear definition of status, and "respect behavior" marked people's status in the group. These values are changing with the younger generation and have weakened the respect for the elderly. With the advent of the Internet, elders may no longer be seen as having the most relevant knowledge for problem solving (Kick, 2001). Children

were raised to become members of a social group, and raising children was a joint responsibility. Children were told from an early age that their behavior reflected on the entire family. Increasingly, families are now nuclear families and older children are caring for younger children. Child care is becoming a problem, and sending children home to the village is less of an option. Modernization has caused an upheaval in men's traditional roles as the importance of fishing and farming has been reduced. Education is geared to cash-oriented urban society rather than communal living and village societies. Young men are less clear about their role, and there are increasing rates of delinquency, alcohol abuse, juvenile delinquency and mental illness (Kick, 2001). The concept of sharing resources has diminished. In a cash-based society, women are viewed as competitors rather than partners. Jobs are scarce and the population is growing.

Education in rural areas is limited and very academically oriented. Most Pacific Islanders do not complete secondary school and some do not finish primary school. The schooling they receive often does not prepare them to live in a mixed subsistence and cash society. Limited basic health services are reducing infant mortality and improving child development, but few resources are available to provide counseling services and needed therapy for children with disabilities. Stresses of having a child with a disability impact the entire family.

See Table 2–11 for ways to include Native Hawaiian and Other Pacific Islander families with children with disabilities.

American Indian and Alaska Native Families

American Indians and Alaska Natives are people who have their origins in any of the original peoples of North, Central, and South America and who maintain tribal affiliation or are attached to the community (Humes et al., 2011). There are several hundred American Indian tribes with 300 separate languages and dialects. Increasingly, American Indians

TABLE 2-11 IMPLICATIONS FOR WORKING WITH NATIVE HAWAIIAN AND OTHER PACIFIC ISLANDER FAMILIES

- Determine the language skills, cultural characteristics, and family values that will impact the child.
- If you need a translator, get parental input on who this person should be.
- Ask parents whom they want to include in meetings and include them.
- Support a collectivist view (if that is the family value) while encouraging children to learn and support peer learning.
- Serve snacks family style and talk about the importance of sharing and taking turns, and ensure parents know this is one of your values.

Source: Mokuau & Tauili'ili, 2004.

are moving into urban communities. The largest group, the Cherokee, comprise about 19 percent of the American Indian population. The second largest group, the Navaho, comprise about 12 percent. Other groups, ranging from 6 to 2 percent, include the Chippewa, Sioux, Choctaw, Pueblo, Apache, Iroquois, Lumbee, and Creek tribes (U.S. Census Bureau, 1995). Their population at the time Columbus landed (1492) was estimated to be about 10 million (Harjo, 1993). See Table 2–12 for more information about American Indians and Alaska Natives.

American Indians and Alaska Natives live mostly in the western region of the United States: California, Arizona, Oklahoma, New Mexico, Washington, Oregon, and Alaska. It is important to know the characteristics of the particular tribe the family belongs to, as there is much intertribal variation and danger in overgeneralization.

About two-thirds of all American Indian family households are composed of married couples, with about 59 percent of mothers not married when they gave birth (National Center for Health Statistics, 2000). Interracial marriage is common. Elders play a special role, and grandparents actively participate in passing on the cultural heritage. Overall, American Indians stress cooperation over competition, and harmony with nature as opposed to trying to control nature. Personal strength is derived from knowing oneself and one's culture. Identity is associated with family roles, responsibilities, and relationships largely passed on by the mother (Kawamoto & Cheshire, 2004). They are adult centered as opposed to child centered, and their time orientation is present instead of future. The 2000 census found that 12 percent of American Indians and Alaska Natives held bachelor's degrees compared to 24 percent of the total population (U.S. Census Bureau, 2002).

TABLE 2-12 STATISTICS AND DEMOGRAPHICS ABOUT AMERICAN INDIAN AND ALASKA NATIVES AND THEIR FAMILIES

- About 3 million people, or about 1 percent of the population of the United States, claim American Indian or Alaska Native origins (Humes et al., 2011).

- Between 2000 and 2010, the American Indian and Alaska Native growth rate increased by 18 percent (U.S. Census Bureau, 2010a).

- American Indians and Alaska Natives have a median age of 30 compared to a median of 41 for the white population (U.S. Census Bureau, 2010a).

- Thirty percent of their population is younger than age 18 compared to 20 percent of the white population (U.S. Census Bureau, 2009b).

- Seventy-three percent of American Indian children under age 6, 0.1 million, live in low-income families in 2009 with 47 percent of these living in poor families (Chau et al., 2010).

- Almost half (44%) of the American Indian and Alaska Native population reported having more than one race in the 2010 census (Humes et al., 2011).

Alaska Natives comprise approximately 16 percent of Alaska's residents and represent a significant segment of the population in over 200 rural villages and communities. Many have retained their customs, language, hunting and fishing practices, and ways of living since "the creation times." Alaska Native people are divided into 11 distinct cultures speaking 20 different languages (Alaskan Native Heritage Center, 2008).

While other minorities have struggled to gain a place in the United States, American Indians have struggled to avoid being eliminated and to preserve their land, water, traditions, and unique legal rights. Unlike other minority groups, American Indians have negotiated more than 600 treaties with the U.S. government and ceded billions of acres of land and untold natural resources (Harjo, 1993).

According to Harjo (1993), assimilation for American Indians has meant cultural genocide. There has been a concerted effort to destroy American Indian languages, traditions, customary laws, dress, religion, and occupations. This was done by encouraging Christian denominations to convert Indian nations, imposing an educational system that separated children from their families and instilled non-Indian values, and by the federal government's breaking up tribal landholding in favor of individual landowners, and taxing the lands.

The Federal Bureau of Indian Affairs controlled education for American Indian children. Traditionally, the schools were boarding schools, located far from the children's homes, with European American educators. The focus of this education was to "de-Indianize" the children. It has not worked. American Indians have, in many instances, not wanted to have their children included, but instead have wanted to foster closer ties within the tribe. They want to improve the quality of education for their children by changing the standard curriculum to be more responsive to another view of American history. Until the 1970s, American Indian children were taught in school that their traditions were savage or immoral (Harjo, 1993). Educators tried actively to change and denigrate their way of life. Their school dropout rates were and still are high.

Some feel that one reason the dropout rate for American Indians and Alaska Native children is higher than for the rest of the population is because of the biased view that educators and textbooks present (Joe & Malach, 2004). For example, many American Indians view Thanksgiving as a day of mourning, not one of cooperation, celebration, and feasting. Remember that cultural diversity may impact the ways in which you celebrate holidays. Of all cultures, U.S. educators tend to misrepresent American Indians the most. See Table 2–13 for ways to include American Indian and Alaska Native families and their children.

IMPLICATIONS FOR EDUCATORS

Reflect on the Thanksgiving holiday and how you might celebrate it in a way that is respectful of American Indians. Think about what you could do in your curriculum to help all children have a greater appreciation of the circumstances of American Indians and Alaska Natives in the United States. Use the Resources at the end of the chapter and the section in the children's bibliography on *American Indian and Alaska Native Families and Children* to learn more about these cultures, and share this knowledge with children.

TABLE 2-13 IMPLICATIONS FOR WORKING WITH AMERICAN INDIAN AND ALASKA NATIVE FAMILIES AND THEIR CHILDREN

- Ask parents whom they want to include in meetings. In some Alaska Native families, the mother's brother takes responsibility for training and socializing his sister's children so that they grow up knowing their clan history and customs. Once who is to be included is established, include and show respect for the entire group.

- Listen to the family's ideas and concerns and acknowledge and incorporate them. Provide emotional support and respect for families.

- Build trust. Many American Indian and Alaska Native families have a history of negative experiences with public agencies and hence distrust them.

- Learn about communication styles. Some families find periods of silence and reflection an important part of their interactions, move at a pace that is comfortable for the family.

- Find out what families want, particularly if they need support in interpreting an assessment and then explaining these results to other family members.

- If families speak English as a second language, offer the skills of an interpreter. Choose an interpreter with the advice of the family,

- sometimes a person from the community is a good choice; in other instances, this might violate confidentiality.

- When you need a lot of information from families, set the stage by telling them you will be asking a lot of questions. Encourage them to ask for clarification if they do not understand and to feel free to consult with others before they answer.

- If you know little about the family's culture, admit it, show your respect, ask them to tell you if you offend them in some way, and make a sincere effort to learn more about the culture.

- Even after arranging to meet with families at a particular time, always check before entering to see if it is a good time; if not, honor their decision and reschedule.

- As families change and grow in their understanding of their child's situation, they may want or need information that they had previously been offered but was ignored. Offer suggestions again, particularly opportunities to talk with other parents.

Source: Joe & Malach, 2004; Alaskan Native Heritage Center, 2000.

White Families

White people are those who have their origins in the original people of Europe, the Middle East or North Africa. (The terms *white* and *European American* families are used interchangeably in this text.) The 2000 census showed people from the following major white groups: German (15%), Irish (11%), English (9%), Italian (6%), Polish (3%), French (3%), Scottish, Dutch, Norwegian, Scot-Irish and Swedish (about 2% each) living in the United States (U.S. Census Bureau, 2000). For more information about white families, see Table 2–14.

Traditional white Anglo-Saxon Protestant (WASP) values include such personal traits as self-control, personal responsibility, independence, individualism, stoicism, keeping up appearances, a "hard work" ethic, and moderation. Complaining is viewed negatively. Increasingly, this dominant culture is embracing the importance of individualism,

especially in gender-related issues. For their children, there is an emphasis on personal development such as being independent, self-reliant, self-assertive, self-controlled, and focusing on individual achievement. In contrast, many Asian and Latin American cultures emphasize interdependence, cooperation, collaboration, and being respectful and loving (Okagaki & Diamond, 2000). There are many subcultures of the dominant culture.

Although there may be a set of values that reflects the dominant culture, it too is heterogeneous and it is just as difficult not to generate stereotypes about whites as it is others. See Table 2–15 for ways of working with white families.

IMPLICATIONS FOR EDUCATORS

Value and respect the culture of others at the level at which they embrace it. Reflect on your experiences in being part of a minority or majority culture. Think about how you would be different if you were part of another culture. Talk to your parents about what they feel is

TABLE 2-14 STATISTICS AND DEMOGRAPHICS ABOUT WHITES AND THEIR FAMILIES

- About 224 million people, or about 72 percent of the population of the United States, are white, non-Hispanic (Humes et al., 2011).

- Between 2000 and 2010, the white growth rate increased by about 6 percent (Humes et al., 2011).

- Whites have a median age of 41 (U.S. Census Bureau, 2010a).

- Twenty percent of their population is younger than age 18 with 80 percent of the white population over 18 (U.S. Census Bureau, 2009b).

- The median income of white families was $54,461 in 2009, whereas for all races of U.S. families it was $49,777 (DeNavas-Walt et al., 2010).

- The poverty rate for white non-Hispanics was 9.4 percent compared to the U.S. rate of 14.3 percent (DeNavas-Walt et al., 2010).

- Thirty-two percent of white children under age 6, 4.2 million, live in low-income families in 2009 and 15 percent lived in poor families (Chau et al., 2010).

- Twelve percent of the white non-Hispanic population does not have health insurance (DeNavas-Walt et al., 2010).

TABLE 2-15 IMPLICATIONS FOR WORKING WITH WHITE FAMILIES AND THEIR CHILDREN

- Speak about issues directly and honestly without using jargon. Be aware of regional differences in terms and vocabulary.
- Expect families to take an active role in their children's education; they want to be informed and have input into the process.
- Acknowledge the possibility of multiple possible causes of disabilities.
- Schedule meetings to accommodate active, complex lifestyles.
- Start and end meetings on time.
- Honor and respect individual differences and preferences among the dominant culture.

Source: Hanson, 2004.

TABLE 2-16 CHANGING STRUCTURE OF THE AMERICAN FAMILY

	1970	2007
Families (with breadwinner; and full-time caregiver)	60%	34%
Married women in the labor force	30%	61%
Married couples with children younger than age 18	40%	23%
Family households	81%	68%
Women living alone*	12%	15%
Men living alone*	6%	12%
Children younger than 18 living with one parent	11%	27%
Births to unmarried women	11%	40%

Source: CDC, 2009; Fields, 2003; Kreider & Elliott, 2009; U.S. Census Bureau, 2002.
*Cohabitating households are included in these figures.

culturally important to them and how that affected how you were raised. Use the Resources at the end of the chapter and the section in the children's bibliography on *European American Families and Children* to learn more about the majority culture, and share this knowledge with children.

Again, a caution is in order: When discussing ethnic or cultural traits, we risk stereotyping people. The intention here is to provide evidence of diversity. Working with families requires good communication skills and sensitivity to the needs and values of all families based on their culture and the circumstances in which they live. Early childhood special educators need to be respectful of families and read the cues the family gives them about what is important and the best way to convey information.

Working with Children with Disabilities in Diverse Family Structures

Before the 1970s, our focus was solely on *children* with disabilities. Although we were aware they lived in families, we rarely considered the fact that children both affected and were affected by their families. We now look at children in the context of their families with increased awareness about the impact of the family's structure, culture, and the environments in which children live and grow. Children with disabilities live in all family types. These variations have implications for children, their families, and how we work with these families. They increase our need to know more about families and to develop the skills to interact with all family members. The American family is changing. However, it is not the structure per se that poses the greatest challenges, but how the structure affects and is affected by children.

Family structure has changed dramatically since 1970. Fewer households have children younger than age 18. Twice as many women are in the work force. Couples are marrying later and are cohabiting before marriage, after a divorce, or as a lifestyle choice. More single women are having children. See Table 2–16.

Family structures are evolving in the United States because of economic and social changes and immigration patterns. In 2004, 70 percent of children lived with two parents, 26 percent lived in single parent families. Seventeen percent of all children lived in blended families (Kreider, 2008). As an educator, expect that the children you work with will come from a variety of family configurations, and ensure that you are prepared to work with and honor this diversity.

● ● ● Children in Separating and Divorcing Families

One variation from the traditional family life cycle comes through separation and divorce. Of white separated women, 91 percent move from separation to divorce within three years compared to 77 percent of Latinas and 67 percent of black women (CDC, 2002). Of these divorces, approximately three-fourths involve children (Berk, 2002), who are likely to be young.

Approximately 50 percent of first-time marriages end in divorce. Twenty percent of these separations or divorces happen during the first five years (CDC, 2002). If the separation or divorce is followed by a period of inept parenting or underparenting by the custodial parent, the loss of the noncustodial parent, a decline in family income, conflict between parents, and residential instability, then the outcome is problematic for any child, but particularly for a child with disabilities. On the other hand, if the divorce is followed by attentive and authoritative parenting, the noncustodial parent is active, the household income remains stable, and there are few additional stressors, then it is likely to have a minimal effect on children (Amato, 2004).

The average child spends approximately five years (almost a third of childhood) with a single parent, usually the mother, but with a growing number of single-parent households headed by men. For many children, this period is followed by new relationships, some informal, such as cohabitation; but after 2 to 3 years, approximately 40 percent of parents remarry and an additional 20 percent are in some type of nonmarital union. About half of these remarriages will result in divorce in about two to three years (Hetherington & Kelly, 2002). When children with difficult temperaments or other challenges have to cope with stressful life events such as family disorganization, divorce, and remarriage, their problems are magnified (Lengua et al., 2000).

Parental conflict does not end with divorce; indeed, it often escalates after a divorce. Conflicts often revolve around issues related to visitation rights and child support payments. Children with disabilities can be caught in the middle of these conflicts. Older children seem to be able to adapt and negotiate, whereas young children, including many children with disabilities, do not have these skills but do experience the stress.

Women are more likely than men to be economically disadvantaged after divorce. The economic well-being of women and children plunges when compared to pre-divorce levels. In addition to the loss of one income, three-fourths of divorced mothers in the United States get less than the full amount of child support they are entitled to or none at all (Children's Defense Fund, 2000). The economic implications of divorce may mean that families have to move from their homes, thus reducing ties with neighbors and friends. After divorce, both parents' social networks become smaller and less dense. Women, especially those caring for children with disabilities, have less time, energy, and economic opportunity to build a new friendship network. Because women typically interact more frequently with kin during the marriage, they are more likely to sustain this support network than men are. Ties to kin may become the major support network if relationships are positive.

Few issues surrounding divorce have generated more concern than those relating to children's adjustment to divorce and its aftermath. It is difficult to make generalizations because the issues are complex. To some extent they are dependent upon the age, sex, and temperament of the child. The period of greatest challenge is from the separation until two years after the divorce. The cognitive immaturity of some children with disabilities makes it difficult for them to understand the issues related to their parents' divorce.

Three major factors impact children's adjustments to divorce: (1) the effectiveness of the custodial parent in parenting the child, (2) the level of conflict between the mother and father, and (3) the relationship of the child with the noncustodial parent. When the custodial parent is effective, levels of conflict are low, and the relationship between the child and the noncustodial parent is maintained, the outcome can be positive for children (Hetherington & Kelly, 2002).

For children, divorce is a loss of a way of life. The predictable patterns of everyday life are replaced by different expectations and life experiences and a profound degree of uncertainty. Household rules and routines change, and a single parent typically experiences task overload as he or she takes on the tasks that previously were shared. Young children are particularly vulnerable, as the people they would turn to most for comfort and to mediate the stress may be unavailable (Wallerstein, Lewis, & Blakeslee, 2000).

You, as an educator, will probably be told about the divorce when the physical separation takes place. This is when parents must make practical decisions about who will be picking children up and what emergency numbers have to be added or changed. Finding out about the divorce may help explain a child's behavior.

IMPLICATIONS FOR EDUCATORS

During the divorce process, young children and children with disabilities frequently regress and lose skills they had previously attained, such as adaptive skills and toilet training. They may want to be held more, or they may want an attachment object such as a blanket that had been given up. They may need extra support trying new activities and materials. Children who had adjusted well to the educational environment may now cry when dropped off and become anxious when they see other children leave and someone is not there to pick them up. It is imperative that early childhood educators know the legal and informal agreements between parents regarding the care of the child. Children with disabilities are almost always in the custody of their mothers.

Children need stability in their early care and education setting. They need familiar toys, familiar adults, and a familiar routine. Their world seems out of control and they seem adrift. Help them choose toys and activities that put them in control, and emphasize this as you talk with them. Be supportive of children's feelings of sadness, fear, and anger. Acknowledge these feelings and find ways to deal with them. Although children may test your limits, they need to know that limits exist. "You look like you are angry. You can kick the ball two more times, but then we need to put it away."

Children need to have divorce explained to them with an emphasis on the fact that it is a permanent change. Use books in the section of the children's bibliography on *Families Who Separate and Divorce*. Read these books to all children, but find time to read these books one on one with a child to help her talk about her feelings. Share these books with families to support them in talking with their children about the process. Support both parents in maintaining contact with their children, and help them use authoritative parenting. It is not helpful if one custodial parent is overly indulgent with the children. Children may feel that both parents would be that way all the time, and it sets up conflict and erroneous ideas.

• • •

Children in Cohabiting Families

By age 30, three-quarters of women in the United States have been married and half have cohabited outside of marriage (CDC, 2002). **Cohabitation** is a living arrangement in which two adults who are not married to each other live in the same setting and have a sexual relationship. Cohabitation is becoming increasingly common. By 1995, 40 percent of women ages 20 to 24 had cohabited. Half of all first unions were cohabiting unions (Bumpass & Lu, 2000). Cohabiting couples become parents when they have a child together, live with children from a previous relationship, or are single women who become pregnant and choose to cohabit rather than marry.

In 2004, 29 percent of all children lived with one or two unmarried parents. Five percent of all children lived with a cohabiting parent (Kreider, 2008). Nearly half of all adults have lived in a cohabiting relationship at some time during their lives, with approximately three-quarters cohabiting before a second marriage. Cohabitation is less stable than marriage. The probability of a cohabiting relationship breaking up within 5 years is 49 percent (marriage is 20%)

and after 10 years is 62 percent (first marriages are 33%) (CDC, 2002).

Two out of five children will live in a cohabiting family during some of their childhood, and 15 percent of children born are the biological children of cohabiting couples (Bumpass & Lu, 2000). Cohabiting fathers spend more time with their biological children than fathers who do not live in the same household, but less time than fathers who are married to the mother. Some adults may want to know the implications of including a child with a disability in a family before committing to marriage. Whether cohabitation is good or bad for children with disabilities depends upon the alternatives.

Cohabiting relationships cut in half the median time (7 to 3.7 years) children live in a single-parent post-divorce household (Bumpass & Raley, 1995). The fact that half of these cohabiting unions do not last (there is either a marriage or separation) increases the number of transitions children with disabilities experience (Seltzer, 2000). Nonmarital cohabitation appears to be difficult for many families and particularly boys. There is more cohabitation among previously married adults than never-married adults. Although this trend is too new to know what it means for children with disabilities, it does mean you are likely to have children in your setting living in cohabiting families.

IMPLICATIONS FOR EDUCATORS

Early childhood settings have to deal with many family structures and provide opportunities for input from parents and significant others. When cohabiting relationships change, children need the stability of a setting that has familiar activities and people. Early care and education settings make individual decisions about whom they invite to conferences and group meetings. It is important to talk with biological parents and determine the roles of adults in a child's life to be sure to include important figures.

Become familiar with the families of the children in your setting. If cohabiting families feel uncomfortable and judged as less than adequate, they may not participate in school-related activities. When you plan activities, think about having children invite a "special adult" rather than specifying a mother or father. Be inclusive rather than exclusive. Build bridges to all families regardless of their structure.

• • •
Children in Blended Families and Stepfamilies

Blended families, formed when remarriage occurs or when children living in a household share only one or no biological parents, can contain stepchildren and their stepparents, **half siblings**, or **stepsiblings** (Kreider, 2008). A **stepfamily** is defined as one in which at least one of the recoupling adults has one or more children from a prior relationship and the children spend some time in the adults' household (Crosbie-Burnett & McClintic, 2000). About half of remarriages include minor children. There are 12 million children living in blended families, 17 percent of all children younger than the age of 18 (Kreider, 2008).

Blended and stepfamilies are complex and highly variable. They include more than one household unit. All family

We know little about the effects of cohabitating families on children with disabilities; the implications are affected by the alternatives for the mother and child.
© Cengage Learning 2012

members are affected emotionally, financially, and legally by the actions of another household. The co-parenting team is large, including biological parents and their respective spouses and/or committed live-in partners. The new extended family includes multiple grandparents and stepgrandparents, and siblings consist of biological siblings, half-, and stepsiblings from both households. Approximately half of stepfamilies have a mutual child. If the child is born after the couple has formed a solid relationship, the birth of the child usually makes a positive contribution to the integration of the family; if before, there will likely be increased stress.

Stepfamilies are different from first-married families in a variety of ways. Stepfamilies form after a process of loss and change. Members of stepfamilies come together at different phases of their individual, marital, and family life cycles. Children and adults have experienced different traditions and ways of doing things. Parent–child relationships have preceded the couple relationship, rather than followed it. One parent may have had extensive experiences with disabilities, whereas the other (step)parent may be trying to learn what the disability will mean for the child and family. Children have a parent elsewhere—if not in reality, at least in memory. About half of children in stepfamilies have contact with their noncustodial parent; therefore, there are shifts in household membership when the children move between households. There is little or no legal relationship between stepparents and stepchildren.

IMPLICATIONS FOR EDUCATORS

Educators have to be open to discussions with children who have siblings "some of the time" or who call their mother by her first name. Conscious efforts must be made to include diverse families in stories and celebrations and to acknowledge many types of families. Including books about stepfamilies and supporting children in making two Mother's or Father's Day presents can go a long way to helping children cope. Also, as an educator you have to be clear on who should receive notices and who should be included in conferences and invited to school events. You also need to know who is to pick up the child and under what circumstances. Your emergency forms should indicate whom to contact and what to do if you cannot reach the identified person.

••• Children in Single-Parent Families

Single-parent families are those with one parent and dependent children. The number of single-parent families has more than doubled since 1970. Approximately 26 percent of children, 19 million, lived in a single-parent household in 2004, with 88 percent of them living with a single mother and 10 percent with a single father. In approximately 10 percent of the families, the mother or father had a partner (Kreider, 2008)

Single-parent families have increased because of divorce, nonmarital childbearing, and cohabitation. Most children raised in single-parent homes grow up healthy and happy. However, children raised in single-parent families face more risks than those raised in two-parent homes. Some problems relate to behavior; for boys, particularly, externalizing problems such as aggression is common. Other concerns involve long-term effects such as increased risk of teen pregnancy. Single-parent homes are more likely to be economically disadvantaged, and single mothers feel the strain of work and parenting (Martin, Emery, & Peris, 2004). In single-mother families, 30 percent lived below the poverty line and 17 percent of single-father households lived below the poverty line (U.S. Census Bureau, 2010b). Children with disabilities increase the stress and the financial demands on the household.

Single-parent families are as diverse as two-parent families. Despite the increased number of single-parent families, there is still a tendency to look at these families as dysfunctional, deviant, or unstable. Society has not focused on the strengths of single-parent families or accepted them as viable family units with variability in style, structure, and values. Given the number of children living in single-parent families, it is important to view their strengths as well as their challenges (Annie E. Casey Foundation, 2006). See Table 2–17 for the number of single-parent families.

ADOLESCENT SINGLE MOTHERS

Adolescent motherhood is a complex and serious situation. Although the national teen pregnancy rate is falling (84.5 pregnancies per 1,000 women ages 15–19), it is still the highest among developed countries. The poverty rate of children who are born to mothers ages 15 to 19 who are not married and did not graduate from high school is 78 percent (Annie E. Casey Foundation, 2006). See Table 2–18 for the number of births to adolescent single mothers.

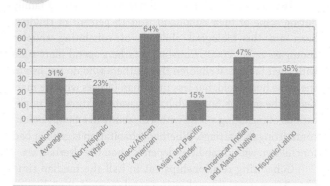

TABLE 2-17   PERCENT OF CHILDREN IN SINGLE-PARENT FAMILIES IN 2004

Source: Annie E. Casey Foundation, 2006.

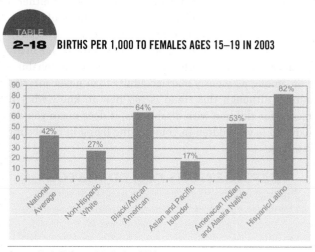

TABLE 2-18   BIRTHS PER 1,000 TO FEMALES AGES 15–19 IN 2003

Source: Annie E. Casey Foundation, 2006.

The move away from the marital dyad is increasing for all families in the United States. In 2000, 79 percent of all teenage mothers were not married at the time of delivery. Grandmothers or other family members often take on parenting responsibilities. This provides a collective responsibility for the child but often adds stress to the household (Annie E. Casey Foundation, 2006).

Many infants born to adolescents experience long-term challenges. They are 50 percent more likely to be born at low birth weight, 50 percent more likely to repeat a grade, and less likely to graduate from high school. If female, she is 83 percent more likely to become a teenage mother. Males are 13 percent more likely to be incarcerated. Regardless of sex, they are twice as likely to be abused or neglected and two to three times more likely to run away from home (Florida State University Center, 1997; Annie E. Casey Foundation, 2006). Early intervention and high-quality early care and education can change these statistics.

Risks do not end with the birth of a full-term viable infant. Only 1 to 2 percent of children are born with disabilities that are identifiable at birth, yet by school age 10 to 12 percent of children are identified as needing special educational services. The interplay among risk factors in early childhood produces poor outcomes. The combination of low birth weight and low maternal education increases by eight times the probability that the child will need special educational services (Florida State University, 1996). Adolescent mothers are less verbal and less supportive of their infants. Negative long-term child development outcomes have been found in the areas of intellectual development, social-emotional development, and school achievement. Opportunities for learning and nurturing missed early in life cannot be fully regained; by 18 months, infants raised in impoverished environments have cognitive deficits that may not be totally reversible (Florida State University, 1996).

IN THE FIELD

Our 21-year-old daughter, Tina, lives with me and my wife, Hannah. Tina gave birth to our grandson Will about 5 years ago. Tina is a single mother and had Will when she was only 16. Hannah and I watch Will while Tina works at the supermarket and takes courses at the community college. She is trying to get ahead and we want to help her. However, taking care of Will has become very difficult for us. Will has autism. I think we have accepted this now. I'm not sure Tina has.

When Will was an infant, we didn't have a lot of trouble taking care of him. We didn't want Tina to marry Will's father, so we agreed to help. Will is in preschool for part of the day, but when he comes home, he runs up and down the stairs for hours. We just can't keep up with him, he moves so fast. Will has trouble communicating and gets angry when we can't understand him. Then he hits himself or us. It's getting to be too much. We tell Tina, but she doesn't want to hear it.

Tina says that she will be able to afford after-school care soon. To me, it seems like soon isn't soon enough. Will is a great little boy and we love him dearly. However, my wife and I have already raised our children, and we don't have the resources or energy to raise Will the way we would like. Will needs more than we can give. I'm not sure we are safe anymore; it's an awful feeling. Tina keeps saying "just a little while longer," but I'm afraid something terrible will happen before this all gets sorted out. I feel helpless and angry at the same time. I wish I knew what to do about all this before it's too late.

IMPLICATIONS FOR EDUCATORS

Take time to talk with young mothers and to learn about their life and their beliefs about child rearing. Do not make judgments. Find out what kinds of support systems they have, both formal and informal. Talk with them specifically about what you do in class and why. Talk about reading to children and why you spend time doing that. Talk about talking to young children even before they can talk. Help them think about fun ways to connect. Try to be matter of fact. Do not tell them how to raise their children, but rather try to help them think about the variables related to raising young children, particularly children with disabilities. Look at the supports you might potentially provide, such as a lending library. If you send homework, send home the supplies that are needed to complete the project. If children come back with incomplete projects, think about the skills you expect parents to have and whether these expectations are realistic relative to time, energy, and academic knowledge.

• • •
Children in Gay and Lesbian Families

Until recently, early childhood educators dealt with sexual orientation by ignoring it. As more people are openly expressing their sexual preferences, the intersection between early childhood education and the gay community must be addressed (Laird, 2003). Several million gay men and female lesbians are parents. Because of the stigma associated with being identified as gay or lesbian, we have little reliable data about numbers of gay and lesbian couples (Kurdek, 2004). Children of these unions often experience discrimination.

Three types of family structures typify gay- and lesbian-headed families: blended families, single-parent families, and couples having children together. As most gay fathers and lesbian mothers became parents through a heterosexual marriage, blended families are the most common type. Approximately 65,500 adopted and 14,100 foster children live with gay and lesbian parents (Gates et al., 2007). Lesbian partners who want to have children in the context of their relationship adopt children or use artificial insemination. This practice is new, and we do not know a lot about how it affects their children's early education (Kurdek, 2004).

Contrary to concerns about children in these relationships, studies have found that children's development does not differ from that of children raised in a heterosexual relationship and that attention, love, and support seem to be more important in rearing children than the gender identity of the parents. Children seem well adjusted and most develop a heterosexual orientation (Chan, Raboy, & Patterson, 1998).

IMPLICATIONS FOR EDUCATORS

Early childhood educators have to explore their own feelings for evidence of homophobia and for the assumptions they make about the children in their classroom. This is an opportunity to look also at gender bias in general and stereotypical sex roles in particular. It is important to teach tolerance and support of those who do not follow traditional gender roles.

• • •
Children in Biracial or Multiracial Families

The term *multiracial* or *mixed-race* identifies people whose ancestors come from multiple races. The term *biracial* refers to having parents or grandparents from two different races. In the U.S. Census, race and ethnicity are self-identified; that is, people who fill out the census decide which race or races they most closely identify with and whether they are of Hispanic origin (ethnicity). There are approximately 7 million people in the United States who identify themselves as mixed race. Half are under 18 years of age (Rockquemore & Laszloffy, 2005). Approximately 3 percent of the population is biracial, a number that increased by 32 percent between 2000 and 2010 (U.S. Census Bureau, 2010a).

Families, schools, and communities may lack a clear understanding of the challenges mixed-race children face. Rockquemore and Laszloffy (2005) argue that healthy racial identity develops over time and through multiple pathways and involves a continuum of possible racial identities. One size does not fit all.

Biracial children have lived in the United States since colonial times. However, it wasn't until 2000 that the U.S. Census allowed citizens to identify themselves as having more than one race. The census found that about 4 percent of children in the United States are multiracial. When looking at projected rates of population change in the Unites States, it is expected that this population will continue to increase.

Of all racial/ethnic groups, this is the fastest growing one. See Table 2–2.

Multiracial families and their children face some challenges monoracial children will not face. Children may be asked whether they are adopted, and they need to be able to answer questions such as, "What are you?" They may choose to answer this question in a variety of ways, including the simple, "I'm a girl. What are you?" Parents and children need support in explaining why they may look different.

Multiracial children do best in settings that have cultural diversity and where children are not forced to choose only one race or ethnic group they can identify with. Children may choose a racial identity based on their physical appearance or on which parent they spend the most time with, or what racial/ethnic group they are currently with (Kareem, 2010).

IMPLICATIONS FOR EDUCATORS

Have a classroom that celebrates cultural diversity. Include books that feature multiracial characters; support children and their families in connecting with other children regardless of racial/ethnic identity; and help children talk about their racial/ethnic identities and what it means to them. Celebrate differences and similarities.

Working with Children with Disabilities Whose Families Face Special Challenges

Regardless of family structure or culture, some families face additional challenges. Some of these challenges increase the risk of having a child with a disability and others make caring for children with disabilities more difficult. For some families, the situations they are in are temporary, whereas for others they are more permanent. Poverty is a leading risk factor for negative outcomes and disabilities for young children.

Children in Immigrant Families

The United States is a nation of immigrants. One child out of every five children in the United States qualifies as a **child of an immigrant parent**. Children are considered to be children of immigrant parents if they are younger than 18 years of age and are either themselves foreign born or were born in the United States with at least one foreign-born parent. This is one of the fastest-growing segments of the nation's child population. In the 1990s, this population of children grew at seven times the rate of native-born children (Capps et al., 2004). In 1900, 80 percent of these immigrants came from Europe, with only about 1 percent coming from Latin America and Asia (U.S. Census Bureau, 1999). Today, about 65 percent of immigrants come from Latin America (Capps et al., 2004).

There were approximately 12 million **unauthorized migrants** in the United States in 2005. Most have entered across the Mexican border (60–70%). Others (25–40%) entered legally but overstayed visas or violated other terms of their admission (Passel, 2006). Undocumented men come to the United States to work, and in 2003, 90 percent of them worked, which is higher than the percent of U.S. citizens or legal immigrants who work (Passel et al., 2004). Over half of the undocumented men (54%) live as married couples or in other family situations (Passel, 2006).

IN THE FIELD

I knew on our first date that José and I were going to get married. My husband is Guatemalan; I'm from Delaware. We met at a bar in a tiny tourist town called Panajachel, in the highlands of Guatemala. He was a restaurant manager, and I was a friend of one of the bands that played there frequently.

We fell in love. The only problem? We lived a continent and several countries apart. So I moved to Guatemala, living there for months at a time for almost three years. But then I realized that I wanted a career. I didn't want to live on $120 a month. And so I suggested that José come to the States and that we marry. Neither one of us thought the journey down the aisle would be quite as difficult as it proved to be. It took my husband almost a year for his visa to be approved. It was denied because papers were out of order, because I didn't make enough money, and because a signature didn't appear to be original.

My husband went to the U.S. Embassy 16 times, lined up, and stood for seven hours in the cold (because, even if you have an appointment, they will only see 100 people a day), waiting for a person who wasn't even a U.S. citizen to tell him "No." There were times when I thought our relationship would crumble—moments when I was so angry that I wanted to scream at my government and ask them what right they have to tell me who I can or can't fall in love with. Instances when both of us said, "This is just too hard."

My parents watched our struggle. They mostly stayed on the sidelines, but near the end they decided to intervene. It had gotten to the point of idiocy. José's visa was being denied for no reason and their little girl was unhappy. Delaware is a small state and my parents had been active in politics. Soon our senators and representative were on a mission to bring José to the United States. It took numerous phone calls, faxes, and emails, but with the help of a friend who is an immigration attorney, and members of Congress, enough pressure was put on the U.S. Embassy in Guatemala that José was granted a visa.

He came to Delaware six days later with a visa for 90 days. If we did not marry during that time, he would have to return to Guatemala and could not come back to the United States for three years. We married one day before his visa expired.

REFLECTIVE PRACTICE | There is much concern about illegal immigrants in the United States. Have you thought much about the process of obtaining a visa to come here legally? How would you feel if you were in this woman's situation? From the first application for the visa to reapplying for a green card that will allow him to continue work in the United States and also visit his family (which he wasn't able to do for three years), this couple paid almost $10,000 in legal fees. Reflect on what that means for immigrant families.

IN THE FIELD

I am an international student from China. Strictly speaking, I am not an immigrant but a "nonimmigrant alien," based on the categorization by the U.S. Immigration Office. Before I came to the United States, I had a stable job in Shanghai (one of the largest cities in China) and was married to my husband, a junior scientist working in a research institute. The idea of seeking better educational opportunities in a western country was very attractive to us. A year after we got married, my husband left for the United States to study at a major university, but we never knew it would take us so long to see each other again.

Within 14 months I made four visits to the U.S. Consulate in China, to apply for a spouse visa. I was rejected the first three times because I was suspected of having immigration intentions. Each time, I cried my way back home and made tearful phone calls to my husband. I was literally hopeless when I went to the U.S. Consulate for the fourth time. Luckily I was granted a visa this time. I was finally able to go to America to see my husband.

A few months after I arrived in the United States, I was also accepted at the university. To enroll as a full-time student, I needed a new visa. The fastest way to obtain such a visa was to apply in a U.S. Embassy or Consulate outside the country. Otherwise it would take several months for a visa to be approved and mailed by the U.S. Immigration Office. I flew to El Paso, Texas, crossed the Mexican border, and obtained my student visa in the U.S. Consulate in Juarez, Mexico. Compared with my previous visa application experiences in China, this trip was easy and delightful!

So far I have studied in the United States for six years, have had a child, and have graduated from university with a Ph.D. If I want to stay in America after graduation, I am allowed one year to look for a job and change my student visa to a different one. If that year expires and I still do not have a decent employer, I will have to leave America. I took the first job that was offered to me because I was afraid I would have to leave.

REFLECTIVE PRACTICE | Both of the previous women have children born in the United States who are citizens. Reflect on these women's experiences. How are they similar to and different from each other? Do you think these are typical experiences? The home language of the children in both families is not English. How do you think this will affect their educational experiences?

Two-thirds of all children with **undocumented** parents (about three million) are U.S.-born citizens who live in **mixed-status families** (Capps & Fix, 2005). Although the children might be eligible for educational services, undocumented adults are not eligible for welfare, food stamps, Medicaid, and most other public benefits (Fix, Zimmermann, & Passel, 2001). In mixed-status families, there is a concern that finding services for a child with a disability will result in the adult's undocumented status being discovered and some of the adults in the family being deported. About 5 percent of children in elementary school had undocumented parents in 2000 (Capps & Fix, 2005).

IMPLICATIONS FOR EDUCATORS

If families have immigrated recently, they may need time to adjust to the culture and to find out how they will meet their basic needs. There may be little energy left to focus on the needs of a child with a disability. Particularly if the family is not legally documented, be clear about your role. Specifically be aware of how it relates to child welfare (you are not there to take their child away) and the United States Bureau of Citizenship and Immigration Services (*La Migra*) (i.e., you will not inform on them). In paperwork, do not reference their status. Educators need to know what resources can be used for both legal and illegal immigrants and what actions might jeopardize their legal status now or in the future. Learn about the immigrants' country of origin and area of the country the family emigrated from. If the area is rural, they may need support childproofing their home and adjusting to other basic issues that are different from their homeland.

REFLECTIVE PRACTICE | Think about your own experiences with immigrant families, especially those who speak English as a second language, those who have not lived here long, and those who may have immigrated illegally. Reflect on your style of interacting with others and establishing trust. Immigration, whether legal or illegal, is a controversial area. Think about your feelings and how you will provide all children with the best possible education.

● ● ●
Children Whose Families Have Few Economic Resources

One of the most pervasive adversities facing children and their families is **poverty**. The human cost of poverty is high, robbing young children of their health, education, hopes and dreams, and even their lives. There is concern over the increasing number of children who live at or near poverty levels. The number of families who are totally dependent upon welfare has fallen from 3 million in 1976 to 960,000 in 2001. However, the number of poor children who are living in families with earned income and no public assistance has risen from 4 million in 1976 to 7 million in 2001. Of all children living in poverty, only 22 percent receive cash assistance (Annie E. Casey Foundation, 2003). See Table 2–19 for the percent of children living in poverty. The 2009 American Community Survey found 14 percent, or 43 million people, in the United States living below their respective poverty thresholds (Bishaw & Macartney, 2010). The number of families living in poverty was 11 percent, 9 million people (U.S. Census Bureau, 2010b).

Using a slightly different measure of poverty, the United Nations compared child poverty rates in the developed world. On this scale, the United States ranked 20th out of 21 countries, with only Mexico having higher rates of child poverty. Another comparison using industrialized nations again found the United States at the bottom of the scale, with only Russia having higher rates of child poverty (Annie E. Casey Foundation, 2003).

Poverty in the United States varies by where families live and the support systems that are available to them. Maryland and New Hampshire had the lowest rates of child poverty at 10 percent; Mississippi had the highest rate at 30 percent. The District of Columbia and Puerto Rico are not ranked as states, but had 33 and 56 percent child poverty rates, respectively (Annie E. Casey Foundation, 2007a). The U.S. Census Bureau (2010b) determines poverty thresholds

TABLE 2-19   PERCENT OF CHILDREN LIVING IN POVERTY BY RACE IN 2009

Non-Hispanic white	12%
Hispanic or Latino	33%
Black or African American	36%
Asian	15%
American Indian	34%
Other	24%

Source: Wright, Chau, & Aratani, 2011.

according to family size and the ages of members. The number of children living in poverty increased by 33 percent between 2000 and 2009 (Wright, Chau, & Aratani, 2011).

America's "fifth child" is the one child in five who lives in poverty. Contrary to public belief, this child is likely to live in a family where at least one adult works. Poverty affects all races of children; however, one in three black and American Indian or Alaska Native children (35%) and one in four Latino children (28%) were poor in 2006 (Annie E. Casey Foundation, 2007b). The poverty rate for children under age18 rose from 19 percent in 2008 to 21 percent in 2009 (U.S. Census Bureau, 2010b). Poor children face risks other children do not face (see Table 2–20).

The number of people living in poverty fluctuates. In reality, many more people are poorer than the poverty rate suggests. Families living close to the poverty line may drop into poverty because of life changes such as an illness, birth of a child, divorce, separation, or disability (Annie E. Casey Foundation, 2005). In 2011, the **poverty line** was $22,350 for a family of four, $18,350 for a family of three, and $14,710 for a family of two. Research suggests that families need about twice this amount of money to meet basic needs (Chau et al., 2010).

Poverty adds to the stress experienced by all families. Families who are forced to spend their resources and energy on survival often do not have additional time or energy to encourage a child with a disability to learn language and other cognitive skills. When this happens, such children are more likely to experience emotional trauma and sustain accidents. Poverty increases the probability that children will be born with disabilities and that disorders that are preventable with timely medical intervention may become disabilities. Families who cannot afford regular medical care may wait until conditions become severe and then seek emergency-room treatment. Nine million children, most of whom live in two-parent homes and 90 percent of whom have a working parent, have no health insurance (Children's Defense Fund, 2007).

TABLE 2–20 RISKS POOR CHILDREN FACE

Poor children are

- twice as likely to be born without prenatal care, have low birth weight, and to die before reaching their first birthday.
- twice as likely to repeat a grade, drop out of school, and require special education.
- more than twice as likely to be abused or neglected.
- frequently tired in school because they can't sleep in their noisy, overcrowded apartment, house, or shelter.
- likely to fare better if they lived in another country. If they lived in 23 other industrialized nations, they would be guaranteed health insurance, an income safety net, and a chance for a parent to stay at home with pay after childbirth.

Source: Children's Defense Fund, 2002, pp. 5, 6.

Poverty increases the probability that risk factors will be present simultaneously in the child, the parent, the parent's informal support system, and the neighborhood. The disadvantages of poverty permeate all of life, from health care and nutrition, to quality of housing and neighborhoods, to educational opportunities. The cycle of poverty is associated with poor maternal nutrition, increased substance abuse by pregnant women, and low-birth-weight infants. These are all potential causes of developmental problems and additional stressors in an already stressed system.

Women with low incomes have the highest rate of depression of any group. Depressed mothers are less responsive and nurturing, less aware of their child's moods, and more restrictive. Children raised in extreme poverty are at risk for developmental problems. The causes are complicated but include poor cognitive/language stimulation, poor nutrition, exposure to safety hazards, and poor health care. Adverse financial circumstances affect the entire family and include increased risk of marital dissolution, family disorganization, physical abuse, and neglect (Annie E. Casey Foundation, 2006). One outcome of poverty can be homelessness.

CHILDREN IN HOMELESS FAMILIES

The number of people who are **homeless** in the United States is a matter of debate. They are a difficult group to identify, and definitions of homelessness vary. Homelessness can be a transient condition or long term. It is estimated that over 1 percent of the population, somewhere between 2 and 3 million people, experience homelessness during a year and that about 700,000 people are homeless on a given night (U.S. Department of Health and Human Services [USDHHS], 2003a). The National Coalition for the Homeless (2009) estimates that 3.5 million people are homeless, of which 39 percent are children.

Many factors contribute to the growing number of homeless: unemployment, increases in the number of people in poverty, the minimum wage level, a decline in public assistance, shortage of affordable rental housing, and housing foreclosures are among them. Other factors that push people into homelessness include lack of affordable health care. For people with few economic resources, a major illness can result in bills they cannot pay, job loss, and then eviction. Approximately 16 percent of the adult homeless have severe or persistent mental illness (U.S. Conference of Mayors, 2005). Domestic violence was cited as a primary cause of homelessness in 50 percent of cities surveyed (U.S. Conference of Mayors, 2005). Many homeless families have experienced high rates of violence and report that family violence was the primary cause of the homelessness. Often the mother took the children and left an abusive situation without time, emotional strength, or financial resources to find another secure place to live. Concern about additional violence may make having a permanent address impossible.

The number of homeless families has increased significantly over the past 10 years. Of homeless families or parts of families, 4 percent lived on the streets, 29 percent lived in emergency shelters, 56 percent lived in transitional housing, and 40 percent lived in permanent supportive housing (U.S. Conference of Mayors, 2008). Most (76%) of the homeless population is single adult males. However, of the homeless whose members include children, 35 percent were headed by males and 65 percent by females (U.S. Conference of Mayors, 2007).

Living on the streets, in cars, campgrounds, or shelters, impacts children and their families. There are physical health problems related to homelessness: colds, tiredness, and feelings of depression are the most frequent health problems. One in 50 children experiences homelessness each year in the United States. These children have high rates of acute and chronic health problems. They are twice as likely to have specific learning disabilities and four times more likely to have developmental delays as non-homeless children (National Center on Family Homelessness, 2010).

Homeless children with disabilities may be hungry and have poor nutrition and increased health problems. Homeless parents may not have safe places to put their children; therefore, there is little opportunity for them to play and explore their environment. For a young child, becoming homeless is devastating. Conditions related to homelessness frequently lead to developmental delays; these are most apparent in emotional, motor, cognitive, and language development. Homeless children may display problems by acting out or exhibiting aggression, depression, inattentiveness, hyperactivity, chronic tiredness, anxiety, and for younger children, regression. From toddlerhood on, these delays will influence later behavioral and emotional problems (Hart-Shegos, 1999).

School-age children face barriers enrolling in and attending school. They may lack clothing and school supplies, and transportation and residency requirements may be challenging as families move. In some cases, it may be difficult to obtain previous school records (National Coalition for the Homeless, 2007). Parental roles may change as families move, and parents may not be emotionally available to their children when they are trying to cope with problems related to food, shelter, and finances. Poverty and homelessness are inextricably tied to the family and community. In many instances, these problems are compounded by violence.

IMPLICATIONS FOR EDUCATORS

Many young homeless children are fearful. They frequently display emotional and behavioral problems, such as short attention span, withdrawal, aggression, speech delays, sleep disorganization, difficulty in organizing behavior, regressive behaviors, awkward motor behavior, and immature social skills.

Increasing numbers of early care and education settings are including homeless children. First and foremost, these programs must feel safe for children. Schedules should be predictable, and there should be many opportunities to use large motor skills and to participate in dramatic play. This is challenging because although many of the children are in programs when their family is in a shelter, rules about how long a family can stay in a shelter vary, and programming is based on unstable funding sources and whether space is available. Some shelters have on-site child care, whereas others use settings within the community. Regardless, early care and education is seen as an essential element in helping young children whose families are homeless.

Children in Violent Environments

No one likes to think about violence and young children. When violence does occur, we want to believe that it is the exception and that it is only reported to make headlines and sell newspapers. When we read these articles, we also want to believe that children don't understand what is happening and therefore won't remember the experiences. Research findings negate such optimistic views (Groves et al., 2000).

Witnessing violence threatens a young child's basic trust in adults. Young children show their reactions in four specific areas: emotional distress, physical complaints, regression, and loss of skills, particularly in the language area (Groves et al., 2000). Restoring the parent–child relationship, where possible, is the primary goal of intervention. The best way to help children is to help their parents. As stress to families increases, the probability for violence increases. Young children are exposed to this violence and frequently are the victims of it. Children *do* experience violence, and it influences their lives. Because they may not have the language to express their feelings, it is the professional's role to comprehend the meaning of this violence for them. In addition to being the victims of violence, children are exposed to violence on television, in their homes, and in the community. The United States is the most violent industrialized nation in the world (Zero to Three, 2007).

Parents who raise children in violent environments may be depressed, sad, and anxious. Adults who are depressed tend to talk to children less and to be less responsive to their needs. They have difficulty controlling their emotions, and their children experience more scoldings and shouts than hugs and kisses. Young children reflect this same depression and smile less and begin to withdraw into themselves. Adults may cope with violent environments in a variety of ways, such as becoming overprotective as a way of keeping their children safe. They might put children to sleep in bathtubs to avoid random bullets and may rarely take them outside to play (Osofsky, 1994; Rice & Groves, 2005).

Young children exposed to violence think about their world differently. Repeated exposure to violence is likely to have an even more significant effect and is likely to be more pervasive as children's understanding of events changes with increasing age. It will be difficult for such children to learn to trust others or to think about their environment as dependable and predictable. Traumatic events in infancy continue to negatively affect social, emotional, and cognitive growth into adulthood. Male children abused or neglected in early childhood were younger at the time of their first arrest and committed twice as many offenses. Being abused and neglected increased the likelihood of being arrested as a juvenile by 59 percent, as an adult by 28 percent, and for a violent crime by 30 percent. Females were also at increased risk of arrest for violence as juveniles and adults (Widom & Maxfield, 2001).

Unlike older children, young children have a very small repertoire of behaviors with which to show their distress. The symptoms children display are related to their age, gender, and circumstances. Some very young children who have been maltreated or exposed to violence withdraw and become depressed; others may become aggressive. Among young children who see parents fight, boys are more likely to become aggressive and girls are more likely to withdraw. Other symptoms may include disrupted patterns of eating and sleeping, fearfulness, and difficulties in attending.

IMPLICATIONS FOR EDUCATORS

Children living in violent environments need to know that early care and education settings are safe. If children cannot feel safe, they cannot participate in activities fully. Part of their energy is spent being watchful and waiting, not engaging. Children learn over time that they are safe and only then become available for learning. Activities need to be repeated to gain control and mastery. Parents need to know that their children are safe before they can be concerned about their development.

Children in Kinship or Foster Care

Sometimes, child rearing becomes so complicated by other stressful conditions, such as physical or mental illness, domestic violence and abuse, alcoholism or drug addiction, that the social service system decides that a child's safety is threatened. In 2005, there were more than 514,000 children in the formal foster care system (ACF, 2007). Many of these children have special needs. Of children between ages 2 months and 2 years in foster care, over half were at high risk for developmental delays or neurological impairments (Vandivere, Chalk, & Moore, 2003).

Abandonment and removal of children from their biological family is occurring more frequently. The increase in the number of children in out-of-home placements is related to increases in substance abuse, AIDS, homelessness, and child abuse and neglect (Green, 2004). Child removal is an emergency response for their safety. **Foster care** is a living arrangement for children when a court decides they cannot safely live at home.

Kinship care occurs when children who cannot safely live at home live in a foster care arrangement with relatives. One reason why kinship care has become the preferred placement is that it can provide continuity and connectedness for children who cannot remain with their parents (Green, 2004). However, kinship caregivers receive less supervision and fewer services than non-kin caregivers do. Kinship foster parents tend to be older, have fewer resources, and be in poorer health. This makes caring for young children a challenge.

Kinship care arrangements can be informal or formal. The most common informal type that takes place outside of the child welfare system is referred to as **private kinship care**. In cases of child abuse and neglect, a caseworker may suggest that a relative take a child rather than the state taking custody. This is a **voluntary kinship care** placement. The most common voluntary kinship caregivers are grandparents. Such children are not considered part of the formal foster care system (Green, 2004). Increasingly, the child welfare system also turns to relatives to act as foster families—**kinship foster care**.

Attachment provides the framework or blueprint for future relationships. The attachment process is affected when children are removed from their homes. Attachment is based on day-to-day interactions and having needs met for physical care, nourishment, and affection. "As a practical guide, for most children between the ages of two and five, a separation for more than two months is upsetting to the degree that it may lead to psychological harm" (Solnit & Nordhaus, 1992, p. 16). Approximately 18 percent of the children in foster care are 2 years and younger. About 25 percent of children are in care for less than 6 months and another 29 percent had spent between 6 and 18 months in foster care (ACF, 2006). Concerns about attachment are one reason why kinship care is often preferred. Families who cannot meet children's basic needs place young children at risk. These young children are in double jeopardy: they live with caregivers who are unavailable to them and place them at risk, yet removing them from their homes may have negative consequences relative to attachment. Kinship care helps young children stay connected to their birth parents.

IMPLICATIONS FOR EDUCATORS

If you have a child who is living with a foster family, talk to the family about the child and what types of support they receive. Find out from them how the child came into the foster care system and the child's relationship with his or her biological parents. Learn whom you should invite to meetings. Children with disabilities are in foster care disproportionately.

Children Living with Grandparents

Grandparents play an important role in caring for children. They frequently provide babysitting, child care, and financial support. The living arrangements when grandparents and grandchildren live in the same household vary. Part of this variation relates to who is the householder, that is, the person who owns or rents the house. When children and their single mother live with a grandparent, the grandparent is likely (79%) to be the householder. Of those living with grandparents, this included 61 percent of black children; 57 percent of white, non-Hispanic children; and 43 percent of Hispanic children. Over half (52%) of black children who lived with their grandparents lived with single mothers and grandparents (Kreider, 2008). Regardless of the reason for this family configuration, 23 percent of parent and grandparent families lived in poverty. When there was no parent present, 33 percent of the grandparent families lived in poverty. Over half (56%) of children living with no parents were living with grandparents (Kreider, 2008).

Increasingly, after a divorce, incarceration, child abuse or neglect, or death, custodial parents turn to the child's grandparents for help. Grandparents typically agree and take on the responsibility of parenting as well as grandparenting. Grandparents or other relatives are raising approximately 1 in 12 children, or 7 million children in the United States, about 10 times the number in the foster care system (Meyersohn & McFadden, 2007). The legal status of the relationship between the grandchildren and grandparents may be challenging. If the grandparents do not have custody, it may be difficult for them to enroll their grandchildren in school, find health care coverage, and access services.

Grandparents also face their own challenges. They may feel saddened by the situation that led to their grandchildren coming to live with them. They may have less energy to care for active children. They may have problems balancing time for themselves and time with their grandchildren. Finances may be problematic. They also bring much strength to the grandparent–grandchildren relationship with their love, maturity, stability, and knowledge of family roots.

IMPLICATIONS FOR EDUCATORS

When grandchildren are living with grandparents, find out the reason for the living arrangement and how long it is expected to last. Talk with grandparents and find out what they want and need from the educational system. If possible, provide them with this information. Expectations for children may have changed since they were parenting their own children. Help them keep up with the times. Tell them about activities or events their grandchildren might participate in. Respect them and their role and listen.

● ● ●
Children in Adoptive Families

The number of children living with adoptive parents in the United States is increasing. According to the 2000 census, there are 2.5 million adopted children living in U.S. households (Kreider, 2003). Of these children, 87 percent were born in the United States. Of the 13 percent who were foreign-born, about half (48%) were born in Asia, a third (33%) in Latin America, and a sixth (16%) in Europe. Korea is the largest single source of foreign-born adopted children and accounted for 15 percent of children younger than age 6, with China contributing 3 percent. Most of the European-born adopted children younger than age 6 (82%) came from Russia and Rumania. Mexico accounts for a third of Latin American adoptions. However, Mexican children have been primarily adopted by relatives or by the union of non-Hispanic whites and Hispanics who adopted stepchildren. Seventeen percent of adopted children were of a different race than their family householder (ACF, 2003).

The situations of many of these children before adoption places them at risk for disabilities. Likewise, children from the United States who are adopted out of the child welfare system have also experienced the trauma of separation and often neglect or abuse before adoption. Over 12 percent of adopted children between ages 5 and 17 have at least one identified disability as opposed to 5 percent of biological children (ACF, 2003).

THE EVIDENCE BASE

When families adopt internationally, they have less knowledge about the health and development of the children than do families who adopt domestically. Internationally adopted children have a range of developmental and behavioral difficulties. Seventy-five percent of children adopted from China had significant delays in at least one domain. Children adopted from Guatemala had similar patterns of growth and developmental delays, but these were milder (Miller & Hendrie, 2000). Of infants and toddlers adopted from Guatemala, those who were raised in foster care had better growth and cognitive development scores than those who were raised in orphanages before adoption. The younger the children were at adoption, the better off they were (Miller et al., 2005).

Families who choose to adopt children have higher incomes and higher levels of education than families with biological or stepchildren (Kreider, 2003). When they adopt children with special needs, they may be better informed than other parents. Families may have more realistic expectations based on education and information prior to the adoption. In addition, they may have a good external support network (Lambie, 2000).

IMPLICATIONS FOR EDUCATORS

Educators may need to support families in developing realistic expectations for their adopted children. This may be particularly true if there are no other children in the family. Children's books about adoption should be included in the classroom literature. Educators should be aware that some projects, such as making a family tree, may be stressful. Educators must also be watchful for social and emotional problems, particularly those relating to trust, self-esteem, and identity. Especially when children are adopted, educators need to be prepared for discussions about race, ethnicity, and culture as well as about adoption itself.

● ● ●
Children in Transient Families

The United States is a highly mobile society. Among the 287 million people (ages 1 and older) living in the United States in 2005, 40 million lived at a different address than they did in 2004. Approximately 14 percent of the population moved between 2004 and 2005. Families move for many reasons. Over 50 percent move because of housing-related reasons, and more than 25 percent gave reasons related to their family (U.S. Census Bureau, 2006). Families who move frequently are diverse and range from migrant families who move with the crops, to military personnel, to high-ranking company executives, to upwardly mobile people following job opportunities (Plucker & Yecke, 1999). Regardless of who they are, they and their children face a common set of problems. They are frequently in a state of leave-taking and arriving at new places. This means not only looking at housing issues and friendship patterns but also involves looking at issues relating to continuity in medical care and educational planning. Socially, families must establish support networks in a new place.

Relocation disrupts social and academic continuity for all children and may impair academic achievement. The reason for the move has implications for children's adjustment. If families move because of significant life changes such as divorce, economic problems, or death of a parent, children's academic achievement is likely to be adversely affected. One reason for the development of the common core state standards in mathematics and English language arts was to increase the curricular continuity for children who relocate frequently.

The importance of family during the relocation process is paramount. Open communication and viewing the move as part of a common goal increases the likelihood that the transition will be smooth. As with other potential traumatic life events, a child's resilience increases when caring adults mediate these experiences. Helping children reestablish familiar routines, and maintaining ties with extended family and friends helps the transition process. Children who can establish a sense of security and routine within two to six months after relocation experience less difficulty in the adjustment process (Hausman & Reed, 1991).

MIGRANT FAMILIES

In some situations, such as those with migrant children, it is tempting for educators to feel that it is not worth getting involved with these children because they will soon move on. There are over 3 million migrant children, mostly Hispanic, who live and move with their families. As a typical family of five, they may earn less than $5,000 annually (Rothenberg, 1998). Children as young as 4 years may be working in the fields. These children tend to enter school later, have difficulty concentrating due to fatigue or illness, attend class irregularly, and have high drop-out rates (Davis, 1997). Migrant Head Start programs, designed to be flexible, serve these children whose families are often isolated from community resources. During harvest they may open at 4:00 A.M. and run until midnight, and may be open seven days a week. They may run for only the six weeks that the families are working in their area. Health, education, and nutritional specialists may follow the children as their families follow the crops (Duarte & Rafanello, 2001).

Lack of prenatal care contributes to the poor physical and mental health of migrant children. Children have high rates of infectious diseases and chronic illnesses. Their greatest strength is their extended family. They often travel together (Duarte & Rafanello, 2001). Although some of the problems faced by migrant children are unique, others are the result of a lifestyle based on frequent relocation and poverty.

MILITARY FAMILIES

Military families provide another unique subset of families who relocate. Military families move about three times as often as their civilian counterparts. Approximately 1.5 million children of military families attend schools other than those sponsored by the Department of Defense (U.S. Department of Defense, 2008). In contrast to other frequently relocating children, those in military families appear to experience few long-term negative effects with recurrent relocation. This may be related to the support systems available to their families. In an effort to help frequent transitions for children, a compact was developed by the Council of State Governments, Department of Defense, and education and military family experts, which addresses common problems that affect military children as a result of frequent moves and deployments. States that sign on to the compact agree to work collectively with other compact states to create uniform practices regarding the transfer of records, course placement, graduation requirements, redundant or missed testing, entrance-age variations, and other transition issues (U.S. Department of Defense, 2008). In an effort to support deployed families with young children, including those with disabilities, Zero to Three has developed a variety

of auditory, visual, and print resources to support families and their children (Zero to Three, 2008).

Interestingly, military families and other families frequently try to move during the summer months so as not to disrupt their children's schooling. Children themselves are less concerned about academic continuity and would prefer to move during the school year when it is easier to establish a social network. In some instances, summer sports may fill the gap for children, if they are allowed to participate. As children increase in age, the social aspects of the move become more important.

IMPLICATIONS FOR EDUCATORS

Early childhood settings should have procedures in place to welcome new children, whether they are entering at the beginning, middle, or end of a school year. Entering children have two transitions: academic and social. Methods of obtaining information from the previous setting have to be in place. Individual Educational Programs and Individualized Family Service Plans may have to be scanned and emailed or faxed to maintain some continuity in programming. If these processes take too long, children will have trouble with the academic transition. Socially, children may need an opportunity to mourn the loss of their previous friends before they are ready to make new friends. They may be tentative and fearful of the new setting or they may adjust quickly. This is difficult to predict because it is impacted by so many variables, including the child and his temperament, how long the family had lived in the previous location, the reason for the move, and even the response of the family and siblings to the move. Some children will need support in joining groups and becoming part of the fabric of the class. If there have been frequent moves, children may even wonder whether it is worth joining the group and becoming attached to the teacher. They need your support in reaching out.

Working with parents who have experienced several moves can be challenging. Many such parents have found that the only way to get services for their children is to be a strong advocate. Most are not trying to be pushy or aggressive but are concerned about the effects of frequent moving. Time lost in not receiving services can accumulate very quickly.

● ● ●

Children Whose Parents Have Disabilities

Parents with disabilities are as diverse as those without disabilities. They may have become disabled after their child was born, or the disability may have preceded the child. As we do with children, we need to view these parents as individuals first and parents second, and then focus on the accommodations necessary to include them. There are approximately 9 million parents with disabilities, or 15 percent of all parents (Through the Looking Glass, 2007). Parents with disabilities face two barriers: physical and attitudinal. Some people judge parents with disabilities as inadequate, and such parents may have experienced discrimination.

SPECIFIC LEARNING DISABILITIES

Given the prevalence of specific learning disabilities, it is likely that you will be interacting with parents who have learning disabilities. By adulthood, most parents know what accommodations they need and may directly ask for them. For example, they might ask you to put things in writing that you might not think necessary. Parents may ask to record meetings so they can play them back when they have additional time to think about what is being said. These parents may seem to be disorganized and have trouble returning forms, signing papers, and remembering special requests. Having a monthly calendar may help all parents. There is a 35 to 45 percent recurrence rate for reading disabilities in families (Shapiro, Church, & Lewis, 2002). It is important to consider that some parents of children with learning disabilities will also have learning disabilities, whether or not they have been diagnosed. Some parents will share their knowledge of their disability with you; others will not.

INTELLECTUAL DISABILITIES

Parents with intellectual disabilities function at a lower level of cognitive understanding than other parents. They may live independently with support from their family or a social service agency. They require support in understanding the changing needs of their child. As an educator, you should provide parents with information that is clear and at a level they can understand. Check the reading level of your written material to see whether it is reasonable to expect parents to comprehend it. Provide very specific information and, where appropriate, drawings or photographs to support the written word. Stress safety issues. Parents with intellectual disabilities may lack complex problem-solving strategies. They may need to be specifically told the importance of playing with and stimulating their child as well as providing custodial care.

Early care and education settings will provide most of the stimulation that children need. Ensure that your program is strong in language and literacy and that children have many experiences in play as a support for problem solving.

PHYSICAL DISABILITIES

Many physical disabilities involve mobility impairments. Parents with spinal cord injuries, cerebral palsy, and other disabilities may use wheelchairs or other mobility aids. Your environment has to be accessible to these parents. Not only do parents have to get into the building, but also you have to consider accessibility to adult restrooms and transportation. You must also consider how you will handle a personal assistant who may come with the parent.

Other types of physical disabilities make parents fatigued or make it difficult to sit for an extended period. Be open and inclusive with families and acknowledge how they have adapted to the tasks of child rearing. Do not exclude these families from participating in the classroom; consider how they can be included.

PSYCHOLOGICAL DISORDERS

Adults with psychological disorders vary as individuals and with the nature and severity of their particular situation. The National Comorbidity Survey found that 49 percent of their respondents (18–60+ years of age) experienced a psychiatric disorder at least once in their life, and 28 percent had had such an experience within the past year (National Comorbidity Survey, 2005). **Comorbidity** refers to the presence of one or more diseases or disorders in addition to the primary disorder.

Men and women differ in the prevalence of particular psychological disorders. Men show higher rates for substance abuse (25% for men compared to 14% for women) and impulse control disorders (29% for men compared to 22% for women). Men are more likely to self-medicate with alcohol and illicit drugs as a method of coping, so their rates may be underestimated, especially mood and anxiety disorders. Women show higher levels of **anxiety disorders** (36% for women compared to 25% for men) and **mood disorders**, which include depression (25% for women compared to 18% for men). Fluctuations in hormonal levels during the female life cycle are related to anxiety and depression. Hormonal changes during pregnancy are also related. During the major childbearing years (ages 18–29), in any given year 22 percent of women are diagnosed with an anxiety disorder, 13 percent with a mood disorder, 12 percent with an **impulse control disorder**, and 13 percent with a **substance disorder**. Overall, 38 percent of adults 18 to 29 years old are likely to have a psychological disorder during any 12-month period (National Comorbidity Survey, 2005).

Some parents with psychological disorders have a paralyzing listlessness, dejection, and overall feeling of helplessness that impact not only them but also their children. Some anxiety and mood disorders manifest themselves in young adulthood. Families may already have young children when parents discover the presence of these disorders.

Adults with psychological disorders may need, in addition to counseling and medication, specialized help in developing and maintaining relationships with their children. The episodic nature of some mental health problems may make relationships particularly difficult. Illness in one parent may contribute to the other partner's problems, or the partner may be able to compensate. Other problems relate to unpredictability and inconsistency. Marital discord is common, as is separation and divorce.

CHRONIC ILLNESSES

Chronic illness affects all aspects of family life. Conditions that affect functioning include epilepsy, diabetes, traumatic brain injury, asthma, chronic fatigue syndrome, HIV, multiple chemical sensitivities, multiple sclerosis, or environmental illness. The particular chronic illness and its severity will affect what parents find difficult and what they are able to do. Learn something about the illness, in particular, whether it is progressive, such as cancer, or life threatening. Find out whether it is episodic—that is, times when a parent may be almost symptom-free and other times when he or she may be incapacitated—and whether the condition is stable. Knowing the course of a particular chronic illness will help you understand the impact on a child, some of the challenges families face in supporting their child, and better ways to work with the family. Families may or may not share this information with you. To the extent that they do, it is important to find out the accommodations they need and follow through with providing them.

SENSORY IMPAIRMENTS

Adults with hearing impairments may wear hearing aids to help their understanding of speech. Depending upon the amount of residual hearing and when they acquired their hearing loss, their own speech may be difficult to understand. If their loss is severe or their identification is with the deaf community, they may use Signed English or American Sign Language (ASL). If they sign, it will be necessary to have a sign language interpreter at conferences or programs that depend on oral language. The parent may know someone she feels comfortable with, or it may be necessary to hire a sign language interpreter. For communication, TTYs (teletypewriters) can be used. Both locations must have the TTY, which consists of a keyboard that has between 20 and 30 character keys and a display screen. TTYs are easy to learn how to use. Text messaging, e-mailing, and instant messaging are beginning to take over, as they are more inclusive.

Adults who have visual impairments vary greatly in their ability to use sight to comprehend their world. They know what works best for them, and the simplest way for you to know is to ask. They may need written communications to be larger and bolder, or they may need information given verbally. Initially the adult may need to be oriented to the building and to where her child's belongings are kept. She should be consulted on how she prefers this orientation and under what conditions. If she uses a service dog, be clear with the children and others that the dog is working and is not there as a pet. Get her permission before approaching the dog.

IMPLICATIONS FOR EDUCATORS

The rights of parents with disabilities are protected under the American Disabilities Act (ADA). Early care and education settings are required to provide reasonable accommodations to them, just as they would for children. The accommodations vary with the parent's particular disability. The first, most obvious step is to learn from parents, their partners, or other service delivery systems that work with these families what accommodations are necessary. Examples of reasonable accommodations vary by general disability area. If more than one disability is involved, more adaptations may be needed.

Educators must challenge their own attitudes and beliefs about disabilities and inclusion. They should also think about the assumptions they make about parents who have disabilities and how they can be included in early childhood programs.

Use the section in the children's bibliography on *Different Types of Families and Their Children* to increase awareness of parental disabilities.

Family–Teacher Collaboration

There is general consensus among all professionals that family–teacher **collaboration** is essential. The first encounter with families sets the stage for family involvement. Collaboration is the dynamic process of connecting families' resources (motivation and knowledge/skills) to an empowering context to make decisions collectively (Turnbull & Turnbull, 1997). Communication is the key to successful collaboration. Families and educators each have history, personal style, and needs that should be acknowledged; each has different concerns, perspectives, and ideas about potential solutions. The communication skills of the teacher can increase or decrease mutual understanding.

• • • Sharing Information with Families

Communication is the process we use to get and give information and is an indicator of interpersonal functioning. Clear communication, both verbal and nonverbal, is essential. Communication includes speaking, listening, reflecting feelings, and interpreting the meaning of the message (Berger, 2004). It is a complicated process because it takes into account not only the words spoken, but also nonverbal information such as the tone of voice and the body language that accompanies the words. The message is also filtered through the values of the receiver and his experiences in the decoding process. Once interpreted, the responder sends a message back, which treads the same complicated path.

Relying only on the content of the spoken word is not effective. Researchers believe that, when interpreting communication, only about 7 percent of the meaning of a conversation is conveyed by the verbal message (spoken word). About 38 percent of the information is gleaned from the way the words are spoken (the vocal and tonal quality of the message); and 55 percent of the meaning is gathered from the visual message—the body language (Miller, Nunnally, & Wackman, 1975). As early childhood professionals, we need to be conscious of these factors and monitor ourselves as communicators.

Knowledge about the communication process indicates that important information be conveyed face to face with parents and that telephone conversations should be limited to nonemotional factual information. In addition to the general communication process, people filter messages through their culture, values, and experiences. Different people may interpret the same information differently.

Collaborating with families is a dynamic empowering process that should be child centered.
© Cengage Learning 2012

Educators who are good communicators

- give their attention to the person speaking, using eye contact and body language, and focus on what is being said.

- listen to parents to gather both the feelings and meaning behind statements. They clarify, reframe or restate parental concerns, and distinguish between factual information and feelings. They do not criticize, moralize, blame, or judge.

- recognize parents' feelings and govern what they say in the context of the relationship they have with the family. They discuss the child's positive qualities before bringing up concerns.

- match their style of giving information and the amount of information they share with the family's ability to handle the information. They do not "dump" all the information on the parents at one time if they feel the parents will not be able to process the information.

- emphasize that concerns are no one's fault. They work together to solve problems and plan for the child's future.

- focus on one topic at a time and encourage families to talk and share information.

- document specific information on both concerns and progress while keeping the focus on strengths.

- become allies with parents, viewing them as partners and working to empower them to help their children (Berger, 2004, p. 208).

Words are abstractions that stand for ideas. They make communication possible but also confound it. Clarity is especially difficult when people from different cultural backgrounds communicate. Context is important in determining the meaning of words. The word *orange*, for example, can be a fruit or a color. The way it is used allows us to distinguish between the two meanings. However, as ideas become more abstract, clarity is more difficult.

COMMUNICATION TECHNIQUES

The first step in the communication process is building **rapport**. Think about rapport as a process. Do you know when you have rapport with the person you are talking to? Reflect on how you know this. Be specific. Keep checking to be sure that rapport is maintained and that there is a sense of synchronicity. Rapport is not possible when there is not trust. Do you trust the other person? Does the family trust you? If not, can you establish trust? This may mean looking at the process and stating what is going on, "When I listen to your questions, I feel that you don't think I can carry through on this. What specifically could I say or do that would increase your confidence in me?" The reply to a question such as this often relates to the past. It may start, "We have been told . . . ." "Other professionals said . . . ." If families have had negative experiences with professionals in the past, you may have to prove that you are trustworthy before rapport can be established.

Until you have some feeling of rapport, it is not useful to try to communicate substantive information. Much rapport building is nonverbal. Even after rapport is established, it can be lost and will need to be reestablished. Unless there is mutual respect and trust between the parties, it is almost impossible to establish rapport.

There are times when you might want to interrupt the flow of conversation. If you are developing an IEP or an IFSP with a family and everyone is feeling very cooperative, you might want to be sure the family looks at the document itself. You might say something like "We have really worked quickly writing Elvira's IEP. Now I want you to think about how this will work for her, how it will fit into your workday, and whether it is what you want." Then give the family the space they need to reflect on the IEP.

If a meeting has been long or complex, it is useful to present a summary at the end. Again, it may start out with "Let me be sure I remember what we agreed to. I will . . . ." If there is an action to be taken, it is also useful to write it down as you speak.

Communication, like other skills, requires practice.

COMMUNICATION TECHNIQUES TO AVOID

There are some ways of communicating that are likely to be counterproductive with parents—or with anyone, for that matter.

Avoid Giving Advice. It is often tempting to give parents advice on how to solve problems, but it is rarely wise. It is appropriate to offer constructive suggestions, but even these should be given with care. Before giving suggestions, follow these steps:

1. Gather enough information about a situation to make the suggestions relevant.

2. Find out about the problem: when it occurs, how frequently it occurs, what parents have already tried to do to solve the problem, and whether these solutions were effective. Try to get as much specific information as possible before you offer any suggestions.

3. Paraphrase your perception of the problem to see whether it is the same as theirs.

4. Support the parents in their efforts to solve the problem by commenting on the solutions they have tried.

If you do find the need to offer suggestions, do so in a casual, tentative, nonjudgmental way. Offer several suggestions (optimally four) rather than just one. If you just give parents one suggestion, they are likely to come back to you and say, "I tried what you said and it didn't work."

Avoid the Word *Understand.* Sometimes educators respond to a family's problem by saying, "I understand exactly what you mean." This response is likely to trigger in a parent thoughts such as, "How can she understand? She isn't me. She doesn't walk in my shoes. She isn't the one getting up in the middle of the night," and so on. People who respond by *understanding* usually convey the impression to others that they really do *not understand*. An empathetic response is far more appropriate: "It must be difficult to get up in the night when you know you have to go to work the next day."

Avoid Judging and Blaming. Although we consciously try not to judge parents, sometimes our language gives us away. When parents feel they are being judged or blamed, they frequently become defensive. Starting out a conversation with "As you know, . . . " is almost always offensive. Using words such as *ought* or *should* also implies judgment. Saying "You should always make sure Darsy takes her medicine" is different from saying "Darsy didn't get her medicine today, and that makes it more difficult for us to work with her." The former statement is likely to evoke a defensive reaction from a parent. This can end up being a no-win situation that could easily have been avoided.

Avoid Mind Reading. Mind reading is assuming you know what another person is thinking or feeling without asking. When a parent says, "Tell me about Elizabeth's day," she is assuming that you can read her mind. If you respond to that statement, you will tell her what you find interesting or what you would want to know if you were the parent. For example, you may tell her the particular activities her daughter enjoys when what she really wants to know is whether she is a "behavior" problem. If she is not, you are unlikely to mention it. If you do not figure out what the parent wants to know, the parent will be dissatisfied with the exchange. It is more useful to help the parent clarify what it is she wants to know than to assume you can read her mind. Do this by asking the parent for more specific information: "I want to talk about the concerns you have. Can you ask me questions about certain aspects of the day?" If the parent persists in wanting to know about what you think is important, you may have to offer her choices: "Would you like to know about her activities, her eating, or how she gets along with the other children? Help me decide where to start." This will usually get a parent to at least state a preference.

Being an active and explorative listener is a good way to avoid mind reading. A parent might ask, "Do you think David is happy here?" To simply say "Yes" doesn't answer the question. It may take some exploration on your part to find out what the parent is concerned about, such as, "Can you tell me more specifically what you want to know?" The parent may say, "I worry because he always cries when I leave him and I wonder if he cries all day." Then you can appropriately respond, "David continues to cry for about five minutes after you leave. A teacher holds him and she walks around the classroom with him as she tries to figure out what may interest him. She typically finds something and he gets involved playing. At naptime he frequently withdraws and gets a little weepy. We rub his back until he settles down. The other difficult time for him is when the other children's parents pick them up. He becomes anxious for you. I can see why you

might think he was unhappy when you only see his most difficult times. Do you have suggestions for ways of comforting him that work well for you that we might try?"

Suppose, on the other hand, you had said, "David really enjoys modeling clay; that keeps him happy for a long time." Although a truthful answer, the parent might come away from the conference feeling that you didn't answer her question (even though she never really asked it).

Much of the communication that takes place between parents and teachers takes place on an individual basis in brief, daily interactions or through brief notes. In addition to these daily exchanges of information, regularly scheduled conferences focus on each child's long-term development. At other times, the parents of all the children in the class may meet with the teacher. Such occasions are times to talk about general philosophy and curriculum issues and inclusion. They also provide opportunities for parents to meet other parents who may become part of informal support networks.

SUMMARY

- Family systems theory and the family life cycle are useful in organizing information about families.
- Educators need to evaluate their cultural competence in the light of changing U.S. demographics.
- Educators need to be responsive to the special challenges some families face in addition to rearing a child with a disability.
- Educators need to be responsive to families with structural, functional, cultural, and ethnic diversity that have children with disabilities.
- Educators need a repertoire of good communication skills to establish rapport with families, gather the information they need, and then summarize the information and clarify action plans.

EDUCATIONAL RESOURCES

Annie E. Casey Foundation has a variety of research and information about current topics, including **Kids Count**, which provides annual benchmarks of child well-being by state and nation. www.kidscount.org/

Beach Center on Families and Disability is a federally funded research and training institute that focuses on the successful functioning of families who have members with disabilities. www.beachcenter.org/

Family Village at the Waisman Center is a global community that integrates information, resources, and communication opportunities on the Internet for persons with cognitive and other disabilities, for their families, and service providers. It is easy to navigate and has resources and links. www.familyvillage.wisc.edu/index.html/

Institute for Urban and Minority Education at Teacher's College provides online publications dealing with the education of minority families. It also provides links to other sites concerning minority families. http://iume.tc.columbia.edu/

National Black Child Development Institute was founded to improve and protect the quality of life of African American children and families. It publishes a variety of materials about parenting and child health. www.nbcdi.org/

National Task Force on Early Childhood Education for Hispanics provides information about the Latino culture and the early education of Latino children. www.ece.hispanic.org/

Native Americans—Internet Resources provides links to a variety of Internet resources about American Indians. www.cumbavac.org/Native_American.htm/

Parents with Developmental Disabilities shares information on the struggles parents face in raising their children. Videos make this site come alive and provide good information for discussing the rights of parents. www.developmentaldisability.org/parents_with_disabilities.htm/

For additional Educational Resources, visit the book companion website for this text at www.cengagebrain.com.

3 Assessment and Evaluation

I probably wouldn't have kept the appointment except that I forgot to cancel it and felt guilty when they called. I'd made the appointment to get Diana's hearing checked several months ago when she was having a bout of ear infections.

Because we weren't worried, my husband went fishing, and Diana, then almost 3 years old, and I went to the audiology clinic. We entered a soundproof room about the size of an elevator, and I sat slightly behind her so she couldn't see me. The audiologist conditioned her to place a ring on a spindle each time she heard a noise. Then the testing actually began. I didn't pay much attention until I realized that I could hear sounds but Diana wasn't doing anything. Then I began to pay close attention. She really couldn't hear the sounds—I could, but she couldn't. I was dumbfounded and didn't have to be told that she had a hearing loss. Next, they tried to get tympanic responses and said that her ear canals had fluid in them. They recommended that I take her to an ear doctor. I heard what they said but didn't really absorb it. All I kept thinking was that I was her mother and I didn't know she couldn't hear. Somehow I should have known.

I was dazed as we left. I couldn't decide whether to take her to the child care center or not. She couldn't hear. Rationally, I knew that she had gone the day before and couldn't hear then either, but now I knew. How could I have let this happen? Where was my husband when I needed him? I pulled myself together and decided, given my current state, that my daughter was probably safer at the child care center than she was with me, and I really needed some personal space. I took her into the center and explained very briefly that I'd just had her hearing tested and that she had a hearing loss of about 60 decibels. I turned as the tears began to come and ran to the car, where I just sat and cried for a while. Then I decided there were a lot of things I needed to do. I went home and made an appointment for Diana with the otologist and cried some more. Then I began to wonder why there was fluid in her ears. What caused it?

I called the pediatric allergist and made another appointment. By now, it was time to go get Diana. I was early, and the director met me at the door and invited me to come in and talk. The tears that were close to the surface welled up again. I felt

© Cengage Learning 2012

ridiculous because it was almost certain the hearing loss was temporary and getting the fluid out of her ear canal would solve the problem, but this knowledge didn't seem to register with me. By the time Diana and I got home, the rest of the family was there, and I thought that now I would have the support I needed.

I told my husband, Jim, and the two older children what the audiologist had said. No one believed me, but as I was preparing dinner, I could hear the older children hiding and calling Diana from another room to see whether she could hear them. The hiding and calling seemed to go on forever. Jim followed me into the kitchen and wanted me to repeat in exact detail everything that happened. He also found the whole thing hard to believe. How could she talk if she couldn't hear? It made no sense to him. The assessment must be wrong. We'd find another audiologist. He'd go with me this time. Probably the best thing that happened to me was that by this point I was too mad to cry.

We finally sat down to dinner, with Diana still being asked questions amid the general uproar of a typical dinner. Midway through dinner, there was a big storm with lightning and thunder that was loud and startled everyone—everyone but Diana. More questions: Did she hear the thunder? What thunder? It came again, but there was no response. Dinner was very quiet after that. I think the family finally realized what I already knew. ✳

The Assessment Process

Many of us have had a nightmare similar to one in which we have a final examination, arrive at the class with only five minutes left to take a two-hour exam, and realize that all we have on is our underwear. Fear and apprehension accompany most testing situations. Even if we have prepared well for the test, we will probably experience some apprehension prior to it. Now, try to imagine the level of apprehension parents might feel when an assessment may indicate that the child of their dreams is no more and that another child has taken her place.

Young children are delightful, unpredictable, and difficult to make conclusive statements about. The child who "acts out" daily is angelic when you ask someone to come and observe; the child who is withdrawn cooperates beautifully during the observer's visit. Parents face similar problems when having their child assessed. A child who shuts his eyes during an eye examination makes it difficult to determine accurately what he sees. If another cries when earphones are put on, it is difficult to determine what she hears. The difficulty in getting representative behavior from children on a scheduled basis makes the role of early childhood professionals important. They can provide baseline information about behavior and how typical it is.

"Assessment is the process of collecting data for the purposes of making decisions about individuals and groups" (Salvia & Ysseldyke, 2007, p. 4). **Assessment** is designed to determine a quality or condition, whereas **evaluation** uses the assessment information to make decisions. Assessment for young children should be broad based and include a wide range of methods such as observations, checklists, rating scales, portfolios, samples, or documentation of children's work as well as criterion and norm-referenced tests. Assessments should be chosen to match children's developmental level and be responsive to their culture and language. Purposes of assessment for young children are as follows:

1. To make sound decisions about teaching and learning
2. To identify significant concerns that may require focused intervention for individual children
3. To provide information programs use to improve their educational and developmental interventions

DAP Indicators of effective assessment practices include these:

- Ethical principles guide assessment practices.
- Assessment instruments are used for their intended purposes.
- Assessments are appropriate for ages and other characteristics of children being assessed.
- Assessment instruments are in compliance with professional criteria for quality.
- What is assessed is developmentally and educationally significant.
- Assessment evidence is used to understand and improve learning.
- Assessment evidence is gathered from realistic settings and situations that reflect children's actual performance.
- Assessments use multiple sources of evidence gathered over time.

- Screening is always linked to follow-up.
- Use of individually administered, norm-referenced tests is limited.
- Staff and families are knowledgeable about assessment (NAEYC/SDE, 2009a, p. 1).

Assessment is a complex topic. Educators have a major role in the early identification of young children with disabilities. The first part of this chapter focuses on using assessment for identification purposes. Children who are receiving special educational services will already have been through the identification and assessment process. When there are concerns about children, but no diagnosis, the assessment process provides four major decision-making points for educators. The initial one is a pre-referral decision.

Pre-Referral Decisions

After the first week of school, you may reflect on the children in your class. Different children come to mind, with different incidents that make them stand out: your mind's-eye snapshot creates what each is like, both high points and those not so high, as well as triumphs and concerns. Sometimes, the concerns focus on a particular child. They start out small but then niggle in the back of your mind, stay there, and grow. The scenario often goes something like this:

Natasha is one of the youngest children when she enters your class. She is not as advanced as the other children, but that is expected. She doesn't seem to catch on as quickly as the other children; she seems small for her age. Informal conversation with her family reveals that she was a preemie, weighing in at only 2 pounds. You casually inquire whether her parents have any concerns. They don't. They did when she was younger, but when she started to walk they knew that she had finally "caught up." Her behavior is a puzzle to you, and your concern increases. You are convinced that there is something different that you should be doing with Natasha, but you aren't sure what.

DAP All of us have some expectations about what typical, or developmentally appropriate behavior is. Trust yourself. Watch the child more closely, noting what bothers you. The first decision you must make is whether a child's behavior is typical for her age. That is, is the behavior that you are observing so different from the norm that it will require different educational methods and materials? There are a variety of ways of making this decision; all require observation, instructional assessment and modifications, and record keeping. You need to be sure you are responding to a pattern of behavior that extends over time. Answer the following questions for yourself:

- What do I need to know?
- How will I use this information?
- What is the most effective way to gather this information?

If you have a system of record keeping in place, use it; if not, some suggestions for informal assessments follow. Observation and record keeping are essential parts of the assessment process.

Record Keeping

There are many different systems of record keeping. Older children have test scores and report cards. Younger children provide more of a challenge. Especially at the beginning of the year, a combination of record-keeping methods is most effective.

IN THE FIELD

When I began my job as an early childhood educator a few years ago, I had little idea about how to keep accurate records about my students' learning. I felt my progress reports were based on limited reliable data. To solve this problem, I asked for help.

I began speaking to colleagues about how they handled record keeping in their classrooms. I soon learned that I did not have to reinvent the wheel. My coworkers helped me learn some easy tips for keeping accurate records on children's learning. They gave me some checklists they used in their classrooms and showed me how to use them. I reprinted these, and my paraeducator and I modified them to work with our children and what they were learning. I also learned that I had to have a schedule that would allow me to track their learning goals on a regular basis. This took some adjustment but soon worked. I learned the importance of keeping checklists on clipboards in appropriate areas throughout the classroom.

I now feel as though I have an adequate record-keeping system. When it is time to do progress reports, I can give an accurate assessment of what each child can do. Good record keeping also allows me to be more reflective about my teaching practices. I now change instructional strategies and activities to fit the needs of each child.

ANECDOTAL NOTES

Probably the most common form of nonsystematic observation involves anecdotal notes. For each child, you might have a card, a page in a notebook, or a folder. In a class of 20, some educators' write notes about 4 children each day. There are some problems with this system: significant events happen to children on "other" days. If your order of writing is random, on Friday you may have put off writing notes on four children because you don't know what to write and what you really want to do is go home. Frequently, going home wins. Additionally, one tends to write about interesting events as opposed to developmentally important information—the age-old conflict between what's cute and what counts. It is useful to note which children you have the fewest notes on and try to figure out why. These may be the children that you need the most information about.

Anecdotal notes are for you. They need not look beautiful and they might include questions your observations generate as well as the notes themselves. Your notes may resemble these:

(4/7) Suzy spilled her milk (more often than the other children?). She did not (cannot? will not?) put a simple puzzle together. She did not sit through group time (bored? over her head?). She played with Nathan in the dramatic play area, but this ended when she couldn't be the baby. She ran to her cubby and stayed there until a teacher helped her reenter the group. (Was this a bad day?) (I better check and see whether anything is going on at home.)

(4/8) Talked to Mom and she said everything was fine at home.

To make anecdotal notes more useful, you might ask yourself why you observe the children. Typically, observations are used to make academic and social decisions. When things are going well, your notes provide information you need for parent conferencing. When you begin to develop concerns about a child, you need to refine your note-taking system and combine it with behavioral observations that target particular children and specific behaviors.

BEHAVIORAL OBSERVATIONS

Behavioral observations are useful ways of recording information on behaviors that draw your attention (such as hitting). They are less useful for an assessment of social patterns and what children are learning. The usual purpose of behavioral observation is to target behaviors that need intervention or that indicate a child's development is not following the usual track. Behavioral observations include information about the situation as well as specific characteristics relative to behavior: duration, latency, frequency, intensity, context, and time (Salvia & Ysseldyke, 2007).

Duration. Behaviors have discrete beginnings and endings. It is relevant to know how long Suzy played in the dramatic play area before leaving and how long she remained in her cubby before a teacher helped her reenter the group. Think about how she spends her time, picturing her in your mind's eye. If you picture her sitting in her cubby, find out how much time she spends there each day. Most digital watches have timers. Use yours for several days to record the amount of time she spends in her cubby. Duration also provides important information about children who wander or who remain at activities for a short or long time.

Frequency. Frequency relates to how often a particular behavior happens. In this case, it is relevant to know how often Suzy goes to her cubby during a day and for how many days. If you record how many times a day she seeks refuge there, and the amount of time she spends each time, you can build a database. Compute a weekly and daily average using the frequency and duration data for the episodes.

Intensity. Intensity has to do with the magnitude or severity of the behavior. Some children whimper, others scream;

sometimes a temper tantrum involves lying on the floor sobbing; other times, screaming, flailing arms and pounding legs. Find some consistent way to calibrate intensity. Perhaps a scale of 1 to 4, where 1 is low intensity, nondisruptive; 2 disrupts a small group of children nearby; 3 disrupts most of the class; and 4 disrupts the entire class and those in the hall or perhaps in adjoining rooms. Adding intensity to duration and frequency data provides additional insights.

Latency. Latency is the length of time between a request and the child's response to the request, for example, the time between asking children to put away their materials and when they actually start to do so. This is a relevant variable when children are asked to do tasks that require higher-order thinking, tasks that require change, and tasks children do not want to participate in.

Context. Context refers to what is happening in the classroom before, during, and after an event. Context provides information about probable causes for the behavior: what influences the duration of the behavior and what role the response to the behavior has in maintaining the behavior. If the behavior occurred during group time, one might explore different possible solutions than if the behavior occurred during **transitions**. It is useful to find out whether behavior is consistent across settings and contexts (Salvia & Ysseldyke, 2007), particularly if you are seeing the same behavior as the parents. If the behavior is consistent across contexts, you need to focus on the behavior itself. If it is inconsistent, there may be something in the environment that is triggering the behavior.

Time. Time refers to when during the day a particular behavior occurs. It is important to note whether the behavior happens at specific times of the day or seems to occur randomly throughout the day.

IN THE FIELD

Ronnie had a temper tantrum every day, from the first day of school. I checked with his mother and found that he "never" had temper tantrums at home. By observing his behavior, I found that he only had one temper tantrum a day; it seemed unrelated to the children he was playing with or the activity itself, and it lasted about 10 minutes and disturbed most of the class. After trying a variety of different interventions, all of which failed miserably, I talked with his mother again and asked her to tell me about a typical day at home. Ronnie's day began about 4:30 A.M., with breakfast at 5:00 A.M. He played until lunch at about 10:00 A.M., took a nap and played, had dinner at 4:00 P.M., and was in bed by about 6:00 P.M. Based on this information, I noted the time of the temper tantrums, 10:00 A.M., and decided that the cause of the tantrums was hunger. I had a snack ready earlier or had an open snack set up at a center where children could eat when they were hungry. The temper tantrums stopped.

Behaviors that are targeted for observation and intervention are those that are harmful to the child or others (hitting, biting), behavior exhibited in an inappropriate context (using an outside voice inside, running inside), infrequently displayed desirable behavior (sharing, taking turns, and other prosocial behavior), and stereotypic behavior that draws negative attention to the child (hand flapping and rocking) (Salvia & Ysseldyke, 2007). Anecdotal notes are typically done at the end of the day; behavioral observations are made during the day and require planning and organization. Behavioral observations focus on particular children and specific behaviors; checklists collect general information on all children in a short time span.

CHECKLISTS

At the beginning of the school year, checklists can help you learn children's names, focus on general patterns of adjustment and behavior, and learn where and how long children play in different areas. Use a checklist such as the one in Figure 3–1 several times during center time for about a week. If there are other adults in the classroom, encourage them to fill out the checklist as well. The recorder initials the form and fills in the time and date. First, divide the room into areas and write a brief description of what is in each area on a given day. (If the dramatic play area is a hospital, note that.) Write the first names of the children in alphabetical

Recorder_____								Time _____		
Unit/theme _____								Date _____		
Activity Areas Checklist										
Child's name	Area	Art	Manipulative	Water/Sand table	Books	Blocks	Dramatic Play	Cubbies	Wandering	Bathroom
	Day's activities									

Instructions: Place a check mark in the areas where you observe child.

FIGURE 3–1 CHECKLIST: ACTIVITY AREAS

Use this form at the beginning of the school year to determine where children are playing, with whom, and for how long.

order on the side. Adapt the form to your needs. When you have perfected it, duplicate and use it.

This checklist (3.1) is most useful at the beginning of the year. After you name each different area, add other areas beyond the heavy line where children might be (bathroom; wandering around; cubbies; therapy, if this is not in the classroom). If events such as these happen frequently, add them to the checklist; if they are unusual, they are not worth including. Indicate the theme, if any, and place a brief reminder of the day's activities below each designated area. Use the checklist by placing a check in the box beside the child's name to indicate where each child is in the room. Use a checklist like the one in Figure 3–1 several times a day. It helps to have it on a clipboard in various places in the room.

Assume that in a week you have been able to fill out this form 10 times. What can you learn from the data you've generated? First, put it all on one form. Some implications are immediately apparent. Some children play in many areas, some in only one or two. You might identify small groups of children who play together. If you haven't noticed them yet, children who appear in the columns after the heavy line (cubbies, wandering, bathroom, other) frequently are of concern. These are children who are walking around without purpose and not engaging in activities, and they probably need your help. At this stage, you are asking more questions than generating answers. If you become interested in how long children are staying at activities, try to use the form at short intervals for a few days, and look at children who are in the same area of the room on at least two consecutive observations as well as those who are never in the same area twice. This allows you to generate some information about interest span. These data, coupled with other observations, begin to give you a foundation for looking at the children in your classroom in a more systematic way. You can do this record keeping and teach at the same time. You may now decide that you need more specific data on some children's skills.

Checklists also help focus attention on specific skills. Some you can more appropriately fill in after school is over. Useful examples and rationale for some of the checklists have been included. Especially with younger children, adding their age (in years and months) to a general skills checklist often is important, as children in a given class have a range of 12 to 18 months in age; for 4-year-olds, this is a fourth of their lifetime. Adding ages to the checklist is a reminder that children are appropriately different. Try to add information to these charts a few times a week. Children who are inconsistent or need work in an area will become more evident. These are the children to observe more closely (see the General Skills Checklist, Figure 3–2).

Transitions are a good time to collect information about children's skills. For example, as children move from a group situation to centers, it is easy to dismiss them while you assess their learning. With planning, you can ensure that all children are successful, and that you have accurate records. If you are concerned with number and letter recognition, consider using the record-keeping forms in Figure 3–3, Checklist: Group Time Transitions. Include color and spatial concepts in your assessment as well. To do this effectively, you can use a calendar for number identification ("Put your finger on the 12 and then you may go to the block area") or recognition ("Tell me the name of this number [point to a number on the calendar] and you may go to center time"). If your calendar is magnetic or is designed in a way that something will stick to it (double-sided tape on the back of the object works), ask the child to put an object in different spatial configurations relative to a specific number on the calendar. ("Put the circle above the number 21.") This exercise allows you to tap both spatial and numerical concepts. You can modify this form to gather information that is important to you. With an alphabet available, you can pose similar tasks. As children learn the capital letters, introduce lowercase letters.

Recorder									

General Skills Checklist

| Child's name | Age yr./mos. | Language | | Approach + or − | Social | | Motor | |
		Receptive	Expressive		Assertiveness interaction child	Assertiveness interaction adult	Small	Large

Key: 1 Above average   2 Average   3 Seems inconsistent   4 Needs work

FIGURE
3-2   CHECKLIST: GENERAL SKILLS

Decide what skills to monitor. Language and motor skills have norms and social skills that relate to inclusion are critical. Use children's age in years and months as it may vary by 12 to 18 months. This span causes a significant difference in skill development and expectations.

Child's name _____

Numbers

	Code	Date	Code	Date
0				
1				
2				
3				
4				
5				
6				
7				
8				
9				
10				

Letter concepts/capitals

	Code	Date	Code	Date
A				
B				
C				
D				
E				
F				
G				
H				
I				
J				

Letter concepts/lowercase

	Code	Date	Code	Date
a				
b				
c				
d				
e				
f				
g				
h				
i				
j				

Spatial concepts

	Code	Date	Code	Date
Above				
Below				
Between				
Inside				
Outside				
Behind				
Under				
At the top				
At the bottom				
Across from				
In front of				
Up				
Down				
Beside				
Beneath				
Nearest				
Right				
Left				

Shapes

	Code	Date	Code	Date
△				
○				
▭				
□				
⬭				

Sizes

Materials: Three sizes of shapes

	Code	Date	Code	Date
Small				
Smallest				
Little				
Littlest				
Medium				
Big				
Bigger				
Large				
Larger				
Largest				

Body parts

	Code	Date	Code	Date
Ankle				
Arms				
Back				
Cheeks				
Chest				
Chin				
Ears				
Elbow				
Eyes				
Eyebrows				
Eyelashes				
Feet				
Fingernails				
Fingers				
Hair				
Head				
Hips				
Jaw				
Knee				
Mouth				
Neck				
Nose				
Legs				
Lips				
Teeth				
Tongue				
Toes				
Thumb				
Waist				
Wrist				

Key: Response
R = Recognition (point to the)
I = Identification (What is this? Where is this?)

Key: Accuracy
+ = Correct
= Correct with help
= Incorrect
NA = Not attempted

FIGURE 3-3 CHECKLIST: GROUP TIME TRANSITIONS

Transitions from group time provide the opportunity to assess and keep records on individual skill levels. Double coding (R+) provides information that a child correctly recognizes a particular item.

Checklists are quick and efficient to use. They can be used on your schedule, include all the children, and can be designed to fit your particular purpose. If you were interested in the quality of children's play, you might design a checklist similar to that in Figure 3–4. The disadvantage is that you have to prepare them ahead of time, and it may take a few attempts for you to develop checklists that fit your needs.

WORK SAMPLES OR PORTFOLIOS

DAP Assessments should be tied to children's daily activities (NAEYC & NAECS/SDE, 2009a). Work samples or portfolios show what young children are doing and can serve as an alternative assessment for children with disabilities of all ages (Salvia & Ysseldyke, 2007). There are many different types of portfolios: Showcase portfolios use a child's best work; working portfolios allow children and teachers to communicate about a work in progress; assessment portfolios are holistic and are scored or rated (Columba & Dolgos, 1995). Portfolios include examples of children's writing, art, and so on; and photographs of projects, including skills children display, friendships, and construction projects. To be useful, the collection of samples should begin the first week of school so you can see growth and also so the children learn that putting some of their products in the folder is part of the system, both yours and theirs. The following guidelines will help you decide what should go in the portfolio. Items or representations should meet these criteria:

- Reflect what you want children to know and learn
- Reflect authentic assessment of what children are expected to do in the real world
- Reflect learning strategies and problem solving
- Show cooperative learning and engaging with peers

- Show patterns of learning and reflection as part of the learning process
- Show the relationship between assessment and instruction (Salvia & Ysseldyke, 2007)

Choose items that meet the above criteria rather than those items that are "cute." Talk to the children about their portfolio and give them the opportunity to add items and reflect on the items that are included. Establish early that there are short- and long-term items for the portfolio. Long-term items would include children's first drawings and paintings of the year, as well as work that illustrates particular skills (or lack of them). Short-term items might be stories that are then replaced by other stories.

Use the portfolio with the children. Let them enjoy their personal growth by looking at work they have done earlier and comparing it to what they can do now. Talk about how much they have learned. Invite a photographer or designer to come to the class, share a portion of her portfolio with the class, and explain its use in her profession.

For each artifact collected, it must be clear what specific curriculum goal the child was working toward and how this work clearly documents progress (or lack of progress) toward meeting the goal. The role of the teacher is to provide commentary about the context and process (Gronlund, 1998). To streamline this process, develop a checklist similar to Figure 3–5.

As children complete tasks such as identifying the letters of the alphabet and placing them in a puzzle, document the number of letters correctly identified and the number of puzzle pieces correctly placed.

In addition to work that is the outcome of various activities, it is important to include work in the portfolio that helps you focus on specific areas such as language, math, science, and so on. You might design some activities

Recorder _____		Time _____ Date _____				
Level of Play						
Child's name	Unoccupied	Onlooker	Solitary	Parallel	Associative	Cooperative

Key: Write initials of playmates in space. For cooperative play, note the leader.

FIGURE 3–4   CHECKLIST: LEVEL OF PLAY

One goal of inclusion is to have children play together. It is useful to know the level of children's play to suggest appropriate peers. A child's level of play is developmental and it is helpful in transition planning. Forms such as this make observations more systematic.
Definitions. *Unoccupied:* Child is not participating in an activity or watching other children. *Onlooker:* Although not participating, the child is actively watching other children. *Solitary:* The child is playing alone with materials that are different from other children's. *Parallel:* The child is playing alone with materials that are the same as other children nearby. *Associative:* Children are playing together but the play is not goal oriented and there is no leader. *Cooperative:* Children are playing together, the play is goal oriented, and there is a leader (Parten, 1932).

Portfolio Artifact Checklist		
Child's name _____	Date _____	
Curriculum goal:		
Activity:		
Initiation:	child	peer	teacher
Task:	new	emerging	mastery
Support:	adult	peer	independent
Involvement:	little	average	great
Time:	short	average	long
Requirements:	not met	met	exceeded

FIGURE 3-5 CHECKLIST: PORTFOLIO ARTIFACTS

in each area that you do consistently several times each year. For example, make up a short story with specific details at the beginning of the year and then have the children draw a picture about the story. (This is not an art project; it is assessment.) Tell the same story about four months later and again at the end of the year. Look for personal growth and also at the level of detail in the drawing across the group. This story should have details, familiar animals and modes of transportation, and a very simple plot. Tell a story something like this:

> One day a dog and a cat met. The dog said, "I like to run, I'll race you home." "Okay," said the cat. "One, two, three go!" The dog raced past the cat. The cat saw a boy on a

Document a child's accomplishments during free play as well as during specific activities designed for assessment purposes.
© Cengage Learning 2012

bicycle. "Can you go fast?" "Yes," said the boy. "Can you catch that dog?" "Sure." The cat jumped on and off they went, up and down hills and across bridges. Finally, they caught up to the dog. The dog was mad. If the cat can play tricks, so can I. He met a horse and asked if the horse could go as fast as the bicycle. The horse said, "Yes." The dog jumped on his back, and off they went. They went through the woods, jumped a stream, and finally caught up with the boy on the bicycle. The boy on the bike hit a rock and the cat fell off. The dog raced by on the horse. The cat shook himself off. The dog said to the horse, "I'm glad we don't have to run as fast now." Just then they saw the cat go flying past on an airplane. "Oh, no!" said the dog. And when he got home, he said to the cat, "Let's race again tomorrow." "Okay," said his friend the cat.

Feel free to use this story or modify it. Having the children draw pictures about the same story over time makes it easier to see change. It is important that the story be original, as some children might know a published story and others not.

Fine and gross motor skills are other areas about which you may begin to gather some systematized data. One way to do this is to have your own (noncompetitive) "Olympics." Develop the Olympic events from criterion-based assessments. One of the most useful is the *HELP for Preschoolers Charts* (VORT Corporation, 1995). The three-page charts are organized by domain areas (social, gross and fine motor, cognitive, etc.) and by age. They also provide a time span during which skills should emerge. The *Learning Accomplishment Profile*, Third Edition (Sanford et al., 2004) also provides relevant information. For 3-year-olds, the Olympic events (with appropriate norms noted) might include these events:

- Broad jump (mark off 2 feet) to the next line.
- Push or pull a wagon to the next line (10-foot distance).
- Walk (10 feet) on a 4-inch-wide taped line.
- Catch a ball thrown from 5 feet away.
- Put the ball down, take two steps, and kick it.
- Gallop back to the starting line.

These are all skills that 3-year-olds are expected to be able to do. The Olympics provides the motivation and learning opportunities that make this part of the curriculum. You have made assessment fun and interesting as well as informative.

IMPLICATIONS FOR EDUCATORS

You now have some ideas about how to collect the informal data you need to confirm or disconfirm your concerns about a particular child, as well as to monitor the development of all the children in your classroom. Use this information in two ways: First, to look at the development of a particular child over time; second, to compare children to a norm or average for the age level you are teaching. Next, look at the birth dates of the children in the class. If there is a child you are concerned about, find other children who are within a month or two of the child's age and compare their work samples and observational results. The intention is not to make judgments, but to see the range of behaviors and to determine whether a particular child is outside of this range. Then compile information from your behavioral observations, checklists, and the child's portfolio. You may decide at this point that the behavior that caught your attention was just the result of a temporary problem; or you may decide that you need additional information to reach a decision. You might begin to generate some hypotheses about what is causing the behavior and how you can modify your curriculum to better meet this child's needs.

As you modify your curriculum and instruction, documentation is extremely important. You have now made a commitment about your concerns and have developed a plan of action. Put your concerns in writing, and list your hypotheses about probable causes. Decide on your modifications, the period in which you will use them, and the outcomes that you expect. If your hunch is right, you will need this documentation for the next step. At this point your concerns may relate to a child who needs additional help in a particular area or to a child who appears bored and needs enrichment. Document your results. If you feel the concern has been dealt with, continue to monitor the situation intermittently to ensure it stays solved. If the problem is still of concern, there is another decision to make: Is it time to call in additional support, to try different methods of remediation or enrichment, or to make substantial changes in the child's program?

● ● ● Response to Intervention

Response to Intervention (RTI), or Response to Instruction (RTI), was a new component of the Individuals with Disabilities Education Improvement Act (IDEA) 2004. It was designed to help children who are struggling when there is a possibility that their problems are due to inadequate instruction or there is not a good fit between the instruction and the child. The hypothesis underlying RTI is that if these children can be identified early and, with appropriate intervention, become successful learners, they will not require special educational services. RTI promotes the early identification of children who may be at risk for learning difficulties (National Research Center on Learning Disabilities, 2007).

RTI is a concept with multiple meanings and implications, but the focus is on the effectiveness of instruction for all children in the classroom, and there is an expectation that all instruction is evidence-based. RTI measures how much all children are learning in core subjects; that is, if there is specific content the majority of the children in a classroom are expected to master, are they learning the material? Children need to be monitored on a regular basis to ensure that learning continues and that it is effective. Although the length of time can vary, six to eight weeks should be sufficient time to determine whether a child is not learning at the expected rate.

IMPLICATIONS FOR EDUCATORS

As you begin your school year, you need to get your assessment system in place early. If school starts on September 6, the expectation is that you will know by November 1 which children need to receive more intensive instruction. Also, you will have spoken with their parents about what you plan to do, how you plan to do it, and found out what parents want to know about the process. How will you be prepared to do this? What do you need to know and do to reach these expectations?

As part of the identification and assessment process, some children will be identified as not learning at the expected rate. Based on their response to instruction, something else needs to be done to ensure their success.

Their instruction must be enhanced, modified, or changed in some way to ensure they will progress at the expected rate. This requirement highlights the circular relationship between instruction and assessment, and the modification of instruction and additional assessment to make data-driven decisions (Salvia & Ysseldyke, 2007). You are trying in the pre-referral stage to eliminate the environment as the source of the problem or as a solution to the problem.

RTI typically has different levels of intensity, or tiers. When children do not succeed, they typically move to the next RTI level, which is more targeted and intensive, and usually provided in small groups. In kindergarten through third grade, reading and mathematics are typically the targeted areas. Some educational settings have formal intervention assistance teams that are designed for this specific purpose; other intervention assistance works on friendship patterns or an informal organization. With these additional sets of eyes and insights, new methods of scientific, evidence-based instruction are delivered and again judged as successful or unsuccessful. Children may remain in this tier for as long as a marking period to determine whether there has been a successful match. RTI requires that children are given repeated assessments of achievements at reasonable intervals and that these results be provided to the child's parents. If the child learns the essential skills, he may return to the previous tier and continue in general education. If the child has not responded to the intervention, a third tier may be utilized that is even more intensified and individualized. If children do not succeed in this tier, parents will be informed and encouraged to seek a comprehensive evaluation, which they can request at any point in this process. Results of the RTI will be one component of the information to be reviewed. RTI is not a delay tactic.

The National Research Center on Learning Disabilities (2007) defines the following features of effective RTI:

- High-quality research-based classroom instruction
- Student assessment with classroom focus
- Universal screening of academics and behavior
- Continuous monitoring of students' progress
- Implementation of appropriate research-based interventions
- Progress monitoring during interventions (effectiveness)
- Teaching behavior **fidelity** measures

Fidelity looks at whether the teacher is being faithful to the intervention that was designed, that is, carrying it out with the level of intensity and stipulations that were recommended. Chapter 8, Children with Specific Learning Disabilities, provides additional information on RTI.

● ● ● Early Intervening Services (EIS)

Early intervening services is also a new component of the IDEA 2004. Although they apply to children in grades K to 12, there is a particular emphasis on children in kindergarten

When a teacher reads to a child one-on-one, she has the opportunity to show the child how the words and sounds go together. By using her finger to identify each word, this teacher is focusing and individualizing instruction for this child.
© Cengage Learning 2012

through third grade who are not identified as needing special education services but who do need additional supports to succeed in the general education curriculum (Office of Special Education and Rehabilitative Services, 2006). Unlike RTI, which focuses on identifying children who may be at risk for specific learning disability, EIS's goal is to prevent significant disproportionality. It is designed "to prevent the inappropriate overidentification or disproportional representation by race and ethnicity of children as children with disabilities, including children with a particular impairment" (IDEA Regulations, 2007). EIS is also concerned with the particular educational settings where these children learn and the incidence, duration, and type of disciplinary actions they receive. States are required to **disaggregate** rates of suspensions and expulsions and to determine whether there are significant discrepancies based on race, ethnicity and disability. A proportion of federal funds can be used to address these problems (IDEA Regulations, 2007). Parents are an important part of the educational process in making decisions about their children.

• • •
Productive Parent–Teacher Conferences

Traditionally, parent–teacher conferences happen two to three times a year. The first occurs near the beginning of the year, the second about the middle of the year, and the third at the end. If there is an expectation that the child will change placements or move to a different setting, another conference

may be used to plan for the transition. Conferences don't just happen. They require planning. Routine conferences use the basic technique known as the "sandwich":

- Talk about the child's positive qualities and how she has adjusted and the developmental strides she is making.

- State your concerns about the child, if there are any, and give concrete examples.

- Conclude on a positive note.

Gather and organize the notes you have about the child, including examples of activities that you plan to share with parents. Give careful thought to the child as an individual, his likes and dislikes, personality traits, temperament, and the special qualities that you enjoy. Be prepared to talk about the child's group participation and how you support this. Have some of his favorite toys or activities available so parents can see them. (This also provides them with information about developmentally appropriate materials they might use at home.) Make a short (5 minutes or less) videotape to show families how their child spends his time. Use digital photographs to support and document developmental gains if they can be pictured. Parents may be particularly interested in friendship patterns. Make parents physically and psychologically comfortable.

CONFERENCING WITH FAMILIES

Establish rapport. Avoid jargon, accentuate the positive, and talk in terms that are specific enough that parents can take action on new information if they choose. Families genuinely want to know what their child does while she is with you. Older children bring home tests and talk about what they do in school. Younger children and those who have few communication skills cannot convey this information, and they may have fewer "products" as examples of their activities. Families want specific information about their child. Routinely share with parents the following types of information:

- *Videotapes.* Show parents how the child spends his day. If the child has behaviors that are of concern and you want to point these out, videotape them so you can show families specifically what concerns you and when it occurs. This helps clarify the context.

- *Photographs.* Use a digital camera to help families share experiences that their child has which cannot be taken home such as a block building, a dramatic play ensemble, or a new skill. These can be e-mailed if families have Internet access or printed on regular paper.

- *Work samples.* Collect samples of the child's work and share these with parents. If there are differences you want to point out to parents, show them the work of another child of a similar age and gender (obscuring the name).

- *Anecdotal records and checklists.* Have available the records (originals and your summaries) you keep on each child to share with families and to document your observations.

Sometimes, as you prepare for a conference, your concerns are heightened and you focus more closely on the child's development.

PREPARING A CONFERENCE ABOUT DEVELOPMENTAL CONCERNS

No one wants to suggest that a child might have a developmental problem; however, at some point, you may have to do so. The role of the educator in this instance is to provide parents with the information they need to make a decision about whether follow-up is necessary, and if so, how to do it. This type of problem-solving conference requires careful preparation, records of observations, and detailed information about interventions that have been tried and their level of success. This section details the formal procedures necessary to make a pre-referral decision and focuses on packaging and presenting information to families.

When you first suspect a developmental problem, you may have only a vague feeling of uneasiness. Trust yourself and think about the steps you need to take to confirm or alleviate your concerns. Watch the child closely, and write down your behavioral observations to determine what is bothering you. These notes are for you and might include the questions your observations generate as well as the observations themselves, for example:

> Shawn seems to have trouble getting along with the other children. (More often than the others) I better start counting. (frequency) (Has this always been true?) Better talk with his mother briefly when she picks him up and his teacher from last year. (context) He cannot (will not?) sustain an activity for over a minute or two. I need to time this. (duration) He doesn't seem to be involved with the activities of other children. (bored? over his head?) Is he enthused about anything? (intensity) Transitions are a problem too. Are there particular times when his behaviors occur? (time)

Does Shawn have an emotional problem? Maybe he does and maybe he doesn't. Your role is to gather additional specific information, not provide a diagnosis. It is the family's decision as to what to do with the information you gather.

Your first goal is to gather the information that you need to either talk with the family, or to dismiss your concern. After you have gathered enough information to determine Shawn's typical or baseline information, generate (and write down) your hypotheses and potential solutions. Modify your program and instructional strategies in response to these solutions, and keep records. Based on what you record, fine-tune what you are doing and keep doing it if you see progress. If you are not seeing positive changes, have another set of eyes look at the child. The director or administrator of the program, principal, or other teachers might have suggestions as well as additional insights and observations about the child (Salvia & Ysseldyke, 2007). Again, modify your interventions and keep records.

Gathering and Organizing Additional Information. If, after further observation and data gathering, you still believe there is a problem, the next step is to talk with the family. Prepare yourself by keeping the following questions in mind: "What do I need to know?" "How will I use this information?" "What is the most effective way to gather and convey this information?" Be creative and thorough as you gather needed information.

To the videotape, photographs, work samples, records, and checklists, add the following:

- *Instructional modifications.* Be prepared to talk with families about the ways you have systematically modified your interventions for their child and the results of these modifications. Document and date these. As you reflect on these, decide whether you have made enough modifications and tried them for a long enough period of time to ensure they had an opportunity to succeed.

- *Informal consultation.* Share with families your initial concern, how you worked through the process, the people with whom you shared your concerns, and the feedback they gave you. Be clear that this was informal, not part of a referral process.

- *Agencies, families, and other professionals.* If families share your concerns, they are likely to proceed further. They will probably ask you for suggestions about referral sources. Think about the types of services that parents may need and have the names of contact people as well as phone numbers. They may want to know about **Child Find** or other agencies that serve young children. They may also want to know about private resources. They may even want to know if there are parents or parent groups that might provide some insights for them. If they have a computer available, you might want to suggest some websites that provide additional information. (See the Educational Resources at the end of this chapter and other chapters that focus on specific problems and disabilities.)

Your role is one of expressing concern, providing information, and helping families develop a plan of action that will support their decision making about their child. This process of confirmation and decision making may require referral services. States provide free evaluations for children ages 3 to 5; many states also provide these services for children age 3 and younger. The Child Find specialist is a contact person who knows the regulations for the state, the services provided, and the cost. Child Find is a good initial source of information.

Know, going into the conference, that this may be the first of a series of meetings. Most families need time to consider what you say and to look at their child in a new light. Give them time as well as information. Although you may have prepared a great deal of information for the conference, you may not use it all at the first meeting. Conferencing is part of a process, and the follow-up is as important as the conference.

CONFERENCING ABOUT DEVELOPMENTAL CONCERNS

Welcome the family, state your general concerns, then get input from the family about their perception of their child's behavior both at home and at school. If they share your concerns and are appreciative that someone else has noticed, the conference will probably move quickly. If they don't share your concerns, you need to find out the basis for their perceptions. These are frequently based on experience with other siblings ("Jack didn't talk until he was 3, and he was always a loner") and/or lack of information about developmental norms or experience with other children. Sometimes learning about developmental norms can influence parents' understanding of the situation and help them differentiate between age-appropriate behavior and that which is not. They may attribute the behavior to particular circumstances ("Dottie's grandmother is in the hospital"). How you proceed depends on the parents' perception of the situation. They may provide you with information that causes you to rethink the issues.

The goal of the conference is to develop a plan of action, which may be for additional observation and new interventions or for a family's following up on the referral process. Who is responsible for doing what, and when you will conference again, should be clarified. You will have to meet again to evaluate what you each have learned. The referral process, if parents make that decision, takes time. It typically starts with a developmental screening; depending on these results, it may move to more specific assessments. Keep lines of communication open and support parents in their efforts. This is a stressful time, and families may be reluctant to talk with others until they know the outcome of the assessment process. Parents themselves may disagree about whether to follow through on the assessment, and this may add to family stress. Support the process and the concerns that parents have. If the parents follow through on the assessment and find that their child is eligible for services under the IDEA, then the focus of concern moves with greater clarity into more formalized family-centered intervention.

Explain your concerns, how you have reached your conclusions, and why you believe the child will benefit from a comprehensive assessment. You need the *information* an assessment provides (not the *label*) to meet this child's needs. If the family does not agree with your concerns and conclusions, this process may take several conferences and some structured observation to help parents see what concerns you. Some families may never agree to an assessment.

If the family agrees to a diagnostic assessment, the exact procedure depends on the age of the child, whether the child is in a public or private school, and the nature of the problem itself. The school psychologist, educational diagnostician, Child Find specialist, or other professionals may assess the child. If concerns are more medical in nature, the child's physician will do an initial assessment and provide necessary referrals.

PROBLEM-SOLVING CONFERENCES

On occasion, you will request a conference with the parents, or they with you, to discuss a specific concern. These conferences are different from the routine conferences or those about developmental concerns. They are problem related and usually have one definite topic. A problem-solving conference should be scheduled when you notice a consistent change in a child's behavior, when his behavior in a specific area deviates significantly from the norms of development, or his particular behavior pattern consistently comes to your attention. These situations involve more than just having a "bad day" or behavior that is expected because of a child's disabilities.

Scheduling the Conference. Arranging a problem-solving conference is a delicate matter. You don't want to alarm parents, but they do need to know the purpose of the conference. The time frame between scheduling the conference and holding the conference should be as short as possible. Parents are likely to be anxious when you request such a conference. Plan what you will say ahead of time. State your concerns generally; for example, you might begin by saying, "I have been observing Kate for several weeks. I'm concerned about the amount of time she spends sitting alone. I have tried to adapt the program to better meet her needs, but she still has difficulty getting involved with activities. She wanders around the classroom. Could we set a time to meet and talk about this?" Parents may push for additional information. Give them general information, but do not have the conference on the telephone. Explain that you have things to show them to help them better understand what is happening before you can jointly work on solving the problem. Schedule the conference as soon as possible.

Conferencing about Specific Problems. As with all conferences, being well prepared is important. In problem-solving conferences, however, much of the preparation has to do with preparing yourself. After you have made your observations and gathered all the information, proceed through the following steps, which require careful thought before meeting with families as they provide guidance for the conferencing process:

* *Welcome the family and state your general concern.*

* *Define the problem.* An important aspect of this part of the conference is to separate facts from assumptions or generalizations. It is important to be specific and precise. To say that Brian "doesn't get along with the other children" is not precise enough. However, knowing that Brian bit Sally while they were both using play-dough and that he hit Juan, knocking him off the tricycle, helps define the problem more clearly. It might be expressed like this: "I'm concerned about Brian's social interactions. In a typical day, he has at least three confrontations with his classmates, which usually involve hitting another child."

* *Express your concern.* At this point, it is useful to express concerns on how the behavior makes you feel: "I am worried that one of the other children will get hurt and also concerned that the program is not meeting Brian's needs."

- *Determine the parents' perception of the situation.* It is useful to describe the problem and express your concerns before you ask the parents how they feel about the situation. Parents may share your concerns or have very different ones. Some parents may respond that they do not view this behavior as a problem ("He is all boy just like his Dad!"). Another parent might be appalled that his son is being aggressive with others and want to "straighten him out at home." It is futile to try to problem solve without knowing how the parents perceive the problem. Although the "facts" might be agreed upon, how the facts are interpreted may be very different.

- *Generate hypotheses.* Ask parents their hypotheses about the child's behavior. In general, behavior doesn't have either a single cause or a single solution. It is wiser to think through the problem fully the first time than to have a second conference over the same issue, having made no progress toward the solution. Problem solving generally involves generating hypotheses about the cause of the problem and potential solutions. Generate some hypotheses of your own before the meeting. If yours are different from the parents', include your concerns in the discussion. Ensure that you and the family have an agreed upon plan of action when the conference ends.

Your role (with family permission) is to share your written data with the specialists of their choice, and to support that person's observations in your classroom. If the family does not agree to an assessment, your role is to continue to provide intensive individualized programming in your class and to use your support network for ideas and interventions. If parents do agree, you move into a set of decisions related to **entitlement**.

Entitlement Decisions

Entitlement decisions are made to determine whether children are eligible for certain types of services. The first step in entitlement decisions is screening.

Screening

To determine whether a comprehensive assessment is necessary, children often go through a screening process whose goal is to identify children at risk for delayed development and who will continue to experience delays and academic challenges without intervention. The underlying assumption behind screening is that children can be divided into two categories: those at risk and those not at risk.

We have all been screened at one time or another. School districts screen children prior to entering kindergarten. Scheduled hearing, visual, and dental screenings are done throughout the school years. Adults are screened for vision and knowledge of driving safety before receiving a driver's license. Children enter the screening process in different ways. Some physicians have concerns about children and encourage parents to have them screened. Some parents themselves are concerned and initiate the process. You, as an educator, may express concerns to parents about their child's need for screening.

Screening instruments vary. Some require highly trained professionals, whereas others use trained volunteers. The goal of a screening instrument is to identify all children who have certain characteristics, called "hits," and none of the children who do not have these characteristics. For screening to be effective, the process has to be simple. That is, it must be easy to complete and quick. It also must be accurate. There have to be clear criteria, and the measures used have to be sensitive enough to identify as many children who have delays or disabilities as possible, as well as specific enough to distinguish between children with and without delays. Measures have to be comprehensive and cost-effective, and must be done in partnership with families. There are three screening outcomes:

- The results look typical; that is, development seems to be proceeding at the expected rate.

- The results are inconclusive, and the child should be monitored or rescreened.

- The results indicate the possibility of atypical development, and the child should be referred for further, more in-depth assessment.

The criteria used in making screening decisions varies from state to state; however, the following concerns are typically addressed in screening decisions: development that is more than 1.75 **standard deviations** below the **mean** (that is, below the 80th percentile), medical history that shows risk, parental concerns, environmental concerns, and professional judgment (Salvia & Ysseldyke, 2007).

For young children, screening should consist of a range of topics and activities that include information about the child's health, physical and motor development, social interactions, emotional expressions, social competence, concept development, and adaptive skills. It should also include an interview with the child's family to provide relevant information about the child's medical history, family health concerns, and the family's concerns and perception about the child's development. Screening is designed to be a brief assessment that identifies children who may have a condition that requires further diagnosis. Screening should not be used as a diagnosis, particularly not with children who are English language learners (NAEYC, 2009b).

If the screening determines that a child is at risk, further assessment is designed to confirm or refute the existence of a problem. Diagnosis is designed to clarify the nature of the problem. Is the problem so serious that intensive intervention is required? Do the interventions need to be designed by specialists? Is a hearing loss the result of fluid in the ear canal, nerve damage, or both? Formal diagnosis is a long process.

Referral is the first step in this process. Parents must fill out specific forms requesting assessment by a team of professionals to determine whether their child's academic, behavioral, or physical development qualifies him for special education services. This team is frequently called a Child Study Team. The makeup of the assessment team varies depending on the age of the child, the particular concern, how the child entered the screening process, and the child's race/ethnicity and language. For example, if the early childhood educator expressed the concern to the family, she would be on the team.

The assessment team must decide whether the child meets the state's eligibility criteria for services by either having a documentable disability or by being gifted and talented. State criteria differ. This is especially true for children from birth to age 3. Additionally, the team must decide whether the child has special learning needs. Children can have a disability and not have special learning needs. Likewise, children can have special learning needs and not meet the state criteria for special services. Children must meet both criteria to receive **mandated services**.

IN THE FIELD

I have concerns with existing screening procedures used to identify preschool children with academic problems. We don't have the benefit of RTI. The measures are not accurate when dealing with at-risk children. Many of the measures are inappropriate for some populations. Several of the children I now work with passed the screening tests at age 3 and later, and yet when they entered kindergarten, were found to have IQ scores in the range of 50 to 55.

My other concern compounds the problem of the poor predictability of screening tools. This concern relates to the inadequate training of teachers to identify developmental problems in the children they teach. Lack of training adds to the problem of identifying children who need early intervention and is a disservice to the children. The earlier these children receive intervention, the more likely they are to overcome their delay.

I have found that taking anecdotal notes and doing observations can help to identify any problems the child may be exhibiting. Assessment techniques should be a part of all programs that train early childhood educators. Assessments assist in meeting children's individual goals but they also help detect problems that screening measures miss. Furthermore, screening children who live in poverty doesn't seem to work. However, when I use my checklists, it is clear that some have a pattern of delays. These children are at risk for academic failure and deserve the best possible services to ensure their success.

I am committed to the children I teach, but they would be so much better off if they had been identified when they were younger. They come to me expecting to fail. I have to spend the first part of the year working on what they know to give them the motivation to begin to work on the material that we are supposed to cover in kindergarten. There has to be a better way to identify these children at a younger age.

DAP GUIDELINES FOR DEVELOPMENTAL ASSESSMENT
Assessing young children is very different from assessing adults or even older elementary school children. It requires different skills for those who are doing the assessment. The following guidelines highlight recommended practices:

- **Assessment should be based on an integrated holistic developmental model.** Children's functioning is interdependent; it is not a collection of isolated areas such as cognitive, sensory, or motor abilities. Assessment should focus on the child's level and pattern of organizing experiences and his functional capacity. It should take into account not only what the child can do and how he does it but also the child's motivation and the context in which the behavior is or is not displayed. It should be gathered in natural settings that reflect what the child knows and can do.

- **Assessments should include multiple sources of information and multiple components gathered over time.** Information from the family and different members of the assessment team obtained in different contexts provides different perspectives and allows a more comprehensive profile of the child to emerge. Assessment is a collaborative process. Sources should be culturally and linguistically appropriate.

- **Assessment requires establishing working alliances with the child and significant people in a child's life.** Professionals must develop rapport and trust with families and respect them as members of the assessment team. This alliance is the first step in the assessment process; it includes the relationships between the family and child, family and professional, and child and professional. It requires families and early childhood educators to learn about assessment tools, what they do, and how they are appropriately used. Decision makers should be aware of the concerns and cautions associated with assessments and young English language learners.

- **Assessment of the child's relationship with her most trusted caregivers forms the base for assessment.** The parent–child relationship forms the blueprint for later relationships to build upon. When this is well grounded, professionals can develop methods of intervention that are congruent with the child's preferences and interaction patterns. Those assessing young English language learners should be bilingual and bicultural. If the parent–child relationship is maladaptive, then it should be a focus of the intervention, whether this involves teaching families new patterns or providing other potential attachment figures.

- **Assessment is appropriate for the child's age and characteristics; what is assessed is developmentally and educationally significant.** Assessment should be aligned with early learning standards and should be broad based rather than focusing on a narrow set of skills. The instruments should be valid for the children based on their age, culture, abilities, home language, and other characteristics.

- **Assessment processes should identify the child's current and emerging strengths and competencies.** The focus is on what children can do, as this forms the basis for intervention. Assessment should increase early childhood educators' knowledge about children, improve the educational program, and identify resources and teaching techniques needed to support learning. Special attention should be given to the language development of English language learners.

- **Assessment is not dependent upon norm-referenced tests.** The use of norm-referenced tests should be limited and provide only part of the information needed about a child's development, such as identifying potential disabilities.

- **Assessment should be viewed as a service.** It is the first step in a potential intervention process, not merely a means for identification and measurement. Assessment should be viewed as an ongoing process that informs intervention and is informed by intervention.

- **Assessment measures and procedures should be relevant and used for their intended purpose.** The measures should be reliable, valid, and unbiased. Those who participate in the assessment process should have extensive and comprehensive training as well as be familiar with the child (Meisels & Atkins-Burnett, 2000; NAEYC, 2009a; NAEYC, 2009b; Salvia & Ysseldyke, 2007).

Post-Entitlement Decisions

When children between the ages of 5 and 9 are identified as needing services, it is frequently because of lack of academic progress. For younger children, it is more likely the failure to reach developmental milestones at the appropriate time. These differences are what must be addressed in curriculum planning. A variety of decisions have to be made: What to teach (content), how to teach it (methods, teaching techniques, or strategies), and realistic expectations (Salvia & Ysseldyke, 2007). Consideration must be given to the setting in which instruction will take place and the additional supports necessary for success. Agreement must also be reached on how to evaluate progress or learning on a regular basis. Chapter 5 of this text focuses on individualized planning.

Issues in Assessment

All children undergo assessment, and assessment and curriculum are inextricably tied together. As a nation we are concerned about what our children are learning (or not learning). The No Child Left Behind Act and IDEA 2004 clarify the federal agenda and concerns about education. The Acts create strong criteria for what children need to know, particularly in the areas of literacy and math. The **Common Core State Standards** have increased these expectations and quantified them. There is a strong focus on reading, particularly for children in kindergarten through third grade who are at risk for reading disabilities (specific learning disabilities). The hope is that early identification of these children will result in interventions using scientific, evidence-based instructional strategies that will increase reading skills and reduce the number of children in special education. The laws increase state and local flexibility in meeting criteria while holding them responsible for failing schools, particularly schools that serve low-income and minority families. Parents have the right to move their children out of "failing schools"

to other public schools, including charter schools (Salvia & Ysseldyke, 2007).

Although No Child Left Behind does not focus on children below kindergarten, it has generated concerns about the increasing academic pressure brought to early childhood settings. If public school educators are being judged on their ability to teach children to read, they want children to enter school with basic pre-reading skills. Skills that may previously have been taught in kindergarten or even first grade are now expected of entering kindergarten children.

Common Core State Standards in English language arts and mathematics have moved expectations even higher. The National Governors Association Center for Best Practices (NGA Center) and the Council of Chief State School Officers (CCSSO) developed these standards. Unlike previous standards that looked at children in the context of their state or nation, these standards are based on the most effective models in the United States and countries around the world. They acknowledge that we live in a global society and that if U.S. students are going to compete, they have to do so internationally. By the end of 2010, 43 states had adopted these standards (Common Core State Standards Initiative, 2010).

Concern about the use and abuse of assessment is not new, and it stems from many different areas: the tests themselves, the testing process, and the use of the test results. Concern about the assessment process is primarily focused on the use and misuse of standardized tests and testing procedures. We are particularly concerned that black and Hispanic children come to kindergarten with fewer skills in math and reading than white children. Differences in vocabulary, letter recognition, and early reading and math skills are apparent by age 3 (Haskins & Rouse, 2005).

THE EVIDENCE BASE

Black and Hispanic children enter kindergarten already behind their white peers. The question is, what is the size of the gap and what does it mean? Because different tests are used to measure learning and readiness, statisticians typically use a tool called the standard deviation for measuring the spread of scores around a bell-shaped distribution. The assumption is that 68 percent of all scores will be 1 standard deviation above or below the mean score and that 95 percent of all scores will be within 2 standard deviations.

- The Early Childhood Education Longitudinal Study, Kindergarten Cohort (ECLS-K), a nationally representative sample of almost 23,000 kindergartners, shows that black and Hispanic children score more than half a standard deviation below white children at the beginning of kindergarten on math and reading achievement.

- The Family and Child Experiences Survey (FACES), an assessment administered to children entering Head Start, shows that Head Start children, disproportionately minorities from low-income families, are already up to 1 standard deviation (15 points on an IQ test) below their white peers in vocabulary, early reading, letter recognition, and early math at ages 3 and 4. Using representative data from ECLS-K, Jencks and Phillip found that about 85 percent of black 3- and 4-year-olds scored lower on a vocabulary test than did the average white child of the same age.

What does a gap of 1 standard deviation mean? According to Rock and Stenner, the 1 standard deviation gap has the following implications:

1. Choosing one white and one black child randomly, the white child will have higher scores 76 percent of the time, and the black child, 24 percent of the time.

2. Eighty-four percent of white children will perform better than the average black child, and 16 percent of black children will perform better than the average white child.

3. If the class is half white and half black, the students in the lower performing group will be 70 percent black and 30 percent white.

4. If the top 5 percent of children are identified as gifted, there will be 13 times more white than black children.

5. If the bottom 5 percent of children are identified as having special needs, 72 percent of the children will be black. (School populations are 17 percent black.)

6. If a reading textbook is written so the average white student has a 75 percent comprehension rate, the average black child will read at 53 percent comprehension.

A gap of 1 standard deviation or even half a standard deviation matters. The reasons for the gap are complex and not well understood. Future research is designed to learn more about this gap and what it means.

Two types of programs hold promise for closing the gap—those that help parents learn the behaviors that promote child development and school readiness, and those that directly teach poor and low-income children school readiness skills, both intellectual and behavioral.

Source: Haskins & Rouse, 2005; Jencks & Phillip, 1998; Rock & Stenner, 2005.

The achievement gap impacts children, families, educators, school systems and our nation. With the increase in the number of children from different cultural/ethnic groups, it is imperative that we figure out how to solve this dilemma.

••• Standardized Testing

As an early childhood professional, you need to be able to interpret the results of standardized tests, convey these results to others and understand how they affect curriculum planning. You should know how standardized

Some children come to school ready to learn while others do not.
© Cengage Learning 2012

measures are selected and evaluated, and the purpose of the measures used.

Standardized tests are used frequently in current educational practice. Overreliance on standardized testing is viewed as a major problem. Although there are many alternatives to standardized tests, these tests are used because they are the same everywhere and so allow comparison (but are not responsive to different program goals); they are inexpensive; and they are relatively fast to give. When properly designed and used, they give information about groups of children that can be compared to a standard (Salvia & Ysseldyke, 2007). Because young children change quickly and their growth may be uneven across domains, standardized tests may over- or underevaluate what children know, and the results may be misleading for some children.

Some assessment characteristics influence the quality of the measure regardless of what is being measured. **Psychometric issues** relate to the quality of the assessment. **Reliability** focuses on the consistency of a measure, that is, the degree to which the scores are dependable, or repeatable. If the measure is reliable, the results should be the same or very close to the same each time it is used. The child who obtains a score of 100 on Tuesday should get the same score or one very close to it on Wednesday. If tests are not reliable, we do not know whether differences relate to the children being tested or the test.

Validity has to do with whether a test measures what it claims to measure. Reliability is related to validity. If you cannot consistently get the same results each time you measure something (reliability), your results cannot be valid. There are many aspects to validity. **Content validity** is concerned with the relationship between the items in the test and the intended use of the test. If your midterm examination for the course using this text consisted of 20 math problems, you would question the content validity of the examination.

Standardized testing is complex—there are many different types of tests for different purposes. Assessment provides us with baseline data. To monitor change, the first thing that has to be established is change *from what*. Initial assessments provide the starting point.

The assessments you are most likely to encounter fall into two broad categories: **norm referenced** and **criterion referenced**. In a norm-referenced assessment, a child's performance is evaluated relative to the performance of other similar children (Salvia & Ysseldyke, 2007). Criterion-referenced measures rely on an absolute standard for determining scores. Children are asked to perform certain tasks, and the score is based on the level at which they perform. **Curriculum-based assessments** are used in schools to determine the instructional needs of children. **Objective-referenced assessments** look at how a child is performing relative to specific objectives that have been designed for that particular child (Salvia & Ysseldyke, 2007).

Achievement tests are designed to measure the content children have learned as a result of instruction. That is, the content of the test ought to reflect what is being taught.

There is concern that this sometimes works the other way around; that is, the content of the curriculum is driven by the content of the test. If educators believe they will be judged by how well the children in their class do on achievement tests, they may "teach to the test." They may also put pressure on the teacher in the previous age/grade level to have children come to their class better prepared. This has resulted in many kindergartens becoming "watered-down" first grades that are developmentally inappropriate for 5-year-old children (Bredekamp & Copple, 2009). In a trickledown effect, programs for 3- and 4-year-olds may be designed to get children ready for kindergarten. Children who do not come to school "ready" influence later test results.

With young children, we are also concerned with **predictive validity**. Predictive validity is concerned with the ability to predict the same or related characteristics in the future. If we identify a child as having delayed language development at age 3, we want to assume that she will have delayed language development at age 8 without intervention. If, however, the child had a language delay at age 3, received no intervention, and was identified as having superior language development at age 8, we would question the predictive validity of the test. This particular issue has arisen with children whose home language is not English and for whom it is a misuse of the test. Early intervention is based on the predictive validity of assessments given at young ages.

CONCERNS ABOUT STANDARDIZED TESTING

There are concerns about standardized testing, whether for screening or diagnosis, and its use and misuse. Some of these revolve around the use of tests to determine school entry. The practices include these:

- Inappropriate use of screening and readiness tests
- Discouragement or outright denial of school entrance to eligible children
- Use of segregated transitional classes (prekindergarten or pre–first grade) for children who are felt to be unready for the class they should be enrolled in
- Increasing use of retention (National Association of Early Childhood Specialists in State Departments of Education [NAECS/SDE], 2000)

These problems seem to revolve around whether children have the capability of coping with the kindergarten curriculum. Many believe that it is not the children who should be capable, but the program that should be flexible, and if the children aren't capable, they should not be denied admission to the place designed to teach them these skills. There is particular concern that male children, those of racial and linguistic minorities, and low-income children are disproportionally denied entrance to school when they are legally entitled to enroll. More disconcerting is that at the end of the primary grades, children who delayed entrance to kindergarten did not perform better than peers who entered on time (NAECS/SDE, 2000).

Although retention seems like a good short-term solution when children are deemed to have not mastered required materials, the long-term consequences must also be addressed. "Children who have been retained demonstrated more social regression, display more behavior problems, suffer stress in connection with being retained, and more frequently leave high school without graduating" (NAECS/SDE, 2000, p. 6).

Some issues regarding assessment have to do with the application of standardized tests to children with disabilities in general and to the child being tested in particular. Assessments results should be used with caution.

• • •
Culturally Sensitive Assessment Procedures

The first step in any assessment process is establishing rapport with both the child and the family. When the people involved are from different cultures, the process is more challenging. Professionals have to be culturally competent, open, and nonjudgmental. To the extent that professionals decide that all children and families should fit a single mold and a single set of interventions is offered, it is likely that many families will refuse to participate. There is no blueprint for cultural competence. However, culturally sensitive screening and assessment procedures start from a family-centered perspective. Professionals need an understanding of the family's values, the group with which the family identifies, and their degree of transcultural identification. Then they need to act and respond in ways that are congruent with this understanding (Lynch, 2004).

Assessments that compare children to a standardized sample (norm-referenced) or on the basis of their mastery of specific skills (criterion-referenced) can result in biased assessment of children from minority cultures and ethnic groups. When using norm-referenced measures, ensure that the norms are recent and that they are representative of the population being measured. If children are from cultural/ethnic groups not represented in the norming group, standardized testing results are questionable and should be interpreted with caution if at all (Padilla & Borsato, 2008).

Assessment is complicated by the fact that knowledge and behaviors valued by one culture are not necessarily those valued in another culture. If tasks are not valued, then it is unlikely that families have encouraged their children to perform them. This often means that children have not had the same opportunities to learn the required skills, an assumption that most standardized assessments make. This can be further complicated when the family speaks a language other than English. Although some assessment tools are translated into languages other than English, they are often imperfect translations and may not have separate norms. Functional assessments can be very useful in finding out what children know and can do.

YOUNG ENGLISH LANGUAGE LEARNERS

Assessing children with limited English proficiency can be a daunting task, especially in the early childhood years. It isn't just about knowing or not knowing the English language, but about demographic, linguistic, and cultural differences. More than three-quarters of the children whose home language is not English speak Spanish (Salvia & Ysseldyke, 2007). Even in these broad groups, children speak different dialects, and those who speak the same language do not necessarily have a shared culture and history. How, when, and why families came to the United States impacts the language proficiency and resources of the parents. To the extent possible, children's assessments must be administered in their home language. Special education is not an appropriate way to deal with children whose only problem is **limited English proficiency (LEP)**.

Some tests may be available in the child's home language. When tests are translated, we assume the child can understand the directions and the questions (which may or may not be true); we cannot assume that the child has had the same experiences as children growing up in the United States. Ideally, those assessing young English language learners are bilingual and bicultural, know assessment, and know the child (NAEYC, 2009b). Or we can just assume that the child has enough language and experience to make the test valid. Or perhaps the best answer: Do not test.

Some children have disabilities that are obvious, regardless of language. This is usually true for sensory and physical impairments. It is more difficult with specific learning disabilities, communication and language impairments, social, emotional and behaviorial disorders, and cases of mild intellectual disabilities. Observations, portfolio assessment, and an interpreter who can provide information about testing and also interview families and find out about the child's experiences may be necessary.

Standardized Achievement Tests and Accountability

Standardized achievement tests are used not only to assess children but also the teachers and schools in which these children learn. Assessing and teaching are inextricably combined. You need to know what children have learned in order to know what they are ready to learn. Accurately assessing young children is more difficult than accurately assessing older children or adults. Inappropriate testing of children can lead to unfair and harmful decisions. The most frequent abuses of testing in early childhood occur when a test designed for one purpose is used for another or when testing procedures appropriate for older children are used with younger children (NAEYC, 2009a).

DAP Although it is apparent that infants and toddlers do not have the language or motor skills to "bubble in" answers, the question arises as to when children do have these skills. According to the National Association for the Education of Young Children (2003):

> Before age eight, standardized achievement measures are not sufficiently accurate to be used for high-stakes decisions about individual children and schools. Therefore, high-stakes assessments intended for accountability should be delayed until the end of third grade (or preferably fourth) (Shepard, Kagan, & Wurtz, 1998, p. 52).

There are specific problems that relate to giving younger children standardized achievement tests. Developmentally, it is difficult for children to sit still for the allotted amount of time, and their depth of knowledge can rarely be tested through this methodology. This brings into question the validity of this type of testing for young children (Popham, 2000). Testing itself is stressful for children. The nature of standardized tests requires that they be constructed so that they discriminate among children. If teachers did a marvelous job teaching an important concept and 98 percent of the children taking the test got the answer right, this question would have little testing value because it does not discriminate. The same would be true if 98 percent gave incorrect responses. Such questions should be removed from the test. Those who construct tests are looking for items that about 50 percent of the children get right (Wesson, 2001). What this means to a young child taking the test is that she is confronted with many items for which she does not yet know the answer.

If teachers become better at helping children learn, to the point that most children have mastered concepts, then questions about these concepts will no longer discriminate among children and will be removed from the test. There is some concern that test developers may choose items that reflect what children learn *outside* of the classroom rather than *inside* the classroom. Such tests may lead to what Wesson (2001) calls the "Volvo effect": higher correlations with family income, education, and occupation than with what goes on in classrooms. Knowing a child's zip code may be a good predictor for how well the child will do on standardized tests.

To the extent that the dominant culture's *outside* experiences help in taking standardized tests, children who come from different cultural and ethnic groups are disadvantaged. And they are disadvantaged in a way such that good teaching cannot make a difference. Young English language learners face additional challenges in the testing arena. As one might predict, in homes where Spanish is spoken, children perform better on test items in mathematics than they do on items that are more heavily language based (Wesson, 2001).

IMPLICATIONS FOR EDUCATORS

With the adoption of the Common Core State Standards, there is a clear message about what children are expected to know and be able to do in mathematics and the English language arts. Assessments are being developed to ensure that these standards are being met. Although these standards begin in kindergarten, concern exists that other areas of the curriculum such as social skills and the fine arts will no longer be an important part of the early childhood curriculum. Many of the experiences that transform children's learning cannot be measured by achievement tests.

Assessment of Children with Disabilities and English Language Learners

Children with disabilities, until recently, were excluded from school reform activities related to curriculum standards and state assessment programs. Measuring educational outcomes for children with disabilities has been inconsistent, at best, among states. The No Child Left Behind Act of 2001 requires all states to report each year on the progress of *all* children. The reporting leads to two types of accountability: **student accountability**, which is designed to motivate students to do their best; and **system accountability**, which is designed to improve educational programs. The focus of federal education reform efforts is at the systems level (Salvia & Ysseldyke, 2007).

If all children are to be assessed, then accommodations must be designed to allow children to participate without compromising the technical aspects of the test. The matter of accommodations for testing individual children with disabilities is covered as part of the IEP and should be used for all testing situations, not just state and national tests. There are four general areas in which accommodations are made:

- Presentation of the test material (oral, interpreter, etc.)
- Response format (oral, computer, etc.)
- Setting (individual or small group)
- Timing/schedule (allowing breaks and more flexible time limits) (Bolt & Thurlow, 2004)

Abedi, Hofstetter, and Lord (2004) found that some strategies to accommodate English language learners were more effective than others, such as modifying the language of test items to reduce low-frequency vocabulary and complex language structure that do not impact the content knowledge being tested. Such modifications did not affect scores of English-proficient students.

PLAY-BASED ASSESSMENTS

Professional organizations, such as the National Association of School Psychologists and Zero to Three, advocate the use of dynamic play-based approaches for the assessment of young children. Transdisciplinary play-based assessment is an integrated approach to assessment, based on research showing that play encourages children's thinking skills, communication and language abilities, movement proficiency, and social-emotional development. It also lends itself to intervention (Linder, 2008a).

To develop a dynamic play-based curriculum assessment, take the following steps:

- First, conduct an ecological assessment. This involves looking at the environments in which the child spends his time, and how he performs in these environments.
- Establish priorities for goals; determine which areas of development hold the greatest potential for intervention and what is most important to families.
- Determine the child's present level of academic achievement (PLAA) and functional performance.
- Identify measurable annual goals in the context of state and professional standards.
- Develop an instructional program (for eligible children, this will be an IEP or IFSP).

- Develop an instructional schedule. That is, answer the question, How will the child's instructional objectives be incorporated into the daily schedule?
- Put the plan into motion and provide the required instruction based on the schedule that was set up.
- Finally, assess the skills learned and monitor the level of attainment, retention, and generalization (Ford & Dahinten, 2005).

Transdisciplinary play-based assessment (TPBA) and *Transdisciplinary play-based intervention* (TPBI) (Linder, 2008a, 2008b) is a curriculum-based, criterion-referenced, assessment and also an intervention system, designed for use by a team of different professionals (early childhood educators, early childhood special educators, physical therapists, occupational therapists, speech-language pathologists) and the parents. Transdisciplinary teams require a high degree of coordination and trust. The goal of TPBA is to look at the child as a whole so that each professional can see her particular area of expertise from the view of others, particularly the family. It is also designed to be a more normal, natural situation in which to assess young children. One professional typically takes the lead while the others sit in a circle and watch, sometimes asking questions or making requests or suggestions. Done well, this is an excellent way for professionals and families to assess and plan for young children with disabilities.

Assessment Teams

There is consensus that it takes a team to educate a child with disabilities. Although it may be called by different names, a child study team decides whether the child meets the eligibility criteria of the IDEA, the designated disability category, and the child's special learning needs. It is important to know what each team member (specialist) does, and there are often many team members. In inclusive settings, most professionals will come into the classroom and work with a particular child or a small group of children. Specialists working in the classroom give educators an opportunity to observe what they do and gain additional skills. They can then help children generalize and transfer the skill that the specialists initiated. Educators and peers have the opportunity to learn about the therapy and to ask questions. In cases where the therapy cannot be done in the classroom, the educator should try to observe the child in therapy and request a description and explanation of the activities that occur during therapy. Specialists can help educators understand how a child's therapeutic needs will affect behavior in the class. Educators need to know how to follow through with the therapists' goals in the class and should invite the therapists to visit the class whenever possible.

Conversely, the early childhood special educator can help the therapist understand what is happening with the child in the classroom and why (specialists may not know why play is important). Educators should also see the specialist as a consultant available to share her expertise concerning any child in the classroom.

Knowing what specialists do is important, especially when you need advice about a problem. The next part of this chapter discusses types of specialists and others who work and plan for children with disabilities. When consulting a specialist, an effective communication strategy is to confirm or clarify points, restate what you think the specialist said in your own words, and ask whether that interpretation is accurate. Demonstrations are often effective. Say "Let me show you, and tell me if I am doing the right thing."

Potential Team Members

Included here is an alphabetical listing of specialists and others who provide services for young children with disabilities, with more detail provided for the less familiar specializations. These specialists are team members who work to meet the holistic needs of the child.

- **Administrators** provide leadership to organizations and are charged with ensuring organizations run smoothly, goals are being met, and the place works. These would include school district–level administrators, school principals, center directors, and others.

- **Child development consultants** usually have a master's degree and are trained in developmental principles and the use of assessment measures for young children. These consultants may work in a home-based setting and provide consultation to families, as well as in early care and education settings. They may serve as a liaison between the parents and a medical or educational setting.

- **Developmental psychologists** know about various aspects of child development and usually have a doctorate degree. They conduct assessments of children and families, and are knowledgeable about behavior management, counseling, and intervention strategies. They use educational and psychological tests to aid in the diagnostic process and are often on the multidisciplinary assessment teams of young children.

- **Early childhood educators** provide care and education for children from birth through age 8. They informally and formally assess children's development, plan curriculum, and select activities and experiences to support children's development in the areas of social-emotional, cognitive, language and literacy, physical/motor, and aesthetics. They may work with children and families in their homes, centers, or schools. Increasingly these educators are graduating from blended degree programs where they also gain skills in early childhood special education and early intervention. They help children learn and generalize concepts and behaviors by using them in a variety of situations.

- **Early childhood special educators** have training in child development, early childhood materials and methods, and special education. Increasingly, there is state certification for this position. These specialists have in-depth knowledge of specific disabilities and strategies for learning and accommodation. They may team-teach with early childhood educators. Increasingly students are earning dual certification in early childhood education and early childhood special education, including early intervention.

- **Educational diagnosticians** usually work under the supervision of a psychologist, testing and observing children referred to them for suspected disabilities. They write the formal reports that are required for special educational services. They can discuss test results with parents and educators and are usually knowledgeable in other areas such as behavior management, counseling, and intervention strategies.

- **Family support workers** offer home-based services to families of children with developmental delays and disabilities. They provide emotional support, assistance with obtaining appropriate services, and information on issues that relate to the child. They also act as advocates for the family and child and assist in coordinating services.

- **Medical specialists** are frequently consulted when children have disabilities. The exact nature of the problem and the complexity of it determine the specialists required. Frequently needed specialists include those in the fields of allergy and clinical immunology; arthritis and rheumatology; cardiovascular diseases (heart); dermatology (skin); endocrinology and metabolism (glandular diseases); gastroenterology (stomach and intestines); hematology (blood); nephrology (kidneys); neurology (nervous system); oncology (cancer); ophthalmology (eyes); orthopedic (bones); otolaryngology (ear, nose, and throat); physical medicine and rehabilitation; psychiatry; surgery; and urology (urinary tract). If specialists focus their specialty on children, the word **pediatric** precedes the specialization, for example, a pediatric rheumatologist.

- **Nutritionists** have training in the area of foods; the essential nutrients for a balanced diet; and the amount

Therapists are important team members who work with children and provide educators with information to modify the learning environment.
© Cengage Learning 2012

of nutrients necessary for energy, maintenance, and growth. They are concerned about all the processes by which the body uses food for energy and growth. Children with feeding problems, food allergies, and children who fail to thrive are likely to have a nutritionist on their team.

- **Occupational therapists (OTs)** work from a developmental rather than a medical base. They hold bachelor's or advanced degrees from an accredited school with course work in biological and psychosocial sciences, foundations of medicine, sensory integration, psychiatry, and prevocational skill development. Their therapy emphasizes vestibular (balance), tactile, **kinesthetic** or **proprioception** (sensory knowledge of one's body movements), and perceptual motor (mental interpretation of sensation and movement based on these sensations) development; fine motor coordination; and self-help/adaptive skills. The therapist's role includes assessment, intervention, and consultation in the areas of adaptive behavior and play, and sensory motor integration. OTs may adapt the environment (limiting distractions, combining gross and fine motor activities, making a task achievable) and provide devices to help develop functional skills such as eating, dressing, playing, and minimizing the impact of a disability.

- **Paraeducators** are paraprofessionals, educational assistants, and instructional assistants designed to aide the teacher or a specific child. They reflect the variety of roles and responsibilities of this member of the special education team. Paraeducators work under the supervision of a teacher or other professional. They have skills and contributions that make them important in the education of young children.

- **Parents and family members** are important specialists. They determine the priorities for their child and family. They know what their child wants and needs and how they want these needs addressed. Families give other team members information on how their child functions at home and help team members see the whole child in the context of the family and the culture in which they live. They update the team on an ongoing basis.

- **Pediatric nurses** are registered nurses who have training in developmental screening tools as well as additional training in family counseling, evaluation, and children. They work out of hospitals, community-based settings, or a state department of health. The pediatric nurse often makes home visits to help parents learn to better care for and meet the medical needs of their young child with a disability, in addition to monitoring the child's health status. These nurses often work with child development specialists for developmental intervention or infant stimulation.

- **Pediatricians** are physicians who specialize in the medical treatment of children from birth to about age 12. They are probably the most familiar professionals for families with young children. Pediatricians may be the first to express concern about a condition or the first person to whom parents turn to express their concerns.

- **Physical therapists (PTs)** are state-licensed health professionals who have completed an accredited educational program, largely medically based, which includes the study of biological, physical, medical, and psychosocial sciences, as well as course work in neurology, orthopedics, therapeutic exercise, and treatment techniques. Physical therapy is directed toward preventing disability, that is, developing, improving, or restoring more efficient muscular functioning and maintaining maximum motor functioning. PTs work with any child requiring **prosthetic** management training; wheelchair mobility training; or measurement for, or use of, other medically prescribed mobility devices. PTs evaluate the child's **range of motion**, posture, **muscle tone**, strength, balance, and gross motor skills. Treatment usually focuses on increasing strength, improving balance skills, and gross motor development. PTs are responsible for monitoring a child's orthopedic needs and assisting the family in obtaining adaptive equipment, if necessary. They provide families and educators with information about optimal ways for positioning and carrying the child for different activities.

- **Physicians** are medical doctors who may be pediatricians, family practitioners, neurologists, or other medical specialists. Their role includes determining medical needs and referring the family to specialists and programs that can provide needed services.

- **Psychologists'** roles vary with the setting and the level of training they have as well as their specialization. A school psychologist is state certified and typically has completed either a master's or doctoral degree in school psychology. Course work varies from state to state but generally includes psychology, counseling, standardized testing and its interpretation, child development, disability studies, and education. Most psychologists must complete an internship or practicum under a practicing psychologist. The duties of a psychologist in a school setting vary with the number of psychologists in the district and their individual skills. Most school psychologists test and observe children referred to them because of a suspected disability. They write formal reports that are required to determine children's eligibility for special education services and may consult with teachers or families to discuss test results or make observations and suggestions. Some psychologists emphasize individual therapy; others work with the child as part of the family unit.

- **Social workers** usually concentrate on the adults in the family unit. They may look at family needs in relation to child rearing or coordinating the social service network. They are knowledgeable about resources and referrals to community services (Medicaid, **respite** care). Social workers usually work in the home and are often the best source of information about the types of intervention families may need. They are trained in family relations, counseling and advocacy skills, and working with agencies. Increasingly, public schools have social workers as part of their staff.

- **Speech-language pathologists** are state licensed and have completed a degree program with an accredited college. Course work includes psychology, education, and anatomy, with an emphasis on speech and language development. The role of the speech-language pathologist in early intervention includes assessment and intervention with oral-motor disorders (difficulties in feeding and swallowing as well as speech production) and communication delays and disorders. Their work relates to social communicative competence during preverbal and verbal development, receptive and expressive language (both speech and nonverbal means of communication), and speech production and perception. Many children with disabilities have associated problems with muscle tone that may affect the movements of the tongue and lips needed for feeding and speech.

IMPLICATIONS FOR EDUCATORS

Once you read and analyze a specialist's report, you must translate it into strengths and challenges for which you can program. The process might work like this: The occupational therapist reports, "Mike fell off the nystagmus board following rotation." After doing some checking in the medical dictionary, you decide that Mike was dizzy! Mike probably needs practice in changing directions and starting and stopping to better develop his sense of balance, which is located in the inner ear—vestibular sense. Now, check with the medical report and parents to figure out why Mike might be dizzy and whether you need to avoid or limit any activities. You might plan creative movement activities with slow turns, as well as working on body awareness, flexibility, and static and dynamic balance.

The role you, as educator, will play on the team is largely determined by how the team defines itself, but your role is always extremely important. You have the opportunity to talk formally and informally with families on a regular basis and to see the child almost every day. Few other team members will have that amount of contact. Assessment operates in a variety of ways: as a multidisciplinary team, an interdisciplinary team, or a transdisciplinary team.

Multidisciplinary Teams

The multidisciplinary team sorts the child's condition into component parts. The parents take their child to different professionals for assessment and intervention, and the professionals then funnel their input back to the parents, primary care physician (and hopefully the service coordinator), who must sort it out. A strength of this model is that people from different disciplines are involved, and parents have more input in the choice of team members (they can choose the physical or occupational therapist they like best). However, separate disciplinary assessments, reports, and goals written by each professional may contribute to confusion, fragmented services, and lack of coordination of services to children and their families.

Professionals may present conflicting diagnostic and intervention strategies. Team members rarely meet, so it is up to parents to decide what to do, whom to believe, or what further information they need. Despite the obvious drawbacks, if there are strong, knowledgeable parents, this type of team has the potential for providing good programming for children. A multidisciplinary team may be the only option available to some families, especially those who live in rural areas. For professionals, this is the least time-consuming type of team as no time need be allocated for interacting with team members, and for many professionals that is an important consideration.

Interdisciplinary Teams

Traditionally, interdisciplinary teams have specified members as a core team and add members as needed. Core team members include those who are directly responsible for the child and who work together to plan, implement, and evaluate the child's educational program. Core members usually include the child's early childhood educator and/or early childhood special educator, paraeducators, therapists, a designated service coordinator, and family members (Snell & Janney, 2000). They meet on a regular basis (e.g., once a month). A **service coordinator** is a designated individual who, in addition to being part of the team, has the specific role of communicating with the family and other team members to set up meetings and convey information. She is responsible for organizing the team and ensuring that outcomes do not conflict with one another, and is the main contact for the family when the assessment process is completed. The IDEA requires that identified children between birth and age 3 have a service coordinator. Parents, if they choose, can function in this capacity. For less involved children, the service coordinator may be the early childhood special educator. For young children who are severely involved, the service coordinator is frequently a pediatric nurse.

It is possible for interdisciplinary teams to have some specialists who do not meet with the group but send in written reports. Drawbacks to this method include problems in communication and interaction when team members do not have comprehensive understanding of the expertise of other team members. Scheduling meetings may be a problem.

Transdisciplinary Teams

Transdisciplinary teams have the highest level of coordination and integration. All members of the transdisciplinary assessment team, including the parents, provide information regarding the child's strengths and needs. Ideally, this process helps each discipline see the interrelationships among developmental areas. What emerges is an individualized program based on the whole child that can be implemented in a setting following the regular routines.

Once the child is assessed, the team develops an integrated service plan and decides on one team member to carry out the plan with the family. One major concept in the transdisciplinary approach is that of **role release**, "a process of transferring information and skills traditionally associated with one discipline to team members of other disciplines" (Rainforth & York-Barr, 1997, p. 19). For example, the PT may coach the speech-language pathologist on working with positioning a particular child and thus functions as the child's speech-language pathologist and PT in this instance. Role release requires trust that another professional will follow through and seek more advice when necessary. A developmental psychologist may work with a child in the areas of OT and speech therapy in addition to psychology. This does not mean that the developmental psychologist has become an instant occupational therapist, but rather that the skills necessary to intervene with this particular child can be transmitted to the psychologist so that the child and family can receive three types of therapy in an integrated approach from one person.

The potential for better communication and more accurate diagnoses exists because parents and professionals can ask questions of each other during the assessment process rather than relying on written reports. This highly desirable approach is also a costly one. Considerable time has to be allocated for sharing, planning, coordinating, and training team members. Coordinating schedules so that all team members are available at the same time necessitates an ongoing regular commitment. However, more agencies are seeing the worth of this model. From parents' perspective, one possible drawback is that once they choose the team, they lose the ability to choose individuals, so that if there is one member of the team they do not like or respect, they must adapt.

Regardless of the makeup of the team, if there is a concern about a child, a conference with the family is necessary. Some conferences are scheduled on a regular basis; others evolve because of developmental concerns or problems.

IMPLICATIONS FOR EDUCATORS

As part of the assessment team, you will often find yourself in the position of needing to get or give information about a particular child. Without meaning to, other professionals may use terms that are unfamiliar to you. Stop and ask them to define words that you don't understand. If you disagree with something that other professionals have written or said, ask them to explain why they made that particular determination. Often if you pair something that you like about what they did or said with something you are concerned about, they will listen more attentively. For example, "I'm very pleased with the progress Victor's been making since he began physical therapy, but I don't understand why it is so important for him to sit with his feet in front of him and his knees up during group time."

Remember, you know the child well. You certainly see the child more often than the specialists, and you have important information to share. It is helpful to be specific and to base your comments on direct observations of the child and your written records. For example:

- When you know that a child can perform some skills that specialists report she did not perform during the assessment, share that information with them. They may still want the child to perform the particular skill for them as well, but your input is helpful.

- Whenever you notice dramatic changes in a child, it is important to report them to the child's family and other professionals on the team especially if they are trying to determine the usefulness or appropriate amount of medication needed. (Also, ask that others inform you when a child's behavior or medication is changed.)

- Keep other team members informed when a child is able to master goals written on her IEP/IFSP. This will let others know that it is time to write new goals and suggest some new activities.

- A child's needs are best met when all individuals working with the child, including parents, educators, doctors, therapists, and child care providers, are well informed.

Program Evaluation

Assessment and evaluation includes program evaluation. Programs must be regularly evaluated to determine whether they are meeting their goals and whether children and their families are benefiting from the program (NAEYC, 2009a). In the past, it was often simply assumed that if children went to school, they were learning. But teachers, like other professionals, must now be more accountable—not only to principals and other administrators, but to children, families, taxpayers, and the legal system.

As with assessing children, multiple indicators of progress are used and all components of a program evaluated. Families and legislators are increasingly concerned about how well educational settings are doing in educating the young citizens of the country, particularly those at risk. Without accountability assessments, it is difficult to know which programs and which aspects of a program are doing well and which are not. Accountability decisions are usually made at the district, state, or national level.

THE EVIDENCE BASE

The emphasis on scientific, evidence-based early childhood educational programs has made us look at programs differently. Previously, there was often conflicting evidence, or researchers came to different conclusions about programs based on the same data. To address these problems, as educators we must become better consumers of evaluation information. The National Forum on Early Childhood Program Evaluation has identified five key questions that should be asked about early childhood programs:

1. Is the evaluation design strong enough to produce trustworthy evidence? (p. 2)

This question really asks, How are children different because they attended xyz program? To answer this question, a comparison group of children who did not attend xyz is needed. Ideally, children are assigned randomly to intervention and nonintervention options. If this is not possible, a comparisons group must be used and the research designed to ensure that the comparison group is similar to those who are attending the program.

2. What program services were actually received by participating children and families and comparison groups? (p. 3)

The way programs are designed and the way the services are actually delivered can differ. Sometimes programs are not implemented as intended or families may not participate in the expected way. It is important to know whether families and children availed themselves of the services offered, that is, how many of the children and families participated and how much service they received. Similar information is needed about the comparison group.

3. How much impact did the program have? (p. 5)

Impact is the difference between the treatment and comparison group on selected outcomes. This is frequently expressed as "effects sizes." In general, the larger the effect size, the better. Program impact may be different for different subgroups of children and for those who used the program more.

4. Do the program's benefits exceed its costs? (p. 7)

If very effective programs have a large effect but are tremendously expensive, they may not be practical. It is a balance between costs and benefits, or return on investment. But return for whom? Is return measured by the quality of life for the participants or by economic productivity and costs for society? In early childhood, the benefits are typically long range and relative to fewer children in special education, fewer children in the justice system, or higher earnings.

5. How similar are the programs, children, and families in the study to those in your constituency or community? (p. 8)

To the extent that you decide to use a particular program or practice you need to find out how similar the children and families served are to the children and families you work with.

Source: National Forum on Early Childhood Program Evaluation, 2007

Using evidence to improve programs is an important part of program evaluation. However, all programs should be evaluated formally or informally on a regular basis.

Informal Program Evaluation

The major reason for evaluating a program is to provide information to those involved with the program about what is working well and what needs attention. One obvious question most programs want to answer is, Does the program meet the needs of the people it serves? The answer to this question requires information. What are the characteristics and needs of the children and families served in the program? Different children in different types of families have different needs, although they may all be in the same program or classroom. Program evaluation needs to be sensitive to both group and individual differences.

It is important to know the purpose of the evaluation at the beginning. When the evaluation is being done to decide whether to continue a program or eliminate it, those involved in the evaluation may have very different agendas. If the purpose of the evaluation is to determine whether early intervention decreased the number of children requiring special education services, then the data necessary for evaluation are very different than if the purpose of the evaluation is to decide which is more effective, full- or half-day kindergarten. Without having decided on the purpose of the evaluation, one cannot proceed in any meaningful way.

Sometimes program evaluation is used to help solve a particular problem a program or class is having. This type of evaluation focuses on a single aspect of a program or a classroom that has been identified as a problem. Although the problems may vary, the procedure for evaluation is similar:

1. Identify the problem in a way that can lead to solutions. "They should not have violence on children's television shows" is not a solvable problem. It is a value judgment. Instead: "Some children watch superheroes on television and come to school and play out what they have seen. How can I set up my classroom to discourage superhero play? What must I develop to regulate this play?" is a solvable problem.

2. Review relevant literature and talk to people in other programs or classes to see how they have dealt with similar problems. (Although problems may seem unique, it is unlikely that you are the first person to encounter the problem.)

3. Develop a system for dealing with the problem. Share this system with all those involved (especially families) and gather their input. Modify the system.

4. Field-test the modified system for an appropriate period of time (perhaps two to four weeks).

5. Evaluate the results, modify the system if necessary, and retest, or keep the system in place.

You may have used this procedure informally, for example, when you were coping with superhero play, and not realized that in reality you evaluated your program as having a problem, explored the dimensions of the problem, looked at what others had done, developed a system to solve the problem, evaluated that solution, and modified your approach.

Some program evaluation is extensive and ambitious. You may be asked to participate in evaluation projects by providing specific input. Some evaluation projects are long range as well as short range. Knowing long-term goals for children can help you focus a curriculum in early childhood.

IMPLICATIONS FOR EDUCATORS

People who fund programs want to know how effective they are, and administrators may need the information to defend programs or to get additional programs or classrooms. Educators, however, may feel threatened by the evaluation process or feel that it is not relevant to them. They may feel that the obligations of teaching alone are already enough. "You hired me to teach, leave me alone and let me teach!" Program evaluation is not likely to succeed without teacher support.

At the very least the process of evaluation must describe the population you serve and exactly what you are doing. All programs and individual classrooms need this minimum information. If you are not clear about what you are doing and why you are doing it, you cannot effectively present your classroom to parents or administrators.

Evaluation is essential to improve programs. Administrators need to know how you evaluate your program and how satisfied you are with the program. To the extent that you are not an active participant in the evaluation process, things that do not satisfy you are unlikely to change, and you may be unhappy in your job. Know that you are one of the stakeholders; you have a vested interest, and you need to know enough about the evaluation process to make it work for you and your program. You also need to be sure the evaluation process does not interfere with your teaching.

The less intrusive and less burdensome the evaluation process is for teachers, the more likely it is to go smoothly and to be completed. You need to remind others the evaluation process is important. Data collected must be used, and the people who collect the data need to be informed of its use.

If you believe that the information you collect is going into a "black hole," you are unlikely to continue collecting it in a careful manner, if at all.

When children have IEPs with measurable goals, these need to be evaluated as well. IEPs should be grouped for evaluation, and you should aim for an 85 percent achievement rate. A dramatically higher rate may show that you aren't stretching yourself or the families; a rate of 50 percent or less means that expectations are not realistic or the program is not effective.

We no longer need to question the efficacy of early intervention because we have "proved" it works. We are now fine-tuning the system. We need to learn about the effectiveness of different models of programming for different populations: What types of services, in what combinations, using what models are most effective? Applied research is now concerned with why a program works or fails to work and for whom it works.

SUMMARY

- Assessment provides the basis for eligibility for special educational services.

- Referral processes begin informally with families or educators having concerns about a child.

- Response to intervention plans are developed. If not successful, screening measures, functional assessments, and standardized tests may be used.

- Information from these measures and the pre-referral process determine whether a child is eligible for special educational services.

- Assessment teams are organized in a variety of ways, depending on the particular team members and the roles that various professionals play.

- Parents are part of all teams that make decisions about placement and instruction.

- Early childhood special educators must learn the roles of other team members and methods of collaboration.

- Programs are evaluated, as well as the children who are in these programs.

EDUCATIONAL RESOURCES

American Psychological Association (APA) has specific sites devoted to testing and assessment. The APA publishes journals and holds annual conferences that relate to assessment as well as other developmental issues. www.apa.org; www.apa.org/science/testing.html/

Association of Test Publishers provides basic answers to why testing is useful. Good site for educators and parents. www.testpublishers.org/

ERIC Clearinghouse on Assessment and Evaluation provides links to tests and test selection kits and information on assessment, evaluations, and research information. Good resource for educators and providers. www.ericae.net/

National Center for Research on Evaluation, Standards, and Student Testing (CRESST) focuses on the assessment of educational quality, design issues, and the use of assessment systems to serve multiple purposes. CRESST conducts research that improves assessment, evaluation, technology, and learning. www.cse.ucla.edu/

National Center on Educational Outcomes (NCEO) provides leadership in including students with disabilities in national and state assessments. The center has an online bibliography with research on the effects of various testing accommodations for students. http://cehd.umn.edu/nceo/

Wrightslaw provides accurate, reliable information about special education law, education law, and advocacy for children with disabilities at www.wrightslaw.com/. It provides information on understanding tests and measurements for parents and explains the law and the meaning of tests. It also links to other sites about advocacy and IEP planning at www.wrightslaw.com/advoc/articles/tests_measurements.html/

For additional educational resources, visit the book companion website for this text at www.cengagebrain.com.

The most difficult thing for me when I first began teaching was to figure out how to set up and run my classroom. I remember going into my room for the first time and seeing this huge pile of stuff in the middle of the floor, containing all of my classroom furniture, desk, and other random materials. I had no idea where to start, so I just dug in and started laying out my classroom.

When I began designing lessons, I realized there was no curriculum to follow and no resource materials to provide ideas. I was overwhelmed! I asked my principal about the kindergarten curriculum; he told me that whatever I wanted to do was fine by him as long as the class wasn't too noisy—not the answer I was looking for. I went to a teachers' store and began gathering and reading resource books for ideas—even ideas about how to begin school on the first day.

I remember being frustrated and thinking that college did not prepare me to design and develop a curriculum. There were very few materials to work with in the room—no manipulatives, construction paper, or even paint. I quickly found out how much my budget was going to be, grabbed all the school's catalogs, and ordered my materials, which made me feel much better.

When we had our first open house, parents thought my paraeducator was the teacher, not me. I looked far too young to be a teacher. That was difficult, and I felt I had to start earning the respect of parents and coworkers who didn't take me seriously because I was so young and new to the classroom. When I held my IEP meetings at the beginning and end of the year, I felt the need to prove myself as a professional and to be seen

© Cengage Learning 2012

as the authority in my classroom. Even after three years in the classroom, parents still refer to my paraeducator as the teacher, a mistake I clear up right away.

The first year ended quickly, but when I look back on those hectic first days, I wonder how I endured the stress. Luckily, I had a very good mentor who helped me when things got hairy and guided me whenever I had questions about IEPs or anything else related to the classroom. I'm thankful to her because I don't think I would have survived without her mentorship and patience. ✳

REFLECTIVE PRACTICE | Do you feel ready to set up a classroom and greet children the first day of school? You probably have additional coursework to take and student teaching. As you continue your education, reflect on this new teacher's dilemma and what you must do and learn to feel more confident on your first day.

Planning Inclusive Curriculum

DAP Developing a program that (1) meets the needs of all the children in your classroom, (2) falls within the guidelines of your current workplace, (3) follows the dictates of both state and federal laws, and (4) fits your personal philosophy and beliefs is a difficult task at best. To do it on a daily basis, year after year, may seem daunting. Given the importance of

the task, it is necessary not only to do it well but also to do it efficiently. Designing a classroom experience that is enjoyable for you and the children, is flexible enough to support both short- and long-term change, and has a flair of creativity is a challenge.

Curriculum involves decisions about how children learn, when learning takes place, and what is to be learned. It requires you to "[i]mplement curriculum that is thoughtfully planned, challenging, engaging, developmentally appropriate, culturally and linguistically responsive, comprehensive, and likely to promote positive outcomes for all young children" (NAEYC, 2003, p. 2).

Some children with disabilities take longer to learn concepts than their peers. They need activities that are self-motivating within a prescribed set of IEP goals. Planned activities and experiences must also cover all the strands that are traditionally part of the developmental domains (cognitive, adaptive [self-help], physical [fine and gross motor], sensory, communication, social, and emotional), and also part of the general curriculum (mathematics, science, English language arts, etc.). Where possible, activities should teach more than one skill at a time.

Including children with diverse abilities in regular classrooms has a legislative base. However, your personal feelings about inclusion will influence how you proceed. Once you are clear about your feelings, you can move on to the next stage and look at the strategies you will use to be inclusive and the personal supports you need to make inclusion a positive experience for all children.

There may be some children and some disabilities you will find easier to include than others. Although all of us like to think we like all children equally, this is rarely true. We may treat children equally, but personal feelings are different. Try to move yourself away from the specifics and figure out the generic aspect of a child or disability that influences you—the part that will be repeated with other children.

Reflective practice is the foundation of competence in early childhood education. It emphasizes the importance of thoughtful analysis and continual revision of effective approaches to teaching and learning. The competent educator is characterized by habits of mind that emphasize critical thinking, experimentation, and openness to change. Reflective practice encourages educators to become confident in applying a flexible array of skills that at times may seem automatic. Understandings are constructed, not given, and these understandings must be continually adapted, revised, and revisited. Reflection is different from description. Reflection requires asking "what if . . . ?" types of questions. Reflection is a complex process that has to be broken down into smaller units and requires a model or an organizational framework that makes clear the steps in the process. Reflection is a skill that becomes more refined with practice; it is a growth experience that leads to continuous improvement in teaching.

Developmentally Appropriate Practice

DAP What is developmentally appropriate practice? How do you know it when you see it? To explain developmentally appropriate practice, the National Association for the Education of Young Children (NAEYC) developed a position paper and guidelines in 1986, updated them in 1987, revised them in 1996, and again in 2009. These revisions reflect new knowledge, particularly in neurobiology; the inclusion of children with disabilities in regular classrooms; and the increasing number of infants and toddlers in group care. They also reflect a field that is changing and a professional commitment to keep up with these changes (NAEYC, 2009a).

Developmentally appropriate practice (NAEYC, 2009a) has three basic components:

1. What is known about child development and learning—referring to knowledge of age-related characteristics that permits general predictions about what experiences are likely to best promote children's learning and development (p. 9).

2. What is known about each child as an individual—referring to what practitioners learn about each child that has implications for how best to adapt and be responsive to that individual variation (p. 9).

3. What is known about the social and cultural contexts in which children live—referring to the values, expectations, and behavioral and linguistic conventions that shape children's lives at home and in their communities; practitioners must strive to understand these in order to ensure that learning experiences in the program or school are meaningful, relevant, and respectful for each child and family (p. 10).

Knowledge about child development and learning requires you to understand patterns of growth and development. Knowing about child development is essential, but it is also necessary to know about the strengths, interests, and needs of the individual child. This knowledge allows you to adapt to and be responsive to individual variations in including children with diverse abilities (NAEYC, 2009a). Knowledge of age-related characteristics helps you predict where children are developing within an age range so you can design experiences and activities and choose materials that are interesting and will also challenge them. Children live in families. Meaningful and relevant learning experiences are respectful of children and their families. They must take into account the children's culture, language, and social context (NAEYC, 2009a).

● ● ●

Principles Underlying Developmentally Appropriate Practice

The principles underlying developmentally appropriate practice are based on what we reliably know about child development and learning. The principles are given below, and a brief explanation follows each principle. These principles influence the beliefs and philosophy of education for all children. Principles of development and learning inform developmentally appropriate practice (NAEYC, 2009a).

1. *All the domains of development and learning—physical, social and emotional, and cognitive—are important and are closely interrelated. Children's development and learning in one domain influence and are influenced by what takes place in other domains (p. 11).*

The younger the child, the closer the curriculum is tied to the child's experiential base. Scholars are focusing more on functional interrelationships among developmental **domains**. Changes in one domain, for example, learning to walk, influence all other domains. Young children need a comprehensive curriculum that interrelates all of the developmental domains. Thinking about multiple domains helps organize learning.

2. *Many aspects of children's learning and development follow well-documented sequences, with later abilities, skills, and knowledge building on those already acquired (p. 11).*

Predictable changes occur in all developmental areas during the early childhood years. Knowledge of these patterns provides the basis for designing the environment and planning for children. Information about developmental patterns helps determine the types of materials to use as well as whether children are showing atypical patterns of development. Knowledge of prerequisite skills helps individualize planning.

3. *Development and learning proceed at varying rates from child to child, as well as at uneven rates across different areas of a child's individual functioning (p. 11).*

All children are unique, yet they share commonalities in their sequence of growth and development. They have individual patterns of strengths, challenges, and interests, and vary in temperament, attitudes, and personality as well as the knowledge base they bring to the learning situation. Individual variation is expected, valued, and planned for.

4. *Development and learning result from a dynamic and continuous interaction of biological maturation and experience (p. 12).*

Development is the result of the interplay between nature and nurture. Children who are born with a genetic makeup that predicts a typical growth pattern may experience developmental delays if they experience abuse and neglect and then become homeless. Likewise children born at risk who have responsive families and early intervention may exceed expectations. Diversity is forcing us to investigate the roles of nature, nurture, culture, and the complex interactions of these.

5. *Early experiences have profound effects, both cumulative and delayed, on a child's development and learning; and optimal periods exist for certain types of development and learning to occur (p. 12).*

Children's early experiences, both positive and negative, affect their development. Isolated events may have a minimal impact, but events, positive or negative, that occur frequently have cumulative, lasting effects. Research supports the idea of broadly conceived *sensitive periods, or cycles*, when the child is more susceptible to change or where the impact of events is more pervasive. Birth to 3 years is the optimal period for the development of verbal language skills. Although children can learn language later, it requires specific intervention and more effort. Information about the relationship between early experience and the brain has focused on early childhood as a "prime time" for development. An enriched environment helps brain cells form synapses and stabilizes these connections to support learning. Genetics may establish the upper and lower limits of development, but the environment determines where within this range a specific trait falls.

6. *Development proceeds toward greater complexity, self-regulation, and symbolic or representational capacities (p. 12).*

Young children learn through hands-on experiences. They begin to acquire symbolic knowledge and move into thinking that can take place in the present, remember the past, and anticipate the future. Children grow in their ability to regulate their own behavior. The adult's role is to present a curriculum that motivates and challenges them, and social situations that require high levels of peer interaction.

7. *Children develop best when they have secure, consistent relationships with responsive adults and opportunities for positive relationships with peers (p. 13).*

Changing social patterns affect families and children. Children need warm, nurturing relationships with family members and other caring adults. When children spend large parts of their day with adults other than their parents, having a trusting relationship with a primary caregiver is essential. Children need to be in environments where they can develop trusting relationships with adults, establish their autonomy, and be empowered to continue to learn. They need to feel safe in early childhood settings both psychologically and physically. Prosocial behavior should be encouraged and supported

8. *Development and learning occur in and are influenced by multiple social and cultural contexts (p. 13).*

We must become more aware of families and culture and the role they play in early growth and development, and assure that curriculum and planning is responsive to this knowledge base. All of us are members of cultures and are influenced by them. Every culture has preferred patterns of child rearing and interprets children's behavior and development in its own way.

9. *Always mentally active in seeking to understand the world around them, children learn in a variety of ways; a wide range of teaching strategies and interventions are effective in supporting all these kinds of learning (p. 14).*

Curriculum continually moves from what children know to the acquisition and consolidation of new knowledge. It moves from what children can do themselves to learning that requires adult scaffolding. Children come to learning experiences with different backgrounds; some have had a variety of experiences, others relatively few. Good curriculum and responsive adults meet children where they are and provide the scaffolding for them to take the next steps. Curriculum and experiences have to be flexible and allow for different learning experiences with the same activity. Experiences must be modified (made easier or more difficult) to meet the needs of children with diverse experiences and abilities. Teachers must have multiple teaching strategies to meet children's different learning styles.

10. *Play is an important vehicle for developing self-regulation as well as for promoting language, cognition, and social competence. (p. 14)*

Most early social interactions center on play and play activities. The quality and level of interaction that occurs among children in play activities develops sequentially, increasing with age and maturation. As children's play develops, their social interactions move from adults to peers. One of the greatest aspects of play is that it is unpredictable. When children play, they do not know where it will lead. They have to respond to what happens. This means they have to put their cognitive processes in gear as well as using their social and emotional skills.

11. *Development and learning advance when children are challenged to achieve at a level just beyond their current mastery, and also when they have many opportunities to practice newly acquired skills (p. 15).*

Environments that support children as active learners encourage the construction of knowledge by offering experiences that are at the edge of a child's knowledge base and that encourage a child to generate and test out her hypotheses. Well-chosen new experiences help children modify, adapt, expand, and reorganize their working model of the world. When educators scaffold learning and help children plan, act, and then reflect on experiences, this process is enhanced.

Children come to understand their world in different ways. Over time, they develop preferred learning modalities and different styles of learning. They represent their world differently and are good at different things. Sometimes this is due to personal experience and preferences. Other times, it is because of sensory or motor impairments. Knowing how children represent their world, adults can present information in ways that make it easier for them to learn; likewise, they can give children opportunities to strengthen other areas.

12. *Children's experiences shape their motivation and approaches to learning, such as persistence, initiative, and flexibility; in turn, these dispositions and behaviors affect their learning and development (p. 15).*

It is as important to know how children learn as well as what they learn. Children who are motivated and eager to learn do better in language arts and mathematics. Motivation is the desire to do something. Teachers can help build motivation by challenging children, choosing activities that have high interest, showing children that they are genuinely concerned about them and their learning, planning for success, and rewarding children when they do well (adapted from NAEYC, 2009a; pp. 10–16).

Strategies for Individualizing Learning

DAP Regardless of content or age, there is a cycle of learning that takes place as new information becomes part of a child's repertoire. This learning framework has four broad aspects: awareness, exploration, inquiry, and utilization (Bredekamp & Rosegrant, 1992).

1. *Awareness* is the initial stage in the learning cycle and grows out of experience. As children notice differences among themselves, questions arise: "Why does Ian have those things on his legs?" "Why is my skin black and Justine's white?" When children are at an awareness

level, they want a simple, straightforward answer. "Ian's legs aren't strong enough to hold him, so he needs braces to help" may be all the child wants to know. Often we tell children more than they really want to know.

2. *Exploration* is the next level and requires children to examine and try to make sense out of an event or experience by exploring materials, gathering additional information, poking, prodding, or doing whatever seems to make sense to the child. Although it is tempting to "explain" the situation, it is rarely useful; children need to find their own meaning for information. Explaining fosters dependency. Asking open-ended questions fosters exploration.

3. *Inquiry* involves the understanding of classes of information, the ability to generalize information, and the ability to call up previous learned information for comparison. Adults can help children with more focused questions at this stage.

4. *Utilization* is a functional level of learning where information can be used in a variety of settings and applied to new information and situations. Children who understand the concept of one-to-one correspondence can count objects accurately and decide that six chairs are necessary for six children to sit on.

This cycle occurs repeatedly as children learn. It is important to know where individual children are in the cycle. When a child encounters information for the first time, he begins at an awareness level. Children with previous experiences may be generalizing the same information. Some children will have less broad experiential backgrounds. They need to be given time to experience and explore before they can be expected to participate in higher level skills. Programs must be designed that allow children to profit from experience at all phases in the learning cycle.

Young children encountering a wheelchair for the first time will go through these stages in the learning cycle. Rent or borrow a wheelchair so children can explore it. Initially, they will be curious about the wheelchair and might want to sit in it and see how it works. This is exploration; they need this time. When they have their own understanding of the wheelchair, try to broaden and generalize this information so they can figure out what activities are difficult or easy to do in a wheelchair and the relationship among wheelchairs, crutches, and walkers. As they integrate this information, have them think about the world outside the classroom, the utility of curb cuts, why bathrooms can be difficult to negotiate, and the problem with table heights. Then help them break down the utility of different constructs by comparing wheelchairs to tricycles and bicycles.

Range of Teaching Techniques

DAP Teaching techniques must be adapted to meet children's learning needs. These techniques range from more directive to less directive, with many degrees in between. The goal is to match the technique to the material being learned and the child who is learning it. *All* teachers need *all* of these techniques.

- *Withholding attention,* or planned ignoring, is frequently used when adults know a child can accomplish a task without assistance, or as part of a behavior strategy for handling undesirable but nondangerous behavior. It can also be employed during the latency period between making a request and the child's response. Be sure to give young children enough time to respond.

- *Acknowledging* reinforces children's behavior by giving children positive attention, particularly when the goal is to have the behavior continue. Done intermittently and for pointing out specific aspects of behavior, it is a useful way to shape behavior. When overused or when acknowledgment is too general, it is less useful.

- *Encouraging* supports effort and persistence, it is different from praising and evaluating.

- *Giving specific feedback* helps children focus on particular aspects of their behavior or project that were well done or need additional work.

- *Modeling,* whether conscious or unconscious, is a way of teaching children which behaviors are appropriate and which are inappropriate. By their actions, adults show children how to interact with others or how to use a new material, rather than telling them.

- *Facilitating* involves providing temporary assistance to a child. This can involve verbal support, such as giving a suggestion for a different way of approaching a problem or reattaching a piece of paper that has come loose. It is specific and time-limited and enables a child to continue independently.

- *Supporting* is similar to facilitating, but it is more general and lasts longer. The goal is independence, but the expectation is that it will take longer to achieve.

- *Scaffolding* is working on the edge of a child's knowledge base. It provides the link between what a child can do independently and what she can accomplish with adult help. It is more directive than the previous techniques in that the adult provides more focus for the child's activity.

- *Creating or reducing challenge* helps expand children's knowledge or meets children where they are.

- *Asking questions* helps children to think differently or more deeply about what they are doing.

- *Co-constructing* involves doing a project with or collaborating with a child. This is a more directive technique and one that is useful when children don't know how to use particular materials. It is also useful to join with children. One can move momentarily from scaffolding to co-construction and back.

- *Demonstrating* is more directive, as the teacher does the project and the children watch. There are times when this is extremely useful and appropriate such as when

there is a correct way to do something, such as writing the letters of the alphabet. Demonstrating is often followed by less directive techniques and the opportunity to practice.

- *Directing* involves telling a child specifically what to do. It also implies that there is a correct way to do something and that a specific outcome is desired (adapted from Bredekamp & Rosegrant, 1995; Copple & Bredekamp, 2009).

An educator's philosophy and the children she teaches reflect how much time she spends using different teaching techniques. Early childhood educators are frequently criticized for being too nondirective to meet the needs of children with disabilities, whereas special educators are criticized for being too directive. The solution is to be aware of the range of techniques and continually move from less directive to more directive techniques as children need more support learning, but then to move into less directive strategies as children begin to master tasks. The goal is an appropriate match so that the strategy that provides the most learning for the child is employed.

Contextual Planning

Planning is dependent upon your philosophy, the setting you work in, the age of the children you teach, and the children who are included in your class. Planning starts with the children you teach. Find out what topics interest them, and then evaluate these topics for the goals and standards children are striving toward, both academic and developmental. Then, think about yourself. Does the topic interest you? What do you know about the topic? What resources do you have to support it? Next, think about its potential for meeting children's Individualized Educational Program (IEP) goals. If you work through this process, the themes or units you choose are likely to be successful.

For young children, the curriculum is based on their individual needs, the places (home, school, child care, or some combination) where they spend time, and the priorities of the child's family. Good curriculum is responsive to the cultural background of the children and their geographic location. For example, if transportation were the theme, a class of children from an urban area studying transportation might graph the number of children who walk to school, take the bus or subway, or are driven by families. Children in a rural agrarian area may focus on cars, trucks, and tractors, whereas those who live near the shore might look at boats and ships, including tugboats, freighters, and container vessels.

Schedules, Routines, and Transitions

Schedules refer to who will do what and when they will do it. The key to schedule planning is flexibility and organizing general time blocks that respond to children's needs. Ideally, timing is flexible but sequences are predictable. This helps children learn what will happen next. **Routines** are events that must be completed on a regular basis and often involve a series of responses. Some routines offer an opportunity for spending time individually with a child and provide chances to communicate. Routines give children a sense of security and trust, as their most basic needs are being met in a consistent caring manner. Thinking about routines as part of the learning environment incorporates planning into the caring aspect of routines.

Transitions are the time between the end of one event and the beginning of another. Transitions offer unique opportunities for growth as well as challenges to educators. This can be the time between activities, the beginning and end of the day, before and after lunch, or moving from inside to outside. Transitions are particularly difficult times for children as well as adults. At home, the times before meals, bedtime, and the like are stressful. As there are many transitions in a single day, and the stress created in these transitions can carry over into the next event, it is important to plan transitions to both increase learning and decrease stress.

The younger the children, the wider the age range of children, or the more children with disabilities, the more likely it is that transition periods will be longer. (Compare the time it takes for a 5-year-old versus a 3-year-old to put on boots and a snowsuit.) With younger children, the transitions may be more obvious to the adult than to the child. Transitions are important learning times for children, as many tasks involve adaptive skills. Teaching these skills (dressing and undressing, toileting, hand washing, eating, and settling for a nap) consumes a large portion of the day. It is sometimes tempting to just do things for children rather than support them in learning these skills. Learning adaptive skills is a legitimate part of the curriculum and should be planned and valued in that light, not just as a daily necessity.

School Readiness Gap

Children differ in the skills they bring to educational settings. Some children have been in child care since infancy;

High-quality preschools are one way to help close the school readiness gap.

others have attended preschool for three years before entering kindergarten; and some have their first large group educational experience entering kindergarten. Some children have fewer educational experiences because their families lack resources. States are required to report assessment information separately for four subgroups: children who are economically disadvantaged, children from racial/ethnic minorities, children with identified disabilities, and children who have limited English proficiency. Many of these children were not included in the assessment system, or if they were, their scores were not reported and not counted. We are concerned that some children come to kindergarten with fewer skills and that the educational system is not closing this gap.

NIEER focused on the school readiness gap of children entering kindergarten, based on family income. They further focused on social skills and academic abilities. It is difficult to define readiness, but increasingly teachers are concerned about not only academic skills but also social skills such as being able to follow directions, communicate needs, listen, and not be disruptive. See Table 4.1.

Achievement gaps occur when one group of children outperforms or underperforms another group and the differences are large enough they could not have happened by chance. When we talk about achievement gaps, we usually use information based on scores on the National Assessment of Education Progress (NAEP). The NAEP is given in grade 4 and 8, in math and reading, in the public schools. It has a scale of 0 to 500. However, knowing about the relationship between race and score does not reveal its underlying cause (Vanneman et al., 2009).

Achievement gaps change for a variety of reasons: the higher performing group stays the same or declines, and the lower performing group increases; both groups increase, but the lower performing group increases more; and so on. It can also change because of population or policy changes.

Although data support the need for children in the lowest income groups to profit from high quality preschools, NIEER noted the differences between the middle 20 percent and the top 20 percent, which represented optimal development, and suggested that they too needed high-quality preschool education. These differences mirror academic abilities of entering kindergarten children (Barnett et al.,2004).

The National Center for Educational Statistics began to keep statistics on this gap, beginning in 1990, for math,

TABLE 4-1   SOCIAL SKILLS OF ENTERING KINDERGARTENERS BY FAMILY INCOME WITH 9.60 AS OPTIMAL DEVELOPMENT

Bottom 20%	8.50
Second lowest 20%	8.85
Middle 20%	9.05
Second highest 20%	9.20
Top 20%	9.60

Source: Barnett, Brown, & Shore, 2004.

and in 1992 for reading. Both black and white students scored higher in fourth grade in 2007 than they did in the early 1990s, and the gap between black and white children has narrowed over that time. However, the gap is still 26 points in mathematics and 27 points in reading at grade 4 (Vanneman et al., 2009).

The achievement gap is present before age 5 and is significant for both race and socioeconomic status in math and reading achievement (GiveWell, 2010). The Early Childhood Longitudinal Study of children who entered kindergarten for the first time in 1998 followed them from kindergarten through grade 3 (Rathbun, West, & Hauskin, 2004). Black third-graders had lower achievement scores than white, Hispanic, and Asian/Pacific Islanders in math, reading, and science. Hispanic third-graders had lower achievement scores in science than whites. Children who lived in families with more risk factors (living below poverty line, primary language non-English, mother with less than a high school degree or GED, and living in a single-parent household) also had lower achievement scores. Achievement gaps between disadvantaged children and those with more advantages widened over the first four years of school attendance (Rathbun et al., 2004). Seven- to 8-year-old children in low-income families are twice as likely to repeat a grade, 3.4 times more likely to be expelled from school, 3.5 times more likely to drop out of school, and half as likely to finish a four-year college (Children's Defense Fund, 2002).

THE EVIDENCE BASE

Economists have a different view of the value of early childhood education. A study done on 11,571 children who participated in Project STAR (Student/Teacher Achievement Ratio) in Tennessee, recently analyzed by economist Raj Chetty and his colleagues, looked at the efficacy of different styles of instruction and intervention. Children placed in smaller classes gained about 5 percentile points; however, this advantage faded by grade 8, as did the effects of high-quality early childhood classrooms. (In a cost–benefit analysis, children in small classes earned $431 more than their peers at age 27, but that equaled the cost of the smaller classes.) However, they found that the benefit of a high-quality kindergarten teacher reappeared in adulthood. One standard deviation increase in teacher quality yielded gains of $12,000 per child, or $240,000 for a class of 20 children (based on U.S. tax records).

Source: Chetty et al., 2010

Standards in Early Childhood Education

We are concerned about the achievement gap, and some see educational standards as a way of closing this gap. Focusing on what children know and are able to do has increased interest in **standards** and curriculum content. Neither early childhood education nor special education had been included in the early part of the standards movement; that has now changed.

Program standards for early childhood have existed for many years. **Program standards** describe the learning environment such as the resources, activities, and instruction. What is being added is **child outcome standards**, that is, what children should know and be able to do, the range

of knowledge and skills they should master. Child outcome standards also describe the habits, attitudes, and dispositions children are expected to develop (Bodrova, Jablon, & Stetson, 2004). Overall, the field is more willing to develop considerations to be addressed in child outcomes than the actual outcomes themselves. NIEER offers the following nine keys to effective preschool standards:

1. Standards should represent values that make sense to children's families and communities.
2. Standards should be evidence-based.
3. Standards should be comprehensive.
4. Standards should be specific, yet still allow flexibility as teachers implement them.
5. Standards should allow for a coherent educational experience.
6. Standards should make sense to teachers and help them with their day-to-day work.
7. Standards must be written in a way that makes it possible to assess whether they are being met in the classroom.
8. Standards documents should distinguish clearly between program standards and outcome standards.
9. Child outcome standards should be designed in ways that offer benefits beyond strengthening accountability (Barnett et al., 2009, pgs. 4–8).

Standards have come to early childhood from the top down. Mandatory testing in third grade has put pressure on teachers in K–2. Kindergarten teachers have noted that the school readiness gap between children who come to school is based on **sociocultural factors**. Kindergarten teachers wanted children to come to school with a required set of proficiencies (Copple & Bredekamp, 2009). Thus they supported preschool standards. The number of state-funded programs for 3- and 4-year-olds (including Head Start) grew in the early years of this century, but in 2008–2009 progress was slower and more uneven. Approximately 25 percent of 4-year-olds were enrolled in state-supported preschools and only 4 percent of 3-year olds. On average, state spending per child enrolled was $4,711 for prekindergarten children compared to $12,039 for children in K–12 (Barnett et al., 2009). When Head Start and special education populations are included as well as private programs, the number of children rises to 74 percent for 4-year-olds and 47 percent for 3-year-olds.

As of 2009, 47 states had comprehensive early learning standards for prekindergarten-age children (Barnett et al., 2009). For many of the standards, there is also guidance on how to use them with children with delays and disabilities and children who are culturally and linguistically diverse (Scott-Little et al., 2007).

The federal government has supported the efforts of professional organizations to develop national standards. This standards movement was part of the Goals 2000: Educate America Act of 1994 and continued with the No Child Left Behind Act of 2001 and the Common Core State Standards Initiative (CCSSI) (2010). The CCSSI is a state-led initiative and currently targets reading and math standards, science is next. At the beginning of 2011, 44 states and territories and the District of Columbia had voluntarily adopted these standards. Because of the number of states adopting these standards, where applicable they will be the standards used in this text. When children with disabilities are included in the general curriculum, they are expected to meet these standards. The expectation is that an IEP will support the individualized instruction needed for children to meet the Common Core State Standards.

Standards in and of themselves are neither good nor bad. Standards can transform the pre-K curriculum even when they do not directly apply to preschool. Early childhood educators are challenged to teach children in a developmentally appropriate way and meet early learning standards, whether the standards are those developed by professional organizations, the federal or state government, or the school district. These standards, plus the 2004 amendments to IDEA, influence the development of Individualized Education Programs and guide and build on each other to develop successful programs with continuity and value for all children in all educational settings. Teacher preparation is crucial. Are teachers prepared to use a standards-based curriculum? It requires us to look at designing activities to help children meet content standards. Child outcomes are first; activities make meeting those outcomes interesting, provide a context, and make them applicable to the real world in which children live and grow.

DAP In all early childhood programs, there are agreed-upon characteristic of high-quality programs. NAEYC and NAECS/SDE have also developed a set of "Early Learning Standards" to acknowledge and improve the professional practices in early childhood education and early childhood special education and to increase public knowledge about the importance of quality in early childhood education.

1. Effective early learning standards emphasize significant developmentally appropriate content and outcomes (p. 1, 2009).

Standards should emphasize all areas of early development learning. Content should be evidence based, important, and meaningful for children's well-being and future learning. Standards should be flexible and support positive outcome for all children, including those who are socioculturally linguistically diverse and those who have delays and disabilities.

2. Effective early learning standards are developed and reviewed through informed, inclusive processes (p. 2, 2009).

Relevant experts should help develop and review the standards. Standards should be clearly defined, shared, and understood by all stakeholders, including families, teachers, and administrators, and should be revised on a regular basis.

3. Effective early learning standards are implemented and assessed in ways that support all young children's development (p. 2, 2009).

Assessment should be connected to important learning and it should be used to benefit children. Standards provide guidance for the curriculum, classroom practices, and teaching strategies. Teachers connect these standards to children's interests and abilities to promote development and learning.

4. Effective early learning standards provide a foundation of support for early childhood programs, professionals, and families (p. 2, 2009).

To implement standards with positive effects requires professional development opportunities for teachers and respectful communications with families. It will also require adequate resources to implement high-quality programs (adapted from Copple & Bredekamp, 2009; NAEYC, 2006b; NAEYC &NAECS/SDE 2009b).

Content or Performance Standards

Some see standards in terms of specific content based on subject matter areas; others see them as the ability to perform certain tasks. In reality, the two are intrinsically related (Kendall & Marzano, 1996). **Content standards** specify what children should know and be able to do; **performance standards** specify at what level children need to know and demonstrate their understanding of the concept to meet the standard, that is, the quality of the child's performance. In elementary school, report cards typically indicate how a child is meeting performance standards. The emphasis of this book is on content standards.

Some organizations do not like the term *standards,* so the terminology varies. Some choose to call them *guidelines.* Head Start has a child *outcomes* framework, whereas others prefer the word *goal.* This text uses goals for preschool and standards for K-12. The intent is to ensure that curriculum is planned and designed to help children master increasingly more complex material in relevant areas.

IN THE FIELD

I once had a student teacher who wanted to do a two-week unit on chocolate. It was well thought out, although the unit had some problems. But I thought that, given what children needed to learn, it was not a wise use of their time. The student teacher pointed out the merits of what she had done, and in many cases she was right. I did not have problems with the activities, but whether it was worth spending two weeks in kindergarten learning about chocolate. I persisted. She was very angry with me. Do you think she was right?

Implementing Standards

Are standards the curriculum? No! Standards guide curriculum, providing parameters about what children should know and be able to do. The standard for "Reading: Foundational Skills" on phonological awareness is *Demonstrate understanding of spoken words, syllables, and sounds (phonemes).* Based on your unit or theme, you choose a story, poem, fingerplay, or rhyme that uses these concepts. You may dismiss children from the group by asking them to name a rhyming word to one you give. And, you would note which children can and cannot do this. Then you reflect on who did not succeed at the task and decide how to work with them, within the context of the unit, to meet this indicator. This also alerts you to look at the bigger picture. This was one indicator of phonological awareness. Does the child know the other indicators for phonological awareness? What about the other language arts standards? Used well, standards help us think about children, their special needs, and their level of competence in important areas of learning.

Different professional groups have written standards, and they include skills that each group feels are most appropriate. When you try to use the standards in curriculum planning, it is clear that they have some commonality that transcends content areas. It is important to maintain a holistic approach to the curriculum and not lose the child or lose sight of the child's special needs in the struggle over the standards the child should meet.

Regardless of the discussion about standards, there is a need to have appropriate content in all domains, a method for determining the order in which this content should be presented, some parameters for the scope of what content is covered, and the determination of some minimal level of performance. At the least, standards can guide our thinking about curriculum. They provide the impetus for continued reflection about developmentally appropriate practices and assessment during the early childhood years.

The Common Core State Standards detail standards in mathematics and the English language arts. Most state standards pay little attention to the creative arts and to social and emotional development, which is a major concern. There are standards developed by professional organizations for some areas of creative arts (visual arts, music, dance, and theater). Because standards for creative arts and physical education are not required, and areas such as social-emotional development do not have standards, there is concern that they will be seen as less relevant and that time spent in these areas will diminish as educators focus on the standards children are required to meet.

Educational standards developed by professional organizations are included by content area. In some cases, just an abstract of the standard is used; in other cases, more details are given. This was done because of the complexity and applicability of some of the standards and because some standards did not include children below kindergarten. I strongly recommend that you read the standards developed, not to jump into the fray over their use, but as part of your reflective learning and growth and to clarify what you believe is important. As a field, early childhood education has not strongly embraced specific standards but has focused on developmentally appropriate practices and play as the base of learning. Overall, standards help ensure that children and youth have the skills and knowledge they need to be prepared for postsecondary education and the workforce beginning in kindergarten. Standards help students, parents, and teachers set clear, realistic, measurable goals that provide an accessible roadmap for all stakeholders (NGA Center & CCSSO, 2010c). The Common Core State Standards focus

on outputs, specifically, what children should know and be able to do at the end of each grade or **grade band**. A person's or group's philosophy determines "how" this knowledge is taught (Kagan, Scott-Little, & Frelow, 2009).

Goals and Standards

This text is written for educators who teach children from birth through age 8. Most of the standards begin in kindergarten. To make the activities more accessible for younger children I have indexed the activities by both goals and standards. Using these together provides information about the general goals and additional information about the aspect of the goal that the standards support. For example, if the goal were *to improve reading literacy* children could meet this goal by using the English language arts standards: Reading: Literature (R:L)

> **R:L 1** Ask and answer questions about key details in a text.
> **R:L 2** Retell familiar stories, including key details.
> **R:L 3** Identify characters, settings, and major events in a story.

Before reading a story you, the teacher, would decide which standards you would plan to emphasize that day. If your goal were to have children ask and answer questions about key details, then you would have to pose questions that meet this standard, and you would focus on the characters and main events. On another day, you might remind children about the story they had read and ask them to retell it or even compare it to another story. The goals present the big picture; the standards remind you of the aspects of the big picture that should be included. Because of the link between standards and curriculum, the order of the goals reflects the organization of the Resource Chapters. The standards are given in Part III before Resource Chapter 1. This makes them easily accessible as you plan for children.

Social Awareness Goals and Standards

There are not national standards in some areas such as social competence, even though it is an important aspect of the early childhood curriculum. Organizations such as the National Institute for Early Education Research (NIEER) recommends, "Include in learning standards the outcomes that preschool programs are expected to achieve for social and emotional development" (Boyd, et al., 2005, p.1). There are standards for social studies.

Social competence involves the ability of the child to successfully select and carry out interpersonal goals. It includes the child's effectiveness in meeting goals, and the appropriateness of these goals in social situations. Different social situations require different competencies. The three major categories of social competence include adult–child interactions, social play relationships, and peer interactions. Inclusive classrooms place high demands on social competence.

Children with disabilities are often expected to have interpersonal competence because of their experience with a wide variety of adults. However, children may be competent with adults on a one-to-one basis because adults do the compensating and adapt their expectations. The same compensation rarely occurs with peers, although it is important. Success with social tasks such as making friends and gaining entry into groups is imperative for all children. Inclusive settings provide opportunities for many levels of play, including complex social play.

> ▶❚❚ TeachSource Video Case
> **Young Children's Stages of Play: An Illustrated Guide**
>
> Watch the TeachSource Video Case *Young Children's Stages of Play: An Illustrated Guide,* in which you'll learn about the stages of play and see children who exemplify these stages while they engage in different curriculum activities. The video can be found in the Early Childhood Education Media Library under Play, available at www.cengagebrain.com.

Mildred Parten (1932) was one of the first scholars to point out the dramatic changes in children's play behavior as they progress through the preschool years. She identified a three-step sequence that we still use to categorize children's play. Children's play typically starts with nonsocial activity and consists of **unoccupied play**, **onlooker play**, and **solitary play**. Later, children move into a limited form of social interaction that Parten called **parallel play**, in which children play near other children using similar materials, but the children don't really influence each other's behavior. She also identified two types of true social interaction. In **associative play**, children are playing together, but the play is not goal oriented. In **cooperative play**, children are playing together, the play is goal oriented, and they have a leader. Although nonsocial play decreases as children increase in age, it continues to be part of children's repertoire throughout their preschool years. What does change is the quality of the nonsocial play, which should reflect children's increasing cognitive maturity. If, however, the nonsocial play is primarily made up of aimless wandering, looking, and repetitive motions, there is some cause for concern. Solitary play in and of itself is not a problem. It is the level of play that is of concern and the ability of the child to join a group if the child chooses to do so.

Social competence is the key to social acceptance. Peers make judgments based on data (Jorge can't climb, looks funny, etc.). Children enter a new group with a clean slate, but they develop a personal social history within the group. Children with disabilities may use strategies for approaching other children that make it difficult to make friends. They are often less socially competent. As clusters of children form, more complex entry skills are required to join groups; if children lack these skills, a reputation for lack of social competence is established, and a pattern of social separation and reduced social status can result. This may result in a child having fewer opportunities to practice social skills. Social networks become narrower and more difficult to enter as children get older; therefore, it is imperative that children learn these skills early.

Children with disabilities face challenges in social play situations. Children with communication difficulties have decreased access to peers, as the ability to communicate is important in developing social competence. These children participate in fewer positive social interactions and use speech less frequently. They are not as successful as their typically developing peers in getting positive responses to their social overtures. They can, however, sustain play and respond to others' social bids (Guralnick et al., 1996). Children with hearing impairments also have trouble joining groups and tend to wait and hover on the edge of an activity (Brown et al., 2000). Children with visual impairments initiate fewer social interactions (Crocker & Orr, 1996). Disorders that affect children's behavior, such as attention-deficit/hyperactivity disorder (ADHD) and autism, lead to difficulties in social situations (DuPaul et al., 2001). Children with ADHD have fewer social skills and display more negative social behaviors than their typically developing peers. Our knowledge about the influence of ADHD on younger children is limited because in the past fewer children have been diagnosed with ADHD during the preschool years. Children with severe developmental delays participate in more nonsocial play even in inclusive classrooms (Hundert et al., 1998).

Given the problems that some children with disabilities have in social relationships, it is useful to try to pinpoint where in the social interaction children are having problems:

- *Gaining attention.* Before a child can join a social group, she has to get the attention of the children in the group she wants to join.

- *Initiating interaction.* Once it is clear to others that the child wants to join, the child must make an overture to the children in the group.

- *Responding to others.* Children need to develop skills that allow others to join their groups.

- *Sustaining interactions.* To participate in ongoing social play children need to be able to continue interactions and develop the give and take necessary for play to continue.

- *Shifting the focus of an interaction.* As play continues and becomes more complex, children need to be able to change roles and refocus the play.

- *Ending an interaction.* Children need to find ways to close interactions rather than just walking away when they lose interest.

Intervention aimed at supporting the social integration of children with disabilities has been approached from two very different frameworks. Educators with strong developmental backgrounds have assumed that physical proximity to other children, plus using open-ended, process-oriented activities in a free play setting, would result in social integration. This has not been the case. Others, from a more behavioral orientation, have observed the lack of social competence and have developed structured skits and specific exercises for children to repeat. The field is still struggling to help children with disabilities learn skills that lead to social competence and an understanding of how to function in today's complex world.

Educators and children interact throughout the day with exchanges of words, gestures, and even positioning. Powerful interactions are different from everyday interactions. **Powerful interactions** are "those in which you intentionally connect with the child while at the same time saying or doing something to guide the child's learning a small step forward" (Dumbro, Jablon, & Stetson, 2011). Powerful interactions build relationships and also help resolve conflicts. The conflict between the child's growing need for autonomy and self-esteem and the adult's need to inculcate values and socially acceptable behavior is classic. Conflict appears first in toddlerhood, and parents and caregivers make intentional or unintentional choices about where they stand. The issues that must be resolved are the forerunners of the conflicts in adolescence and even in later adult life. When put in perspective, especially if one believes that conflict resolution patterns learned as toddlers set the groundwork for adolescence, some solutions are more expedient than others.

THE EVIDENCE BASE

The National Prekindergarten Study of almost 4,000 prekindergarten classrooms was published by the Yale University Child Study Center. One report from this study looked at the number of prekindergarten children who were expelled.

> *Results indicated that 10 percent of prekindergarten teachers reported expelling at least one preschooler in the past 12 months. Nationally, 7 preschoolers were expelled per 1,000 enrolled . . . 3 times the rate for K–12 students. Rates were highest for older preschoolers and African Americans, and boys were over 4½ times more likely to be expelled than were girls (p. 1).*

Source: Gilliam, 2005.

REFLECTIVE PRACTICE | To the extent that preschool programs expel the children who most need to learn social competence, children are not likely to develop these skills, and their behavior will continue to be problematic. What solutions do you see for teachers and children? How might you help children learn social skills and increase their social competence and self-esteem?

SOCIAL COMPETENCE GOALS

Social competence goals focus on broad areas that are designed to help children function well and to include and understand others.

- To improve self-concept
- To increase awareness of roles people play
- To broaden concepts of family
- To increase inclusion
- To increase awareness of individual differences and similarities

IMPLICATIONS FOR EDUCATORS

There are no standards for social awareness and social competence. Does that mean social competence and social awareness are not important? No! If standards focus educational practices, what do you expect will happen to areas that lack standards?

Successful social inclusion of children with diverse abilities requires thoughtful planning and programming. Give the same consideration to social competence as you do for math or language and literacy. Think about the learning cycle and use this to plan for social inclusion: work from awareness to exploration, to inquiry, to utilization. Start by increasing the awareness of all children about differences, including cultural and ethnic differences and disabilities.

Setting classroom rules and behavioral expectations is as important as the arrangement of the classroom, particularly when working with children who may have behavioral challenges. Children need to learn appropriate behavior, social competence, and positive character traits. The behavioral expectations and classroom routines you set for the children in the first few weeks of school will affect how well your classroom runs the rest of the school year.

When developing rules for the classroom, you should consider three or four rules that are very important to you and phrase them in a positive manner. Then, on the first day of school, have a class meeting with children to discuss other rules that they feel are important. Help children to come to an agreement about which rules deserve to be classroom rules, and phrase them positively. Add these to your rules chart in both word and picture form. As children have played a role in developing the rules, they should feel a sense of ownership for both the rules and the classroom. When establishing classroom rules in this manner, children are more likely to respect and follow the rules, especially if you adhere to them consistently.

Take this opportunity to teach, model, and role-play the rules in appropriate situations. For example, if one rule you and the children have chosen is "Listen quietly when the teacher speaks," you will want to model and discuss how one listens quietly; discuss and role-play situations in which this rule applies; and finally, practice as a whole class. Practice each rule consistently the first few weeks of school and reinforce children who follow the rules. Practice the procedures for lining up at the door, washing hands, changing centers, and walking in the hallway. Discuss why those routines are important and give specific feedback to children. By practicing, modeling, discussing, and role-playing rules and procedures, children know what to expect from you and their environment. Once these are established, you will have more time to focus on other areas.

● ● ●
Social Studies

Social studies is an aspect of social awareness in the early childhood years. Social studies is a subject matter area with specific activities and learning, but also one in which observation and modeling are important learning tools. Children need to learn about their own culture and cultures of their

Children need to develop global connections and have experiences that study people, places, and environments.
© Cengage Learning 2012

classmates; they need to learn about the people and places and the environments in which they live and work; and they need to learn that they are part of a global society.

The National Council for the Social Studies (1994, 2008) developed national standards for social studies. There are 10 social studies standards. For the standards and complete information about them, go to The National Council for the Social Studies at www.socialstudies.org. These standards are available in Part III before Resource Chapter 1.

The revised standards include information that children should learn during the early elementary years. Learning expectations for each standard are identified, and information is provided on the purpose of the standard, key questions for exploration, knowledge, processes, forms, and products (National Council for the Social Studies, 2008). This additional information makes it easier for early childhood educators to adapt some of the content for younger children. Also provided are snapshots of practice to show how to implement the standards in the classroom.

Several related areas included under social studies during the early childhood years—geography, civics and government, and history—also have standards. See the Educational Resources at the end of this chapter for additional information about these areas.

Taken together, the social studies goals, standards, and principles require early childhood educators to take a close look at how they present the social studies curriculum, an area that is frequently neglected in early childhood. It takes a skillful teacher to implement social studies goals and standards in a developmentally appropriate way.

SOCIAL STUDIES GOALS

- To increase cultural awareness
- To increase social studies concepts

IMPLICATIONS FOR EDUCATORS

Although the social studies standards provide guidance on what to teach, it is up to the early childhood educator to determine how to teach the content. Ensure that the content reflects an anti-bias approach and includes the roles of men, women, and different cultural/ethnic groups. Allocate time for children to ask questions, explore, and experiment. Support children in generating additional solutions and alternative explanations for behaviors. Encourage children who are ready to think in a broader context.

In early childhood, some aspects of social studies are taught through daily organization and decision making: deciding what to name the new goldfish, what to do when someone knocks down the blocks, and how to share special materials. This is all part of the social learning that occurs at this age.

As children and their families enter your classroom, they learn something about how you respond to inclusion and how you teach social studies. They will look at the pictures and bulletin boards to see whether they represent the cultures and languages of the children you teach as well as those in the community and the world. They will look at the books on display to see whether you support a bias-free approach or whether you reinforce racial and gender stereotypes. They will evaluate the room to determine whether it allows diversity in play. As their eyes wander, they will note whether the dolls represent the diverse cultures reflective of the children and how you will promote equity. They will look for the possibility of

language differences, not only Spanish or Chinese, but also American Sign Language and Braille. They might even note whether there are pictures and books about children with disabilities. All children need to feel they are part of the class. It is important that children become aware of themselves as unique human beings and as children who are similar to, as well as different from, others.

Children learn social competence through the situational aspects of behavior. Behavior that is appropriate in one situation or time is not necessarily appropriate in another. Children in the process of learning to take turns wonder whether they will get their turn if they postpone it or let someone ahead of them. If they do lose their turn, they will be less likely to take turns in the future. Start with your setting. Help children feel comfortable both indoors and out. Take short walks in the area. Focus some part of your curriculum on the community itself as well as communities in general—why we have them, what they do, and how they help the people who live there. Discuss the differences between rural and urban communities.

Field trips are one of the most common ways of making abstract ideas concrete for young children. Resource people can be invited to visit, and resource media such as film, television, compact discs, DVDs, and the Internet can also be used to include the social studies standards in your curriculum.

English Language Arts Goals and Standards

Learning to communicate and understand communications is one of the major tasks of childhood. Learning language is a dynamic process that is affected by the language heard and the way that adults respond to emerging language. In situations where children have rich language models and are supported in producing speech, they are more open to new opportunities to expand their language skills. In addition to a strong experiential base to provide something to talk about, children also need to feel the urge to communicate. If no one listens and responds, children are less likely to talk. Children who spend many hours watching television have little incentive to talk because television is a noninteractive media.

Common Core State Standards for English Language Arts and Literacy in History/Social Studies, Science, and Technical Subjects

The 2004 amendments to the IDEA and the Common Core State Standards for English Language Arts (NGA Center & CCSSO, 2010a) place particular emphasis on the role language arts and literacy plays in many subject matter areas. Speaking and listening, reading, writing, and language although highlighted individually, are interrelated and interdependent. Although there are designated English language arts activities, language and literacy should be part of all curriculum areas.

You will note that the goals and standards for language and literacy appear in social studies, math, and science as well as in English language arts.

Speaking and Listening

Speaking, or expressive language, is a major component of the early language and literacy curriculum. To match language and literacy activities to the level of the children in your class, it is important to know each child's present level of language functioning. This can be compared to what the typical child of that age can say (vocabulary and **mean length of utterance**), and can also provide a guide for the types of activities that increase children's vocabulary and sentence length.

There is some professional debate about the role language plays in learning. Some focus on children's active role in language learning as they construct language (and knowledge) for themselves to meet their needs to communicate. The child is viewed as a producer of knowledge, not a recipient of it (Piaget, 1967). The process itself is interactive. Others place more emphasis on the social function of language and view speech as a vehicle for self-organization (Vygotsky, 1978). The core of young children's language and literacy development is to convey meaning through speaking and writing and to interpret meaning through listening and reading. Whether children invent language or use it as a vehicle for social interaction, it is an important part of the development of communication and knowledge. The role of the teacher is to ensure that children have a rich base on which to build communication skills and to support children in using these skills.

Listening is a relatively recent addition to the language arts and literacy curriculum. It was obvious to most people that children learned to talk and must be taught to read and write, but listening was taken as a given. The belief was that all children knew how to listen; they just needed to "pay attention."

Listening is a complex component of learning. It involves hearing that allows for auditory identification and discrimination. There is both a short- and long-term memory component. Listening or auditory processing is also part of attending and sensory motor integration. If you ask a child, "What is your name?" the child must hear the question, interpret the meaning, formulate an answer, and respond to the question. We do not assume children are listening unless they respond to our requests.

Listening, or at least making sense out of what is heard—taking in information—has a developmental base. It is the role of the adult communicator to match the language base of the child. The following list highlights the steps in moving along the listening continuum:

- No information intake via language. Initially, the verbal aspects of language (words) have no meaning for children; they use nonverbal cues by looking at what is being done or the tone of the voice to gain information.

- Information intake if language is clearly related to the experience. This is like a play-by-play broadcast: adults put into words what children are seeing or experiencing.

- Information intake if language complements or extends the ongoing experience.

- Information intake if language complements or extends the context of the experience, that is, paints a broader scene.

- Information intake if language complements or extends a topic or activity a child has initiated.

- Information intake if language reminds the child of past familiar experience and extends that experience.

- Information intake if language is about a new topic the child has neither experience with nor any particular interest in (French, 1996).

Much teaching in public schools concerns topics that some children may have had little experience with, and perhaps no interest in. If children have not had these experiences, they may not gain information through listening.

As with speaking, children are most likely to develop good listening skills if you are a good model. If you always repeat what you say, children learn *not* to listen the first time. When you are listening to a child, *listen*. Although we don't often think of listening as a school subject, children spend more of their school time listening than doing any other single task. They listen to the teacher, they listen to peers, they listen to the intercom, and they listen to recorded sounds. For younger children, we have fingerplays that help them "zip their mouths closed" so they can listen, or they put on their "listening caps." The goal is to have the children be quiet. Despite the preparation for listening, the focus is still on speaking rather than the skills involved in listening. One of the questions we as teachers must evaluate is "how much of what we say is worth listening to?" Would we be willing to sit spellbound for several hours each day listening to boring information? For children to practice good listening skills, they need something stimulating to listen to. Interest helps them focus on listening as a process.

● ● ●
Reading

Educators are becoming more interested in and concerned about literacy. There is agreement that no one teaching method or approach is likely to be effective for all children all the time and that every teaching method should build on what children already know and should include both direct teaching of key literacy skills as well as incorporating these skills into play (NAEYC & IRA, 2005). There is also agreement that the teacher is an important variable. Your enthusiasm for reading and for valuing it as a skill is important as children struggle to learn this complex task. Although the formal teaching of reading usually begins in elementary school, early literacy skills, which set the foundation for beginning reading, begin in infancy. The International Reading Association (IRA) and the National Association for the Education of Young Children (NAEYC) issued joint position papers about learning to read and write. The following statements are based on those position papers (IRA & NAEYC, 1998; NAEYC & IRA, 2005).

Children come to school with diverse literacy experiences. Some children have been exposed to many different types of reading materials at home or in an early care and education environment; others come with few literacy experiences. Reading builds on what children know and can do.

Phase 1: Awareness and exploration (infancy though preschool)

During this phase, children are exploring the environment and building the foundations for learning to read and write (IRA &NAEYC, 1998). Reading to infants, toddlers, and preschool children establishes a literacy-rich environment. Ask preschoolers questions about the characters and the plot, and have them retell the story. Expose children to concepts about print. Help them connect written and spoken language. Label materials in your classroom, and model how the label helps you know what something is. Help children understand that there is a systematic relationship between letters and sounds (alphabetic principle). Linguistic awareness develops through rhyming activities such as nursery rhymes. **Phonological awareness** *is the child's understanding and awareness that speech is composed of identifiable units, such as sounds, syllables and spoken words. During the preschool years, direct training in phonological awareness is inappropriate. Sensitizing children to sounds that form predictable patterns while allowing them to enjoy being read to is more appropriate.*

Phase 2: Experimental reading and writing (kindergarten)

Kindergarten children are developing basic concepts about print and are beginning to engage in and experiment with reading and writing (IRA & NAEYC, 1998). In kindergarten, one focus is on enhancing children's vocabulary, which can be achieved by having children listen to stories, if children are asked predictive and analytic questions before and after reading the story. It is not something that happens automatically. Repeated readings seem to help children extract the way different genres are structured. Reading then becomes an interactive experience, not a listening activity. Language-experience stories help children clarify the concept of word. Writing down what children say helps focus on the connection between speaking and writing, but also on the fact that there are spaces between words; different words have different letter configurations; and words differ in the number of letters they have. Letter naming is an important first step in literacy, and by the end of kindergarten children are expected to recognize and name all upper- and lowercase letters of the alphabet. Phonemic awareness (connecting the sound to the letter) follows, but it takes time and practice. Rhyming words can be used to extend children's vocabulary. Some children develop phonemic awareness through reading. However, approximately 20 percent will not without additional training (IRA & NAEYC, 1998).

Kindergarten children will read some words and are building a sight vocabulary. The relationship between reading and writing ability is a strong one at this age. Children can engage in independent reading and writing. By the end of kindergarten, children's print concepts should

include following words from left to right and top to bottom, and understanding that words are separated by spaces in print (NGA Center & CCSSO, 2010a). Children are learning to segment spoken words into individual sounds and blends. Strong programs in early literacy are not as obvious in preschool and kindergarten as they are in the primary grades.

Phase 3: Early reading and writing (first grade)

Children are beginning to read simple stories and write about meaningful topics (IRA &NAEYC, 1998). Reading instruction in the primary grades is often based on a basal or literature anthology series. Successful approaches to reading have "some type of systematic code instruction along with meaningful connected reading " (IRA & NAEYC, 1998, p. 7). Children are building a sight word vocabulary as teachers introduce new words and teach spelling strategies. As children are learning to read, their reading is likely to be slow and deliberate, but as they become more confident, their fluency increases, as does their comprehension. Attempts at punctuation and capitalization are becoming part of their writing. Reading and writing are used for a variety of purposes. Children need to be read to as well as practice their reading skills.

Phase 4: Transitional reading and writing (second grade)

Children are beginning to read more fluently and to write using simple and more complex sentences. Good readers use metacognitive strategies that help them prepare for what they are going to read. Then they read and reread a passage and ask questions if necessary. Children need to practice reading to others. They also profit from integrating reading and writing. Children can now write stories and poems and use other forms of writing. They can read a range of texts, and their writing has become part of a process of writing, editing, and proofing. They can spell more difficult words and have new spelling strategies. Invented spelling, although still acceptable, is phasing out as spelling instruction is increasing the number of words children can spell accurately.

Phase 5: Independent and productive reading and writing (third grade)

Children continue to refine and extend their reading and writing skills and modify them to suit varying purposes and audiences. Third-graders should be capable fluent readers who have a range of strategies to draw meaning from text (IRA & NAEYC, 1998). Identification strategies are becoming more automatic, and writing and spelling, easier and more accurate. Instruction is not solely focused on teaching children to read and write, but using reading and writing as tools to learn other material.

Some children have difficulty learning to read. Although this book suggests many activities to make learning the underlying concepts of reading more fun, it is your role to put the magic in reading. The best way to do that is to read to children. Read to children even after they can read. Their ability to read and what they enjoy hearing are on different levels. My favorite third-grader announced after the first week of school that she liked all her teachers but one, the librarian. When asked why, she said, "She doesn't read to us." Reading is difficult; it should be learned because of the elation of reading, not the drudgery and discipline of learning letter sounds and blends.

To be fluent and effective readers:

* Children need to be exposed to a wide range of print and nonprint material to acquire information about themselves and the world they live in. Literature should include stories, dramas, and poetry, whereas informational texts should include literary nonfiction (such as biographies), scientific, and technical texts.

* Children need to develop a wide range of strategies to use texts, including knowledge of the English language and life experience.

* Children need to learn the structure and conventions of language and to adjust their language usage (written and spoken) to their purpose and audience.

* Children need to use a wide range of strategies as they write for different audiences and purposes.

* Children need to apply their knowledge of language structure and conventions (spelling, punctuation) to create, critique, and discuss written material.

* Children need skills in conducting research; that is, they need to identify a topic; pose problems; gather, evaluate, and synthesize data from a variety of sources; and communicate this knowledge to an appropriate audience.

* Children need to be able to use a variety of information technologies (libraries, databases, videos, the Internet) to obtain and synthesize information and to convey it to others.

* Children need to respect diversity in languages and communication patterns.

* Children with limited English need to use their first language to increase their competency in English and to understand content.

* Children need to be part of a literacy community.

* Children need to use spoken, written, and visual language to accomplish their purposes (adapted from IRA & NCTE, 1996; NGA Center & CCSSO, 2010a).

Determining the level at which a child is reading is sometimes challenging. We typically use grade level equivalents. That is, a child who is reading at a grade level equivalent of 2.4 is reading at the level we would expect a child in the fourth month of the second grade to read. The problem is that these units are not equal-interval units. You cannot conclude that a child who moves from 2.4 to 2.9 has grown in reading the same amount as the child who moved from 3.4 to 3.9 (MetaMetrics, 2011). The Lexile (L) scale helps solve this problem as it is an equal-interval scale. Moving from 450L to 500L is the same as moving from 550L to 600L. Many states are in the process of developing assessments that show children's reading levels in lexils. Lexil measures are designed to show text at which a child can read independently at a 75 percent comprehension rate. This matching is designed to challenge, but not frustrate. The Common Core State Standards Initiative does not include kindergarten or first grade in its lexil bands. Children in second and third grades are expected to read and comprehend texts from 450L to 725L and stretch up to 790L (MetaMetrics, 2011).

Writing

A classroom that provides the space, materials, time, and rewards for writing is a classroom in which children will write. Although we think of writing as beginning later than other communication skills, such thinking is due more to our inability to interpret the writing of children than to their lack of interest. From the time a toddler picks up a marker and puts the first stroke on the page, that child has become an author. Over time, with appropriate materials and encouragement, that author will go from scribbling, to drawings that may contain letters or words or tell a story, to writing words using invented spellings, to fluent writing that may involve editing and publishing. Although some information about writing was included in reading, this section highlights other relevant areas.

For children with fine motor problems, learning to write is challenging. Some of the challenge is in the writing itself, not the conceptualization. Support children in the way you teach writing by using a variety of tools, adaptive grips, and computers. Reading and writing support each other. Help children see this connection.

One of the first things that children want to write is their name. However, even before children can write, they need to see you write. As you write, verbalize for the children why you are writing: "I am writing your name on the paper so I know that it is yours." "I am making a list of the things we need at the store so I don't forget." "I am writing a note to your mother so that she knows why you have a bandage on your finger." Children need to be aware of the purpose of writing from an early age. If a classmate is sick, suggest that the children write a get-well note to her. In the age of the Internet and cell phones, it is still important that children appreciate the value of writing.

Writing, like most other skills, progresses through developmental stages. Thus, writing a name, for example, typically progresses from "scribbling a name; writing a name in mock letters; copying a name; writing a name that is illegible; writing a first name legibly, but misspelled; writing a first name correctly with some letter reversals; writing a first name correctly; writing a first name with last initial; writing a first and last name legibly and correctly spelled" (Lamme, 1985, pp. 48–49).

The requirements necessary for writing vary with age. Very young children need both stand-up and sit-down places to write (Lamme, 1985). For young children, a chalkboard with large chalk, an easel with thick markers, or just a large piece of paper taped to a wall or any other flat surface can be the base for a mural so that writing is a social event.

Although children can write almost anywhere, having a designated place in your classroom increases the likelihood that they will do so. Choose tables large enough for at least two and no more than four children. Tape alphabet letters on the table so each child can refer to them as she writes. Think of writing as a social process, not an isolated experience. Children can ask each other questions about their writing. After writing, children need an audience for their written work if they choose to share it. An author's chair, where children can read to others what they have written, is part of the process.

As children become more experienced writers, the materials should be more diverse. The writing center should be equipped with a variety of paper: manila paper, paper with wide lines that cover the entire sheet as well as some with lines that cover only half the sheet (allowing space for illustrations), and plain white paper. Add paper that is folded in half, small notepads, paper cut into interesting shapes, colored paper, and even stationery. Rubber stamps allow children to print their own stationery. Almost any light-colored paper will do; it is having a variety that is important. The writing tools should be selected to match both the paper and the children using them. The youngest children (18 months to about 3 years) need water-soluble markers and large crayons or crayons with knobs on the top. They also need large paper. As children gain experience and proficiency, add thin markers and pencils that have erasers, as well as a supply of interesting erasers. A pencil sharpener is a must; the small handheld ones are fine if they don't "walk home." Colored pencils add interest also. As children get older, you might add some of the writing and illustrating media that are more difficult to control, such as oil pastels, chalk, watercolors, and charcoal. One solution is to place the writing center near the art area so that children can freely use art materials to illustrate their writing.

Computers should be part of or near the writing center. Writing and drawing on the computer supports writing as a process, and certain materials can help make that possible. Rewriting is often slow for children, so they need to have scissors and tape available for changes as well as the support of computer software. Glue or paste is also helpful, as well as a stapler, hole punch, and brads to hold pages together (provided there are not younger children around). Add a ruler, gummed stickers, and other accessories. Although you might have all of these materials available, it is not necessary to have them all out at any one time. The particular materials and accessories used can vary with the theme or unit that is being studied and even the season of the year.

Children and adults use the computer to word-process written work rather than to write it out by hand. This is particularly helpful for children with fine motor problems and specific learning disabilities. Because of this, it is important to separate your writing goals from your penmanship goals. Children do need to learn to write; however, when the content is the goal, I believe children should use whatever method helps them put their ideas into a print format. Computers with two chairs, so friends can support each other, should be located near the writing table, with appropriate software.

Language

It is imperative that children have a vocabulary large enough to express their wants and needs and to enable them to understand the wants and needs of others. Children must also learn the rules that govern how language is used. Understanding language enables them to function effectively in their environment. Most professionals feel that children use their own language system to make guesses about words they cannot read. The more specific and complex their language is, the better their guesses will be as they learn to read.

Vocabulary acquisition and use is an important part of all subject matter areas, and these areas should be used to actively build vocabulary. Children also need to learn the conventions of standard English such as how to ask questions, use prepositions, make plurals, and use complete sentences. They should be capitalizing the first word in a sentence and ending sentences with appropriate punctuation.

Language and literacy is a particular concern in early childhood special education as many children, particularly those with communication disorders and specific learning disabilities, struggle in this area. Having a broad understanding of the principles involved in learning to communicate effectively helps you design curriculum and identify children who are not learning at the expected rate.

ENGLISH LANGUAGE ARTS GOALS

- To improve expressive communication
- To improve listening skills
- To improve knowledge of the structure of language
- To improve receptive communication
- To improve reading literacy
- To increase vocabulary acquisition and use
- To increase respect for diversity in modes of communication
- To use diverse print and nonprint sources and genres
- To increase phonemic awareness
- To improve writing literacy
- To increase comprehension
- To follow directions
- To improve memory skills

IMPLICATIONS FOR EDUCATORS

Children do not automatically become literate. It takes careful planning and instruction to support young children as they learn to speak and build their vocabulary, to listen and follow directions, and to become fluent readers and writers by the end of the early childhood years. Building vocabulary is particularly important in early childhood. Think about how you can teach to ensure that the children you teach learn at least one new word every day and that they can use that word in appropriate contexts. Think about how much you and other adults talk in the early childhood classroom. Particularly, think about English language learners and how much they will learn by listening (or not listening). Evaluate your expectations about how children learn and how much of the day they will listen. Think of methods you can use to make information more relevant by tapping into prior knowledge and by presenting information in a variety of formats.

Look at the skills needed for reading, such as letter recognition, phonemic awareness, segmenting words into sounds, and decoding printed text. Think of ways of teaching these skills to instill in children a love of reading while making learning these necessary skills fun and interesting. Reflect on the 20 percent of children who may not learn to read easily. How will you identify these children before they come to see themselves as struggling readers and what will you do to help them?

Writing is a difficult skill for many young children. Reflect on how you can provide opportunities to support children's interest in writing as they work to master the skills. Think of ways to make language and literacy important to children and how to integrate language arts into other curriculum areas.

Discovery Goals and Standards

Discovery describes both curriculum and an approach to a curriculum area. The approach is one of *doing* math, *doing* science, and *working* with technology. This is not drill and practice, but developing an understanding of underlying concepts.

● ● ● Mathematics

Mathematics is an area that causes concern for many people. When young children have trouble remembering math facts, adults usually try to intervene, perhaps by getting flash cards or writing numbers for children to count, copy, add, or subtract. Such an approach is rarely effective, even though the facts are reviewed over and over again.

Some children with specific learning disabilities find math particularly challenging. Building a strong sensory motor base helps them as they move into the more abstract

Using puzzles helps children analyze the characteristics and properties of geometrical shapes.
© Cengage Learning 2012

areas of mathematics. Finding out specifically what children know and starting there recognizes the sequential qualities of mathematics.

Mathematics experiences in early childhood settings should concentrate on number (which includes whole number, operations, and relations) and geometry, spatial relations, and measurement, with more mathematics learning time devoted to number than to other topics. Mathematics process goals should be integrated in these content areas (Mathematics Learning in Early Childhood, National Research Council, 2009).

MATHEMATICS PRACTICE STANDARDS

Mathematics Practice Standards focus on the ways educators should engage children in the study of mathematics. The first four practice standards are based on National Council of Teachers of Mathematics (NCMT) process standards (NCTM, 2003). The process standards—problem solving, reasoning and proof, communication, connections, and representation—apply to all grade levels; the expectation is that the standards will receive different emphasis at different grade levels.

The remaining practice standards are based on the strands of mathematical proficiency *Adding it Up* (National Research Council, 2001). Although there are some differences in the approaches, the underlying theme is that previous mathematics instruction in preschool and elementary school lacked depth and that children have not become fluent and proficient in needed skills. The new *Practice and Content Standards* are designed to change this (NGA Center & CCSSO, 2010b). There is a far greater emphasis on understanding and reasoning than on memorization.

Children and youth should be able to do the following:

1. Make sense of problems and persevere in solving them: children can explain the problem to themselves and look for an entry point to solve it.

2. Reason abstractly and quantitatively: children can decontextualize (abstract the underlying concepts and represent them symbolically using objects or other means), then contextualize (bring the concepts back to referent and perform the required actions) to solve problems.

3. Construct viable arguments and critique the reasoning of others: children can explain what they have done, why and in what way a particular solution is better than other options using objects, diagrams, drawings, or actions.

4. Model with mathematics: children can use mathematics to solve everyday problems.

5. Use appropriate tools strategically: children can use manipulatives, pencil and paper, and other concrete models to solve mathematical problems.

6. Attend to precision: children can discuss the meaning of symbols and use clear definitions to support their reasoning.

7. Look for and make use of structure: children look for and identify repeating patterns or structures, and they can sort and identify shapes by the number of sides they have.

8. Look for and express regularity in repeated reasoning: children can see repetitions and sort out the underlying concept (NGA Center & CCSSO, 2010b).

MATHEMATICS STANDARDS

The standards are a balanced combination of procedure and understanding. Children who lack understanding will rely too much on procedures and will lack flexibility in considering analogous problems. The mathematics standards that identify what children should know and be able to do at the end of kindergarten are given in Part III before Resource Chapter 1. I would strongly encourage you to look at all the grade level standards at www.corestandards.org/the-standards/mathematics.

In kindergarten, instructional time should focus on (1) representing, relating, and operating on whole numbers, initially using manipulatives; and (2) describing shapes and space. Children should use numbers to represent quantities, count objects, arrange and rearrange objects and count and recount them, compare set sizes, and eventually write equations to represent the numbers in sets $(2 + 3 = 5)$. Children should be able to use geometric ideas and vocabulary to describe their physical world. They should be able to name two-dimensional objects such as squares, circles, and triangles and three-dimensional shapes such as cubes, cylinders, and spheres (NGA Center & CCSSO, 2010b).

DAP The National Association for Education of Young Children and National Council of Teachers of Mathematics identify characteristics of high-quality mathematics education for children 3 to 6 years. In these programs, educators attempt to do the following:

- Enhance children's natural interest in mathematics and their dispositions to use it to make sense of their physical and social worlds.

- Build on children's experience and knowledge, including their family, linguistic, cultural, and community backgrounds; their individual approaches to learning; and their informal knowledge.

- Base mathematics curriculum and teaching practices on current knowledge of young children's cognitive, linguistic, physical, and social-emotional development.

- Use curriculum and teaching practices that strengthen children's problem-solving and reasoning processes as well as representing, communicating, and connecting mathematical ideas.

- Integrate mathematics with other activities and vice versa.

- Provide ample time, materials, and teacher support for children to engage in play, a context in which they explore and manipulate mathematical ideas with keen interest.

- Actively introduce mathematical concepts, methods, and language through a range of appropriate experiences and teaching strategies.

- Support children's learning by thoughtfully and continually assessing all children's mathematical knowledge, skills, and strategies (NAEYC & NCTM, 2002, p. 3).

MATHEMATICS GOALS

- To improve number sense and numeration
- To improve geometric and spatial sense
- To improve measurement concepts
- To improve estimation skills
- To identify and understand patterns and relationships
- To improve knowledge of whole number operations and computations

Science

Science is a process, a way of knowing about the world. Science "facts" will change, but the process of generating these facts is relatively stable. Science is both knowledge about specific phenomena and the strategies or processes used to collect and evaluate the information. Science is inquiry; it goes beyond observation. Science is divided into particular areas such as physical science, life science, and earth and space science. The application of science to human problems (technology) is also part of science (Center for Science, Mathematics, and Engineering Education (CSMEE), National Science Education Standards, 1996).

Children need to develop a respectful curiosity about the beauty, orderliness, and balance of the world. They need to develop skills to gather data, organize it so information can be classified and hypotheses can be generated. These hypotheses need to be tested through experimentation and the results recorded. The last step in the process is sharing and applying the knowledge gained.

Children need the opportunity to explore materials on their own, with minimal adult supervision. Initially, they should be asked questions such as "What do you think will happen?" "What else could you try?" Such questions help children explore materials and learn about their properties. Your goal is to have children discover as many properties as they can and to encourage their discovery of more subtle aspects of materials. Give as little guidance as possible to promote the most learning. Children are not just learning facts; far more important, they are learning how to learn.

Science is particularly relevant to children with disabilities. Much of what we know about disabilities is based on science and we hope to discover more through the scientific process. Some children may need support in being curious about their world, and others may need parts of their world brought to them.

SCIENCE GOALS

- To improve observational skills
- To improve classification skills

- To improve cause-and-effect reasoning
- To improve generalization skills
- To increase knowledge of the natural world
- To make predictions

To learn more about the National Science Education Standards go to www.nap.edu/openbook.php?record_id=4962&page=R1.

• • •
Technology

Technology, simple and sophisticated, promises opportunities that were not available 30 years ago. Technology is part of today's life. The question is how to use it in a developmentally appropriate way as an optimal learning experience for children. Computers offer children a source of communication and a way of exerting control over their environment. Children can make a plan, carry it out, and see the outcome of their actions. Children need to be exposed to a variety of technologies, including computers, the Internet, e-mail, digital cameras, recorders, calculators, cell phones, electronic pads and tablets, smart phones, the Wii, and so on. In early childhood technology should be a social experience. Computers should have at least two chairs around them for children or be in a place where a child and adult can work together. Software chosen should facilitate the interactive use of technology (NAEYC, 2006c).

Adapting computers to serve as a resource for children and developing applications for people with disabilities is an important part of the field's growth. Technology can be customized for children with severe physical or sensory impairments by using switches, voice and music synthesizers, robots, and other peripherals. Apple has created a section in its store called "Special Education" and has built in specialized applications in its iPad, iPhone, and iTouch products for people with disabilities; new tablet applications are being developed by other companies as well.

The key to using technology in early childhood is selecting appropriately designed software and modifying the hardware to be responsive to the developmental needs of the child. The criteria for evaluating software set forth in the *Haugland Developmental Software Scale and the Haugland/Gerzog Developmental Scale for Web Sites* are useful for determining the developmental appropriateness of websites and software. Both scales have 10 criteria that are ranked. A summary of the criteria follows:

1. *Age appropriateness:* Think about the age of the children. Regardless of the computer, would you expect children this age to do these types of activities? The focus is on one or more valuable learning objectives. Do the teaching methods meet the needs of children rather than requiring the child to adapt to the software or website? Any software used should support curriculum objectives and standards.
2. *Child control:* The computer is only a tool. Control should be with the child. She should set the pace and

return to the main menu when she desires. There should be visual or verbal prompts to assist her as she moves throughout the site.
3. *Clear instructions:* How easy are the instructions for young children who do not read? To the extent that directions are dependent on the teacher reading to the children, children are being taught dependence in a medium that should foster independence. Directions should be simple, precise, and verbal, or have picture choices.
4. *Expanding complexity:* Software should be flexible. It should be designed to provide increasingly challenging, not solely repetitive, tasks and it should have the potential to teach powerful ideas.
5. *Independence:* The goal of using computers is to make children independent of adults. Software must be selected to support this concept. Using a computer independently or with peers supports self-esteem, confidence, and learning. Computer usage does not diminish the teacher's responsibility to supervise computer activities; it means that the teacher's role is to enrich and expand learning, not choose and load the software. Children should be encouraged to work together to solve problems.
6. *Nonviolence:* Violence in software is a particular concern because frequently it is the child who initiates and controls the violence. Children are not just *seeing* it; they are *doing* it. Children don't personally experience the results of violent behavior when they use software. When they restart the software program, everything and everyone is as good as new. This is not true in real life. Software can and should enhance positive social values both on the screen and off.
7. *Process orientation:* Computers are discovery oriented media; the reward is in the process.
8. *Real-world model:* In the real world, houses are larger than children and eyebrows fit on faces. Look at the software to see whether the images on the screen reflect this orientation. Children need to learn how the real world works; software should present accurate information.
9. *Technical features:* Graphics and sound should support the program. Cluttered designs and too much sound detract. The programs and DVDs should load and download quickly. Software and websites should be colorful and allow children to control the animation. It is important that programs be consistent so children learn that when they do X, Y happens. Printing allows children to share their experiences, use their results in off-computer applications, and put together a portfolio. Software should also allow children to save their work so they can start where they left off as opposed to starting at the beginning again.
10. *Transformations:* Computers have the potential for making changes at the stroke of a key. Children can

make designs and re-create them without the redraw-ing necessary in other media.

The final element of this scale is an anti-bias deduction, which is designed to ensure that software accurately reflects the diversity of the global society in which children live (Haugland, 2002).

DAP Much of the software that is on the market for young children is not developmentally appropriate. In 2006, the National Association for the Education of Young Children issued a revised position statement entitled Technology and Young Children—Ages 3 through 8. They believe that "Educators must use professional judgment in evaluating and using this learning tool appropriately; applying the same criteria they would to any other learning tool or experience" (NAEYC, 2006c, p. 1). They offer the following guidance for using technology with young children:

- Used appropriately, technology can enhance children's cognitive and social abilities.

- Appropriate technology is integrated into the regular learning environment and used as one of many options to support children's learning.

- Early childhood educators should promote equitable access to technology for all children and their families. Children with special needs should have increased access when this is helpful.

- The power of technology to influence children's learning and development requires that attention be paid to eliminating stereotyping of any group and eliminating exposure to violence, especially as a problem-solving strategy.

- Teachers, in collaboration with parents, should advocate for more appropriate technology applications for all children.

- The appropriate use of technology has many implications for early childhood professional development (NAEYC, 2006c).

Use websites like www.childrensoftware.com for their reviews of software for both home and school.

To make traditional computers work, children must be able to implement a single keystroke. Without this skill, typing looks like this: *ppppppppppppppp*—and the computer cannot interpret it (the sensitivity of the keyboard can be controlled to make this easier). Once children can make a single keystroke, they need to build keyboarding skills. These skills involve learning to locate keys, reading and selecting from a menu, and giving commands. Additionally, children must learn about the computer itself and how to make it run. They also must develop the necessary fine motor and sensory integration skills. Computers have tremendous potential for positive change for children with diverse abilities, but they need adult scaffolding to make the system work. As we begin to think about the area of computing with children, it too has a set of standards that relate to what children should know and be able to do.

Technology expands children's worlds especially when it is a shared experience.
© Cengage Learning 2012

The International Society for Technology in Education (ISTE) took the leadership in establishing the National Educational Technology Standards. They first identified categories that apply to all students regardless of age, including these:

1. Creativity and Innovation
   Children can think creatively and develop products and processes using technology. They can apply what they know to generate new ideas, create original works, use models and simulations to explore complex issues, and identify trends.

2. Communications and Collaboration
   Children can use digital media and environments to communicate and work with others, including those at a distance, to support their own learning and that of others. They can interact, collaborate, and publish with peers and others, using a variety of digital environments and media.

3. Research and Information Fluency
   Children use digital tools to gather, evaluate, and use information. They plan strategies to gather information and locate, organize, and analyze information from a variety of sources and media. They evaluate and select information sources and digital tools, process data, and report results.

4. Critical Thinking, Problem Solving, and Decision Making
   Children think critically to plan and conduct research, manage projects, solve problems, and make decisions using appropriate digital tools. They can identify and define problems, ask significant questions, plan and manage activities to find a solution. They can collect and analyze data to make informed decisions and explore alternative solutions.

5. Digital Citizenship
   Children understand human, cultural, and societal issues related to technology. They practice and advocate for responsible use of information and technology, and they have a positive attitude toward using technology that supports collaboration and learning.

6. Technology Operations and Concepts
   Children understand technology concepts, systems, and operations. They can select and use applications, troubleshoot problems, and use what they know to learn new technologies (adapted from ISTE, 2007a).

The expectation is that by the first or second grade, children should be able to recognize a website and work in that site using links. They should be able to use the basic tools of a browser to go forward, back, and home. By grades 3 or 4, they can be expected to recognize the components of a URL (website address) and to access a website by using a URL. They should be able to use a children's search engine (such as Yahooligan) to find information. Additionally, they should be able to send and receive e-mail. Appropriately used, technology holds the potential for helping all young children, particularly children with disabilities. Your role is to help children see technology as a natural part of everyday life.

TECHNOLOGY GOAL

* To improve technology skills

IMPLICATIONS FOR EDUCATORS

It is important that children develop positive attitudes toward mathematics, science, and technology and view themselves as competent in these areas. During their early years, children learn about math informally. Adults help children connect their experiences to mathematical knowledge. Educators set the stage by providing children access to books and stories with numbers and patterns, and they integrate mathematics with music and language. They provide children with opportunities to count, sort, categorize, match, make sets, and so on. They help children make comparisons and learn the language of mathematics. Math includes activities such as counting, measuring, using blocks, playing board games, and so on. Children need opportunities to solve problems and talk about their solutions. Both computers and calculators play a role in learning mathematics. Children need to learn when and how they are best used.

Children sometimes know more about math than is conventionally tested. Teachers need to use a variety of assessments to find out what children know so they can plan appropriately for each child. Numbers and operations form the basis for most mathematics curriculum, whether it is using them to solve simple problems, such as how many crackers we need so each child has one, or complex data analysis. Numbers are for more than counting. Children need to know that numbers can be represented with objects or numerals, how to use numbers and operations to solve problems, and that numbers are part of a rule-based system.

Children write numbers less frequently than they write letters or words, so they may be less skillful in writing numbers than letters. Reversals of numbers in the preschool years are common, with the numbers 2, 3, 6, 7, and 9 the most frequently reversed. These numbers continue to be reversed even after children are consistently writing all of their alphabet letters correctly (Lamme, 1985). In addition to signaling inadequate left–right orientation, reversals may be one sign of a problem with patterns and relationships.

Exposing children to informal science and experiences is not enough to build necessary concepts, but it is a necessary first step. Many activities in this area require at least two days and often more. The second time the materials are out, some children will continue to explore the materials; others will need more structure to expand their explorations. It is important that children view science as part of their world and that they see cause-and-effect relationships rather than "teacher magic."

Think about the discovery standards. What qualities make them relevant and good examples of best practice? As you think about the mathematics you will do in the classroom, how do the standards guide what you will plan and expect from children? How much time do you allocate for math and science? What concepts might you support in other curriculum areas? What can you do in your teaching to help children see themselves as scientists? To build scientific concepts, your curriculum has to support the process. What will you do to ensure this happens? Why do you think science has such a strong discovery base? Think about how you will use technology to put children in charge of technology, not the other way around. Children are intrigued with technology. However there are concerns about the types of technology children use and what they learn from it. How will you choose software wisely for young children, and what advice will you give parents as they support their children in this area?

Wellness Goals and Standards

Wellness is an overriding concern for all children. It goes beyond the lack of illness to a way of looking at well-being. Children who are hungry, live in unsafe environments, and struggle with tensions at home may not come to school ready to learn. They may lack energy, motivation, or attention. School should be a safe haven for children, one in which they can feel free to devote their energy to learning.

• • •

Health and Safety

Health and safety are areas of study as well as states of being. When young children become aware of what it means to be unhealthy and have the knowledge and vocabulary to describe their symptoms, there is less likelihood of serious, undetected illness. When they learn to recognize signs of danger and act appropriately, the environment will be less threatening. Children need to refine their awareness and skills in these areas. Only children who are healthy and feel safe are free to enter into your program fully. Children learn basic health practices as part of routines (such as washing their hands after toileting and before snack).

The Joint Committee on National Health Education Standards (2007) developed the *National Health Education Standards: Achieving Health Literacy*. "Health literacy is the capacity of an individual to obtain, interpret, and understand basic health information and services and the competence to use such information and services in ways which are health-enhancing" (p. 12). Young children achieve health literacy through experience and related learning activities. In early childhood, most of the emphasis is placed on the development of a healthy lifestyle, including good hygiene and nutrition, the prevention of infectious diseases and injuries, and participating in structured and unstructured physical activity.

The Joint Committee on National Health Education Standards (2007) developed national Health Education Standards (NHES). The standards are written expectations for what children should know and be able to do from Pre-K through grade 12. Only the standards related to Pre-K through grade 2 are detailed in Part III before Resource Chapter 1. The standards relate to personal, family, and community health.

HEALTH AND SAFETY GOALS

- To improve health literacy
- To improve safety concepts
- To improve adaptive skills

Physical Education

Becoming physically active at an early age sets the stage for future physical activity, participation in sports, and the enjoyment of being physically active. The National Association for Sport and Physical Education (NASPE, 2010b) published the second edition of its national education standards in 2010. The content standards are for *all* children. The role of the teacher is to include *all* children in meeting the standards.

Physical activity can be categorized as locomotor, manipulative, and nonmanipulative:

- Locomotor skills include crawling, creeping, walking, running, hopping, jumping, skipping, galloping, and sliding.
- Manipulative skills include grasping and reaching, throwing, catching, striking, kicking, dribbling, volleying, and trapping.
- Nonmanipulative skills include turning, twisting, rolling, balancing, transfer of weight, stretching, and curling.

No formal measures of physical fitness are recommended in grades K–3; rather the emphasis is on physical activity and health-related fitness. Recommendations for physical activity for infants and toddlers are given in Chapter 7. The National Association for Sport and Physical Education (2010a) recommends five physical activity guidelines for preschoolers:

1. Preschoolers should accumulate at least 60 minutes of structured physical activity each day.
2. Preschoolers should engage in at least 60 minutes—and up to several hours—of unstructured physical activity each day and should not be sedentary for more than 60 minutes at a time except when sleeping.
3. Preschoolers should be encouraged to develop competence in fundamental motor skills that will serve as building blocks for future motor skillfulness and physical activity.
4. Preschoolers should have access to indoor and outdoor areas that meet or exceed recommended safety standards for performing large-muscle activities.
5. Caregivers and parents in charge of preschoolers' health and well-being are responsible for understanding the importance of physical activity and for promoting movement skills by providing opportunities for structured and unstructured physical activity.

Structured physical activity for young children is "planned and directed by the parent, caregiver, or teacher and is designed to accommodate the infant, toddler, or preschooler's developmental level" (NASPE, 2002, p. 18). When physical activity is adult directed, children obtain significant amounts of moderate and vigorous physical activity (Ward, Saunders, & Pate, 2007). **Unstructured physical activity** is "child-initiated physical activity that occurs as the child explores his or her environment" (NASPE, 2002, p. 18).

During the preschool years, children should be encouraged to practice movement skills in a variety of activities and settings. Instruction and positive reinforcement is critical during this time to ensure that children develop most of these skills before entering school (NASPE, 2010a).

The guidelines for children ages 5–12 define physical activity broadly and include exercise, sport, and dance as well as other movement forms.

1. Children should accumulate at least 60 minutes, and up to several hours, of age-appropriate physical activity on all, or most days of the week. This daily accumulation should include moderate and vigorous physical activity, with the majority of time being spent in activity that is intermittent in nature.
2. Children should participate in several bouts of physical activity lasting 15 minutes or more each day.
3. Children should participate each day in a variety of age-appropriate physical activities designed to achieve optimal health, wellness, fitness, and performance benefits.
4. Extended periods (periods of two hours or more) of inactivity are discouraged for children, especially during daytime hours (NASPE, 2010c).

Most children do acquire **fundamental movement skills** in unstructured physical activity. However, they never achieve an advanced level without instruction, practice, and encouragement that is available only in structured physical activity (NASPE, 2002). Early skills provide the foundation on which later skills are built. Children who lack these skills often choose not to participate in physical activities as they get older and games become competitive (Graham, Holt-Hale, & Parker, 2005). For both structured and unstructured physical activities to happen, they have to be incorporated into the schedule and embedded in routines and transitions.

PHYSICAL EDUCATION GOALS

- To improve locomotor skills
- To improve manipulative skills
- To improve nonmanipulative skills
- To improve physical fitness
- To improve motor planning

Sensory Motor Integration

Fine motor skills involve the coordination of small muscles found in the hands and fingers. These muscles are usually used in coordination with one of the senses (eye–hand coordination). The development of these skills, which begins in infancy, is necessary for writing, manipulating small objects, adaptive skills (buttoning), and most artistic endeavors.

There are no standards for this area, but it is a necessary part of the curriculum in early childhood.

Developmentally, the large muscles of the trunk and arms have to develop in order to provide the stability that allows the use of the small muscles of the hands. If a kindergarten child worries that she will fall out of her seat, it is difficult for her to use her small muscles to write the alphabet. If children are having challenges with small motor development, first try to determine whether the problem is a small motor one or indicates a lack of stability in the large muscles. Occupational therapists are the experts for children who have problems with sensory motor integration. To work on these needed skills, provide children with opportunities to develop finger strength though manipulating clay and playdough, puzzles and other manipulatives to help eye–hand coordination. Crayons and chalk of different sizes help develop prewriting and drawing skills.

SENSORY MOTOR INTEGRATION GOALS

- To increase body awareness
- To improve fine motor skills
- To improve sensory motor integration

IMPLICATIONS FOR EDUCATORS

We are concerned about health and safety-related issues. Health literacy helps us focus on the broader aspects of health. Given the level of childhood obesity in the United States, it has become a pressing issue. Think about how you would arrange a schedule to include the recommended amounts of structured and unstructured physical activity in an early childhood program. How will you go about rethinking physical activity in light of the standards and guidelines given, and how might you look at sensory motor integration problems in a new light?

Creative Arts Goals and Standards

All children are creative. Some are more creative than others. Some children are more creative in one area than in other areas. As children interact with the environment, the responses they get to their creative efforts play a large part in their creative development.

As children get older, they are increasingly rewarded for convergent thinking; they also need to be supported in divergent thinking. The world is changing too quickly to predict the kinds of knowledge children will need in 20 years. They have to develop processes that allow many potential solutions and methods for figuring out how to solve problems. This approach to problem solving begins now. Children who know only how to acquire facts and who are rewarded for conformity and neatness may not be equipped to solve tomorrow's problems.

What is creativity? Creativity is a process of thinking, acting, or making something that is new or different. It doesn't mean that a person has to be the first one to produce a product, but it does mean it is a new experience for that particular person.

The creative process can be thought of in two stages. The first is the thinking or idea stage: children play with what they want to do in their mind. The second stage is the implementation stage. This is the "doing" stage: children try

The visual arts help children display what they know and can do through color, texture, and mood and then reflect on their work.
© Cengage Learning 2012

out their ideas. This process is probably best thought of as a circular rather than a linear process, as children change their thinking and actions as they get feedback from the process.

Children gain many benefits when their creativity is fostered. Rewarding creativity helps develop a positive self-concept. It supports children's finding alternative solutions to problems and expressing their own ideas. Children learn to take risks to develop new skills and also learn about their own uniqueness. These are particularly positive qualities for children with diverse abilities.

Educators can support creativity in two major ways: by supporting the creative process itself and by providing the time, space, and materials necessary to foster creativity. The Consortium of National Arts Education Associations (1994, pp. 122–127) developed national standards for arts education, including the visual arts, music, dance, and theater. To see all of the content and achievement standards for the arts, go to www.nacdnet.org/education/contests/poster/2009/National_Standards_for_Visual_Art_Link_To_State_Dep. The arts are a mainstay in the early childhood curriculum. The visual arts offer opportunities for individual participation as well as for being part of a group.

Visual Arts

Visual arts for young children are messy, fun, and exploratory. They range from squashing sponges and watching how much paint drips, to rolling and pounding playdough; from gluing paper, cloth, and macaroni, to coloring or scribbling with water-based markers, chalk, or crayons. But it is also about reflecting on one's art and evaluating it. Art results from actively engaging materials. It is not making something that looks like everyone else's; nor is it gluing precut objects in the same place as does everyone else. Art is an experience, a process. The best art may never hang on the refrigerator door. It may remain in the child's mind.

At 12 months, children can begin to do simple art projects. By 3 years, these projects begin to have more structure and children can tell you about them. With increasing age, products become more important, and this is the time when reinforcing the process aspect is imperative. If children decide they don't draw well, they may decide not to draw. Some children will have better products than others. However, the process is as important as the product in early childhood.

Art helps young children understand the properties of materials. Children's first response to any new medium is one of exploration. What can it do? What are the limits? What do I like to do with it? Curiosity abounds. Allowing children to explore these differences and helping them figure out the variables to test is far more useful than explaining to them that objects stuck with glue will stay when turned upside down, whereas paint is unlikely to hold objects together. They learn thin paint runs down a page faster than thick paint. Help children to reflect on what they have done. Discuss illustration and the relationship between text and pictures.

VISUAL ARTS GOALS

- To increase visual arts concepts
- To increase creativity

● ● ●
Music

Music can be soothing or stimulating; it can promote social activity; it can be used anytime anywhere. Traditionally, music has not been integrated with the rest of the curriculum. It has been restricted to a "music period" and taught without any goal beyond the vague one of teaching children music. Music can be used to meet a number of educational goals. It can teach and reinforce skills that are part of other curriculum areas.

Musical experiences should match the developmental level of the child. By age 3, children have favorite songs and can recognize some tunes. They may want to add words or motions to songs for a new verse. They learn longer songs. By age 4, children participate in singing games and more actively participate in selecting musical experiences. With increasing age, children can sit longer and enjoy songs and dances that have rules (Mayesky, 2002). By age 7 or 8, children can read the words to songs. Some children begin formalized music training during the early childhood years.

Music is an academic field with its own standards established by the Music Educators National Conference. This organization has a very child-centered approach to learning. Their standards are based on the following beliefs:

- All children have musical potential.
- Children bring their own unique interests and abilities to the music learning environment.
- Very young children are capable of developing critical thinking skills through musical ideas.
- Children come to early childhood music experiences from diverse backgrounds.
- Children should experience exemplary musical sounds, activities, and materials.
- Children should not be encumbered with the need to meet performance goals.
- Children's play is their work.
- Children learn best in pleasant physical and social environments.
- Diverse learning environments are needed to serve the development of many individual children.
- Children need effective adult models (Consortium of National Arts Education Associations, 1994).

Music is a multisensory experience. Music can foster learning skills without sacrificing the goals and objectives or the standards of a music education program. Children learn new words and develop memory skills as they recall songs from one time to the next. They develop a sense of rhythm as they sing and listen to music.

The overlap of music and listening skills is obvious. Children learn to differentiate pitch, rhythm, and intensity. As children become older, they enter into some of the more visual aspects of music, such as visually discriminating the musical notes and symbols and then integrating this information into auditory output. Pairing music with movement supports sensory integration. The mood of the music can set the pace for the movement.

MUSIC GOAL

- To increase music concepts

● ● ●
Movement and Dance

Movement helps children become aware of their bodies. This awareness helps them express feelings and moods, improve self-control, and learn how to relax at will. Children discover ways to relax and to work off excess energy. Movement activities develop rhythm and balance. Movement and dance can provide sensory integration and an opportunity for creativity and expression.

Creative movement and dance are particularly helpful for children with behavior and emotional disorders as they can participate without fear of being judged. Dance allows you to meet children with autism where they are and help them into more functional movement patterns.

Movement and dance are not child-sized versions of calisthenics with a "no pain, no gain" philosophy. They are ways young children learn how their bodies work. Creative movement is a personal statement about one's inner self. This is what differentiates it from functional movement, which usually has a practical purpose such as running to get a ball. Dance supports classroom management and obesity prevention. Get music with a fast beat and have a dance party. Have children jump, reach, march, or move as you call out each child's name for attendance and then continue moving as you count the number of children in the class. It helps get the wiggles out.

MOVEMENT AND DANCE GOALS

- To move creatively
- To understand dance

●●●
Dramatic Play and Theater

Dramatic play is spontaneous, self-expressive play through which children can learn to understand themselves and their relation to others and to the world around them. In dramatic play, children construct a world in which they can make up for defeats and frustrations and can experiment with different ways of working out fears, feelings, and uncertainties. Dramatic play can help children grow in social understanding and cooperation; it provides a controlled emotional outlet and a means of self-expression.

Dramatic play for young children starts out with what they know best: domestic scenes. Children cook, clean, care for babies, leave for work and return, have visitors, and so on. They begin with familiar roles. A second theme is superimposed upon the first and involves a rescue mission. The baby is sick, someone has fallen and broken a leg, and the children focus their play around solving the problem presented. Once solved, a new "problem" is likely to occur. The third theme is sudden threat. A monster appears to carry off a victim, wild animals threaten to attack, and villains must be beaten off. Children reenact these themes over and over again. The setting changes, and with increasing age, the play becomes more sophisticated, but the themes remain. The play itself often is chaotic, violent, noisy, and difficult to manage. It sometimes involves children who "don't want to play" as unwilling victims. This sometimes falls in the category of war play. Before the mid-1980s this play grew out of children's experiences and needs. Broadcasting deregulations in 1984 allowed toys to be directly linked to television programs. By 1987, 80 percent of all children's television programming was done by toy companies (Levin & Carlsson-Paige, 2006).

As children reach the elementary years dramatic play can move into theater where children can write a script, assign roles, make props, direct a play, reflect on the process, and then do it again with variations.

The Consortium of National Arts Education Associations (1994) developed content standards in the area of theater. They can be seen in Part III before Resource Chapter 1.

DRAMATIC PLAY AND THEATER GOALS

- To play creatively
- To perform roles

IMPLICATIONS FOR EDUCATORS

With standards and legislation so clearly focused on literacy and math, there is concern that the creative arts will systematically be eliminated from the curriculum. The arts provide a lifelong means of expressing feelings and gaining enjoyment. The arts allow children to be part of a group while expressing their feelings and creativity without being judged different or strange. Children can react to art and talk about the characteristics that appeal to them in a particular work as well as in their own art. Children can explore materials and express themselves in a visual form, and they can look back at past artwork and see what changes have occurred.

To support the visual arts in your program, schedule time for children to paint, draw, glue, color, and use dough or clay each day. Do *not* provide a model for the children to copy. When children request a model, help them visualize what they want to draw, and emphasize the process, not the product. Discuss the relationship between art and fine motor development. Teach academic tasks like letter printing or coloring within the lines for other times. Show interest in what the children are doing and display everyone's original artwork regardless of quality. Instead of asking, "What did you make?" say, "Tell me about your picture."

Audiovisual equipment can be used both as a source of creativity and as a method of capturing creativity so that it can be shared or viewed at a later time. Consider videotaping a creative movement experience or the dramatic play area and then showing it to the children. Children can use digital cameras and record the events of a field trip with photographs. Encourage children to record their voices and play them back, or record the group singing and then listen. Children are intrigued with technology. Use it to encourage and support creativity.

Music supports language development, especially for children with fluency disorders, and is a way of building memory and vocabulary for children with specific language disabilities. As children vocalize sounds and words, they may create new verses to familiar songs. Music is also a social experience. Include music from many cultures, folk music, classical music, and contemporary selections. Think about music both as a content area and what music can teach children. Reflect on its overlap with reading and math and how it supports those areas as well as having its own standards. Creative movement has no right or wrong movements, but the potential for moving can encourage children to think about situations and integrate that cognitive information with what their body does. Reflect on how you can use this knowledge to support movement and learning. Together, music and movement provide many opportunities for sensory motor integration.

You can use dramatic play as an index to measure children's development. By observing dramatic play, you can assess small and large motor coordination, language development, social skills, concept formation, and developmental progression. Adding theater ties in reading and writing with performance. Reflect on dramatic play and where it fits in with the standards movement. If early childhood theory supports children learning through play, how do you see the amount of time devoted to play changing based on standards? Do you think you can justify play as a way of meeting standards? Be prepared to defend the time spent on creative arts in the early childhood curriculum and why they should be maintained.

Play

DAP This chapter has been devoted to curriculum and standards. Please do not lose sight of the value of play for children. Play contributes to children's pleasure and enjoyment and helps them regulate their emotions, thereby supporting health and well-being. Play helps children learn to respond to the demands of an ever-changing environment. Play changes the architecture of the brain. It is a self-protecting process that enhances children's adaptive capabilities and resilience (Lester & Russell, 2010).

Play is not a luxury, but a fundamental right for children. Play can help mitigate the effects of severe stress. Children need time and space to participate in play and playfulness. It is up to adults to promote play and to set up conditions that allow the flexibility, predictability, and security for children to play. Although play requires adult supervision, it should not have adult interference. Play is not frivolous; it is a necessary part of children's lives that needs to be planned for and acknowledged (Lester & Russell, 2010).

SUMMARY

- Curriculum planning involves the relationship between one's personal philosophy and developmentally appropriate practices and standards.
- States and professional organizations have developed standards in most curriculum areas.
- Standards impact education for *all* children.
- Social awareness is a broad area that looks at the child and the world in which he lives. Social studies standards focus on the child and near and far communities and how they work.
- Language arts and literacy have been influenced by the development of the Common Core State Standards in the English language arts.
- Discovery focuses on the mathematics, science, and technology curriculum and uses a hands-on approach to learning content and the underlying principles of theses areas.
- Wellness emphasizes a commitment to health and physical activity and fitness.
- Creative arts support creativity and experiencing many different media. The combination of music and movement leads to an integration of sensory experiences.
- Educators translate goals and standards into developmentally appropriate activities and an integrated curriculum that is flexible enough to meet the needs of all the children.

EDUCATIONAL RESOURCES

Bookshare is an online library of digital books for people with print disabilities funded by the U.S. DOE, Office of Special Education Services, which makes these books available to children with visual impairments, physical impairments, and specific learning disabilities. www.bppkshare.org

Center for Civic Education is designed to promote responsible citizenry and understanding of the democratic process. It has developed National Standards for Civics and Education. It also provides lesson plans and other learning materials. www.civiced.org

Common Core State Standards Initiative (CCSSI), started by the National Governors Association Center for Best Practices and the Council of Chief State School Officers, used global standards to develop core standards in mathematics and the English language arts and literacy in history/social studies, science, and technical subjects for children in kindergarten through grade 12. www.corestandards.org

Early Connections: Technology in Early Childhood Education is a website that provides research, information, and best practices regarding technology use to benefit children through age 8. www.netc.org/earlyconnections/index1.html

Learning Works for Kids turns video games into playtime that focuses on real-world improvements in working memory, planning, organization, focus, self-control, self-awareness, flexibility, and time management.

International Society for Technology in Education provides the National Educational Technology Standards and information on the standards for students and teachers. http://cnets.iste.org

MetaMetrics provides information about lexils and has a search engine where you put in a book title and are provided with the lexils.

National Association for Music Education provides information on music standards and additional information on how to meet these standards. www.menc.org

National Center for History in the Schools is dedicated to improving history education in K–12 schools via its challenging, yet easy to use, curricular materials, and assisting with the professional development of K–12 teachers. For the grade band K–4, the standards address historical thinking and content standards. www.sscnet.ucla.edu/nchs/

National Council of Teachers of Mathematics provides information on the mathematics standards as well as ideas for lessons at different levels that incorporate mathematics into the curriculum. www.nctm.org

National Council for Geographic Education provides information on geography standards, *Geography for Life, National Standards*, developed in 2008, as well as lesson plans for teachers and ideas to implement these standards by developmental levels. www.ncge.org/

National Council for the Social Studies helps social studies educators teach students the content knowledge, intellectual skills, and civic values necessary for fulfilling the duties of citizenship in a participatory democracy. Its mission is to provide leadership, service, and support for all social studies educators. www.socialstudies.org/

Project Intersect at The Institute for the Study of Exceptional Children and Youth, University of Maryland, looks at how special education and charter schools coexist and expands the knowledge base in special education and related services. www.education.umd.edu/Depts/EDSP/ProjectIntersect/index.html

Public Broadcasting Service has a link, "From the Start," which contains teaching ideas (lesson plans and activities) linked to PBS shows, organized by grade level and topic. www.pbs.org/teachers/

Yahooligans is a searchable index on the Internet that focuses on content designed for children.

For additional educational resources, visit the book companion website for this text at www.cengagebrain.com.

5 Individualizing Planning

I left for the meeting alone at 7:00 A.M. Jack wanted to come, but with three kids, someone had to get them off to school. I arrived at the school for my first individualized education program (IEP) meeting. I wasn't sure what to expect, but I knew there would be a lot of *them*. Having gone through all the assessment and evaluation procedures, we were convinced that Charlene had a learning disability. More specifically, she was probably dyslexic.

After the introductions (where was her classroom teacher?), they gave me the IEP. I was appalled, as I thought this was something we did together. I would talk about what Charlene could do and liked to do, and then we would figure out how to use what she could do to help her learn to read. It seemed clear that they did not want my input because the form was typed and there were seven copies of it (one page of her IEP is shown in Figure 5–1).

© Cengage Learning 2012

I tried to get myself back together and at least look at the information on the form. The annual goal was fine. We too wanted her to improve her reading skills. The rest of the form made little sense. It was like a code that teachers use to keep parents out. How could I ever tell whether she mastered the critical objectives for her grade when they were given as 01, 02, and so on? When I looked at the evaluation procedure, it said that she was to get at least a 75 percent accuracy rate. Why not a 100 percent? How were they going to teach her to read: structural analysis, phonics, and kinesthetics? How individualized was that? What had they been doing up till now—trying osmosis? I was not a happy camper. Then I looked at who was responsible. Staff! What if I have a question? Do I call up the school and say, "Hello, I'd like to speak to staff to see whether my daughter is mastering her cm 04s yet?" Again, I tried to get my act together.

I asked them what they liked most about my daughter. There was silence. The educational diagnostician finally spoke up. She was the only one in the room who could even recognize Charlene. I asked where Charlene's classroom teacher was. They said she wasn't necessary as they began to explain why Charlene would be better off in a special education class. I explained that my husband and I had both observed in this class and didn't find it appropriate for our daughter. After some discussion, they said that there was a marvelous teacher at another school in the district who would just love to have a little girl like Charlene in her class, and they were sure it could be arranged to bus her to that school. At this point, the meeting seemed meaningless. As I got up to leave, someone reminded me that I hadn't yet signed the IEP. I left the meeting without signing it. I wondered if that meant that Charlene didn't have a disability.

REFLECTIVE PRACTICE | The IEP meeting described above happened in 1988. Do you think the process has changed and is more family friendly today? How would this meeting be different if it happened now? How could you make it different?

Planning for Individual Children

In the years since 1988, the laws and the educational system have changed. Current laws more clearly support the decision-making role of parents and keep most children, especially those like Charlene, in regular education classrooms. These changes have impacted classrooms and how we prepare teachers. All teachers now have to be prepared to teach all children.

DAP We no longer believe that "one size fits all." The concept of individualization is strongly supported by law, and individualized planning is a mainstay of early childhood special education. The idea of appropriateness comes

Student _Charlene_	School _West End School_		Page _2_ of ____			

Annual goal _1.0 To improve reading skills_

Short-term objective	Criteria and evaluation procedures	Specific educational services	Dates		Staff responsibilities	
			Begin	End	Name	Position
1.0 Charlene will master four critical objectives for grade. _Reading vocabulary_ _Comprehension_ VC 01 CM 01 02 02 03 03 04 04 05 05 06 06 07 _Study/ references_ _Sentences_ SR 01 SN 01 02	1.0 —Teacher test —Textbook test —Observation } at least 75% accuracy —Other Methods to include: —Structural analysis —Phonics —Kinesthetic	Level I	11/88	6/89	Staff	

Parent's signature

Teacher's signature _Ms. Vandivere, E.D._

FIGURE 5–1   ANNUAL GOAL FROM CHARLENE'S INDIVIDUALIZED EDUCATION PROGRAM (IEP)

from developmentally appropriate practices and looks at whether planning is appropriate for the particular child based on her age and culture. If a child with a disability reads at a pre-first-grade level but is 8 years old, the content of the reading material should reflect the child's age, whereas the reading level should match the child's ability. To understand planning for children with disabilities, you must understand the laws that guide this planning: Individuals with Disabilities Education Acts (IDEA). The rules set forth by the IDEA determine which children are eligible for services, the sources of paying for these services, the roles parents and professionals play in deciding which services should be offered, how frequently they are given, and where the services are delivered.

The IDEA requires that all children identified as eligible for special education services have an individualized plan for their education. Infants and toddlers have an individualized family service plan (IFSP) and children three and over have an individualized education program (IEP) to guide adults when they work with these children. This plan is an acknowledgment that each identified child needs individualized special educational services and supports to learn. Family goals and expectations for their children are part of the plan.

Individuals with Disabilities Education Acts

The Individuals with Disabilities Education Acts (IDEA) are a set of laws that ensure services to children with disabilities throughout the United States. The IDEA governs how states and public agencies provide special education, and related services to more than 6.6 million eligible children and youth with disabilities in 2007–2008. This is 13 percent of the public school enrollment (National Center for Educational Statistics, 2010). The IDEA has four parts.

- Part A defines the terms used in the law.

- Part B gives money to states to provide special education and related services for eligible children and youth (ages 3 to 21 years) with disabilities. Section 619 of Part B focuses on services for preschool children (ages 3 to 5 years). When professionals in the field talk about services for children ages 3 to 5, they might refer to them as either "619" or "Part B."

- Part C provides for early intervention programs for infants and toddlers with developmental delays or disabilities, or those at risk, and their families. The shorthand for services for children from birth to age 3 is "Part C."

- Part D helps state education departments and other agencies improve how they work with children and youth with disabilities.

The IDEA 2004 defines key terms and concepts and sets minimum federal standards that must be met to achieve **compliance**. The following definitions apply to children from birth through age 8 and those who educate them. This information is organized conceptually here rather than as it actually appears in the law.

● ● ●
General Definitions

The first thing to establish is whom we are talking about. The IDEA 2004 defines each of the disability terms used. Rather than defining them all here, some are defined in the chapters where they are covered.

A **child with a disability** is a child with an intellectual disability, hearing impairment (including deafness), speech or language impairment, visual impairment (including blindness), serious emotional disturbance, orthopedic impairment, autism, traumatic brain injury, other health impairments, or specific learning disabilities who needs special education and related services (U.S. DOE, 2006).

There is concern about mislabeling young children, and the term **developmentally delayed** allows for the provision of services rather than requiring a more specific diagnosis, such as learning disability or intellectual disability, for children ages 3 through 9 (U.S. DOE, 2006). The expectation is that during these years the delay will have responded to early intervention, or a more specific diagnosis will have been established. States vary in how they use this provision of the law.

Special education means specially designed instruction, at no cost to parents, to meet the unique needs of a child with a disability, including instruction in the classroom, the home, hospitals and institutions, and other settings; this includes physical education (U.S. DOE, 2006).

The area of related services is an interesting one. The goal of related services is to ensure that children are available for a free appropriate public education (FAPE), and its provisions are designed so schools are not providers of medical services, but do provide supportive services. For example, school personnel could help set the volume and check the batteries, but not adjust the electrical stimulation levels of cochlear implants nor pay for doing so (Mandlawitz, 2007).

Related services cover transportation speech-language pathology and audiology services, interpreting services, psychological services, physical and occupational therapy, recreation, including therapeutic recreation, social work services, school nurse services, rehabilitation counseling, orientation and mobility services, and medical services, to assist a child with a disability to benefit from special education; they include the early identification and assessment of disabling conditions in children (U.S. DOE, 2006).

The law defines what is meant by a free appropriate public education (FAPE) as

special education and related services that are provided at public expense, under public supervision and direction, and without charge; meet the standards of the State educational agency; include an appropriate preschool, elementary school, or secondary school education in the State involved; and are provided in conformity with the individualized education program (U.S. DOE, 2006)

The increasing role of assistive technology in supporting children with disabilities is acknowledged in the law, as is the need for educational institutions to provide and maintain these devices and provide training on their use. An **assistive technology device** is any item, piece of equipment, or product system, whether acquired commercially off the shelf, modified, or customized, that is used to increase, maintain, or improve functional capabilities of a child with a disability. On a case-by-case basis, children may use school-purchased assistive technology devices at home or in other settings if doing so is on the child's IEP. **Assistive technology services** helps a child with a disability in the selection, acquisition, or use of an assistive technology device and the training or technical assistance for the family and educators.

Part C defines the aspects of the law that relate to **infants or toddlers with disabilities**.

The term *infant or toddler with a disability* means a child under age 3 who needs early intervention services because she is experiencing appropriately diagnosed developmental delays in one or more of the areas of cognitive, physical, communication, social or emotional, and adaptive development, or she has a diagnosed physical or mental condition that has a high probability of resulting in developmental delay. States, at their discretion, may include at-risk infants and toddlers. Identified infants and toddlers must receive an educational component that promotes school readiness and incorporates preliteracy, language, and numeracy skills. Parents receive a written notification of their rights and responsibilities (U.S. DOE, 2006).

Other definitions and parts of the IDEA are discussed where they apply in the text.

Requirements of the IDEA

Sections of the IDEA require states to do a variety of different things to ensure that children with disabilities are provided with the services they require and the safeguards they need. Following are highlights of some of these requirements:

Identification. States must make extensive and well-publicized efforts to screen and identify all children and youth with disabilities. Child Find agencies typically fulfill this role.

Least Restrictive Environment. To the maximum extent possible children must be educated in the least restrictive environment (LRE) that is consistent with their educational needs and as much as possible with typically developing children.

Due Process. Parents' informed consent must be obtained before a child is evaluated, labeled, or placed. Parents who disagree with the school's decision have the right to mediation and to an impartial due process hearing.

Mediation. In an effort to resolve issues between families and schools without requiring a due process hearing, the IDEA supports mediation.

Highly Qualified Special Education Teachers. Highly qualified teachers (HQT) apply to special education teachers teaching core academic subjects in public elementary or secondary schools. Fully certified general education teachers who earn full special education certification or licensure are considered new special educators teachers for purposes of HQT. Teachers must have state certification as special education teachers and be qualified in the subjects they teach. These content area requirements are the same as they are for regular education. There are alternative routes to certification (U.S. DOE, 2006). To see the full requirements, go to www.idea.gov.

Individualized Education Program Teams

Individualized education program (IEP) teams are responsible for the identification, assessment, design, and implementation of the individualized program. The federal law provides information about the people who need to be on this team, their respective roles, and necessary skills. The IEP team is composed of the child's parents, at least one regular education and one special education teacher, and a representative of the local educational agency who is qualified to provide or supervise specially designed instruction to meet the unique needs of children with disabilities, including knowledge of the general education curriculum and the availability of resources of the local educational agency. A person who can interpret the instructional implications of evaluation results must be included. And, at the discretion of the parent or the agency, other people who may contribute, and the child, if appropriate (U.S. DOE, 2006).

The IEP team can be a formidable group. Parents have an extremely important role as they are the ones who will ultimately accept or reject the IEP. Regular education teachers are required because children are included in regular classrooms. The special education teacher or consultant is part of the team. Someone on the team must have the authority to commit resources; for example, if the team wants to have an assistive technology device included in the IEP, someone must have the authority to say the school system will pay for it. There is a requirement that at least one person on the team know specific instructional techniques for this particular child, as well as a person who is knowledgeable about the general curriculum. Someone on the team must understand and be able to interpret evaluation results. There is an option for others to be part of the team at the request of either the parents or the educational setting. The goal is to have all the stakeholders on the team. Some team members might fulfill multiple roles.

Additional IEP team members frequently include specialists who work with the child, but they can also include advocates, representatives of agencies and community programs that the child has attended or might attend, friends, previous teachers, parents of children with disabilities, or anyone the family or school feels would provide information, emotional support, and practical assistance.

One of the initial responsibilities of the IEP team is to ensure that parents understand the process itself and their rights under the law. Team members have the responsibility to talk with families about the range of services and service delivery settings available and to arrange for meeting times and locations that are convenient for families and other team members. The IEP meeting organizes and evaluates information about the child that has been gleaned from assessment data and other sources. It provides an opportunity for parents to talk about their child's strengths and their desires for their child. The IEP meeting also is a time to develop individualized criteria for assessing progress toward goals, giving family-initiated outcomes and goals priority, and to explore necessary accommodations for children to be part of the general curriculum.

IN THE FIELD

I had a boy named Jake, who had severe intellectual disabilities, in my 4-year-old class. His older brother and sister are developing typically, and his sister Jane is in the gifted and talented program. His parents are well educated and hold good jobs.

Most of the time Jake's parents are calm and giving. In fact, they gave the school a computer and each classroom some toys. However, when it was time for an IEP meeting, Jake's father's demeanor changed dramatically. He sent a note saying he had a list of things he wanted addressed at the meeting and persons he wanted to attend. I was able to get the various people to the meeting, but as far as his list went, he would not tell me anything except that he wanted a certain car seat for Jake to use on the bus. Needless to say, I reflected a lot on my teaching and wondered what I was not doing for this child and his family.

At the IEP meeting, Jake's father had a checklist in front of him and referred to it frequently, making remarks like, "Only 16 more things to address." For me, it was very intimidating. Eventually, the IEP meeting ended, and because his father had not asked for anything too unreasonable, the school district was able to accommodate the family's desires in Jake's program. I assumed that Jake's father was happy and it would be smooth sailing for the rest of the school year. It was smooth until the time came for the home visit.

Immediately after I scheduled the home visit, the daily notes in the communication book had a different tone. Mr. Taylor was critical of the way I ran my classroom and of the methods I used to teach his son. He also felt that we were not providing Jake with everything that he was entitled to, specifically, a portfolio. Mr. Taylor added that he was not afraid to get his lawyer involved and he had done it before.

Before the home visit, I sent home a copy of the functional curriculum to show Mr. Taylor how I was teaching, based on the curriculum goals and Jake's IEP. Additionally, I explained that a portfolio was not officially started until kindergarten but that I would be willing to bring the portfolio of Jake's progress that I was keeping. I let him know that I was open to suggestions and would be willing to incorporate his ideas. At the home visit, I took time going over everything I had sent home. My teaching and organizational methods were explained as well. Mr. Taylor seemed to feel better.

For the next few months, Jake's parents seemed happy with the program. When it was time for school to end and Jake to go on to kindergarten, his father started writing not-so-nice notes again. He questioned our motives for sending Jake to kindergarten and not retaining him. Mr. Taylor threatened to sue because the assistive technology referral from the IEP was taking too long. Again, I explained the philosophy of the program and why the assistive technology was taking longer than expected.

After the year ended, I really started to think about Jake and his family. It occurred to me that the only time his parents had issues with the school was before a transition and before a meeting directly related to Jake and his progress. I think scheduling these meetings really triggered some emotions for his family. They started to think about all the things that Jake will not be able to do and how they are going to accommodate him later in life. I believe that if we had a school social worker who could help families, many of their threats would end. Instead of taking their feelings out on the teachers and school, they would be able to handle them more appropriately and effectively.

Individualized Education Programs

When a child is identified as having a disability, certain procedures and requirements must be followed. Federal and state laws determine many of these procedures. All states must individualize programming for eligible children with disabilities. Information about the IEP is given first.

The IDEA requires that an IEP be designed *in writing* for each child with a disability, and as noted, the program must be developed *jointly* by teachers, specialists, parents or guardians, and, if possible, the child. Putting the program in writing is meant to ensure that it will be carried out and that there is agreement about its contents.

The 2004 amendments to the IDEA require that the IEP include the following information:

- A statement about the child's *present level of academic achievement* (PLAA) and functional performance
- *Measurable annual goals (MAGs)*, including academic and functional goals
- Information about a child's *progress* toward meeting the annual goals, which must be provided at the same time as regular report cards
- *Special education and related services* and supplementary aids and services, based on evidence-based research to the extent practical
- Expected participation with children without disabilities and the extent to which a child is *not participating* has to be explained.
- Appropriate *accommodations* or modifications necessary to measure the child's academic achievement and functional performance on state and district assessments
- If using an *alternative assessment*, why, and why the alternative assessment selected is appropriate
- A projected *time frame* or date for services and modifications to begin and the anticipated frequency, location, and duration of these
- *Transition services*, which must be included when a student is age 16

No additional information is required to be included in a child's IEP beyond what is explicitly mentioned in the law (U.S. DOE, 2006). To see the actual law, go to http://idea.ed.gov.

Parents have the right to examine all relevant school records regarding the identification, evaluation, and educational placement of their child, which enables them to examine the data on which decisions are based. Parents are entitled, on request, to see test results and receive copies of reports. Families are equal members of the IEP team and are invited to all team discussions of their child; access to data encourages them to actively participate in the IEP process. Therefore, documents should be free of jargon (or, at least necessary technical terms should be defined) so that all team members can understand them. Families need to know the current laws that regulate this process and what is considered best practice in the field.

The school district must provide parents with information *in writing,* in a language they can understand, about the identification, evaluation, and placement of their child. The parents must be notified in writing of contemplated program changes as well. In the past, some parents were not informed when their children were placed in or removed from special education classes.

In developing a child's IEP, the IEP team considers the strengths of the child, the goals and concerns of the parents, and the results of the evaluations of the child. As you are learning the elements of an IEP, you may ask yourself, "Is all this worth the effort for just one or two children?" Yes! In the process of complying with these legal requirements, you can learn a great deal about individualizing instruction for all children and about getting the maximum benefit from the resources you have. For other children in the class, especially those you have some concerns about, you can incorporate the planning and principles used to design an IEP.

The U.S. Department of Education designed a model IEP form that provides guidance about how the form should look and how to ensure that the needed elements are included. This form (Figure 5–2) documents the legal requirements for each section. Although states use this model to ensure compliance, most states have developed their own forms.

▶❚❚ TeachSource Video Case

Bobby: Serving a Student with Special Needs in an Inclusive Elementary Classroom

Watch the TeachSource Video Case *Bobby: Serving a Student with Special Needs in an Inclusive Elementary Classroom,* in which you will see a first grader with Down syndrome who is fully included along with other students with special needs in the regular classroom. The video can be found in the Early Childhood Education Media Library under Special Education, available at www.cengagebrain.com.

• • •

Requirements for Annual Goals

The 2004 reauthorization of the IDEA no longer requires measurable instructional objectives or benchmarks as part of the IEP for most school-age children. This decision was made in an

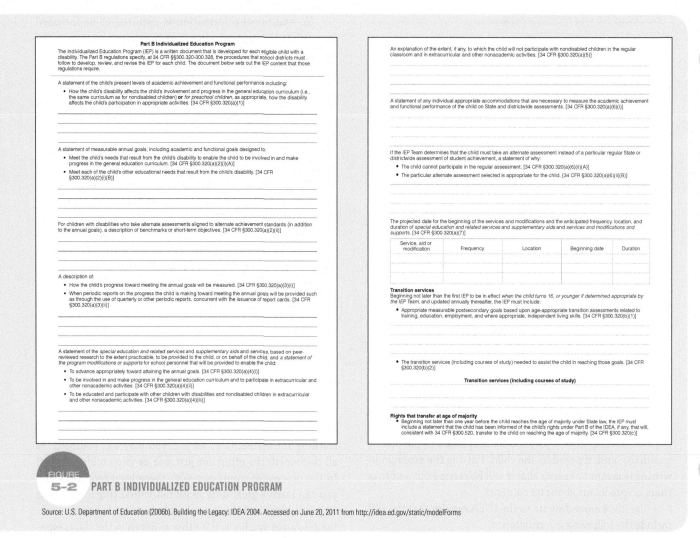

FIGURE 5-2   PART B INDIVIDUALIZED EDUCATION PROGRAM

Source: U.S. Department of Education (2006b). Building the Legacy: IDEA 2004. Accessed on June 20, 2011 from http://idea.ed.gov/static/modelForms

effort to reduce paperwork. Rather, the annual goal is measurable and is tied to state standards for each grade level. State standards provide the needed guidance for instruction. They are specific and reflect the scope and sequence used for all children in a grade level. Families of children with disabilities are concerned about how they will know whether their children are learning the required material if objectives and benchmarks are eliminated. They worry that if state standards are used to meet annual goals, there will be no individualization of instruction, because the state standards apply to all children.

IMPLICATIONS FOR EDUCATORS

Think broadly about measurable annual goals, standards, and the scope and sequence that support the attainment of these goals. Be prepared to tell families how you know their children are progressing toward their annual goals and the techniques you are using to individualize instruction.

WRITING ANNUAL GOALS

Annual goals are statements of long-range, measurable behaviors. They are based on the child's strengths and areas of need, both informal and formal assessments of the child, developmentally appropriate practice, knowledge about the child's developmental profile, and regular educational

standards. Annual goals relate to particular developmental/educational areas such as gross or fine motor development, language and literacy, mathematics, and so on. Within each domain, they are more specific. An appropriate annual goal in the area of mathematics, based on the Common Core State Standards for kindergarten mathematics, could be *Counting and Cardinality: Know number names and the count sequence.* Thus, by the end of kindergarten children are expected to write the numbers 0 to 20 and to count objects up to 20 and write the appropriate numeral. The standard is the same for all children; the individualization is how teachers go about teaching the standards. For preschool children, this could be broken down into prerequisite skills such as *tracing the numbers 1 to 5, copying the numbers and writing them without prompts; matching sets of objects that number between 1 and 5 with the appropriate numeral.* As children gain these skills, the numbers would increase to 10. See Activity 3–1 for *Matching Symbols* as an example of any activity to support learning required math concepts.

The first step in writing annual goals is to determine what a child can do independently and what he can do with scaffolding.

book, discussing who wrote it, and asking whether they know what the word *author* means. You might discuss the illustrator as the person who drew the pictures and inquire whether the children know what an illustrator is and does. Before you begin reading, you might ensure that children know words they may not be familiar with, and you might check these words again as you go along. When you finish reading, you could talk with the children about what type of literature the book represents and how they know.

Think of the IEP as a useful system of keeping track of information about children, and help families to think about it that way as well. As you talk about annual goals, discuss what you do in the classroom to ensure the child meets the goals, as well as the types of experiences families might work into their routines at home that would enhance their child's learning. (Setting the table can teach simple patterns and relationships.) Families may not be aware of underlying math concepts and might not think of table setting as supporting math. Reaching annual goals is a team effort, and all members of the team can help the child attain these.

After the child's present level of academic achievement and functional performance is determined, the IEP team must develop measurable annual goals. Research on the quality of IEP goals for young children shows that in the past many of the goals and objectives have been poorly written, with little attention to the context or activity in which the skill will be taught. Also, many goals were not developmentally appropriate, nor did they target functional skills. **Functional skills** are those skills the child needs to function independently in the environment and that can be taught during activities in the classroom or in routines at home (Grisham-Brown & Hemmeter, 1998). Rather, many IEP goals reflected isolated skills. If children with disabilities are to be included, IEP goals must be written in such a way that they can be part of the ongoing curriculum.

• • •

Choosing Annual Goals

To develop goals for an individual child, you need to know the demands of the school setting (or other settings where a child spends his time); that is, What is the child required to do? You need to find out the child's family's priorities for his skill development and behavior. Determine where the child is in developmental sequences and expected behaviors as the child progresses.

Family priorities may be very different from the ones you might set for a child. A family might want their child to have friends and play with other children. Your goals might revolve around specific communication skills. Although on the surface these look different, it may mean that the communication skills you focus on are those that are likely to increase communication with peers and the ability to join groups. If a family wants to toilet train a child, and you see fine motor skills as a priority, again, practice fine motor skills in the context of toileting. Before writing goals, the family along with the IEP team must identify the skills that are critical for a particular child.

DETERMINING CRITICAL SKILLS

Although critical skills for each child will differ, the following guidelines offer a way of thinking about skills that are useful for all children. Identify skills that, for example,

• are emerging or are present in some contexts but not in others.

Write annual goals that increase the probability that children will develop the skills they need to function independently in the world in which they live.
© Cengage Learning 2012

PRESENT LEVEL OF ACADEMIC ACHIEVEMENT AND FUNCTIONAL PERFORMANCE

The child's present levels of academic achievement and functional performance (PLAA) provide the starting point for developing annual goals. The child's disability and how this affects her involvement and progress in the general education curriculum must be taken into consideration as well. For preschool children, the emphasis is on developmental milestones, functional performance, and pre-academic skills. Annual goals are the educational focus for a year, so they are broad, but measurable.

IMPLICATIONS FOR EDUCATORS

Where does one begin when writing goals? The only way to answer that question is to know what the child is presently able to do in different development and content areas. With older children, achievement tests are often used to provide this information; with younger children, it is more challenging. If English language arts were on the IEP, a potential annual goal for a kindergarten child might be "to increase reading comprehension." The next step would be to look at the expectations for kindergarten children given in the Common Core State Standards for English Language Arts, which include such things as these:

• Ask and answer questions about unknown words in a text.
• Recognize common types of texts (storybooks, poems).
• With prompting and support, name the author and illustrator of a story and define the role of each in telling the story (CCSSO, 2010).

These standards provide you with a lot of information about what you should be doing to increase reading comprehension. After you have selected a book to read, you might begin by showing the children the title of the

- will permit the child to participate in daily routines and become more independent.
- will allow the child to accomplish the greatest number of tasks.
- the child is highly motivated to learn.
- the family wishes the child to learn.
- will support the child's participation in future environments.

Annual goals for school-age children are related to academic skills and behaviors based on the regular education curriculum and the state standards. For children ages 3 to 5, they can be developmental skills that will have an impact on educational ability. Standards and state-developed performance indicators provide guidance for these goals. The annual goals mentioned in this text are necessary developmental skills based on the Common Core State Standards and those developed by professional organizations. All measurable goals should be based on the child's present level of academic achievement and functional performance.

WRITING MEASURABLE GOALS

Measurable goals are written in such a way that anyone can read them and tell whether the child is making appropriate progress toward attaining them. To help satisfy this empirical requirement, there are rules for writing measurable goals that include identifying it, describing the behavior that shows the goal is being met, and establishing criteria for acceptable performance.

With young children, the measurable part is a challenge. This is difficult because you must be able to measure (see) what is done. This means that some words—such as *understand, know, appreciate, try, feel, discover,* and *think*—should not be used. Early childhood special educators have more difficulty writing measurable goals than other educators because young children have a smaller repertoire of behaviors. Traditional words—such as *write, list, translate, read, predict,* and *compare*—represent skills children may not have achieved. A starter list of words that allow skills to be measurable follows:

point to	order	name	color
match	say	pick out	copy
select	label	choose	dramatize
tell	repeat	find	dictate
set up	define	jump	cut out
state	look at	run	count
arrange	draw	hop	
locate	circle	walk	

The evaluation criteria are also challenging. How well or how often does a goal have to be achieved for you as the teacher to decide that it has been mastered? In education, we frequently decide a child has to be correct four out of five times to have mastered a particular goal. This is 80 percent. Because of human variability, it is unwise to anticipate a 100 percent performance, even when you think this can be achieved. For a variety of reasons, children often decide not to comply with requests. You have to build flexibility into your evaluation criteria. You must also give some thought to what you specifically need to do to figure out whether the goal has been achieved. How will you know it is 80 percent of the time unless you allow the child at least five trials? (You can convert four out of five trials to 80 percent; if you choose 90 percent you have to use ten trials.) Will this get "old" for you and the child? Think about it before you write it down.

Goals should have enough flexibility to allow for individual differences and lend themselves to variety in programming. Once you begin to think more broadly about the goals themselves, you should expand that thinking to the settings where potential behaviors can happen. Children need many opportunities to practice these goals and their prerequisite skills. Think about how to build them into routines in the classroom and into the routines that the child's family already uses. Inclusion of a goal in several settings increases the probability that the skill itself will be generalized, as well as the opportunities the child has to practice the skill.

As you reflect on writing and implementing annual goals and their prerequisite skills, it becomes clear that it is much simpler to write trivial goals than important ones. Furthermore, some of the qualities you value most are almost impossible to put into measurable terms, for example, empathy, creativity, cooperation, joy, and interest. Finally, it is clear you will have to develop a system of record keeping to determine whether goals have been met or are in the process of being met.

Setting priorities, or deciding what to do first, is sometimes difficult. Parents' choices and children's preferences are primary considerations. However, parents may not be aware of the many steps it takes to accomplish a particular goal. If parents want their child to read, yet the child cannot identify letters and letter-sound relationships, you should be prepared to help parents understand the need for some prerequisite skills—and that "learning to read" is not a measurable goal as stated. This doesn't mean that you dismiss the goal as inappropriate; it means that it may take a long time to reach, and you and the parents have to be clear about prerequisite skills that lead to the attainment of the goal. Additionally, the goal should be reframed so it is measurable. An important and measurable goal would be for the child *to read at the beginning second grade (2.0) level as measured by the STAR (Standardized Test for the Assessment of Reading) Early Literacy test.*

Find out the family's priorities, and then ask about each annual goal: How difficult will it be in the future if the child does not learn a certain skill? The more the child will need this skill, the higher the priority you assign the annual goal and its prerequisite skills, and the more time designated to work on meeting it. Goals should reflect knowledge of child development, the child's abilities, and the goal's importance.

EMBEDDING ANNUAL GOALS

The process of embedding goals and their prerequisite skills requires you to identify when and where a child's goals will be addressed in the classroom and who will be responsible for teaching the required skills. To embed annual goals successfully, you might try the following:

1. Identify the structure of the day, including the daily schedule, routines, transitions, and activities or experiences.

2. Review each child's IEP or IFSP and annual goals.

3. Identify possible times during each day when a child's goals can be incorporated into the program.

4. Starting with the child's present level of academic performance and functional behavior (PLAA), determine the next steps in the process by breaking the goal down into prerequisite skills.

5. Determine what types of activities—specify *which*—can be planned during the identified routines to foster the acquisition of the necessary skills. The more frequently you include aspects of goals in daily routines and transitions, the greater the likelihood of meeting the goals.

6. Determine what teaching strategies best support the acquisition of these skills.

7. Decide which adults in the classroom are going to support the child learning these prerequisite skills, and ensure that they are aware of both the skills and the teaching techniques necessary for their acquisition.

8. Ensure that the adults discuss the child's learning and chart his accomplishments so that needed skills increase in complexity or are replaced with different prerequisite skills.

9. If more than one child has an IEP in your classroom, or you have closely embedded your goals within the routine of the program, it is useful to include aspects of the goals in the daily schedule. Put the skills you plan to meet for each child across from the designated routine and code the objectives from each child's IEP that you plan to meet. If you embed skills in the activities that you plan, be clear what skills you are going to emphasize for different children as part of the planning process (Pretti-Frontczak & Bricker, 2004).

Schedule	Saul
Arrival	A.2 Respond to "yes/no" questions
	A.3 Respond to "tell me about" questions
	Stella
	B.2 Name members of the class
	C.1 Initiate communication with peers and adults

REFLECTIVE PRACTICE | Notice how easily these skills fit in with regular routines and planning. What it takes is a reminder to do this everyday on a regular basis. The questions vary in content, but not in intent.

DAP Goals and their prerequisite skills can be incorporated into activities. You need to think in terms of the underlying principles of how children learn developmentally appropriate practices, and how you plan for children. Think in terms of particular activities and also types of activities that support the skills children need. If children are struggling with reading, one aspect of reading is vocabulary. If the goal is "to increase vocabulary acquisition and use," this can be done through such activities as 2–3 *Synonyms*, 2–14 *Hurricanes*, 2–27 *Mind Mapping*, and 2–45w *Greek Myths*. Goals are met when adults build skills into each day multiple times and in multiple contexts.

Part Three of this text is designed to help you embed annual goals and their supporting skill in activities. The numbers given above are for activities that are designed to increase vocabulary. The goals and activity numbers detail additional activities that support this goal. You have to decide which activities to use in what particular progression and how to vary them to meet an individual child's needs.

With increased emphasis on academic areas, some of the skills that make children available for learning, such as social competence, are becoming rare on IEPs. Whether or not children's goals include skills related to self-regulation and social interactions, they are important aspects of school competence. If children have trouble joining groups, then a plan must be developed to scaffold joining groups. Families, educators, and specialists should participate in developing and carrying out the plan. Although this skill cannot logically be carried out as part of a transition, it can be scaffolded several times each day, thus providing opportunities for social interaction. It is up to adults to design environments to promote active engagement, learning, participation, and membership (Wolery, 2005). To program inclusively, you must meet the learning needs of all children who are functioning at a variety of developmental and academic levels, not just those for whom you have an IEP.

IN THE FIELD

As a first-grade teacher in an inclusive classroom, I have often struggled with how to embed the teaching of IEP goals into the regular routine of my classroom. When I began teaching, I simply had a paraeducator pull the children receiving special education services out of the general class lesson to teach a particular IEP goal. This did not seem fair. However, I continued this practice for several years until I realized that this was not truly inclusion.

After taking a graduate class that focused on inclusion, I learned many ways to embed IEP annual goals into the classroom. I actually incorporated the skills and goals into classroom instruction by adding these to my lesson plans and found time to make each IEP goal fit in with the general curriculum. During every unit, I identified which activities lent themselves to teaching the skills needed for the annual IEP goals.

Further, I identified what routines and schedules had to be changed and which would work with the skills I needed to teach. I used my para's help to involve all children in an activity instead of pulling out the children with disabilities; at times, the para worked on IEP goals within the whole-class activity. I also had to identify different teaching strategies to help each child achieve her goals.

Having really focused on embedding the IEP goals into the regular curriculum, I realize that I am teaching more effectively in this inclusive classroom. Now I know that I am truly planning for the individual needs and differences of each child.

Universal Design for Learning

Universal design for learning (UDL) is a research-based educational framework that promotes the development of flexible learning environments that can accommodate individual learning differences. It means that instructional materials and activities are designed so that children with wide differences in their abilities can achieve learning goals. Universal does not mean "one size fits all." Instead, it is meant to underscore the need for multiple means of representation, expression, and engagement to meet the needs of children with diverse abilities (Meyer & Rose, 2005).

The 2004 amendments to the IDEA emphasize this concept as a way of supporting the learning of all children. This is achieved by using flexible materials and activities that allow children to display their learning in a variety of ways. The materials and activities are designed this way from the beginning; they are not additions or modifications. Flexible digital media makes it easier to provide these multiple alternatives and customize teaching and learning. Although technology can make the process easier, the underlying concepts apply to all areas. Information should be accessible and support skill development, and above all, what is learned should be important (Stahl, 1999).

More specifically, UDL helps educators accommodate individual differences by providing (1) multiple means of representation of the information presented, to give learners various ways of acquiring information and knowledge, (2) multiple and modifiable means of expression and control, to offer learners alternatives for demonstrating what they know, and (3) multiple or modifiable means of motivation or engagement, to tap into learners' interests, challenge them appropriately, and motivate them to learn (CAST, 2007; Rose & Meyer, 2005; Stahl, 1999).

Research in neuroscience has shown that each brain processes information in a different way. The way we learn is as individual as our DNA or fingerprints. Universal design for learning is one way of doing this.

THE EVIDENCE BASE

Research at the Center for Applied Special Technology has identified three primary brain networks and the roles they play in learning:

- Recognition networks involve gathering facts. These look at how children identify and categorize what they see, hear, and read. Identifying letters, words, or sounds are recognition tasks—the "What" of learning.
- Strategic networks are used in planning and performing tasks. How children organize and figure out how to perform new tasks (motor or cognitive). Expressing ideas and solving math problems are strategic tasks—the "How" of learning.
- Affective networks are the ways in which children are engaged and motivated. How they are challenged, excited, or interested. These are affective dimensions—the "Why" of learning.

UDL principles help educators reflect on their teaching for individual differences in each of these three brain networks.

Source: Center for Applied Special Technology, (CAST) 2007

IMPLICATIONS FOR EDUCATORS

As you think about applying the principles of universal design to activities and materials that support annual goals, remember:

1. Choose activities that use as many senses as possible (vision, taste, touch, hearing, smell). Be clear that these senses are available for both input and output of learning experiences.
2. Choose activities that reinforce goals but have many variations. Repetition helps children master a concept, but repeating the same activity is boring. If you are working to improve measurement concepts, have children measure both wet and dry materials (water, cooking oil, coffee beans, cornmeal, etc.). Have many different types of measuring devices, and talk with children as well as show them the relevance of being able to measure materials. This provides a broad base for learning about a variety of concepts including measurement, as well as fitting into a variety of themes that support generalization and contextual learning.
3. Use variety when presenting the same information. Color, for example, can be shown through clothing, painting, bingo, gelatin, and nature walks, to name just a few.

Record Keeping

Good record keeping is indispensable for implementing an IEP. Much of your record keeping will be similar to that described in Chapter 3 on assessment. However, for children with an IEP, in addition to the records that you keep on all the children, you must keep records on children's progress toward meeting annual goals, as well as state standards.

A one-page outline that corresponds directly to the child's annual goals and the skills needed to meet these will be a reminder to ensure that children have many opportunities to practice skills and that you are keeping track of their progress on a regular basis. In an outline report, numbers and key words identify the goals (Figure 5–3). Plus and minus signs and checks are helpful shorthand for daily notes.

Figure 5–4 shows how anecdotal notes can be used for record keeping. The choice of how you keep records is yours, but you must keep records.

IEPs are individualized plans, but as you plan for your class, it is important that you include all the children's goals in your planning on a regular basis. To do this, it may help to put goals on one planning form, such as the one illustrated in Figure 5–5. You may have one chart such as this with all the child's goals stated in a generic sense and then individualized to fit into your class routines (Pretti-Frontczak & Bricker, 2004).

As you plan an activity or unit, think about children's IEP goals. Determine which of them can be met during an activity. Then, focus on flexibly designing the inputs and outputs to meet the goals. Finally, determine how accessible the materials, equipment, procedures, instructional style, or peer behaviors you plan to use ensure that the child's goals are being met in the context of what all children are learning.

Implementing an IEP in a Theme

DAP Themes make learning fun and facilitate children's understanding. They are a means to an end, but not the end itself. Focus on how themes support the content of

Name	Tinea B.	Evaluation criteria		Date	Date	Date
				10/13/11	10/20/11	10/27/11
1. Fine Motor						
1.1 Stringing beads		10 beads		2 beads	2 beads	
1.2 Copy shapes		3 of 5 correct		2 shapes	3 shapes	
1.3 Block tower		5 blocks high		3 blocks	4 blocks	
2. Language concepts						
2.1 Colors		6 of 8	R	3 red, yellow, green	3 red, yellow, green	
2.2 Numbers		1 to 5	E	1, 2	1, 2	
2.3 Prepositions		6 of 8	R	on, under	+ in	

Key: E = Expressive
R = Receptive

FIGURE 5-3 CHECKLIST: WEEKLY IEP REPORT

There are a variety of ways of keeping records. Some teachers like checklists, where as others prefer anecdotal notes. Both work.

the general curriculum. Start with your learning goals. If an annual goal were literacy based, a theme would provide guidance and continuity for the books you read, the topics children write on, and the vocabulary words they learn. Children are excited and motivated about themes that grow out of their interests and are presented in a developmentally appropriate way.

In many ways, the theme makes some of the planning easier. The vocabulary to stress is more obvious and more easily reinforced because it is maintained for at least a week. As children expand their concepts, use analogies to help them learn. The purpose of theme-based planning is contextual learning. Children can learn more, faster, and in greater depth if materials are related and relevant.

Tinea B. 10/20/11

Fine motor: T. is still demonstrating needs in this area. She can now build a 4-block tower, copy three shapes, △○□ Bead stringing is not improving. I think I'll try sewing cards and see whether that helps.

Language: T.'s language has improved since September. Sentences have 3 to 5 words. She can identify red, yellow, and green when I give her a pair of colors and ask her to show me (red). We are working on blue. She can say the numbers 1 through 5, but I'm not sure it means anything. It is sort of like singing the alphabet song. She can follow one-step directions containing the prepositions: on, under, in. Starting to work on beside.

FIGURE 5-4 ANECDOTAL RECORDS: WEEKLY IEP REPORT

This figure contains the same information as Figure 5–3, but in an anecdotal format

IMPLICATIONS FOR EDUCATORS

The principles of contextual learning can be applied to the home as well. If parents want to work on language concepts at home, they can use the house for context. Have parents decide what they will do in each room of the house to help children learn contextually. Make a chart similar to that in Figure 5–6, but instead of having developmental domains, have rooms of the house. In the bedroom, children might learn the names of clothing; in the kitchen, eating utensils and foods; in the living room, furniture. Parents are more likely to remember if they can put the chart on the refrigerator instead of in a notebook. Change charts as children master concepts.

Discipline and the IDEA

Discipline is challenging in many settings, particularly when children with identified behavioral problems are involved. The 2004 amendments to the IDEA modified appropriate disciplinary actions for children with disabilities. The goal is that the same rules apply to children with and without disabilities. Schools decide on a case-by-case basis whether to change a placement for a child who violates the code of student conduct. Children can be removed from their current placement to an appropriate **interim alternative educational setting (IAES)** or another setting, or suspended for not more than 10 school days. Additional removals of not more than 10 consecutive school days during the school year for other incidents are possible as long as these do not constitute a change of placement.

One questions that relates to discipline is whether the behavior experienced is a manifestation of the child's disability. Whether it is or not, when a child is removed from a setting, she must continue to receive educational services to help her progress toward IEP goals and participation in the general education curriculum. As appropriate, she also must receive a **functional behavioral assessment** and behavioral

Child	Communication	Cognitive	Gross motor	Fine motor	Social skills
Ali	B.1 Request desired transportation objects.	C.2 Identify different methods of transportation.			A.1 Initiate conversation with a peer about transportation.
Mario	A.1 Respond to a yes/no question about transportation.			B.1 Move small trains and buses on a path.	
Carol	C.2 Respond to "what" or "how" questions about transportation.			A.1 Move from a lying down to a sitting position and maintain that position while using transportation manipulatives.	

FIGURE
5-5   EMBEDDING CHILDREN'S OBJECTIVES IN A THEME-BASED CURRICULUM

intervention services and modifications. There is a concern that children who are removed from school because of behavioral problems will also experience academic failure. If the removal is a change of placement, the IEP team determines appropriate services for the new location.

One requirement of the process is to determine whether the conduct was a **manifestation of the disability**. It is considered to be a manifestation of the child's disability if the conduct in question was caused by the child's disability or was the direct result of the local educational agency's failure to implement the IEP (U.S. DOE, 2006). If the IEP is not being implemented, the school (local educational agency) must remedy this problem. If the behavior is related to the child's disability, the IEP team must either conduct a functional behavior assessment (FBA), if this has not been done previously, and implement a **behavioral intervention plan (BIP)** or review the previous plan and modify it as needed. The child then returns to her previous placement unless the violations involved weapons, drugs, or serious bodily injury, or there is agreement that the placement should be changed.

Functional Behavioral Assessments and Behavior Intervention Plans

The IDEA focuses attention on the connection between behavioral problems and learning in the creation of IEPs. Analyzing this connection involves assessing the function of problematic behavior. Understanding what a student gains through her actions is critical to behavior modification efforts. The functional behavioral assessment (FBA) involves determining the cause of a behavior in order to formulate an appropriate intervention. It reviews how a child functions in different settings such as school, home, and in the community, and uses this information to develop a plan that addresses the underlying causes of problematic behavior

(Mandlawitz, 2007). IEP teams use a variety of techniques to investigate whether biological, social, affective, and/or environmental factors contribute to the origin, maintenance, or cessation of the targeted problematic behavior.

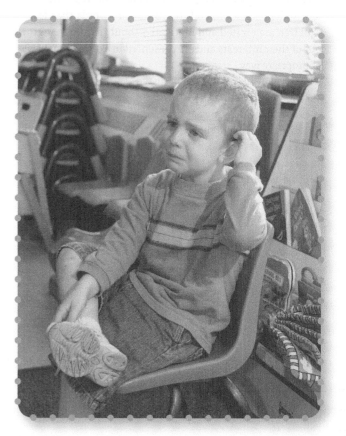

Most children test rules some of the time. When a child has a disability, it is important to determine whether the behavior is a manifestation of the disability or is related to the environment.
© Cengage Learning 2012

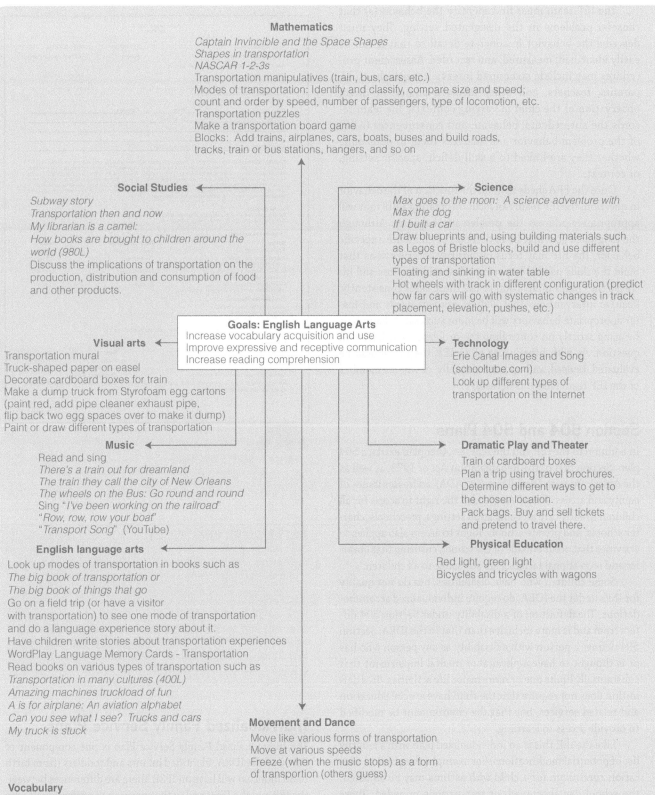

Mathematics

Captain Invincible and the Space Shapes
Shapes in transportation
NASCAR 1-2-3s
Transportation manipulatives (train, bus, cars, etc.)
Modes of transportation: Identify and classify, compare size and speed;
count and order by speed, number of passengers, type of locomotion, etc.
Transportation puzzles
Make a transportation board game
Blocks: Add trains, airplanes, cars, boats, buses and build roads,
tracks, train or bus stations, hangers, and so on

Social Studies

Subway story
Transportation then and now
My librarian is a camel:
How books are brought to children around the
world (980L)
Discuss the implications of transportation on the
production, distribution and consumption of food
and other products.

Science

Max goes to the moon: A science adventure with
Max the dog
If I built a car
Draw blueprints and, using building materials such
as Legos of Bristle blocks, build and use different
types of transportation
Floating and sinking in water table
Hot wheels with track in different configuration (predict
how far cars will go with systematic changes in track
placement, elevation, pushes, etc.)

Goals: English Language Arts
Increase vocabulary acquisition and use
Improve expressive and receptive communication
Increase reading comprehension

Visual arts

Transportation mural
Truck-shaped paper on easel
Decorate cardboard boxes for train
Make a dump truck from Styrofoam egg cartons
(paint red, add pipe cleaner exhaust pipe,
flip back two egg spaces over to make it dump)
Paint or draw different types of transportation

Technology

Erie Canal Images and Song
(schooltube.com)
Look up different types of
transportation on the Internet

Music

Read and sing
There's a train out for dreamland
The train they call the city of New Orleans
The wheels on the Bus: Go round and round
Sing "*I've been working on the railroad*"
"*Row, row, row your boat*"
"*Transport Song*" (YouTube)

Dramatic Play and Theater

Train of cardboard boxes
Plan a trip using travel brochures.
Determine different ways to get to
the chosen location.
Pack bags. Buy and sell tickets
and pretend to travel there.

English language arts

Look up modes of transportation in books such as
The big book of transportation or
The big book of things that go
Go on a field trip (or have a visitor
with transportation) to see one mode of transportation
and do a language experience story about it.
Have children write stories about transportation experiences
WordPlay Language Memory Cards - Transportation
Read books on various types of transportation such as
Transportation in many cultures (400L)
Amazing machines truckload of fun
A is for airplane: An aviation alphabet
Can you see what I see? Trucks and cars
My truck is stuck

Physical Education

Red light, green light
Bicycles and tricycles with wagons

Movement and Dance

Move like various forms of transportation
Move at various speeds
Freeze (when the music stops) as a form
of transportion (others guess)

Vocabulary

Types of transportation
Train (station), bus (station), airplane (terminal, hanger), car (garage), boat (marina, slip, dock)
Freight train, passenger train, subway
School bus, city bus, long distance bus
Sedan, station wagon, convertible, SUV, truck
Speedboat, tanker, tugboat, sailboat

THEME PLAN: TRANSPORTATION

FIGURE
5-6

The IEP team must first identify the behavior(s) that cause(s) problems in the designated setting. They must describe the behavior in concrete detail so that it can be easily identified, measured, and recorded. Assessment procedures may include structured interviews with the child, parents, teachers, and other involved adults, or direct observation of the child in varying contexts. The team records the antecedents, behavior, and consequences (ABC) of the problem behavior and analyzes them to determine whether they are linked to a skill deficit, specific setting, or context.

Once the FBA sheds light on the function of the behavior in question, the IEP team can focus on creating a BIP that will appropriately address the problematic behavior. Although the long-term goal may be to decrease or eliminate a specific behavior, the BIP may focus on positive interventions that build the skills needed to perform desired behaviors and increase the child's motivation to use these skills consistently. Positive interventions that address student needs and foster appropriate behaviors will be more successful than plans focusing strictly on controlling the problematic behavior in question. As with other areas of an IEP, the BIP should be evaluated, revised, and updated annually, or when a member of the IEP team feels it is necessary.

Section 504 and 504 Plans

In addition to the IEP and the IFSP, another plan exists, a 504 plan. Section 504 of the Rehabilitation Act of 1973, as well as the Americans with Disabilities Act (ADA), addresses issues of equity and access. The ADA extended the right to access for all children to early care and education settings, preschools, charter schools, and private schools. Right to access also applies to activities that occur outside of the school, ensuring that libraries and recreational facilities are accessible to all children.

Some children who have disabilities, but do not qualify for IEPs under the IDEA, do require individualized accommodations. The definition of a disability under Section 504 differs from and is more inclusive than that in the IDEA. Section 504 defines a person with a disability as any person who has or is thought to have a physical or mental impairment that substantially limits one or more major life activities. This definition does not require that the child have special education and related services, but that the environment be modified to provide access to learning.

Like the IEP, this is an individualized plan with a lengthy list of potential modifications. For example, the physical education curriculum for a child with asthma may be adjusted, the school day shortened, or rest periods provided. There may be a tutor provided at home if the child is out of school frequently. There may be changes in classroom management, curricula, or instructional procedures to accommodate these children. Like the IEP, these are individualized plans designed to make school accessible to all children. Included here is a sample 504 plan so that you can see the ways in which it might be used, and how it differs from an IEP (see Figure 5.7 for a sample 504 plan).

FIGURE 5-7   SAMPLE 504 PLAN

REFLECTIVE PRACTICE | Children with special health care needs may need 504 plans to accommodate limitations in energy, problems relating to the environment, and ways to make learning accessible. They do not need special instructional methods as much as accommodations to allow them to come to school and for continuity of instruction. How would you feel about having a child with a 504 plan in your class? What if a child had an episodic illness such as asthma or cancer? What about epilepsy? Would you have to learn new techniques? These 504 plans can impact a very different part of the educational system, and they require you to develop different skills and ways of thinking.

Individualized Family Service Plans

The Individualized Family Service Plan is one component of Part C of the IDEA. Identified infants and toddlers (from birth to 36 months) will have an IFSP. There are differences between the IEP and the IFSP, and in the approach of professionals who work with infants and toddlers and their families. The purpose of the IFSP is to identify, organize, and facilitate the attainment of families' goals for their infants and toddlers and for themselves to support their children. The process of interacting and joining with families in their exploration of their strengths and goals for themselves and their infants and toddlers may be more important than the IFSP itself. The IFSP requires professionals to add new skills to their repertoire and to go beyond the traditional boundaries of their disciplines. In many ways, the IFSP addresses not only intervention in the infant or toddler's development but also the relationship between families and professionals. The family-centered model is based on collaboration and partnership. Relationships depend upon mutual respect, understanding, and empathy. In a family-centered approach, parents and professionals are viewed as equals. This is a very different perspective from when professionals were seen as the experts who had both knowledge and power. Now the family defines the role the professional will play, which can be active or passive and may change over time. The professional's role is to empower families to make the choices that best fit their current strengths and needs.

DAP The central idea of an IFSP is that services should be family based instead of child based. The IFSP changes as the family and child change, because the process and resulting product are *family-driven*. Families decide what they want as outcomes on the IFSP. Four major themes are part of the recommended practices:

1. Shared responsibility and collaboration
2. Strengthened family functioning
3. Individualized and flexible practices
4. Strengths- and assets-based practice (Trivette & Dunst, 2005)

These themes provide professionals with a framework for thinking about and supporting families. Although it is the process that is important, sometimes the product tells us about the process. Because infants and toddlers are not the same as small preschoolers, the IFSP does not have the behavioral focus of the IEP.

Content of the IFSP

The IDEA determines the requirements of the IFSP, and it specifies that the early intervention services must include a multidisciplinary assessment and a written IFSP to be developed with the family. The IDEA stipulates the following relative to the content of the IFSP.

The individualized family service plan shall be in writing and contain statements about the following:

1. The infant's or toddler's present levels of physical development, cognitive development, communication development, social or emotional development, and adaptive development, based on objective criteria;
2. The family's resources, priorities, and concerns relating to enhancing the development of their infant or toddler with a disability;
3. The measurable developmentally appropriate outcomes expected to be achieved for the infant or toddler and the family, including preliteracy and language skills, and the criteria, procedures, and timelines used to determine progress toward achieving the outcomes as well as whether modifications or revisions of the outcomes or services are necessary;
4. The specific evidence-based early intervention services necessary to meet the unique needs of the infant or

toddler and the family, including the frequency, intensity, and method of delivering services;
5. The natural environments in which early intervention services will be provided, and a justification if any services will not be provided in a natural environment;
6. The projected dates for initiation of services and the anticipated length, duration, and frequency of the services;
7. The identification of the service coordinator who will be responsible for the implementation of the plan and coordination with other agencies and persons, including transition services;
8. The steps to be taken to support the transition of the toddler with a disability to preschool or other appropriate services (U.S. DOE, 2006).

The IDEA stipulates also that the contents of the IFSP shall be fully explained to the parents, and informed written consent from the parents shall be obtained prior to the provision of early intervention services described in the IFSP. If the parents do not consent to a particular early intervention service, that early intervention service will not be provided.

- Child assessment refers to reviewing an infant and toddler's pertinent records (health status and medical history), observing the child and assessing him to identify his unique strengths and needs, including his level of functioning in cognitive and physical development, which includes vision and hearing, communication development, social or emotional development, and adaptive development. These assessments must be based on objective criteria and must include informed **clinical opinion**.
- Family assessment, typically a voluntary personal interview with the family, involves the identification of the family's resources, priorities, and concerns, and the supports and services necessary to enhance the family's capacity to meet the developmental needs of the family's infant or toddler with a disability, as determined through child assessment.
- Service needs assessment, if the infant or toddler qualifies as *a child with a disability*, including reviewing the assessment of the child and family as well as pertinent records and observations to identify the early intervention services appropriate to meet the child's unique needs in each developmental area.
- Evaluating the assessments of the child and the family to determine whether the child is eligible for services and her continuing eligibility (Keilty, Walsh, & Ziegler, 2007; U.S. DOE, 2006).

IFSP Process

Although all agencies will have slightly different procedures, eligibility criteria, and organizational frameworks, it is expected that the process will be something like this:

1. Families are referred to early intervention services by a physician or agency, or are self-referred.
2. Families then talk about their likes and dislikes, wants and needs, preferences, and priorities. This may be

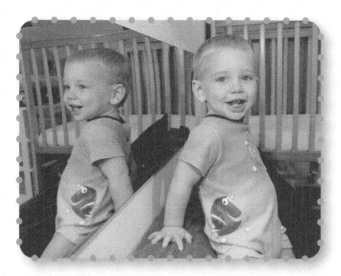

Infants and toddlers need to be observed in their natural environments as part of the assessment process.
© Cengage Learning 2012

the first time they have been asked what *they* want for their family as well as for their infant or toddler. They may need support to think about the needs of the family instead of just those of the infant or toddler, and this process may take more than one meeting. Because families' preferences set the stage for the IFSP, giving them the time they need is vital.

3. In assessment planning, the information gathered is analyzed to clarify the family's preferences for involvement and their priorities for both the family and child. Information about the infant or toddler's characteristics and additional information from other assessments should be included. One role of the service coordinator is to help support the family in deciding on their role and their level of participation. Families have an active voice in the assessment process, scheduling the assessment, determining appropriate assessment measures, and when and how the assessment information will be shared. Planning the assessment around the parents' work, the child's most alert time, and the schedule of professionals can be a challenge. Parent's participation in the process makes the assessment more accurate and more relevant.

4. Before formal child assessment begins, it is imperative to determine the parents' perceptions of their infant or toddler. Find out what they consider to be their infant's or toddler's strengths and needs, likes and dislikes, what their specific areas of concern are, and what they want for their child. It is often useful to find out what a typical day is like in the family; be sure to include all family members to understand how they share roles, as well what role the infant or toddler plays in the family.

5. Child assessment serves different functions at various points in the process. Initially, the assessment focuses on determining whether the child meets the eligibility criteria for Part C. Information is also necessary to develop the IFSP.

6. Identification of family values and preferences involves clarifying with families what aspects of their family life are relevant to their infant or toddler's growth and development. There are a variety of measures available to help families identify their strengths, needs, resources, and supports, and they come in many different formats. However, the most efficient way to learn about what families want and how they want to participate is to ask them. If they want further clarification, offer them some options.

Agreeing on the desired outcomes to meet child and family needs requires the interpretation and synthesis of formal and informal assessment information in light of the family's priorities. It may involve some rethinking and will certainly necessitate choosing among strategies, activities, and services to meet desired outcomes. Do not assume all families with a child with a disability have the same needs, wants, desires, or values. IFSPs are designed to be a family-based collaboration with a specialist to achieve a set of desired outcomes. When this does not happen, the results can be devastating to families and children.

IN THE FIELD

I was concerned about Bobby's language and decided to take him to Child Development Watch for an assessment. It was horrible. I have never had such a bad experience in my life. I called to get an appointment and waited to hear from them. They called on Friday to confirm the appointment for Monday. I decided not to say anything even though they scheduled it right at his naptime.

It didn't go well. Bobby and I were the first people there. It was a doctor's office with all kinds of cabinets and stuff. He was tired and he played with the stroller until we put it outside. Then they gave him toys and instead of doing what they asked, he would put the toys in the cabinets.

There was a developmental nurse and a speech-language pathologist. The speech and language person could not get him to engage. They called him Bob, my husband's name, and then they said he didn't respond to his own name. I was getting upset and I forgot to tell them that we called him Bobby. I would have told them if they had asked if he had a nickname. They gave him the Peabody Picture Vocabulary Test, but they couldn't get him to sit still to look at the pictures. He kept pulling at my hand because he wanted to go home. We were there for over two hours and we were both exhausted. When we got home, he slept for three hours.

They kept saying things like, "Well, we know he's different." And, "He likes music; maybe he could do something in that." He's only 2 years old and they are already feeling that he's not going to make it. They didn't listen to anything I said. I had already told them that he doesn't do what you tell him to do. But in 10 minutes, she "knew" what was wrong with him. She kept pooh-poohing everything I said he could do. I was irrelevant in a doctor's room. Just because something happens in one situation does not mean it is true in all settings. The environment was producing some of this.

I was frustrated. I knew that he had some problems, but not all the problems they were saying. I told them that he could go down four stairs independently (we have a split-level) so they took him to the top of this long dark staircase, and the speech-language pathologist stood at the bottom of the stairs and called to him. He shook and cried and grabbed me, and she only said, "Well, sometimes we see what we want to see when it is our child." I know he is not perfect—his temperament makes it difficult for him to sit still, but he is just 24 months old and he needed a nap. He knows what he wants to do and he does it. I do a lot of incidental teaching at home. He moves to learn, because he is not a sitter. Bobby likes to play with his toys by running them on the couch or windowsill. When he was playing with the toys there, they said to me, "Don't you ever put toys on the floor for him?" Of course I do. What did they think? This was a strange place and his style is to explore it all.

When he is free to explore, he is like this. He likes his stroller and when we go to the grocery store, everyone in the store knows him. I went there for eight years before we had Bobby, and I never knew anyone. They say things like, "Here comes the boy!" Everyone knows him. He really likes grown-ups, especially the grandpas and uncles, and tries to get their attention. Sometimes I'll hear him belly laughing and see some guy down at the end of the aisle making faces at him. He's very outgoing.

They gave me the results right there. They said they would give me the results in writing later, but they wanted me to know right away so we could get started. He is 24 months old, and they said his adaptive skills were at 24 months; his cognitive skills were only at 11 months. He got 2 out of 12 questions on the Bayley. His receptive language was at 10 months and his expressive language at 13 months. His fine motor skills were at 10 months and gross motor skills, 21 months. His social and emotional skills were at 18 months.

I was devastated. I cried for two weeks and then I got angry. They wouldn't listen to me. They felt they knew more about my son than I did. They told me he needed a neurologic evaluation and gave me a card telling me when it was scheduled. They didn't even ask me if I wanted one. They told me he needed speech and language therapy, occupational therapy, and a feeding evaluation (I guess that was because I said he was a picky eater). He also needed a hearing test. That was supposed to be done that day as well, but when we went to the audiologist, she looked at us and asked if I was really worried about his hearing. I said I wasn't. She asked how likely it was that Bobby would cooperate. I said he wouldn't. She suggested we come back on another day.

I walked out of there shaking like a leaf. I wanted to shout, "How can you do this to parents?" I wanted to throw up for a week. My God, is there nothing you can do for me? If we give kids early intervention, they can do more. Is there no hope? Kids are not a textbook. We know more now and how to help them better, but that was not how I felt when we left. We are doomed. I kept saying, "Don't worry about the tests; they are just test results." I felt like I needed to defend him. At 2 he looks like everyone else because they are all throwing tantrums. It is very disturbing; these people are going to identify all the kids who need help. Their goal seems to be to scare people. They do not say things like, "Based on what we see today ..." or "He qualifies for help," because he does need help. I wanted someone to affirm what I was feeling. I wanted them to do it at my house. This felt like a medical diagnosis rather than trying to figure out what we could do to help him learn. I had sought them out because I was concerned about his language development. I didn't need this.

REFLECTIVE PRACTICE | Reflect on how this assessment process compares with what you have read about the IFSP Process and recommended practices. If you were the mother, what would you have done? What could the professionals have done differently that would have changed the outcome for both the mother and Bobby? What conclusions can you draw about Bobby and how he functions in his world? Think about his scores on the Bayley Scale of Infant Development III. Where do these scores place him developmentally?

The IFSP's expected outcomes should be the changes that families want for themselves and their child. The IFSP does require a statement of what is going to occur to produce the desired outcomes. Because it is developed collaboratively with parents, it may require new skills for professionals. The IFSP should reflect the values and priorities of the family, not the professionals. The role of professionals is to help families identify relevant strengths and provide assistance in meeting goals. Professionals need to use listening and interviewing techniques as well as negotiation skills, and they should also know the resources available in the community.

Implementing the IFSP requires another round of decision making. Families need to know the range of options available to them in order to decide which of the options best fit their needs. This range should start with the options that the family would choose from if their infant or toddler did not have a disability. If the parents' first choice is that the toddler should be in the same family child care home as his older sister, that should be the first option explored. If this setting is chosen, the question for the team becomes how to support the toddler in that setting. Assistance might include the provision of necessary related and support services as well as training, technical assistance, and perhaps specialized equipment for the family child care provider.

Different families have different desires. For some, placement in an early care and education setting is most appropriate; for others, a home-based program or even a segregated early intervention program will best fit the family's needs. Or families may find that a combination of these options works best. The role of the professional, particularly the service coordinator, is to ensure that families make choices from the full range of options. Facilitating linkages among professionals, available resources, and program options is a major role. Creativity is required to meet families' needs.

Young children change quickly. Informal IFSP reviews have to be made on an ongoing basis, and more formal ones should be called for when necessary. At the beginning, reviews should be made early for troubleshooting, if necessary. The IFSP must be evaluated annually with a formal review every six months.

IFSP Case Studies

Families are different. Case studies have been included to help clarify these differences and the roles necessary for positive interaction. Because the IFSP process is more flexible than the IEP process, all the relevant parts of the IFSP for one child and portions of IFSPs for other children have been provided. Presented here are a variety of formats, as there is no set form. The first IFSP is for Bobby (Figure 5–8). You read about his Child Development Watch experience in the *In the Field* section included previously in this chapter.

REFLECTIVE PRACTICE | Think carefully about this IFSP. Consider the discrepancies between the test results and the parents' concerns. If this 2-year-old were in your classroom, what concerns would you have? How would you plan to work with this toddler to support his needs and his parents' concerns? How would you decide to work with the differences between the assessment information and the parent's concerns as reflected in the IFSP? What do you see as Bobby and his family's strengths?

FIGURE 5-8 INDIVIDUALIZED FAMILY SERVICE PLAN

Section 4. Developmental strengths and concerns for the child plan — Date: 9/18/11 — Child's name: Bobby

Present levels of functioning	Strengths/resources	Concerns/needs/priorities
1. Cognitive (thinking and solving problems): Date: 8/14/11; Age at evaluation: 24 months; Test tool: Bayley Scale of Infant Development III; Developmental age: 11 months	1. Will repeat an activity to get a laugh. Very inquisitive—wants to know how things work. Good problem-solving skills. Loves books. Imitates adult activities—engages in imaginary play.	1. None
2. Adaptive (self-help skills): Date: 8/14/11; Age at evaluation: 24 months; Test tool: Early Learning Accomplishment Profile; Age: 24 months	2. Can pull off and put on pants. Uses a spoon; learning to use a fork. Can brush teeth. Can put on shoes.	2. None
3. Social/emotional (interacting with others): Date: 8/14/11; Age at evaluation: 24 months; Test tool: Early Learning Accomplishment Profile; Age: 18 months	3. Great sense of humor. Does things to make people laugh. Good socially. Gets along with others at preschool. Can be independent and he engages in parallel play.	3. None
4. Communication (understanding and using language): Date: 8/14/11; Age at evaluation: 24 months; Test tool: Preschool Language Scale 4th Edition; Receptive language: 10 months; Expressive language: 13 months	4. Makes his needs known by making sounds, pointing, eye contact, some signs, and can use some words. He seems to understand what is said. He has just started singing. No problem with food textures—balanced diet—loves fruit and eats meat.	4. Bobby should be saying more at this age and we would like Bobby to express himself appropriately.
5. Physical (large body movement and ability to use hands): Date: 8/14/11; Age at evaluation: 24 months; Test tool: Bayley Scale of Infant Development III; Fine motor: 10 months; Gross motor: 21 months	5. Good gross motor skills—runs, jumps, kicks ball—loves to roughhouse. Can unlock and open sliding glass door. Colors. Puzzle play is emerging. Plays with play dough. Loves to dump/pour—loves to play with water.	5. None to motor skills but have concerns about sensory integration.

Section 5. Health strengths and concerns for the child plan — Date: 9/18/11 — Child's name: Bobby

Present levels of functioning	Strengths/resources	Concerns/needs/priorities
Primary care physician	Dr. Amy Groll	
Vision:	Vision was tested: appropriate	
Hearing:	Tested 9/8/11: appropriate	None
Nutrition:	Picky eater—but has a balanced diet—takes a vitamin—typically two	
Significant medical findings: Cognitive Communications Motor		

Section 6. Strengths and concerns for the family plan — Date: 9/18/11 — Child's name: Bobby

Current family information	Strengths/resources	Concerns/needs/priorities
Bobby currently lives at home with his mother and father and two dogs.	Supportive family with some family in the area and others in Florida.	None
	Mom gets to work part-time and be at home with Bobby.	

Section 7. Child and family outcomes plan — Date: 9/18/11 — Child's name: Bobby

Major outcomes (to address concerns/needs priorities)	Steps toward outcomes	Review dates/outcomes
1. Bobby will speak at an age-appropriate level.	1. Refer for speech and language therapy. Parents will convey all of the wonderful things they are doing.	
2. We will explore sensory integration	2. Refer to an occupational therapist for a sensory integration evaluation. Mom will read Raising Your Spirited Child.	

THE DEE FAMILY

The Dee family consists of a single mother with six children. The mother, a full-time homemaker, is pregnant with twins. The two oldest children have been identified as having specific learning disabilities and receive special education services. Alvin is 18 months old and attends a child care center full-time, along with his 2½-year-old brother. Alvin was observed informally at the child care center, where the DelCare staff were holding an in-service training. Upon learning about developmental norms, a child care provider became concerned about Alvin and asked whether she should talk to his mother. At 18 months, Alvin was not walking, standing, eating independently, or talking. He had strong temper tantrums, had to be fed, and used a bottle. He had limited social interaction skills and few purposeful play skills.

Public health nurses visited the family. They made appointments for the family, but the mother did not keep them (sometimes appointments conflicted with one another; sometimes she forgot). The mother reported that all the children have behavior problems. The family lives in a rural area and transportation is a problem. The mother feels overwhelmed. The father is available, but not living in the home.

The amount of the father's child support payments makes the family ineligible for Temporary Aid for Needy Families (TANF); however, his payments are frequently late or too little. Although there is no money for utilities, heating bills are $400 in the winter months. The children experience frequent illnesses, but the mother cannot locate a doctor willing to treat the children because no local doctor will accept new Medicaid patients; therefore, illnesses go unattended.

A graphic outline of the coordination services facilitated by the DelCare staff among the family, the early care and education center, and the service providers is shown in Figure 5-9. Initial involvement with this family required assisting the mother in meeting her priorities, including getting financial assistance for child care, food, and utilities. This assistance was gained through agencies listed under the Economic services and Charities categories and included accessing emergency utility funds, budgeting help, applying for special needs child care funding, and accessing the regional food bank.

Once basic resource issues were attended to, the mother became more receptive to tackling child issues. Arrangements were made to have the two younger boys assessed for intervention purposes. The family was channeled to an Early Childhood Center for an evaluation. Developmental evaluation results indicated Alvin was functioning at 5 to 10 months below his age expectations, and his brother had a significant language delay. The Early Childhood Center assisted in the provision of speech and language therapy and behavioral intervention. Therapy was provided at the child care center; behavioral intervention was provided at home with consultation. The public health system was accessed for evaluations including the hearing clinic, vision clinic, and medical clinic. Transportation was arranged when possible, and efforts were made to prevent appointment conflicts. Initial contacts with the family focused on meeting basic needs.

Meetings were set up between the child care center and service providers to facilitate a coordinated intervention program. The child care center was able to implement activities involving language stimulation and behavioral management. When the mother did not come to the meeting, the early childhood consultant made a home visit to gain input and share the information. The result of these efforts was a coordinated intervention system for Alvin (see Figure 5–10 for a portion of Alvin's IFSP).

Service coordination for the Dee family was complex. It required an unusual variety of skills on the part of the service

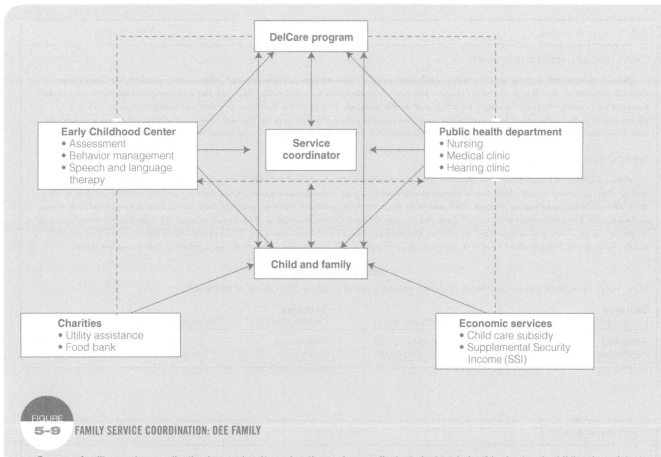

FIGURE 5-9 FAMILY SERVICE COORDINATION: DEE FAMILY

For some families service coordination is complex. It requires the service coordinator to be knowledgeable about early childhood special education and also public and private services and resources. When service needs are complex family needs may take priority over child needs.

coordinator in addition to a broad knowledge of available community resources, far beyond that expected of most early childhood educators.

THE MONROE FAMILY

The Monroe family consists of a two-income professional couple and their two biological children and one daughter from the husband's previous marriage. Their youngest child, Cathy, was diagnosed with Down syndrome at birth and enrolled in a large child care center when she was 5 months old. Currently, she is 29 months old and is functioning at levels of 10 to 12 months in all areas. The Monroes heard about the early intervention program from another parent at a workshop sponsored by the Parent Information Center and contacted the DelCare program staff. When services began, the Monroe family had their daughter enrolled in a child care center, but were not satisfied with the level of care. The Monroe family located a family child care provider who agreed to participate in training and also enrolled their daughter in an early intervention program two afternoons a week. (Transportation provided by the early intervention program made this possible.)

The family is functioning well. The parents are aware of their daughter's disability and are seeking ways to provide her with the best opportunities possible. Their concerns have been to find the best public school option for Cathy and to plan wisely for her future. Staff provided the family with information on financial planning for families with children with disabilities. A staff member attended the family's meeting with the school district as part of the transition process to public school services. She also observed potential classrooms and talked with the teachers.

The service coordinator made a few visits to the early intervention site to coordinate the services Cathy was receiving there with the care she received at the family child care provider's home. She arranged for Cathy's physical therapist to visit the family child care provider to demonstrate positioning and carrying techniques. In the beginning, monthly home visits were scheduled, but once Cathy's program was in place, visits were replaced by monthly telephone contacts at the family's request (Figure 5–11).

Some families need far less coordination than others. They are aware of their personal resources and those in the community. However, they too need to have a service coordinator, especially as children transition from one setting to another. Such families might find an informal narrative statement of their strengths/resources and desired

Child's name: Alvin Dee	DOB 4/8/10	Date 10/10/11

Child's strengths and functioning levels:

Alvin is a relatively happy undemanding child who seems to be able to occupy himself. His mother reports that he enjoys watching television but has a "terrible temper" like the other children in the family. She has not encouraged him to stand or walk because he is easier to care for when he stays put in the playpen. He likes his bottle so she has encouraged him to use it. He shows some initial interest in toys but this is only momentary and if in the crib he throws them out. At the child care center he can focus on toys for 2 to 3 minutes with adult support. He can hold his bottle and will crawl toward it when hungry.

Family's strengths, concerns, and priorities:

Alvin's mother is a full-time homemaker. She is concerned about all the children but her priorities now relate to basic needs rather than whether or not Alvin has a developmental delay. She is concerned about them turning off the utilities as it is getting cold. The children need warm jackets. She wants to keep the two younger children in child care but is afraid her benefits will run out and with her pregnancy she doesn't have the energy to care for them all day. She needs money for some basic expenses and information on money management as well as the services she might have available. She would like to focus on skills that will make Alvin more independent as she is worried about the time she will have to devote to his care once the twins are born.

Child assessments

Note: There have been few assessments as Alvin's mother's priorities are in other areas at this time.

Skill area Language	Chronological age	Functional level	Skill area Developmental	Chronological age	Functional level
Receptive	18 months	12 months (9–13)	Mental age	18 months	13 months (11–16)
Expressive	18 months	8 months (6–9)	Motor age	18 months	9 months (6–11)

Child's name: Alvin Dee		Date 10/10/11				

Major outcomes	Supports/ resources	Action plan	Comments	Family eval. Date	Status
Alvin's receptive language will improve	*Mrs. Dee, siblings, Ms. Taylor (teacher) Mr. Janis (service coordinator)*	*Mrs. Dee and his teacher Ms. Taylor will make a list of words and concepts that would be most useful for Alvin to understand. Then Ms. Taylor will develop a plan. Mr. Janis will show Mrs. Dee and the other children how to use it at home.*		*10/10/11*	*1*
Alvin's expressive language will improve	*Mrs. Dee, siblings, Ms. Austin (speech therapist) Mr. Janis*	*Mrs. Dee and Ms. Austin (speech therapist) will generate a list of words based on Mrs. Dee's priorities and Ms. Austin will refine the list based on the difficulty of the words and sounds and suggest alternatives for important ones if necessary. Ms. Austin will develop a plan and Mr. Janis will convey, model, and monitor the plan at home and in the child care setting.*		*10/10/11*	*1*

Family evaluation status: 1 = Implementation not yet begun   2 = Outcome partially accomplished; continue current strategies
3 = Outcome partially accomplished but need different strategies   4 = Outcome partially accomplished but needs practice
5 = Outcome predictably accomplished to family's satisfaction

5-10 INDIVIDUALIZED FAMILY SERVICE PLAN: ALVIN DEE

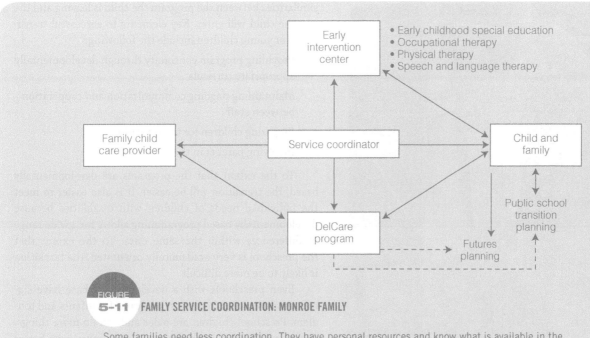

FIGURE 5-11 FAMILY SERVICE COORDINATION: MONROE FAMILY

Some families need less coordination. They have personal resources and know what is available in the community. A service coordinator is helpful especially during transitions.

outcomes the most workable for them. Figure 5–12 is part of the Monroe family's IFSP.

Family Goals

Some families do not want family goals included in the IFSP; others feel having stated outcomes for the family can help them justify what they need but frequently neglect. Figure 5–13 shows family goals for a couple who want to spend more time together.

Transition Planning

Moving from one educational setting to another can be stressful. Increasingly, kindergarten is not the first

---

Individualized Family Service Plan

Family's strengths, concerns, and priorities

The parents are aware of Cathy's disability and are actively planning for her present and future. They are willing and able to read and understand complex material and participate actively in both short- and long-term planning for Cathy.

Their long-term goal is to find the best public school placement for Cathy. Their other major concern relates to long-term financial planning.

Because they both work they would like the service coordinator to coordinate services between early intervention and the family child care provider. More specifically, they would like to help the family child care provider understand the importance of positioning for Cathy. They would also like some references on long-term financial planning.

FIGURE 5-12 INDIVIDUALIZED FAMILY SERVICE PLAN: MONROE

---

educational setting young children encounter. Most children have had previous experience with "school." Based on the requirements of the IDEA and common sense, we have begun to look more critically at the transition from one setting to another and what this means for children, families, educators, and related service providers. For children with disabilities, the transition from infant and toddler programs (Part C) to preschool programming (Part B, Section 619) has regulations in the law. It is a move from discretionary services into mandated services that changes eligibility requirements and entitles children to a free appropriate public education. However, the principles underlying transition planning are the same for transitions between other settings such as preschool to kindergarten or between grade levels.

Transition planning begins when toddlers are about 28 months old to allow time for exploring options, determining the most appropriate placement, and working on the skills necessary to make the transition a smooth one. To support children in transitions, infant and toddler and preschool teachers need open communication patterns throughout the year. Teachers, families, and children should visit potential programs. Joint in-service workshops can facilitate the development of both informal networks as well as the exchange of information.

The critical goal for transitioning toddlers is to provide the support and skills necessary for them to have a successful experience in the new setting. They should approach preschool with motivation and openness to new experiences that validate their growing achievements and confidence. If toddlers are to approach this setting positively, parents too

Transition planning is challenging as it requires all involved to learn about different people and to develop new skills and encounter new challenges.
© Cengage Learning 2012

similarities between the program the child is leaving and the one the child will enter. Key elements to successful transitions for young children include the following:

- Providing program continuity through developmentally appropriate curricula
- Maintaining ongoing communication and cooperation between staff
- Preparing children for the transition
- Involving parents in the transition

To the extent that the programs are developmentally based, the transition will be easier. It is also easier to meet the individual needs of children with disabilities because developmentally based programming allows for a wide range of differences within the same class. To the extent that the preschool is very academically orientated, the transition is likely to be more difficult.

Even preschools with a developmental base have significant differences from most programs for infants and toddlers. Preschool children are older and can do more things. They are interested in the broader community, have better gross and fine motor skills, and play for longer periods at associate and cooperative levels of play.

must feel confident about their child's ability and the ability of the setting to meet their child's needs.

The IDEA sets forth transition requirements for toddlers moving from infant and toddler programs into the mandated programs that begin at age 3. To ensure a smooth transition, the lead agency has some specific responsibilities. It will, for eligible children, (1) notify the local educational agency that the child will soon be eligible for preschool services; (2) with the approval of the family, convene a conference among the lead agency, the family, and the local educational agency not less than 90 days before the child is eligible for the preschool services, to discuss services that the child may receive (U.S. DOE, 2006). For children who are no longer eligible for services, the lead agency will, with the approval of the family, make reasonable efforts to convene a group to discuss the appropriate services that the child may receive (U.S. DOE, 2006).

DAP The written transition plan looks something like Figure 5–14. For teachers to support the transition, they have to know the individual child and the differences and

---

Family Goals/Outcomes

1. Goal/Outcome: Lee and Joe will spend more time together as a couple.

Objective: They will be together alone for an outing 1/month

    Strategy: Ask Joe's mom or friend to babysit

    Persons responsible: Lee and Joe

    Criteria: They go out 1/month

    Review date: 1 month

2. Goal/Outcome: Lee will be provided with more information on prognosis of microcephaly

Objective: To obtain information about microcephaly and on children with microcephaly, especially long-term effects.

Strategies:
1. Ask questions of medical personnel involved with Justin (i.e., pediatrician, pediatric neurologist, or early intervention program).
2. Provide reading material on specific disability.
3. Provide phone number of Parent Information Center, where Lee may talk with other parents as well as get information she wants

Persons responsible: Lee and Celeste (service coordinator)

Criteria: Parent is satisfied with information she obtained

Review date: 3 months

FIGURE 5–13 **INDIVIDUALIZED FAMILY SERVICE PLAN: FAMILY GOALS/ OUTCOMES**

Transition Plan

Child: _____   Expected transition date: _____

Service coordinator: _____   Target receiving site: _____

Reason for transition: _____

Transition event	Person responsible	Dates achieved	Comment
1. Parents informed of possible options	Service coordinator		
2. Receiving agencies contacted	Parents Service coordinator		
3. Parents visit agencies	Parents Service coordinator		
4. Transition conference to determine appropriate placement	Parents Service coordinator Receiving agency Intervention team		
5. Transfer of records	Receiving agency Sending agency		
6. Written transition plan developed	Parents Service Coordinator Receiving agency		
7. Placement	Parents Child Receiving agency		
8. Follow-up	Sending agency Service coordinator		

FIGURE 5-14 TRANSITION PLAN

▶❚❚ **TeachSource Video Case**

Preschool: IEP and Transition Planning for a Young Child with Special Needs

Watch the TeachSource Video Case *Preschool: IEP and Transition Planning for a Young Child with Special Needs*, which reviews how child care providers should be advocates and role models for children. The video can be found in the Early Childhood Education Media Library under Special Education, available at www.cengagebrain.com.

Preschools that include children with disabilities may be public or private. They may be part of the public school system, Head Start, early care and education centers, church preschools, or family or center child care. The group size is typically larger and the number of teachers per child is smaller. Time schedules may be more strictly adhered to because there may be only one time when specific groups of children can use the playground, or they may have a schedule for "specials" such as gym or music.

IMPLICATIONS FOR EDUCATORS

Early interventionists prepare for the transition by visiting preschools, perhaps sharing a snack with the children, or by making a videotape of what happens in preschool. It is important that you show toddlers several different preschools if you do not know the school or class they will be entering or if they will go to different preschools. Because teachers may be moved or hired as late as August, this exposure is a good idea, even if you feel confident you know what will happen. Talk about the differences and similarities between preschool programs and between preschool and infant and toddler programs.

Encourage parents to visit the preschool class they would like their child to attend. They may want to visit early in the year (October) to get a feel for the expectations teachers have of incoming children and then perhaps visit all the classes during the latter part of the school year to look at teaching styles. Some schools are responsive to suggestions from parents about particular teachers with whom they feel their child would do well, whereas others are not. Most are willing to listen to why certain teachers might be a mismatch.

Talk with parents about which records they want forwarded and which they do not. Tell parents about the other children in the class or children that you know who will be attending the same setting. Encourage parents to invite such children over to play, and perhaps arrange a time when parents could get together to talk as well. Be sure that parents know what their rights are and help them stand up for them, if necessary. If a child was served under Part C (from birth to age 3), at the parent's request, the Part C coordinator or other representative can be present to ensure a smooth transition.

SUMMARY

- IEPs are designed with measurable annual goals that are tied to state standards for the education of all children.
- Technology is being used to support children with disabilities.
- IFSP focuses on the strengths and resources of the family as well as the child.
- Transition planning is important because children transitioning from Part C to Part B of the IDEA are identified earlier.

EDUCATIONAL RESOURCES

Association for Persons with Severe Handicaps (TASH) is an advocacy organization that disseminates information to improve the education and independence of those with severe disabilities. www.tash.org

Disability Rights Education and Defense Fund (DREDF) provides information, technical assistance, and referrals on laws and rights. (510) 644–2555, (510) 644–2626; ADA Hotline: (800) 466–4232; www.dredf.org

IDEA: Building the Legacy of IDEA 2004 is designed as a one-stop shopping site for information about the IDEA. This site is sponsored by the U.S. Department of Education and is an ideal place to keep current on the law and its regulations. http://idea.ed.gov

National Center to Improve Practice in Special Education through Technology, Media and Materials provides information on the effective use of technology; video profiles of children using assistive and instructional technologies, both high and low tech. It provides links to other special education and technology resources. www2.edc.org/NCIP/

SERI Inclusion Resources is a good site to start with as it provides essential information plus links to other resources. www.seriweb.com/inclu.htm

For additional Educational Resources, visit the book companion website for this text at www.cengagebrain.com.

6 Prenatal Development: Typical and Atypical

He sat on the floor of the cement terrace, a joint dangling between his fingers, his eyes full of tears, as he began his story. "I was so stupid," he said. "Laura and I would get drunk and high and then we would just do it. I never thought of condoms; I never thought of consequences. When you're in college, you're studying, you're partying, and that's your world. I didn't know . . . no, I did know, but I didn't care if she got pregnant . . . that's what abortions were for. But then she did and everything changed. . . .

"I didn't know she was pregnant until the third month . . . and we kept partying and having sex, night after night, until she finally told me. I remember we'd done coke the night she told me. And afterward I drank and drank; I just couldn't believe she was pregnant . . . I didn't even really know her. All I knew was that she refused to have an abortion and that I was going to be a father."

"What did I know about being a dad; it's not like I had the best childhood. But I knew that babies cost money . . . and that was something I didn't have and Laura wanted us to live together, to be together . . . . All I had wanted was sex . . . not a relationship, just sex."

"Anyway, Laura went to the gynecologist, and stuff. Everything was going okay. I thought that at least the baby would be normal and maybe life wouldn't be so bad. I got my head together, quit school. I started working and getting ready for the big B."

"But four months later . . . Laura went into labor and the baby was born three months premature. I can't say that Carena was a beautiful baby . . . no baby is beautiful with tubes and IVs and stuff. She was so little, and deformed . . . and at that moment I regretted every time I had ever slept with Laura. I wanted a different life and it seemed that the nightmare was just beginning.

"Doctors explained that my little girl would probably never walk, would never be able to eat without tubes, and might never sit up. A normal life was completely out of the question for Carena.

"The doctors' bills for Carena were incredible. Seventy percent of my paycheck went to paying for her health care. Laura stayed home with the baby and got up every time Carena cried. I tried, I really did, but I couldn't bond with my baby, and I started to hang out at bars more . . . I couldn't deal with the

© Cengage Learning 2012

two women in my life, one who I didn't love but had to support because she was the mother of my child and the other the baby girl who I couldn't understand.

"Life hit an all-time low when Carena became really, really sick when she was 18 months old. The doctors told us she was going to die and pushed us toward hospice to help us. Laura was hysterical and never slept. She worried constantly that Carena was in pain, and when she wasn't worrying, she was grieving."

"I didn't know what to do. I discovered that I loved my baby, but at the same time it was a relief to know that she wouldn't have to suffer anymore. Now that she's dead . . . it's hard. Laura and I have nothing joining us . . . but I feel guilty about ending the relationship . . . and then I still grieve for Carena and also for the way life might have been. I wish I'd used a condom . . . but maybe it was good. For two very short years, I learned how to be a dad to a very special little person." ❖

REFLECTIVE PRACTICE| Building and maintaining relationships is challenging. Men and women frequently respond to the birth of an infant with a disability differently. How would you work with this family before Carena's death? How would your work with this family change after her death? Do you think Laura and Robert's relationship continued?

Pregnancy

The United States does little in the way of educating its young women and men to think about the life skills and healthy living habits needed before, during, and after pregnancy. When pregnancies are planned, the prospective mother and father can make positive changes in their lifestyle. Such conscious decisions are crucial because prenatal development dramatically impacts the infant.

A healthy lifestyle is a positive step, but it does not guarantee a successful pregnancy outcome; however, it should be a goal of all prospective mothers and fathers. Many prenatal risks can be prevented; others can be monitored or managed. Planning gives a woman time to ensure that her diet meets the nutritional demands of pregnancy. It provides time to stop using tobacco, alcohol, drugs, and caffeine, and to avoid harmful environmental exposure. These decisions are designed to increase the probability of having a normal, healthy baby. Unfortunately, some prenatal risks are unknown, cannot be prevented, and may not be discovered until birth or after.

Many factors influence the development of the fetus before birth: the genetic matter that forms the fetus, the environment in which the fetus grows and develops, and the developing fetus himself. These factors interact to shape the developing organism.

The time from conception to birth, called **gestation**, usually lasts 40 weeks, or about nine calendar months, most commonly thought of as three trimesters. This is an outside-looking-in approach. Here, we focus on periods that are more significant to the developing organism: the **germinal**, **embryonic**, and **fetal** periods. This approach still breaks the nine months into three periods, but the duration of each is different: the germinal and embryonic periods correspond to the first trimester, and the fetal period to the remaining two trimesters.

Germinal Period

Each of us starts out as a single cell, the ovum, or egg. To develop from this single cell into a person, several processes have to take place: first, the egg has to be fertilized by a sperm; cells divide and increase in number, then differentiate to create different body parts (skin, bones, heart, etc.); finally, the cells initiate the systemic function of metabolism.

Women are born with all of their reproductive cells. About 2 million eggs or immature **ova** are present in a female's ovaries at birth; however, only about 500 to 600 are used. The mature unfertilized ovum is the largest cell in the female's body—about the size of the period that ends this sentence. The ovum is large because of the nutrients it contains, which nourish the cells during their initial growth and development. Approximately once a month during a female's reproductive years, an egg ripens, is pushed from the **ovary**, the female reproductive organ, drops into one of the **fallopian tubes**, and is available for fertilization. If the egg is not fertilized in 10 to 14 days, the woman's menstrual flow begins, washing away the egg and the lining of the uterine wall. This cycle repeats itself on a regular basis unless fertilization takes place (Haffner, 2007).

Although females are born with immature eggs, males do not begin producing sperm until puberty and continue into old age. Sperm are composed of a large head and a long tail. The head contains the cell nucleus, and the tail, or flagellum, is used for propulsion. During intercourse, hundreds of millions of sperm are mixed with seminal fluid and deposited into the female vagina. Sperm travel the remaining length of the vagina and push through the cervix into the uterus. Midway into the menstrual cycle, mucus secretions of the vagina and the thinning of the cervix make it easier to penetrate, so fertilization is more likely. Women are fertile for approximately five days before ovulation and the day of ovulation, which is the day that conception is most likely to occur (Haffner, 2007).

Once in the **uterus**, the sperm must travel to the correct fallopian tube and then swim up the tube to meet the egg. Only about 200 reach the fallopian tubes. Sperm must travel approximately 7 inches to reach the egg, a journey of about an hour. When one sperm penetrates the outer layer of the egg, the successful sperm prevents others from penetrating the egg. The unsuccessful sperm die within 24 hours (Haffner, 2007). Once inside the egg, the sperm's tail detaches, and the nucleus from the sperm and ovum migrate toward each other and then unite, creating a **zygote**. Fertilization restores the number of **chromosomes** in the cell to 23 pairs and initiates cell division, or **cleavage**. In humans, of the 23 pairs of chromosomes, there are 22 twin chromosomes called autosomes and one pair of sex chromosomes. Chromosomes are very long continuous pieces (or molecules) of DNA that contain many genes and other regulatory material. The sex chromosomes are designated X for female and Y for male. The sex of the child is determined by the father. If the child is a girl, she will have two X chromosomes; if it is a boy, he will have an X and a Y chromosome.

All of the cells in the body divide, but at different rates ranging from once every 10 hours for skin cells, to once a year for liver cells (Batshaw, 2007). All cells except sex cells divide through the process of **mitosis**, by which a cell duplicates its genetic information (DNA) and generates two identical cells. These two daughter cells are formed from one parent cell and are exact replicas of the original cell. Cells also divide through **meiosis**. Meiosis is more complicated than mitosis and results in more abnormalities. Unlike mitosis, where two identical daughter cells are formed, during the first division in meiosis the chromosomes that come from the mother and father intertwine, allowing genetic material to be exchanged.

Meiosis recombines the 23 chromosomes from each parent and fuses them with the set from the other parent to make the 46 chromosomes necessary for sexual reproduction. This union results in four daughter cells (Batshaw, 2007). This complexity increases the likelihood of genetic disorders, but it also enables children to be similar to, but not exactly like, their siblings.

The fertilized cell continues to replicate itself. By three to four days, this solid mass is called a **morula**, the earliest stage of development, and its cells continue to multiply as it moves down the fallopian tube. After five days, fluid begins to accumulate between the cells, and it begins to change in size and shape, becoming a **blastocyst**. The blastocyst is the second stage of development, with an inner and outer cell mass. Once in the uterus, it rests for about two days before it attaches. This is the formal beginning of pregnancy (Haffner, 2007).

Following ovulation and fertilization, hormonal changes begin. Levels of **progesterone**, a hormone that supports pregnancy, increase and that, in combination with other hormonal changes, causes the lining of the uterus, the **endometrium**, to become thick, spongy, and ready for implantation, as its glands and blood vessels increase in number and size. The **placenta**, formed from the endometrium, supplies the embryo with oxygen and nutrients and takes away wastes.

Of all fertilized eggs, only about half survive and reach the uterus; the body reabsorbs the others. Although it is possible for the blastocyst to implant, or attach, itself to the uterine wall in many places, it normally does so in the upper back portion of the uterus. The site of implantation is critical. If the blastocyst attaches itself to the bottom of the uterus it may cause complications in the delivery, or the placenta may detach too early.

Until implantation is complete, about 12 days after conception, the developing organism, called an **embryo** from the time of implantation through eight weeks, absorbs nutrients directly from the mother's cells. During the time leading up to implantation, a woman may not even suspect that she is pregnant. Her suspicions usually begin once her menstrual flow is due but does not occur. The embryo produces a hormone, **chorionic gonadotrophin**, which prevents the mother from menstruating.

Exposure to **teratogens** during the germinal period usually leads to a spontaneous abortion or does not impact the embryo at all. There are so few cells at this stage, it tends to be all or nothing (Haffner, 2007).

••• Embryonic Period

The embryonic period lasts from week 3 to week 8 after fertilization. The five weeks of the embryonic period are crucial. For the embryo to survive, a complex infrastructure must be developed to protect and nourish the growing organism. These changes are generated through cell differentiation. Although the cells were originally unspecialized, the membranes now begin to develop into three distinct layers: the **ectoderm**, which evolves into skin, spinal cord, and teeth; the **mesoderm**, which becomes blood vessels, muscles, and

bones; and the **endoderm**, which develops into the digestive system, lungs, and urinary tract (Batshaw, 2007). The changes they evoke include thickening of the uterine lining, the development of the placenta, the **umbilical cord**, and the **amniotic sac**. The amniotic sac consists of a pair of tough, thin membranes that hold the embryo and then the fetus during pregnancy.

The placenta is a highly specialized disk-shaped organ through which the embryo makes functional contact with the wall of the uterus. The embryo is connected to the placenta by the umbilical cord, which is hose-like and contains blood vessels. The **amnion**, a sac-like membrane filled with a clear liquid called **amniotic fluid**, allows the embryo to move freely within the uterus and protects it from injury.

The mature placenta develops rapidly after implantation and covers about 20 percent of the uterine wall. There is a fetal and a maternal portion of the placenta, and although these intertwine, they do not intermingle. Once implantation is completed, the embryo experiences a period of rapid growth, receiving nourishment from the mother's blood through the placenta, which is more efficient than absorbing nutrients from the mother's cells.

A placental barrier keeps the blood supplies of the mother and embryo separate. Even though small molecules can pass through this barrier, large molecules cannot. The exact exchange of substances is complex, but in general, nutritive materials from maternal blood—oxygen, water, and salts—cross the placental barrier and digestive waste products and carbon dioxide from the developing embryo can cross back the other way toward the mother. However, large molecules, like red blood cells, most bacteria, maternal wastes, and many dangerous toxins and hormones, cannot pass.

Earliest development occurs in the head, brain, and sense organs, followed by the trunk area (**cephalocaudal**). After two months of gestation, the head accounts for about half of the total body length; by birth, the head comprises about one-quarter of the newborn's body length, whereas in adults, the head is only about 10 percent of a person's height. Growth moves from the middle outward. Structures that are near the **midline** of the body, such as the spinal cord and heart, develop before the arms and legs, which develop before the fingers and toes (**proximodistal**).

The rate of growth is faster during the embryonic period than at any other time: all body tissues, organs, and systems develop. While all this is happening, a woman may not yet realize that she is pregnant. For this reason, many physicians recommend that women who are planning to become pregnant begin taking prenatal vitamins and that all women of childbearing age take folic acid to protect against **congenital malformations**, medical conditions that are present at birth. The embryo is very susceptible to the influences of disease, alcohol, drugs, radiation, and other substances. Exposure to teratogens during this period usually leads to structural abnormalities or miscarriage (Haffner, 2007).

During the second month, the embryo becomes markedly less curved and the head increases in size; a face develops, with a primitive nose, eyes, ears, and upper lip; and the neck lengthens. The tail-like projection almost fully disappears. Fully formed, but extremely small, arms and legs, hands and feet, and even fingers and, toes appear. The heart and circulatory system begin working, and, by the end of the second month, the kidneys take over the function of concentrating and excreting urine. Although not yet functional, digestive and respiratory systems develop. The reproductive system also forms. A skeleton of cartilage develops, as do some finer features such as eyelids. The embryo is recognizable as a human being by the end of the second month of development, although it is somewhat strange looking (Haffner, 2007).

Fetal Period

The developing organism becomes a **fetus** when all the major structures and organs have been formed, about eight weeks after fertilization. The early part of the fetal period is characterized by the development and growth of true bone. During the third month, the main organ systems (cardiovascular, neurologic, digestive, etc.) are established and differentiated. The fetus is about 3.5 inches long and weighs about an ounce. By the fourth month, with the fetus growing to about 6 ounces and measuring 10 inches, the mother can begin to detect movement. Tissues and organs continue to develop; the heart can be heard with a stethoscope or by placing an ear on the mother's abdomen. During the fifth and sixth months, there are more refinements in development (fingernails) and continued growth. By the end of the sixth month, the fetus is about 12 to 14 inches long and weighs about 1.5 to 2 pounds. With the support of neonatal intensive care nurseries, infants born at 22 weeks or later are considered viable (Lowdermilk & Perry, 2003).

The major function of the third trimester is fetal weight gain. The fetus starts storing fat, and life support functions develop more fully. The brain continues to develop rapidly. The lungs begin to be capable of some limited gas exchange. The fetus grows to about 20 inches in length, usually weighs between 6.5 and 8 pounds, and is ready to be born (Lowdermilk & Perry, 2003).

> ▶❚❚ TeachSource Video Case
> **0–2 Years: Prenatal Assessment**
> Watch the TeachSource Video Case *0–2 Years: Prenatal Assessment*, in which you'll see how ultrasound is used to estimate fetal age, position and growth of baby, and health of placenta. The video can be found in the Early Childhood Education Media Library under Infants and Toddlers, available at www.cengagebrain.com.

Multiple Pregnancies

Usually the female releases only one ovum at a time. If two mature eggs are released and they are both fertilized (by separate sperm), fraternal, or **dizygotic twins**, will develop. The term dizygotic refers to the fact that there are two zygotes

as well as two amnions, two chorions, and two placentas. Genetically, fraternal twins are no more alike than other siblings. They are the result of different eggs and different sperm, yet they share the same uterine environment.

Identical, or **monozygotic twins**, develop from a single fertilized ovum that divides into two separate embryos. These twins will be of the same sex and have the same **genotype**. The cell division resulting in monozygotic twins usually occurs between four to eight days after fertilization. When this division is early, there will be two amnions, two chorions, and two placentas that may be fused (Lowdermilk & Perry, 2003).

In 1980, the rate of twinning was 1 in 53 per 1,000 live births; it rose to 1 in 32 births per 1,000 live births in 2007 (Martin et al., 2010). The twinning rate rose 70 percent between 1980 and 2004 but has remained stable since then. The rate of triplets and other higher-order births was 149 per 100,000 live births; this birth rate climbed more than 400 percent between 1980 and 1998, and after that was showing a gradual trend downward (Martin et al., 2010). Multiple gestations accounted for over 3 percent of all births in 2002 (Brown & Satin, 2007). The incidence of fraternal twins varies with the age of the mother, whether there were previous births, racial background, and the use of assisted reproductive techniques. Mothers having babies later and the use of fertility drugs increase the number of multiple births or multifetal gestations. When couples use in vitro fertilization, more than one embryo is typically implanted.

Regardless of the number of fetuses, all are governed by the principles of heredity and genetics.

Heredity and Genetics: Just the Basics

Heredity influences the growth and development of human beings. It was once believed that hereditary factors were the only influences on development. Research has since indicated that this is not true (Travers, 2006). The genetic makeup within each individual plays a strong role in dictating specific developmental outcomes. The color of our eyes, our potential height, the size of our feet, the color of our skin, and even the diseases that plague us are influenced by the genes we inherited from our biological parents. However, the environment also plays a role in the expression of many genes. Most traits that humans are interested in are not located on a single gene, but are actually the result of interactions among different genes and the environment. Personality and intelligence fall into this category. Genetics is a complex field, and knowledge about inheritance patterns varies with particular traits.

Chromosomes

The human body is made up of approximately 100 trillion cells, including skin cells, liver cells, nerve cells, and so on. In the center of most of these cells (but not blood cells), a nucleus encloses the cell's genetic material, deoxyribonucleic acid (DNA). A watery substance called cytoplasm fills the rest of the cell. DNA is formed in thread-like double-helix strands called chromosomes and contains the genetic blueprints, or instructions, for development (Batshaw, 2007). Its main

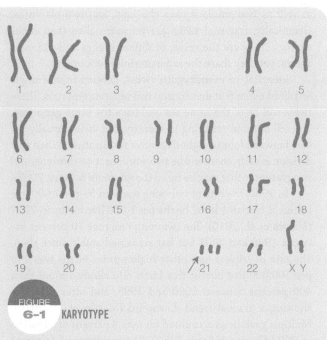

FIGURE
6-1 KARYOTYPE

This is a simplified karyotype of a boy (see X Y chromosomes) with Down syndrome. Note the three chromosomes on the 21 pair.

role is the long-term storage of information. Humans have 46 chromosomes arranged in 23 pairs, numbered for identification. Chromosomes 1 through 22 are called **autosomes** and are nonsex chromosomes. Although different in size, each is a matched pair. The 23rd pair of chromosomes is the sex chromosomes: the larger female chromosome in the shape of an X, and the smaller male chromosome that looks like a Y with a short tail. Females have two XX chromosomes, whereas males have an X and a Y (National Human Genome Research Institute, 2007). During the **metaphase** state of cell division, the chromosomes can be seen as distinct cell bodies that can be counted and grouped, a process called **karyotyping** that is used in the identification of some disabilities (see Figure 6–1).

Chromosomal errors account for 3 to 5 percent of disabilities that are identifiable at birth. The actual number of these problems is much higher; approximately 25 percent of eggs and 3 to 4 percent of sperm have an added or missing chromosome. Approximately 95 percent of fetuses with these chromosomal disorders do not survive to term (Batshaw, 2007). Most chromosomal abnormalities occur during cell division: meiosis. Damage can happen to parts of a chromosome or to the whole chromosome. There are two basic types of chromosome abnormalities: numerical and structural (Figure 6–2).

NUMERICAL ABNORMALITIES

In numerical abnormalities, one chromosome from a pair is missing or a chromosome pair has an additional chromosome. In most instances, this results in a miscarriage. When it does not, infants have developmental disabilities (Roizen, 2007).

STRUCTURAL ABNORMALITIES

There are different kinds of structural abnormalities. Listed are some cases:

- A portion of the chromosome and hence the genetic information is missing (deletions).
- Genetic material may be duplicated, which results in extra genetic material (duplication).
- A portion of the chromosome can break off, turn upside down, and reattach (inversion).

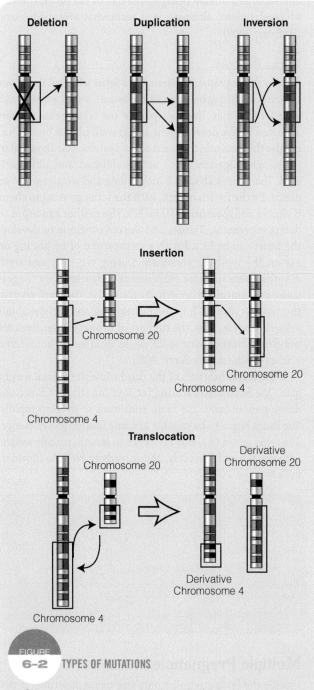

FIGURE
6-2 TYPES OF MUTATIONS

Chromosomes can mutate during cell division. In some cases information is deleted, duplicated twice, or inverted. In other cases, parts of chromosomes are traded or inserted on a different chromosome. (Courtesy of the Human Genome Project)

- Information that should be on one chromosome is put on a different chromosome (insertion).
- Parts of two chromosomes are switched (translocation) (National Human Genome Research Institute, 2007) (see Figure 6–2).

Most chromosomal abnormalities are accidental and are present in the egg or sperm at the time of fertilization.

IN THE FIELD

We hadn't planned on my getting pregnant. We weren't married and we were struggling with the decision. Although we had lived together for eight years, we just couldn't make that final commitment. It wasn't like there was anyone else. It was just that we both did things that annoyed the other. However, it was clear that I was pregnant.

At first, we decided not to tell anyone until after the first three months. But after a visit from my parents, I told. I was really feeling guilty because I didn't plan to get pregnant. I was drinking and not taking great care of myself when I found out. I spent a lot of time feeling guilty because I couldn't undo those first few weeks.

I liked the doctor. She was a woman and seemed to care a lot about me and understood some of my concerns. They did some routine blood work and then she wanted me to have an ultrasound. It seemed early to me. Although I had never been pregnant, I had many friends who were. Actually, I was worried about my biological clock, and I figured this was why the ultrasound was done. I was concerned listening to the conversation, when they were talking about the neck and that it was thick or something. It seemed strange to me.

Then, the unthinkable happened. Just when we were beginning to cope with the idea of having a baby, I had a miscarriage. It was awful, not so much physically as emotionally. Having just accepted being pregnant, I was no longer pregnant. When I talked to the doctor, she told me that one of the things she had been concerned about was the possibility that the baby might have had Down syndrome. She'd been about to suggest an amniocentesis. This hit me hard. She said that one reason I had the miscarriage was that he had a problem. It was a he. What if he had had Down syndrome? What would I have done? I know how I feel about this issue, but I don't know how I feel about it when it is me.

• • •
Genes

Chromosomes are made up of genes. Each chromosome has between 250 and 2,000 genes, containing genetic material (DNA) that directs the body through the developmental process, one protein at a time. The human genome contains about 30,000 to 40,000 genes. The mapping of the human genome in April 2003 facilitated the study of hereditary diseases and the identification of single-gene disorders (National Human Genome Research Institute [HGP], 2007).

Genes have two core functions: they serve as a reliable template, or blueprint, for development, and they have a transcriptional function. As a template, some genes regulate the development and functioning of the body, while others make specific products such as enzymes and hormones. Their transcriptional function is less well-known. The transcriptional function allows the gene to impact the structure, function, and other biological characteristics in which it is expressed (Jensen, 2006). Every cell has the genes for your whole body. However, only a small portion of the gene is activated in a particular cell: Only the kidney-related function

Children with Down syndrome are active participants in inclusive classrooms.
© Cengage Learning 2012

of a gene is activated in the kidney cell, and the other parts of the gene are repressed. It is gene expression that translates genetic information into action. Everyday factors such as emotional states, stress, exercise, and nutrition influence gene expression. The environment in which one lives and how one feels can impact gene expression, which is the cause for concern about toxic environments and the basis for early intervention. Although genes provide the blueprint, just as with the blueprint for a house there can be modifications later. Brain structure, for example, is highly experience dependent (Jensen, 2006).

A **mutation** is a change in a gene that occurs by chance. Some changes or errors are irrelevant; there are enough checks and balances in the system to take care of them. Other changes, like those in the gene itself, disrupt subsequent steps. About 1 percent of the population has a congenital malformation caused by a single-gene defect (Batshaw, 2007).

A genetic mutation can lead to a genetic disorder (Batshaw, 2007). The larger the gene affected, the greater the probability of a mistake. Older parents have higher mutation rates. Some mutations occur spontaneously, whereas others are related to radiation, chemicals, and viruses (HGP, 2007). The most common mutation is called a point mutation, where a single chemical is replaced with another chemical. In sickle cell anemia, a single substitution in the DNA base tells the cells to produce valine instead of glutamic acid at one spot on the hemoglobin protein. This leads to a painful disability where red blood cells are shaped like sickles instead of disks.

Now you have a basic understanding of how chromosomes and genes work and the role they play in development. The next step is to put this knowledge into the context of heredity and the children who may be in your classroom.

● ● ●
Genetic Transmission

Before getting into this, let's talk about the language of genetics. When we talk about genetics, we use a lot of prefixes. Breaking the words down makes it easier to understand what we are talking about. Let's start with the prefix *homo*. Homo means the *same*. Think about words you know that begin with homo. *Homogeneous* is an adjective that generally means composed of the *same* kind of parts. We homogenize milk to break up the cream so the fat globules are all the *same* size. And we are *homo sapiens* because we are all the *same* species.

Obviously, there is a flip side to this: *hetero,* which means different. Heterogeneous groups are different from each other. The term zygote is used for the developing individual who was created by the union of the egg and sperm. Think about eye color. Both the mother and father contribute a gene (or genes) related to eye color. If they both contribute the *same* eye color (both blue) the child will be **homozygous** for that trait. If they contribute different colors (brown and blue) the child will be **heterozygous** for that trait. Armed with this information, let's tackle heredity.

Two basic concepts help you understand how inheritance patterns work: how genes are passed from parents to children and the dominant and recessive characteristics of genes. Genes always occupy a specific location on a chromosome. The genes for eye color from each parent are in the same location on their respective chromosomes. Although the genes are in the same location, they may be for different eye colors.

Let's start with the assumption that you have blue eyes (we'll get to brown eyes soon). Your blue eyes are somewhat of a mystery because both of your parents have brown eyes. If you inherited the same genes, from each parent (blue eyes) you are homozygous for that trait. If you inherited different codes (brown eyes from one parent and blue eyes from the other) you would be heterozygous for the trait and you would have brown eyes. So, obviously this didn't happen. Something else is going on.

We use capital letters (A) to indicate dominant forms of genes and small letters (a) to indicate recessive forms. There are two ways to be homozygous: you can inherit two dominant (AA) genes or two recessive (aa) genes. Knowing you have blue eyes, your parents have brown eyes, and that brown eyes are dominant, we know that you received recessive genes from both your parents. We also know that your parents are heterozygous for eye color. When there is one dominant and one recessive gene in a pair (Aa), the individual is heterozygous.

The basic genetic makeup of an individual transmitted from the specific genes of the parents at conception is called a person's genotype. This is the sum total of the genes transmitted to you from your parents and the genes that you will pass on to future generations. However, you can't tell a person's genotype by looking at her. The observable characteristics of an individual, both biological and behavioral, are a person's **phenotype**, which is partially the result of the interactions within the genotype of dominant and recessive genes. However, phenotypes can be determined by multiple genes and influenced by environmental factors. The distinction between genotype and phenotype is important in understanding genetic transmission (see Figure 6–3).

Because genes can be either dominant or recessive and there are two different types of chromosomes, three different inheritance patterns are possible: autosomal dominant, autosomal recessive, or X-linked. The X-linked refers to those genes on the sex (X Y) chromosomes. Single genes control some of these characteristics (unifactorial inheritance). Single-gene disorders are caused by a change (mutation) in one gene. There are over 6,000 identified single-gene disorders. Although each individual disorder does not affect very many children, when grouped together they account for about 1 in 300 births (CDC, n.d.c.). Other disorders are caused by a variety of factors (multifactorial inheritance), including genes interacting with the environment.

AUTOSOMAL-RECESSIVE DISORDERS

There are approximately 1,700 different autosomal-recessive disorders (McKusick et al., 2005). Generally, dominant genes determine traits. However, if an infant receives a dominant gene (A) for a particular autosomal-recessive disorder from one or both of her parents, she would not inherit the recessive disorder. For a child to inherit this type of disorder, she must receive an abnormal-recessive gene (a) from both her father and her mother. The child would therefore be homozygous (aa) for the autosomal-recessive trait. Autosomal-recessive disorders typically relate to enzyme disorders.

AUTOSOMAL-DOMINANT DISORDERS

Autosomal-dominant disorders relate to structural abnormalities in the individual. Unlike someone who is heterozygous (Aa) for an autosomal-recessive disorder (and would therefore only be a carrier and not have the disorder), those who are heterozygous for an autosomal-dominant disorder, will be a carrier of *and* be affected by the disorder.

There are approximately 4,500 autosomal-dominant disorders that have been identified (McKusick et al., 2005). If only one parent has a dominant gene (Aa) for an autosomal-dominant disorder the probability that the child will have the disorder is 50 percent. However, the probability is also 50 percent that the child will not be affected and not be a carrier (aa). If both parents were heterozygous for the trait, the pattern would predict that the child has a 50 percent chance of having the disorder, a 25 percent chance of being unaffected, and a 25 percent chance of receiving two copies of the dominant gene. If the child receives two dominant genes (AA), the disorder will be more severe and may result in death. Autosomal-dominant disorders affect men and women equally and most frequently involve structural

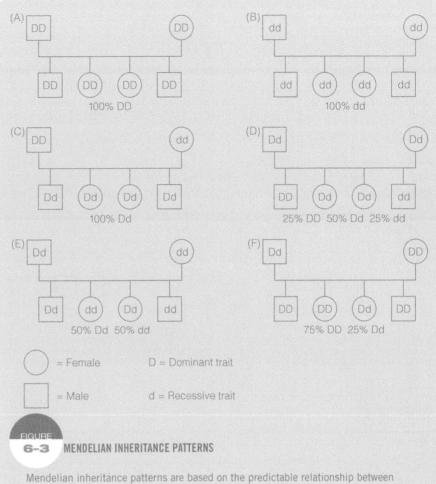

FIGURE
6-3 MENDELIAN INHERITANCE PATTERNS

Mendelian inheritance patterns are based on the predictable relationship between dominant and recessive genes on the autosomes. These patterns determine the probability of someone with a dominant or recessive gene disorder passing the gene on to the next generation.

(physical) abnormalities. About half of these disabilities result from mutations (Batshaw, 2007).

X-LINKED DISORDERS

Approximately 900 X-linked disorders have been identified. X-linked disorders typically result in physical disabilities and cognitive impairments (McKusick et al., 2005). These disorders are passed between generations by carrier mothers. That is, these disorders are carried on the female sex chromosome (X) and typically involve mutations of genetic information that are found on this chromosome. These disorders occur mostly in males because the pairing of the XY chromosomes means that there is no second X chromosome in males to cover the problem. Approximately 25 percent of males with intellectual disability and 10 percent of females with specific learning disabilities are affected by X-linked disorders (Batshaw, 2007). (See Figure 6–4 for the outcomes.)

• • •
Multifactorial Inheritance

Genes from one or both parents may interact with each other and may be affected by environmental factors. The multifactorial causes of disabilities are less well-known than those caused by single genes. These factors are more challenging to identify and beyond the scope of this book. Many common congenital malformations are a result of multifactorial inheritance, such as cleft palate and neural tube defects. Depending upon the number of genes affected, these malformations can be mild or severe. In families in which this pattern of inherited disorders occurs, it usually favors one sex more than the other. Many traits not related to disabilities are also inherited in this way. Height is an obvious example of multifactorial inheritance. It is a result of genetics but also environmental factors such as diet.

• • •
Genetic Counseling

Genetic counseling is the process of advising individuals about the consequence of a disorder, the probability of developing and transmitting it, and ways in which the disorder can be prevented or ameliorated. Different individuals provide genetic counseling, depending upon the complexity of the situation. Most obstetricians and others such as family doctors, nurses, midwives, and social workers feel

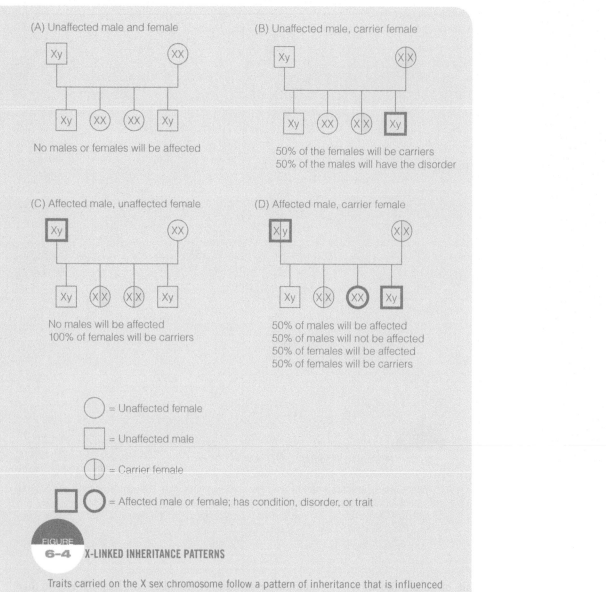

(A) Unaffected male and female

No males or females will be affected

(B) Unaffected male, carrier female

50% of the females will be carriers
50% of the males will have the disorder

(C) Affected male, unaffected female

No males will be affected
100% of females will be carriers

(D) Affected male, carrier female

50% of males will be affected
50% of males will not be affected
50% of females will be affected
50% of females will be carriers

◯ = Unaffected female

▢ = Unaffected male

⊘ = Carrier female

▪ ● = Affected male or female; has condition, disorder, or trait

FIGURE 6-4   X-LINKED INHERITANCE PATTERNS

Traits carried on the X sex chromosome follow a pattern of inheritance that is influenced by the sex of the offspring.

comfortable providing information about chromosomal abnormalities and common conditions that follow the Mendelian pattern. Beyond this, they may refer individuals to a clinical geneticist.

Genetic counseling before conception can often identify genetic disorders within a family and the risk of occurrence. The goal is to reduce the probability of serious life-threatening disorders occurring or reoccurring in the same family. Parents who have or have had a child with an inherited disease might seek genetic counseling before deciding to have more children. Genetic counseling might be particularly appropriate for couples from groups with a high incidence of an inherited trait; women older than 35 years of age; individuals who have had excessive exposure to drugs, chemicals, or radiation; and close relatives (first cousins) who plan to marry (Schonberg & Tifft, 2007).

Often genetic counseling begins with a family tree, genogram, or pedigree that carefully identifies people in the family who may have the disease or are carriers of the disease. This pedigree includes close family relatives and is done over several generations. For genetic counseling to be effective, hereditary information obtained must be precise and comprehensive enough to make an exact diagnosis or estimate of risk. Decision making lies with the individual receiving the information. Genetic counseling should be nondirective and supportive, and can happen before conception or be part of the prenatal screening process. The most common reason for obtaining genetic counseling is advanced maternal age. The risk of chromosomal abnormalities increases markedly after age 35.

● ● ●
Fetal Therapy

The ultimate goal of prenatal diagnosis is to prevent severe disabilities by treating them before birth. Although fetal therapy is an exciting field, it is so new that there are many complications. Because of these complications, work is being done primarily in areas where the child's early death is almost a certainty or when the fetal condition will worsen as the pregnancy progresses (Schonberg & Tifft, 2007). Prenatal screening serves a variety of purposes. When results of diagnostic tests show that the developing fetus has a major abnormality, parents must make a decision about whether the fetus will be carried to term or the pregnancy will be terminated.

The Developing Brain

Brain development begins shortly after conception and the brain grows at an amazing rate. The fetus doesn't start with a small brain that just gets bigger and fills up with information. The brain is made up of nerve cells called neurons (Figure 6–5). Most of a newborn's brain cells (neurons) are formed during the prenatal period. The brain grows in layers; because of their fast rate of growth, the layers begin to fold over each other and become the **neural tube**. The head portion of the neural tube becomes the brain and the tail portion, the spinal cord (Haffner, 2007). The **central nervous system (CNS)** consists of the brain, the spinal cord, and the nerves that control voluntary and involuntary body functions. The development of the CNS affects the actions of the muscles, glands, and organs of the body as well as motor and cognitive activities. If something interferes with the development of neurons, the specialized nerve cells that make up the CNS, the child will experience delays in development.

> **TeachSource Video Case**
>
> **Infancy: Brain Development**
> Watch the TeachSource Video Case *Infancy: Brain Development*. Look at the characteristics of brain cells (neurons) to understand the growth patterns of these cells, and look at regions of the brain and how specific regions of the brain regulate particular behaviors and emotions. The video can be found in the Early Childhood Education Media Library under Infants and Toddlers, available at www.cengagebrain.com.

Neurons are different from each other in physical and biochemical features. Brain cells are like all other body cells in that they contain a nucleus and cytoplasm. However, they are not the rounded shape we think of. Instead, they have an **axon**, a long snake-like fiber, which reaches out from the cell body and conducts electrical impulses away from it. **Dendrites** are short spider-like branched projections of a neuron that conduct electrical impulses to the cell body. The tip of each axon, the **growth cone**, provides guidance for the growing axon and helps it reach its destination. As axons grow, the number of spines along the surface of the dendrites increases, allowing for more elaborate and sophisticated communication between neurons. Individuals with intellectual disabilities have fewer dendritic spines (Yaun & Keating, 2007).

The axon of one neuron does not actually touch the dendritic spine of another neuron; there is small space between them called a **synapse**, of which there are two types: chemical and electrical. Electrical synapses are closer together, and communication among the cytoplasm of the neurons makes electrical transmission rapid and bidirectional (Yaun & Keating, 2007).

With chemical synapses the gap between the neurons is larger. Transmissions stop at the end of the axon, where there are small vesicles in the neuron that hold neurotransmitters. (See Figure 6–6.) **Neurotransmitters** are chemicals that relay, amplify, or modulate electrical signals between cells, affecting the postsynaptic cell by either exciting or inhibiting it. The signal is unidirectional (Yaun & Keating, 2007). Exposure to teratogens such as drugs, alcohol, radiation, intrauterine infection, and poor nutrition can derail this process.

If this transmission process seems long, complicated, and laborious, with many steps, it helps explain why speed is important. Infants have immature dendrites and the process is very slow. It takes a long time for them to perceive

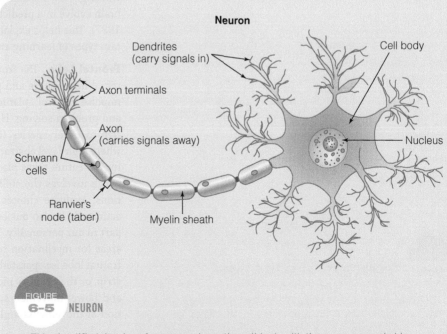

Neuron

FIGURE 6-5 NEURON

This simplified drawing of a neuron shows the cell body with the axon surrounded by the myelin sheath and the dendrites. (Courtesy of the Human Genome Project)

sensation, send a message to the brain, process it, return with a message, and respond. This is why infants seem to react in slow motion.

Neurotransmitters play an important role in this transmission process. Each neuron uses specific neurotransmitters. There are many different neurotransmitters; some of the most important include **serotonin**, **dopamine**, and **norepinephrine**. The neuron's neurotransmitters are stored in pouches, **synaptic vesicles**, which border the synaptic membrane. When a depolarizing electrical current passes through the presynaptic membrane of the axon, these pouches open and release the neurotransmitters. The released neurotransmitters move across the **synaptic cleft** to the postsynaptic membrane of the dendrite with an excitatory or inhibitory neural impulse, much like an on–off switch. Each neurotransmitter also has an inactivator that can stop the transmission (McDowell, 2004).

Problems related to neurotransmitters are implicated in a variety of disabilities. Depending on the timing and nature of the problem, the child might develop a specific learning disability, autism, or a neurologic disorder such as epilepsy, or schizophrenia. In general, the earlier the derailment occurs, the more severe the effects (Jensen, 2006). Many of the drugs that are used to treat these disorders as well as seizures, movement disorder, and depression act by altering specific neurotransmitters, their receptor sites, or what happens to the neurotransmitters that are released but not needed for the transmission (Yaun & Keating, 2007).

The sequence and timing of brain formation are crucial. Neurons must be in the right place, at the right time, with the right information. To do this they need the support of **glial cells**. In addition to the 100 billion brain cells, there are at least 10 times that many glial cells. Almost 90 percent of the brain is composed of glial cells that provide support and protection for neurons (Koob, 2009). Some glial cells are able to move around the brain consuming dead neurons; others

form the myelin sheath around neurons; and others direct information flow as they come into contact with various genes, which define the neuron's identity, location, and mission (O'Shea, 2005). A lot more is known about neurons than glial cells. Like neurons, glial cells have electrical potential, communicate with neurons, and respond to and release neurotransmitters (Koob, 2009). As brain cells migrate, they can receive "misinformation" from glial cells and die, or they can go to the wrong place, at the wrong time, and form the wrong synapses.

● ● ●
The Cerebral Cortex

The cerebral cortex is the outer layer of the **cerebrum**, the largest part of the brain, and plays an important role in memory, attention, thinking, language, consciousness, and perceptual awareness. It resides in both hemispheres of the brain (Kandel, Schwartz, & Jessell, 2000). Looking at the brain in cross section, there are two distinct regions: the **gray matter** and the **white matter**. The gray matter contains nerve cell bodies, whereas white matter contains myelinated axons, which are covered in a protective fatty coating of glial cells, called a **myelin sheath**, that surrounds the axons of many neurons. The myelin sheath allows the rapid conduction of nerve impulses. Axons of newborns have little or no myelin. Development of the myelin sheath is necessary for the development of voluntary fine and gross motor movement. Myelination allows the newborn to move from the primitive reflexes present at birth to the ability to walk, run, and pick up small objects.

THE FOUR LOBES OF THE BRAIN

The brain is divided into two hemispheres (left and right) and four regions, or lobes: the frontal, parietal, occipital, and temporal lobes. Each of the four cortical lobes is responsible for specific activities and functions (Al-Chalabi, Turner, & Delamont, 2006), and each has many folds, which do not mature at the same time. The brain releases chemicals in waves, which govern maturation; therefore, different areas of the brain evolve in a predictable sequence (Jensen, 2006; Shore, 1997). This helps explain why there are prime times for certain types of learning and development (see Figure 6–7).

Frontal Lobe. The **frontal lobe** lies at the front of each cerebral hemisphere and plays a role in reasoning, judgment, impulse control, planning, language, memory, emotions, and problem solving. Humans have large frontal lobes relative to other species (McDowell, 2004). The frontal lobe, where high-level abstract thinking, planning, and organizing for the future takes place, is the seat of **executive function**, which involves the ability to recognize consequences of actions, evaluate choices, and suppress unacceptable social actions. It is also our emotional control center and plays a part in our personality. The frontal lobe is one of the slowest areas for myelination to be completed (Jensen, 2006). The frontal lobe is separated from the parietal lobe by the **motor strip**, or the **primary motor cortex**, which controls all bodily and bowel movements, including the planning and execution of movements and the intricate muscles necessary for

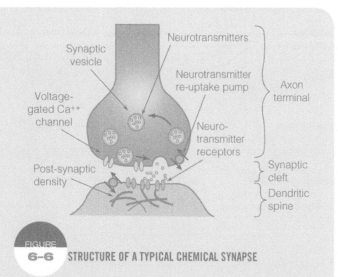

FIGURE
6-6   STRUCTURE OF A TYPICAL CHEMICAL SYNAPSE

Neurotransmitters transmit signals from the axon of one neuron across the synaptic cleft to the dendrite of another neuron.

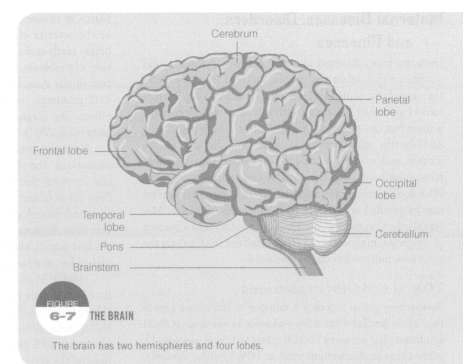

FIGURE
6-7 **THE BRAIN**

The brain has two hemispheres and four lobes.

speech, such as the tongue, and fine motor coordination, as well as muscles in the shoulders, knees, and trunk (Yaun & Keating, 2007). For motor activity to occur, a nerve impulse is sent from the primary motor cortex down the **pyramidal** (also called **corticospinal**) **tract** that connects the cortex to the spinal cord, and ultimately to the appropriate muscles. The corticospinal tract is a massive collection of long motor axons that run between the brain and the spinal column. Damage to either the motor cortex or the pyramidal tract can result in spasticity or seizures.

Parietal Lobe. The **parietal lobe** is located behind the frontal lobe and above the occipital lobe. It integrates sensory input from the different modalities with other stimuli. There are distinct areas for vision, hearing, and smell. The parietal lobe also houses the sensory areas of perceived touch, pressure, temperature, and pain (McDowell, 2004). Children with visual-perceptual problems and trouble with fine motor coordination, including children with specific learning disabilities and ADHD, may have abnormalities in this area of the brain (Yaun & Keating, 2007).

Temporal Lobe. The **temporal lobe** is below the parietal lobe and is involved with sensation and communication. It contains the primary auditory cortex, which is involved in hearing and also enables higher level auditory processing. The underside of the temporal lobe supports complex visual processing such as face recognition. The **limbic system**, also located in the temporal lobe, consists of the structures of the brain involved in the emotions associated with memories and motivation. The limbic system reacts to stress and controls emotions (McDowell, 2004). The hippocampus and amygdala are small structures at the base of the temporal

lobe, and are part of the limbic system. The **amygdala** controls emotions that are fundamental for self-preservation, the "fight or flight" response. It is the center for basic feelings, particularly fear and sexual response, and plays a crucial role in control of major emotions such as love and rage. The **hippocampus** plays an important role in memory, the ability to learn new information rapidly, and processing and packaging the context of memory (McDowell, 2004).

Occipital Lobe. The **occipital lobe** is at the back of the head and houses the primary visual receptive cortex and the visual processing center of the brain. Damage to this area causes defects in the visual field (Yaun & Keating, 2007).

BRAIN STEM

The **brain stem** is the lower part of the brain that connects to the spinal cord. Although small, all the nerve connections from the motor and sensory systems pass through the brain stem. The brain stem controls reflexive and involuntary activities such as blood pressure, heart rate, regulation of body temperature, breathing, and other autonomic processes. It is made up of the midbrain, pons, and medulla oblongata. The **midbrain** serves as the nerve pathway of the cerebral hemispheres and contains auditory and visual reflex centers. The **pons** plays a role in relaying messages in the brain. It controls arousal and regulates respiration. The **medulla oblongata** is the lower portion of the brainstem and deals with autonomic functions (Yaun & Keating, 2007).

Some parts of the brain are not involved in either movement or sensation. Called association areas, they are believed to give individuals personality and a sense of humor (McDowell, 2004). In addition to genetics, other conditions influence the developing brain.

Maternal Diseases, Disorders, and Illnesses

There are many different maternal diseases, disorders, and conditions that affect the unborn infant. Pregnancy alters the natural course of some infectious diseases. Group B streptococci are rarely associated with infection in nonpregnant women but can cause infectious diseases during pregnancy. Additionally, some noninfectious chronic diseases of the mother, such as diabetes, may require different management techniques because of the physical demands of pregnancy. With good prenatal care, negative effects of these risk factors may be avoided or cured, or birth outcomes improved. Maternal infection and chronic illness account for 3 to 4 percent of congenital malformations (Hill & Haffner, 2002). Only the most common conditions are discussed.

••• TORCH and Other Infections

Researchers group together a number of infectious agents that cause similar disabilities and refer to them as TORCH syndrome. The acronym TORCH refers to toxoplasmosis (T); other congenital infections such as HIV, syphilis, varicella, and others (O); rubella (R); cytomegalovirus (C); and herpes simplex virus (H). When a mother contracts one of these agents, the infant may be born with visual or hearing impairments, damage to the central nervous system (CNS), or heart defects (Bell, 2007).

TOXOPLASMOSIS

Toxoplasmosis is caused by one of the most common protozoan parasites in humans, *Toxoplasma gondii*, contracted through the fecal matter of cats, infected meat, or protozoan eggs. Most people with toxoplasmosis are asymptomatic. Prevention is the best strategy—pregnant women should stay away from cats. If they have cats, they should determine their exposure to the protozoan before becoming pregnant. An estimated 4,000 cases of toxoplasmosis occur each year (Montoya & Liesenfeld, 2004). Infants are usually asymptomatic at birth, but many will have neural pathway impairments. Other impairments can result in cerebral palsy, including hydrocephalus or microcephalus, intellectual disability, visual and hearing impairments, and other problems such as anemia, low birth weight, and liver and spleen enlargement.

OTHER INFECTIONS

Syphilis is a venereal disease that once appeared to be virtually eradicated with the advent of antibiotics. However, it is becoming a problem again, with 30 cases per 100,000 births in the United States (Bell, 2007). If it is detected and cured with antibiotics before the 16th week of pregnancy, there are few adverse effects. A single injection of penicillin can prevent 98 percent of congenital cases. The particular spirochete (*Treponema pallidum*) that causes syphilis is passed from human to human and can cross the placenta. Before penicillin, 60 percent of infected infants were stillborn, died during the first month, or had severe brain damage (Golden,

Marra, & Holmes, 2003). The risk to the fetus is influenced by the severity of the infection. Many affected infants die before birth or shortly after birth. Those who live have a variety of problems, from skin rashes and edema to malformation of the eyes, hearing impairment, growth retardation, CNS problems, seizures, intellectual disability, and other effects. The diagnosis of syphilis is dependent upon blood tests (Bell, 2007).

Varicella, or chicken pox, has been associated with malformations. The abnormalities it causes are less severe and less common than most other uterine infections. When it does occur (about 2% risk), it results in limb, facial, skeletal, and neurologic abnormalities. There is a vaccine for this virus. Women should determine whether they have had chicken pox; if not, they should be vaccinated before they plan to become pregnant.

Human immunodeficiency virus (HIV) is a retrovirus that infects cells in the immune system making it vulnerable to infection (Bell, 2007). The HIV virus can be transmitted in utero, during delivery, or through breast milk. Active treatment with zidovudine (ZVD) in pregnant women has reduced the vertical transmission of HIV.

Approximately 25 percent of infants born to mothers with HIV infection will become infected without intervention. Aggressive treatment with a highly active antiretroviral treatment (HAART) is recommended as soon as infants are diagnosed. If it is suspected, infants should be tested within 48 hours of birth, at 1 to 2 months, and again at 4 to 6 months. If negative at 6 months, the infant has a 99 percent chance of not being infected with HIV. HIV enters the CNS in the early stages of infection. It damages the neurons and glial cells, making children vulnerable to developmental brain injuries as well as the typical opportunistic infections of childhood (Bell, 2007).

RUBELLA

During a two-year period in the United States in the 1960s, there were 11,000 fetal deaths and 20,000 infants were born with birth defects caused by rubella. With vaccination and surveillance programs, these occurrences have been reduced to now about 20 infants a year (Atreya, Mohan, & Kulkarni, 2004). Rubella is caused by a virus that is transmitted through body fluids, including mucus and saliva. If a woman is infected during the first trimester, there is a 90 percent rate of fetal damage, including hearing and visual impairments, heart defects, cataracts and malformed retinas, brain calcification, CNS damage with long-term neurologic impairment, and thyroid dysfunction (Bell, 2007).

CYTOMEGALOVIRUS

Cytomegalovirus (CMV) is a virus from the herpes family, a double-stranded DNA genome of more than 200 genes, and the most common cause of intrauterine infection. Infections of adults and children are asymptomatic or flu-like, with few or no side effects. A majority of adults (50–80%) are latently (hidden, inactive) infected. It occurs in 1 percent of live births, but only 1 in 1,000 of these infants will have

CMV disease. The greatest risk is to women who acquire a primary CMV infection during the first half of pregnancy. The most common effect of CMV disease is CNS damage. Of initially asymptomatic infants, approximately 10 to 15 percent will develop a sensorineural hearing loss, significant intellectual disability, and behavior problems. Overall, the most common symptoms are progressive hearing loss and intellectual disability (Bell, 2007). Women of childbearing age should be tested for CMV exposure; if not immune, they should avoid infection. A vaccine is being researched but is not yet available.

HERPES SIMPLEX VIRUSES

The herpes simplex virus (HSV) causes a variety of diseases in humans from "fever blisters" to genital infections. Orolabial herpes is primarily a disease of childhood. Adult herpes is transmitted through sexual contact. About 5 percent of neonatal HSV infections happen in utero, with 85 percent occurring during the birthing process (a cesarean delivery is recommended). The remaining 10 percent are acquired from environmental sources (Bell, 2007). Like CMV, herpes is difficult to diagnosis because about 50 percent of the women do not have genital lesions. There is no cure for these infectious diseases. However, if it is known that a woman has CMV or herpes, the pregnancy can be managed in such as way as to reduce the probability of neonatal infection. Without proper management, the outcomes are much less positive. Untreated, the infant mortality rate is 70 percent. Antiviral therapy reduces this to about 30 percent. Even with treatment, infants are likely to have CNS involvement and may have blindness, deafness, or significant intellectual disability (Bell, 2007).

OTHER CONGENITAL INFECTIONS

Some congenital infections such as influenza, mononucleosis, malaria, parvovirus, and enterovirus result in increased maternal anemia, low birth weight, intrauterine growth retardation, premature deliveries and infant mortality, but they do not seem to cause fetal malformations (CDC, 2007c).

Group B Streptococcus. Group B streptococcus (GBS) is one of the most common infections in the developed world. It was recognized in the 1930s and 1940s as a cause of postpartum infection, but it was not until the 1970s and 1980s that the impact of the mother's infection was related to the prevalence of the **perinatal** infections in infants. Although not part of TORCH infections, Group B streptococcus is a leading cause of **sepsis**, a serious blood infection, and **meningitis** during the first two months of neonatal life. Meningitis is an infection of the fluid and lining (membranes) of the brain and spinal cord.

Approximately 30 percent of pregnant women have GBS in their genital tract, and 1 to 2 percent of their infants develop blood poisoning (sepsis). When this occurs, there are two patterns. In about half of the cases, the infant becomes ill in the first week of life. The newborn may get sepsis, pneumonia, and meningitis. In other cases, the onset is later (a week to several months after birth), with meningitis more common (CDC, 2007e).

Women should be screened routinely between 35 and 37 weeks gestation for this infection. If GBS is discovered, the infected woman is treated with antibiotics. Because GBS can cause women to have a fever during labor or their membranes to rupture 18 hours or more before delivery, women who experience these symptoms should also be screened for GBS, and if it is detected, the infected women should be given antibiotics before birthing (CDC, 2007e).

CHLAMYDIA

Some sexually transmitted diseases (STDs) pose serious threats to the fetus. One of the most common, yet least well-known, is chlamydia, the most commonly reported bacterial sexually transmitted disease in the United States. The Centers for Disease Control and Prevention (CDC) estimate that 3 million people are infected each year (CDC, 2006a). The infection is silent: three-quarters of the women who have the disease have no symptoms. Chlamydia is potentially highly destructive and difficult to diagnosis. The fetus is most likely to be affected during the birthing process. Outcomes range from conjunctivitis (eye inflammation) to pneumonia, but there is also an increased risk for HIV infection, prematurity, stillbirths, and infertility. Chlamydia is responsive to antibiotics (CDC, 2006a). Overall, 26 percent of female adolescents (14–19 years of age) in the United States, about 3 million females, are infected with one or more STDs (CDC, 2006a).

• • •

Maternal Weight and Weight Gain

The fetus is dependent upon the mother for all of his nutrition. Her diet is his diet. Prepregnancy weight is a given and not amenable to change. There are few standards by which to evaluate weight as a risk factor. When a woman is either significantly overweight or underweight before becoming pregnant or when the weight gain during pregnancy is too low or too high, there is concern (Lowdermilk & Perry, 2003). Women who are overweight are more likely to have high blood pressure, hypertensive disorders, problems regulating blood sugar and insulin, and urinary tract infections.

Gestational diabetes, a form of diabetes that affects pregnant women who have never had diabetes, is probably caused by hormones produced during pregnancy. Overweight women are also likely to have infants who are large for their **gestational age**. The risk for overweight women of having a child with a major problem present at birth (congenital) is double that of a woman in the normal weight category (Prentice & Goldberg, 1996). Dietary manipulation is not advocated during pregnancy as it is viewed as having no benefit to the mother at this time and may be harmful to the fetus.

Weight gain during pregnancy is a common concern for many women. A pregnant woman needs to consume about 300 additional calories a day (Haffner, 2007). Recommended weight gain is dependent upon the appropriateness of the prepregnancy weight. For a single fetus, the recommendation would be between 25 and 35 pounds. Overall, a weight gain of about 17 to 20 percent in body weight is the goal (Abrams, Altman, & Pickett, 2000). Thus a woman with a prepregnancy weight of 100 would be considered fine even if she gained only 17 to 20 pounds, whereas a woman weighing 150 pounds might expect to gain 26 to 30 pounds. If the mother is underweight, she should gain between 27 and 40 pounds, and if overweight, at least 15 pounds and up to 25 pounds (Lowdermilk & Perry, 2003).

Optimal rates of weight gain depend on the stage of the pregnancy. At the beginning of pregnancy, the weight gain is primarily in the mother (amniotic fluid, placenta, breast tissue, extra stores of fat, blood, and fluid). By the third trimester, the fetus is gaining the weight. During the first trimester, a woman may gain about 5 pounds. In the second and third trimesters, it may be about a half a pound a week.

Chronic Maternal Illnesses

Some women become pregnant already having conditions that may affect the fetus; in other situations, the pregnancy itself can precipitate risk conditions. Pregnancy causes complex metabolic changes in a woman that can alter previously controlled conditions, such as diabetes, lupus, cardiovascular disorders, anemia, and hypertensive disorders. These conditions affect both the mother and the child.

DIABETES MELLITUS

Women with diabetes do not produce enough insulin. Before insulin was discovered in 1921, little was known about diabetes or its effects on pregnancy. The use of synthetic insulin has resulted in higher pregnancy rates in women with diabetes, but managing insulin during pregnancy is challenging. Pregnancy influences the amount of synthetic insulin a women needs. Early in pregnancy, diabetic women may have periods of **hypoglycemia** because of the fetuses' heightened demands for glucose (sugar). Hypoglycemia is having lower than normal amounts of sugar (glucose) in the blood. Hormones produced by the placenta alter the mother's metabolism and, in general, increase her need for insulin. Changes in the mother's metabolism produce periods of maternal **hyperglycemia**, high levels of sugar in the blood. Uncontrolled diabetes can place the fetus at risk; too much sugar (glucose) results in large babies (excessive fetal growth) and places the infant at risk for hypoglycemia at birth when less insulin is required. Controlled diabetic women who receive optimal prenatal care do well; those whose diabetes is not controlled or who do not receive this level of care are more likely to experience sudden and unexplained stillbirths and an increased risk for major birth anomalies (Brown & Satin, 2007).

HYPERTENSIVE DISEASES

Some women (1–5%) have **hypertension**, or elevated blood pressure, before conception or before 20 weeks of gestation. Hypertension is blood pressure that is chronically elevated (greater than 140/90 mmHg) (Brown & Satin, 2007). These women may have high blood pressure because of personal heredity factors, excessive weight, or medical problems. Hypertension is one of the most common medical complications of pregnancy. These women are monitored carefully because the fetus is at risk for intrauterine growth deficiency and premature rupture of the placenta.

When hypertension develops after the 20th week of gestation and is accompanied by an accumulation of fluid in the tissue (**edema**) and protein in the urine, it is called **preeclampsia**. This form of hypertension occurs most frequently in first pregnancies and complicates 7 percent of pregnancies (Creasy, Resnik, & Iams, 2004). The cause of preeclampsia is unknown, but for women with this condition the risks are the same as those for women who enter pregnancy with high blood pressure. Preeclampsia is a concern for the fetus because there may be a low blood supply to the placenta, which is the fetal source of food and oxygen (Haffner, 2007). If preeclampsia is not treated, seizures (**eclampsia**) may develop. In some cases, labor will be induced or a cesarean section performed if the mother's life is threatened by the probability of having seizures.

IN THE FIELD

As soon as they knew I was having twins, they told me to expect to have a cesarean. The babies weren't due until October, but I was ready to have them in August; I felt like a beached whale. Me, who likes to swim and hike; me, who eats organic food and takes such good care of myself. I gained 70 pounds. Can you believe it? The doctor was so pleased with me and I was so miserable.

They became concerned about my blood pressure during the seventh month. By the beginning of the eighth month, I had to see the doctor twice a week. His nurse would take my blood pressure. He would come in and shake his head and then send me to the hospital for blood work and a urine sample. It took hours, and I began to dread sitting in the hospital just waiting and waiting.

The third time we went through this, we were sitting and sitting and sitting. Me, with my fat tummy and swollen feet, trying to find a way to get comfortable. I told my husband we should just leave. Suddenly there was all this activity, and I knew something was wrong. I looked around to see what all the commotion was about and realized they were heading our way. Apparently, my test results suggested that I could easily go into seizures. We didn't go home to pick up my nicely packed bag; we went directly to the operating room. Less than an hour later, I was the mother of twins.

Trauma and Abuse

Approximately 10 to 20 percent of women experience some form of trauma during pregnancy (Cunningham et al., 2005). Motor vehicle accidents, falls, and assaults cause the most common form of blunt trauma to the abdominal area. The most likely outcome is preterm labor, which occurs in as many as 28 percent of the cases (Brown & Satin, 2007). The placenta can become detached, placing the mother and fetus at risk.

Teratogens

Teratogens are nongenetic, extraneous substances implicated in causing death, malformations, growth deficiency,

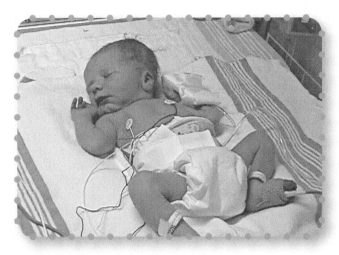

Teratogens affect the fetus through the mother and may result in growth deficiency or functional deficits.
© Cengage Learning 2012

or functional deficits in the developing fetus. Common teratogens include alcohol, nicotine, and prescription and illicit drugs. The effects of many specific teratogens are known. Some teratogens have more effect at specific times during prenatal development, whereas others have debilitating effects throughout fetal development. This section focuses on the major teratogens that directly affect the fetus.

Among pregnant women, 5 to 10 percent abuse alcohol, 20 percent smoke cigarettes, 10 percent use marijuana, about 1 percent use cocaine, and 0.5 percent use opiates. Three-quarters of individuals who abuse one substance are likely to abuse others as well (Center on Addiction and Substance Abuse, 1996). Polydrug use makes it difficult to determine the exact impact of a specific substance on the fetus. Additionally, pregnant women who use drugs rarely have adequate prenatal care or good nutrition, and they may have STDs.

Alcohol

Alcohol use during pregnancy is the most common cause of preventable intellectual disability. Alcohol is abused more than any other drug in the United States. In the United States, and in many parts of Europe, fetal alcohol spectrum disorders (FASD) are the leading cause of intellectual disability. They are more frequent than Down syndrome, spina bifida, or fragile X syndrome. Fetal alcohol syndrome (FAS) is the most severe end of fetal alcohol spectrum disorders. Although prevalence varies among different populations, the CDC estimate that FAS occurs in 0.2 to 1.5 births per 1,000, and that FASD is approximately three times that rate, putting it at 0.6 to 5.5 per 1,000 live births in the United States. Combined, they constitute 0.8 to 7 cases per 1,000 live births (CDC, 2007a).

FAS is defined by four criteria: maternal drinking; prenatal and postnatal growth deficiency (low birth weight and poor muscle tone); facial anomalies (thin upper lip, flat mid-face, short nose, low nasal bridge, small head, droopy

eyes); and brain damage (CNS dysfunction, irritability, hyperactivity, attention deficit, and intellectual disability) (Wunsch, Conlon, & Scheidt, 2002). The timing of alcohol consumption affects fetal outcomes. If alcohol abuse occurs during the first trimester of pregnancy, there is an increased probability of miscarriage, and the physical signs of FAS are likely to be present. Binge drinking early in pregnancy produces the worst birth outcomes (Burbacher & Grant, 2006). Alcohol abuse during the second trimester affects physical and intellectual growth, but there are no physical malformations. If abuse occurs in the third trimester, cognitive development alone is impaired. Children exposed to alcohol show learning and behavioral problems and poor impulse control.

In a survey of American mothers, about 30 percent reported drinking alcohol at some point in their pregnancy (U.S.DHHS, 2003). When a pregnant woman drinks alcohol, her blood alcohol content and that of her fetus increases. They increase at the same rate, but the blood alcohol level of the fetus remains high longer because the mother's liver must remove the alcohol from her own blood before removing the alcohol from the fetus. The ethanol in alcohol crosses the placental barrier and goes into both the fetus and the amniotic fluid. Ethanol impairs the placental function of channeling essential nutrients to the fetus and also interferes with carbohydrate metabolism, resulting in growth retardation. By causing fetal malformations through chemical imbalances, alcohol affects the cells and the DNA of the fetus. Alcohol also affects fetal breathing and therefore levels of oxygen in the blood. If a woman drinks one drink per day throughout her pregnancy (270 days) she will have exposed her fetus to 135 ounces of pure alcohol. This would be the equivalent of feeding the baby 16 bottles (8 ounces each) of pure alcohol (Burd, n.d.a).

Nicotine

Exposure to tobacco smoke is the number one preventable cause of low-birth-weight infants. The birth weight is directly proportional to the number of cigarettes smoked per day or the length of time a woman is exposed to passive smoke (Klesges et al., 2001; Wunsch et al., 2002). If a woman smokes one cigarette per day throughout her pregnancy (270 days), she will have exposed her fetus to 13 full packs of cigarettes. If she smokes 10 cigarettes per day, it is equivalent to 1,305 full packs of cigarettes (Burd, n.d.[b]). Approximately 25 percent of pregnant women smoke (Fried et al., 2003). The CDC found that 3 to 13 percent of women not covered by Medicaid smoked during pregnancy compared to 14 to 38 percent of women on **Medicaid** (CDC, 2005d). Medicaid is a health insurance program for individuals and families with low incomes and few resources, funded by the state and federal government and administered by states. A recent CDC study showed that the less education a woman had, the more she was likely to smoke during pregnancy. That same study also showed that white women are far more likely to smoke than black, Latina, or American Indian women (CDC, 2005d).

THE EVIDENCE BASE

Women who smoke during pregnancy are 83 percent more likely to deliver a low-birth-weight infant, 129 percent more likely to have an infant who will die from SIDS, 30 percent more likely to deliver an infant with respiratory distress syndrome, and 41 percent more likely to have an infant with a perinatal respiratory condition (Marks et al., 1990). In 2003, 12 percent of all women, 13 percent of Latinas, and 20 percent of black women who smoked during pregnancy delivered a low-birth-weight baby (U.S. Preventive Services Task Force, 2003). Up to 8 percent of all neonatal deaths in the week after birth are due to problems related to the mother smoking during pregnancy (CDC, 2005d). Smoking is correlated with education: 2 percent of college-educated non-Hispanic white women smoked during pregnancy, whereas 43 percent of non-Hispanic white women with 9 to 11 years of education smoked during one of their pregnancies (U.S.DHHS, 2004).

Specific counseling tailored for pregnant women increases smoking abstinence rates during pregnancy and leads to increased birth weight. Of women who received less than 3 minutes of physician counseling, 11 percent quit; of those receiving 3 to 10 minutes, 12 percent quit; and of these receiving over 10 minutes of counseling, 19 percent quit. In 1996, maternal smoking accounted for 2 percent of all neonatal medical expenditures, an estimated $367 million dollars. Pregnant smokers incurred an additional $704 in health care costs (in 1996 dollars) (Berg, 2003). Clinical trials show that $6 in health care costs is saved for every $1 invested in smoking cessation programs for pregnant women (Campbell, Rosenthal, & Chattopadhyay, 2006)

When a woman smokes during pregnancy, the carbon monoxide from her bloodstream crosses the placenta and reduces the amount of oxygen available to the fetus. The nicotine causes the blood vessels to become smaller (constrict). In response to this, both maternal and fetal heart rates increase and fetal movement decreases. Cigarette smoking also interferes with the assimilation of essential vitamins and minerals. Nicotine has been found in breast milk, although the impact on the infant has not been well documented. Long-term follow-up suggests impaired intellectual and emotional development has occurred. Infants born to smoking mothers are more likely to display hyperactivity and impaired school performance. Prevention involves explaining the risks of maternal smoking and advising women to stop or at least reduce the number of cigarettes they smoke.

Almost 60 percent of U.S. children between 3 and 11 years, 22 million children, are exposed to **secondhand smoke**. One in four of these children live in households with at least one smoker (U.S.DHHS, 2007). Children whose parents smoke have more respiratory illness, bronchitis, and pneumonia than children of parents who do not smoke. The California Environmental Protection agency estimates that secondhand smoke caused 430 children to die of sudden infant death

syndrome (SIDS), was responsible for 202,300 asthma episodes and 790,000 ear infections that required medical attention (U.S.DHHS, 2007). Children of fathers who smoked were twice as likely to develop cancer in adulthood as those whose fathers did not smoke (Huncharek, Kupelnick, & Klassen, 2002).

IN THE FIELD

As a special educator whose school draws from a mostly low socioeconomic area, I know that many of my students' parents smoke. While I knew that this could cause respiratory problems, I always held my tongue when I conferenced with these adults. I am young and I don't want to be judgmental. However, on one occasion I scheduled a conference with the mother of one of my students. I knew she was pregnant. Ethically, I felt I should talk to her about smoking and its dangers during pregnancy. I thought about this as I watched her outside my window having her second cigarette while she waited for the school buses to leave. Smoking is not allowed on school grounds, but the signs did not seem to deter her. I didn't want the conference to start off badly, so I didn't mention it as she put out the cigarette before she entered the school.

In the days before the meeting, I had learned that this mother lived in a very poor trailer park; she had one other child in addition to Ellen, who was in my class. My colleagues told me that she herself had attended this school and had dropped out at 16. They remembered that she had learning problems, but that had been in the days before we knew much about learning disabilities. Her school experiences had not been positive.

The mother was very polite during our meeting and seemed very interested and concerned about Ellen. She wanted to know whether she could do anything to help her. We discussed how she could help her at home. I wondered if she would be as happy to help her unborn baby by quitting smoking.

Throughout the meeting, all I could look at was the pack of cigarettes hanging out of her purse. I wanted more than anything to tell her about the dangers of smoking, not only for Ellen but also for the unborn baby. Because of her economic situation, I figured she did not receive the best prenatal care. Also, I surmised that she didn't know much about the dangers of smoking to unborn babies because she probably never completed crucial high school classes, such as health education. I never got up the nerve to bring up the topic. To this day I think about it.

• • •
Drugs

Drugs are another commonly abused substance. Of pregnant women who use drugs, some use illicit drugs, whereas others use only prescribed drugs. In the United States, the Food and Drug Administration (FDA) is considering methods of testing drugs to collect information about their effects on pregnant women in order to provide information about safety. The FDA currently uses potential fetal risk as its criterion for establishing guidelines for prescribing drugs to pregnant women. General concerns related to drug use during pregnancy are birth defects, spontaneous abortion, preterm labor, low birth weight, and fetal death. Drugs taken by the mother pass through her system to the fetus via the placenta. Some over-the-counter drugs such as aspirin can cause problems. Aspirin interferes with blood clotting and leads to increased bleeding. High doses of aspirin can lead to more serious problems.

ILLICIT DRUGS

Some pregnant women are recreational drug users (those who use narcotics sporadically), and others are addicted (they have a tolerance to the narcotic and show signs of withdrawal when they stop using it). When pregnant women were asked if they had used illicit drugs during the past month, 10 percent self-reported that they had (Substance Abuse and Mental Health Services Administration [SAMHSA], 2005a). The actual incidence of use during pregnancy is much higher, ranging from 10 to 32 percent depending upon whether the results are based on self-report or urine testing (Mason & Lee, 1995; SAMHSA, 2005a; Huestis & Choo, 2002). If a pregnant woman uses illicit drugs, the specific drugs and the magnitude of use must be determined. Women are routinely asked about their drug use, but about 25 to 50 percent deny using drugs even when they know they have just given a urine sample that will be tested for drug use (Mason & Lee, 1995). Given their desire for social acceptance, the expectation is that the higher numbers cited above are more accurate. The price for the infant is high. More that 75 percent of infants who have been exposed to drugs in utero will have major medical problems compared to 27 percent of unexposed infants (Huestis & Choo, 2002).

Marijuana. Marijuana is the most commonly used illicit drug among middle-class women of childbearing age and, after alcohol and tobacco, is the most commonly used drug during pregnancy. Of young adults between 18 to 25 years, 17 percent state that they have used marijuana in the past month (SAMHSA, 2005b). It is estimated that 10 percent of pregnant women use marijuana. More use it in the first trimester than in the third, but these rates vary throughout the population.

Marijuana increases the carbon monoxide level in the blood. Carbon monoxide levels while smoking a "joint" are five times higher than those found during cigarette smoking (Wunsch et al., 2002). There is some indication that infants of marijuana users might be born preterm and have low birth weights; however, this is not conclusive. Effects after birth are that the infants cry more and are difficult to console. There is disagreement about the effects of marijuana on the development of the fetus. When confounding variables of race, education, income, marital status, and alcohol and tobacco use were controlled, many previous findings about the detrimental effects of marijuana did not hold up (Kandall et al., 1999; Lester, 2000). Prenatal marijuana exposure did not appear to have an important impact on postnatal development when it was used in isolation.

Cocaine. Cocaine is one of the most frequently used illicit drugs and one of the most addictive. Of young adults between 18 and 25 years, 2 percent state that they have used cocaine in the past month (SAMHSA, 2005b). Although its use is not as prevalent as alcohol and marijuana, fetal exposure occurs in 1 to 3 percent of pregnancies (Chiriboga,

1996). Although this drug is generally labeled "cocaine," it may take many forms; the concentrations vary; and it is used in different ways: inhaled, smoked, free-based, or injected, making conclusive statements about its effects difficult.

Cocaine effects are both direct and indirect. Cocaine affects the CNS as a stimulant and causes the blood vessels to constrict, which decreases the amount of blood and oxygen that can reach the fetus. The lack of blood and oxygen circulation then interferes with fetal development and the effect is magnified if the mother also smokes cigarettes or drinks alcohol. Structural defects associated with cocaine use are caused by the interruption of the blood flow to developing structures or previously developed structures (Covington et al., 2002). Cocaine has been associated with prematurity and low birth weight as well as neurobehavioral abnormalities (Wunsch et al., 2002). It can also cause contractions of the uterus and premature birth or spontaneous abortion. The constriction of the blood vessels can result in growth retardation, intracranial hemorrhage, malnutrition, reduced oxygen, and microcephaly (Espy, Kaufman, & Glisky, 1999).

Children who have been exposed to cocaine prenatally are at biological and environmental risk. However, these risks may be overstated. With differences in instruments used in testing and inconsistencies in results, it is difficult to reach conclusions. Some of the differences that appear shortly after birth fade by 7 months or so (Wunsch et al., 2002). Other abnormalities are not apparent until school age (Singer et al., 2002).

Opiates. Opium and its derivatives (heroin, morphine, and codeine) can be ingested, injected, or absorbed through mucous membranes. Heroin addiction has decreased since the 1990s. Most heroin users administer it intravenously because of the immediate effect. The only drug available to treat pregnant heroin-addicted women is methadone. This can be taken orally, is long acting, and helps women maintain fairly consistent blood oxygen levels. The use of other opiates tends to produce rapid swings from intoxication to withdrawal, and this adversely affects the fetus. The most common signs of neonatal narcotic withdrawal syndrome in infants reflect the disregulation of the CNS and include irritability, restlessness, sleep disturbances, sweating, vomiting, diarrhea, high-pitched cry, tremors, seizures, **hypertonicity**, and uncoordinated sucking. Withdrawal symptoms are more severe and prolonged for methadone than heroin (Haffner, 2007).

• • •

Environmental Teratogens

Many factors found within the environment of the pregnant mother can affect the developing fetus, including radiation, hyperthermia, mercury, and lead. Prenatal environmental factors account for 2 to 3 percent of disabilities (Hill & Haffner, 2002) and often lead to congenital malformations. For infants, exposure to environmental toxins during the first few days after conception seems to have an all-or-nothing effect. That is, the embryo either dies or is unaffected. Later in the pregnancy, these toxins may affect the size of the fetus, either causing microcephaly or low birth weight. There are individual differences in susceptibility to these toxins as well as a threshold effect. Below a certain level, some toxins may not be harmful.

RADIATION, MERCURY, AND LEAD

Radiation is energy in the form of waves or particles and is one of the most common toxins. Although low doses have been found not to be harmful, the effect of radiation depends on the amount and timing of exposure. During the first weeks of pregnancy, the embryo is either unaffected or its effects are lethal. During the next two months, if not lethal, exposure to radiation produces growth retardation. During the second trimester, excessive radiation can cause central nervous sensitivity, microcephaly, and eye abnormalities. Pregnant women should avoid X-rays when possible. All females should wear lead capes when exposed to X-rays to protect their supply of eggs from radiation.

Maternal exposure to mercury can lead to severe disabling conditions in the infant, including cerebral palsy, congenital malformation, and intellectual disability. Methylmercury is a heavy metal that is found in some fish; however, other nutrients in seafood may mitigate its potential adverse effects (Davidson & Myers, 2007). Regardless, the population in general and pregnant women in particular, have been advised to limit fish consumption to not more than twice a week, especially "oily" fish such as tuna, bluefish, and swordfish.

Ingestion of **lead** during pregnancy has been shown to cause brain damage in infants. Prenatal exposure to lead also predisposes children to develop ADHD (Stein et al., 2002). Lead is also a heavy neurotoxic metal that accumulates in soft bones and tissue. Lead levels as low as 10 micrograms per deciliter are associated with lower IQ scores. Fetal exposure to many different environmental pesticides, cleaners, paints, and other toxic substances increases the risk for developmental disabilities.

THE EVIDENCE BASE

High levels of lead affect the cardiovascular, renal, and liver systems and can produce neurological complications that can result in disability or death. The neurological complications are irreversible. A rise in blood lead level from 10 to 20 **micrograms per deciliter** (μg/dL) reduces a child's IQ by an average of two points. It is estimated that 310,000 children between 1 and 5 years have elevated lead blood levels. The prevalence of such elevated blood levels has declined 98 percent since 1976–1980. Critical factors were the reduction of lead-based paint in homes, lead-soldered pipes, leaded gasoline, and industrial emissions.

The estimated life cost for a birth cohort of 5-year-olds (children born the same year) was estimated at $43.4 billion in 1997 (Landrigan et al., 2002). Because of falling blood lead levels since the late 1970s, it is estimated that the average IQ of children in the late 1990s was on average 2 to 5 points higher. Each IQ point raises worker productivity about 2 percent. The estimated economic benefit in 2000 dollars for each year's cohort of 2-year-old children ranges from $110 to $319 billion (Grosse et al., 2002). The cost of blood lead screening averages $30 per specimen. Children at risk for lead exposure should be screened at or before 12 months of age and again at 24 months if the risk continues. The main treatment is to stop exposure by removing the environmental or dietary source of lead

Source: Brown & Chattopadhyay, 2006.

REFLECTIVE PRACTICE | Evidence about the effects of lead were used to make societal changes. Although there is concern about the welfare of children, it is sometimes the economic impact that is the impetus for change. How do you feel about that? Do you believe that one of the reasons universal preschool may be implemented is because it is cost-effective, not because it is good for children?

Hurricane Katrina brought a lot of the concerns about environmental toxins to the fore, including concerns about carbon monoxide because of power outages, the chemicals in floodwaters, and even the use of insect repellent. Not enough studies have been done to know whether DEET is safe for pregnant women (CDC, 2007b). It should not be used on infants.

HYPERTHERMIA

Exposure to high temperatures (over 102°F), especially during the first trimester, is related to neural tube defects (Liptak, 2002). In hyperthermia, the body absorbs more heat than it can get rid of, so body temperature rises. Because of the dangers of hyperthermia, spas and hot baths are not recommended for pregnant women.

SUMMARY

- All human beings start as a single cell containing the genetic information that shapes that individual and the genetic material that individual will pass on to future generations.

- Sometimes there are problems in the process of cell division and chromosomes may be added, lost, or moved to different locations.

- A variety of different screening methods are used to identify prenatal disorders and help families understand what these conditions mean.

- Some developmental disabilities can neither be prevented nor diagnosed prenatally.
- In utero, the fetus has predictable patterns of development.
- Biological factors, teratogens, and maternal diseases, disorders, or illnesses can interfere with prenatal development.
- Biological factors such as maternal malnutrition and chronic illness impact the developmental trajectory.
- Teratogens such as alcohol, nicotine, and drugs, as well as environmental teratogens, interfere with development.
- Most infants are born without developmental disabilities.
- With advances in knowledge about brain development and early intervention, children born with disabilities face new opportunities.

EDUCATIONAL RESOURCES

Centers for Disease Control and Prevention is a government funded source that contains a wealth of health information and up to date information about a variety of diseases and conditions. www.cdc.gov/

Kids Health supported by the Nemours Foundation is a nonprofit organization supporting child and family health. It has an extensive searchable database on issues relating to prenatal development and risk factors, as well as other information. It has places for parents, teens, and children. www.kidshealth.org/

National Human Genome Research Institute supported by the NIH provides educational materials including definitions, a talking glossary, and fact sheets as well as information about the Human Genome. www.genome.gov/

National Library of Medicine (NLM) is part of the National Institutes of Health and is the national resource for all health-related materials. (888) 346-3656; www.nlm.nih.gov/

National Organization for Rare Disorders, Inc. (NORD) is a clearinghouse for information about rare disorders (e.g., inborn errors of metabolism). It encourages research, represents people with rare diseases, and educates the public about these diseases. www.nord-rdb.com/

Smart Moms, Healthy Babies was developed by UMHS Health Education Resource Center and the Women's Health Resource Center to provide information about pregnancy, prenatal testing, and a variety of conditions that affect fetal development. www.smartmoms.org/

For additional resources, visit the book companion website for this text at www.cengagebrain.com.

Inclusive Early Childhood Education

Part II focuses on educating children with disabilities in inclusive settings. It begins with a chapter on infants and toddlers and details some of the conditions that place them at risk. It also provides information on the role that experience plays in shaping the brain and discusses the curriculum in general as well as ways of including infants and toddlers with delays and disabilities.

Chapters 8 through 19 each focus on including children with a particular disability (such as intellectual delays, specific learning disabilities, or a visual impairment), or a special need (such as English language learners or children who are gifted and talented) in educational programs. Each chapter provides a definition of the disability or special need; information on the prevalence and cause; and on assessment and early identification. All chapters include guidelines, curriculum adaptations, and additional educational resources.

7

Infants and Toddlers At Risk

We were older parents—I was 34 years old—so I asked my obstetrician about some of the newer tests. He told me I was healthy and in good shape, and I shouldn't worry. I decided not to. My water broke in the middle of the night. I went to the bathroom, Jack laid towels on the floor and called the doctor. He said we should come to the hospital. When we arrived, Jack calmly asked the nurse, "Is she pregnant?" They told him to sit down for a few minutes. They swept me away, telling him they would be back for him in a few minutes.

We had decided to try to have the baby as naturally as possible. I knew about fetal monitors and decided if it lost the heartbeat, Jack would "lose it," so I refused the monitor. We had the baby in the birthing room of the hospital. Having gone to the birthing classes, my husband was helping me breathe. Later, a nurse commented that what we were doing was asthmatic breathing as my husband has asthma. I had what I later learned was "back labor." That meant it hurt all the time, not just when the contractions came. I had to put my hand on my stomach to feel the contractions.

I was tired. After 20 hours of labor, I overheard the nurses say that I was "only 8 centimeters dilated." Given my feelings about medication, the doctor apparently resigned himself to the idea that I would hold out. He told me to push; the nurses murmured; I pushed. I might have had better luck pushing a car toward a wall 10 feet away. At some point I heard my husband and the doctor talking as the face emerged; they were guessing about whether it would be a boy or girl. I was outraged. I pushed again. It was a girl.

They held her up and I looked. She had the right number of fingers and toes and they put her to my breast. I was cold and trembling, but elated. She looked so perfect. I felt wonderful. I had entered the hospital about 4:30 a.m. I am not a hospital person and wanted to leave.

My obstetrician released me the next day but said only the pediatrician could authorize my daughter's release. He

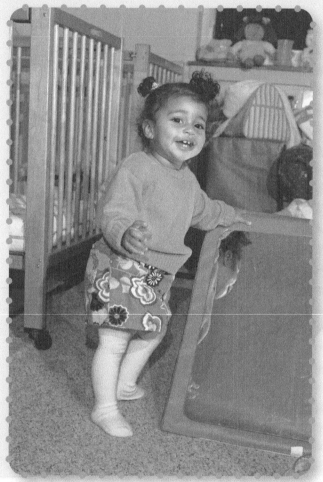

©Cengage Learning 2012

did. As we were leaving the hospital they stopped us—they needed a name. When we told them we'd get back to them, they made it very clear that there would be a lot of complications if we didn't name her. My husband filled out the papers, and as we got in the car I asked him what he had named her. ✳

Labor and Delivery

The move from pregnancy to giving birth is dramatic, and one that brings many biological, social, and emotional changes to mothers and fathers. The process of giving birth to a baby, which has changed dramatically over the centuries among industrialized societies, has remained quite personal for millennia. New methods of fetal monitoring and delivery practices have made childbearing safer for both mother and infant. Complications during labor and delivery account for less than 10 percent of cases of severe childhood disabilities (Brown & Satin, 2007).

Dating a pregnancy is a crucial step in prenatal care. A pregnancy is full term if the baby is delivered between

38 and 42 weeks. About 85 percent of women deliver within 7 days (before or after) of their due date. The fetus is still small enough to fit through the birth canal and mature enough to cope with the extrauterine environment. Deliveries before 38 weeks are consider **preterm** and those after 42 weeks are **postterm**.

Most of the factors that cause labor to begin are chemical in nature, and the expectant mother is unaware of them. Some chemicals like **oxytocin** stimulate uterine contractions; others such as **epinephrine** cause uterine relaxation. Basic knowledge of the roles of different chemicals has allowed doctors to control the onset of labor to some degree. However, they are still uncertain about the role of *every* chemical or the interactions between chemicals.

An early sign of labor is **lightening**, which is the initial descent of the fetus and uterus into the pelvic cavity. The decrease of pressure makes breathing easier. This is followed by **engagement** as the fetus moves farther down the pelvic cavity into position for birth, with his head low in the mother's abdomen and close to the mother's cervix. As the cervix thins and dilates, tiny blood vessels break and give the mucus a bloody appearance, which may be seen on a mother's underwear as bloody spots. Also, the mother's "water" may break. This is the clear amniotic fluid that surrounds and protects the fetus while he is in the womb. **Contractions**, or the movement of the muscular walls of the uterus that push the fetus through the birth canal and out of the woman's body, may also alert her to the impending birth. Initial contractions may be cramp-like and come at irregular intervals. With time, these contractions become more intense, regular, and closer together.

The process of bringing an infant into the world is called **labor**. Most women who have had children approve of the name for this dynamic personal experience. Labor is defined as regular uterine contractions leading to progressive cervical changes. Technically, it involves discharging the fetus, placenta, and umbilical cord from the uterus.

The **first stage of labor** begins with the onset of regular contractions and continues until the cervix is completely dilated (about 10 centimeters). Uterine contractions and the fetal heart rate are monitored. A normal fetal heart rate ranges between 120 and 160 beats per minute, and varies within these limits during childbirth. A fetal heart rate that slows beneath this range is cause for concern, and unless the cause is found and the heart rate returns to the normal range, the delivery is made by cesarean section, forceps, or vacuum extraction, depending on considerations of safety and expediency (Brown & Satin, 2007).

During the **second stage of labor**, the constriction of the abdominal muscles and the straightening of the fetal body push the fetus into the birth canal. Each contraction also decreases the placental blood flow for a short time. For most fetuses, this decrease is not a problem. However, **hypoxia** (deprivation of oxygen to the brain) may be a problem for premature or at-risk fetuses. Contractions also compress the umbilical cord and the fetal head. When the fetal head encounters the pelvic floor, the chin tucks, presenting a smaller diameter for the descent. The fetus then rotates and the head extends to permit passage through the vulva. The crowning head, then face and chin, are delivered. While awaiting the next contraction, the obstetrician applies suction to remove fluid from the newborn's mouth and nose. Following the delivery of the head, the fetus rotates, allowing the shoulders and the rest of the body to pass out of the birth canal. The umbilical cord is then clamped and cut (Lowdermilk & Perry, 2006).

The **third stage of labor** involves the separation and expulsion of the placenta, or afterbirth, which happens about five minutes after the birth of the baby (Lowdermilk & Perry, 2006).

A **cesarean section** is the delivery of the fetus through an incision in the abdominal wall and uterus. The purpose of the cesarean birth is to support the life and health of the mother and the fetus. A fast delivery is particularly important when the fetal supply of oxygen is diminished (Lowdermilk & Perry, 2006).

Newborns at Risk

Complications arise from a variety of sources related to the health of the mother, the placement of the placenta, the presentation of the fetus, multiple gestations, and birth injuries. Many of these conditions result in preterm labor and delivery. Preterm births account for 85 percent of complications around the time of birth (Norwitz, Robinson, & Challis, 1999; Lowdermilk & Perry, 2006).

At birth, infants must make the transition from the dark, watery womb that was warm and constant (almost 99°F) to a world of variable temperatures, light, and air. The wet infant enters the world with a large surface area and little body fat, which is why he needs to be warmed immediately. He must move from a pulmonary (lung) and cardiovascular (heart and blood vessels) system dependent on the mother and the placenta to one that is independent. The passage through the birth canal usually rids the lungs of fluid, and the first cry usually inflates the lungs. The chemical surfactant helps the lungs maintain their shape (Gaitatzes, Chang, & Baumgart, 2007). The pattern of blood circulation changes at birth, allowing the lungs to oxygenate the blood. These changes are tenuous during the first few hours and even days after birth. When the umbilical cord is clamped, additional circulatory changes allow the blood to pass through the liver for detoxification before entering the infant's heart. The transitions are challenging for a full-term infant; prematurity can make the birth process daunting for the newborn.

The **infant mortality** rate is the number of infants dying before 1 year of age, per 1,000 live births. In the United States, this rate is comparatively low: 7 per 1,000 live infants in 2009 (World Bank, 2011). Of infants who die during the first year, more than half die during the **neonatal period** or first four weeks of life (Hoyert et al., 2001). See Table 7–1. **Morbidity** refers to the occurrence of complications such as disease, disability, and chronic illness.

TABLE 7-1 INFANT, NEONATAL, AND POSTNEONATAL MORTALITY RATES, BY RACE OF MOTHER IN THE UNITED STATES IN 2006

	Mortality Rate per 1,000 Live Births		
Race of Mother	Infant	Neonatal	Postneonatal
All races	6.7	4.5	2.2
White	5.6	3.7	1.9
Black	12.9	8.7	4.2
Hispanic	5.4	3.7	1.7
American Indian or Alaska Native	8.3	4.3	4.0
Asian or Pacific Islander	4.6	3.2	1.4

Source: Mathews & MacDorman, 2010.

Both term and preterm infants are at risk for morbidity and mortality, but the nature and the frequency of conditions varies.

Some infants are born with conditions that place them and their future development at risk. The purpose of this section is not to identify all such conditions, but rather to increase your awareness of them and to help you think about how these conditions will impact how you will educate and care for these infants and toddlers.

Birth weight and **gestational age** are used in determining neonatal risk. The preterm infant comes into the world at a disadvantage. The immature organs may not be ready to perform the necessary tasks of independent living. Neonates weighing less than 2,500 grams (5½ pounds) are considered *low birth weight (LBW)*; those weighing below 1,500 grams (3⅓ pounds) are *very low birth weight (VLBW)*; and below 1,000 grams (2¼ pounds) *extremely low birth weight (ELBW)*. See Table 7–2.

The relationship between gestational age and weight is an important one. Infants who are born **small for gestational age (SGA)** are particularly at risk. These are infants whose birth weight is below the 10th percentile for their gestational age. Infants below the fifth percentile are particularly at risk. The size of the infant indicates fetal growth retardation unless the infant is simply genetically small. An infant born at 40 weeks gestation age and weighing 4 pounds would be considered small for gestational age, as he ought to weigh about 7.5 pounds. If born at 34 weeks gestational age, he would just

TABLE 7-2 CLASSIFICATION OF NEWBORNS BY BIRTH WEIGHT

Grams	Pounds	Classification
2,500–4,000	5½ to 8¾	Typical birth weight
1,500–2,500	3⅓ to 5½	Low birth weight (LBW)
1,000–1,500	2¼ to 3⅓	Very low birth weight (VLBW)
Less than 1,000	Less than 2¼	Extremely low birth weight (ELBW)

be considered low birth weight and preterm, as his weight would be appropriate for his gestational age. About half of SGA infants are attributable to maternal illness, smoking, or malnutrition (Rais-Bahrami & Short, 2007). SGA infants are at greater risk for complications.

Preterm and Low-Birth-Weight Newborns

Thirteen percent of infants are born before 37 weeks and 8.1 percent are born weighing less than 5½ pounds (National Center for Health Statistics, 2007). Preterm births and low-birth-weight babies occur in 11 percent of all pregnancies, yet they account for the majority of **neonatal deaths** and almost half of all neurodevelopmental disabilities that are present at birth (Hoyert et al., 2001). These figures are not distributed equally: the percent of black low-weight births (13) is 72 percent higher than any other group and the infant mortality is almost double the national average (13) (Mathews & MacDorman, 2010). The most common causes for low-birth-weight newborns are maternal infections and adolescent mothers, or both (Rais-Bahrami & Short, 2007).

Being born too soon means that not all systems are ready. Premature infants face risks that other infants do not face. Their immature immune system makes them more susceptible to infection. They have problems regulating body temperature, coordinating sucking and swallowing, and absorbing nutrients; they may not breathe regularly, and their hearts may not beat rhythmically. They also look and sound different than term infants. They typically have fine hair, or *lanugo*, over their body (disappears by 38 weeks); their skin is more translucent and has a reddish tinge because the blood vessels are closer to the surface; and they may lack breast buds, skin creases, and cartilage in their ear lobes. They may be floppy because their muscle tone is not well developed. Preemies may appear passive and disorganized (Rais-Bahrami & Short, 2007).

RESPIRATORY PROBLEMS

A premature infant's respiratory system does not work as easily or predictably as that of term babies. Their lungs may not expand because of the lack of the chemical **surfactant**. Supplemental oxygen is given to infants until their system can produce enough surfactant. In more serious cases, infants are given surfactant replacement therapy, which works almost immediately (Rais-Bahrami & Short, 2007).

CARDIOVASCULAR PROBLEMS

For some premature infants, necessary changes in the circulatory system do not take place. One of the most important is the closure of the ductus arteriosus, which the fetal circulatory system used to bypass the lungs. In **patent ductus arteriosus**, which affects about 30 percent of premature newborns, this closure does not take place. A higher blood oxygen level stimulates closure, but if the premature infant has respiratory distress, the opening may not close. This exacerbates the problem of oxygenating the blood. Medication exists to stimulate closing of this duct (Rais-Bahrami & Short, 2007).

NEUROLOGICAL PROBLEMS

The preemie is also troubled by an immature central nervous system (CNS) that controls respiration and circulation. Getting oxygen into the lungs is a challenge. **Apnea** is a respiratory pause of 15 to 20 seconds; **bradycardia** is a fall in the heart rate to below 80 to 100 beats per minute. Apnea and bradycardia are problems for about 10 percent of low-birth-weight infants. The smaller the infant, the more likely the problem is to occur (Rais-Bahrami & Short, 2007). Although apnea of prematurity is not a major predisposing factor for SIDS, infants who have persistent episodes of apnea and bradycardia are sent home from the hospital on an **apnea monitor**. Theses monitors sound an alarm if the infant stops breathing.

IN THE FIELD

I had an emergency C-section and Harvey only weighed 5 pounds 2 ounces at birth. I was in my 34th week. He was in the neonatal intensive care unit for a week. We begged to bring him home. They finally agreed after we had taken a course in infant cardiopulmonary resuscitation, CPR. He came home with an apnea monitor. It has been a nightmare. I feel like I have my own little corner of the world. One of us sits here and watches him day and night. I watch during the day and we take three-hour shifts at night. We know we can't keep doing this, but now it is the only way we have any peace. I know the monitor would wake us up as it is loud, but it is so scary. What if we didn't wake up—what if we didn't get to him in time? I heard about a woman who took a shower and didn't hear the monitor; her baby died.

It goes off all the time, but then he starts to breathe again or his heart beats or whatever is supposed to happen does. Only once did we have to use CPR. They told us that he self-stimulates. I guess that means if his heart stops for too long, it will starts itself again. But the fear is always there, because he is connected to a machine. I can't decide whether it gives me comfort or anxiety.

Premature infants' blood vessels are very fragile. Problems occur when the blood vessels that go to the ventricles break. Most preemies have some degree of **intraventricular hemorrhage (IVH)** within a few hours after birth. Intraventricular hemorrhaging is bleeding into or near the normal fluid spaces (ventricles) of the brain. The lower the birth weight and the younger the gestational age, the greater the probability of hemorrhaging. When hemorrhaging is limited, there are no adverse outcomes. Severe hemorrhages lead to neurological impairment such as cerebral palsy and intellectual disability. Ultrasound is used to diagnose and classify intraventricular hemorrhage. Medication is used to reduce the incidence of IVH (Rais-Bahrami & Short, 2007).

OPHTHALMOLOGICAL PROBLEMS

Retinopathy of prematurity (ROP) occurs when abnormal blood vessels grow and spread throughout the **retina**, the tissue that lines the back of the eye. These fragile blood vessels can leak, scarring the retina and pulling it out of position, which causes the retina to detach, resulting in visual impairment and/or blindness. This occurs most frequently in newborns weighing 2¾ pounds or less (National Eye Institute, 2006).

GASTROINTESTINAL PROBLEMS

Many low-birth-weight babies cannot coordinate the sucking reflex and swallowing mechanism. This coordination is possible by about 32 weeks gestation. Before this, the infant wears himself out sucking without getting the necessary calories and nutrients. A special high-caloric formula or tube feeding may be used to help these babies. Some premature infants have a life-threatening intestinal disease called **necrotizing enterocolitis**, which may be cured by managing feeding and suctioning; however, in about half of the cases surgery is required to remove the diseased section of the bowel. Additionally, preemies often have problems with **gastroesophageal reflux**; the contents of their stomach regurgitates into the esophagus. Treatment involves medication and positioning the infant so his head is higher than his feet when sleeping (Rais-Bahrami & Short, 2007).

OTHER PHYSIOLOGICAL PROBLEMS

Some problems directly relate to prematurity; others relate to the infant herself. Preterm neonates are more susceptible to problems such as **hypothermia**, hypo- and hyperglycemia, **anemia**, and **jaundice**. Hypothermia occurs because the preemie does not have much subcutaneous fat and her higher ratio of body surface to body weight causes faster heat loss. Premature infants have smaller reserves of **glucose** (sugar), which puts them at risk for hypoglycemia. This may cause lethargy, vomiting, and seizures. These infants have early feedings, their glucose levels are monitored, and glucose may be administered intravenously. An immature liver may cause **bilirubin** to build up in her system, giving her a yellow, jaundiced appearance. Treatment involves phototherapy. The newborn's eyes are shielded and she is put under a light source. Anemia decreases the oxygen-carrying capacity of the red blood cells and may be treated by transfusion or medication (Rais-Bahrami & Short, 2007). Premature newborns are assessed to determine whether they could profit from early intervention and to help their parents understand their behavior.

Neonatal Assessment

The most widely used neonatal assessment tool is the Neonatal Behavioral Assessment Scale (NBAS) developed by T. Berry Brazelton in 1973, revised in 1984, and again in 1995 (Brazelton & Nugent, 1995). It is used with infants from the first day of life up to two months. The scale evaluates the infant's potential for self-organization and his ability to control his state of arousal (alertness) as a response to the environment. The NBAS focuses on four major areas: the **autonomic system**, the motor system, **state regulation**, and social interaction (Brazelton & Nugent, 2005).

The measure is based on several key assumptions:

- Newborns have nine months of experience to draw on.

- Infants are capable of controlling their behavior to respond to their environment.

- Infants communicate through their behavior.

• Infants are social beings who shape and are shaped by their caregiving environment (Brazelton & Nugent, 2005).

Unlike most previous measures, the NBAS is an interactive assessment, and the role of the examiner is to draw out the neonate's organizational skills and strengths. The emphasis is on establishing the newborn's capacities and limits, especially as they affect interactions with a caregiver. The infant's best scores are used, rather than his average performance. The examination takes 20 to 30 minutes and the examiner does the testing with the infant's parents or guardians, who help the examiner assess the infant's level of skill. The examiner must be knowledgeable about infants. The assessment assesses the infant's capabilities and determines whether she may need extra caregiving in some areas (Brazelton & Nugent, 2005).

Some of the first challenges newborns face are regulating their temperature, breathing, and other parts of the autonomic system. High-risk infants may spend most of their energy just doing this and not have energy left over for other developmental tasks. They may be overtaxed by noise and visual stimulation. Infants also need to inhibit random movements and control their activity level. Swaddling helps infants control random movements.

State regulation is the next challenge. **State** is the term used to describe levels of consciousness that range from quiet sleep to active crying. The ability of the infant to control her state determines how available she is to respond to her environment. The examiner looks at an infant's state, state changes, and the predominant state of the infant during the assessment process. Some infants can ignore stimulation or **habituate** to it. Caregivers must evaluate the environment and regulate the amount of stimulation if infants cannot.

Finally, the ultimate developmental task: social interaction. The examiner looks at how infants respond to faces, voices, and even a ball. Because the parents or guardians are

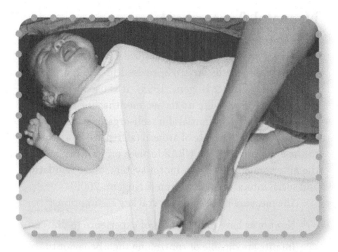

When infants get out of control and cannot calm themselves, swaddling helps them get organized and lowers their state of agitation.
Penny Low Deiner

present at the assessment, they see what their infant can do. The examiner gives them a profile of their infant that they can use to better care for her (Brazelton & Nugent, 2005).

Long-Term Implications of Prematurity

Medical risk factors are the best predictors of developmental risk during the first year, whereas environmental risk factors are more useful predictors at older ages. Socioeconomic factors have a significant impact on the predicted outcome for all at-risk infants. Problems of developmental delays and neurological problems are greater for very low-birth-weight infants whose mothers are 17 years or younger, have less than a high school education, and are not married, than for infants born to middle-class families with more resources (Moore, 2003). Limited parental resources (money, transportation, education, etc.) can exacerbate the problems of coping with a premature infant. In addition, premature and low-birth-weight infants have a far greater risk of being abused by parents or caregivers during childhood even when social class is held constant (Sullivan & Knutson, 2000).

The possibility of developmental delays also looms. Overall, there is a correlation between birth weight and developmental delay: the lower the birth weight, the greater the probability of a developmental delay. Delays are more likely to appear in the perceptual-motor areas than in verbal areas (Allen, 2002; Msall & Tremont, 2002). **Perceptual-motor development** is the ability to mentally organize and interpret sensory information and respond to it. Birth weight itself is not the major factor, but rather the complications such as hemorrhaging and other medical risk conditions.

Infants born prematurely typically develop at a rate based on their expected due date, not their birth date. Their motor skills lack the coordination of infants born at term. Most infants who weigh 3⅓ pounds or more at birth show few differences from their peers by age 5. The prognosis is not as positive for infants who were born very premature or those who weighed less than 3⅓ pounds. By age 2, some of these toddlers show signs of attention-deficit/hyperactivity disorder (ADHD) and language delays that are often precursors to learning and behavior problems. Infants born weighing less than 2¼ pounds are at even greater risk. Approximately a fourth of these children will be identified as having delays or developmental disabilities in intellectual and/or motor development (Rais-Bahrami & Short, 2007). Carefully assessing infants at risk over time, as well as working closely with their families, is necessary, because risk factors are cumulative and interactive. One must evaluate both the infant and the socioeconomic and familial factors that influence developmental outcomes. Without assessing biological and environmental factors, it is not possible to determine whether intervention will be helpful or appropriate.

Early intervention programs have positive effects on child outcome, but intervention is not a cure. Many children will continue to need speech and language therapy, special education, and supports for behavioral and emotional development through their school years to maintain gains from early intervention (Guralnick, 2005).

● ● ● Developmental Risk

Caution should be used before labeling a child as developmentally at risk, and when this labeling is used, it should consider not only the child, but the family as well. Before deciding that an infant is "at risk," it is important that the term be clarified and that parents understand the criteria used to determine risk and know how their child's situation will differ based on this label. As children change, grow, and develop, risk should be reevaluated.

The term *at risk* does not mean that a child will inevitably be delayed or affected, but rather that the probabilities are higher than normal. Children can be placed in this category because of biological conditions, the family in which they live, or the physical environment in which they are raised. Children with established biological problems (e.g., Down syndrome) and who may be functioning within the normal range at an early age are considered "at risk" for later developmental delays, because experience has shown that their rate of development will be slower.

Families have the potential for increasing or decreasing child risk. Families who abuse or neglect their infant or toddler put them at medical, psychological, and educational risk. Infants born prematurely and infants with disabilities are particularly vulnerable to abuse and neglect. On the other hand, families who love and respond to their infants, spend time playing with them in developmentally appropriate ways, and keep the infant safe and healthy decrease child risk.

Environments can also cause infants and toddlers to be at risk. Some environments are conducive for developing motor delays or patterns of behavior that make learning difficult. Substandard housing, crowded conditions compounded by poor nutrition, and lack of medical treatment increase the risk of developmental problems among young children. Environments that reduce risk are settings where infants and toddlers can safely and freely explore inside and outside, a wide selection of toys and materials are available for them to play with, and adults support and facilitate play and learning.

Experience and the Brain

At birth, the infant's brain is still under construction. As children grow, the number of neurons remains stable, but each one becomes bigger and heavier due to the increasing number of dendrites. The key task in early development is the growth of these connections in the brain. One neuron can connect to as many as 15,000 other neurons (Yaun & Keating, 2007). Experience is the architect that determines how blueprints are turned into reality. Brain development is an interplay between the genes the child was born with and the experiences he has. These early experiences shape not only the child's behavior, but also the architecture of the child's brain.

Unlike other primates, who are born with the brain more completely formed, three-quarters of the human brain develops outside the womb. This is both an asset and a liability. How the brain develops is based on the interplay of nature and nurture. It seems obvious that trauma, disease, and abuse and neglect can change the brain. However, positive influences can change the brain as well. An enriched, stimulating environment can change infants' brains not only in the area of cognitive development but in social development as well (Jensen, 2006).

> ▶❚❚ **TeachSource Video Case**
> **Piaget: Sensorimotor Stage**
> Watch the TeachSource Video *Piaget: Sensorimotor Stage*, after which you will be able to describe Piaget's sensorimotor stage. The video can be found in the Early Childhood Education Media Library under Child Development, available at www.cengagebrain.com.

The brain runs on **glucose**. Glucose is a simple sugar that cells use as a source of energy. Neurons cannot store glucose like body cells can. This is one of the reasons children's eating breakfast is related to school performance. Between birth and age 4, the cerebral cortex's use of glucose rises to more than twice the level of adults' brains and stays that way for 10 years (Chugani, 1998). Young children also have higher levels of some neurotransmitters. Children are biologically primed to learn. Some areas of their brains are getting hardwired. The brain responds constantly and swiftly to conditions that promote (or inhibit) learning. Brain activity surges when a child addresses a difficult problem, but it is virtually nondetectable when a problem is easily solved (Shore, 1997). Increased metabolic activity in the frontal cortex during the second half of the first year coincides with the ability of the infant to form attachments.

The process of connecting and strengthening neurons takes place after birth. The brain's ability to change and recover lost functions is remarkable during the first 10 years of life. The brain develops sequentially, so the connections that are necessary to process basic information are wired before the connections that allow more complex information to be processed. If basic connections are not wired properly, higher levels of learning are more difficult (Zero to Three, 2008). Early intervention takes advantage of the brain's development and plasticity. These are prime times for optimal development as the brain is particularly efficient at specific types of learning. In physiological terms, there are times when the brain's neurons create synapses more efficiently and more easily than at other times. This requires not only energy and neurotransmitters but also space.

The young child's brain has amazing plasticity, or **malleability**; that is, if one area of the brain is damaged another part may be able to take over the function. For example, if a young child loses her language skills due to a stroke, she may recover these language skills, because the brain cells move this function to another area of the brain. This is more likely in a younger brain than an older one. In a young brain, there are areas of the brain that are not yet committed to a particular function. There is an overproduction of synapses that are not in use and not yet designated for a particular use (Jensen, 2006).

Although we use the plasticity of the brain to enhance the development of children, negative early relationships can lead to a lifelong limited ability to regulate the intensity, frequency, and duration of primitive states such as rage, terror, and shame and are related to antisocial behavior and personality disorders. Factors that increase the activity or reactivity of the brainstem (chronic stress) or decrease the moderating capacity of the limbic or cortical areas (neglect) will increase the child's aggressiveness, impulsivity, and capacity to display violence. Violent behavior is most likely to occur when there is lack of stimulation to the cortex and overstimulation of the limbic system. Brief stress challenges infants to cope and learn self-regulation; repeated exposure to overwhelming stress damages the developing brain (Zero to Three, 2008). Knowing how the brain develops helps you plan better and more effective activities and learning environments.

IMPLICATIONS FOR EDUCATORS

Early intervention is based on the malleability of the brain and methods of changing neural pathways to benefit children. To get the brain to pay attention, we must teach in a way that is congruent with positive brain development.

- Children must be active participants in their learning. (The brain doesn't change from observation.)
- Experiences must be novel, challenging, and meaningful for children to learn. (The brain doesn't change by repeating what children already know, meaningless experiences do not produce change.)
- Experiences must have both complexity and coherence. (The brain doesn't change from chaos or boring experiences.)
- Children need to strive for attainable goals. (The brain does not form new synapses when uncomfortable and overwhelmed.)

A trip to the beach provides a variety of interesting and novel sensory experiences for young children who grow up in urban areas.
Penny Low Deiner

- Children learn in the context of positive social relationships. (Unsafe environments cause the brain to be overvigilant and develop synapses that do not support learning.)
- Children need good nutrition to grow their bodies and their brains. (Too little or too much food is not good for the brain.)
- Children need time and repetition with minor variations. (The brain rarely changes by just one experience unless the experience is traumatic.) (Jensen, 2006).

The potential for early intervention is high. Individual experiences specifically designed for young children can help them develop new capacities and change their brain. Using the principles given, think about how you could design an experience for a child that you think will change his brain. Start small: look at what the child is playing with and decide what you could do to add a novel touch. You can and will make a significant difference in children's brains. Identifying and working with children who need additional support during early childhood and working within these prime times can and does make a difference.

Early Learning Guidelines

Early learning guidelines, or learning standards, describe what infants and toddlers should know and be able to do during specified age ranges. Early learning guidelines (ELG) have the potential for optimizing development by creating awareness about the importance of the first three years and by helping parents and caregivers understand the processes underlying development (Gebhard, 2010). Infant and Toddler Guidelines should align vertically with pre-K and K–12 content standards in a way that highlights the foundational aspects of learning in the first three years. This alignment should not be viewed as a push down of content standards, but rather a building up. They should align horizontally with the standards in the assessment system. Guidelines are not a curriculum, but they should align with curriculum. Almost all states (85%) focus on common developmental domains: social and emotional, language and communication, cognitive development and general knowledge, physical development and motor skills, and approaches to play and learning (Petersen, Jones, McGinley, 2008). This text uses these domains to organize the activities in Resource Chapter 6.

Within these broad developmental domains, learning expectations or benchmarks must be defined to ensure that infants and toddlers are progressing. Benchmarks are more specific and move beyond traditional milestones such as first steps and first words. They should be written in a way that is meaningful to diverse cultural, ethnic, and linguistic populations and be inclusive of children with special needs. The learning expectations should have discrete and observable indicators and be clearly stated (Petersen et al., 2008). States are in the process of developing Quality Rating and Improvement Systems (QRIS), and many are finding ways to embed the early learning guidelines into this system (Gebhard, 2010).

Curriculum for Infants and Toddlers

DAP Because infants and toddlers change and grow so quickly, their curriculum must change and grow with them. There are no agreed-upon national standards for the number or age groups for children from birth to 3 years. The goal of all such divisions is to divide infants and toddlers into age groups based on meaningful criteria. Different organizations divide them up differently; some use a single grouping (birth to 36 months). Others, such as the National Association for the Education of Young Children (Copple & Bredekamp, 2009) and Zero to Three (2008), use three overlapping groups to guide the curriculum. This text uses their guidelines.

- Young Infants: Birth to 9 months
- Mobile Infants: 8 to 18 months
- Toddlers: 16 to 36 months

From birth until about 9 months, the focus is on developing a sense of security. With mobile infants (8 to 18 months), internal needs focus on moving and exploration. Between 16 and 36 months, the toddlers' need to explore is replaced by a drive to define the self. "Interactions and negotiations with others lead to learning about themselves as independent, dependent and interdependent beings" (Lally & Mangione, 2006, p. 17). The role of the educator and interventionist must change with the infants' development. With toddlers, the adults' role is setting boundaries to help them learn about themselves and the societal rules that govern interactions. Adults must be supportive while providing security for the toddler and enforcing boundaries that are set.

Including Young Infants: Birth to 9 Months

Young infants need to feel secure and to build a base of predictable, warm, loving relationships to support their exploration and learning (Zero to Three, 2008). Experiences and materials for very young infants are chosen because they are interesting to look at or listen to. By about 2 to 3 months, infants begin to reach for and grasp small toys. For infants older than 3 months, materials and experiences are designed to withstand active exploration, particularly mouthing, as well as constant washing. For infants to practice skills, having a variety of similar toys is helpful, and varying their use is the key for planning. Observe infants and respond to their changing skills.

The nonmobile infant is dependent on the adults in her environment to choose developmentally appropriate experiences. Planning is very individualized and developmentally based. Activities, usually one-on-one, are planned for a particular infant, and are executed when that infant is interested. Because of the individualistic nature of planning, including young infants with disabilities requires few adaptations. Infants have such a small repertoire of behaviors that a single activity with variations can be repeated until the infant reaches another developmental level. For example, Activity 6–2, *Tummy Time*, can be repeated many times, simply by carrying the infant in different ways and pointing out different sights.

Planning for young infants is more holistic than planning for older children. Their ability to attend to a task is dependent on their state, and your ability to choose the appropriate time and activity to engage them. The ability to excel as a teacher is dependent on accurate observations of the infant, knowledge of development, and the ability to bring these two sets of information together. Figure 7–1 depicts this process of materials-methods interaction, part of how you teach young infants.

The best materials are those that encourage active involvement of the infant. Active involvement differs; just looking is active involvement for a very young infant, but not for an older infant. Many interventions for infants are variations on caregiving routines or are implemented during routines. Build interventions into routines. It is important to think of routines as teaching opportunities and to vary them; otherwise care can become solely custodial.

Routines are events that must be completed on a regular basis and often involve a series of responses (Ostrosky et al., n.d.). Much of the time spent providing care to infants is made up of important and essential routines such as changing diapers, preparing meals, giving bottles, or helping infants settle down for a nap. These routines offer important opportunities for spending time individually with an infant and provide chances to communicate how much you like that infant by making eye contact, talking, singing, imitating the infant's sounds, or saying nursery rhymes. Routines give infants a sense of security and trust, as their most basic needs are met in a consistent and caring manner. Routines are part of the learning environment. If infants have an individualized family service plan (IFSP), the goals

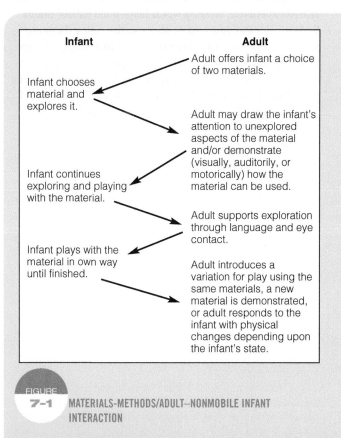

FIGURE 7-1 MATERIALS-METHODS/ADULT–NONMOBILE INFANT INTERACTION

for the infant should be planned for and incorporated into routines. Tying intervention to routines ensures that there are many opportunities during the day for intervention to occur.

The learning environment changes during the day as infants are picked up and carried, rocked in a rocking chair, walked outside in a stroller, set to bask on a blanket in the shade, or play on a floor. Their environment should contain both soft and hard elements, such as pillows and mirrors. Infants like bright, high-contrast colors and interesting patterns to look at. They need cheerful, friendly pictures of infants, children, and adults hung at different levels. The learning environment should include equipment and materials that are developmentally appropriate, and these materials should be organized in a useful way so that they are readily available, but rotated so they are not all out at once.

The interaction of development, experiences, and learning is the foundation for planning for young infants. The infant's development is the given; the adult selects experiences or activities within the infant's **zone of proximal development**, and when the match is accurate, learning takes place. This learning is then "grooved" to a level of mastery through variations of the experiences, and new and more complex experiences are introduced with adult scaffolding.

Adults must choose appropriate materials to support infant learning. Young infants need materials of different textures, colors, weights, and sizes and that can be held, dropped, thrown, mouthed, and shaken. They also need books and an adult to read to them. Reading is a wonderful shared experience. Hearing words helps build babies' brains. Cuddle babies as you read to them as this helps them connect your voice and the closeness of you to reading. Choose books about familiar routines with simple repetitive phrases or words. Choose vinyl or cloth books with few objects on a page. Expect that they will be grabbed, chewed, and dropped and that they will need to be disinfected regularly.

IMPLICATIONS FOR EDUCATORS

If you want to play with a 6-month-old infant, start by observing him. He is sitting on the floor and you notice that he looks at a particular toy. Voila! You get the toy and hold it slightly out of reach (motor). You encourage him to reach for it. Tell him what it is (cognitive) and verbally support his exploration of the toy (language). When he tires of the toy, show him a different way to use it (cognitive). He led; you followed (social).

Think about the process you used. You did not expect him to get the toy because you knew he could not crawl yet, but his sitting was stable enough that he could lean, reach, and manipulate the toy (physical/motor). You supported his choice of object and you provided him with experiences responsive to his interests (emotional). You encouraged his exploration by talking about what he was doing (language) and provided additional ways to play, which enriched his cognitive experience. Reflect on how this interaction is respectful and responsive to infants' development. Think about the types of interactions that are intrusive. How would you expect infants to respond to these?

Now, look at the activities in Resource Chapter 6. Choose one based on your knowledge of what infants can and like to do. Try it out. Challenge yourself to think of variations for tummy time. Also think about how much time infants are spending in car seats, swings, and other "containers." What can you do to decontainerize these infants and support their development?

●●●
Including Mobile Infants: 8 to 18 Months

Planning for mobile infants is different from planning for either young infants or toddlers. Mobile infants want to explore, investigate, and experiment! Developmental milestones emphatically mark this transitional time: the first step and the first word! Mobile infants have a growing sense of self and an increased interest in their peers. However, they also have a strong attachment to the adults they love and may feel vulnerable when they are gone (Zero to Three, 2008). They are interested in listening to adult language but may not be happy around unfamiliar adults. These powerful feelings reflect their new levels of understanding and knowledge. Sitting is old hat; creeping and standing are replacing crawling. Walking is emerging, to be followed by the infant's version of running.

Receptive language far outstrips expressive language. Mobile infants are moving from one- to two-word utterances, and their vocabulary is increasing. There are often long babbled sentences that "ought" to make sense, but it is as if they are in a different language. Adaptive skills are emerging as children want to dress and feed themselves—although they may be happier undressed, and self-feeding is often messy. Emotions are becoming more specific. There are smiles and hugs for affection, anxiety at separation, and anger at people and objects that do not do what they are "supposed" to do.

Mobile infants have a heightened awareness of the world around them and the ability to explore more of that world, but they lack experience. Planning concentrates on the consolidation of emerging skills and building a foundation of trust in the world around them. Adults are responsible for setting the stage for mobile infants' play. To provide quality play experiences, adults must arrange time, space, materials, and preparatory experiences. Mobile infants need space to play in order to practice emerging large-motor skills. A good program has areas for mobile infants to create messy art work, a dramatic play corner for simple familiar play (variations on housekeeping), a block corner for constructive play, a cozy book and language area for quiet reading, a fine motor manipulative area, and a sensory area for exploring the properties of materials.

Mobile infants need a combination of materials and experiences that are nearby. Toys should be arranged on low shelves so they can go to them and choose the ones that attract them. Be sure that toys are accessible, as mobile infants will creep to an area, sit, make a choice, and then play. Be prepared that this process may be repeated several minutes later (if that long). When the infant initiates the choice of materials, play will probably take place on the floor; if an adult prepares an experience, older infants may be at a low table, but it should be their choice to be there.

Mobile infants learn through active exploration of materials and objects. They learn using all their senses. They continuously absorb the sights and sounds of the world around them, whether events are planned or happen spontaneously. Building on what they have previously learned, they add new ideas, words, and thoughts. This building process results in learning when adults provide the scaffolding.

Mobile infants need more than nice toys and equipment to play with. They need to have warm, caring interactions with adults. Knowledgeable adults join the infant's play and expand it through imitation, modeling, and scaffolding. They demonstrate and talk about cause and effect. If a mobile infant is using playdough, the adult might expand the play by initially manipulating the playdough and then making a pancake, snake, or little balls out of it. The infant can decide whether to add these actions to his repertoire of playdough behaviors.

Read to infants. The more stories they hear, the more words they will have been exposed to, the more resources they will have as they begin to talk, and the more interest they will have in learning to read themselves. Mobile infants may have definite book preferences. They are interested in turning the pages and may start pointing to objects. Board books are a good addition. Choose interactive books that have mirrors, fur, or other interesting textures. Choose simple repetitive texts with clear realistic pictures or photographs. If you have baskets of toys children can play with, be sure to add some sturdy books.

IMPLICATIONS FOR EDUCATORS

Encourage mobile infants to interact with each other. Their concept of interaction may differ from your expectations, but allow infants to explore. Your role is to keep the interactions positive and support the achievements of all infants. Model appropriate behavior for mobile infants, and encourage empathy and prosocial behaviors in children, enlisting these methods:

- Say the infant's name. This serves as a marker for getting her attention. Then tell her what she has done in short, simple language, and that it pleases you.
- Be responsive to cues from mobile infants that indicate understanding, interest, frustration, or fatigue.
- Provide many opportunities to manipulate and explore objects and materials. Give mobile infants time to explore materials before expecting them to use the materials.
- Provide experiences that are developmentally appropriate for the skills and goals of each mobile infant.

● ● ●

Including Toddlers: 16 to 36 Months

With predictable mobility, mobile infants move into toddlerhood. Toddlers are focused on understanding who they are. Developing their sense of self has them using their communication skills to assert their independence and establish control of their world. They begin to pick up cultural messages about who they are and how they are both different and the same as others (Zero to Three, 2008). Other changes that occur between 16 and 36 months are also dramatic. Toddlers move from tentative walking to running, climbing, jumping, and twirling around. They learn to throw and sometimes catch a ball, to pick up small objects with their fingers, to scribble, and to feed themselves. They learn to

dress themselves in clothing that is easy to put on and take off, and most learn to use the toilet. They can talk and are learning to share and take turns. They know they can impact their world, and they want to. Most of all, they are learning about themselves.

Toddlers use two-word phrases and finally full sentences. By their second year, most toddlers are capable of holding conversations with adults. With the advent of language skills, play becomes richer and more imaginative. They begin to "pretend play" with toys and imitate the adults in their world, often playing "Mommy" or "Daddy." They begin to understand themselves as separate individuals with rights and privileges; however, they are only beginning to see that others have these same rights. They are more aware of their own feelings than the feelings of others. This is the stage of increasing independence and possessiveness. You'll hear exclamations such as "Mine!" and "Me do it!" and "No!" as children try to assert control over their environment. They notice other children in their world and struggle with building social play skills; they are sometimes eager to share toys with another child and sometimes hoard all the toys.

Toddlers are emotional beings who are learning to identify, label, and demonstrate their feelings. They display a range of emotions, from pure delight to utter frustration and sadness, from open curiosity and gregariousness to extreme shyness, from happy cooperation to obstinate noncompliance, and from tender love to hurtful anger. Physical development has slowed down, but language, cognitive, social, and emotional developments are in full swing. It is a period of rapid changes and amazing growth. Toddlers need adults who can accept the inconsistencies in their behavior with loving care and serenity.

Toddlers are challenging to adults in different ways than infants. Some adults feel very comfortable working with toddlers, watching a person unfold and develop, with all of the trials and tribulations that are inherent in the process. Others prefer to care for infants; they like the dependency of children of this age more than the budding autonomy of toddlerhood.

Planning curriculum and setting up learning environments for toddlers is different from planning for young or mobile infants. Although developmentally based, planning for toddlers is typically experience related and organized along more traditional subject matter. A good toddler curriculum provides toddlers with choices of experiences. Toddlers play with what interests them at any given moment and might reject a particular experience an adult has planned. If given choices, the toddler can choose the toys or materials she wants to play with from the preselected, developmentally appropriate experiences the adult provides. This is most easily accomplished by having low open shelves with safe toys that toddlers can use. Choices also provide toddlers with the opportunity to assert their independence and autonomy. Choosing for oneself builds self-esteem.

Good toddler curriculum provides experiences that are self-paced and open-ended. A toddler is finished playing when he wants to leave an area. Forcing or coaxing a toddler to "finish" his art project only causes frustration for the adult and the toddler. Toddlers have different interests and attention spans. Some toddlers paint for 20 minutes; others, for 20 seconds. The same toddler might paint for a long time one day and not show any interest in painting the next.

Reading and experiences with books should happen every day. Reading to toddlers builds the foundational skills for later independent reading. Reading to toddlers expands their vocabulary and helps them connect letters to sounds and to understand that letters can represent words. When you read, do it expressively, dramatically. Talk about the illustrations, and ask toddlers questions about the characters in the story and the plot. Some teachers use reading as a large group experience, whereas others prefer it as a small group time. Listening is not easy for toddlers. The goal is for them to love books and to want to read independently and it is often easier to be positive and supportive of toddlers in a small group. Fingerplays and music can work well with a large group of toddlers because they are actively involved.

Music is part of the toddlers' world. It is fun and requires props. Because music uses many different parts of the brain, it forges neural pathways and supports the development of reading and math. Use short songs that are repetitive and some that have hand motions to go with them. Include instruments such as bells, rattles, and tambourines. Music can make transitions easier. The National Association for Music Education (2008) has developed content standards for children 2 to 4 years:

- Singing and playing instruments
- Creating music
- Responding to music
- Understanding music

Young toddlers are building a mathematics vocabulary and understand concepts such as "more." Although they can say numbers, the sequence might not be accurate, and their understanding of the meaning of numbers needs practice. Ask children to give you a specific number of blocks (1 to 5), and then identify what you have been given. Make it a game. Count with children while they walk or go up and down steps. Sing counting songs. Encourage children to stack blocks and use simple puzzles. Use words like *big* and *little* and *fast* and *slow*. Encourage toddlers to order objects by size and match by shape.

> **TeachSource Video Case**
> **Infants and Toddlers: Cognitive Development and Imaginative Play**
> Watch the TeachSource Video *Infants and Toddlers: Cognitive Development and Imaginative Play*, which demonstrates ways in which children's cognitive development begins to take shape, through imaginative play with various objects and play scenario. The video can be found in the Early Childhood Education Media Library under Child Development, available at www.cengagebrain.com.

IMPLICATIONS FOR EDUCATORS

Toddlers learn through sensory, creative, physical, and problem-solving experiences. Experiences are the building blocks of planning. As you think about experiences, consider areas of development and how these can be incorporated into your plan in a developmentally appropriate way. One way to do this is to label the different areas of the room, for example, dramatic play or language arts. Allocate space for sensory play, easel painting, creative arts, playdough, simple dramatic play, books, blocks, music, language, and manipulative experiences. There should be enough materials for toddlers to use without causing undue frustrations; that is, there should be at least duplicates of popular toys and enough other materials so sharing is not a problem. Some things toddlers need are listed here:

- Warm, personal contact with adults (verbal and nonverbal) who are active, enthusiastic, and enjoy playing with toddlers
- Experiences that are mostly self-directed and a few that are teacher directed, including active physical play
- A comprehensive program that includes developmentally appropriate experiences that meet the interests of individual children as well as the group. Planning includes physical, emotional, social, language, creative, sensory, and cognitive areas of development
- A regular and stable schedule that allows for flexibility in meeting the needs of toddlers, including planned times for quiet and active periods
- Consistent rules and guidance techniques that preserve self-esteem
- Opportunities to play alone, near peers, with peers, and with adults
- A safe classroom environment that encourages active play

Including Infants and Toddlers with Delays and Disabilities

Some infants are vulnerable because of their environment or their biological makeup. Infants born to parents living in poverty, those born prematurely, and those who do not weigh enough are at risk for developmental disabilities (Guralnick, 2004). Some infants are doubly vulnerable, as they have identified disabilities and other risk factors.

States differ in the eligibility criteria they use for early intervention services. We classify infants as having a developmental delay rather than trying to pinpoint a specific disability unless a specific disability is apparent such as Down syndrome. Unless the infant is being monitored because of risk factors, or the delay is serious, it is unlikely that an infant will be identified before 9 months. It is often unclear whether delayed development is just an individual growth pattern and the infant will "catch up" in his own time or whether the delay is of a more permanent nature. However, if an infant cannot hold his head up when on his tummy or cannot push up with his arms by 3 months, encourage parents to consult their pediatrician or contact the local Child Find. Infants identified as having a developmental delay can have an early intervention team and an IFSP. This team provides guidance in planning for these infants.

Toddlers are becoming aware of the ways in which they are similar to and different from each other. It is the skill of a sensitive teacher that determines the long-term outcome of this awareness. Children look to you as a model. Examine your feelings about including young children with disabilities in early childhood programs. Also, reflect on your feelings about having children from different ethnic, racial, and language backgrounds, and your expectations based on gender, to discover whether you have personal values that might make working with some children difficult and that you need to reexamine.

If you pity toddlers with disabilities or are overprotective or condescending toward them, the other children will react the same way. If you celebrate only holidays that a majority of the children share, then those who have different beliefs may feel excluded. If you always choose boys to go to the block area and expect girls to use the dramatic play area, you are supporting stereotypic gender differences. Awareness is important for *all* children. Toddlers are egocentric. They need support in viewing events from another's perspective.

Adults can successfully facilitate the inclusion of infants and toddlers with disabilities into their programs if they plan to meet the individual needs of all the children in their group. Sometimes special toys or materials are needed to support a toddler with a disability in learning a new skill. Often, all the children in the program can use the special toys. By including young children with disabilities in a setting, there is potential gain for all children.

● ● ●
Infants and Toddlers with Developmental Delays and Intellectual Disabilities

For infants and toddlers the category of developmental delays is a broad one and will include some children who will later be identified as having other disabilities and some whose development has moved into the typical category.

YOUNG INFANT: BIRTH TO 9 MONTHS

Early intervention can change the trajectory of development, and it begins shortly after birth with disorders such as Down syndrome or fetal alcohol syndrome. Accommodations are easy to implement because working with infants is so individualized. Early intervention increases the probability that low birth weight and premature infants will catch up to their peers. Use infants' adjusted age for planning. A 5-month-old who was born two months prematurely is appropriately planned for as a 3-month-old infant.

Infants born prematurely have an especially limited repertoire of skills, so having a variety of materials at the same developmental level is important. Although many low-birth-weight infants catch up with their peers, at this young age there are predictable differences. The cues that these infants give are often subtle. With practice, these can be interpreted and responded to.

- Provide a visually stimulating environment, particularly mobiles, until the infant begins reaching and grasping. (Watch the infant—what is stimulating to some is overstimulating to others.)

- Monitor premature infants' level of stimulation. An active early care and education setting may tax their system. If infants become fussy and irritable, try less, as opposed to more, stimulation, decreasing it as much as you can. Swaddling is a good way to help them get organized.

- Use variation and repetition of experiences, especially those that intrigue the infant; it is likely to take these infants longer to "groove" an idea or skill.

- Help premature infants establish a pattern of wake and sleep.

- Help disorganized premature infants become more organized. Remember they often cry six hours a day. (Full-term newborns cry two to three hours a day for several months.) Colicky crying typically begins right after feeding, and frequent burping helps. Random patterns of crying are difficult to interpret. They may be just a discharge of excess energy, boredom, or overstimulation.

- Encourage the efforts that all infants make.

MOBILE INFANTS: 8 TO 18 MONTHS

With increasing age, differences among infants become more apparent especially in the motor and language areas. Infants with developmental delays may have deficits in a variety of areas so that a particular disability is not yet apparent. Mobile infants with intellectual disabilities may also have deficits in other areas, but it is clear that intellectual functioning will be involved. Some modifications in your planning and activities are required, but these are minor and usually easy adaptations. Depending upon the specific infant, you will want to emphasize some areas more than you do for other infants. Embedding these needed skills into routines ensures that they are taught.

- Use simple, direct language and directions.

- Break down difficult activities into small steps. (For example, if you are playing with pop beads, start with two and see whether the infant can pull them apart. It is far easier to pull them apart than to put them together.)

- Model what you want the infant to do. Then give her a turn and support her attempts at imitating you. Reflect on her response and decide how effective your scaffolding was. That will determine your next response.

- Emerging skills need to be honed by working on variations of that skill. If the infant has learned to roll an orange rubber ball, then have her roll a tennis ball, a wiffle ball, a yarn ball, a soccer ball, a football, a beach ball, and any other balls you have.

- Keep activities short. Infants with developmental delays have short attention spans and need more support and redirection. They may need more cues to interact with materials.

TODDLERS: 16 TO 36 MONTHS

Involve toddlers actively in the learning process, but expect to repeat this process with variations many times for learning to take place. Have toddlers crawl *under* the table when you are teaching that concept. When a toddler is using an obstacle course, point out that he is *under* the ladder. You may need to use more direct teaching rather than assuming the toddler will discover what to do or learn from observing others, and provide additional scaffolding.

- Keep a consistent daily schedule so toddlers will know what will happen next. Provide a picture chart to support the schedule.

- Limit choices to two or three experiences during free play, or provide some guidance in choosing appropriate experiences.

- Add cues such as carpet squares to indicate where toddlers should sit.

- Provide safe outlets for the release of excess energy and feelings. Toddlers may need punching bags, dance parties, or silly time to use up excess energy.

- Sequence tasks from easy to hard to match the toddler's developmental level. Use **backward chaining** where appropriate.

- Be specific about rules for experiences and post these with pictures. Show the toddlers the rules as well as telling them.

- Toddlers with developmental delays may have a limited repertoire of behaviors, and modeling can increase this repertoire. Point out the salient features you want them to attend to.

- Help toddlers organize their experiences. For example say, "What will you do first?" and "What comes next?"

Infants and Toddlers with Mental Health Challenges

Infants with social and emotional disorders cover a broad area, and with young children it is sometimes difficult to accurately identify all of the important variables. These problems and disorders fit in the broad area of infant mental health and at these ages are frequently related to attachment, sensory integration, and self-regulation. Experts in infant mental health recommend that infants and toddlers be referred for mental health services if their behavior:

- Has changed markedly or the child has become difficult.

- Makes positive satisfying interactions with others difficult.

- Takes place in multiple places and is observed by multiple people.

- Persists over a long time (Parlakian & Seibel, 2002).

YOUNG INFANTS: BIRTH TO 9 MONTHS

Developing secure long-term relationships helps infants feel safe and emotionally secure. When infants do not develop this sense of security, it may manifest in feeding or sleeping issues, lack of attachment, or inappropriate response to touch. These infants may cry more and be more difficult to comfort or not make eye contact, and generally seem unhappy. They may truly be.

- Help infants develop secure relationships with their caregivers.

- Actively explore the types of problems infants may be having, from allergic reactions to formula and gastrointestinal reflux, to living in an environment where their needs are not being met either physically or emotionally.

- Look into both internal and external sources of stress and do what you can to decrease the stress.

MOBILE INFANTS: 8 TO 18 MONTHS

Secure relationships give mobile infants the curiosity to explore their world. Sometimes sensory input makes this difficult. The goal of programming is to identify an infant's internal response to sensory input and then to program in a way that is compatible with their internal being. Children can have either high or low sensory thresholds and, within these limits, some overreact to small stimuli, whereas other children try to avoid stimulation. Consult with families, a psychologist, and/or an occupational therapist on the best ways to adapt programming to include mobile infants with mental health challenges in your program. Look at the "goodness of fit" between the child's needs and your environment (Williamson & Anzalone, 2001).

- For mobile infants with a very low threshold for sensory input, the littlest thing can bother them, such as a tag in their clothing. They are distractible, their affect is often negative, and they may be impulsive. If a child is overly sensitive to stimuli, evaluate your environment in this respect. A loud heating and cooling system or other children playing noisily may disturb mobile infants with this type of social-emotional disorder.

- Other mobile infants with low thresholds for stimuli may try to avoid sensory input. They are often quiet and hypervigilant, scanning the environment for someone who might come too close or touch them. Respect the infant's concerns and create areas that are safe for him to play in without other children getting in his space. Be sure to find ways of letting this infant know you like him. Verbal support such as saying "Brett, I'm glad to see you this morning" is wiser than a hug. When you do touch the infant, do it firmly.

- Some infants have high thresholds of arousal. These mobile infants may be difficult to arouse and may miss opportunities because they do not engage. Their affect may appear flat or depressed. We often miss these infants because they are "good." A light touch may alert these infants. Loud music with a varied intensity might get their attention as well.

- Other infants with high thresholds seek sensory input. They may be impulsive and take risks for the sensory feedback. They can become overexcited. These are the mobile infants who pull up on shelving, not to see what is on the shelf, but to get to the top. For these children, classical music is a good choice, and swinging and rhythmic rocking decrease stimulation. A pacifier also can decrease sensory input.

Mobile infants desire different levels of sensory input. Decrease the sensory input if infants become concerned.
© Cengage Learning 2012

Identifying mobile infants and meeting their needs is a challenge and takes skill. Too often, these children are not identified as having a genuine problem, but are seen as unusual or difficult children.

IN THE FIELD

Laura had difficulties with feedings around 3 weeks of age. She would cry for food and then when drinking her bottle, she would scream and claw at the bottle as if in extreme pain. My husband and I took her to the doctor who diagnosed Laura with gastrointestinal reflux. The solution was to hold her high on an incline when feeding her, give gas relief drops, and try to get as much air out of the bottle as possible before feeding. This alleviated some of the crying, but not all.

She continued to cry while eating for six more weeks. This was extremely stressful to me. Listening to her cry for hours on end was frustrating and anguishing because I could not do anything about it. She hurt, so I hurt. When she began eating solid foods, she no longer cried when drinking her formula, but now made strange noises when eating the baby foods. The noises sounded as if she were not enjoying the food, but she never made any gestures to avoid the food or refused to eat it. This continued from when she was around 6 months old to a little over 2 years of age. I think there was something else going on. I attribute this behavior to her having sensory integration issues. She had problems with loud noises and too many people in one room. She had extreme responses to new and different environments and adults she didn't know getting too close to her. Her response would be to cry and try to escape. This was difficult for both of us.

TODDLERS: 16 TO 36 MONTHS

Toddlers who do not have healthy early relationships may seem lethargic and show flat affect, they may "self-stimulate" (for example, rocking back and forth for sensory input). Some toddlers may become aggressive and hit or bite others without provocation. A predictable, safe environment helps toddlers become better organized and provides stability. Toddlers need adult support, warmth, and attention. They may have the same problems as mobile infants, related to sensory integration and self-regulation.

- Provide toddlers with many opportunities to run, jump, climb, and swing in a secure environment.

- Develop, with the parents, a consistent plan for handling disruptions and targeting behaviors to concentrate on.

- Give toddlers positive feedback and help them develop the skills necessary to enter small groups and play with others.

• • • Infants and Toddlers Who Are English Language Learners

A child's sense of identity evolves from his cultural background. The infant's first language, or home language, is the language that the infant heard and overheard her parents speak before and after her birth (Genesse, Paradis, & Crago, 2004). Infants and toddlers exposed to two languages at the same time are called **dual-language learners** (Genesse et al., 2004).

YOUNG INFANTS: BIRTH TO 9 MONTHS

Young infants depend upon familiar schedules, routines, and relationships to feel safe. To the extent that these are extremely different, infants can become confused and disorganized. Creating some level of continuity is important, and yet challenging, when the infant's home language is not English. It is more of a challenge when neither the parents nor the caregivers are fluent in a common language. In situations where many infants come from homes where the caregivers do not speak English, it is imperative to have at least one child care teacher who speaks the home language. Although it is helpful to send important information home in both English and the home language, it may not be possible. Additionally, adults may not be literate in either their home language or English.

- Find out about the infant's routines at home and, if possible, ensure there is continuity between home, early care and education, and/or intervention settings.

- Be honest about your desire to communicate with families and be creative about making this happen. Find out from parents what works for them.

- Use photographs and videotapes of the infant or toddler to enhance communication.

- Celebrate the ways in which infants and families are alike and different.

MOBILE INFANTS: 8 TO 18 MONTHS

Locomotion makes all infants able to explore their world. This provides greater potential for learning as well as greater challenges. If families are recent immigrants to the United States, they may have come from regions where the threats to a mobile infant's safety were very different. Mobile infants in immigrant families are more likely to live in crowded housing (more than one person per room) and in households that include people in addition to their parents and siblings (Hernandez, 2004). Crowded conditions may make it difficult for mobile infants to explore their environment safely.

Evaluate the learning environment to ensure it is supportive of the children in the setting. The early childhood classroom provides messages about what the program values and who is valued, from what hangs on the walls to the experiences educators offer. Bilingual/bicultural teachers are a tremendous asset in language learning and in communicating with families. Research supports infants' ability to learn two languages simultaneously. Settings make choices about supporting second language learning, depending on the goals and philosophy of the program and available resources (human and material).

- Provide information about childproofing environments and child safety for mobile infants.
- Ensure that mobile infants are encouraged to explore their environment. Provide safe places to crawl, creep, and explore.
- Play CDs that celebrate different cultures, languages, and styles of music.
- Sing songs and use fingerplays in the language of the infants in the setting.
- Develop effective ways to communicate with families. This may include sharing photographs as a method of communication and assessment.

TODDLERS: 16 TO 36 MONTHS

As mobile infants move into toddlerhood, language becomes a more important vehicle for communication and learning. Supporting early language learning is an important aspect of all early childhood programs. When toddlers are learning two languages, the process is more challenging, but also more rewarding. How this process actually works is dependent on how particular programs are set up. In some settings, toddlers spend their day in an environment where the second language is used. Depending on the multicultural commitment of the program, there may be few cultural supports for children whose first language is not English. This situation is both stressful for toddlers and not supportive of the home language; it devalues the home language. Culture and language are part of the curriculum for toddlers.

Ideally, programs have bilingual educators who are representative of the languages and cultures in the setting. It is easier to build relationships and to understand schedules, routines, and transitions in the home language. If one teacher speaks each toddler's home language and other teachers speak English, all children are immersed in a rich language environment. However, this may not be possible where children speak five or six different home languages and no educators can speak the language. If toddlers are not taught in their home language, then it is imperative that the setting reflect the cultures of the toddlers who attend. A play-based environment and small groups support language learning. A long large-group time in one language does not support language-learning goals, in addition to being inappropriate for toddlers (DeBey & Bombard, 2007).

As toddlers are learning two languages, there may be words they know in one language but not in the other. It is natural for them to use the words they know from both languages (**code switching**). As you talk with them, include the words they are trying to learn. Provide a language-rich environment.

- Provide board books in the home language and picture books that show different cultural and ethnic groups.
- Support both the home language and English in the classroom; do not comment when toddlers switch between English and another language.
- Encourage families to talk with you about what they want for their toddlers.
- Discuss childproofing the house, given the toddlers' increased mobility skills.
- Provide time for active play inside and outside.

Infants and Toddlers with Physical and Neurological Impairments

The *Back-to-Sleep* campaign began in 1994 to reduce the risk of Sudden Infant Death Syndrome (SIDS). Overall, SIDS rates have declined by more than by 50 percent (NIH, 2010a). However, infants no longer get the 12 hours of "tummy time" they used to get during sleep, as now children are put to sleep on their backs instead of on their stomachs. Lying on their stomachs stretches and strengthens the back and neck muscles that are needed for infants to reach motor milestones. The number of infants experiencing motor delays is increasing, and lack of tummy time is a contributing factor. One in 40 babies is diagnosed with an early motor delay, and 400,000 babies a year are at risk (Pathways Awareness, 2008). Pathways Awareness Medical Roundtable is trying to establish standards for tummy time. It supports having children attain at least one hour of tummy time per day by the time an infant is 3 months old. This should not be all at once, but spaced throughout the day (Pathways Awareness, 2008).

Some motor delays and physical disabilities involve damage to the central nervous system. Although these cannot be cured through early intervention, alternative pathways may be developed through exercise, massage, appropriate positioning, and the use of prostheses.

YOUNG INFANTS: BIRTH TO 9 MONTHS

It is difficult to identify young infants with physical impairments until they begin to miss developmental milestones unless they have a condition that is diagnosed at birth.

- Provide toys that are interesting to look at and listen to.
- Bring objects to the infant and experiment to see whether there is a way she can hold or control the object herself.
- Use soft or textured objects that are easy to grasp.
- Use toys with suction cups so the toys stay in one place if the infant has coordination problems.

MOBILE INFANTS: 8 TO 18 MONTHS

Mobile infants with physical impairments need materials that support the development of their large and small muscles. When other children are beginning to crawl and walk, it is important that you think about other forms of mobility, such as a creeper of some kind. Scaffold motor tasks. Talk to families and other professionals working with the infant to find the best way to do this. Holding and positioning children with physical impairments is important. Specific information should come from the infant's family or the physical or occupational therapist.

- Encourage mobile infants to use all the movements they are capable of.
- Be alert to subtle movements that indicate communication of thoughts or feelings.
- Moving muscles is both an internal and external process. Infants whose muscles do not move as they want can observe other children moving in ways they want to move. They can use these models for motor planning and visualization.
- Support children's exploration of materials. Ensure that they can reach, touch, and explore the materials.
- Talk with the families and therapists about positioning. Infants should be positioned based on the task they are trying to accomplish.

TODDLERS: 16 TO 36 MONTHS

Toddlers need materials that encourage the development of large- and small-motor skills and to work on the skills that have potential functionality for them. The adult's role is to provide an adequate supply of a variety of materials that encourage functional movements and reflect a developmental progression for skill building. The nature of the disability will determine the most appropriate accommodations.

- Use adaptive equipment to support toddlers' participation.
- Use larger, lighter versions of manipulative toys.
- Be aware of equipment in the classroom that can easily tip or roll.
- Encourage adaptive skills by attaching a carry-all or basket to the child's walker, or have the child wear a back or front pack if he is using crutches.

- Encourage toddlers to use their motor skills. Children may shy away from art or manipulative experiences because these are difficult for them. It is your job to make these areas fun and intriguing.

• • •
Infants and Toddlers with Hearing Impairments

Be aware of infants who pull on their ears. They may pull on their ears because they discovered them or because their ears hurt. Some infants begin to have middle ear disease at a young age. Also be alert to infants and toddlers who don't seem to respond to sound appropriately and infants who stop babbling around 6 months.

All children need exposure to language. If a child's home language is American Sign Language (ASL), this needs to be respected and included in the curriculum as you would any other language. Learn as much ASL as you can and use it correctly. It confuses young children when you make motions with your hands that look like they are signs but are really just made up or random signs. Integrate ASL across the curriculum if that is what families are teaching their infants and toddlers. Infants with identified hearing impairments who are in families that use American Sign Language (ASL) see signs in much the same way hearing infants hear conversations. With the support of parents, these signs should be encouraged as one would encourage babbling. Early intervention can help infants and toddlers use residual hearing. Increasingly, we are using signs with all infants as a method of communication before they have the coordination to speak. Take advantage of this opportunity to teach all infants and toddlers conventional signs.

YOUNG INFANTS: BIRTH TO 9 MONTHS

With most states adopting hearing screening of newborns, more infants with hearing impairments are identified earlier. Once identified, they are likely to be prescribed hearing aids as young infants.

- Support infant's signs and learn the meaning of gestures that the infant and his family typically use for communicating.
- Offer stimulation through other senses in addition to hearing: sight, smell, taste, and touch.
- Find out what residual hearing the infant has, what the hearing aids supplement, and what you should do in the context of this knowledge.

MOBILE INFANTS: 8 TO 18 MONTHS

If a hearing impairment has not been identified at birth, it is often during this period that it is suspected. When infants and young toddlers do not meet milestones in the area of speech and language, they are referred for a hearing evaluation. Consult with the child's family and the speech-language pathologist for additional information on how to accommodate and adapt your programming. The degree and cause of the loss determine the needed accommodations. Families decide how they plan to have their child educated and the form of language they wish to pursue.

- Use vision and visual cues as input sources with appropriate verbal information. Show the infant what you want her to do. Model behavior.

- The sense of hearing and balance are related. Give infants many opportunities for experiences that require and develop balance.

- Provide activities that encourage the infant to use the hearing she has. Find out what the infant is most likely to hear and incorporate these sounds into your curriculum.

- Sing songs and use fingerplays that have motions to go with the words. If you can sign songs in ASL, do so. If not, ensure that the motions are not confusing to a young child learning ASL.

- Be aware of extraneous noise in the classroom. Hearing aids amplify all sound, so the infant may actually have a hard time concentrating on specific sounds if there is loud background noise.

- Use signs with all infants to communicate some information. Many infants who do not have hearing impairments do not have the language skills to tell you what they want or need.

TODDLERS: 16 TO 36 MONTHS

Families decide how they want their toddler to be taught communications skills. Your role is to support this decision. When possible, incorporate the toddler's preferred communication mode into regular experiences. If a toddler has a profound hearing loss, the family may decide to have a cochlear implant during this time.

- Remove barriers that may block the child's vision of the classroom, provided such removals do not create runways. Encourage toddlers to look over activity choices before deciding what to do.

- Encourage toddlers to attend to a speaker's face. Look at the toddler when you talk to her, and remind the other children to do the same. "Look at Sofia when you talk to her; it makes it easier for her to understand you."

- Place the toddler in a good visual position during small group time or snack time—across from you, and not looking into the sun.

•••
Infants and Toddlers with Visual Impairments

In infancy, the role of vision is to motivate and guide behavior. It also plays a major role in incidental learning, and it extends the infant's world beyond his reach. Because infants with severe visual impairments do not use eye contact to express and maintain interest, caregivers must use other senses to motivate infants and toddlers to explore their world.

YOUNG INFANTS: BIRTH TO 9 MONTHS

Unless an infant has a severe visual impairment, it is not likely to be identified at this age. Intervention begins in early infancy for infants with severe visual impairments. It is important in preventing **blindisms**, or secondary autistic-like behaviors. Physical stimulation is necessary during the critical periods of ages 2 to 3 months and 7 to 9 months in order to develop attachment behaviors.

- Find out the infant's degree of vision and under what distance and lighting conditions she sees best.

- High-contrast colors such as black and white are usually easiest to see and developmentally appropriate for this age.

- Use real three-dimensional objects to support concept development.

- Work through the infant's strengths by offering stimulation through other senses: sound, smell, taste, and touch.

- Keep in verbal contact with the infant as she will use your voice to know you are near if she cannot see you. Be sure to identify her by name when you talk to her.

- Provide as much verbal stimulation as the infant can adapt to.

MOBILE INFANTS: 8 TO 18 MONTHS

With the advent of locomotion, infants with visual impairments may need additional accommodations. Consult with a vision and orientation and mobility specialist about room arrangement, appropriate experiences, and so on. These specialists have information about long-term expectations for the child, that is, whether the child will read using large print or Braille, and other useful information.

- Use materials that make sounds when manipulated. Toys that make a noise when they move help children focus on and reach for them.

- Help children locate sound. Make a noise, and when the child turns to the sound encourage him and give him the noisemaker. Verbally encourage him as well. "Friedrich, I can't fool you. You know where that noise is coming from, don't you? Here is the ball." This supports locating skills through sound.

- Use whatever sight the mobile infant has available. If she can make distinctions only among toys with high contrast like black and white, be sure you have some.

- Locomotion is challenging for infants with visual impairments. They frequently walk later than other children and they often use **hitching** as a means of locomotion instead of creeping or crawling. (Children hitch when they scoot on their bottom while using their legs for propulsion.) This is very adaptive, as they run into things with their feet, not their head.

- Provide materials such as large manipulative toys that require two hands or activities that prohibit self-stimulation behavior, if this is a problem.

TODDLERS: 16 TO 36 MONTHS

Help the toddler locate the different areas of the room and help her develop safe ways to get to each (no toys lying around). Keep these areas consistent to encourage independent movement. Providing consistent routines helps children know what to expect and supports their independence.

- Be aware of the toddler's location in the room.

- Use objects the toddler can feel and pair words with the objects she is feeling. "Chunga, this is a ball. Feel how round it is. Drop it and it bounces back up." Use of pictures of objects is dependent upon the child's level of vision.

- Be aware of lighting needs. Some toddlers see better in dim settings. If she sees better in some lighting conditions than others, adapt your classroom.

- Use language that is comfortable for you. Don't eliminate the words "see" and "look" from your vocabulary, but describe what you see to the child in the most concrete way you can.

- Work with the family and an **orientation and mobility specialist** to ensure that the toddler has an environment that meets her needs.

Adapting Materials for Infants and Toddlers with Disabilities

Most of the toys and materials you would use for any infant or toddler can be used with infants or toddlers with delays and disabilities; others may require minor modifications. If there are major modifications, families or specialists will typically provide this equipment or the information for adaptation. If there is no need to modify an experience, don't. When modifications are necessary, the toys and materials should be appropriate for the child's developmental level and chronological age, promote age-appropriate social and communication skills, and do not interfere with regular routines or call undue attention to the child. Although alternative activities may be used, they should be interesting, varied, and available to all the children in the class. In reality they are activities that are good for all children, not just alternative activities. Adaptations are useful to all infants and toddlers who are challenged by any activity.

- Deflating beach balls slightly makes it easier for infants and toddlers to catch them than regular rubber balls.

- Hang toys above an infant or toddler who is not moving independently but can reach for and grasp toys. Hang them from the upright handle of an infant seat, above a changing table, or (if you are ambitious!) attach a pulley to the ceiling and hang toys from a rope. The use of the pulley allows you to adjust the height of the toys. Be sure that this equipment is strong enough to be safe when infants grasp and pull toys.

- Glue magnetic strips onto the back of toys with several parts (such as simple puzzles). Use a cookie sheet as a base. Moving the pieces and taking them on and off the cookie sheet provides some resistance.

- Cut pop beads open and put them over small handles, such as those on a jack-in-the-box, to make them easier to hold. Foam hair curlers can be placed over paint brushes or crayons.

- Experiment with different adaptations to see what works. Remember infants and toddlers change and grow quickly, so monitor and evaluate adaptations to ensure they are developmentally and socially appropriate and are still necessary.

- Use suction-cup toys because they stay put when a child who is working on eye–hand coordination manipulates them.

- Add Velcro wrist bracelets to rattles or small noise makers to help infants who are unable to hold them independently.

- Use pop beads or bristle blocks to practice putting things together; but for a child who needs to work on strength, pulling them apart is great.

- Inflate toys partially to make them easier to grasp.

- Place Dycem (a nonslip plastic) on the table to keep toys from rolling away and to anchor cups and plates. You can also put Dycem on chair seats to keep children from slipping off.

- Connect a toy to a capability switch (a device the child uses to manipulate something). The child activates the switch and something happens, encouraging cause-and-effect reasoning. Capability switches are very sensitive and will respond to slight movements from

Some toddlers have to be taught skills for approaching other children and how to maintain play once contact has been initiated.
Penny Low Deiner

any body part. Switch selection should be based on the mobile infant's or toddler's most consistent and reliable body movement. There are switches that will respond to sipping or puffing, voice, sideswipes, pinches, touch, movement of the tongue, chin, nose, and so on. Lighted switches help children with hearing impairments; others are gravity sensitive so that tilting a body part will activate them. Any body movement that creates a shadow can activate photosensitive switches. Switches can control robots, trains, fire engines, pigs, bears, and rabbits. They can be attached to music boxes, toy radios, toy TVs, and tops. They help children with disabilities gain control over their world.

Individualizing Planning

Individualized planning is a circular process. It starts with a designated outcome: What the infant's or toddler's family and early childhood educators want the child to know and be able to do. For example, if a goal for a toddler is to increase his receptive vocabulary, one of the first steps in the process is to decide when and how frequently you are going to incorporate this goal into your programming. Start with routines. They occur several times each day, ensuring that the child has many opportunities each day for practice. Identify the routines and the types of receptive language that can logically be a part of each. When the toddler arrives at school, you might decide to comment on articles, colors, and patterns of clothing. You might say, "You have a *shirt* on today. Let me look at that *shirt*. I like the buttons on your *shirt*." As the toddler's receptive vocabulary increases, this might change to "Let me see what *shirt* you are wearing today," with the expectation that the toddler will show off his *shirt*. If the toddler can do this successfully, you know this technique works to build receptive language. When you share this information, it is useful to identify both the techniques you are using and the vocabulary and receptive language you are supporting.

To broaden the context of receptive language, you might think of including a broad-based theme such as "my family and me," and then incorporate the words you want the child to identify into that theme, to increase contextual learning. If you are interested in children learning household words, you might set up the dramatic play area as a house, choosing the specific household items based on the receptive language you plan to teach. Then consider how you will incorporate the teaching into the play. You might begin by verbally labeling the objects for the infant or toddler and demonstrating what each does. Support the mobile infant or toddler using the objects and again verbally labeling the objects and what the child is doing. Finally, request that the child discriminate between the desired object and others: "Show me the blanket." "Can you wrap the baby in the blanket?"

THE EVIDENCE BASE

The age at which infants and toddlers begin early intervention (EI) influences the outcome. The National Early Intervention Longitudinal Study (NEILS) had a sample of 3,338 infants and toddlers who entered early intervention before 31 months of age and their families. One aspect of the research focused on the process of getting into the early intervention system and beginning to receive services. Table 7–3 shows the data, given in months, from when families were first concerned about an infant's health or development until the IFSP was developed. Both the mean (arithmetic average) and median (the middle figure, meaning that half of the infants and toddlers were younger and half older than the month given) are included. Looking at the differences between when parents were first concerned about their infant's development and when they had an IFSP on the average (mean), it took 8 months with a median of 12 months. This means that half of the families waited for more than a year between their initial concerns and their infant receiving services based on their IFSP. This time varied by disability as well.

The differences between the mean and the median are significant. It is clear that some children entered early intervention early and others much later. This is particularly true for the difference between first concerns and the development of the IFSP. In trying to sort out this problem, the researchers divided the infants and toddlers into three groups: developmental delay, diagnosed condition, and risk condition (see Table 7–4). For children with risk conditions it took 6 months; for those with a diagnosed, condition, 7 months; and for those with a developmental delay, 9 months.

Approximately three times as many infants and toddlers with developmental delays received early intervention services. However, on average, infants and toddlers with developmental delays did not have an IFSP until they were 20 months old, whereas infants with diagnosed conditions or risk conditions had an IFSP at 9 and 8 months respectively. Adults did not become concerned about their infant's delays until they were 11 months old, whereas adults were concerned about the health of those with a diagnosed or at risk condition at 2 months.

Source: Hebbelere et al., 2007.

REFLECTIVE PRACTICE | Look at Tables 7–3 and 7–4 carefully. A child's entrance into early intervention is dependent upon someone noticing a problem, perhaps something very subtle in the infant's or toddler's development. How will you hone your skills to be aware of developmental differences that may require early intervention? What do you think caused the difference in ages among the groups? What is the significance of the mean and the median?

TABLE 7-3 AGES FOR IDENTIFICATION OF INFANTS AND TODDLERS AND SERVICE PROVISION

Situation	Ages in Months Mean	Ages in Months Median
First concern about health or development	7	4
First diagnosis or identification	9	6
First looked for early intervention	12	11
Referral received by early intervention program	14	14
Age at which IFSP was developed	16	16
Number of children	3,056–3,235	3,056–3,235

TABLE 7-4 IDENTIFIED DELAYS, DISABILITY, OR RISK AND AGE

Situation	Mean Age in Months		
	Developmental Delay	Diagnosed Condition	Risk Condition
First concern about health or development	11	2	2
First diagnosis or identification	13	4	3
First looked for early intervention	16	6	5
Referral received by early intervention program	18	8	6
Age at which IFSP was developed	20	9	8
Number of children	1,826–1,923	638–675	436–463

Implementing an IFSP

The initial development of the IFSP and figuring out whether it is accomplishing its goals is a circular process. It works something like the process illustrated in Figure 7–2. You might begin by identifying the desired IFSP outcomes and framing them in the context of the theme you are working on. You then determine the procedures you will use to implement the goal, choose the appropriate materials, and implement the experiences or activities with the infant or toddler. Once implemented, you reflect on the effectiveness of the process. If it was effective, you would use it again with variations until the infant or toddler reaches the desired level of performance. If the process was not effective try to determine the aspects that were not working well, modify them, and use the activities again. Once you have perfected the process add new activities.

Once you have worked through this process on an individual basis several times, you will begin to get a feel about the match between what the infant or toddler can do and the goals that were set. You share these new insights with the team and let them know that you are working toward achievable goals, or, if things are not progressing, that the goals themselves might need to be modified.

Because so much of infant and toddler programming is individualized, incorporating the goals of the IFSP into your daily plans is relatively easy. Including goals in routines and transitions ensures that they are included on a daily basis and support contextual learning. Serving a cut-up fresh fruit snack is an easy way to help children practice using a spoon. Likewise, talking about body parts and pointing to objects is easy when a child is arriving: "You needed to wear a sweater today to keep your arms warm. Please hang your sweater in your locker." "Show me what you have on your feet. What are these?" You can easily incorporate these steps in your planning, but you need to remain deliberate and intentional about what you are doing and why. Schedule when you will work on specific outcomes with a toddler. Short-spaced work is more effective than attempting to sit a toddler down for half an hour and "do it all."

Because routines take up so much of the day, it is often useful to develop a chart like the one in Figure 7–3, which focuses your attention on the goals themselves as well as when and how you plan to implement them. Generalize this concept to home and other settings.

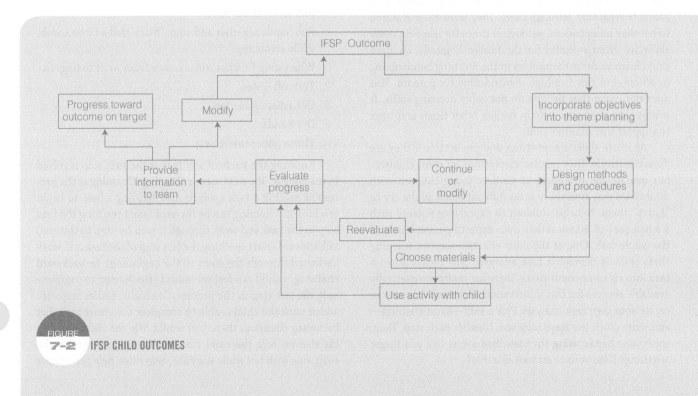

FIGURE 7-2 IFSP CHILD OUTCOMES

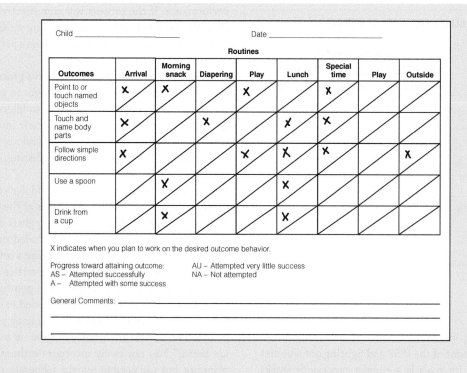

Child _____　　　　　　Date _____

Routines

Outcomes	Arrival	Morning snack	Diapering	Play	Lunch	Special time	Play	Outside
Point to or touch named objects	X	X		X		X		
Touch and name body parts	X		X		X	X		
Follow simple directions	X			X	X	X		X
Use a spoon		X			X			
Drink from a cup		X			X			

X indicates when you plan to work on the desired outcome behavior.

Progress toward attaining outcome:　　　　AU – Attempted very little success
AS –　Attempted successfully　　　　　　　NA – Not attempted
A –　　Attempted with some success

General Comments: _____
_____
_____

FIGURE 7-3　EMBEDDING GOALS AND OBJECTIVES IN ROUTINES

Because so much of infant and toddler curriculum revolves around routines it s essential to incorporate their IFSP goals into these routines. A chart such as this one makes it clear what the desired outcomes are and when they will be addressed.

ADAPTIVE SKILLS

The development of adaptive skills is important for the growing independence of infants and toddlers and in the long term reduces the amount of time parents and early childhood educators spend in caregiving. Parents and children often have conflicts regarding self-help skills. They want their children to be more independent, yet logical times for learning these skills are often stressful for the family. Logically, children could learn to dress themselves in the morning before going to school, but this is a high demand time for parents. This does not mean that parents do not value dressing skills. It means they need your help in finding other times and ways to support this adaptive skill.

Adaptive skills are repetitive and predictable if they are done effectively. They require adaptations for some children, but overall, the procedure is similar. Young children with disabilities may find these tasks difficult when adults try to "hurry" them. It helps children to experience success with a small part of a task rather than expecting completion of the whole task. One of the most effective ways of teaching these skills is through a **task analysis**. This breaks down a task into its component parts. There are many commercially available sources for this information. However, it is easy to create your own task analysis. Pick a skill—hand washing—and write down the steps involved. Number each step. Then, wash your hands using the identified steps. Did you forget anything? Does your chart look like this?

Goal: Wash hands independently

1. Push up sleeves (if necessary).
2. Turn on water.
3. Press the liquid soap container.
4. Rub soap on hands.
5. Rub hands together and sing, "Mary Had a Little Lamb" while scrubbing.
6. When song finishes, rinse hands from wrist to fingers.
7. Turn off water.
8. Get a disposable towel.
9. Dry hands.
10. Throw paper towel away.

Knowing the parts of any task is the first step involved in teaching it. The next step is chaining. **Chaining** is the process of making a task analysis and deciding where to begin teaching it. Chaining can be forward (start teaching the first step in the task and work through it step-by-step to the end) or backward (start teaching the last step of the task and work backward through the steps to the beginning). In **backward chaining**, a child can feel successful after having to complete only the last step in the process. Gradually, earlier steps are added until the child is able to complete the entire task. For backward chaining, then, you would *help* the child push up his sleeves, *help* the child turn on the water, *help* use the soap, *sing* with her while she rubs, *help* rinse, *help* get a paper towel, *help* dry hands, and *teach* the child how to throw away the paper towel. You would then say something like, "Cheri, now put the towel in the trash. Great job! You did that by yourself." Praise the child for doing it well. When Cheri can predictably throw the towel away, you would teach her to dry her hands. For some tasks to begin at step one is discouraging because the teacher, not the child, accomplishes the final step. Task analysis is useful in making you aware of the steps involved in a particular task. It also becomes clear what the prerequisite skills are. If a child lacks the prerequisite skills, it is doubtful that the task will be completed.

Guidelines DAP

1. *Discuss important issues.* Provide an atmosphere where issues about race, culture, gender, and disability can be freely discussed. Young children are becoming aware of these differences. Toddlers learn respect and caring for others who are different from themselves by modeling adults' interactions with the child.

2. *Support diversity.* Provide activities, materials, and curriculum planning that allow children to learn about differences by firsthand experience. If a toddler wears braces, the other children may want to try on the braces. Under supervision, and perhaps with the support of a physical therapist, children can explore and experiment with braces and other adaptive equipment, but they should not be the child's actual aids. The goal is to create awareness and to have a positive, rather than a negative, experience.

3. *Teach ways to cope with unkind words.* Teach specific ways of handling situations involving staring or making unkind remarks. Make toddlers aware of how children who are stared at feel. If other children tease or make unkind remarks about a child with a disability, serve as the child's ally. Stop the teasing and explain that words can hurt people's feelings. Give correct information: "Camille is not stupid. It just takes her longer to learn new things." Over time, help children build the skills necessary to stand up for themselves. Teach all children socially acceptable ways of learning about others.

4. *Teach how to approach others.* There are specific skills used in approaching others and entering groups; some children do not know these skills.

5. *Facilitate social inclusion.* Help infants and toddlers find roles to play and facilitate adaptations and accommodations that allow children to play together.

6. *Keep a consistent daily schedule.* Infants and toddlers know what will happen next when the sequence is consistent. Provide a picture chart to support the schedule.

7. *Add cues.* Carpet squares or marks on the carpet indicate where toddlers should be.

8. *Limit the potential for distraction.* During small-group experiences, seat the child with a disability close to you and facing away from busy areas. If you have large group activities with older toddlers, they should be limited to 5 to 10 minutes.

9. *Use planned energetic play.* Provide safe outlets for the release of excess energy and feelings. Lead toddlers in jumping, marching, or dancing for two to three minutes frequently during the day.

10. *Use a variety of teaching techniques.* Match your teaching techniques to the information you want the child to learn and the particular infant or toddler. Mobile infants and toddlers often learn appropriate behavior by imitating others.

11. *Use shaping.* Help shape a mobile infant or toddler's behavior by breaking an activity down into smaller steps and then leading the toddler through progressively more of the steps, providing many prompts until she can do the task independently.

12. *Use fading.* The opposite technique of shaping is fading. As the mobile infant or toddler begins to master a skill, gradually give fewer cues and less information so that he becomes more responsible for doing the skill independently.

SUMMARY

- The first three years of life pose risks and potential that will not appear again.
- Risks for infants increase if they are born too small or arrive too soon. They may have problems in a variety of systems: respiratory, neurological, cardiovascular, gastrointestinal, and ophthalmological.
- Physical and motor skills develop at a rapid rate during the first three years.
- The brain itself is not fully developed at birth and, through interacting with the environment, some parts of the brain become hardwired while unused synapses are pruned.
- The central nervous system gains maturity and speed in the transmission of impulses.
- Infants' and toddlers' rates of development are assessed, and interventions are prescribed if development is delayed.
- Good programming provides varied opportunities for all infants and toddlers to meet early learning guidelines, and children with disabilities can practice identified goals as they incorporate them into daily routines and themes.

EDUCATIONAL RESOURCES

Child Care and Early Education Research Connections offers many up-to-date resources, including new research and policies about issues related to child care and early education. www.childcareresearch.org/

Child Find has a variety of resources for the early identification of infants and toddlers who may have developmental delays or disabilities. www.childfindidea.org/

Child Trauma Academy (CTA) is a not-for-profit organization that works to improve the lives of high-risk children through direct service, research, and education. One particular focus is children who have experienced abuse and neglect.

Early Head Start National Resources Center at Zero to Three, supported by the Administration of Children and Families, has a variety of information available about Early Head Start as well as health and safety and useful multimedia. www.ehsnrc.org/

Healthy Child Care America sponsored by the American Academy of Pediatrics (AAP) has resources for parents and early childhood educators. www.healthychildcare.org/

High/Scope Educational Research Foundation supports an Infant-Toddler Curriculum based on the principle that children learn best through direct, hands-on experiences with people, objects, events, and ideas. Learning and development are anchored by long-term, trusting relationships with caregivers. Adults scaffold further learning as they interact with infants and toddlers throughout the day. www.highscope.org/

March of Dimes provides information about birth defects and related newborn health problems.

Pathways Awareness Foundation has produced an inexpensive compact disk, *Is My Baby OK?* which highlights typical and atypical development in the young infant. It also has other resources. www.pathwaysawareness.org/

World Bank Early Child Development focuses on early childhood from a global and economic perspective. It has resources and links to international and regional sites, and data from international organizations. www.worldbank.org/children/

Zero to Three provides information and advocacy for professionals and parents for children from birth to age 3, including links to resources, training, and conferences. www.zerotothree.org/

For additional resources, visit the book companion website for this text at www.cengagebrain.com.

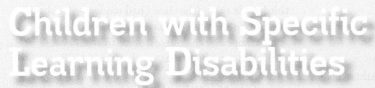

Children with Specific Learning Disabilities

8

I never thought that I would have to call a lawyer to see that my daughter got the education she deserved. I was wrong. I would like to share my experience with you, in the form of letters I sent, to show how far we have come—or have not come. The first letter was written to her second-grade teacher in November; the second letter, a year later, was to update our lawyer. ❋

November 8, 1986
Dear Mrs. Brown,

We appreciate being able to talk with you about Pat. We know you will have many conferences during the day, and we thought it would help if we could share our major concerns with you before the conference. We would like to know whether our perceptions of the problems are the same as yours and also which of our solutions are feasible.

We would like to concentrate on the area of *reading*. We appreciate and notice that you are going out of your way to help Pat learn to read and we also notice that she is consciously trying hard. However, she is not learning at the level her ability suggests is appropriate. (Our assumption is that she is average to above average in intelligence.) We have tried to figure out why she is not performing at grade level.

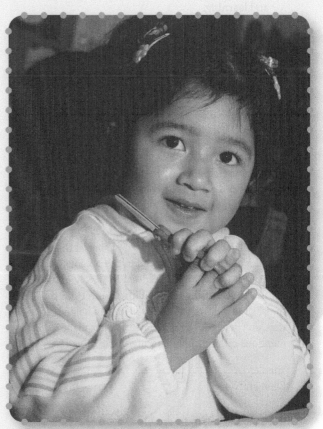

©Cengage Learning 2012

1. Problem: Hearing. As part of Pat's allergies, her ears fill up with fluid. When this happens she experiences a 50–60 dB bilateral conductive hearing loss. This condition can change on an almost daily basis. We had tubes placed in her ears when we discovered the condition. They were replaced once. After that, the medical decision was that they were probably not necessary, as the medication she was taking should control the condition.

   Given Pat's history of hearing losses, is it possible to use a different basal reading series or a different approach to teaching her reading? I would not expect you to do this in your classroom. However, could/should she be part of some reading group even in another class? Could you suggest something that you feel would not interfere with the program that is used in the class? We could do this at home so that she could experience some success.

   Potential Solutions: A diagnostic workup would be needed to determine whether or not this is a problem.

2. Problem: Dyslexia. Pat has many of the characteristics commonly associated with dyslexia. She still has letter and number reversals. Although reversals may be common until age 7, she is getting to the stage when she should be outgrowing this. She is left-handed and many children who are dyslexic are lefties (at least that is what people have told me). She appears to be bright, but still does not grasp the essentials of reading, and in math seems to have particular problems with one-to-one correspondence.

   Potential Solutions: Again, she would need an educational workup similar to the one mentioned above, but with a particular test designed to pick up dyslexia. If the results were positive, she would need a specific educational program for dyslexia.

   There may be other potential problems, and probably other solutions you can suggest. Those mentioned above occurred to us as possibilities.

We are not concerned that Pat is not in the "highest" reading group, but rather that she learn at a pace she can feel good about.

We would appreciate any help you can give us regarding your perceptions of Pat's reading problems, as well as potential solutions. Our biggest concern is not Pat's lack of achievement, but rather the struggle she is going through. We want to find ways to maintain her current enthusiasm for school and learning.

Sincerely,
Ellen and Jim Hastings

The second letter was written to their lawyer in December. Pat was in third grade.

December 21, 1987
Dear Mr. Hart,

An update on Pat as requested. I have also enclosed copies of the child study team meetings that we attended and a copy of the letter and attached information we received today from the cluster coordinator.

I would like to add just one word of special thanks to you. For a long time I believed in the school system and that it works for all children. In the "ivory tower" approach, I guess I wasn't willing to entertain the idea that I should go ahead on my own. You helped me see that, so whatever the outcome, this has made a tremendous difference in Pat's life.

Thanks.
Ellen and Jim

Re: Teacher assignment

After talking to you at the end of August, I called the office of Mrs. Truck (the principal) on August 25th to make an appointment sometime during the week of August 29th. The secretary told me that this was not possible, but that she would try to get Mrs. Truck to call me. She called on August 30. I briefly explained the problem and, after a long lecture on the problems of having parents request teachers and so on, I was told, and I quote, "I have been in special education for 18 years. Your daughter is not identified and I will call Special Services to see what I *have* to do for her." I called the cluster coordinator the next day and explained to her what happened. (It appeared that she expected my call.) She felt that I should talk with the superintendent about the situation. She agreed to call him and to prepare him for my request. I called but did not get him on Wednesday and left a message. I called again on Thursday and did not get him but after I told the secretary my name, she told me "you got what you wanted" and hung up.

I decided to take Pat to school the first day just to see what was happening. I took her to Mrs. Lee's third grade room (the class I had requested) and she was not on the list. Mrs. Lee graciously added her and I stopped by the nurse's office to see if I could get a class list to see what was happening. Given Pat's recurring illness, I knew the nurse well. Pat was assigned to Mrs. Nola's class. I retrieved Pat, apologized, and took her to Mrs. Nola's classroom (either teacher was fine with me). She has been in Mrs. Nola's classroom since.

Re: Memorandum of agreement concerning Pat Hastings, Grade 2, East Park School

I met with Pat's teacher, Mrs. Nola, on September 20, 1987, at my request. At that point, I began to talk with her about the letter of agreement you had written to the school district. She had not seen it nor did she know that it existed.

Dr. Cole called the evening of September 21 to set up an appointment for a child study team conference. The conference was held on 10/27/87. Relative to that conference the following is in place:

- Pat will not get Project Assist, the reading help we requested, as it is not in the school and will not begin until January; however, the reading resource teacher, Mrs. Fewell, feels that Pat should not be in the program as so many other children have a greater need for the service.
- The reading resource teacher, Mrs. Fewell, learned about the letter of agreement at the conference (10/27/87). She said that she can do nothing for Pat as she is now reading at grade level and all of the children she works with are below grade level.
- She is continuing to receive instruction in the District basal reading series.
- The report card appears to be the measure used to determine her progress.

Re: Current status

Currently, Pat has been changed into the highest reading group. Her classroom teacher, Mrs. Nola, expressed some concern about this move and worried that her grades in reading would go down. Her first marking period grades are all As. Her reading, spelling, language and math are all at the 3.1 level.

What have we been doing?

We have developed a rigorous and intensive therapy program for Pat in addition to the academic work we do with her. Homework is a struggle. Jim and I take turns. We also try to read to her at least a half an hour a day. She struggles so much with learning to read that we want her to experience the joy of books, thus making the struggles worth it for her.

Perhaps I should give you the rationale for what we have done. I started to do a lot of reading on sensory integration. I found that the brain is programmable up until about 8–10 years. The more I read, the more I was convinced that her problem was dyslexia and something they call "clumsy child syndrome." I decided to focus on her postural stability/flexibility, balance, and motor planning and control. (This was based on the occupational therapy report.) I tried to think of fun ways to begin to work on these and, given her age, time was not on our side. I guess I am telling you all of this because we are putting a tremendous amount of time, energy, and money into this and I think we are getting amazing results. The school system seems totally uninterested in what we are doing.

Project Assist is based on the Orton Gillingham theory of dyslexia. Both Jim and I have taken the training. The course is 4 hours a week for 10 weeks. Although we don't formally sit Pat down on a daily basis, we do use the techniques to teach her spelling and to help her with her reading.

Sensory Motor Therapy: This is the occupational therapy that Pat gets 30 minutes each week. Our Blue Cross/Blue Shield pays for that. With driving time, that is about an hour a week of our time.

Recreation: This is one of the related services listed in the rules and regulations, and it is through the interpretation of the occupational therapy report that the additional evaluations were completed and the specific recreations chosen.

Therapeutic Horseback Riding: We had Pat evaluated for this program and found, through the occupational therapy evaluation, that this particular program should help her in the area of balance. They are also working on the rotational skills she needs while she is riding. This is a half hour a week at the state park. It is officially through 4-H. We pay $14.00 for each lesson and with driving time; it takes 2 hours a week.

Ice Skating: As I analyzed Pat's evaluation, I thought that as a sport, ice skating had the potential to help her in all of the six areas she has needs in:

- Monitor response to movement
- Postural stability/flexibility
- Balance
- Gross motor planning and control
- Fine motor planning and control
- Tactile and kinesthetic perception.

I have worked with her skating coach to emphasize that the skating is not competitive, but to work on related issues. With lessons and practice, she currently skates 5 to 6 hours a week. Between the lessons and the ice time, this costs about $40.00 a week. Since an adult has to take her and stay with her during this time, in parent time this is about 7 to 8 hours a week.

Is it worth it? Yes! However, my concerns are twofold. In many ways, I am the one who both diagnosed and remedied the problem. I don't think most children have parents with this knowledge. The tragedy is that what I have found about Pat is that some of her problems can be permanently helped through what we are doing. Others could be as well, but when the brain can no longer be programmed in this way, the only thing that therapy can do is teach compensatory skills. I think the school system has failed to identify the problem.

The second area that is still of concern to me is that she is currently functioning very well in a regular third grade class. If she were identified as having dyslexia she would not be in that placement. We know she has a disability. We are not in denial, but we are unhappy about the range of services offered by the school if we allow her to be identified.

Interestingly, now the school seems convinced that there is nothing wrong with her. We, however, feel that we have a lifetime challenge.

Again, we thank you for your time and effort on our behalf.

REFLECTIVE PRACTICE | The situation described above happened in 1986–1987, before the parts of the IDEA supporting children in their natural environments were emphasized, and at that time dyslexia was not acknowledged as a disability under the law. Think about the time commitment this family made to their daughter's education. Reflect on what they did and how they used normal recreational experiences to support her development. Think about what you might do in a classroom to support children with specific learning disabilities, in addition to what is required by the IEP. What will you need to know about what other professionals do in order to work with them effectively?

Specific Learning Disabilities

Children with specific learning disabilities are as smart as their classmates, but one or more of their information processing systems do not work efficiently, making academic work challenging (LD OnLine, 2007). Most children with learning disabilities struggle with learning to read.

In 1969, the federal government recognized learning disabilities as a group of disabilities requiring special educational services. However, diagnosis was medically based, and many children did not qualify. Teachers saw children who should be learning, but were struggling, as a major problem. In the educational community, these children were labeled "underachievers." Some saw this perplexing problem as a "school disability" because children seemed to be fine before they went to school and then began having problems. The assumption was also that when they got out of school, they would be fine. We know far more about specific learning disabilities than we did 50 years ago, and we are still learning.

Defining Specific Learning Disabilities

In addition to not agreeing on the actual nature of specific learning disabilities, confusion also resulted from different definitions used by the educational, legal, psychological, and medical fields. It seems easier to determine what learning disabilities *are not* rather than what they *are*. This is further confounded because learning disabilities can coexist, or be **comorbid**, with other disabilities. It is estimated that about 10 to 40 percent of children with specific learning disabilities (SLD) have other disabilities, including attention-deficit/ hyperactivity disorder (ADHD), conduct disorder, oppositional defiant disorder, major depressive disorder, and others (APA, 2000; Silver, 2002).

The clearest agreement seems to be that specific learning disabilities are neurologic in nature and impede a child's ability to store, process, and produce information. The federal government's definition of SLD governs academic programs and determines our estimates of the number of children with specific learning disabilities. Not all children with specific learning disabilities qualify for special education services.

> According to IDEA 2004,
> *specific learning disabilities (SLD) is a disorder in one or more of the basic psychological processes involved in understanding or in using language, spoken or written. It may manifest itself in an imperfect ability to listen, think, speak, read, write, spell, or do mathematical calculations. SLD includes such conditions as perceptual disabilities, brain injury, minimal brain dysfunction, dyslexia, and developmental aphasia; it does not include a learning problem that is primarily the result of visual, hearing, or motor disabilities; intellectual disability; emotional disturbance; or environmental, cultural, or economic disadvantage. (U.S. Department of Education [DOE], 2006)*

The National Joint Committee on Learning Disabilities (NJCLD) has a broader definition that looks at the lifetime implications of learning disabilities.

> *Learning disabilities is a general term that refers to a heterogeneous group of disorders manifested by significant difficulties in the acquisition and use of listening, speaking, reading, writing, reasoning, or mathematical abilities. These disorders are intrinsic to the individual, presumed to be due to central nervous system dysfunction, and may occur across the life span. Problems in self-regulatory behaviors, social perception, and social interaction may exist with learning disabilities but do not by themselves constitute a learning disability. Although learning disabilities may occur concomitantly with other handicapping conditions (e.g., sensory impairment, mental retardation, serious emotional disturbance), or with extrinsic influences (such as cultural differences,*

> *insufficient or inappropriate instruction), they are not the result of those conditions or influences. (NJCLD, 1990, p. 1)*

The American Psychiatric Association (APA) uses the term *learning disorders*. In their *Diagnostic and Statistical Manual of Mental Disorders*, 4th ed., Text Revised (DSM IV-TR), the APA defines learning disorders in the following way:

> *Learning disorders are diagnosed when the individual's achievement on individually administered, standardized tests in reading, mathematics, or written expression is substantially below that expected for age, schooling, and level of intelligence. The learning problems significantly interfere with academic achievement or activities of daily living that require reading, mathematical, or writing skills. (APA, 2000, p. 49)*

The term *specific learning disabilities or disorders* is used because there are different types of learning disabilities, most of which fall into three broad academic categories: reading disorder (dyslexia), writing disorder (dysgraphia), and arithmetic disorder (dyscalculia). Because of the overlapping aspects of speaking, listening, reading, writing, and mathematics, as well as the brain functions that support these skills, some children have problems in all of these areas (LD OnLine, 2007).

Prevalence of Specific Learning Disabilities

The federal government began keeping records on children with SLD during the 1976–1977 school year. At that time, 8.3 percent of children in the public schools were identified as having a disability. Of these children, 1.8 percent had a specific learning disability. In the 2007–2008 school year, 13.4 percent of children were identified as having a disability, with 5.2 percent of these children having a specific learning disability. The number of children identified with specific learning disabilities reached a high of 6.1 percent in 2000–2001 (National Center for Educational Statistics [NCES], 2010). This caused concern and required educators to look at how children were identified and what could be done to prevent this problem. The rate has been dropping consistently since then (see Table 8–1).

There are few estimates of how many preschool children have SLD. Many professionals believe SLD exist during the

TABLE 8-1   PERCENT OF CHILDREN WITH DISABILITIES, SPECIFIC LEARNING DISABILITIES, AND INTELLECTUAL DISABILITIES

Year	Children with Disabilities	Children with Specific Learning Disabilities	Children with Intellectual Disabilities
1976–1977	8.3%	1.8%	2.2%
2007–2008	13.4%	5.2%	1.0%

Source: National Center for Educational Statistics, 2010.

preschool years, or precursors to the problems are present. When the focus is on prevention, identifying children during the preschool years is worthwhile, especially if interventions could prevent children from being labeled SLD in elementary school (Coleman, Buysse, & Neitzel, 2006). Changes in the early identification system are moving into the area of prevention, with the preschool and early elementary years being viewed as a time to support young children in learning the skills they need before they experience failure.

Causes of Specific Learning Disabilities

In many cases, the causes of learning disabilities are not known, although we do have some clues and discoveries are occurring at an ever-increasing rate. Two fundamental ways of looking at the causes of learning disabilities are the medical model and the educational model. The medical model looks for causes in the child's biology and the makeup of the CNS. The educational model focuses on the interaction of the learner and the environment, and looks at changing the learning environment and using behavioral reinforcement to shape behavior.

Scientists are providing insights into how biological factors cause learning disabilities. Growing evidence supports the role genetic influences play in some learning disabilities. Since the mapping of the human genome in 2003, investigations into genetic causes of SLD have increased. A 35 to 45 percent recurrence rate for reading disabilities in families suggests SLD can be inherited and relate to family genetics (Shapiro, Church, & Lewis, 2002).

Other hypotheses are that learning disabilities are the result of subtle disturbances in the functions and structures of the brain—some "faulty wiring" in its cortex. The problem becomes obvious when the miswired area of the brain is needed to process certain information (Silver, 2002). Intervention, then, involves developing learning strategies to compensate for these problems, which show up as SLD in children.

Although efforts to pinpoint the causes of SLD continue, that they are real is accepted, and it is understood that a child with an SLD will often need more time, understanding, and encouragement from educators. Indeed, educators may need to concentrate efforts on preliminary assessments of a child suspected of having a learning disability.

Early Identification of Specific Learning Disabilities

Early signs of potential learning disabilities appear during the preschool years, seen in pronunciation problems, slow growth in vocabulary, and a lack of interest in listening to stories and in telling them. These children also have poor memory for routines and have trouble learning numbers, the alphabet, and the days of the week. They often show signs of restlessness and lack the ability to persist at tasks, particularly those they do not enjoy. They may have trouble sitting still and employing self-help skills. They have trouble with

tying shoes, buttoning buttons, and getting zippers to work. Overall, they appear to be clumsy. They may be reluctant to draw, especially if they have received negative feedback about the relationship between what they think they have drawn and others' perceptions. They may show difficulty playing with peers and demonstrate weakness in other social skills. They also have problems with learning directionality (left and right).

Although it is difficult to identify children during the preschool years who may later be identified as having SLD, there are some areas that signal risks for later academic problems:

- *Perinatal conditions:* low Apgar score, low birth weight, 24 hours or more in a neonatal intensive care unit, difficulty sucking and swallowing;
- *Genetic or environmental conditions:* family history of learning disabilities or language problems, limited exposure to language, exposure to environmental toxins, being adopted, living in poverty;
- *Attention and behavior:* distractibility, impulsivity, hyperactivity, perseveration (constantly repeats actions or ideas) and problems with change;
- *Delays in reaching developmental milestones;*
- *Cognitive skills:* not understanding means–end relationships, object permanence, or lack of symbolic play;
- *Language comprehension and expression:* limited receptive and expressive vocabulary, immature syntax, speech that is difficult to understand, little spontaneous communication, and trouble following directions;
- *Literacy skills:* fewer objects and colors named, limited print awareness or interest in print, little phonological awareness (rhyming);
- *Perceptual-motor skills:* problems with fine motor skills (e.g., coloring, cutting, stringing beads) and gross motor skills (e.g., hopping, running, jumping) (NJCLD, 2006).

Before the 2004 amendments to the IDEA, it was difficult to identify a child with a learning disability until he was in second or third grade and had experienced failure. States identified children with learning disabilities by looking at the difference (discrepancy) between a child's IQ on a standardized intelligence test and the child's academic achievement, by comparing the child's mental age from the intelligence test to the grade-age equivalent of a standardized achievement test. States developed formulas for how far a child had to be behind to qualify. In some states, if the child's achievement scores were two years below his mental age, the child was identified as having a learning disability.

There are a variety of problems with this practice, including these:

1. The discrepancy requirement made it virtually impossible to identify young children as having a learning disability.

2. Discrepancies may exist for a variety of reasons that may or may not relate to having a learning disability.

3. The discrepancy model required that children have repeated experiences with failure until the gap between IQ and achievement was large enough to meet the criteria for identification.

4. Disproportionately, children from diverse cultural and ethnic groups were identified as having specific learning disabilities.

5. Children who fail academically often develop behavior problems, low self-esteem and have problems with peer relations.

6. IQ scores are not good predictors of a child's ability to recognize words and do phonological decoding—the basic skills involved in reading (Coleman, Buysse, & Neitzel, 2006; Shapiro, Church, & Lewis, 2002).

It became clear that if the goal were to prevent so many children from being identified as having SLD, then the criteria would have to change. According to IDEA 2004, states must have procedures for identifying children with specific learning disabilities that do not require the use of a severe discrepancy between intellectual ability and achievement for making such a determination. They must permit the use of a process based on the child's response to scientific, research-based intervention as well as permit the use of other alternative research-based procedures for determining whether a child has a specific learning disability (U.S. DOE, 2006).

> ▶❚❚ TeachSource Video Case
> **Learning Disabilities**
> Watch the TeachSource Video Case *Learning Disabilities*, in which the mother of three children with learning disabilities gives her perspective on how to live with and diagnose children with a learning disability. The video can be found in the Early Childhood Education Media Library under Child Development, available at www.cengagebrain.com.

The following criteria are used to determine whether a child has SLD. The child does not achieve adequately for his age or to meet State-approved grade-level standards in one or more of the following areas, when appropriate instruction has been provided:

- Oral expression
- Listening comprehension
- Written expression
- Basic reading skills
- Reading fluency skills
- Reading comprehension
- Mathematical calculation
- Mathematical problem solving

If a child does not make sufficient progress to meet age/grade-level standards in one or more of these identified areas when using a process based on the child's response to scientific, research-based intervention, then additional assessment must be completed. The child's pattern of strengths and weaknesses in performance, achievement, or both, relative to age/grade-level standards must be documented. To ensure that underachievement is not due to lack of appropriate instruction in reading or math:

- Data must demonstrate that the child was provided appropriate instruction in regular education settings, delivered by qualified personnel; and
- Data-based documentation of repeated assessments of achievement at reasonable intervals, reflecting formal assessment of student progress during instruction, which was provided to the child's parents.

The public agency must promptly request parental consent to evaluate the child to determine whether the child needs special education and related services, and must adhere to the specified time frames (U. S. DOE, 2006).

The regulations ensure that the child is observed in her learning environment (including the regular classroom setting) to document her academic performance and behavior in the areas of difficulty. The team must use information from an observation in routine classroom instruction and monitoring of the child's performance that was done before the child was referred for an evaluation, or after the child has been referred for an evaluation and parental consent is obtained.

For children less than school age, a group member must observe the child in an environment appropriate for a child of that age (U.S. DOE, 2006).

The law also specifies the documentation needed to determine whether a child has SLD. The documentation to determine a child's eligibility for services under the IDEA must contain information about

- Whether the child has a specific learning disability;
- The basis for making that determination;

Children must be observed in their natural environments.
©Cengage Learning 2012

- Relevant behavior and the relationship of that behavior to the child's academic functioning;

- Educationally relevant medical findings;

- Whether the child is making sufficient progress to meet age/grade-level standards or the child exhibits patterns of strengths and weaknesses in performance, indicative of SLD that are not caused by visual, hearing, or motor disability; mental retardation; emotional disturbance; cultural factors; environmental or economic disadvantage; or limited English proficiency;

- The child's response to scientific, research-based intervention including the instructional strategies used and the student-centered data collected;

- Documentation that the child's parents were notified about the State's policies regarding the amount and nature of student performance data; strategies for increasing the child's rate of learning; and the parents' right to request an evaluation.

- Each group/team member must certify in writing whether the report reflects the member's conclusion (U. S. DOE, 2006).

These changes are a result of the passage of the 2004 amendments to the IDEA. This model makes it possible to identify young children with SLD. The first criterion is that the child must have had "appropriate instruction in reading and math" (appropriate is based on the child's age). Obviously children who have had little or poor instruction cannot be expected to learn reading and math. The second criteria is that the process must be based on the "child's response to scientific, research-based intervention." These criteria have given rise to the concept of early intervening services (EIS) and response to intervention (RTI).

IN THE FIELD

My son, Rob, was identified last spring as having a learning disability. I had always known that Rob learned differently than other children and was happy when his problem was identified so he could receive services to help him.

Unfortunately, Rob's problem didn't only consist of a learning disability. Since the time Rob was an infant, I have had many problems with Rob's behavior, both in and out of school. One of Rob's most disturbing behaviors is his inability to follow directions and complete simple chores. It seems that he simply forgets what he has to do. Rob is easily distracted. He has trouble completing a task and concentrating on what he is doing. I took him to a doctor to find out if he had ADD or ADHD, but he didn't. He also seems awkward and a bit clumsy. He constantly had skinned knees from tripping, and other children laughed at him. Because this makes him feel bad, he quit participating in the games and sports he used to play. I know he is young, but I see him starting to gain weight.

I asked for a meeting with Rob's teacher to see if she had some ideas for me. I learned that some of Rob's behavior problems are normal for children with learning disabilities. I really thought it was just that he couldn't learn to read and struggled with math. I didn't realize how much it affected other areas of his development. This has helped me deal with these behaviors differently. Knowing that these are normal characteristics for kids with learning disabilities has made me a better parent. I learned that he is not being naughty, and now I try to help Rob instead of losing my cool. If only I could teach the rest of the family.

Early Intervening Services

Early intervening services (EIS) are designed for children in kindergarten through grade twelve (with a particular emphasis on K–3) who are not identified as needing special education services but who need additional academic and behavioral support to succeed in the general educational environment (U.S. DOE, 2007b).

EIS funds can be used to provide professional development to enable personnel to deliver scientifically based academic instruction and behavioral interventions, including scientifically based literacy instruction and instruction on the use of adaptive and instructional software; and to provide educational and behavioral evaluations, services, and supports (U.S. DOE, 2006).

THE EVIDENCE BASE

The United States is concerned about the reading ability of all young children. The National Assessment of Educational Progress (NAPE) provides a measure of how children are doing at specific grade levels.

Percent of public school 4th graders at or above Proficient on the NAPE in 2009

Academic Areas	White	Black	Hispanic	Asian/ Pacific Islander	American Indian/ Alaska Native	Total
Reading	41	15	16	48	22	32
Mathematics	50	15	21	61	23	38

These scores have remained stable since 2007. They raise concerns about what all public school children are learning and particular concerns about black, Hispanic, and American Indian and Alaska Native children. Of the children assessed 48 percent were eligible for free or reduced price lunch. There has been a significant increase in the number of children in this category since 2003.

Source: U.S. DOE, 2011.

REFLECTIVE PRACTICE | In fourth grade, only 32 percent of children are proficient in reading and 38 percent in mathematics. Disproportionately, some groups of children are not successfully mastering the skills they need to succeed. These discrepancies were one reason for looking more carefully at what children in the general education curriculum were learning; we must ensure that all children are learning at the expected rate without having to identify special learning needs.

Response to Intervention

The acronym RTI is used to refer to response to intervention or response to instruction. **Response to instruction** is used to refer to core programming or what is happening everyday to all students. Response to intervention refers to responses that are made when there are major or substantial changes in programming for some or all students (Salvia & Ysseldyke, 2007). The RTI model for school-age children allows and supports early and intensive intervention before children fail. The underlying assumption of RTI is that early intervention holds the potential of preventing academic problems for children with learning difficulties. It emphasizes the general curriculum and holds potential for helping all children (Coleman et al., 2006).

There is general agreement that the model is a tiered approach and that the first tier is regular education and the top tier is special education. There is less agreement about the middle tier(s) (Reschly, 2005). The bottom of the tier or the foundation of the triangle is high-quality instruction for all children. The assumption is that 80 percent of children in a class should be making progress at the expected rate. If this were not true then the intervention would be to improve the quality of the classroom instruction until this goal is met. Tier one is also designed to determine which children need additional instructional interventions to progress at the expected rate (Coleman et al., 2006). The second tier is targeted to the small group of children (about 20%) who did not make adequate progress in tier one. Teachers intervene with these children using differentiated instructional methods such as modifying the curriculum, using small-group instruction, standard treatment protocols, or other methods of presenting material in different ways that support learning and have a research base. It is expected that an additional 15 percent of children will progress at the expected rate with these modifications in instruction. A small portion of the children, perhaps 5 percent, will not make sufficient progress with these modifications and will move on to the next tier. These children will receive intensive individualized interventions. If this intensive instruction does not produce learning at the expected rate, the children are referred for formal evaluation (with parental consent) (Reschly, 2005). The approach is a collaborative one between classroom teachers, parents, and specialists that uses assessment data to guide curriculum, teaching, and interventions.

Children can move in an out of tiers depending upon their reading level. In a first grade classroom using RTI you might find children in small groups with some reading books, others with headphones listening to a book as they read along with it. Other children may be playing word games with each other while still others use individualized computer or electronic tablet applications.

An emerging body of literature says that RTI is a potentially effective method of identifying children at risk for learning disabilities. However, less agreement exists about which intervention strategies are most effective and how RTI could be implemented for 3- and 4-year old-children. Little information is available about children who have problems in areas other than reading (Coleman et al., 2006). RTI presents an instructional approach for identifying school-age children who are at risk for learning disabilities. It provides intervention without the need to label children until it becomes clear that they need individualized instruction and that they are likely to meet the IDEA criteria for SLD.

To establish the evidence base, a research synthesis on response to intervention was conducted. It showed that specialized interventions could potentially either help children learn the skills they need or prevent the occurrence of learning disabilities. Research results varied based on who delivered the intervention, how long children participated, the intervention approach used, the outcome measures, and even the function of RTI (Coleman et al., 2006). However, most of the studies focused on children in grades 1 to 3 rather than preschool children. Additional research with preschool children is necessary to expand the research to younger children and to answer questions about some of the important variables such as which instructional methods, for which children, and for how long, produce what outcomes.

THE EVIDENCE BASE

The Committee on the Prevention of Reading Difficulties in Young Children (1998) looked at letter identification skills of 1,000 kindergarten children who were designated as at risk in kindergarten (the bottom 10%)—that is, the children who did not know their letter names—and who were in the bottom 20 percent of teacher's ratings in first grade (did not have letter-sound knowledge). This method correctly identified 63 children as having reading disabilities and falsely identified 37 children. Based on these data, the Committee hypothesized that if children do not know letter names by January of their kindergarten year, this may be a sign that reading problems will be present. If a child gets to first grade and does not have letter-sound knowledge, this also signals reading difficulties

Source: American Federation of Teachers, 2004.

REFLECTIVE PRACTICE | Screening mechanisms, even ones as simple as these, are the first step in the assessment process and the basis on which RTI help can prevent reading disabilities. With this information, teachers can begin to target children in kindergarten and move into an RTI that will increase children's probability of learning to read before they experience failure in first grade. If you plan to teach 3- and 4-year olds or kindergarteners and first-graders, how would this knowledge impact your assessment and teaching practices?

Professional organizations, including the Learning Disabilities Roundtable (2002) and the National Joint Committee on Learning Disabilities (NJCLD) (2006), recommend that preschoolers be screened for early language and readings skills just as they are for vision and hearing.

> ▶❚ TeachSource Video Case
>
> **Response to Intervention: The Three-Tier Model in a Preschool Environment**
>
> Watch the TeachSource Video Case *Response to Intervention: The Three-Tier Model in a Preschool Environment*, in which you will see RTI in action in an early childhood classroom. The video can be found in the Early Childhood Education Media Library under Special Education, available at www.cengagebrain.com.

Recognition and Response

Recognition and Response is an early intervention system being developed for preschool children at risk for specific learning disabilities. It has its base in the RTI movement, but applies the principles to younger children and the contexts in which young children grow and learn (Coleman et al., 2006).

The essential components of the Recognition and Response system include the following:

- An intervention hierarchy (three tiers)
- Screening, assessment, and progress monitoring
- Research-based curriculum, instruction, and focused interventions
- Collaborative problem-solving process for decision making (Coleman et al., 2006)

Recognition and Response is similar to RTI in its tiered approach. Tier 1 focuses on the early childhood research-based curriculum, to ensure that most of the children (about 80%) are making progress at the expected rate. Children who are not progressing move to tier 2, where educators provide interventions and curriculum modifications, requiring minor adjustment to classroom routines, to this targeted group of children. For example, before a story is read to the entire group, a small group of children who are not making progress at the expected rate would be gathered. The story might be discussed briefly to activate prior knowledge; vocabulary might be reviewed; or other strategies would be used to make the experience more meaningful. As with tier 1, decisions are guided by assessment. Tier 3 provides more intensive individualized instruction. A teacher might work one-on-one teaching rhyming concepts, letter recognition, or whatever the assessment shows that the child needs. If children do not make adequate progress in tier 3, they would be referred for formal testing (Coleman et al., 2006).

Program standards and guidelines have been developed to guide early care and education practice. High-quality early care and education settings are expected to construct and implement a thoughtfully planned comprehensive system of curriculum that aligns with early learning guidelines and program standards, and make sound educational decisions for all children (NAEYC & NAECS/SDE, 2006). Providing high-quality early learning environments requires money and expertise. An effective Recognition and Response system makes even greater demands. Looking at a combination of state, local, federal, and Temporary Assistance for Needy Families spending, approximately $4,134 per child is spent for preschool; for Head Start, it moves up to $7,860; and for children in K–12, it is $11,286 (Barnett et al., 2007). When we look at the preschool year as having the possibility for prevention of learning disabilities, we examine the allocation of resources, teacher–child interactions, and how children are spending their time during the preschool years. Recent economic difficulties at all governmental levels will make increased spending on high-quality early learning environments especially difficult.

THE EVIDENCE BASE

Measuring quality in early child classrooms is challenging. It is easier to count ratios, class size, and qualifications than what is going on in the classroom. One major research effort involved 240 randomly selected state-funded pre-kindergarten programs in six states, with more than 900 pre-K children who were representative of over 211,000 pre-K children participating in the sites. Overall, the class size and teacher–child ratios met or exceeded standards. The pre-K teachers, on average, were better educated and better paid than teachers in non-school settings (FPG, 2005a).

Although two of the states in the study (Georgia and New York) were moving toward universal pre-K, most of the children were either from poor families or were those at risk for learning delays. A large proportion of the children's mothers (42%) had only a high school education or less and 23 percent of the pre-kindergarteners spoke a language other than English at home (FPG, 2005a).

Researchers developed two measures of quality that looked at "Emotional Climate," which "indicates how positive, sensitive, and responsive the classroom is" and "Instructional Climate," which "indicates how well time, materials, and teacher–child interactions are managed to optimize children's learning (FPG, 2005b, p. 21).

Trained observers spent two days in each classroom, using the SNAPSHOT, a measure that looked at the main intended activities, the content areas the child was engaged in, and the frequency of teacher–child interactions. Overall, children spent the most time (13%) in social studies, which included dramatic play and blocks, closely followed by literacy (12%), art and music (9%), science (8%), motor (7%), and math (6%). However, 44 percent of the time the child was engaged in none of these. Teacher–child interactions were also coded. Distressingly, there was no teacher–child interaction during 73 percent of the time children were in preschool. Teacher-child interaction was minimal 18 percent of the time, with elaborated interactions coded only 8 percent of the time. These occurred mostly during whole-group activity. Routine interactions occurred about 1 percent of the time. Teachers devoted only about 3 percent of the time to helping children move from less complex to more complex understanding of math and literacy, and less than half of the children experienced this (FPG, 2005c). What were the children doing? They spent a lot of time waiting in line or eating.

Sources: Frank Porter Graham (FPG) Child Development Institute, 2005a, b, and c.

REFLECTIVE PRACTICE | If prevention of learning disabilities is going to move to preschool, how do you see that happening? What will have to happen to preschool programs and curriculum? What will you do to change your pattern of interacting with children and supporting literacy and math in a developmentally appropriate way?

The Recognition and Response system is being designed to help preschool teachers identify children who are not learning at the expected rate and who require more focused intervention. It can provide guidance by offering teaching strategies and approaches for monitoring and evaluating the effectiveness of instructional approaches. The Recognition and Response system is expected to be beneficial for children enrolled in all types of prekindergarten programs, including child care centers, family child care homes, Head Start, and private and public preschools. Because of its research base, it also has the potential to improve the quality of early childhood programs for all children (Coleman et al., 2006). However, if teachers spend little time interacting with children, and much of children's time is spent in waiting, the potential will not be realized.

The overarching goal of the Recognition and Response system is for teachers to use assessment as part of an integrated instructional system to make improvements in the general early education program and to plan more focused interventions for children who may be at risk of developing learning disabilities and who require additional supports to learn (Coleman et al., 2006, p. 33).

Young children who are at risk for learning or reading disabilities require a carefully planned environment that supports their development and helps prevent learning difficulties from occurring later. Protective factors include high-quality responsive learning experiences and the availability of multiple supports if children are identified as having a problem. However, protective factors do not rule out the possibility of a child actually having a disability.

IMPLICATIONS FOR EDUCATORS

We know techniques that support all children in learning to read and that can be incorporated into the early childhood curriculum.

- Before reading a story, activate prior learning. After reading a story, discuss it. Stop some stories and see whether children can anticipate what might happen next. Have children retell stories using the pictures as clues. Have children "play read" books. Share your joy of reading with them and continue to read to them.
- Teach children about the structure of books and the vocabulary that goes with it. They need to know the title of a book (after you have read it) and to point to it on the book itself. They need to know where the story begins. Additionally, they need to know the front and back of a book, the first and last page, and the bottom and top of the

page. Children need to be able to find individual words and to point to words as you read. (This is best done individually, with a child on your lap.)
- Help children recognize rhyming words. Many nursery rhymes have rhyming words at the end of lines. Change one of the words and see whether the children notice. If they understand the concept of rhyming, see whether children can generate rhyming words to match those you say.

Children also need to be taught about parts of words and how sounds blend into words. If their name has more than one syllable, this is a place to start. Say the first syllable and pause before saying the second: Mi-chael. Sometimes, compound words help children get the idea: playground, bed-room, air-plane. Don't belabor this, but do introduce it regularly.

A beginning phonetic skill is the association of initial sounds with objects or pictures. Begin with small objects and initially agree on what each is called (apple, cup, key, pencil, toothbrush). Then, ask the child to give you the object that begins with the sound /a/ (be sure it is the *sound*, not the letter name). Make it a guessing game: "I'm thinking of something that begins with /p/. What am I thinking of?" Then, ask for the remainder of the items. Ask for some more than once, and put the items back so the child cannot use the process of elimination. Then, have the child be the "thinker" (teacher) who requests the information. Start with real objects, then use pictures for some sounds that are difficult to find objects for.

Foundation skills and motivation are important in learning to read. To help determine a child's skill level, read a book with a known lexile level that should be within the child's reading range:

- Read the book with the child one-on-one. Choose a simple yet unfamiliar book with clear illustrations. Ask the child what the book is about. (Does the child use the illustrations and other clues to make a guess?) Read the story together with the child. Can the child use context to make sense of the story? Does the child go back and reread part of a sentence once she has worked out the meaning? Does the child hesitate over misreading? Can the child comment on characters and events in the story? Children need to learn to use contextual cues combined with the knowledge of phonemes to figure out what a word might be. If they don't have these skills, you need to teach them while you read to individual children. If the book is too difficult, find one with a lover lexile level and repeat the process.
- Keep records for each child on the alphabet letters the child can identify (upper- and lowercase) and their single letter sounds as well as the number of words in their word bank. Look carefully at the children who are in the lowest 20 percent. Something is not working for these children and they are going to need more individualized and intensive instruction in this area.

It is often difficult for children with specific learning disabilities to interpret what they see (visual perception). A child may not be able to judge size, shape, location, movement, and color because to the child these properties keep changing. Because of the difficulty children have in sorting out foreground and background, they often focus on irrelevant details. It is difficult for them to recognize similarities and differences (visual discrimination). Their problems are magnified when they try to learn to recognize numbers and letters, as the differences are slight. The letters that are reversible are especially difficult (*b, d*), as are the ones with "tails" (*p, q, j, g*). See Activity 2–22, *Alphabet Lotto*.

Visual tracking is the ability to focus the eyes on one point and then move them rhythmically from side to side, up and down, and diagonally. Some children have jerky eye movements or move their whole head instead of just their eyes. Part–whole relationships (visual closure) cause problems. The children may have trouble identifying missing parts; a picture of a three-legged chair appears normal to them. They may have trouble remembering what they see. (Place four objects on the table, cover them,

Signs of learning disabilities are apparent during the preschool years. The use of recognition and response during these years may prevent some specific learning disabilities.
©Cengage Learning 2012

remove one, and ask them to name the missing one.) Poor visual memory also makes it difficult to remember sequences. Needed memory skills can be built by games that require children to remember the original order of objects that have been moved. See Activity 3–35w, *Changing Objects.* Teachers can use the following methods to support visual skills:

- Play visual tracking games by having children follow a flashlight or pointer with their eyes.
- Hide objects or pictures so they are partially visible and have children find them.
- Help children learn to observe detail. Have children think about the parts of a flower while they are looking at it, and then from memory.

Assessment of Specific Learning Disabilities

Although many professionals are reluctant to identify young children as having learning disabilities, there may be indications in young children that learning is not progressing in some areas at the expected rate, including these:

- Delays in speech and language development
- Lack of motor coordination
- Problems with perceptual reasoning
- Immature social interactions and achievement
- Premath and preliteracy skills (NJCLD, 2006).

More specifically, young children who struggle with reading often have problems with phonemic awareness (the ability to identify and manipulate the sounds in words), and they usually have a small **sight vocabulary** (words they can read without sounding them out).

If Recognition and Response or RTI are not successful, the formal assessment process begins. There is agreement that assessment must be multimodal. It typically includes the use of standardized tests of intelligence and standardized achievement tests combined with teacher ratings. Although the exact battery of tests may differ, testing should include the eight areas identified in IDEA (2004) (oral expression, listening comprehension, written expression, basic reading skills, reading fluency skills, reading comprehension, mathematics calculation, and mathematics problem solving) (Salvia & Ysseldyke, 2007).

Cognitive functioning (IQ) and executive function should also be assessed. In the past, formal assessment did not begin until a child's reading age was significantly below grade level. If we do not intervene with children who are having problems reading before the third grade, the probability of successful remediation drops to about 25 percent (Shaywitz & Shaywitz, 1991). Early intensive remediation has a much higher probability of success. Hence, the 2004 IDEA supports identifying all children with early reading problems and using RTI to prevent future reading problems for most children.

The National Joint Committee on Learning Disabilities (2006) recommends a four-step ongoing assessment:

1. *Describe learning problems prior to referral for formal assessment, particularly as they relate to a child's strengths and problems.* This step involves interviewing key participants, gathering and analyzing information, observing the child in the classroom, and looking at alternative explanations for the problem. It also focuses on monitoring the interventions and accommodations and their effectiveness.

2. *Identify children as having learning difficulties by looking at the information from step 1 and deciding how pervasive and severe the problems are and how they relate to other areas of development.* If the decision is made to proceed, a comprehensive evaluation should be conducted. Information should include the areas of listening, speaking, reading, writing, reasoning, and mathematics. Decision making should be sensitive to both over- and underidentification by looking at linguistic and cultural differences, adequacy of general instruction, and the occurrence of other disabilities.

3. *Determine eligibility for special education and related services that involve a collaborative decision-making process, taking into account the requirements of the IDEA.*

4. *Bridge assessment to specialized instruction and accommodations by using the information gleaned from the entire assessment process to develop an IEP.* The IEP should be responsive to the child's current strengths, weaknesses, and learning styles, with input from parents, educators, and therapists.

Formal assessment of learning disabilities is likely to include a measure of cognitive functioning, such as the Wechsler Preschool and Primary Scale of Intelligence–III (WPPSI–III; Psychological Corporation, 2002). The WPPSI–III has two scales: one for children ages 2 years and 6 months to 3 years and 11 months. The other scale begins at 4 years and goes to 7 years and 3 months. Both scales have verbal and performance subtests as well as some supplemental subtests. The Wechsler Intelligence Scale for Children–IV (WISC-IV; Wechsler, 2003) is used for children from age 6 years to 16 years and 11 months. The WISC-IV provides a full-scale IQ as a measure of general intellectual functioning. It also provides four index scores: Verbal Comprehension Index, Perceptual Reasoning Index, Working Memory Index, and Processing Speed Index. The index scores provide information about aspects of general intelligence that are helpful in understanding how a child views his world.

Achievement tests are used frequently in education settings to evaluate knowledge and understanding in different curricular areas. Some tests are administered to groups, whereas others must be administered individually. Some serve as screening tests and others are diagnostic devices. Some focus on a single content area such as reading or math, whereas others cover multiple areas. Some are norm referenced, whereas others are criterion referenced (Salvia & Ysseldyke, 2007). The appropriate measure is selected based on how it will be used. The Iowa Tests of Basic Skills-C (ITBS; Hoover, Dunbar, & Frisbe, 2007) includes subtests for children in kindergarten through grade 8. Applicable subtests include vocabulary, word analysis, reading/reading comprehension, listening, language, and mathematics. For kindergarten and first grade, the tests are untimed and read aloud by the teacher.

Some measures are specifically designed for reading. The Woodcock Diagnostic Reading Battery (WDRB; Woodcock, 1997) has 10 subtests that focus on reading, which are combined to provider cluster scores, and can be used for children ages 5 and older. The subtests include letter/word identification, word attack, reading vocabulary, passage comprehension, incomplete words, sound blending, oral vocabulary, listening comprehension, memory for sentences, and visual matching.

Teacher rating scales can be informal or formal. The Conners Rating Scale-Revised (CRS-R; Conners, 2000) is an observational measure used by teachers (there is also a parent's version) to rate children's behavior. It looks at factors such as daydreaming/inattention, hyperactivity, conduct problems, anxiousness/fearfulness, and social cooperation. The actual battery of tests will be determined by the child's pattern of strengths and weaknesses, and the school and examiner's preferences.

Informal assessment methods may involve having a child read a particular passage that has a known age-to-grade-level equivalent and noting the mistakes the child makes. In the hands of a skilled educator, this can be a good assessment tool; in the hands of a less sensitive educator, it may be meaningless information.

Additional assessments include trained observers and a behavioral event sampling that targets behaviors in specific situations. Peer rating may also be used, as children with SLD often find peer relationships challenging. Overall, the goal of assessment is to focus on the particular problems and strengths the child shows and to develop an individualized curriculum to work through the strengths to build needed skills. The most common specific learning disability and the one we know the most about is dyslexia.

Dyslexia or Reading Disability

Developmental **dyslexia**, or reading disability, is the most common type of learning disability. Developmental dyslexia is a chronic, persistent condition and one that is both familial and heritable. Boys are more frequently diagnosed (60% to 80%) than girls (APA, 2000). The American Psychiatric Association (APA) (2000) estimates that 4 percent of the school-age population, or four out of five cases of learning disorders, relate specifically to reading.

The Board of Directors of the International Dyslexia Association (2002) has adopted the following definition of dyslexia.

> Dyslexia is a specific learning disability that is neurobiological in origin. It is characterized by difficulties with accurate and/or fluent word recognition and by poor spelling and decoding abilities. These difficulties typically result from a deficit in the phonological component of language that is often unexpected in relation to other cognitive abilities and the provision of effective classroom instruction. Secondary consequences may include problems in reading comprehension and reduced reading experience that can impede growth of vocabulary and background knowledge.

This is clearly a medical definition of dyslexia, but it is one that is supported by genetic research and how the brain works. Reading is a dynamic complex process that changes with experience. Early reading instruction focuses on **decoding**.

Children with dyslexia have problems with the decoding process. They seem unable to segment the written word into its phonologic elements. The phonologic-deficit hypothesis for dyslexia posits that children with dyslexia have a neurological inability in this area. This is supported by functional brain-imaging studies that show differences in the temproparietal brain regions between those with dyslexia and those without (Shaywitz & Shaywitz, 2005). This area of the brain is used to analyze the written word, a process called decoding. This lower-order linguistic block prevents access to higher-order linguistic skills. Until children can decode and identify words, they cannot look at meaning and comprehension. Their skills in other areas of language (syntax, semantics, etc.) are comparable to their peers.

In their framework for developing evidence-based practice in early literacy, Dunst and colleagues (2006) have identified overlapping areas of skills necessary for reading. These skills and variations of them can be categorized as print-related skills, linguistic processing skills, and visual processing skills (Dunst, Trivette, & Hamby, 2007) and are predictors of later decoding, spelling, and comprehension (see Table 8–2). Although the skills are necessary for early literacy, a shotgun approach to teaching all of these skills is not supported by the evidence. Rather, interventions that focus on one skill or a set of interrelated targeted skills are more likely to be effective (Dunst et al., 2007).

Further research on the efficacy of reading instruction practices showed that active reading experiences were most effective with 3- and 4-year-olds, and shorter reading episodes (15 minutes or less) were more effective than longer ones (Dunst et al., 2007).

▶❚❚ TeachSource Video Case

Collaborating with School Specialists:
An Elementary Literacy Lesson
Watch the TeachSource Video Case *Collaborating with School Specialists: An Elementary Literacy Lesson*, in which you will see one school specialist help a classroom teacher. The video can be found in the Early Childhood Education Media Library under Child Development, available at www.cengagebrain.com.

IMPLICATIONS FOR EDUCATORS

Children need a literacy-rich environment and need to be read to. Do you think there are better ways to read to children? Obviously, it is best to be expressive and to choose books that are at children's developmental level, but are there techniques that work better than others, especially for

TABLE 8-2 PRINT, LINGUISTIC, AND VISUAL LITERACY SKILLS

Print-Related Skills	
Alphabetic Knowledge	Ability to recognize and name letters of the alphabet and translate graphemes (units of print) into units of sound (phonemes).
Print Awareness	Ability to recognize that print has rules and properties based on the written language, and what children can see in print they can say.
Written Language	Ability to represent ideas or concepts in a printed or written format consisting of letters, words, and sentences.
Linguistic Processing Skills	
Phonological Awareness	Ability to recognize, manipulate, and use sounds as distinct from meaning. Includes rhyming, blending, and segmenting sounds into syllables and words.
Oral Language	Ability to understand the rules for combining sounds and organizing sounds into words and words into sentences, as well as understanding the meaning of words and using words to communicate with others.
Listening Comprehension	Ability to understand the meaning of the spoken word by decoding words and sentences and making meaning of what is heard.
Text Comprehension	Ability to understand the meaning of the written word by decoding words and sentences and making sense of what is read.
Visual Processing Skills	
Visual Memory	Ability to remember visual representations such as letters, words, and pictures.
Visual Motor Skills	Ability to integrate visual information with fine or gross motor skills.
Visual Perceptual Skills	Ability to accurately interpret what is seen and make it meaningful.

Literacy experts, literacy centers, and professional organizations have identified the print-related skills and the linguistic processing skills as important for reading literacy. The visual processing skills do not yet have that level of research support.

Sources: Dunst et al., 2006; Dunst et al., 2007; Robyak et al., 2007.

children who may struggle with reading? Involving the children themselves in the process matters. It starts with the child and his interest in the topic as the basis for the book choice. Then comes the "how" question, which appears to be more important than the sheer amount of reading (Trivette & Dunst, 2007). In *shared reading*, an adult reads a book to one child or a small group of children. In *interactive shared reading*, the adult reads a book to a child or a small group of children and asks *Who/What/Where/When/How* questions. In *dialogic reading*, the adult and child switch roles so the child learns to become the storyteller, with adult support. The adult functions as an active listener and questioner. Both interactive shared reading and dialogic reading are more effective than shared reading. Reading for 15 minutes or less is more effective than reading for 30 minutes or more (Trivette & Dunst, 2007).

In *guided reading*, the teacher introduces a book and guides the children through it. Take the children through a "book walk" or a "picture walk." Have children think about the story and what will happen in the book. Introduce key vocabulary in the context of the story and discuss reading strategies. Children then read the book independently, with a partner or in a small group. The goal is to make children successful readers. After they have read the book, the teacher discusses the book with the children to assess their level of understanding. The children then reread the book.

Activating prior knowledge is a strategy you can use with all reading strategies. You can teach children this strategy to help them remember new information, especially in reading. Before reading a story, ask children what they know about the subject of the story (one of the *Who/What/Where/When/How* questions). For example, if you are reading a story about a picnic, ask children whether they have ever been on a picnic and what they remember. Have children share with the class their descriptions of previous picnics. When reading, refer back to what the children said about picnics or their own experiences with picnics. They will make connections between what they already know and the new information. As a result, they will be more likely to remember the story or the new information.

REFLECTIVE PRACTICE | As you think about reading, do you expect parents to read to their children? Do you expect in-class reading to be a large-group activity? How might knowledge of the effectiveness of different reading styles influence what you tell parents about reading to their children and how you spend your time reading in the classroom? How can you use this information to develop an early reading program for young children? Where would you start? How would you plan to focus your intervention?

Dysgraphia, or Disorder of Written Expression

Dysgraphia is also a neurological disorder, generally characterized by the profound inability to form meaningful symbols. The child with dysgraphia produces distorted or incorrect letters in her attempt to write (National Institute of Neurological Disorders and Stroke [NINDS], 2007). Many children who are identified as having dysgraphia also have dyslexia. A disorder of written expression is more than just poor handwriting (which would be classified as a developmental coordination disorder); it involves problems related to grammar, punctuation, and poor paragraph organization, as well as excessively poor handwriting. There is some evidence that perceptual motor and language deficits may be part of this disorder. Prevalence rates for dysgraphia are difficult to establish because it is almost always accompanied by other learning disorders (Richards, 1999). It is seldom diagnosed until the end of first or second grade, when children are required to do more writing (APA, 2000). See Table 8–3 for signs of dysgraphia.

Fatigue and frustration impede the child's learning process and may lead to low self-esteem. It is not that the child cannot learn, but that so much time may be spent on the writing process that much of the information is missed. The child is able to associate sounds with meaning, and therefore able to develop appropriate verbal skills; however, sound-letter recognition appears to be lacking in many children who have a writing disability.

There are a variety of strategies used to help children with dysgraphia; the most important consideration is finding the strategy that best fits each child's needs. Some children's handwriting will improve with additional instruction. Other children do better when they are provided with alternatives to written expression (NCLD, 2008).

In many educational settings, children with dysgraphia use word processors. Although computers are a great aid to children with dysgraphia, understanding and time are still the greatest gifts a teacher can give.

TABLE 8-3   SIGNS OF DYSGRAPHIA

Illegible, slow handwriting (in spite of appropriate time and attention given to the task by the child) and tiring quickly while writing
Inconsistencies—mixtures of points and curves; improper use or mixture of upper- and lowercase; irregular size, shape, or slant of letters
Unfinished words or letters, or omitted words in sentences
Inconsistent position on the page with respect to lines and margins, messy and unorganized
Inconsistent spaces between words and letters
Poor fine motor skills
Problems copying
Tight, awkward pencil grip and body position
Avoidance of writing or drawing activities
Saying words out loud while writing
Problems with syntax, structure, and grammar
Problems organizing thoughts on paper
Large gap between expressive language and what is produced in writing

Sources: International Dyslexia Association, 2003; National Center for Learning Disabilities, 2008.

Dyscalculia, or Mathematics Disorder

The neurobiological evidence of **dyscalculia** is evolving, but it is challenging as different types of math skills require different brain functions that activate different brain areas (Shapiro et al., 2007). Dyscalculia seems to be genetic and heritable in nature. The parietal lobe is implicated in the cause of this disorder, although other areas of the brain can compensate for this impairment in some children (Shapiro et al., 2007). It is frequently found in combination with reading disorders or disorders of written expression (APA, 2000). The number of children identified with a mathematics disorder fluctuates between 1 and 6.5 percent of the children enrolled in school (APA, 2000; Geary, 1999). Like dyslexia, dyscalculia is identified by mathematical ability that is significantly below that expected, given the child's age and intellectual level. It is seldom diagnosed before the end of first grade. For children with high IQs, it may not be identified until fifth grade or later (APA, 2000).

Dyscalculia is the inability to understand the processes associated with mathematical calculation and reasoning. Like other learning disabilities, it has little to do with IQ, motivation, or other factors that might influence learning. Although there are many aspects of math relating to problem solving, measurement, time, and so on, it is defined by lack of mastery of mathematical facts and lack of fluency in calculations (Jordan, Hanich, & Kaplan, 2003). Children with dyscalculia may never grasp the fact that $5 + 7 = 10 + 2$, or that $4 \times 6 = 24$. These children will work feverishly for years, using everything from fingers to pieces of paper, to assist them in their quest for the correct answer to a math problem, without understanding that the problem calls for subtraction and not addition.

Identifying dyscalculia is challenging, because there are more variations in mathematics instruction than in teaching reading. Poor math skills may be related to lack of adequate instruction. If this is the case, RTI should impact these children. Mathematics encompasses a variety of skills and neurological processes. Some of these skills may be impaired and others not (Shapiro et al., 2007). Some children may have problems with math because they have a reading disability or because of lack of executive function and inattention, which causes mathematics to be problematic. Of a sample of children with dyscalculia, 17 percent also had a reading disability and 26 percent had ADHD (Gersten, Jorden, & Flojo,

2005). Although the inability to decode the written symbols of math is part of dyscalculia, it goes far beyond that. Dyscalculia also includes the inability to understand the visual-spatial aspects of math and the language of math. Dyscalculia affects children in very different ways. One child may not be able to add; another may be able to add; however, division is a notion that is simply unattainable. Some have problems similar to dyslexia, such as approaching problems in a left to right manner, forgetting to carry, or misplacing signs or digits (Shalev, 2004). Far more is unknown about math disorders than is known about them. As is the case with all SLD, research continues to find ways to improve the quality of life and education for children with these disorders.

THE EVIDENCE BASE

The ability to determine what mathematical difficulties are persistent and lead to mathematical disorders is the first step in early identification. If these learning needs could be identified early, then interventions could be designed to prevent failure in math. A sample of 411 kindergarten children in six schools, who used the Trailblazers kindergarten math curriculum, were assessed for number sense, which includes counting, number knowledge, and number operations.

Based on a battery of number sense tests, they found three distinct classes of skill and growth curve for children in kindergarten who they followed into first grade: low/flat (139 children), middle/steep (173 children), and high/flat (102 children). In low/flat patterns, children come to kindergarten with few skills and show little improvement. In middle/steep patterns, children come with some skills but show rapid learning. High/flat patterns show children coming to kindergarten with most of the needed skills, but not acquiring many additional skills.

The researchers tracked children's development of number sense at four points during kindergarten and into first grade. Although almost all children learned some math skills, 50 percent of low-income children were in the low/flat category. These children came to kindergarten with fewer skills in number sense and gained very little in kindergarten and first grade. Low-income kindergarten children showed almost no growth in solving story problems, from the beginning of kindergarten to the end of the year. A similar pattern was observed in number combinations. Gender differences were small but emerging, with boys showing an advantage over girls; these differences extended into first grade. Reading proficiency at the end of kindergarten predicted performance on all number sense measures. Children who began kindergarten at an older age and were more advanced in reading at the beginning of kindergarten continued that advantage. Screening children for number sense in kindergarten might be a way of identifying children who may struggle with math and could also be an opportunity to provide intervention. Based on their research the investigators developed a 33-item streamlined assessment tool for identifying number sense in children.

Sources: Jordan et al., 2007; Jordan, Glutting, & Ramineni, 2008.

IMPLICATIONS FOR EDUCATORS

Because the push for children learning to read is so strong, there is concern that less time and energy will be devoted to mathematics and those who struggle with math. Evaluate how your curriculum approaches mathematics. In the research cited, children in free and reduced-cost lunch programs entered kindergarten with fewer skills in the area of number sense. They had particular problems in the area of story problems and number combinations. With this knowledge, what might you do to help children in these areas either as prevention or intervention? Engaging young children in simple number games helps build number sense.

Processing Disorders

Processing disorders, whether auditory, visual, or kinesthetic/tactile share some common elements. Often elements of these disorders overlap with the specific learning disabilities discussed. Some are concerned that if children learn to read with the support of RTI, specialists will believe that they have solved the child's learning disability and that the processing problems children have will not be dealt with. Processing, or **perception**, is the cognitive process in which the information received from the senses is organized and interpreted by the brain. Perception is dependent on motivation and memory. Once information enters the brain, it must be placed in the correct order or sequence, understood in the context in which it was used (abstraction), and then integrated with other information that is also being processed (organization) (Silver, 1995).

Some children can process information but can't integrate the information to form a whole. As long as they are asked for specific pieces of information, they can answer questions (e.g., "What was the mother's name?"). But they often miss the big picture (e.g., "What was the story about?"). Their lack of organization is frequently general: Their desks are a mess; they forget to take things home or bring them back; they might do work but can't find it to turn it in; they forget their lunch or snack; and so on.

Children with specific learning disabilities often have problems processing auditory, visual, or kinesthetic/tactile information.
©Cengage Learning 2012

Once information enters the brain, it must be stored (remembered). The brain stores information in different ways. The two most important for learning are short- and long-term memory. Short-term memory is limited temporary storage, perhaps five seconds at most; for example, looking up a phone number and then walking to the phone to dial the number. Distractibility makes short-term memory difficult. Long-term memory is more permanent and seemingly unlimited. Retrieving information from long-term memory requires remembering where the information was stored; much like remembering what label you put on a document in your computer. Many children with processing problems have a haphazard labeling system. They function better using divergent retrieval (talking about a topic they generated) rather than convergent retrieval (answering a question).

Usually, the child's ability to transfer information is good. This is one reason why contextual learning is so important; it gives children a system for not only learning but also storing information. Rote learning and isolated facts tend to be stored randomly; this may account for the unevenness of responses in memory tasks. Memory may also be affected by whether the input was visual or auditory. The inability to remember information or effectively retrieve it limits sequential problem solving (Shapiro et al., 2007).

Activating prior knowledge works by connecting new information in a story or lesson to information already stored in long-term memory, the new concepts are also likely to "hook onto," or be stored, in long-term memory. Children will therefore remember and understand stories and other lessons to a greater degree.

Activating prior knowledge can also be used in other domains such as science. If you are teaching about tigers and want children to remember that all tigers have a different set of stripes, first discuss the children's own unique fingerprints. This concept has something to do with themselves and is probably already in the long-term memory. Then, when you introduce the concept of each tiger's unique stripes, children will have a previous concept to latch onto and will be more likely to remember and understand the new concept.

Teach older children about activating prior knowledge. Simply tell them that before they learn about a new concept or read any story, they should think about what they already know about the subject or story or what they have experienced. You may want to tell them that by doing this they are getting their brains ready to remember new information from the lesson. You might even show them a simple diagram of what this might look like (Figure 8–1), explaining that for the little bits of information not to drop out (be forgotten), they have to join up with other information to get into long-term memory.

Executive function involves the ability to maintain appropriate problem-solving procedures to attain future goals and to sustain working toward those goals. It is a broad area that involves planning, organization, time management, working memory, and **metacognition**, including self-monitoring and self-evaluation skills (Dawson & Guare, 2010). Other skills that are necessary to move along the path to meet goals include response inhibition, emotional control (self-regulation of affect), sustained attention, task initiative, flexibility, and goal-directed persistence (Dawson & Guare, 2010). The need for executive function increases with age, particularly when more independence is required.

When children's executive functions are impaired, they are less able to wait for a turn, and they have problems inhibiting responses that involve self-control and delayed gratification. They struggle with formulating sequential plans. They also have problems encoding the information that is relevant for current or future problem solving (e.g., they may focus on shoe color rather than facial expression). Executive function involves being aware of the skills, strategies, and resources to call upon in order to perform tasks efficiently and effectively, and having the self-regulation to complete tasks (Shapiro et al., 2007). Children lacking these skills may use the first solution that occurs to them and may make errors because they are more interested in just finishing (if they do) rather than doing something correctly.

Auditory Processing Disorders

Auditory processing happens when the brain recognizes and interprets sound. A disorder occurs when something in the brain interferes with this process. **Auditory processing disorders** have a variety of names, including central auditory processing disorder, auditory perception problem, and even "word deafness." Children with processing impairments are unable to integrate auditory stimulation despite having normal hearing. For these children, the learning of meanings,

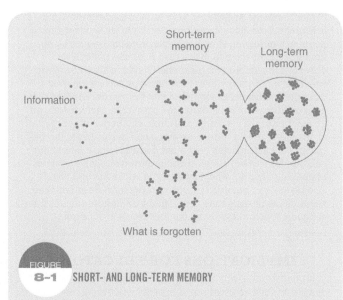

FIGURE 8–1   SHORT- AND LONG-TERM MEMORY

The brain receives an enormous amount of information. If this information seems random or not related to other information it is dropped out of short-term memory. To retain information, move it to long-term memory, and store it so it can be retrieved it needs to be connected to other information the child knows. Interactive reading activates prior knowledge and helps children make connections to new information.

sound combinations, and the specific order of words is flawed; hence, the child's internal models of language are inaccurate (Stuart, 2007).

Auditory discrimination is the ability to detect differences among sounds. Children with processing problems often have trouble recognizing differences in sounds or words, hence what you say is not necessarily what they hear. Some children have difficulty distinguishing subtle differences in sounds and confuse words like *plan* and *plane*, *play* and *place*, hence they often misinterpret meanings. They also have problems identifying the rhyming elements of words.

Auditory memory requires children to keep in mind what was said. Sometimes, children forget the beginning of a sentence by the time you get to the end of it. The second request in two-step instructions may not be remembered. Some children have problems with **auditory sequencing** and **spatial awareness** as well as the parts of speech that relate to position such as prepositions (*in, on, over, under, beside*). Children with sequencing problems may hear and understand a story, but they confuse the sequence of events; they don't know what comes first or last. They may be able to say the letters of the alphabet, days of the week, or months of the year in order, but they can't tell you what letter comes after *l*, the day that comes before Monday, or the month that follows July. If they can, they will start with the beginning of the sequence and go through it until they come to the needed information.

Children may also have problems focusing on a single voice, such as the teacher's, when there is background noise like children talking, a CD playing, or even the heating or cooling system running. Listening is more challenging in noisy environments or with complex information (National Institute on Deafness and Other Communication Disorders [NIDCD], 2004). We often accuse these children of not listening or not doing what they are told, when, in reality, they may not have heard us accurately.

The cause of congenital auditory processing disorders is usually unknown. The most common cause of acquired language disorders is traumatic brain injury. The part of the brain that is injured will determine the severity as well as the type of the disorder. Auditory processing problems may appear alone or they may be associated with other language impairments, dyslexia, or developmental delays. Children with auditory processing problems often have additional problems related to sounding out words, spelling, vocabulary, and reading comprehension. See Table 8–4. These children are particularly difficult to identify because they pass all the traditional auditory screening tests and they usually have typical intellectual development. Because of the elusive nature of auditory processing disorders, a medical diagnosis begins by ruling other things out, the most obvious of which is hearing loss. Testing is complex, but there are standardized tests designed to identify these children. Audiologists may suggest ways to adapt the listening environment to improve the child's learning.

Visual Processing Disorders

Children who have visual processing disorders confuse visual input. Although a variety of specific visual problems are identified, these can and often do overlap. **Visual discrimination** involves noticing small differences in colors, shapes, objects and letters. Children with visual processing disorders have difficulty identifying letters of the alphabet and confuse such letters as *b, d, p,* and *q*. They might read *pat* as *tap*. They also struggle with **visual figure-ground discrimination**. It is difficult for them to focus on a particular aspect or figure as distinguished from the entire page. In reading, they might skip words or lines. In games like "I Spy" or "Where's Waldo" where children are to find one object in a picture with many details, they are unlikely to find it (National Center for Learning Disabilities [NCLD], 2009).

Some children have problems with **visual sequencing**, or the ability to see the order of symbols, letters, words or images. This leads to skipping words or lines in reading and in understanding mathematics problems. They may have problems with auditory sequencing as well.

Visual memory involves both short-term and long-term memory. **Visual closure** allows children to recognize an object from a partial or a limited view. It focuses on part–whole relationships. Children with problems in this area have trouble putting multipiece puzzles together. **Spatial relationship** problems relate to organizing the child's position in space. The child might confuse left and right or misjudge distance. At a younger age, visual perceptual problems might be displayed in visual-motor tasks such as putting puzzles together, catching or hitting a ball, jumping over a rope, and related activities that require visual motor coordination.

Sensory Processing Disorders

Knowledge of sensory processing disorders or sensory integration disorders is based on the pioneering work of A. Jean Ayers (1972). It has been expanded and extended by others

TABLE 8-4 CHARACTERISTICS OF CHILDREN WITH AUDITORY PROCESSING DISORDER

Children with auditory processing problems have some of the following challenges:
• Paying attention to and remembering information presented verbally
• Carrying out multistep directions and auditory sequential memory
• Listening
• Processing information quickly
• Learning in general, and reading comprehension, spelling, sounding out words, and vocabulary in particular
• Behaving appropriately in different situations
• Understanding language; they confuse syllable sequences and find it hard to increase their vocabulary

Source: Herer et al., 2007; NIDCD, 2004.

(Williamson & Anzalone, 2001). Although sensory processing disorders are not as widely accepted as other areas of specific learning disabilities, such knowledge makes a contribution to understanding children and some of the challenges they face.

The tactile system is the largest sensory organ and covers the body and the external surface of the internal organs. Young children can either over- or underreact to tactile stimulation. Children who are hyposensitive may not feel pain from bumps and bruises, and also may not be able to manipulate materials well. Children who are hypersensitive may avoid tactile input and not want to be held or cuddled; they may not participate in tactile activities such as sand and water play. Vestibular information helps to regulate attention as well as posture and balance. Children who don't process enough information about their own movements may have trouble maintaining balance and need to spend conscious energy just to stay sitting in a chair. Those who process too much movement information may become fearful or overstimulated. Occupational therapists are the major specialists in this area.

Guidelines

The following guidelines should be useful when including children with specific learning disabilities. Two key words to keep in mind are *consistency* and *preparation*.

1. *Be consistent.* Establish class rules and classroom management/guidance techniques and use them consistently. Also keep the daily schedule and sequence of the program the same.

2. *Prepare for questions about changes in the routine.* Announcement of a change may set off a flood of questions. The third time you hear the same question, you might respond, "I hear your concern about the trip to the museum. You are asking that question a lot. Can you tell me the answer?" If the child cannot give you the answer, give the child the words and then ask her to tell you the answer.

3. *Keep the classroom orderly and organized.* Use color coding or numbering of bins and shelves to identify groups of materials.

4. *Give frequent feedback.* Verbal feedback may be the least salient. Find out what works, but try visual (e.g., smiles, stickers) and tactile (e.g., a touch, a hug) feedback.

5. *Use self-correcting materials.* These materials provide feedback to the child. In a simple puzzle, if the child tries to put the square where the circle should be, it will not fit. It is immediate and will not embarrass the child.

6. *Move from simple to complex.* Begin with simple activities dealing with one concept, and move to more complex concepts as the child seems ready; for example, move from *taking turns* to *friendship,* from *counting* to *estimating.*

7. *Give directions simply.* Make directions simple, brief, and clear, and state them in a positive manner, with eye contact maintained. If necessary, give them a step at a time. "It's cleanup time" may not be enough. Try "Put the doll clothes back in the drawer;" when that is completed, continue with "Put the dolls in their bed," and so on. When the child has done as you requested, be sure to reinforce the behavior: "I liked the way you folded the doll clothes and put them away." A specific and concrete reinforcement is more effective than a general one such as "good job."

8. *Check for prerequisite skills.* If a child has problems learning a particular task, check whether she has mastered the prerequisite skills. If a child can't pick out the square from a group of circles, she probably can't find the *p* among similar looking letters.

9. *Use concrete objects when teaching.* Count children, fingers, boys, girls, windows, and teachers—but don't just count. Count for a purpose that you share with the children. Use manipulatives such as blocks to count during activities. Each child can touch her own manipulatives as she counts.

10. *Identify learning styles.* Most children have a preferred way of learning information (visual, auditory, or kinesthetic/tactile). It is helpful to know and use the child's preference, or use all three:
    - *Visual.* Have a poster in the block corner demonstrating the proper and improper use of blocks. Put a big red "X" through those that are not safe.
    - *Auditory.* Tell the child, "Blocks are for building. You may not throw the blocks."
    - *Kinesthetic/tactile.* Take the child to the block corner and show him what to do; then have him demonstrate the appropriate behavior to you.

11. *Provide processing time.* Be cognizant of processing problems in all learning styles. Give children time to process verbal, visual, and kinesthetic information.

12. *Use differentiated instruction.* Provide children of different abilities and learning styles with similar, but different, tasks to teach the same lesson. This will allow children with different abilities to learn the same concept in a manner appropriate for them. This also works with different learning styles.

13. *Teach rules.* At the beginning of the year, teach your schedule, rules, and procedures. Model and practice these with the children. Have children develop some of the rules. This allows children a sense of ownership in the classroom.

14. *Provide varied learning experiences.* Teach the same concept in many different ways numerous times. Teach body awareness through art, movement, listening, music, and health activities.

15. *Alternate quiet and active times.* Children need periods of quiet time and relaxing activities as well as active or

hands-on work. Some children may also need to take a few minutes "off" between activities. Have some times each day when children participate in structured moderate to vigorous activity.

16. *Use planned energetic play.* Provide activities that encourage movement, especially during large-group times. Don't expect children with SLD to sit as long as their peers might. Have children march or jump for the number of children in the class. Jump and count or do calisthenics and count. This works well at the beginning of a group time.

Group time is often a difficult time for all children; for children with SLD it can be more challenging. Experiment to find out what works best for you. Seat children in a semicircle and place the child with a learning disability across from you, where you can easily maintain eye contact. Have children who are good role models sit on either side of the child. Be sure to rotate these children so they take turns.

Sometimes, children with SLD need more structure in learning tasks than is typically provided in early childhood classrooms. A skilled teacher can provide more structure and individualize learning tasks. Use the basics of RTI:

1. *Assess* the child's knowledge base in the specific area.

2. *Describe* the procedure, what is going to happen, giving the child a rationale for the procedure.

3. *Model* the procedure. As you demonstrate, state aloud the procedure and the thought processes.

4. *Use verbal rehearsal.* Have the child state the procedure aloud.

5. *Practice* the "easiest version" of the task with your assessment and feedback.

6. *Modify* the task to make it more difficult until it reaches age/grade expectations. Provide assessment and feedback.

7. *Evaluate* the child's learning and begin generalization.

8. *Promote generalization* so the child becomes aware of situations and strategies for using the learned material.

9. *Communicate* with the parents. Change can take place daily, and knowing that a child had a "good day" may be the support a parent needs.

Curriculum Adaptations

Children with specific learning differences require some adaptations. Children's needs determine the particular adaptations you use and the emphasis you place on specific areas. If you adapt your programs to include children with SLD and meet their needs during the early childhood years, you may prevent a secondary disability, such as oppositional defiant disorder, that may be based on repeated social and academic failure. Help children build necessary academic and social skills so they can meet the continuing challenges of the educational system.

SLD is not a single problem but rather a combination of problems. SLD is diverse. Be alert to patterns of behavior and clusters of needs that indicate areas to concentrate on. (If a child is clumsy, has poor eye–hand coordination, and has balance and rhythm problems, concentrate on working with this child in the motor skills area.) Keep in mind the developmental level of the child. (Is the attention span really short for a 3-year-old?) Look for uneven development characterized by average to above-average development in some areas, but noticeable developmental lags in other areas. (The child can discuss trains, the roles of the various people on the train, and how trains work, but cannot put a toy train beside, in front of, or above a block.)

Social Awareness

All children need to form relationships with other children and adults. They need to be aware of how they are similar to and different from others. Encourage children with SLD to use a variety of solutions to problems; they have a tendency to get stuck. They require guidance and practice. The skills of taking turns and sharing are especially critical.

Children should be taught concrete methods for dealing with problems. For example, if children have a "small" problem, such as another child is not giving them a turn, they could be taught to ask politely and remind the child, evoke the rules about sharing, compromise on different ways of taking turns, or ignore the problem and do something else. For a "big" problem, they can be told to speak to a trusted adult. Children are growing up in a global world. They need to learn about different people, places, and environments as well as about themselves. Some of the activities in Resource Chapter 1 are especially designed to support children who have specific learning disabilities; Activities 1–37w, *One More*, and 1–44w, *Feelings*, help all children learn more about how difficult it can be to accomplish certain tasks and may set the stage for understanding individual differences.

Social Competence

Identifying learning needs early benefits both you and the child. Once children have already experienced failure, you have to deal with poor self-esteem in addition to the specific learning disability. Help children become aware of their strengths.

1. Increase body awareness and value the uniqueness of each child. Children with SLD often show poor knowledge of their body, whether they are asked to label parts on a doll or identify a body part of their own.

2. Highlight children's creativity and divergent thinking.

3. Help children feel they are part of the group. Appreciate their uniqueness as human beings and the contributions they make to the group.

4. Help children become aware of the situational aspect of socially acceptable behavior. In the classroom, there are rules that all children need to abide by.

5. Help children develop skills to be part of a group some of the time as well as skills to be and do things alone.

Social Studies

Social studies can be used to create awareness of other people, the roles they play, and how people have adapted over time and in different cultures and environments.

1. Set up a "society" in your class based on the strengths and needs of the children: "Gina will take the messages to others because she is a good runner. Barbara will print the messages. Kenzi will call us together because he has a good strong voice."

2. Explore varied occupations such as plumber, computer programmer, baker, physicist, producer, professional athlete, and pest exterminator. Let the children's interest guide your choices. Be sure to give an unbiased non-sexist presentation of occupations.

3. Talk about how decisions are made in the classroom and rules are set. Encourage children to explore the democratic process and learn the skills to adapt when their choice is not the one chosen.

English Language Arts

There is concern about the language and literacy development of the children in our schools. There are too many children who do not communicate effectively or read and write at the level that today's society demands. Some question whether all of the children who are identified as having dyslexia are truly dyslexic or whether they have not been taught well. Good preschool programs that provide different levels of intensity of instruction to children can provide a solid foundation for reading. This may mean you assist families and caregivers to increase their interactions with all children. Encourage interactive book reading, conversations, and trips to the store, library, and playground to stimulate cognitive and linguistic development. If families have few books, develop a lending library.

Children with dyslexia will find this a particularly challenging area. Make it a positive experience. Sequencing activities and memory games may be difficult for some; making auditory distinctions is difficult for others. Children with dyslexia will need more practice than others in literacy skills. If these skills are difficult, they may try to avoid them. Emphasize activities that intrigue them while teaching the necessary skills at the same time. Your job is also to provide excitement and motivation.

Speaking and Listening

Encourage children to verbalize their feelings as well as to communicate ideas. When they do not have the words, provide them. Help them build the vocabulary they need to ask and answer questions and to describe the people and places in their environment

1. Support children in their verbalizations with picture cues. Ask children to tell you about specific items in a picture. This helps focus their attention as they talk.

2. Give children a sequence of pictures that displays a familiar action, such as getting ready for bed, and have the children sequence the pictures and tell you what is happening.

3. Give children pictures of the sequence of your day at school and have children put these in order and describe the sequence.

4. Play a sentence completion game, such as "I draw with a . . . ." To make it more difficult, ask what else they can draw with.

5. Play "Say What I Say." You can make sounds, words, sentences, or nonsense. See Activity 2–28, *Say It.*

6. Play rhyming games to increase children's phonological awareness. See Activity 2–57w, *Rhyming Words.*

7. Play word games. See Activities 2–3, *Synonyms*; 2–59w, *Same and Different*; and 2–30, *Never.*

Listening is made up of many different auditory skills. Give children practice following your directions by showing what they mean both with their own body and with a block or doll. Choose topics that are of particular interest and reinforce their attempts at communicating. Work to increase attention span and concentration. Shorten sentences and give directions one step at a time.

1. Play games such as "Find the . . . ."

2. Play direction-following games such as "Simon Says," and "Mother, May I?" Give directions such as "Put the block under the table" for practice with prepositions. Add steps. Don't eliminate children who make mistakes; they are the ones that need the most practice.

3. Play musical chairs. Don't eliminate any chairs; this is a listening game.

4. Use sound tapes and have the children identify the sounds. See Activities 2–34w, *Sound and Tell*, and 2–38w, *Sound Cues.*

5. With the child blindfolded or looking away, have the child guess who is talking or where in the room the person is speaking. See Activity 3–18, *Where Is It/Who Is It?*

Reading

Because many children with SLD have problems learning to read, it is imperative to make language arts enjoyable. To be motivated, they need to know reading can and *will* be fun. Begin by building strength in literacy skills. Children are expected to be ready to read when they are about 5 or 6 years old. However, some children don't seem to be ready when their peers are. This doesn't mean that reading instruction should be delayed; it means it may have to begin in a different place. Challenge, but don't overwhelm, children with the necessary visual and auditory skills that are prerequisites to reading. (*Note:* There are many different approaches to teaching reading. It is beyond the scope of this book to decide among these. However, the basic foundation skills given here are a place to start. A reading specialist will provide additional help.)

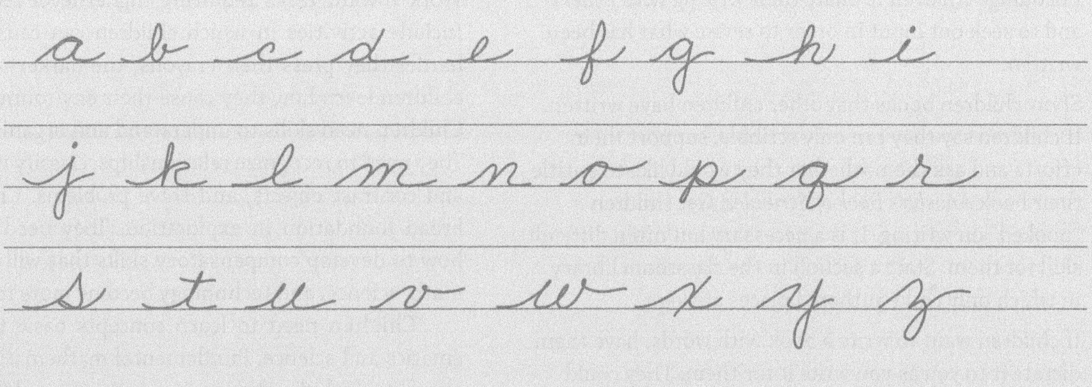

a b c d e f g h i

j k l m n o p q r

s t u v w x y z

FIGURE 8-2 LOWERCASE CURSIVE LETTERS

In this system of cursive writing all of the letters begin on the line. This helps children who cannot remember where to start to form letters.

During the early development of reading:

1. Take children on a "book walk" before reading the story. Look at the pictures and make predictions about the story.
2. Read to children at their interest level, not at the level at which they read. Read both literature and informational texts.
3. Have children put words they can read in a word bank or personal dictionary.
4. Play memory games such as "Concentration" with increasing numbers of cards. Identify and match shapes and colors before proceeding to letters and numbers. See Activity 2–22, *Alphabet Lotto.*
5. Have a set of wooden numbers and letters. Encourage children to feel the letters and numbers with the first two fingers of their dominant hand and match them to outlines of the same letters.
6. Play sequencing games using picture cards.
7. Encourage children to read by having a wide selection of books available on many different reading and lexile levels and on many different topics, including books that have only pictures as well as reference books.
8. Have a quiet, private reading area with comfortable seating, where children can get away to look at books alone or with others.

Reading books can be entertaining and enlightening for children. When you read to children, choose the books carefully, introduce them to the children, and read them with interest and expression, and interactively. Remember to ask the *Who/What/Where/When/How* questions before, during, and after reading.

1. Choose books that deal with individual differences and ask children to compare books on that topic.
2. Tell and read stories, rhymes, and poems so that the children's only cues are auditory. Consciously work on building phonemic awareness.

3. Make reading interactive. Ask children questions about the book you have read, and relate the answers to other situations and books.
4. Remember when you read to identify the author and illustrator and to comment on the structure of the book (especially for informational texts).

Writing

Most young children love to write until someone tells them they aren't "really" writing or that they can't spell. Seeing oneself as an author during the early childhood years provides some insulation for the future.

Writing involves legibility (someone has to be able to read what is written), fluency (writing flows smoothly without breaks within words), and speed. Some problems in this area relate to lack of stamina (poor muscle strength) and lack of fine motor coordination. Left-handed children have additional problems.

There is disagreement about whether children should begin with script (printing) or cursive (joined writing). Those who favor script look at the relationship between reading and writing and feel that it strengthens this connection. Others feel that if children are likely to have problems writing, one shouldn't waste time on teaching them to print when it is easier to write in cursive. This decision belongs to you and the educational setting in which you work. One method of teaching cursive has all the lowercase letters start on the line. This helps children with spatial problems. If they have learned script first, they can print the capital letter and follow with this method of cursive (Figure 8–2).

1. Set up a writing center and stock it with a variety of writing instruments (e.g., pencils, fine and thick colored markers, crayons) and many types of paper to write on (e.g., plain and colored, cards, envelopes). Talk about writing and its many purposes. See Activity 2–25, *Writing Center.*

2. Encourage children to share their writing with others and to seek out input in order to revise what has been written.

3. Show children books that other children have written. If children say they can only scribble, support their efforts and ask them whether they would like to entitle their book *Anasha's Book of Scribbles*. Get children "hooked" on writing. It is a necessary but often difficult skill for them. Start a section in the classroom library in which only child-authored pieces are kept.

4. If children want to write a book with words, have them dictate it to you as you write it for them. They could also "write" it verbally on a tape recorder, to be transcribed later, or have them type it on a computer.

5. Encourage collaborative writing and research projects that use a variety of digital tools to produce and publish writing.

● ● ●
Language

Help children learn the conventions of standard English when they speak or write. Play word games using words with multiple meanings as a way of building vocabulary. Help children find synonyms and learn the more subtle distinctions among words.

1. Encourage children to "read" the books they write to others. Let them know that writing is a process that includes writing, editing, rewriting, and publishing. When children are not pleased with their work, talk about editing. Use this as a way of discussing capitalization and punctuation. This is also a way to deal with spelling, as it is an obvious time to correct it and it provides a lifelong skill of not stopping with a first draft.

2. As children become concerned about spelling in their written work, write out the words they need to spell on cards and develop a spelling bank. Put the words in the bank alphabetically. Looking words up that are in alphabetical order is challenging for children, but it ties together the reading and writing process.

3. Encourage children to write stories on the computer and then spell-check, share, edit, and print them.

Discovery

Children with specific learning disabilities may not have as much general knowledge as other children. This is especially true in the area of cause-and-effect relationships. They may not understand that it is hotter in the sun than in the shade or that if you don't water plants, they will die.

Children need practice in logical reasoning. Demonstrate first with objects and then by drawing attention to the child's own behavior that it is possible to make predictions about what will happen. In this way, children will gradually improve cause-and-effect reasoning skills. Start with short, obvious examples, such as putting weights on a balance.

Work toward tasks requiring higher-level reasoning skills. Include activities in which children can cause change: the harder they press their crayons, the darker the color. Help children learn how they cause their environment to change. Children need skills to understand and organize their world. They need to recognize relationships, classify items, compare and contrast objects, and solve problems. Children need a broad foundation in exploration. They need help learning how to develop compensatory skills that will serve them as math, science, and technology become more formalized.

Children need to learn concepts basic to both mathematics and science. Fundamental mathematics and science concepts include observing, comparing, classifying, measuring, and communicating. Process skills support children in learning new information through concrete experiences (Charlesworth & Lind, 2009). Use real materials and situations. For children with dyscalculia, work on number sense, including counting, one-to-one correspondence, estimation, and copying and extending patterns.

Technology can help compensate for many skills that challenge children with SLD. Help them explore and feel comfortable with many different types of technology.

● ● ●
Mathematics

Help children develop a sensory motor experiential awareness of math. *Doing* math, not just looking or hearing about it, is the key.

1. Use concrete objects, manipulatives, to teach number sense and numeration, and employ as many variations as you can think of. Use snack time and food (e.g., raisins, whole grain cereal, small whole grain crackers) for teaching these concepts: same/different, numbers, sets, equal, one-to-one correspondence, and more/less/same. (Somehow, children learn faster when another child is going to get "more" than they are!) Play Activity 3–7, *100's Game*.

2. Play number concept games, such as counting objects, naming numbers when shown the number, matching numbers to groups of objects, and games that require matching, sorting, and selecting numbers, colors, or pictures. Use charts, lists, and graphs to organize and classify information. See Activities 3–1, *Matching Symbols*, and 3–2, *Spacey Dots*.

3. Create situations where children must use mathematical reasoning to solve problems: "What if you run out of large blocks and you need to make another wall the same length as the first?" Discuss relative length. See Activities 3–38w, *Variations on Blocks*, and 3–46w, *Variations on Cuisenaire™ Rods*.

4. Play size comparative games with children: "Give me the big ball" or "Give me the biggest triangle."

5. Help children identify, construct, and predict patterns and relationships of colors, objects (e.g., shoe, shoe, sock, shoe, shoe, sock), and numbers. Have a pattern party.

6. Emphasize the vocabulary children need to communicate mathematical concepts (two- and three-dimensional geometric shapes, relative size, numbers themselves, spatial relationships, and measuring).

7. Have children keep a math journal in which they write about math problems and triumphs.

8. Give large-grid paper to children to help them complete math computations.

9. Work with children on math story problems and have them play them out to make them more concrete.

Science

Science activities can create enthusiasm in children with SLD if a discovery approach is taken. Children can use science concepts to organize and understand their world.

1. Use science to teach general information, such as cause and effect (e.g., the relationship between temperature and the state of water: liquid, steam, ice); the relationship between structure and function (e.g., how snakes move); continuous and discontinuous properties (e.g., pitch, and how it changes on various instruments from water glasses to violins); and diversity (e.g., how leaves of various trees are alike and different). See Activities 3–20, *Goop*, and 3–50w, *Water Tones*.

2. Let children examine items (e.g., orange, cup, mirror) and describe as many details of the item as they can (e.g., color, shape, size, texture, function, parts). This is a great way to teach comparison. Two items are alike in some ways and different in others.

3. Because children with SLD often have gaps in their knowledge, remember to repeat the learning cycle (awareness, exploration, inquiry, experimentation, and utilization) when you introduce new ideas and concepts and tie it to previous knowledge.

4. Teach children science process skills and the basics of the scientific method.

Technology

Computers have infinite patience and inexhaustible energy, and they don't get upset with children who forget. Some programs are even designed to support children as they get closer to the right answer or have increased their scores, no matter where they started. Computers are under the control of the children who use them. They can be turned off or on as the child desires. This is empowering to children who are in charge of so little. Computers and electronic tablets with appropriate applications can provide personal instruction to children at a speed that suits their learning process and in a time frame that accommodates the child's attention span. Children can proceed at their own pace.

By age 3 children can begin to use technology and discovery-based software with the help of an adult or an older peer. To be effective and developmentally appropriate, technology must be planned for and be a part of the curriculum. Plan for children to use all their senses when working with technology. Software and technology use should support educational goals. Think carefully about the experiences you want children to have or the learning goals you want to support, and select software and applications to encourage these learning experiences.

1. Choose software that is compatible with the child's learning needs, supports her interests, and is open-ended. Ask open-ended questions about children's work. Ensure that two or three chairs can fit around the computer and plan activities that require cooperation.

2. Although older children might profit from some of the drill and practice in the areas of spelling and math, for younger children the idea that computers are interactive and that children can learn cause-and-effect (if–then sequences) reasoning is far more compelling. Talk with children about what is happening on the screen. "When you click the mouse here, the person moves."

3. Becoming comfortable with technology at a young age is critical for children with SLD. Computers can compensate for poor handwriting and check spelling, and some programs can analyze grammar and composition.

4. Software can support emerging literacy skills by helping to link words to pictures. Children can create their own stories (on the computer, an electronic tablet, or dictated into a tape recorder) and illustrate them.

5. Software can help children work on emerging math skills such as patterning, classification, seriation, and numerical relationships.

6. Software can influence behaviors such as cooperation and motivation and how children interact with each other.

7. In inclusive classrooms, technology is an excellent tool for individualizing instruction.

Wellness

All children need to find ways to be safe and healthy in their world. Children with SLD are at risk because of poor motor planning skills, and problems in processing information about their environment. They may also experience complications when understanding directions or taking appropriate actions during an emergency. They may show an impaired ability to integrate information about space and distance in relation to their movement.

Children need to refine the movements of both their large and small muscles in addition to coordinating these muscles with information they receive from their senses. Children with SLD need to develop a physically active lifestyle. It is critical that children develop strength in their core muscles to provide trunk stability as a prerequisite for doing fine motor skills. Children who are not good at these motor activities may avoid them. It is the teacher's role to support children, but also to make activities so intriguing that children want to participate.

● ● ●
Health and Safety

Children with SLD may have had many prior experiences with health care professionals. They may have had a history of early ear infections and may have been seen for mild trauma care. Their difficulty following safety directions and poor sensory motor integration places them at risk.

1. Teach children who to talk to about being lost (a mother with a child may be a good choice) and then to state their name and information parents want them to give in this situation.

2. Talk about injury prevention. Help children see the relationship between actions and results (e.g., what may happen if someone runs in front of a tricycle or bicycle).

3. Talk about the health problems common to children (colds, ear infections, stomachaches, headaches) and ask children to identify the symptoms of each. Talk with children about ways to prevent illness, and how illnesses are treated. See Activities 4–1, *Symptoms*, and 4–35w, *What Would You Do If?*

● ● ●
Physical Education

Children with learning disabilities may have been late (or at the end of the normal age range) in reaching motor milestones. Some lack body control and rhythm. While walking or running, these children appear disjointed. They get where they want to go, but they are inefficient and don't move smoothly. Some lack necessary fundamental motor skills such as hopping, jumping, and skipping. Before children can participate in fine motor skills, they must be able to stabilize the large muscles in their trunk and shoulders. Obviously, some activities that are challenging for preschool children are too easy for children in first grade. Extract the principles behind the activity and adapt it to the developmental levels of the children you are teaching. The following activities are designed to strengthen the core muscles of the neck and trunk:

1. Have children crab walk (using hands and feet with stomach toward ceiling) to get items and carry them back on their stomach. Vary the type of walking and the way they hold the object on their return.

2. Play crab soccer with a small group of children or have children try to keep a beach ball up in the air using their feet while maintaining the crab position. This is challenging.

3. Do bent-knee sit-ups and give children puzzle pieces that they reach for with each sit-up.

4. Tie a rope between two stable objects and have the children lie on a scooter on their back and pull themselves from one end to the other. See Activity 4–16, *Obstacle Course*.

5. Have children lie on their backs and throw beanbags at a target. Then have them do the same thing while lying on their stomachs. You might provide a bolster for under their chest to increase their range.

6. Encourage children to draw on a chalkboard at shoulder level.

7. Include activities that develop the lateral muscles of the trunk: crawling and climbing. Children can't control a tool such as a crayon or pencil until the lateral muscles are sufficiently developed. See Activity 4–36w, *Variations on Creeping and Crawling*.

To increase balance skills, try the following:

1. Play "Freeze and Thaw" but have children hold their position for five seconds or more.

2. Tape a line on the floor and have children do a variety of activities while staying on the line: pick up puzzle pieces, catch beanbags or beach balls, walk forward toe/heel, backward heel/toe, tiptoe, and so on. See Activity 4–29, *Variations on Balancing*.

3. Tape a square onto the floor and have children hop on two feet while staying in the square, then on one foot. Play catching and throwing games with the child staying in the square. Play hopscotch.

Some children will have problems with tasks that require bilateral movement (using both arms and hands at the same time), such as lifting or throwing. Cross-lateral movements (using opposite arm and leg at the same time), such as crawling, may be difficult. It may be hard for them to control their

Motor coordination and planning are challenging for some children with specific learning disabilities.
©Cengage Learning 2012

balance while moving, and they may frequently trip, bump into things, or drop things. They may also have poor spatial orientation and may find the relationship of objects to each other difficult to understand. They may not know how high to step to get over an object or how to fit their body under a rope. These children also have trouble catching a ball, especially if it bounces first. It is difficult for them to decide when the ball will reach them and how high the ball will be when it does. Hence, they rarely catch it.

Some children will need your encouragement to participate in large motor activities. Plan opportunities both indoors and outdoors for children to practice large motor skills, including these:

1. Help children develop concepts of space and direction by having them pace off distances, or see how far they can run in five seconds compared to walking or crawling.

2. Have children do variations on skills that they already know: walking, jumping, throwing, rolling, and crawling. See Activities 4–13, *Variations on Jumping*; 4–14, *Variations on Running*; 4–38w, *Variations on Hopping*; 4–18, *Variations on Throwing*; and 4–44w, *Variations on Body Rolling*.

3. Use underinflated beach balls as well as large balls to increase the possibility for successful throwing and catching.

4. Help children learn sequencing by using the large muscles of their body. Design an obstacle course that children must do in sequence. After the child can successfully navigate the two or three obstacles in sequence, add another obstacle.

5. Help children become physically fit. Preschool children need an hour of structured, moderate-to-vigorous physical activity each day. Put on the music and plan four- to eight-minute dance parties several times a day. Build these into your routines and transitions. These work well before group times because they help children settle down. For the activities to be effective, children need to dance (or jump, march, etc.) until they are breathless. (Monitor children who have asthma or other special health care needs to ensure they do not do more than is safe for them.) See Activity 4–17, *Fitness Course*.

6. Help all children understand and respect differences among children who participate in physical activities.

● ● ●
Sensory Motor Integration

Children get information from their senses—including touch, sight, sound—and from movement, body awareness, and the pull of gravity. The process by which the brain organizes and interprets this information is sensory integration. The integration of this information with motor activities is called **motor planning**. For some children, motor planning is easy and natural, but children with SLD may find it difficult. When this process is disordered, children may have problems in learning new skills. They may under- or overreact to touch, movement, sight, or sound; they may be clumsy or appear careless; their activity level may be inappropriate; and this combination may lower children's self-esteem. Motor planning skills increase when children do such things as fingerplays and songs that require sequential motions. Obstacle courses in which children move through different types and sizes of objects require planning, as does using different parts of their body to keep an object in the air. Children also work on motor planning when they do variations on familiar activities like rolling, walking, and hopping, and when a particular pattern is requested (e.g., two steps forward, one to the side). Ask children to march in a circle with their eyes closed, and so on. Have children work their way through mazes. Motivation plays a critical role in sensory integration. Children must be actively involved and exploring in a goal-directed way to become efficient organizers of sensory information. If the activity is not goal directed, it does not increase motor planning.

1. Roll playdough into logs, make letters, and help the child spell his name or initials.

2. Play "Hot and Cold." Hide an object and have the child try to find something by telling the child whether she is hot (close to the object), hotter (even closer), or cold (going away from the object).

3. Play "Do What I Do" while sitting still. You do something (e.g., clap twice, tap your head with one hand, and hit your thighs with both hands). The children imitate what you do. Play "Follow the Leader" as well. See Activity 4–27, *Mirroring*.

4. Include activities that require children to use both sides of their body at the same time, such as underhand throwing or catching a large ball with both hands, hopping or jumping with both feet together, clapping, and doing jumping Jacks or Jills.

5. Include activities that require children to use both sides of the body alternately, such as going up steps with alternate feet on each tread, climbing a ladder, riding a tricycle, walking a line or balance beam, running, walking, and skipping. Place a string or tape on the floor in various configurations (e.g., straight, curved, with angles) and have the children walk on this.

6. Include activities that require children to cross the **midline**, the imaginary line through the center of the body, which divides it into right and left sides. Have children throw balls or beanbags while standing sideways to the target. Have them touch the toes of the opposite foot while standing. See Activity 4–22, *Hand Clapping*.

7. Encourage children to draw a design on paper (with adult support) and then make this design with blocks or other small manipulatives.

8. Teach children yoga and how to take deep yoga breaths.

All young children need practice in fine motor skills. Children with specific learning disabilities may need extra motivation in this area. They may avoid small motor activities. However, they need the practice, and it is your role to make it fun. Children whose fine motor skills are poor are clumsy in handling small objects that require finger and wrist movement. They may not be able to button, snap, or tie. An underdeveloped **pincer grip** may make it hard to pick up small items.

1. Flick a ping-pong ball into a container placed on its side, using the index fingers, thumbs, and then other fingers.

2. Squeeze a bulb syringe so that the air pushes a ping-pong ball across the table. See whether the children can get the ball to cross a line for a goal.

3. Roll putty or playdough into a log shape, place it around the fingers, and spread the fingers to stretch the playdough; include the thumb. Make small balls by rolling the playdough between the first two fingers and the thumb.

4. Use different sizes and shapes of rubber bands to encircle geoboards and objects.

Coloring inside the lines and pasting in a specific area may be difficult. Cutting with conventional scissors can be challenging. Large crayons, large chalk, and simple designs all help. Your concern is to ensure that children experience success in this area so that they do not quit trying.

1. Pick some activities that may especially intrigue a particular child. If the child likes cars, provide a car drawing to color. Provide a maze for small toy cars to follow. Have the child practice lining the cars up in specified patterns. Magnets can be used to attach metal cars to a jellyroll pan.

2. Have children practice adaptive skills like buttoning, snapping, and tying. Discuss the pride of being able to "do it myself." Plan extra time so this is functional—before going outside, when coming inside, or when going to the bathroom. See Activity 3–8, *Caterpillars*.

3. Encourage children to participate in board games that combine fine motor skills with other skills; such games include bingo, dominos, checkers, and Chinese checkers. See Activity 5–10, *Board Game*.

4. Use hand and finger puppets to increase dexterity.

5. Have a variety of different types of scissors available (including left-handed ones), so children can choose scissors that will enable them to cut. Ensure that you include scissors with small holes for small children, spring-loaded scissors, scissors with four finger holes (so the teacher can help), and scissors attached to a block (so that a child only needs to press down on the scissor handle).

6. Supply smaller materials that connect together in a variety of different ways to improve fine motor skills. Have a large supply so children can work together.

Creative Arts

Creative arts provide an opportunity to practice skills in a safe place before using them elsewhere and to learn more about the world. Children with specific learning disabilities may find an emotional release in the visual arts, an opportunity to integrate the visual and tactile senses and to make a creation that will not be judged by others as right or wrong.

Music can help improve sensory motor integration; adding movement and dance helps children express emotions and increase body awareness. Use dramatic play and theater to help children become more aware of roles and feelings. Help them express caring and happy feelings as well as sad, angry, and unhappy ones. As holidays and special events are stressful for some children, playing them through may help.

Visual Arts

For children with specific learning disabilities, the major focus of art should be on the *process*, not the product, while encouraging children to evaluate their own work and the work of others. Allow children freedom to be spontaneous and creative. When they begin to feel that their work should "be something" or look like something specific, and the emphasis is on a product, the potential for failure is greater.

1. Use large paintbrushes; these require less eye–hand coordination than small brushes. As children become skillful with the large brushes, add smaller ones.

2. Use colored marking pens, which are easier to use than crayons, because either light or heavy pressure leaves an impression. As children become skillful, add crayons, chalk, and colored pencils.

3. Make your classroom an attractive place. Use reproductions of art to connect art to culture and the real world of artists.

4. Give children time to explore a wide variety of art materials and techniques. Help them build the vocabulary that supports art—colors, shapes, textures, techniques.

5. Use art to develop children's observational skills. Help them think about art and how it is created, by asking questions. "What did the artist use to make the creation you are displaying? What are the processes involved?"

6. Tie illustrations in books to the art you have encouraged children to think about. Don't make models for children, but do teach them techniques to control the medium with which they work.

Music

Music contributes to a child's physical, aesthetic, and intellectual development. It provides pleasure and creative experience, develops auditory skills, encourages physical development, and increases the range and flexibility of the voice. Use a wide variety of musical experiences: listening, singing, moving to music, and playing instruments.

1. Have a variety of different instruments available. Help children explore and evaluate the sound of an instrument when it is held and played in different ways. See whether they can identify the instruments they know in a recording. See Activity 5–20, *Zin! Zin! Zin! A Violin*.

2. Incorporate music and language experiences; have children make up new verses to songs. Play unusual instrumental recordings and ask children to describe what they imagine while listening. See Activity 5–11, *Mood Songs*.

3. Put stories to music. Have children choose background music for stories; encourage them to think about how the mood of the music relates to their story.

4. Have children make musical instruments (e.g., glasses with different amounts of water, coffee-can drums, and wax paper over combs). As they participate in this process, they will gain an understanding of how sounds are made, where they come from, and how to change them. See whether they can make sounds with different parts of their body.

5. Introduce children to the concepts and vocabulary of music, including pitch, loudness, tempo, and duration. See Activity 5–14, *Conductor*.

6. Expose children to music of various genres, styles, time periods, and cultures.

Movement and Dance

Movement that is not judged on quality, but rather on creativity, offers potential for children with specific learning disabilities. Children can experiment with movement and dance and their interpretation of what it should be like without being judged. Movement also provides an opportunity for sensory integration.

1. Have the children walk through imaginary substances, such as gelatin, deep sand, flypaper, a swamp, or quicksand. Have others guess what the substances are.

2. Combine music, movement, and dance to give children the opportunity to translate an auditory stimulus (e.g., music on a CD) into movement. Be sure to discuss the mood of the stimulus and the types of movement or dance this mood evokes.

3. Have a daily dance party using music from different cultures, and encourage children to explore different types of dancing.

Dramatic Play and Theater

Dramatic play allows children to try out roles and the potential to work through new experiences. It also gives them the opportunity to rehearse new roles and to be in control. Theater combines writing a script with performance and the option for changing roles.

1. Help children play through special or stressful events such as field trips, visits to the doctor, and so on. Discuss what could happen as well as what behavior is expected of them. (You gain some insight into what children expect to happen.) See Activity 5–27, *Doctor's Office*.

2. Discuss emotions beyond just being happy and sad. Discuss how others know how you are feeling. Have the children pretend to open a package that contains something they really want. Have children role-play various social interactions.

3. Encourage children to play the role of therapists or medical professionals and pretend to tell other children what to do. Provide them with the necessary supports.

4. Choose a book and have children translate the story into a play. Help them write the script and then perform it. Include a variety of roles. Encourage children to perform it again, changing roles.

Routines and Transitions

Some children with SLD dislike change. Special school events can be stressful, and children may have trouble handling feelings of anticipation. In addition to the challenges, transitions provide another opportunity for helping children feel the same as others, yet unique as individuals. Be sure children understand what you want them to do during transitions, especially at the beginning of the school year. Routines and transitions, a difficult time for many children, make up approximately 20 percent of the school day. Structure them well and ensure that they are times of learning.

1. Plan enough time to prepare children for the upcoming transition; try a warning of "five more minutes" or singing a particular song. Tell children about the next activity and the motivating aspects of it. Use code words, songs, or visual cues to help children anticipate transitions.

2. Employ auditory or visual cues to signal change in the daily routine itself. Let children know specifically how and what needs to be done to move to the next activity.

3. Reinforce and acknowledge a child's completion of an activity.

4. Without being obvious about it, dismiss children with SLD early in the transition; this should be thought of as prevention, not favoritism.

5. Use transitions to increase body awareness and feelings of being part of the group: "All children with brown eyes and black hair may *jump* to their centers."

6. Play the "I'm thinking of someone" game to dismiss children: "I'm thinking of someone with blond hair, blue eyes, and a striped top. Yes, Lisa, you can get your coat."

7. Ask children math facts or spelling words; they can get in line after giving answers.

8. Use planned energetic play (PEP) during transitions to help children burn off calories and focus. Play music (3- to 5-minute songs) with a fast beat and model different ways of moving to the music. Keep your movements in the moderate to vigorous range.

SUMMARY

- Children with SLD are the largest category of children identified as needing special education services.
- Early intervening services and response to intervention were designed to ensure all children were progressing in the general education curriculum and to decrease the number of children identified as having SLD.
- Dyslexia, dyscalculia, and dysgraphia are SLD; of these dyslexia is the most prevalent SLD and the best understood.
- Children with SLD often have auditory, visual, or sensory processing disorders.
- Children with SLD may need more support, more structure, fewer distractions, and require more direct teacher literacy instruction.

EDUCATIONAL RESOURCES

Center for Early Literacy Learning (CELL) is a research-to-practice technical assistance center funded by the U.S. DOE. CELL's goal is to promote the adoption and sustained use of evidence-based early literacy learning practices in early childhood education. www.earlyliteracylearning.org/

Division for Learning Disabilities (DLD), Council for Exceptional Children (CEC) concentrates its efforts on specific learning disabilities, producing a journal and newsletters. They also have state divisions. www.dldcec.org/

Dyslexia, The Gift is a site maintained by the Davis Dyslexia Association International and has information about dyslexia and other learning disorders, and is great for parents and teachers.

Handwriting without Tears provides resources and information on handwriting and literacy.

International Dyslexia Association focuses exclusively on helping children with specific reading and language learning disabilities. It has publications for parents, educators, and physicians. www.interdys.org/

LD OnLine offers information on learning disabilities for parents and educators, as well as children and adults with learning disabilities. This site is well organized and easy to navigate. www.ldonline.org/

Learning Disabilities Association of America (LDAA) is a nonprofit organization of volunteers, including individuals with learning disabilities, their families, and professionals. This well-organized site has fact sheets and online publications. www.ldanatl.org/

National Center for Learning Disabilities provides information, referrals, and resources for children and adults with learning disabilities. This is a good site for parents, adults with learning disabilities, professionals, and children (teens) dealing with learning disabilities. www.ncld.org/

For additional resources, visit the book companion website for this text at www.cengagebrain.com.

9

Children with Social, Emotional, and Behavioral Disorders

I wonder about Julie. She used to be such a happy, outgoing little girl, and now it seems like she'd rather sit in her locker than do anything else. Even the other children notice it. They ask me what's wrong with Julie. I'm probably overreacting; after all, what could be wrong with a 4-year-old?

REFLECTIVE PRACTICE | That's a good question. What could be bothering a 4-year-old? As you contemplate your own problems and worries, the things that might bother a 4-year-old seem so inconsequential that you may decide the child's concerns are not worth worrying about. Therefore, you tell the child not to worry. That's like a millionaire telling you not to worry about your inconsequential rent, bills, and so on. Your response would probably be a silent or spoken "You don't understand."

To go back to Julie, she has lost interest in everything, including playdough, which used to be her favorite activity. Trying to interest Julie in the playdough is one way you show her you don't understand. Julie has been spending more time just sitting in her locker, and that worries you. Rather than enticing her away, you show concern by saying, "Julie, *I'm* worried because you are sitting in your locker and not playing with the playdough and talking with your friends the way you usually do." Compare the preceding statement with this one: "Julie, *you* shouldn't be sitting here in your locker, especially when I put out your favorite activity." In the first instance, you make an "I" statement, which reflects your concern about the situation. It requires nothing of Julie, not even a response. In the second statement, you seem to be both judging and blaming Julie for her behavior. "*You* shouldn't" really means "*she* shouldn't because *I* don't want her to." You would be better off admitting your discomfort than blaming it on her. After expressing concern, give the child permission to talk about her feelings: "Sometimes when I'm sad I want to be alone. I wonder, are you sad about something now?" While still expressing concern, you can offer an opportunity, or invitation, for Julie to talk.

Whether or not she responds, the next move is to tell her how you are willing to help while giving her some control over the situation: "Would you like to talk about how you feel? (Pause) I can listen now. I'd like to come and sit beside you for a few minutes whenever I can. Is that okay with you?" Be careful not to make an offer you can't follow through on. Don't offer to sit beside the child all morning even if you think that would be helpful. Your duties as a teacher make an "all morning" offer impossible to fulfill.

Is Julie just having a temporary bad time? If you were her teacher what approach would you take? How would you go about finding out what the problems are?

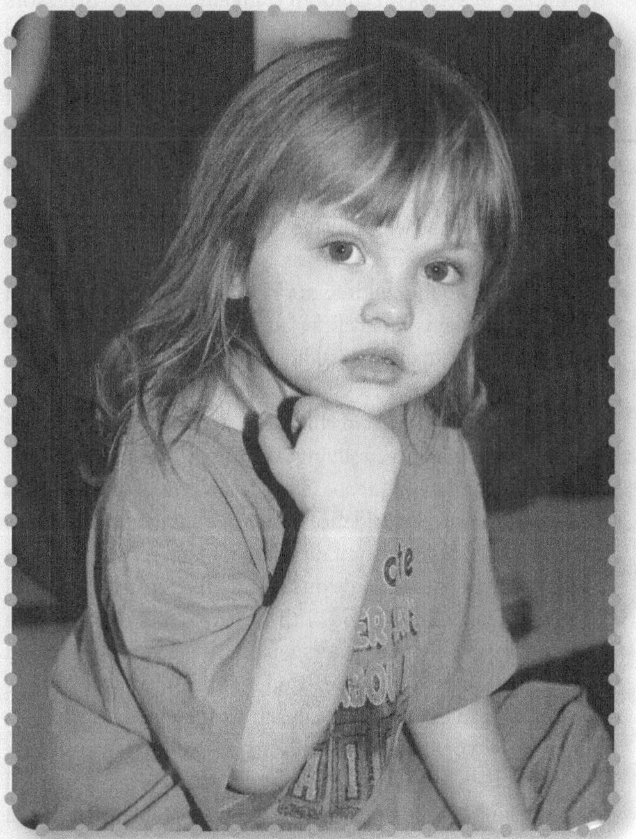

Social, Emotional, and Behavioral Disorders

Increasingly, children come to educational settings with the stress that is part of living in a struggling family. Both parents may be working and trying to balance work and family issues. Some families may be living in poverty, going through a separation or divorce, or just too stressed to cope with life due to situational or maturational crises. Educators have the opportunity to help children by modifying the learning environment to meet children's needs as well as helping children develop skills to cope with these diverse situations.

Helping children deal with mental health problems has not traditionally been a school responsibility. However, current thinking is that all school personnel should be part of a team engaged in an effort to help children develop coping skills to live with stressful situations. Teachers are key figures because they see children daily. They need the training to provide psychological first aid to children, but, this is no longer enough. There must be a follow-up system to open lines of communication among the home, school, and mental health agencies.

Stress can be viewed as an event or a pileup of events that is perceived as threatening and for which the child does not have the resources to cope. Developmentally, older children might cope with events that are stressors to younger children. Sensitive adults can serve as mediators in lessening the impact of stress on children (Finkelhor, 2008). Stressors can be caused by a variety of different situations. The child determines the definition of stress, and the impact of the stress is related to the coping strategies and resources of that child. For example, one might believe that a child who has just moved with his mother to an apartment because of a marital separation would feel stressed. If they moved because the father was abusive and now they feel safe, this actually may have reduced stress.

Stress for young children can be internal, arising from such factors as gas pains in a colicky infant, a painful ear infection in a young child, or the episodic pain of a child with juvenile rheumatoid arthritis. Stress can also result from external factors such as being placed in child care, the arrival of a new sibling, domestic violence, or living in a distressed neighborhood.

Stress can be unique, based on a single situation such as an injection, a single incidence of sexual abuse, or a fire. Stress can also be habitual, chronic, and cumulative, such as living in poverty with a parent who consistently uses drugs or alcohol or abuses the child. A child with a chronic illness may have pain so continually that others tend to see it as the norm and forget that the pain is still real and stressful to the child.

Stress can be overt or covert. Overt stress, such as a home fire or a death in the family, may create fewer problems because others are aware of the situation and are a potential resource for helping the child cope with the problem. Children can talk about their fears and others can respond. When stress is covert, others may not know about it; it may be a family secret. Habitual abuse of a child is typically not talked about with others. If children are threatened, particularly by adults to whom they are entrusted, they have no one to mediate the situation and few resources to cope. Sometimes it isn't clear whether stress is real or imaginary. From the standpoint of the child, that is irrelevant; the child's perception of stress is very real. For children, stress may result in irritability and disorganization. Children who have developmental disabilities may have mental health disorders related to that particular disability in addition to being vulnerable to the same range of stressors and illnesses that typically developing children encounter (Robb & Reber, 2007).

Defining Social, Emotional, and Behavioral Disorders

Social, emotional, and behavioral difficulties exist on a continuum ranging from short-term problems that may produce acute, disruptive, and challenging behaviors to long-term serious mental health problems and disabilities (O'Brien, 2005). The level and duration of disruption distinguish among social, emotional, and behavioral problems and disorders. Disorders in this area are divided in a variety of different ways. **Social disorders**, or anxiety disorders, focus on issues related to attachment, separation, and social situations. **Emotional disorders** focus on mood disorders. **Behavioral disorders** focus on disruptive behavior (Robb & Reber, 2007).

Social, emotional, and behavioral development should include the emergence of an accurate and positive sense of self and the ability to develop and maintain meaningful relationships with other children and adults. Children with social, emotional, and behavioral problems experience an abrupt break, a slowing down, or a delay in the development of these processes.

Social, emotional, and behavioral actions are difficult to classify accurately. Some children have not had the opportunity to learn expected social and school-related skills. Other children have had to learn early how to fend for themselves to survive in their environment. Because of their cultural and ethnic heritage, some families have values and expectations for their children different from traditional white middle-class values. Children's emotional and behavioral development should be evaluated in the context of their early environment. Children with emotional and behavioral problems and disorders occur in all ethnic groups and at all socioeconomic levels.

According to the IDEA 2004:

> Children with an emotional disturbance *exhibit one or more of the following characteristics over a long period of time in a way that adversely affects a child's educational performance, and the inability to learn cannot be explained by intellectual, sensory, or health factors. The child is unable to build or maintain satisfactory interpersonal relationships with peers and teachers and displays inappropriate types of behavior or feelings under normal circumstances. This can be a general pervasive mood of unhappiness or depression, or a tendency to develop physical symptoms or fears associated with personal or school problems. Emotional disturbance includes schizophrenia but does not apply to children who are socially maladjusted* (U.S. DOE, 2006).

All of the disorders discussed in this chapter fall into the emotional disturbance category of the IDEA. I use the term *problems* to refer to less serious social, emotional, and behavioral situations that are very real but that would probably not meet the requirements of the IDEA. The section on social, emotional, and behavioral *disorders* describes those that would probably meet the requirements of the law.

Some behavioral problems are more common at certain stages of development. When they appear during expected periods, they are considered typical behaviors. When these behaviors persist beyond expected ages and/or the behaviors become excessive in nature, they are considered emotional and behavioral disorders. Definitions related to specific psychiatric disorders are given in the text where the disorder is described, as well as in the glossary.

Prevalence of Social, Emotional, and Behavioral Disorders

There are no universally accepted criteria for determining which children have social, emotional, and behavioral disorders. This chapter acknowledges the emotional aspect of the problem but focuses on the disordered behavior. As you might assume, if we cannot define the term we do not have a good idea of how many children fit the definition. Much of what is diagnosed is a matter of the degree to which behaviors occur. It is almost always subjective and falls in the category of **clinical judgment**.

The National Center for Educational Statistics (2010) report for children between 3 and 21 years of age found that 0.9 percent of children in the public schools eligible for services under the IDEA were identified as having an emotional disturbance in 2007–2008. This rate has been relative stable since 1976–1977, when it was 0.6 percent. Prevalence rates vary by disorder and will be given with the discussion of that disorder.

All children have problems sometimes; the length, severity, and unacceptability of the behavior determine whether a problem is a disorder. Some behavioral problems are learned behaviors that affect children's ability to participate in activities with adults and other children. They are considered situationally specific responses; examples include attention-seeking behavior, pinching, and temper tantrums. Emotional and behavioral disorders involve pervasive changes in the child's behavior and mood states exhibited across many situations and settings. They interfere with interpersonal relationships and with development and learning, and can be harmful to the child and others.

Classification of Social, Emotional, and Behavioral Disorders

Professionals concerned about social, emotional, and behavioral disorders are primarily in the field of mental health (e.g., psychologists and psychiatrists). The focus of mental health for young children has been on prevention and an attempt to identify long-term risk factors. This fast-growing field is different from adult mental health and has been multidisciplinary from its inception.

One of the challenges to the profession is the task of classifying disorders in this area. Problems must be classified within a developmental orientation, because young children change so quickly that what is normal at one time may be atypical at another. Classification must also be done with an understanding of the dynamic exchange among the child, the family, and the environment. This requires a systemic and multigenerational point of view.

Several different organizations have developed classification systems, including the American Psychiatric Association

(APA), the World Health Organization (WHO), and Zero to Three. The APA (2000) has a section devoted to disorders first diagnosed in infancy, childhood, or adolescence. This text uses the categories developed by the APA and information from Zero to Three. Only the most prevalent problems and disorders are discussed.

Causes of Social, Emotional, and Behavioral Disorders

The causes of most social, emotional, and behavioral disorders are complex interactions among biological factors, including genetics; the environment in which the child lives and grows; and psychosocial factors (Robb & Reber, 2007). Problem behaviors that are restricted to a few environments are likely to be caused or maintained by specific contingencies in those particular environments. Those that are generalized across many environments have multiple causes, may have a biological base, and are more difficult to modify (Salvia & Ysseldyke, 2007).

Overall risk factors, including the child, the family, the school, and the society in which the child lives, predispose children to these disorders. The complexity of human behavior, the range of potential influences, and the diversity of behaviors represented by behavior disorders preclude simple answers.

Child Factors

The temperament of a child influences the way he relates to the world. Children with difficult temperaments are likely to show more behavioral problems and are more likely to be referred for treatment for aggressive behaviors and tantrums (Chess, 1990). Although not all children who are aggressive during early childhood develop behavioral disorders, behavior in early childhood is one predictor of later disruptive behavior disorders. Evidence suggests that neuropsychological deficits and difficulties early in life place a child at risk for subsequent conduct problems and delinquency (Moffitt, 1993).

Childhood behavior disorders tend to be relatively stable over time. If young children show consistent patterns of **antisocial** and **aggressive behaviors** toward others, it is unlikely that they will just "grow out of it" (Kazdin, 1995). These children become antisocial youths and adults. A well-developed pattern of antisocial behavior during the early school years is perhaps the single best predictor of adolescent delinquency, and, in turn, the best predictor of adult criminality (Walker, Ramsey, & Gresham, 2004).

Academic deficiencies and below-average intellectual functioning are associated with disruptive behavior disorders. The association does not necessarily mean that academic dysfunction represents a risk factor, but that reduced time at school (e.g., truancy and expulsion) and less attention from teachers may lead to poor academic performance (Walker et al., 2004).

Some types of maladaptive behaviors are found primarily among children who have severe and profound levels of intellectual disability, and may be the direct result of biochemical abnormalities (Robb & Reber, 2007). Overall, children with intellectual disabilities have higher levels of psychiatric disorders. Gillberg and colleagues (1986) found 57 percent of children and youth with mild intellectual disability and 64 percent of those with severe intellectual disability met the diagnostic criteria for having a psychiatric disorder.

••• Family Factors

Looking at the long-term effects of family factors is challenging, because families are changing. Older data focused on separation and divorce and the effects of these disruptions on child behavior. Newer data also focuses on single mothers and cohabitating families. (Waldfogel, Craigie, & Brooks-Gunn, 2010), sometimes referred to as fragile families. **Fragile families** consist of children who are born to unwed mothers and who live the first part of their lives with a single mother who is not living with a boyfriend or partner. Mothers in fragile families tend to be younger and less well educated than married parents. Children living in fragile families have fewer resources available to them.

In 1960, 5.3 percent of births were to single mothers. By 1980, it was 18 percent, and in 2007 this figure reached 40 percent. Overall, 60 percent of births to women ages 20–24 were nonmarital (Ventura, 2009) (see Table 9–1). In the past, the majority of unmarried mothers were teenagers. In 2007, teenagers (ages 15–19) accounted for 23 percent of nonmarital births, down from 50 percent in 1970 (Ventura, 2009). In the twenty-first century, adult women ages 20 and over account for much of the increase in nonmarital births.

Cohabitating partner families consist of a mother who is residing with a partner to whom she is not married. Although there are two adults in cohabitating families, they tend to be less educated than those in married families and to have a lower income. Additionally, they are less likely to share their income than married families. In cohabitating couple families, if the father is not the biological father, he tends to invest less time with the children. Single mothers or mothers in cohabitating relationships report having more depression, and mothers experiencing instability in their relationships (whether dating or cohabitating) report more stress and engage in harsher parenting (Brown, 2004).

Parental disciplinary practices and attitudes influence child behavior. In homes of children with disruptive behavior disorders, punishment practices have been found to be extreme. These children are also more likely to be victims of child abuse and to be in homes where domestic abuse is evident (Robison, Frick, & Morris, 2005). Although severity and consistency of punishment contribute to aggressive behavior, some evidence suggests that parental punishment may be a response to child aggression rather than an antecedent to it (Robison et al., 2005). Parents of antisocial children are less likely to monitor their child's whereabouts or to make arrangements for child care when they are temporarily away from home. In general, the quality of the parent–child relationship is low, and there appears to be less warmth, affection, emotional support, and attachment (Robison et al., 2005). Research has consistently demonstrated that unhappy marital relationships, interpersonal conflicts, and aggression characterize the parental relations of delinquent and antisocial children. Whether the parents are cohabitating, separated, divorced, or married, the extent of discord and overt conflict is associated with the risk of disruptive behavior disorders and childhood dysfunction (Cummings & Davies, 2002; Nichol, Stretch, & Fundudis, 1993).

Socioeconomic disadvantage can be viewed as a risk factor. Poverty, overcrowding, unemployment, receipt of social assistance, and poor housing are among the salient measures of socioeconomic disadvantage that increase family risk for disruptive behavior disorders and delinquency. The effects appear to be enduring. However, once all other associated features are controlled, the precise role of economic issues is not always clear.

Young children are dependent upon the adults in their world to fulfill their basic needs; they are vulnerable in ways that older children are not and can easily become victims of inappropriate adult–child relationships. As children grow and develop, they both acquire and lose characteristics that put them at risk for atypical social development (Finkelhor, 2008). In an effort to move beyond the literature that focused solely on child abuse and neglect and to find a developmental framework for viewing social situations in which children are at risk, Finkelhor (2008) proposed the concept of "victimization." He saw the need to develop a means for understanding social traumas within a developmental framework.

The most clearly dependency-related form of victimization is neglect (Finkelhor, 2008), and parents and caregivers are the adults responsible for such neglect. Even when others are aware of neglect, it is the parents' responsibility to care for their children. Young children are also victims of child abuse, homicide, and abductions by parents.

This view of victimization uses the disruption of developmental tasks of childhood as a basis for understanding vulnerability (Finkelhor, 2008). Development of attachment to a primary caregiver is a major social task of infancy. Victimization interferes with this task when the caregiver perpetrates the abuse. The result is disorganized attachment, and the expectation is that the effects of this insecure attachment will be carried into later phases of development and other relationships. There may also be physiological alterations in endocrine functioning and neurologic processes

TABLE 9-1	BIRTHS TO UNMARRIED WOMEN BY AGE IN 2007

Age	Percent
15–17	93
18–19	82
20–24	60
25–29	33

Source: Ventura, 2009.

that permanently affect cognitive and behavioral development (Putnam & Trickett, 1993). Infants and toddlers who have been maltreated show more symptoms of anxiety and depression in adulthood (Kaplow & Widom, 2007).

Preschool children are capable of mental representation, and they develop the ability to dissociate. **Dissociation** is a mental state where certain thoughts, sensations, or memories are compartmentalized because they are too overwhelming for the conscious mind. Therefore, children fantasize, developing imaginary playmates, and deny things they clearly have done. Young children use dissociation as a defense mechanism and can develop chronic patterns of dissociation, such as memory loss, a tendency for trance-like behavior, and auditory or visual hallucinations (Putnam, 1991; Macfie, Cicchetti, & Toth, 2001).

Assessing the results of victimization for young children is different than for adults. When adults are victimized, they typically display posttraumatic stress symptoms that are relatively short term and primarily affect the behavior associated with the experience. Young children also show such behaviors as fearfulness, nightmares, avoidance of violence on television, fear of adults who resemble the offender, and fear of returning to the place where the victimization occurred (Finkelhor, 2008). Almost all traumatic situations result in some increased sense of fearfulness. In addition to traditional posttraumatic stress symptoms with very young children, victimization interferes with normal developmental processes. Although specific developmental problems vary, the effects of victimization and exposure to a variety of violent events can result in impaired attachment; separation anxiety; problems relating to others; poor peer relationships, often in the form of aggression toward peers, with lack of remorse; and problems coping with stress and anxiety (Briere, 1992; Cicchetti & Lynch, 1993; Lynch & Cicchetti, 2002). Within family relationships, deviant mother–child or father–child relationships, no father in the home, mental health problems of the parent(s) or other family members, and deviant parental relationships were viewed as factors that placed children at risk (Aronen & Arajarvi, 2004).

School Factors

Characteristics of some schools place children at risk for disruptive behavior disorders. Schools that use and support harsh discipline and provide poor child supervision place children at risk. For many children, school is no longer a safe haven.

Teachers who are not aware of different behavioral, disciplinary, and communication styles of different ethnic and socioeconomic groups in their classrooms can misperceive and misunderstand children's behaviors. Lynch (2004a) identified ways in which teachers may misinterpret or respond inappropriately to a child's behavior:

* *Perceiving behavior problems that do not exist.* Many African American children express emotions much more intensely than white children; teachers may assume children are much angrier than they really are.

* *Not noticing problems that do exist.* Teachers who are not tuned in to the ways students from other cultures communicate can miss a request for help or assistance. For example, some Asian American children believe that to ask for help would insult their teachers.

* *Misunderstanding the causes of children's behavior problems.* Educators may mistakenly attribute different causes to behavioral problems that are culturally determined. A teacher may assume that an Asian child who smiles when reprimanded has no respect for authority. Asian children tend to "camouflage" their embarrassment by smiling.

* *Using inappropriate techniques to deal with children's behavior.* Even when teachers recognize that a child's behavior problem might be culturally determined, they may still respond inappropriately. Hispanic parents tend to speak more politely and indirectly when they criticize or discipline their children. If teachers are gruff and direct with children, the children may see this as indicating they are not worthy of a proper relationship.

THE EVIDENCE BASE

Character education is a newcomer to curriculum interventions. It emphasizes concepts such as respect, fairness, caring, responsibility, trustworthiness, and citizenship. The What Works Clearinghouse looked at 93 studies in this area. Eighteen studies of 13 programs met their review qualifications—7 without reservations and 11 with reservations. The program that had the highest evidence rating for success was Positive Action. Positive Action is designed for children in kindergarten through grade 12. It uses 15-minute lessons designed to be taught several days a week throughout the school year.

Children participating in the Positive Action program improved an average of 19 percentile points in areas such as being supportive, friendly, and helpful; honest, rule abiding, and respectful; and fighting less. Interestingly, the children's standardized achievement scores in reading and math increased an average of 16.5 percentile points. Positive Action has no lessons designed in these areas.

Source: What Works Clearinghouse, 2007.

REFLECTIVE PRACTICE | How do you explain the increase in math and reading when there was no instruction in these areas? What do you think this means in the broad context of education?

Societal Factors

Society's social and economic problems spill over into the schooling process and greatly complicate the task of educating young children. We are a violent nation. The United States has the highest rates of violence of all industrialized nations, and children and youth are more involved in violent behavior at ever younger ages (APA, 2000). The cost of disruptive behavior disorders is high. First, there are the personal costs to the child. These children are often victims of abuse, neglect, and insensitive caregiving. The children tend to victimize others. They may use coercive acts to attain short-term gains, but they experience long-term losses. They are victimized by their own behavior and need assistance to break out of this

School may not feel like a safe place for some children.
©Cengage Learning 2012

behavior pattern. Schools and teachers play a pivotal role in this process (Walker et al., 2004).

Societal problems related to bias and discrimination are concerns in identifying children with disruptive behavior disorders. A disproportionate number of male, black, and Hispanic children are in special education, and they are especially overrepresented in the category of emotional disturbance (IDEA, 2004). Ultimately, nearly all behavioral standards and expectations—and therefore nearly all judgments regarding behavioral deviance—are culture bound; value judgments cannot be entirely culture free.

Early Identification of Social Problems and Disorders

All children need social skills to succeed in life. Social skills and emotional intelligence, confidence, curiosity, self-control, cooperation, communication, relatedness, and intentionality are crucial aspects of school readiness (Willis & Schiller, 2011). The identification and detection of atypical social development is difficult with young children. Diagnosis includes a subjective judgment of what is inappropriate. Assessment must consider cultural and child-rearing differences. The first signs of atypical social development are identified as children try to master basic developmental skills or social responses. There is concern when an infant cannot be comforted, a toddler does not talk, a child continues to show extreme anxiety

around strangers, or a child does not demonstrate any responsiveness to adults. These responses are warning flags for social development.

Shyness and Selective Mutism

All children like and need to be alone some of the time. Children who are alone most of the time or who seem uncomfortable when they are with groups of people cause concern.

Occasional **shyness** is expected, and typical of children who are slow-to-warm-up. It is characterized by an ambivalent approach–avoidance quality. Shyness is different from wariness and social disengagement; those behaviors do not share the ambivalent characteristics of shyness. In young children, shyness is often in response to new adults and is often characterized by thumb sucking or alternately smiling and hiding. Avoidance of gaze, an unwillingness to respond to friendly social overtures, and even blushing are also associated with shyness.

Children learn some aspects of shyness; some appear to be culturally based; and others are genetic. When shyness is a temporary solution to a novel or overwhelming social situation, it may be adaptive. Extreme shyness may be related to poor self-image or lack of social skills. Shy children may not be noticed and may not have the opportunities or skills to interact with other children or to gain an adult's attention (Hyson, 2004).

Selective mutism may be an extreme form of shyness, if the child displays different behavior in the family setting (APA, 2000). In selective mutism, the child can talk and is familiar with the spoken language, but does not talk in specific social situations, such as school, when there is an expectation that the child will talk. It cannot be diagnosed during the first months of school (it must last at least a month) and interfere with the child's social and academic development.

Shy children need to be given time to warm up in new situations. They may need to be taught skills for joining peer groups and given support in feeling good about themselves and the talents they have to offer. They need the subtle support of caring adults who encourage them, but don't take over and act for them. Shy children may need to learn skills to gain access to groups and maintain group membership. Children who grow up in authoritarian families are more likely to be shy. Caregiving styles that support democratic decision making and respect may help young children; making children feel attractive, supporting them in small groups after teaching them social entry skills, and teaching them muscle relaxation games helps.

Fear, Phobia, Anxiety, and Anxiety Disorders

All children are fearful at times. Sometimes this begins with a single incident such as being frightened by a dog. This fear may then generalize to all dogs and perhaps to all animals—in extreme cases, even to pictures of animals or animal crackers. When the focus is on a single object, place, or situation (e.g., dogs, school, going to a sleepover), it can be the beginning of a phobia. These passing fears are normal in children; it is their persistence and ability to limit the child's daily routine that are of concern.

A **phobia** is a marked and persistent fear that is excessive or unreasonable, and set off by anticipating, seeing, or coming into contact with the object or situation. For example, a child may be afraid of dogs. Upon seeing a dog, or even a photograph of a dog, the child may cry, tantrum, freeze, or cling (APA, 2000). Children try to avoid these situations. A phobia is not typically a major problem unless it interferes with academic functioning or social activities.

A **social phobia** involves a marked and persistent fear of situations that expose a child to strangers or to situations in which she feels she might be embarrassed, for example, a birthday party where the child may cry, have a temper tantrum, freeze, or shrink away from unfamiliar people. This child might be afraid to go to school, speak up in class, use the restroom, or eat in the cafeteria. To be considered a social phobia, the behavior must last for at least six months and take place in multiple settings, but not at home with familiar adults (Robb & Reber, 2007).

Anxiety is more generalized. Children worry, become upset easily, and may become extremely anxious about participating in new activities. They may be worried that they cannot do things right and may become perfectionists. They may have more problems than other children at their developmental level in distinguishing between the real world and the one that is make-believe. Monsters may be very real and a threat to them. Transitions and unstructured situations may increase their anxiety. Fear of new experiences may delay their mastery of new skills and interfere with their memory and concentration. Help anxious children by giving them clear explanations of what is happening and what is expected, and reassure them about your confidence in their ability to cope. These children need praise and support and may be oversensitive to criticism.

Anxiety disorders are among the most common disorders and are associated with feelings of emotional uneasiness, fear, and maladaptive worry. A **generalized anxiety disorder** is excessive anxiety and worry about a variety of things and results in fatigue, restlessness, difficulty concentrating, irritability, tension, and sleep disturbance. Generalized anxiety is more prevalent than had previously been thought; however, these disorders are difficult to diagnose (Robb & Reber, 2007).

Posttraumatic stress disorder can result from exposure to an extremely traumatic stressor, such as when the situation involves actual or threatened death or serious injury. It may involve feelings of intense fear, helplessness, or horror. In young children this may result in disorganized or agitated behavior (APA, 2000), and they may repeatedly reenact the experience. They may have physical symptoms such as stomachaches and headaches. They may feel that they won't live to grow up. Increasing numbers of children experience this disorder.

Posttraumatic stress disorders are classified based on the number of events: a single event (acute, single) or a connected series of traumatic events (chronic, repeated). A child who was in an automobile accident, broke her arm, and had to be taken to the emergency room would be expected to have short-term disturbances such as nightmares and would probably be fearful of riding in cars for a time. A child who is repeatedly abused or neglected is at risk for more pervasive interference with developmental tasks.

●●●
Attachment and Attachment Disorders
Some children fail to develop secure attachment patterns with adults. They do not respond as expected to social stimuli. They may be irritable and not easily comforted, and may dislike affection and withdraw. As infants they may have difficulties in their signaling systems that interrupt the early attachment process. They may cry continuously, have a piercing scream, arch their bodies to physical touch, and show no response to soothing interactions from adults. They may have poor eye contact and lack interest in social interaction. They are frequently described as "difficult" children. The presence of these behaviors can cause adults to think the child does not like them. They may also find it unpleasant to be around the child due to these behaviors. The result may be the failure of the adult and the child to develop secure attachment.

ATTACHMENT
Attachment is the development of the human bond between infants and adults. The underlying assumption of attachment is that young children use attachment as an internal working model for relationships. Its purpose is to make the relational world more predictable, meaningful, and shareable (Bretherton, 2005). Attachment has been studied in more detail than any other early childhood relationship. For the attachment process to operate efficiently, the infant must have information about himself and the attachment figure. He needs to know how likely the other is to respond as environments and conditions change. By the end of the first year, the infant has a considerable amount of knowledge about his world and organizes this knowledge to form a "working model" that includes models of self and adults in interaction with each other (Bowlby, 1989). The infant uses these models to plan his behavior. When caregivers abuse or neglect infants, or when the relationship is disrupted by events such as death or foster care placement, the model may become inaccurate and does not function as intended (Dozier, Dozier, & Manni, 2002). The more accurate and adequate the infant's model, the better adapted his behavior.

▶❚❚ TeachSource Video Case
0–2 Years: Attachment in Infants and Toddlers
Watch the TeachSource Video Case *0–2 Years: Attachment in Infants and Toddlers*, which demonstrates attachment forms through reciprocation between child and caregiver. The video can be found in the Early Childhood Education Media Library under Child Development, available at www.cengagebrain.com.

STAGES OF ATTACHMENT

Attachment develops in several stages. **Indiscriminate attachment** is present from birth to approximately 3 to 6 months. The infant enjoys being handled, being approached by people, and engaging in social interactions. Once the infant develops the ability to identify familiar adults (3 to 4 months), the process of **discriminate attachment** begins. During this stage, children show a marked change in social behavior. They respond differently to one (or a few) familiar individuals than they do to strangers.

The third stage builds on earlier attachment behaviors but is characterized by the infant's initiative in seeking proximity and contact with the attachment figure. This is referred to as **active initiation** and begins around 8 or 9 months (Ainsworth, 1969). Patterns of attachment in children appear to be far more stable over time than specific behaviors. However, they are less stable for infants from economically vulnerable families or in families where mothers entered into employment during the attachment process. It appears that the mother–child relationship has to be renegotiated at this time. The picture emerging is one of developmental complexity (Sroufe et al., 2005). Infant attachment alone does not predict later relationships, but in context provides important information. Secure attachment histories provide a base for toddlers to accept parents' limit setting. When there is insecure attachment or anxious attachment, parents have greater problems setting limits and boundaries, and providing the support for the struggles that children have with autonomy (Sroufe et al., 2005).

One way of looking at attachment is through the "strange situation" developed by Ainsworth in 1963 and still used today. It works something like this:

- A mother and child (between ages 12 and 24 months) enter an unfamiliar room that contains two chairs and a few appropriate toys for the child to play with. The mother stays with the child for three minutes and then leaves.

- A stranger enters and stays for three minutes.

- The mother returns, and the mother and infant are reunited (Honig, 1993).

Much of our knowledge about attachment is based on research done using the strange situation.

TYPES OF ATTACHMENT

Four different types of attachment have been identified.

- **Secure attachment.** Young children showing **secure attachment** protest at being left alone or with a stranger in an unfamiliar place. They may show the obvious distress of crying or fussing, disruption of play behavior, or unwillingness to be comforted by a strange adult. When the parent returns, the child calms quickly, seeks proximity, and returns to play and exploration. Parents of securely attached children appear to be sensitive and responsive to their child's signals. Children who are securely attached seek out their parent for comfort when they are scared, hurt, or hungry. These children use their parents to help them settle down (Dozier, Dozier, & Manni, 2002).

- **Avoidant Attachment.** Young children who display **avoidant attachment** neither protest when their parent leaves, nor immediately acknowledge her return. Rather, they become busy exploring the surroundings and making overtures toward the unfamiliar adult. At first glance, these look like mature behaviors. However, most feel that this is a strategy for dealing with the stress of separation rather than lack of stress per se. It is viewed as an organized defensive strategy. Parents of these infants tended to minimize or dismiss the importance of attachment and to avoid confronting negative affect. When children come to their parents because they are scared, they may be told "There is nothing to be scared of," or "You have to grow up—this is silly," or "Don't bother me." If parents consistently do not comfort and reassure their young child, she learns that they do not respond to her concerns. She may look and then turn away, based on her memory of previous experiences. The child's behavior may be adaptive for the situation she is in (Dozier, Dozier, & Manni, 2002).

- **Resistant Attachment.** Toddlers displaying **resistant attachment** are distressed at separation from the parent and contact her when she returns, but the contact is one of anger. They don't seem to be comforted by the parent's return and don't seem to be able to resume play. This behavior has been interpreted as the child's response to inconsistent caregiving. Parents of ambivalent children showed similar ambivalent feelings about their own parents and appeared preoccupied with attachment relationships (Dozier, Dozier, & Manni, 2002). Avoidant and resistant attachment patterns are seen as organized consistent strategies of response to stress that are adaptive for the young child in some situations.

- **Disorganized/Controlling Attachment.** Young children with **disorganized/controlling attachment** lack a consistent pattern in response to stress. This behavior is typically in response to caregivers whose behavior is frightening to them, which can occur for a variety or reasons. The toddler's concern can be based on fear of abuse or neglect, or it can be in response to threats of abandonment. Children's responses may be idiosyncratic but typically include alternations of approach and avoidance of the parent. These children lack an organized way of seeking comfort and security when stressed. Their parents appear stressed and seem to be dealing with unresolved loss or trauma. Parents who are depressed, abusive, alcoholic, or having serious psychosocial problems may respond in ways that frighten young children and make them unable to respond in a consistent way. Some researchers feel that these children are at the greatest risk for later psychopathology (Dozier, Dozier, & Manni, 2002).

Children with both avoidant and resistant attachment have figured out a system that works for them—not ideal, but workable. Children with disorganized/controlling attachment are vulnerable for both internalizing symptoms such as anxiety and depression, as well as externalizing symptoms such as acting out (Lyons-Ruth, 1996).

Reactive Attachment Disorder. Failure to develop appropriate attachment patterns may lead children to withdraw or shun social interaction. They may exhibit cranky and whiny behaviors. Social responsiveness may be limited. These children fail to develop appropriate interaction patterns with adults and peers, and do not respond as expected to social stimuli. The combination of these behaviors typically results in further isolation, as both adults and peers tend to ignore or dislike these children and refrain from interacting with them.

Although rare, children who experience markedly disturbed and inappropriate social relatedness can be diagnosed with **reactive attachment disorder** of infancy or early childhood (APA, 2000). The main characteristic of this disorder is the lack of social relatedness that occurs before the age of 5. There are two different types: inhibited and disinhibited. In the inhibited type, the child does not express age-appropriate signs of social responsiveness. The child does not respond appropriately to social interactions and may be excessively inhibited, hypervigilant, or show approach–avoidance responses. In the disinhibited type, the child is indiscriminately social, relating to strangers with excessive familiarity, but showing no selectivity in attachment figures.

Reactive attachment disorder is caused by extreme neglect and grossly inadequate or inappropriate caregiving. Children with this disorder respond well to positive nurturing and caregiving. Although the emphasis in intervention is typically on parent–child relationships, it is possible that a child who is distressed in an early care and education setting would show a disorder in this category. Adults can be helped to read children's cues more accurately and respond to them quickly, as well as increase the order and predictability in the child's environment and the availability of a primary caregiver.

Separation Anxiety Disorder. As the name suggests, anxiety results from separation from familiar people, usually parents, or from leaving home. The reaction is excessive and usually occurs regardless of the general intellectual level of the child. **Separation anxiety disorder** and generalized anxiety are strongly associated (Warren, 2004). Separation anxiety may be a precursor to adult anxiety.

All young children react to separation. Some children cry; others want their parent to stay; some withdraw and some act out; some hesitate to enter a new setting and, when left, keep returning to the door; some look stressed; and some bring attachment objects. It is the recurrent excessive distress upon separation, and persistent and excessive worry about losing or having harm befall the attachment figure that characterize this disorder. It may involve sleep disturbances,

both not wanting to go to sleep as well as having nightmares about separation. It may involve physical symptoms such as vomiting, headaches, or nausea upon separation or knowledge of separation (APA, 2000). The condition must last at least four weeks to be considered a disorder.

IN THE FIELD

When you teach 2-year-olds, you expect separation problems. We have a goodbye window where children can watch their parents leave and look in anticipation of their return. We have had some difficult separations, but none in the same category as Rebecca. She started school in September, and her mother stayed in the classroom with her on the first day, which is pretty typical. The next day, her mother planned to leave, but Rebecca protested so violently that her mother stayed. I tried to coach the mother to have her say goodbye, leave for five minutes, and then return so Rebecca would get used to the separation. She cried the whole time her mother was gone. The next day, Rebecca came with her father. This was more difficult, and we again tried the five-minute routine. The family was desperate for her to be in school because they were expecting another child in several months. Rebecca's father did mention that she and her mother were very close. Rebecca didn't even like her mother to close the door when she went to the bathroom. And although Rebecca had her own room, she cried to the point that she either slept with her parents or one of them slept with her in the double bed in her room. Her father said they were always tired. As long as he stayed and talked with us, Rebecca was fine. When he left, she cried. We tried variations on leaving, bringing attachment objects, and everything else we could think of. It was difficult to tell at the beginning whether this was a power struggle or a genuine separation anxiety disorder. By the end of the fourth week, we were all exhausted. We had a parent–teacher conference and mutually decided that Rebecca would be withdrawn from the program. I suggested that some family counseling might be helpful. They were noncommittal. I feel a bit guilty, but I felt like the other children were paying such a high price, and I really thought that I had done all I knew how to do. This situation required more skill than I had.

• • •

Eating and Eating Disorders

Many children go through stages in which eating certain foods is problematic, often more a problem for adults than for children. Typical eating problems involve "finicky" eaters who go through phases when they will eat only certain foods like hot dogs, peanut butter and jelly, and candy. They may refuse to eat most table foods, and they may eat on the run, grabbing an apple slice or cracker. For most children, these finicky habits are just phases that they experience and pass through.

For some children, eating problems are more severe and can lead to nutritional problems that affect development. Some infants develop a pattern in which they refuse to eat, turning their head away from nursing, the bottle, and cereal. As we are learning more about children's eating behaviors, it appears that food allergies may play some part in the child's behavior. Infants who are allergic to milk or soy formulas may be diagnosed as "failure to thrive," when in reality the child has an allergic reaction to the food offered. In recent years, more children seem to be developing severe food allergies.

If children have eating problems, a medically based approach such as blood tests to determine food allergies should be suggested. If the child is allergic to particular foods or additives, a special diet can be recommended. Ensuring that children are not hungry, reinforcing appropriate eating habits, establishing consistent eating routines, and suggesting behavior modification techniques can help to overcome most eating problems. However, some children fall into the category of "failure to thrive."

FAILURE TO THRIVE

Malnutrition is caused by inadequate caloric intake, calorie expenditures that exceed caloric intake, or the body's inability to use the calories for growth and development (Eicher, 2007). The most frequent cause of **failure to thrive** is that the infants do not get enough food. It is, in effect, more of a symptom than a diagnosis (Beker, Farber, & Yanni, 2002). In infancy, it also means deficits in nutrients to the brain and diminished physical energy for exploring and learning. Malnutrition reduces the number of brain cells.

Failure to thrive can be a result of organic (biological) or nonorganic (psychosocial/behavioral) reasons, or the interaction of these. It is more common among children living in impoverished environments, but not exclusive to them. In these cases, it may relate to lack of available food, lack of parent knowledge, or lack of parental involvement. It can also be related to the child's refusal to eat or willingness to eat only certain foods. Children with developmental disabilities are disproportionately represented in infants who fail to thrive (Isaacs, 2007). As children become older, around 2 years, failure to thrive is less of a problem because children can obtain food for themselves by asking for it or finding it in the home.

Early Identification of Emotional Problems and Disorders

Although the basic processes by which children learn about and develop emotions are similar, there are vast individual differences in their display of emotions and emotional states. **Temperament** is one aspect of emotional development that has received much attention. Each child has a unique personality, part of which is his or her temperament, which affects how a child relates to the world.

• • • Temperament

All children exhibit the following characteristics to some extent; the extremes characterize children who show emotional and behavioral vulnerability. The pattern of these dimensions makes up temperament. Thomas, Chess, and Birch did some of the pioneering work in this area in 1968.

> **▶❚❚ TeachSource Video Case**
>
> **0–2 Years: Temperament in Infants and Toddlers**
>
> Watch the TeachSource Video Case *0–2 Years: Temperament in Infants and Toddlers*, which demonstrates how infants have unique characteristics and temperaments at birth. The video can be found in the Early Childhood Education Media Library under Child Development, available at www.cengagebrain.com.

Temperament Dimensions. Temperament includes the child's predictable pattern of response and preferences, made up of the following dimensions:

- **Activity Level.** This refers to the amount of time a child is active or not active. Children who are always on the go and can't sit still are at one end; children who are inactive and just sit are at the other extreme.

- **Regularity.** All children have an internal biological clock that can be either regular or unpredictable. For those children who are *very* regular (they get up at the same time, eat at the same time), it is important to look at the match between adult expectations, programmatic demands, and the child's typical pattern. To the extent that these are mismatched, these children can be more difficult than the unpredictable child. Unpredictable children do not have a strong internal rhythm.

- **Approach–Avoidance.** Children have a typical response to new experiences. The extremes are to approach without caution or to avoid at all costs through crying or clinging to adults. Most children approach new experiences with some degree of caution. For children who have had many or recent new encounters that were painful, the avoidance response may be predominant.

- **Adaptability.** Some children find it easy to adapt to change; others find it very difficult. Children who are change resistant find new routines, a substitute teacher, a new sibling, or even a new child entering the class extremely stressful. Especially at celebrations, holidays, and transitions, slow-to-adapt children need extra time and support.

- **Physical Sensitivity.** Some children are aware of slight changes in the environment; others respond only to major physical changes. Children who are highly sensitive can become overstimulated by too much noise, touch, light, and so on. They need support in regulating their environment.

- **Intensity of Reaction.** Many situations evoke reactions in children; the intensity and length of the response in relation to the event are what must be evaluated. One child may cry violently for 20 minutes when another child takes a toy, whereas another child may fuss only briefly.

- **Mood.** Children have a range of moods that are a balance of happy and less positive moods. Some children are in a predictable mood most of the time; others vary considerably. Children who are predictably negative may make adults feel guilty or angry. Rather than receiving the extra attention, love, and support they need, these children may be avoided.

- **Persistence.** Persistence is the amount of time a child attends to or persists with a task, and can be related to how difficult the task is and how interested the child is in it.

• **Resistance/Distractibility.** Resistance measures the ability of the child to return to an activity after an interruption. Resistance focuses on longer breaks for such things as toileting. Distractibility relates to momentary interruptions and how the child reacts to extraneous stimuli. Distracting sights and sounds cause some children to lose concentration, whereas others can continue.

Table 9–2 provides a method of assessing temperament.

TEMPERAMENT STYLES

Thomas and his colleagues (1968) have organized these dimensions of temperament into four basic temperament styles: flexible, feisty, fearful, and typical.

1. *Easy or flexible children* (40%) are those who rate moderate in intensity, adaptability, approachableness, and rhythmicity, and have predominantly positive moods. They are usually calm and predictable and tend to eat and sleep on a schedule, although they can adapt the schedule to some extent. They smile frequently, typically approach new experiences positively, and show little negative emotion. These children tend to be easygoing and highly sociable. They adapt quickly to change, and have low-to-medium intensity of reactions. Their biological rhythms are regular; they are (or were) easy to toilet train; and they sleep through the night. Chess and Thomas (1977) classified about 40 percent of their sample as easy children.

2. *Difficult or feisty children* (10%) are at the other end of the temperament scale. Difficult children often display negative emotion. They cry a lot and are fearful or withdrawn in the face of new experiences. They are unpredictable, have mood shifts, and are easily distracted. Although they set their own eating and sleeping schedule, it is not predictable (Chess & Thomas, 1990). They shift states quickly and may go from sleeping to screaming in seconds. These children are slow to adapt and change, are nonrhythmic, have intense reactions, and often have negative moods. Their biological rhythms are irregular, and they have difficulty sleeping through the night; toilet training also is a challenge. They are typically movers: they crawl, walk, or run, rarely staying in the same place for long. They are less sociable than other children. Chess and Thomas (1977) found about 10 percent of their sample to be difficult or feisty children.

3. *Slow-to-warm-up or fearful children* (15%) share some of the characteristics of difficult children. They initially appear to have the characteristics of difficult children,

TABLE 9-2 ASSESSMENT OF TEMPERAMENT

Activity Level						
Quiet	1	2	3	4	5	Active
Regularity						
Regular	1	2	3	4	5	Irregular
Approach–Avoidance						
Approach	1	2	3	4	5	Withdrawal
Adaptability						
Adaptable	1	2	3	4	5	Slow to adapt
Physical Sensitivity						
Sensitive	1	2	3	4	5	Not sensitive
Intensity of Reaction						
Low intensity	1	2	3	4	5	High intensity
Predictable	1	2	3	4	5	Not predictable
Mood						
Positive	1	2	3	4	5	Negative
Persistence						
Long attention	1	2	3	4	5	Short attention
Resistance						
Returns to task	1	2	3	4	5	Does not return
Distractibility						
Not distractible	1	2	3	4	5	Highly distractible
Total						
Temperament Style: Flexible; Feisty; Fearful; Typical						

Circle the number that best represents the child's behavior, add the columns and then circle the child's temperament style.

Children with easy temperaments are flexible, moderate, and usually in a positive mood.
©Cengage Learning 2012

but do not show the intensity or persistence. Initially, their response to new events is negative, but, given time, they do in fact "warm up," although it takes them longer to adapt than easy children. They have negative moods, but the intensity is low or mild. They can have either regular or irregular biological rhythms. Fifteen percent of Chess and Thomas's (1977) sample fell into this category.

4. *Typical children* (35%) did not fall into any of these categories and were classified as typical.

A child's temperament is sometimes a challenge to adults. Some parents find it comforting to know that children are born with different temperaments and that they are not the cause of their child's temperament. Temperament affects the child's development because it impacts how the child approaches her environment, as well as how the environment responds to the child. Difficult children and easy children evoke different responses from adults, although they don't get the same response from all adults. The key is the interaction pattern between the child and the adult, or the "goodness of fit" (Thomas & Chess, 1980).

GOODNESS OF FIT

The concept of goodness of fit looks at the match between the expectations and interactions of the adult and the child's behavior in relationship to these expectations. A parent or educator who is up and on the go, wants to do things and not sit around, and isn't disturbed by crying and temper tantrums might be delighted with a difficult child and find an easy child boring. A parent or educator who is patient and has a cautious approach to new ideas may find a slow-to-warm-up child enchanting, whereas with either a difficult or easy child, she may feel overwhelmed or unnecessary. It is not possible to evaluate children's outcomes on temperament alone. Chess (1983) stresses that the interaction between the adult's expectations and the child's responses is a key factor in assessing the quality of the adult–child relationship. Concern focuses around children who are "slow to warm up" and those with difficult temperaments, who need extra adult understanding but who may actually receive fewer positive responses from adults who do not understand and know how to work with them.

IMPLICATIONS FOR EDUCATORS

Educators should be observant of and responsive to children's temperament. The goal is not to change their temperament (which is genetic and not likely to change), but to work with children in ways that are supportive of their development. This means finding time to give the easy child attention, supporting the fearful child as she learns to join groups, and setting limits and finding ways to help the feisty child gain skills in self-regulation. It also means acknowledging that young children do have issues that impact their emotional and mental health, and being knowledgeable about the resources to support these children.

Using Table 9–2, observe and record the behavior of a particular child for parts of several days, or as long as you feel you need to in order to establish a pattern. If possible, ask the child's parents for their input about the child's temperament. Compare your observational results with their perceptions, and reflect on the similarities and differences. Identify the child's temperament style. Decide how this might impact your programming for this child or a child with his temperament. Now do the same thing for yourself. What is your temperament style? Which children do you like to teach most? Which children are you most comfortable working with? Which children are most difficult for you? Which children have the best goodness of fit in your teaching? Once you know this, do some hard thinking about children who may not fit as well. Both the adult and the environment should be as flexible as possible to include children of all temperament types.

● ● ●

Introversion, Extroversion, and Mood Disorders

Children differ in how introverted or extroverted they are. Children who are introverted need more time to be alone, whereas children who are extroverted like lots of social interaction. Respect the rights of children to be introverts, but be wary of a pattern of excessive withdrawal, characterized by the inability to develop relationships with parents or peers, inactivity, excessive social isolation, and lack of affect. Children may have a favorite place in the room where they feel safe. When approached, they may react by moving away and not interacting. If these characteristics occur individually or in combination, there is a cause for concern. Children may need to be taught social skills and reinforced for social initiatives. Consistent lack of interaction will cause a child to miss experiences that lead to improved social competency, better self-esteem, and increased overall development. Settings that emphasize warmth, caring, and consistency can help children overcome feelings of insecurity. Children who are withdrawn learn from observation. If they are not part of the group, ascertain what they can see from their vantage point, and maximize their opportunity for learning.

There are three significant mood disorders: **dysthymia**, **depression**, and **mania**. Dysthymic disorder is characterized by being sad or "down in the dumps." For children to be identified, this has to persist for a year. This becomes the way the child is in the world and is associated with poor eating or overeating, low energy, low self-esteem, poor concentration or difficulty making decisions, and feelings of hopelessness (APA, 2000). These symptoms can go unrecognized because they are so chronic. Major **depressive disorders** can appear as a single event or a repetitive series of discrete episodes. They are more obvious than dysthymia, and more extreme. The differences are based on severity, chronicity, and persistence (APA, 2000). Children who are depressed emotionally withdraw, have little interest in the activities of daily life, have problems sleeping and eating (failure to gain expected weight), have poor concentration, often feel worthless and guilty, and may have thoughts of death or suicide. In young children, it can also be seen as an irritable mood.

A **manic episode** is characterized by an abnormally and persistently elevated, expansive, or irritable mood. This is accompanied by inflated self-esteem; little need for sleep; being talkative, flighty, and distractible; and excessive involvement in pleasurable activities that have a high potential for painful consequences (APA, 2000). **Bipolar disorder** is a condition where a child has episodes of mania and also periods of depression. Bipolar disorder has a strong hereditary base, and symptoms can emerge in infancy or early childhood. In retrospect, mothers report that their children were difficult to settle, slept erratically, and seemed extraordinarily clingy. Even at a young age, they had uncontrollable tantrums out of proportion to the issue, and just the word *no* could trigger these episodes. Some children with ADHD may have early-onset bipolar disorder or this may be in addition to ADHD (Child and Adolescent Bipolar Foundation, 2002). When bipolar disorder begins in childhood, it may be a different and possibly a more severe form of the illness. It is often characterized by a continuous, rapid-cycling, irritable, and mixed symptom state that may co-occur with disruptive behavior disorders (Robb & Reber, 2007). At this point, no separate criteria exist for diagnosing children with bipolar disorder. The concern is that early intervention might help and that as the symptoms worsen, the child becomes progressively impaired.

Overall, children with emotional disorders are either too sensitive or not sensitive enough to the stimuli in their world. Their sensory systems over- or underreact to stimulation, and sometimes they do so inconsistently. Their functional development is uneven; that is, they may walk within the normal time range, but not talk. Children who talk may have an appropriate vocabulary, but not use it to convey meaning in a conventional sense. They may confuse words that are associated (e.g., hat and coat) or use unique code words when most children have replaced these with conventional words. They may have favorite toys they want to use and find it difficult to use others or to change tasks. Their body language communicates isolation and confusion, often lacking a social smile, eye contact, and social approach skills.

They may use their bodies in unusual ways (e.g., rocking, flapping) but also as a way of comforting themselves. Some children also use their bodies to express strong feelings by banging their head against the wall or floor and hitting or biting themselves until they are stopped. They don't seem to function in an integrated way. It is difficult to develop an accurate picture of these children, as they are difficult to assess. Educators need to be firm and kind and, above all, consistent. Keep routines the same and favorite toys and materials in the same locations. Educators should keep in contact with families on a daily basis.

IN THE FIELD

Communication with parents is key! I found that each day I was writing home to parents basically the same information, and it was taking up a lot of time. I modified a "Daily Report" from a fellow teacher to send home. On the daily report, there is space to circle what the child ate at school, the activities and therapies in which she participated, and what her mood was like. Each day, the paper goes home with the child, and the parents are expected to complete the same type of information on the back of the paper and return it to school. I really like knowing what the children did at home the previous night so we can talk about it at school the next day. In addition to this, we also send home a communication book, in case the parent or teacher has a question or comment.

Early Identification of Behavioral Problems and Disorders

Before deciding whether you think a child has a behavioral problem, look at the child's environment, lifestyle, and the demands of the program. Young boys in particular need time to be physically active and participate in active hands-on learning and play. To the extent that early childhood programs support a teacher-directed academic-scripted curriculum, boys are more likely to have behavior problems. They enter the classroom less developmentally mature than girls in social-emotional development and literacy skills (Gropper et al., 2011). There is also a difference between being "streetwise" and having a behavior problem. Some children may have *learned* to be aggressive as a way of surviving. I have taught children who would not have made it safely home if they had followed the same rules I enforced in our classroom.

IN THE FIELD

A 6-year-old inner-city boy once told me: "Lady, you wouldn't last one hour on my block." I responded, "Germane, you're right. In fact, I probably wouldn't last five minutes."

Assertiveness is a valuable asset for children. When it moves into aggressiveness, it causes concern, particularly if it becomes the child's typical way of interacting with others. Aggressive children hurt others with or without provocation. Some children become aggressive under stress; when they cannot get what they want, they explode. They use aggression as a means of communication, but what are they trying to communicate? Children who are aggressive may be fearful and anxious and use aggression as a way of responding to an inner self that also feels hateful and suspicious. These children often have poor self-images. Trying to identify the situations that provoke aggressive behavior is one place to start. However, it isn't useful to waste time on what you cannot change. You can, however, control where the child sits in the classroom, the children you sit next to him, as well as the space available for large motor activities. You need to set and enforce the boundaries of acceptable behavior in your classroom.

Start by gathering information by behavioral observations, including information about the situation as well as specific characteristics relative to behavior: duration, latency, context, frequency, intensity, and time (Salvia & Ysseldyke, 2007). You want to answer the questions: "When, where, and how often does the behavior happen?" and "What causes or triggers the behavior?" You will also need to answer questions that are more specific to the particular situation:

- *Who is the victim*? Is the victim anyone who happens to be there, or is it usually a particular child or a certain few children? If it is a variety of children determine whether they are mostly boys or girls; bigger or smaller; older or younger; aggressive or timid. Or are the victims adults?

- *How does the child act after the behavior*? Does the child deny the behavior or admit it? Does the victim's crying upset the child (if that is what happened)? Does the child get upset if the victim returns the behavior (bites or hits back)? Does the child look to see if an adult is watching before proceeding with the behavior? Does the child walk away? Or does the child apologize and show concern for the victim?

Children who are aggressive in early childhood are at risk for loneliness and lack of peer support. A high level of aggression is predictive of serious problems in adulthood. Children with these behaviors may continue a cycle of violence, including severe punishment of their own children, domestic violence, and antisocial and violent criminal behavior (Lewin, 1999). Bullying is one of the common forms of aggression children face.

Bullying

Bullying is aggressive behavior. It is intentional, repeated over time, and based on a real or perceived imbalance of power or strength. According to the Multidimensional Bullying Identification Model (Marini, Fairbairn, & Zuber, 2001), there are three components to bullying: the characteristics of bullying, types or forms of aggression, and roles involved in bullying. Bullying is purposefully used with the intent to control and harm, psychologically or physically, and the behavior is repetitive and secretive. It usually occurs in areas that lack adult supervision (Olweus, Limber, & Mihalic, 1999). The bully puts substantial effort into concealing bullying from parents and teachers. The harm that results from bullying is recurrent. Victims fear the bullying because they know that it will happen again. This is a significant and devastating aspect of bullying. A power differential between the bully and the victim is a component of bullying behaviors. The power from bullying can be knowledge of the victim's sensitive issues or vulnerabilities, higher intelligence, or better physical strength. This power creates fear, anxiety, and intimidation in the victim (Marini et al., 2001).

Characteristics of children who bully:

- Impulsive, hot-headed, dominant
- Easily frustrated
- Lack empathy
- Have difficulty following rules
- View violence in a positive way
- Boys who bully tend to be physically stronger than other children (Health, Resources and Services Administration [HRSA], 2010)

Bullying can be physical, social, cognitive, or emotional in nature. The most common type of bullying is physical. Physical contact between the victim and bully includes kicking, hitting, shoving, hair-pulling, or punching. In social bullying, a group or gang of peers picks on a particular child. Other types of bullying use verbal threats or insults or nonverbal gestures such as glares or hand gestures to cause harm to the victim. Excluding peers from play or spreading rumors is another form that bullying can take. The goal of this bullying is to exclude or isolate the victim. Talking about someone, spreading rumors, and making obscene phone calls or texting are just a few examples of emotional bullying (Marini et al., 2001) (see Figure 9–1).

The final component of bullying looks at the roles children take during a bullying situation. The three specific roles are bully, victim, and bystander. Each one is affected by and part of the act of bullying (Marini et al., 2001). The role of bully is the perpetrator or instigator who directly or indirectly causes harm, physically or psychologically to the victim. Bullies tend to choose victims who are significantly weaker cognitively and socioemotionally (Marini et al., 2001). Victims, on the receiving end of the bullying behavior, can commonly be described as insecure with low self-esteem, socially isolated, lonely, and having deficits in psychological and physical strength (Olweus, 2001). Bystanders are the largest group in the bullying situation, but may not be directly involved.

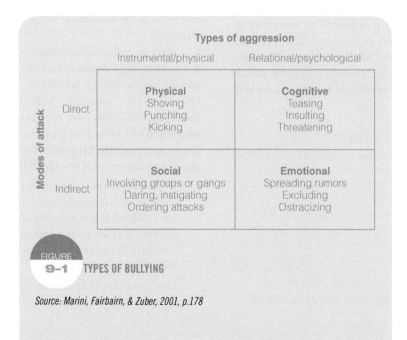

FIGURE 9–1   TYPES OF BULLYING

Source: Marini, Fairbairn, & Zuber, 2001, p.178

Their contribution to the bullying situation can range from detached observer, to supporters of the bully or defenders of the victim (Olweus, 2001). Although bullying seems like a minor problem, it negatively impacts the lives of many children.

Of the behavior disorders that occur in early childhood, those identified by the American Psychiatric Association in DSM-IV-TR (APA, 2000) are **oppositional defiant disorder**, **conduct disorder**, and **disruptive behavior disorder not otherwise specified**. These disorders may co-occur with other disorders but are characterized here as single disorders to highlight their characteristics.

> ▶❚❚ TeachSource Video Case
>
> **School Age: Emotional Development**
>
> Watch the TeachSource Video Case *School Age: Emotional Development*, to see a lesson that teaches children about bullies, and how caregivers can reach bullies and victims. The video can be found in the Early Childhood Education Media Library under Child Development, available at www.cengagebrain.com.

Oppositional Defiant Disorder

The essential feature of oppositional defiant disorder (ODD) is a recurrent pattern of defiant, disobedient, negativistic, and hostile behavior toward authority figures (APA, 2000). This behavior is evident before age 8 and typically begins in the home but appears in other settings as well. For some children, it is a precursor to a conduct disorder. Depending upon the population studied and the methods used, the prevalence rate ranges from 2 percent to 16 percent (APA, 2000).

Beneath the observed behavior is a child who does not know how to deal with the discomfort or pain of stress. Children with oppositional defiant disorder project their problems onto others and do not take responsibility for them: Someone else always starts the fight, and the adults are at fault. Children who externalize stress do not accept responsibility for their actions; therefore, they do not appear anxious or depressed, even though the adults around them do (Silver, 2004). These children are difficult to help because they see others as the source of their problem.

Oppositional behavior is common in preschool children and should be diagnosed with care. Oppositional behavior should be markedly greater and more persistent than expected by developmental norms. Depending upon the age of the child, these characteristics play out in different ways. During the preschool years, these children often have difficult temperaments with high reactivity and are difficult to soothe. They frequently have high levels of motor activity. They may have low self-esteem or overinflated self-esteem. As they reach school age, they show low frustration tolerance and precocious use of alcohol, tobacco, or illicit drugs as well as changeable moods (APA, 2000). ODD is more common in boys than girls until puberty, but equals out after that. As expected, there are frequent conflicts with parents, teachers, and peers. Boys have more confrontational behaviors and more persistent

DIAGNOSTIC CRITERIA FOR OPPOSITIONAL DEFIANT DISORDER

A. A pattern of negativistic, hostile, and defiant behavior lasting at least 6 months, during which four (or more) of the following are present:
1. often loses temper
2. often argues with adults
3. often actively defies or refuses to comply with adults' requests or rules
4. often deliberately annoys people
5. often blames others for his or her mistakes or misbehavior
6. is often touchy or easily annoyed by others
7. is often angry and resentful
8. is often spiteful or vindictive

Note: Consider a criterion met only if the behavior occurs more frequently than is typically observed in individuals of comparable age and developmental level.

B. The disturbance in behavior causes clinically significant impairment in social, academic, or occupational functioning.

Source: American Psychiatric Association, 2000, p. 102.

symptoms (APA, 2000) (see Table 9–3 for diagnostic characteristics of ODD).

There are some familial patterns that relate to children having ODD, such as at least one parent with the disorder or a related disorder such as a mood disorder, conduct disorder, or attention-deficit/hyperactivity disorder. It is also more frequent with maternal depressive disorder, but it is not clear whether this is a cause or result (APA, 2000). The occurrence is also higher in families with serious marital discord and inconsistent caregiving, and in families where harsh, inconsistent, or neglectful child-rearing practices are common (APA, 2000).

In some instances, the oppositional behavior only occurs in the home setting, and it is more evident with familiar adults and peers, making diagnosis difficult. Usually children with ODD do not consider themselves defiant, but see their behavior as a legitimate response to unreasonable demands or circumstances.

Children with ODD show persistent stubbornness, noncompliance to requests, and an unwillingness to compromise or negotiate. They deliberately and continually test limits. These children frequently ignore requests, argue, and do not accept blame for misdeeds. In fact, they often blame others for their mistakes and are angry, spiteful, and vindictive. They deliberately annoy others, but this is usually done verbally, not physically. These behaviors interfere with their social and academic functioning.

IN THE FIELD

The most difficult child I ever taught was a 6-year-old boy with defiant behavior. His antisocial behavior kept many of his classmates from playing with him, and this led to his inability to make and keep friends. He was in a vicious cycle.

Justin hated school, he hated home, and he especially hated women in authority. He would swear and kick if he were told to do something he didn't want to do. He wanted to love and he wanted to be loved, but he didn't have the social skills to do so. Justin was a loner and had a difficult time fitting in. Children and adults avoided him and kept a safe distance.

We quickly learned that Justin hated change and that he did not like to be interrupted from an activity. We arranged the classroom so that we could decrease the likelihood of an outburst during transitions. We always gave Justin a countdown so that he could prepare himself. A five-minute warning was used and then we basically counted down. This gave him time to get accustomed to the change.

Because children can select the centers they want to play in, we knew that Justin would always go to the art table first and get "hung up" on the activity. We modified his self-selection by stating that he had to do three other centers first and then he could spend as much time as he wanted at the art table.

We have an open snack so children can eat when they want to. It is one of our centers. We always kept snack last for him because he had a difficult time eating with other children. He could handle two or three, but five were overwhelming. Most of our children like to go to snack first or second, so the majority of the children were done before Justin ate.

We learned to recognize the signs when Justin was going to get out of control. By getting to know his behaviors, we could often distract him or remove him before he would lose his cool.

Justin needed a structured environment. We made sure that he knew exactly what was expected during the day. After meeting with his parents several times, it became evident that Justin had no set routines at home. His house was chaotic. He seemed to relax in a structured environment. He liked knowing that a certain type of behavior would result in a particular consequence. Justin liked consistent rules and discipline. We always had to pick up the pieces after a long weekend or winter break.

Justin hated waiting times but he loved fingerplays. During transitions, we always kept him busy until the last possible minute. When we had to wait in line for buses or other such necessities, I often asked Justin what he would like to sing or which fingerplay he wanted. If he didn't get to pick, I stood close to him so that he would not feel left out.

Justin was a ball of fire during circle time. He constantly pushed or leaned on children. I quickly learned that he liked to have his back scratched during sitting activities. This really calmed him down. Of course, you cannot provide that constantly, but Clifford (stuffed dog) helped, as did other children. Once during a lesson, I noticed two of my very bright young children sitting beside Justin. Justin was attending and very calm. I was glad to see that and I continued my lesson with ease. I started to notice that this little boy to the right of Justin and the little girl to the left of Justin were putting their hands behind his back. I thought that they were holding each other's hands behind him or poking Justin to agitate him. I continued my lesson, watching curiously what was going on. I soon realized that both children were rubbing Justin's back together in a very pleasant way. I was so pleased to realize that Justin may have finally made some friends.

I believe that the most important way to deal with a difficult child is to get to know that child. You must be patient and try to figure out what will work. Be positive, because change is difficult, and the child may be living negativity daily. It is also important to be positive with the parents. They are probably sick and tired of hearing how terrible their child is. It may be a difficult road to follow, but it is worth the journey.

• • •
Conduct Disorder

The essential aspect of a conduct disorder is a repetitive and persistent pattern of behavior that violates the basic rights of others and does not follow rules or age-appropriate societal

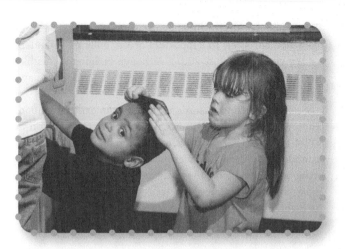

Children with conduct disorders repeatedly and persistently violate the basic rights of others.
©Cengage Learning 2012

norms. The American Psychiatric Association (2000) identifies four specific areas of concern: aggression to people and animals, destruction of property, deceitfulness or theft, and serious violation of rules.

Conduct disorders have increased in frequency and are higher in urban areas. Prevalence rates vary widely and are reported ranging from 1 to more than 10 percent of the population (APA, 2000). There are concerns that children will be identified as having a conduct disorder when their undesirable behaviors actually have protective value. The occurrence of conduct disorder is higher in males than females and has become the most frequently diagnosed condition in both outpatient and inpatient mental health facilities for children (APA, 2000). This text only deals with the childhood-onset type (Table 9–4).

Children with conduct disorders show little empathy and have little concern for the feelings, wishes, and well-being of others. They frequently misperceive the intentions of others and respond with aggression, which they feel is justified, but which may not be an accurate representation of the situation. Although there is bravado displayed, these children usually have low self-esteem. Conduct disorders are most frequently diagnosed in adolescent children (Robb & Reber, 2007). In addition to a diagnosis of conduct disorder, children may have other disorders.

• • •
Disruptive Behavior Disorder Not Otherwise Specified

Disruptive behavior disorder not otherwise specified (NOS) is usually diagnosed when it is clear there is a significant impairment, but the behavior does not meet the requirement for a conduct disorder or oppositional defiant disorder (APA, 2000).

This diagnosis may be given because the behavior itself is not severe enough to meet the qualifications of a conduct disorder or oppositional defiant disorder because not enough of the criteria are met (e.g., a child was physically cruel to people and animals, but does not display a third criteria), or

9-4 **DIAGNOSTIC CRITERIA FOR CONDUCT DISORDER**

A. A repetitive and persistent pattern of behavior in which the basic rights of others or major age-appropriate societal norms or rules are violated, as manifested by the presence of three (or more) of the following criteria in the past 12 months, with at least one criterion present in the past 6 months:

Aggression to people and animals

1. often bullies, threatens, or intimidates others
2. often initiates physical fights
3. has used a weapon that can cause serious physical harm to others (e.g., a bat, brick, broken bottle, knife, gun)
4. has been physically cruel to people
5. has been physically cruel to animals
6. has stolen while confronting a victim (e.g., mugging, purse snatching, extortion, armed robbery)
7. has forced someone into sexual activity

Destruction of property

8. has deliberately engaged in fire setting with the intention of causing serious damage
9. has deliberately destroyed others' property (other than by fire setting)

Deceitfulness or theft

10. has broken into someone else's house, building, or car
11. often lies to obtain goods or favors or to avoid obligations (i.e., "cons" others)
12. has stolen items of nontrivial value without confronting a victim (e.g., shoplifting, but without breaking and entering; forgery)

Serious violation of rules

13. often stays out at night despite parental prohibitions, beginning before age 13 years
14. has run away from a parental or parental surrogate home at least twice (or once without returning for a lengthy period)
15. is often truant from school, beginning before age 13 years

B. The disturbance in behavior causes clinically significant impairment in social, academic, or occupational functioning.

Conduct Disorder, Childhood-Onset Type: onset of at least one criterion characteristic of Conduct Disorder prior to age 10 years.

Severity:

- **Mild:** few if any conduct problems in excess of those required to make the diagnosis, and conduct problems cause only minor harm to others.
- **Moderate:** number of conduct problems and effect on others intermediate between "mild" and "severe"
- **Severe:** many conduct problems in excess of those required to make the diagnosis, or conduct problems cause considerable harm to others.

Source: American Psychiatric Association, 2000, pp. 98–99.

because the behavior has not lasted for 12 months. When it is clear that a child's behavior impairs his social and academic life, and the behavior is persistent, the goal is to get the child help, and a diagnosis of disruptive behavior disorder allows that to happen. With intervention, the diagnosis may be changed or removed, or it may show the clearer pattern of conduct disorder or oppositional defiant disorder.

Comorbidity

Comorbidity literally means an additional "morbidity," or disability. Disruptive behavioral disorders rarely occur in isolation. Some disorders result from the same underlying causal factors, such as dysfunctional family processes, and may lead to both depression and disruptive behavior disorders. Likewise, there may be a relationship between two disorders such as ADHD and conduct disorder. That is, the ADHD disrupts the family functioning, leading to a conduct disorder. It is important to recognize that comorbidity is the rule rather than the exception for children with disruptive behavior

disorders. More importantly, the co-occurring conditions are important because they influence how we treat and educate children with these disorders.

ADHD is the most common comorbid diagnosis for children with conduct disorder. Children with both ADHD and conduct disorder are at high risk of developing substance abuse problems, antisocial personality disorder, and being involved in criminal activity compared to children with just ADHD (Pliszka, 2003). Given this possible trajectory, early intervention is imperative. The ADHD is likely to be treated with stimulant medication, but behavioral disorders respond better to behavioral therapy (Robb & Reber, 2007). Other common comorbid disorders with conduct disorder include depression and anxiety disorder. The comorbid condition has to be acknowledged, and educational programming must take this into account to be successful. Interventions must not focus on simply eliminating or reducing the conduct problems but also on providing treatment for the comorbid conditions.

Assessment of Social, Emotional, and Behavioral Disorders

Social, emotional, and behavioral development is influenced by many factors. Assessment is necessary to determine whether children's development in this area is harmful to themselves or others or whether it is displayed in inappropriate contexts. There are a variety of ways of assessing problem behavior. Systematic observation of children in natural settings is one of the best ways. When this must be quantified, rating scales or checklists are used because they offer more structure to the assessment and provide focus. Mental health professionals typically use interviews to gain insight into behaviors and issues that are troubling. There are standardized measures as well (Salvia & Ysseldyke, 2007). Often a variety of these measures are used to provide a broader perspective of the situation.

One of the most frequently used assessments of child emotional/behavioral functioning is the Child Behavior Checklist series, which has profiles for children 2 to 3 years old (Achenbach, 1992) and for children ages 4 to 18 (Achenbach, 1991). For the youngest children, behaviors are divided into internalizing and externalizing problems, sleep problems, and **somatic problems**. The assessment is divided into sections that look for competence as well as problems. For older children, additional items relate to social and school functioning, and problems in the areas of social, thought, and attention.

The Devereux Behavior Rating Scale—School Form (Naglieri, LeBuffe, & Pfeiffer, 1992) is a 40-item scale that can be completed within five minutes and helps evaluators determine whether a child's behavior falls within the normal range or whether a child might be experiencing an emotional or behavioral disturbance. The scale focuses on interpersonal problems, inappropriate behavior/feelings, depression, and physical symptoms/fear.

Models for Understanding Disruptive Behavioral Disorders

How you approach children with behavior disorders will depend upon the theoretical model used to determine the cause of the disorder and how the family decides to treat the disorder. For example, if they believe in a **biophysical model**, they would believe that the cause of the problem lies within the child. This model typically has a medical base. The expectation is that the cause of the disorder is genetic, developmental, neurologic, biochemical, or temperamental. The solutions are primarily medical (often psychopharmacological), and your role would be to daily monitor the prescribed interventions and serve as a liaison with families and specialists.

In the **psychodynamic model**, the focus would be on helping the child in the development of his personality and the process of emotional growth and change. This model would see therapy, including group therapy and class meetings, as the preferred approach. Your role would be to promote a humanistic and therapeutic school environment in which affective issues and personal growth are as important as academic success.

An **ecological model** would focus on the interaction of the child with others in the environment. It would view deviance from a culturally relevant perspective and acknowledge that behaviors and traits that are deviant or abnormal in one setting (school) might be relevant and highly desirable in another (the street). The model implies that it is meaningless to discuss problems of behavior in isolation from the contexts that define the behavior as a problem. Behavior is viewed as disturbing rather than disturbed, and the emphasis is placed not only on the child but also on the individuals and factors in the child's immediate environment. Your role would be to assess and hopefully use your influence to intervene in the various environments in which the child lives and interacts, such as the home, school, classroom, community, and so on.

Behaviorists view disturbed behavior as learned responses that are subject to laws that govern all behavior. Behaviorists assert that the only difference between most disordered behaviors and normal behaviors are the frequency, magnitude, and social adaptiveness of the behaviors; if certain behaviors were less frequent, less extreme, and more adaptive, they would not be labeled disordered. Classical or operant conditioning and social learning are the three major divisions of the behavioral model. Because behaviorists place the utmost importance on the setting in which the behavior occurs, and on the events immediately preceding and following the behavior, your role would be to manipulate environmental events to support change in behavior. You would use methods such as **shaping**, **modeling**, and **contingency contracting** to increase desired behaviors and **extinction**, **reinforcement** of incompatible behaviors, and punishment to decrease undesirable behaviors. You would keep track of and record this information using checklists, rating scales, and observation.

In many instances, some aspects of several of these models are combined. For example, someone using an ecological model can develop a home behavior management program using behavioral principles.

IN THE FIELD

At the beginning of the year, my children help me draw a paper plate puppet to show what I look like when I am happy and when I am "grumpy." The happy side shows me smiling, eyes open, hair neat. Then I write "Happy Teacher" on the plate. On the other side we draw what I look like when I am mad (grumpy). My face is red, eyes squinted, hair is a mess, and I write "Grumpy Teacher" on the plate. We then talk about what happens when the "grumpy teacher" comes to class: no treats, shorter recess, observer chair. We then attach a craft stick and hang it on the chalkboard with a magnet. When some children do not respond to verbal directions, I ask them if they want the grumpy teacher to come visit. I then hold the puppet to my face and we see if I am happy. It sounds crazy, but it works. It also lets them know that I do not like it when I need to use my grumpy tone, and they need to change their behavior.

Behavior Management/Guidance

Children with social, emotional, and behavioral disorders, whether temporary or long term, need a warm, relaxed, and secure environment. They need to be accepted as they are, with the educator's attention focused on the behavior that has to be modified. Allow children to work at their own pace. Until children can cope with the world, they may not have the energy to forge ahead academically, even if tests show they have the ability.

When children have social, emotional, or behavioral problems or disorders, it is important to fine-tune your classroom management techniques. Be consistent, set clear limits, and state the necessary rules as briefly and directly as possible. However, be prepared to reinforce rules that you have. Make children aware of both positive and negative consequences. *If you cannot enforce a rule, don't make it a rule.*

If a rule states that children who play with the blocks must help to clean them up, you must know who played there. If a child is reluctant to help, you should say, "Mia, you played with the blocks, so you have to help clean them up." If there is no response, you might make an offer: "It's time to pick up the blocks. Do you want to do it by yourself, or would you like me to help you?" If necessary, physically help Mia by opening her hand, placing a block in it, closing her hand, walking with her (or carrying her, if need be) to the block shelf, and helping her deposit the block in the right place; then thank her for helping. The rule was not that children had to clean up *all* the blocks. Time and physical limitations might make such a rule unenforceable. The children are only required to *help,* and even one block put away is a help.

When a child does something that you want continued, reinforce the child's behavior. Decide what specific behavior you want to reinforce (such as sitting through group time). Tell the children they can have or do something they value if they do the specific behavior you've decided on. The trick in using reinforcement is to discover what is rewarding to a particular child. Encouragement, attention, a hug, or some time alone to read in the book corner may be the answer for different children. Make your best guess and then try it. (If the positive behavior continues, you are doing something rewarding.)

When dealing with children with social, emotional and behavioral problems, be cautious about being demonstrative at first. Some children find hugging and even high-fives frightening, and some find it difficult to handle praise. Some children may not consider a hug or praise at all rewarding. An obvious ploy is to ask a child what he finds rewarding and do what he likes. Some children will prefer rewards that you don't personally like. Start with rewards you both agree are acceptable until the behavior is established. Then decide how to change the reward system. If the child finds food rewarding and you want to use verbal encouragement, use the following procedures: When Doyle does well, verbally encourage him, and then give him food he desires. Over time, increase the time span between when you verbally encourage him and when you give him the food. Then, gradually stop giving him the food at all, but continue to verbally encourage him when he does a behavior that you want to continue. With this principle, called **operant conditioning**, you present the new reward just before you present the old one that you know works but you want to change.

Reward children's behavior each time only until the behavior becomes established; then reward intermittently. This is the way to have desired behavior continue. If you *always* reward behavior, then forget a few times, the child will decide you don't want that behavior to continue—if you did, you would keep rewarding it as in the past. (Note that the child's age and cognitive level will influence your decision about reinforcement. Some children who are young either chronologically or developmentally may not "get it." Be prepared to be flexible.) Intermittent reinforcement is a proven method for establishing a new behavior. (Regretfully, the same principle works in reverse for setting limits. If you uphold the limits sometimes and not others, the children will *always* test them. It is important to always reinforce limits!)

If you think a child is acting out to get attention, purposefully ignore the behavior—*providing the behavior isn't dangerous to the child or other children.* Make a mental note to give attention when the child does something that is desired. Give the child cues for acceptable ways of getting your attention: "If you want me to watch you while you use the computer, you have to ask and I'll come over."

The problem in an inclusive setting is how to deal with all the children. What if another child complains that when he paints a lovely picture all he gets is a hug? You have to talk about differences. You should talk about the fact that for some children, some things are difficult that for other children are easy. Then enlist the children to find rewards that are reinforcing for all. If what Sean really wants to do is play with Steven, will Steven play with him for 10 minutes? This can be a win–win situation of inclusion rather than exclusion.

Demonstrating behavior in situations, modeling, is also effective, but it can be a double-edged sword. Children tend to model meaningful people, which in a classroom means they will probably model you over classmates or volunteers (and model parents over you). You are always on display. If you combat aggression with aggression, you may then serve as an aggressive model for children regardless of your intentions. Be a good model by behaving in ways you would like the children to copy. If you don't want children to yell at each other, then you must talk in a normal voice even when you are angry.

Alerting children before they are expected to do something, **cuing**, is another effective means of changing behavior. You use cuing when you flick the lights to tell the children it is cleanup time. More specifically, if Amy looks longingly at Nancy's truck, warn her by saying, "Ask Nancy whether she is using the truck." Don't wait until Amy has clobbered Nancy and then say, "Nancy was using the truck. It hurts her when you hit her." If you can anticipate that the child is about to do something undesirable, try to act *before* it happens. When you sense trouble, just moving into the area may prevent a child from misbehaving. Giving a child a "teacher look" is another way to cue a child that something the child is doing or plans to do is not appropriate. These nonverbal techniques (e.g., frowns, eye contact, throat clearing) are most effective when a child is just beginning to act out. To work, they require a relationship with the child and eye contact.

When these approaches don't solve the behavior problem, you must take a more systematic approach to changing the behavior. Write down the information that you gathered through informal observation. Then check with the parents to see whether the behavior is happening at home. Gather some baseline data on frequency. That is, if hitting is the problem, wear an apron with a pocket and keep a paper and pencil in it. Put a mark for each time the child hits during the day. (This can be adapted for whatever behavior is the problem.) You can get more elaborate and write down the time, place, victim, and reaction if you want. However, the first step is determining how often this behavior occurs. Do this for three days in a week and put it on a chart. Mark where you begin to intervene. By using a chart such as that shown in Figure 9–2, you can tell whether you are making a difference. If necessary, you can show the parents your documentation of the problem.

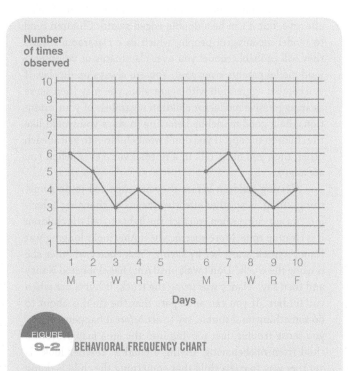

Days

**FIGURE
9–2   BEHAVIORAL FREQUENCY CHART**

The chart shows a pattern of occurrence that appears to be high at the beginning of the week and decreases toward the end of the week. More data would be needed to see if this is accurate. If accurate it can be used to generate hypotheses about potential causes.

There is one area that I think should be part of the guidelines you use with the children, but I feel conflicted about it. Many people feel that a child who hurts another child should apologize. My problem is this: When a child tells me he isn't sorry he hurt Allen and he'd like to do it again, I am not clear what to do. If I make him apologize, then I am teaching him to ignore his own feelings. On the other hand, I believe that an apology is an appropriate response. My compromise has been to find out what the child is sorry about and require the apology, but not the expected one. For example, "I'm sorry I have to sit in the thinking chair because I hit Allen." This is obviously a compromise, but consider it.

To be effective, all educators and paraeducators must use the same procedure when rules are not followed. This is particularly true when someone is hurt. Consistency works and must be established before the behavior becomes a problem. One scenario might look like this:

1. Quickly check on the victim. If possible, have another adult do this.

2. Tell the aggressor firmly but quietly that you will not tolerate the behavior (think through this statement so you know exactly what you will say ahead of time). For example, as you are walking with the child to the thinking chair, say, "I will not allow you to hurt other children." Ask the child how long he needs to sit in the thinking chair to get himself back together. (Children have little concept of time, so their responses may not make a lot of sense, but you want the children to learn techniques of getting in control of themselves, and this is part of the process.) If the child's response is unrealistically long, state that you will set the timer for a specific time and then you will come to check on her.

3. Note the time or set a timer, turn your back on the child, and walk away. Do not talk to the child or make eye contact with the child during this time. If other children approach the child, simply state, "TR needs to be alone for a few minutes. He needs to think about what he has done."

4. Thinking time needs to be developmentally appropriate for the child. A useful guideline is one minute for each year of the child's age: two minutes for a 2-year-old, four minutes for a 4-year-old, and so on. (Although this seems like a short time to adults, a child's perception is very different. It is far better to keep the time short than to deal with the child's behavior during a long "thinking time.") In addition, children who have developmental delays may need shorter times than their chronological age would dictate.

5. When the time is up, go to the child and ask, "Are you ready to get up now?" If yes, talk with the child about what happened very explicitly. If no, give the child another minute or so. If the answer is no again, tell the child you will help her get ready. Then take the child to a private area and talk about what happened. This is the time to talk about the incident. It is imperative that children know exactly what they have done wrong

and why it is not allowed; the specific incident has to be addressed. The goal is to bring closure to the incident so that both you and the child can continue your day without this hanging over you.

If particular children are especially difficult, remember that you can get help: You don't have to solve all problems on your own. Sometimes, someone outside of your setting can be more objective about the situation than you are. Ask another teacher or an administrator to observe the situation and offer suggestions. Or seek the advice of a school or community mental health professional.

Positive behavior management requires respectful treatment of all children. Your consistent modeling of respect for the children in your care is probably the most powerful behavior management tool you have. Positive relationships between adults and children and among children are the foundation for each person's feeling good about herself. Children who feel loved and respected are more likely to help and follow your rules.

IMPLICATIONS FOR EDUCATORS

Teach all children the Turtle Technique. Although there are many variations, the basic steps to teach the child are the same.

- First, you must recognize your feelings to know that you need to use the technique.
- Then think, "Stop." Cross your hands over your chest, go inside your shell, and take three deep breaths.
- Come out of your shell when you are calm, say what the problem is and how you feel, and think of a solution.

Initially you will be the one to issue the command "turtle." When this is done often enough, children learn to do it themselves.

Your goals are to strengthen or reinforce appropriate behavior and to redirect inappropriate behavior. Let's start with the strengthening goal. It is easy to reinforce children who do the right things. A smile, a "thank-you," a hug, or even a token reward works, but with children who don't do the right things, where do you start? Start with a principle called **successive approximation**. Reinforce the child at each step that brings her closer to the goal. For example, if a withdrawn child like Julie sits in her locker and cries during group time, encourage her when she doesn't cry. Then encourage her when she progresses to sitting on a chair beside her locker, a chair at a table, a chair nearer the group, a chair behind the group, then on the floor a little separate from the group, and finally with the group. Reward each stage, but don't expect her to go directly from her locker to the middle of the group. This process may take days, weeks, or perhaps months. Discuss with Julie where she'd like to sit. After you and she reach an agreement, reinforce behavior that conforms to the agreement. As children do things that more closely approximate the desired behavior, keep intermittently rewarding that behavior until you achieve the goal.

Guidelines

One important thing you can do for children with social, emotional, and behavioral problems is to help them accept themselves as good individuals with behaviors that need to be changed. The most effective way to do that is to teach children to control the behaviors that cause other children to avoid them and to provide successful experiences for them.

1. *Structure the environment for behavioral success.* Have a sensory area with water, sand, or other materials to relax a tense child. Have a punching bag and playdough to release aggressive feelings. Arrange traffic patterns to prevent congestion and long runs; make lighting less harsh; and remove toys or objects that create problems. (Make a rule that if a child brings a gun-like toy from home, it must stay in the child's locker and should not return.) Balance active and less active activities. Give children choices and warn them before changes.

2. *Plan very motivating activities.* Especially at the end of the day or before lunch, this helps children be more cooperative and feel more in control.

3. *Maintain consistent rules and discipline.* Set limits and enforce them. Write them down for yourself, tell the children, and post them both in writing and in picture form. For example, draw a stick figure of a child with a block in a raised hand and put a large "X" over it. Place the picture in the block area. Your reminders for yourself might be to be positive and to say, "You may build with blocks, but you cannot throw them." If necessary, add, "If you throw a block again, you will need to pick somewhere else to play." If the child throws the block again, follow through. Physically guide the child to pick up the block and return it. Then help the child move from the block area and help him choose another area to play in. Repeat the rule: "Blocks are for building, *not* throwing." Make as few limits as possible, but if children violate these, there need to be natural and logical consequences.

4. *Teach rules and procedures at the beginning of the year.* Although you may feel this is a waste of instructional time having children understand the rules and procedures saves instructional time in the future.

5. *Have a consistent plan that all educators and paraeducators use to respond to particular types of behavior.* Deal with situations directly and at the time they occur.

6. *Communicate clearly, using language the child can understand.* Be specific about your expectations. A child's definition of sharing the blocks may be very different from yours. Ask questions to determine the child's perceptions. For example: "Which blocks are you sharing with Misha?" (The child points to three small blocks.) "You need to give him some of the big blocks too, so you each have some. Help me count yours. Now count Misha's."

7. *Teach children to distinguish between feelings and behavior.* Teach prosocial behavior and social interaction skills. Support children in practicing these skills with small groups of children who accept different behaviors. Use stories, dramatic play, and puppets to teach ways of expressing positive and negative feelings.

8. *Give children choices.* If a child is acting out or not following directions, give him the choice of doing whatever it is you are asking or, for example, sitting in the thinking chair for a few minutes.

9. *Learn more about the children in your class.* Watch how each child waits for a turn, plays with others, and interacts in a small group. Learn to read children's body language. Be aware of who is sitting beside whom. Some combinations of children provoke trouble. Intervene before a conflict occurs.

10. *Control children's behavior by obtaining and maintaining eye contact, standing close by, or gently touching the child.* Use positive, firm, supportive language.

11. *Intervene early.* If a child cannot cope with a situation, take her out of it early, before it worsens. If children are having problems playing together and your several solutions to sharing aren't working, say, "There are too many children in the dramatic play area now. Who would be willing to play in another area?" If no one volunteers, ask a child. If that doesn't work, close down that area for the day.

12. *Insert activity breaks.* If you have a long story or listening time and some of the children are having problems listening, change the pace. Break for something active; put on some music with a beat and dance to a song with a strong beat for three minutes then come back to the story.

13. *Keep waiting times to a minimum.* When it is unavoidable, make waiting interesting by singing songs, doing fingerplays, and so on. Often, behavior problems develop when children are unoccupied and expected to wait for long periods.

14. *Evaluate the structure and sequence of the class day,* especially if children seem to have problems at the same time each day. If large-group time is at 10:30 a.m. and this is a bad time for the children, consider rearranging the schedule so that the class is outside at 10:30 a.m. and in group time at 9:30 or 11:30 a.m.

15. *Evaluate yourself and the children objectively.* Are there particular behaviors that "bug" you? What is your temperament style? What are the matches or mismatches between the children you find most difficult and your own temperament? What can you change about your own behavior?

16. *Mediate.* Children rarely think about how what they do affects others. Help children see the other's point of view and support them in learning the negotiation skills necessary to work together.

17. *Give children a warning.* Sometimes children do not realize what they are doing is wrong or irritating. For example, children may not realize they are tapping on the floor while you are reading to them or humming while you are discussing a lesson.

18. *Make four positive statements for each negative or corrective one.* Count! It may seem to you that you are being positive, but the reality may be different. Make positive statements to children's parents on a regular basis.

19. *Be patient.* Change is difficult, both for children and adults. When you become discouraged, try to think of *one* time when the desired response occurred. If even that does not work, pretend it did and think through the result. The struggle is long and hard, but the development of children is worth it.

20. *Overall, simplify, shorten, and structure activities.* Plan to specifically teach skills other children might learn informally. Make learning meaningful and be respectful of children's work.

21. *Use timers.* If timers have a visual component, children can see how much time they have left.

22. *Use behavior management techniques.* If children are asked to do a task they don't want to do (e.g., cleaning up), follow it by something they like. "First we are cleaning up, then we'll have snack."

IN THE FIELD

If a child is having a bad day, I take him aside and ask him whether he wants his pals to help him be good. If he says yes, we ask the class to give him a thumbs-up when they see him being good and a thumbs-down when the behavior is inappropriate.

Curriculum Adaptations

The number and degree of adaptations depend on each child's needs. Your awareness of short-term needs will greatly aid the child's long-term adjustment.

If you use a thinking chair ensure that the time is developmentally appropriate.
©Cengage Learning 2012

Social Awareness

For children with social, emotional, and behavioral disorders, social awareness is paramount. Some children may not be as tuned into the world around them as they need to be. These children need their classroom and community to be familiar and safe. Do a lot of preparation for field trips, as well as doing follow-up. Make sure you have plenty of adults on trips so that all of the children can be safely supervised. Take care to keep routines a consistent part of the program for all children. Some of the activities in Resource Chapter 1 are specifically designed to support children who have social, emotional, or behavioral disorders. Activities such as 1–2, *Family Book*, may help children who are having separation problems. Activity 1–38w, *Share Your Feelings*, encourages children to talk with others about how they feel and learn ways to share feelings.

Social Competence

Children need to feel good about themselves. Before children can learn to control their feelings, they must become aware of their emotions. It is important to ask a child how she feels: "When I see you wandering around the classroom, I wonder how you are feeling." Help children learn that they are the only ones who know how they feel. Once children are aware of feelings, they can be taught to express them. If you, as a teacher, accept the feelings and don't judge them, then the children will probably continue to talk. If children are told that it is silly or stupid to feel the way they do, they are likely to quit talking about how they feel.

1. Talk to individual children about their similarities to other children; at the same time, talk about what makes them unique (e.g., hair, skin, eye color, and so on).
2. Include children's names in songs and stories.
3. Have children share some of the great things that happen to them. (Children may need support in sharing, and for these great things to happen at school, your help may be required as well.)
4. Help raise a child's self-esteem by mentioning to the class a particular skill she does well or something she has accomplished. Your statements should be sincere. Do this for all children.
5. Building good character is difficult. Children who demonstrate good character traits such as honesty, respect, fairness, and so on, should be rewarded.

It may seem clear to you by this point that including some children with social, emotional, or behavioral disorders will be a challenge. You are right. Children need help to feel that they are part of the group. They must be aware of individual differences, know the other children, and know that they too are accepted and belong, even when they are isolated or have conflicts with others. Plan some activities that don't demand a great deal of social interaction yet allow children to see themselves as part of the group. For example,

have each child paint or color an area of a mural, or have each child contribute a page to a class book.

1. Discuss appropriate behavior with the entire class. Point out when a child is engaging in an appropriate behavior. This will be helpful in prompting children with social, emotional, or behavioral problems to engage in the behavior. Keep your eyes open for children with social, emotional, and behavioral disorders to "catch them being good." It is important to point out good behavior at the beginning of the year.
2. Talk to children about aggressive or withdrawn behavior (or whatever specific problem you have), and discuss the dimensions of that behavior: how people behave when they feel different ways. The purpose is to discuss the behavior, not the child, and to generate alternative behaviors.
3. Ask all the children to think about times when they felt or acted a certain way (e.g., aggressive, withdrawn). If they don't respond, ask them to pretend what it would be like. Encourage them to role-play the different general behavior patterns. Then ask them how they felt when they were role-playing the behaviors. (They will usually say "lonely," "angry," "mad," and so on.) Ask them what they really want from others when they feel that way. Talk about how children can help each other. Give them the words: "I'm feeling lonely; may I play with you?" Some children may not be willing to include others in the play. Help them with the skills of negotiation: "You can play when we finish this game"; "You can watch and we'll talk to you." All children need skills to include others and to request inclusion.
4. Ask other professionals for help with building social skills and appropriate behaviors and friendships in your inclusive classroom. Often a guidance counselor or child development specialist is willing to come to your classroom to teach lessons on a specific problem (such as name-calling or swearing). This colleague may also spend time targeting a child's specific behavior problems.
5. Send a child to the "Chill Out Corner" if it looks like his behavior is becoming unacceptable. In this corner, provide short, meaningful, easy activities. When the child calms down, let her return to the group. Some children know when they need to chill out and will actually ask to go. This is prevention; it is not the "thinking chair."

Social Studies

As children move into the preschool and elementary years, interactions with peers and the global community become more important. Discuss issues related to power, authority and governance, and how they work in the classroom, school, and community.

1. Talk about many different types of families: those with one or two children, those with many children, those with single parents, step- or blended families, families

with relatives living in the home, mixed racial families, families that are cohabiting, families with two mothers or two fathers, and families with adopted or foster children. Emphasize the functional components of families.

2. Expand the concept of families by talking about different roles family members have: mother, friend, daughter, teacher, and sister. Help the children see their own various roles: son/daughter, friend, brother/sister, student. See Activity 1–13, *Photograph Story*.

3. Talk about people, places, and environments and their implications for learning and behavior. (Note that some children may be frightened of police or doctors because of a previous experience with them.) Role-play such situations as being lost, seeing a fire, and visiting a friend. Follow this up with having some helpers visit the class (children usually like the K-9 police squad the best).

4. Include many different people when telling a child to complete a project with an adult. If you only mention parents, you may be leaving much of the family out of the picture. Do, however, know who can legally sign permission slips. Learn the caregivers of the children in your class and include these roles when you speak of family. Respect all family structures; don't leave children feeling awkward or left out.

English Language Arts

Help children develop the skills to talk about situations they find difficult and the feelings these situations bring about. Through literature, children can learn how other children have dealt with similar feelings and situations. Children with social, emotional, and behavioral disorders require a vocabulary that helps them verbalize their feelings and communicate with others.

Some children may have learned to tune out their environment because it seemed negative, irrelevant, or scary. They will need your help in learning how to tune you in and listen again. Writing and illustrating are potential outlets for feelings and expression. Help children take advantage of these.

● ● ●
Speaking and Listening

Although children with social, emotional, and behavioral disorders speak, they may need to learn to focus on using language for social interaction.

1. Teach the vocabulary for expressing feelings. Use words the child understands: *mad, sad, happy, tight, hit, tense, excited*. Expand on these words to place them in a preventive framework: *before, going to be, want, ready to*, and so on.

2. Encourage children to use words to solve problems: "May I play in the hospital with you? I could be the nurse."

3. Demonstrate words, especially those associated with feelings. Pretend to be a statue or model. Have the children tell you how to arrange yourself to show a specific emotion. Give them some clues about the areas to address: "I'm angry. Should my hands be open or closed? Should I look up or down? How should my mouth be?"

Use listening to increase children's awareness of their behavior.

1. Give children short, simple, and specific one-step directions until they can predictably follow them.

2. Reassure children with your words and your tone of voice.

3. Tell children what to do, followed by what not to do. Children with social, emotional, and behavioral problems need both. Give children feedback about their behavior: "Walk more slowly. You are walking too fast." (Put a hand on the child and walk with him.)

4. Think about the content of what you are saying and whether the child has the experiential background for understanding.

As many listening experiences happen during group time, be aware of some of the inherent problems for children in groups.

1. Seat potentially aggressive children between non-threatening children. However, keep a careful eye out for warning signs of aggression. (Always placing a child next to an adult externalizes their control and contributes to dependency.) Rotate the children so that it is not always the same children sitting next to each other.

2. Call on a child who is very active, or mention the child's name to help focus attention. (Do this for all the children, but mention that particular child's name more frequently, if necessary.) Keep activities short and focused, give directions frequently, and intersperse moderate and vigorous physical activities with those that require only listening. For example, count the number of children in the class, then jump once for each child's name. Then, do it again.

3. Give children the opportunity to talk, but don't force them to respond. Tell them that you will not call on them unless they give a particular signal such as raising a hand, or allow them to say "pass" if they are uncomfortable or don't know an answer.

4. Encourage children to participate as they show signs of becoming part of the group.

● ● ●
Reading

Mastering reading and readiness skills requires children to make fine auditory and visual distinctions. Although the needs of all children are similar when learning to read, choose subject matter that is relevant to the adjustment needs of the child. See the Children's Bibliography for suggested books.

1. Distinguish and label facial features. Play "Lotto" by matching faces (Figure 9-3). Even in simple line drawings, focus attention on the face and help children attach feelings to expressions.

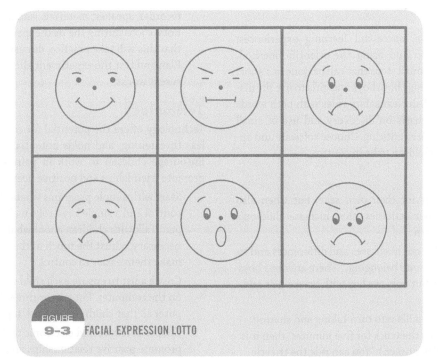

FIGURE 9-3   FACIAL EXPRESSION LOTTO

2. Read aloud a story that has a pertinent problem situation. Stop before the problem gets solved, and ask the children to predict what the characters will do to try to solve the problem. Then, ask the children what they would do to solve the problem. Compare their ideas to what the characters do to solve the problem, and discuss it.

3. Read stories dealing with angry feelings and peer conflict. Encourage children to ask and answer questions about the reasons for the conflicts and additional potential solutions.

4. Select stories that have problem situations pertinent to the children in the class. Compare and contrast the characters in the stories.

5. Tell stories about a child who learns to deal with feelings: "Once upon a time, there was a girl named . . . , who . . . ." (Be careful not to pinpoint a particular child or social/emotional/behavioral problem.)

Writing

Like other fine motor activities, writing is challenging for some children. Some children may find it easier to convey ideas graphically than verbally, or by using a word processor rather than a pencil.

1. Have a variety of materials available, especially large paper and large markers and crayons.

2. Help children focus on the communicative aspect of writing as opposed to the fine motor skills.

3. Encourage their efforts and call children authors and illustrators. Have them share their work with others. All communication in any media should be encouraged.

4. Scribe, or write, children's stories as they tell them. Let them revise and edit this way. Help children use computers to write, edit, and illustrate their stories.

5. Give older children a **rubric** for how the work will be graded. If the emphasis is on content, write the rubric so no or few points are deducted for spelling and grammar mistakes.

6. Begin a communication journal with children. This provides a private outlet for children to share their feelings. Use the journal to practice specific forms of writing such as letter writing, poetry, and so on.

7. Cut pictures of people and situations out of magazines (those with obvious themes are easiest). Have the children write, dictate, or draw a story about what might have happened and how the people involved may have felt. Encourage children to ask and answer questions about their writing and the rationale for their decisions. Invent a variety of endings, and discuss which aspects of situations could change.

Language

Children need to build a vocabulary to express their feelings, wants, and needs.

1. Have children discuss moods and the words that are used to characterize moods. Write language experience stories using moods as themes. Discuss what might happen to make children feel different ways.

2. Help children focus on a topic for their writing pieces. Then, during a writing conference, help them choose the correct form for what they want to write, and teach them how to use this form. Point out the conventions of standard English usage.

3. Help children explore word meanings and how similar words have slightly different meanings and connotations. As they write and talk, encourage them to build their vocabulary to make it more specific and interesting.

Discovery

Children need positive, successful learning experiences. Encourage participation and using the scientific method. Break tasks down into small steps that can be done in a short amount of time. Encourage both boys and girls to use the discovery area, but establish clear safety rules with both words and pictures. The emphasis on discovery and use of small groups may make this area enticing. Choose software and applications that allow children to be in control.

Mathematics

Math skills are taught for their own sake, but when also incorporated into other activities, they increase children's awareness of using math.

1. Use math to point out likenesses and differences and to create a sense of group belonging: "There are *three* boys with brown hair, but only *one* boy with brown hair and a red shirt."

2. Incorporate math skills into turn taking and sharing: "You can play with the truck for five minutes, then it is Lance's turn." (Set a timer.) "You can ride the tricycle around the play yard four times, then give it to Carlos." (Incorporate children into the waiting process by helping them count the four trips.)

3. Use simple card games like "Go Fish" to encourage peer interaction.

4. Encourage children to use manipulatives to sort, count, and create word problems or equations.

5. Create math problem-solving activities for children to work on in small groups. This promotes peer interaction and cooperation. You may want to teach, model, and practice guidelines for working together in a small group. If children can read, post these guidelines in words; if not, add pictures of the guidelines.

6. Do not play whole-group competitive mathematics learning games.

Science

A discovery approach has great potential for teaching science to children with social, emotional, or behavioral problems. They can be doing what they prefer, yet still be included.

1. Help children to understand cause-and-effect relationships as they learn the physical properties of materials: "Ice cubes melt when they get warm." Help them to think about this in relation to their behavior and consequences.

2. Encourage children to make predictions about experiments before they actually do them: "What will happen to the balance when you put the cup on it? Now, let's try it and see." Eventually, you can expand this skill to making predictions in personal interactions.

3. Teach children how to perform an experiment while working in a group to promote cooperation and peer interaction. Assign jobs for children in each group:

recorder, speaker; materials, and doing the experiment. Rotate jobs during the next experiment. Remember that this will take practice, discussion, and modeling. Plan and test the experiment ahead of time to make sure it works.

Technology

Technology offers the potential for communication, may be less threatening, and holds potential to build social skills. Encourage children to work in pairs on the computer to promote friendships and positive peer interactions.

1. Start with simple programs where the children are in control and a single keystroke makes something happen. Talk with children about what they are doing. If necessary, adjust the touch of the computer keys to make them easier to control.

2. Create a list to ensure each child gets a chance to work on the computer. Put two or three chairs at each computer so that children can work together.

3. Choose software and electronic tablet applications that promote positive relationships and social skills, *not* software or applications that support violent behavior.

4. Take pictures of children with a digital camera when they are part of a group or doing something you want to reinforce. Talk about the pictures with the child. Encourage children to use the camera to take photographs and share them.

Wellness

Children need to feel safe, trust the environment, have nutritional needs met, and develop relationships with caring adults and peers to be available for learning. Children need to become more aware of their bodies and the relationship between their feelings and what they do with their bodies. They need to recognize tension and learn how to release tension in a way that doesn't infringe on the rights of others. Children need to know how their bodies feel just before aggressive interactions; once this knowledge is attained, you can help children learn to substitute other behaviors. Children need to become aware of their bodies before they can control them.

Motor activities help develop gross and fine motor skills and provide opportunities for peer interaction. Help children learn to monitor their level of activity. Children with social, emotional, and behavioral disorders can use large motor activities as a way of venting energy and participating in a group experience. A noncompetitive environment allows you to individualize activities without focusing attention on a particular child.

Health and Safety

Help children learn that your classroom is a safe place. Provide predictability and consistency so children can plan on what will happen.

1. Help children develop independence and self-esteem by teaching adaptive (self-help) skills. To teach dressing,

use buttoning and zipping frames as well as natural opportunities such as coming to school and going home or outside or when playing with large dolls. Teach children hygienic toileting behaviors.

2. Provide children with a variety of experiences with different nutritious foods for snacks and lunches and help them learn to use different eating utensils.

3. Use cleanup time to help all children feel that they are contributing members of the group. Create a sense of responsibility for keeping the room neat.

4. Teach lessons on nutrition, and have healthy snacks for the children to eat. Talk about the importance of drinking milk and water (not juice or soda) and eating fruits and vegetables and lean protein.

5. Teach simple safety lessons about fires, electricity, stoves, and more. Children may not receive these important lessons at home. See Activity 4–34w, *Not to Eat*.

6. Make personal safety lessons part of your curriculum. Such lessons might include discussions about good and bad touch. The guidance counselor, nurse, or child development specialist may be helpful with these

Group time may be difficult for children with behavioral problems.
©Cengage Learning 2012

topics. See Activities 4–9, *Traffic Sign Hunt*, and 4–10, *Warning Sounds*.

Physical Education

Teach children to use large motor play to run off excess energy and frustration. The benefits are obvious to adults who clean house, jog, or work out in a gym when angry or upset. Children have yet to learn this. Prevent the need for discipline by encouraging children to run, climb, or ride tricycles. Encourage them to play hard until they are tired, breathless, but not exhausted.

1. Do some large motor activities early if children have a long ride to school. Work on developing fundamental motor skills.

2. Make exercise an important part of the school day. Plan 60 minutes of structured moderate-to-vigorous physical activity for preschool and elementary school-age children (30 minutes for toddlers) in an all-day program. "Structured" means that the activity is planned, as you would plan a literacy lesson; that you are responsible for ensuring that it happens; and that you participate with the children. Young children do not have the stamina to do 60 minutes at one time, so exercise should be spaced throughout the day. Incorporate three to four minutes of vigorous activity into classroom routines.

3. Structure some outdoor time to ensure that children actually participate in moderate to vigorous play. Children with emotional and behavioral problems may become overly rough during unstructured recess. Your presence and structuring some of the time decreases these problems.

4. Consider adding a punching bag or an inflatable Bobo doll to your room. When children feel like hitting something, encourage them to hit the punching bag—hard. Comment positively on this behavior: "You really can hit that punching bag hard." (A commercial punching bag that is on a spring attached to a wooden base can be moved to different locations, even outside. Be sure to develop rules about its use.)

Sensory Motor Integration

Children need practice integrating sensory information. Some children are hyper- or hyposensitive to touch, sound, or other sensory input.

1. Encourage children who are hypersensitive to touch to wear a sweater or jacket when contact is likely. Designate personal space, and be sure all children know the rules of the game before you start. Stop the game, if necessary, to remind children of the rules. It is imperative that children feel safe.

2. Avoid competitive games, especially chase-type games. Add a cooperative, or at least noncompetitive, component to games.

3. Adapt games so children are not eliminated.

4. Be sure children have good control of their hands and fingers before expecting them to control tools. Build this strength through using clay, spray bottles, hole punches, holding on while swinging, and so on.

5. Use cold water and add ice cubes for variation for children who are hyposensitive. Warm water has a calming effect and is useful for hypersensitive children.

6. Encourage children to increase their body awareness and knowledge of how their body feels at various points in time. See Activities 4–28, *Freeze*, and 4–30, *Tense Me*.

Be aware of the timing of small motor activities. If a child is already feeling frustrated, problems connected to small motor development may increase the frustration. However, children should not just avoid what they find frustrating; rather, educators need to provide motivation, encouragement, and support for children.

1. Encourage the independent use of small motor materials when children can concentrate on them most easily. At other times, promote success by making the activity more interesting or easier, or shorten the time expectation.

2. Use a wide variety of materials, including some of the *large* small motor toys designed for toddlers.

3. Help children learn both self-control and a sense of completion. If a child appears frustrated, help the child finish the step of the task that she is doing, label for the child what this step is (e.g., "After you add the eyes, we'll put the puppet away"), and then tell the child that she can finish it another day. Children need to understand that they should finish tasks (often they don't finish), but not necessarily all at one time.

4. Include materials in your fine motor area that children find motivating. These will vary with the group of children but often include tangrams, puzzles, and manipulatives. Making small motor practice fun decreases discouragement.

Creative Arts

Encourage children with social, emotional, and behavioral disorders to use the arts as a way of expressing feelings. Strong feelings can be expressed through the use of bold colors, pounding clay, and tearing paper. Draining angry feelings in these ways helps children keep themselves in control. Use music to help children relax (play soft music at rest time) and to release feelings (encourage them to beat a drum to express anger). Provide plenty of movement and dance activities. As long as there are no right or wrong movements, children can participate and learn about their bodies. Dramatic play can help children work through their fears and anxieties about specific issues. If talking directly about situations produces anxiety, have the child dress up and pretend to be someone else or talk through a puppet. Use written scripts to help children play different roles.

Visual Arts

The visual arts can teach children about their bodies and how to express their feelings.

1. Use activities that incorporate the child's body or name. Make body pictures by tracing the outline of the child on a large sheet of paper. Have the child color and cut it out to make a life-sized paper doll. Use water to paint the child's shadow on the sidewalk. Use face- or body-shaped paper for painting or coloring. Make a *Name Book* about the children and what each child does and likes. Add a photo of the child doing the activity to the book. Make posters or books using pictures of the children in the class. Do foot or hand printing or painting. See Activity 5–4, *Hand Print Mural*.

2. Help children use three-dimensional art media such as clay to work through feelings. Let them pound, roll, and tear clay.

3. Encourage children to paint their feelings and to use the paintings to talk about these feelings. See Activity 5–44w *Mood Colors*.

4. Start with "clean" messy activities such as playing in water if children are reluctant.

5. Encourage children to use art programs and games on the computer. These are motivational and allow children to express themselves through art. Help children print their creations to take home or hang in the classroom.

6. Have children create simple picture books about themselves. They become the author and illustrator of a book about themselves, their lives, and their feelings.

7. Encourage children to paint or draw their negative feelings while they are in the "Chill Out Corner."

Music

Music can be used to teach the relationship between feelings and sound. Combined with movement, it is good for energy release.

1. Match the beat of the music to the children's activity. If you want to calm them down, start out with a vigorous tune and work toward a slow one. Make a tape or compact disk of selections ranging from very loud and active to quiet and restful. Record only a part of each piece, rather than the whole piece, so that the recording is not too long.

2. Use familiar songs to promote a sense of predictability in a changing world. Teach new songs after singing old favorites.

3. Encourage children to request particular songs. Particular rhythms can be enjoyable to children with social, emotional, and behavioral disorders.

4. Talk about the different moods that music conveys and how different music can make people feel. See Activity 5–11, *Mood Songs*.

5. Play classical music during quiet activities. This may help keep some children stay on task and promote a calm atmosphere.

Movement and Dance

Children need to learn to control their bodies, be aware of their internal feelings, and develop socially acceptable behaviors that respond to these feelings. Movement and dance provide an outlet for feelings.

1. Help children learn to tense their bodies like wooden soldiers and to relax like rag dolls. See Activites 5–21, *Rag Dolls*, and 5–26, *Relaxation Stories*.

2. Teach children that dance can be a way of letting out emotions or releasing energy. Play a variety of music with different rhythms for children to dance to.

3. Help children learn how much space they require to avoid bumping into each other during movement activities.

4. Incorporate a child's characteristic behavior such as hand flapping into a set of motions done to music. Do this in a way that helps the child feel part of the group but that doesn't draw attention to him: "Flap, flap, flap your hands, flap your hands together." Then do something that is incompatible with hand flapping: "Clap, clap, clap your hands, clap your hands together." Ask for other suggestions.

Dramatic Play and Theater

Dramatic play can be used to help children build successful peer relations and work out fears about specific issues. Theater helps shape experiences in a way that can be repeated.

1. Help a child who wants to play with another child or a group of children but does not know how to join the group. You might join the group with that child, play until the child becomes involved, and then slowly lessen your own involvement.

2. Arrange some times when only two or three children may use a specific area at one time if a child is reluctant to play with a large group of children.

3. Let children see how they fit into the various roles and relationships in a family, school, store, hospital, or fire station. Encourage them to try different roles.

4. Help children reenact fearful experiences in a supportive class atmosphere, where they can come to grips with the experience. Read the story of the "Three Little Pigs." Help children convert this into a play with a script. As children play the role of a pig, have them make a safety rule when the wolf knocks on the door; for example, never answer the door without asking who it is (looking through a window); call 911 if the Big Bad Wolf is breaking into the house or hurting someone; don't take candy (drugs) from the Big Bad Wolf (stranger); don't run off with the Big Bad Wolf (stranger). Videotape the role-play and encourage children to draw or paint it.

5. Encourage children to talk about things they are afraid of, and discuss what to do in various situations such as seeing a snake or getting stung by a bee. You may need to include some areas that you will need some preparation for, such as what to tell children about domestic violence and drug dealing, and how to remain safe when drugs and alcohol are being abused in the family. This helps children gain some control and some strategies as well as the knowledge that they are not alone.

6. Use puppets as a way for children to talk indirectly about experiences.

7. Have play telephones available. Children may talk more freely when not face-to-face with their partner. Encourage them to write, type, or draw feelings and share them with someone.

8. Watch and listen to children's dramatic play to help guide them to act appropriately in certain situations.

Routines and Transitions

Transitions are difficult for many children. Consider the number of transitions in the day. Can any of them be eliminated (e.g., can you have an "open" snack that is available during free play rather than a specified time when all children must participate)? Keep transitions to a minimum. Provide warnings before they happen and support for children who have difficulty with them. Incorporate planned energetic play into routines by having children dance or move to a song for three to five minutes.

1. Follow a regular routine for arrivals, departures, and moving among activities. If the adults are disorganized, the children will feel even more confused.

2. Gradually reduce the support you offer during routines, to match the child's learning.

3. Some children have a difficult time coping with noise and movement and have little internal sense of time. For them, transitions may be incomprehensible and overwhelming. Adult support is necessary during these times until the child adjusts.

4. Use transitions to single out children and build their self-esteem. When you dismiss children from large-group time or while you wait for others to join the group, try these methods:

   • Singing the children's names

   • Calling last names or initials (children often are not aware there are so many different ways of referring to themselves)

   • Describing an important event or fact about the child

   • Calling children by hair color, eyes, or type of clothing, and so on

5. Practice, teach, and model routines and transitions. Focus on this at the beginning of the year, but continue throughout the year.

6. Be prepared for challenging behaviors at these times and develop a plan for intervening.

SUMMARY

- Social, emotional, and behavioral problems and disorders exist on a continuum ranging from short-term problems that produce acute disruptive and challenging behavior, to serious mental health problems.
- Intensity of reaction and duration influence the continuum.
- Social disorders, or anxiety disorders, focus on issues related to attachment, separation, and social situations.
- Emotional disorders focus on mood disorders.
- Behavioral disorders focus on disruptive behavior.
- Attention-deficit/hyperactivity disorder (ADHD) is the most common comorbid condition.
- Interventions involve helping children learn self-regulation skills, and helping adults, educators, and parents learn behavior management skills.

EDUCATIONAL RESOURCES

American Psychiatric Association offers information for both professionals and parents. The site is well organized and allows for searches on specific subjects. Including press releases on mental health subjects. www.psych.org/

National Alliance for the Mentally Ill (NAMI) is a nationwide network for family advocates on behalf of individuals with severe and chronic mental illness. It has local chapters and publishes and annotates books and pamphlets. Many resources are available. www.nami.org/

National Mental Health Association refers individuals to local affiliates, directs a research program, a public information program, and acts as a liaison with governmental and private organizations. It has specific information for children and families. www.nmha.org/

Pendulum Pages is a nonprofit source for information on bipolar mood disorders. www.pendulum.org/

Research and Training Center (RTC) on Family Support and Children's Mental Health is designed to promote the transformation of mental health care by increasing knowledge of supports, services, and policies that build on family strengths; are community-based, family-driven, and youth-guided; promote cultural competence; and are based on evidence of effectiveness. www.rtc.pdx.edu

Stop Bullying Now is part of the government's campaign to increase knowledge and awareness of the problems related to bullying. It has tips and activities for parents and children. www.stopbullyingnow.hrsa.gov/

What Works Clearinghouse (WWC), established by U.S. DOE's Institute of Education Sciences provides educators, and the public with a source of scientific evidence of what works in education. WWC reviews and reports on studies of interventions (education programs, products, practices, and policies) in selected topic areas including early childhood. www.ed.gov/about/offices/list/ies/ncee/wwc.html

For additional resources, visit the book companion website for this text at www.cengagebrain.com.

Children with Attention-Deficit/Hyperactivity Disorder

10

Jack was the firstborn in a family with six children. He was a very happy baby. I stayed home with him while his father went to work. Jack developed a little on the early side through infancy. He was a curious toddler. He was given developmentally appropriate toys, many of which we made. Jack was allowed to explore our small home. He often opened cupboards to pull out Tupperware or pots and pans, and played quietly in the living room where all breakables were kept out of sight and the electric outlets were plugged with safety caps.

In the summer, he played in a small swimming pool while I sat close by. He really enjoyed picking strawberries from the home garden at 2. Although Jack was very active, he cooperated with a schedule that included nap times and 10 to 12 hours of sleep each night. He ate well and grew steadily, although he remained at the tenth percentile for height and weight. His most outstanding feature was an insatiable appetite for climbing. The higher he could go, the happier he was. He seemed to be "all boy." He was controllable, but very active. If Jack missed his normal naps or nightlong sleep, he was very restless, "bouncing off the walls."

Although he never attended a childcare or early education setting, he did attend Sunday nursery school, where he was noted as being well behaved, but a "wanderer." He liked walking around the room and touching things. By age 5, it was clear that Jack really preferred balls, bicycles, running, and jumping to paper and pencil (which he liked for about 5-minute stretches). We decided to delay school for a year because his birthday was in late summer, making him one of the youngest children in the classroom. I often "wondered" whether Jack might have attention-deficit/hyperactivity disorder (ADHD) or whether he was just "all boy" and slow to mature. Because I had grown up with a child with severe ADHD as a neighbor, and because Jack slept peacefully through the night and took naps, I thought "no."

Jack was in private school through the fourth grade, home-schooled for four years, and entered the public school system for the first time as a freshman in high school. Most

teachers really liked him, and he was cooperative, but he was *always* losing things and flustered; he didn't complete assignments; and, for the first time, he failed a class: math. At first, the teachers thought he was lazy, unfocused, or just too busy with sports and girls to accomplish the tasks required of high school. But as time went on, he did not get along well with the kids on the soccer team, received low grades for incomplete work and test scores, and just generally appeared to be helpless and increasingly depressed. He didn't want anyone to do the work for him or help him with it; he just let things go. During Jack's junior year in high school, we finally turned to our pediatrician for help. Jack's younger brother was also struggling in school: easily distracted and inattentive, with poor grades and difficulty with social behavior. I began investigating attention-deficit/hyperactivity disorder. Jack seemed to fit the bill for ADHD (hyperactivity), whereas his younger brother was being diagnosed with ADHD (inattentive) and possibly with a learning disability. There was also a family history of schizophrenia and bipolar disorder two and three generations back. Both boys were prescribed Adderall, with great results in schoolwork and behavior. I still have some worries about the side effects, but right now I have put that aside.

REFLECTIVE PRACTICE | Many times, parents are the ones to seek a diagnosis, which often occurs *after* a child has entered school, and sometimes not even until high school. Educators also may be the first to suggest a screening for attention-deficit/hyperactivity disorder (ADHD) or possibly a learning disability when children struggle to progress (or even "tune out") in the educational setting. Mild or moderate cases of ADHD can look normal, especially in young boys. Although some girls with ADHD do exhibit hyperactive behaviors, more often they are seen as "dreamy" or "air headed." Some educators and educational settings make it easier for children with ADHD to survive in the classroom. Nontraditional educational settings such as home-schooling or schools specifically designed to work with children in nontraditional ways may prolong a diagnosis or make it unnecessary. Both boys mentioned in the vignette were diagnosed with ADHD, but they did not have the same symptoms. The second child was not as active, but was much more obviously "lost" in the classroom. He also has a learning disability, which is common among children with ADHD. The same medication was prescribed for both boys and produced positive results for each of them. Because the understanding is that the problem is caused by neurotransmitters in the brain, the medicine worked for both boys. How do you think this scenario would have been different if these boys had been in an early care and education setting during their early childhood years? When would their behavior have called attention to their learning needs? What would you have had to do to help identify their learning needs before they failed?

Attention-Deficit/Hyperactivity Disorder

Although attention-deficit/hyperactivity disorder (ADHD) is one of the most prevalent neurodevelopmental/mental health disorders in childhood (Glanzman & Blum, 2007), there is still some debate about whether the disorder actually exists. The consensus seems to be that it does in fact exist, even though there is not an objective, conclusive test for it. Because children identified with ADHD are at greater risks for academic, behavioral, and social problems, and early identification and intervention helps improve these outcomes, most scholars want to move on from this debate and serve children who seem to be vulnerable to academic risks (Weyandt, 2007).

Defining ADHD

ADHD has had many other names in the past and has many variable characteristics today. This makes it difficult to give a simple definition but reflects both its complexity and our gradual understanding of the symptoms, causes, and interventions for ADHD over the years. The changes in terminology over time provide clues as to how we can and cannot define ADHD. In the 1950s and 1960s, **minimal brain damage** was coined to address the symptoms of inattention, impulsivity, and overactivity in children. This inferred that brain damage was the cause. This "damage" could not actually be identified, so the term was changed to *minimal brain dysfunction*, again inferring a biological base in the child's brain, but not necessarily one caused by damage to the organ. By the mid-1960s, doctors focused on the hyperactivity of these children, so the name changed to *hyperkinesis*. In the 1970s, the term was changed to *attention-deficit disorder* as focus was moved from activity to the short attention span as the primary condition. The *Diagnostic and Statistical Manual of Mental Disorders, 4th ed., Text Revision* (*DSM-IV-TR*) (APA, 2000) uses the term *Attention-Deficit/Hyperactivity Disorder* and identifies four subtypes: predominantly inattentive type,

predominantly hyperactivity-impulsivity type, combined type, and not otherwise specified.

To be identified as having ADHD according to APA (2000), specific criteria must be met:

ADHD, Combined Type, requires six or more symptoms of inattention and six or more symptoms of hyperactivity. Most children and adolescents with the disorder have the combined type.

ADHD, Predominantly Inattentive Type, requires six or more symptoms of inattention and fewer than six symptoms of hyperactivity-impulsivity.

ADHD, Predominantly Hyperactivity-Impulsivity Type, requires six or more symptoms of hyperactivity-impulsivity and fewer than six symptoms of inattention.

ADHD, Not Otherwise Specified (NOS), is used for children who have a significant impairment but do not meet the criteria for the other subtypes.

The symptoms have to have persisted for at least six months to a degree that is maladaptive and inconsistent with the child's developmental level, and the behaviors must happen frequently (APA, 2000). Table 10–1 summarizes the symptoms of inattention and hyperactivity-impulsivity.

Children with ADHD do not meet the criteria for special educational services because they are diagnosed with ADHD. It must be shown that they also have an inability to learn using regular educational methods. Children with ADHD who meet the criteria for specific learning disabilities may be categorized as having SLD; if children's behavior interferes with their ability to learn, they can receive services as children with emotional disturbances. However, most children with ADHD can meet the criteria for "other health impairments."

When ADD or ADHD is a chronic health problem that results in limited alertness that adversely affects educational performance, and special education and related services are needed, it is covered under the IDEA. "Limited alertness" includes a heightened alertness to environmental stimuli that results in limited alertness with respect to the educational environment (IDEA, 2004).

Children who are not eligible for services under the Individuals with Disabilities Education Act (IDEA) may be eligible for accommodations under Section 504 of the Rehabilitation Act. This act defines a disability differently and refers to a physical or mental impairment that limits one or more major life activity. Academic performance is a major life activity for children and youth. Section 504 is not an education act and does not provide additional funding for qualified children. However, it does protect their rights to reasonable accommodations, and they may have a 504 accommodation plan rather than an IEP.

TABLE

10-1   DIAGNOSTIC CRITERIA FOR ATTENTION-DEFICIT/HYPERACTIVITY DISORDER

Symptoms of Inattention	Symptoms of Hyperactivity-Impulsivity
• Fails to give close attention to details or makes careless mistakes in schoolwork	• Fidgets with hands or feet or squirms in seat
• Has difficulty sustaining attention in tasks or play activities	• Leaves seat in classroom or in other situations
• Does not seem to listen when spoken to directly	• Runs about or climbs excessively in situations where it is inappropriate
• Does not follow through on instructions and fails to complete schoolwork, chores, or duties (not due to oppositional behavior or failure to understand instructions)	• Has difficulty playing or engaging in leisure activities quietly
• Has difficulty organizing tasks and activities	• Is "on the go" or often acts as if "driven by a motor"
• Avoids, dislikes, or is reluctant to engage in tasks that require sustained mental effort (such as schoolwork or homework)	• Talks excessively
• Loses things necessary for tasks or activities (e.g., toys, school assignments, pencils, books, or tools)	• Blurts out answers before questions have been completed
• Is easily distracted by extraneous stimuli	• Has difficulty waiting for his turn
• Is forgetful in daily activities	• Interrupts or intrudes on others (butts into conversations or games)

Source: American Psychiatric Association, 2000.

Prevalence of ADHD

The American Psychiatric Association (2000) criteria estimated that between 3 and 7 percent of the school-age population have ADHD. Prevalence rates vary depending upon the population assessed, the exact definitions used, and who is doing the rating. Nolan, Gadow, and Sprafin (2001) found a prevalence rate of 15.8 percent when teachers rated children ages 3 to 18. Prevalence rates were higher for African American children (40%) than white children (14%); other studies had similar findings (Reid et al., 2001). This may suggest that black children, particularly black males, are at risk of overidentification (Weyandt, 2007). It is difficult to decide whether the number of children identified with ADHD is increasing, because the diagnostic criteria have changed, confounding comparisons. The Centers for Disease Control and Prevention (2005a) estimated that 4.4 million youth ages 4 to 17 have been diagnosed with ADHD by a health care professional. In 2003, 8 percent of school-aged children were reported to have an ADHD diagnosis by their parent (CDC, 2005a). Males are more frequently diagnosed with ADHD than females. In 2003, half of those identified as having ADHD—2.5 million youth ages 4 to 17—were receiving medication treatment for the disorder (CDC, 2005a).

Causes of ADHD

Using family, twin, and adoption studies, researchers have found that ADHD is both familial and heritable. Some aspects of ADHD are more heritable than others. A research team in the United Kingdom (Paloyelis et al., 2010) found a genetic relationship between reading difficulties and inattention symptoms. These genes are different from those that contribute to general cognitive ability. Child-specific environmental factors also contributed to this relationship. The study showed high heritability for these traits.

Kuntsi and colleagues (2005) estimated that between 60 and 90 percent of children with ADHD inherited it from their parents. No specific gene or combination of genes has been identified as causing ADHD, but there is much research being conducted to look for such a connection. Many studies have found a relationship between genes involved in the production, regulation, and functioning of the neurotransmitter dopamine and behaviors related to ADHD (Asherson, Kuntsi, & Taylor, 2005). Dopamine is involved in the ability to modulate attention and behavioral regulation in the frontal cortex. Norepinephrine, another neurotransmitter, plays a role in orienting attention and regulating alertness, also in the frontal cortex (Glanzman & Blum, 2007).

Clearly the cerebral cortex of the brain is involved; the limbic system, the **basal ganglia**, and the **reticular activating system** are involved in ADHD (Silver, 2004). As scientists learn more, they may be able to identify the specific sites and neurotransmitters causing the problem.

Conditions that predispose a child's brain to develop ADHD include prenatal exposure to lead, alcohol, nicotine, and possibly cocaine; prematurity or low birth weight; brain infections; and certain genetic syndromes. Complications during labor and delivery and infancy also seem to impact the brain, but how this happens is not clear (Glanzman & Blum, 2007).

The frontal lobe of the brain processes incoming stimuli and coordinates it with appropriate responses. This part of the brain in children with ADHD is different in subtle ways, and this area of the brain may be compromised (Glanzman & Blum, 2007). Neuroimaging technology has enabled researchers to compare the brain activity of individuals with ADHD to those who are not identified. They can also see the effect that specific medication has on parts of the brain. Specifically, they have found that certain structures in the right prefrontal region of the brain are smaller in individuals with ADHD. Interestingly, maturation in these circuits continues into the third decade of life, which could account for the fact that many children with ADHD show progressive improvement in symptoms as they enter their 30s and 40s (Castellanos et al., 2001).

Many people assume that because glucose is the energy source used by the brain, excess sugar would lead to excess brain activity, perhaps leading to hyperactivity. Empirical studies have not found food additives or sugar to be a cause of ADHD. Allergies to specific foods and dyes and reactions to refined sugar are not supported by scientific evidence in spite of the advocates who claim they affect the attention and behavior of young children (Weyandt, 2007).

Effective parenting makes a difference in all children. Lack of parenting skills does not cause ADHD; however, it can exacerbate the condition. Researchers have found that difficult children tend to evoke more commands and negative feelings from parents. Consistently following through to conflict resolution is difficult. A child with ADHD may challenge parents more often and with greater intensity. Conduct disorders and oppositional defiant disorders are more common in children with ADHD than in the general population, further confounding the relationship between parenting and ADHD. The presence of these disorders in children stresses the parenting process. However, all children diagnosed with ADHD will not look alike due to comorbidity, personality, temperament, and environmental influences. We have tantalizing pieces of the puzzle related to ADHD, but we have yet to find all of the pieces and know what the puzzle will look like when it is put together. Educators find themselves trying to assemble this puzzle, beginning with questions about whether a child might have ADHD.

> ▶⏸ TeachSource Video Case
> **Mysteries of the Brain: Unlocking the Secrets of ADHD**
> Watch the TeachSource Video Case *Mysteries of the Brain: Unlocking the Secrets of ADHD*, in which you'll see how brain studies are becoming one tool in diagnosing ADHD. The video can be found in the Early Childhood Education Media Library under Special Education, available at www.cengagebrain.com.

Early Identification of ADHD

It is unlikely that children from birth to age 3 would be identified as having ADHD as it is difficult to determine the difference between very active infants and toddlers who are displaying developmentally appropriate behaviors for their age and those who might have ADHD. However, the peak age of onset is between 3 and 4 years of age. Yet most children are not referred until the early elementary years.

During the preschool years, power struggles between parents and children escalate. Predictable patterns of eating and sleeping have not emerged, and sometimes toilet training has not been completed. Characteristics of ADHD during the preschool years frequently lead to judgments of immaturity. Whenever this label is used, the question should be asked, "Is the child immature or does he display some characteristics of ADHD?"

Although there is a lack of agreement about what ADHD actually looks like in preschool children, they are increasingly being diagnosed and treated for this disorder (Connor, 2002). Key factors in children being diagnosed in the preschool years are listed here:

- The child displays symptoms of inattention and hyperactivity-impulsivity very early and at a much more severe level than is developmentally expected.
- Symptoms are apparent in a variety of contexts (school and community), not just the home.
- Symptoms continue after a developmental stressor (the birth of a sibling) (Connor, 2002).

There are other warning signals in the medical realm. Children later identified as ADHD have frequent ear infections; there is also a high incidence of allergies, asthma, and other respiratory problems. A child's inability to master specific age-expected tasks may have been unnoticed or attributed to immaturity.

If pediatricians began to routinely screen for children with difficult temperaments, we could begin to provide parents with resources to increase their competence in parenting, whether or not the child was later identified as having ADHD. To the extent that families, educators, or caregivers become anxious, irritated, and angry with these children because of their inability to manage their behavior, problems will be exacerbated.

When children with ADHD spend tremendous amounts of energy keeping themselves under control during school hours, they may let it all out when they come home. Battles ensue over homework, chores, mealtime, bedtime, and so on. As children get up to face another day, they dawdle to keep from having to go to school while parents are trying to get themselves off to work and other children off to school as well. It may be only 8:30 a.m., but parents may feel that they have already put in a full day's work. The ability to identify young children who are at risk for ADHD would increase the quality of life for the children, their families, and the schools.

THE EVIDENCE BASE

A nationally representative Canadian study followed 10 cohorts of approximately 1,000 children ($N = 10,658$) over six years. They identified three distinct developmental trajectories of children between ages 2 and 11, based on their physically aggressive behavior.

- About a third of the children (31%) rarely used physical aggression as toddlers and used virtually no physical aggression by preadolescence.

- The majority of the children (52%) showed moderate physical aggression as toddlers but used it infrequently by preadolescence.

- One sixth of the children (17%) followed a high stable trajectory of high levels of physical aggression that continued on into preadolescence. Analysis found that these children were more likely to be boys and from low-income families where the mother had not completed high school and reported using hostile/ineffective parenting strategies.

Source: Cote et al., 2006.

REFLECTIVE PRACTICE | The results of this study identify a group of children, as young as toddlers, who are at risk for developing physical aggressive behavior and characteristics of ADHD that will continue on into preadolescence. How does this knowledge affect your response to these children, and what might you talk with their parents about? What could you do to change this trajectory?

IMPLICATIONS FOR EDUCATORS

As an educator, you and the child's family are likely to be part of the early identification process. Thus, knowledge of the identification process and characteristic behaviors is important. Identifying children with ADHD is difficult because during the early childhood years many of the characteristics of ADHD are characteristics of typically developing children. It is more a matter of degree than whether a behavior is present. However, children with *difficult* temperaments may be at risk. Children who have a high activity level and do not adapt well to changes in the environment, and who have intense reactions, unpredictable routines, and difficulty sleeping and eating, are challenging to even the most competent parents.

Three-year-olds who are very intense in their reactions to the environment, particularly when these reactions are usually negative, are of concern. Also, children identified as having speech and language problems are at risk for ADHD. Other at-risk children are those who lack good problem-solving strategies as well as those who cannot delay their response to an inviting stimulus, whether a toy another child has or a cookie. These children don't seem to develop the early skills necessary for making and keeping friends. Children who are impulsive, noncompliant, and fearful may also be at risk, as are children who seem unable to plan or accept limits. Motor clumsiness may become apparent as children take over more responsibility in dressing, toileting, tying shoes, cutting, coloring, and writing.

As children reach elementary school, some of the characteristics of ADHD become more apparent and the implications more obvious. The demands on children to perform specific skills at specific times and in specific ways may be daunting to the child with ADHD. Teachers give tests and grade them and send the results home on report cards (if they wait that long). Some children do not perform well in school, often fail to finish assignments, may become disruptive in class, may experience poor social relations, and may be easily frustrated. They may have a very short attention span and show some aggressive or even oppositional behavior. Such children frequently are moved to the lowest math and reading groups.

Girls with attention-deficit/hyperactivity disorder may appear lonely, dreamy, or like they are just not paying attention.
©Cengage Learning 2012

If they become disruptive, they lose instructional time because they are in the principal's office. The hyperactive child may become a bully. The inattentive child may be perceived as weird. Because of impaired social skills, the inattentive child (frequently a girl) may be lonely, isolated, and lack friends. Organized extracurricular activities begin to play a role in children's development. For some children, sports such as soccer and baseball may be an opportunity for success and acceptance. For others, it will be another area of failure and rejection. Look at the whole child in the context of where he lives and grows before you reach any hypotheses you want to follow up.

Assessment of Attention-Deficit/Hyperactivity Disorder

Most professionals use multiple measures to tap into the various aspects of ADHD. These include behavioral rating scales; structured interviews; measures of attention, hyperactivity, and impulsivity; and structured observations (Smith & Corkum, 2007).

Most clinicians use the diagnostic criteria developed by the APA (2000) and published in the DSM-IV-TR as the starting point for diagnosis. A history will typically be gathered from the parents. Parents, early childhood educators, and others who have observed the child's behavior in different settings may be asked to fill out formal observation scales. There are a variety of formal rating scales and behavior checklists used to help in this process, including the Conners

3 (Conners, 2009); the ADD-H Comprehensive Teacher's Rating Scale (Ullman et al., 1996); and the Child Behavior Checklist for Ages 4–18 (Achenbach, 1991). These tools are useful, because teachers and others may have different views of behaviors, and the child may display different behaviors in different settings. Early childhood educators view the child in the context of the children in the classroom, whereas the parents may see the child only in the context of the home and with siblings or neighborhood children. Additional information would be obtained by interviewing the child and from his self-report, a medical/neurologic examination, and a psychoeducational assessment (Stein et al., 2002). The different perspectives add both confusion and information.

In addition to the information obtained in the checklist, the focus should be on three tasks:

1. The child's ability to seek out what he wants and then attend to and focus on it.
2. The child's ability to maintain this focus.

3. When finished, the child's ability to stop attending and to move on to something else (Sliver, 2004).

IMPLICATIONS FOR EDUCATORS

As a teacher, you may be one of the first to suspect that a child may have ADHD. The question is, When does a child exhibit enough of the characteristic behaviors for a long enough time for you to talk with the parents? Before approaching parents, look at the cultural background of the family and learn something about the family's expectations. Information about any child should be evaluated within the context of the family and the culture.

If further information sheds no light on the behavior, observe the child over a span of time to get a representative look at his behavior. Then construct a simple behavioral checklist that focuses attention on areas identified by the APA as criteria for identifying children with ADHD. First, decide how much a particular behavior describes the child on a given day. Then note the behaviors that you observed to form that opinion. Do this for several days, and ask other adults in the classroom to do the same. Also observe one child of the same gender who is about the same age, whom you think is developing typically. Your form may resemble Figure 10–1.

ADHD: Inattention	Perceived frequency	Date	Actual frequency*
1. Makes careless mistakes	M S R		
2. Does not follow through	M S R		
3. Disorganized	M S R		
4. Loses things	M S R		
5. Inattentive	M S R		
6. Distractible	M S R		
7. Does not seem to listen	M S R		
8. Avoids challenging tasks	M S R		
9. Forgetful	M S R		
ADHD: Hyperactivity–Impulsivity	M S R		
10. Fidgets, squirms	M S R		
11. Leaves large, small group activities	M S R		
12. Runs, climbs excessively, inappropriately	M S R		
13. Trouble playing quietly (books, manipulatives)	M S R		
14. Seems always "on the go"	M S R		
15. Talks excessively	M S R		
16. Blurts out answers	M S R		
17. Trouble taking turns, waiting for turn	M S R		
18. Interrupts, butts into activities and conversations	M S R		

Date	Observation	Description
	Antecedent	
	Behavior	
	Consequences	
	Comments	

Key:
M = More than other children, frequently
S = Sometimes, same as other children
R = Rarely, less than other children

*Use numbers to count actual frequency and put numbers in the comments section and clarify the antecedent behavior, the behavior itself, and the consequences.

FIGURE 10–1   ADHD OBSERVATION FORM

When children's behaviors are irritating or cause problems in the classroom, it is sometimes difficult to sort out their actual occurrence from perceived occurrence. Before you begin using a form such as Figure 10–1, start by reflecting on your class as a whole and then the particular child relative to the class. Then fill out the perceived frequency in Figure 10–1. Over the course of several days or a week, look at the relationship between your perceptions and the actual occurrences and the behavior itself, what preceded it, and what happened afterwards. These insights will provide information to respond to questions and to develop a plan of action.

Your observations should be systematic, and the behavior observed should have necessary detail: "Sheila knocked over the juice while reaching for the crackers with her left hand." Write down the details as you see them. Keep your facts objective. The most important part of observing is looking for patterns. You will have to observe for several days or weeks to get enough data for patterns to emerge. Whether or not you decide to talk with the parents about your observations, you will have a more accurate picture of the child. This information is useful in targeting program goals.

It is also useful to include peers in the evaluation process, as ultimately it is the peers who will decide who they are willing to include in their play, as well as who they choose to be friends with. Teachers may accept some aggressive behavior as being part of the syndrome a child has, whereas peers are less forgiving—hitting is hitting!

• • •
Medical Treatment of ADHD

When a child is referred to a medical professional, the process focuses on four aspects of the diagnosis: (1) the symptoms of ADHD, (2) whether other conditions might be causing the symptoms, (3) comorbid conditions, and (4) associated conditions that might not have enough symptoms to be diagnosed but could interfere with the child's life and should be part of the treatment plan (Glanzman & Blum, 2007). Although the process may vary, it should be a multimethod assessment (Weyandt, 2007). The presence of associated problems must also be explored.

Many factors can cause children to have symptoms similar to ADHD. A number of physical and psychiatric problems should be ruled out before a diagnosis of ADHD is made. Inattentiveness, impulsivity, and underachievement can be found in children with emotional and behavioral disorders and those who are depressed. Children should have a medical examination to rule out medical issues such as sensory problems, motor disabilities, seizures, thyroid disease, allergies, intellectual disability, and pervasive developmental disorders (Glanzman & Blum, 2007).

The evaluation team for determining ADHD usually involves the family, the family physician or pediatrician, a child psychologist or psychiatrist, a neurologist, a family counselor or therapist, and an educator. More informants increase diagnostic certainty (Weyandt, 2007). Accurate diagnosis is important because it dictates follow-up treatment. It is important to rule out conditions that mimic ADHD.

Although a direct cause for ADHD has not been found, there is agreement that it has a physiological base and that some of the problems are related to neurotransmitters. In addition to educational interventions, about half of children identified with ADHD also have a pharmacologic intervention (CDC, 2005a).

MEDICATION

Twenty years ago, medication was considered a last resort for treating ADHD. Today, medication is recognized as a first line of treatment for children with ADHD, and the emerging consensus is that medication should be used sooner rather than later. A greater variety of drugs are now prescribed. More precise diagnostic practices enable individually tailored multimodal approaches that combine the use of medication with

behavioral interventions (Weyandt, 2007). Stimulant medications are most commonly prescribed for children with ADHD.

Let's begin with the medication itself and how it works. **Stimulants** increase the level of arousal of the central nervous system (CNS). Although this may seem strange, research suggests that children with ADHD are underaroused and that their hyperactivity is a way of increasing arousal (Weyandt, 2007). Stimulant medications interact with the biogenic amine transporters (dopamine, norepinephrine, and serotonin). Their actions increase the availability of these neurotransmitters, primarily dopamine (Stein et al., 2002). Research shows positive effects of stimulant drugs on decreasing impulsivity and hyperactivity. The short-term and intermediate-term effects remain positive. The long-term effects are not as well studied (Glanzman & Blum, 2007).

There are primarily two kinds of stimulants: **methylphenidate stimulants** and **amphetamine stimulants**. Although similar, they act on the brain in slightly different ways. The methylphenidate stimulants block the dopamine transporter; because there are fewer available transporters, there is increased dopamine at the synapses. The amphetamines work by increasing the release of biogenic amines in general. Methylphenidates (Ritalin, Concerta, Metadate, Methylin) are the most commonly prescribed stimulants for children (Zito et al., 2003). Most stimulants are available in two forms: short acting (given twice or more a day) and sustained release (given once a day). The sustained-release form can be given to a child before he goes to school. This eliminates the need to have medication taken at school and ensures some confidentiality. The dosage and type of stimulant used should be individually determined (Weyandt, 2007). Medication is increasingly being prescribed for preschool children (Zito et al., 2000).

EFFICACY OF MEDICATIONS

There are few studies of the efficacy and safety of stimulant medication for preschool children. With school-age and older children who have average intelligence, the drugs have been effective. However, parents in particular are concerned about the side effects of taking stimulant medication. The major side effects include weight loss, sleep disturbances, headaches, stomachaches, and mood changes (Weyandt, 2007). There is some concern that preschool-age children might be more susceptible to the side effects than older children (Connor, 2002).

If stimulant medication is recommended for a child, it typically starts with a low dose and is increased gradually (over the course of a week or several weeks) until a response is evident or until side effects develop. Other protocols use different dosages and compare the results. During this time teachers may be asked to fill out daily or weekly behavior rating forms. (The teacher does not know the medication regimen.) Often one week on and one week off are compared. Stimulants work immediately; they do not need to build up in the body. Families need to make decisions about when they feel the benefits of medication outweigh the concerns. Some children do not receive medication after school, on weekends, and during the summer. This is particularly true if a child's rate of growth begins to decelerate. Children need to be monitored on a regular basis (every 3 to 6 months) to ensure proper growth and nutrition and to determine whether the medication is still required (Glanzman & Blum, 2007). Although the short-term benefits seem to be well documented, many questions remain about the long-term effects.

IMPLICATIONS FOR EDUCATORS

As an educator it is important that you know when and if the medication has been taken and how long it is likely to be effective. You should also know about the specific side effects and what to look for. Families make decisions about whether their child should be on stimulant medication, and the medical community tries to select the most appropriate medication for the child. Your role is to observe the child and provide accurate feedback about the child's behavior in the classroom.

IN THE FIELD

As a special educator who teaches 7- and 8-year-olds, I have worked with many children with ADHD. I have learned to work with most of these children very successfully over the years. Nikki, a student in my class, displays all of the symptoms of ADHD without the hyperactivity. Nikki often loses focus during lessons and cannot work on an assignment or an activity for a sustained period of time. She also has problems keeping her hands out of her desk. Nikki's main difficulty, however, is staying focused during reading and writing times; she usually only sits quietly.

Nikki also has a minor learning disability, but I feel that her attention problems are seriously affecting her grades and learning. She cannot pay attention long enough to master new concepts and skills. As a result, I have contacted her parents and discussed the issue with them. Nikki's mother mentioned that it takes about four hours a night to complete homework—and this is when she sits right by Nikki's side. (Most other children report completing the homework in less than an hour.) Nevertheless, they downplayed any concern and said that sometimes Nikki just doesn't feel like doing work. I suggested they take Nikki to the family physician and to mention my concerns. I even sent home an ADD/ADHD checklist that they could also take to their physician; the checklist did substantiate my theory that Nikki had a problem with paying attention. However, the doctor visit never happened.

Nikki's parents will not consider the fact that Nikki may have ADHD. Even after mentioning the subject at our many meetings, the parents have not acted in any way to help their daughter. Nikki's father did once mention that he did not believe in medication for children. I wanted to scream out loud at him, "If your daughter had diabetes, would you provide her with insulin?" To me, ADHD is the same as any other disease or disorder. This child will continue to suffer, learn less, and get very poor grades until these parents decide to help their daughter. I feel a mind is being wasted.

REFLECTIVE PRACTICE | How do you feel about the use of medication for young children who may have ADHD? Do you think this teacher is justified in her feelings? What might you do in her situation? How would you respond to a parent who asked you about the efficacy of using stimulant medication on her 6-year-old child who was diagnosed with ADHD? Could you explain to her how it works?

• • •
ADHD, Comorbidity, and Associated Problems

When children have more than one disability, the disabilities are referred to as comorbid, or coexisting. Comorbidity requires that children with ADHD meet the criteria for diagnosis for ADHD and also the criteria of the other disorder. There are cases in which children experience anxiety or impaired learning, but the criteria for the second disorder are not met. Researchers estimate that as many as two-thirds of children diagnosed with ADHD also have at least one other condition. Because of the numerous conditions that can coexist with ADHD and their implications for education, it is important to identify these as well. Approximately 30 to 50 percent of children diagnosed with ADHD also have an externalizing or disruptive behavior disorder (Waxmonsky, 2003).

There is considerable overlap with ADHD and mood disorders (depression, anxiety); estimates range from 14 percent to 83 percent. Overlap with bipolar disorder is only now being studied, and estimates range from 10 percent to 20 percent. Anxiety disorders occur in about 25 percent of children with ADHD. There is debate about the overlap with specific learning disabilities, and these estimates range from 10 percent to 40 percent (Spencer et al., 2000; Glanzman & Blum, 2007; Weyandt, 2007; Kronenberger & Dunn, 2003). Although these disorders may accompany a primary diagnosis of ADHD, they also are found alone or in various combinations without ADHD.

Children with ADHD have challenges monitoring their behavior. This inability to prioritize and inhibit responses interferes with their academic achievement. They may also have problems in the area of sensory motor integration, which interferes with the development of adaptive skills and the attainment of skillful locomotion. There is also overlap with reading disability (Paloyelis, 2010).

- **Academic underachievement** is one of the markers of ADHD during the school years.

- **Executive function** is the system within the brain that uses cognitive control and future-oriented processes to make decisions (Shapiro, Church, & Lewis, 2007). It underlies good organization. Children who have problems in executive function have trouble organizing and prioritizing information, sustaining attention, planning, self-monitoring, and inhibiting responses (Shapiro et al., 2007). Academically, they are underachievers, even if they have a high IQ (Denckla, 2003). They acquire skills but do not use them effectively. (See Chapter 8 for a more detailed discussion of executive function.)

- **Developmental coordination disorder**, or just clumsiness in general, may make a child the last chosen for teams and may make sports a challenge. This also places children at greater risk for accidental and non-accidental injuries. Children may get themselves into difficult situations more frequently and have fewer skills to get out. Some of their behaviors may irritate adults and peers and put them at risk for abuse (Stein et al., 2002).

- **Adaptive skills** may be slower to develop; rather than waiting for children to perform certain tasks, parents may decide that it is just easier to do it for them. This is a good short-term solution but has serious long-term implications.

- **Impulsiveness** means acting quickly, without planning and thinking about the consequences of actions. Impulsive children seem to have a short fuse. They act before they think, and they rarely learn from past experience because they don't give themselves time to reflect on previous experiences and their outcomes.

- **Distractibility** is having problems attending to a task. Children's attention and even their bodies seem to be drawn elsewhere. They do not have the ability to redirect their attention back to the original task once their attention has wandered. Children's seeming disinterest and inability to complete tasks is not always a disadvantage; sometimes, they notice new connections and come up with imaginative solutions to problems.

- **A short attention span** means children do not stay at tasks for long. They may not finish tasks or get satisfaction from them.

- **Inability to follow directions** can relate to a lack of understanding the directions or understanding, but then forgetting, what was asked.

- **Hyperactivity** is excessive activity or motion that is not goal oriented. Children seem distracted by and need to respond to all environmental stimuli. Even when sitting, children are not quiet; they may twitch, jerk, or rock. As they get older, the hyperactivity may be displayed in nonstop talking as well as nonstop moving. The hyperactivity is chronic and unrelated to specific events.

- **Hypoactivity** is too little activity. Children appear to move in slow motion. They may seem listless, bored, or sleepy. Every movement seems to require a lot of effort.

- **Perseveration** is starting a task without the ability to stop. A child rolling a playdough snake may roll snakes all morning long if not interrupted. It is as if the child is not capable of refocusing attention once it has been focused: The child can't change channels. This may be a way of coping with distractions.

- **Awkwardness** is clumsiness where children frequently bump into things or people, knock things over, and trip over their feet or other objects.

- **Social problems** may occur because children may do things that irritate others. They are more likely than other children to be in conflict with their peers. They have difficulty recognizing social cues and using social skills. They don't read others' body language accurately and hence make wrong assumptions and act inappropriately.

- **Family problems** indicate a lack of social skills in the home as well as in school. Children's frustrations and failures affect families and family relationships. Parents may disagree on how to cope with troubling behavior, causing additional stress on relationships. Siblings

may feel that there is a double standard applied to behavior and chores. Even as they begin to understand about ADHD, they may feel both guilt and anger (Shapiro, Church, & Lewis, 2002; Shapiro et al., 2007; Silver, 2004).

Overall, in evaluating a child with ADHD, one has to take into account the child's developmental level, the context in which she lives, and the possibility of both a variety of comorbid disabilities and the reality of those that are problematic but do not reach criterion.

Developing a 504 Accommodation Plan

Children with disabilities recognized by the IDEA are entitled to an individualized education program (IEP). Children with ADHD are not included in the disabilities served under the IDEA. They may receive special education because of comorbid conditions (e.g., specific learning disabilities or emotional disorders) or under "other health impairment" (IDEA, 2004). If these conditions do not exist, a child may qualify for a 504 Classroom Accommodation Plan. The definitions of disabilities that receive services under the Rehabilitation Act of 1973 are different from those in the IDEA. ADHD is included because it is a "physical or mental impairment which substantially limits a major life activity" (learning).

There is a three-step process for creating a classroom accommodation plan (Blazer, 1999).

1. *Talk with the parents and child.* Children as young as 5 years of age can be included in creating their 504 plans. They often know better than others what would make school easier. Provide parents with some guidance on the types of accommodations available under Section 504.

   - **Physical accommodations** may include posted class rules, color codes, preferential seating, reorganized work space, an extra seat or table, a standing workstation, a quiet area to study, and so on.

   - **Instructional accommodations** may include repeated and simplified directions with additional directions provided in written form; individualized homework assignments that reduce the volume of work and extend deadlines, alternative assignments, an extra set of textbooks; and assignments requiring technological learning aids (e.g., tape-recorded assignments, word-processed assignments, and multisensory manipulatives).

   - **Behavioral accommodations** may include positive reinforcement, verbal or written feedback, reward systems and incentives, private signals, role-playing, and clearly articulated rewards and consequences for actions; and promoting leadership and accountability with assigned jobs that can be performed well (e.g., line leader). They need clearly defined goals with incentives and reinforcements (through student contracts, an incentives chart, and reward system), and communication among parents and teachers (phone calls, e-mail, daily or weekly book or diary, etc.).

Use a form that children are familiar with, such as a webbing, a chart, or a poster, and have children decide what they want and what would make it easier for them to learn (Figure 10–2). Children may keep this form (perhaps laminated) so they know the accommodations to which they are entitled.

2. *Teacher input/agreement.* This is a more formal step that is written by the teacher(s) and appropriate school personnel. It involves not only listing the accommodations but also determining whether they are achieving their purpose. Teachers provide input about the accommodations they are currently using, how successful they are, and what is still challenging. If, for example, the teacher has allowed the child to do her spelling homework on the computer and spell-check it, and

the child is getting 100 on the Friday spelling test, the accommodation would be considered very effective. On the other hand, if the child continues to fail the spelling test, a different accommodation would be needed. The effectiveness of an accommodation is related to child outcomes. Children with ADHD are not expected to learn less; they may need to approach learning by a different route.

3. *Parent follow-up, coordination, and advocacy.* At this point, the parent formally sends a letter to the school requesting a 504 Classroom Accommodation Plan. Included in this request are the accommodations developed by the child, the family, and the educators. Once agreed upon, this becomes part of the child's permanent file and will not have to be renegotiated each year, just modified and updated.

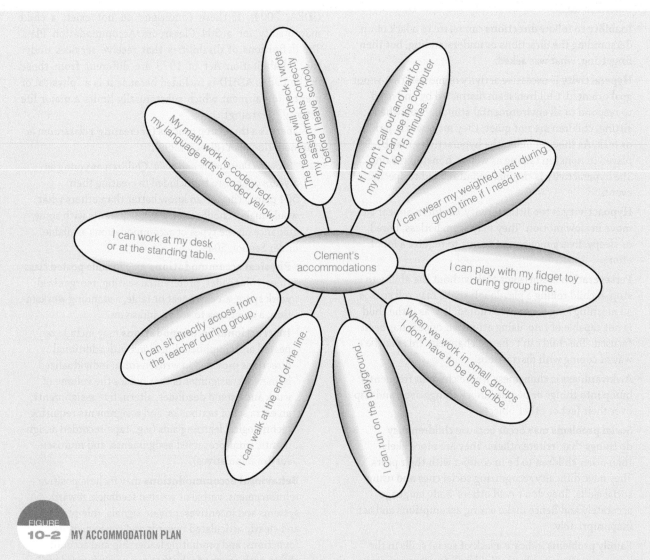

FIGURE 10-2 MY ACCOMMODATION PLAN

This is an accommodation plan for Clement, a 6-year-old, in first grade, who has been diagnosed with attention-deficit/hyperactivity disorder, hyperactive/impulsive subtype. Using a format that children are familiar with helps them become more independent in their learning and ensures that if there is a substitute teacher that they will receive their needed accommodations.

Intervention Strategies

There is no cure for ADHD, but just as there is a multimodal assessment plan, there is also a multimodal intervention plan. Intervention typically involves parent education in behavior management; an appropriate educational setting (typically, with a teacher who knows behavior management techniques); individual and family counseling when necessary; and, frequently, medication.

Education and training of parents of children with ADHD is an essential component of most intervention plans. Informed parents are more likely to comply with medication regimens and pursue effective child management (Glanzman & Blum, 2007). Educators also need training in modifying their classroom behavior management methods. Consistency between home and school in behavior management is a tremendous asset for the child. Techniques focus on maintaining the child's attention on tasks, improving behavior, teaching organizational skills, and adapting programming to specific learning disabilities if they coexist (Glanzman & Blum, 2007).

Intervention should be multimodal. The intervention team may need to act like detectives, assembling clues to provide ideas about effective intervention strategies. Start with the setting itself. Look at the child's strengths and where he functions most competently. Although children will vary, see Table 10–2 for what this might look like for a child with ADHD.

Although these variables may not always be under your control, it is important to think about them and know that children are facing challenges. Space should be arranged to offer children opportunities to work individually, in small groups, or in large groups. Ideally, the classroom provides a variety of well-defined learning-action stations. If children have coexisting conditions, look at the guidelines for those conditions to expand your teaching strategies.

Behavior Management/Guidance

Discipline, or classroom management, is rarely easy; including children with ADHD presents additional challenges. Because their behavior is inconsistent, it is difficult to know whether these children are refusing or are unable to behave as requested. (Parents have the same dilemma.) Children often take medication in the morning before school. It takes about half an hour for it to work, which may mean that mornings are a challenge for families. Children with ADHD, even young ones, can control the family. If they want attention and aggressive behavior gets attention (even if it is negative attention), their need will be rewarded.

Behavior management plans have two basic assumptions.

1. Rewarding desired behavior is more effective than punishing undesired behavior.
2. Agreeing on what behaviors are acceptable and unacceptable, and on a consistent response to the behaviors is critical (Silver, 2004).

The first step is to collect information. One easy model to use is the ABC chart. The chart should always have the time and date noted and then the ABC components:

A   the **A**ntecedent (what happened before the behavior occurred)

B   the **B**ehavior

C   and the **C**onsequences of the behavior (Silver, 2004).

If parents are also doing the recording, have them do it separately. The same goes for teachers if there is more than one in the classroom. Table 10–3 shows a typical ABC chart.

As data are collected, patterns should emerge. They may be related to time of day, specific antecedent behaviors leading to predictable unacceptable behaviors, a change in routines, medication wearing off, and so on. Data often cluster to make an impossible list more possible. Most unacceptable behaviors fall into one of three categories: physical abuse

TABLE 10-2 STRENGTHS AND CHALLENGES FOR CHILDREN WITH ADHD

Strengths	Challenges
One-on-one	Group times
Familiar/frequent recurring tasks/situations	Novel tasks/situations
Frequent feedback	Infrequent feedback
Immediate consequences	Delayed consequences
Noticeable consequences	Less obvious consequences
Supervised work	Unsupervised work
Morning	Afternoon
Self-paced tasks	Tasks paced by others
Quiet environment	Noisy environment
Smaller class	Larger class

TABLE 10-3 ABC CHART FOR DARIA

Date/Time	Antecedent	Behavior	Consequences
10/6/11			
10:30 a.m.	Don't know	Had a temper tantrum screaming, fell on floor	Moved furniture out, redirected children
11:00 a.m.	S. took her book (end of clean-up)	Bit S.	Time out, 5 minutes, & talked to her
11:20 a.m.	Spilled juice	Knocked pitcher to floor	Had her clean it up

Look for the pattern in Daria's behavior. Although the antecedents and consequences varied, her behavior was physical.

(e.g., hitting someone, breaking things, or threatening to do so); verbal abuse (e.g., yelling, cursing, taunting); and non-compliance (not completing a task or complying with a request) (Silver, 2004).

Once the patterns have been identified, an initial behavior plan is designed. The family, including siblings if any, and educators should be part of the plan. The plan involves rewarding positive behavior and withholding rewards for negative behavior—every time it happens. For children the day is too long to be one unit. It should be divided up into three or four time units, such as (1) from getting up until getting to school, (2) from getting to school until lunch, (3) from lunch until getting picked up or leaving school, (4) from returning home until bedtime. Remember, the purpose is to reward positive behavior.

The use of "time out" for children with ADHD has its proponents and opponents. If used, it should be only one of a variety of methods of guidance, and there should be clear guidelines as to when it is the most appropriate alternative. If removing a child is necessary, I prefer the concept of "thinking time," which involves removing the child from the ongoing activities to a specified location off to one side of the room or playground. It is designed to give children time to think about what happened and regain their self-control. The child may know better than the teacher when he is back in control. Ask him. Then ask the child three questions before allowing the child to leave the thinking area: (1) "What happened?" (2) "What should you have done?" (3) "What will you do next time?"

Guiding the child in ways to handle issues for the next time is beneficial. However, until the child is emotionally available, it is a waste of time. It may take children five to ten minutes to emotionally recover to the point that they can think about what happened (Goleman, 1995). This is the time to talk with them about their behavior, the choices they made, and what they could do differently. Help them think about alternatives. Ultimately, the goal is to have the child do the thinking before the action.

When a child is out of control, it may be necessary for him to leave the classroom. This option should be used as just one of the tools in behavior management/guidance. Its effectiveness is diminished when used continually or exclusively. It also reduces the number of social interactions that occur between peers. Using incentives, behavioral reinforcers, and modeling opportunities may be more effective.

IMPLICATIONS FOR EDUCATORS

The development of a behavior management/guidance plan is part of the multimodal method for working with children with ADHD. If you already have a plan that works, use it. There are a variety of ways to plan. Some educators successfully use logical consequences. For example, if a child knocks all the plastic blocks off a table, he needs to help pick them up; if he spills milk, he should help clean it up. (If the child spills milk persistently and purposefully, you might try not giving any more. If the child is thirsty, give him water.) Impulsive children who act before they think and only then remember the consequences of their actions may not profit from this approach. A combination of the two methods often works best. You want the child to learn internalized self-control and to stop inappropriate behavior.

Think about the purpose of challenging behavior. Is it something that starts out as fun that children do not know how to end, or it there an underlying cause?
©Cengage Learning 2012

Some teachers use a token reward system. This involves token rewards for appropriate, or on-task, behavior and loss of token rewards for inappropriate behavior. It is important to find out what is rewarding to the child. If the reward is irrelevant, there is no incentive to work toward it. The best rewards are those that involve time with adults. Food is not a good reward. For young children, using stickers or stars often works. The child may earn the right to borrow a favorite book, have 5 minutes of special one-on-one time with the teacher, or whatever that child finds rewarding. If your system does not seem to be effective, see whether there are unexpected snags. All systems need fine tuning once they are in place.

Make sure your consequence is not rewarding, or the behavior will continue. It is important to think about what behaviors are being rewarded and whether or not those are the ones you want to continue. Develop a system to ensure that you move to intermittent rewards to establish the behavior.

IN THE FIELD

I once taught a little girl who was particularly disruptive during group time. I had a student teacher take her out into the hall when she acted up. Instead of decreasing, the disruptive behavior increased, and it began to occur closer to the beginning of group time. I decided to see what was happening. The next time Andrea created a disturbance, I took her out into the hall. Once there, she told me to sit down, plopped herself in my lap, and said, "This is the book I want to read today." She then hauled out her book, and I read it. Now I knew why this child disrupted my group! The next day, Andrea went to the hall with *no* book, and the student teacher was instructed to ignore her. By the end of the week she sat through most of group time!

● ● ●
Working with Challenging Behaviors

Challenging behavior is difficult for teachers to deal with. However, it is not the same for all teachers. What is challenging behavior for one teacher may not be challenging behavior for another, and vice versa. Challenging behavior is behavior that makes teachers feel inadequate because they don't know how to deal with it (Marion, 2002).

Ignoring challenging behavior (especially when you think that getting attention is the child's purpose) is ideal when it works. However, it doesn't always work, and it is inappropriate if the child is doing something dangerous or is hurting others. Then, removing the child from the situation is probably the best solution, but it is only the first step in the process.

As with all behavior, it is important to look for patterns and to try to examine the roots of the challenging behavior. The first thing to consider is developmental level. Is the behavior appropriate for the developmental age/level of the child? It is difficult for young children to take the perspective of others and to understand that it hurts to get hit. Young children typically focus on one thing at a time, and that may be getting the toy they want. Or is there a skill that a child needs that he lacks? Some children have unmet needs. If the child needs attention, is this the only way he can get it? Is this the only way he knows how to get it? Look at the context (the environmental aspects) of the situation. Does the environment support this behavior? Look at the room arrangement, the available activities, and the sequence of activities to determine whether these contribute to the behavior.

Satiation is another way of dealing with challenging behavior. The child is made to continue a behavior when he no longer wants to. This is particularly effective for something physical, like falling off a chair. If a child is required to sit down, fall off, and get up repeatedly, this behavior loses its charm. To discourage acts that are likely to be contagious in a classroom, satiation may be more effective than ignoring.

IMPLICATIONS FOR EDUCATORS

Figure out specifically what you want. Often it is easier to know what we don't want than what we do want. If the problem is cursing, what do you want? Obviously, you want it to stop. Is there an appropriate place for a child to curse? Is there a safe place for this to happen? If you can provide an uninteresting place for a child to go, this may be part of your solution (after you have tried a variety of other things that you hoped would work). It is important to teach the child that behavior is situational and that there are things you can say and do in some situations but not in others. Be creative. The more skills you have, the fewer challenging behaviors you will encounter.

It is important, however, to be able to differentiate between children whose behavior challenges you and requires educational intervention, and children who need therapy. You are probably not a therapist, but you should know how to get the support of one. Be authoritative, unrelentingly positive, and reflect on your behavior and your practice with challenging behaviors (Marion, 2002).

Guidelines

1. *Seat a child with ADHD in the area where the teacher spends the most time.* If children sit in rows, place the child close to the front, with his back to the rest of the class to keep other children out of view; surround the child with good role models (ensure that this does not become a problem for these children or rotate seats), and seat the child away from distractions such as noisy pencil sharpeners, heat and air-conditioning units, or open doors and windows.

2. *Assign a child with ADHD two chairs or a chair and a standing work place.* When children are required to sit in chairs, he can move between them (within reasonable limits). Allow the child (or any child) to sit astride the chair (backward); this will keep the chair from rocking or tipping and provides a more stable base.

3. *Present information from a location where physical and visual reinforcement can be maintained.* Do not have a group activity in a place where the child can look outside and see others playing. Children's ability to selectively ignore stimuli varies. Reducing external visual and auditory distractions is usually helpful.

4. *Keep the classroom orderly and organized.* This can be done through color coding or numbering bins and shelves.

5. *Keep lessons brief and fast-paced, and break up information into manageable "chunks."* Present information sequentially, a step at a time rather than all at once. Model tasks to make them easier to follow and improve recall.

6. *Decrease waiting and increase on-task time.* Plan ahead.

7. *Encourage cooperative/collaborative learning.* Have children work in small groups with a common goal.

8. *Require a daily assignment notebook.* Make sure each child correctly writes down all assignments each day. If a child is not capable of this, help her. Sign the notebook daily to signify completion of homework assignments. (Parents should also sign.) Use the notebook for daily communication with parents. For younger children, teachers may write the comments to the family and include children's illustrations or photographs of what they did during the day.

9. *Modify assignments as needed.* If the child has an IEP, use the information to determine the child's specific strengths and challenges. Provide extra time and opportunity for certain tasks. Children with ADHD may work slowly. Do not penalize them for needing extra time. Make sure you are assessing knowledge and not attention span. If a child has a 504 plan, base modifications on the plan.

10. *Decrease frustration.* Stress, pressure, and fatigue can break down children's self-control and lead to poor behavior.

11. *Give feedback frequently, using visual, verbal, or tactile methods.* Verbal reinforcement is often the least salient. Find out what works and use it.

12. *Avoid ridicule, criticism, and sarcasm.* Remember, children with ADHD have difficulty staying in control.

13. *Enforce classroom rules consistently.* Have preestablished consequences for behavior. Remain calm, state the infraction of the rule, and avoid debating or arguing with the child. Administer consequences immediately, monitor and support appropriate behavior frequently, and then move on.

14. *Determine the child's preferred learning style.* Get information from educational, psychological, and/or

neurological testing to determine whether the child has a preferred learning style (auditory, visual, kinesthetic), and use this information to frame instruction.

15. *Decide which of the smaller characteristics typical for children with ADHD you can ignore* (fidgeting, swaying, rocking, etc.). Try redirecting behaviors you cannot ignore into more purposeful actions. This may take some creative planning. If fidgeting during groups time is something you want to address, provide all children with "stress balls" to fidget with during group time. Initially all children will probably use them over time; however, some children will continue to use them, whereas others will not.

16. *Ensure belongings are labeled.* As homework plays a larger role, if parents can afford it or the school is willing, obtain a second set of books. This means the child has a set at home to do her homework and that she can also write in the book or highlight it. For some children, this is a very effective learning strategy.

> ▶❚❚ **TeachSource Video Case**
>
> **Including Students with High Incidence Disabilities: Strategies for Success**
>
> Watch the TeachSource Video Case *Including Students with High Incidence Disabilities: Strategies for Success,* in which you'll see how a veteran teacher accommodates the learning needs of all the students in her elementary inclusion classroom. The video can be found in the Early Childhood Education Media Library under Special Education, available at www.cengagebrain.com.

Curriculum Adaptations

Children with ADHD require some adaptations. For those with impulsivity and hyperactivity, it may be in the area of increasing the time available for learning and helping them focus on tasks. The social skills necessary to do cooperative learning may have to be taught. In general, the accommodations are behavioral in nature or are designed to support the child's organization and minimize distractions. Because so many children with ADHD have coexisting conditions, these should also be taken into consideration when adapting the curriculum. See curriculum adaptations for those disabilities as well.

Social Awareness

All children need to form relationships with others. The skills of taking turns and sharing are especially critical. The behavior of children with ADHD is variable; they are often unaware of how they feel, and so they need to identify their feelings and learn to control them while developing a sense of self-worth and group belonging.

Impulsiveness is one of the hallmark traits of ADHD. Children with ADHD have poor self-control, which negatively affects their behaviors in the classroom and also with their peers, impacting their social development. Social and organizational skills that we take for granted may have to be

specifically taught. Experiences in starting and stopping an action on a signal and in self-pacing or regulating their responses will help children develop self-control. Learning of this nature can be initiated in the classroom, provided some activities have definite starting and ending points. Practice the starts and stops on a signal. Visual and tactile clues will help the child mark passages of time.

Some of the activities in Resource Chapter 1 are specifically designed to support children who have ADHD. Activities such as 1–37w, *One More*, help children think of many different solutions for a problem. Activity 1–44w, *Feelings*, helps children identify their feelings. Activity 1–46w, *I'm Thinking of*, is like the game "20 Questions," where children ask yes–no questions until they can answer the question. This increases children's awareness of not having enough information.

● ● ●
Social Competence

Help children feel comfortable about seeking assistance (many children with ADHD will not ask for help). Gradually reduce the amount of assistance, but keep in mind that these children need more help for a longer time than a typically developing child. Evaluate your own behavior: Do you reward more than you discipline? This ratio impacts self-esteem. Support children immediately for any and all demonstrations of good behavior until those behaviors are well established. Encourage children in a variety of ways; change rewards that are not effective in motivating behavioral change. Teach the child to reward herself. Encourage positive self-talk ("You did very well remaining in your seat today. How do you feel about that?"). This encourages the child to think positively about herself.

Children need to increase their awareness of their own feelings and those of others. They also need experience in differentiating between feelings and behavior: "It's okay to be mad at Sara; it is not okay to hit her." Help children learn to express both positive and negative feelings in socially acceptable ways. They can run, poke playdough, or hit a punching bag. They need to consciously decide how they will deal with their feelings. They may also need to learn expressions and gestures that show others that they are happy and like them, and may need help making and keeping friends. Social skills are the foundation of being a successful part of groups and establishing friendships. These skills develop during the early childhood years and lay the foundation for social relationships throughout life.

1. Work on identifying feelings. Help children learn the specific facial configurations of different emotions. Go beyond happy and sad to angry, hurt, surprised, scared, jealous, embarrassed, and so on. Discuss when children might have these feelings and what they want to happen.

2. Encourage children to make books about their feelings: "When I felt … ." See Activity 1–44w, *Feelings*.

3. Support positive self-talk: "I can … ," "I like … ," and "I'm good at … ."

4. Use vignettes, puppets, and dolls to pose social problems to children, and ask what they might do if they were the child in the vignette. Get at least four responses for each scenario. As you get each response, consider it from the children's point of view, and discuss how they might feel. Have children role-play. The goal is to help them develop a repertoire of skills for assessing and joining groups, and for figuring out which skills to apply under what set of circumstances.

5. Once children have figured out how to join the group, a different set of skills is necessary for maintaining group membership. Teach these as well.

All children need to feel they belong. They need to appreciate and learn from differences as well as similarities. They all need to feel that they contribute to the group.

1. Help children view events from various perspectives. Increase children's awareness of the uniqueness of self.

2. Support children as problem solvers. Encourage children by sharing problems about broken crayons, markers that dry out, and other current problems. As children begin to see themselves as problem solvers, begin to talk about problems in the classroom, and brainstorm about how these problems might be resolved.

3. As children play with others, teachers should help them see others' perspectives and the consequences of social actions.

• • • Social Studies

Children construct their understanding of the world based on their experiences. They try out their ideas in social situations and get feedback: positive or negative. Sometimes objects or events challenge the child's working model of his world and he is then forced to adjust the model and alter the mental structures that support that sociocultural model (Copple & Bredekamp, 2009). Children should be presented with diverse social situations and a culturally rich classroom to get an accurate working model of the global world in which we live. As concerns about school violence increase, it becomes imperative that we teach children about their immediate social world as well as the larger one in which they will live and grow.

1. Emphasize group belonging and the courtesy extended to other group members: property rights, space to play, and including others. Discuss how children feel when they are not included, their toys are taken, or their space is invaded. Also, discuss ways of dealing with these feelings.

2. Talk to children about oral histories and why they are important. Ask children about their own oral histories with questions like "What do you remember about being little?" "What stories does your family tell about when you were little?" "Are these stories written down?" Invite children to talk to their parents and

Reading instruction is individualized, with some children listening to books as they follow along with the printed version.
©Cengage Learning 2012

grandparents about their memories and to record or write their responses or to ask adult family members to do so. Encourage children to expand on this and to talk and write about family customs and the holidays they celebrate.

English Language Arts

Communication is important to all children. This is the information age. Communication, whether spoken or written, formal or informal, English or another language, on paper or electronic, is the cornerstone for conveying information. Children need skills in both expressive and receptive language. These skills develop in the context of social interactions and are based on the child's cultural experience. Effective communicators master the skills of both speaking and listening in the context of turn taking. Some children with ADHD have problems with the listening part. For children with a high activity level, having to *just* listen may seem close to punishment. Children also need to develop print awareness and skills in reading and writing.

• • • Speaking and Listening

Help children with ADHD develop the words to connect their speech and language to their behavior. Encourage them to use **self-talk** as a way of regulating and making sense out of their behavior. Support them in learning to talk through situations based on anticipating what may happen and as a way of reflecting on what did happen.

1. Encourage children to ask questions, help them focus their questions, and support their listening to the answers.

2. Encourage children to restate directions for each other.

3. Support children's speaking by active listening.

4. Paraphrase and summarize what children say.

5. During group times, use physical signals to help children organize their bodies as they listen. A carpet

square or "X" made with masking tape may help. As children become more competent, replace these with verbal reminders. Children need to learn to control their bodies without external cues, so they don't become dependent on them.

Listening is difficult, especially for children who are ready to move. Gain the child's attention before speaking. Speak slowly, but not so slowly that it is exaggerated. When giving directions to children with ADHD, maintain eye contact and make verbal instructions clear and concise. Be consistent with daily instructions. Simplify complex directions. Avoid multiple commands. Make sure children comprehend the instructions before beginning the task. If they don't, repeat instructions in a calm, positive manner. Recognize when a child is tired and give her a break. This may be the wrong time for concentrated listening.

1. Use gestures when they support what you are saying but are not distracting.
2. Use words that guide behaviors such as *first*, *next*, and *last*, and help children pick these out while they listen.
3. If children don't seem to understand, restate what has been misunderstood, rather than repeating all of the information.
4. Check for comprehension by asking the child questions; then go to a new topic.

Reading

Children need to be literate in many aspects of reading and they need to learn about the function that written language serves. They need to know about **environmental print**, such as road signs, price tags, schedules, familiar logos, and so on. **Occupational print** might be a menu for a waiter, health records for a medical professional, or a blueprint for a builder. **Informational print** is found on calendars, newspapers, informational texts, and reference books. **Recreational print** is used for leisure, such as stories, novels, magazines, and poetry. Children need to be exposed to a variety of print sources and to understand their functions.

1. Help children identify the characteristics of pictures and photographs and discuss what is happening in them. Give children time to formulate their answers. Add to the picture by saying such things as "What do you think will happen if someone appears and … ?"
2. Help children reflect on their feelings after a book has been read. Encourage them to think about what they might do if they were one of the characters in the story. See whether they can remember a similar story and how the characters were both the same and different.
3. Encourage children to respond to reading through the arts, dramatic play, building, and so on.
4. Provide opportunities for children to learn a sight vocabulary. Begin with their names. Read books with

low lexile ratings, and then have children read the story to you.
5. Expose children to a variety of **genres**, the categories of language used to classify form and content. Genre is shaped by the purposes of the writer and the needs of the audience. It helps children know what to expect. Stories are an important genre during early childhood, but children should also be exposed to story telling, poems, rhymes, and informational texts.

Books can be entertaining and enlightening for children. Choose them carefully and read them interactively with interest and expression.

1. Keep books short until children become accustomed to listening to them. It is better to read a 5-page story that the children sit through attentively than to read a 20-page story with 20 interruptions.
2. Use stories that support participation. Children can move the flannelboard characters to follow the story, as well as make predictions about what will happen.
3. Read stories in small groups, where you can individualize the story and your attention. Ask children questions about how the illustrations support the text.

Writing

Encourage children to think of themselves as authors. Writing is a difficult, complex task. And initially, there is little satisfaction until others can read what is written. Support prewriting skills as well as alternative writing procedures like word processing. Have a variety of materials (pencils, markers, crayons, rubber stamps, papers of many sizes and colors, cards, etc.) so children can find materials that both appeal to them and are easy to use.

1. Support children's attempts at writing. Like language, writing is culturally based. If children see a written language other than English at home, their writing may look different from children who have seen only written English.
2. Attach a visual strip of letters and numbers to the writing area or, as children become older, each desk so that children have a visual model.
3. Teach children how to use the index finger of the nonwriting hand to identify the letter or word they want to copy.
4. Place an arrow → on the left corner of the writing desk, and have the child put his paper below the arrow. Explain that you move in the direction of the arrow.
5. Encourage children to use the keyboard if they find writing to be a laborious process. Children can use software such as My First Amazing Diary (ages 5 to 9) with which they can fill in facts and answer questions as well as write. It gives some structure and variety to the writing experience. As children reach age 8, there are many programs that teach typing and other forms of writing. See Activity 2–26, *My Diary*.

Language

Help children develop the vocabulary to express their frustrations and to use language to do this effectively.

1. If children want to write but have trouble with spacing, draw a space on the paper for each letter or word. Point out the first word in a sentence, put two lines under it, and talk about capitalization. Help children use punctuation at the end of sentences. This is easier if they know what they want to say, because you can space out the letters and the distance between words more accurately.

2. Choose stories that deal with feelings, including hostile or unhappy feelings as well as happy ones. Point out the vocabulary used in the story and how it relates to the character's feelings. See the Children's Bibliography.

Discovery

Children are curious about their world. They want to understand it and how their actions impact it. Discovery needs to be integrated all through the curriculum, especially dramatic play. The underlying concepts of math and science can be found throughout the early childhood classroom. Number symbols can be on price tags, play money, shoe sizes, or rulers. You can count the grocery store items purchased, chairs at the table, or the number of items at the sand or water table. Children can count and classify blocks, beads, or buttons. They can put them in sets and add or subtract them. They can even write out and solve simple equations. Part–whole relationships can be taught as children slice an apple or eat a piece of whole-wheat pizza. Use science and math processes to help children grasp the sequences of behaviors and also the consequences of actions, including those that may be unsafe.

Children learn about science through cooking or by watching a liquid turn into a solid, observing what happens when heat is applied, or watching ice melt. Science and math are all around. Children can be helped to remember the sequence of activities through the use of a digital camera. Computer software and the Internet can bring science to children. They can visit the Exploratorium in San Francisco (www.exploratorium.org) or the Franklin Institute Science Museum in Philadelphia (www2.fi.edu/), even if they live in North Dakota.

Mathematics

Mathematics is crucial for problem solving. The goal is depth of understanding of the concepts that underlie mathematics, as opposed to the memorization of facts. Children can work in groups on problems generated by both the teacher and the children. Math has to be real for young children.

1. Provide running commentary whenever possible to help children make connections between mathematics, the language of math, and its use in the real world: "You drank half of your water." "You have one piece of cheese yet to eat." "We have two empty chairs at this table."

2. Help children develop concepts of patterning and seriating, starting with simple repeating patterns (e.g., red, yellow, red, yellow), not only by showing them blocks but also by looking at clothing for check patterns and more complex patterns like plaids. See whether children can repeat these patterns with blocks or Unifix Cubes. Help them see the utility of patterns in their daily life as a method of organization.

3. Provide children with picture sequences of the class routine. Ask children what is going on in each of the pictures. Then mix up the sequences in silly ways ("Go home *before* you come to school," "Wash your hands *before* you go to the bathroom") and talk about this with children. Help children develop sequences in their own behavior, for example, with an after-school sequence that incorporates getting necessary work done and going outside to play (or vice versa).

4. Teach children the vocabulary of time (such as *age, morning, soon, next, calendar, weekend*), and use time informally by incorporating it into art (e.g., drawing a night picture) and social studies (e.g., special occasions and holidays). Encourage children to use timers outside, to see how far they can run before the timer goes off, or in dramatic play. Again, use time as an organizational device. Setting a timer to work on a particular project provides boundaries and may make tasks doable. Consider the developmental level of the child as you consider the time span. It is better to get great concentration for a short time than to struggle to keep it for a longer time. Gradually increase time concepts based on positive experiences.

Science

Like math, science is often crucial for problem solving. Discovery is an accurate description of science during the early childhood years, and perhaps after. Children need to learn the basic processes of science, such as observing, comparing, classifying, measuring, and communicating. These extend into inferring, predicting, hypothesizing, and defining and controlling variables (Charlesworth & Lind, 2009). This is the early childhood version of the scientific method.

1. Encourage children to use their senses in isolation and combination. Observation involves all of the senses. Children need to become accurate observers. Encourage children to look at photographs and pictures in books and to tell you what they see. Help them look for additional items in the picture. You want children to pick up details as well as the major event. Then make them into picture *detectives*, using clues to interpret what is going on in the picture. Do the same thing with hearing; encourage them to close their eyes. As you play a piece of music, have them describe what they hear. Talk about tone, tempo, and pitch. Using their kinesthetic sense, have children reach into a bag and describe the object in the bag, or

have them choose between two objects and ask them to describe the objects. Keep the task simple and short at the beginning. Support the development of specific vocabulary.

2. Classification skills underlie both science and math skills. For children with ADHD, one purpose in teaching these skills is to help keep children safe. Classify food-type items as to whether they are safe to eat or drink. Classify people who are safe to talk to if a child is lost. Think about the environment and what is geographically and culturally safe. Classify behavior as safe (e.g., piling blocks) and unsafe (e.g., throwing blocks).

3. Cause and effect reasoning, or learning the predictable consequences of events, is important. It may help children develop inner controls and control impulsivity in some situations. Encourage children to answer questions such as "What happens if . . .?" "What could you do about . . .?" "Is there anything else you could do?" And, if possible, have them test out their responses. Help children think through actions before performing them and predicting the consequences.

4. Children will give incorrect answers and make inaccurate predictions. One way to handle this is to frame it as part of the scientific method. Talk about the scientists who work to come up with solutions and often get many wrong answers before they get the right one. Help children see mistakes as a natural part of the learning process.

••• Technology

Technology offers children opportunities to explore, learn, and play, either alone or with friends. It enables them to have a sense of control and do extraordinary things. They can make decisions, change decisions, and develop the skills to work cooperatively with others. Technology can capture moments that children want to remember; digital pictures can support children's memories of events and allows them to share with their families what they have done at school. Technology supports many accommodations for children with disabilities: speech synthesizers allow the computer to talk to the child, switches can take the place of the keyboard, and alternative keyboards can be used. Touch windows can control the computer, electronic tablets are a good size and very portable. Children like technology. We, as adults, may have our doubts, but children do not share them.

1. Modify computers and other input devices to meet the needs of the children in your classroom.

2. Identify software and websites that support children's learning. Share this information with families if they have computers at home. If they do not have computers at home, encourage families to go to the public library and use their computers.

3. Encourage children to use a word processor or computer for schoolwork. Help them use spell and grammar checks as a way to learn which words they have misspelled, to see their mistakes, and to learn the accurate spelling and use of words.

4. Use a digital camera to enhance children's memory skills and to encourage complexity in their development. Instead of children just building with blocks, see whether they can replicate what they built in the past and then decide on the changes they want to make.

5. Use a digital camera to talk about perspective taking. Start with the concrete. Take a picture of a child from the front, back, and each side. Print the pictures. Talk about the differences from each angle. Use this to transition into talking about behavior. Take pictures of a child with a toy or material and a picture of a child who wants this toy or is grabbing it (or use other situations that occur in your classroom). Have children pose for these pictures so you are not singling out children who engage in this behavior. Talk about the picture from each child's perspective. The power in this technique is that it is immediate; it uses the children in your classroom to illustrate the points you are making, and it does not involve the specific children who typically engage in such behavior. Use this technique to talk to the class at a time when the children are not emotionally involved in what is going on.

6. Many well-known magazines and programs have websites designed for children:

   • *National Geographic* has a kids' section. (www.nationalgeographic.com/)

   • *Owl Kids* is a science site for children and *OWL* is a Canadian nature magazine for children younger than age 8. (http://owlkids.com/)

   • *Reading Rainbow* is designed to encourage a love of books and reading among children ages 4–8. (http://pbskids.org/readingrainbow/)

This is just a small sample. There are many more and many categories of sites as well. See the Educational Resources section at the end of the Resources chapters.

Wellness

Moving is part of life. Movement increasingly comes under the child's control and gradually become more efficient and skillful. Children learn adaptive skills, allowing them increasing independence and control of their bodies. With independence comes increased risk. As children move farther and faster, they can place themselves in situations in which they need to make judgments about what is safe and healthy. Children need to be aware of specific practices that place them at risk. They need to learn to use the muscles in their bodies in concert with their senses to explore their world.

Health and Safety

This is an important curriculum area for children with ADHD, who, even at an early age, may have seen a variety of specialists, perhaps had an electroencephalogram (EEG) and taken medication, and who may have some fears about health professionals. Children must cooperate in medical testing and report their reactions to medicine they may be taking, so developing good rapport between children and medical personnel is important. Increase body awareness so children can locate body parts and then respond about how specific parts feel. Teach children about nutrition and junk foods.

1. Work on traffic signs and teach children to control impulsive behavior that may lead to accidents. Use activities such as 4–2, *Stop and Go*, and 4–33w, *Warning Signs*, to teach children about safety signs and their implications for behavior.

2. Talk about injury prevention. Help children see the relationship between actions and results (e.g., what may happen if someone runs in front of a tricycle, bicycle, or car).

3. State and post class safety rules, especially those in which children could be hurt (e.g., standing on chairs and tables, running with scissors, throwing things).

4. When children initially engage in some unsafe practice, such as climbing the fence instead of the jungle gym, make your limits clear but situational: "*At school*, you may not climb on the fence. If you want to climb, you may climb on the jungle gym." Be prepared to reinforce this statement physically if necessary: Help the child climb down from the fence and walk her over to the jungle gym.

5. Integrate food preparation into the curriculum through snacks and lunch. Discuss nutrition. Help children learn about the relationships among growth, food, and health. Include cultural variations of good food. Use familiar and unfamiliar foods. Serve fruits and vegetables for snack that the children help prepare (e.g., use Activity 3–30, *Fruit Kabob*).

6. Discuss where foods grow, and compare fresh foods with canned or frozen foods. Talk about food additives and food allergies. See Activity 3–23, *Food Forms*.

7. Talk about common health problems of children (colds, ear infections, stomachaches, headaches), and ask children to identify the symptoms of each. Talk with children about ways to prevent illness and how illnesses are treated.

8. Talk about healthy lifestyles and the need for nutritious eating and exercise. Discuss the role of doctors and the medicines they prescribe in helping children stay healthy and helping them return to health after they have been sick.

9. Ensure your snacks are nutritionally sound. Evaluate them based on calories and nutrition. Add low-fat cream cheese to crackers or rice cakes, and put cut-up vegetables on them to make faces. In a group snack, children might eat this, whereas they may not at home. Dip fruit or vegetables in yogurt or low-fat salad dressing. Make choices that are good for all children.

Physical Education

Children can use large motor activities to release frustration, tension, and anger. If they do not do this independently, encourage them. Participating in physical activities helps children develop feelings of belonging to a group. Practice fundamental motor skills. Children need many and varied opportunities to practice.

1. Obtain a punching bag and encourage children who feel like hitting to hit the bag (not just to hit it once or tap it lightly, but to hit it hard and frequently).

2. Provide balls for throwing and kicking. Encourage children to kick the ball and then run after it and kick it again, or to kick the ball at a target like a plastic milk bottle. See Activities 4–39w, *Target Bounce*; 4–18, *Variations on Throwing*; and 4–40w, *Variations on Dribbling*.

3. Spot children who are using equipment to climb high. Teach them safety rules. Ensure that the surfaces beneath equipment children could fall off of are safe.

4. Encourage cooperative sports.

5. Motor skills need to be practiced and, over time, refined and mastered. They develop in a predictable order. Incorporate these skills into your everyday planning. See Activities 4–14, *Variations on Running*, and 4–38w, *Variations on Hopping*.

6. Help children develop a physically active lifestyle. Lifetime habits can be developed during the early childhood years.

Many children with ADHD find small motor skills such as cutting challenging.
©Cengage Learning 2012

• • •
Sensory Motor Integration

Sensory motor integration requires children to use the information they receive from their senses to understand where their body is in space, to understand what is heard in the environment, to coordinate both sides of their body, to develop fine motor skills including eye–hand coordination, to process movement, and to respond to touch. Sensory integration encompasses quite a list, but it is possible to modify the level of sensory motor integration required in many activities. Before you modify an activity for a child, decide on the value of the activity. Is this something the child really needs to learn how to do, in and of itself, or is it a basis for later essential skills? If it is important, then modify the activity to allow the child to participate; if not, let it go.

1. Observe the skill level of the children by playing simple games that children should have the skills to do. If they cannot, try to analyze where in the system the process is breaking down. If it is in understanding the directions, give them directions one at a time. If it is motor planning, model or physically help children move through the actions.

2. Children come with different skill levels. Focus children who are more advanced in a skill on the next step in the developmental process. If children can catch large balls, then decrease the size of the ball for these children. If children are struggling with a skill, coach them. Although almost all children learn basic motor skills, they do not perfect them without coaching. Activities that are too easy or too difficult tend to elicit disruptive behavior.

3. Find out from children what is more important to them: the process or the outcome. If the outcome is important, use this knowledge to build their motivation and persistence. Help children understand the steps necessary to achieve the outcome, and support the accomplishment of each step in the process.

4. Use activities that require coordinating both sides of the body, such as hand clapping. Provide opportunities for hands and fingers to work together with Legos, pop beads, stringing beads, sewing, cooking, woodworking, and so on.

5. For some children, organizing personal belongings is challenging. Try to limit the number of items children have at school. Talk about strategies for organizing personal belongings.

6. Encourage children to pour at the water table. The emphasis here is on accuracy. Can they pour different amounts of sand, seeds, or liquid from a pitcher into a smaller container? This requires them to use eye–hand coordination and to control the force and angle of their pouring.

7. As children develop prewriting and writing skills, have them practice in a variety of ways: writing on sand, aluminum foil, using stencils, and so on.

Small motor skills are challenging for many children. Developmentally, the large muscles of the trunk must first have developed in order to provide the stability that allows the use of the small muscles. Small muscles are used for writing and for manipulative and adaptive skills.

1. Teach adaptive skills in naturally occurring situations. Allow time for children to learn the skills—they are part of the early childhood curriculum.

2. To the extent that fine motor skills are challenging, ensure that children participate in these activities. This is the only way the skills will develop. Have children participate for several short times over the course of the day.

3. Encourage children to use their fine motor skills in a variety of positions, such as standing, sitting, and lying down. Vary heights of tables.

4. Use adaptive equipment to make skills easier. Adaptive handles on scissors, spoons, and pencils make them easier to hold, but consider this an interim step. As children become more proficient, gradually stop using the modification.

5. Integrate fine motor skills into program areas that children enjoy. If children like technology, they will be motivated to develop the skills necessary to use it. If children particularly like dramatic play, then include activities that require fine motor skills as part of what is going on in that area.

Creative Arts

Creative arts allow children to develop and practice necessary skills and movements in a safe way. An emphasis on creativity encourages children to think outside the box and allows them to explore and take chances; because there is little possibility for failure—differences, yes, failure, no—creative arts allow children to experiment and practice.

• • •
Visual Arts

Children should be exposed to a variety of art forms and processes. They need to work on individual projects and to be included with others on murals and collages. They need to see art and learn about artists. They need to look at illustrations in books and learn about illustrators. Help children see themselves as artists and illustrators.

1. Talk about art—not just about the picture, but about what they like and don't like about a particular picture. Bring in sculpture to share with them. If possible, bring in very good art (in books, reproductions, or from the Web) and compare it to other art (not art that children create, but not from well-known artists either). Ask the

children to talk about what they have learned, and ask whether they want to incorporate any of the ideas into their own art.

2. Use three-dimensional materials such as clay and playdough. These can be good for releasing tension and are reusable and easily stored; they are available on short notice.

3. Include some art materials that accommodate expansive work. Have children color or paint on very large paper without restrictions, or they can use fingerpaint on the table and then lay paper over the paint and press down to make a paper "print" of their picture.

4. Encourage art that does not require cutting with scissors or precise fine motor skills. Tear paper, or use larger brushes, bigger paper, markers, sparkle glue, and so on. See Activity 5–35w, *Torn Paper Flowers*.

Music

Music is an essential part of who we are as a people and as a nation. It is also a way to explore other cultures. Music is a field of its own, yet it provides many opportunities to learn about other areas. Integrating music with other curriculum areas encourages the development of concepts and provides interesting and varied ways of practicing skills.

1. Paint to music. Be sure the music has a distinctive mood. Talk about this with the children. Ask how it influenced the colors they chose and what they painted. See Activity 5–44w, *Mood Colors*.

2. Sing songs with motions (e.g., "My Bonnie Lies Over the Ocean," "Hey, Betty Martin") and those that create body awareness (e.g., "Put Your Finger in the Air," "Head, Shoulders, Knees, and Toes"). See Activity 5–16, *Sequencing Songs*.

3. Introduce music and songs that are stylistically different from traditional "American" music. Include chants, bells, drums, and so on. Help children focus on the differences and similarities. Or listen to music that depicts natural events that may be less familiar to children. They might listen to the CD *African Rainforest* by Putumaya Kids, available at www.putumayo.com/en/putumayo_kids.htm and draw pictures of what they think the sounds represent.

4. Include music from different parts of the United States and from different cultural/ethnic groups. Help children think about the differences in the music and why the specific groups might have developed different music.

5. Sing songs to practice vocabulary. Listen to the song first so that you know what words children will need to know, and go over them briefly before singing the song. For example, sing along with "Shake Something," which uses the vocabulary words: shake, up and down, round

and round, bend and unbend, twist back and forth, side to side, fast and slow. "Circle Game" practices the spatial vocabulary: around, inside, out of, over, above, below, to the side, between, behind, in front, forward, backward, under, through. Both of these songs are on the CD titled *Getting to Know Myself* by Hap Palmer, available at http://cdbaby.com/cd/happalmer21.

6. Use music to release energy. If bad weather has kept children indoors, play salsa music or a Sousa march.

7. Use music to help children settle down. If children are excited before a quiet time, encourage them to march, then jump, then twirl, and repeat it all again for 3 to 5 minutes. When they are tired help them relax with some "easy listening" music.

8. Encourage children to find patterns in the songs they sing at group time. In the song "Good Morning," the pattern is AAB: "Good morning, good morning, good morning to you." The CD title is *We All Live Together*. "Number Rock" on the same CD includes counting forward and backward by Greg and Steve.

Movement and Dance

Encourage children to move for a particular purpose or in response to a stimulus such as music. Creative movement requires children to take an experience that is familiar to them and to interpret it with their bodies.

1. Encourage children to dance to music with different tempos. Include dances and music from a variety of cultures and those that are stylistically different (e.g., waltz, country line dancing, ballroom dancing, tango, calypso, hip hop). Help children analyze the differences.

2. Show children ice melting and have them be ice that is melting in the sun. Or they could be a snowman that melts. You can also have them freeze. Talk about the fact that this is a gradual process, and have them think about what parts melt or freeze first and why.

3. Do animal walks. Talk about the characteristics of different animals and how they move. Discuss the relationship between movement and body type (e.g., turtle vs. cheetah) and how movement is adaptive.

4. Encourage children to think about different surfaces and how they would walk through or on them (e.g., sand, water, a mattress, a hot surface, a very cold surface, a slippery surface, a gooey surface, a moving surface). Have children think about how they will move, and then have all children demonstrate their version of it. Talk about the characteristics that influence their choices. Have them think about the shoes they might like to have as they traverse these surfaces.

Dramatic Play and Theater

Dramatic play and theater support children in learning about their world in an environment in which they can be in control. They can rehearse new roles and replay familiar ones. They can camp in a tent, construct a beaver dam, or play "house." Children's interests and the teacher's philosophy drive the area. Play can be spontaneous or in response to a script.

1. Encourage children to build structures for various climates and uses. Ask them to suggest supplies they need for the construction area, such as fabric, dowels, netting, and so on, to build their structures. Examples of some designs children could make are listed here:

   - A house for a climate that is hot and rainy
   - A school in a climate where it is almost always cold and often dark
   - A store where the temperature changes seasonally

2. Help children role-play different medical roles and what these professionals do and look for. Provide the necessary supports. Incorporate technology using websites such as www.uniquely-adhd.com/add_adhd.html to provide pictures of the brain.

3. Talk about plays and how they differ from television and other screen productions. Encourage children to make books into plays.

Routines and Transitions

Routines and transitions are challenging and often a difficult time for children. Structuring them well helps children with ADHD.

1. Employ auditory and visual cues to signal changes in the daily routine.

2. Decrease the number of required transitions as much as possible; plan those you must have carefully.

3. Try using code words, songs, or visual cues to help the child anticipate and make the transition.

4. Prepare children for upcoming transitions. Try a warning of "five more minutes" or a song to begin the transition.

5. If children need to take medication, build it into a routine or transition so it is seen as a natural part of the day.

6. Let the child know specifically how and what needs to be done to move to the next activity. Express positive reinforcement and recognition of the child's ability to finish and make the transition.

SUMMARY

- Children with ADHD may have problems with attention, hyperactivity, and/or impulsivity.
- Somewhere between 2 percent and 7 percent of children are identified as having ADHD.
- ADHD is primarily an inherited genetic problem related to neurotransmitters.
- Medication is one intervention used for some children with ADHD.
- Many children with ADHD have comorbid conditions such as learning disabilities or emotional disorders, and these must be included in the intervention plan to meet the child's needs.
- Children with ADHD who meet the criteria for "other health impairments" will have an IEP.
- Children with ADHD may have a 504 accommodation plan.
- ADHD is difficult to diagnose because the behaviors that mark ADHD are typical for young children.

  Effective interventions include behavior management plans both at home and at school.

EDUCATIONAL RESOURCES

American Academy of Child and Adolescent Psychiatry is a public service for professionals and families to support the understanding and treatment of children with developmental, behavioral, and mental disorders. www.aacap.org/

Attention Deficit Disorder Association provides national information on education, research and public advocacy but little information on young children. www.add.org/

Children and Adults with Attention Deficit Disorder (CHADD) emphasizes family and community support, as well as encourages scientific research. It is a great resource for parents and professionals with many fact sheets and provides many useful links. www.chadd.org/

School and Me with ADD! is a national organization that supports parents, teachers, and children with attention-deficit disorder, with special pages for home-school interactions. www.add.org/main/kids/school.htm/

For additional resources, visit the book companion website for this text at www.cengagebrain.com.

Children with Communication Disorders

11

I didn't talk as a young child. Well, I said things, but no one could understand what I was saying. My sister Mary was 10 months older, and they would use her to interpret what I was saying. I am one of five children, each separated by about a year. I am the middle child. I remember the debate over whether I'd be allowed to go to preschool. I also remember people being so mean and teasing me, saying, "Can't you speak English? Are you speaking German?" At the time, I neither knew what "German" meant nor "English," but how they made me feel came across loud and clear. I did not speak for a long time, even when I had needs. I showed someone. Often my parents didn't have the time to wait and told me, "Just say what you want." Then I did without.

I don't know why they finally decided to take me to a specialist. With five kids, we rarely saw doctors of any kind. What's interesting is how they arrived at the conclusion that I was not "retarded." My receptive language skills were not in sync with the expressive ones. I not only misplaced words but apparently mixed up letter placement as well. I do not remember going back for any type of follow-up therapy. Apparently, knowing that I wasn't "retarded" was all they were concerned about.

I remember, vividly, stopping before I opened my mouth and thinking of the action and the steps involved before I could tell an event in the right order; it wasn't that I didn't know the order, but I skipped to the end and then returned to the next thing. I felt I was living in a world where I could produce sounds, but not put them in an order that could be understood.

Because I could not get the words out, I was unable to defend myself when blamed for stuff I didn't do. The more stressed out I became, the worse things got. I remember trying so hard and knowing exactly what I wanted to say. I would try but get these blank stares, and I would have to wait until Mary got home from school to translate, if she felt like it. When my parents took the time to tell me to "slow down," rather than "hurry up, we don't have all day," I had time enough to order the words or letters, once I knew which sounds went with what words.

The last time the other kids on the block teased me about my speech was when I clobbered Pammy Pantalo over the head with Anne's book bag. She had been teasing me so much and was much larger than me. Anne, my oldest sister, was in kindergarten, and I was about 3. After a number of remarks like

©Cengage Learning 2012

"Look at the baby; she can't even talk yet—can't talk, stupid, stupid, stupid," I took Anne's red-and-black-plaid book bag and hit her over the head with it. I distinctly remember her mother bringing Pammy to the house and wanting to speak to Mom. I hid behind the stairwell until her mother accused my sister of picking on her charming Pammy and wanted to know why Anne didn't pick on someone her own size. (Our family was tall; Pammy was average from what I can remember.) When Mom ordered Anne to come and "'fess up," Anne said, "Oh that wasn't me. I gave Paula my book bag because I would have missed, and I knew she would hit her." When Pammy's mother found out it was me, she dragged Pammy home, scolding her daughter for making her look stupid, because I was so much younger and not even Pammy's size yet. I guess I learned early that I needed to stand up for my rights. I remember well the loneliness and isolation. It helps me still today to read aloud to no one, or to the dog if I find my mind racing.

I remember needing to put a great deal of effort into talking. Gram would help by repeating what she thought I was trying to say, or part of it, and asking me to fill in the blanks. When we moved to Maryland, I was placed in speech class, but that had more to do with my strong New York accent—compounded with the Irish brogue I learned from Gram—and specific sounds I couldn't say. I was relieved that two other kids in my class, both boys, had the same problem. We all froze up when asked to read to the rest of the class. All through third grade we encouraged one another. None of us had a problem understanding one another's "skip talk." ❈

Communication

Some children come to school as "talkers." They immediately want to know why they are in school, why they can't go outside now, where the crayons are . . . until you think you may change your profession if you hear one more question. These children stick in your mind from day one. Then there are the children who appear shy and immature and of whom you probably still won't have a clear picture even after a few weeks. This group is difficult, as it is hard to determine whether these children choose not to communicate or do not have the ability to communicate. A third group is composed of children who have a diagnosed language or communication disorder.

One of the first questions to ask when you are concerned about communication is, Can this child communicate in an age-appropriate way that can be understood by others? Then think back over events of the week. When you dismiss the children from group time by the color of their clothes, does this child need to be prompted? When you give simple directions, can this child follow them? How about more complex directions? Does this child volunteer comments? Does the child speak up during group time? When this child speaks, can you understand most of the words or only some of them? Given free choice, does this child seek out activities requiring language, or does he avoid them? How can you tell whether the child falls in that wide range called typical or whether he has an impairment?

The next concern relates to your observation: Is what you hear representative of the child's speech? Children are very adaptable in their communication styles and use language differently when talking with a peer than they do with an adult. They also adapt their speech to situations. Young children's language in school differs from that at home. When at home, the child typically displays more frequent, longer, and more balanced conversations over a wider range of topics than she does at school. Children who are quiet at school may be nonstop talkers at home. Given this, it is important to find out from a child's family how representative the speech is that you are hearing.

Defining Communication Disorders

I have purposefully used *language*, *communication*, and *speech* as if they were interchangeable. Although there is much overlap, there are also some important distinctions. **Communication** is the process by which information is transmitted between two or more individuals. It involves a sender, who encodes information, and a receiver, whose job it is to decode the information. This information can be verbal or nonverbal, symbolic or nonsymbolic, widely understood or colloquial, human or nonhuman. **Language** has functions other than communication. It is a cognitive tool that is used to organize information and influences thinking and memory skills. **Speech** is an aspect of language: spoken language. Disorders of spoken language include speech disorders, articulation disorders, and fluency disorders.

According to IDEA 2004:

Speech or language impairment is a communication disorder, such as stuttering, impaired articulation, a language impairment, or a voice impairment, that adversely affects a child's educational performance.

The American Psychiatric Association (APA) (2000) is more specific than the IDEA. They identify expressive language disorders, mixed receptive-expressive disorders, phonological disorders, and fluency disorders.

Expressive Language Disorder

Although the actual diagnostic features vary with age, the APA identifies an **expressive language disorder** as one in which the child's expressive language development is substantially below the norms for a child's age, based on a measure of nonverbal intellectual capacity and receptive language development. These requirements ensure that it is viewed separately from an intellectual disability, a speech-motor or sensory deficit, linguistic differences, or environmental deprivation. Symptoms of an expressive language disorder include limited vocabulary, making errors in tense, having problems recalling words, and using sentences that lack length and complexity, based on the age of the child. And these problems interfere with academic or social communication (APA, 2000).

Mixed Receptive-Expressive Disorder

In a **mixed receptive-expressive language disorder** both receptive and expressive language are below the norms on standardized tests. In addition to the characteristics described for expressive language disorders, children with receptive language impairments have difficulty understanding words and sentences or specific types of words. Because the development of expressive language is dependent upon receptive language, a purely receptive language disorder is almost never identified. What differentiates this disorder from the expressive language is the comprehension deficit (APA, 2000). Communication disorders vary depending upon the severity and the age of the child; to be classified as a disorder, they must interfere with academic or social communication.

Phonological Disorder

Phonological disorders involve errors in sound production, use, representation, or organization, based on the child's age and dialect. In some cases, one sound is substituted for another, or sounds are omitted from words, and these phonological problems interfere with academic or social communication. Phonological disorders were formerly called developmental articulation disorders (APA, 2000).

Fluency Disorder

A fluency disorder, or stuttering, is a developmentally inappropriate disturbance in normal fluency and the time patterning of speech, and interferes with academic or social communication (APA, 2000).

TABLE
11-1 SPECIFIC COMMUNICATION DISORDERS BY TYPE, APPROXIMATE AGE AND PERCENTAGE OF CHILDREN AFFECTED

Type of Disorder	Age	Percent of Children
Expressive language	Birth to age 3	10–15
	School age	3–7
Mixed receptive/expressive	Preschool	5
	School age	3
Articulation/phonological	6- and 7-year-olds	2
	17-year-olds	0.5
Fluency (stuttering)	Children	1
	Adolescents	0.8

Source: APA, 2000.

Prevalence of Communication Disorders

Problems with the overlapping of categories of communication disorders impact our ability to identify how many children actually have communication disorders. In 2007–2008, 13.4 percent of children were identified as having a disability. Of this group, 3 percent had speech or language impairments and received services through the IDEA (NCES, 2010).

The APA (2000) estimates are based on age and type of impairment. Although the ages they use are not exact, they show developmental progression and the effectiveness of development and intervention in ameliorating these disorders. See Table 11-1.

Causes of Communication Disorders

Communication disorders can have a genetic, neurological, structural, physiological, psychological, emotional, or cognitive base (Stuart, 2007). They can be related to late maturation or an unstimulating environment and also to cultural and language differences. Although English is the primary language of the United States, there are regional differences, and dialects such as African American English, which use a different set of linguistic rules. In addition, English language learners must be considered.

Communication is a complex process that involves different regions of the brain that regulate, integrate, and formulate communicative messages (Stuart, 2007). Communication is also dependent upon the lungs, larynx, vocal cords, throat, nose, mouth, lips, and other body parts. Communication involves many areas of the brain, some more than others. Broca's speech production area is in the frontal lobe; Wernicke's speech comprehension area is located in the temporal lobe (Yaun & Keating, 2007). Problems in any of these areas can cause a speech or language problem.

Sound enters primarily through the ear and travels through the auditory nerve to the auditory cortex, which

signals Wernicke's area, where the neurons for combinations of sounds are activated. Neurons can store a variety of information about a particular sound combination. If the combination were "book," the neurons might have a visual representation of a book, whereas other neurons might store more conceptual or functional information about books. These ideas would then be transmitted to the speech area of the brain, Broca's area, converted into patterns of motor movement, and referred to the motor strip, which then sends the impulses for the muscle movements needed to produce sound (Hegde, 2001).

The two most common organic causes of language delays are intellectual disability and hearing impairment. Brain damage, also organic, can interfere with a child's ability to receive, understand, remember, and recognize communicated information. These types of disorders are referred to as receptive language disorders. The child can hear adequately and has no expressive disorder, but the messages, once heard and transmitted to the brain, encounter interference, and the message is not understood.

Physical disabilities can also affect both speech and language development. Motor impairments that prevent children from becoming involved with their environment—that is, they are unable to actively manipulate materials and receive sensory input—will result in fewer experiences to build semantic language skills. Children with these impairments may be delayed in language acquisition and will require assistance in acquiring the knowledge or experiences to compensate. Physical disabilities can also affect the oral motor structures and musculature of the body. These children are capable of developing language but may be unable to verbally express themselves in ways that others can understand. Alternative methods must be developed for these children to express and communicate their thoughts and wishes.

Emotional disturbances can lead to language delays. Young children who exhibit moderate and severe emotional disorders often have problems with language expression. Emotional disorders may slow a child's development of expressive language skills or stunt the development of an inner language with which to think about received information. Some children with emotional disorders may develop their own language form, one that is unintelligible to others. Children with autism and severe psychotic disorders typically demonstrate severe language disorders, even though they may not experience speech difficulties.

Early Identification of Communication Disorders

Early identification of children with communication delays is critical. Communication plays an important role in children's cognitive development, social interactions, and overall well-being. Children with communication delays may also be at risk for other developmental disabilities that affect school performance.

Unless it is related to a high visibility disorder, such as severe intellectual disabilities or neuromotor abnormalities, it is difficult to diagnose a communication disorder at an early age. Communication disorders are high-incidence, low-visibility disorders and are often not identified in very young children. Because communication has such a strong developmental base, knowing age-appropriate behavior is essential.

Shortly after birth, infants begin to coo, and by 4 to 6 months they have added babbling and laughing to their repertoire. Babbling changes over the next six months and by a year the child may have one or two words. Over the next year, he begins to say more words, put two words together, and ask questions. About a fourth of his speech is comprehensible to nonfamily members (Hulit & Howard, 2006).

▶❚ **TeachSource Video Case**

2–5 Years: Language Development in Early Childhood
Watch the TeachSource Video Case *2–5 Years: Language Development in Early Childhood*, in which you can see how, at about 2 years of age, children's vocabulary expands greatly. The video can be found in the Early Childhood Education Media Library under Child Development, available at www.cengagebrain.com.

Toddlers can answer routine questions, say the names of familiar objects in pictures, and identify body parts on a doll as well as on their own body. They like to ask "what" questions and have a vocabulary of about 50 words. Once children hit the 50-word mark (at about age 18 months) they tend to experience rapid growth in vocabulary, especially nouns (Hulit & Howard, 2006). Young children need many opportunities to build vocabulary in the context of learning.

Two-year-olds who speak fewer than 10 words and cannot comprehend simple directions should be referred. By age 2½, concern arises about children with very limited vocabularies, those who have no phrases of two or more words, those who cannot answer simple questions, and those whose speech is entirely unintelligible (Wang & Baron, 1997). About half of their speech should be comprehensible to nonfamily members.

By age 3, children should be able to point to pictures of familiar objects when they are named, identify objects when told their use, and understand questions relating to what and where. The average child has a vocabulary of 250 to 900 words (Wang & Baron, 1997). They understand and can use negations such as "no," "not," "can't," and "don't," and they enjoy simple stories again and again and again. Expressively, they can name many common objects and use language as a way of communicating thoughts. They usually enjoy using language, gain satisfaction from expressing themselves and being understood, and show frustration when they are not understood. They understand and use abstract words such as "up," "down," "now," and "later." They are beginning to refer to themselves as "me" instead of using their proper name. Words are combined into short phrases, and they are starting to ask primitive questions.

By age 4 children's understanding of relationships is increasing. They use words like "because" and contingencies such as "if" and "when." They also understand size comparatives (e.g., large–larger). They are beginning to understand the vocabulary of time (e.g., tomorrow) as well as the concept of "pretend." Children are beginning to ask questions for information and for social contacts. They use simple sentence structures and can repeat at least one nursery rhyme. They are beginning to use the simple future tense, "I will," as well as pronouns that refer to others (she, his, theirs, etc.). They love new words, and their vocabulary should be increasing rapidly. All of their words should be intelligible, and their vocabulary should have grown to about 1,200 to 1,500 words (Hulit & Howard, 2006).

Preschool children talk a lot—not always to tell or ask something important, but to seek attention and companionship. They love silly language. They employ a variety of sentence structures and use almost all pronouns appropriately. They can explain why they want to do something a certain way as well as asking "when," "how," and "why" questions (Hulit & Howard, 2006).

Three-year-olds who cannot engage in simple conversation, have no short sentences, and whose speech is largely unintelligible are of concern (Wang & Baron, 1997). When 4-year-olds have difficulty learning new concepts, explaining events, and following two-step directions, there is concern. Likewise, when their speech is unclear or they are still simply echoing speech with no complete sentences, a referral is indicated (Wang & Baron, 1997).

Between 5 and 6 years of age, children demonstrate many pre-academic skills. They are curious and ask many questions. They use complete sentences and give full information, and thus need opportunities to talk with someone who is interested and who will listen attentively. They use different verb tenses and have a vocabulary of about

Children who have good social language may be challenged by the demands of academic English as they reach the elementary school years.
©Cengage Learning 2012

2,000 words. By the time children enter kindergarten, they demonstrate academic skills and function at an adult level in understanding communication. They understand increasingly more complex vocabulary, which should have grown to about 2,600 words. Language structures are mastered and are being refined for irregulars. Children are adding reading and writing to their communication skills.

There are distinctions between social and academic English. Children who may not have been identified earlier may be referred for an evaluation because of these distinctions. Language at school relies less on the context of environment and less on the content of past conversations and events. Elementary school teachers do most of the talking, giving children fewer opportunities to initiate conversation. Teachers also have less knowledge than parents about individual children. Finally, the school culture may make demands on the child that are not parallel to the home culture.

Assessment of Communication Disorders

Language is a very personal thing, and language styles are different depending on the individual and her cultural or ethnic identification. Certainly, we would expect language differences in children who are learning English as a second language. However, there is also much variation in individuals who are native English speakers. Previously, some children who did not speak and write standard American English were diagnosed as having a language disorder (Salvia & Ysseldyke, 2007). The 2004 amendments to the IDEA are designed to ensure that this does not happen. Although there is debate about acceptance of nonstandard English, there is agreement that children who speak nonstandard English should not be classified as having a language disorder. In some instances, there are regional as well as cultural uses of language. Think of such terms as *hotdog, frankfurter,* and *wiener.* If only one of these is an acceptable answer on a language assessment, then some children are penalized not for their lack of vocabulary, but for using a regional label.

● ● ●
Informal Language Assessment

If you are concerned about a child's speech and language, begin informally. First, look up the child's birth date. This alone might resolve the problem. If this child is one of the youngest in the class and your basis for comparison is older children, the difference between them may be a developmental one that will disappear with time. In early childhood, even a few months has a considerable effect. As a further check, find out whether this child was premature and is developmentally even younger.

If you are still concerned, assign the child to a small group with several others who are close in age. (Do not include children who are cognitively delayed or advanced.) When doing language activities, note who volunteers the most and least often. Take language samples from each child and compare them for sentence length, sentence structure, vocabulary, concepts, and articulation (note omissions, distortions, or substitutions of sounds). An easy way to obtain language samples is by recording small-group time. Do this on at least two occasions to allow for a child's having a bad or good day. If the child is in the top to middle of this group, there is probably no cause for concern. If the child is at the bottom, continue gathering information.

As you continue your observations, note how the child uses materials not related to language, both the number of different materials and their appropriateness. This information will help you decide whether the child is delayed in other areas. If so, the child's speech and language problems may have an underlying cause such as a developmental delay or lack of an experiential background.

The next step is to determine the gap between the child's comprehension and production of language. During the early childhood years, children have a greater ability to understand language than to speak it; you are looking for a significantly wider gap between the two than is expected.

After carefully observing the child alone and with others, if you still feel there is a problem, schedule a conference with the parents. Alert them to your concerns, and then accept whatever they say. Your goals in the first conference are to gather more information and to begin to make the parents aware of your concerns. Schedule a class visit for them in about two weeks; if this isn't possible, make a videotape to show them. Have them observe (or show them) their own child with an age-mate, just as you did. At your second conference, discuss and compare their observations with your own. (Their opinions may have changed as they became more conscious of their child's speech and language and listened more carefully.)

Consider making a home visit. Between 28 and 60 percent of children with communication disorders have a sibling or parent who also has problems in this area (Fox, Dodd, & Howard, 2002). You will have an opportunity to watch and listen to the family interact more informally. You may learn that the child's speech or language is modeled after the family pattern, which means you are unlikely to convince the parents there is a problem. If you still feel the problem exists, discuss it. Even if parents do not share your concerns, there is still much you can do within the classroom to foster this child's speech and language development.

If the parents agree the child has a problem, you might suggest that the child be assessed. The family physician is probably the best choice to begin, as there may be a medical reason for the problem. The physician might then refer the child to an audiologist to test hearing, to a speech-language pathologist, and/or to a psychologist for testing in social and intellectual development.

No matter how the parents choose to obtain further information about the child's needs, there will be a lag between your initial concern and a final conclusion. Young children can be difficult to assess, test results may be inconclusive, and many times the decision is made to "wait and see." In the meantime, your role is to help this child in your classroom.

Formal Language Assessment

The goals of assessment are to determine whether, in fact, there is a communication impairment and in what area or areas this disorder lies. The next step is to determine the goals for intervention and then to establish a plan to meet those goals and implement the plan. The final component is to develop a method for monitoring progress toward goals.

To determine whether a child has a communication and/or language disorder, speech-language pathologists typically use standardized tests. Most tests differentiate among receptive language, comprehension, and expressive language production (Salvia & Ysseldyke, 2007). *The Test of Language Development, Primary*, 3rd ed. (TOLD-P: 3; Newcomer & Hammill, 1999) is a norm-referenced, individually administered test used for children ages 4 through 8. It measures expressive and receptive language, identifies children's language strengths and weaknesses, progress in language development, and language problems. *The Goldman-Fristoe Test of Articulation,* 2nd ed. (GFAT-2; Goldman & Fristoe, 2000), one of the most frequently used tests to assess phonology, is a norm-referenced test designed to measure articulation for persons 2 through 21 years of age.

There are some concerns with the assessment of language:

- One is whether the formal assessment actually reflects the child's spontaneous language. Testing situations may be new and frightening for children. To the extent that children's response to this situation influences their language, the measure will not be an accurate reflection of their spontaneous language.

- A second concern relates to the use of standardized tests of language. The step from getting the results of a language test to generating goals and ways to implement them is a large one. Parents may want to focus on a fundamental social vocabulary to allow them to better understand what their child wants and needs. Speech-language pathologists may want to work on particular articulation problems or other specific areas of language, whereas educators may feel the most appropriate goal is to increase the number, complexity, and length of children's sentences in spontaneous conversation.

- A third concern of assessment is whether the child being assessed has the same characteristics as the sample on which the measure was standardized; in other words, are test norm results valid for this child? If not, then it is difficult to figure out exactly what to do (Salvia & Ysseldyke, 2007).

THE EVIDENCE BASE

The Peabody Picture Vocabulary Test III (PPVT-III) is a measure of receptive language, frequently used for screening, because it is short, easy to administer and score, and correlates with intelligence scales. The Expressive Vocabulary Test (EVT) is a measure of children's expressive one-word vocabulary, often used in conjunction with the PPVT-III to measure expressive language. There is some concern that these measures might be biased against certain groups. To examine the bias issue, 210 children (ranging in age from 4 to 5.2 years) attending public prekindergarten programs (one rural, one urban) were given the PPVT-III and the EVT within the first 45 days of the school year. Although an item analysis of the PPVT-III did not find evidence of ethnic bias, there are concerns that some groups of children will not score as well as others. Using the PPVT-III as a diagnostic measure, 24 percent of African American children were identified as having a significant vocabulary problem as compared to 4 percent of European American children. For mothers who had a high school education or less, 24 percent of the children were identified as having a significant vocabulary problem as opposed to 4 percent for mothers who had a bachelor's degree or some college.

Using the EVT, only 5 percent of African American children were identified as having a significant language problem, and no European American children were identified. For mothers who had a high school education or less, 4 percent of the children were identified as having a significant vocabulary problem as opposed to 1 percent for mothers who had a bachelor's degree or some college.

Sources: Restrepo et al., 2006.

REFLECTIVE PRACTICE | Why does this matter? The concern is that African American children and children whose mothers have a high school education or less may be misdiagnosed as having a potential language disability if the measure of language used is the PPVT-III. What does this information mean in your classroom, and how will you identify children and evaluate the results of these measures? How can you use this evidence to inform your practice?

Language Delays and Disorders

Language does not develop in isolation, and the interaction between language and cognitive development is difficult to unravel. There are also many ways of classifying language disorders. Some look at the rate and sequence in which language develops, whereas others focus on the cause or related conditions, and still others break language down into subsystems (phonology, morphology, syntax, semantics, and pragmatics). In general, a child's language is impaired when there are deviations in the formation, expression, or understanding of language.

All children have to learn the rules of the language they speak. We rarely think of this aspect of language if we have grown-up hearing people using these rules correctly. Rules govern the form and function of language.

Children with language delays have normal or close to normal speech and language form and function (phonology, grammar, semantics, and pragmatics) but are delayed in their development. A language delay can include a general delay in all dimensions of language, or it can relate to skills in specific areas, such as semantics or syntax. Children with language disorders are impaired in their ability to generate or interpret language, and their speech may be impaired.

Rules about form determine which sounds and words are combined to express meaning. The form of any language relates to the rules that govern **phonology** and grammar (Stuart, 2007). **Phonemes** are the smallest units of a language that distinguish meaning (vowels and consonants). The meanings of c*at* and c*ap* are distinguished by the phonemes /*t*/ and /*p*/. Phonology uses the rules for combining types of phonemes, pauses, and stress to form words (Stuart, 2007). One phonemic rule of the English language is that *q* is always followed by *u*. Other rules relate to whether vowel sounds are short or long. Children who lack phonemic awareness and word analysis skills have problems coding and decoding words.

Grammar is concerned with the rules for using the smallest units of language that contain meaning (*morphemes*) and word order (*syntax*) to convey meaning. Some children have problems with grammar because their language role models do not follow the standard grammatical rules; others, because of organic challenges.

Morphemes are words or meaningful word parts. **Morphology** looks at how adding or deleting parts of words change their meaning. An example would be the difference between *disorder* and *order*, or changing *book* to *books*. **Prefixes** and **suffixes** are morphemes. Knowledge of the role of morphemes in language is important in building vocabulary. If the child knows the word *friend*, that can serve as the base for understanding *friendly*, *unfriendly*, *befriend*, *friendship*, and so on.

Syntax refers to the linguistic rules that govern the arrangement of words into phrases or sentences and the relationship among these elements in a sentence—that is, how words are put together. Syntax establishes the requirements that all sentences have a subject and verb, and that different word orders change the meaning; for example, "André hit the ball" is different from "The ball hit André." Children with aphasia have problems in this area.

Semantics relates to the intent and meaning conveyed by words, phrases, and sentences. Semantics has a cognitive base and involves underlying skills such as memory, mental imagery, and concepts (Stuart, 2007). Sometimes children have problems in this area because of lack of an appropriate knowledge base.

Pragmatics relates to rules that govern the use of language in personal situations and social interactions. The emphasis is on the functional use of language rather than the mechanics of it. Children need language to convey their needs to others and to interact with them.

There are two major categories of language disorders: those that are present from birth (**congenital**) and those that arise after a child has been developing language at a typical rate (**acquired**). Congenital language disorders usually have some organic base. Hearing loss is a primary consideration.

Specific Language Impairment

Despite variations in the timing of language acquisition, as with motor and cognitive development there are major milestones that occur in a predictable sequence. When milestones are not reached, there is concern about delayed language development or specific language impairment.

Specific language impairment (SLI) is a disability in which children are delayed in saying their first words. Children with SLI acquire language along the same developmental patterns as typically developing children, but the acquisition of skills occurs slowly over a longer period of time. SLI occurs when children's language maturation is 12 months behind their chronological age, and affects approximately 7 percent of children but is rarely diagnosed. Children with SLI do not have a severe communication problem. However, they may not begin to talk until they are 3 or 4 years old, and when they do, they use immature grammar and simple sentence structures (NIDCD, 2009b). Their language does not catch up, even in adulthood. Because SLI tends to run in families, scientist have searched for and recently found a gene (KIAA0319) that plays a key role in SLI. Exactly what this gene or family of genes does is not clear, but KIAA0319 also plays a role in reading disabilities. Early identification and targeted interventions have the potential for changing these children's trajectory when the brain's neural pathways are open to change (NIDCD, 2009b).

Aphasia

Aphasia, caused by damage to one or more of the language areas of the brain, can happen at any age but is typically the result of traumatic brain injury (e.g., from an automobile accident or a blow to the head) or a brain tumor (NIDCD, 2008). Brain damage occurs when blood doesn't reach part of the brain so brain cells, deprived of oxygen and nutrients, die. The disorder impairs the expression and understanding of language as well as reading and writing (NIDCD, 2008). Some children with aphasia have mild problems; for others, problems are severe.

The area in which the brain is damaged determines the nature of the particular problem. Damage to the temporal lobe usually causes fluent, or Wernicke's aphasia. Children with fluent aphasia may speak in long sentences that have no meaning and may include nonsense words and jargon, making it difficult to make sense out of utterances. Children also have difficulty understanding the speech of others. As the part of the brain that controls body movement is not affected, their motor skills are age appropriate (NIDCD, 2008).

Children with nonfluent, or Broca's, aphasia, have damage to the frontal lobe of the brain, making speaking difficult; they often speak in short phrases and omit words. Children with Broca's aphasia usually understand the speech of others and may become frustrated at their inability to communicate effectively. Children may also experience weakness on the right side of their body or paralysis in their right arm or leg, because the frontal lobe plays a role in motor movement (NDCID, 2008).

Because aphasia results from injury to the brain, a neurologist may be the first medical person to diagnose it. The child would then be referred to a speech-language pathologist. The goal of therapy would be to restore language abilities as much as possible; help the child learn and use language; and, if necessary, teach compensatory skills and alternative methods of communication.

IMPLICATIONS FOR EDUCATORS

Encourage any type of communication: speech, gesturing, pointing, drawing, texting, and other forms of technology. Give the child time to talk, and do not correct his speech. Include the child and ask for his opinions as part of the class when appropriate. Minimize distractions. Shorten and simplify your language, but not to the point that it attracts attention to the child. If the child has trouble understanding language, support your language with gestures, pointing, drawing, pictures, or whatever else that might work. Use technology to support communication.

Speech Delays and Disorders

The production of speech sounds involves the manipulation of the mouth, tongue, cheeks, and throat, along with the shaping and control of air, to produce specific vowel and consonant sounds. Problems with any one of these variables can result in atypical sound production or a speech disorder. In general, a child's speech is impaired when it deviates so far from the speech of other children that it calls attention to itself, interferes with communication, or causes the child to be self-conscious.

Speech is the verbal means of communicating. Speech consists of the following:

- *Articulation*—how speech sounds are made (e.g., children must learn how to produce the "r" sound in order to say "rabbit" instead of "wabbit").
- *Voice*—use of the vocal folds and breathing to produce sound (the voice can be abused from overuse or misuse and can lead to hoarseness or loss of voice).
- *Fluency*—the rhythm of speech (hesitations or stuttering can affect fluency).

When a person is unable to produce speech sounds correctly or fluently, or has problems with his voice, then she has a speech disorder (ASHA, 1997–2011c).

Speech Sound Disorders

All children make mistakes when learning new words. Some of this is developmental, based on when children are able to produce certain sounds. By age 8, children should be able to make all of the sounds required for English correctly. (All sounds have an age range when children should be able to make them correctly.) When children continue to make mistakes past this time, the child may have a speech sound disorder. **Speech sound disorders** include problems with articulation and **phonological patterns** (ASHA, 1997–2011b).

Articulation Disorders

Articulation is the ability to produce, orally, any one of a variety of vowels, consonants, and/or vowel-consonant blends. The inability to produce these sounds can be developmental or physiological: lack of tongue or mouth control, oral musculature difficulties, or the result of a hearing loss or other disability. Articulation disorders occur when sounds are omitted, added, distorted, or substituted. These changes make it difficult for children to be understood (ASHA, 1997–2011b). Take, for example, *spaghetti:*

paghetti	*s* is omitted
spaghettiti	extra *ti* is added
speghetti	*a* is distorted to *e*
basaghetti	*ba* is substituted for *p* and put at the beginning

Articulation errors can happen at the beginning, middle, or end of a word. They may be the result of indistinct articulation. Slow, labored speech and rapid, slurring speech are both articulation problems. Some articulation problems are a natural part of a child's development or may result from a dialect the child has grown up with. Although children may outgrow some problems, therapy is indicated in other instances.

Phonological Process Disorders

Phonological processes are sound patterns in speech. In phonological process disorders, there are particular patterns of sound errors that are repeated. These are usually sounds that are made in a specific part of the mouth. For example, consistently substituting sounds made in the front of the mouth /t/ for those made in the back of the mouth /g/, hence *gas* become *tas*. Another sound pattern error is only saying one consonant sound in words that begin with two consonants (e.g., *peech* for *speech*) (ASHA, 1997–2011b).

A speech-language pathologist evaluates children for speech sound disorders. An evaluation would probably include the evaluation of the oral mechanism to ensure the mouth is working properly, an articulation test, and an evaluation of general language development to determine communication functioning (ASHA, 1997–2011b).

Voice Disorders

Voice disorders involve abnormal production and/or absence of vocal quality, pitch, loudness, resonance and/or duration of speech for a child's age or sex (ASHA, 1997–2011b). The cause can be attributed to physical, learned, or psychological problems. Vocal disorders, particularly hoarseness, occur frequently, in 6 to 23 percent of school-age children. If untreated, voice disorders can lead to lifelong communication impairments and impede social and academic performance (Faust, 2003).

Children's *pitch* should be appropriate for their age, sex, and size; mismatches can lead to social and emotional difficulties. *Volume* concerns the children's ability to monitor the loudness of their voices; hearing loss can result in a child's using a louder voice than normal. *Quality* refers to the general character of the voice, such as hoarse, nasal, breathy, or normal. Extremely harsh or hoarse quality speech can be related to vocal cord nodules or excessive screaming; nasal quality speech can be the result of cleft palate disorders. *Duration* refers to how much or little a child talks. Most problems encountered in voice disorders are treatable medically or through speech-language therapy.

Fluency Disorders

Fluency disorders are the abnormal flow of verbal expression that is characterized by impaired continuity, smoothness, and rhythm that may include labored speaking. The most common fluency disorder is stuttering. Stuttering occurs when the normal flow of speech is interrupted by abnormal repetitions, hesitations, and prolongations of sounds and syllables and avoidable struggle behaviors. Associated with stuttering are characteristic body motions such as grimaces, eye blinks, and gross body movements (Stuttering Foundation, 2007).

One or more of the following characterizes stuttering:

- Sound syllable repetitions
- Sound prolongations
- Interjections
- Broken words (pauses within a word)

Children with fluency disorders may experience tension when speaking.
©Cengage Learning 2012

- Audible or silent blocking (filled or unfilled pauses in speech)
- Circumlocutions (word substitutions to avoid problematic words)
- Words produced with an excess of physical tension
- Monosyllabic whole-word repetitions (e.g., "I—I—I see him") (APA, 2000, p. 69).

Four factors contribute to the development of stuttering:

- *Genetics.* Over half of those who stutter have a family member who does also.
- *Other speech and language problems or developmental disabilities.* These increase the likelihood of stuttering.
- *Neurophysiology.* Research shows that people who stutter process speech and language in different areas of the brain than those who do not.
- *Family dynamics.* High expectations and fast-paced lifestyles play a role in stuttering (Stuttering Foundation, 2007).

Approximately 20 percent of children go through a stage of development when they stutter enough to concern their parents (Stuttering Foundation, 2007). The incidence of stuttering is highest between ages 2 and 4 and ultimately affects 4 to 5 percent of children. During these ages, there are equal numbers of boys and girls affected. However, girls are more likely to recover without assistance, so the ratio of boys to girls at later ages is approximately 3 to 1. Most children recover within 6 to 36 months after the stuttering was first noticed (Zebrowski, 2003). It is estimated that less than 1 percent of adults stutter (NIDCD, 2002d).

Most children experience some dysfluency between ages 2 and 5. In normal dysfluency, there is no struggle and the dysfluency is effortless. Normal dysfluency is also situationally specific. It increases when children talk with someone who speaks rapidly, when language use is more formal, or when children ask questions, use more complex sentences, or use less familiar words. Dysfluency is episodic and may occur because the child is upset, anxious, under pressure to communicate, or has a lot to say.

The question is, When should a child be referred to a speech-language pathologist based on stuttering? Young children who stutter may recover naturally without intervention, so there is some reason to wait and look for changes in the child's speech. If after six months there are not significant improvements, or if the child shows signs of becoming distressed by the disorder, the child should be referred. During the early childhood years, treatment for stuttering is very effective and can result in children speaking as if they have never stuttered (Onslow, 2000). See Table 11–2 for ways of working with children who stutter.

Childhood Apraxia of Speech

Childhood apraxia of speech is a motor speech disorder. Children have trouble saying what they want to say consistently or correctly. This problem is not based on weakness

TABLE

11-2   GUIDELINES FOR WORKING WITH CHILDREN WHO STUTTER

Do not imply that stuttering is a bad habit.
Do not tell a child to stop and start over or to stop and think what to say.
Do not help a child with words he is trying to say. Wait for the child to get it out for himself.
Do not tell a child to talk slowly unless she speaks too rapidly to articulate.
Do not tell a child to talk faster, in a low voice, high voice, to swallow, to take a deep breath first, and so on.
Do not call on a child when he doesn't volunteer or when he is tired or harassed.
Do not call stuttering to a child's attention if she does not know she stutters.
Do not pretend a child's speech is normal if he is aware of his stuttering.
Do not make the tempo of home and school life too strenuous.
Do not make a child compete for a chance to talk; let her have a turn at activities or during group discussions.
Do not require a child to participate in competitive activities that require rapid verbal responses (reading flash cards, spelling bees, etc.).
Do not let other children feel they can "catch" stuttering. Stuttering is not a disease.

Sources: Guitar & Conture, 2007; Rind & Rind, 2003.

or paralysis of the muscles necessary for speech; rather, the brain has problems planning the coordination and movement of the necessary muscles. The child knows what she wants to say but her brain can't get the message through to muscles (ASHA, 1997–2011a).

Childhood apraxia of speech (CAS) is present at birth. As infants, these children do little or no babbling and have difficulty imitating sounds and words. They may have limited vowel and few consonant sounds. Children speak later; their language does not follow the typical pattern of children with delayed language development (NIDCD, 2002b). They frequently leave out or substitute incorrect sounds in words. And—frustrating for them and others—their speech errors are unpredictable and inconsistent. Additionally, they may not accurately vary the rhythm, stresses, and inflections that are used to convey meaning. Together, these problems result in a small vocabulary, incorrect grammar, and difficulty organizing spoken information. These problems frequently spill over into reading, writing, spelling, and math.

Children have better receptive language than usable speech (NIDCD, 2002b). Spontaneous speech is unusual and difficult to understand. CAS affects more boys than girls. The cause of CAS is unknown. Some believe that it is a neurological disorder; however, brain imaging has not found differences in the brains of children with CAS. Children with CAS frequently have family members who have communication disorders or learning disabilities, suggesting that genetics may play a role (NIDCD, 2002b).

Diagnosis is difficult because there is no single factor or test that is used and no agreement on the significant symptoms that define the disability. Much is left to clinical judgment. Like most disabilities, CAS can vary from mild to severe (NIDCD, 2002b). Some children may need the help of alternative or additional communication methods.

Augmentative and Alternative Communication

Some children have such severe communication disorders that spoken communication is not a long-range option for them. **Augmentative communication** is an alternative communication system that is used to supplement the expressive communication skills of a child, either temporarily or permanently. Augmentative and alternative communication (AAC) is categorized in two ways: unaided and aided. Unaided communication systems use only the child's body to communicate. Sign language, gestures, vocalizations, and facial expression are examples of unaided communication. Aided communication methods employ tools or equipment such as picture communication boards, object symbols, and high- or low-tech speech-generating devices to help the child expressively communicate (Stuart, 2007).

To work effectively, aided augmentative communication must be designed for each individual child. Creative software designed for microcomputers is greatly impacting augmentative communication and has tremendous potential. Even for young children, the use of touch-sensitive control pads can facilitate communication. Voice synthesizers are relatively inexpensive and plug into the printer port of most computers. Rather than printing what is typed, the synthesizer "speaks" it. If the child touches the color red on an adapted keyboard, the word *red* is said. There are also electronic tablet applications that provide auditory output.

Children may use a variety of AAC systems, depending upon the activities they are participating in, the situation, and how familiar they are with the people involved. Speech-language pathologists play an important role in deciding on the most effective system and in helping children learn to use it.

IMPLICATIONS FOR EDUCATORS

Language modeling techniques can be used at any time in the early childhood classroom. They can be used with all children throughout the day to stimulate language. If the concern is with infants and toddlers, use parentese. **Parentese** is a way of speaking that has a slower rate of speech and exaggerated intonation and stress, with more variation in pitch and loudness. It uses a limited vocabulary with short, simple sentences. Parentese helps focus the infant's attention on language, and the same words are repeated frequently enough for the toddler to understand their function as well as learn the words themselves. This is a tremendous help to the infant or toddler who is trying to figure out when speech stops and starts and the role different words play (Hulit & Howard, 2006).

Use **parallel talk** to give words to the child's behavior. As the child plays, describe what the child is doing, seeing, or hearing. In self-talk, you describe what you are doing while the child watches. Like parallel talk, it is an effective way to model vocabulary and grammatical forms.

Expansion is the process of extracting the meaning of a child's utterance and putting it into a more complex form. For a child using telegraphic speech such as "Me go," the expansion might be "Where do you want to go?" or "Are you ready to go now?" The objective is to provide a language model, not just answer "okay." **Extension** involves putting the child's statement in a broader context, that is, extending the meaning of the phrase. If a child says "Me go out," you might respond, "If you want to go outside, you need to put your coat on." Using these techniques is particularly effective as the child has initiated the "conversation" and is prepared to listen to the response, as it is meaningful to him. You can also extend children's language through intonation and emphasis (e.g., "What do you want to *do* outside?"). Expansion and extension encourage children to use more complex language structures (Hulit & Howard, 2006).

You can stimulate language either directly or indirectly. In **indirect language stimulation**, you provide labels for objects, people, and actions, without requiring the child to respond. In **direct language stimulation**, you question the child about what is happening. These questions should be phrased in such a way that the child cannot answer with a "yes" or "no."

In **repetitions**, you repeat all or part of the child's phrase. This is a good strategy when a child has made an incorrect utterance. You repeat the utterance, correcting the mistake. **Fill-ins** require the child to complete the statement. This is frequently done when reading a familiar story or when dealing with rhyming words or analogies.

Guidelines

If a child has been diagnosed with a communication disorder, read the child's file. Talk with the parents and gain their perspective in addition to having formal IEP team conferences. Find out what the diagnosis means to the child's total development. (Is the language delay part of another disorder?)

Ask the child's speech-language pathologist when she expects to be in your classroom and the kinds of activities you can do that would be helpful. Whether a child has an official diagnosis or not, you must assess where in the language process the problem is, its severity, and how you will adapt your programming to meet this child's needs. As you listen to children throughout the day, look for their most and least comfortable times with speech. Most children show a pattern. Although each child's situation will be different, the following guidelines are helpful:

1. *Use simple, concrete language and lots of repetition.* Simplify your grammar and vocabulary and use shorter sentences. Children will have fewer problems processing information in this form. If you talk fast, slowing down your rate of delivery may help.

2. *Ask few direct questions, especially during group times.* Questions place high demands on a child for speech, even when the response requested is just a short one.

3. *Allow children, on occasion, to "pass" answering a question* if they feel uncomfortable or cannot verbalize the answer. This will reduce fear of embarrassment and may lead to more interaction in the long run.

4. *Give short, simple, clear directions.* Start with one-step directions; gradually work up to more complex directions. If necessary, have the child repeat or verbally "walk through" the directions before doing an activity.

5. *Use appropriate "wait time"* when asking children a question. Some children need more time to form or articulate their answers. Don't rush answers.

6. *Plan for language development.* Set aside time each day that specifically emphasizes language development. (The activity may vary, but the intent shouldn't.)

7. *Encourage children's desire to communicate.* Increase their interest in themselves and their environment. Find out what children find interesting. If a child with a communication disorder likes biking, discuss the topic with her. She may be eager to talk about a subject that is important to her.

8. *Provide a secure, consistent, well-organized environment.* Set up activities to provide noncompetitive peer interaction.

9. *Include children with communication disorders in group activities.* Children need not have a speaking role if that provokes anxiety. Nonverbal group participation may be a prerequisite to verbal participation. Participation with puppets may come before communication without props.

10. *Create a need for speech.* If the child uses gestures instead of speech, deliberately (but not obviously) misunderstand briefly, and name other objects. Before the child becomes frustrated, give the child what was requested, but use the word in one- or two-phrases or sentences. Gradually increase the number of misunderstandings and incorrect guesses until the child is slightly frustrated by your "stupidity."

11. *Give a lot of running commentary.* Give a play-by-play description of what either you or the child is doing. One way that children learn to talk is by listening and imitating.

12. *Be a good listener.* Give the child your undivided attention, or explain that you cannot listen then, but will soon. Arrange to do that as soon as possible.

13. *Reward the child for correct speech*, but do not criticize lack of speech or incorrect speech.

14. *Model good speech and language.* Rephrase what children say to reinforce appropriate speech and to let them know that you care about what they are saying.

15. *Differentiate between speech and language, and reinforce appropriately.* For example, you might tell a child, "I'm glad you want to tell me about your picture. I'm having trouble understanding what you are saying. Can you tell me with different words?"

16. *Post rules and routines with pictures and/or words.* Reinforce learning through visual and tactile experiences.

17. *Structure lessons to provide children with more successes than failures.*

18. *Reinforce spontaneous language* independently of the quality of the speech. Respond to the meaning of children's communications.

19. *Help children develop the skills to handle teasing independently.* Some children may imitate speech problems or make fun of the way others talk. Do not reinforce the children, and tell them clearly that you find their behavior unacceptable. The imitation problem is usually a short-term one that goes away without reinforcement, but teasing may continue indefinitely.

Language and cognition are related. For children to use their language, they need something to talk about. Expand children's awareness of the environment. Lack of stimulation may be a factor in underdeveloped language. Children cannot be expected to talk about something they have no knowledge of. Remember the learning cycle—awareness, exploration, inquiry/experimentation, and utilization—and provide children with opportunities for different levels of learning.

Curriculum Adaptations

Children with communication disorders require few curriculum adaptations. Rather, they may need some areas of the curriculum expanded to meet their needs.

Social Awareness

Children with communication disorders may not have good skills at joining groups. Help them develop the language necessary to be included. Think about the priorities in language development: broadening language skills through field trips, followed by language experience stories. This sequence supports both the social studies and language aspects of the experience. Work on vocabulary to go with the actions. As children's vocabulary expands, help them become more detailed and specific in their speech. Some of the activities in the Resource Chapters are specifically designed to support children who have communication disorders. Activities such as 2–48w, *Tongue Twisters*, help children learn that some things are difficult to say. Activity 1–43w, *Talking*, demonstrates different ways of talking and some resulting frustration if children are not understood.

Social Competence

As children learn more about themselves, their self-awareness increases. They may need support to use their language

skills to communicate their wants and needs. As they build skills, teach them ways to be assertive.

1. Incorporate a broad base of communication skills into your curriculum to increase children's awareness of differences in communication. Include different written and spoken languages, American Sign Language, computers with voice simulators, communication boards, and so on.

2. Talk to children about how they would communicate if they couldn't speak. Discuss communication boards, and have children make their own communication boards. Discuss what to include, and talk with them about what is important to be able to communicate. Then discuss the limitations and the frustrations of not being understood and especially how the person who is not understood might feel.

3. Help children learn about their body, how it reacts in different situations, and how this impacts their speech and language. (How do they feel when asked a question in a group situation when they don't know the answer? When someone calls them names?) Talk about how children can handle these situations. Initially, the plan may involve your intervention; however, as children learn and grow, they should take increasing responsibility.

4. Use fingerplays to stimulate body awareness. Those that involve the face and mouth area are especially beneficial.

Children with communication disorders may not seek out other children; they may play alone or near other children. Encourage cooperative play so that children can learn to interact comfortably with peers. When they do play with others, children with communication disorders are rarely leaders; they often receive instructions from classmates rather than giving them, and because they are often reluctant to argue with the leader as others might, they may end up with the least desirable roles. It is important for all children to feel they belong. Children need to know they are all similar in some ways and different in others. Language may be an area in which they are different.

1. Have children play with language, perhaps by mispronouncing an unfamiliar word or a word in another language. Ask children how they feel and how they would feel if others criticized or made fun of them. Ask them whether they would try to pronounce the word again and how they would feel.

2. Discuss the importance of taking turns in language as well as on pieces of equipment. Point out that sometimes people need to wait for others to have time to say what they want to communicate. It is important for them to wait, as well as for you.

3. Use books without words.

4. Have a discussion with the whole class about teasing and treating others appropriately. Do not focus on

Talk about language differences and similarities, verbal and nonverbal communication, and ensure that all children are included.
©Cengage Learning 2012

speech, but on being respectful in general. Many children, especially older children, will understand that this also pertains to speech disorders.

Social Studies

Speech and language skills can be integrated into the social studies curriculum through conversation and role-playing. Help children identify similarities and differences throughout the immediate environment, the region, and the country, as well as globally. Your goal is to promote the concept of diversity. At the same time, you are promoting the children's awareness of differences and similarities in speech and language.

1. Talk about different languages, some of the commonalities and differences in language and culture, and how one might feel if he didn't speak the same language as others in the classroom.

2. Discuss names and naming traditions in different languages and cultures. Some common names translate well: John in Spanish is Juan; in French, Jacques; in German, Johann. However, there are some names for which there are no equivalents. Discuss these as well as how names are passed down in various cultures.

3. Make a tape recording of people from different regions in North America (with the characteristic accents). If possible, have them all say the same sentences so that the children can more readily grasp the differences. Make a similar tape of people from different countries or those for whom English is a second language. Have a person who speaks another language come to class. See Activity 1–20, *Visitor*.

4. Help children act out situations that require roles that have different speech patterns associated with them,

for example, teacher, police officer, father, mother, and baby.

5. Teach lessons that introduce children to famous figures such as Helen Keller. Introduce sign language, Braille, and other methods of communication such as pantomime. Talk about communication in languages other than English. Help children to get a more global concept of communication.

English Language Arts

English language arts is the area most emphasized for children with communication disorders. Communication skills cannot be viewed in isolation, but rather are related to the acquisition of all language skills. Children who do not acquire a complex expressive sentence repertoire are at high risk for problems in reading and writing, which are language-based skills.

In particular, children need to develop and refine listening, attention, and memory skills. Language arts can be used to increase spontaneous language as well as to develop readiness skills. Check with the child's speech-language pathologist for specific advice and additional activities. For children who need work on specific speech sounds, read stories and ask questions that require them to practice those sounds. Some children have articulation problems because they do not have good speech models. Their speech reflects what they hear, so it is important that you provide a good model for them. Highlight the interrelationship between expressive and receptive language, and reading and writing. Provide children with firsthand experiences, followed by discussions and opportunities for internalizing concepts and expanding key ideas. Using a farm as an example, you might do the following activities:

- Visit a farm.
- Generate a language experience story about the trip to the farm.
- Read a book about a farm and have a variety of books about farms available for individual reading at different lexile levels.
- Play farm animal and farm machinery lotto.
- Sing "Old MacDonald Had a Farm."
- Learn about different types of farms. Discuss the equipment and animals on these farms and their purpose, and imitate the sounds that farm animals make.

These suggestions are ordered on the principles that children learn contextually rather than in isolation, and they learn the concrete before the abstract; thus, gradually increasing exposure to a concept increases the depth of learning.

Speaking and Listening

Children with communication disorders may speak only when absolutely necessary. Speaking in front of others may be a threatening experience for these children. When asked questions in a group situation, they may respond with a shrug or "Don't know." It is easier for them not to know something than to risk ridicule by the other children. Encourage speech in one-on-one situations and in small groups before you work on large groups. Which speech skills to emphasize will depend on the needs of each child; areas include fluency, voice, resonance, and articulation, especially as they relate to intelligibility of speech. Provide many opportunities to practice in nonthreatening situations. Speaking requires practice and information to communicate.

1. Use puppets to encourage children to talk. Give the child cues to encourage speaking when necessary. As children become more confident, have them play together using the puppets.

2. Have telephones available, and encourage children to talk on the telephone with you and with each other.

3. Practice reading poems and rhymes out loud from a poster, the board, an overhead projector, or a computer with a projector. This will enhance reading and speech skills. Use activities such as 2–3, *Synonyms*, and 2–60w, *Word Associations*, to expand vocabulary.

4. Have the whole class write a story or letter together, which you record on a large piece of lined paper. Read these aloud as a whole group.

5. Include poems that match a current language arts theme. Make these appropriate for the children, and have them practice reading these at home and out loud to you, on an individual and group basis, to promote fluency. Ask questions about poems to promote comprehension.

6. Do not correct a child's speech in front of the other children. They may not speak up again. Correctly rephrase what they say, and encourage their good content or answers.

7. Use fingerplays to encourage group participation as children can speak in a group as well as participate in the motions. The motions also provide visual cues that help children understand the words. Fingerplays that rhyme are good for ear training. Those that have the sounds the child is working on are particularly useful.

Provide varied listening experiences to help children discriminate and associate sounds. Read books to expand the child's world, as well as to provide an opportunity to practice different sounds. Begin with stories about familiar events, including books about children, families, and animals.

1. Read books such as Dr. Seuss books that emphasize specific sounds and have a small vocabulary, as well as those that emphasize rhyming.

2. Read stories and do fingerplays that have rhymes, until the children are familiar with them. Then read the stories with pauses to let the group fill in the rhyming word. Children also enjoy nonsense rhyming games. You say a word and have the children call out real and made-up rhyming words for you to write on the board.

3. Encourage children to use listening centers and follow along in a book.

Reading

Young children with communication impairments are likely to have difficulty learning to read. While they are concentrating on pronunciation, their comprehension of the reading material goes down. Their reading rate may be slower than average, and their phrasing may be poor. Reading may become so unpleasant, they try to avoid it whenever possible. Particular care should be taken to develop their reading literacy skills to forestall these problems.

When you teach reading, you will most often use visual and auditory means. Children need to see and say letter sounds and blends regardless of where they are positioned in the word. Ear training, the ability to listen well, is one prerequisite that children with speech and language disabilities may find difficult to master, yet it is essential to the development of literacy.

Matching and sorting tasks can be either perceptual or conceptual in nature, or a combination. Perceptual matching requires the children to match like letters to each other. They don't need to know what the letters stand for. When the task is a conceptual one, the children are required to abstract the idea and generalize it to another instance, for example, when going from lowercase letters to uppercase letters or when going from script (printing) to cursive. Conceptual matching can be used not only in reading literacy but also in other curriculum areas. Examples of both are presented in Figures 11–1 and 11–2.

A picture file set up in a flexible format allows for later expansion. Make a file for consonant sounds: beginning, medial (middle), ending consonant sounds, and consonant blends (e.g., *bl*ouse, pu*mp*kin, sta*nd*) (see Figure 11–2). Children rarely have problems with vowels. Organize the sets alphabetically and store them in four file boxes. Once you have developed the four basic sets, you are prepared for a variety of activities.

1. Have children find all the pictures with a specified beginning sound. (When ending an activity, call out the sounds in alphabetical order. The pictures will automatically be organized for putting away.) Do the same thing for beginning consonant blends. Repeat the process for the middle and final position. When you introduce this activity, you might have the name on the front of the card; the activity is easier when the child can match the initial letters as well as the sound. See Activity 2–56w, *Body Sounds*.

2. Set out four picture cards, three of which have the same ending sounds; say the words; and then have the children identify the one that is different. Gradually give the children more responsibilities, thereby increasing the level of difficulty. You might have the children say the words, have them create sets for each other, and so on.

FIGURE 11-1   PICTURE FILE CARD

A picture file can be used to identify words as well as beginning, medial, and ending consonant sounds.

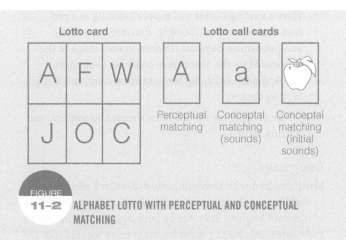

FIGURE 11-2   ALPHABET LOTTO WITH PERCEPTUAL AND CONCEPTUAL MATCHING

Alphabet Lotto with upper- and lower-case letters and initial sounds provides important literacy skills.

3. Make sound books. Introduce one sound at a time, and write the sound at the top of a piece of paper. Have the children find pictures of objects that have that sound and paste the pictures on the page. When the child has a page for each sound, make it into a book. Encourage children to share their book with others.

4. Use variations on lotto and bingo to teach letter recognition (see Figure 11–1). When children can match identical letters, add pictures as well as lowercase letters to the game. Play activities such as 2–21, *Sound Bingo*, and 2–22, *Alphabet Lotto*.

5. Make a set of alphabet cards, or use letter tiles with multiple copies of each letter. Encourage children to play games and make words.

6. Facilitate the development of letter memory or letter sounds by making two sets of the "Lotto" call cards and playing "Concentration." Start by turning four to six pairs of cards face down. If this is too easy, add more pairs.

7. Create or buy games for learning centers that focus on learning words and vocabulary. For example, you may want to use "Sight Word Bingo" or have the children play games in which they create words using word families.

8. Make a word wall of popcorn words. These are words that "pop up" everywhere such as colors, numbers, and pronouns. The goal is for them to "pop" into the child's head.

9. Incorporate reading into other areas where children need to read informational text to complete a project. Support the written word with pictures or drawings.

10. Read tests out loud to children with communication disabilities or to English language learners if you want to know about comprehension rather than reading skills.

11. Read children a variety of books, and talk about different types of texts, when each would be the most useful or enjoyable, who wrote and illustrated them, and the various parts of different types of book.

Writing

The focus in early writing is on meaning. If the initial focus on written work is on the spelling and punctuation, young writers can become discouraged. Allowing children to spell creatively (how it sounds or looks to them, regardless of accuracy) increases their fluency and allows writing to serve as an outlet for children who are not comfortable speaking. Correcting children's spelling as they are just beginning to write causes some of the same problems as correcting their speech. If the task becomes onerous, children try not to participate; if children do participate, they take as few risks as possible.

Writing provides both challenges and solutions for children with communication disorders. First, they have to establish the connection between the written and spoken word. Do this informally by pointing out to children that you cannot see words if their hand is over them, or that you cannot read the book if it is upside down. Write down what they say, but do not hesitate to ask them to slow down, pointing out that you cannot write as quickly as they can talk. Use language experience stories, and support all of children's attempts at writing regardless of the quality of the letters or the spelling.

1. Write children's names on their papers and point out to children that you do this so they will not get mixed up. If you forget who made them, you can look at the name.

2. Support children's verbalizations by writing down what they say and then reading it back to them. Again, point out the advantage of a written language by reading what the children said at a later date.

3. Discuss writing as a symbol system, and point out that the English language uses the alphabet most are familiar with, but some other languages do not. Illustrate these. Have the children create a syllabary (a type of dictionary); they can decide on the written configurations that stand for words or syllables and can use this to write to each other. (In this instance, spelling is irrelevant.)

4. Have a writing center and support writing as a process that involves authorship, illustration, editing, and publishing. Support children in each stage of the process. Place the center near available computers. See Activities 2–12, *Authors and Illustrators*, and 2–25, *Writing Center*.

5. Scribe or write for a child when measuring content, not writing skills.

• • • Language

Many children with communication disorders need support in building vocabulary and understanding the conventions of standard English. They need a language-rich environment and contextual clues to make language more meaningful.

1. Help children learn the names for the body parts that are involved with speech.

2. Say a simple sentence and have children "walk" through the sentence by being big for the capital letter at the beginning of the word, taking a step for each word, jumping over the space between words, and stopping at the period. If the end punctuation is an exclamation point, have them jump up and down.

3. Show older children how to use spell and grammar checks as part of their writing and editing.

Discovery

For children with only speech problems, the discovery area is not likely to be different from that for other children in the classroom. Like others, these children need to start with concrete experiences to learn best. Emphasize the vocabulary that goes with the experiences of learning math and science: longer, shorter, more, less, the same, equal, one more, and one less. Children can learn through science how sounds are made and which parts of the body are involved in making various sounds. They can learn to use objects such as a feather or pinwheel to observe the effect of their breath. Technology offers an opportunity for communicating without the need for speaking, while it can also reinforce communication.

• • • Mathematics

Children with communication problems usually have math skills comparable to their classmates. They often enjoy math, as it can be learned with a minimum of speech. Math, then, can give these children a feeling of achievement.

1. Use math concepts to facilitate speech and language development. Have children count and sort objects that make sounds and objects that don't. Have them count the number of times a sound is made.

2. Make number books by having children cut out a specified number of pictures beginning with the same sound. You might have, for example, one /T/, two /R's/, three /S's/, four /B's/, and so on.

3. Apply the math vocabulary (e.g., big/little, more/less, equal) to sounds and body awareness. Tell children to make their bodies take up as much space as they can, then as little. Have them find pictures of an animal with a big tail and one with a little tail. Do those animals make big/loud sounds or little/soft sounds?

4. Present pictures of geometric shapes, and have children draw these shapes in the air. Once they have shown they understand by tracing the shapes with their hands, have them outline the shapes with their jaw, head, tongue, and finally by moving only their eyes. Discuss the characteristics of the shapes and how they are different.

5. Put a word wall up in the classroom that includes math words. Practice saying these words with the whole class, and send a copy home. Include definitions on the copy you send home.

6. Compare the chest measurements of children after they inhale and after they exhale. This can be done with string or measuring tape; string is more effective with younger children because they can see which string is longer. Discuss why the measurements change, and then do it again.

• • • Science

Science can enhance children's understanding of the mechanics of speech and language. Although fewer verbal skills are required by science than by some other subjects, interest is usually high, and science can stimulate language use.

1. Teach some anatomy, especially the organs that produce sound (lips, tongue, teeth, throat, diaphragm, etc.).

2. Put up a word wall in the classroom that includes science words. As with math, practice saying these words with the whole class, and include the words and their definitions for children to take home.

3. Use mirrors to help children see the articulatory organs while exploring the concept of mirror images (reversals).

4. Discuss the sounds different animals make and how they make them. (Crickets, for example, rub their legs together.) Have children experiment making sounds by using different body parts (e.g., clap, stomp, slap thighs). Make a recording of animal sounds, and pair the picture of the animal with the sound.

5. Talk about how sound is made in nature (e.g., thunder, water moving, wind) and how humans make noise (e.g., music, talking, working). Discuss how noise cues us about what is happening in our environment. These sounds may be presented on tapes or compact discs. Use pictures to present the sounds; the visual reinforces the aural learning.

6. Discuss the properties of air and its function in speech. Use a beach ball or fan to make air more tangible.

Technology

Computers require no verbal input, yet are capable of verbal output. Children who will later depend on technology for communication should be interacting with them from the preschool years on. Most computers are designed with internal features that can be modified to make them easier for children to use. The manufacturers have this information and willingly share it. Use digital cameras, electronic tablets, cds, dvds, and videotapes or tape recorders to communicate information.

1. Have a computer with a voice synthesizer in the classroom so children can become familiar with it.

2. Help children become familiar with computers. If necessary, modify a keyboard to match the child's needs. See Activities 3–64w, *Alphabet Keyboard*, and 3–29, *Computer Bingo*.

3. Encourage children to learn that technology is part of their life and that they are in control of technology.

4. Encourage children with communication disorders to regularly play on the computer with another classmate. They often will be eager to play, will speak while playing, and may develop friendships.

5. Take digital pictures and use them to talk with children and to share information with families.

6. Videotape field trips and class experiences so you can reflect on experiences with the children.

7. Use electronic tablets and appropriate applications.

Wellness

Work on language skills that will increase children's safety and/or auditory identification of warning signals. Use large motor activities to build self-esteem and to support children's inclusion. Talk about their skills and what they are doing.

Sensory motor activities support the communication process by increasing body awareness. They provide opportunities for communication, but are not dependent on it. Supply words for what children are doing in the motor area. Focus fine motor activities on those movements associated with speech, such as breath control and lip and tongue action, in addition to those necessary for visual discrimination, writing, and adaptive skills. Help children increase their body awareness, particularly to learn when they are tense. Many speech problems increase with tension.

Health and Safety

Speech and language production requires the coordination of muscles from the waist up, the speech organs, and the brain. It is one of the most complicated human processes. Children need to be made aware of the body parts involved. Listening to someone who has nasal congestion helps children learn the nose's function; a sore throat demonstrates the throat's contribution to speech.

Teeth—Discuss how to care for teeth. Invite a dentist to visit the class. As children lose their baby teeth, discuss what sounds become difficult. Have them discover the role teeth play in making sounds.

Jaw—Use scissors to illustrate the hinge-like action of the jaw. Have children use their fingers to feel the bones and muscles as they drop their jaw. Again, experiment with sound as the jaw lowers and rises.

Tongue—Do tongue exercises with the class. Let the children use mirrors to watch their tongue move. Have them pair off and watch each other. Make it fun.

Vocal Cords—Have children place their hands on their throat to feel the vocal cords vibrate. See whether they can feel a difference in sounds. Use a rubber band to show how the vocal cords work, stretching it tight for high sounds and only slightly for low ones.

1. Teach children the language of safety: Stop/go (red/green), fast/slow, quickly/slowly, carefully, quietly, and so on. Children not only need to know the words but also need to have a sensory motor understanding of the behaviors.

2. Teach children how to talk about their needs and wants. This is one of the reasons for language. Also, tell children how to verbalize that they need help or have a problem.

3. Go on imaginary walks with children to demonstrate language safety concepts. Children need to know that moving quietly means walking on tiptoes very carefully without talking. See Activity 4–9, *Traffic Sign Hunt*.

4. Talk about voices and how they are used and where they are used appropriately. Talk about what happens when children shout, scream, or talk loudly for too long.

5. Discuss times when it is appropriate to scream or speak loudly. Also, discuss times when it is appropriate to speak quietly and wait for your turn to talk. Introduce "6-inch voices"; this means speaking as if you were 6 inches tall during quiet times.

6. Help children learn about the various health problems related to the speech-producing parts of the body, how to describe their symptoms, and what is typically done about them.

7. Blow objects like a ping pong ball or a pinwheel to help develop the muscles of the mouth, to give children practice in closing off the palate and throat, and to teach breath control. Your role is to make this fun.

Physical Education

Using large muscles is usually a pleasure and should be encouraged. Because children's language problems rarely interfere, this may prove to be one of their strengths.

Playing together with blocks and trains provides many opportunities to communicate and few demands.
©Cengage Learning 2012

1. Use large motor play to foster a sense of group belonging.
2. Help classmates see children's strengths in this area.
3. Play cooperative, not competitive, games. As cooperative play increases, children talk more to each other.
4. Play structured games outdoors to give children with communications differences a chance to be part of a team and to participate with a group, without high language demands.
5. Include games using balls, from playground balls to soccer balls to beach balls. See Activity 4–20, *Circle Ball*.

Sensory Motor Integration

Children need to listen in coordination with seeing, hearing, and touching.

1. Use activities that pair listening skills with visual or tactile skills: "Turn the page when you hear the tone."
2. Use activities that help establish a hand preference (e.g., coloring, turning nuts on bolts, eating). (It is irrelevant which hand is preferred.) Play hand-clapping games. See Activity 4–22, *Hand Clapping*.

Children need to focus on the small muscles of their body; eye movements are necessary for reading, the hand and fingers for writing, and the facial muscles for speaking.

1. Start with large writing tools, and then provide many opportunities for children to pick up small items to develop finger strength.
2. Encourage children to draw or scribble by providing a variety of paper and drawing utensils and many varieties of manipulative toys.
3. Have children make funny faces and describe them, and then have the other children copy them. Encourage them to use many different facial features.

Creative Arts

Creative arts offer children the ability to develop skills, with much less emphasis on the specific product. Children may become so absorbed in the creative arts that they forget their reluctance to talk as they discover they want to share their work with others. Music can provide a non-threatening atmosphere for using expressive language. Through music, you can encourage children to attempt speech and to imitate other children and adults. Include songs and activities that concentrate on sounds that are difficult for them to produce. Movement and dance allow children to participate without speech and also provide the potential for increasing body awareness. Through dramatic play, children can practice situations before encountering them. They can use puppets, talk on the telephone, or dress up and pretend they are another person as they participate in situations that provide the opportunity for communication. With theater, they can write the script and direct the play.

Visual Arts

Visual art activities provide a nonverbal way of expressing feelings and working off energy.

1. Help children learn to recognize differences in how pencils, crayons, markers, paint, and chalk sound, feel, look, and are used.
2. Encourage children to talk about their pictures (not in response to "What is it?" or, as a naïve graduate student once asked a 3-year-old, "What does this picture represent to you?"). Start out with a comment such as "I like the way you use red in this picture." That's an invitation—you may have shown enough interest to get a response. You might ask, "Does your picture have a story?" Be prepared for the fact that it may not!
3. Have children create pictures or art together, such as murals or collages. Children may talk when working on a task they can make a real contribution to.
4. Encourage children to use drawing and painting to communicate feelings or events in their lives and talk about them if they choose.
5. Show children murals and discuss how they have been used to express feelings and opinions people could not talk about.
6. Make puppets for use in dramatic play. Often, shy children will vocalize more with puppets.

Music

Music requires children to develop and use different vocal patterns. Both blowing into instruments and singing stimulate the palate and musculature of the mouth. Because some speech problems don't carry over into singing, this vocal activity can be especially rewarding.

1. Have children make musical instruments to develop listening skills. Make paper plate tambourines filled

with beans or rice. These can be played in a group as well as paired according to the different sounds they make. Have children make and use musical instruments that emphasize mouth movements. See Activities 5–19, *Making Tambourines*, and 5–49w, *Reeds*.

2. Help children become more aware of their voices as they whistle, hum, and sing high and low, loud and soft. Help them note tension in the lips and the feel of air coming in and out. Help them relate what they learn to speaking.

3. Using music provides a natural way to teach the concepts of high and low. Reinforce the concepts by having the children stretch their bodies high for the high notes, crouch low for the low notes, and be somewhere in between for the middle notes.

4. Hold notes for long or short periods of time to increase breath awareness and improve breath control. See Activity 5–14, *Conductor*.

5. Sing, as the rhythm of music also applies to speech and language, especially for children who are dysfluent. Interestingly, children can often sing things they cannot say. To create more awareness of rhythm, you can have children lower their jaws (as if chewing), or even click tongues to a rhythmical pattern.

6. Sing action songs that allow children to participate whether or not they know the words. Actions provide visual cues for learning the words.

7. Play compact discs to enhance listening skills, and ask children questions to help them comprehend the content and purpose of the music.

8. Use simple musical instruments to play along with a recorded song.

●●● Movement and Dance

Use movement to increase body awareness (especially of speech organs) and to provide relaxation.

1. Have children pretend to be clothes fluttering on the line in a gentle wind. To relax the throat and neck, have the children drop their heads forward (chin toward chest). Have the wind pick up a bit and then die down. Talk with children about the differences in the strength of the wind and their implications. Use a variable speed fan if children seem to have trouble understanding the concept, and hold a piece of clothing in front of it as you change the speeds. Be sure the fan is one that is safe for children.

2. Encourage games, like charades, and movements that use pantomime and discuss how frustrating it is not to be understood.

3. Dance to music and interpret the mood or rhythm of the dance.

4. Use movement to help children relax. See Activities 5–21, *Rag Dolls*, and 5–26, *Relaxation Stories*.

●●● Dramatic Play and Theater

Dramatic play and theater provide safe outlets for energy and an opportunity for children to try out roles without fear of judgment. They also allow children to be a part of a group.

1. At the beginning of the year, the dramatic play area should be an easy, familiar, nondemanding place. Children may drift toward this area, as it represents a tie with home. (This is particularly true of younger children.)

2. Children may be fearful of new situations and the demands they may make on their language skills. Take advantage of dramatic play and theater to have children rehearse potential experiences beforehand to gain knowledge of what to expect and how to use a script as a guide in playing roles.

3. Puppets encourage speech in a nonthreatening way. Play a recording of characters with very distinctive speech patterns (such as Donald Duck and Mickey Mouse) as a way of reassuring children that puppets can and do sound different.

4. Join children in dramatic play, and take a minor role in their play. This allows you to facilitate some children's play without obvious intervention.

Routines and Transitions

As children end one activity and prepare to go on to another, there is often some confusion. Turn the confusion into opportunities for learning by taking advantage of routines and transitions to build language.

1. Combine movement and sound to help children get from one area to another: for example, "Walk like a duck and quack as you go to a center." Ask children to walk as quietly or to make as much noise as they can while going to the learning center of their choice.

2. Increase body awareness and sense of self. Dismiss children by having them make a particular sound.

3. Ask children to line up by asking them questions about words and letters.

SUMMARY

- Approximately 20 percent of all children who need special educational services have a communication disorder.

- Communication includes the ability to make and understand language, speech and speech sounds; change meaning; use language in a social environment; and understand and use words appropriately.

- It is challenging to identify speech and language problems because of the developmental nature of communication.

- Assessment of language development is both formal and informal.

- Language delays and disorders include specific language impairment and aphasia.
- Speech delays and disorders include speech sound disorders, articulation, phonological processes, voice disorders, and fluency disorders.

EDUCATIONAL RESOURCES

Ablenet provides a mail-order catalogue of communication aids; they also produce videotapes and conduct technology workshops. www.ablenet.org/

American Speech-Language-Hearing Association (ASHA) is a website divided into specific information for professionals, and the public. The alphabetic index aids in finding specific topics. www.asha.org/

Australian Stuttering Research Centre provides reports on research related to preschool children and stuttering. http://sydney.edu.au/health_sciences/asrc/

Center for Applied Linguistics is a national and international research and resource center in the application of linguistic science for social and educational problems. www.cal.org/

National Stuttering Association has information for parents, professionals, adults, teens, and children. It is easy to navigate and offers information on books, newsletters, and conferences on stuttering. www.nsastutter.org/

Stuttering Foundation of America offers many online resources to help parents, professionals, adults, and children deal with stuttering. The information is plentiful, and there are links to international programs. www.stuttersfa.org/

For additional resources, visit the book companion website for this text at www.cengagebrain.com.

12

Children Who are English Language Learners

I live in fear. Every time I pull out of the driveway, I wonder whether the police will stop me for driving without a license. I can't set up a bank account. I worried when I registered Diego for school because I don't have a social security number. I am undocumented.

For me the risks of being deported are worth it. My country was engulfed in a civil war when I came to the United States. The war disrupted not only the economy—so much so that unemployment was higher than 60 percent in my village and those that found work only made $2 a day—but also made traveling, going to the market, or even attending church services unsafe. Death was a way of life, and a day didn't pass when we didn't hear that someone we knew—a friend, a family member—had either been found dead or had simply disappeared.

I was 18, and my 9-month-old daughter Hannia and I were starving. I walked from Guatemala to the border of Mexico with the help of a coyote. There I train-hopped through Mexico, dodging gangs and the unforgiving wheels of the train that claimed more lives than I care to remember. It took two harrowing months to get from Villa Nueva, Malacatán, Guatemala, to Houston, Texas.

I stayed in a shelter in Houston—Casa Juan Diego—until I had enough strength to work. Then I found employment as a nanny, tending to other children as I wept for the child I'd left behind.

Two years later, I fell in love with a man from El Salvador. He had also fled a civil war and knew what it meant to live in fear—his friends had been shot or tortured by guerrillas. He fled El Salvador, knowing he would never return—and left with a heavy heart, knowing he was leaving his teenage daughter behind. We married in Houston but soon found work to be scarce. So we moved to the east coast, where jobs were plentiful in the poultry industry.

I think the schools are good here, but it is hard for me to know because I speak little English and there is no one at the school who speaks Spanish. My son, Diego, broke his glasses, and he needs them for school, but we don't have enough money to buy new ones. He gets headaches and has trouble seeing the board. In Texas, the children qualified for Medicaid, but in Delaware the requirements are different. We

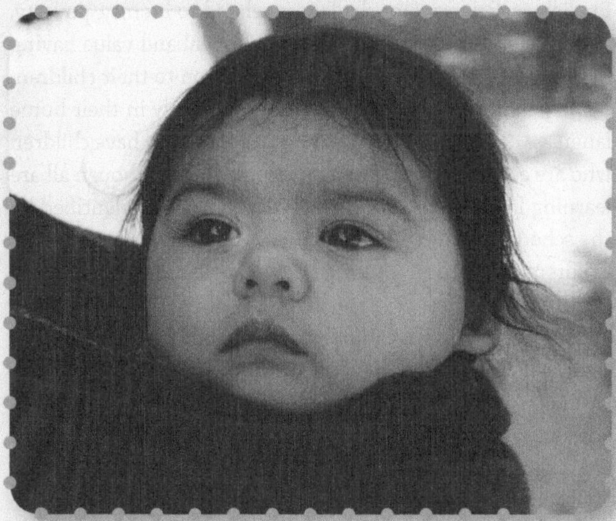

Penny Low Deiner

are trying to save the money to buy Diego new glasses, but with two U.S.-born children here and two children still overseas, it is difficult.

I have not seen Hannia for 10 years. It's hard to be a mom over the phone. You can't hold your daughter or kiss her good night. I dream that one day she will be able to come to the United States. Hannia lives with my parents. They are in their 80s, and my mother has diabetes. I wonder what will happen to her when they die. I cry when I think about her.

Maria, our youngest, is 3, and she stays home with me. I thought about Head Start, but I am too afraid to enroll her. Diego is 6. He is having problems in school, and we can't help him because we can't communicate with his teachers or understand his homework. Kindergarten was okay, but a struggle. I know he is a smart boy, but first grade is difficult for him. He is trying to learn English. They want to test him to see whether he has a disability. They keep sending papers home. Even when the papers are in Spanish, they don't make any sense to me. I wish there were someone at the school I could talk to. I want him to learn English and succeed; that's why we came here. I didn't think it would be so hard.

REFLECTIVE PRACTICE | Children come to school with different cultural and linguistic experiences. Their families too bring different challenges and experiences to the teacher–family partnership. How would you work with this family? What resources do you, the school, and the community have to include children whose home language is not English and whose mother is undocumented?

English Language Learners

English language learners (ELL) are children who have had experience with a language other than English. As a group, these children are diverse. Although 76 percent speak Spanish at home, as a group they speak more than 460 different languages (U.S. DOE, 2008) and have a tremendous range of educational needs. Some parents with limited proficiency in English are highly educated and provide their children with excellent role models in their home language. Other parents with limited English proficiency face challenges related to literacy, poverty, and legal status. Some parents are bilingual and value having two languages, and want to pass this gift on to their children. Some parents cannot read or write proficiently in their home language or English. Not all of these families will have children who are considered English language learners, although all are learning English. In addition to children who are identified by the schools as limited English proficient there are many more children whose home language is not English, and the number is increasing.

As defined in No Child Left Behind and Title III, the goal for English language learners in early childhood education through grade 3 is to prepare them to achieve the same high academic standards that all children are expected to meet. The challenge is the lack of a shared, well-articulated vision to accomplish this (Leos & Saavedra, 2010). The National Assessment for Education Progress in Reading and Mathematics found the achievement gap for ELL children in the fourth and eighth grades to be about 30 percent lower than their English proficient peers (National Center for Educational Statistics, 2009a, 2009b).

Children who are English language learners (ELL) have problems speaking, reading, writing, and understanding English, which interferes with their ability to learn academic information. The first school-related policies for these children began in 1968 and are currently covered in Title III of the No Child Left Behind Act of 2001. The word *bilingual* has been removed from the law and the Office of Bilingual Education and Minority Language Affairs has become the Office of English Language Acquisition, Language Enhancement, and Academic Achievement for Limited English Proficient Students (OELA). The mission of this office is two-fold:

- To provide national leadership to help ensure that English language learners and immigrant students attain English proficiency and achieve academically
- To assist in building the nation's capacity in critical foreign languages (OELA, 2008).

Historically, English language learners have been excluded from the statewide assessment process. However, with the passage of the No Child Left Behind Act, states are required to show that all children are making yearly progress toward reaching the "proficient" level on states' language arts, mathematics, and science assessment by 2014. No Child Left Behind requires states to assess the English proficiency of English language learners annually. Limited English proficiency is viewed as a temporary condition. The expectation is that these children will learn English and that once they have reached proficiency, they will no longer be classified as limited English proficient and hence will meet the same requirements of No Child Left Behind as their peers whose first language is English (U.S. Government Accountability Office [U.S. GAO], 2006a). The requirements of No Child Left Behind hold the potential for improving the education of young English language learners, because they are required to learn the same content and pass the same assessments as other children, and the schools are held accountable for their English proficiency. This may lead to more of an investment in early education programs with strong educational underpinnings in order to serve these children and to begin to close the achievement gap before kindergarten.

Defining English Language Learners

Language is one of humanity's highest achievements. All civilizations have developed a symbol system that allows them to express their ideas and concepts, share their feelings and emotions, remember the past, discuss the present, and plan for the future. However, cultures have varied in the approaches they have taken to language and literacy. The written forms of language are as diverse as the spoken ones. Language and literacy served different purposes and social functions at different times and in different places. In the past, the ability to encode and decode written language was reserved for those with privilege and power. However, in highly literate societies, the ability to read and write affects all people's lives on a daily basis (Ada, 2002).

The No Child Left Behind and the Individuals with Disabilities Educational Opportunity Act of 2004 use the term *limited English proficiency* (LEP). There are a variety of other terms that are also used to refer to this category of children: *English as a second language* (ESL), limited English speaking (LES), second language learners (SLL), potential English proficient, and *non-English speaker*. I have chosen to use *English language learners* or *English learners* as I feel this designation is more positive than the term used in the federal law. It also supports the concept that some children may be learning English as a third or fourth language. In this text, *English language learners* or *English learners* refers to children who are learning the academic English that is used in schools in the United States for teaching and learning (Houk, 2005).

There is a difference between being able to use a language socially and use it academically. Socially, it is enough to be able to be polite and greet others, say thank you, and ask and respond to requests about concrete situations. Academic language requires a far more complicated set of skills. Academic language requires the ability to understand abstract thought, to use inductive and deductive reasoning, and to create and critique ideas and concepts (Fineberg, 2002). Think about how many years you studied English in school. According to most research, it takes more than six years for non-English-speaking children to compete academically with their English-speaking peers (Ada, 1993). Although they learn to speak the language before this, to be able to use English as a tool for learning requires in-depth knowledge not only of speaking and comprehension but also reading and writing.

Young children who are just learning language have a fragile hold on their home language, and if their language development is not supported, they can lose their home language. Parents who speak limited English use their home language to hand down traditional family values and to communicate within the home. Loss of the home language can be damaging to children's self-esteem and may make mastery of their home language and English more difficult (Fineberg, 2002).

IN THE FIELD

I came to the United State at the age of 23. After more than a decade in this country, I still speak English with a Chinese accent. When I was pregnant with my son, I had planned to teach my son the Chinese language, which is spoken by a fourth of the population on earth. I asked my family in China to send me children's books so that I could read to him even before he was born. I wanted to make sure that he would immerse himself in the Chinese language and culture. My plan was to speak and read to him only in Chinese. Good plan, right? Good luck to me.

It was not too difficult in the beginning. When he was little, I could read him anything and he would not protest. I have read all the Chinese children's books and classics that my dear sister could afford to send me. I read to him while he was nursing and before bedtime, and I sang to him in Chinese. He was happy to hear my voice. Those were the happy, easy days. I was so sure that my son would be speaking Chinese as his first language.

My husband, who is not Chinese, however, speaks to my son only in English. Even though English is not my husband's first language, he is more comfortable with it than his mother tongue, which is Urdu. I think that my husband's intention is to make sure that our son will speak English without a foreign accent like us. We have been teased and frowned upon more times than we care to remember.

My son is 2½ years old now. Every morning he greets me in English, asks for his breakfast and milk in English, and wants to watch the Barney DVD. I think his first word was "DVD," and his second was "TV." When I drop him off at the child care center, he will not respond to me unless I talk to him in English. All day long, he spends his time in an English-speaking environment. When I pick him up and start to converse with him in Chinese, he only responds to me in English. Then it starts—my desperate effort to engage my son in Chinese for a few hours before he goes to sleep. I know that he understands my Chinese because he can follow my commands and smiles at my praise of his good behavior. But somehow, it is so difficult to get him to speak the language. When I try to read to him bedtime stories in Chinese, he will cover his head with the blanket or cover my mouth with his hand. By the time he falls asleep, he may have heard about 10 minutes of Chinese spoken to him.

Every night I feel frustrated and wish that I had spoken a few more words in Chinese to my son. Now he can speak English in full sentences, but only phrases in Chinese. What happens to the assumption of acquisition of the "mother tongue"? He seems to pay more attention to me when I speak English. To be fair, I do speak English all day long until I pick him up from child care. How can I expect him to speak Chinese since I don't speak it very often myself?

Despite the resistance on my son's side, I am still very committed to teaching him Chinese. The majority of the rest of the world can speak more than one language. Why can't we? In the meanwhile, I am just going to press on and not give in. It feels almost like a battle between my son and me. The problem I am facing is that there is no nearby environment where my son can practice Chinese. I just have to keep trying and not lose faith. When I have the time and money, I will take him back to China to spend a few months with my family. Perhaps he will pick up the language quicker this way.

I do hope that we can get more encouragement from society. Every time when I speak to my son in Chinese, the child care providers would ask me what I said. I do not want to appear rude or inconsiderate; therefore, I do not speak to my son in Chinese in public any more. It is also extremely difficult to find any books or videos in Chinese. These are the difficulties I am facing. The challenges are mine, and forward-minded shall I be.

REFLECTIVE PRACTICE | How do you feel about raising children bilingually? If you were in this child care setting, how would you respond to this mother's language dilemma? As you think of yourself as a professional in the field, what do you believe about bilingualism in early childhood? As you think about the possibilities of bilingual education, where do you place yourself?

Prevalence of English Language Learners

The United States is a nation of immigrants, many of whom came as English language learners. In the nineteenth and twentieth centuries, the large number of immigrants caused concern and fear. The second wave of immigration began in the mid-1960s. In 1960, Hispanic, Asian, and mixed race children and youth made up about 6 percent of all U.S. children; in 2011, that share is about 30 percent. The number of black children rose slightly to 14 percent, and the number of non-Hispanic white children dropped from 81 to 56 percent. Non-Hispanic white children are expected to be 40 percent of all U.S. children by 2050 (Passel, 2011).

Children from Latin America face rising anti-immigration sentiment. Beginning in 1975, public school districts in Texas were allowed to charge tuition to undocumented students. Few did, but the supreme court ruling in *Plyler* v. *Doe* in 1982 denied states' right to exclude children of **illegal immigrants** from public schools, saying it would hurt children who could contribute socially and politically to the United States and would help to create a subclass of people vulnerable to unemployment and crime (Olivas, 2004).

In 1980, because of the Mariel boatlift that brought younger and poorer Cubans to Dade County, Florida, the voters passed an anti-bilingual ordinance that prohibited spending money or supporting any language other than English or promoting cultures other than mainstream U.S. culture (Saracho & Spodek, 2004). In 1994, California passed Proposition 187, making it illegal for children of **undocumented immigrants** to attend public schools. The federal courts ruled Proposition 187 unconstitutional. In 1998, California voters overwhelmingly approved Proposition 227, which eliminated the state's bilingual education programs and required that all instruction be conducted in English. Arizona passed a similar law, Proposition 203, in 2000 (Saracho & Spodek, 2004). The education of English language learners is controversial.

Immigration is changing the child population of the United States. It is difficult to put a firm figure on the soaring number of immigrant children in the schools, particularly the number of children with limited English proficiency.

Estimates are that one in five U.S. children have an immigrant parent and one in four low-income children have an immigrant parent (Urban Institute, 2010). Since 1998, English language learners and immigrant students have been the fastest-growing student subgroup in the United States, and increase annually at a rate of 10 percent (Fry, 2008). In 2000, there were 10.5 million **immigrant children**—that is, children of **foreign-born parents** and children of **immigrant parents**—enrolled in grades K–12. This is an 84 percent increase in a 10-year period (Hood, 2003). During 2007–2008, there were over 5.3 million English language learners, or 10.6 percent of K–12 public school enrollment (Calderón, Slavin, & Sánchez, 2011). The Urban Institute estimates that from 1990 to 2006 the number of immigrants rose from 20 million to 37 million (2010). From 2000 to 2010, the nation's white population grew by 1.2 percent, while the growth rate for Hispanics and Asians was 43 percent (Frey, 2011a). The rapid growth of the Hispanic population is related to a high and sustained level of immigration, the large number of young adults who are in their family-formation years, and the relatively high fertility rate among Hispanic women (primarily immigrants). The expectation, based on the 2010 census is that white children will be a minority before 2020, and the country will be "minority white" before 2042 (Frey, 2011a). White 3-year-olds comprise less than half (49.9%) of all children this age. This is the youngest age for which data is available (Frey, 2011b). Between 1990 and 2000, the number of students classified as limited English proficient increased by 105 percent, whereas the overall student population increased by only 12 percent. Children of immigrants are the fastest-growing child population; half of them do not speak English fluently (Calderón, Slavin, & Sánchez, 2011). According to the 2000 U.S. Census, nearly one in five people, or 47 million U.S. residents age 5 and older, spoke a language other than English at home.

Economically, politically, and socially, English language learners, Hispanic children in particular, will play an important role in the nation's future. In 2000, there were 106 workers for every 100 nonworkers. It is projected that by 2050 there will be only 90 workers for every 100 nonworkers (Toossi, 2002). Given the projected number of Hispanic children, they and their education are critical for our nation's future. Most young Hispanic children were born in the United States and hence are U.S. citizens. It is important that they become informed, engaged citizens with skills that promote their strengths.

IN THE FIELD

In 2000–2001, 6 percent of the children in my school were identified as having limited English proficiency (LEP). By 2007–2008, that number had grown to more than 40 percent. This makes for very different demands on my staff. Unfortunately, my budget is decreasing. Seven years ago, funding was $530 for each LEP student. It has dropped to $212, and that doesn't cover the need. I have to use local money and take resources away from other children to support this program. I keep moving money around to hire the teachers I need for the LEP children. I apply for grants for before-school and after-school instruction and to help in the summer. I think I spend more time writing grants and begging for money than I do being principal. We have to change how money is allocated or we are going to have a massive population of limited English proficiency children and no money to serve them or the other children.

We place LEP children in different classes, depending on what they need. If children have very little English, they are placed in self-contained classrooms for first and second grade, with Spanish as the language of instruction. We use a small-group pull-out program for some children from the regular class whose comprehension is good but who need additional help, usually in reading and writing English. What we are doing works, but I don't know how much longer we can keep doing it.

Causes of English Language Learners

Children are born into families, and their culture determines what language will be spoken. Shared behavior helps children know how to act with others and establishes broad social patterns that determine what is appropriate or not appropriate in a particular culture. Culture and families are adaptive, creative, and dynamic (Perez & Torres-Guzman, 2002).

Schools, in general, have not done a good job teaching children who are from different linguistic, cultural, and social backgrounds. Studies have documented apparent discrepancies in the levels of referral and placement of LEP children in special education (IDEA, 2004). In 2004, students with limited English proficiency performed below progress goals in two-thirds of the 48 states that reported data. There are some problems obtaining separate test results for limited English proficient students. There is also concern that the U.S. Department of Education is using flawed data to distribute funds to states to support English language learners (U.S. GAO, 2006a). Most English language learners spend their time in regular classrooms with teachers who do not think they are prepared to meet their needs (Calderón, Slavin, & Sánchez, 2011). In addition to looking at the achievement gap, we need to look at teacher preparation.

Children of Immigrant Parents

One out of every five children in the United States is an immigrant or the child of an immigrant parent (Capps, Fix, Ost, et al., 2005). Children are considered to be **children of immigrant parents** if they are younger than 18 years of age and are either themselves foreign born or were born in the United States with at least one foreign-born parent.

PLACE OF ORIGIN OF IMMIGRANT FAMILIES

In 1900, 80 percent of immigrants to the United States came from Europe, with only about 1 percent coming from Latin America and Asia (U.S. Bureau of the Census, 1999). Today immigrants come mainly from Latin America. See Table 12–1 for the place of origin of current immigrant families.

GROWTH AND LOCATION OF IMMIGRANT CHILDREN IN THE UNITED STATES

In the 1990s, the population of immigrant children grew at seven times the rate of native-born children (Capps, Fix, Ost, et al., 2005). Although immigrants make up 11 percent of the total U.S. population, children of immigrants make up

TABLE	PLACE OF ORIGIN OF IMMIGRANT PARENTS OF CHILDREN
12-1	**YOUNGER THAN AGE 6**

- 64% (3.7 million) Latin America and the Caribbean
  - 39% (2.3 million) Mexico
  - 25% (1.4 million) other Latin American and Caribbean countries
- 23% (1.4 million) Asia
- 7% (423,000) Europe and Canada
- 6% (363,000) Africa and the Middle East

Source: Capps, Fix, Ost, et al., 2005.

22 percent of the 23.4 million children younger than age 6 in the United States and 20 percent of children ages 6 to 17 (Capps, Fix, Ost, et al., 2005). Most of the growth of the Hispanic population today is because of births to U.S. families rather than immigration (Frey, 2011a).

Two-thirds of children of immigrants are concentrated in six states: California, Texas, New York, Florida, Arizona, and New Jersey. However, immigrants are increasingly moving to other states. Regardless of the state they live in, many Hispanic children and their families are residentially segregated from whites, reinforcing segregated school patterns (Frey, 2011c).

THE EVIDENCE BASE

Five states educate over half of the English language learners in the United States: Arizona, California, Florida, New York, and Texas. Data from these states were used to look at the role schools play in the English learner achievement gap. In all five states, English learners were much less likely than white children to score at or above the state's proficient level.

About half the elementary schools in the nation educate English language learners. However, almost 70 percent of English learners are enrolled in 5,000 public schools. This is 10 percent of the nation's 50,000 elementary schools. Although these schools served 70 percent of English learners, they accounted for only 13 percent of elementary school children (Consentino de Cohen, Deterding, & Clewell, 2005). These schools are identified as "High-LEP" schools. They are mostly located in urban areas, where there are a majority of English learners. Many of the children are economically disadvantaged, embedding the discussion in the context of poor, minority, immigrant-serving urban schools. The other 30 percent of English language learners are educated in "Low-LEP" schools, in which they are a minority population. (Remember, the U.S. Department of Education uses the term *limited English proficiency*, hence LEP.)

There are significant differences between High-LEP and Low-LEP schools in principal and teacher demographics, training, and experience. With the exception of Florida, the High-LEP reporting schools tend to be located in central cities; the schools themselves are larger and serve more children; there is a higher child-to-teacher ratio, they have more children qualified for free or reduced-price lunch; and they have fewer white children.

When English learners and white children attend the same schools, the differences in proficiency are less. In Arizona, the differences in white and English language learners overall is 35 points, but this dropped to 27 points for children in Low-LEP schools. In California, the difference scores dropped from 32 to 21 points. Math proficiency rates are lower for LEP-reporting schools for all children who attend the school, not just English learners. Overall, English language learners do better in schools with enough white children to report the results of white children separately and sufficient black children to report the results of black children. English learners' math achievement scores are lowest when schools report the results of English language learners and black children but there are insufficient white children to report white results.

Source: Fry, 2008.

REFLECTIVE PRACTICE | Reflect on the implications of high- and low-LEP schools and what this means for the education of all children. What are the implications of segregated neighborhoods that are reflected in high-LEP schools? We frequently think about individual children and classrooms, but rarely the influence that schools per se have on children. What does this information mean in a practical sense? Will this influence the schools you might want to teach in? How do school populations impact children's education, and what might be done to bring about change?

The rapid growth of this population of young children in many different states has moved the concern about educating immigrant children from a small number of states and cities to a national concern (Capps, Fix, & Passel, 2002).

STATUS OF IMMIGRANT CHILDREN

Most young children in immigrant families are born in the United States and are American citizens (93%); 7 percent of children younger than age 6 have foreign citizenship. See Table 12–2 for the status of children younger than 6 years of age. The status of other family members is more complex. Most of these children live in mixed-status families with one or more noncitizen parents (Capps, Fix, Ost, et al., 2005).

Half of the children of immigrant parents, younger than age 6, have a parent who came to the United States during

English learners come from many different countries and different cultures and have different levels of skills in English and their home language.
©Cengage Learning 2012

TABLE 12-2 STATUS OF CHILDREN YOUNGER THAN 6 YEARS OF AGE BORN TO IMMIGRANT PARENTS

- 19% are citizen children of naturalized citizen parents.
- 48% are citizen children of legal noncitizen parents (permanent residents, people who have been granted asylum, and those with work permits).
- 26% are citizen children of undocumented parents.
- 4% are legal noncitizen children (children who came to the United States due to a parent's work, people who have been granted asylum, or those awaiting citizenship).
- 3% are undocumented noncitizen children.

Source: Capps, Fix, Ost, et al., 2005; Schmidley, 2003.

the past 10 years. Of these children, 86 percent have only foreign-born parents (Capps, Fix, Ost, et al., 2005; Schmidley, 2003). You might ask why this matters. It matters because many federally funded programs are not available to legal immigrants until they have lived in the United States for 5 years or longer. If one member of the family is undocumented, the family may fear dealing with federal agencies even though the child is eligible for services. It also means that the home language may not be English.

Children whose parents have limited English proficiency face not only language barriers, but also health barriers. Parents with limited English proficiency are three times more likely than parents who speak English well to have children in fair or poor health. Of parents who report that they speak English not at all, 27 percent were uninsured (Flores, Abreu, & Tomany-Korman, 2005). Children of immigrants face other challenges as well. Ninety-six percent of children from Central America and Haiti have been separated from one or both parents for a few months to a few years. Separations place children and mothers at risk for depression and other illnesses (Suárez-Orozco, Todorova, & Louie, 2002).

Immigrants from Southeast Asia (Vietnam, Cambodia, and Laos) are primarily refugees. These children are likely to have nontraditional family structures because of the death of family members in war or refugee camps. They have complex living arrangements and may create fictive kinship networks they consider family (Landale, Thomas, & Van Hook, 2011).

Some immigrant groups come with a competitive advantage. Not only do Asian immigrants' children have more educated parents, but also school personnel have been willing to invest in their education. In contrast, the children of Latin American immigrants have greater socioeconomic disadvantages and also stereotypes that marginalize them in schools (Crosnoe & López Turley, 2011). Children of Latin American immigrants have lower levels of school readiness than other groups of immigrant and nonimmigrant children (Reardon & Galindo, 2009). However, although they scored lower in math, they were rated higher by their teachers in work habits than those of the same socioeconomic status (Crosnoe & López Turley, 2011).

The major challenge facing the largest Latin American immigrant population, Mexicans and their children, is their limited opportunity for economic integration. On average, Mexican immigrants have completed about 8½ years of education. Additionally, limited English proficiency and unauthorized legal status limits employment opportunities. One result is that 34 percent of Mexican children immigrants are poor (Landale, Thomas, & Van Hook, 2011). Almost half of Mexican American children live in families with mixed legal status, where children are citizens and at least one parent is not here legally. This situation is true for 13 percent of Asian immigrant children and 14 percent of European immigrant children (Fortuny & Chaudry, 2009).

Undocumented immigrants face the possibility of deportation. One solution to illegal immigrants is to raid worksites and catch, punish, and deport workers. This practice has increased sevenfold between 2002 and 2006 and is expected to continue rising. The majority of the individuals seized had no criminal violations other than being in the country illegally. Many of the individuals were not allowed to communicate with their families or lawyers before being transported to out-of-state detention centers or deported (Castañeda, 2007). The reason for including this information is not political; it is to raise the question "What happens to the children?"

For every two persons arrested, one child is affected, and most of the children are under 10 years of age. Millions of children are at risk of being separated from their parents. After a large-scale raid, community members try to arrange for the children. These children and families face severe financial hardship. Adults are often afraid to go to the grocery store to buy necessities. Some hide in homes and basements and do not send children to school for days or weeks. Children experience feelings of abandonment, fear, social isolation, and anger. Family friends and teachers noticed changes in children's behaviors immediately after the raids. In serious cases, they may experience separation anxiety, depression, posttraumatic stress disorder, and even suicidal thoughts (Castañeda, 2007; Perreira & Ornelas, 2011).

Early Identification of English Language Learners

A child's first language, or home language, is the language that the infant was first exposed to, the one she heard and overheard her parents speak before and after her birth (Stechuk, Burns, & Yandian, 2006). Infants and children exposed to two languages at the same time are called **dual-language learners** (Genesse, Paradis, & Crago, 2004).

● ● ●
Dual-Language Learners

We know more about the development of monolingual children than bilingual children. At 24 months, monolingual children average 200 to 300 words in their expressive vocabulary. By about 30 months, this grows to 400 words (Hulit & Howard, 2006). One explanation for the child's ability to acquire so much information about so many words is the concept of **fast mapping** (Carey & Bartlett, 1978).

In fast mapping, when a child first encounters a new word, she uses the surrounding language and the context to gain some clues about the meaning of the word. She stores these bits of information. When the word is next encountered, the child adds to her knowledge base about the word. This process works best when children hear the same word over a period of time. Drilling a child on a word is not effective because the context within the drill is the same each time, and it is more difficult for the child to extract the bits of information necessary to form meaning. What this means in the context of word knowledge and vocabulary building is that children may have bits and pieces of information about a word, but not a complete understanding of it (Hulit & Howard, 2006). This is why so much programming for children is theme or unit based and why culture and context are important for children learning a first or second language.

Adults often believe that learning one's home language is effortless and that trying to learn two languages would get in the way of learning a single language. These beliefs may be wrong. Infants exposed to two languages babble and use the same number of vocalizations as monolingual infants (Oller et al., 1997). Children who have good language models in two languages meet the same milestones as monolingual children relative to first words, two-word utterances, and the achievement of 50 words. Children's vocabulary was similar and they spoke in the language of their communication partner (Petito et al., 2001). There are different ways to count vocabulary. When the vocabulary of a bilingual child is counted, the vocabulary in each language is counted, then combined for a total. This may actually be an underestimation if the child knows the translational equivalents (e.g., *zapatos* in Spanish and *shoes* in English) of many words.

There is some concern that young children do not understand that they are learning two languages. This is especially true when they code-switch, or mix, the two languages. As children are learning two languages, there may be words they know in one language, but not in the other. It is natural for them to use the words they know from both languages (**code-switching**). However, their switches are grammatically correct. Think about your language. What if you wanted to use the word *simultaneous*, but you couldn't think of it, so you said "at the same time." That is how young children code-switch. They use a word they know in one language to substitute for a word they don't know in the other. As their vocabulary grows, this becomes less frequent. As you talk with them, include the words they are trying to learn. Provide a language-rich environment.

Young children who are raised in a bilingual environment may show language delays. Communication differences based on learning English as a second language should not be confused with communication disorders. Children who speak languages other than English can have language delays. However, it may take a native speaker, ideally a

bilingual speech-language pathologist, to pinpoint areas of concern.

● ● ●
Second Language Development in Young Children

The changing demographics of the early childhood population demand that educators have some knowledge about second language acquisition and culturally sensitive instruction as well as first language learning (Hepburn, 2004).

Some aspects of second language acquisition are the same as first language learning; others differ. The stage the child is in may determine the most appropriate teaching strategies. Carrera-Carrillo and Smith (2006) identify five stages in second language learning with the corresponding developmental process and appropriate teaching strategies:

- *Preproduction.* When children start the second language learning process, they understand few words and may have no verbalizations. To show they understand, they do such things as nod or shake their head, point to objects, or categorize them. Children need a language-rich environment, including many different and varied learning and listening opportunities with an emphasis on physical movement, art, and music. Mixed ability groups work well as does shared interactive reading.

- *Early Production.* Children have limited comprehension and can use one and two word responses. They can identify people, places, and things, repeat some language, and listen with greater understanding. Context helps children understand the meaning of language. This is the time to ask *Who/What/Where/When/How* questions, give either–or choices, and ask yes–no questions. Encourage children to label and actively manipulate objects. Before shared reading or other activities that are new, activate children's prior knowledge to provide a context for learning and ensure that the reading is interactive.

- *Speech Emergence.* Children have good comprehension and can make simple sentences that may have errors but are understandable. This is the time to build vocabulary, define new words, and describe people, places, and events. Encourage children to retell information in their own words. Teachers should move to more open-ended questions as well as modeling, restating, enriching, and expanding children's language. Continue to provide and use context in learning and create language experience stories and books. Small groups work well.

- *Intermediate Fluency.* Children at this stage have excellent comprehension and few grammatical errors. They can express and defend views, behaviors, and actions. They can negotiate with others and give their own opinions. Teachers can begin to use larger groups and provide more complex language. Children should actively participate in the writing, editing, and publishing process with appropriate reference materials.

- *Advanced Fluency.* Children have oral and written language comparable to native English speakers of the same age. Teachers continue to use and support an integrated language arts program.

In reality, although the stages have been identified, there is little evidence to support a separate set of "second language" learning experiences for young children (Stechuk, Burns, & Yandian, 2006). However, if you reflect on the stages, they are very similar for all young children learning language.

In addition to language development, there is interest in finding out how children best learn to read. This was challenging because there are far fewer studies to be evaluated. Ultimately, the National Literacy Panel cited the same reading skills (phonemic awareness, phonics, fluency, vocabulary, and comprehension) as being needed regardless of the language of instruction (Leos & Saavedra, 2010).

International Children Adopted into English Speaking Homes

The number of children living with adoptive parents in the United States is increasing. According to the 2000 census, there were 2.1 million adopted children living in the United States (Administration for Children and Families [ACF], 2003). Of the 13 percent who were adopted from foreign countries, about half (48%) were born in Asia, a third (33%) in Latin America, and a sixth (16%) in Europe. Korea is the largest single source of foreign-born adopted children and accounts for 15 percent of adopted children younger than age 6, with China contributing 3 percent. Most of the European-born adopted children younger than age 6 (82%) came from Russia and Rumania. Seventeen percent of adopted children were of a different race than their family householder (ACF, 2003). Although adopted from different countries, most adopted children share one commonality: They are English language learners. Their situation is different from children whose home language is their first language. These children face both language and cultural differences.

We may not think of the challenges these children face as English language learners. They are leaving familiar surroundings and immediately thrust into an environment where the language and culture is unfamiliar. We know little about how these children best learn English as a second language.

> ▶❚ TeachSource Video Case
>
> **Modifications for a Culturally and Linguistically Diverse Student in an Inclusive Elementary Classroom**
>
> Watch the TeachSource Video *Modifications for a Culturally and Linguistically Diverse Student in an Inclusive Elementary Classroom*, in which you'll see Christina, a fourth-grader with some fine motor deficits who has come to the United States from the Ukraine. Her teacher and her mother describe her rapid progress in acquiring English and the various interventions, including sign language, manipulatives, and visual aids, that have been put in place. The video can be found in the Early Childhood Education Media Library under Special Education, available at www.cengagebrain.com.

Supporting Second Language Learning

Some children come to school proficient in their home language but with no knowledge of English. These children can express themselves at home, get their wants and needs met, and communicate their joys and sorrows. They come to school and must not only master the content of the curriculum but also learn English and a new set of cultural expectations. They may feel different. They have lost some of their identity—personal and cultural—and their ability to express themselves. There is concern that these young children may find the totality of this experience overwhelming and withdraw.

There are a variety of ways in which adults support children's language learning. One strategy is that of *saying* the word in English and in the child's home language. For example, if a child were playing with a train, the adult might point to the train and say, "tren"(Spanish) and then say, "train." This may be followed by a request *asking* the child, "Can you say train?" A response to this question is hopefully followed by reinforcing statements such as "That's close—good for you!" or "You certainly can." At a later time, there might be follow-up about the train where the adult *talks about* the properties of the train or the phonemic aspect of the word: "This train is moving on the track. I wonder where it is going?" Or, "Train starts with the sound /t/ like your name: /t/rain,/T/omas." Other times, adults *define* the word: "All of this [*gesturing*] is the train. This front part of the train that makes it move is called the engine. It pulls the other cars. The last car is the caboose." Sometimes adults *explain* a word by adding details and tying them into the children's experience: "When you come to school, you cross over the railroad tracks. Have you ever had to stop and wait for a train to pass? Some trains are long and others are shorter. Some of the trains go very fast, but others seem to go back and forth and they take a long time. But, all of the trains have to stay on the track. They can only go where there are train tracks" (Han et al., 2005). Obviously, your use of these techniques is dependent upon the age of the child, the child's interest in the topic, and your assessment of the child's language skills.

Speaking is one aspect of language. An academic language also requires reading and writing. To be successful readers, children need to have a stock of about 6,000 root words by grade 2. To achieve this requires them to acquire about two new word meanings per day from age 1 (Biemiller & Slonim, 2001). If children do not have a strong English vocabulary, they are unlikely to become successful readers. So, an important part of early childhood education for all children who are English language learners is the development of vocabulary, particularly root words.

Root words are common words and are defined as basic vocabulary as opposed to rare words that are specific and used infrequently. A root word is a real word and one you can make new words from by adding prefixes and suffixes. For example, the root word *use* can become *useful, useless, using, user, usable, misuse, used,* and so on. Together these words form a word family. **Word families** share the same root word, part of the spelling, and have a shared meaning. Using word families is a way of increasing vocabulary. One responsibility of the adults in all children's environments is to ensure that there are many opportunities for the development of vocabulary and that the adult and child jointly focus their attention on the same object or event at the same time (Owens, 2005).

Assessment of English Language Learners

The intent of the IDEA (2004) is to ensure that children's abilities, not just their English, are tested. It reads:

> *Materials and procedures used to assess a child with limited English proficiency (must be) selected and administered to ensure that they measure the extent to which the child has a disability and needs special education, rather than measuring the child's English language skills.*

However, it is difficult to assess young English language learners. Even if assessments are translated, they are not necessarily equivalent. A word that is difficult in English may not be the same level of difficulty in other languages (U.S. GAO, 2006b). Children may be given accommodations to help in the testing situation or an alternative assessment. These too may impact the validity of the measure unless it can be demonstrated that the assessments are equivalent. No Child Left Behind requires that LEP children be provided with reasonable accommodations and be tested "in the language and form most likely to yield accurate data." If children have been in U.S. public schools for three years or more, language arts must be assessed in English. States must establish English language proficiency standards and these standards must be aligned with academic content standards. They are required to measure all English language learners' oral language and skills in reading and writing English annually from kindergarten through grade 12 (NCLB, 2001).

IMPLICATIONS FOR EDUCATORS

It takes approximately two years for children to become socially competent in a language and five or six years for academic competence. Thus, it is unlikely that children who are English language learners will be academically competent during the early childhood years. What further confounds the issue is that children may know information in one language and not in another. For example, if a child whose home language is Spanish attended an English-only preschool at ages 3 and 4 and the assessment is given at the entrance to kindergarten, what language should the child be tested in? He might actually know colors and numbers and other things better in English, but if a question involved problem solving or complex thinking, he would do better in Spanish. Look at the results of testing very carefully in the context of what you know about the child and his language development, and make decisions based on multiple sources of evidence gathered over time, not just test scores.

English Language Learners in Early Care and Education

High-quality early childhood education holds the potential for helping all young children enter kindergarten with skills to get along with others and the reading and math skills that are vital to success in kindergarten and beyond. They particularly benefit low-income children and those at risk of school failure. Children born to immigrant parents face multiple risks that would make participation in quality early childhood education programs beneficial, yet these children are less likely to participate in these programs than native-born children (Matthews & Ewen, 2006).

Quality early childhood programs can help children increase school readiness and accelerate language acquisition as well as serve as a transition to public school. They also increase the probability of identifying children with special needs and starting early intervention. In programs with a broad array of services, families might participate in literacy programs, improve their English, and gain skills that increase their employment opportunities (Matthews & Ewen, 2006).

Although early care and education hold the potential for both short- and long-term gains, immigrant children are less likely to participate. Structural barriers include affordability, availability, and access, as well as language, bureaucratic complexity, distrust and fear of government programs, and cultural preferences for parental care (Karoly & Gonzalez, 2011). Four factors explain the lower use of nonparental or center-based care: higher poverty rates, low parental education, more two-parent families, and Hispanic origin (Karoly & Gonzalez, 2011).

School readiness covers more than academic performance, and many of these skills make children available for learning. Preschool can help immigrant children adapt to a sociocultural environment that is different from home. Children can learn the rules and norms of a school setting, how to play cooperatively with diverse peers, and how to relate to adult authority figures outside the family. It is difficult to quantify the benefit immigrant children receive from preschool. One confounding variable is that parents who provide more parental support at home are also more likely to send their children to preschool (Karoly & Gonzalez, 2011).

When comparing the quality of the preschool programs that immigrant children and native-born children participated in Karoly and Gonzalez (2011) did not find significant differences among programs. However, the overall quality of preschool programs for all children raised concerns.

Children of immigrants face multiple risks. Approximately 29 percent of young children of immigrants live in households that are below the federal poverty level and another 27 percent have incomes between 100 and 200 percent of poverty (Capps, Fix, Ost, et al., 2005b). Of U.S.-born citizens of young children, only 8 percent of parents have less than a high school degree compared to 30 percent of children of immigrants. Over half of all young children of immigrants have at least one parent who has limited English proficiency and almost one-third live in homes that are linguistically isolated. Homes are considered **linguistically isolated** if no one older than the age of 13 speaks English fluently or exclusively (Capps, Fix, Ost, et al., 2005).

TABLE 12-3 PERCENT OF FOURTH-GRADE CHILDREN BY ACHIEVEMENT LEVEL FOR READING AND MATHEMATICS

	Reading Grade 4	Math Grade 4
English Learners		
Advanced	1	1
Proficient	6	11
Basic	21	43
Below basic	73	46
White Children		
Advanced	10	7
Proficient	30	40
Basic	35	42
Below basic	25	11
Black Children		
Advanced	2	1
Proficient	11	12
Basic	29	47
Below basic	59	40
Hispanic Children		
Advanced	2	1
Proficient	13	18
Basic	29	48
Below basic	45	33

Source: National Assessment of Educational Progress, 2005.

available immediately. Long waiting lists cause families frustration after they have reached a difficult decision, and children who have to wait may not be enrolled (Vesely & Ginsberg, 2011).

Mexico is the country of origin for 39 percent of immigrant families with young children. The next country, India, accounts for 2.8 percent of immigrant families with young children (Capps, Fix, Ost, et al., 2005). Three- and 4-year-old children of Mexican origin and children of native-born families with Mexican origins have the lowest preschool enrollment of any group of immigrants. This is also true for kindergarten enrollment (Matthews & Ewen, 2006). Because Mexican immigrants constitute such a large proportion of the immigrant population, the experiences of children of Mexican immigrants drive national trends among all young children of immigrants (Capps, Fix, Murray, et al., 2005).

THE EVIDENCE BASE

Fry analyzed data from the National Assessment of Educational Progress (NAEP), begun in 1969. He looked at a sample of about 172,000 fourth graders to document these findings. By fourth grade, 35 percent of English learners are behind in math and 47 percent are behind in reading when compared to their white counterparts (see Table 12–3). The gap between white children and all other children in math is apparent. The number of children classified as English language learners begins to decrease in second grade as children exit programs that are designed for English learners and move into other classrooms. This pattern continues in every grade thereafter.

Source: Fry, 2007.

REFLECTIVE PRACTICE | Look at the numbers in Table 12–3 carefully. What do they tell you about what all children have learned or not learned in school during the early childhood years? Do some subtraction. How far behind white children are the other groups identified? What does this mean relative to what you do in the classroom and how you teach children?

Mothers in immigrant families are more likely to be married but not work. They are more likely to stay home with their children, and, like all nonworking mothers, their young children are less likely to be in early care and education settings. Children of immigrants are less likely to participate in any type of nonparental care arrangement than children who are born of citizens of the United States (Matthews & Ewen, 2006). Children of immigrants compose 22 percent of children younger than age 6, yet they compose only 16 percent of children attending preschool (Capps, Fix, Murray, et al., 2005). Additionally, federal restrictions and fear of government makes these families less likely to use public benefits and may increase the hardships associated with poverty.

Some early childhood programs have outreach components to neighborhoods with a high population of immigrant families. They target parents who are interested in learning more about child development but not yet ready to place their children in a preschool program. They may include playgroups that meet in a community park. Families learned about the play groups through door-to-door recruitment and immigrant friends with children who participated. If families show interest in more formal preschool programs, enrollment should be

Although there is agreement that children of immigrants should become proficient in English, there is less agreement about how that should be done.
Penny Low Deiner

Educational Approaches for English Language Learners

If we believe that education is the key to success in a global society, then how do we educate English learners to ensure they too have the right keys? One key is literacy, another a more global curriculum, and others may include changes to how instruction is delivered, parent involvement, professional development, and the effective use of technology (Brennan, 2010).

Language is an important vehicle of communication and learning. Supporting early language learning is an important aspect of all early childhood programs. When children are learning two languages, the process is more challenging, but also more rewarding. How this process actually works is dependent on how particular programs are set up. In some settings, the children spend their day in the second language. Depending on the multicultural commitment of the program, there may be few cultural supports for children whose first language is not English. This situation can be both stressful for children and not supportive of the home language; in fact, it devalues the home language. Culture and language are part of the curriculum for young children. See Table 12–4 for a summary of different ways in which programs teach English language learners.

In addition to the overall structure and methods of teaching English language learners, the use of multifunctional learning devices has the potential for playing a major role in how children are taught. English has many words with multiple meanings, such as orange. The meanings are different even though the word is spelled the same way. I can eat an orange or I can wear an orange dress. Words such as these are difficult for English learners. Using devices such as electronic tablets, children can see an orange fruit and someone eating an orange, wearing an orange dress, or stacking an orange block; hear someone pronounce the word *orange*; and create a recording of their voice saying orange (Brennan, 2010).

The Internet has the potential to connect English language learners to information and to people. As children move through the early childhood years, they can access online self-paced tutorials in many languages (Brennan, 2010).

IMPLICATIONS FOR EDUCATORS

Ideally, programs have bilingual educators who are representative of the languages and cultures in the setting. It is easier to build relationships and to understand schedules, routines, and transitions in the home language. If one teacher speaks the children's home language and other teachers speak English, all children are immersed in a rich language environment. This way both teachers are considered pure language models (Carrera-Carrillo & Smith, 2006). However, this may not be possible in settings where there are five or six different home languages. In some cases, no educators speak the child's language or are from her culture. If children will not be taught in their home language, it is imperative that the setting reflect the cultures of the children who attend. A play-based environment and small groups support language learning. A long large-group time in one language does not support language-learning goals (DeBey & Bombard, 2007).

Regardless of the philosophy of the program, children and their families need to be valued and feel positive about their home language and their culture. They need to be encouraged to communicate and never threatened. Code-switching should be accepted and not criticized. Children live in homes and need to be supported in learning their home language, particularly if that is the way they communicate with their parents and extended family.

Think about the different types of program options and the implications of No Child Left Behind. Also, think about your own preparation to teach

---

TABLE 12–4 METHODS OF TEACHING ENGLISH LANGUAGE LEARNERS

Structured immersion: The entire day is in English, with little support or use of the child's home language; the goal is for children to learn English. Research has shown that this slows down academic learning and achievement.

Culturally and language-enriched environments: Although the entire day is in English as in the structured immersion program, there is an effort made to increase the linguistic and cultural awareness in the classroom.

English as a Second Language (ESL): The entire day is in English, with an emphasis on teaching the English language during specific school periods or having children pulled out of the classroom once to several times a week for additional supplemental English language instruction or to help with specific content areas. This is the second most common approach used in the United States.

Dual immersion bilingual education: This format uses both English and another language. Depending on the program, approximately 50 percent of the day is in English, with times or days specified for each language. The goal is for English language learners and English-proficient children to become bilingual.

Early-exit or transitional bilingual education: This approach supports the child's home language to teach both English and academic subjects as well as emphasizing English language development and academic learning. Children are usually in these programs for one to three years. This is the most common model used in the United States.

Late-exit or developmental bilingual education: This method emphasizes full bilingualism by varying the amount of instruction given in the home language as children progress academically in their knowledge of English and subject matter areas. Children are in these programs for approximately six years before moving into a more traditional English-based classroom. This model shows the highest academic achievement in the long term.

Dual-language programs: This approach supports children in developing proficiency in their home language and in English. Typically, one teacher, a native English speaker, teaches in English, and the other teacher, a native speaker of the home language, teaches in the home language in a culturally and language-rich environment.

Sources: DeBey & Bombard, 2007; Saracho & Spodek, 2004.

English language learners and how comfortable you would be teaching in these different models. What do you think will be the most popular models based on the requirements of No Child Left Behind?

THE EVIDENCE BASE

The Institute of Education Science convened an expert panel to summarize and evaluate the evidence available on teaching literacy to English language learners in kindergarten through fifth grade. They identified five essential concepts and have provided recommendations on how to implement these concepts as well as information on the level of evidence that supports the practice.

1. *Screen and monitor progress.* Conduct formative assessments to screen for reading problems and monitor progress (*evidence strong*). Children need to be assessed in the areas of phonological processing, letter and alphabetic knowledge, and word and text reading. These data can be used to identify children who require additional instructional support.

2. *Provide reading interventions.* Provide intensive, small-group reading interventions for English language learners at risk for reading problems (*evidence strong*). Reading interventions should be timely, occur in a small group format, be provided in addition to the regular reading, and cover the five components of reading: phonological awareness, phonics, reading fluency, vocabulary, and comprehension. Instruction should be fast-paced, explicit, and direct.

3. *Teach vocabulary.* Provide extensive and varied vocabulary instruction throughout the day (*evidence strong*). Essential content words should be taught in depth, and children should have opportunities to acquire vocabulary from a language-rich setting. Instructional time should address the meaning of common words, phrases, and expressions not yet learned.

4. *Develop academic English.* Develop academic English competence beginning in the primary grades (*evidence low*). Academic English focuses on the formal aspects of the language, including understanding the structure of language and the precise way in which words and phrases are used.

5. *Schedule peer learning.* Schedule regular peer-assisted learning opportunities, including structured language practice (*evidence strong*). Students of different ability or proficiency levels should work together on structured academic tasks at least 90 minutes a week. These activities should be designed to allow children to practice what has been taught and to extend it to their learning.

Source: Gersten et al., 2007.

The brains of all children ages 3 to 8 are biologically primed to learn language(s) in a way that affects cognitive capacity. The key to academic English is not just the acquisition of the academic vocabulary but also the ability to develop and manipulate, even play with language(s) in its various forms. This is what will make a long-term difference in children's achievement. Language development impacts brain development and comprehension in children ages 3 to 8 years. English language learners have three distinct sets of skills they have to develop simultaneously to learn academic English and become lifelong learners and thinkers:

- *Language acquisition* is the process part. Language learners must learn the vocabulary of the language(s) they will speak and ways to increase their vocabulary by understanding the principles underlying language acquisition.

- *Language development* teaches the roles and rules of language, and the underlying structure of how language works, when to use what aspects of language, and how to manipulate language in its various forms.

- *Reading* is the product. Teaching reading skills alone will not solve the achievement gap.

A major question that has been the focus of teaching English learners is what the language of instruction should be. Recent federal policies have restricted the amount of time that children can be taught in their native language. Perhaps this question needs to be reframed. What may matter most is the quality of the instruction (Calderón, Slavin, & Sánchez, 2011).

Barnett and colleagues (2007) compared an English immersion program with a two-way bilingual immersion approach for randomly assigned 3- and 4-year olds in a high-quality preschool program. Children in both approaches gained skills in language, emergent literacy, and mathematics. The assessments that were conducted in English showed no differences between the groups. However, the dual immersion program showed large gains in Spanish vocabulary. In a global economy, bilingualism has many potential advantages. English-speaking children also improved their Spanish, with no loss of English language learning.

● ● ●
Comprehensive School Reform

A different approach for improving outcomes for English language learners is comprehensive school reform. Success for All (SFA) is an approach that has been adapted for English learners and the adaptations have been evaluated for effectiveness. SFA provides extensive professional development and coaching for teachers. It has well-structured curriculum materials that emphasize phonics in K–1, cooperative learning, and direct instruction in comprehension and vocabulary at all grade levels (Calderón, Slavin, & Sánchez, 2011). The SFA approach uses frequent assessment and regrouping as needed as well as small group or one-on-one instruction for struggling readers. Their *Bilingual Program* teaches reading in Spanish in K–2, and then transitions students to English beginning in grades 2 and 3. SFA's *Structured English Immersion* adaptation supports reading with vocabulary development strategies. Research has found positive effects for English language learners and other language-minority students (Calderón, Slavin, & Sánchez, 2011).

Calderón and her colleagues identified eight elements that have been found to be effective from preschool through grade 12 regardless of how English learners are taught.

1. *School structure and leadership:* Schools must collect formative data on learning, teaching, attendance, behavior, and other identified outcomes. They must have a system for preventing and solving problems and monitoring solutions. Staff development must be intensive and ongoing. Leadership must provide a clear method for

organizing, motivating, and guiding children. Leaders must have information, monitor the quality of teaching and learning, and hold staff responsible for shared goals.

2. *Language and literacy development:* Vocabulary is the foundation for success for English language learners. Children in poverty hear about 615 words an hour; middle-class children, about 1,251; and children of professionals, about 2,153 (Hart & Risley, 2003). Vocabulary is a significant predictor of reading comprehension and difficulties. Children must also be taught the key components of reading (phonemic awareness and processing, phonics, fluency, vocabulary, working memory, word-level skills (decoding and spelling), and text comprehension and skills such as scanning, skimming, summarizing, and making inferences (August & Shanahan, 2008). Explicit vocabulary instruction requires exposure to words in multiple forms to ensure understanding, and when possible, an equivalent word in the child's home language. For most students word recognition means being able to read the word. For English learners, it also means remembering the meaning of the work.

3. *Cooperative learning.* Working in small mixed ability groups helps English learners speak and learn from peers.

4. *Professional development.* Teachers found that hands-on practice with techniques they could use in their own classroom and personalized coaching were most helpful.

5. *Parent and family support.* Parents need to feel that they play an important and meaningful role in school decisions that impact them and their children. Schools can offer workshops about helping children at home, behavior management and financial planning in the family's native language if possible. There should be many opportunities for informal communication. Opportunities to provide health, mental health, and social services at school should be possible, as well as information about immigration problems and adult literacy.

6. *Tutoring and other interventions for struggling readers.* One-on-one tutoring by well-trained certified teachers who use a structured phonetic program is most effective. Cooperative learning and small group tutoring are effective ways to reduce the number of children who need one-on-one tutoring.

7. *Monitoring implementation and outcomes.* Student outcomes as well as each element of a program need to be monitored. This may require a facilitator. Counselors are available who speak the student's language and who are knowledgeable about the problems should be available.

Although school reform is needed at all levels there are compelling reasons to begin in the early childhood years

when children's needs are more manageable and educators are teaching new skills rather than focusing on remediation (Crosnoe & López Turley, 2011). Education has long been seen as the road to upward social mobility and economic success for immigrant families and their children. For some it has worked well, others have encountered discrimination, disadvantage, and barriers that reinforce social stratification and inequity (Crosnoe & López Turley, 2011).

Multicultural Education

Multicultural education encompasses all of the issues young children encounter in their lives that can potentially create stereotypes and bias: race, ethnicity, abilities and disabilities, language differences, class, gender, age, religion, and so on (Williams & Cooney, 2006). Multicultural education uses age-appropriate materials and activities, incorporating the strengths of children's families and communities to enrich the curriculum.

Multicultural education can take place at a variety of levels. Morey and Kitano (1997) identify three levels of curriculum transformation: exclusive, inclusive, and transformed.

The *exclusive* level has a low level of diversity with a focus on the four "F's"—food, folklore, fun, and fashion—basically, the tourist approach. The *inclusive* level adds diversity content but focuses on comparing other cultures and knowledge to the majority culture. A variety of methods are used to relate new knowledge and for children to construct their own knowledge and to think critically with peers about issues related to diversity. The *transformed* curriculum challenges traditional views and encourages the reconceptualization of issues and new ways of thinking. Diverse perspectives are shared and problem solving is the focus. Moving from an exclusive to a transformed curriculum is a developmental process for both teachers and children (Kea, Campbell-Whatley, & Richards, 2006). Utilizing children's literature is certainly a key, as is inviting families not only to come to class but also to provide input into the decision-making processes.

> ▶❚❚ TeachSource Video Case
> **Multicultural Lessons: Embracing Similarities in Preschool Education**
> Watch the TeachSource Video Case *Multicultural Lessons: Embracing Similarities in Preschool Education,* in which Literacy Coach Shelly Outwater and teacher Erica Layte explain their approach to multicultural education in an early childhood classroom. The video can be found in the Early Childhood Education Media Library under Multicultural, available at www.cengagebrain.com.

Guidelines

The modifications that you will need to make in your classroom depend on the needs of the particular children you have and your approach to teaching English learners. The following guidelines are divided into two sections. The first includes guidelines and techniques to support culturally sensitive instruction as a context for teaching English language learners. It includes some information on working with families, particularly those who have come to the United States recently. The second section provides guidance on how to develop and use specific strategies for language acquisition.

• • • Culturally Sensitive Instruction

The early childhood classroom constantly provides messages about what the program values (and who is valued), from what hangs on the walls, to the curriculum teachers implement with the children. Regardless of the particular approach used, the programs should support a multicultural philosophy. The question is, How would you would know one if you saw one, and how could you ensure that all classrooms support multicultural values? Williams and Cooney (2006) suggest a culturally sensitive approach.

1. Promote sensitivity and appreciation for cultural diversity. If children do not feel safe and develop positive relationships, they will not be available for learning.

2. Focus on many different cultural groups through literature, music, and environmental planning.

3. Instill creative and critical thinking skills.

4. Value families' cultural and linguistic practices and do not try to "fix" them.

5. Respect and learn about the children's culture and how they spend their time at home.

6. Understand what is important to parents in terms of cultural values.

7. Ensure that pictures, photographs, and artifacts represent diverse racial, ethnic, and ability groups.

• • • Interacting with Families

1. *Provide information about childproofing environments and child safety.* When children become independently mobile, families may need to learn ways of keeping their children safe.

2. *Develop effective ways to communicate with families.* This may include a translator or teachers developing additional skills in the language of the children in the class if no teachers speak the languages of the children.

3. *Use a digital camera and photographs to share with families what their child is doing during the day.* Encourage families to bring you (or e-mail you) photographs about how they do things at home. If they do not have a camera, loan them one if possible. Photographs give you a common ground on which to base a discussion, even one that may consist of a lot of nodding and smiling.

4. *Value all languages spoken in the classroom,* whether or not you can speak them. As children are learning first words, learn with them. Ask parents to write down the words children know and how they use them. Develop your own pronunciation code.

5. *Ensure that children are encouraged to explore their environment.* Provide safe places indoors and outdoors for children to play.

6. *Ensure that the music, books, toys and materials available reflect the cultures of the children* in addition to the dominant culture.

• • • Second Language Acquisition

1. *Determine where children are in language learning* relative to speaking, listening, reading, and writing. Do this for both their home language and English.

2. *Label objects in the classroom in the languages the children speak.* Color-code the labels so that each language is in a specific color. As you add labels, point these out to all children. Help children connect the written and spoken word.

3. *Support teaching and learning with visual cues.* Use real objects, pictures, photographs, role-playing, maps, and diagrams to help set the context of learning. Knowing what is being talked about helps English language learners make better guesses about content and language and helps increase vocabulary. Post class rules in written and picture form. Model, show, and demonstrate a variety of ways of doing things.

4. *Make language more understandable* for children by using simpler speech, shorter sentences, and slowing your rate of talking. Use children's names when you talk to or about them. Avoid using slang or idiomatic expressions unless you plan to teach the children what they mean.

5. *Repeat and restate language, enunciating clearly, and emphasize key words.* Check frequently to see whether children actually comprehend what is happening. Have children demonstrate their understanding of directions.

6. *Pair children and use cooperative strategies for teaching and learning.* Teach children how to work together using verbal and nonverbal strategies. Ensure that all children's ideas are valued and respected. Pair children with different ability levels or different levels of English proficiency. Rotate the pairs.

7. *Focus on the meaning and comprehension of language rather than correcting grammatical errors.* Developmentally, young children do not understand the structure of language, even when they use it well. Modeling language until children self-detect and self-correct is more useful.

8. *Build vocabulary.* Create opportunities throughout the day to increase children's vocabulary. Give children the words for what they are doing, how they are doing it, and what they are doing it with. Know children rarely learn a word the first time they hear it.

9. *Provide language instruction in small groups.* Short language-group times highlight the importance of

both languages. If some children are struggling with particular concepts, use small groups to focus on these concepts and explicitly teach them.

10. Do not use drill and practice.

Curriculum Adaptations

The number and degree of adaptations depend upon the children in your classroom, including the diversity of languages and language skills, and the program philosophy. A thematic approach to content instruction may help English language learners learn content as well as usable vocabulary.

Social Awareness

As children in classrooms are diverse in background and ability, spend time developing a community of learners. Help children have a forum to share artifacts that shed light on their joys, passions, experiences, and home culture. Despite obvious differences, one conclusion relates to how much children are the same. Some of the activities in the Resource Chapter 1 are specifically designed to support children who are English language learners. Activity 1–4, *Foreign Languages*, increases awareness of other languages. Activity 1–16, *International Snack*, introduces children to a variety of different foods.

Children who do not have the language skills to negotiate entering a group may be tentative about joining groups.
©Cengage Learning 2012

Social Competence

Children need to feel good about themselves, their families, and their culture. They need to be part of social interactions and to be valued as individuals.

1. Provide time for children to learn about themselves and their culture.

2. Help all children feel positive about their speech, language, and communication skills.

3. Encourage children to communicate, whether in their home language, English, or a combination of the two.

Not speaking the same language is a barrier to inclusion. It is also a concern relative to discrimination. Children who are English language learners need not only to be included but also to be valued as contributing members of the group.

1. Use many centers and small group experiences as language is learned, so children can be included in a group. Use few large groups and keep them short.

2. Play with a child using similar toys or materials. If he leads, expand on what he is doing, and add an innovation to see whether he will follow. Join the child first nonverbally, and then talk about what is going on.

3. Pair children for some activities. Encourage children to be "coaches" and "players." Pair them based on expertise and experience; then reverse the roles.

4. Celebrate ways in which children and families are alike and different.

Social Studies

We are all members of a global community. Including English learners stretches us to learn about different cultures and environments, and different ways of being in the world

1. Create a cultural democracy in which children's language and cultural differences are viewed as a resource, not a liability.

2. Educate children about social justice.

3. Discuss with children how decisions are made in the classroom and in non-classroom environments such as governmental agencies.

4. Show children safety signs or other significant signs they are familiar with (stop, go, bathroom, etc.) in another language. Talk about how confusing and even scary it might be to not understand spoken or written language. Expand this to talk about immigrants to the United States and children with dyslexia.

5. Talk about spoken language and how difficult it might be to communicate and meet one's wants and needs if one can't understand what is being said. Again, bring this back to the classroom and children who speak English as a second language and children who have auditory processing problems.

English Language Arts

Create a literacy-rich environment that includes multicultural materials, resources, and interactive learning. Partner with families to identify their language goals for their child and the interface of their goals with the program. Use books that are multicultural and nonsexist, showing different family structures, races, and ages, and include individuals with disabilities. Include books with families of various cultures living in the United States (see Children's Bibliography). Have a variety of books in the classroom and include some books in Spanish, Chinese, and other languages, including Braille. As you work with and observe children who are English learners, look at both their English language proficiency and how well they are reading.

Speaking and Listening

Learning to speak academic English is a challenge. It requires a language-rich environment and a commitment to teach English more intentionally even during the preschool years.

1. Provide language input. In some Latin American cultures, children are expected to learn by modeling the behavior of others. These children may not have been exposed to as much spoken language as European American children.

2. Use visual cues, repeat and restate language, and match language to children's level of learning.

3. Support both the home language and English in the classroom.

4. Support children's talking and do not comment when they switch between English and their home language.

5. Use small conversational groups where children are expected to talk and receive feedback on how to use their skills.

6. Talk to children about topics they are interested in, and revisit these topics on different occasions.

7. Help children learn to compare words across languages. A simple conversation may include the following exchange:

   Teacher: "Que es esto?" (pointing at a book)

   Child: "Es un *libro*."

   Teacher: "En Ingles es un *book*."

8. Invite a non-native English speaker to talk to the children about her culture and language.

9. Teach all children to speak Spanish or another foreign language.

Being expected to listen when you cannot understand is difficult, and being one of a few who does not understand makes it more difficult. Children quit listening if they are put in frequent situations where they cannot understand most of what is happening.

1. Provide many opportunities throughout the day for children to listen to language. However, most of this should be one-on-one or in small groups.

2. Learn to read the children to see whether they are agreeing because everyone else is or because they understand what is happening.

3. Pair what you are saying with a physical response. Ask children to do something: follow directions, stop or go, turn, twirl, sit down, and so on.

4. Provide multiple opportunities for children to respond to questions.

5. Play games like "Simon Says."

Reading

Learning to read is a challenging task for all children. To be learning English and learning to read at the same time is even more challenging. Support all children as they are learning to read by reading to them at their level of interest and understanding rather than the level at which they can read independently.

1. Label materials in the classroom in the languages of the children in the setting.

2. Provide books in the home language, and help children read them to each other.

3. Provide bilingual visual and word dictionaries so children can look up new words.

4. Use picture books that show different cultural and ethnic groups, and have children make up stories to go with the pictures.

5. Teach phonological processing by helping children identify the individual sounds that make up words (phonemes) and identifying the words that those sounds combine to make See Activities 2–21, *Sound Bingo*, and 2–56w, *Body Sounds*.

6. Provide multiple opportunities for children to read words and sentences in small groups or with a peer.

7. Give clear feedback about errors when it is part of formal language learning.

8. Read many different alphabet and number books.

Writing

Provide many opportunities to write and many examples of why writing is a necessary and useful skill. Show examples of many different types of written work. Include examples of different alphabets such as the Chinese and Cyrillic alphabet (base for Slavic languages including Russian), and even Braille. Discuss the different purposes of writing.

1. Encourage children to use thinking maps and webbing as graphic organizers for their work. See Activity 2–27, *Mind Mapping*.

2. Have children air write letters with the large muscles of their dominant arm. Pair this with the letter name and the sound of the letter. As children become better at this, have them write whole words. See Activity 2–58w, *Air Writing*.

3. Set up a writing center with a variety of writing tools and different types of paper. Include an English alphabet as well as others in the languages of the children in the class. Have bilingual picture dictionaries.

4. Writing in some languages such as Chinese is almost an art form. Discuss this with children and provide examples.

5. Encourage children to use the computer to write. Help them learn about some of the supports the computer can provide, such as spell checking, grammar, and other languages using various fonts.

Language

1. Teach the alphabet and letter sounds. See Activities 2–22, *Alphabet Lotto*; 2–20, *Letters and Sounds*; and 2–53w, *Alphabet Line*. Include letters from the languages the children in the class speak. Include the Spanish /ll/ and /rr/. Also, look at how different punctuation marks are used, and talk about the role of accent marks.

2. Introduce new vocabulary (root words) that is relevant to the child. Help her learn to use prefixes and suffixes to make new words. See Activities 2–3, *Synonyms*, and 2–57w, *Rhyming Words*.

3. Create a bilingual word wall.

Discovery

English learners do less well in math than their native-born peers and need to be supported to learn the necessary skills. They need to become intrigued with science and the potential it holds for change and solving global problems. They also need to become competent users of technology to be part of the information age.

Mathematics

English learners need to be taught the language of math as well as the computational skills. Word problems are particularly problematic for all young children. Children need the skill to use math, not just do math.

1. Teach the math vocabulary (*numbers, plus, all, round, square,* etc.) so children become familiar with the terms and what they mean. See Activity 3–44w, *Big and Little Pairs*.

2. Use manipulatives to teach math. Also use intentional informal opportunities to teach math skills, such as one-to-one correspondence during snack and when putting blocks away. See Activity 3–38w, *Variations on Blocks*.

3. Use visuals to teach math concepts. Use graphs and charts. See Activities 3–1, *Matching Symbols*, and 3–2, *Spacey Dots*.

4. Talk about symbols and abbreviations, and ensure that children know what they mean before being expected to use them.

5. Give children practice in writing numbers. All children write numbers far less frequently than letters.

6. Sing songs about math and read stories about math (e.g., counting books).

Science

Children need to learn about the world they live in, how it is changing, and what the implications of those changes are. They need the skills of astute observers, and from these observations the ability to classify information and generalize it.

1. Show as well as tell children what is happening. Demonstrate science, do experiments, and encourage children to participate in the experiments.

2. Support science through experimental learning, field trips and other experiences to establish a common experiential base to work from. Language experience stories, as well as diagrams of what the children found interesting, can follow.

3. Use illustrations and graphics to teach concepts.

4. Use word study and word sorts to help children expand their vocabulary in a particular science area and their understanding of relationships within that area.

Technology

Technology is an important resource and knowing how to use it is a necessary skill. If children come from families in which there is little technology in the home, they will need to develop these skills at school.

1. Help children gain the skills they need to independently use the keyboard effectively. In addition to contributing to keyboarding skills, this also is a motivation for alphabet learning. See Activities 3–64w, *Alphabet Keyboard*; and 3–29, *Computer Bingo*.

2. Use computer programs that support children's learning, but not those that provide just drill and practice, particularly in areas of English language and math.

3. Choose interactive programs children can control. They need to learn cause-and-effect reasoning and that they can cause the computer to do something.

4. Encourage children to work on the computer in pairs. Given the variety of skills the computer requires, it is a great way to teach and learn and to help children develop friendships.

5. Use free educational software in other languages such as Spanish. One company, Educational Freeware, also has many children's programs that run in Spanish, as well as software that teaches Spanish and other languages.

6. Take photographs of children with a digital camera so they can share with their family what they have been doing and learning in school.

Wellness

To be available for learning, children need to feel safe, trust the environment, have nutritional needs met, develop relationships with caring adults and peers, and feel that they and their family and culture are respected. Culture impacts the food they eat, the games they play, and maybe even how safe they feel.

Health and Safety

The legal status of children and their families impacts their health and safety. If families are here without documents, they are often reluctant to seek medical care until children become very sick. Even if families are here legally, if they are recent immigrants, they may not be eligible for many social and medical services.

1. Find out what children eat at home and check to see whether there is anything that you are serving that could be problematic for them because of dietary or religious reasons.

2. Observe what children wear. If they come dressed inappropriately for the weather, they may have lived previously in a different climate or may not know about (or have) appropriate seasonal clothing or concerns related to sun- and windburn. See Activity 4–31w, *Seasonal Clothing*.

3. Teach children what safety signs mean and what to do when they see them. Do not just tell them, but play games in the classroom and outside where they must respond to different signs and warning sounds. See Activities 4–2, *Stop and Go*; 4–9, *Traffic Sign Hunt*; and 4–10, *Warning Sounds*.

4. Teach children body parts and some medical terms so that if they are sick they can describe what part of them hurts and how much. This is particularly important if their parents have limited English and the medical professional does not speak their language.

Physical Education

Provide time for active play inside and outside, especially if children live in crowded housing conditions.

1. Find out about the sports that are played in the child's country of origin and the fundamental motor skills needed to participate. Think about how you can support these skills if they are not part of your traditional program.

2. Plan to incorporate 30 minutes of structured moderate to vigorous activity into your day, especially if children do not have safe places to play at home.

3. Ensure children get opportunities to develop fundamental motor skills such as ball handling. See Activities 4–18, *Variations on Throwing* and 4–41w, *Big Balls*. Children also need locomotor skills; see Activity 4–14, *Variations on Running*.

Sensory Motor Integration

Combining information from the senses and translating this information to motor activity is an important part of many academic and sports activities, requiring both hemispheres of the brain to work together to accomplish tasks.

Some experiences that are familiar to children growing up in the United States are new for English language learners.
©Cengage Learning 2012

1. Encourage children to play "Follow the Leader" and other games where children can lead and follow. Pair children and have them take turns. See Activity 4–27, *Mirroring*.

2. Talk with children and show them photographs of people carrying objects on their head and back, and in slings, wraps, and pouches. Encourage children to try a variety of ways of carrying different objects, to evaluate their effectiveness. See Activity 4–24, *Balance It*.

3. Help children develop their tactile sense by matching materials and identifying objects without seeing them. See Activities 4–42w, *Feely Bag*, and 4–11, *Pick-a-Pair*.

Fine motor skills are necessary for writing, keyboarding, and adaptive skills. Find a variety of interesting ways for children to practice these skills.

1. Ensure that puzzles are multicultural and nonsexist. Include some with and without knobs, and use simple form boards as well as multipiece puzzles.

2. Be sure that the dress-up clothing you have available has the type of fasteners children are most likely to encounter and that some of the clothing is

representative of the types children in the class might wear. Build vocabulary by talking about the clothing children are putting on and taking off. See Activity 3–8, *Caterpillars*.

3. Encourage children to play with and use a wide variety of tools for a particular purpose. Tools can be paintbrushes or crayons used in art or tweezers and needlenose pliers to pick up small things, or forks and chopsticks to eat with. Include the vocabulary necessary for children to identify all the tools used.

Creative Arts

Encourage children to share their culture through creative arts. Ensure that you have the necessary materials and equipment to allow this to happen. Evaluate your visual arts materials, as well as music—singing, playing, and listening, and the equipment you have for dramatic play to ensure that it reflects the global community, particularly the cultures of the children in your class.

Visual Arts

Show children a variety of art and sculpture from different countries. Encourage them to look at the style of painting as well as the particular type of paint used. Ask them questions about the art to help focus their attention on its particular features. Show them different types of visual art, such as murals, and talk about how murals are used to document events and even to protest.

1. Make a mural with children. Decide on the topic of the mural, what its purpose is, and how they can each contribute to the mural.

2. Have children make handprints, and talk about similarities and differences in their prints. See Activity 5–4, *Hand Print Mural*.

3. Talk about different countries, different climates, and how structures are related to where they are built. Choose a country and find out about its climate and, using papier-mâché, create a community for that country, with each child contributing to the community. See Activity 5–1, *Creature*.

4. Show children rubbings from temples, churches, and other surfaces, and discuss how and why they are made. Have children identify objects in the classroom that would be interesting to make rubbings of. See Activity 5–3, *Crayon Rubbing*.

5. Look at the relationship between celebrations and art. Identify relevant celebrations, talk about their significance, and help children use art to celebrate an occasion such as Dia De Los Muertos or the Chinese New Year. See Activity 5–6, *Chinese New Year Dragon*.

Music

Music is a multisensory experience. It can teach listening skills and help develop vocabulary and basic concepts.

Children can be part of a group or can perform individually. Music is also part of culture and language. Musical notation may be new to many children, and learning the meaning of that symbol system and integrating it with auditory output is a great literacy skill for all children. See Activities 5–12, *Color Notes*, and 5–18, *Notes Collage*.

1. Use tapes CDs and DVDs that celebrate different cultures, languages, and styles of music.

2. Sing songs and say fingerplays in more than one language.

3. Ensure that the music you play reflects the languages and cultures of the children in the class.

4. Use music (e.g., singing and compact discs) to support play and language learning.

5. Help children learn about the musical instruments used in different cultures and how they are played. Use maracas, castanets, and other instruments.

6. Teach children the hand signals that conductors use when they lead an orchestra. Talk about the rhythms of music and the rhythm of different languages. See Activity 5–14, *Conductor*.

7. Sing songs with movements. See Activity 5–52w, *Movement Songs*.

Movement and Dance

Movement and dance encourage children to move in response to ideas, music, or imaginary circumstances. This challenges children to find different ways to move and to get in touch with their body.

1. Pair music and movement and have a dance party. Be sure to include traditional dance movement from different countries. Demonstrate dancing from different eras as well as different styles: swing, jitter bug, tango, line dancing, and so on.

2. Provide props to support movement, such as scarves and fans that can be twirled and waved.

3. Increase body awareness by moving different body parts in different ways and at different speeds.

4. Read books such as *African and Asian Dance* by J. Bingham, N. Gamble, and A. Solway, (Chicago, IL: Heinemann Library, 2008). Talk with children about different styles of dance, including choreography, performance and presentation, history, costumes, and music—and then, dance!

Dramatic Play and Theater

Use dramatic play to help make the unfamiliar familiar. Provide safe places for children to learn about experiences they might encounter and to replay those they have encountered. Use theater to expand children's knowledge.

1. Set up the dramatic play area in a variety of different ways. If children want to play through medical experiences, set it up as a doctor's or dentist's office. See

Activity 5–56w, *Dentist's Office*. If children are interested in stores, have a grocery store, shoe store, clothing store, and so on. See Activity 5–28, *Shoe Store*. If children are interested in food production, have a sushi bar, teahouse, taco stand, and so on.

2. Have a variety of clothing available for children to try on. Help children explore different types of traditional dress, and talk about the utility of clothing and why people wore that clothing. Also look at the fabric the clothing is made of and why particular types and colors of fabric are used in some places and not others.

3. Ensure that the dolls are male and female and ethnically diverse, and that other **huggables** represent the cultures of the children.

4. Use scripts to introduce children to different roles and customs, and encourage them to use the Internet to find additional information.

Routines and Transitions

Children depend upon schedules and routines to feel safe. To the extent that these differ wildly, children can become confused and disorganized. Creating some level of continuity is important and yet challenging when the child's home language is not English. It is more of a challenge when neither the parents nor the caregivers are fluent in a common language. Create a bilingual learning environment by learning helpful phrases in the child's home language that support daily routines and transitions. Routines and transitions emphasize the social aspects of language.

In situations where many children come from homes where the caregivers do not speak English and speak a common language, it is imperative to have at least one educator who speaks the home language. Although an obvious strategy is to send important information home in both English and the home language, it may not be possible. Additionally, adults may not be literate in either their home language or English.

Be honest about your desire to communicate with families and be creative about making this happen. Find out from parents what works for them. Provide children with their own take-home learning tools that support their native language and English (Hepburn, 2004).

1. Use routines to build adaptive skills and the language that goes with what the child is doing. For example, there is a natural time to say (and point), "That is your hat. You are putting on your hat."

2. Use meal and snack time to initiate purposeful communication and to communicate expectations, for example, "Good! You are using your spoon."

3. Routines are also the source of indirect experiences as children listen to conversations of other children as well as observe other adult–child interactions.

4. Use transitions to teach prepositions such as *on, under, in front of, behind,* and so on.

SUMMARY

- The number of English language learners is increasing dramatically.
- English language learners speak over 460 languages; however, almost 80 percent speak Spanish.
- Many English language learners live in immigrant families. When a family member is undocumented, children are likely to be poor and have fewer academic skills.
- Accurate assessment of English language learners is challenging because children may not have had the same language or the same experiential base.
- Educating English language learners is a controversial area.
- Regardless of educational methods, the classroom should be language rich, and teaching should be culturally sensitive.
- Comprehensive school reform might be needed to increase the learning of all children, but particularly English learners.

EDUCATIONAL RESOURCES

Early Child Development (ECD) by the World Bank focuses on early childhood from a global and economic perspective. It has links to international and regional sites and resources, and links to data and statistics from various international organizations. www.worldbank.org/children

Future of Children is a collaboration of the Woodrow Wilson School of Public and International Affairs at Princeton University and the Brookings Institute. The 2011 spring volume (21) is devoted to immigrant children. It is available online at http://futureofchildren.org/

International Reading Association (IRA) lists culturally diverse books for children and provides professional development resources. IRA has position statements on reading instruction, as well as resources on teaching strategies for teaching in diverse classrooms. www.reading.org/

National Center for Cultural Competence (NCCC), based at Georgetown University, is dedicated to increasing the capacity of health and mental health programs to design, implement, and evaluate culturally and linguistically competent service delivery systems. It has checklists for self-assessing one's cultural competence. www11.georgetown.edu/research/gucchd/nccc/

For additional resources, visit the book companion website for this text at www.cengagebrain.com.

Children with Autism Spectrum Disorders

The most difficult child I ever taught was severely autistic. Carlos was 4 years old, with no language skills. We were unsure of his mental abilities because he often refused to do any type of class work. He was a very heavy child and often threw temper tantrums that resulted in him throwing himself onto the floor and screaming. Carlos could not handle any type of change in his routine and often had a tantrum if we altered anything in our class schedule.

This was Carlos's first experience in a school setting, and he had a difficult time understanding that there were rules and consequences for inappropriate behaviors. At school, he was given breakfast, lunch, and a snack. He would only eat peanut butter and jelly sandwiches and refused any other foods. Carlos only drank milk and would often tantrum if he did not have his "usual" lunch.

We developed a picture exchange system for communication. Carlos had never been required to use any form of communication; when he wanted something, he either pointed or simply grabbed. By the end of the year, Carlos understood that he needed the pictures to get what he wanted rather than being his usual bossy and demanding self. He also understood that his picture schedule would keep him aware of upcoming events throughout the day, so he was prepared.

Carlos's mother was a single parent with two other children. I often did respite care for her after school because her parents refused to watch him because of his behaviors. Carlos would come home with me and we would play with whatever held his interest. Once, I left the room to use the bathroom, and I thought I had locked all the doors in the house, but he found one that was open. When I went back into the room, he was not there. I looked all over the house, yelling his name, but because he wouldn't speak, I got no response. I lived on a little back road, and he loved going to the playground behind the house. I quickly went there, but he was nowhere to be found. I was in such a panic and was totally flustered when I saw him walking near my driveway. I quickly checked for any scratches or injuries and, thankfully, there were none. Carlos was laughing

©Cengage Learning 2012

and didn't seem bothered. I brought him in the house, gave him a huge hug, and made him a big peanut butter and jelly sandwich, his favorite.

Working with him was difficult because he was the most violently temperamental child I have dealt with, and I would be physically exhausted by the end of the day. There were many funny incidents that occurred with Carlos that I can now look back on and laugh about, but at the time they seemed terrible. Even though I used to pray for his absence the next day at school, I still wonder how Carlos is doing and hope that he is improving year by year. That year I learned many things from Carlos. I needed to be patient and to give him space when he needed a break, and to be more understanding than frustrated when he refused to do activities. ✳

Autism Spectrum Disorders

The term **autism spectrum disorders (ASD)** refers to a continuum of neurodevelopmental disorders related to impairments of social interaction, communication, and narrow repetitive patterns of behavior (Matson & Minshew, 2006).

The American Psychiatric Association (2000) uses the term **pervasive developmental disorder (PDD)**, which includes **autism, Asperger's syndrome, Rett syndrome,** and **childhood disintegrative disorder. Pervasive developmental disorder–not otherwise specified (PDD-NOS)** is used as a classification when symptoms are present but do not meet the criteria for a particular category. These disorders are grouped because they share an essential feature of all pervasive developmental disorders (PDDs): impaired social reciprocity. Children with these disorders also have problems with communication and repetitive behaviors. The social limitations usually result in limited play skills. PDDs may co-exist with other disorders, and there is often some degree of intellectual disability (APA, 2000; Hyman & Towbin, 2007).

There are many unanswered questions about autism spectrum disorders. To answer some of these questions, the **Combating Autism Act of 2006** was signed into law on December 19, 2006. It mandates the expansion of autism research, the development of a national research agenda, and the education of physicians and the public about autism, with the goal of early identification and intervention.

Defining Autism Spectrum Disorders

The IDEA 2004 defines autism as follows:

Autism is a developmental disability significantly affecting verbal and nonverbal communication and social interaction. It is evident before age three and it adversely affects a child's educational performance. Other characteristics include repetitive activities and stereotyped movements, resistance to environmental change or change in daily routines, and unusual responses to sensory experiences. These behaviors are not caused by an emotional disturbance.

The American Psychiatric Association (2000) has developed diagnostic criteria for autistic disorder. To be diagnosed with autistic disorder, its onset must be before age 3, with abnormal functioning in one of the following areas: social interaction, language as a communication skill, or symbolic play. To meet the criteria, the child must display six or more items from the list in Table 13–1, with at least two coming from A and one each from B and C.

The diagnostic criteria for Asperger's syndrome requires that there is not a general or significant delay in language, but the disturbance does cause problems in social, occupational, or other areas of functioning. Additionally, children must display at least two criteria from A and C, given in Table 13–1.

The term pervasive developmental disorder–not otherwise specified (PDD–NOS) is a source of confusion for parents and professionals. It is a vague designation that does not have specific criteria. Some use it as a diagnosis for children who have a basic impairment in relating and communicating, but do not meet the criteria for autistic disorder. Others use it when it is not clear whether the criteria (before age 3) have been met or when the child's case is too "mild."

Greenspan and Wieder (2006) particularly object to the label pervasive developmental disorder. They prefer to use the term **neurodevelopmental disorders of relating and communicating**. They feel that this term more accurately defines the regulatory-sensory processing problems with the

TABLE 13–1 DIAGNOSTIC CRITERIA FOR AUTISTIC DISORDER
A. Qualitative impairments in social interaction
• Marked impairment in using multiple nonverbal behaviors such as eye-to-eye gaze, facial expression, gestures, and body postures to regulate social interaction
• Inability to develop appropriate peer relationships
• Lack of spontaneous sharing of enjoyment, interests, or achievements with others
• Lack of social or emotional reciprocity
B. Qualitative impairments in communication
• Delay in, or lack of, spoken communication
• Inability to use speech to initiate or sustain conversation
• Stereotyped and repetitive use of language or idiosyncratic language
• Lack of spontaneous make-believe play or social imitative play
C. Restricted, repetitive, and stereotyped patterns of behavior, interests, and activities
• Preoccupation with stereotyped patterns of interest (intensity or focus)
• Adherence to specific nonfunctional routines or rituals
• Stereotyped and repetitive motor mannerisms (e.g., hand flapping)
• Preoccupation with parts of objects

Source: American Psychiatric Association, 2000.

significant developmental delays and dysfunctions that derail the child's ability to relate and communicate.

Greenspan and Wieder's research (2006) shows a different pattern of development from that noted by the American Psychiatric Association (2000). Their research shows children having seemingly normal development for about the first 12 to 15 months. At this time, the toddler begins to show oversensitivity or becomes less reactive to sounds and touch. Language development stops and existing language seems forgotten. Greenspan and Wieder (2006) see these behaviors as falling along a continuum rather than fitting into clear diagnostic categories. They see each child as having a unique profile relative to sensory reactivity, sensory processing, muscle tone, and motor planning or sequencing.

Prevalence of Autism Spectrum Disorders

Autism and related disorders are more frequently diagnosed than in the past. It is not clear whether this is due to increased frequency, newer definitions of autism, or an increased ability to diagnose autism spectrum disorders (PubMed Health, 2010c). The Centers for Disease Control and Prevention (2010a) estimate the rate is between 1 in 80 to 1 in 240 people, with an average of 1 in 110. Autism is four times as likely to occur in boys than girls. ASDs occur in all socioeconomic, ethnic, and racial groups (CDC, 2010a).

In 1997–1998, 0.1 percent of children with disabilities (12.3%) were receiving services for autism under the IDEA. This percentage has increased steadily. In 2007–2008, 0.6 percent of children with disabilities (13.4% of all children) were receiving services for autism under the IDEA (NCES, 2010). The number of children diagnosed with autism and served under IDEA increased by more than 500 percent between 1995 and 2005 (U.S. Government Accountability Office, 2005).

Causes of Autism Spectrum Disorders

Autism spectrum disorders (ASD) encompass a variety of different disorders, and there is not a single etiology. There seems to be general agreement in the field that there is a biological base and a significant genetic influence in ASDs (CDC, 2010a; Hyman & Towbin, 2007). Autism is linked to abnormal biology and chemistry in the brain (PubMed Health, 2010c). Scientists have isolated several abnormalities on chromosomes 2, 7, and 15 associated with ASD (Muhle, Trentatcoste, & Rapin, 2004). There is interest in the role of neurotransmitters, particularly serotonin, in children with ASD. In Rett syndrome, the relationship is clearer as it is associated with a mutation of a gene on the X chromosome. It is predominately seen in girls because male infants usually die (Huppke & Gartner, 2005).

Although it seems clear that genetic influences are an important risk factor, environmental factors influence gene expression. Research also shows that autism tends to run in families, although not in a clear-cut way. Siblings of children with autism have a higher rate of autism than expected in the general population (CDC, 2010a). If one twin has autism, the other twin has a 65 percent chance of having autism, and others will show some autistic symptoms (Hyman & Towbin, 2007).

Advances in diagnostic testing, including the **comparative genomic hybridization (CGH)** array, have allowed scientists to identify subtle duplications or deletions of genetic materials (Hagerman, 2007). These changes affect the development of synapses early in development, or synaptic plasticity and environmental responses. Mutations in genes that guide inhibitory and stimulatory connections also contribute to autism. Environmental stimuli such as emotional trauma can impair synaptic connections, and targeted educational programs can enhance synaptic connections (Hagerman, 2007).

There are some drugs that, if taken during pregnancy, can increase the probability of having a child with autism. **Thalidomide**, a drug used in the 1950s and 1960s to treat morning sickness, and valproic acid are two such drugs (CDC, 2010a; Newschaffer et al., 2007). Clearly, our environment has changed with both natural and artificially created toxins. Pregnant women and children are exposed to pollution, nuclear waste, food additives, household chemicals, and pesticides at levels no other generation has faced (Interactive Autism Network, 2007). There is no single, simple answer.

There are a number of possible causes that have been suggested but lack scientific research as proof, including diet, digestive tract changes, mercury poisoning, the body's inability to use vitamins and minerals, and vaccine sensitivity (PubMed Health, 2010c). There has been a lot of controversy about whether the measles, mumps, and rubella (MMR) vaccine caused autism or whether the ethyl mercury–based preservative **thimerosal** that was used as a preservative for pediatric vaccines before 2001 could be associated with the rise in cases of ASD. At this point, there is not scientific documentation for a causal relation between these variables, although clearly some parents believe this is true (Hyman & Towbin, 2007; PubMed Health, 2010c).

IN THE FIELD

Our son has autism. He was a marvelously well-developing toddler until he had his MMR. Several weeks after he had his vaccination, his behavior began to change. He quit talking and looking at our eyes and became self-absorbed. We told his pediatrician, who made light of it. His older sister was very advanced for her age, and he told us not to make comparisons. We didn't; we worried. We talked to people. My wife is a nurse, and she began to talk to people and we began to believe that Tony was developing autism. We changed pediatricians. We told our new pediatrician that we believed our son had autism and that it was caused by the thimerosal in the MMR. Over time, and with a lot of observations, surveys to fill out, and so on, he eventually diagnosed Tony with autism. We were angry and we now talked to other parents who were angry. At first we were so consumed with our anger that we almost forgot about Tony. We were going to get lawyers and sue. We were going to march. We were going to do all kinds of things. Then it hit us that as we were focusing on our anger, our son was slipping farther and farther away from us.

Finally, we refocused and used our energy on learning to teach children with autism. We decided that applied behavior analysis made the most sense for us. My wife got the training and then we started. We really thought about what we wanted for Tony and then how to get it. Depending on the year, we spent between $60,000 and $100,000 doing the training. That isn't counting our time (daughter included) and the friends that came to help. I haven't changed my mind about what I believe caused my son's autism, but I did change how I used my time and money.

Greenspan and Wieder (2006) feel the environment triggers the disorder and that two events derail the child's development between 16 and 24 months. The first is the child's emerging capacity of higher-level presymbolic, symbolic, and cognitive functioning. If these new capacities are built on a weak foundation, the child is overwhelmed, and he regresses in the areas of self-regulation, behavioral organization, interpersonal patterns, motor control, and language abilities. At the core of this regression is a weak capacity for intentional two-way affective communication. Although this alone may impact development, a second event that stresses the child, such as the loss of a caregiver, a parent's return to work, or the birth of a sibling, may also be overwhelming. The more difficult the child becomes, the more frustrated the parents feel.

THE EVIDENCE BASE

As we move toward more evidence-based decision making, it becomes clear that in some instances we lack evidence. The Centers for Autism and Developmental Disabilities Research and Epidemiology (CADDRE) Network is undertaking a 5-year multisite collaborative study: The Study to Explore Early Development. The goal of the study is to identify what might put children at risk for autism spectrum disorders and other developmental disabilities. The study is focusing on three main areas:

1. Physical and behavioral characteristics of children with ASDs, children with other developmental disabilities, and children without a developmental delay or disability
2. Health conditions among children with and without ASDs
3. Factors associated with a child's risk of developing ASDs

The study will include 2,700 children, ages 2 through 5, and their parents, in six states. The study looks at the following factors:

- Reproductive and hormonal features of mothers
- Smoking, alcohol, and drug use during pregnancy
- Parents' occupations
- Sociodemographic features
- Genetic features
- Biomarkers
- Physical and behavioral characteristics
- Infection and immune function, including autoimmunity
- Select mercury exposures
- Gastrointestinal features
- Sleep features
- Hospitalizations and injuries

Source: CDC, CADDRE, 2010; to keep updated about this research go to www.cdc.gov/ncbddd/autism/seed.htm.

Early Identification of Autism Spectrum Disorders

Identification of children with autism spectrum disorders is determined by their behavior in three areas: social reciprocity, communication, and repetitive behaviors. Concerns arise when infants do not babble by 12 months, do not gesture (e.g., wave "bye-bye") by 12 months, do not say single words by 16 months, do not spontaneously say two-word phrases by 24 months, or lose language or social skills at any age (PubMed Health, 2010c). Additional concerns include delays or abnormal functioning in social interactions, not using language as a tool for social communication, and not participating in symbolic or imaginative play (APA, 2000).

One finding that may help in the early identification of infants is that their pattern of brain growth, as measured by head circumference, shows a different pattern than other children. Although normal at birth, brain growth accelerates between 1 and 2 months, and 6 and 14 months (Courchesne, Carper, & Aksoomoff, 2003). There are a variety of theories about the impact this has on development. One theory focuses on the synaptic pruning process, where synapses that are used remain and those that are not used are pruned. If this pruning does not happen, then the neural structure of the brain may be disorganized (Mundy & Burnette, 2005). In addition to differences in brain structures, there also seem to be differences in the connections between various parts of the brain. The lack of abilities that are most characteristic of autism, social interactions and language, require a high degree of integration among various parts of the brain (Minshew et al., 2005).

Most parents of children with autism suspect that something is wrong with their toddler when she is about 18 months old and begin to seek help by the time the child is age 2 (PubMed Health, 2010c). Parents often notice lack of speech by 15 to 18 months. However, deficits in the areas of communication can be noted earlier in prespeech behavior. Infants lack appropriate gaze and the turn-taking pattern that characterizes adult-infant communication. They do not respond to their name or recognize their parents' voices, yet they are aware of environmental noises. They also don't have a gesture system that typically supports vocalizations. Approximately 25 to 30 percent of infants with ASD begin to say words, and then stop speaking and using gestures between 15 and 24 months. Although children may regress based on environmental stressors, ASD should be one of the possibilities considered (Johnson, Myers, & the Council of Children with Disabilities, 2007).

Parents seem less aware of the social aspects of children's early development than motor milestones. Infants with ASD do not seek connectedness; they seldom make eye contact and ignore their parents' bids for attention. They seem content being alone. Deficits in joint attention are one of the most distinguishing characteristics of very young children with ASDs (Johnson et al., 2007). Toddlers with autism also have problems with pretend play, social interactions, and verbal and nonverbal communication (PubMed Health, 2010c). The importance of early identification and early intervention is imperative. If children are identified early and intervention is begun, the outcome for children and families can be positively impacted.

Assessment of Autism Spectrum Disorders

Assessment begins with a multimodal view of the problem. There is no biological test for autism. Assessment may begin with a family medical history, a detailed history of the child's social development, and general information about the family and how it functions. Typically, the child's hearing and language development are assessed. A test of intelligence is used to determine overall cognitive functioning. More information is obtained through a neurologic examination, an **electroencephalogram (EEG)**, and blood studies (Hyman & Towbin, 2007).

Observations of the child are made in different settings at multiple times. Rating scales are often used to assist and organize evaluation information. Scales like the Childhood Autism Rating Scale (CARS; Scholar, Reichler, & Renner, 1993) rely on comprehensive observations and are summative for children older than age 2.

The Autism Diagnostic Interview-Revised (ADI-R; Lord, Rutter, & Le Couteur, 1994) focuses on five different areas: (1) opening questions about parents' or caregivers' concerns;

(2) early and current communication skills; (3) social development and current play skills; (4) repetitive and restricted behaviors; and (5) behavioral problems. Questions were added that are designed to differentiate between different disorders on the spectrum. Mothers typically serve as the informants, and the interview takes 60 to 90 minutes to complete and requires someone who is a competent interviewer and knowledgeable about ASD (Matson & Minshew, 2006). This is often used in conjunction with the Autism Diagnostic Observation Schedule-Generic (ADOS; Lord et al., 1989, 2000). This tool has eight standardized tasks the examiner and child participate in. During the tasks and throughout the observation, the examiner rates the child's behavior as within normal limits (0), infrequent or possible abnormality (1), or definite abnormality (2). These tools are used with children during their preschool years.

Because of the importance of early intervention, many see waiting until the preschool years for a diagnosis as too late. Although parents become concerned about their child's behavior sometime after their child's first birthday, children are rarely assessed by a pediatrician or psychologist for ASD until their second or third birthday or later. The Checklist for Autism in Toddlers (CHAT) was developed as a screening tool to be used by parents and pediatricians at the toddler's regular 18-month check-up (Baron-Cohen, Allen, & Gillberg, 1992). A modified version, the M-CHAT (Dumont-Mathew & Fein 2005), is a screening tool for children ages 18 to 36 months.

Although there are batteries of tests used in the early identification process for other disabilities, mental health professionals have relied primarily on unstructured clinical interviews and clinical judgment, based on guidelines from the American Psychiatric Association's *Diagnostic and Statistical Manual of Mental Disorders*, 4th ed. (Text Revision) (APA, 2000) to make decisions (Matson & Minshew, 2006). In general, medical testing is not helpful, although a detailed medical history should be taken and other potential causes of the behavior ruled out. One major concern with the diagnosis of autism is differentiating it from other disorders.

Autism Spectrum Disorders

Like most children with disabilities, children on the autism spectrum have different disabilities and different levels of involvement. Disorders that are considered part of the autism spectrum include autism, Asperger's syndrome, Rett syndrome, and childhood disintegrative disorder and pervasive development disorder–not otherwise specified

● ● ●
Autism

Autism was first described by Kanner (1943) as infantile autism. He documented with detail and accuracy children's lack of interest in people, stereotypic behavior, and problems with language. Given Kanner's sample of 11 children, he did not believe that autism had as high an overlap with intellectual disability as today's research supports. His research also led to a misunderstanding of the parent–child relationship. The reciprocal nature of parent–child relationships was

Children with autism are often more interested in playing with things than peers.
©Cengage Learning 2012

not explored, and reports looked to parents' psychopathology as one of the causes of autism, identifying, for example, the "refrigerator" mother who could not relate to her child. Recent research (Wamboldt & Wamboldt, 2000) found that although family problems can exacerbate child problems, it is often the other way around. Autism is not caused by lack of parenting skills.

Children with autism are usually identified when they are toddlers or during the preschool years. As infants, their characteristic behaviors may seem unusual, but by age 2, the failure to develop nonverbal aspects of social behavior (e.g., facial expression, looking at the speaker) and lack of interest in peers become apparent. Deficiencies in communication skills are also noted, particularly the lack of spontaneous communication and the inability to use language symbolically. If there is language, it may be immature or idiosyncratic so that only those familiar with the child know what is meant.

● ● ●
Asperger's Syndrome

Asperger's syndrome (AS) is a developmental neurobiological disorder in which children have a marked deficiency in the area of social skills. Children have problems with social interaction, social communication, and social imagination, that is, flexible thinking and imaginative play. Parents usually sense something is wrong by the time the child is about 3 years old (National Institute of Neurological Disorders and Stroke [NINDS], 2011c). Not meeting social milestones is one of the first markers. Unlike children with autism, children retain their language skills. Because they may become preoccupied with a particular object or subject, they can be misdiagnosed as autistic. Unlike autistic disorder, there is usually little intellectual impairment, and initial language acquisition follows the predicted pattern. There is considerable overlap between the diagnosis of high-functioning autism (no intellectual disability) and Asperger's syndrome (Hyman & Towbin, 2007).

Some children with AS may not be diagnosed during the early childhood years because they mask the severity of their difficulties with social interaction with verbal skills. Asperger's syndrome may not be diagnosed until school age, when the social demands of the classroom make the symptoms apparent (Hyman & Towbin, 2007). Three to four times as many boys as girls are diagnosed with AS. The actual incidence of AS is not well established, but estimates are that two out of every 10,000 have the disorder (NINDS, 2011c). Diagnosis is complicated for a variety of reasons. There is no standardized diagnostic screen for AS. Additionally, some doctors do not believe Asperger's syndrome is a distinct disorder. They see Asperger's syndrome as being the high-functioning end of autism spectrum disorders and feel it should be labeled as high-functioning autism. Some professionals use the terms *Asperger's syndrome* and *high-functioning autism* interchangeably (NINDS, 2011c).

Children with Asperger's syndrome have three core characteristics: poor communications skills, obsessive or repetitive routines, and physical clumsiness. Doctors rely on the following core behaviors for a possible diagnosis of AS. Problems in at least one of the areas of communication and socialization or repetitive, restrictive behavior must be present before age 3.

- Abnormal eye contact
- Aloofness
- Failure to turn when called by name
- Failure to use gestures to point or show
- Lack of interactive play
- Lack of interest in peers (NINDS, 2011c).

Although children with Asperger's syndrome may have perfect spoken language, they often use language in a way that tends to be formal and even pedantic. The use of language will set the child apart from others. The child's voice may lack expression and rhythm and have an odd inflection or be a monotone (NINDS, 2011c). They often lack the ability to monitor the volume of their voice based on their surroundings. Children also have problems getting meaning from the tone of someone else's voice. They have problems interpreting nonverbal communication and may understand others in a very literal way. To say "I could have died laughing" would be very confusing to the child because you are not dead. Children also fail to get the implied meaning of language. If you said, "The telephone is ringing" the child wouldn't understand that you intend to answer the phone or that you may want someone else to answer the phone. Children may need a visual signal to know that you are unhappy with their behavior, as they may not pick it up from your tone of voice.

A child with Asperger's syndrome may have an all-absorbing interest in something his peers find unusual. The child's obsessive interest in a particular topic or object excludes all others. The child seems driven to know all he can possibly know about this topic, and it is all the child wants to talk about or do. Children have trouble with transitions and change. They want things to stay the same. He may have a schedule or routine that he insists be observed. This may be anything from a bedtime ritual to how he puts on his clothes. He is limited in his ability to think and play relatively. He also has problems in generalizing and in transferring skills from one setting to another. Organization is a challenge. A child may have problems getting all his belongings together or finding his way around. Writing and drawing neatly is also problematic, as is finishing tasks.

Children with Asperger's syndrome often have difficulty in motor skills. The child may be clumsy and awkward in his movements. Children may have delayed motor skills development and motor clumsiness. This particularly affects skills that require sensory motor integration such as catching a ball, peddling a bike, or climbing a jungle gym. These children may also have an uncoordinated walk that is bouncy or stilted (NINDS, 2011c).

Children with Asperger's syndrome may be socially isolated, but this rarely bothers them. They may become tense and distressed when they are trying to cope with the approaches and social demands of others. Because of their narrow interests and lack of social reciprocity, they make few friends.

> **▶‖ TeachSource Video Case**
>
> **Autism in Girls**
>
> Watch the TeachSource Video Case *Autism in Girls*, in which you'll see how autism affects girls of various ages socially. The video can be found in the Early Childhood Education Media Library under Special Education, available at www.cengagebrain.com.

IN THE FIELD

My brother Paul was born in 1962. We knew he was different, slow, his speech was weird, but we lived on a small farm in Alberta, Canada. When my parents tried to enroll him in school, he was not admitted. He worked some on the farm, but mostly he stayed at home and cleaned things. It took him a long time, but he loved to clean. Canada passed new laws about children with disabilities, and in 1978, when Paul was 16, he entered school for the first time. Our family grows them big. At that time Paul was almost 6 feet tall and weighed close to 160 pounds. He was formally tested and identified as having Asperger's syndrome. He was placed in a first-grade class. Can you imagine? He cried, he fought—he didn't want to go to school and the school didn't want him. He scared the teachers and the children.

He was then enrolled in a residential school in Edmonton, about two hours away. He lived with my aunt during the week. We expected him to have adjustment problems, and he did. However, when he started defecating in all of the corners of my aunt's house, she had had it. He was once again home on the farm. My father died when Paul was in his 30s. At his funeral, I told my stepmother that I would have Paul spend a week with me as soon as I could arrange it. About two months later, Paul came to visit me. When the week was up, I called to make arrangements to take him back to my stepmother. She said that she had packed his things up and she planned to have them delivered to me, and that he would be staying with me. That was 20 years ago, and he is still living with me.

● ● ●

Rett Syndrome

Rett syndrome is a neurodevelopmental disorder that begins with a period of normal development through the first 6 to 18 months of life. Then there is a deceleration of head growth resulting in intellectual disability. There is progressive neurologic involvement, which results in the loss of purposeful hand skills (replaced by hand-wringing or hand-washing behavior) and spasticity in the legs. Social engagement is lost. The child has a severe impairment in both expressive and receptive language, and has a poorly coordinated gait and trunk movements. The disorder eventually stabilizes. In toddlers, it has the same characteristics as other autistic disorders; however, by preschool age, the differences are evident. Rett syndrome has only been diagnosed in females and is much less common than autism (Hyman & Towbin, 2007).

Rett syndrome is caused by a mutation in the MECP2 gene on the X chromosome (Huppke & Gartner, 2005). This gene contains instructions for the synthesis of the protein MECP2, which is needed for brain development and tells other genes to turn off or stop producing their own unique proteins. Girls have two X chromosomes, so only about half of the cells in the nervous system use the defective gene. Boys with the MECP2 mutation die shortly after birth (NINDS, 2011e).

There are four stages to the syndrome.

- *Stage I, Early Onset.* The disorder may be somewhat vague and autistic-like if noticed. Infants may show less eye contact and there may be gross motor delays. This stage lasts for a few months and possibly up to a year.

- *Stage II, Rapid Destructive Stage,* begins between ages 1 and 4 and lasts for weeks or months. During this time, the characteristic hand movements such as wringing, washing, clapping, or tapping appear, head growth slows, and rapid or gradual purposeful hand skills and spoken language are lost.

- *Stage III, Plateau or Pseudo-Stationary Stage,* begins between ages 2 and 10 and can last for years. **Apraxia**, motor problems, and seizures are prominent, but the child may show more interest and alertness, and some behavioral skills improve. Girls may remain in this stage for most of their lives.

- *Stage IV, Late Motor Deterioration Stage,* can last for years or decades and is characterized by reduced mobility (NINDS, 2011e).

Childhood Disintegrative Disorder

The essential feature of childhood disintegrative disorder (CDD), as the name implies, is a marked regression in multiple areas of function, following a period of at least 2 years of normal development. After 2 years, but before 10 years, the child loses previously acquired skills in the areas of expressive and receptive language, social skills, and adaptive behavior, including bowel and bladder control, motor skills, and play skills (APA, 2000). At some point, the disorder stabilizes, leaving children with many of the characteristics of autism (Hyman & Towbin, 2007). CDD is usually associated with severe intellectual disability. It is a very rare condition and no single cause has been identified.

Pervasive Developmental Disorder–Not Otherwise Specified

The diagnosis PDD–NOS does not meet the criteria for a diagnosis of autism or pervasive developmental disorder, but it does represent a functional impairment. It is referred to as a **subthreshold condition**. Children diagnosed with PDD–NOS are a heterogeneous group that may have comorbid symptoms of cognitive, language, and behavioral symptoms in addition to symptoms of autism (Hyman & Towbin, 2007). These children typically are identified later than children with autism and are less likely to have intellectual disability. Whether or not a child is diagnosed with autism or PDD–NOS, the treatment and interventions are individualized but essentially use the same principles.

Associated Conditions

There is a close connection between autism and intellectual disability, which confounds diagnosis. It is estimated that two-thirds to three-quarters of children 3 to 10 years of age with autistic disorder also have intellectual disability (Yeargin-Alsop et al., 2003). The overlap appears to be only about 40 percent with preschool children (Chakrabarti & Fombonne, 2001). The developmental trajectory of this group of children who have autism but do not have intellectual disability can be greatly impacted. With early intervention during the preschool years to improve language, play, and the motivation to socialize with peers, they will appear more like children with Asperger's syndrome than autism (Attwood, 2007).

Sleep disturbances are very common in children with ASDs, with 50 percent to 70 percent of children reported to have problems in this area. These appear most problematic during the preschool years but persist for many years (Wiggs & Stores, 2004). Approximately a fourth of children with autistic disorder also have epilepsy (Tuchman, 2000).

Characteristics of Children with Autism Spectrum Disorders

Like all children, children with ASD have a variety of characteristics with a range of severity. Some of these behaviors are close to what other children their age might do, whereas others are more severe. There are three central domains affected: social, communication, and behavior.

Social Reciprocity

Social interactions form the core of getting along with others. Social interactions are complex. They involve being able to read and respond accurately to the cues of others. These social skills emerge as children learn about themselves as individuals and, eventually, about the thoughts and feelings of others. Children with ASD are inept at learning these skills. They may not respond, have limited responses, or be clumsy in their attempts. Thus, they do not have good social interaction skills. Overall, depending upon the level of involvement, they

- show little interest in making friends and playing with other children; are indifferent to peer contact.
- rather play alone than play with others.
- have difficulty being with and interacting with peers.
- not imitate behavior or model what other children or adults are doing, even when this is one-on-one.
- not show age-appropriate play behaviors.
- not make eye contact.
- not smile at people or family members.
- have difficulty interpreting social cues.
- seem unaware of the existence of other people and may not respond to family members differently than unknown adults.
- show socially and emotionally inappropriate behaviors (Attwood, 2007; NINDS, 2011a,c).

Communication Skills

Children with ASD have some degree of communication impairment. Expressive language may show more **echolalia** (repetition of what is spoken) than spontaneous speech. Personal pronouns are often confused. Speech may be high pitched and have an unusual rhythm and intonation pattern (Hyman & Towbin, 2007). Receptively, children may have problems with more complex communication. Traditionally, they are visual learners. Overall, depending upon the level of involvement, they may

- have delayed speech development.
- have difficulty maintaining a conversation, even if they have good speech skills.
- reverse pronouns such as "I" and "you."
- have echolalic speech or "parrot" words others say, either immediately or after a delay.
- have little or no imagination, cannot understand symbolic or creative interactions, and cannot pretend.
- misinterpret literal or implied meanings.
- not use traditional symbolic gestures such as waving; have limited facial expression.
- not communicate well with words or gestures.
- have expressive language that may be superficially perfect and formal (Attwood, 2007; NINDS, 2011a,c).

Stereotyped Behavior

Children with ASD don't know how to play, especially when children get into pretend play. They often get into rituals, routines, and schedules, but spontaneity is beyond their capability. They often become upset if their routines are disturbed. They may display stereotyped movements and self-stimulating behaviors such as arm flapping, pacing, running in circles, rocking, hand waving, and so on. They may have sleep disturbances, mood changes, and unusual

responses to sensory input. Overall, depending upon the level of involvement, they may

- be passive or physically inactive and may not respond to requests.
- have a narrow range of interests to the exclusion of other activities.
- be picky eaters.
- throw temper tantrums when there is not an obvious cause.
- behave aggressively and may physically attack others.
- practice self-injurious behavior such as head banging or eye gouging.
- have a compulsive need for routines that affects themselves and others (Attwood, 2007; NINDS, 2011a,c).

IN THE FIELD

Children with autism can be challenging to teach, which is what makes their success that much sweeter! Knowing what to teach preschool children with autism is very important. Some parents may want academic rather than functional skills on their child's individualized education program (IEP). I cannot stress enough the importance of functional skills. If a child has not already mastered these skills, then she should be working on them. The critical skills include responding to yes–no and choice questions, using the bathroom, dressing, attending to personal appearance, having mobility in familiar locations, eating without drawing attention, occupying self while waiting, responding to greetings, requesting what she needs, indicating when a task is finished, and gaining attention. When teaching children these critical skills, teachers must present them in a functional way. Having a child get dressed just because it is 10:00 a.m. and that is what you do in school at 10:00 a.m. is not functional, but having a child change into "messy play clothes," or having children practice dressing themselves after going swimming, is very functional.

Instructional Models

There is no one universally accepted way to teach children with ASD, although almost all professionals believe that early intervention is essential and that this intervention should be intensive, continuous, and multidisciplinary (Hurth et al., 1999). Most agree that early intervention for children with autistic spectrum disorders should have a high degree of structure; materials must be presented in a planned, predictable manner, and environmental stimulation needs consideration (Gammeltoft & Nordenhof, 2007). However, professionals disagree over how this should happen. Educational approaches are diverse, and there does not seem to be compelling information to support one particular method. All, however, agree that intervention needs to be early and individualized. For many families, the cost of specific interventions is out of their reach.

Some professionals believe that children with ASD should be included in regular classrooms, whereas others feel that this is inappropriate. Still others feel that early intervention must be individualized and segregated but that children do need to be included as they get older and/or for some part of the day, although maybe not the entire day. The programs and methods detailed below are designed primarily for segregated programs and focus on individualized planning.

Applied Behavior Analysis (ABA), the Lovaas Method

Lovaas (1987) developed a model of intensive, comprehensive one-on-one training. It involves teaching many discrete lessons. Children usually start a 40-hour-per-week program at age 2. The approach is based on principles of behavior modification. It uses a model of introduction, prompting, and behavior reinforcement. The curriculum focuses on language, academic skills, and social behavior. Although not as simple as this, the approach involves the following steps:

- Decide on the behavior you want to change, replace, or initiate. Take a baseline (how frequently does it occur, what happens before it occurs, when and where does it occur).
- Make a hypothesis about the purpose of the behavior you want to change or replace. State the goal in positive terms (what the child will do, *not* what the child will not do). Think about the components of the behavior.
- To initiate behavior, break the goal down into its component parts, and design a drill. Speech is a good place to start.
- After each intervention, use positive reinforcement. Because drills are short and frequent, rewards must be small and fast and something the child finds reinforcing, such as food, hugs, verbal praise, and so on. Some programs use negative reinforcers for undesired behaviors.
- Assess the effectiveness of the intervention and modify it if necessary. (Waltz, 1999)

This is a very intensive program and most frequently is home-based and run by parents who are trained in the method, with family, friends, and students as volunteers. Generalization of the skills learned is an important component of the treatment plan. Schools, too, use variations on this approach.

IN THE FIELD

Data collection is a very important part of evaluating a child's programming. Classroom staff must collect data on each IEP goal one time per week to determine how well the child is progressing. If the child is not progressing, the team has to review the data to decide what changes should be made in how goals are presented. A data sheet should include, at the very least, the name of the child, goal or benchmark, key, reinforcement schedule, and parameter details. We also include the initial stimulus, target stimulus, error correction procedure, task format, prompt strategy, and the target level. Data collection can be very time-consuming and works best when it is built into the daily classroom routine. For example, many children have hand washing as an IEP objective. Because children have the opportunity to wash their hands at least three times per day, data should be taken at one of those times. Do not just decide out of the blue that you are going to take a child to wash his hands just because you need to collect data.

Reinforcement is very important for children's success. Before an activity, each child should have the opportunity to choose what he wants to work for. You will often hear me say in my classroom, "If you want _____,

then you need to _____." It's amazing the change in behavior I find when children are reminded of what they can receive if they complete a task. It is often difficult for some parents to realize the effectiveness of this approach. Of course, fade the reinforcement as much and as quickly as possible. If a child does a good job and likes pretzels, don't give him 10 pretzels; one is just fine. We have to remember that adults need reinforcement, so why wouldn't children?

Treatment and Education of Autistic and Related Communication-Handicapped Children (TEACCH)

Treatment and Education of Autistic and Related Communication-Handicapped Children (TEACCH) was established in the early 1970s by Eric Schopler at the University of North Carolina, and was one of the first disorder-specific educational programs that developed an intensive, structured, coordinated approach to developing communication abilities for children with autism. The approach involves parents as cotherapists and uses behavioral strategies to enhance communication and social interactions. It heavily supports the use of visual organizers and cueing (Mesibov, Shea, & Schopler, 2005).

IN THE FIELD

I implement some TEACCH strategies in my classroom. Each day, I assign children "basket work," which is basically an individual work system. Work systems should always answer four questions: (1) what work, (2) how much work, (3) when is the work finished, and (4) what's next? Basket time allows the children to work independently on tasks with a work schedule. I have set up "basket work" so that each child has a sentence strip with three cards on it. The child takes the first card on her strip and matches it to a basket that is found in the same place each day. When the child returns to her desk and completes the work in the basket, she places it in a "finished" basket and gets the next card on her strip. These steps continue until the child has completed all her tasks. On the strip, after the third card, is a picture of a preferred activity. The children know that when they have completed all three tasks, they can participate in the preferred activity. I usually have the children complete basket work while I am working with children individually. Basket work is also a good activity for the kids to work on when they first arrive in the morning, while I am reading communications books and taking children to the bathroom. It is exciting to see the children progress from completing one task with assistance to completing three or four tasks independently for 15 minutes or more!

Shoebox tasks, or task boxes, are wonderful to use in basket work. These activities can be made using shoeboxes (what else?) and Velcro. To make a task box for a child who needs to improve fine motor skills, attach an ice cube tray to the top of the box and then place 1-inch cube blocks inside each of the cube holders. Cut a hole in the shoebox for the children to put the cubes into. The child has to use a pincer grasp to take the block out of the ice cube tray and put it in the hole. Children know the task is complete when all of the blocks are gone. When cleaning up, simply take the ice cube tray off the top of the box, put it in with the blocks, and it is done. I like shoebox tasks because they contain all the materials in the box, so there is no need to go searching around for the manipulatives you need. It is also nice that you can use your imagination to make the task boxes meet the needs of your children. You can also purchase shoebox tasks online at www.shoeboxtasks.com. I think they are rather expensive, but you can also use the website just to get ideas for making your own task boxes.

Infants with autism appear to be developing typically until about 12 to 18 months, when they fail to develop nonverbal aspects of social behavior and lack interest in toys and people as well as the communicative aspects of language.
©Cengage Learning 2012

Developmental Individual-Differences Relationship-Based Approach

Greenspan and Wieder (2006) developed the developmental individual-differences relationship-based (DIR) approach. They identified six fundamental developmental skills they feel should form the foundation of all intervention:

- The dual ability to take an interest in the sights, sounds, and sensations of the world and to calm oneself down
- The ability to engage in relationships with other people
- The ability to engage in two-way communication
- The ability to create complex gestures, to string together a series of actions into an elaborate and deliberate problem-solving sequence
- The ability to create ideas
- The ability to build bridges between ideas to make them reality-based and logical (Greenspan & Wieder, 1998, pp. 3–4)

Greenspan and Wieder (2006) place autism spectrum disorders in the broader context of neurodevelopmental disorders of relating and communicating (NDRC). They have proposed four types of clusters, or clinical subtypes, that they feel have implications for diagnosis and treatment,

based on four developmental pathways that characterize how individuals process information:

- Sensory modulation—the ability to modulate or regulate sensation as it is coming in
- Motor planning and sequencing—how we act on our ideas or what we hear and see
- Auditory processing and language—the way in which we receive information and comprehend and express it
- Visuospatial processing—the ability to make sense of and understand what we are seeing (Greenspan & Wieder, 2006, p. 236)

Their approach is very different from a behavioral approach but just as intensive. Children and their parents engage in emotional interactions that use emerging but not fully developed capacities for communication and relatedness. Working from this philosophy, they feel that intervention should "involve children in dynamic, emotionally based, problem-solving interactions that are likely to foster abstract thinking and the very ability to generalize itself" (Greenspan & Wieder, 1998, p. 478). The intervention, sometimes called "Floor Time," begins with establishing attention, engagement, and intimacy, and then moves on to two-way communication, feelings and ideas, and logical thinking (Greenspan & Wieder, 2006). In a comprehensive program, they see spontaneous, follow-the-child's-lead floor time happening 8 to 10 times a day with 20- to 30-minute sessions in addition to semistructured problem solving and spatial, motor, and sensory activities. They are far more optimistic about outcomes for children but feel that approaches that do not pull the child into spontaneous, joyful relationship patterns may intensify rather than remediate the problem (Greenspan & Wieder, 2006).

Assistive Technology

Much of the focus of assistive technology for children with ASD is on augmentative and alternative communication. Parents themselves can make some of these devices, and children are able to point to pictures to let others know about their wants and needs. These are typically single-meaning pictures, and many pictures are needed. A core vocabulary of just a few hundred words covers 85 percent of most communication. Some of the communication devices actually "talk," and with current technology there is even a choice in the voice that will be used. Increasingly, children with autism are using electronic tablet applications to communicate.

▶‖ TeachSource Video Case

Tyler: Augmentative Communication Techniques for a Kindergarten Student with Autism and Language Issues

Watch the TeachSource Video Case *Tyler: Augmentative Communication Techniques for a Kindergarten Student with Autism and Language Issues*, in which his teacher and speech-language pathologist describe how visual strategies can be used to help students. The video can be found in the Early Childhood Education Media Library under Special Education, available at www.cengagebrain.com.

Many schools use the picture exchange communication system (PECS), which is commercially available. The pictures in this system are specifically designed to represent words and concepts. PECS was developed in 1985 to teach children and adults to initiate communication. It has seven phases and works well with approaches that use behavior analysis. Briefly:

- *Phase I:* Teaches children to initiate communication by exchanging a single picture for a highly desired item.
- *Phase II:* Teaches children to be persistent communicators by actively seeking out their picture and traveling to someone to make a request.
- *Phase III:* Teaches children to discriminate among pictures and to select the picture that represents the item they want.
- *Phase IV:* Teaches children to use sentence structure to make a request in the form of "I want . . . ."
- *Phase V:* Teaches children to respond to the question "What do you want?"
- *Phase VI:* Teaches children to comment about things in their environment both spontaneously and in response to a question.
- *Phase VII:* Teaches children to expand their vocabulary, using attributes such as colors, shapes, and sizes in their requests (Frost & Bondy, 2002.)

IN THE FIELD

I cannot say enough about the importance of communication skills. The most common reason that adults with disabilities are fired from jobs is their lack of communication skills. The picture exchange communication system (PECS) can be used not only with children with autism but also with children who have other disabilities. Children beginning to learn to communicate via PECS start with requesting a desired item by placing a picture of the item in an adult's hand, with full assistance. Gradually, assistance is faded, and children are presented with a variety of pictures from which they need to discriminate what they want. Children go on to use an "I want ___" sentence strip and often use the sentence strip as a visual cue for how to request an item.

One key thing to remember with PECS is that adults should not be asking children what they want; rather, the child should initiate communication with the adult. Children begin PECS training with requesting because they will find it motivating to receive an item they have asked for. Once a child becomes proficient at requesting, staff will begin helping the child to comment on things in the environment. Having previously taught at a school that did not implement PECS, I can vouch that children who have learned the PECS as an alternate form of communication have enjoyed many more opportunities at school, home, and in the community. If a child is having a tantrum and I don't know why, it is very nice to know that if I gesture toward the communication book, the child can usually tell me what it is he or she wants.

THE EVIDENCE BASE

This synthesis of practice-based research focused on the effectiveness of the picture exchange communication system (PECS) for improving the functional communication skills of children with autistic spectrum disorders. Eleven articles (13 studies including 125 participants) met the selection criterion.

In all of the studies, participants who received PECS training experienced positive gains in functional communication skills.

The most commonly reported outcomes included (1) successful use of PECS as a communication tool (100% of studies); (2) an increase in overall level of communication and language (62% of studies); (3) an increase in spontaneous language/speech imitation (46% of studies); (4) an increase of initiations of communication (31% of studies); and (5) an increase in mean length of utterance (23% of studies). Studies that included follow-up assessments found that the gains were maintained at posttest.

Source: Tien, 2008.

REFLECTIVE PRACTICE | This research synthesized the studies that had been done using PECS to determine the effectiveness of this particular approach to teaching language skills to children with autism spectrum disorders. Researchers set up selection criteria, analyzed the studies, and then proposed rival explanations. They looked at threats to internal validity, such as observational coding and the fact that the changes could be related to maturation, and ruled out these possibilities. They concluded that PECS is a good tool for teaching functional communications skills for children with ASD and that it can be easily integrated into the school and home. Tien (2008) cautions that these results cannot be generalized to other disabilities. As you look at yourself as an educator who uses evidence-based research, what does this mean to your practice? How might you use this information? What does it suggest about ways to determine best teaching methods?

Therapies and Interventions

A variety of different therapies are used with children with ASD. Speech-language therapy is a major intervention for children with ASD. The issue typically involves lack of speech and functional communication skills.

For children with ASD, an occupational therapist (OT) develops an individualized program based on the particular child and her needs. It might focus on helping the child learn to suck through a straw, put on and take off clothing, and work on balance and developing the vestibular sense. The OT might also work on building up specific muscles, teaching techniques for self-relaxation, and techniques for dealing with sensory overload. Occupational therapists also work with body awareness, using massage and brushing the limbs. Most children with ASD will need occupational therapy; some will need physical therapy to work on issues like gait problems, low muscle tone, strengthening muscles, and other related issues.

Sensory Integration

Sensory integration is the process by which individuals receive information from their senses, process that information, and then act on it. Some feel that one of the problems that children with ASD have is interpreting the world around them. Sensory integration problems can be fundamental because they interfere with the development of basic skills.

Children demonstrate individual variations in how they interpret and respond to their world. They have different thresholds for sensory awareness and, to further confound things, these levels change relative to their levels of stress and fatigue. People can also have a low threshold for some things and a high one for others. If you are concentrating on reading this book, you may not hear approaching footsteps until someone is beside you. If, however, you are listening for someone to come, you might pick up the footfalls much earlier. According to Myles and colleagues (2000) there are five stages in the sensory integration process. In real life, the process happens so quickly, it seems like a single action.

- *Registration* refers to awareness, the point at which we know we have touched or smelled something. Until the input registers, it cannot be acted upon.

- *Orientation* can occur after we are aware of the stimulus. This typically results in a shift of attention—from the book to the footsteps.

- *Interpretation* takes place as we relate what is happening to our past experience. What does this mean? If nothing, the response may end.

- *Organization* occurs in the brain to determine what response will be made.

- *Response* will be executed based on the brain's interpretation and organization.

Modulation is the ability to regulate responses in the context of what is happening. If there is an exam the next day, you might continue to read the book. If you are reading ahead, you might benefit by taking a break with a friend. To stay awake driving, you might sing, open the window, or chew gum. When you arrive at your destination, you might read a boring story or play soft music in order to calm down to make sleep possible.

Effective sensory integration processing feeds into motor planning, or **praxis**, which is necessary to respond and execute motor actions. This is particularly important in analyzing new actions and in adjusting to variations in old ones. It involves the cognitive process of representing the action, knowing where the body is, starting the action, proceeding with the necessary sequence of steps, making adjustments, and then knowing when the action is over. Something as simple as getting out of different chairs requires praxis. Think about how you would get out of a deep, low-slung chair as opposed to a straight-backed wooden chair. Different motor planning and adjustment is required.

Some children have ineffective sensory processing. They have trouble learning to ride a bike. Some children may refuse to wear some types of clothing that feel uncomfortable, due to their unusual responses to sensory input. They may experience unpleasant sensations when others do not. Children with ASD often have unusual sensory reactions, which vary with the sensory input involved.

Children with ASD tend to have reactions either greater or less than one would expect from the situation. This has to do with the central processing of the child's brain. The hypersensitive child's brain registers sensation too intensely, which causes the child to misinterpret information (Kranowitz, 1998). He may view a touch as a life-threatening blow and

hence try to avoid being touched. Children who are hyposensitive are underreactive. This child's brain registers too little sensation, so the child seeks stimulation to maintain a "normal" arousal level. This child may be constantly touching and feeling things. He needs to act but may lack coordination and organization. He misses cues other children get and may not understand nonverbal cues. Some children are a combination of hyper- and hyposensitive. This can vary with the particular stimulus, or it can vary with the place or time of day (Williamson & Anzalone, 2001).

IN THE FIELD

Children with autism need sensory input. It is a good idea to set aside a specific time each day to incorporate sensory activities into your classroom. The most common thing to do for sensory time is to play at the bean/sand/rice/water table. Although this is a great idea and fun for them, there are many other types of sensory activities that are much more beneficial for the kids. For example, children in my class love the "hot dog game," which is when they lie on a sleeping bag and we roll them up tightly. They also enjoy vibrating pillows and having their back, arms, legs, hands, and feet brushed with a fingernail brush or surgical cleansing brush. To get children moving more, try having them bounce on a therapy ball or jump on a trampoline. Oral-motor stimulation can occur when a child brushes his teeth with an electric toothbrush, or by using straws for pudding and applesauce. Some occupational therapists recommend using a weighted vest with children. I have found this to be very helpful. The vest will be on the child for 15 to 20 minutes and then off for 15 to 20 minutes. The times will vary depending on the child. The weights used should be no more than one-tenth of the child's body weight, but you need the help of an occupational therapist to get started and do it right.

TACTILE

Children with ASD can be overreactive (hypersensitive) or underreactive (hyposensitive) to tactile stimuli.

Tactile Hypersensitivity. Children who are hypersensitive to touch, sometimes called tactile defensiveness, often refuse to participate in messy activities. They may only wear certain clothing (e.g., dresses that fall from the shoulders), or certain fabrics (e.g., cotton), or only clothes that have been washed in a certain detergent. They may have problems with some food textures. They may not feel safe when close to other children because they don't want to be touched. Work with these children and their families. Some children need to wear sweaters or jackets so they can modulate the experience of touch. Find out what type of touch is best tolerated.

Tactile Hyposensitivity. Children who are hyposensitive to touch may not notice touch until it is firm or intense. Children may not react to scrapes or bruises or know when or how they received them. They may touch others in line or even lean on them and not know it or understand the problem. If hyposensitivity is accompanied by low muscle tone, these children may be clumsy and tire easily, becoming exhausted after physical activity. They may run into the door jam as they walk through the door. Because they need sensation, they may crave tactile input, which may result in hitting or biting themselves. Or they may bite their fingernails to the quick or prefer tight clothing (Myles et al., 2000).

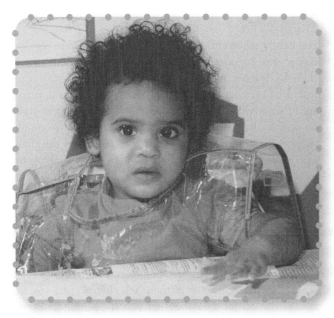

Children with autism can be tactilely defensive and approach sensory experiences tentatively, if at all.
©Cengage Learning 2012

VESTIBULAR

The vestibular system is involved with movement, posture, vision, balance, and coordination between the sides of the body.

VESTIBULAR HYPERSENSITIVITY

Children who are hypersensitive have a low tolerance for activities that involve movement. They like their feet on the ground. They don't like to play games that involve changing direction or speed, or require other than upright body positions. Children who have problems in this area may not participate in sports and may have problems with some requirements in physical education. Some school tasks are challenging, such as copying from the board and keeping their place when reading. The child may move his whole body rather than just his head to look at something.

Vestibular Hyposensitivity. Children who are hyposensitive often rock back and forth in their chair. They are clumsy and have trouble starting and stopping movement. They cannot sit still. They wiggle and constantly reposition themselves (Myles et al., 2000).

PROPRIOCEPTION

This system helps us keep our balance and rebalance based on feedback from our muscles and joints. It also helps us move, sit, and hold things. When the proprioception system is not working well, children may slump, display left–right confusion, and have problems completing obstacle courses. Fatigue is common.

VISUAL

Compared to other sensory systems, vision is a relative strength for children with ASD. With concentration and motivation, this system usually works well. It is difficult, however, for children with ASD to maintain both concentration and motivation.

IN THE FIELD

Children with autism are visual learners and need visual supports throughout the school day. Children often respond better to a picture symbol that displays "sit down" than to the verbal command "sit down." It can be hard to limit your "verbage" (verbal garbage)—basically it is easy to talk too much, leaving children completely lost. For example, instead of saying, "Johnny, you need to sit in your chair like your friend Matt," it's much better to simply say, "Sit," or better still, show the child a "sit" picture. Visuals can be easily implemented into morning circle songs as well. For the song "If You're Happy and You Know It," teachers should have on hand pictures of various actions so the children have a visual representation of the actions they are expected to follow. This works best if the pictures are made on a large scale, laminated, and bound into book format in the order you sing. (Digital cameras are a godsend.) Organization and preparation is very important when teaching preschoolers in general, especially preschoolers with autism. The last thing you'll have time to do right before an activity is gather a bunch of different pictures from a variety of places!

AUDITORY

Children with autistic spectrum disorder do not seem to process auditory information the same way that other children do. Children with ASD typically have unusual sensory preferences. Three- and 4-year-old children with ASD do not show a preference for parentese or child-directed speech over acoustically modified nonspeech (Kuhl et al., 2005).

Auditory Hypersensitivity. Loud noises can be unbearable to some children. Even small noises can be irritating. Some children cannot tolerate specific sounds, and others have problems with noises that seem quiet to us.

Auditory Hyposensitivity. Some children seem not to hear what is going on around them, not even when their name is being called. Others seem to drift off in the middle of a conversation.

GUSTATORY

The sense of taste can be problematic for some children with ASD. They often have strong likes and dislikes.

OLFACTORY

Apparently, many children with ASD have a type of olfactory sensory sensitivity (Myles et al., 2000). Schools have many smells, from cafeteria smells to the cleaner used to mop the floors, to the unique body odor each of us possesses. For some children and adults, these smells can be overpowering and even problematic.

Medication

Medication may be considered as part of a treatment program for specific target behaviors or comorbid conditions. Stimulant medications might be used if the child has symptoms of hyperactivity or inattention. If there is concern about neurotransmitters, serotonin reuptake inhibitors might be used to treat repetitive behavior. Other medication is being researched, but medication is not seen as a cure for ASD (Hyman & Tobin 2007, NINDS, 2011a).

Inclusive Settings

People have very different feelings about the inclusion of children with ASD into regular classrooms. Although most feel that children should spend *some* time in a regular classroom, many feel that only children with mild impairments should be significantly integrated into inclusive classrooms. They feel that the structure and organization most children with ASD need cannot be provided in an inclusive setting. Others disagree. Regardless of location, many experiences for children with ASD require more structure and a clearer purpose than those for other young children.

Organizing games for children with ASD is different from planning games for other children. If the game involves social interaction, it has to be set up for that to happen. Playing is vital to children's social development. However, playing is not spontaneous for children with autism, but must be organized and planned. Gammeltoft and Nordenhof (2007) suggest thinking through the following:

- *Where will the game take place?* Choose a table or some place that can be delineated using tape or mats.

- *What are we sharing?* Children need to know exactly what they will be doing and for how long. Begin with several short games rather than one long one.

- *Who is playing the game?* It may be easier if another child initiates the play. Give participating children numbers, and have the child with number one begin the game.

- *Whose turn is it?* A cap may be used to identify whose turn it is at the beginning.

- *How should materials be handled?* Be clear where materials belong and how they should be used.

- *Where does the game start and end?* Clear indicators help determine when the game is completed.

IN THE FIELD

For young children with ASD, acquiring play skills is very important. Children need to be taught to play appropriately with a variety of toys. This is especially important if a child is in an inclusive classroom with typical peers. Play skills are best taught in a systematic manner by first selecting a new toy or activity; establishing objectives; analyzing the task; teaching one step at a time; and finally, gradually expanding the play period. Cause-and-effect play skills should be taught first. Toys in this category include pop-up toys, rain sticks, bubbles, and so on. Closed-ended activities may be taught next. These activities are puzzles, shape sorters, stringing beads, and so on. Open-ended activities (e.g., playing with play-dough, blocks, dolls, dress-up clothes, and paints) may be more difficult for children to learn because there is no end product or sequence. Visual supports may help with open-ended activities. Children can be given a doll and clothes along with a picture of a doll all dressed and then be told to dress the doll like the picture. Or children can be given a visual model to guide them in stacking blocks to make a bridge or a train. Once a child has developed a repertoire of play schemes, the child is ready to move on to parallel play activities where he is expected to play with his own toys beside another child, and finally the child should progress to group play activities.

Support Personnel

Frequently, when children with ASD are included in regular classrooms, support staff are included as well. This means that the teacher not only has additional support for the child who is in her classroom, but that she also has to manage other adults in her classroom. In general, support staff do one of the following things: they provide one-on-one support for a particular child; for the children in the class who have special needs, either directly or by making or modifying special curriculum materials; or for the delivery of curriculum.

Support staff have the potential for enriching the classroom, but also of stigmatizing the child. It should be clear in what way the support staff will make a difference, and what form it should take. To determine this, teachers, parents, and children should be consulted. Sometimes the greatest support can be to modify lessons to include children with special needs or to collect data about what is happening. In other instances, team teaching is the goal. It is important for all to know the goal of additional support and to agree about what is needed. This goal impacts the job description of the individual, the required training, the status, and the expected support. Thus, the role of the support person can take shape in many different ways. This person can be a consultant, an observer, a problem solver, a person who sits beside the child, and so on. What is important is what the role is relative to the teacher and that it be clearly defined and agreed upon by all. The role of the support person should also be clear to all children in the classroom.

IN THE FIELD

Children with autism do best when their time is structured. They do not do well with a lot of downtime. File folder activities work well with children. Because they are easy to make, the file folders can be adapted to meet the individual needs of children. File folder books can be purchased at teacher supply stores, but I have found them to be too challenging for most of my children, so I make them myself or ask one of my support staff to help. We use colored file folders, index cards, library book pockets, and stickers/stamps/picture symbols. For example, if you have a child who is working on matching numbers, you can make a file folder activity. Begin by gluing or stapling eight library pockets on a file folder. On the pocket you can place number stickers, number stamps, or just write the numbers the child is working on matching. On the index card, write the same numbers, or use stamps or stickers, whatever was on the pocket. Laminate all materials, cut them apart, and the student is ready to match. If your school does not have the library book pockets, you can use index cards in place of the pockets. I attach the loose card to the cards glued on the folder with Velcro so I can check the child's work before the cards end up all over the floor.

As was said before, children need a structured school day. In addition, they need predictability. Providing children with a picture schedule gives them both. Children with autism have trouble with transitions because they don't know what to expect next. Tantrums and noncompliance due to difficulty with transitions is dramatically reduced if a picture schedule is used consistently. Some people may question the use of schedules, stating that children become too dependent upon them. I usually respond to such questions by asking people what they would do without a calendar, which usually puts things in perspective for them.

Depending upon ability, some children come to the table for the arts. I have a mini-schedule that shows children that they will first color, then cut, then glue. Many parents find schedules useful at home as well. Educators should visit homes to teach families how to incorporate a schedule and to determine what picture cards are needed.

Guidelines

DAP Autism spectrum disorders cover a wide range, with different levels of involvement; however, the following guidelines are useful in working with all children with ASD. The particular child you are working with and the setting he is in will determine the way in which you will use these guidelines.

1. *Ensure visual and auditory congruence.* When you discipline or correct a child, show him your facial expression and say, "Look at my face. Am I happy?" "Look at Tyrone's face. He is sad; you just hurt him." It is very confusing for a child if you use your "happy face and voice" when you are telling him something negative.

2. *Make auditory messages congruent with task.* When you need to discipline a child, use a stern voice so she knows you are not happy. Then find a child who is doing something good and use your happy voice to offer positive reinforcement. This way children know that you are not mad at the entire class. Once the child's behavior has changed, immediately "catch him being good" and provide positive reinforcement so he knows that the entire day is not ruined because of one problem. This also forces you to deal with the situation and move on.

3. *Define tasks.* Make clear the meaning of any task. Don't assume that a task, situation, activity, or event is clear to a child. Try to see it from his perspective.

4. *Define the child's role.* Alert the child to her role in tasks, situations, or events. Even if she is clear about what is happening, she may not understand her role in the event.

5. *Teach tasks as a series of simple steps.*

6. *Forewarn children.* Some children with ASD are tactilly sensitive; therefore, you need to check with them to ask if they want a pat on the back. Ask, "Are you ready for a pat on the back for being good?" This allows the child to have control of the situation and also get used to positive touch. Use deep pressure where possible. Encourage the child to initiate touch.

7. *Be explicit.* Don't assume that the context will help make the meaning of directions clear. Don't assume, for example, that if you have a table set up with large paper and markers, the child will know he is expected to draw.

8. *Identify beginning and end points of tasks.* List the steps involved in the task, or have pictures or diagrams.

9. *Use visual clues.* Pictures help highlight meaning.

10. *Help children generalize knowledge.* Build in opportunities for children to generalize what they know. Vary the materials they use to achieve a particular goal. Help children use skills in different situations.

11. *Activate previous knowledge.* When presenting new material, identify the main point and make connections between previous knowledge and skills explicit; help children see the whole picture rather than just the details.

12. *Individualize instruction.* Remember that each child is different and what works for one child may not work for another. Children themselves are also variable, so what works for a child one day may not necessarily work another day.

13. *Present tasks visually.* Make expectations clear and highlight the important information.

14. *Be patient.* Learning and relationships take time to build.

15. *Provide reinforcement for behavior.* Children need frequent reinforcement using whatever system works for that child.

16. *Engage children's attention actively* in highly structured activities.

17. *Provide visual or physical boundaries* for sitting (tape, carpet squares, etc.) or working at a table (e.g., divide individual work areas using tape).

18. *Provide fidget items.* Give children a fidget item to play with as they listen. This can be a pillow, a stuffed animal, a stress ball, or something related to what is going on.

19. *Have a predictable schedule.* Warn children when the schedule will change.

20. *Eliminate visual distractions.* Assess your room for visual distractions such as cluttered walls or work surfaces. If the play space is visually confusing or complex, modify it to decrease visual distractions.

21. *Eliminate auditory distractions.* Check the room for auditory distractions such as noise from the street, hall, or playground. In some cases, there is nothing you can do about these distractions. If you can predict the timing of auditory distraction; however, try to schedule your class to make these times less problematic.

Curriculum Adaptations

Curriculum adaptations involve relating your interpretation of class activities to children with ASD and focusing the children on their specific tasks and roles. Including children with ASD in your class may challenge some of your beliefs about how children should be taught. Some of the recommendations given are different from what I would do if I did not include a child with ASD. For example, I am against giving children models to copy in art; however, that is one of my suggestions for a child with ASD. For children who cannot picture what a picture looks like, provide an example. Some of the suggestions may be a stretch for you. Know they are available as additional resources if needed. Think about yourself and what you believe. You need to be calm, positive, consistent, and to maintain your sense of humor!

Social Awareness

It is difficult to think about teaching levels of social behaviors that we have never needed to learn. They are just part of who we are. For children who have ASD, this is not true. They have to learn what we take for granted. We cannot just deal with the surface behaviors, but need to get to the fundamental deficits. Social skills need to be specifically taught. Learning the social skills necessary to be included in a classroom is a demanding and stressful task for a child with ASD. It may take so much concentration that the child is not available for academic learning. Give children time to get to know you and the other people in the classroom and school. Don't expect too much too fast.

● ● ●

Social Competence

DAP All children need to develop self-knowledge. They need to have some understanding of themselves before they can understand others. Help children gain this knowledge by providing feedback about what the child likes and dislikes and what he does well.

1. Use specific strategies to develop the child's sense of self.

2. Help children become aware of their own feelings and beliefs and then those of others.

3. Help children think of themselves as problem solvers; use visual methods of promoting self-reflection and self-recognition.

4. Teach children to make choices.

5. Teach children how to respond to criticism.

Children with ASD are being placed in regular classes; the challenge is to include them. Adults must make conscious efforts to guide them so that children play together. Educators must explain behavior that other children might find unusual. Children need simple explanations and adult models.

1. Understand that for a child with ASD, being part of a classroom is a challenge.

2. Teach children to identify emotions as physical, auditory, and visual expressions. Draw their attention to the emotions of others. Be specific. Clarify why another child may be having these emotions.

3. Teach other children how to approach and interact with a child who has ASD.

4. Identify what children like and dislike socially, and use this information when including the child and helping other children to include her.

5. Be sure the child does not become a victim of teasing, exclusion, or other more subtle forms of relational violence.

6. Focus on individual similarities and differences and what children like and dislike. Use this as a frame for discussing why there may be different rules for different children and why some children are taught differently than others.

7. Engage children in the problem-solving process. Let them help decide what is reinforcing and what they can do to facilitate the education of all the children in the class.

8. Allow all the children to be alone some of the time. Talk about why children want to be alone.

9. Expect to teach basic social skills such as taking turns, sharing, waiting in lines, and working in small groups.

10. Teach children a specific script to repeat if they bump or annoy another child.

11. Draw the child's attention to the use of gesture, facial expression, eye direction, and proximity as social cues that convey meaning. Identify specifically what these mean.

12. Do not assume that children can identify your intentions from your behavior.

● ● ●

Social Studies

DAP Social studies is a challenging area for children with ASD. Because of the subtle and pervasive nature of these disabilities, those who work with them must provide a level of scaffolding that is more extensive than other children need.

1. Meet the child at his level of social understanding—you need to start where the child is, not where you expect him to be.

2. Research with children the different ways people communicate in different cultures and how these came about.

3. Discuss the ways technology facilitates communication among people both near and far.

Children with autism spectrum disorders can become overwhelmed with social interaction and change and are unable to adapt to deal with situations.
©Cengage Learning 2012

English Language Arts

Communication is the foundation for social interaction. It is also an area that is very challenging for children with ASD. It is not that they cannot speak; it is that they do not use speech for communication. In addition to building language skills, children need to develop the intentional use of speech for communicating with others, particularly peers.

Speaking and Listening

DAP Children with ASD need support in initiating and maintaining a conversation, and in developing techniques for understanding the meaning of conversation. Think about their communication level rather than their ability to speak.

1. Teach children how to use language socially; specifically teach such skills as making eye contact, entering a group, listening to replies, and responding to others.
2. Be aware of the difference between a child's ability to use language and his ability to communicate. They are two different functions of speech and children may be on very different levels for each.
3. Use concrete simple language.
4. Give instructions one at a time. If necessary, support these with visual cues.
5. Keep your facial expression and gestures clear, simple, and congruent with your speech.
6. Teach metaphors and be aware of them in your own speech.
7. Help children vary their tone and volume to match situations.
8. Support self-talk to encourage task completion if this does not interfere with other children. Teach children to do this quietly.
9. Encourage peers to be involved in the picture exchange communication system if this is what children use.

Children with ASD may have trouble listening, so be sure to use facial expressions and gestures to support what you are saying. Encourage children to look for nonverbal cues and body language.

1. Teach children to listen and not interrupt.
2. Give children time to respond.
3. Develop a code so that if the child does not understand she can tell you without disrupting the class and calling attention to herself.
4. Support children's auditory discrimination skills by playing games such as bingo, comparing sounds, associating sounds with the sources that made them, and so on.
5. Warn children if an unpleasant noise will occur, so they can prepare. If the noise cannot be eliminated, try exposing the child to the noise in small increments or for limited periods. Pair the noise with a preferred activity or use another more pleasing noise (e.g., music) at the same time.

Reading

DAP Reading can be both an individual and a group activity. Preview books with children. Help them connect what is in the book with the real world.

1. Read books about being different.
2. Read children books about children who have autism. Use this as a springboard to talk about ASD. See the Children's Bibliography.
3. Teach stories using picture sequence cards. Draw the child's attention to the cause-and-effect aspect of a book, identify the plot, and make the motives of the characters in the story explicit.
4. Use social stories to help children learn necessary social skills.
5. Use social skills stories. Carol Gray has developed a social skills program using social stories for children with autism. These stories describe social situations in terms of relevant social cues. There are now many social skills books available or you can make your own. Gray provides information about writing social stories on her website at www.thegraycenter.org/social-stories.

IN THE FIELD

I find social stories beneficial for the children I teach. Books of social stories can be purchased, or the classroom team can write a social story, based on the needs of the children. The suggested formula to use for writing a social story is three to five descriptive and perspective sentences and one each of directive and control sentences. A descriptive sentence explains who, what, where, and/or why. An example of a descriptive sentence would be, "My teacher changed her mind in school today." A perspective sentence describes the feelings and reactions of others in a situation. For example, "This means that she had an idea but then had a different idea." A directive is an individualized statement of what the child needs to work on. An example would be, "I will work on staying calm when my teacher changes her mind." The last type of sentence found in a social story is a control sentence. A control sentence could be, "When my teacher changes her mind, I can ask to take a break to give me time to adjust to the new idea." Due to their complexity, social stories work best for higher functioning children. Some teachers write their own social stories and illustrate them with photographs of the children in situations corresponding to events in the story. When I use pictures of the children, they feel a stronger connection to the story.

6. Read joke books. Try to cultivate a sense of humor.
7. Help children extend their understanding by using pictures to predict what will happen or to add context.
8. Read informational texts as well as literature.
9. Use computer programs to support learning. Programs such as Edmark's Reading Program Software Series, Levels 1 & 2 (Riverdeep) for grades K–3 is designed to help children with developmental disabilities and those who are learning English as a second language. It helps children practice words used in basal readers. The software is very straightforward with few multimedia perks, which is good for children with ASD.
10. Adapt books specifically for ASD children.

Writing

DAP Encourage children to write, either with a pencil or through word processing. An inability to think creatively may impede children's progress in writing. Use a copy of the alphabet, pictures for each letter, and small pictures that can be used instead of words.

1. Encourage children to write about real things they have experienced, then introduce a "What if ... ?" to help them extend their thinking and writing.

2. Start with the child's interests, even if they are narrow, and build from there. If it is animals, use this, and extend it into where they sleep, what they eat, and so on.

3. Give children a visual cue, such as a picture to write about.

4. Have children trace and copy letters. Help children form letters and connections between them and the sounds they make.

5. Break crayons into small pieces so children cannot hold them with just their fingertips. When using pencils add different grips or use deep pressure on the palm of the child's hand (rubbing it with your thumb) before the child writes.

6. Support children in writing their own social stories.

7. Help children write in the air, on textured surfaces, and with a variety of tools. See Activities 2–58w, *Air Writing*, and 2–54w, *Sand Printing*.

Language

DAP Helping children build a vocabulary to get their needs met and to be able to comment on their world. Both are important aspects of language.

1. Build a vocabulary that allows exceptions. Try to use words such as *most* or *sometimes*. If you *always* eat lunch at school and then have a half day, children become upset. "*Sometimes* when we have to wait, we sing." Work with children on this concept to build the idea of several alternatives.

2. Develop a core vocabulary (with parental input) and systematically teach it.

3. Use a topic children are interested in to build vocabulary.

Discovery

Make math, science, and technology concrete. Use practical examples and emphasize the utility of the process. Take advantage of technology to help children. Use a digital camera to take pictures to help the child structure his environment. Technology can also provide support in the area of organization. A computer can take some of the tedium out of writing while providing visual support, and electronic tablet applications for children with special needs can make a tremendous difference in children's lives as long as the adults are technology literate.

Mathematics

DAP Make math relevant to children. Use objects and pictures that are of interest to children to teach math. If children are interested in trucks, they can sort them by color, size, material, function, and design. They can count them, pair them, and even add them. If you include people with the trucks, you can do one-to-one correspondence. Children with ASD need to apply math. The more you teach it as part of problem solving and relating to real issues, the more likely math will be useful.

1. Asking the same question over and over can be frustrating, so turn it into a math lesson. Decide on a limit of times the child can ask (perhaps three times) and have her chart this. When she asks again, refer her back to the chart.

2. Teach children the language of math. Write the words on cards. Have children sort cards and identify different words that often go together (e.g., multiply, times; add, sum).

3. Teach math concepts visually and with three-dimensional objects.

4. Use word problems with pictures and manipulatives.

Science

DAP Science is not about memorizing isolated facts, but about making observations; asking questions; and gathering, organizing, and analyzing data. Framing science in this way makes the process more challenging and more beneficial to children with ASD.

1. Use observation as a fundamental skill. Have children observe their environment on walks, on the playground, in the classroom, and at home. Help children use observational skills to anticipate events so they can be prepared for them.

2. Help children sharpen their observational skills by identifying the main idea and the supporting parts (e.g., car: wheel; tree: roots, branch, leaves). Connect this information to previous learning.

3. Encourage children to make charts and lists as methods of organizing information.

4. Discuss how different animals communicate without using words. If you have animals in your classroom,

teach children how to hold and stroke them. Some feel that because animals do not talk but do communicate, children with ASD who do not have useful communication skills will find the relationship therapeutic.

Technology

DAP Technology can be a tremendous asset in working with children who have ASD. Your ability to think about creative uses of technology can support their learning and ability to function in the classroom. Technology can help children handle change. It can be modified to the needs of particular children and it can support their learning (with infinite patience). It also provides opportunities for children to work together. The task is defined and children can be together without a great demand for social interaction.

1. Explore a variety of assistive technologies, and encourage children to use technology to help with writing, spelling, grammar, and so on.
2. Use a digital camera as a support for sequencing activities and the events of the day.
3. Use the computer and programs such as PowerPoint to present material to the class. This can provide visual support and if there is a sequence, the child can recheck the necessary information independently. If the family has a computer, you can e-mail the presentation to the family so they know what you are teaching and can support the concepts at home.
4. Encourage children to develop their own website. Use an easy program such as Complete Web Studio or Sierra On-line (Havas). This supports children's learning and their self-concepts.
5. Use programs such as Sammy's Science House (Edmark) pre-K–2 program, which helps children with part–whole relationships in "The Workshop"; they can also sort plants and animals at "The Sorting Station."

Wellness

Children may need support to participate in physical activities. They may avoid them because of concern about being touched, anxiety about their skill level, or to avoid unpleasant sensations. Be sure the environment provides opportunities and safe places to vigorously exercise and to calm down.

Health and Safety

DAP Health and safety are particularly important areas for children with ASD. If children are more tuned into themselves than to their surroundings, they can place themselves in dangerous situations. Their concern with the textures of foods as well as personal likes and dislikes may make eating a balanced diet a challenge. Some health and safety practices that other children learn from observation have to be specifically taught.

1. Teach techniques of grooming, toileting, and adaptive behaviors. Children may need a visual sequence or checklist to ensure that all the steps are completed.
2. Encourage the use of Velcro fasteners or large buttons. Be sure that children look at what they are doing.
3. Find one food a child likes and present it in a different form. If the child likes fruit, try fresh, dried, and canned fruit. Add small amounts of different fruits in very small bites.
4. Work on fine motor skills and using eating utensils to eat. Encourage activities that use the mouth, such as blowing bubbles, blowing through a straw, blowing ping-pong balls across the table, and so on.
5. Teach self-care practices: "After five bites, wipe your mouth with a napkin."
6. Evaluate the environment for safety. Is the outside area fenced? How close is traffic? What are the surfaces made of under the equipment?

Physical Education

DAP Activities in this area should be more structured, especially if there is an unstructured recess or outdoor playtime. Without support, the child may be isolated and merely stand around, as opposed to playing.

1. Organize cooperative games or games where there are no winners or losers.
2. Use obstacle courses, and using a digital camera and printer, provide pictures of the next piece of equipment with a child, demonstrating how to move through that piece of equipment.
3. Provide children with "large motor breaks" where you encourage all children to work the wiggles out.
4. Support underlying concepts of physical fitness, and provide opportunities for children to participate in activities that will develop these skills.

Sensory Motor Integration

DAP Organizing sensory information so that it can be regulated and acted upon challenges all young children. Some children require a great deal of assistance in processing sensory input and achieving the levels of self-regulation necessary to explore and interact with their environment. Children respond to their environment in unique ways. The guiding principle is "to modify the environment to provide motivating, sensory-enriched surroundings that require repeated, complex coordinated action by the child" (Williamson & Anzalone, 2001, p. 106).

1. Make your environment as fragrance free as possible if children have problems with scents. Use unscented detergents and shampoos. Don't wear perfumes or aftershave lotions.
2. Have a swing or rocking chair available for children to use. Use beanbag chairs if children need stability to read or to do fine motor activities.
3. Vary traditional activities. Have children walk across or jump on a mattress or crawl over and around cushions.

4. Give children with ASD the time and opportunities to repeat and practice, even if the behavior may appear perseverative, and then introduce variations.

Children, especially those with low muscle tone, may need to develop strength in their fine muscles. To do this, they need to use them. The trick is to find things they enjoy doing so that practice is fun.

1. Hide objects that need to be found in putty, clay, or playdough to develop finger strength.

2. Encourage children to use their hands in a variety of different textures such as birdseed, sand, and so on. (If children may eat the materials, use rice and beans instead.)

3. Support children in using their hands to explore materials, especially to hold objects with one hand and investigate them with the other.

Creative Arts

Children with ASD are rarely creative on their own. They need adult support to play and pretend. They need to be encouraged and provided with more structure than other children. Rather than the child generating the script, the adult may have to provide the script and help the child work through it. Because of the children's deficits, you have to work with them very differently than you do with other children. You need to be more directive in areas where you would normally follow the child's lead.

Visual Arts

DAP Encourage exploration of a variety of media. Allow children to approach tentatively, and find ways to increase their exploration of new and different materials. Start with what they like and what is familiar, and add variations a little at a time.

1. If a project has several steps or if it is the first time the child has used a particular media, show the child a model or picture of the end product so the child knows what is expected or possible.

2. Introduce activities in which children can participate by using just their fingertips, such as fingerpaint or lotion. As children become comfortable with various textures, encourage them to use their whole hand, and then both hands.

3. Encourage children to use putty, clay, and playdough.

Music

DAP Use music to create a mood, help focus attention, and help children get in touch with the auditory world.

1. Add music to tasks to give them a beginning and an end.

2. Sing songs with children's names and reinforce the child for responding to his name.

3. Experiment with using background music in the classroom. For some children, this is calming.

4. Sing songs with motions.

5. Provide pictures of some of the things you sing about.

6. Add visual cues to sequencing songs.

7. Encourage children to use percussion instruments, such as drums, to maintain a beat, and then change the rhythm.

Movement and Dance

DAP For children with ASD, the best thing about creative movement is not that it is creative but that movement is not judged; even repetitive and self-stimulating movement is acceptable.

1. When you do creative movement, do join children in their idiosyncratic movements, and then introduce variations on that movement. Change the rhythm, range of motion, speed, and so on. Bring the movement up to a more conscious level.

2. Have children dance to music. Discuss the music first, and how it relates to the type of movements or how dancing is different with different kinds of music.

3. Provide pictures and have discussions if you want children to move in specific ways. Try to make pretense as real as possible.

Dramatic Play and Theater

DAP Children with ASD do not pretend-play well. This is something they have to be taught.

1. Teach children to pretend-play and help them discriminate between what is pretend and what is real.

2. Role play. One way of managing change is to make it more familiar. If you are going to do something new and different, role-play it. Point out the salient features.

3. Write a script and play it with the children. Provide specific directions on how things are done.

Routines and Transitions

DAP Transitions are difficult for many children. For children with ASD, they loom even larger. Use the child's strengths to help with transitions.

1. Have as few transitions as possible.

2. Have a predictable routine that you keep as consistent as possible.

3. Introduce change gradually.

4. Use visual supports to manage change. Provide children with a picture sequence of the day. As each part of the day is completed, have the child take that picture off the sequence.

5. Give children time to prepare for change. A specific signal about five minutes ahead of time is useful.

6. Ask the child to be first or last when it is necessary to line up.

7. Select a locker or cubby for the child that is at the end of the row to decrease unintentional physical contact.

8. Consider having children do jumping jacks or touch their toes before or during a walk in the hall.

9. Develop a system to ensure enough space between children when they walk.

IN THE FIELD

We have a mailbox outside our classroom. Every day, we check for mail from our friend Myron the Mouse. Myron is at home sick and is unable to come to school. His sister, Myra (a white stuffed mouse who sits in class on her own carpet square) comes to school and goes home each day to tell Myron what she has learned. Each day, Myron writes a letter, reviewing what we have learned, asking questions, and most importantly, telling the children whether there are any changes in the schedule. (Myra sneaks around the class at night so she knows things before Mrs. Wells does, for example, when we have assemblies, or any change in the schedule.) Several aspects of this strategy work well: Myron tells the children when there is a change, so it is not Mrs. Wells's fault that things are different, and Myron uses question marks and exclamation marks. The children count the different punctuation marks and then determine whether he is "more excited" or whether he has more questions. To recognize an exclamation mark, we say, "The line was so excited, it jumped up and down on the period." We then make simple math sentences. They love this! Myra will be included in our class photo this year. Last year we forgot her, and they were upset.

SUMMARY

- Autism spectrum disorders include autism, Asperger's syndrome, Rett syndrome, childhood disintegrative disorder, and pervasive developmental disorder–not otherwise specified.

- The essential feature of all ASDs is impairment in social reciprocity, communication, and repetitive behaviors.

- Children with ASD require more structure in their environment and more one-on-one instruction to learn skills.

- Teachers need consistency in behavior management and a good understanding of sensory motor integration issues to work effectively with these children.

- Advances in early identification and early intervention have made a tremendous difference in the lives of children with ASD and their families.

EDUCATIONAL RESOURCES

Augmentative and Alternative Communication (AAC) assists people with severe communication disabilities to participate by providing access to a wide range of information and resources related to AAC. http://aac.unl.edu/

Autism–PDD Support Network has a large website with information on diagnostic criteria, the IEP process, and helpful hints for working with schools and specialists. It also provides information about state agencies.

Autism Research Institute provides information about current research projects and methods of working with individuals with autism. www.autism.com/index.asp/

Autism Society of America answers many common questions about autism, particularly those related to causes, types, and diagnosis. It also looks at different approaches to teaching autistic children and reports on news and events related to autism. It provides links to state resources and local chapters. www.autism-society.org/

Do 2 Learn provides picture schedules and tips on how to structure your classroom, pictures that you can print, and children's games.

First Signs website provides a wealth of vital resources, covering topics from healthy development, to concerns about a child; and from the screening and referral process, to treatments for autism spectrum disorders. www.firstsigns.org/

Interactive Autism Network (IAN), a project of the Kennedy Krieger Institute, is funded by Autism Speaks. IAN's goal is to facilitate research that will lead to advancements in the treatment, cure, and prevention of ASDs. It provides information about current research and findings in the area of autism. www.ianproject.org/

Tinsnips—Special Education Resources for Autism contains tools for teachers of children with ASD, related developmental disabilities, and children with special needs. www.tinsnips.org/

Treatment and Education of Autistic and Related Communication Handicapped Children (TEACCH) provides information on a structured program that integrates methods and services in a systematic way.

For additional resources, visit the book companion website for this text at www.cengagebrain.com.

14 Children with Intellectual Delays and Disabilities

Watching André, you would guess him to be one of the youngest children in the class, yet he is actually one of the oldest. He rarely has much to say, and what he does say is difficult to understand. His parents say they are not talkers, and they understand him and are not worried. I thought by 4 years old more of his speech should be understandable. He doesn't seem to get involved in his play and plays alone most of the time. Most things seem difficult for him. It's hard for him to sit through our group time and he rarely participates. He struggles with adaptive skills, but with help and time he usually succeeds. His parents say he dawdles, so they just do things for him. Many things seem to be beyond him. He just seems like he is developing more slowly than the other children. He is not as animated and seems confused. I've tried to talk to his parents, but when I bring up these issues, they don't seem concerned and often don't follow up. I really can't decide whether it is just the environment he lives in or whether he's not as capable of learning as the others. Or is my program not matching his knowledge base? ❋

REFLECTIVE PRACTICE | How do you feel about André? A majority of children who cause concern for teachers look like other children but don't seem to be learning as quickly in one or more areas. We are not as accurate in identifying children with mild delays as we are children with more serious delays. It may not be until a child enters an intellectually demanding environment that adults become concerned about his level of functioning. On what basis would you decide to follow up with children like André?

Courtesy of Penny Low Deiner

Intellectual Delays and Disabilities

Professionals today are reluctant to classify young children as having an intellectual disability. The requirements for this diagnosis are more stringent than they have been in the past. Misdiagnosis is a concern because of the stigma attached to this particular label and because of the overidentification of children from ethnic/cultural minorities (IDEA, 2004). Concern relates to the child developing a poor self-concept, the negative views of others, and the belief that intellectual disabilities are a socially constructed condition. That is, children who are relatively high functioning do not *become* "intellectually disabled" until they enter school. Are these children really intellectually delayed or is this an example of the **achievement gap** and middle-class values? Because of such concerns, some children who in the past were classified as having a mild intellectual delay are now classified as having a specific learning disability or are not identified. We no longer view an intellectual disability as a permanent condition.

Defining Intellectual Delays and Disabilities

Intellectual disability is a failure to meet age-appropriate **neurodevelopmental milestones**, based on the typical sequence of development in the areas of language, motor, and social-adaptive development (Batshaw, Shapiro, & Farber, 2007). Most children with intellectual disabilities follow the same sequence of cognitive skill acquisition as other children, but their rate of acquisition is slower.

Intellectual disabilities is a broad term that can refer to children of all ages and with varying degrees of differences in cognitive development. The term *intellectual disability* is preferred, and you will not see the term *mental retardation* used except when referring to the work of others or for historical reference.

The American Association on Intellectual and Developmental Disabilities (AAIDD) has developed the following definition:

> *Intellectual disability is a disability characterized by significant limitations both in intellectual functioning and in adaptive behavior, which covers many everyday social and practical skills. The disability originates before the age of 18 (AAIDD, 2010b).*

Adaptive behavior consists of three types of skills:

1. Conceptual skills, including language and literacy; number, time, and money concepts; and self-direction

2. Social skills, including interpersonal skills and the ability to solve social problems, as well as self-esteem, taking social responsibility, obeying rules, and the ability to avoid being victimized

3. Practical skills focusing on the activities of daily living and occupational skills (AAIDD, 2010b).

AAIDD stresses that professionals should

- evaluate limitations in present intellectual and adaptive behavior functioning within the context of the person's age, peers, and culture;

- take into account the person's cultural and linguistic differences as well as communication, sensory, motor, and behavioral factors;

- recognize that limitations often coexist with strengths within an individual;

- describe limitations so that an individualized plan of needed supports can be developed; and

- provide appropriate, personalized supports to improve the functioning of a person with intellectual disability (AAIDD, 2008, p.1, 2).

Previously, the definition of intellectual disability was based almost exclusively on IQ scores. Now, although an IQ of 70 to 75 or below is considered below average, there is consensus that additional measures must be used to verify these results and that the results should be reviewed by a multidisciplinary team.

According to the IDEA 2004:

> *Mental retardation means significantly subaverage general intellectual functioning, existing concurrently with deficits in adaptive behavior and manifested during the developmental period, that adversely affects a child's educational performance.*

As with many other disabilities, intellectual disability is further divided into levels. These are based on the theoretical assumption that intelligence is normally distributed. The levels generally indicate the intensity of services that are needed for the child and are assigned after formal assessment of the child's intellectual and adaptive functioning skills. A traditional breakdown of the levels of intellectual disability is given here. Because of the error of measurement of the assessment instruments, we assume that scores can

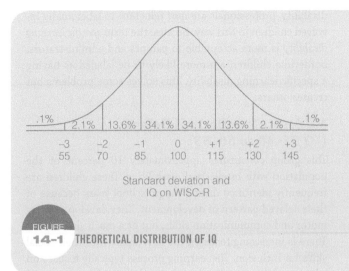

Standard deviation and
IQ on WISC-R

FIGURE 14-1 THEORETICAL DISTRIBUTION OF IQ

vary by about 5 points, so we use a range (i.e., an IQ of 70 may be 65 or 75, given the error of measurement.

Using only IQ as a way to determine intellectual functioning assumes that 95 percent of the population is in the "average" range, with 2.5 percent on either end being above or below "average" (see Figure 14-1). Some question the validity of using IQ to determine intellectual disability, especially with young children, because of the poor predictive validity of infant psychological tests and concerns related to cultural bias. The American Psychiatric Association (APA, 2000) continues to use IQ scores. The American Association on Intellectual and Developmental Disabilities focuses their subcategories on the patterns and intensity of supports people will need. This is a move away from looking at disability to ability. In this text, the definitions of the subcategories given combine the two approaches. The designated categories are determined by the APA categories, but the focus is on the needed supports.

Mild Intellectual Delays (IQ 50–55 to 70–75)

Children in this category used to be referred to as educable mentally retarded (EMR). This category constitutes about 85 percent of children with intellectual disabilities (APA, 2000). Children develop sensory motor, social, and communication skills during early childhood, but these may be consistently at the lower range of the developmental norms. These children generally attend regular early care and education settings and neighborhood public schools, and may be identified as needing additional educational services during the early elementary years. Their learning process is usually slower than other children's, often requiring concrete learning procedures with the focus on learning basic academic skills. With intermittent supports, most will live independently in the community and hold jobs after schooling is completed (AAMR, 2002).

Because schools have been criticized for improperly identifying minority children as having an intellectual disability, professionals are now reluctant to label mildly involved children in this way. Because the term *specific learning disability* is more acceptable to parents and administrators, borderline children are more likely to be labeled as having a specific learning disability. This solves some problems but creates others.

Moderate Intellectual Delays (IQ 35–40 to 50–55)

This group constitutes approximately 10 percent of the population with intellectual disabilities. These children are frequently identified during the preschool years because of their delayed pattern of development. They develop sensory motor and communication skills, but at a much slower rate. There is increasing focus on the development of their social skills for inclusion. The learning process typically focuses on adaptive skills, functional academic skills, and prevocational skills. Individuals require limited support (AAMR, 2002). Our past expectation was that these children would reach an academic attainment level of about second grade (APA, 2000). Again, as children are identified during the early years, the success of early intervention makes us question these expectations.

Severe Intellectual Delays (IQ 20–25 to 35–40)

This category constitutes approximately 3 to 4 percent of people with intellectual disabilities. Children are identified as infants or toddlers and may not reach early communication and physical/motor milestones until their school years (APA, 2000). Their learning may progress to learning some sight words and survival skills. These children need extensive support (AAMR, 2002).

Profound Intellectual Delays (IQ below 20–25)

Children who are classified as having profound intellectual delays constitute approximately 1 to 2 percent of people with intellectual disabilities. They are delayed in all areas of development and require intensive services and pervasive supports. They usually have an identifiable neurologic condition that accounts for the intellectual disability (APA, 2000). Identification occurs early, and intervention generally focuses on self-help or adaptive skills, mobility, and basic cognitive development. As adults, they can perform uncomplicated vocational tasks and live in supervised settings (AAMR, 2000).

Prevalence of Intellectual Delays and Disabilities

Given our difficulty in defining intellectual disability, it is not unexpected that prevalence figures vary. They are dependent upon the definition used, the method of assessment, and the population studied. The identification figures peak at 10 to 14 years of age, when most children with mild impairments have been identified (Yeargin-Allsopp, Drews-Botsch, &

TABLE
14–1 PERCENT OF CHILDREN RECEIVING SPECIAL EDUCATIONAL SERVICES BY YEAR

	1976–1977	1980–1981	1990–1991	2007–2008
Specific learning disabilities	21.5	35.3	45.2	39.0
Intellectual disabilities	26.0	20.0	11.3	7.6

Source: National Center for Educational Statistics (NCES), 2010.

Van Naarden Braun, 2007). Overall, intellectual disabilities occur more frequently in boys than girls. Approximately 12 to 16 of every 1,000 school-age children have an intellectual disability, or about 1 in 83 children had an IQ of 70 or below in 2000 (Centers for Disease Control [CDC], 2008b).

During the 2007–2008 school year, 7.6 percent of the children receiving special educational services were identified as having an intellectual disability. This is in contrast to 1976–1977, when 26 percent of school children in special education had intellectual disabilities. (National Center for Educational Statistics [NCES], 2010). Look at Table 14–1 to see the relationship between children identified as having intellectual disabilities and specific learning disabilities. It seems clear that there is a relationship between the two in how children are being classified. There is also overlap with Asperger's syndrome.

Causes of Intellectual Delays and Disabilities

Intellectual disability can be identified anytime before a child turns age 18. Some causes occur before a child is born, such as those that are genetic in nature. Other causes happen during pregnancy and can relate to the way embryonic or fetal cells divide and grow. Cells can be affected by alcohol or infections like rubella. Other problems can happen during the birthing process, such as lack of oxygen to the infant's brain. Some problems happen after the child is born, and these can be caused by infections such as meningitis or measles (National Dissemination Center for Children with Disabilities [NICHCY], 2004). In general, the earlier the cause the more severe the effect (Batshaw et al., 2007).

Causes of intellectual disabilities fall into two overlapping categories. Children who fall in the mild category (about 87%) (NICHCY, 2004), those needing intermittent supports, are most frequently from families of lower socioeconomic status and have fewer environmental resources; parenting may be neglectful or abusive, and there is less likely to be a biological cause. Disabilities that require more extensive supports, those in moderate to profound categories, are usually linked to biological causes (Batshaw et al., 2007). These account for about 13 percent of children with intellectual disabilities (NICHCY, 2004). Many causes of intellectual disability are not known.

The causes of mild disabilities are known in less than 50 percent of children identified. When the intellectual disability is severe, a biological cause can be identified in about three-quarters of the cases (Aicardi, 1998). When the causes of intellectual disabilities are known, approximately 5 percent are hereditary, such as Tay-Sachs disease. Another 30 percent are due to chromosomal mutations during the development of the embryo (for example, Down syndrome trisomy 21), or to damage to the embryo due to toxins (such as alcohol, drugs, or infections). Another 10 percent occur during the fetal period and include such problems as malnutrition, trauma, hypoxia (lack of oxygen), and prematurity. After birth, another 15 to 20 percent are related to environmental influences such as neglect and lack of stimulation, as well as related disorders such as autism. Approximately 5 percent are related to infections such as meningitis, traumas such as head injuries, and lead poisoning (APA, 2000).

The environment in which a child is raised is a big factor in facilitating intellectual development. Some limitations may be present that prevent a child from acquiring specific intellectual skills such as advanced abstract thinking abilities. Appropriate stimulation and early intervention are key ingredients to a successful educational program.

In the past, intellectual disabilities present at birth were viewed as a given, a nonpreventable disability. Increasingly, causes of intellectual disability are preventable. Some prevention is based on health procedures that ensure that children receive inoculations in a timely manner (CDC, 2005d). Others relate to accident prevention and environmental stimulation. The fastest-growing prenatal causes of intellectual disability are preventable.

Children experiencing intellectual disabilities are as different from each other as those who have more typical developmental patterns.

Early Identification of Intellectual Delays and Disabilities

Depending on the level of the impairment, intellectual disabilities are identified at different times during early childhood. Concerns may arise because infants were born prematurely, had low birth weight, or there were **perinatal** complications (Batshaw et al., 2007). During the first months of life, inadequate sucking, floppy or spastic muscle tone, and/or lack of response to visual or auditory stimuli cause concern. Infants may show little interest in the environment and not be as alert as other infants. As infants grow older, they may reach developmental milestones later than expected. It is often unclear whether this is just an individual growth pattern and the infant will "catch up" in time or whether the delay is of a more permanent nature. The most obvious signs of intellectual disability are that children are slower to talk than other children, may seem immature, and may also have been slower to walk (after 15 months) (Batshaw et al., 2007). They may have a short attention span, and some are highly distractible. Language skills are delayed, as are basic daily living skills (feeding, toileting, and dressing). Children with more severe delays lack social interaction skills, motivation, and

a striving for independence. Infants and toddlers exhibiting extremely delayed development or for whom there is a known cause may be diagnosed before age 3. Because of the success of early intervention, if you suspect delayed development, talk with parents and support their seeking medical and educational intervention.

Mild delays may not be noticed during the preschool years, although you may begin to suspect something as you watch these children. Perhaps a 4-year-old with a mild delay acts more like a 3-year-old. Preschool children with intellectual delays have a slower rate of learning, poor memory skills, poor generalization skills, and lack higher-level learning strategies (NICHCY, 2004).

Even during preschool, children with moderate cognitive impairments show noticeable delays in intellectual development, especially speech and language, and motor development. They may need assistance in self-help skills. They may not be toilet trained, or if they are, they may not be able to manage taking off and putting on their clothes independently. In some cases, these children will look different from other children (if they have fetal alcohol syndrome). In other cases, they won't. A 4-year-old needing limited support may act more like a 2-year-old. Most likely, parents will know that their child has a cognitive delay. Children needing extensive support show marked delays in all areas of development and,

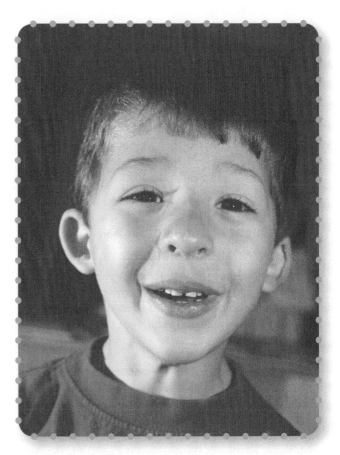

Sometimes intellectual disabilities are suspected because they are part of other syndromes.
©Cengage Learning 2012

at the preschool level, have few verbal communication skills. They may communicate using sign language.

IMPLICATIONS FOR EDUCATORS

Increasingly, children needing extensive supports are being cared for and educated in regular early care and education settings. Some children may be in inclusive settings for part of the day and in a setting designed for intensive early intervention for the other part of the day. However, in both settings the emphasis is on developmentally appropriate curriculum, fundamental academic skills, and adaptive skills that support the development of independence. Social skills are stressed to foster peer interaction.

During the early elementary years, the focus is on literacy skills and abilities that are prerequisites for later learning. These include behaviors such as learning to sit and attend to teachers, following directions, and learning the names of the letters of the alphabet. Children with intellectual delays need practice developing fine motor skills, which are necessary to hold a pencil and cut with scissors. They will need continuing support on adaptive skills and developing skills to interact with peers. The focus is frequently on fundamental academic skills that are necessary in life as well as skills that allow them to communicate.

IN THE FIELD

My son Roberto was identified as a toddler with delayed development. I feel that he has received some of the best early intervention possible. I kept thinking that he would catch up, but he did not. Then I struggled to accept a diagnosis of intellectual disability. At first it seemed so cruel, but I finally realized that it is something I must deal with. Since I have gotten divorced, I worry more about money and the future. While I am blessed to have Roberto in my life and love him dearly, I wonder what will happen to him if anything happens to me. My husband Tomas left because he couldn't deal with our son. Would Tomas raise Roberto?

My main goal now is to help Roberto receive the best education possible. I am happy to say that Roberto receives all the support he needs in his classroom from his teacher and therapists. I don't see them as much as I used to, but it seems to be working. He is learning to use his small muscles better and is easier to understand. What is important to me is that he is so much better at dressing himself and can even go to the bathroom alone. He is getting too old to bring to the ladies' room with me, so going out with him was getting to be a problem.

In the next few years I hope that Roberto will learn the skills to live independently. I truly worry about his future and his happiness. I wonder if Roberto will ever be able to live on his own.

Assessment of Intellectual Delays and Disabilities

There are two major aspects in the assessment of intellectual disability: intelligence and adaptive behavior. Adaptive behavior in young children focuses on self-help skills; in young adults it is on the ability to understand currency, pay bills, and so on.

Assessment of Intelligence

The assessment of intelligence is a controversial issue. What is intelligence? We can't see it, hear it, or agree on a definition. We use the concept of intelligence to explain differences in behavior.

Two major dimensions relate to the accuracy of measuring intelligence in very young children; the first has to do with issues relating to the test, and the second is the child herself. In general, when we talk about intelligence testing for children under age 3, we don't end up with an intelligence

quotient or IQ; rather, we talk about a developmental assessment and a **developmental quotient**, or **DQ**.

One reason for assessing an infant is to determine whether there might be long-term problems that could respond to intervention. In this case, the concern is the test's ability to detect problems that have potential long-term negative outcomes. Infant developmental tests do a good job of identifying infants and toddlers with severe and profound delays. They are not as effective in identifying infants and toddlers with mild to moderate delays.

One critical issue concerns the relationship between scores obtained on infant developmental tests and intelligence tests given at a later age. What we consider intelligence in infancy is not the same as intelligence in elementary school children or adults; different patterns of cognitive activities constitute intelligence at different ages.

Norm-referenced measures such as the Battelle Developmental Inventory, 2nd edition (BDI-2; Newborg, 2005) and the Bayley Scales of Infant and Toddler Development, 3rd edition (Bayley III) Screening Test (Bayley, 2005) often form the core of a diagnostic assessment. These measures are used to get an overall picture of the infant or toddler and to determine whether further, more specialized assessment is necessary. Given the lack of high-quality screening measures for young children, norm-referenced measures may also serve a screening purpose. These measures are standardized and require a trained examiner.

As children increase in age, other assessments are used. For children older than 2 years, the Stanford-Binet Intelligence Scale, 5th edition (SB5; Roid, 2003) may be used. During the preschool years, the Wechsler Preschool and Primary Scale of Intelligence–III (WPPSI–III; Psychological Corporation, 2002) is an option. School-age children may be evaluated using the Wechsler Intelligence Scale for Children, IV (WISC-IV, Wechsler; 2003).

Criterion-referenced measures such as the Learning Accomplishment Profile, 3rd edition (LAP-3; 2004) for children 36 to 72 months and the Early Learning Accomplishment Profile, 3rd edition (E-LAP; 2002) for children birth to 36 months, are often used after screening and diagnosis have been completed. These tests are useful in curriculum planning and in measuring increments of development.

Regardless of the test, one measure alone should never be the only source used to determine whether a child has an intellectual disability. Such information must be amplified by additional information from behavioral observations, medical history, and families to gain a more accurate picture of a child's functioning.

Assessment of Adaptive Skills

To classify someone as having an intellectual disability, a test of intelligence and a test of adaptive behavior are required. This information is also useful for curriculum planning.

Assessment of adaptive skills relies on the report of a respondent or observer. In the case of young children, this is primarily their parents and/or caregivers; for older children, a teacher might also be a source. The respondent is expected to be both truthful and knowledgeable in answering questions about the child's behavior. Having more than one respondent helps reveal the situational aspects of behavior (home and school).

The Vineland Adaptive Behavior Scales, Second Edition (VABS II; Sparrow, Cicchetti, & Balla, 2005) is an individually administered scale for people from birth through 90 years. There are three forms of the VABS, one each for parents, caregivers, and teachers. They vary in the amount of information obtained about the child's development. However, all three forms assess communication, daily living skills, motor skills, socialization, and maladaptive behavior.

The AAMD Adaptive Behavior Scale–School: 2 (ABS–S2; Nihira, Leland, & Lambert, 1993) is a norm-referenced scale for persons 3 to 21 years old. It looks at five main factors: personal self-sufficiency, social adjustments, personal adjustment, personal-social responsibility, and community self-sufficiency.

A child must be well below average in *both* measured intelligence and adaptive behavior to be identified as having an intellectual disability. We now believe that with appropriate early intervention, some children will no longer have an intellectual disability. For children with mild intellectual disabilities (those needing intermittent supports), a cognitive delay is often their only impairment. Children needing more supports are more likely to have other disabilities such as cerebral palsy, speech and language impairments, sensory impairments, seizure disorders, psychological or behavioral impairments, and specific learning disabilities (Batshaw et al., 2007). These may make it challenging to accurately identify children and the supports they need.

Intellectual Disabilities and Syndromes

Of the many different identified intellectual disabilities and syndromes, only the most common are detailed here.

Down Syndrome

Down syndrome, named after John Langdon Down, the first physician to identify the syndrome, is the most frequent genetic cause of mild to moderate intellectual disabilities (National Institutes of Health [NIH], 2010b) and was one of the first syndromes associated with intellectual disabilities. Prevalence of Down syndrome increases with maternal age. At age 30, a woman has about a 1 in 900 chance of conceiving a child with Down syndrome. Those odds increase to about 1 in 400 by age 35 and rise to about 1 in 12 by age 49. Therefore, the incidence of Down syndrome is dependent upon the maternal age distribution and age-specific pregnancy rates. Currently, it is stabilized at 1 per 800 live births (Roizen, 2007; NIH, 2010b).

▶❙❙ TeachSource Video Case

5–11 years: Developmental Disabilities in Middle Childhood

Watch the TeachSource Video Case *5–11 Years: Developmental Disabilities in Middle Childhood*, in which you will see how some children show significant maturation delays or "exceptionalities." The video can be found in the Early Childhood Education Media Library under Special Education, available at www.cengagebrain.com.

Children with Down syndrome are typically identified at birth because of characteristic features that include a small, relatively flat head, an upward slant to the eyes, and a short, broad neck. The ears, mouth, feet, and hands are relatively small; fingers are unusually short and broad; and there is a simian crease on the palm of the hand (Roizen, 2007). Chromosome analysis determines whether Down syndrome is an accurate diagnosis.

Children with Down syndrome reach motor milestones later than other children, walking independently or speaking their first words around age 2. Language delays become evident during the preschool years. Most of the motor problems are overcome by school age, but the cognitive challenges become more obvious. With the success of early intervention and educational inclusion, some children with Down syndrome do exceedingly well. Some have graduated from high school and are seeking advanced vocational training.

Children with Down syndrome have an increased risk of abnormalities in almost every organ system (Roizen, 2007). They usually have decreased motor tone and appear floppy. Feeding problems may occur because the tongue is usually thick. Almost half of the children have congenital heart disease, vision problems such as **cataracts**, **amblyopia**, **refractive errors**, or **strabismus**; hearing problems (often related to chronic middle ear infections); or structural problems with the ear itself (Kids Health, 2008a). Although this list may sound long and negative, most of the problems are treatable. The vision problems respond to corrective lenses, and most of the problems that relate to the heart and gastrointestinal system are solved through surgery or medication. Most children with Down syndrome are included in regular early care and education centers and in the public schools. Researchers are looking at the possibility of medical interventions and treatment strategies (NIH, 2010b).

IMPLICATIONS FOR EDUCATORS

Children with Down syndrome are usually enrolled in an early intervention program by 3 months of age. Initial intervention may focus on maintaining antigravity postures, such as sitting, and working on other motor skills, if the young child has low muscle tone. Children with Down syndrome usually respond to educators who arrange tasks sequentially, and break up complex tasks into smaller and simpler ones. A speech-language pathologist often helps with feeding as well as speech and language.

Fragile X Syndrome

Since its recognition as a genetic disorder, fragile X is the most common inherited cause of intellectual disability worldwide (Down syndrome, although genetic, is not inherited) (Meyer, 2007). An unusually large number of genes critically important to brain development, nerve cell functioning, learning, and memory reside on the X chromosome (Inlow & Restifo, 2004). In Fragile X, there is an abnormality in the X chromosome that causes the bottom tip of the large arm to become threadlike and "fragile." It is one reason why more males have intellectual disabilities than females. It is estimated that 2 to 6 per 1,000 live births have X-linked intellectual disabilities (Stevenson & Schwartz, 2002).

Children with intellectual disabilities are active participants in the activities of inclusive classrooms.
©Cengage Learning 2012

delays may have learning disabilities or behavior problems (Meyer, 2007).

Unless suspected, children with fragile X are often difficult to identify in early childhood because they may meet developmental milestones; however, their ability to meet milestones on time gradually declines. There are some behavior patterns that are typical of children with fragile X. Although all the behaviors alluded to are typical of young children, it is the frequency, duration, and intensity that indicate a problem. When excited or frustrated, children may flap their hands or bite them or have other autistic-like behaviors such as a fascination with spinning toys or other unusual objects. Speech patterns are unusual, and speech may be high-pitched, repetitious, and cluttered. They may be hyperactive or inattentive, with low levels of frustration tolerance, which can lead to temper tantrums. Sensory integration issues are common, and children often become overwhelmed with noisy environments. Some may react defensively to light touch (Meyer, 2007).

IMPLICATIONS FOR EDUCATORS

Be aware of some of the challenges that children with fragile X face and of the behaviors that characterize this disorder, as early childhood educators may be the first to suspect a disability. Work through the strengths of children with fragile X. They tend to process information as a whole rather than step by step, and they have good visual matching as well as adaptive functioning. They may have problems with executive functioning and sequential learning (Loesch et al., 2002; Meyer, 2007). Look for autistic-like behaviors. Provide children with functional skills as well as academic challenges, and match their level of learning with an enriched environment.

● ● ●
Fetal Alcohol Spectrum Disorders

Alcohol ingested by a pregnant woman can have a variety of physical and neurodevelopmental effects on the developing fetus, ranging from death of the fetus to physical malformation, intellectual disability, or learning and behavior problems. This range of disorders is known as fetal alcohol spectrum disorders (FASD) (CDC, 2006b). Fetal alcohol syndrome (FAS) is the most severe of these. Children with FAS have three characteristic anomalies: intrauterine and postnatal growth deficiency, including low birth weight and poor muscle tone; facial anomalies (thin upper lip, flat midface, short nose, low nasal bridge, small head, droopy eyes); and central nervous system (CNS) dysfunction, including irritability, attention deficit, hyperactivity, and intellectual disability (CDC, 2006b). The most severe effects happen early in the pregnancy and are related to maternal binge drinking (four or more drinks) (Davidson & Myers, 2007).

The prevalence of FAS and related disorders is difficult to estimate for a variety of reasons. One is the ability to confirm exposure to alcohol during fetal development. Depending upon the population studies, estimates range from 0.2 to 1.5 per 1,000 live births for FAS and three times that frequency for FASD (CDC, 2006b). One of the most frustrating aspects of FASD is that, theoretically, it is 100 percent preventable. The benefit in human terms is an obvious improvement in

The problem in fragile X is a chemical one. The FMR1 gene influences the expression of many other genes. FMRP, a protein essential for early brain development, is inactivated in fragile X . Both males and females can have the full mutation or a permutation that is more variable and less severe (Meyer, 2007). The overlap of fragile X and autism is an interesting one that has the potential for helping researchers understand both conditions better. Approximately 2 to 6 percent of children with autism spectrum disorder have fragile X syndrome; the cause is the fragile X gene mutation. About a third of children with fragile X show some degree of autism. Fragile X is the most common single gene cause of autism known (National Fragile X Foundation, 2008).

Although there are common physical features, these are not pronounced during childhood. Delays are apparent in cognitive ability, communication, behavior patterns, and low muscle tone. Approximately 80 percent of males with this syndrome will have mild to moderate intellectual disability (Loesch et al., 2002). These children are likely to be identified as infants or toddlers. Most females do not show the significant delays that are apparent in males. Children having fragile X who don't show intellectual quality of life. Moreover, because society bears the cost of raising children with FAS through the health care and educational systems, there would be huge economic benefits also.

THE EVIDENCE BASE

Using data from North Dakota, it was estimated that the health care costs for a child with FAS were $2,842 annually compared to children without FAS, which were approximately $500 a year. Assuming these costs are stable between birth and 21, health care costs alone run about $50,000 more than that of a child without FAS. Prevention of one case of FAS per year for 20 years results in a cost savings of $491,820. If one were to take into account the costs of special education and foster care, and then add in potential costs (or savings) by corrections and mental health, the potential savings grow tremendously with each prevention of FAS.

Source: Klug & Burd, 2003.

Children with FAS often have feeding problems, which can lead to failure to thrive. As young children, they tend to be short and thin, although they are likely to attain a typical height and weight. Developmental delays become apparent early, particularly in the area of speech and recall. Motor delays may occur, primarily showing themselves as clumsiness and lack of fine motor coordination (Wunsch, Conlon, & Scheidt, 2002). Although children with FAS display a range of IQ scores, most of them fall in the mild intellectual disability range. Part of their intellectual challenges is in the areas of planning, sequencing, self-monitoring, and goal-directed behaviors. These can lead to problems in routine activities such as self-help skills and can appear as behavior problems. Behavior problems such as hyperactivity and impulsivity are common. Children with FAS may also display oppositional defiant disorder, or they may have a conduct disorder with increasing age.

Children with FASD tend to function in the borderline average range and have fewer behavioral problems. Their impairments are subtler. In school, they seem to have particular difficulty with reading and math. They do not necessarily have the overall delay that is often associated with intellectual disability (Wunsch et al., 2002).

IMPLICATIONS FOR EDUCATORS

Children who are exposed to alcohol prenatally often live in families that have problems nurturing their children. In addition to inborn risks, children are often raised in homes where there is biological, psychological, and environmental risk. Infants and young children in such an environment are at increased risk for abuse and neglect. Many children will be placed in foster care for this reason. Others will enter the foster care system because their parents died of alcohol-related causes, such as cirrhosis of the liver, car accidents, suicides, and overdose.

IN THE FIELD

My daughter, Grace, couldn't have children, and she and her husband desperately wanted a child. They considered many alternatives and finally decided on a private adoption. They hired a lawyer who specialized in adoption, sold their boat, got a second mortgage on their home, and waited. They received the call when they were on vacation. They flew back to New York City in the midst of a raging snowstorm, rented a car, and started into the city. It took them five hours. My daughter kept calling, reminding them that one of the conditions of the adoption was that they could speak with the birth mother before she left the hospital.

The birth mother assured her that the baby's father was Dominican, even though the baby boy was blond with blue eyes. (Grace's husband is Cuban.) She also said that she didn't use drugs or alcohol while she was pregnant (another condition). The weather made going home impossible, so they checked into a hotel that was close by with provisions the hospital had given them. I called and my daughter was deliriously happy. The baby was beautiful. Her husband was downstairs with the chef trying to figure out how to make formula (thank God, the chef had children). And the baby was crying. Grace didn't know much about babies, but I'd had four children. I started to worry when he was a week old. By the time he was in preschool, he was identified as having neurological problems that affected his behavior and his learning. They said he had fetal alcohol effects. I was angry that the birth mother had lied about the father and about drinking. I kept telling my daughter she should do something. But she loves him.

Intellectual Delays

Studies consistently show that mild intellectual disability without a known etiology or cause is highly correlated with lower socioeconomic status. Children born to women who have fewer resources are more likely to have had little prenatal care and poor nutrition and are less likely to have received social and cognitive nurturing in early childhood. Women who haven't completed high school are four times as likely to have children with mild developmental delays (Mendola et al., 2002). African American children are twice as likely to be categorized as having mild developmental delays; this may be related to assessment issues or the disproportionate number of African American families who live below the poverty line, or both.

Another way of framing concerns related to children with mild developmental delays is to focus on the **achievement gap**. The achievement gap refers to the difference between groups of children based on **gender**, race/ethnicity, ability, and socioeconomic status and their scores on educational measures. Overall, black and Hispanic children and those children whose families have few resources are at a disadvantage in school compared to white middle-class children. By the time African-American and Latino children reach fourth grade, on average, they are almost three academic years behind their white peers (NCES, 2009b). With the exception of residential instability, black and Hispanic children have a greater probability of experiencing hardship than white children (Duncan & Magnuson, 2005). Racial and ethnic differences mirror differences in family socioeconomic status. However, children of all races/ethnicities who are eligible for free/reduced lunch are approximately two years of learning behind those children who are not eligible (McKinsey & Company, 2009).

Although there is clear agreement that the achievement gap exists, there is less agreement about the cause of it. The No Child Left Behind Act of 2002 was designed to close this gap. We are also concerned about school readiness. We know that what happens to children before they reach school age has a profound impact on their later achievement (Rouse, Brooks-Gunn, & McLanahan, 2005).

Children who participate in early care and education programs come to school more ready to learn. Early intervention services have improved the expected outcome for children with mild developmental delays (Batshaw et al., 2007), and they have the potential for narrowing the achievement gap. However, the children who seem most in need of these services may be the least likely to get them.

THE EVIDENCE BASE

To the extent that early intervention in the form of high-quality preschool could influence outcomes for children whose families are "poor," the question is, How many of them attend preschool? Data from the 2005 National Household Education Survey provided information on preschool participation but made no attempt to measure quality. The data are interesting and the differences between 3-year-olds and 4-year-olds is quite revealing.

Overall, children in poverty have lower participation rates in preschool than families who make more money, with families making between $20,000 and $30,000 having the lowest rates. These are the working poor. Despite the compensatory efforts of government to support these families, almost half of 4-year-olds and the vast majority of 3-year-olds do not participate in preschool. It is not until income levels rise to more than $85,000 that over half of 3-year-olds attend preschool (see Figure 14–2).

Another way to look at concerns is based on a mother's education (see Figure 14–3) and relates both to the concept of valuing early childhood education and the level of stimulation that one might expect in the home environment.

There is a strong link between a mother's education and preschool participation. The children who could be expected to gain most from high-quality preschool programs are the least likely to attend. These may well be the children who are identified as having mild intellectual delays when they reach kindergarten. Moreover, families in which the mother dropped out of high school have children who are likely to reach kindergarten with two years less of high-quality preschool than those of mothers who went to college.

A third way of looking at preschool participation is by race/ethnicity. Clearly, Hispanic children are less likely than other children to attend preschool (see Figure 14–4). Data suggests that lack of access is the most likely reason for this low rate.

Source: Barnett & Yarosz, 2007.

IMPLICATIONS FOR EDUCATORS

When children who live in impoverished environments are identified as having intellectual disabilities, they need a program with many hands-on experiences. You cannot assume that they have been exposed to the same experiences as other children. Do not assume that they are incapable of doing a task until you ensure that they have the necessary prerequisites to participate. These children need to go on field trips and to experience a variety of materials and media. They need to role-play and to have good language models. They need an enriched environment. Do you believe that lack of participation in high-quality preschool programs might be one reason why some children come to school and are identified with mild intellectual delays?

Instructional Strategies

In general, teach from simple to complex. Be specific! Where appropriate, simplify information, but not to the point that it loses its meaning. Use a variety of teaching techniques.

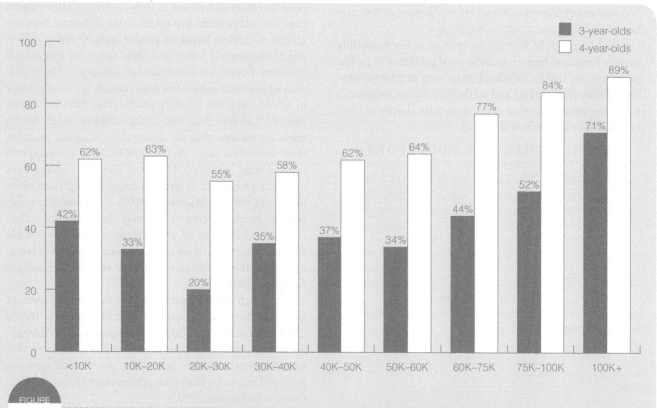

FIGURE 14-2 PRESCHOOL EDUCATION PARTICIPATION BY INCOME, NATIONAL HOUSEHOLD EDUCATION SURVEY, 2005

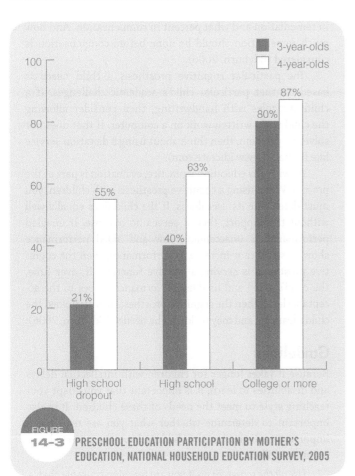

FIGURE 14-3 PRESCHOOL EDUCATION PARTICIPATION BY MOTHER'S EDUCATION, NATIONAL HOUSEHOLD EDUCATION SURVEY, 2005

Task Analysis

A task analysis is the process of breaking a task down into its component parts, sequencing these, and then teaching them. A great deal has been written on the use of task analysis. However, if you understand the basic principles involved in a task, you can do the task analysis yourself. Start with something the child must do frequently, like putting on a coat. Apply your task analysis. Is there any change? If, after your task analysis, the child still has a problem, review your analysis for both order and possible missed steps. Change it and try again.

Figure 14–5 presents a sample task analysis, including a filled-in chart that shows the child's progress. Task analysis and tracking of progress should be done on a weekly basis.

Backward Chaining

In some cases, the technique of backward chaining is useful. Using the example of putting on the coat, offer the most help with the first steps and the least help with the last step in the chain. The first step you would expect the child to do without assistance is step 8 (zip up the coat). This means the child gets some satisfaction for task completion instead of needing help to finish. (Backward chaining is easier when the component parts are of about equal difficulty.)

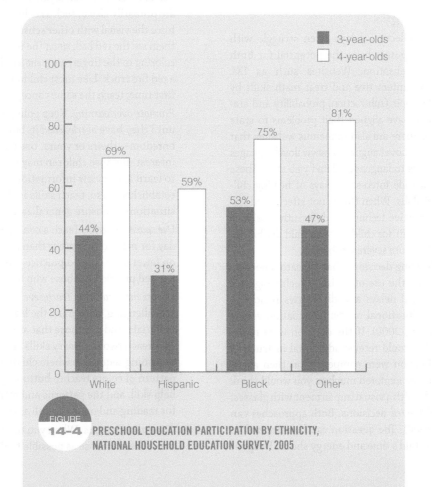

FIGURE 14-4 PRESCHOOL EDUCATION PARTICIPATION BY ETHNICITY, NATIONAL HOUSEHOLD EDUCATION SURVEY, 2005

	M	T	W	TH	F	M	T
1. Take coat off hook.	P	V	V	V	N	N	N
2. Put coat on floor, inside up.	P	P	V	V	N	N	N
3. Stand at neck of coat.	P	P	V	V	V	N	N
4. Bend over.	P	P	P	V	V	N	N
5. Put hands in armholes.	P	P	P	V	V	V	V
6. Flip coat over head, pushing arms into armholes.	P	P	P	P	V	V	V
7. Start zipper.	P	P	P	P	V	V	V
8. Zip up coat.	P	P	P	P	P	P	P

Be sure to praise the child for his efforts.

Key: P = physical help
     V = verbal help
     N = no help

FIGURE 14-5   TASK ANALYSIS AND TRACKING CHART

Modeling

Teachers may need to model a particular behavior while verbally describing it. Provide opportunities for the child to practice, and verbalize what the child is doing; also, provide reinforcement and specific feedback.

Assistive Technology

Children with mild intellectual delays often struggle with reading and math. Computers have the potential for both remediation and compensation. Websites such as IXL (www.ixl.com/math) are interactive and treat math skills by grade level and also by topic (subtraction, probability and statistics, time, etc.). They have aligned their problems to state standards. IXL is free. There are also numerous websites that support reading such as iLoveLanguages (www.ilovelanguages.com/) that provide links to language-related web sites. These computer examples provide interesting ways of helping children learn grade level skills. When this is not effective educators need to look at assistive technology differently. Assistive technology is very different for children with mild disabilities than it is for those with more severe disabilities.

One of the underlying decisions that educators need to make when considering the use of assistive technology for children with intellectual delays and disabilities is how to best meet children's educational needs: remediation versus compensation (Edyburn, 2000). If the decision were remediation, then the child would receive additional instruction in an area. If the decision were compensation then assistive technology would be explored much as you would think about providing a child with a visual impairment with glasses. These need not be either/or decisions. Both approaches can be used (Edyburn, 2000). The question can be reframed to ask what percent of a child's time and energy should be spent

in remediation and what percent in compensation. And how much remediation should be done before compensation is considered (Edyburn, 2006).

The particular cognitive prosthesis a child needs is based on that particular child's academic challenges. If a child struggles with handwriting, then consider allowing the child to do written work on a computer. If that does not solve the problem, then think about using a dictation service like iDictate (www.idictate.com).

As with any educational practice, evaluation is part of the process. When using a cognitive prosthesis with children, you must determine its usefulness. If the child does equally well without the support, then it serves no purpose. If unaided performance is unacceptably low and aided performance shows a significant increase in performance, then the cognitive prosthesis is serving a positive function. If, over time, the child's aided and unaided performance moves to the acceptable level, then the cognitive prosthesis has scaffolded the child's learning and may no longer be needed (Edyburn, 2006).

Guidelines

Because it takes longer for children with intellectual delays and disabilities to learn, it is important that you adapt your teaching style to meet the needs of these children. It is also important to determine whether what you are teaching is important and whether the children have the expected prerequisite skills.

1. *Use all the senses.* Even if you are teaching concepts that are primarily visual, such as colors, have children reinforce the visual with other sensory experiences. Have them *see* the red ball; *sit on* the red square; *add* red food coloring to the fingerpaint; *eat* a red tomato; and *listen* to a red fire truck. Like most children, they don't learn the first time; teach the same concept in different contexts.

2. *Promote overlearning.* Keep going over the same concept until they have *overlearned* it, but not to the point of boredom—theirs or yours. Use variations to maintain interest. Because children may easily forget, they need to learn and review information until it is firmly established. Also, teach skills in different areas and situations to ensure generalization.

3. *Use spaced practice.* Teach a concept for a short time each day for many days, rather than for a long period of time on fewer days. Spaced practice is more effective than massed practice, as those who "cram" for exams know.

4. *Choose materials that teach several skills.* Because learning is challenging, determine the learning value of specific materials, and use those that are most efficient or those that teach two necessary skills at one time. For example, buttoning sequences where children must duplicate a pattern of colors teaches buttoning, a necessary self-help skill, and the patterns and relationships necessary for reading and math, as well as color names.

5. *Generalize concepts.* When you teach concepts, try to make them as close as possible to the setting where

they will be used. Keep activities relevant, short, and to the point. Be clear with directions. Be wary of cute shortcuts. One school I visited decided to teach children to say "three-teen" instead of thirteen because it was easier. Some of those children are now about "three-teen and five-teen," and their peers make fun of them when they say how old they are.

6. *Use many examples.* If you use only one example when teaching the concept *orange*, it is likely that the children who learn this one example of orange will have difficulty generalizing to other orange objects and fruits.

7. *Reinforce appropriate behavior.* Set your sights realistically. Reinforce effort and steps accomplished toward a goal. Don't wait until the goal is accomplished, or the child may lose motivation.

8. *Focus on essential skills.* Don't try to teach the whole curriculum at a lower, slower, simpler level. Rather, concentrate on what is important for children. What skills will be essential later for the children that need a base developed now? Depending on the child, you will teach basic academic skills and also functional living skills and/or vocational skills. Teach safety and health skills necessary for wellness. Children need to learn to wash hands after toileting, not to get into the path of moving objects (whether swings, tricycles, or cars), and to wear clothing appropriate for the weather.

9. *Teach vocabulary.* Children need the vocabulary to express basic wants and needs whether they learn words or signs or use a communication board. They need a way to communicate that they are hungry, thirsty, tired, or need to go to the bathroom. Practice on a daily basis. Incorporate vocabulary learning into all curriculum areas.

10. *Use universal design.* Provide activities that can be used at many different levels by individuals and groups of children and provide adult scaffolding to support children's learning.

11. *Evaluate Progress.* Evaluate the progress of children with intellectual delays and disabilities against their own development, as well as in the context of the general curriculum and what all children in the class are learning.

Curriculum Adaptations

Adapting the curriculum, in general, consists of simplifying some tasks, focusing on essential tasks and omitting others, and including tasks that other children may learn more informally through incidental learning.

Social Awareness

Children learn about themselves and their environment by building on familiar experiences. Begin with them and their immediate surroundings—family and school—then expand into the larger community. Help children evaluate situations, including your classroom, relative to their health, fitness, and safety. Focus on making all children part of the group and teaching them social skills that will be appropriate throughout their lives. Some of the activities in the Resource Chapter 1 are specifically designed to support children who have intellectual disabilities. Activity 1–22, *Our Town*, provides a concrete way for children to think about the community.

• • •
Social Competence

All children need to be contributing members of the class. As you help children join groups, model and teach the skills they need, gradually fade your support so children will not be dependent on your intervention.

Children need to learn about themselves and others. Teach children the names of their body parts, using songs as well as direct instruction and questioning. Remember, you want to include all children: Do not act surprised when a child with intellectual disabilities can do something, or praise him inordinately.

1. Teach children the courtesies of everyday living. Ensure children know how to greet you (say "Hello" and look at you while they say it). They also need to learn to use "Please" and "Thank you" appropriately and not to interrupt conversations.

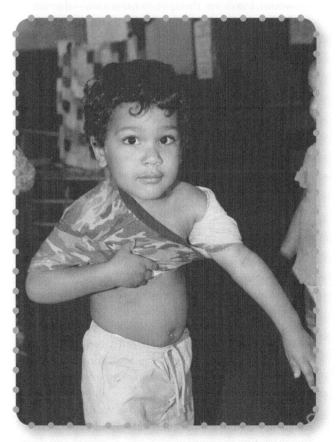

Build time in the curriculum to teach adaptive behaviors when they would naturally occur.
©Cengage Learning 2012

2. Give children tasks they can do.

3. Have easy and difficult, but age-appropriate, options available so children can easily participate in group play. Mix age groups for some activities if this is possible.

4. Help develop a positive self-concept by pointing out to the child and others what she can do and how much she *has* learned, just as you do with all children. Be truthful.

5. Focus on and support strengths where possible. Use these to work on necessary challenges.

6. Support children's expansion of learning at the level at which they are capable.

7. Support children as they learn age-appropriate adaptive skills.

• • •
Social Studies

Like all children, those with intellectual delays and disabilities need to learn about the community in which they live. Concentrate on roles the children may need to know or can readily identify.

1. Discuss the roles of police, firefighters, and mail personnel. Go on field trips to see them at work, and then follow up with role-playing. Be practical. Have children mail letters or postcards home to see their address. Talk about the implications of writing the wrong address.

2. Help children learn about many different roles—cafeteria worker, bus driver, therapist, to name a few—they are likely to encounter. Have them play games in a one-on-one situation with a teacher or paraeducator. Discuss how the teacher also learns from these specialists.

3. Explore varied occupations. Be sure to include *some* occupations that require limited skills. It is important that a range of occupations be included and that they all be valued.

4. Take children on field trips to different areas in the community. Teach skills they need to interact in the community. Encourage parents to take children on the bus, to restaurants, and to the library. Teach prerequisite skills for these trips.

English Language Arts

Language, both expressive and receptive, may be one of the child's most challenging areas, but it is one of the most essential. Children with intellectual disabilities have smaller vocabularies and use simpler sentence structures than their peers. Their language may be difficult to understand and used less frequently than that of other children. Lack of competence in communication can lead to frustration and may result in crying, hitting, or other means of nonverbal communication.

Provide time for extra repetitions of vocabulary and help generalize words to a variety of situations. Children will need time mastering the concept of a symbol system and developing a functional vocabulary. They may need to repeat and copy sounds before these become connected to words. These skills may be learned in conjunction with such necessary small motor skills as patterned eye movement (left to right), following a line of print with a finger, and turning pages. Children need to practice these skills, and it is your role to motivate them and capture their interest. Do this in short periods, and be sure prerequisite skills have been attained before going on to more difficult tasks. Children with intellectual disabilities may just be mastering the initial stages of reading and writing during the early elementary years. Ensure the prerequisite motor skills have been developed when children experience difficulties,

Children who have intellectual disabilities need first-hand experiences to translate into language and literacy. They need to build a strong experiential base. Start with the concrete and gradually work toward the more abstract. Children need to explore balls, roll, throw, and kick balls before stories about balls make sense.

• • •
Speaking and Listening

Like all children, those with intellectual delays and disabilities depend on communicating with others to have their needs met.

1. Encourage children to communicate in any way they can. Start conversations with an obvious frame of reference: "I like your hat." Photographs or videotapes taken during field trips can be used later to help children talk about what happened on the trips. They can also sequence pictures. A sequence of a trip to the apple orchard might look like this:

Picture 1:	Getting into the cars
Picture 2:	Arriving at the orchard
Picture 3:	Eating apples at the orchard
Picture 4:	Taking off coats back at school, with the apples in the picture

Using a digital camera allows you to show the sequence quickly without having to wait for film to be developed. Printing the photographs on regular paper rather than photographic paper saves money.

2. If you are going to set up a grocery store in the dramatic play area, take a field trip to a grocery store (or encourage parents to do so) so children have this experience to build on. Point out the similarities in the two situations.

Listening is difficult. Where possible, use props. Speak clearly at a normal speed with simple, direct statements.

1. Provide concrete examples of the items that you are talking about so children can both see and hear the information.

2. Give the child practice following one- and two-step directions.

3. Be sure that children understand the interactional quality of listening and speaking and that they don't see listening as a passive experience (as they might with television).

Reading

Children with intellectual disabilities require more practice to develop early literacy skills. Build a solid base and do not spend so much time on rote drill and practice that children lose interest in learning to read. First establish basic skills, and then use these skills to teach the integration of higher-level skills. At the beginning, use short, simple stories that have a familiar theme. Remember, the group experience may be new to children.

1. Use stories with repetition, rhythm, and rhyme, such as Dr. Seuss books like *Go, Dog. Go!* If you have the resources, start a read-at-home program. Send books home and have children read and reread them with their families.

2. Animal stories with big pictures and few words, alphabet and counting books, and those with simple rhymes are good.

3. Before you read a story, discuss the meaning of some words. For example, before reading the story *Caps for Sale*, establish that caps are hats.

4. Use flannelboard stories. They have simple plots and children can participate in the story and repeat it as they manipulate the pieces.

5. Read to children one on one and follow the words with your finger so children develop the connection between written words and reading. Make reading fun and exciting. Read more books rather than fewer.

Writing

Writing begins with marks on the page and ends with the understanding of a complex symbol system. Work initially with the fine motor aspect, as the symbol system will take time.

1. Help children enjoy the process of making marks on paper. Give them a variety of tools (crayons with knob ends, large markers, thick chalk) to mark with and varying sizes of paper, cardboard, and poster board to mark on.

2. Have large wooden alphabet letters available. Spell out the child's name and have the child trace the letters with two fingers (index and middle fingers of dominant hand).

3. Have children imitate you as you make large arm circles in the air with the dominant arm, first in one direction and then the other. When children can make circles, begin to air write letters with your arm (it is important that this is a large motor activity). See Activity 2-58w, *Air Writing*, for more details.

Language

Children need to learn the rules of English (how to make plurals, how to ask questions, and so on). They also need to enlarge their vocabulary to express their needs.

1. Work on vocabulary. Start with a nucleus vocabulary that focuses on the child. Teaching body parts teaches not only vocabulary but also body awareness as well. Next, focus on health care, the family, clothing, and aspects of the school and home environments. Emphasize nouns and verbs first. They are essential for communicating needs. If necessary, begin with words that allow children to express their basic needs and wants, including words such as *yes, no, thirsty, hungry, please, bathroom*, and *tired*.

2. Use simple nursery rhymes and rhyming in general to develop vocabulary.

Discovery

Support the discovery approach with verbalizations about the process. Allow time to repeat experiences and to do variations on themes. Help children generalize knowledge. As activities become more challenging, ensure that they can be done at different levels. Children with intellectual disabilities will need concrete experience even after their peers are dealing with more abstract concepts. Use real objects that can be touched and manipulated. Modify the keyboard of the computer or be sure children have prerequisite skills such as the ability to use a single keystroke before expecting them to interact with computers.

Point out similarities and differences within classification systems (e.g., cars and trucks both have wheels). Increase attention span by programming for what the child likes and encouraging the child for staying with projects to completion. However, don't avoid areas that are challenging, as this may be where he needs the most practice. Make it interesting.

Mathematics

Children with intellectual disabilities need a foundation in basic mathematical skills to function in society.

1. Teach number concepts, such as counting, with real objects that can be moved or touched. Count children, blocks, chairs, and tables. Use an abacus and relate the beads back to real objects. See Activity 3–33w, *Abacus*.

2. Choose math experiences that also teach other skills. Pegboards are useful for facilitating small motor skills while teaching counting and one-to-one correspondence. Pegboards can also be used to teach sequential patterns and relationships. You can make up a pattern and ask the child to copy it, identify the pattern, and then count the number of pegs used in the pattern. Stringing large wooden beads offers a similar opportunity for learning about numbers and patterns while also teaching eye–hand coordination. Geoboards are also useful for teaching counting, area, and multiplication.

3. Use real objects such as cups, napkins, and fruit pieces to teach one-to-one correspondence. A good activity for snack time is to have a child put a glass and piece of fruit or vegetable in front of each chair (children

without something to eat or drink usually make this known, and thus you have a teachable moment).

4. Code your classifying and matching tasks by number (use 1 for easy tasks, 2 for more difficult, and so on). This means that all the children can do the same activity but at different levels. Provide a variety of levels of classifying activities such as these:

   (a) Sort identical objects from a mix: round beads from crayons, or wooden clothespins from small wooden blocks.

   (b) Group the same objects by size: big from small, plastic clips or big blocks from small ones.

   (c) Sort the same objects in different colors: red from green beads, or red from white blocks.

   (d) Group the same objects with differing shapes: round from square from cylindrical red beads.

   (e) Have a mix of objects that can be grouped in two or more ways. First, demonstrate the system and have the child follow it; later, encourage the child to group and regroup independently. A mix of large and small cars of different colors, large and small blocks of different colors and shapes, and large and small beads of varying colors and shapes may all be sorted into two containers of large and small—three containers if they sort by object, and more if they sort by color.

Within each step, you can make the task more difficult by adding more objects, colors, sizes, and shapes. Start with 2 items and work up to perhaps 10. A more difficult version is grouping different objects by color, size, and shape. After children have classified the objects have them count the objects.

Science

Science should focus on first-hand knowledge and give information that is relevant for future learning and well-being.

1. Use field trips, especially those dealing with nature and the environment, to teach children about the world around them.

2. Discuss the seasons and the predictable changes that occur with the changes in nature.

3. Encourage children to test simple cause-and-effect reasoning. State a relationship and have the child test it. "The color is darker if you press harder" may be obvious to you, but children may not realize they cause the change systematically.

4. Tie science lessons to safety knowledge. Science lessons can also provide an important opportunity to teach everyday living skills, such as the relationship between being out in the sun and getting a sunburn (if you don't use sunscreen), and stopping the spread of germs by processes such as hand washing.

Technology

Technology holds great potential for teaching cause-and-effect reasoning, and its "patience" with repeated learning is infinite.

Provide children with first-hand experiences, and use the moment to teach needed skills.
©Cengage Learning 2012

1. Look at various keyboard options and choose those that best meet the child's needs.

2. Choose software carefully. It needs to be developmentally appropriate and simple to operate.

3. Encourage independent use of the computer itself. This is tremendously impressive to others. Parents may be encouraged and surprised that their child can turn on and operate a computer. Some of the skills are easy and sequential, and some of the software (especially with picture menus) is very user-friendly.

4. Encourage children to work at the computer in pairs.

Wellness

Children with intellectual disabilities may have had fewer experiences in these areas. Plan activities that are at the child's developmental level, with variations to allow mastery and more challenging ones to provide growth. Children need simple as well as more complex activities and many opportunities for practice. Begin with relatively large objects with few pieces: program for success. Try to include as many adaptive skills as you can (dressing boards, doll clothes with Velcro fasteners, and so on).

Health and Safety

It is important for children to make good health habits part of their routine. Teach skills such as toileting, washing hands, blowing and wiping their nose with a tissue, eating with utensils, and grooming, if necessary.

1. Teach safety skills. Emphasize dangers with the greatest likelihood of occurrence and those that are most dangerous, such as traffic, electrical outlets, fire, and poison. Teach safety signs, warning signs, and warning words. See activities such as 4–2, *Stop and Go*, and 4–10, *Warning Sounds*.

2. Concentrate on building good food habits. Help children learn to choose healthy snacks like water and milk, vegetables, fruit and low-fat yogurt rather than juice and soft drinks and cookies and crackers.

3. Role-play with children what to do if they get lost. Have them memorize safety information.

4. Break complex skills down into simple tasks the child can do. Teach the necessary skills in different curricula.

Physical Education

Large motor skills help develop stamina and increase body coordination and awareness. Provide opportunities for children to participate in skills that require locomotion (creeping, running), manipulation (throwing, bouncing, catching), and stability (stretching, rolling, balancing). Encourage children to develop game skills (kicking, throwing, catching, jumping, batting). Participation in cooperative games where no one wins or loses and no one is eliminated works best.

1. Emphasize basic fundamental motor skills and their variations; walking forward, backward, sideways, fast, slow, and so on.

2. Help children build physical stamina by daily participation in moderate to vigorous activity, active games, and an active lifestyle.

3. Use large, lightweight blocks, which are easy to manipulate.

Sensory Motor Integration

When you plan for fine motor play, think of the skills that both help the child develop the necessary small muscles in the body and serve as a foundation for later skills. Provide opportunities for children to use motor skills in coordination with their senses.

1. Provide a variety of objects so that the child can practice many styles of grasping, manipulating, and releasing.

2. Use many different materials that require fine motor skills (formboards, pegboards—rubber ones for strengthening finger muscles—plastic blocks, or beads that fit together). Start with relatively large, toddler-size objects. Gradually add more pieces and smaller objects (be sure they cannot be swallowed). Use this opportunity to teach color and number skills also. Have children sort and group various materials.

3. Provide a variety of pencils, crayons, and brushes of different sizes. Short or broken crayons encourage an appropriate writing grasp. Larger implements are easier to grip. Add grips, tape, or foam curlers to make them easier to hold. (An occupational therapist can provide advice on these accommodations.)

4. Teach adaptive skills such as buttoning and snapping.

5. Provide materials and activities that require the use of two hands: clapping, putting together snap-construction toys, and placing large blocks in containers. Include some that require different motions of each hand (such as a jack-in-the-box, where a child must hold the box with one hand while turning the knob with the other, lacing beads onto string or pipe cleaners, and lacing cards with various-sized holes (some large and easy to string, others small).

6. Provide puzzles with different levels of difficulty. Puzzles with knobs attached to the pieces are easier to manipulate.

Creative Arts

As long as there is no competition and children are not required to do the "same" thing, children with intellectual disabilities need few accommodations in this area. Through the manipulation of various art media, they can learn about texture, shape, and size. If you use costumes, provide some realistic ones. Encourage children to move their whole body to bold music. The practice of moving and dancing and the opportunity to be part of the group is important.

Visual Arts

Art for young children should focus more on the process than the product. Children learn by doing, especially if a thoughtful teacher is providing guidance.

1. Use a variety of art media.

2. Cutting is often difficult; it may be helpful to use easy-grip or "training" scissors with a loop or a spring handle or tear paper. See Activity 5–35w, *Torn Paper Flowers*.

3. Encourage children to participate in the visual arts each day. Provide feedback on what they do and how they are doing it.

Music

Music can be used in a variety of ways. Repetition makes it easier for children to learn songs. Teach families songs so children can hear and sing them at home as well.

1. Use music to teach basic concepts such as numbers, colors, and body parts.

2. Expand a child's vocabulary and increase auditory memory through music.

3. Use music to help children establish a rhythm pattern. Vary the pattern so that children can learn to match it.

4. Increase self esteem and create a sense of group belonging by using songs that call children by name.

Movement and Dance

Movement is a must for all children. Nonjudgmental movement is an added plus. Support all attempts at movement. Dancing is an easy way to build in physical activity and let everyone have fun. Dancing is a lifetime sport.

1. Play music that has an obvious beat and encourage children to move.

2. Model moving specific body parts. Be sure to move these parts long enough so the children know the part indicated: "Everybody move your arms in circles."

3. Help children recognize speed by having them move quickly or slowly. Children gain sensory motor integration as well as necessary concepts through movement.

4. Have frequent dance parties to get children up and moving.

• • •
Dramatic Play and Theater

Dramatic play is a way to make strange experiences more familiar and is a good way to teach appropriate behavior. Having scripts that include all children makes theater inclusive.

1. Visit a real store, then set up a play store (department, grocery, pet). Play through the essential features. Setting it up for one or two days isn't enough; keep adding features throughout the week so it doesn't get boring.

2. Playing theater with other children provides the child with information about how roles are played in society. Children, especially those with disabilities, may be given little realistic feedback, yet feedback is necessary for their development. Directors can provide feedback as part of the play. It can be realistic without being judgmental. Acknowledge reality, but help children think about alternatives.

3. Play should be concrete with realistic props. Children with intellectual disabilities are typically less imaginative than their peers. Have a lot of props available to facilitate play: a garage, for example, needs cars, trucks, a block structure, hose, gas pumps, and so on.

Routines and Transitions

Routines and transitions can be used to promote independence and prevocational skills as well as teach colors, numbers, and body awareness.

1. Have a sign-in and sign-out board. Use this for roll call some days. Have children find their own nametag and put it on or move their name card from one side to the other, or use place cards to designate seating.

2. Dismiss children at a time when they can get the help they need with toileting and dressing.

3. Use transitions to reinforce concepts the child has learned. For example, call children to line up after they have correctly spelled a word or answered a math question. Vary the difficulty of the questions to match what the children are learning.

4. Allow time for transitions so children can be successful. It is easy for children with intellectual disabilities to get distracted and to feel rushed when others are waiting.

5. Sitting too long for the sake of sitting is not a useful skill for any child. Use finger plays or listening games while other children are finishing, or teach children to independently get and use readiness materials (puzzles, books, or small motor materials) while they wait.

SUMMARY

- Intellectual delays and disabilities are conditions that can be changed or modified through early intervention.
- Infants and toddlers are identified by missed motor and language milestones, the quality of their movements, and their lack of interest in the environment.

- Preschool children are identified by a short attention span and poor memory skills.
- School-age children may not have readiness skills necessary to pursue learning at the expected rate.
- Milder cognitive delays are identified later.
- Children must have delays in both intelligence and adaptive skills to have an intellectual disability.
- Intellectual disabilities are caused by both genetic and environmental factors.
- Children with intellectual disabilities may need more repetitions and more direct teaching techniques such as task analysis, backward chaining, and modeling.

EDUCATIONAL RESOURCES

American Association on Intellectual and Developmental Disabilities (AAIDD) is a national organization for professionals interested in the general welfare of people with intellectual disabilities and the study of causes, treatment, and the prevention of intellectual disabilities. www.aaidd.org/

ARC of the United States is an advocacy organization with a strong commitment to meet the needs of those with intellectual disabilities and their families. www.thearc.org/

Centers for Disease Control and Prevention (CDC) developed *Learn the Signs. Act Early* as a way to help families and early childhood educators identify typical developmental milestones and those that, if missed, should be followed up by talking to the child's doctor. It provides many recently developed materials and multimedia in English and Spanish. www.cdc.gov/ncbddd/actearly/index.html/

Education Equity Project is a civil rights organization whose mission is the elimination of the racial/ethnic achievement gap in public school by ensuring that each classroom has an effective teacher, empowering parents, and accountability. www.edequality.org/

Family Village is an organization that integrates information and resources on the Internet for people with disabilities and their families. www.familyvillage.wisc.edu/

The Future of Children is a collaboration between the Woodrow Wilson School of Public and International Affairs at Princeton University and the Brookings Institution. All of its publications focus on issues that are important to children and their future. www.futureofchildren.org/

National Down Syndrome Society provides information about Down syndrome, including the topic of inclusion. www.ndss.org

National Fragile X Foundation provides information about fragile X and supports research to better understand whom it affects and how it affects them. www.fragilex.org/html/home.shtml/

Pregnancy and Alcohol is a nonprofit site sponsored by the University of Wisconsin that provides information about pregnancy and the use of alcohol as well as information about fetal alcohol syndrome and related conditions. http://pregnancyandalcohol.org/index.asp/

For additional Educational Resources, visit the book companion website for this text at www.cengagebrain.com.

Children Who Are Gifted and Talented

Chevaneese stacked blocks before her older brother did. She walked early and she spoke in sentences when other toddlers were still saying one or two words. Chevy was smart. But being labeled as "gifted and talented" eventually became more of a burden than an accolade.

"I've always had more stress in my life because I was 'smarter,'" she said. "Teachers put me in groups with 'trouble-makers' and 'nongifted' children, somehow hoping my influence would encourage them." But making Chevy the example, and letting everyone know that she was smarter than others, strained relationships with her peers. "Many children would purposely not interact with me, and if I received a less than perfect grade on something, taunts of 'Why did you get that grade if you're so smart?' followed," she said.

This caused her to not only regret her "smartness" but also feel emotionally unstable. "There's a serious problem when you get sick and you're scared to miss school for fear you'll get behind," she said. ❄

©Cengage Learning 2012

Gifts and Talents

Sometimes we focus so much on children's differences, we forget that regardless of their ability or disability, they have the same needs as other children. If we are committed to inclusion and equal educational opportunities for all children, then what do we do about children who are intellectually advanced in their development? Some see gifted children as a precious national resource that is being wasted. Others feel that these children should be able to succeed very well without special services. Gifted education has been criticized as being "elitist," not open to children from diverse ethnic groups, those with disabilities, and those who exhibit gifts and talents in only one area.

In the current educational climate, the energy of the nation is focused on closing the gap between learners who have access to resources and those who do not. No Child Left Behind has helped focus this commitment and also made clear the emphasis on math and reading literacy. The 2004 amendments to the IDEA also focus on literacy, particularly providing early intervening services for children who are not progressing at the expected rate. Standards have been developed to ensure that children learn appropriate content. However, little is said about developing a conceptual framework to understand how gifted children learn, how and what they should be taught, and how schools should be supporting their development (VanTassel-Baska & Stambaugh, 2006).

Some feel that No Child Left Behind leaves gifted children behind, or that no child is allowed ahead.

Many feel that the instructional needs of gifted and talented children are not being met; that is, there is little curricular differentiation to accommodate their learning needs. Further, few preservice teachers are receiving training to teach gifted and talented children. We are more concerned that teachers who have children with disabilities included in their class have the appropriate training to meet the needs of these children. We are apparently less concerned about training teachers to include gifted and talented children. Perhaps the general education curriculum should be reconceptualized to include the diversity of all children.

Some feel that gifted and talented children can appropriately be thought of as disadvantaged because of the lack of legislation concerning their needs and rights; the lack of government guidance relative to training teachers, and provision of services; and the lack of funding for these children.

Defining Gifts and Talents

In many ways, what is valued is related to the sociohistorical time and the culture in which one is raised. In a society where people hunted for food, an individual who shot more accurately and from a greater distance than others might have been considered "gifted." In industrialized nations, we value other skills. In the past, we identified individuals as gifted only after they had made major contributions to society (George, 2003). In early childhood education, the goal is to identify children in order to provide them with a developmentally appropriate education. This is not necessarily an accelerated curriculum, any more than we try to slow down the curriculum for children with intellectual disabilities. It is a curriculum designed to meet the child's needs.

Definitions of giftedness typically involve at least two processes: a large information base and the cognitive processing skills needed to assemble, control, and work with this information (Wingenbach, 1998). That is, gifted children are aware of the knowledge they possess and know how to process that information efficiently. Additionally, they can communicate this information well in speaking and writing. They have good problem-solving skills and creative ideas.

There is no federal mandate for individualized education to meet the needs of this population. Individual states decide whether to have programs for them. The following definition is based on the Jacob K. Javits Gifted and Talented Students Education Act (1988) as part of the Elementary and Secondary Education Act

> *Children and youth with outstanding talent perform or show the potential for performing at remarkably high levels of accomplishment when compared with others of their age, experience or environment.*
>
> *These children exhibit high performance capability in intellectual, creative, and/or artistic areas; possess an unusual leadership capacity, or excel in specific academic fields. They require services or activities not ordinarily provided by the schools.*
>
> *Outstanding talents are present in children and youth from all cultural groups, across all economic strata, and in all areas of human endeavor.*

The problem is that giftedness, intelligence, and talent are fluid concepts that look different in different contexts and different cultures. Furthermore, there is not a universally agreed upon definition. Conservative definitions are based on high IQ scores; more liberal definitions include multiple criteria and even multiple intelligences (National Association for Gifted Children [NAGC], 2008).

The National Association for Gifted Children (2008) sees the development of ability as a lifelong process with various factors either enhancing or inhibiting the development and expression of abilities. In early childhood, the focus is on a rapid rate of learning compared to other children or exceptional performance on tests or other measures of ability.

By adolescence, high levels of achievement and motivation are the primary characteristics of giftedness.

Gifted individuals are those who demonstrate outstanding levels of aptitude (defined as an exceptional ability to reason and learn) or competence (documented performance or achievement in top 10 percent or rarer) in one or more domains. Domains include any structured area of activity with its own symbol system (e.g., mathematics, music, language) and/or sensorimotor skills (e.g., painting, dance, sports) (NAGC, 2008).

Prevalence of Gifts and Talents

In the United States in 2006, 6.7 percent of the public school population was identified as gifted and talented. Table 15.1 provides information about the distribution of identified children by sex, race/ethnicity.

There are cultural and ethnic differences in the proportion of children who are identified as gifted and talented. This raises contentious questions about whether there are gender and racial-ethnic differences in mental ability or whether there are underserved gifted populations (Smutny, 2003). It also brings into question the measures that are used to determine giftedness as well as intellectual disability.

This text uses terminology and classifications to indicate the degree to which a child differs from the norms, thus identifying the degree to which children's development is delayed (mild, moderate, severe, or profound) or the level of supports a child needs (intermittent, limited, extensive, or pervasive). An IQ, as a measure of rate of cognitive development, also suggests the degree to which children with advanced intellectual development are developing differently from their peers. For example, a moderately gifted child with an IQ of 133 and with a chronological age of 6 has a mental age of 9; and an exceptionally gifted 6 year old with an IQ of 160 has a mental age of approximately 11. This first-grader would be expected to be able to understand content at the level of children in sixth grade. Some suggest that it would be useful to develop some standardized

TABLE 15–1   PERCENT OF GIFTED AND TALENTED CHILDREN IDENTIFIED IN THE PUBLIC SCHOOLS IN 2006 BASED ON GENDER, AND RACE/ETHNICITY

United States	6.7
Female	7.0
Male	6.3
White	8.0
Black	3.6
Hispanic	4.2
Asian/Pacific Islander	13.1
American Indian/Alaska Native	5.2

Source: National Center for Educational Statistics, 2008.

terminology and classify children based on IQ in the following way:

IQ 130–144	Moderately gifted
IQ 145–159	Highly gifted
IQ 160–179	Exceptionally gifted
IQ 180+	Profoundly gifted

In a normal distribution, approximately 1 child in 20 in a given population would be moderately gifted; 1 in 1,000, highly gifted; fewer than 9 in 100,000 could be classified as exceptionally gifted; and fewer than 1 in a million as profoundly gifted (Gross, 1993).

Because the number of moderately gifted children is so much greater than highly, exceptionally, and profoundly gifted children, most school programs for the gifted are designed based on the characteristics, learning styles, and needs of this group (Gross, 1993). These programs rarely take into account that a child with an IQ of 190 is as different in ability level from a child with an IQ of 130 as the child with an IQ of 130 is from the child with an IQ of 70 (Gottfredson, 2003). See Table 15–2 for behaviors that may indicate advanced cognitive development in early childhood.

Causes of Gifts and Talents

There is debate about the causes of special gifts and talents. Information from brain research clearly shows that the potential for giftedness is biologically rooted; however, it is also clear that the environment into which one is born shapes not only the child's expression of giftedness but also the brain itself (Shore, 1997). The brain's growth is dynamic. Appropriate stimulation increases the amount of dendrite branching in the neurons, which in turn increases the child's ability for complex thinking and the ability to see interconnections (Yaun & Keating, 2007).

The family a child is born into affects the child in two major ways: Families provide the stimulation that enables children to gain essential knowledge, skills, and mental strategies, and they transmit values and attitudes related to learning and achievement (Jackson, 2003). Biological parents also supply the child's genetic makeup.

Studies have shown some similarities among parents of young children identified as being gifted or talented. The families placed a high value on achieving. The parents introduced the child at an early age to the area in which he eventually excelled, and it was frequently an area in which at least one of the parents had talent. The child's special skills began developing in the context of home activities through informal parent teaching. Parents were involved in the child's outside activities and made sure that the child practiced. Genes and environments work together in ways that are almost impossible to disentangle (Jackson, 2003).

Children who are gifted vary based on developmental differences and general categories such as these:

- Abilities and aptitudes
- Achievement
- Academic background
- Culture and identity
- Effort and motivation
- Interests, learning styles, and creative opportunities (Reis & Renzulli, 2009).

Early Identification of Gifts and Talents

Unique gifts and talents are a developmental phenomenon. Young children who display these gifts often show both general and unique patterns of strengths. One of the concerns that many have is the stability of the IQ over time.

TABLE 15-2 EARLY IDENTIFICATION OF CHILDREN WHO ARE GIFTED AND TALENTED

- May demonstrate a high level of language development
- Uses advanced vocabulary and/or develops early reading skills
- Asks many specific questions and seriously listens to the answers
- Has an unusual capacity for memory and a greater amount of knowledge, which is well organized and accessible, and unusual retention of information
- Has a mature and perhaps even subtle sense of humor
- Is exceptionally curious intellectually, has a passion for learning
- Is interested in cause-and-effect relationships but may view these relationships differently than adults
- Has a long attention span for activities of his own choosing, great powers of concentration
- Has a high energy level; may be restless in mind and body, intense
- Knows many things that peers are unaware of and is aware of issues at a deeper level
- Learns in intuitive leaps
- Is sensitive to emotional issues at an early age; empathizes, may have concerns about death, anger, love, pain, and so on
- Is eager to try new activities and/or perform familiar activities in new ways
- May develop a passion for a particular area of interest
- May be bored in a classroom designed for typically developing children
- Prefers the company of older children and adults
- Has an accelerated pace of thought, rapid learning rate, extraordinary speed in processing information
- Has the ability to comprehend concepts and whole ideas and to identify the underlying structures and patterns in ideas and relationships
- Has the ability to synthesize and think abstractly from a young age
- Has unevenness in development, which may make him vulnerable to social isolation
- Has periods of intense concentration
- Demonstrates talent in the arts

Sources: Clark, 2002; George, 2003; Koshy, 2002, NAGC, 2006.

In general, from about ages 6 or 7 through adulthood, stability is the rule rather than the exception (Gottfredson, 2003). Before school age, there is more variability. Parents are often the first to recognize gifted behaviors in preschool children. So the question is, What is gifted performance in early childhood? Sternberg and Zhang (2001) identified five qualities they consider to be requirements of gifted performance:

1. It must be excellent relative to the performance of same-aged peers or others who have had the same amount of instruction.
2. It must be rare among same-aged peers.
3. It must be demonstrable or measurable on some reliable and valid assessment.
4. It must be productive or have the potential for productivity.
5. It must have some societal value.

Initially, these qualities may not seem to be applicable to young children. However, if one considers the way a child's behavior changes his environment, it is more apparent. The infant who talks early and well has dramatically different social opportunities than the infant who does not yet speak. The child who reads independently and fluently at age 5 has access to very different information than a 5-year-old who does not yet read (Jackson, 2003). Early identification of young intellectually advanced children focuses primarily on early language development and positive, motivationally relevant behaviors.

Because children are gifted or talented does not necessarily mean that their growth or development at young ages is different from other children's. However, because of *uneven* development, young children, especially, may appear to have deficits when in reality they are developing physically at a normal pace but not at the same pace as their intellectual development or their particular configuration of gifts and talents. Young children with exceptional intellectual resources may have a greater than average need for emotional, social, and other nonintellectual capabilities to successfully cope.

We know little about the developmental course of giftedness until children have actually displayed these characteristics and we consequently identify them. The Fullerton longitudinal study provides an exception; it chose a sample of 130 healthy 1-year-olds. Some of the children at later ages were identified as gifted, whereas others were not. Hence, the study was in a good position to make comparisons between the two groups (Gottfried et al., 1994; Gottfried, Gottfried, & Guerin, 2006).

Verbal skills are one area where developmental differences are likely to be most apparent. The Fullerton longitudinal growth study found significant differences between gifted and nongifted children in receptive language at age 1, and differences in both receptive and expressive language were consistent from infancy onward. These were the major differences found in the early years; some questioned whether the high scores in the language area accounted for

the differences in intellectual performance that were found at 18 months and continued (Gottfried et al., 1994).

The rate of development of children with advanced intellectual development is different during the preschool years; that is, their particular pattern of gifts and talents develops more rapidly than that of nongifted children. Very young gifted children also appeared to be different in the testing situation itself, showing "significantly greater goal directedness, object orientation, attention span, cooperativeness, positive emotional tone, and responsiveness to test materials" (Gottfried et al., 1994, p. 105). These characteristics are relevant to motivation and might be considered gifted motivational behaviors; they could be used as one means of identifying young gifted learners (Gottfried et al., 2006). If so used, the inclusion of some children with disabilities and English language learners might increase. Other indicators include great attentiveness, ability to concentrate, intense interest and curiosity, and delight in the unexpected (George, 2003). It was not until age 8 that the children in the study were given an IQ test and designated as intellectually gifted or nongifted. Of the 107 children still in the study, 20 children (19%) had IQs of 130 or more. These children also had a development index (DQ) of 130 or greater when they had been tested at ages 1½ and 2 years. They were more advanced in their receptive language as early as 1 year of age and continued to score consistently well in both receptive and expressive language. Parents also noted these differences. Teachers found them more competent in the classroom. From infancy through the early school years, intellectually gifted children had superior cognitive mastery and academic intrinsic motivation (Gottfried et al., 2006).

Overall, the behavioral and emotional adjustment of children with advanced cognitive development is not distinguishable during early childhood (Gottfried et al., 1994). Advantages in the cognitive realm were not associated with disadvantages in other areas of development, although some display superior social reasoning (but not necessarily superior social behavior) and adaptive functioning.

In general, children with advanced cognitive development have physical development that is ahead of same-age children with lower IQs, but this may be due to social class differences more than any other variable. Their coordination seems similar to that of their age mates. To the extent that very gifted children are accelerated in school (e.g., starting first grade at age 4), their physical development may appear slower because the comparison group is actually a year or two older. Relating to others in an appropriate way is often difficult, as the child can feel (and is) different. Additionally, their tendency to choose older children as friends focuses attention on their relatively immature physical development (Gottfried et al., 1994). These differences often increase the probability of their choosing noncompetitive types of physical activities.

There is a great deal of interest in the interaction of these young children with their family and family environment. Research findings in this area have been consistent since the 1920s. Gifted children are predominately first-born or only children. Most children with advanced intellectual development have been in consistently stimulating environments from infancy through their early elementary years (George, 2003). Their environments respond to the child's demands by providing early culturally and intellectually stimulating activities. Their families are able to provide stimulating environments in part because the families are typically of high socioeconomic status, with highly educated parents. Parents are typically involved, responsive, and nurturing and have high educational aspirations for their children (George, 2003).

Children identified as having advanced intellectual development are significantly more likely to enter school at an earlier age and are not likely to be retained at any grade level (Gottfried et al., 1994; Gottfried et al., 2006). Their teachers characterize them as working harder, learning more, and being better behaved than their nongifted counterparts. In general, they are more adapted to the demands of school. Being extensively read to in the early years is consistently associated with advanced intellectual development. Academically, these children excel and frequently skip grades during these years or are placed early into kindergarten or first grade.

As children move more clearly into the academic world, some who were not previously identified will be noted. It is not just what they do, but how they go about doing it. Gifted children seem to grasp the essence of the problem or situation or can relate the situation to an analogous one. They may skip steps in the process or are intrigued by finding alternative solutions. Again, their persistence, high ideals, self-discipline, and independence are noted (George, 2003).

Children with advanced cognitive development can be difficult because they do not fit the norm. They are often highly curious, beyond just being interested in things. They are interested in details and ask many questions. They have a broader knowledge base than their peers and may become bored, especially during group instruction. They may be intense and highly critical, argumentative. They work with information by manipulating it, as opposed to just remembering it. They like mysteries and complexities and enjoy learning. They may have unusual or silly ideas and make keen observations (George, 2003).

They may seem to be more emotionally stable, but they are not invulnerable to life circumstances. They may feel that they are different from others, but at young ages they are not completely aware of the cause of the differences; they may feel superior because they are "smart." However, they may have fewer skills in peer relationships.

Interestingly, although there is a strong belief that young children with disabilities should be identified early and that early intervention is effective, this belief has rarely been applied to gifted and talented children. Sankar-DeLeeuw (1999) found that only half of the primary teachers responding to the survey thought that gifted and talented children should be identified during the early years of school.

Gifted young children are often intrigued with reading and writing and have a large vocabulary.
Courtesy Penny Low Deiner

Assessment of Gifts and Talents

Some feel that high intelligence alone is not enough, that giftedness is an interaction among above-average ability, creativity, and sustained interest. Currently, we are moving away from using IQ as the sole method of identifying giftedness, just as we are moving away from it as the only way of identifying children with intellectual disabilities toward the concept that there are multiple talents or intelligences (George, 2003).

STANDARDS The National Association for Gifted Children has developed gifted programming standards. Standard 2 addresses assessment.

Standard 2: Assessment

Description: Assessments provide information about identification, learning progress and outcomes, and evaluation of programming for students with gifts and talents in all domains.

2.1 Identification. All students in grades P–12 have equal access to a comprehensive system which allows them to demonstrate diverse characteristics and behaviors that are associated with giftedness.

2.2 Identification. Each student reveals his or her exceptionalities or potential through assessment evidence so that appropriate instructional accommodations and modifications can be provided.

2.3 Identification. Students with identified needs represent diverse backgrounds and reflect the total student population of the district.

2.4 *Learning Progress and Outcomes.* Students with gifts and talents demonstrate advanced and complex learning as a result of using multiple, appropriate, and ongoing assessments.

2.5 Evaluation of Programming. Students identified with gifts and talents demonstrate important learning progress as a result of programming and services.

2.6 Evaluation of Programming. Students identified with gifts and talents have increased access and show significant learning progress as a result of improving components of gifted education programming (NAGC, 2010, p. 9).

A more global definition of giftedness opens the door for a variety of specific areas in which unique talents might be displayed. Despite broadening of the definition, the most frequently used means of identifying gifted children is intelligence tests: the Stanford-Binet Intelligence Scale (5th ed.; Roid, 2003), the Wechsler Preschool and Primary Scale of Intelligence–III (WPPSI–III; Wechsler, 2002), or the Wechsler Intelligence Scale for Children IV (WISC-IV; Wechsler, 2003), where they would exhibit an IQ of approximately 130 or higher.

State and local definitions of children who qualify as gifted and talented vary. How these terms are defined determines who is included or excluded. It is one of the most controversial areas of education, and a difficult one. Depending on the definition and method of testing, children with other special needs can be included or excluded from this group.

Labels of all kinds are misleading and infer that children can be neatly divided into groups. This applies to children identified as having gifts and talents as well as those with intellectual disabilities. Generally speaking, these labels suggest variations along a continuum we refer to as intelligence. All agree that individuals vary in abilities. It is the arbitrariness with which we divide up the continuum and label individuals that is of concern. This is particularly true when we label young children as either "slow" or "fast" and use this label to project future achievement or lack thereof. In general, we look at children's present level of functioning as a prediction of future abilities. In cases where there are major changes in a child's life, we cannot accurately predict future progress.

There is general consensus that multimodal testing is necessary to identify children who are gifted and talented. Most recommend a combination of testing (intelligence, achievement, creativity), observations of parents and teachers, work samples, a portfolio, and so on. A professionally administered individual intelligence test is traditionally part of the battery. These measures are well designed, normed, and validated. They allow for observations by a well-trained examiner. It is useful to look not only at the total score but also at the profile.

An IQ score reflects what a child has already learned and hence is a "static" approach to assessment. Another view of assessment tries to assess problem-solving ability, the interactive "dynamic" quality of learning potential. Vygotsky's (1934/1987) theory and methodology focuses not on what children can do independently but on what they can do with adult support or scaffolding. He labels this their zone of proximal development (ZPD). To use the ZPD as an assessment paradigm, children are presented with a series of problem-solving tasks that they cannot solve independently. The child is asked to solve the first task but is told that assistance will be available. An adult then provides hints, suggestions, and repeated trials necessary for the child to solve the problem. Once the child has mastered the problem-solving strategies, he is presented with analogous and increasingly difficult problem-solving tasks. The evaluation then focuses on the child's ability to generalize and adapt the problem-solving strategy. The less help the child needs on the more difficult tasks, the broader the child's ZPD. Children with higher ability have broader ZPDs (Kanevsky, 1992).

Portfolios

Because of concern with the underidentification of children from minority groups, those with disabilities, and those from less affluent families, measures such as portfolios are being used in the identification process. In some classrooms, portfolio assessment is used with all children.

A portfolio is a collection of a child's work selected by the child (with younger children, and at the beginning of the year, there is more teacher input). These artifacts provide information about the child's attitudes, motivation, level of development, and growth over time (Salvia & Ysseldyke, 2007). The portfolio also provides important information for individualizing planning for children and conferencing with parents. Portfolios are useful for assessment for a variety of reasons, including the following:

- Portfolios are child driven.
- Portfolios involve a process of *collecting, selecting,* and *reflecting.* Teachers provide the guidelines for selecting (e.g., "Something you have done very well."). Children then reflect on their choice and add an artifact to that part of the portfolio. Children can dictate their reflections, or write or word process them with the understanding that creative spelling is acceptable. If children want to choose three-dimensional creations, then children or teachers can photograph the artifact (ideally with a digital camera so the child can choose the appropriate view and perspective). Again, the child reflects on her choices.

Gifted Motivation

Gottfried and his colleagues have proposed another dimension of giftedness: Gifted motivation. Based on IQ scores, children who are motivationally gifted were not necessarily intellectually gifted. Only 8 children in their sample were both intellectually and motivationally gifted. Using their data, Gottfried and Gottfried (2004) proposed the construct of gifted motivation. "Gifted motivation applies to individuals who are superior in their strivings and determination pertaining to an endeavor. Hence, motivation in the extreme is considered gifted just as is intellectual performance in the extreme" (Gottfried, Gottfried, & Guerin, 2006, p.437). Gottfried and colleagues believe that motivational giftedness should be considered as a criterion in the process of selecting children into gifted and talented programs and that teaching children to be motivated learners may be as important as teaching them academic skills (Gottfried et al., 2006). Motivationally gifted children were more environmentally engaged and requested more cognitively relevant extracurricular activities from their families. These findings lead to the concept of motivational giftedness. Motivationally gifted children were noticed to be harder working and learning more than their peer comparison group. None dropped out of school, and they were more likely to enroll in college and, at age 24, graduate school (Gottfried et al., 2006).

Multiple Intelligences

Gardner's (1983, 1993, 1999) work on multiple intelligences has raised questions about intelligence itself and how we assess it. For many years the assessment of intelligence has been based on the assumption that there is a single "g" factor as espoused by Charles Spearman (1863–1945). Tests such as the Stanford-Binet were based on this premise. About the middle of the century, David Wechsler (1896–1981) successfully proposed that there were two abilities underlying intelligence: verbal and performance. The Wechsler intelligence tests reflect these areas (2002, 2003). The latest revision of the Stanford-Binet test also acknowledges at least two aspects of intelligence because it measures verbal and nonverbal abilities as separate subscales (Roid, 2003).

Acceptance of Gardner's ides of multiple intelligences would require major changes in assessment processes. Some feel that a multiple intelligences approach to the identification of children with gifts and talents would increase the number of poor children, children from ethnic minorities, and children with disabilities who would be identified (George, 2003). They also feel that the information gleaned from the assessment process could serve to guide curriculum.

In some children, the potential for advanced cognitive development is identified early; in others, it is only apparent later in their development. Tests assume that children have had the same opportunity to learn. When this is not true, the tests may be biased. Many children who come from a home with lower socioeconomic status or who are English language learners may not be identified as gifted because they have not had the same learning opportunities as others. Likewise, children from different cultural backgrounds as well as those with disabilities are more difficult to identify. Tests that focus on divergent thinking and creativity have the potential for identifying some of these children (George, 2003). Gardner (1993) initially proposed seven intelligences where special talents may exist, and one more has been added, naturalist intelligence (Gardner, 1999). All children have a unique blend of these intelligences:

talented children are especially advanced in at least one intelligence area.

The characteristics for multiple intelligences were gleaned from the following authors: Fisher (1998); Farnan (2009); Gardner (1983, 1993, 1999); George (1997, 2003); Goleman (1995); Pierangelo and Giuliani (2001); Koshy (2002); Porter (1999); Reyes-Carrasquillo (2000); and Saunders and Espeland (1991).

Verbal-Linguistic Intelligence

Verbal-linguistic intelligence refers to the ability to appreciate and understand the various functions of speech and language and use language with sensitivity and clarity. Children appreciate the order, meanings, and rhythm of words. Decoding words and the rules of grammar is often a game. They like to invent new languages and play with words. They have extensive vocabularies and like to communicate. These children

- speak and read early.
- have accelerated literacy skills in stories, poems, drama, and writing.
- use advanced vocabulary.
- employ longer and more advanced sentence structures (use words like *however* and *although*).
- make up elaborate, coherent stories and fantasies.
- describe experiences with unusual depth and accuracy.
- memorize and recite stories and poems.
- prefer books with more words and plot than pictures.
- may be bilingual or interested in learning a second language.
- are interested in language in its many forms.

Logical-Mathematical Intelligence

Scientific reasoning, a love for abstraction, understanding of numerical patterns and problems, and an interest in mathematical operations characterize logical-mathematical intelligence. These children use logic, deduction, and reasoning and are good problem solvers. They are interested in categorizing, hypothesizing, experimenting, and developing arguments and in graphing, counting, and manipulating numbers. They are fascinated by how things work. Young children talented in logic and mathematics

- use advanced mathematical skills.
- use highly original reasoning.
- ask a series of logical questions focused on solving a problem.
- apply reason to solve concrete and abstract problems.
- enjoy using hands-on tools such as Cuisenaire rods, Uniflex cubes, blocks, puzzles, and an abacus to solve logical-mathematical problems.
- enjoy computer games and applications related to logical-mathematical reasoning.

Musical-Rhythmic Intelligence

Musical-rhythmic intelligence refers to the ability to use musical elements (pitch, timbre, rhythm, timing, and tone) at an unusually sophisticated level. Some children may have perfect pitch and the ability to identify a wide range of musical scores when only a few bars are played. They enjoy creating and listening to music. Musically talented children are intrigued with and notice sounds in their environment. Musically talented young children

- are highly motivated to practice and perform music.
- enjoy and frequently request music-related activities.
- respond emotionally to music even without clues from lyrics (might report that certain music makes them happy).
- can identify familiar songs by hearing the tune.
- sing in tune or close to it and can match pitch within their range.
- may sing to themselves and have good pitch.
- can identify the sounds of a particular instrument.
- prefer poems with sound and rhythm over narrative stories.
- dance, move, and clap in time with musical patterns and rhythms.
- have an excellent memory for melodies, music, and musical scores.
- show skill in reading music, singing complex songs, or playing difficult passages.
- are interested in composing music.

Visual-Spatial Intelligence

Visual-spatial intelligence is the ability to perceive the visual world accurately and then recreate that visual experience in art or graphics. It involves mental imagery and the ability to manipulate and transform images. These children are adept at puzzles and other spatial problem-solving activities. Visually talented young children

- show advanced drawing, painting, and sculpting with both technical skill and fine detail.
- remember in detail items, places, and pictures they have seen.
- have advanced eye-hand coordination.
- show attention to texture, color, and balance.
- respond emotionally to photos, paintings, or sculpture.
- share feelings and moods through drawing, painting, or sculpture.

Psychomotor-Kinesthetic Intelligence

Psychomotor-kinesthetic intelligence refers to the ability to control one's body or body parts skillfully. These children move expressively (as in dance) and are good at both informal and organized games and sports. Young children with psychomotor talents

- are skillful at movements such as running, jumping, climbing, dancing, and other movement activities.
- have an accurate and relaxed sense of both static and dynamic balance (hopping on one foot, walking a narrow line, balancing a beanbag).
- use gestures, body movements, and/or facial expression to show or mimic emotions and ideas.
- can adapt motor skills in game situations.

Intrapersonal Intelligence

Intrapersonal intelligence is the ability to form an accurate model of oneself and use this model effectively to evaluate situations. It involves detecting and distinguishing one's feelings. These children understand themselves well and know their own strengths and weaknesses. Young children with intrapersonal intelligence

- are aware of their needs, problems, and emotional state and can identify their emotions.
- can express their perceptions and understandings through speaking and writing.
- can understand the cause of feelings.
- can recognize the difference between feelings and actions.

Interpersonal Intelligence

Interpersonal intelligence focuses on the ability to recognize and distinguish the moods, intentions, and motivations of other individuals. These children often emerge as effective leaders and organizers. They are empathetic and sensitive to the needs and desires of others. Young children with interpersonal intelligence:

- interact easily with both children and adults.
- are sought out by other children for play.
- are able to enter an already-playing group of children and be accepted.
- can influence other children toward their goals (positive or negative).
- understand cause-and-effect as it relates to behavior and consequences.
- recognize when their behavior yields certain predictable results.
- can take another child's perspective.
- are better at resolving conflicts and negotiating disagreements.
- can motivate and organize peers toward their goals (positive or negative).
- have strong leadership abilities.
- have a sense of justice and fair play for themselves and others.

Naturalist Intelligence

Naturalist intelligence is the ability to discriminate among living things, including humankind, plants, and animals as well as other features of the natural world such as clouds and rock formations. In the past, this ability had great survival value. It involves a kind of pattern recognition that is valued in certain sciences. Today this ability may enable individuals to discriminate among makes and models of cars or even sneakers. Young children with naturalist intelligence

- are interested in pets and concerned about their care.
- are curious about nature and look for and collect plants, bugs, rocks, or other natural objects.
- are interested in identifying plants and gardening.
- enjoy the outdoors and outdoor activities such as hiking, camping, and fishing.
- are curious about the human body and the way it works.
- may enjoy cooking.
- are interested in electricity and magnets and the way things work.

••• Other Intelligences

Gardner and his colleagues are exploring the possibility of additional intelligences, including existential intelligence, the ability to reflect on the philosophical questions about life and death.

Children Who Are Twice Exceptional

Some children with gifts and talents also have coexisting disabilities, hence are twice exceptional. The number of children in this category is difficult to determine accurately, although estimates are about 300,000 in the United States (Baum & Owen, 2004). The National Education Association (2006) estimated that, of the 6 million students with specific learning disabilities, ages 6 to 21, who received educational services under the IDEA in the 2000–2001 school year, approximately 6 percent were also academically gifted and need their unique learning needs met.

There is no tracking system for children who are twice exceptional. Sometimes only one aspect of a child's learning is recognized; that is, the child might have a specific learning disability but, because of his cognitive abilities, performs at grade level, so the learning disabilities are not identified (Nicpon et al., 2011). Likewise, children with specific learning disabilities may have significant difficulties in learning to read and expressing their ideas in writing. They may show significant weaknesses in organization and in processing input. "They are not 'slow-thinkers'; they are 'slow-receivers'" (Peer, 2000, p. 69). They may also have difficulty with short-term memory. These characteristics make it challenging to identify them as gifted. Further confounding identification is that these children use their strengths to compensate for their limitations. Hence, they may appear to be average learners, with neither the giftedness nor the learning disability identified.

Children with specific learning disabilities and other disabilities may feel stressed as they become aware of the differences between their level of thinking and their ability to show others what they can do. If identified as having a specific learning disability, the focus typically moves to remediation—a focus on the deficits rather than on an overall picture of the child. The academic emphasis becomes a multisensory approach to teach reading, spelling, grammar, and perhaps math. This approach "requires regular, detailed teaching, review, practice and overlearning" (Peer, 2000, p. 71). The approach is often successful in increasing the skill level of the child, but does not address the area of giftedness and, if not creatively done, may "turn off" the gifted learner. The child's areas of strength may not be identified, and hence alternative modes of processing information are not encouraged. A strengths-based approach presents material at a high academic level in a way that is accessible to the child while at the same time spending time working on areas of deficit. However, the emphasis is not on the deficit, but rather on ways to compensate. For children with dyslexia, technology can play a key role. Computers can read to those who need it and word processing can meet the needs of others (Peer, 2000).

Children with ADHD may need behavioral intervention, yet what is reinforcing for a gifted child with ADHD may be very different from what is reinforcing for children who are not gifted. They may have problems with sustained attention but may enjoy a challenge and may have high untapped levels of creativity (Nicpon, 2011).

Children with behavioral and emotional problems present another challenge. Their problems interfere with concentration, motivation, and task completion, resulting in underachievement. Families who do not understand the educational system well can compound these factors. Teachers may become so focused on a child's behavior that their expectations for the child are low and they are critical of the child. Behavioral and emotional problems are complex and may require therapy and medication as well as educational interventions. The focus is on finding educational tasks that the child is motivated to do using her strengths.

For children with physical and sensory disabilities, the challenge involves removing the physical barriers of the disability to the greatest extent possible by using adaptive technology and focusing on the child's strengths.

Culturally Diverse Children with Gifts and Talents

Public schools can be daunting places for both children and parents, especially those with limited English. Parents may not be aware of the opportunities for their children to participate in programs for the gifted and talented, and children may be working so hard learning English that their other gifts and talents are overlooked. Children with limited English proficiency are underrepresented among children who are identified as gifted and talented. A variety of factors contribute to this problem. Certainly, one factor is the assessment process itself. In addition to the obvious language-related issues, culture plays an important role in deciding which skills are valued. No tests are culture free. To the extent that a culture values social skills and nonverbal abilities over cognitive skills and verbal abilities, children from that culture are less likely to be identified as gifted and talented in the United States. Identification processes that use a broader definition of intelligence, such as Gardner's (1983, 1993, 1999) multiple intelligences or Gottfried and colleagues' motivationally gifted concept, are more likely to identify these children. Embedding cultural factors in the specific ways in which gifts and talents are expressed may also help identify some children (Lopez, 2000). Using multiple referral sources (e.g., teachers, parents, and peers) and multiple measures of intelligence and creativity, formal and informal, increases the probability of identifying children. Some teachers tend to see white children more positively and are less likely to refer African American and Hispanic children for gifted programs than white children. The difference in referrals is statistically significant and close to a full standard deviation (Tenenbaum & Ruck, 2007). Teachers and other school personnel may need training in cultural diversity to better understand the beliefs that underlie what is valued in different cultures (Fletcher & Massalski, 2003).

THE EVIDENCE BASE

Mentoring Mathematical Minds (Project M³) was designed to identify children in grades 3 through 5 who are capable of handling advanced mathematical concepts. By broadening the selection process to use more than IQ scores and selecting children based on nonverbal math ability, including such things as spatial sense and reasoning as well as teacher recommendations, the number of black and Hispanic children included in the program was increased. The project teaches math concepts several years beyond grade level standards. Early results show promise. Children have made significant gains on standardized math tests compared to control groups, and lower-income children have made the greatest gains. Children in the program also did well in the district-level math assessments.

Other researchers identified five categories that contributed to the successful identification of culturally, linguistically, ethnically diverse, and high-poverty children who could profit

Using gifted motivation and multiple intelligences may help identify culturally diverse children with gifts and talents.
©Cengage Learning 2012

from gifted and talented programs. They include modified identification procedures and program support systems such as identifying high-potential children and providing advanced work prior to identification; selecting curriculum designs that support children from culturally, linguistically, and ethnically diverse groups, and those who live in poverty, building home-school partnerships; and using program evaluation practices that highlight student success.

Sources: Briggs, Reis, & Sullivan, 2008; O'Neil, 2006.

IMPLICATIONS FOR EDUCATORS

Teacher identification plays a strong role in deciding who gets into programs for the gifted and talented. Reflect on the characteristics of children who are gifted and talented. How might these characteristics be different for children from different cultures and ethnic groups? How might you change your ideas if they do not include children from these groups?

Loyalty may confound identification. To the extent that the child feels she must emulate the majority culture when its standards and values are different from those of her family and culture, the child may suffer a conflict of identity. If the child moves in the direction of the majority culture to achieve success, she may begin to feel that she does not belong anywhere. She is "too Brazilian to be American and too American to be Brazilian." She may feel that she is not accepted at home or at school. If a child is singled out for her individual achievement in cultural groups that value affiliation, she may feel isolated and rejected (Bailey, 2000).

Using noncompetitive activities and some group work, and privately supporting children may help. Also, lending support to children who span more than one culture by helping them understand what behaviors are acceptable in particular social-cultural situations may assist children and help them build positive relationships with gifted children from other cultures, whether or not the child has been identified as gifted (Bailey, 2000). Teaching all children social-emotional skills and knowledge of other cultures should be included in curriculum at all levels (Goleman, 1995). Working with therapists or school counselors may help some children. A more individualized selection of books for certain children may prove useful as a springboard for discussion. Mentors from a child's culture may provide the child with both emotional support and a role model. As children increase in age, the computer can help children learn at their own pace, one based on individual ability and interest, while providing relative anonymity.

Instructional Strategies

A variety of strategies are used to meet the needs of children with gifts and talents. As with other diverse abilities, professionals support different positions. Some feel that children with gifts and talents should be included in the regular classroom to the maximum degree possible and that teachers of gifted and talented children should support regular teachers in providing an appropriate learning environment for these children. The key issue here is whether regular classroom teachers can provide an exciting and stimulating environment for children who can achieve at 3, 4, or 5 years or grade levels beyond their peers (a similar issue to what we face with children with intellectual disabilities). The record from the past in this regard is discouraging. If this *can* be done, it doesn't appear to have been done well, and some feel that separation, especially with increasing age, is desirable. If regular classrooms could be designed to meet the needs of all children, including gifted children, then all children would profit. However, we do not seem to be doing that well. Although colleges and universities increasingly are requiring preservice teachers to take courses on teaching children with disabilities, few require such courses for the gifted and talented.

 The Gifted Education Programming Standards provides some guidance for setting up the learning environment and curriculum planning. In addition to providing student outcomes for these areas the NAGC provides the evidenced-based practices. They are too long to include here but can be accessed at www.nagc.org.

• • •

Standard 1: Learning and Development

Educators, recognizing the learning and developmental differences of students with gifts and talents, promote ongoing self-understanding, awareness of their needs, and cognitive and affective growth of these students in school, home, and community settings to ensure specific student outcomes.

1.1 Self-Understanding. Students with gifts and talents demonstrate self-knowledge with respect to their interests, strengths, identities, and needs in socio-emotional development and in intellectual, academic, creative, leadership, and artistic domains.

1.2 Self-Understanding. Students with gifts and talents possess a developmentally appropriate understanding of how they learn and grow; they recognize the influences of their beliefs, traditions, and values on their learning and behavior.

1.3 Self-Understanding. Students with gifts and talents demonstrate understanding of and respect for similarities and differences between themselves and their peer group and others in the general population.

1.4 Awareness of Needs. Students with gifts and talents access resources from the community to support cognitive and affective needs, including social interactions with others having similar interests and abilities or experiences, including same-age peers and mentors or experts.

1.5 Awareness of Needs. Students' families and communities understand similarities and differences with respect to the development and characteristics of advanced and typical learners and support students with gifts and talents' needs.

1.6 Cognitive and Affective Growth. Students with gifts and talents benefit from meaningful and challenging learning activities addressing their unique characteristics and needs.

1.7 Cognitive and Affective Growth. Students with gifts and talents recognize their preferred approaches to learning and expand their repertoire.

1.8 Cognitive and Affective Growth. Students with gifts and talents identify future goals that match their talents and abilities and resources needed to meet those goals (e.g., higher education, opportunities, mentors, financial support) (National Association for Gifted Children, 2010, p. 9).

• • •

Standard 3: Curriculum Planning and Instruction

Educators apply the theory and research-based models of curriculum and instruction related to students with gifts and talents and respond to their needs by planning, selecting,

adapting, and creating culturally relevant curriculum and by using a repertoire of evidence-based instructional strategies to ensure specific student outcomes.

3.1 Curriculum Planning. Students with gifts and talents demonstrate growth commensurate with aptitude during the school year.

3.2 Talent Development. Students with gifts and talents become more competent in multiple talent areas and across dimensions of learning.

3.3 Talent Development. Students with gifts and talents develop their abilities in their domain of talent and/or area of interest.

3.4 Instructional Strategies. Students with gifts and talents become independent investigators.

3.5 Culturally Relevant Curriculum. Students with gifts and talents develop knowledge and skills for living and being productive in a multicultural, diverse, and global society.

3.6 Resources. Students with gifts and talents benefit from gifted education programming that provides a variety of high quality resources and materials (National Association for Gifted Children, 2010, p. 10).

At the student level, the main modifications that are used in early education to accommodate gifted learners include accelerating the pace of instruction; enrichment, which refers to a broader, more varied educational experience; or extension, which is a deepening of the curriculum. Enrichment and extension may be done together.

• • •

Acceleration

Acceleration is a process of moving through an educational program at a faster rate than usual or at a younger age. The assumption underlying acceleration is that some children learn at a consistently faster pace than others. As curricula become more rigid, there is the potential for a mismatch between children's abilities and the subject matter presented.

Because of the range and types of acceleration options, it is difficult to be for or against them. Advocates for acceleration argue that it provides increased efficiency and effectiveness of instruction. They see it as providing bright students with appropriate educational opportunities, and continuing challenges that will maintain their enthusiasm and excitement for learning. Some see it as a necessary first step in meeting the needs of gifted children (VanTassel-Baska & Stambaugh, 2006). Those opposed to acceleration are concerned about possible gaps in general knowledge. They are also concerned that children who show academic excellence at young ages may not maintain this level of performance and that the accelerated demands may be too great for the young child's experience and sophistication. That is, the programming is not developmentally appropriate and children do not have enough time to play, indoors or outside. There is some concern about later social maladjustment as students reflect on lost opportunities. Some are worried about the effect of acceleration on emotional adjustment, with concerns about friendship patterns, increased pressure, and lack of outlets for expression, as well as reduced opportunities for extracurricular activities. In a survey study of primary teachers, only 7 percent supported the early school entrance of gifted children (Sankar-DeLeeuw, 1999). However, longitudinal studies continue to show positive results in cognitive development from acceleration and no negative impact on social and emotional development (Colangelo, Assouline, & Gross, 2004).

There are many different types of acceleration. Children can be admitted to kindergarten prior to the age specified. They can skip a grade. They can be placed in classes where two or more grade levels are combined. They can have subject or content matter acceleration, that is, be placed at a more advanced grade level for one or more subjects (e.g., a kindergartner going to first grade for reading and math) (VanTassel-Baska & Stambaugh, 2006).

For children identified as having gifts and talents during the preschool years, certainly the most frequent option is early admission to kindergarten. This is viewed as the least disruptive option for children who are intellectually advanced and within six months of the usual entry age (Koshy, 2002). Studies show that children who were *selected* for early school entrance, were within a year of the school-entrance age, and were considered mature for their age have performed well. Some feel that acceleration itself is not enough and that an enriched curriculum must be offered as well (Feldhusen, Van Winkle, & Ehle, 1996). When early school entrance is seen as the most appropriate way to provide acceleration, the following areas should be considered:

- Is the school willing to accept the child?
- Is the classroom flexibly structured and the teacher willing to include the child?
- Will any learning gaps be filled?
- Does the child have the necessary fine motor skills?
- Does the child have the prerequisite reading readiness skills?
- Does the child want to go to school?
- Do the parents want the child to go to school?
- Is the child comfortable being one of the youngest children?
- Is the child socially and emotionally ready for school?
- Is the child average or large for his or her age?
- Has the child had previous experience in school settings? (Baggett, 1992; George, 2003; Koshy, 2002; Porter, 1999).

At times, rather than accelerating a particular child, small groups of gifted children may be placed together.

Cluster Grouping

Cluster grouping involves placing a small group of identified children together in a classroom. By placing these children together, they are included in the classroom but have the opportunity to do more complex learning as a group (Winebrenner & Devlin, 1998) and can support each other as they learn. This has the potential of meeting the learning needs of this group of children while they are in the regular classroom. This is not designed to replace other programs but is a way of ensuring that gifted children get their learning needs met. Depending upon the size of the school, clusters can be of all eligible children or they can be based upon a concept such as Gardner's multiple intelligences.

Teachers of cluster groups work at both compacting the regular curriculum and differentiating it. Enrichment minicourses can help children investigate topics of interest to them. All children are empowered when topics are designed around their interests. As a community of learners, they can develop critical thinking skills, new knowledge, and the ability to work as a team (Schlichter et al., 1997).

IN THE FIELD

As a second-grade teacher in an inclusive program, I have struggled to provide quality extension activities for gifted and talented children in my room. Even though I tried to enrich instruction for the children with advanced development, I felt as if I weren't providing them with quite enough "push." I eventually came up with a system that worked.

I decided to add more centers to my program. I added a center that would be especially appropriate for children with advanced development. At the same time, these children could receive more individualized instruction with the paraeducators to help reinforce skills or teach unique concepts.

I assigned a learning activity to all the children in my classroom but changed the activity slightly for different levels of children. For example, if the class were studying fruit, I would group students homogeneously and assign them to an appropriate activity. Everyone would be studying fruit, yet at a level that was appropriate. This allowed children with disabilities and children with gifts and talents to all work on the same topic while learning at the level each needed. I feel that through careful planning and reflection, I have improved instruction not only for children with gifts and talents but also for all of my students. I just wish I felt as confident in this area as I do when I plan for the children with disabilities.

Differentiated Curriculum and Instruction

Curriculum that is differentiated for each child builds on past achievements, presents challenges that allow for additional achievements, provides opportunities for success, and removes barriers to participation (George, 2003). Like universal design, this system involves devising tasks that are appropriate for a range of abilities. It does not require labeling children; it does require meeting individual children's needs. Overall, the goal is to raise the achievement of all children and to ensure that all children achieve their personal best performance (George, 2003).

There is no single strategy for differentiation; rather, it is an approach that adapts the content, process, and concepts across subject matter areas to meet the advanced children's needs (NAGC, 2010). For children who are gifted, it involves broadening the curriculum to include information that is not traditionally part of the curriculum at a particular level. George (2003) suggests that one consider the following factors before choosing a method of differentiation:

- Is the method flexible enough for children to develop at their own pace?

- Does the method support the acquisition of higher-order thinking skills?
- Is the method both intellectually stimulating and emotionally protected?
- Is the method likely to alienate a child from peers or provide information that will be repeated later?
- Does it foster teamwork or individual differences?

For children with gifts and talents, many aspects of their curriculum are differentiated with enrichment of the general curriculum. Many enrichment programs use a model that increases awareness of higher-order thinking skills. Bloom's (1985) taxonomy, for example, moves from lower-level to higher-level thinking skills: knowledge, comprehension, application, analysis, synthesis, and evaluation. The goal is to go beyond comprehension to ensure that children have the opportunity to use higher-level thinking skills. That is, it is not enough that a 5-year-old can name several different dinosaurs (knowledge) or make a chart showing the different sizes of dinosaurs (comprehension) or even compare those who are carnivores to those who are not (application). Children who are gifted and talented should be challenged to predict what might have happened if dinosaurs had not become extinct (analysis), write a play about life when dinosaurs lived (synthesis), or debate theories of causes for dinosaurs having become extinct (evaluation).

Other methods of adding depth to the curriculum include the design of in-depth integrated units. Units designed for gifted and talented children profit from an overarching theme around which long-term study can be organized. Longer units and fewer of them allow greater depth. Obviously, these themes must be chosen carefully; some considerations include those listed here:

- Importance of topic and sufficient depth and breadth
- Application to other learning areas
- Assumptions about prior knowledge
- Inclusive gender, cultural, and ethnic awareness
- Outcomes in terms of products and process
- Assessment and evaluation (Walker, Hafenstein, & Crow-Enslow, 1999)

Instruction has to be differentiated. Teachers must have multiple ways of structuring lessons to challenge each child at the appropriate level and to assess differentiated curriculum and instruction. Assessment also has to be differentiated. Some children who are gifted and talented may require off-level or above-grade-level tests to accurately assess what they have learned (NAGC, 2010).

Partnering with Families

Parents play a crucial role in the life and education of all children. They are their child's first and ongoing teachers, and they are vital sources of information and support as well as an invaluable resource for understanding their children. Parents

are role models for their children. It is important that parents are empowered with knowledge, skills, and resources to support their developmentally advanced child (Moon, 2003). Teachers and families need to work collaboratively to support children's education. This is particularly true when parents have limited English and there is the possibility that the child moves into a miniature adult status because of advanced verbal skills. Gifted children need parents, and parents need the support of teachers as they make decisions about their child's education so that these decisions are congruent with both the family's values and the child's abilities (Moon, 2003).

The general principles of good parenting apply to parents of children who are gifted and talented. However, the challenges to parents make this problematic. Children with advanced language skills can challenge parents on issues of independence and control at an early age. Their reasoning abilities and problem solving may place them in situations they do not have the maturity to cope with. Their advanced development in one area can foster inappropriate expectations in other areas and frustrate both children and parents.

IMPLICATIONS FOR EDUCATORS

During the early years, encourage parents to devote time and energy to language, help their children use their imaginations, and read stories interactively and discuss them with their children. Support parents in learning about the educational system and how it works. A positive parent–teacher relationship shows parental respect for the educational system. It is a way of showing that parents openly value education and learning. Every day parents must walk a fine line between high expectations and putting so much pressure on a child that he feels like a failure even when he succeeds. This is particularly difficult when children's development is uneven and expectations generalize so that children are expected to do well at everything, even tasks that do not interest them or that they are incapable of performing.

- Develop a regular method of communicating with parents. This can be through short conversations when children are picked up or dropped off, telephone calls, or e-mail.
- Keep parents informed about the units and themes in your classrooms. If there is an appropriate community component, tell all parents about it.
- Encourage parents to initiate communication if their child does not want to come to school or appears bored and uninterested in school or seems to be unusually stressed.
- Provide parents with a list of children's books and other materials that are developmentally appropriate, yet academically challenging, for their child.
- Provide parents with resources for themselves as parents to better understand the challenges in raising a gifted child.

Guidelines

Children who are gifted and talented need your help in stretching and adapting the curriculum to include and challenge them. Use your creativity to make variations on activities and to increase the cognitive demands while at the same time ensuring these children are part of the group. Emphasize similarities and differences in all children without making value judgments.

1. *Use open-ended activities.* Plan some activities that will take several weeks and that can go in many directions.

Ensure that what children start can remain in place until the activity has ended. It often takes more than 1 day to increase complexity.

2. *Develop independent work habits.* Don't equate independence with isolation. Children come to school to learn with and about other children. Your challenge is to plan activities with a range of difficulty that allows all the children in the class to participate and learn at their particular ability level.

3. *Teach socially acceptable ways of dealing with emotions.* Many times children are frustrated if they know they are different and learn things more quickly or if what they can do does not keep pace with their understanding.

4. *Provide variety and depth.* Activities and experiences that allow children to explore and find areas of interest are essential, but also allow children to concentrate their energy in one area to a depth that satisfies them.

5. *Emphasize both how and why something occurs.* Go beyond what is happening to help children focus on why and to ponder how to make things happen differently.

6. *Emphasize group and individual problem solving.* Learning to work in groups is an important aspect of problem-based learning. All children need the skills to participate in group problem solving as well as individual problem solving, and even to reflect on the differences.

7. *Encourage higher-level thinking skills.* Go beyond knowledge and comprehension to emphasize analysis, synthesis, evaluation, and problem solving.

8. *Use less repetition and a faster pace.* Give children important problems to solve.

9. *Offer a high degree of complexity.* Increase the number and variety of materials, processes, and outcomes.

10. *Support different learning styles:* Allow children to choose and use different learning modalities to complete assignments.

11. *Provide flexibility in the pace at which learning opportunities are provided* to enable some children to benefit from acceleration and others the opportunity to explore a topic in depth.

12. *Give children opportunities to develop advanced literacy skills* while at the same time ensuring that the reading material is developmentally appropriate.

13. *Expose children to advanced concepts in an age-appropriate way.*

14. *Provide caring environments that support healthy risk-taking behaviors.*

15. *Require divergent thinking.* Provide children with activities that require divergent thinking; have them think about "what if" things they take for granted will *not* happen such as if the earth stopped turning, rain didn't fall, or didn't quit falling, and so on.

There are many ways to encourage divergent thinking and creativity. The easiest is to tell children to be creative—obvious, yet it does work.

1. *Regard creativity as a process.* Encourage different ways of doing things, regardless of the results (which may look far worse than another child's more traditional product).

2. *Value creative achievement in comparison to a personal norm, not a universal one.* If a product or process is new for a child, it is creative for that child, whether or not society would see it in that light. On the other hand, if a child can use materials well and is not doing so, do not reward such behavior; question it.

3. *Reward creativity.* Verbally support children who come up with new ideas. Ask about how things could work in different ways.

4. *Encourage children to ask questions and to explore materials.* Provide new and varied materials to peak children's interest.

5. Ask questions that stimulate creative thinking. Here are some useful questions:
   "What do you think about . . . ?"
   "What (who) interests you?"
   "What can you say about this?"
   "Is there anything here worth thinking about?"
   "Do you have any ideas?"
   "Does this remind you of anything?"
   "What ground rules do we need to set up?"
   "Does this stretch your brain a little or a lot?"
   "Does this look (sound, feel) interesting?"
   "What else can you make out of this?"
   "What would you like to rearrange?"
   "Do you see any other possibilities?"
   "What can we do with this? What else?"
   "Where should you (we) start?"
   "What's funny about this?"
   "Can you change this to make it something else?"
   "Can you use this in a different way?"
   "Start your mind working on this, but don't tell me for a minute."

6. *Encourage children to make the commonplace different.* Do not always ask what things are or require that products have a specific purpose.

7. *Accept failures as a natural part of the learning process.* Provide a safe, well-organized, but flexible environment where children feel safe about making mistakes and testing hypotheses.

8. *Use toys and materials with fewer details.* Encourage children to add or imagine the needed details. Support children in creating a play scenario with scenery, script, and more.

There are a number of practices you should strive to avoid with children who are gifted and talented. You want to encourage creative thinking, not discourage it. The following responses and procedures are great discouragers.

1. *Avoid putting pressure on children for conformity.* This does not mean the children should be excused from following class rules, but rather that they should not be judged as strange because they think differently. Tell children why something must be done. Whether gifted or not, children like to have reasons for what must happen, and it increases the probability that the directions of a task will be completed.

2. *Avoid emphasis on traditional gender roles.* This tends to discourage creativity for both boys and girls because it narrows both roles. All children need exposure to varied nontraditional and nonsexist roles.

3. *Avoid pressuring children to succeed.* In a success-oriented culture such as ours, failures present problems. Fear of failure prevents many children from being creative.

4. *Avoid insistence on regimentation.* Having regimented activities that cannot be expanded or contracted, or requiring all children to finish projects in a specified amount of time, discourages children with advanced and delayed intellectual development. Be flexible with time limits to allow for the creativity of the process.

5. *Avoid highly structured materials.* Materials that do it all—that are brightly colored, move, make noise—don't leave as much room for imagination as those that allow the child to create the movement, function, and noise.

6. *Avoid using disparaging phrases.* Refrain from making comments that discourage creativity, such as "Don't be silly." "It won't work." "That's not our problem." "Don't be so sloppy." "Do it the way I said to." "What's the matter with you?"

Judging children or their activities often discourages creativity. Parents are also in a position to encourage or discourage creativity.

IN THE FIELD

My class of 4-year-olds was making reindeer out of clothespins, which required them to glue the wooden pieces together as well as add a nose and eyes. Tony proudly displayed his finished product, and I said, "Tell me about it." He explained how all the other kids' reindeer had two eyes but he wanted his to only have one. I told him that there was a special name for a

race of men-giants who had one eye right in the middle of their forehead: Cyclops. We looked it up in the dictionary. Tony went home and proudly told his father about making the reindeer. His father predictably asked, "Where is the other eye? All reindeer have two eyes!" To which Tony responded, "Not mine, mine is a Cyclops." The father looked it up in the dictionary and brought Tony and the reindeer into school early the next day. "We have to speak," he said, handing me Tony's Cyclops. "What is this? If my son is going to make a reindeer, it has to have two eyes, not one." I could almost feel Tony's hurt feelings. He was crushed that something he was proud of was maligned. Tony's father and I agreed that Tony would have time to make another reindeer with two eyes, just like all the other kids. He could keep his Cyclops, and I could try to encourage creativity, but Tony would also conform when necessary. "Well, what about the other kids?" the father asked. I replied that the other children would also be given a chance to make another reindeer and that if they wanted to put three eyes on them, that would be allowed.

Tony was embarrassed after his father left and needed some reassurance. I told him that in life there are different ways to do things. He replied, "Yeah, but with my dad I'll always be making two of something: one for him and one the way I want it to be."

Curriculum Adaptations

Activities for young children who are gifted and talented need to be more varied, cover a broader range of materials, be done in greater depth and with an emphasis on higher-order thinking skills, and offer the possibility for an individualized focus.

Social Awareness

Encourage children to practice developing social skills. Although gifted children may have greater understanding of how to solve interpersonal problems in the abstract, generating solutions and implementing them are different skills. They need to practice both. Some of the activities in the Resource Chapter 1 are specifically designed to support children who are gifted and talented, for example, Activities 1–13, *Photograph Story* and 1–6, *Family Flags*.

Social Competence

All children need to feel good about themselves. Children with advanced development, although ahead of their peers in many ways, often hold themselves to high standards that are difficult to live up to. Children who are very good in one area may expect to be good in all areas and when they are not, they quit participating.

1. Support children with realistic feedback about their performance.

2. Encourage children to try new activities and take risks in areas where they may not excel.

3. Help them learn the skill of supporting other children in areas of strength and in asking for support from their peers in other areas.

4. Encourage children in all areas of development, not just those they are good at.

5. Encourage children to take leadership roles within the classroom and school.

All children want to be included and accepted. Highlighting both similarities and differences helps all children belong.

1. Have children complete the following statements individually and talk about the differences in answers in a small group with a sensitive adult.

   "I feel happy when . . ."

   "I feel sad when . . ."

   "I am frightened by . . ."

   "I get angry when . . ."

   "I feel proud when . . ."

   "I am like others because . . ."

   "I am different from others because . . ."

2. Talk about children's similarities and differences, but emphasize all people have strengths as well as limitations. Use yourself as an example.

3. Decide upon some character traits you would like all children in your classroom to display. These might include respect, self-discipline, determination, fairness, and so on. Concentrate on a different character trait each week or month. Have children reflect on themselves relative to the trait and whether it is one of their strengths.

Social Studies

Social studies can cover traditional and nontraditional roles and occupations and provide information on unusual ways of doing things. Design lessons that give children an understanding of themselves, their role in society, and in the global world in which they live.

1. Cook foods from many different countries and eat them in traditional ways. Tempura and fried rice can be eaten with chopsticks, fondue with a long fork, and so on. Discuss the food and the utensils used and how they are adapted.

2. Explore varied occupations such as plumber, computer programmer, baker, physicist, linguist, professor, investment banker, producer, professional athlete, and pest exterminator. Let the children's interest guide your choices. Be sure to give a nonsexist presentation of occupations and value all occupations.

3. Help children make maps of the area around the school and learn the basic elements of a map (such as legend, scale, direction). Have them find a treasure using a map.

4. Show children pictures of different types of housing and houses around the world and discuss how they are adapted to different regions.

5. Discuss the role that rules play in your class and talk about laws and the need for laws, why people should obey them, and the need for someone to enforce them and why.

6. Help children learn to take different perspectives. Read books such as J. Scieszka's *The True Story of the Three*

Little Pigs (London: Puffin, 1996), in which the wolf got into trouble because he had a cold.

7. Have children put themselves in the roles of historic or famous people. Ask the children what they would have done.

English Language Arts

This is often an area of strength for children who are identified as gifted and talented. It is also a familiar activity for children, who usually enjoy being read to and may read independently. Reading is a strength in itself, as well as the basis for learning many academic subjects, and should be encouraged. Your job is to refine, expand, and enrich children's language skills as you continue to instill a love of reading and writing.

Speaking and Listening

Help children use descriptive, colorful, precise speech and make word pictures for people.

1. Encourage fluency and flexibility in verbal interchanges. Encourage colorful phrases, vivid descriptions, and analogies.

2. Encourage brainstorming. Do not make value judgments or belittle odd responses, because children will then refrain from making comments freely.

3. Help children think creatively and then translate their thinking into expressive language by giving them situations to talk about:

   "Describe your life as a 6-year-old bicycle."

   "You are a gingerbread mix about to be made and then baked. How would you feel (when made and eaten)?"

   "You are a camera. What kind of pictures will you take? How do you work?"

4. Encourage children to learn new vocabulary words by providing a life perspective that allows for differences; teach concepts such as *some, sometimes, often, frequently,* and *rarely.*

5. Encourage children to expand their speaking by *substituting* a person, place, time, or situation. If they were talking about the *beach,* how would the event change if it were the *desert*? Have them imagine being on a savannah in Africa or a pass in the Andes in winter. They may have to do some research to support their imagination.

6. Make a "Word Graveyard" on a bulletin board and list words that are used too often in speech and writing. Also make a bulletin board of more exciting, creative, and expressive words to use.

7. Teach a second language.

Reading

Read to children even when they are capable of reading independently. Read "chapter" books. Children's development is uneven; what conceptually intrigues them is often beyond their reading level. Also, provide books children can read independently as well as ones with creative illustrations.

1. Ask questions to evoke creative responses after reading a story or poem and compare this story with another one, and talk about the authors and illustrators.

2. Have a wide range of recorded books available for independent listening at learning centers. Such materials allow you to individualize programming while supporting inclusion.

3. Stop at a critical point when reading a story and ask the children to make up an ending. Then compare their ending with the one the author wrote. Pose different circumstances and see whether children can make the characters respond to these.

4. Dramatize stories, songs, and poems. Provide props.

5. Have children generate stories to go with the pictures in wordless picture books.

6. Have a box of words that can be made into different compound words (clothes + line = clothesline; sun + light = sunlight). When possible, have drawings on the back.

7. Have children match labels on boxes to a shopping list, and categorize boxes and cans of food by type.

8. Teach children to use prior knowledge before reading and to use interactive strategies during reading. This will allow children to read more complex material.

9. Visit the library and discuss not only its books and other materials (e.g., newspapers, computers, copiers, CDs, DVDs, large print books, audiobooks), but also the events the library sponsors. Discuss how the library is organized and how people get library cards and borrow and return items. Set up a lending library in your class. Follow up by sending a note home to parents about your visit, and encourage them to join the library if they are not already members.

● ● ●
Writing

Many children are fascinated by writing and by thinking about themselves as authors.

1. Encourage children to write their own stories. Have a tape recorder available for them, or write stories they dictate. Some children may want to word process their stories. Support creative spelling. However, if the spelling is too creative, you may have to ask the child to "read" the story to you.

2. Encourage writing as a joint project. Have children share ideas and help each other, as well as provide adult support. Encourage children to use mapping to organize their ideas. See Activity 2–27, *Mind Mapping*.

3. Help children make their personal timeline and note important events in their lives. Children are more likely to remember how old they were rather than the actual year.

Age	Important Event	Memories
0	I was born	None
2	We moved	I don't remember much
3	Sister born	I didn't like her, and everyone made a fuss over her and ignored me.

Help children think about their past and what they remember about it. Then encourage children to journal as a way of documenting the present.

4. Encourage children to use a writing journal. Give them time to write and support them in writing on any subject that interests them. They can use the journal as a way to correspond with you and/or with other children. This supports appropriate social skills and may even start new friendships. See Activity 2–26, *My Diary*.

5. Help children think of themselves as writers and publishers. See Activities 2–18, *Publishing*, and 2–50w, *Book Making*.

● ● ●
Language

Help children understand the conventions of standard English. Encourage them to learn not just vocabulary but the nuances of the language.

1. Help children learn more descriptive words and encourage them to paint word pictures (e.g., instead of using *walked*, to use *sauntered, ambled, tramped, marched,* etc.). Then have the children walk across the room depicting that type of movement. Have them use a thesaurus to find additional descriptors.

2. Teach children about Braille and sign language as forms of reading and writing.

3. Talk with children about some of the rules that govern the English language, and briefly discuss those rules. Talk about rules in general and their utility, and compare English to other languages.

Follow up a trip to the fire station with block building and language experience stories.
©Cengage Learning 2012

Discovery

Exploring the environment in a realistic way encourages discovery. Children can learn the scientific method, expand to theoretical concepts, and move to more abstract levels. They can learn to use reference materials and the Internet to encourage and support problem solving and to have access to materials that are not available in the classroom.

Mathematics

Math activities should be manipulative and game-like. Help children establish basic number sense and numeration then move with children in directions that intrigue them. Help them think about math as a method of problem solving, give them the vocabulary to communicate about math, and help them with mathematical reasoning. Be sure to support boys and girls equally; stereotyping discourages girls from developing strong math skills.

1. Help children recognize patterns and relationships in their environment. Teach them the use of "pair" for a single object—pair of scissors, pair of pants, pair of glasses—and explore their ideas about why this label is used and what else they could use it for.

2. Have children count a wide variety of objects: raisins, blocks, children, and sets made up of manipulatives of different shapes and sizes.

3. Have children group and count by sorting and classifying: seven red buttons, three yellow buttons. Help them discover whole number operations such as addition and subtraction, and relate this to hierarchical classification as well as base 10:

   Furniture

   7 Beds + 3 Chairs + 2 Tables = 12 Pieces of Furniture (one 10 + 2 ones = 12)

   Once children understand the basics of base 10 thinking, use larger numbers.

4. Teach fractions through incidental learning as the occasion arises: half an apple, a quarter of a sandwich. Give children the entire object. They can count the pieces, put them back together to make the whole, and take them apart again. Measuring tasks are easily done at a water table, in the sandbox, or when making cocoa, gelatin, or a fruit salad. Encourage children to think about units of measurement, the different ways things are measured (e.g., weight, volume, temperature), and how this is done. Use both American measures and the metric system.

5. Use **rebus** recipe cards, and have children read the recipe and make different items. Encourage children to change the proportions of simple recipes and discuss the results. Children can create their own recipes or use one from a children's cookbook. See Activity 3–30, *Fruit Kabob*, for more ideas.

6. Teach some of the more unusual geometric shapes, as well as the relationship between three-dimensional and two-dimensional ones: oval/egg, circle/ball/globe, combinations of shapes (e.g., triangle and rectangle), cylinder, pentagon, and trapezoid. Help them describe, model, draw, and classify these as well as combine them to make other shapes.

7. Facilitate individual work in math concepts by having children use an abacus, Cuisenaire rods, Montessori-type materials (beads of 10), and Unifix cubes. These materials help children discover, experiment, and manipulate information rather than simply memorize facts. See Activities 3–7, *100's Game*; 3–33w, *Abacus*; and 3–46w, *Variations on Cuisenaire Rods*, for additional ideas.

8. Have children figure the next number in progressions.

9. Provide activities that involve mathematics with the scientific method. This connects math and science.

Science

Science provides the structure for gaining new experiences and developing reasoning skills. Encourage children to hypothesize and make predictions. Present problems that are inherently interesting from the child's perspective. Encourage children to observe closely what they do while solving a problem and document it. Help children learn to apply what they have learned by teaching them to see patterns, principles (general), and applications (particular) in science.

1. Use familiar concepts such as the wind, the sun, and water. On a windy day, make observations of the wind's effects. Draw on the children's experiences with the wind and their reaction to it. Share with them the tingle of the skin, the watering of eyes, the tossing of hair, and the bracing and turning of the body to cut through the blowing wind. Have them observe how clothes on a line are pushed by the wind and the differences in the way people walk facing the wind or with the wind at their back. Watch the surface of a pond or puddle as wind blows over it; watch rain change direction when the wind changes; listen to the sound of the wind. Reenact scenes from a windy day. Have children take a pretend walk on a windy day and have other children guess the direction and strength of the wind. Demonstrate a weather vane or windmill. Discuss machines that create wind such as hair dryers and electric fans. Demonstrate how seeds travel with the wind. Blow a small boat across a pan of water. Blow ping-pong balls across the table, then try to blow a tennis ball. Make pinwheels or kites. Talk about the relationship between wind and temperature and the wind chill factor. Read informational texts about the wind, check the Internet for additional information, and look up wind in reference books. Talk about the role the wind plays in hurricanes.

2. Visit an orchard and pick apples. Explore the parts of the apple. Experiment with the effects of heat and cold on apples. Have children predict what will happen

when apples are cooked. Compare the tastes of apple-sauce, baked apples, apple juice, apple butter, and dried apples. Find out what happens when you drop apples and bruise them.

3. Provide firsthand experiences and add depth to the experience by talking about where different animals live, how they protect themselves and their young, how and what they eat, and how they are adapted for their environment. Have children invent animals for particular climates or conditions, such as a lightweight animal with large, flat feet to live near quicksand. Provide informational texts, Web access, and reference books.

4. Help children focus on a particular problem they are interested in such as pollution. Make a mind map to look at contributing factors to the problem (see Activity 2–27, *Mind Mapping*). Have children use the resources in the classroom and Internet to learn more about pollution, and then revise your mind map. Encourage children to hypothesize about potential solutions and persist in generating various solutions to the problem, starting with what they can do as individuals in the classroom. Bring in an environmentalist. Show children how to use information that was obtained to make increasingly more accurate predictions regarding outcomes.

5. Encourage children to use the scientific method before they actually do a task: state the problem; form a hypothesis; observe, experiment, gather, and record data; interpret data; and draw a conclusion. Have them determine whether their hypothesis was right or wrong, and then speculate about why it was accurate or the parts that were inaccurate. Then have children make new hypotheses to further test their thinking.

Technology

Technology allows children to work independently yet capture an experience to share by using a digital camera and downloading or printing the picture. Use tape recorders to capture stories told by the children. Technology holds unlimited potential for children with gifts and talents. Software can be chosen to enhance the development of children and can be tailored to their individualized learning needs in a developmentally appropriate way. Computers support independent and small group learning as well as providing the necessary scaffolding to enable children to perform tasks they could not master independently. The key is the ability of the adult to choose appropriate software and match it to the needs and desires of the child. Mobile software such as electronic tablets can support children's learning and be available to a small group of children working on a project.

1. Integrate computers into the curriculum—don't think of them as a stand-alone feature. Use software that allows children to make choices and be in charge, to control the flow and direction of the program and not merely respond.

2. Use a speech synthesizer to verbalize each letter or word the child inputs. Have the child write a story on the computer, complete with pictures.

3. Encourage children to work at the computer in pairs or small groups.

4. Choose software or applications that become increasingly complex as the children learn the basics and move on.

5. Teach children how to identify, select, and use a variety of developmentally appropriate software packages.

6. Teach children how to use a digital camera to save or share experiences or creations with other children and adults.

7. Encourage children to record stories or to leave messages for each other on a tape recorder or cell phone.

8. Encourage children to have e-mail pen pals from other countries or other places in the United States (with adult supervision).

Wellness

Children with gifts and talents, unless these lie in the motor area, will have motor skills closer to their chronological age than to their mental ability. Their ability to plan what they want to do may exceed their ability to do it. This is especially true for a child who is one of the youngest members of the group. There is a tendency for children who are not good at motor skills to avoid them. Children need your support to participate.

Health and Safety

Health and safety are important because children's curiosity and experimentation can lead to problems. The "What happens if I swallow a penny?" or "Will I bubble like the washing machine if I eat detergent and jump around?" syndrome can have dangerous side effects. (A trip to the poison control center can be stimulating, but it is best to avoid making it.) Children must learn to check with adults before exploring some things. They also need feedback on how to report their specific feelings if they are sick, and a clear understanding that this is not the time to be creative.

1. Help children read labels and sort items based on whether or not the contents are safe to play with. Add new items and help children learn to classify unknown objects as "not to be played with" and "not to be eaten." Don't use food for art.

2. Discuss the safe use of simple tools such as hammers and screwdrivers. Have safety goggles available and discuss why they are used.

3. Talk about safety devices (e.g., helmets, seat belts, safety glasses), their use, and what can happen if you don't use them.

4. Discuss where different foods grow and compare fresh foods with canned or frozen foods. Introduce foods that are from other parts of the country or other parts

of the world. Talk about the nutritional value of food and the concept of organic food.

5. Talk about nutrition and discuss why it is important to eat at least five different fruits and vegetables a day. Talk about the colors of fruits and vegetables and the nutrients they supply. Make shopping lists of items to get at the grocery store, and chart the categories of items they plan to purchase.

Physical Education

Help children understand that some things they can conceptualize are difficult to carry out. Ensure children develop fundamental motor skills to allow them to participate in games and sports.

1. Create an imaginary obstacle course. Have a child climb, dodge, or wade while other children try to guess what the obstacles are. Then have everyone do it.

2. Have children walk through imaginary substances, such as mud, deep sand, sticky paper, a swamp, or a hot sidewalk. Have others guess what the substances are and join in.

3. Have the children help create an obstacle course either inside or outside. Check for safety before children actually use the course.

4. Help children invent their own scenarios to play outside on jungle gyms and other large pieces of equipment. This is also a way of improving social skills.

5. Do yoga on a regular basis.

6. Plan so that all children are participating in moderate to vigorous physical activity daily.

7. Discuss physical fitness and talk about ways to become more fit. Talk about NASPE's recommendation of accumulating at least 60 minutes of structured and 60 minutes of unstructured physical activity a day. Talk about the difference between structured (teacher leading and participating) and unstructured physical activity (children actively playing). As a group, decide how much moderate to vigorous activity they are getting in the classroom and include some individual variations. Talk about how to increase this (e.g., by jumping once as each child's name is called or with 3-minute dances), and incorporate suggestions into the school day. Make plans for getting both structured and unstructured physical activity at home. Individualize the plans and encourage children to use the plan for a week. Record their results and then discuss what worked and didn't work and how they might change their plan to make it work better.

Sensory Motor Integration

Provide opportunities for children to have a variety of experiences that integrate motor skills with visual, hearing, and kinesthetic experiences. Make activities so intriguing that children want to participate.

1. Introduce children to some unusual sensory experiences that seem to defy logic or change states. Have them help you make goop (equal parts of cornstarch and water) and silly putty (one part liquid starch to two parts glue), and then play with the products they make. Help them think about the process of making and using these materials and why they are unusual. See Activities 3–20, *Goop*, and 3–51w, *Flubber*.

2. Encourage children to experiment with a variety of media, and relate this to their control of the media and the outcome (e.g., crayons vs. markers, watercolor vs. poster paint).

3. Have children compare their outcomes when they use brushes (in varying degrees of thickness), crayons (e.g., thin, thick, cone-shaped), or paint (in a variety of densities), encourage children to think about the implications of shape, size, and density on their final product.

Small motor skills may be challenging if children's fine motor skills have not kept pace with their cognitive abilities. Through creative planning, motivate children to use and refine these skills.

1. Have a wide variety of materials and an abundance of them (two or three sets instead of one) so that children's creations are not limited by scarcity of materials.

2. Encourage children to plan and make predictions before they begin manipulating the materials: "How many blocks do you need to make the foundation?"

3. Use short pieces of heavy yarn or string to teach children knots and simple macramé.

4. Bring in a bicycle and have the children help change the tire. Discuss air, volume, and shape. Then change the tire on a wheelchair or wagon to expand the concept.

Creative Arts

Children can define problems, seek solutions, and explore their own creative interests.

Visual Arts

Encourage children to explore their world through the visual arts. Introduce activities that allow children to make their own decisions and exert some control over their world.

1. Set up art activities with enough space to enable children to work freely either alone or in small groups. Show children art from around the world. Talk about artists and sculptors and show their work.

2. Have children draw themselves as a "creature" that is either very large or very small. Discuss with them what they could do as the creature that they can't do as a human, and look at the drawbacks this creature would have based on size and configuration. See Activity 5–1, *Creature*.

3. Learning in the visual arts is predictably developmental. Younger children are interested more in the

process; as they grow older, the outcome is more complex and more important. Do not stifle creative growth by imposing adult standards on children; however, don't praise work that is mediocre for a particular child. Encourage children to evaluate their own art.

4. Repeat activities such as easel painting or making collages, and vary the shape, size, and kind of paper you use as well as the color and texture of the materials.

5. Encourage children to choose colors and to predict what new colors will be made by mixing colors (paint or food color). Add white and black to paint so that children can experiment with shades of color as well.

6. Do art projects with several steps, like crayon etching. (Color a design with a light crayon, color over the design with black crayon, then etch with a popsicle stick. Use tough paper that resists tearing.) Try again with crayon and paint: light-colored crayon, dark paint. Discuss why the paint doesn't adhere to where the crayon is. See Activity 5–3, *Crayon Rubbing*.

7. Teach children Origami, Japanese paper folding, which helps children translate ideas into three-dimensional objects.

8. Repeat activities with variations and help children explore the differences. Fingerpaint made with liquid laundry starch, cornstarch, whipped soap, and commercially bought fingerpaint. Add texture to fingerpaint with sand, salt, coffee grounds, glitter, and confetti.

9. Use tie-dyeing as an art and problem-solving activity. The children can put small blocks on material (or on a white T-shirt) and then make a knot with short pieces of heavy thread. The complexity of the design will depend on each child. Tie-dyed material can later be used in a sewing project.

10. Help children critique their own artistic outcomes as well as those of other artists. Discuss the dimensions of art and how different artists emphasize these dimensions.

11. Have children write about or discuss the meaning and feelings they get from famous paintings. Go to www.famouspainter.com and learn about the lives and art of such painters as Pablo Picasso, Salvador Dali, Michelangelo, Leonardo da Vinci, and Vincent Van Gogh. Then have them analyze one painter and paint like that painter.

Music

Music can contribute much to a child's physical, aesthetic, and intellectual development. It provides pleasure and creative experience, develops auditory skills, encourages physical activity, and increases the range and flexibility of one's voice. There should be a wide variety of musical experiences: listening, singing, and playing musical instruments.

1. Have a variety of different musical instruments available. Help children explore and evaluate the sounds of an instrument when it is held and played in different ways. See whether they can identify instruments in a recording. Talk about how instruments are alike and different (if you don't have the instruments, use photographs). Bring in acoustic and electric versions of the same instruments and have a musician play them. Have children choose an instrument and respond to "If I were (the instrument), I would. . . ." Make a class book from the responses.

2. Combine music and language experiences; have children make up new verses to familiar songs or make up their own songs. Play short parts of unusual instrumental recordings, and ask the children to describe what they imagined while listening.

3. Put stories to music and have children choose background music. Paint to music.

4. Have children make musical instruments (e.g., shoe box guitars, oatmeal box drums, waxed paper and comb). Help them understand how sounds are made, where they come from, and how to change them. Help them experiment with making sounds with different body parts (e.g., clapping hands, stomping feet, strumming finger across lower lip). See Activities 5–19, *Making Tambourines*, and 5–49w *Reeds*.

5. Introduce concepts of pitch, loudness, and duration by singing echo-type songs.

6. Play a variety of music, including classical, rock, jazz, blues, country, folk, big band, rap, and so on. Talk about how different music is made and help children reflect on their feelings and what they liked and didn't like when they listened to different pieces.

7. Use music that reflects different ethnic/cultural groups. Particularly listen to lyrics that tell a story.

8. Encourage children to select music to go with particular themes.

Movement and Dance

Encourage children to take advantage of the creative opportunities in movement and dance to express themselves through their body. Give them the freedom to explore this motor area.

1. Encourage a feeling of group belonging and at the same time foster creative movement. Have children "hold up the roof." Children "strain" together to hold up a pretend roof; they gradually let it down and then push it back up again. They can be ice cubes melting in the hot sun or a balloon deflating. Play "people machines" with or without noises. Repeat such creative movement experiences until the children are comfortable enough to experiment with their bodies and are interacting with each other.

2. Introduce children to some of the classics such as *The Story of Peer Gynt*, with the recording of the *Peer Gynt Suite* by Grieg; "Cinderella," with the recording of *Cinderella* by Prokofiev; "Hansel and Gretel," with excerpts from the opera *Hansel and Gretel*

by Humperdinck; stories about troubadours and Meistersingers, with excerpts from *Die Meistersinger* by Wagner; the fairy tale "Nutcracker King," with Tchaikovsky's *Nutcracker Suite*; and "Mother Goose," with the *Mother Goose Suite* by Ravel.

• • •

Dramatic Play and Theater

In the dramatic play area, too much may be worse than too little. Use props such as dolls and dishes with few details. Provide enough props to create ideas, and then challenge children to create and design props they need. If you provide all the necessary props, children will not improvise and exercise their creativity.

1. Have a small-group planning session to set up a store. Discuss the props needed, how to get them, and when the store should go into business. Create the store and evaluate its success. Use play money and a cash register and/or calculators. Write signs and prices for the store's specials. Make coupons for matching and literacy skills.

2. Plan a train or airplane trip. Look at maps to determine where to go. Have the children investigate weather conditions, how long it will take to get there, and what they will do there. Take the class to a travel agency that is willing to answer their questions and provide schedules and brochures. Be sure to include places where the children and their families are from.

3. Have children set up their own health food store. They can make veggie burgers, baked potatoes, and chicken out of construction paper or papier-mâché. Have them decide who will be the manager, cook, order taker, bagger, and customers. It can also be tied into cooking and snacking.

4. Help the children set up a small tent (outside, if possible). Discuss aspects of camping and backpacking, including the equipment, and take a "hike."

5. Add materials to the block or dramatic play areas to encourage children to write scripts, make props, and put on their play. Then do the play again with different children playing different roles.

6. Talk with children about the differences among theater, movies, and television. Invite a theater group to put on a short play for the children.

Routines and Transitions

This is a good time to individualize programming while not drawing attention to a specific child.

1. Use multistep directions during transitions.

2. Provide an early warning for transitions or agree that some projects don't need to be cleaned up daily but can be set aside to be continued the next day.

3. Have a center available for all children who finish early. This center should include choices of diverse, creative activities for different learning styles.

SUMMARY

- It is difficult to identify children with gifts and talents before age 3.
- Development of children who are gifted and talented is affected by their genes and their environment.
- Children who are gifted have a high general intelligence; children who are talented may be talented in only one area.
- The profession is divided over the best way to educate children who are gifted and talented.
- Acceleration allows gifted children to start school early, skip grades, or have advanced placements in some subjects.
- Enrichment expands and enhances the environment to increase the breadth, depth, and scope of children's knowledge and focuses on abstract thinking.
- Children who are gifted and talented may be included in the regular classroom or separated into special classrooms for all or part of the day.

EDUCATIONAL RESOURCES

Association for the Gifted, Council for Exceptional Children is a national professional association that promotes the welfare and education of children and youth with gifts, talents, and/or high potential. www.cectag.org/

Gifted Child Society is a nonprofit organization that sponsors activities designed to help gifted children, their families, and educators. Its website is organized into specific information for children, parents, and professionals. www.gifted.org/

GT World is an on-line support community for parents of gifted and talented children. It provides definitions, on-line materials, and many other resources of interest to parents and professionals. http://gtworld.org/

Harvard Family Research Project is designed to develop and evaluate strategies to promote the well being of children, youth, families, and their communities. They provide research updates for a variety of topics. www.hfrp.org/

National Association for Gifted Children is a national advocacy group for gifted children and provides standards for those who teach the gifted. It has great resources for parents and professionals and is well organized. www.nagc.org/

National Foundation for Gifted and Creative Children provides information for parents, professionals, and children. Information includes pen pals, brochures, reading lists, message boards, testing and referrals, and links to other sites. www.nfgcc.org/

Odyssey of the Mind—Mastery Education Corporation sponsors competitions for gifted children that encourage cooperation and creativity and has ideas for activities and other resources for gifted children. www.odysseyofthemind.com/

For additional resources, visit the book companion website for this text at www.cengagebrain.com.

Children with Special Health Care Needs

Mary was diagnosed with Down syndrome shortly after she was born. Like many others, she also had a heart condition, but this was not what would take Mary's life. I had followed her since infancy and visited on a weekly basis. Mary was an only child and both parents loved her very much.

When Mary was about a year old she would pull to stand and then start to cry. Initially, we thought it was because she didn't know how to get down and was afraid to fall. But when we looked at her face, she seemed to be in pain and she would always fall to one side. At first, the physician said this was normal for children with low muscle tone. A few weeks went by and bruises started to appear. The family went back for further medical consultation.

With tears in their eyes, the parents met me at the door; the father had taken off work to share the news. "Mary has leukemia. They say she only has six months to live and we have to decide what type of treatment to do. Please help." I went in and we sat on the couch. Mary greeted me as she always did, with a huge smile, and crawled up in my lap with one of her toys. I'll never forget that day or the ones that followed. We are supposed to accept death as part of life. I had been through the death of other children and I had accepted it. I also realized that what parents and children need is not detachment, but, as the parents pleaded, help. I assured them I would be there to support them through any decision they made, but they would have to make the decisions, not me. Mary would be loved until the day she died, but it was a roller coaster of chemotherapy, radiation, and long hospitalizations, accompanied by many tears, mine included. The hospital staff was wonderful, offering emotional support and counseling for the family, making provisions for visitation whenever possible. When Mary died, her parents called and said that they were going to bury her out of state in a family cemetery and they would call me when they returned.

They did call and wanted me to come for a visit. They said that I had been part of Mary's life since birth and felt it only right that I be part of her life in death. I reluctantly agreed. I dreaded the visit at first, but it was one I'll never forget and always treasure. The parents had taken pictures of the funeral and of the grave. Some may think this morbid, but they were so tender

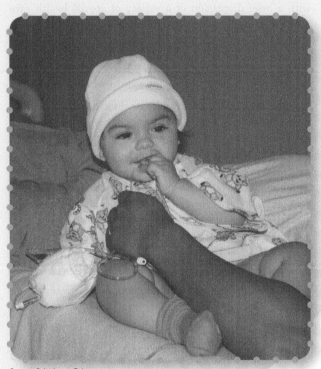

Courtesy Paige Lauren Deiner

and filled with love. Each parent dealt with Mary's death differently. Her mother wanted to take part in the funeral preparation; her father wanted little to do with it. But they respected each other's wishes. They went into detail about the service, and I listened, cared, and realized that I needed closure as well. And to think that these parents had no obligation to share anything with me. Her mother said, "No one can know if we will be alive tomorrow, but we do know we are alive today. We know that Mary was loved each day of her life and gave that love back in her short life. Thank you for going through the process with us." "You know," added her father, "you have been part of our family through the years as well, and we appreciate your understanding."

We may not be able to change things, but we can sincerely care, and there is nothing wrong with showing that care, while having a healthy balance of detachment when needed. I have learned more from families like Mary's than they probably ever learned from me; but we shared, we cared. ❋

Special Health Care Needs

All children will experience sickness during their developmental years. For some children, it is constant ear infections or colds, whereas others fight pneumonia and meningitis. However, some children are born with special health care needs, whereas others acquire chronic health impairments. Understanding how special health care needs affect the child's development and ability to learn is an essential task for all early childhood educators. This chapter provides you with a brief discussion of a variety of special health care needs and their implications for early childhood educators. It also provides guidelines to help you meet the needs of the children and curriculum adaptations that are designed to include children with special health care needs in the classroom.

Special health care needs pose different types of challenges for early childhood professionals. They may make us reassess our boundaries with families, look more carefully at our own role in the early intervention system, and even reflect on our personal beliefs. We may be intimidated by the terminology and feel inadequate because of our lack of medical background. However, the skills of an educator are an essential part of any team that works with children who have special health care needs.

Defining Special Health Care Needs

Health impairments interfere with normal growth and development. They continue for a long time, are likely to entail a prolonged convalescence, and may result in death. According to the American Academy of Pediatrics, "Children with special health care needs are those who have, or are at increased risk for, a chronic physical, developmental, behavioral, or emotional condition and who also require health and related services of a type or amount beyond that required by children generally" (McPherson, Arango, & Fox, 1998).

Special health care needs can be defined on two levels: categorical and functional. A categorical definition (e.g., juvenile diabetes) determines whether the condition falls within stated guidelines; the functional definition looks specifically at the child and how she is affected. In most cases, the categorical definition is used for reporting purposes and the functional definition for curriculum planning.

Unlike other disabilities that directly affect the child's ability to gain or process information, most health impairments interfere with the child's learning by decreasing the body's energy, its ability to remove waste, or its ability to grow. Some special health care needs shorten the life span, whereas others do not. Many are potentially life threatening. Some have periods of activity and remission. In some cases, the condition is progressive, getting increasingly worse, or it weakens other body systems, making the child more susceptible to other illnesses.

Children with special health care needs will be in the hospital more frequently than most other children, miss more school, and spend more time convalescing at home.

Special health care needs are covered by the IDEA if they interfere with the child's ability to learn.

> *Other health impairments limit strength, vitality, alertness, or heightened alertness to environmental stimuli limits alertness in the educational environment. They are chronic or acute health problems such as asthma, attention deficit disorder or attention deficit hyperactivity disorder, diabetes, epilepsy, a heart condition, hemophilia, lead poisoning, leukemia, nephritis, rheumatic fever, sickle cell anemia, and Tourette syndrome; and they adversely affect a child's educational performance (IDEA, 2004).*

If the health impairment does not interfere with the child's educational performance, children's civil rights are protected under Section 504 of the Rehabilitation Act (1973) and the Americans with Disabilities Act (2008). Children with health impairments cannot be discriminated against in admission to early care and educational settings, and *reasonable accommodations* must be made. However, people frequently differ about what they think is reasonable.

Children who are eligible for accommodations under Section 504, but require no special educational services, may have a 504 Plan. A child with a 504 plan does not have to have an identifiable disability under IDEA but requires some accommodations. (For example, a child allergic to peanuts may require a peanut-free area at lunch and specific hand washing for all children.) This plan is less complex than an IEP or IFSP. It may be only one page; however, it requires a team determination, including an administrator or designee, and must be signed by the parents or guardian. The focus is primarily on the modifications or accommodations required and the person responsible for overseeing and/or implementing the modifications. Like the IDEA (2004), Section 504 provides families with the right to due process if they feel their rights have been violated.

Prevalence of Special Health Care Needs

It is difficult to estimate how many children have special health care needs. At a practical level, when looking at children served under the IDEA, in 1976–1977, 8.3 percent of children in the public schools were classified as receiving educational services; of these, 0.3 percent had other health impairments. In 2007–2008, their numbers rose to 1.3 percent (U.S. DOE, 2010). However, this number does not include children who have special health care needs that do not need educational accommodations. The National Survey of Children with Special Health Care Needs estimated that 12.8 percent of children in the United States have special health care needs (van Dyck et al., 2004). Also remember that children with ADHD, when covered under the IDEA, may be placed in this category. It is likely that this accounts for some of the rise in numbers. Because a chapter was devoted to children with ADHD they are not included in this chapter.

The special health care needs population is increasing not only because of children with ADHD, but because there are more children with chronic illnesses and they are living longer due to better identification procedures and technological advances. Insurance and health care programs designed to meet these children's ongoing needs are not increasing.

Causes of Special Health Care Needs

The cause of specific special health care needs varies. Some result from infections, genetic factors, environmental influences, as well as prenatal and perinatal influences and factors that happen after birth. Some special health care needs are congenital and other conditions are acquired during the child's development from accidents, illnesses, or unknown causes. When a cause of a particular health care need is known it is included under that particular health care need. Although these conditions vary widely, children with special health care needs have some common characteristics that influence their quality of life.

Early Identification of Special Health Care Needs

The age at which an illness is diagnosed impacts the family. When an illness is diagnosed in infancy, the family may more easily integrate into their lifestyle the restrictive diet, complex medication regimen, frequent hospitalization, or dependence on technology. The child may know no other way of being in the world because the adjustments made in the family were done when he was so young. Children may have developed relationships and behavior patterns that allow them to adjust well until the challenge of adolescence. On the other hand, children first diagnosed as having a chronic illness at age 7 or older may be angry about the ways they must change their activities and interact with their peers.

A child's age also impacts her understanding of the illness and the degree of dependency the child has on her family. Young children rarely have an accurate idea about how their body functions and how the prescribed medical treatment relates to their wellness. The health impairment itself may be fairly clear; however, the effects on the child's social and emotional interactions present a far more complex situation. The child's knowledge about her health condition will be based on her age, what she has been told, and what she has overheard or surmised. This information may not be complete or necessarily accurate. It is important to find out what the child knows and to ensure that the needs of the child are met without further complicating the environment.

Some characteristics of special health care needs interact with a given family in ways that make the illness easier or more difficult to cope with. Rolland (2002) has developed a typology of chronic illnesses and disabilities based on their psychosocial demands. These are broad areas that impact families and children. In reality, the demands are on a continuum, with the anchor points used for descriptive purposes. This is a functional approach that groups chronic illnesses and disabilities according to key biological similarities and differences that have significant implications for children,

their families, and the professionals who work with them. Chronic illnesses and disabilities are not static; they have predictable patterns of development (Rolland, 2002).

• • •
Onset

Illnesses can be divided into those that have *acute* onset (such as a traumatic brain injury) and those that are more *gradual* (such as cystic fibrosis). In situations of acute onset, or where a gradual condition was not identified until an acute stage was reached (cancer), the family must rapidly mobilize itself to cope with the situation. All of the decisions and changes that must occur are compressed into a short time span. Families who have flexible roles, good crisis management and problem-solving skills, and who can call upon formal and informal support networks will manage an acute onset chronic illness better than others. When the onset is gradual, families have more time to adjust and accommodate to lifestyle changes.

• • •
Course

Chronic illnesses have three predictable patterns: progressive, constant, and relapsing/episodic (Rolland, 2002). A *progressive* illness (e.g., cystic fibrosis, muscular dystrophy, AIDS) is one where the child has symptoms of the illness and these symptoms progress in severity. There are no times when the child is symptom-free, and the progression of the illness requires constant adaptation on the part of the family. There are increasing caregiving demands and requirements to learn new caregiving tasks as the illness progresses. Families can "burn out" from the demands of care. At some point families may have to make fundamental changes in their worldview to cope with the child's illness. Families may see their life mission as caring for the child and define success as keeping the child alive. If the illness is terminal, the family may see itself as a failure when the child dies, even though it was inevitable. A disability that progresses slowly (e.g., muscular dystrophy) may challenge the family's stamina, whereas a disease that progresses more quickly (e.g., brain tumor) may result in an overload of stress through the constant demands of adaptation and decision making.

A health impairment or disability that has a *constant* course after stabilization, such as a spinal cord injury or Down syndrome, is more predictable. Once a level of functioning has been determined, there is more stability over time. Once families have learned the skills needed, family members cope with the particular circumstances and adapt these to the growth and development of the child.

Some illnesses, such as asthma and hemophilia, are *relapsing* or *episodic*. Times when the child is symptom-free (or almost symptom-free) alternate with times of flare-up. Strain on the family in this instance revolves around the changing demands of crisis/non-crisis situations and the continual uncertainty of when a crisis might occur. Crisis may be brought on by stress, either positive or negative. Flare-ups may occur at holidays, birthdays, marker events such as the first day of school, and vacations, times when families are already coping with change.

It is often useful to ask the parents what they have been told about the expected course of the illness and the potential triggers that move it from a chronic state to an acute one. Find out what the family itself has experienced over the course of the illness and how they coped with it. Although an episodic illness may not be as severe as others, it can be the most challenging psychologically (Rolland, 2002).

Sometimes, children with special health care needs fall between the cracks in an educational system. Schools that are flexible and responsive may alter a child's day by making it shorter, making breaks for medication unobtrusive, and reducing the demand for physical activity. Episodic illnesses are the most difficult. If a child is in school 10 days, out for 5 days, back for 3, out for 8, and so on, it is difficult to keep continuity in learning. Most schools require that a child be out of school for a particular length of time before becoming eligible for homebound instruction. A child with an episodic illness may never be out long enough to qualify, yet over time may miss a great deal of school. Some school districts have an attendance policy that automatically fails children who miss more than a particular number of days. In one district where we lived, if a child missed 28 days in an academic year, that child automatically failed the year. Such policies have implications for children with special health care needs and their families. The parents may have to be involved with bureaucratic red tape to obtain a waiver of school policy for their child, and they will almost certainly have to add home schooling to their workload. The Internet has the potential for solving some of these problems.

Outcome

The extent to which a chronic illness is fatal or will shorten a child's life span has an impact on families. The expectation is that a child with allergies will live a normal life span, whereas there is the expectation that a child with AIDS will not. Other illnesses, such as cancer, can be life threatening. Some illnesses such as cystic fibrosis, juvenile-onset diabetes, and hemophilia may shorten a child's life span.

All cultures and families give rights and privileges to those in the role of "patient," especially when the illness may be life-threatening. Those who are unsympathetic to this situation are often viewed as cold and unfeeling. Some children take advantage of this situation, called **secondary gain**, to avoid tasks they dislike, or to get special but unnecessary advantages. Different members of the family and team who work with a child may have very different views on the actual level of threat. It is useful to find out what different individuals believe about the child's prognosis (Rolland, 2002).

Incapacitation

The severity of the illness or involvement in more than one area also impacts the family. In young children, the severity of a particular illness may be unknown. Incapacitation results from impairments in different domains: intellectual functioning (e.g., fragile X), sensation (e.g., visual disability), movement (e.g., juvenile rheumatoid arthritis), decreased energy production (e.g., heart problems), disfigurement (e.g., severe burns), and may be exacerbated by social stigma. There is no direct correspondence between the amount of incapacitation and stress on the family. In fact, families often have the greatest stress when the disability is mild to moderate but the demands for care are ambiguous or unusual. That is, it is difficult for families to decide what they should do and how they should do it (Seligman & Darling, 2007).

Knowledge about the attributes of an illness or disability, that is, the onset, course, outcome, and incapacitation helps early childhood educators work with families and children in a meaningful way. Regardless of the particular illness, there are predictable phases of an illness.

Phases of Illness

With chronic illness, particularly when the expectation is that the parents will outlive their child, the time phases of the illness are important variables.

CRISIS

The crisis phase of a chronic illness begins when symptoms of the illness appear and includes the time when families are struggling to find out what is wrong with their child. It continues through the diagnosis and into the initial adjustment phase (Rolland, 2002). This is an unsettling time when families have to adjust to a new reality. They need to develop skills to work with a health care team, learn a vocabulary to understand their child's diagnosis, and accept the implications of that diagnosis as well as treatment-related procedures. They need to learn illness-related symptoms that accompany acute episodes and develop a flexible family system that is based on an uncertain future.

CHRONIC

The chronic phase is the time span, long or short, between the initial adjustment period and the time when the issue of terminal illness prevails. This is the long haul. Many parents, when asked, say they live it a day or hour at a time. Some families pull together and reorganize as a normal family in unusual circumstances; other families have less functional responses (Seligman & Darling, 2007).

TERMINAL

The final phase is when the inevitability of death dominates family life. Families then must deal with issues surrounding separation, death, grief and mourning, and the resumption of their family life (Rolland, 2002). Not all chronic illnesses shorten the life span, so some families may not move into the terminal phase. Different chronic illnesses bring different concerns and impact the child and family in different ways, but the impact of special health care needs is always present to some degree. Often, hospitals or community agencies will offer seminars on death and dying that may be helpful for educators and parents to attend. They may also have workshops for children including siblings.

Partnering with Families

Families, particularly parents, play many different roles during different phases of a child's illness. They are often expected to take on the role of clinician, in addition to the traditional parental role. They perform daily much of the therapy that the specialists prescribe each week or month. They monitor the child's health, seeking medical help in acute phases. When medical treatment is required, they are the ones to chauffeur the child to and from the appointments. Extra work and responsibility may tax the parent-child relationship. Mothers seem to have the most stress. They may become overly concerned about the child's daily activities, along with managing the rest of the family, and may become frustrated and angry.

Siblings, too, feel the stress and may feel neglected if their relationship with their parents has been disrupted, and then may experience guilt at feeling that way. They may show signs of irritability, social withdrawal, jealousy, guilt, behavior problems, anxiety, low self-esteem, and academic underachievement (Seligman & Darling, 2007). Older siblings may feel resentful that the family does not have enough extra money to buy them trendy clothing, go out to eat, or to go on vacations. These problems are very real and exacerbate an already stressful situation. Long-term planning and resource management are major issues in coping with changes.

THE EVIDENCE BASE

A telephone survey involving families of 13,792 children younger than 18 years identified 7 percent of the children as having special health care needs or disabilities. The definition of disabilities for the survey was "the presence of a limitation in age-appropriate social activities, such as school or play, or receipt of specialized services through the early intervention or special education programs." They were interested in finding out the differences in health services use and health care expenditures for children with disabilities including those with special health care needs and those without.

Children with disabilities and special health care needs have more health care expenses than children without these needs. Children with disabilities, including special health care needs accounted for 23 percent of the total health care expenditures for 1999–2000 while constituting only 7 percent of the

children. Interestingly, these health care expenditures were not uniform. The median health care expenditure for children with disabilities was $462, whereas families in the highest 10 percent income bracket spent $4,940 or more on health care for their child. The highest 10 percent accounted for 65 percent of all health care expenses for children with disabilities. They also reported paying $644 or more in out-of-pocket expenses. Low-income families with a child with a disability were 19 times more likely to exceed 5 percent of their family income on health care. Families with an insured child with a disability spent 51 percent less of their income on health care than did families without insurance. See Table 16–1 for additional comparisons.

Source: Newacheck, Inkelas, & Kim (2004).

REFLECTIVE PRACTICE | Clearly families who have children with special needs and disabilities spend more on health care. What do you think these figures mean for national health care policy and for families and children with disabilities and special health care needs? At a practical level, how do you think health care differs for children with special care needs in high and low income brackets? Reflect on how family income impacts the services the children receive and what it means to their quality of life.

A family's physical, emotional, and financial resources may be severely taxed as they attempt to cope with the effects and limitations imposed by a child's long-term condition. Families whose income places them just over the eligibility level for assistance programs may find themselves more financially strapped than others who qualify for federal or state aid. Some parents have even been advised to divorce in order to fall within the income limits for single parents. Beyond the strictly medical costs, there are many out-of-pocket costs such as transportation to clinics, meals that are eaten outside the home, babysitting for well children, toys and trinkets after procedures for the child who is ill, and lodging if hospitals are too far from home to make commuting practical. Additionally, the care requirements may keep one adult family member, usually the mother, out of the job market. Single mothers who work often lose jobs because they miss so much work. Conversely, some family members

TABLE 16-1 COMPARISON OF CHILDREN WITH AND WITHOUT DISABILITIES AND SPECIAL HEALTH CARE NEEDS

Category	Children with Disabilities & Special Health Care Needs	Children without Disabilities	Comparison
Hospital days	464 days/1000	55 days/1000	8 times higher*
Physician visits	4.6 visits/year	1.9 visits/year	2 times higher*
Nonphysician professional visits	3 visits/year	0.6 visits/year	5 times higher*
Home health provider days	3.8 days/year	0.04 days/year	95 times higher*
Prescriptions	6.2 meds/year	1.8 meds/year	3 times higher*
Health care expenditures	$2,669/year	$676/year	4 times higher*
Out-of-pocket expenditures	$297/year	$189/year	1.5 times higher*

Differences are statistically significant.

Source: Newacheck, Inkelas, & Kim, 2004.

may feel chained to their jobs because they are afraid if they leave their job the child's preexisting condition will prevent health insurance coverage in a new job.

Although children's special health care needs may vary, early childhood educators should use universal precautions and protective barriers with all children.

Universal Precautions and Protective Barriers

One challenge in early childhood settings is keeping children healthy and keeping disease from spreading. Because it is not possible to know who is potentially infectious, the following precautions were recommended by the Centers for Disease Control and Prevention (CDC). "Universal precautions," as defined by CDC, are a set of precautions designed to prevent transmission of human immunodeficiency virus (HIV), hepatitis B virus (HBV), and other blood-borne pathogens when providing first aid or health care. Under universal precautions, blood and certain body fluids of all patients are considered potentially infectious for HIV, HBV, and other blood-borne pathogens (CDC, 1996). Those that apply to early care and education settings follow.

Universal precautions should be taken routinely when there is bleeding (such as a nosebleed), a cut from a fall, vomiting, and even when children need to blow their nose.

- Wear disposable gloves when you come in contact with body secretions, including blood, stool, urine, and vomit, and when nonintact skin is anticipated. Avoid hand-to-mouth/eye contact when finished. Remove and dispose of gloves and wash your hands.

- Children who are sick and vomit need your love, care, and attention. Talk to them soothingly and pat their head while someone brings you gloves and probably a blanket.

If a sick child is not upset, he can walk to the bathroom; if the child is upset, wrap him in a blanket and carry him. You need a layer between you and the sick child.

- Wash all toys and surfaces that have come into contact with bodily fluids or stools with disinfectant such as household bleach (1:10 to 1:100 dilution). Wash all toys and books infants have used, as they may have been mouthing or dribbling on them.

- Cover all open wounds until a scab is formed.

- Use single-use disposable tissues for runny noses and dispose of them immediately in a secure receptacle. Never share tissues. Have children deposit used tissues in a wastebasket. Don't do it for them, and don't pick them up off the floor. If you need to pick them up, use another tissue and wash your hands.

- Wash your hands when you arrive at the center, when you come in from playing outdoors, and before preparing food, eating, or feeding a child. Wash them after toileting (yourself or a child). When you wash them, use liquid soap, make a heavy lather, and wash under running water for at least 10 seconds, particularly around the nails and front and back of the hands. Rinse by holding hands so the water flows from the wrists to the fingertips. Dry hands with a paper towel, then use the paper towel to turn off the faucet and discard (adapted from CDC, 1996, NAEYC, 2006a).

Nonwater-based sanitizers are also effective and in some instances may be used instead of hand washing. Although these precautions are designed for adults, children also need to wash their hands. To help them wash for 10 seconds (which can seem like an eternity) have them sing a song as they wash. Time the song. One verse of "Mary Had a Little Lamb" takes about 10 seconds.

Educators should wear disposable gloves when they come in contact with any body secretions, including when helping a child blow his nose.
© Cengage Learning 2012

Using these precautions reduces the risk of spreading communicable diseases.

Categories of Special Health Care Needs

Descriptions of the most common special health care needs follow. Remember, you are *not* expected to be an expert on every health impairment, but you do need to be aware of their characteristics and how they will influence your curriculum. In the past, as many as 80 percent of children died from infectious diseases such as tuberculosis, small pox, dysentery, pneumonia, typhoid fever, and diphtheria (Leung, 2003). With the advent of improved housing conditions, sanitation, a good water supply, and medical treatment, these diseases are no longer a major cause of death in developed countries. The special health care needs discussed in this chapter are chronic illnesses and are presented in alphabetical order. Those that you are more likely to encounter are given in greater detail.

••• Allergies

An allergy is a sensitivity to something that most other people find harmless. An allergic reaction is an inappropriate immune response. The risk of inheriting an **atopic disease**, such as allergies (e.g., **allergic rhinitis**) or asthma, is 50 percent when at least one parent has the condition (Lemanek & Hood, 1999). Allergies and asthma are determined by multiple factors including gender, race, genetic predisposition, environmental influences, and even the timing of exposure (Leung, 2003).

Allergies affect a child's development, behavior, learning, and relationships with others.

- Allergies account for one-third of all chronic health conditions that occur during the preschool years.
- About 35 percent of children with allergies have been diagnosed and treated.
- About 10 to 24 percent of the population has serious allergies, while another 26 percent experience minor allergies.
- Immunological diseases account for nearly 1 out of 10 office visits to pediatricians.
- Most allergies begin in childhood.
- Allergic rhinitis is the most common allergic disease in the United States, affecting up to 40 percent of children.
- Some allergic rhinitis is seasonal, caused by environmental changes (e.g., pollen). Although symptoms vary in occurrence and severity, symptoms are often worse in the morning. Children with perennial allergic rhinitis have a chronic condition that may be triggered by such things as pet dander and dust (American College of Allergy, Asthma, and Immunology [ACAAI], 2008).

Allergens fall into four general categories based on the site of contact:

- *Inhalation:* These substances are airborne and are taken into the body through the mouth and nose: plant pollen, fungi spores, mold, dust, feathers (down), animal dander, and perfume fall in this category.
- *Ingestion:* These substances, food and medication, are taken into the gastrointestinal tract. Five foods account for the majority of children's food allergies: cow milk, soy milk, soy, peanuts, and wheat (Sicherer, 1999). Seafood is another frequent allergen but it is less problematic in early care and education settings. Some oral drugs are common offenders: aspirin, sulfa drugs, and penicillin.
- *Skin contact:* These substances come in contact with the surface of the skin: ingredients in cosmetics, starch, wool, some detergents, poison ivy, sumac, and oak, animal scratches, pollen, and latex may cause allergic reactions.
- *Injection:* These substances enter the body through the skin by needle, like penicillin, or through stings and bites from mosquitoes, bees, and other insects, and can cause allergic reactions.

Although allergies vary, allergic reactions have some common characteristics (see Table 16–2).

IN THE FIELD

Jean Marie had a number of ear infections as a child and we had tubes placed in her ears. They seemed to drain continually. Then it occurred to me. A trip to the allergist provided the obvious answer: Allergies! She was young, cried through the testing, and at some point the physician decided that it wasn't worth it: Jean Marie reacted to everything.

So, we began to adapt. At first I didn't think it was going to be a big deal. Everybody I knew had allergies. My husband had asthma; I had problems with hay fever. We started in her room. We took out the rug, we took down the curtains, and all her stuffed animals went to live in the attic. We made a platform for her bed and the mattress was covered with plastic. We bought more sheets. They had to be changed every day. We bought more

TABLE 16-2 SIGNS OF ALLERGIC REACTIONS

Nose
Frequent runny nose (clear discharge), nasal itching and stuffiness, sniffling, rubbing the nose, frequent nosebleeds, frequent sneezing (four or five times in a row), wrinkling up the nose
Mouth, Chest, and Airways
Dry hacking cough, wheezing, mouth breathing, shortness of breath or rapid breathing, chest tightness; in food allergies, itching or swelling of the lips, tongue, or throat; tightness of the throat with hoarseness, nausea, and vomiting
Eyes
Red puffy eyes, rubbing the eyes, dark circles under the eyes, watery eyes
Skin
Skin irritations and rashes, pain, itching, swelling, hives, eczema

Source: Asthma and Allergy Foundation of America, 2008.

clothes—if it went over her head once, it was "dirty." And, we changed the way we ate. No chocolate, cheese, milk or milk products, peanuts, tomatoes, corn, and so on. The corn was actually the worst because so many things are sweetened with corn syrup. Going to the grocery store was a new experience. It took twice as long because I had to read all the labels.

And then, of course, there were the allergy shots. Every Thursday afternoon at 4:00 we went to the doctor's office. Waiting was the worst. She would tell them her name and then we would sit, I would read to her, she would whimper. Then the call came. The whimpering changed to crying, and then it was over. Everyone was telling her it didn't hurt and that it wasn't that big a deal. Perhaps it wasn't to them. Then she would sit on my lap and I would talk to her. (You had to wait 15 minutes to be sure she did not have a reaction.) It got better, but every week it was an hour and a half of her life and mine.

She started to sleep through the night and the black circles under her eyes disappeared. We struggled through birthday parties with chocolate cake (I brought a white cupcake for her), visiting friends whose houses were not allergy-free (most children came to our house to play), and wanting a pet (we settled on a turtle after several chameleons died). I assume the situation will get better, but, from where we now stand, the long haul still looks pretty long.

An allergic reaction works something like this: The first time the allergy-prone person runs across an allergen (e.g., ragweed), he makes large amounts of ragweed IgE **antibody**. The IgE molecules attach themselves to **mast cells**. The second time that person has a brush with ragweed, the IgE-primed mast cell will release its powerful chemicals, and the person will suffer the wheezing and/or sneezing, runny nose, watery eyes, and itching of allergy (Schindler, 1997). Most reactions occur within seconds or minutes after exposure to the **allergen**. The reaction can be mild or serious, confined to a small area of the body or may affect the entire body. **Anaphylaxis** is a sudden severe reaction that occurs within minutes of exposure, can get worse very quickly, and may lead to death within 15 minutes if not treated. Symptoms include anxiety, confusion, difficulty breathing and swallowing, fainting, light-headedness, and dizziness in addition to others (PubMed Health, 2010a).

THE EVIDENCE BASE

Pediatric Allergies in America surveyed about 500 parents of children under age 18 with allergies and a comparison group of 500 parents of children without allergies. Parents verified that their child had been diagnosed with nasal allergies and experienced them or had been treated for them in the past 12 months.

- Seventy-six percent of children with nasal allergies said spring was the worst time of year for allergies.
- Forty percent of children with allergies had allergies that interfered with the child's sleep, only 8 percent of children without allergies had sleep problems.
- Twenty-one percent of children with allergies indicated that allergies limited the child's activities, compared to 11 percent of parents of children without allergies.
- Forty percent of children with allergic rhinitis reported that this allergy interfered with their school performance compared to 10 percent in the comparison group.
- Forty-six percent of children with allergic rhinitis had headaches and ear and facial pain although the most bothersome symptom was a stuffy nose (27%).

- Forty-eight percent of children with allergies used prescription medication to treat allergy symptoms.
- Fifty-seven percent of those using medication changed medications because of the side effects, and 15 percent stopped taking the medication altogether.

Source: American College of Allergy, Asthma, and Immunology (2008).

Food allergies are a worry. One food allergen that causes concern in early childhood settings is peanuts and peanut butter. Although very few children have allergies that are severe enough to be life threatening, many children do have reactions that cause swelling and breathing difficulties (an asthma-type reaction). In a severe reaction, an immediate injection of epinephrine will save the child's life. Most children who are allergic to peanuts know that they are. The problem is in the hidden sources where peanut oil is used in the preparation of products, or peanut butter is used as a thickener—again, a very low-level ingredient in a product. Children who are highly allergic can react by breathing the fumes of someone eating peanut butter and also by directly touching someone who has not washed her hands after eating peanut products. Some allergists feel that the claims are an overexaggeration, but parents of children with allergies are concerned. Many schools have peanut-free zones in the cafeteria. Some airlines are peanut free. Other food allergies, especially unusual ones, cause concern.

IN THE FIELD

I walked into the facility's child care center and stopped as I stared at a 3-year-old child eating a banana, smearing the yellow goopy stuff all over her face. I turned to leave—but the child care provider saw me and started talking to my little girl.

"It's okay," she said. "Go enjoy your workout."

"I know this sounds weird, but I'm a little scared to leave. My daughter has a horrible allergy to bananas. If someone just touches a banana and then touches her she breaks out in hives, and then her eyes swell shut and she starts to wheeze."

"We deal with allergies all the time. Don't worry," the provider responded.

"All right, but I need whoever is going to watch her to scrub their hands before they pick her up," I said. "And she can't play with the little girl who is eating the banana."

The provider smiled at me. She reassured me that they deal with allergies all the time and there would be no problem. I walked away and met a friend to swim. We chatted about work and life as we swam lap after lap, but about 20 minutes into our workout, I looked at her and said, "I can't do this."

I explained about the bananas, jumped out of the pool, took a fast shower, and ran back to the child care center with the Benadryl in my hand. The banana-eater had left. Serena was on the other side of the center playing quietly. She looked happy and symptom free.

I felt both relieved and guilty. Of course, other children have allergies and I should have trusted the center to deal with my child's problems, but I still worry. I feel like I can do everything in my power to prevent allergic reactions at home, but it's very hard to do that out in public—especially when it's not a normal allergy, like to peanuts, but rather an odd one.

In addition to food, insect bites can be problematic and even fatal for some children. A bee sting often results in localized swelling and redness, which indicates only a mild allergy. A serious allergic reaction causes more generalized swelling and/or hotness about the face and neck, followed by difficulty in breathing and more severe bodily reactions. A sting to a severely allergic child can result in death if treatment is not immediate. If families know their child is allergic to bee stings, they will usually tell you and provide information on what to do, and perhaps even provide an "epi pen." This is a vial of epinephrine that can be given by injecting it into the large muscle of the thigh. The child will still need emergency care, but the injection will provide more time to get it (Medline Plus, 2007a).

IMPLICATIONS FOR EDUCATORS

You play an important role in the diagnosis of allergies in young children and their treatment plan. Learn the signs of typical allergies described in Table 16–2. Ask all parents whether their children have known allergies of any kind or if they suspect they might, based on family history. The information will help you screen lunch and snack menus, choose a class pet (or not), and prepare in advance against insect bites and other potential allergens encountered during field trips. Find out what reaction the child is likely to have, what you should do if the reaction occurs, and what the side effects of the child's medication are.

Evaluate your classroom in light of what you have learned. If you have children who are allergic to airborne substances, you will need to increase your awareness of the chemicals used to clean the classroom, and to think about how and when the room is cleaned. Unless you dust first and then vacuum, dusting typically only redistributes the room's dust. The vacuum cleaner needs to have a good HEPA filter or it also only redistributes the room's dust. If possible, avoid carpets with high pile; use dustless chalk; wash "soft" toys frequently; and, in general, make the area cleanable: Put toys away so that surfaces can be cleaned.

If possible, avoid serving foods that are more likely to elicit allergic reactions. Plan around food allergies so that all children may be included in food-related activities. Be alert for unusual reactions to food, and report any unusual reactions to parents. Have a written emergency plan for all children with known allergic reactions. In addition, have contact information and a plan for all children, because you may be the first to encounter a severe allergic reaction.

● ● ●
Asthma

Asthma is a lung disease that makes breathing difficult. Typically, as you breathe in, air (oxygen) enters your lungs. Your mouth and nose rapidly warm and moisten the air to prevent it from injuring the delicate lining of the airways. They also trap large particles (e.g., dust, pollen, mold, smoke, spray) and other particles that could injure the lungs. Air then goes through smaller airways. These airways are like branches on a tree; there are millions of small airways that carry oxygen to tiny air sacs called **alveoli**. Airways have a delicate lining that is coated with a thin layer of mucus, like the nose. Some particles are trapped by the sticky mucus and eventually removed. Tiny cilia (hair or whip-like structures) move the particles toward the nose and mouth. They are coughed or sneezed out or swallowed. Muscles surround the airways, and it is the contraction of these muscles that selectively directs the flow of air (American Lung Association, 2011c).

Asthma is a chronic inflammatory condition of the bronchial airways that carry air to the lungs. This inflammation causes the airways to overreact, producing too much mucus and swelling. This obstructs the airways, causing chest tightness, coughing, and wheezing and also severe shortness of breath and low blood oxygen. Prolonged airway inflammation can lead to airway remodeling resulting in lung scarring (American Lung Association, 2011c). Because children's airways are narrower than adults', triggers that may cause only slight problems for adults can create more serious problems in children. In children, asthma attacks can appear quickly with severe symptoms (PubMed Health, 2010b). Asthma breathing problems happen in episodes or attacks, but the inflammation underlying asthma is continuous (American Lung Association, 2011b).

Asthma prevalence rates doubled from 1980 until the late 1990s and have remained high (Akinbami, 2006). Most children who have asthma have symptoms before age 5 (American Lung Association, 2011c). Additionally, 75 to 80 percent of children with asthma have significant allergies. One out of four Americans has asthma or allergies, making asthma the most common chronic disease of childhood, affecting more than 1 child in 20, about 7.1 million children under age 18. It is more common in children (9.6%) than in adults (7.7%) (CDC, 2009a). Among children ages 5 to 17, asthma accounted for an estimated 14 million lost school days and is the most common cause of school absenteeism due to chronic disease. Asthma is the third leading cause of hospitalization among children and accounts for a fourth of emergency room visits (Asthma and Allergy Foundation of America [AAFA], 2011).

There is a strong genetic component to asthma. If one parent has asthma, there is one chance in three that each child will have asthma. This increases to 7 in 10 children if both parents have asthma (AAFA, 2011). Respiratory infections in infancy and early childhood can damage the lungs, with long-term implications for asthma, as can exposure to viral infections, allergens, and other irritants. There is no cure for asthma; it is managed through prevention and medical treatment (American Lung Association 2011c).

There are two types of asthma: allergic asthma and nonallergic asthma. Although both types of asthma have similar symptoms (coughing, wheezing, shortness of breath or rapid breathing, and chest tightness), the causes are different. Allergic asthma is triggered by inhaled allergens such as pet dander, pollen, mold, dust mites, and so on. Inflammatory triggers cause smooth muscle contraction and inflammation. Allergic asthma is the most common type of asthma. In nonallergic asthma, although the symptoms are the same, the asthma is triggered by anxiety, stress, exercise, cold or dry air, hyperventilation, viruses, and other nonirritants. The immune system is not involved in this type of asthma (AAFA, 2011). Some children have both types.

A child's initial acute asthmatic response happens within the first 10 to 20 minutes after encountering a trigger. An antigen binds to a specific immunoglobulin-E surface of the mast cell, and histamines are released, causing bronchospasms. Inhaled **bronchodilator** medications offer quick relief by relaxing the muscles *around* the airways. Short-acting bronchodilators are thought of as quick relief, rescue, or emergency medicines and are a necessary part of asthma management. The longer one delays in administering the quick relief medication, the worse the asthma attack becomes. There are long-acting inhaled bronchodilators that are used in combination with anti-inflammatory asthma medicine (American Lung Association, 2011b).

Anti-inflammatory medication prevents attacks by reducing the swelling and mucus production *inside* the airways. The anti-inflammatory drugs must be taken even if no symptoms are present. These are prescribed for children who have mild persistent, moderate, and severe asthma. Anti-inflammatory medications are the cornerstone for daily routine medical management. If taken consistently, even when the child has no symptoms, they are usually effective (American Lung Association, 2011b).

Children are usually given inhaled anti-inflammatory medication. The device most frequently used with infants and young children is a **nebulizer**, which children frequently refer to as a "breathing machine." It allows them to take the medicine in a mist form and helps ensure the correct dosage. As children get older, they may use a **metered-dose inhaler with spacers**. The inhaler dispenses a set amount of medication with each puff, making it easy to get the correct dosage; however, children have trouble coordinating their breaths to the burst from the inhaler. The spacer attached to the metered-dose inhaler holds the medication, which allows children to inhale it in a few breaths. This allows medication to be adjusted to prevent an attack (AAFA, 2005). Children who take steroids must be monitored carefully. The lowest possible dose should be given. Depending upon a child's specific symptoms, different configurations of medicine are used. Children older than 5 years also frequently use peak flow meters that measure how well the lungs are expelling air.

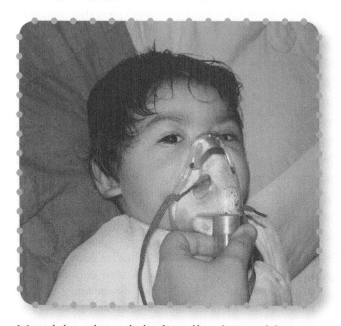

Infants who have asthma or other breathing problems often use a nebulizer to deliver needed medicine.

Courtesy Penny Low Deiner

IMPLICATIONS FOR EDUCATORS

One of the most important things for teachers to know is when a child is having an asthma attack, how severe it is, and what to do about it. The child's treatment is based on the severity of the symptoms and the degree of the airway obstruction. Every child has an early warning system that signals an attack is coming. Each child's pattern is unique, but good observation can identify the pattern, and teachers can learn to see, hear, and feel what is happening. Early identification helps prevent symptoms from becoming severe.

All children with asthma should have a written asthma action plan. This plan details personal information about the child's asthma symptoms, medications, any limitations, and specific instructions about what to do when an asthma attack occurs and what to do if the child does not improve when the plan is followed (American Lung Association, 2011a).

In a *mild* asthma attack, the breathing is mildly difficult and only slightly faster than usual; there is some wheezing, coughing, shortness of breath, or tightness in the chest. There is no "drawing in" of the muscles between the ribs; the child is alert and aware of the surroundings, can speak at his typical level, and skin color is good. If you can identify the source of the problem, remove or handle it (e.g., if the child is exposed to cold dry air, bring the child inside) (American Academy of Pediatrics [AAP], 1995; American Lung Association, 2006).

In a *moderate* asthma attack, the breathing is moderately difficult and faster than usual; there is wheezing, coughing, shortness of breath, or tightness in the chest. There is a slight to moderate "drawing in" of the muscles between the ribs. The child is alert and aware of the surroundings, can speak with difficulty, and skin color is good or may be pale. Reassure the child by your tone of voice and your confident attitude that this is something that can be taken care of. The child will look to you to decide how "bad" it is. If you can relax, he will (AAP, 1995; American Lung Association, 2006).

In a *severe* asthma attack, the child struggles to breathe; breathing may be very fast or very slow and labored. The chest and neck are pulled or drawn in with each breath. The child may become drowsy, has trouble walking, speaks with great difficulty, stops playing and can't begin again, and skin color is poor and the lips or fingernails are gray or blue (AAP, 1995; American Lung Association, 2006). If this happens, follow the asthma action plan, which probably involves taking the child to an emergency room immediately.

If you don't have asthma, but want to know how an asthmatic attack feels, pinch your nose closed and breathe through a drinking straw for a few minutes. Like the child with asthma, you may feel that you can't get enough air into your lungs. The longer you continue, the more pronounced the feeling.

If you teach children with asthma, you need to work with parents to be prepared for an asthma attack. Mild attacks can usually be handled with a child's regular medications and a break, or rest time, to recover. A note should be sent to the parents and, if possible, the trigger identified. It is expected that the child will remain in school, but activities will be monitored. Moderate attacks are more problematic and dependent upon the effects of the bronchodilator. I would notify the parents and not expect the child to remain at school. Severe asthma attacks require emergency treatment. Because asthma attacks occur with little warning, they may be frightening to the child who is having one, as well as to the other children. Children with asthma can remember prior attacks, and these may trigger feelings of anxiety, which can influence perceptions of future attacks. Attacks are most likely to come in the early morning hours. Children usually have prescribed medication (inhaler) to take. You need to have it available and to know how to help the child use it. Generally, the most comfortable positions for the child having an attack are sitting backward, straddling a straight chair, or planting the elbows on the knees. These positions are the easiest for breathing. Lying down flat is not helpful and in some cases may actually be harmful.

Most children with asthma are allergic to common allergens. If possible, have the floor of your room damp mopped rather than swept and eliminate rugs or curtains. If not possible, have the room vacuumed at night so that dust can settle. Try to balance strenuous activities with less strenuous ones.

Bleeding and Clotting Disorders

Bleeding and clotting disorders are umbrella terms for a range of medical problems that result in poor **blood clotting** and continuous bleeding. When a child has a bleeding disorder, he has a tendency to bleed more easily and longer than others, to bruise easily, and is particularly prone to nosebleeds. The problem with bleeding disorders works something like this. When there is an injury, the blood vessels constrict (get smaller). Then tiny cells called platelets bunch together to stop the bleeding and then other factors, as many as 20 different plasma proteins or blood clotting factors, join to plug the clot. The clot strengthens by a complex chemical process to form a substance called **fibrin** that stops the bleeding. The clot dissolves as the wound heals. When any of these proteins, platelets, or factors do not work as they should or are missing, individuals bleed longer than usual. The disorder itself is determined by the specific factor missing. Some bleeding disorders are inherited and are present at birth, whereas others are developed because of specific illnesses or treatments.

The bleeding disorder can be a result of defects in the blood vessels or from abnormalities in the blood clotting factors or in platelets. Blood clotting, or coagulation, controls bleeding, that is, it changes blood from a liquid to a solid. Von Willebrand disease is the most common bleeding disorder and is found in about 1 to 2 percent of the population of the United States. It is the result of a deficiency in the body's ability to make a protein that helps blood clot (the von Willebrand factor) and occurs equally in males and females. It is more noticeable in women due to heavy menstrual periods and after childbirth (National Hemophilia Foundation, 2006d).

Hemophilia is an inherited bleeding disorder (X chromosome–linked) that affects about 20,000 people in the United States, or 1 in 5,000 male births. It results from deficiencies in blood clotting factors that can lead to internal bleeding. The median age for diagnosing children with mild hemophilia is 36 months; for moderate hemophilia, it is 8 months and for severe hemophilia, 1 month (CDC, 2010e). Treatment involves injecting the missing clotting factor into a child's vein. The regularity and amounts are dependent upon the child's size and the severity of the disease. The major concerns are not bleeding to death from a minor cut, but rather internal bleeding into the joints of the long bones (knees, ankles, elbows). Internal bleeding involving the head, cerebral hemorrhage, may lead to complications that can result in permanent neurologic damage or death. This is now rare.

The flip side of bleeding disorders are clotting disorders, or **thrombophilia**. In this case, defects in one or more of the clotting factors in blood cause the formation of potentially dangerous blood clots (thrombosis). Approximately 5 to 8 percent of the population of the United States has one

of the clotting disorders. More than 60,000 Americans die each year from thrombophilia (CDC, 2005b), which also is an inherited condition. The symptoms relate to the part of the vascular system where they occur and the extent to which the clot breaks off and travels to another part of the body, for example, the lungs (pulmonary embolus) or the brain (embolic stroke) (National Hemophilia Foundation, 2006c). The expectation is that most children with blood or clotting disorders will lead normal, functional lives if some prudence is exercised.

IMPLICATIONS FOR EDUCATORS

Safety is a prime concern for children with bleeding and clotting disorders. Prevention is the first course of action. Evaluate your classroom for sharp edges or obstacles that a child might bump into. Tape or glue foam pads to the edges, and remove furniture that isn't necessary. Look at push toys and determine how stable they are. Choose tricycles and other moving equipment that are stable and close to the ground as children are developing their skills. Ensure that children wear helmets when riding. Set rules about roughhousing and physical fighting and enforce them for all children. Use noncompetitive physical activities to reduce the dangers of overexertion and injury. Children can run, but don't have them run a race to see who wins.

Work with parents to encourage the child's safety by doing such things as sewing padding into the knees and seat of the toddler's pants to reduce bruising. As children get older, wearing athletic elbow- and kneepads can deal with the same problem. Children need to wear shoes and high-top sneakers or boots to provide support and added protection (National Hemophilia Foundation, 2006a). Talk with parents about their ideas for dealing with safety issues related to the child himself and the classroom. Jointly decide whether there is any equipment the child cannot safely use (e.g., a high climber).

Respond quickly to children with bleeding disorders. If a child has a small surface cut, it will usually respond to typical first aid. Take universal precautions. Put on gloves, wash the cut, apply pressure, and then bandage. The following are signs and symptoms that internal bleeding may be occurring:

- The child complains about tingling, bubbling, stiffness, or he uses a restricted range of motion in any limb.
- The child's joints are swollen or warm to the touch.
- The child refuses to use a limb, limps, or favors one arm or leg more than usual.

Find out what parents want you to do based on the level of the child's injury. Develop a written action plan and ensure that everyone knows what it is. Contact parents immediately if the child has a blow to the head, neck, or abdomen (National Hemophilia Foundation, 2003c).

Children with bleeding disorders need clear and consistent rules and the freedom to pursue their own interests and ideas. When children are young, they can tell you when they are not feeling well, but it is up to the adult to try to figure out the cause. If older children see adults react to bleeding with worry, fear, or frustration, the child may not tell adults about what is happening until the pain becomes unbearable. Respond in a matter-of-fact way to information about bleeding (National Hemophilia Foundation, 2006b).

Cancer

Cancer is an umbrella term for a group of diseases related to the uncontrollable growth of cells; new cells are made when the body doesn't need them and they don't die when they should. Cancer is treated with surgery, radiation, chemotherapy, bone marrow transplants, or a combination of these.

The prognosis depends on how early the disease is detected, what type of cancer it is, and which systems are affected. Children diagnosed with cancer are typically referred to medical centers that have multidisciplinary teams of cancer specialists (National Cancer Institute, 2011).

Each day in the United States, 46 children are diagnosed with cancer. One in 330 children will develop cancer by age 20, and the number is rising. Cancer is the number one disease killer of children between infancy and age 15, more than AIDS, cystic fibrosis, and muscular dystrophy combined (Candlelighters, 2007a). Approximately 3,317 children under age 15 were diagnosed with cancer in 2010 (Leukemia and Lymphoma Society, 2011). Although the incidence of cancer has increased slightly over the past 30 years, the five-year survival rates have improved from 60 percent in 1975 to 89 percent in 2002 for children younger than 15 (National Cancer Institute, 2011).

Leukemia is the most common type of cancer in children birth to 14 (31%). Leukemia is a type of cancer that affects the blood and bone marrow (the spongy center of bones where bloods cells are formed) (Leukemia and Lymphoma Society, 2011). The abnormal cells are called leukemia cells and grow out of control. They eventually spill out of the bone marrow into the blood. They continue to multiply, and eventually there are so many of them that they crowd out not only the other **white blood cells** but the **red blood cells** and **platelets** as well. This impacts the body's ability to protect against disease, carry oxygen, and clot blood. Therefore, the child looks pale, is prone to infection, and bruises easily (Candlelighters, 2007a).

Signs and symptoms of leukemia include the following:

- Tiredness, lethargy, weakness, paleness, dizziness
- Easy bruising (black and blue marks for no apparent reason), unusual bleeding, frequent nose bleeds
- Aches in back, legs, joints, headaches
- Mild fever with or without infection
- Frequent infections
- Night sweats
- Irritability (Candlelighters, 2007a; Leukemia and Lymphoma Society, 2007)

There are different types of leukemia based on the course of the illness and the type of white cells affected. Acute forms get worse quickly; chronic, more slowly. The white cells that can be affected are the **lymphoid** and **myeloid cells**. Although all types can happen in children, the most common type, acute lymphoblastic leukemia (ALL), accounts for about 75 percent of leukemia in young children and 23 percent of all cancer diagnosed in children younger than age 15 (National Cancer Institute, 2011). Acute myeloid leukemia (AML) accounts for about 20 percent, with the other forms making up 5 percent (Candlelighters, 2007b). The incidence of ALL among children ages 2 to 3 years is approximately four times greater than that for infants and nearly 10 times greater than that for adolescents aged 16 to 21 years old. The incidence of ALL is substantially higher for white children than for black children, but highest in Hispanic children. Children with Down syndrome have an increased risk of developing leukemia (National Cancer Institute, 2011).

The acute form of leukemia progresses rapidly and, without treatment, life expectancy would drop to a few weeks or months. With drugs and bone marrow transplants, the life expectancy for children with ALL has been increased, and 91% percent of children under 5 years old have survived for five years (1999–2006). For AML, the five-year survival rate for children under 15 is 61 percent (Leukemia and Lymphoma Society, 2011).

Chronic leukemia progresses more slowly, but it is less amenable to cure. Treatment of children with any type of cancer is complicated and requires intensive supportive care, such as blood transfusions, managing infectious complications, and also emotional, financial, and developmental concerns; this treatment is usually headed by a **pediatric oncologist** and in cancer centers or hospitals with the necessary pediatric supportive care facilities.

Chemotherapy uses anticancer drugs that are taken as pills, liquids, injections, or intravenously to kill or slow the growth of abnormal cells and to replenish normal cells. For children, the side effects of the chemotherapy can be more devastating than the actual disease. The disease itself is invisible, but bodily changes are very apparent and perhaps even frightening. Children have difficulty tasting food and eat little. They may crave salt and not want meats or sugar products. The drugs affect hair follicles and their hair falls out. Because of the risk of infection, their activities may be limited.

Radiation therapy, which is usually combined with chemotherapy, uses high-energy X-rays, radium, and other ionizing radiation sources to destroy cancerous cells. The procedure is not painful; however, the room in which the therapy takes place can be frightening to children. The child is not radioactive during the treatment or after it. Side effects include some skin damage to the treated area, hair loss, nausea or vomiting, diarrhea, sleepiness, and in some cases long-term intellectual disability or hearing loss.

A **bone marrow transplant** may be used if a suitable donor can be found. In this case, healthy bone marrow is injected into the child's bloodstream and enters the bones where it hopefully begins to produce healthy cells and platelets.

Brain cancers account for about 15 percent of pediatric cancers and are the second most common type of cancer in children. Because the brain controls learning, memory, the senses, and so on, symptoms vary depending on the location of the tumor. Treatment of pediatric brain cancers is very complex. Surgical removal of the tumor is not always possible; it may be inaccessible, or removal could be life threatening. Even a benign tumor in the brain can be life threatening. It is more complicated because of the blood–brain barrier, which, in most cases, is helpful; in this instance it is not, as it prevents some chemicals from entering the brain and reaching the tumor. The prognosis depends on the type, grade, and size of the tumor, and its location in the brain (Candlelighters, 2007b).

Neuroblastoma is a rare cancer that forms in the nerve tissue of the sympathetic nervous system. It usually begins in the adrenal glands, which sit on top of the kidneys. It is often present at birth but is most often diagnosed in early childhood when the child begins to show symptoms of the disease. By the time the doctor has found the cancer, it has usually spread to other parts of the body (Candlelighters, 2007b).

IN THE FIELD

When Betty was about 2½, she had a cold and we took her to the doctor. Because it was near the holidays, we wanted to make sure our celebrations weren't interrupted with too may coughs. The doctor became alarmed when she felt her spleen. After some tests and attempts at trying to be "normal" for our 7-year-old, we discovered that Betty had neuroblastoma. That was how our roller-coaster ride with cancer began. I don't know where it will end. They operated to remove the cancer and then the chemo began. We know she is likely to have a hearing loss because of the chemo cocktails, and some neurological problems; if we are lucky, a learning disability. Chemo cocktails are like eating lead paint with a few other heavy metals thrown in for good measure. She has lost her hair but fell in love with her latest hot pink baseball cap. Not surprisingly, she has gotten clingy and does not want to be away from us. Life is a priority. When the girls are good, I'm good; when they're not, I'm not. We are truly dancing with the devil. (*Note:* In 2011 Betty was 8 years old and in the third grade, and she has passed the five-year mark with few identified problems.)

IMPLICATIONS FOR EDUCATORS

The word *cancer* is scary at any age but particularly with young children. Children need information, but the information they need depends on their age. The main concern for children younger than age 5 is separation from their family, fear of abandonment, and fear of loneliness. They understand that they don't feel well, but they don't understand the disease. They are very egocentric in their thinking and try to relate the illness to a particular event or action. They need to be reassured that they did not do anything to become sick and that being sick is not a punishment.

Children 5 to 10 years old have fears relating to physical injury and bodily harm, and perhaps even awareness of death. It is important to be honest with children, as their imaginations can do more harm than the facts. Answer the questions they ask; their questions may be very different from the questions you as an adult might have. Use analogies to help children understand that the "good" medicine is fighting the "bad" cells. Children like to be reassured that everyone is trying to make them better. Children who have been treated for cancer are at risk for long-term neurocognitive impairment. The specific treatment influences the risk; female children are at greater risk than male children. Children may experience general or more specific functional deficits.

Discipline should be normal at home and at school. Adequate nutrition for growth is a problem because the drugs decrease appetite. (In some cases, the drugs must be reduced so that the child's appetite can improve.) Be sure snacks and lunches are nutritious, as these children cannot afford empty calories. School, despite the dangers of infection and possible taunting by peers, has great psychological value to both the child and the family. Realistic hope is the greatest asset a family can have. Being honest and open is important. However, if a child is in a terminal phase and has a prognosis of two months, it is *not* helpful to deny this.

Children typically regress when they are sick. In general, the last skill learned will be the first skill lost. Parents find this distressing. Providing creative media such as art and dramatic play possibilities that allow them

to work through their fears and concerns is helpful. The child is in a world where she feels out of control, so situations where the child can be in control and make decisions are helpful. If possible, let the child decide what she wants to eat, what she wants to play with, and what she wants you to help with.

●●●
Childhood Arthritis

Childhood arthritis is baffling and professionals do not agree on the name, the cause, or the definition. *Juvenile rheumatoid arthritis (JRA)* is the most common term used in the United States and it is also the most common form (CDC, 2010b). JRA is an autoimmune illness where the body's immune system mistakenly attacks and destroys health body tissue. It may begin with a swollen knuckle, a spiking fever, or an unexplained rash. To be classified as JRA, the child must experience continuously active arthritis of one or more joints for at least six weeks, with no other demonstrable disease, and be younger than age 16 (CDC, 2010b). Because of definitional issues prevalence estimations vary. JRA affects approximately 80,000 children in the United States under age 18 or as many as 294,000 at some point between 6 months and age 18 (CDC, 2010b).

Children with JRA will experience joint inflammation until the immune system self-corrects. This generally takes a year or two. Sometimes, this remission is permanent; sometimes, the system makes the mistake again and the child will again have painful inflamed joints. Occasionally, the mistake is only partially corrected, and in a small number of cases the problem does not correct itself. When the disease is in remission, the joints return to normal or nearly normal size.

There are three types of JRA. The types are based on the number of joints affected, how seriously they are affected, and the length of time they are expected to be affected: oligoarticular (50%), polyarticular (40%), and systemic (10%) (CDC, 2010b). In addition to the expected arthritis, children can also have fevers, rash, fluid around the lungs, heart conditions, and enlarged liver and spleen.

In **oligoarticular JRA**, four or fewer joints are involved. These joints may be painful, stiff, or swollen. Children with oligoarticular JRA may have an infection of the eye (iris) that can lead to blindness, so they should see an ophthalmologist on a regular basis (Kids Health, 2008b).

Polyarticular JRA involves five or more joints. This is more serious because more joints are involved; they are more likely to be seriously involved; and it is likely to persist longer. It affects both large weight-bearing joints and small joints: commonly knees, hips, ankles, feet, and neck as well as wrists and elbows (Kids Health, 2008b). Children may experience chronic tiredness, poor appetite, a low-grade fever, growth retardation, and anemia. Polyarticular JRA affects twice as many girls as boys (Leet, Dormans, & Tosi, 2002).

Systemic JRA begins with a high fever that occurs intermittently for days or weeks (another immune system mistake). The spectrum of involvement and severity in systemic onset JRA is broad and difficult to predict at the onset of the disease (Kids Health, 2008b).

Children with JRA are treated with a combination of medication, physical therapy, and exercise. The goals are to relieve pain and inflammation and to slow down or prevent the destruction of joints and to promote optimal growth and development in all areas, Mild JRA is usually treated with nonsteroidal anti-inflammatory drugs (such as ibuprofen); more severe JRA usually requires other medications such as methotrexate (Kids Health, 2008b). The goal of physical therapy is to keep the **range of motion** and flexibility in the joints and to build strength and endurance. Exercising a painful joint can be distressing for both children and parents. Over time, parents may have trouble paying for the medication; there is often parent-child conflict over the exercise regimen; and parents may burn out.

IMPLICATIONS FOR EDUCATORS

One of the most disturbing aspects of JRA is the pain and its management. Children may be taught self-regulatory methods such as progressive muscle relaxation, meditative breathing, or guided imagery as ways of managing the pain. Give children time to express their feelings. Include relaxation stories and other techniques in your regular repertoire of teaching (see Activity 5–26, *Relaxation Stories*).

A child with JRA may be tired or irritable and lack muscular strength. Allow the child time to do things. Realize that the child is probably in some pain. (The drugs reduce inflammation and pain, but don't cure them.) The child should not participate in competitive sports, in activities that continuously use the same joints, or in jarring, twisting play. Children need to maintain a regular exercise program that includes walking, swimming, and bicycling. Children need to warm up muscles by stretching before using them, which should be fun. The long-term impact on a child's quality of life can be considerable.

• • •

Congenital Heart Defects

Congenital heart defects include structural problems, acquired damage, and heart rhythm disturbances that are present at birth. These defects are usually diagnosed in infancy. Nine out of 1,000 births will have some type of congenital heart defect, most of which are mild. There are at least 18 distinct types of heart defects. Although heart defects are assumed to be genetic, only a few genes have been linked to heart defects. Infants with heart defects have low blood pressure and may have difficulty breathing, feeding problems, and poor weight gain (American Heart Association, 2011).

The heart begins to develop shortly after conception. During development, structural defects can occur, involving the walls and valves of the heart, and the arteries and veins near the heart. These defects can be relatively minor such as tiny "holes" between chambers of the heart or more severe such as the complete absence of a chamber or valve (American Heart Association, 2007). Congenital heart defects disrupt the normal flow of blood through the heart by slowing it down, having it go in the wrong direction or to the wrong place, or blocking it completely.

Congenital heart defects are the most common type of major birth defect. Many of these defects are mild and require no treatment. However, heart defects are the major cause of death from birth defects in the first year of life, with twice as many children dying from heart defects than

from childhood cancer, over 91,000 lives (American Heart Association, 2007).

It is more difficult to identify a heart problem in a child than in an adult. Shortness of breath when feeding or crying, tiredness or sweating during feeding, blueness of the lips and fingernails that becomes more obvious when the child is crying or involved in a physical activity, and slow growth are indications of a possible heart problem (American Heart Association, 2011). Minor defects are often diagnosed on a routine medical checkup and rarely cause symptoms.

Heart murmurs are heard frequently in children. When listening to the heart through a stethoscope, the normal sound is "lub-dub, lub-dub" which is the opening and closing of the heart valves. Sometimes there are extra sounds or "murmurs." These sounds are soft and variable in healthy children, but loud with a specific timing and location when there is a heart defect. Heart murmurs are harmless for most children. In other cases, restricted activity or heart surgery may be required.

Children who have either heart or lung problems are frequently given an exercise (stress) test to see whether they can safely exert themselves at the same level as other children their age without showing abnormal heart rhythms or interfering with the supply of oxygen reaching the heart. Based on the results of these tests, appropriate inclusive educational programs can be planned.

IMPLICATIONS FOR EDUCATORS

Although these children may need some limitations in their activity, this is generally not a problem if you let children rest when they are tired. If you avoid strenuous competitive games, children need not exert themselves unduly to win. It's important for you to be responsive to children's needs within a framework that requires them to learn responsibility. For example, if a child says he is too tired to help pick up the dolls he played with, encourage the child to rest for a minute or two before cleaning up. If the child is genuinely tired, shorten the activity time or increase the variety of less active choices. Children need to both participate and be included. If children are tired, they can sit and hold the box while other children place toys in it, or they can sit and place toys on shelves. Help them find quiet ways to help and be part of the group.

• • •

Cystic Fibrosis

Cystic fibrosis (CF) is an inherited disease caused by a defective recessive gene that causes the body to produce abnormally thick and sticky mucus. This results in life-threatening lung infections and serious digestive problems (PubMed Health, 2010d). CF affects approximately 30,000 children and young adults in the United States. It occurs in 1 of every 3,900 live births in the United States, resulting in about 1,000 new cases each year. It is more prevalent in whites than in African American or Asian children. To be born with CF, both parents must be carriers of this recessive gene, or it is a mutation. The problem occurs on chromosome 7. An estimated 1 in 29 Caucasian Americans have the CF gene. The carriers have no symptoms of the disorder (PubMed Health 2010d).

The defective CF gene causes the body to produce abnormally thick, sticky mucus, due to the faulty transportation of sodium and chloride (salt). When this mucus clogs the lungs, it makes breathing difficult. It also collects bacteria that cause inflammation and can lead to infection. The mucus blocks the digestive tract and pancreas, stopping the digestive enzymes that break down food and provide nutrients for growth from getting to the intestines. Children with CF need to take enzyme capsules with their meals to help with digestion.

Most children with CF are diagnosed by their second birthday (70%). A blood test is available to help detect CF or a sweat test is used. There are more than 1,000 mutations of the CF gene, so symptoms vary, but in general they include the following:

- Salty-tasting skin
- Persistent coughing or wheezing, pneumonia
- Fatigue
- Weight loss, or failure to gain weight normally; delayed growth with a good appetite
- Diarrhea and/or stools that are greasy, difficult, or foul-smelling
- Recurrent respiratory infections (PubMed Health, 2010d)

Treatment is multidisciplinary. Because CF is a complex disease that affects so many parts of the body, it requires specialized knowledge. There are 115 CF Foundation–accredited care centers nationwide. There is no cure for CF, but treatment, therapy, and proper nutrition go a long way to improving the quality of life for children with CF and their families. The use of airway clearance techniques helps to clear the lungs. Medications such as mucus thinners, antibiotics, anti-inflammatory drugs, and bronchodilators make breathing easier.

Families who have children with CF face two major strains on their resources: time and money. The requirements of treatment and caring for the equipment may take two hours a day, and, the child's life is dependent upon the family's willingness and ability to do that. The average life span for people with CF who live to adulthood is 35 years (PubMed Health, 2010d). Although costs vary from one family to another, most families feel the financial strain of paying for necessary medication and frequent hospitalizations.

IMPLICATIONS FOR EDUCATORS

Monitor developmental progress as you would any other child. Provide and support social opportunities in an enriched environment. Support the child who takes prescribed medication before eating. Develop a plan for maintaining contact when the child is sick. See that the child is encouraged to bring up phlegm, not stigmatized for doing so. Some signs of emotional difficulty to look for in the child are depression and withdrawal, fear of death, fear of losing control (dependence), and acting out. Have an emergency plan. Provide matter-of-fact explanations for other children: "Leroy has trouble breathing, like you do when you have a cold, only Leroy has this all the time. His tummy hurts as well."

• • •
Diabetes Mellitus: Types 1 and 2

Diabetes mellitus is one of the most frequent chronic diseases affecting children and youth and the frequency is increasing. Next to obesity, it is the most common metabolic disorder in children and youth. The food we eat is broken down into chemicals, including a simple sugar called glucose. For glucose to get into cells, insulin must be present to "unlock" the cells in order to allow glucose to enter and fuel them. Insulin is a hormone made by the pancreas. Why insulin is problematic for some individuals remains a mystery; however, the key to solving the mystery is related to both genetics and the environment (Knip, 2005).

There are approximately 25.8 million people in the United States (or 8.3% of the population) who have diabetes. Of these people, 18.8 million have been diagnosed and 7 million people are unaware that they have the disease. Diabetes has no cure. The discovery of insulin has literally made the difference between life and death for people with diabetes (Diabetic Foundation, 2011). Regardless of the type of diabetes, the goal is to manage the disease by developing a predictable relationship among the child's diet, insulin, and exercise.

DIABETES MELLITUS TYPE 1

Type 1 diabetes is an autoimmune disease in which the body does not produce insulin because of the destruction of the insulin-producing beta cells of the pancreas. Approximately 151,000 children and youth have diabetes and each year, more than 13,000 children and youth are diagnosed with type 1 diabetes (CDC, 2010c). In children from birth to age 9, the

Children with Type 1 diabetes need to eat at similar times each day and have predictable food exchanges.
© Cengage Learning 2012

prevalence is highest in white non-Hispanic children at 1 per 1,000 (CDC, 2010d). Researchers agree that type 1 diabetes develops through the interaction of genes and one or more environmental triggers (Juvenile Diabetes Research Foundation International [JDRF], 2003). Certain genes called HLA markers are associated with diabetes risk. These markers can be identified at birth. Although genetic, 90 percent of children who develop type 1 diabetes have no relatives with the disease. This information is particularly troubling because type 1 diabetes has increased an estimated 3 percent each year over the past 50 years (JDRF, 2003).

Although type 1 diabetes is an autoimmune disease with a genetic base, the environmental factors that trigger the beginning of the disease are elusive. It can begin in infancy, but the peak incidence occurs during puberty (American Diabetes Association, 2003). Once triggered, the body's immune system kills the insulin-producing beta cells in the pancreas, and the symptoms become apparent. Symptoms include one or more of the following:

- Extreme thirst
- Frequent urination
- Drowsiness, lethargy
- Sudden vision changes
- Increased appetite, constant hunger
- Sudden weight loss
- Fruity, sweet, or wine-like odor on breath
- Heavy, labored breathing, tiring easily
- Itching
- Slow healing of cuts and scratches (JDRF, 2003; National Diabetes Information Clearinghouse, 2007)

It is possible for children to have no obvious symptoms. Some of the symptoms mimic the flu, making the diagnosis difficult. The onset of diabetes in children is usually more swift and severe than it is in adults. Children become very sick very quickly, and if treatment does not begin right away, they will lapse into a life-threatening coma. Insulin injections are necessary for almost all children with diabetes. The injections must be given daily and are probably the most hated part of the treatment. Urine testing (usually before breakfast and dinner) or blood testing may be necessary each day. This procedure is embarrassing for a child striving toward independence. Charting the test results provides the basis for changes in insulin dosage and gives clues to why some diabetics go out of control. When children are old enough, they are encouraged to do the injections themselves.

However, insulin pump therapy is changing how medication is given to adults, children, and even infants and toddlers (Children with Diabetes, 2007). The insulin pump is a small computerized device about the size of a pager and is worn on a belt or placed in a pocket. The pump is attached to the child with a thin plastic tube that ends in a small, flexible plastic cannula or tube. The cannula is inserted through the skin (usually in the abdomen or buttocks) and taped in

place. It must be changed every 48 to 72 hours (Marschilok, 2004). Pumps deliver insulin in two ways: basal insulin and bolus doses. The basal insulin is delivered in steady short-acting doses throughout the day and provides about half of the day's total insulin requirements. For the bolus doses, the user pushes a button and decides how much is needed. Bolus doses are given at snack or meal time, or to lower blood sugar when it is too high (Marschilok, 2004). The advantage of the pump is that it can deliver insulin in precise predictable doses on a continuous basis. It holds several days' supply of insulin, and the pump can be individually programmed to meet a child's needs. Additionally, it can be adjusted if the child is ill or more physically active than usual. It also provides flexibility in allowing children more freedom in when, what, and how they eat (Marschilok, 2004). Obviously, if a child is on an insulin pump, educators will need to understand how the pump works and how to handle situations that may require assistance.

Although most insulin-dependent diabetics are on a "free" diet, it is by no means unstructured. The free exchange system used by adults is often used with children. The free exchange system divides foods into six groups based on calories and grams of carbohydrates, proteins, and fats. Thus, if the child is allowed one bread exchange, the choice of any one of the following could be made: a piece of bread, one-half cup of cereal, two graham crackers, one-half cup of mashed potatoes, or one-fourth cup of baked beans. The number of exchanges is individually determined, and parents will tell you what exchanges the child requires. This will affect what you offer at snack and how much the child eats. The child's activity level will also influence his balance of food and insulin.

Children with diabetes are allowed to have slowly digestible sweets like ice cream, but are not allowed to eat candy bars and other carbohydrates that burn quickly. (An exception to this rule occurs when the child needs quick sugar to avert an insulin reaction.)

The concern is when the insulin level of a child with type 1 diabetes is out of control. Hypoglycemia occurs when the level of blood sugar (glucose) is too low. It is relatively common and occurs when a child has injected too much insulin, eaten too little food, or has exercised without ingesting extra food. Symptoms include fatigue, shaking, cold sweats, dizziness, double vision, and nervousness. If caught in the early stages, providing a drink of juice, or food with sugar will usually help almost immediately. Severe hypoglycemia can result in seizures or unconsciousness, called insulin shock (Medline Plus, 2007b). Hyperglycemia occurs because the blood glucose (sugar) level is too high and the child is typically dehydrated. If this continues and glucose is not available, the body begins to break down body fat. When body fat is broken down, **ketones** (the byproducts of fat metabolism) build up in the blood and spill over into the urine. This may be how type 1 diabetes is first diagnosed. The signs include such things as frequent urination and thirst for a day or more, fatigue, nausea and vomiting, muscular stiffness or aching, rapid breathing, and fruity breath. If caught in the beginning stages, rehydration is the first goal (Medline Plus, 2007b). Obviously, if conditions move into more extreme stages, this is a medical emergency, as it can lead to diabetic coma. As with asthma, there should be a written diabetes action plan developed with the family.

Diabetes Mellitus Type 2

Diabetes mellitus type 2 is a metabolic disorder that results from the body's inability to make enough insulin or to use it properly. It is primarily characterized by insulin resistance, relative insulin deficiency, and hyperglycemia. In the past, this type of diabetes was called adult-onset diabetes. However, a growing number of children and adolescents are developing type 2 diabetes. The prevalence rate is 1.7 per 1,000 for U.S. children and youth between birth and 19. Because this is a new phenomenon, we do not have accurate statistics or even common agreement on when a child has type 2 diabetes. However, reports indicate that 8 to 45 percent of children with newly diagnosed diabetes have type 2 diabetes (American Diabetes Association, 2003). Children diagnosed with type 2 diabetes are usually between 10 and 19 years old, obese, have a family history of this disease, and have insulin resistance (CDC, 2010c). Increasing numbers of younger prepubescent overweight children are being identified. In one clinic, a 5-year-old boy was diagnosed with type 2 diabetes. Obesity precedes type 2 diabetes and may cause disabilities in people who are genetically predisposed to it.

IMPLICATIONS FOR EDUCATORS

Children with diabetes need a predictable relationship between food intake and energy output. Having snacks and meals at about the same times each day helps. The content of the snacks and meals should provide about the same food exchanges. The child need not eat the same foods every day, but the foods should be of equivalent groups and values.

Because of the possibility of insulin reaction, you must always have a source of quick-burning sugar available. Some traditional quick sugar sources are orange juice, soda, a sugar cube, and small chocolate bars. Most children have some warning signs, but young children may not be able to identify these. The child may be dizzy, shaky, trembling, or having an emotional outburst before the insulin reaction begins to occur. Know what the child's favorite sources of sugar are; you need to offer something especially tempting because the child may not feel like eating. Always carry a sugar source on a field trip. If you miss the warning signs and the child becomes unconscious, do not try to get the child to drink, because choking might result. Discuss emergency measures with parents and have a jointly written diabetes health care plan. It should address the specific needs of the child and provide specific instructions on the following issues:

- Blood glucose monitoring
- Insulin administration (if necessary)
- Meals and snacks, including food content, amounts, and timing
- Symptoms and treatment of hypoglycemia (low blood sugar)
- Symptoms and treatment of hyperglycemia (high blood sugar)
- Testing for ketones and actions to be taken based on results (American Diabetes Association, 2003)

The parents should supervise and regulate the child's insulin and diet, and they can usually accommodate most situations if they know about them ahead of time. Send them a list of your snacks for the week or month, or at least post them on a bulletin board for the parents to check when they drop off or pick up their child. If another child will have a birthday party

with cupcakes, tell the parents. A child with diabetes can have one too, if it is planned for. The child should wear a medic-alert bracelet or locket at all times.

• • •
Epilepsy and Other Seizure Disorders

Seizures are brief, stereotyped unpredictable events that alter states of consciousness in different ways. They are abnormal electrical discharges in the brain. Symptoms depend on the part of the brain involved and typically cause unusual sensations, uncontrollable muscle spasms, and loss of consciousness. They occur frequently in childhood, and isolated seizures are associated with fever or acute illness. They are not seizure disorders. Seizures are a disorder of neuronal transmission and brain network interactions (Weinstein & Gaillard, 2007).

Febrile seizures, relatively common in children younger than age 5, can occur when a child develops a high fever, with the temperature rising rapidly to 102°F or more. During a seizure, most children lose consciousness and shake. A child could become rigid and twitch on one side of the body. Although frightening, most febrile seizures are short and harmless (NINDS, 2011b). They are not part of the epilepsy syndrome, and about 5 percent of children between 3 months and 5 years of age experience them. About 80 percent are simple febrile seizures that are brief symmetric tonic or clonic-tonic events that occur once during an illness. Complex febrile seizures are more prolonged or reoccur during an illness, and they may serve as indicators of other central nervous system problems (Weinstein & Gaillard, 2007).

Seizures occur in the brain and must be understood in the context of the brain and how it works. A seizure "involves the abnormal extensive and concurrent firing of a large population of cortical neurons. This results in the interruption of usual brain-generated electrical signals, leading to an abrupt change in the person's behavior" (Weinstein & Gaillard, 2007, p. 440). The firing may continue until excitatory neurochemicals are used up or until it is extinguished by inhibitory neurochemicals, which usually occurs in seconds to minutes. Seizures occur more frequently in children younger than 6 years of age, and in old age.

IN THE FIELD

I thought Selena was playing when she had her first seizure. As her head fell back, I waited for the smile and giggle that usually accompanied that movement. Instead, I watched her eyes roll back in her head and her body go limp. It lasted just a few seconds, but it scared me. I called my husband over to watch her and prayed that what I'd seen was just in my imagination.

Selena laughed and cooed. She didn't exhibit signs of a seizure at all. So I decided that I had just "seen something" that looked like a seizure. But as we dropped her off with her babysitter, Debbie, so we could go to a restaurant opening that I had to attend for work, I couldn't help but feel apprehensive. "If Selena starts acting weird, call me," I told Debbie, not wanting to worry her, but unable to shake the feeling that something was very wrong with my baby girl.

Halfway through the entrée, my cell phone rang. "Leslie, it's Debbie." Her voice sounded shaky. "I need you to come pick up the baby, and I think you should take her to the emergency room. She's had four seizures in the past hour."

"We need to go," I told my husband, flagging down our waiter and then dropping a $20 on the table when he didn't come fast enough with our bill. I called our pediatrician during the five-minute drive to our babysitter's house—he agreed with Debbie. Selena needed to go to the emergency room.

Our hospital experience was a disaster. We spent the night in the emergency room. First, they placed us in a room with a kid with meningitis, and then with a child with a violent viral infection. The nurses wouldn't tell us what was going on. No doctor appeared. Selena would have a seizure and we'd call the nurse, but she wouldn't come to check on her.

I finally snapped. I told the nurses that if they could not be responsible for caring for my child, they should send us home. I explained that my child had come in with seizures and was going to leave in a coffin if they weren't more careful about whom they put her in a room with, how they did procedures, and what sorts of medicine they administered.

We were moved to a private room. The pharmacy director came upstairs and spoke to us about the medicine they were administering. Two doctors appeared at our door, and I believe I made that nurse cry.

For five days, I refused to leave the hospital. My husband would go home to get food or take a nap, but I would not leave my daughter's side because I had so little trust in the hospital. When the neurologist told me Selena was going to have to stay on phenobarbital for up to a year but that he had no conclusive cause of her seizure, the journalist in me kicked in.

I called my friends in the newsroom and got them to look up everything they could find on phenobarbital, and then seizures. I asked them to cross-reference the medicine Selena was taking for allergies and the occurrence of seizures. I work in a profession where we dig for information and where we know how to do it fast.

Within a couple hours, my cell phone was ringing. Selena's allergy medicine had an ingredient in it that is known to cause seizures in children younger than age 2, our health reporter said. My phone rang again. The over-the-counter version of that medicine had been taken off the market two weeks before; my source said it was because it caused seizures.

I breathed a sigh of relief. My child was having a reaction to a medicine her newly acquired and severely misinformed allergist had prescribed. I felt happy, but convincing her doctors, even with the reams of information my friends had provided, was not easy. They said she had to stay on phenobarbital—even though I now knew it caused developmental problems, made Selena a tyrant, and when she wasn't fussing, made her incredibly sleepy.

The physician told me that I wasn't a doctor and couldn't diagnose my own child. As more and more of the drug dripped into her veins, I felt defeated. I knew they were wrong. I started dropping the dose of phenobarbital as soon as we got out of the hospital. I discontinued the use of all the other medications the allergist put her on. The seizures stopped.

I went back to my pediatrician to explain my theory and he listened. He said he thought I was right but wanted us to go to a different neurologist for confirmation. I did, and he kept her on phenobarbital for a month while we awaited the results of the tests. By that time, we'd run out of our prescription and I told my husband I wouldn't refill it.

When we got the test results back, the doctor said my theory had been right. Selena is allergic to pseudoephedrine, a key ingredient in a prescription her allergist had prescribed.

My daughter took a potentially damaging antiseizure medicine that she didn't need for three months, because some "highly qualified" doctor hadn't kept up on the research—or apparently read the newspaper. Her mistake cost us more than $1,000 in medical bills and our insurance company more than $10,000, and put my daughter through a lot of unnecessary pain and suffering.

Sometimes I wonder whether Selena would still be taking that drug and suffering its consequences if I weren't a reporter. I had resources at hand that most parents don't, and the mom in me told me to follow my gut, not

what a doctor said. I fought tooth and nail for my daughter. I wasn't nice to incompetent nurses and I made no friends in the hospital, but I got what I needed for my child.

REFLECTIVE PRACTICE | What happens to the children whose parents do not have the resources, intuition, or the desire to fight for what they believe for their children? Do their children follow doctor's orders? What do you think about this mother? She thought she knew more about her daughter and the problem than the medical profession. Do you think she had the right to override their advice? What would you have done?

Epilepsy is a brain disorder in which clusters of nerve cells, or neurons, in the brain sometimes signal abnormally. Somehow the normal pattern of neuronal activity becomes disturbed, causing strange sensations, emotions, and behavior; or sometimes convulsions, muscle spasms, and loss of consciousness. It has many possible causes: illness, brain damage, or abnormal brain development. Epilepsy may develop because of abnormal brain wiring, an imbalance of neurotransmitters, or some combination of these factors (NINDS, 2011d).

Epilepsy occurs with increased frequency in children with developmental disabilities. Epilepsy is defined as a condition involving two unprovoked seizures separated by 24 hours (Weinstein & Gaillard, 2007). For most children, this is a condition that resolves itself over several years. For some children it is a chronic condition. Children with epilepsy often have learning disabilities and behavioral challenges, but so far we do not know whether problems in brain development cause these problems (as well as the epilepsy), or whether recurrent seizures cause these problems or add to them (Weinstein & Gaillard, 2007). Epilepsy syndromes are seizure disorders, but each has different clinical features and characteristic electroencephalogram patterns.

The effect of the seizure depends on the location of the cells and how far the discharge spreads. Seizures take many forms, but there are two major classifications: generalized and partial. Understanding the seizure type helps to explain the child's behavior and often determines the types of educational and behavioral intervention needed.

Generalized seizures account for about 35 percent of pediatric epileptic disorders. They do not have an identifiable focus and impact both hemispheres of the brain, affecting widely spread cortical areas of the brain simultaneously. The cause is usually genetic. During the seizure, the child will have decreased motor activity or vigorous abnormal motor behaviors (Weinstein & Gaillard, 2007).

Absence seizures (formerly called *petit mal seizures*), a type of generalized seizure, are often inherited and begin between 3 and 12 years of age. They are characterized by glazed eyes, eye blinks, and/or changes in muscle tone. They last less than 30 seconds, cannot be interrupted by touch, and can happen hundreds of times a day (Weinstein & Gaillard, 2007). When a child is having a seizure, he can be injured by falling down stairs, or by walking into the path of an oncoming vehicle. The child is also not available for learning during seizures.

Partial seizures account for over half of all seizures. A simple partial seizure can begin anywhere in the brain and is limited to a small region of one hemisphere, and normal alertness is maintained. If it is sensory, children may experience an **aura**, a telltale sensation before the seizure. Complex partial seizures spread and alter consciousness. They usually start with auras or abrupt alterations in behavior. Children with this type of seizure will have the same aura before each seizure. Depending upon the length of the aura, there may be time for some intervention. Partial seizures may spread and become secondary generalized seizures. Children's movements slow and become purposeless during complex partial seizures. Depending upon the part of the brain in which the seizure originates, the child may appear agitated or may display unusual repetitive behaviors, such as eye blinking, lip smacking, facial grimacing, and groaning. These are caused by the brain's inability to plan and process motor and sensory input (Weinstein & Gaillard, 2007).

Some seizures have prominent motor components and can be brief or prolonged. A group of seizures called *drop seizures* cause abrupt changes in muscle tone. Both myoclonic and atonic seizures fall into this category. In these types of seizure, the child loses postural control.

Myoclonic seizures are brief, single, rapid contractions of muscles that may be repeated and can involve isolated muscle groups or more general muscles of the trunk and limbs. Some are subtle, with just head nodding, whereas others cause sudden flexion or bending backwards that almost seem to pull the child over.

In **atonic seizures**, the muscle tone is lost, which can lead to falling. Although the loss of consciousness may be brief, the child cannot protect himself during a fall (Weinstein & Gaillard 2007). Head injury is an obvious concern, and children may wear helmets to protect themselves. These kinds of seizures are very disconcerting for young children, and they may cry whether or not they are hurt.

Tonic-clonic seizures (formerly called *grand mal seizures*) are the most disturbing to observe. They may begin as either a partial or generalized seizure. These seizures have two components. In the clonic state, there is repetitive, rhythmic jerking of extremities, with slow and rapid components. In the tonic state there is sustained stiffening, perhaps jaw clenching. The loss of consciousness may lead to an unprotected fall. Either the tonic or clonic aspect of the seizure can occur first, followed by the other. During a seizure, respiration may sound raspy; an unusual cry, blueness, and incontinence may follow the seizure (Weinstein & Gaillard, 2007). Tonic-clonic seizures account for about a quarter of seizures overall (Kotagal, 2000). A period of sleep is required for the child to recover, and she will rarely remember the event. Although rare, prolonged seizures—those lasting more than 15 to 30 minutes without full return to consciousness—are considered a medical emergency. The concern here is that irreversible changes to the brain may occur.

Seizures are managed in a variety of ways, and parents must make decisions they feel are in the child's best interests. The first step is to determine whether the child has epilepsy and the seizures will reoccur. Treatment begins after a second unprovoked seizure. Some families choose to use antiepileptic drugs (AEDs). These drugs work by manipulating neurotransmitter activity. Families, in consultation with medical personnel, should evaluate the possibility of the reoccurrence of seizures and the potential side effects of the drugs. The most common side effects are those that impact the motor and cognitive areas of the brain. They include sleepiness, decreased attention and memory, difficulty in speaking, an unstable gait, and double vision. The side effects may occur when the drug is started but may then go away, or they may reoccur when dosages are increased. If side effects persist, the quest is for another drug that will regulate the seizures without side effects. There is additional concern that such drugs may have long-term adverse effects on learning, even after the drug use has been discontinued. They affect other body systems, and children can have allergic reactions to some (Weinstein & Gaillard, 2007). The complex decisions concerning drug treatment include determining the correct dosage and decisions about if and when drug therapy can be stopped.

Antiepileptic therapies do not always rely on medication. Some physicians find that a diet very low in sugars and carbohydrates, one that forces the brain to utilize fat rather than carbohydrates for energy, will alter neurotransmitters. Other therapies focus on making sure the child gets enough sleep and identifying and eliminating triggers. If a child's seizures do not respond to these interventions, surgery may be an option, depending on the number and severity of seizures, and their impact on the child's and family's lives.

IMPLICATIONS FOR EDUCATORS

Seizures are both embarrassing and frightening for the child having them, as well as the children who witness them. Children with seizures may be anxious, have a poor self-concept, and feel rejected and socially isolated. In early childhood, the social and emotional consequences of seizures may be the most devastating effect.

Seizures are primarily a medical problem. The management of seizures in the classroom, however, involves educational decision making. The first thing to do is to talk with the child's family and find out as much as you can about the type of seizures the child has, their frequency and length, whether they are set off by identifiable environmental stimuli, and how the child reacts when having a seizure. You should also have a written epilepsy action plan and follow it for any child who is identified as having epilepsy.

Obviously, it is important to know the first-aid procedure for seizures. The following information is adapted from the Epilepsy Foundation recommendations. It starts with *stay calm*. You can't stop a seizure once it starts. Absence seizures require no immediate action. For tonic-clonic seizures, if the child is upright, help move him to the floor, loosen clothing, and remove any nearby objects so he doesn't strike his head or body against them. Put something soft under his head. Turn the child's face to the side so saliva can flow out of the mouth, but don't otherwise interfere with movements. (A person having a seizure cannot swallow his tongue.) Time the seizure with your watch. Don't be alarmed if the child stops breathing momentarily, and don't put anything in the child's mouth. When the movements stop and he is relaxed, cover him and allow him to rest or sleep until he is ready to get up. Notify the child's parents that a seizure has occurred. Call for emergency medical services if the child has not had prior seizures; if the child has diabetes, heat exhaustion, or a head injury; if the seizure lasts more than five minutes, a second seizure follows, or it is unusual in some way (Epilepsy Foundation, n.d.). The child needs to be observed until fully alert, and teachers should provide reassurance and comfort. If the child has become incontinent, he should be helped unobtrusively to change his clothing and then allowed to rest. When ready, he should be encouraged to rejoin his classmates.

In addition to knowing first-aid procedures, you should note the length of the child's seizure and what the child was doing when the seizure took place. You should know the medication the child takes and its possible side effects.

Again, you are the model; to the extent that you are calm and matter-of-fact, the other children will be as well. If children ask you questions, answer them honestly, but simply: "Sometimes Sibyl's brain has too much energy. Her body is affected by this energy. Once the energy is gone, she is tired and wants to rest." Children who have tonic-clonic seizures are obvious to all children in the classroom. You should keep a towel and washcloth and a change of clothing for the child in your classroom.

●●●
Hepatitis

Hepatitis is an inflammation of the liver caused by a virus, which manifests itself in a number of different ways. **Hepatitis A (HAV)**, often referred to as yellow jaundice, an acute liver disease, is caused by the hepatitis A virus. It is common among the very young and elderly. A fecal to oral pathogen causes HAV; HAV is spread through food or water that was contaminated by a person with the virus. It is best controlled through proper implementation of appropriate hygiene practices and usually resolves itself after several weeks. The CDC (2010f) recommends a hepatitis A vaccination for all children, starting at 1 year of age.

Hepatitis B is a liver disease caused by the hepatitis B virus (HBV) and is spread through infected blood. The disease can be mild or chronic, and can last for a few weeks or lead to long-term liver disease or liver cancer. Approximately 90 percent of infected infants and 30 percent of infected children under age 5 become chronically infected with HBV. The CDC (2010g) recommends that children be vaccinated for Hepatitis B and pregnant women screened for the virus.

Hepatitis C requires more discussion than A, B, D, or E due to the rise in number of reported cases and the severity of the illness. Hepatitis C (HCV) is the most common chronic contagious blood-borne pathogen in the United States. Approximately 3.2 million people are infected (CDC, 2011a). Initially, most identified cases were due to exposure of health care providers who came into contact with contaminated blood. Sixty to 70 percent of newly infected people are asymptomatic, so people might not be aware of the virus. HCV-infected women can spread infection to their infants. The risk is greater if the mother is co-infected with HIV. The rate of transmission can be as high as 19 percent (CDC, 2011a). Through the proper use of universal precautions already discussed in this chapter, the risk of infections to educators and other children from hepatitis C is low and can be controlled. Only 1.5 percent of long-term spouses of individuals with chronic HCV infection developed HCV. There is no effective vaccine for hepatitis C (CDC, 2011a).

Although blood testing is reliable, it should not be conducted during the first 18 months of life, as the mother's antibodies may still be protecting the infant (CDC, 2008a). Families may be reluctant to disclose their child as a person with HCV for fear of discrimination. It is important, however, for parents to know as soon as possible whether their child has HCV, because if cirrhosis or carcinoma develops, the child will need to be placed on a waiting list for a liver transplant. Hepatitis C is the leading indication for liver transplants (CDC, 2008a).

Hepatitis D is a serious liver disease similar to hepatitis B. It is uncommon in the United States and there is no vaccine for HDV. The disease only occurs if someone already has HBV(CDC, 2009b).

Hepatitis E is a serious liver disease caused by the hepatitis E virus (HEV) that usually results in an acute infection. It is typically caused by fecal-contaminated drinking water. Although rare in the United States, it is common in developing countries. There are no current approved vaccines for hepatitis E (CDC, 2009c).

IMPLICATIONS FOR EDUCATORS

Viral hepatitis is primarily spread through direct contact with human blood or contaminated food or water. It can be spread in a household through sharing personal items that might have blood on them. Sneezing, hugging, coughing, sharing eating utensils or drinking glasses, or casual contact cannot spread it. As an educator of young children, it is imperative that you take the time to follow good, sound, and safe hygiene practices. You may not know whether a child in your class has HCV. For those who work with infants, remember that tests are not reliable until the child is at least 18 months old. Children with hepatitis need no special programming, just support of their social development and inclusion in the group.

●●●
Human Immunodeficiency Virus

Human immunodeficiency virus (HIV) has caused massive concern in health care and social systems. Although the number of people living with HIV (more than 1 million) is increasing, the number of new infections is relatively stable. Children with newly diagnosed HIV infection acquire it primarily from their mother (CDC, 2007d).

Between 120,000 and 160,000 women in the United States have HIV, and a fourth of these women do not know it (CDC, 2007d). This places them at risk for passing the virus to their infants. HIV testing is recommended for all pregnant women (AIDS info, 2010). Approximately 25 percent of infants born to mothers with HIV infection will become infected without intervention. Prenatal counseling and testing for HIV; the provision of perinatal antiretroviral prophylaxes; cesarean section births for HIV-infected women; and HIV-infected mothers using formula instead of breast-feeding can reduce the incidence of pediatric infection to 2 percent (CDC, 2007d, AIDS info, 2010). If HIV is suspected, infants should be tested at 14 to 21 days, at 1 to 2 months, and again at 4 to 6 months, using virologic HIV tests. If the test is negative at age 6 months, the infant has a 99 percent chance of not being infected with HIV (Bell, 2007).

Infants born to HIV-infected mothers should receive liquid AZT for 6 weeks. AZT not only helps the infant but also helps prevent mother-to-child transmission of HIV (AIDS info, 2010). Children who are infected with HIV may have a wide spectrum of illnesses, depending on the degree of immune system dysfunction. The advent of a vaccine against *Streptococcus pneumoniae*, and the use of antibiotic prophylaxes against these infections, has also helped improve the outlook for children with HIV. However, children are still at risk for bacterial infections that can cause complications. *Pneumocystis jiroveci* pneumonia, is a severe illness that children with HIV or AIDS may get. Children with normal immune systems who are infected with this germ don't get pneumonia, but children whose immune systems are badly damaged by HIV can get it. Pneumocystis jiroveci pneumonia is the most common serious infection among children with AIDS in the United States (CDC, 2007g).

Medical advancements have made tremendous differences in the quality of life for these children. However, compliance is an issue. To work, the medications have to be taken. If started and then discontinued, some medications can lead to a drug-resistant mutant HIV. There are a number of reasons why the medication routine is not adhered to: the large number of pills, the inconvenient schedules for taking them, uncomfortable side effects, poor understanding of the need for the medication, taste, and caregivers who do not follow through. Once started, the therapy must be monitored both for compliance and to ensure that appropriate drug quantities are taken (Bell, 2007).

Many children with HIV infection have some form of central nervous system dysfunction. These may be mild or more significant when there is not compliance to the regime. Children may have learning disabilities and expressive language disorders, impairments similar to cerebral palsy, and seizure disorders. Some children will lose the skills they have acquired as the disability proceeds if left unmonitored (Bell, 2007).

The HIV severe neurodevelopmental impairments of the 1980s and 1990s are now less common in the United States, but they are replaced by more subtle risks, such as learning and attention disorders. Overall, infants born to women who are infected with HIV typically are of lower birth weight and length than their counterparts. They have IQ scores that fall in the low–average range even when other things are factored out (Bell, 2007). Infants with HIV should have developmental assessments on a regular basis. If they are found to have delays, they are eligible for early intervention services. Children exposed to HIV have much to gain from early intervention.

Another area of concern for children with HIV is the risk for multiple placements outside the home if their parents become unable to provide a consistent and nurturing home for them as they become more ill with their own HIV infection.

IMPLICATIONS FOR EDUCATORS

Having a child with HIV infection in the classroom poses two serious questions: one relates to the disclosure of HIV status, and the other relates to infection control. Because of fear of discrimination, some parents do not tell their children that they have HIV infection, so the child himself may not know. Most states have decided that the teacher does not have the need to know whether a child in her class has HIV, the rationale being that risks to others are not great enough to violate a family's rights. Even if teachers receive this information informally, they are not allowed to disseminate it.

The next obvious question, then, is, "How great is the risk?" There are no documented cases of person-to-person transmission of HIV in child care centers or schools. No special precautions have to be taken other than routine hand washing. Universal precautions should be used with all blood-related incidents because of all blood-borne diseases. The exposure of a child with HIV to other, more contagious, infectious diseases may pose greater risks. Identifying infectious disease breakouts early, and informing parents, is good practice under any circumstances.

No single person or system can be responsive to the complex needs of children with HIV infections. Ideally, teachers work with health care providers as part of an interdisciplinary team to meet children's health, educational, and social needs.

● ● ●
Overweight and Obesity

The prevalence of children who are overweight and obese in the United States has increased markedly in the past three decades. Only Colorado and the District of Columbia had obesity rates less than 20 percent, and nine states had obesity rates at or over 30 percent (CDC, 2011c).

The calculations to determine children and youth's level of obesity are slightly different than they are for adults. For children, the BMI is determined using height and weight. This number is then plotted on the CDC BMI-for-age growth charts to obtain a percentile ranking. This then compares the BMI to other children of the same age and gender. See Table 16–3.

The results of the National Health and Nutrition Examination Survey (NHANES) confirm an increase in the number of children who are obese (CDC 2011b). See Table 16–4. Obesity in childhood is difficult to reverse. Overweight children have a difficult time keeping up with their friends. They cannot run as far or as fast or climb as high. The social and emotional costs are great.

When NHANES first began collecting data from 1971–1974, 5 percent of the children and youth were obese. The number has risen to 17 percent in 2008 (CDC, 2011b). Levels

More children are becoming overweight and obese at an earlier age because of more sedentary activities and less moderate to vigorous activity.
© Cengage Learning 2012

16-3   BMI WEIGHT STATUS CATEGORIES AND PERCENTILE RANGE

Weight Status Category	Percentile
Underweight	Less than 5th percentile
Healthy weight	5th percentile to less than 85th percentile
Overweight	85th percentile to 95th percentile
Obese	Equal to or greater than the 95th percentile

of obesity also vary with race and income. One in seven (14.3%) low-income preschool children are obese, but that number appears to be stabilizing. See Table 16-5.

Individuals' weights are determined by the amount of energy they put into their body in the form of food and the amount of energy they expend in the form of physical activity or energy. If the amount of energy individuals put into their body is equal to the amount of energy they expend, then weight is maintained. If more energy is put into the body than is expended, weight gain occurs. Weight loss occurs when the amount of energy expended is greater than the amount of energy put into the body. To maintain healthy weight, individuals must learn to balance intake and expenditure.

IN THE FIELD

At one point in my life, when I was younger, more naïve, and perhaps more creative, Beth was in my 4-year-old class. The problem was that we had an open snack area at one of the centers, and Beth came in and went directly to the snack center and ate most of the snack. Other children came later and there was nothing left for them. Had Beth been undernourished, I might have dealt with this differently, but Beth was overweight. I was initially subtle and talked about sharing equally, taking turns, exploring all the centers, but it was ineffective to say the least. I had heard about family meetings and class problem solving but had never tried it. With little thought, I decided to broach the topic of snack. At a group time I said, "I'm concerned about the snack center because by the time some of you get there, there isn't anything left."

I called on a child who had dutifully raised his hand and he said, "Yeah, Beth eats it all." I was unprepared for this directness and unable to think of a way out. Everyone was nodding. I hadn't thought they noticed. "Well, I said, what do you think we should do to make sure everyone gets a snack?" The first response was "Kill Beth." Well, obviously, I was out of my league. I described Beth's good points and tried to refocus the discussion. The children were adamant. I had started this and apparently I would have to finish it. We agreed that killing Beth was not an acceptable solution.

16-5   PERCENT OF PRESCHOOL CHILDREN WHO WERE OBESE IN 2008 BY RACE/ETHNICITY

Race/Ethnicity	Percentage
American Indian and Alaska Native	21.2%
Hispanic	18.5%
White	12.6%
Asian or Pacific Islanders	12.3%
Black	11.8%

Source: CDC, 2011b.

The children came up with a variety of solutions and then settled on one. We had a chart that showed which children were responsible for certain activities during the day (leading the line, setting up snack, etc.). Remember that Beth is sitting here during this. I was wishing I had decided to become an accountant like my father wanted. The children's decision was that Beth should be put on the chart and that one child should be assigned to watch Beth each day so that she didn't eat the entire snack. I was mortified, but I had backed myself into a corner that I couldn't get out of. So, we put Beth up on the chart and children were assigned to watch Beth on a rotating basis.

I had apparently missed a lot. Beth had no friends and no one to play with. The children on the roster were conscientious and played with her. She became more a part of the classroom and began to play with others. The snack problem was solved. She was later diagnosed with Prader-Willi syndrome (a disability that includes behavior problems and an insatiable appetite). This explained our problem. The parents were concerned and knew something was wrong, but no one seemed able to tell them what it was.

REFLECTIVE PRACTICE | Children are observant and they know what is going on in a classroom. Although Beth's problem eventually worked out well, in retrospect what do you think this teacher could have done to control this situation better? How might you have handled it and gotten a positive outcome? Do you feel this was an acceptable solution?

Because many factors contribute to obesity, finding a "cause" for it is not possible, but it is possible to identify behaviors that contribute to energy imbalance.

Energy intake. Nutrition—energy input—during the first three years of life helps determine children's growth patterns and body weight (Stunkard et al., 2004). Eating habits established during these years may program preferences into the brain that influence adolescent and adult nutrition (Mennella et al., 2006).

A high percentage of children's food preferences are formed as early as age 2 to 3 years. French fries are the most common vegetables consumed by toddlers. Some type of dessert, sugared sweets, or a sweetened beverage were consumed by almost half of 7- to 8-month-olds, and this percentage increased with age. Eighteen to 33 percent of infants and toddlers consumed no discrete servings of fruits or vegetables on a given day (Fox et al., 2004). As educators, we need to be mindful of this information.

By the time children are 5 years old, they are consuming most of the foods of the adult diet of their culture. However,

16-4   PERCENT OF CHILDREN WHO WERE OBESE FROM 1976 TO 2008 BY AGE

Ages (years)	1976–1980	2007–2008
2–5	5%	10.4%
6–11	6.5%	19.6%
12–19	15.0%	18.1%

Source: CDC, 2011b.

children eat what they like and leave the rest. Therefore, food preferences are especially important determinants of the food intake of young children. In a classic study, Birch (1980) found that when preschool children were provided opportunities to observe other children choosing and eating vegetables (that they themselves did not enjoy), preferences for and eating of the disliked vegetables increased. With the potential of peer modeling, early childhood settings have the opportunity for making nutritious foods available to children and providing models for consuming them.

During the early childhood years, children are capable of learning to like and accept a variety of foods. In addition, repeated opportunities to taste a food increased acceptance. At least 8 to 15 exposures may be necessary before the food is accepted (Birch, 1996). Skinner and colleagues (2002) also found children's preference for a food or flavor increased with repeated exposure. They found that foods introduced after age 4 were less likely to be accepted by children.

If children have had juice for breakfast, then they should not have it again during the school day. Children 12 to 24 months should drink either whole milk or water. Children older than 24 months should drink 1 percent or fat-free milk or water. From 1 to 3 years, at least one-fourth cup of fruits and/or vegetables should be offered at each meal and snack. By age 3, this quantity increases to half a cup (Nemours Health and Prevention Services, 2008).

Physical activity—energy output—promotes growth and development and provides the foundation for enjoying physical activity later in life (Heinzer, 2005). Children's physical activity can be either structured or unstructured. Structured physical activity for young children is planned and directed by an adult. When physical activity is adult directed, children obtain significant amounts of moderate and vigorous physical activity (Ward, Saunders, & Pate, 2007). Adults can also coach children to increase their skill level. Unstructured physical activity is naturally occurring, child-initiated physical activity. Both structured and unstructured physical activities are essential for children. The level of physical activity children participate in is affected by their weight. Overweight boys were significantly less active than normal-weight boys during the preschool day (Trost et al., 2003).

A sedentary life style that is characterized by lack of moderate and vigorous activity, and excessive screen media use (television, videos, computers) is associated with increased risks of childhood obesity (Jago et al., 2005). Children ages 6 and younger spend an average of two hours a day with screen media. They primarily watch TV and videos (Rideout, Vandewater, & Wartella, 2003). For children as young as 3 years of age, the amount of TV viewing along with amounts of physical activity were significant predictors of BMI (Jago et al., 2005). Among 2,761 children aged 1 to 5 years in New York state, those who were black or Hispanic and those with a TV in their own bedroom were at greater risk of becoming overweight. Preschool children with TVs in their bedroom watched an additional 4.8 hours of TV or videos every week (Dennison, Erb, & Jenkins, 2002).

Watching an excessive amount of television both decreases activity level and increases children's requests for advertised foods. Children who watched television more frequently were also more likely to eat high-calorie, low-nutrient food, ask their parents to purchase advertised foods, develop poor eating habits, become overweight, develop eating disorders, and have elevated cholesterol levels (Byrd-Bredbenner, 2002). Watching television has both direct and indirect effects. Half to two-thirds of commercials during children's programming are about food (Comstock & Scharrer, 2003). The most common food advertisements during children's shows are for presweetened breakfast cereals and high-sugar foods. There are virtually no advertisements for vegetables, fruits, protein-rich food, and unsweetened breakfast cereals (Byrd-Bredbenner, 2002). Children younger than 6 years of age cannot distinguish between commercials and programming. They do not understand that the purpose of commercials is to persuade them to buy something or to ask their parents to do so (Johnson & Young, 2003). They simply know they want the advertised product. Food advertisements aimed at children entice them with more than just the food.

Approximately one-third of food advertisements offer prizes, and most of the advertisement focuses on the prize. If children associate getting rewards and prizes with eating fast food and snacks, they are less likely to see the benefit of consuming healthier foods (Byrd-Bredbenner, 2002).

The desire for advertised foods begins at an early age. Children as young as age 2 are more likely to choose advertised foods (Henry J. Kaiser Family Foundation, 2004), and brand preferences start in preschool and continue to strengthen through elementary school (Johnson & Young, 2003). These various influences create additional challenges in helping children establish healthy weights from an early age.

Obesity causes an increased risk of health problems in early childhood and later. Increases in asthma and sleep disorders occur early. Risks for type 2 diabetes, heart disease, high blood pressure and high cholesterol, liver disease, orthopedic complications, and mental health problems can occur later. However, although many of these diseases take years of damage to develop, obese children develop them at a younger age than their parents would despite advances in medicine (Daniels, 2006).

IMPLICATIONS FOR EDUCATORS

Educators need to help children get more in touch with their bodies. When children tell us they are not hungry and we require them to eat or finish the food on their plate, we are teaching them not to respond to what their body is telling them. We need to evaluate our own practices related to eating and the nutritional quality of the food served in early care and education settings.

To help children establish healthy eating habits, adults should choose meals and snacks wisely. Adults determine what foods young children have available to eat. Children need a variety of fruits, vegetables, whole-grain foods and bread, fluid milk products, and meat and meat alternatives, including some unsaturated fat (U.S. Departments of Health and Human Services and Agriculture, 2005). Water should be available and children should be encouraged to drink water when they are thirsty.

Snacks provide about 25 percent of young children's daily energy intake (Skinner et al., 2004). Snacking can help children learn self-regulation by showing them how to maintain their metabolism. A stable metabolism can help children feel less hungry and thus may prevent them from overeating at meal times. To make snacking effective, snacks and meals should have balance, variety, contrast, color, eye appeal, and nutritive value. Snacks are also beneficial because they provide an opportunity to introduce new foods (U.S. Department of Agriculture Child and Adult Care Food Program, 2002).

Think about how your snack choices will support all children's healthy eating. Go beyond juice to serving water or fat-free milk. Replace crackers with strawberries dipped in low-fat yogurt, whole-grain pita with hummus, low-fat cottage cheese with fruit, and steamed or fresh vegetables dipped in fat-free sour cream. Children like to dip. However, they each need their own dipping cup.

Children who are overweight exercise less than other children. They seem to be able to do single, nonrhythmic activities like climbing, but have problems with repeated rhythmic activities like running. Playing loud music with a distinct beat during activities helps them improve this skill. To help burn calories and tone muscles, these children should be encouraged to participate in moderate to vigorous levels of activity in bursts of three to five minutes as many as 10 times a day. They and their parents also need education on nutrition. Praise and other noncaloric rewards should be used, never sweets. Early childhood educators should embed structured and unstructured physical activities into daily schedules and routines.

• • •
Sickle Cell Disease

Sickle cell disease (SCD) refers to a group of painful inherited disorders that affect the red blood cells. It is typically found at birth during routine newborn blood screening tests. Red blood cells are normally shaped like a doughnut with a hole in the middle that does not go through completely, and they have a life span of approximately 120 days. In sickle cell disease, cells take on a crescent, or sickle shape; are more rigid and sticky; and have a life span of about 10 to 20 days (Carroll, 2000, CDC, 2010h). This impairs the oxygen-carrying capacity of the cells, is conducive to clogging, and can lead to anemia. The result is pain and chronic fatigue. Frequent blood transfusions are necessary to replace destroyed red blood cells. The only cure is bone marrow/stem cell transplant (CDC, 2009e). Children with severe forms of the disease may die in childhood or early adulthood from a blood clot, which prevents oxygen from reaching the brain, or infections (CDC, 2010h). **Hemoglobin**, a substance in red blood cells that makes the blood red in color and carries oxygen to all parts of the body, is also problematic in SCD.

In the United States 70,000 to 100,000 people have sickle cell disease. One in 12 African Americans is a carrier of the sickle cell gene, and the disease affects 1 in 500 births. The disease occurs in 1 out of every 36,000 Hispanic American births (CDC, 2010h).

There are four common types of SCD:

- HbSS, or sickle cell anemia, occurs when a child inherits two sickle cell genes (SS), one from each parent. This is the most severe form of the disease.
- HbSC, sickle beta-plus-thalassemia, occurs when a child inherits one sickle cell gene (S) and one gene for an abnormal type of hemoglobin (C). This is typically a milder form of the disease.
- HbS, beta thalassemia, occurs when a child inherits one sickle cell gene (S) and one gene for beta thalassemia, another type of anemia. These symptoms can be mild or severe depending upon they type of beta thalassemia inherited.
- HbAS, or sickle cell trait, occurs when children inherit one sickle cell gene (S) and one normal gene (A). They will not have symptoms of the disease but can pass the disease on to their children (CDC, 2009e).

In sickle cell disease, children lack hemoglobin A; there is only sickle hemoglobin, hemoglobin S. The actual proportion of the sickle-shaped cells varies from child to child. The higher the proportion and the earlier the symptoms appear, the more severe the disease is likely to be.

Anemia is a complication that can cause tiredness, irritability, dizziness, trouble breathing, and slow growth. Taking iron supplements is not helpful as there are not enough oxygen-carrying red blood cells. Blood transfusions are used to treat anemia when it becomes severe. Infection is a major concern and the leading cause of death in children with sickle cell disease. Children should get the traditional vaccines given in early childhood as well as some extra ones, including flu shots and pneumococcal vaccine. The advent of the "pneumonia" vaccine has increased life expectancies for children with sickle cell disease (CDC, 2010h).

IMPLICATIONS FOR EDUCATORS

Young children with sickle cell disease are more prone to crises and hospitalization than are older children. Crises are precipitated by a variety of circumstances: infection; chilling; dehydration; strenuous exercise; sweating; and cold, damp weather. Use this knowledge to take preventive measures. Children with sickle cell disease need nutritionally dense foods. Plan snacks and lunches to meet these needs. They also need to drink a great deal of fluid, especially water. Encourage children to drink more by having fluids readily available, and ensure that there is easy access to the bathroom. Fatigue is a major factor, as children tire easily and a general lassitude is often present. Be aware of the balance of active and quiet activities in the classroom. Be sure to alternate these activities and to have alternative activities that are not physically demanding. Stress cooperation, not competition. Help children build a good self-concept.

• • •
Tourette Syndrome

Tourette syndrome is a neurologic disorder whose essential features are repetitive involuntary motor or vocal tics. A **tic** is a sudden rapid, recurrent, nonrhythmic, stereotyped motor movement or vocalization (NINDS, 2011f). **Simple tics** involve sudden brief, repetitive movements that use a limited number of muscle groups such as eye blinking, shoulder shrugging, throat clearing, sniffing, and so on. **Complex tics** are distinct, coordinated patterns that involve several muscle groups and may be a combination of simple tics such as facial grimacing combined with a head twist and shrugging a shoulder. They may actually appear purposeful such as hopping, bending, or twisting. Complex vocal tics involve words or phrases. The most distressing tics are those that result in self-harm either physically (e.g., punching oneself in the face) or social-emotionally such as uttering swear words or repeating the phrases of others (NINDS, 2011f). The behaviors may seem voluntary and purposeful, but they are not.

Tics are typically worse with excitement and anxiety and better in calm and quiet periods. Motor tics typically precede vocal tics and simple tics precede complex tics. First symptoms occur in the head and neck area and may proceed to the trunk and limbs. The peak period for tic severity is during the early teen years, and then it shows signs of improvement, with approximately 10 percent lasting into adulthood (NINDS, 2011f). Children with Tourette syndrome may also have other neurobiological problems such as ADHD, SLD, depression, or anxiety disorders.

The early symptoms typically begin between 7 and 10 years of age but can start as early as age 2 (APA, 2000). It is estimated that 200,000 children have the most severe form of Tourette syndrome, with 1 in 100 children exhibiting milder and less complex symptoms such as chronic motor or vocal tics or transient tics of childhood (NINDS, 2011f). To be diagnosed with Tourette syndrome, the tics must occur many times a day over a period of more than a year, with the child never being tic free for a period of more than three consecutive months. The tics must not be the effects of medication or of another medical condition (APA, 2000). The causes of Tourette syndrome are not known, but are likely to be complex, with research showing abnormalities in certain regions of the brain, the circuits that connect these regions, and neurotransmitters.

IMPLICATIONS FOR EDUCATORS

Because of the involuntary nature of tics, children need experiences where they have some control. They need to see themselves in positions where the environment responds to them rather than the other way around. Many children will not display tics during the early childhood years. If they do, the involuntary nature of their tics should be acknowledged. It is important that the other children in the classroom understand that the behavior is not under the child's control, and that they learn to ignore it and continue playing.

Guidelines

Children with special health care needs cover a wide range of needs and impairments. They may require you to learn new information and develop skills that are medical in nature. Use the following guidelines to help accommodate these differences and to support children in their growth and development:

1. *Use activities that allow children to be in control*, or adapt activities so that children have more control. Let the children decide what color(s) of fingerpaint they want to use, whether they want one dab or two, and where they want these on the paper.

2. *Encourage the children to do as much as possible for themselves.* Actively support age-appropriate independence.

3. *Arrange the class schedule so that vigorous activities are followed by less strenuous ones*; during strenuous activities, provide rest periods that are built in for everyone and alternative ways for doing activities.

4. *Be flexible in scheduling the day* so that if children have to leave for medical procedures, this can become part of the routine. If you accept the children's therapy and its importance, it will be easier for them. Some children find a full day tiring, especially when they return after an illness. If possible, have them come for part of the day.

5. *Plan activities that are open ended* and do not require excessive amounts of time to complete, or ones that can be completed at home. Because some children may work more slowly and miss more school than others, they may decide not to start things they never expect to complete.

6. *Be a good observer.* Watch for mood changes, as these are often cues to well being. Be aware of the child's body language. Often, a child will grimace or give other signs that will alert you to possible pain or arouse concern about the level of medication the child is taking. Young children have trouble recognizing and verbalizing their needs; you can help them.

7. *Find out as much as you can about the illnesses children have and how it affects them.* Talk to parents, therapists, and medical personnel, read books on the subject, and check the Internet. Be informed about children's diet, physical restrictions, medication, possible side effects of the medicine, and the behaviors that indicate a chronic illness might be moving into an acute phase.

8. *Find out what a child has been told about her illness and its implications.* Be prepared to respond to comments such as "I don't want to play with you. You have leukemia. You're going to die." You need to know how the parents are dealing with the concept of death and exactly what they call the illness. Even with that knowledge, handling the situation is not easy. Young children are not capable of abstract thinking. Death is not viewed as permanent. This doesn't mean, however, that they are any less fearful of it. Although the child's classmates may seem unfeeling, they are only displaying curiosity and lack of knowledge.

9. *Help children learn about the implications of their special health care needs.* Verbalize for them what happens under certain circumstances: "You are allergic to peanuts. If you eat them, it will be hard for you to breathe. There are other things that are crunchy like peanuts

that you can eat. These are sunflower seeds. I like them."

10. *Provide an open atmosphere where children can discuss fears and problems.* One thing that children know is that if it is taboo it is bad. Be honest when you do not know an answer; say you don't know and then find out the answer. In general, don't tell children more than they ask. They are the best guides about what they need to know.

11. *Develop a plan for keeping in touch with absent children.* You could send get-well cards through the mail or use e-mail. Another child could deliver an audio- or video-tape. The child could be called on the phone by other children or by using the computer with appropriate software (find out good times to call or let the child phone school). Send home a "fun bag," or develop a lending library of books and toys. The best plan is tailored to both your situation and the child's needs.

12. *Provide accommodations.* Certain illnesses require adaptations such as free access to the toilet, extra time for task completion, special food for snacks, scheduling time to take medication, and so on. Provide it.

13. *Play cooperative games.* Classroom stress can bring on crises in some chronic illnesses (e.g., asthma, diabetes). Do not play competitive games. Make the classroom as pressure free as possible.

14. *Prepare children for events.* Special events (e.g., holidays, birthdays, field trips) may lead to flare-ups, as there is almost always some psychosomatic element in the timing or severity of acute bouts. Talk about what is likely to happen. This is a time to watch for stress-related reactions.

15. *Learn to recognize warning signs of emergencies.* Discuss with parents what they want you to do in case of an emergency, and develop a written plan that has contingencies. If you are to call, call when you suspect something is wrong—do not wait for full confirmation. Tape the numbers near the phone you will use. Know the location of the nearest emergency room and the fastest way to get there. Take a first-aid course; be sure it includes the Heimlich maneuver and cardiopulmonary resuscitation (CPR).

Curriculum Adaptations

Children with special health care needs require few curriculum adaptations as long as they are allowed to work at their own pace. While working in each curriculum area, help children feel included in the group, and focus on improving their self-concept.

Social Awareness

Many children with special health care needs have been hospitalized. They may have concerns about doctors, hospitals, and separation from their parents. One of the most frightening aspects of hospitalization is the feeling of being out of control. Giving them knowledge about the roles of professionals, including physicians, is empowering. They need to develop social skills and methods of keeping in touch with peers when they cannot attend school. Some of the activities in the Resource Chapter 1 are specifically designed to increase children's awareness of special health care needs (Activities 1–23, *Medical Tools;* 1–24, *Doctors;* and 1–27, *Emergency Room*).

Social Competence

Because most children with special health care needs look like other children, adults may not understand or remember their challenges. As they may have periods when they are fine and periods when they are not, others wonder if it is just a game they are playing. They may be misunderstood at school. They may not be able to participate in some strenuous activities. Because of frequent absences, it may be difficult for them to build relationships with other children and to complete projects. Children may not be fun to be with if they are experiencing pain or side effects from drugs. Teachers may have to remind other children of these circumstances.

1. Help children become more aware of their feelings and learn to express them. Give them the skills to work through them. See Activity 1-38w, *Share your Feelings,* for additional ideas.

2. Have children make a list (an adult can write it) of what they can do and like to do. Focus on the positive.

3. Help children think about what makes them happy and how they can use this knowledge when they become sad or fearful.

Children who have spent a long time convalescing in the hospital or at home may have had few opportunities to learn how to play with other children. They may not function at an age-appropriate level in areas such as cooperating with others, sharing, and turn taking. They may have fewer skills in joining and being part of groups.

1. You are a model of the behaviors that are necessary for children to join groups. To the extent that you never join groups, you don't model this behavior and it is more obvious when you try to include a child with special health care needs. Suggest roles that need filling or parts that they could play. However, accept the reality that this sometimes does not work, and openly explain to children that this is the way it is. If this happens frequently, you may need to use a different strategy and focus all children on how to include others.

2. Your role should be one that changes over time. Children may initially need your active support. However, supporting them when they have the ability to act on their own creates dependency and decreases growth.

3. Emphasize ways of approaching others.

Social Studies

Although our concern about children with special health care needs focuses on medical practice and settings, children spend most of their life in the community. Children need to know and role-play not only traditional occupations but also variations, and they need to learn about people, places, and environments.

1. Help children play the roles of public health nurses who visit homes, itinerant teachers who educate children who cannot attend school, and social workers or others who may serve as a support system to families.

2. Include discussions of cultural variations and the role of extended family as well as alternative medical sources.

3. Help children understand the interconnectedness of the community in which they live. Include information about water, electricity, and waste disposal, and the consequences if the community does not address these needs.

4. Help children draw and fill in a map of the route from the classroom to the nurse's office (if that is where they go). If hospitalized, remind children that they can learn about an unfamiliar place using the skill they have in map making. Include other significant places in the map.

English Language Arts

Children need to be able to communicate. Some children with special health care needs will lack the experiential basis for language because they have spent time in restrictive settings. Parents may have limited children's opportunities, both because of the illness itself and because most illnesses weaken children and increase their susceptibility to contagious diseases. In addition to expanding their overall language base, children need to develop the vocabulary to express their fears and concerns and increase their understanding of the situations they may face. They need to be aware of their symptoms and how to label them, know their body parts, and be able to put the two together to give accurate information about their current state of health. Children may have consciously tried not to listen or found that adults did not expect them to listen, so they quit paying attention. Adults often forget that there may be so much attention to other areas of learning that listening is neglected, or that although children listen, they may not understand what they hear. Reading offers the child an escape into other worlds of learning. Writing affords children the opportunity to express and share feelings, even when those they want to speak with are not present. It also provides a way of remembering important information.

• • •
Speaking and Listening

Encouraging children to speak about nonthreatening experiences provides the groundwork for talking about experiences that they perceive as sad or scary.

1. Take field trips to the florist, bakery, post office, and radio station to help children gain firsthand experiences they may be lacking because of their special health care needs (be sure the places you plan to visit will not trigger an episode for a child).

2. Exchange language experience stories when children are out of school for extended periods. Have children write stories about "Going to the Hospital" or "Things I Can See Out My Window." Include illustrations or use pictures from a digital camera.

3. Send a "Get Well Soon" audio- or videotape or e-mail to the child. Have children who want to share tape a message. If this is set up as an activity area, put a picture of the child beside the tape, and encourage the children to talk to her. (Be prepared to edit the tape before it is sent.) The child who is ill may wish to send an answering tape back. See Activity 1–36w, *Get-Well Cards* .

4. Encourage children to ask questions. Show children pictures of situations and ask them to describe what is happening in the picture; help them ask questions about what specific objects are, how they are used, and about what will happen next.

5. Show children pictures of scenes (beach, grocery store, hospital, doctor's office, classroom, etc.), and ask them how they would feel if they were part of the picture. Show pictures with moods that may be interpreted in a variety of ways. After one child has responded, ask whether others feel differently, and have them describe their feelings. Ask children what they need to change in the picture to change a negative feeling to a positive one (e.g., have a parent present, hold a stuffed animal).

Children frequently are expected not only to listen but also to understand and follow through on adult requests, especially if these come from medical personnel. Children need skills in following directions and in asking for clarification when they do not understand what is required.

1. Play "Simon Says" and include requests that frequently occur in medical situations: "Say, 'Aahhh,'" "Take a deep breath," "Open your mouth wide," and so on. Using similar phrases, put them together and have children perform a series of tasks involving their body: "Open your mouth, take a deep breath, and breathe out slowly."

2. Make a listening tape of hospital sounds. This will make a strange place a bit more familiar. If the child has to stay in bed, make a listening tape of things one might hear from bed and find out what the sounds mean.

3. Consider the appropriateness of what you are doing if children become inattentive listeners, but also consider health issues such as fatigue and illness.

4. Have a listening center where you have appropriate books as well as recordings of those books. Help children develop the skill of independent listening, so if they are out of school for an extended period, they have a familiar activity they can participate in. Children can use headphones and safely listen while not bothering others if the equipment has sound level governors so the children cannot make the sound so loud that it affects

their hearing. Because your collection of CDs, DVDs, and books is likely to be more extensive than any family's, plan a system for loaning children their favorites.

Reading

Reading books is a great way to make the unknown a little more familiar, to help children know they are not the only ones with fears, and perhaps to help put themselves and their situation into perspective. Choose stories that relate to the specific situation the children you are teaching might face (see the Children's Bibliography). Reading requires not only cognitive readiness, but also an experiential background, so that the reading content makes sense. Part of your role is to develop creative ways to give children the experiential background they need to read and comprehend.

1. Read stories about children in hospitals.
2. Read stories about children or animals who are different.
3. Read or record a story the children are familiar with. Make some obvious mistakes (change words, locations, outcomes, etc.) and have the children find your mistakes.
4. Use DVDs, Internet sources, and technology to bring experiences to children.
5. Listen to the child's spoken language. If children have not had opportunities for speaking and listening that others have had, build these skills as part of your literacy program.
6. Help children focus on the relationship between printed and spoken language.
7. Encourage children to gain some control over their world through sequencing activities, especially ones that may hurt or are frightening: "First, we go to the doctor's office. Then I tell them my name, then I wait. Then I get my allergy shot, and then I wait some more. Then I get checked for a reaction, and then I can go home." This makes the injection one of a series of events rather than the total focus.
8. Expose children to a wide variety of written materials. Read and recite many different types of children's books, poetry, fingerplays, and so on. It is useful, especially if what you are reciting is new to you, to have the words available in case you forget them. Point out to the children that you are doing this and why.
9. Have children match line-drawn faces showing different expressions. Then talk about what these people might be feeling or doing.
10. Play hospital or medical Lotto.
11. Use informational texts about the body and its parts and how it works.

Writing

The writing process requires that you help children develop the small motor skills and eye–hand coordination necessary to write, build a desire to write, and connect writing with reading.

1. Make writing part of many different curriculum areas; for example, in dramatic play, encourage children to write prescriptions for the dolls who are sick.
2. Have children keep a chart about what happens to the sick doll. Discuss with children why they might do this and how this helps ensure accurate information when different people care for the doll.
3. Have some of the children make a picture menu of what the choices are for snack, and then let them find out from the other children what they want from the menu. (Be sure you have enough so that children can have what they request.) After each child "writes" his name on his menu, distribute menus to children's places at the table along with their "orders." Because of the quality of the writing, it is likely that some of the orders will be wrong. Talk about the fact that mistakes happen in all restaurants, and discuss what to do about them.

Language

Children with special health care needs need to learn the vocabulary that is used in their special needs area and to describe their feelings and symptoms accurately to become safer and more independent.

1. Teach the names of body parts, both external and internal, and what each body part does. Focus on the ones that are most relevant to the children you teach.
2. Teach children numbers, colors, and shapes, and then help them apply this vocabulary to the medicine they must take (e.g., number of breaths they take on an inhaler).
3. Build a vocabulary that relates to being tired and the relationship between activity level and tiredness, with an emphasis on when to stop activities. Help them tune into the vocabulary that relates to exercise (heart rate, breathing, etc.).

Discovery

Children need support in investigating the world around them and in making sense out of it. They need to sort, classify, and develop the vocabulary to express themselves. They need to *do* this, not simply be told about it. The lives of children with special health care needs are linked to medicine and scientific discoveries. Their understanding of the scientific process can help them look at the implications of taking medicine versus not taking it. They can also explore and learn about their body and how it functions. Make math real and relevant. Technology can allow children to stay in touch with their classmates even when they are home. Software programs that are used at school may also be used at home. Some children with special health care needs use technology to help them move or breathe. Placing technology in the context of learning about health impairments normalizes special health care needs.

Mathematics

Build sensory motor concepts by actively interacting with manipulatives like blocks, Cuisenaire rods, Uniflex blocks, and pegs. Then move on to more abstract number concepts. Make math relevant. Children need to know how many pills they must take and when. This is a step toward independence as well as toward learning number concepts.

1. Use three-dimensional objects like unit blocks to teach basic math concepts; do not rely on rote memory.

2. Use music and rhythmic activities to reinforce math concepts (e.g., clap four times).

3. Have children sort and classify familiar pieces of medical equipment (e.g., cotton balls, tongue depressors, bandages of different sizes and shapes, gauze). They can even make mathematical equations out of these materials and write out the equation (e.g., 3 cotton balls + 5 cotton balls = 8 cotton balls). When there are larger numbers, help them understand the base 10 system.

Science

Because most children take medicine to alleviate symptoms, it is important to develop their cause-and-effect reasoning skills. They need to understand why they should take the medicine even when they feel well.

1. Plant seeds. Discuss conditions for growth. Put some plants in the dark. Do not water some. Discuss the implications of the various conditions and "treatments." See Activity 3–17, *Terrarium*.

2. Help children make predictions. Help them apply this skill to their particular situation: "I have trouble breathing when I run fast. If I run slower, I can run farther."

3. Help children learn about the seasons of the year, especially if they directly affect their state of health. Discuss with them how we prepare ourselves for seasonal change as well as how this happens in nature. Have children talk about the seasons' effects on them: "I can't walk as far in the winter when it is cold and windy." They need to develop this type of causal thinking.

Technology

The computer has many applications for children with special health care needs. It requires little energy to use; it is hygienic, self-paced, and available when the child wants to use it, and it's portable and interactive. Other technologies, such as digital cameras, can allow children to share anything from artwork to pictures of what is happening at home or in the classroom, electronic tablets and their applications are even more portable and support learning. E-mail and the Internet open up even more possibilities.

1. Encourage children with special health care needs to become familiar with technology. They need to establish some control over their world, and they can do that with a computer or electronic tablet. Regardless of how

Children need to be in control of the technology they use.
© Cengage Learning 2012

rudimentary their skills, the potential for cause-and-effect reasoning is present.

2. Use a communication board or computer equipped with a simple switch and a scanning program or an electronic tablet to allow children to make their needs known.

3. Loan or recommend to parents software that will help children learn some of the concepts you are teaching if children are out for an extended time.

4. Help children frame some of the equipment they use as technology.

5. Help children participate in interactive recreation through technology. (Traditional "arcade" games typically require good fine motor coordination but are timed, which is not helpful.) Computerized board games such as checkers and "Monopoly" exist, as well as many other commercially available games.

Wellness

All children need to learn to keep their bodies safe and healthy. They need to learn what they can and cannot do. If they become knowledgeable about their bodies and how they function, children may be able to prevent acute episodes by learning to recognize symptoms and/or avoiding situations likely to cause acute episodes. This knowledge will, in turn, make children feel more in control and help them move toward independence. Children with special health care needs must develop as much strength and endurance as they can. Respect their limits, but encourage them to participate in large motor activities. Young children will rarely overextend themselves if programming is individualized so children can set their own limits. Opportunities for sensory motor integration are essential. Small motor activities are easily adaptable for quiet play and can be used to pace the day. Try to think of variations and new materials that will keep children interested. Be aware of the weather, especially when it is windy or very cold or hot.

These extremes may cause children to tire quickly. Have some quiet activities outside also.

Health and Safety

Health and safety should be emphasized. Children need to learn about foods, those that are good for them and those they must avoid, as well as safety practices.

1. Work on the food groups, which foods are in each, and how the body uses different foods. Use the food pyramid for kids and look at the games and other supports at www.mypyramid.gov/kids/index.html.

2. Use illustrations to explain what happens when people eat food they are allergic to.

3. Teach good hygiene practices to prevent contagious diseases, such as covering their mouths when coughing and sneezing, or coughing into their shoulder or elbow if nothing else is available. Children should always wash hands after toileting and before eating; when coming in from outside; after using a tissue; and, of course, when they are dirty.

4. Help children analyze situations for potential injuries and talk about what can be done to prevent injuries.

5. Talk about healthy lifestyles.

Large Motor

Children with special health care needs may find large motor play challenging. Find ways of allowing different amounts of time for activities if children are not self-regulatory.

1. Keep activities noncompetitive and pressure free.

2. Emphasize the quality of movement, not speed.

3. Modify some games to reduce the distance to be traveled or slow the pace by having children walk, not run. Institute intermissions. (All children must clap 10 times between events.)

4. Have children jump on a trampoline (or mattress with dust cover). This improves drainage of the respiratory tract.

Sensory Motor Integration

Children need experience coordinating their senses. If they have not had sufficient opportunity to do this, you need to provide more activities that make them aware of their bodies and where they are in space.

1. Give verbal directions for motor activities and see whether the children can follow them. Once you have ascertained that they can, change the directions slightly.

2. Play games with beach balls that require little effort but a fair amount of coordination and integration.

3. Toss, balance, or catch beanbags. They are adaptable to the classroom as well as other settings.

4. Incorporate yoga into your daily schedule starting with "Take a deep yoga breath." See Activities 4–25, *Yoga-Breathing*, and 4–26, *Yoga Poses*.

5. Clap to music, songs, or in a pattern (sequence)—especially when the hands cross the midline, the right and left hands take turns, and a partner is added—it is a challenging activity that can be used in a variety of circumstances.

Small motor play is not physically taxing and can therefore be a potential strength builder. Many activities that fall into this category use materials that can be placed in jellyroll pans. These can serve as storage trays and can also be used in a wheelchair, on the floor, or in bed.

1. Choose toys that are washable and can be disinfected.

2. Use a variety of small motor toys. Children need practice in this area, and without sufficient variety they may become bored before they acquire the necessary skills.

3. Include materials that are typically used in medical settings (e.g., cotton balls, tongue depressors, small flashlights) to help children view them in a different context.

Creative Arts

Children with special health care needs may express concerns and fears through the arts that they are unable or unwilling to express otherwise. The arts also can be used as a way of releasing energy and emotions. Music can provide a good transition between home and school. Use slow music when children appear to be tiring. If a child is out of school for an extended period of time, send a musical greeting or a recording of new songs the children are learning so the child can come back to school knowing the words and thus feel included. Help children use dramatic play and theater to better understand their world and to play through situations they may find scary. Children may be very competent at role-playing and can provide leadership while working through some of their own feelings.

Visual Arts

The visual arts are both a means of creative expression and a tension reliever.

1. Concentrate on the process. If you can convince children to use arms and fingers they might not otherwise use, you are succeeding. As the process becomes easy, focus on variations.

2. Use many three-dimensional art materials. The initial goal is manipulation, not a final product.

3. Use art materials that require varying amounts of fine motor skills and strength.

4. Paint to music and then talk about how the music influenced the painting. Encourage children to think about how they might use music to influence their moods. See Activity 2–44w, *Mood Colors*.

Music

Music contributes much to a child's physical, aesthetic, emotional, and intellectual development. It provides pleasure and creative experience, develops auditory skills, encourages physical development, and increases the range and flexibility of one's voice. Provide a variety of musical experiences: listening, singing, moving to music, and playing instruments.

1. Have a variety of different instruments available. Help children explore and evaluate the sounds of an instrument when it is held and played in different ways.

2. Incorporate music and language experiences by having children make up new verses to old songs. Play instrumental recordings and ask the children to describe what they imagined while listening. See Activities 5–15, *Bumblebees*; and 5–45w, *Clouds*.

3. Use music for exercise, self-expression, listening, and keeping time. See Activity 5–11, *Mood Songs*.

4. Introduce concepts of pitch, loudness, and duration.

5. Teach songs with colors and numbers: "Who Has Red On?" "Ten Little Children."

6. Sing songs that call children by name.

7. Use chants, especially if children (or adults) are self-conscious about singing.

8. Put stories to music. Have children choose background music for stories, and discuss why the particular music is appropriate.

Movement and Dance

Movement helps children internalize their ideas about the world and their ability to respond to it.

1. Have children toss beach balls into the air and hum or sing one note until the ball touches the floor.

2. Do movement exploration activities, especially those that emphasize relaxation skills. See Activities 5–21, *Rag Dolls,* and 5–53w, *Movement Exploration*.

3. Combine movement and dance with short music selections so you can change the mood of the music.

4. Dance to music.

5. Select a body part (or combination) and have the children move it back and forth at a slow tempo; then add more body parts until the children are dancing.

Dramatic Play and Theater

Dramatic play and theater, given appropriate props, allow children to act out fears and gives them control over frightening situations. Help children write scripts about situations they may encounter.

1. Hospital: Set up a hospital. Talk about being scared, about strange hospital sounds, about being left alone. Talk about the emergency room: Discuss the script that might be written about going to an emergency room. Emphasize the sense of urgency, but allow the child to be in control. Extend the concept and encourage children to build a hospital, using blocks in conjunction with the dramatic play area.

See Activities 1–23, *Medical Tools*, and 1–27, *Emergency Room*.

2. Doctor's office/clinic: Talk about routine visits and visits when children are sick. See Activity 1–24, *Doctors*.

3. Surgery: Discuss operations. Allow the children to operate on dolls to "fix" them. Make finger casts so that children can learn that having a cast put on is not a painful process.

Routines and Transitions

Transitions are often difficult times. Children who are wary of adults and who may not trust them have a particularly difficult time. Reentries into the classroom require separation from important people. Also, after a period of being absent, children may feel uncertain about their acceptance and about you. They need your support. This may be a time when children feel helpless or abandoned. They may feel hurt that they are being left again or afraid that you will hurt them. A routine helps this transition.

1. Have a predictable arrival schedule, with one adult assigned to be the "greeter." At least during difficult transitions, have that be the same person each day.

2. Have the same adult help the child leave the setting and briefly talk about what will happen the next day, with the expectation that the child will return.

3. Encourage children to become more independent when they feel comfortable—but *not* until the issue over separation has been resolved.

4. Make the end of the day positive. Summarize positive things about the day with the expectation that the next day will be even better.

5. Remind children with special health care needs about transitions especially if they move more slowly than the other children.

6. Dismiss children early from the group to provide time for children to take necessary medication. Other children are less likely to notice because there is a lot going on during transitions and taking the medicine is likely to happen if it is part of the routine.

SUMMARY

- Special health care needs can have many different manifestations; however, some of the characteristics are similar across illnesses.

- Children and their siblings may not understand the illness and its implications.

- Families may have a difficult time coping with the medical requirements, pain, and financial obligations of an impairment.

- Some special health care needs occur gradually, others abruptly; some are acute and go into remission, some are chronic, and others are episodic.

- The age of onset and the degree of incapacitation impact both the child and family.
- There are many different special health care needs. Some children with special health care needs will be covered under the IDEA; others can receive accommodations under Section 504.
- Early childhood educators must learn about particular impairments, how they affect the child, what the child knows about the impairment, and what to do in emergency situations.

EDUCATIONAL RESOURCES

American Cancer Society has information divided into categories: parents, survivors, and professionals. The site also allows you to search by specific cancer types. www.cancer.org/

American Heart Association contains information about children and heart disease as well as teaching tools. It is a good resource for professionals, parents, and children seeking information about heart disease and strokes. www.americanheart.org/

American Lung Association provides a variety of information about lung diseases, including fact sheets. It is a good website for professionals, parents, and children, and allows the user to search for information about any lung disease, including asthma and tuberculosis. www.lungusa.org/

Arthritis Foundation provides answers to basic questions about arthritis and has a section about children and arthritis. It also has tips for teachers, information for parents, and tips for coping with arthritis. www.arthritis.org/

Asthma and Allergy Foundation of America (AAFA) has basic materials designed for parents and teachers, about chronic health conditions, including information on children's allergies and asthma. www.aafa.org/

Candlelighters Childhood Cancer Foundation (CCCF) provides information about cancer, support groups, and counseling for families. It has local chapters worldwide. http://candlelighters.org/

Centers for Disease Control and Prevention (CDC) provides information on many diseases, and is a great tool for professionals, parents, and children. It is a good starting point for gathering information, data, and statistics about special health care needs in general, and provides web links for additional information on specific illnesses and diseases. www.cdc.gov/

Epilepsy Foundation of America (EFA) is well organized and has a great section called the "Answer Place," which is organized by topic and by audience. www.epilepsyfoundation.org/

Juvenile Diabetes Research Foundation International (JDRF) was started by parents with the expressed purpose of finding a cure for diabetes and its complications through research. It is a good source for up-to-date research. www.jdf.org/

National Dissemination Center for Children with Disabilities, funded by the U.S. DOE, serves as the central source of information about the IDEA and No Child Left Behind (related to children with disabilities) and provides research-based information on effective educational practices, fact sheets about specific disabilities and many other resources and services in both English and Spanish. www.nichcy.org/

National Institute of Neurological Disorders and Stroke (NINDS) provides up to date information about how the brain works and information about different neurological disorders. www.ninds.nih.gov/

For additional resources, visit the book companion website for this text at www.cengagebrain.com.

Children with Orthopedic and Neurological Impairments

17

Greg was a preemie. He seemed to be doing well, but there were always qualifiers. I finally asked the doctors what was wrong. They told me Greg had cerebral palsy. I asked them how long they had known. They were sheepish and said "for a while." They just hadn't confirmed it yet. I wanted to know what we should be doing about it while they made up their minds. Acceptance was a problem, but in some ways it was a relief. Now I could start to do something about it. I was more than just an overanxious mother.

Early intervention was a godsend. I began to learn how to work with Greg, and I felt like I was making a difference. I am not sure how Greg's disability played into the divorce, and I am not sure I am really ready to look at that today. Today I am discouraged and feel hopeless and helpless.

I have never faced a harder time in Greg's life than I am facing today. Going from infant to young adult in a school setting is far easier than the challenges he faces as an adult. Greg will graduate in May and would like to obtain a full-time job. I'm not sure he will be successful. Our educational system failed to teach him any real skills. Because of his physical disability, he can't take a physically intensive job. Because of his spastic speech, his present employer (part-time) will not give him a job working with the public. Greg is not extremely bright, so he can't go for one of those brainy jobs either.

I had hoped that the school would have been more involved in the community by adopting a co-op program, one where the school and employer would have worked hand in hand. The school would have supplied the training and the additional aid that the employer did not have time or resources to provide. Instead, the school system pushed Greg out the door so that they would have one less student to fret over. It's scary. We weren't prepared for this.

REFLECTIVE PRACTICE | Do you think about long-term implications as you teach children in the early childhood classroom? What do you think the obligations are to prepare children for their life after school? Is this a school problem, a parent problem, or a society problem?

Orthopedic and Neurological Impairments

Neurological impairments are those that affect the nervous system, the brain, and the spinal cord. The neurological impairments addressed in this chapter are those that result in orthopedic problems. Some orthopedic impairments relate to problems with the neuromuscular and musculoskeletal systems: the muscles, bones, and nerves of the body (Escolar, Tosi Rocha, & Kennedy, 2007).

©Cengage Learning 2012

Defining Orthopedic and Neurological Impairments

Disabilities included under orthopedic and neurological impairments are those in which nerves and muscles don't respond in a coordinated way. They include movement disorders such as developmental coordination disorder and correctable orthopedic impairments. Neurological impairments include cerebral palsy, neural tube defects, spinal cord injuries, and traumatic brain injury. Musculoskeletal conditions include absent limbs and muscular dystrophy.

Orthopedic and *neurological impairments* are umbrella terms for a variety of different conditions and classifications. According to the Individuals with Disabilities Education Improvement Act (2004):

> *Orthopedic impairments are severe and they adversely affects a child's educational performance. They include impairments caused by a congenital anomaly, by disease (e.g., poliomyelitis, bone tuberculosis), and from other causes (e.g., cerebral palsy, amputations, and fractures or burns that cause contractures).*

When a disability has several aspects, such as cerebral palsy, which has a neurological base (abnormality of the immature brain) and orthopedic complications, classification is difficult. This text, and presumably your classroom, will take a functional approach to concerns such as these. It really doesn't matter what you call it; what is relevant is what the child knows and can do.

Prevalence of Orthopedic and Neurological Impairments

The federal government began keeping records on children with orthopedic impairments during the 1976–1977 school year. At that time, 8.3 percent of children in the public schools were identified as having a disability. Of these children, 0.2 percent had an orthopedic impairment. In the 2007–2008 school year, 13.4 percent of children were identified as having a disability, with 0.1 percent of these children having an orthopedic impairment. This percent has remained relatively stable over the years (National Center for Educational Statistics, 2010).

Causes of Orthopedic and Neurological Impairments

Orthopedic impairments can have a variety of causes. Lack of oxygen in the child's brain either while the mother is pregnant or during birth can cause physical impairments. Diseases that affect the brain, such as meningitis and encephalitis, and prolonged high fevers can also cause permanent brain damage. Poisoning and other conditions can lead to lack of oxygen in the brain, as well as head, neck, and back injuries, which sometimes cause paralysis or abnormal movement patterns. Some chronic health problems such as arthritis and muscular dystrophy may ultimately result in physical impairments, but because such impairments usually occur only after repeated acute attacks, they are less likely to be apparent during the early childhood years. Automobile accidents and other injuries can also cause impairments. Causes that relate to specific impairments are discussed under that impairment.

Bones, Muscles, and Nerves

Knowledge of how we move and the importance of muscle tone in movement aid in understanding some of the problems children with physical limitations encounter. Bones form the skeleton of the body. Muscles are attached to bones by **tendons**. To move, we increase the tension in specific muscle groups. When two different bones come together, they form a joint; **ligaments** attach these bones. Because we are concerned about both type and quality of movement, there are a few more terms involved. **Flexion** refers to bending a joint or joints. If your elbow is flexed, your hand is near your shoulder. Extension is the opposite and means to straighten or stretch a joint. If your arm is extended, the elbow joint is straight.

The range of motion is the amount of movement present around a joint. The range of movement of the elbow is usually a little less than 180 degrees. Children may also be challenged by skills that require **rotation**, the ability to twist a part of the body. Rotation is of primary importance

in learning to write because writing requires rotating the wrist. A **contracture** is a shortening of muscle fibers, which is almost always irreversible. A contracture nearly always decreases the range of motion of a joint (Escolar et al., 2007).

The **midline** of the body is an imaginary line that runs vertically through the middle of the body, dividing it in half. This is also called the **median plane**. We are interested in movements that move toward or away from the midline. When motion moves away from the midline, the movement is referred to as **abduction**; movement toward the midline is called **adduction**. Organs or body parts that are closer to the midline are called **proximal** and those that are farther away are called **distal**. The trunk of the body is proximal, whereas the fingers are distal. It is very different for muscular weakness to be in pelvic, trunk, and shoulder areas than in the hands. Children with weak proximal muscles have trouble getting up from sitting, climbing stairs, and playing on the jungle gym. Children with weak distal muscles often trip because they don't lift their feet high enough when walking and have trouble holding a pencil, using scissors, or doing precise fine motor activities for a long time (Escolar et al., 2007). **Superior** means up or above, whereas **inferior** means below. The head is superior, whereas the feet are inferior.

Muscle tone is the ability of the muscle to respond to stretch, whereas **muscle strength** is the force that muscle exerts (Escolar et al., 2007). When muscle tone is too high (tight) children overreact to normal stimuli. This is called **hypertonic** or **spastic**. Spasticity is the inability of the muscles to relax. Children with spastic cerebral palsy have voluntary movement, but it is often stiff, jerky, and inaccurate. When muscle tone is low, children have a response under what is expected, and they appear floppy or **hypotonic**. Many children with orthopedic and neurological impairments have problems with muscle tone. Muscle tone also affects the small muscles of the mouth and face that involve communication. **Athetosis** refers to random, writhing, involuntary movements, especially of the hands. **Ataxia** implies irregular, uncoordinated muscular movement, especially in walking.

IMPLICATIONS FOR EDUCATORS

Although this may seem like a vocabulary lesson, when other professionals talk about and write reports about children with orthopedic and neurological impairments, they use these terms. If you need to understand them further, they are all in the glossary. Let's focus on muscle tone for a minute. To get a better idea of the implications of muscle tone, lie with your back on the floor, tense all of your muscles (make fists, squint your face, tense your legs, trunk, and back), and try to sit up. You will find that your movements are jerky and stiff and that you probably cannot sit up. Now relax. Let your arms become floppy as you pretend to be a rag doll. Try to sit up without tensing any of your muscles. That doesn't work either. The first situation will give you an idea of the problems children with hypertonic (spastic) muscle tone face; the second, hypotonic (floppy) muscle tone. How do you feel at this point? You have only done this for a short period of time. Children who have high muscle tone, in particular, become fatigued.

If children have high, low, or inconsistent muscle tone, you can expect that they will have difficulty with many gross motor activities. The biggest issue with young children is establishing trunk stability. Try to write while constantly moving your upper body. To the extent that you move it too far and overbalance, your concern is with falling, rather than your penmanship. The focus of much early therapy is stabilizing the large muscles.

For a better understanding of rotational problems, attempt to take the lid off a container while keeping your fingers and wrists stiff. (Try handling classroom materials and doing all classroom procedures with stiff muscles to see how difficult each task is for children. In general, hard objects are more difficult to handle than soft, small more difficult than larger, and slippery more difficult than rough.) Your awareness of the child's strengths and needs and your creativity and willingness to try things that are different are the key to good programming for children with orthopedic impairments.

Early Identification of Orthopedic and Neurological Impairments

Understanding the underlying principles of growth and development allow us to make predictions about whether a child's growth and development falls within the typical patterns. We use a variety of signs and symptoms to identify impairments that relate to the growth and development of muscles, bones, and nerves.

Missed motor milestones are one of the markers we use to identify children with orthopedic impairments. In general, children with increased muscle tone (spasticity) will have delays in all **antigravity positions**. They may roll over or even "flip over" close to the expected time, but they will not sit unsupported and may not walk until about age 4. Children who have low muscle tone (hypotonic or floppy) may stand with support or cruise holding onto furniture, but they lack the trunk stability for independent walking and so will remain in this stage for a longer time. Because of small motor delays, children may have problems with self-feeding and dressing. Grasping objects using the pincer grasp (thumb and index finger) is difficult, as is eye–hand coordination.

Severely involved children may also experience delays in language and problem-solving abilities. In general, receptive language is better than expressive language (especially if a child's motor involvement effects the muscles of the speech-producing organs); however, it is sometimes difficult to tell how much children understand because they may not have the physical ability to complete requested tasks. Because many developmental tests for infants and toddlers have motor components, it may be difficult to determine a child's level of cognitive functioning.

By preschool age, children with physical limitations may have a difficult time keeping up with their peers. Differences are becoming more apparent to the child as well as to the other children. As children get larger and heavier and even more determined to be independent, some of the self-care tasks become more difficult. By this age, the pattern of gross and fine motor skill is clearer so the aim of intervention is to maximize a child's potential by capitalizing on what the child can do. Children may profit from adaptive equipment. If children are frustrated by a lack of ability to communicate, a simple communication board or a picture communication system (PECS) might help (children can show what they want if they cannot tell). Using PECS or a communication board does not discourage children from speaking.

As children enter elementary school settings, they become part of a larger community. Kindergarten and first grade demand more fine motor coordination. Some children find that assistive technology can compensate for lack of control in fine motor skills.

IMPLICATIONS FOR EDUCATORS
It helps to be honest about abilities and limitations and to praise work that is praiseworthy. Although you can and should support effort, it should be clear that that is what you are supporting. Tell a child he worked hard controlling the crayon to make the drawing, but, if he is 6 and the drawing looks like the advanced scribbles of a 3-year-old, do not tell him it is a great drawing. Children need help in developing a positive self-concept at a time when new awareness about differences and the value of a beautiful body are becoming part of the child's social world.

Assessment of Orthopedic and Neurological Impairments

In general, impairments are assessed or classified by severity, type, and the parts of the body that are involved. Children with *mild* impairments can walk (with or without crutches, walker, or other prosthetic device), use their arms, and communicate well enough to make their wants and needs known. They may take more time doing things, but with adaptations can do what most other children can. Their problems involve mostly fine motor skills. Children with *moderate* impairments require some special help with locomotion and need more assistance than their peers with self-help and communication skills. Children with *severe* impairments are usually not able to move from one place to another without the aid of a wheelchair. Their self-help and communication skills are usually challenging.

Types of Orthopedic and Neurological Impairments

There are many different types of orthopedic and neurological impairments. The focus of this section is in understanding the impairments and what they mean in the early childhood classroom. The impairments are given alphabetically.

Absent Limbs
Some children are born with deformed or absent limbs. These conditions can be caused by genetic or environmental influences (e.g., drugs or chemicals). When congenital, the problem usually occurs during the early gestation period when limb development occurs. Young children can also have limbs surgically removed because of injury or disease. Prosthetic devices are available to assist in replacing missing limbs. There is a difference in philosophy about the age at which children should be fitted with an artificial limb or prosthesis. Some believe that children should be fitted almost immediately. They feel that the younger a child gets an artificial limb, the easier and more natural the adjustment is. Others feel that children should not be fitted for devices until they are

older, when they are better able to use the device, have better control, and can take better care of it. Regardless, fit is very important, in terms of both comfort and the ability to use the device. A prosthesis must be adapted as the child grows.

IMPLICATIONS FOR EDUCATORS

You need to have some basic understanding of how the prosthesis works in case the child needs help making adjustments and so that you can plan activities that do not frustrate the child. Being accepted as a whole person is extremely important, so don't refer to the prosthesis as the child's "bad" arm or leg. If you notice abnormal postures or motor patterns developing, discuss them with the parents and physical therapist. Exercising the joints nearest an amputation is important; also ask for information about that from the parents, medical professionals, and therapists.

••• Cerebral Palsy

Cerebral palsy refers to a group of neurologically related motor disorders that come in many varieties and severities. "Cerebral palsy is a disorder of movement and posture that is caused by a nonprogressive abnormality of the immature brain" (Pellegrino, 2007, p. 388). In cerebral palsy, the neurological mechanisms of posture, balance, and movement are disorganized.

CAUSES OF CEREBRAL PALSY

Premature births, especially those that occur before 28 weeks, and problems during pregnancy account for the majority of cases of cerebral palsy (Pellegrino, 2007). The number of children with cerebral palsy is about 2.0 to 2.5 per 1,000 births (Winter et al., 2002); premature infants comprise 40 to 50 percent of this group. Very low-birth-weight babies are the most vulnerable. A major cause of prematurity-related cerebral palsy is hemorrhaging in the brain. The hemorrhaging injures the white matter of the brain (the axons and their myelin sheaths) (Pellegrino, 2007). Brain imaging techniques are useful in identifying the location of the damage. Term infants who are diagnosed with cerebral palsy are often small for gestational age and may have experienced birth asphyxia or congenital malformation of the central nervous system (CNS), or they may be one of a multiple gestation. Infection during pregnancy can also cause cerebral palsy (Pellegrino, 2007).

Children are often identified as having cerebral palsy when they do not walk by 15 months. Children who do walk have an unusual gait that may reflect scissoring (increased muscle tone in the inner thigh pulls the legs in toward the middle) or toe walking (because of tightness of the calf muscles and Achilles tendon).

IN THE FIELD

Sari is one of eight children and a twin. Her mother, Carol, is 25. Carol spends her entire day trying to feed, change, or pick up after the children. The two oldest children are in school. This leaves six at home, including Sari, who has cerebral palsy; she is very spastic. Early intervention began with home visits shortly after her birth. This was difficult, because Sari's mother had little time to pay attention to what I was saying as she tried to watch the other children. Carol's education was limited, and she didn't seem to understand what she had been told about Sari. The only thing she remembered was that Sari had "CP" and she "would never be normal."

She sometimes referred to Sari as "the freak"; the other children picked this up and teased her for as long as I can remember.

Because Sari's medical treatment was very involved, she had many appointments for intervention. Some were missed because the family couldn't afford gas for the car, couldn't get a ride with someone, or couldn't find someone to watch the other children. Home visits were the mainstay of her program. Sari was a fussy child and cried frequently, but, interestingly, she almost always cried when her mother yelled at one of the other children. There were few toys; those that were there were broken. As Sari's spasticity slowed her movements, she could rarely reach a toy before someone else had snatched it up. Sari had a short attention span, and her mother was happy if she were sleeping and not crying. She had to be fed slowly as she choked easily, and she would usually spill the juice or cereal as her movements were clumsy and shaky and she didn't have a high chair to give her the support she needed. However, she didn't lack verbal stimulation or visual variety with the other children around. But she never had to speak, as someone always spoke for her. By 8:00 in the morning, when I came each week, Sari's mother was totally exhausted and at her wit's end.

A diagnosis of cerebral palsy had been made shortly after birth, but a full evaluation was not completed until Sari was about 6 months old. Although Sari's mother and I were part of the evaluation team, I never thought they valued our input. I came for my regular home visit after Sari's mother had received a copy of the evaluation. Carol was in a deep depression and didn't want me to come in. I persisted. I wanted to know why things had gotten worse. After a while, she told me. The team had written in their report that Carol "was a mother who neglected the needs of her child." She was trying as hard as she could just to cope through the day. Her husband worked all the time and even when he was home, he was little help. Her family lived out of state; his family "couldn't care less." Carol admitted that she had been suicidal at times. We talked more. By the time my home visit was over, my head was splitting and I wondered how anyone could survive such a lifestyle. Carol was doing the best she could with the resources she had available to her. As I was about the same age as this mother, I only wondered if I would have done as well in the same situation. To call this "case" a challenge was putting it mildly. I again thought of my job description, which never mentioned this type of family. It was time to become adaptive and creative as well as respectful and compassionate. I could leave and go home to a quiet, organized lifestyle and this mother could not.

EARLY DIAGNOSIS AND TREATMENT

For newborns who are at high risk for developing cerebral palsy, such as premature and very-low-birth-weight infants, close neurodevelopmental monitoring identifies cerebral palsy early. However, screening tests traditionally used with infants by the medical profession may not identify children with cerebral palsy during the first year. Often, the absence of primitive reflexes, abnormal muscle tone, and resting positions (an extended arched position for high tone and a rag doll position for low tone) give clues to the possibility of cerebral palsy (Pellegrino, 2007). Some children with cerebral palsy also have sensory impairments, speech disorders, and delayed development. Accurate developmental testing is challenging.

The question about the usefulness of medication for children with cerebral palsy has not been answered definitively. Some children with spasticity and rigidity have found drugs such as diazepam (Valium) useful, whereas others feel the side effects of drowsiness and excessive drooling outweigh the benefits. Newer therapy allows for the direct delivery of antispasticity medication (baclofen) directly into the spinal fluid, using a concept similar to the insulin pump used in diabetes. In this case, a disk-shaped pump is placed under the skin of the abdomen and a catheter is tunneled below the skin around to the back, where it is inserted through the lumbar spine into the **intrathecal** space. The disk has a reservoir that can be refilled with a needle inserted into the reservoir (Pellegrino, 2007).

Surgery is sometimes part of the treatment process. Selective **posterior rhizomotomy** is used to reduce spasticity in some children with spastic diplegia. In this procedure, surgeons cut the motor fibers that cause the greatest spasticity. Spasticity is reduced, but there may be some degree of motor weakness. Orthopedic surgery may be used to increase the range of motion by lengthening the heel cord or partially releasing the hip adductor muscles. Surgeons also monitor and treat **scoliosis** (Pellegrino, 2002).

The goal of intervention is to maximize the children's functioning and minimize disability-related problems. Orthotic devices, primarily braces and splints, are used to prevent contractures of specific joints, provide stability, control involuntary motion, and maintain range of motion (Pellegrino, 2007). Contractures decrease muscle joint mobility. Muscles that remain in shortened positions for prolonged periods are at risk of contractures. Splints and braces are used to position limbs and joints to prevent contractures. The most commonly prescribed orthosis is a short leg brace (ankle-foot orthosis) that prevents the shortening of the heel cord (Pellegrino, 2007). Most splints and braces made for young children are custom-made of plastic materials that are molded directly on the child. These must be modified as the child grows, or they become both nonfunctional and painful.

Positioning is another key to preventing impairment. Because children spend a lot of time sitting, it is important that they sit in the most beneficial position. This is often not the easiest or most comfortable for teachers to manage. If you hold a child with cerebral palsy in your lap, have the child's legs straddle one of yours and hold the child around the middle. If the child sits on the floor, sitting cross-legged is not recommended; instead, have the child sit with legs in front and together. If the child has variable muscle tone the legs should be bent at the knee, if the muscle tone is tight the knees should be straight and the legs out in front. Sitting in a "W" position with knees forward and a foot on either side of the child's bottom is particularly disadvantageous for children with orthopedic impairments and is not recommended for any child.

TYPES OF CEREBRAL PALSY

Cerebral palsy is typically classified by the motor impairment and the extremities involved. In spastic **hemiplegia**, there is involvement of the upper and lower extremities on the same side of the body, with the arm more affected than the leg. If the motor neurons on the right hemisphere were affected, the problem would be on the left side and vice versa. In spastic **diplegia**, the whole body is involved, although the

Sitting for an extended time with legs in a "W" position should be discouraged for all children but especially those with cerebral palsy.
©Cengage Learning 2012

legs more so than the arms. This is the type most associated with prematurity. Spastic **quadriplegia** involves all four limbs. Head control may be poor, and in cerebral palsy there is usually impairment of speech and eye coordination. This also indicates wider cerebral dysfunction, and children may also have intellectual disability, seizures, and other medical complications (Pellegrino, 2007).

IN THE FIELD

We wanted to have a child so badly and finally I got pregnant. We were so excited, and then labor started way too soon, at 24 weeks. He weighed less than a pound and a half. The medical personnel didn't ask me whether I wanted them to take extraordinary measures to save him; they just did. He spent his first year two years in the hospital. I went to visit him every day. I spent almost all of my time learning how to take care of him. The minute he was born, I dedicated my life to him. I gave up my life for his; my health too.

Ravi has spastic quadriplegia because of increased muscular tension. He cannot control his bowels or urine flow. He cannot sit up without assistance; additionally, he cannot walk, talk, or voluntarily move his muscles. He has epileptic seizures that happen mostly at night. He has permanent brain damage. Ravi also has a tracheotomy; he breathes through a tube that was surgically inserted in his trachea. He is fed through a "stomach button," which is a gastric tube that carries food directly to his stomach, although he eats some food as well. He can shake his head "no" and says "augh" for yes, and he has a heart-stopping smile. He has a partial IEP.

When we brought him home, Ravi required 24-hour-a-day care. I had some nursing help. Because of that, I think of our days in shifts. The first shift is 7:00 a.m. to 3:00 p.m.; the second shift is 3:00 p.m. until 9:00 p.m.; and the third shift is 9:00 p.m. until 7:00 a.m. I usually have nursing help for the third shift so I can sleep. Ravi's conditions over the years have worsened, but the medical system still expects me to take care of Ravi. I am scared and I feel unqualified.

My doctor says my health has deteriorated, and a lot of it is because I am so stressed because of caring for Ravi. I have an ulcer. I have really bad reflux that needs surgery, but I can't get it because I have no one to take care of Ravi. The same is true for the two broken bones in my feet. I have migraines, irritable bowel syndrome, and chronic fatigue syndrome. My body can't take much more. My husband helps some, but he is away at work most of the day and he does a lot of traveling. It really isn't his thing.

The nursing company told me that I would only have four days of nursing support in the whole month of January. I couldn't do it. I have gone 48 hours without sleep, but that is as far as I can go. My husband is having an affair and said he is leaving. I asked him to help me one last time. On December 26th, we took Ravi to the children's hospital (he had been here 44 times in the past year and seven months). I brought his favorite toys, some clothes, and food as well as his medical supplies. We left him in the emergency room with a note saying I could no longer care for him.

REFLECTIVE PRACTICE | What would you do if you were asked to testify as an expert witness in this case? What would you say? How do you make sense out of what happened?

Note: *The parents were arrested the next day and charged with a misdemeanor: child abandonment. Actually I was the expert witness. Hours before the case went to court the parents agreed to a year's probation. The couple divorced, and the father lost his job because of the publicity. Ravi was placed in medical foster care, and his family was only allowed limited visitation.*

Spastic cerebral palsy is the most common type of cerebral palsy. The abnormalities in the brain pathways originate in the gray matter of the brain. The motor cortex or pyramidal tract of the brain is damaged, resulting in limb muscles that are very tight and difficult to move (spastic). Voluntary movements are often jerky and inaccurate. Voluntary motion is present but may be labored. Infants who are hypotonic often later develop spasticity.

In **dyskinetic** cerebral palsy, the damage is outside the pyramidal tracts and has different implications. The whole body is affected, and patterns of muscle tone change from hour to hour, or day to day. Children have more problems sucking, swallowing, drooling, and speaking than children who have the spastic form. Again, the variable muscle tone makes it difficult to develop the stability needed for sitting and walking. Children may have rigid muscle tone while awake and normal or decreased muscle tone in sleep. Involuntary movements are often present (Pellegrino, 2007). In one type of dyskinetic cerebral palsy, **choreoathetoid**, there are rapid, random, jerky movements (the *chorea* part) combined with slow, writhing movements (the *athetosis*). In

dystonic cerebral palsy, children have rigid posturing centered in the trunk and neck. There is one predominant level of muscle tone and a lot of involuntary posturing.

Ataxic cerebral palsy is characterized by abnormalities in voluntary movement. Children who walk use a wide base and have an unsteady gait. They have problems controlling their hands and arms accurately when reaching, and often overshoot the targeted item. They also have problems with the timing of their motor movements. Balance and controlling the position of the trunk and limbs in space are challenging. Children can have increased or decreased muscle tone (Pellegrino, 2007). In **mixed cerebral palsy**, children have damage to both the pyramidal and extrapyramidal areas of the brain and can have symptoms of both types (i.e., rigidity in the arms and spasticity in the legs).

IMPLICATIONS FOR EDUCATORS

Children with cerebral palsy typically have individualized programs with a combination of consultative, home-based, or center-based intervention. The most common method of physical and occupational therapy used with young children who have cerebral palsy is neurodevelopmental therapy. The goals of this therapy are to normalize muscle tone and enhance the development of normal movement patterns during functional activities. Early childhood educators would be expected to incorporate handling techniques into the child's routine as well as provide opportunities to practice newly acquired skills. There is some question about the carryover of these techniques, and newer techniques are taking more of a systems perspective and looking at the environment, motivation, and requirements of the task, cognition, and other aspects of the situation that might produce lasting changes in motor behavior. During the early years, problems related to mobility tend to receive the most attention. As children are included in regular elementary school classes, some of the associated learning and sensory problems may receive greater attention and adaptation.

• • •
Correctable Orthopedic Impairments

A variety of relatively short-term orthopedic problems are dealt with during the early childhood years to facilitate normal future growth. These conditions usually require surgery, bracing, casting, and physical therapy. The prognosis is generally good if the condition is treated at an early age. If not treated, these problems result in some degree of orthopedic impairment.

Bowlegs and inwardly rotated feet are common when a child first begins to walk. They are usually cured by normal growth. In extreme cases, however, braces, casts, and/or surgery are used to correct the problem. Clubfeet are usually treated with casts, splints, and physical therapy or surgery. Flat feet may be treated with arch supports or corrective shoes. Congenital hip problems result from improper fit of the femur in the socket joint of the hip treated by a webbed brace, traction, cast, or surgery. Usually, hip problems are treated in infancy. In severe cases, they can have long-term implications.

IMPLICATIONS FOR EDUCATORS

The prognosis for these correctable orthopedic impairments is very good, yet from the child's perspective, the restriction of movement is frustrating. Some children need a lot of help expressing their anger. Prepare children for medical procedures, discuss their fears and feelings, help them express emotions while they are physically restricted, give them activities they can participate in, and try to explain the purpose of the medical treatment in terms they understand.

Developmental Coordination Disorder

It is difficult to decide whether a child has a movement disorder. With physical problems such as a congenital hip, clubfeet, or bowed legs, we expect children to have motor problems, and we provide medical and educational intervention. Some problems are less obvious. We are becoming concerned about children who are clumsy. Although it is difficult to agree on a definition of clumsy, most of us know a clumsy child when we see one. Increasingly, children who have problems controlling their movements are recognized as having special needs. Like other areas, such as specific learning disabilities, there is confusion about terminology.

Developmental coordination disorder (DCD) is used synonymously with the terms **clumsy child syndrome** and **developmental dyspraxia**. With minor variations, these terms all refer to the same group of children. This text uses the terms *developmental dyspraxia* and *developmental coordination disorder (DCD)* depending upon the source of information. This diagnostic category focuses on the relationship between age-expected norms and children who are delayed in reaching motor milestones (walking, running, etc.) or who drop things, are clumsy, do poorly at sports, and often have poor handwriting. As children grow older, there is concern about the relationship between motor coordination, and academic achievement and the activities of daily living.

It is estimated that approximately 6 to 10 percent of children between 5 and 11 years old have some degree of DCD (APA, 2000). Developmental dyspraxia affects children in different areas of development. It affects more boys than girls (Dyspraxia Support Group of N. Z. Inc, 2007a). It is a chronic condition that continues into adolescence and adulthood. There is no apparent etiology or cause of DCD. To be identified as having DCD, children must have the following characteristics.

- Motor coordination is substantially below expected motor milestones, or the child is clumsy in the performance of motor tasks.
- The level of performance must be great enough that it interferes with either academic achievement or the performance of tasks of daily life.
- The disturbance is not due to a medical condition such as cerebral palsy.
- If the child has an intellectual disability, the motor problems are in excess of those expected because of the intellectual disability (APA, 2000).

Dyspraxia is a hidden disability; the child looks like other children; however, he finds it far more difficult to accomplish the same tasks that others achieve with little effort (Dyspraxia Support Group of N. Z. Inc, 2007b). Clumsy children have been a concern to many over the years. Dr. Samuel Orton (1937), who focused most of his work on dyslexic children, was interested in the problems of physical awkwardness. He decided that lack of motor coordination could reflect a motor planning problem or could be caused by

problems with visual perception. He felt that motor dysfunction was multidimensional; that is, that children who were awkward at running also labored over printing and writing. He was concerned that poor motor coordination also led to feelings of social inferiority and low self-esteem. He believed motor awkwardness was one of the six most common developmental disorders and felt it was a most debilitating condition (Dyspraxia Support Group of N. Z. Inc., 2007b).

One problem is that when we look at clumsiness, it is a "soft sign." Soft signs require clinical judgment as opposed to something like a temperature, which is a finite number (102°F) and has diagnostic value. Also, some children display generalized awkwardness, whereas others are clumsy relative to only one task such as writing or balance. Many agree that the clumsy child syndrome is made up of several subclassifications, including children with and without academic problems. In some children, the problem seems to be immaturity; in other children, it is longer lasting. The literature indicates that early remediation is more likely to succeed than just waiting; mild problems are more correctable than moderate ones; and given the current state of knowledge, it isn't clear which problems will change because of maturation and which ones will not. If problems are not dealt with until middle childhood, there may be a negative emotional overlay to the problems themselves. Children may develop poor self-concepts because of constant feedback about dropping, spilling, running into things, knocking things over, and so on.

IN THE FIELD

"Anne, can you help me set the table for dinner?" Anne's mom asked. "Coming mom—give me two seconds," Anne replied. A few seconds later, Anne's mom heard the pitter-patter of footsteps followed by an anguished, "Owww!" "What happened?" asked Anne's mom, stifling a sigh. It seemed that every time her youngest daughter moved, there was some "ouching" involved. She couldn't remember a day without dealing with tears or at least sniffles from Anne's frequent accidents. Sometimes she marveled at how her daughter injured herself just walking or setting the table.

"I'm okay, mom. I just tripped," announced Anne as she appeared in the doorway. "Good. I'm glad you didn't hurt yourself," said Anne's mom, placing a plate into Anne's hands. "Remember, two hands." Anne walked to the table as her mom asked, "How was your day, honey?" "It was okay," Anne answered, taking another plate from her mom. "What happened to make it just okay?" "Stuff," said Anne reluctantly. "What kind of stuff?" inquired her mom. "I fell out of my chair, spilled milk all over Jeremy, tripped up the stairs, broke my science project—everybody laughed at me, even Ms. Rubenthal, the substitute—and I got sent to Mr. Theran's office 'cause I screamed at everybody," she said in one breath.

"It sounds like you had a really bad day. Mr. Theran called me today and said that you were really upset. I can see why. He said you talked about your feelings about people laughing at you and accidents." "I don't like it when people laugh at me, Mom. . . . I get so mad at them, I want to scream and yell and cry. . . . I hear the mean things they say all day," replied Anne, putting the last plate on the table.

"Is there something that we could do so they wouldn't laugh so much?" asked her mom. "Could you talk to Ms. Dublin and tell her that I don't like it when she and her substitutes laugh at me?" Anne asked. "I could do that. I will make an appointment with her tomorrow. Is there anything you could do to try to have fewer accidents at school?" her mom asked, handing Anne the forks. "Mr. Theran suggested that maybe we could talk about some things to do so that you might not have so many accidents. He also said he would like to meet with you once a week. How would you feel about that? Do you feel safe talking to Mr. Theran?"

Anne looked out the window for a few seconds before responding. She began in a quiet, almost introspective voice, "It would be okay with me to talk with Mr. Theran once a week; he's nice and he listens and he didn't make me feel bad for screaming. But if other people know, they'll make fun of me, so I'd like to see him during lunch 'cause then I could eat with him and I don't think he'd be so mad if I spilled things."

Then Anne's mom took the cups out of her daughter's hands and placed them on the table. She wrapped her arms around Anne, hugging her close, and whispered in her ear, "I'm sorry you had a bad day. But you know what? I love you, accidents and all."

Some clumsy children such as Anne are diagnosed as having developmental coordination disorder (DCD) or developmental dyspraxia. *Praxis* is a Greek word that describes the learned ability to plan and then carry out sequences of coordinated movements to attain a goal. When *dys* is used as a prefix it means "bad or abnormal." Hence the term *dyspraxia* means "abnormal praxis." Children who have dyspraxia have trouble with learned, voluntary, skilled movements such as buttoning buttons, handwriting, using a fork, and speaking clearly. Pervasive problems in the area of motor planning lie at the heart of all of these problems (Dyspraxia Support Group of N. Z. Inc., 2007a). Praxis is the ability to organize activities in new and creative ways. It links brain and behavior to help us plan and function in our world and has three components:

- **Ideation** is the understanding of sensory information about objects: what they feel, taste, look, and smell like; what shape they are; how much they weigh; whether they roll or stay put; and so on. To follow through with ideation, a plan of action is needed.

- **Motor planning** involves sending the ideation information to the parietal lobe of the brain to work out how to move one's body to do what is wanted. This involves a person recalling the sensory information about the objects and information about himself, then planning the sequence in which muscles should work. When the plan is made, motor neurons are sent out to execute the plan.

- **Execution** is carrying out the plan. Muscles can only contract or relax, and the motor neurons tell the muscles what to do, for how long, and in what sequence. When the motor plan is made, messages go to different parts of the brain and then to the muscles to carry out the actions (Dyspraxia Support Group of N. Z. Inc., 2007b).

These actions are interdependent. Praxis is developmental. Praxis at age 2 is different from praxis at age 5 because more connections have been made and used in the brain, allowing for more complicated plans and actions. Dyspraxia is a disorder of praxis. Somewhere in the sensory information collection, storage, planning, and execution of actions there is a malfunction. Although praxis focuses on learned

Children with dyspraxia may work with an occupational therapist to help them develop motor planning skills.
©Cengage Learning 2012

behavior, there is a biological component (Ripley, 2001). The cause of dyspraxia is the physical inability of the brain's neurons to effectively communicate movement instructions to the body's muscles. It may affect specific areas of growth such as large motor skill development or areas of fine motor skill development such as verbal communication, where the tongue, lips, and larynx must work together to form the sounds of the language. It is not a unitary disorder; each child is affected in different ways and to a different extent, and the same child may be different on different days. It may be the only disorder a child has or it may be part of other disorders such as specific learning disabilities.

Tasks that are considered enjoyable by many, such as coloring or riding a tricycle, may be extremely difficult for the child with dyspraxia. It is understandable, then, that children with dyspraxia may exhibit the characteristics of a frustrated immature child. As is often the case in children with specific learning disabilities, children with dyspraxia usually have normal intelligence. They are capable of understanding what needs to be accomplished and cognitively develop at an age-appropriate rate. Once again, the problem area is the brain's inability to effectively communicate with the body. Children with dyspraxia may develop low self-esteem and behavior problems because of the amount of stress, anxiety, and failure they experience.

Developmental dyspraxia is difficult to diagnose. It must be done in the context in which the child lives and learns. It is dependent upon the demands of the environment and the child's ability to meet these demands and the adult's ability to tolerate errors as well as the child's ability to cope. It may not become apparent until the child's impaired planning and execution are overtaxed or the environmental demands are higher and less tolerant (Dyspraxia Support Group of N. Z. Inc., 2007a).

Once a skill or action is learned well enough, then praxis is no longer required. Praxis is part of the learning process. So the goal of treatment is to teach the child praxis—to form ideas for trying new things and using familiar things in new ways, that is, to plan actions and execute them. Treatment is a team approach and the treatment is very individualized depending upon the child and the demands of the environment. It is likely to include an occupational therapist who would focus on sensory integration; a speech and language therapist who will work on sounds and speech muscles; a psychologist who looks at cognitive development and learning ability; an early childhood special educator who may focus on helping the child in specific areas that are challenging; the classroom teacher whose expectations may need to be adjusted; and above all, parents who teach many skills children need to grow and learn. A child with dyspraxia will not grow out of it; the disability is a lifelong tribulation (Dyspraxia Support Group of N. Z. Inc., 2007b).

IMPLICATIONS FOR EDUCATORS

Children with dyspraxia may find it difficult to learn new things, concentrate, speak clearly, get dressed, play sports, organize ideas, or think quickly. They may need more time and more practice to develop new skills. Try to figure out where a child's major problem lies. Is it that the child doesn't understand a request, can't figure out how to do the action, or can't perform the action? Then, scaffold that area for the child. New tasks may be threatening because she can't figure out how to sequence all the actions even though she can perform all the skills. Try to sequence new tasks for her. Break down instructions into smaller simplified steps.

Children who are clumsy need to be encouraged to participate in motor activities. They need experience with motor planning in situations where they are likely to succeed and be supported. In general, to require motor planning, a task must be goal directed. For example, just walking requires little motor planning, whereas to walk to the other end of the room, put on a hat, and skip back requires far more motor planning. Likewise, an obstacle course requires a child to motor plan. Because diagnosis is dependent upon the fit of the child and the environment, you are likely to have children who have dyspraxia and have not yet been identified. The demands of kindergarten and early elementary school may challenge the child's praxis.

● ● ●
Muscular Dystrophies

Muscular dystrophies is an umbrella term for a group of chronic, progressive disorders that affect the voluntary muscles. It is an inherited X-linked disorder caused by a genetic mutation, which results in the absence of a critical protein, dystrophin, which stabilizes the muscle membrane during contraction (Escolar et al., 2007). When this protein is deficient, muscles degenerate. The most common type, Duchenne muscular dystrophy, is not usually detected until a child is between ages 2 and 5. The child may experience excessive muscle cramping when exercising and begins to fall down frequently, due to muscle weakness (Escolar et al., 2007). It affects approximately 1 in 3,300 male births (Jeppesen et al., 2003). The muscles closest to the center of the body, those of the hip and shoulder area, are affected first, with the muscles in the fingers being affected later. A toddler may have problems turning over to get up. The result is gradual weakness and decline in muscle strength and health. The child's intellectual functioning is not affected, although most children with this disability have lower than average intelligence. The process, which can occur quickly or slowly, leads to increased disability and death (usually in young adulthood).

We do not know how to correct the metabolic disorder or halt the progression of the disease. The earlier the symptoms appear, the more severe the disease is likely to be and the earlier death will occur. Toddlers will have a waddling gait, fall frequently, have trouble getting up, climb stairs with difficulty, and they may walk on their toes. They will typically be able to walk during early childhood. As more muscles deteriorate and the child becomes weaker, a wheelchair is necessary. Once the disease has started, there is no remission, and its progress over time is predictable. Patience and emotional support are an essential part of dealing with the everyday frustrations that face the child and family.

IMPLICATIONS FOR EDUCATORS

Children with muscular dystrophy have normal feeling in their limbs, even though they cannot always move them (unlike a child with a spinal cord injury, who may have little or no feeling in the limbs). They cannot hold onto you very well because of muscular weakness, so be sure you are holding them securely before you pick them up. Don't lift them under the arms; because of weak shoulders, the arms may fall through your hold. Remember that the neck muscles may be very weak, so support the head when going from sitting to lying. Make sure the child has side supports when sitting. Children often depend on armrests to help hold themselves upright. As children get older and heavier, get someone to help you move the child; a two-person transfer is almost always safer for a child with muscular dystrophy. Find out from parents and physical therapists the most advantageous way to move the child. Although too much exercise is painful, appropriate stretching exercises are helpful (be sure to consult the parents and physical therapist to find the right exercises). Because the child's physical activities are limited and added weight is a problem, a low-calorie diet is recommended.

Blowing and breathing activities maintain the chest muscles. Snacks and lunches should be planned with the child's diet in mind. At preschool age, this child looks weak, not ill, and hence may be made fun of. Work to develop both the child's self-esteem and peer relationships. School, especially at an early age, is invaluable psychologically for both the child and the parents. The child poses few problems at this age. Therapy focuses on minimizing contractures, maximizing muscle strength, and learning to compensate for weaknesses. It becomes progressively more difficult for children with muscular dystrophy to stand and walk. They need to keep their legs well stretched; a goal is to keep the child walking as long as possible. Children may also have learning disabilities and developmental delays, and may need individualized educational programs to meet their educational needs (Leet, Dormans, & Tosi, 2002).

● ● ●
Neural Tube Defects

Neural tube defects is an umbrella term that refers to a group of congenital malformations of the vertebrae, spinal cord, and brain. The three major neural tube defects are spina bifida, encephalocele, and anencephaly (Liptak, 2007). The most common is **spina bifida**.

In spina bifida, there is a split in the **vertebral arches**. This separation can be isolated such as in individuals with **spina bifida occulta**, who have no symptoms and may not even know they have a split. Approximately 10 percent of the general population has this hidden separation (Liptak, 2007).

Some infants are born with a membranous sac over the spinal cord, called a **meningocele**. If the spinal cord itself is not entrapped, these children are usually symptom free.

The form of spina bifida that we typically think of as spina bifida is called **meningomyelocele (or myelomeningocele)**, where the spinal cord is malformed and children show an array of symptoms. The fluid-filled sac protrudes through the spine of the newborn above the defect in the vertebral column; it looks like a flat bubble on the infant's back and contains the malformed spinal cord. The nerves below the protrusion do not develop properly, leading to loss of sensation and paralysis below the site. Surgery is done within several days to remove the bubble, protect the exposed nerves from physical injury, and prevent infection. The surgery does not impact the neurological functioning of the child (Liptak, 2007).

Encephalocele, another neural tube defect, involves a malformation of the skull that allows a portion of the brain to protrude. This can be at the back of the brain in the occipital region or at the front. If at the back, children usually have intellectual disabilities and **hydrocephalus** (excessive fluid in the brain cavities), spastic diplegia, and/or seizures. If at the front of the head, such as the forehead, the impact is more variable (Liptak, 2007). **Anencephaly** is a more severe malformation of the skull and brain, and no neural development occurs above the brainstem. About half of these fetuses are spontaneously aborted, and those who live rarely survive infancy (Liptak, 2007).

CAUSES OF NEURAL TUBE DEFECTS

The problem that causes neural tube defects occurs prenatally by 26 days after conception, when the **neural groove** folds over itself to become the **neural tube**, which becomes the **spinal cord** and vertebral arches. If during this process the neural groove does not close completely, the spinal cord is malformed and the child has some form of neural tube defects (Liptak, 2007). There appears to be a genetic component and also environmental factors related to the development of neural tube defects. Treatment with folic acid during the first 12 weeks of pregnancy has been successful in decreasing the occurrences of neural tube defects. Because half of all pregnancies in the United States are unplanned (CDC, 2007e), folic acid supplements have been added to some grains, but the amount is not optimal.

The presence of neural tube defects can be diagnosed by levels of alpha-fetoprotein in the mother's blood serum during the 16th to 18th weeks of pregnancy. If detected, this is followed by a high-resolution ultrasound focusing on the fetal head and back. Approximately half of couples choose to terminate pregnancy based on confirmation of neural tube defects (Forrester & Merz, 2000). In the United States, the prevalence of meningomyelocele is approximately 60 in 100,000 live births; anencephaly, about 20 in 100,000; and encephalocele, about 10 in 100,000 (Rader & Schneeman, 2006).

There is considerable diversity in the degree of motor delay children with spina bifida may have. Although frequently late to roll over, most use belly crawling as a method of locomotion. Children's mobility is dependent on the location of the lesion. In general, the higher the level of the meningomyelocele, the more muscle weakness and the greater the impairment in ambulation.

The vertebrae of the spinal cord are divided into three major areas (see Figure 17–1). Starting from the bottom, there is the coccyx (tailbone), which is connected to the **sacrum**, which has five parts; the sacrum in turn connects to the lowest lumbar vertebra, and then there are 5 **lumbar vertebrae** (L), 12 **thoracic vertebrae** (T), and 7 **cervical vertebrae** (C). The closer the injury is to the head, the more severe the injury. Each vertebra supports an important bodily function.

Children with myelomeningocele are usually incontinent and cannot tell when they are wet. During the preschool years, incontinence is not a significant problem because the child can wear diapers. The parents and surgeons make decisions about how to manage this problem. This is frequently done with a technique called clean intermittent bladder catheterization (CIC). Parents make the decision how to handle this, which may include timed potty sitting after each meal. Bowel and bladder continence is a realistic and critical part of a child's development.

IMPLICATIONS FOR EDUCATORS

Intervention begins in infancy. In the sensory motor area, therapists are concerned with maintaining the range of motions of the joints, developing strength, and working toward standing and ambulation. Children with neural tube defects have decreased strength and sensations, so special care must be taken to protect their lower limbs. Their bones may not be as strong as they should be and are prone to fractures. Be alert for things that might cause skin problems, such as water that's too hot, sunburn, and insect bites. Children can develop skin sores or decubitus ulcers on weight-bearing surfaces and not know it, as they are not sensitive to pain. Socks should be worn in wading pools and shoes should be worn if the child is walking or crawling (Liptak, 2007).

Many children with spina bifida are allergic to latex. The reason is unclear, but the reaction can be life threatening. Toys that contain significant amounts of latex, such as rubber balls, should be avoided, and band-aids

Some children with spinal cord injuries are in wheelchairs even during the preschool years.
©Cengage Learning 2012

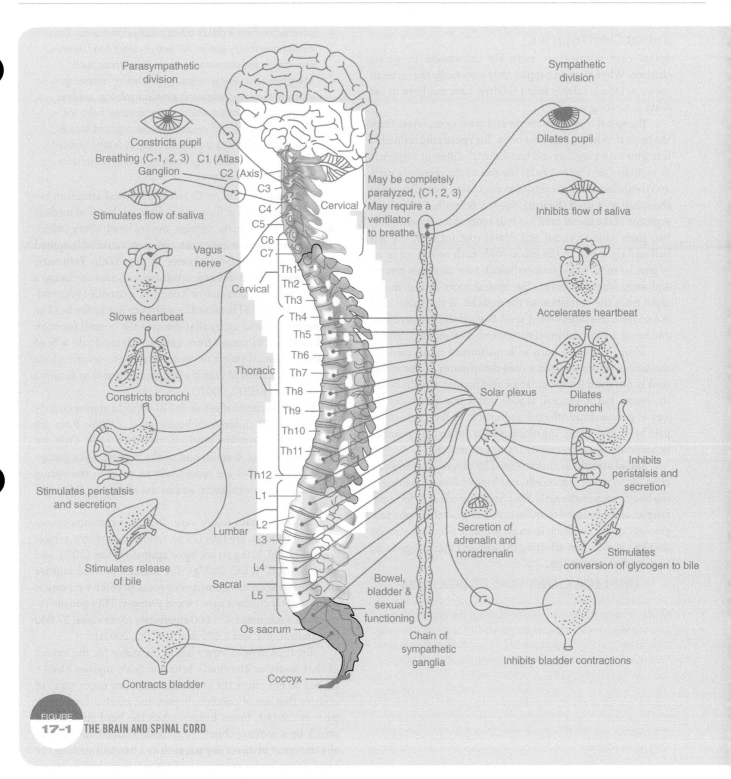

Parasympathetic division

Sympathetic division

Constricts pupil

Breathing (C-1, 2, 3) C1 (Atlas)

Ganglion

C2 (Axis)

C3

Stimulates flow of saliva

C4

Cervical

C5

C6

C7

Vagus nerve

Cervical

Th1

Th2

Th3

Slows heartbeat

Th4

Th5

Th6

Constricts bronchi

Thoracic

Th7

Th8

Th9

Th10

Th11

Stimulates peristalsis and secretion

Th12

L1

L2

Lumbar

L3

Stimulates release of bile

L4

Sacral

L5

Os sacrum

Contracts bladder

Coccyx

Dilates pupil

May be completely paralyzed, (C1, 2, 3) May require a ventilator to breathe.

Inhibits flow of saliva

Accelerates heartbeat

Solar plexus

Dilates bronchi

Inhibits peristalsis and secretion

Secretion of adrenalin and noradrenalin

Stimulates conversion of glycogen to bile

Bowel, bladder & sexual functioning

Chain of sympathetic ganglia

Inhibits bladder contractions

FIGURE 17-1 THE BRAIN AND SPINAL CORD

and ace bandages should not be used. Talk with parents and therapists about alternatives.

Most children with meningomyelocele have IQ scores in the low–average range. However, they frequently have problems that will eventually be labeled as specific learning disabilities. They may have impairments in perceptual skills, organization, attention span, memory, speed of motor responses, and hand function. They also may have problems with executive function

and adaptive skills. These learning problems are challenging. As children grow, concerns related to bowel and bladder control present health problems as well as social problems. To prevent urinary infections, children need to drink liquids; this, of course, increases the need to urinate. If this cannot be controlled beyond the preschool years, it becomes problematic for the child. Supporting children in developing a positive self-concept and feelings of autonomy and independence is imperative.

Spinal Cord Injuries

Spinal cord injuries are relatively uncommon in young children. When they do happen, they are usually the result of motor vehicle accidents when children have not been in car seats or wearing seat belts.

The spinal cord sends motor and sensory messages from the brain to other parts of the body. The spinal cord is divided into four major regions and has about 25 different segments or sections (see Figure 17–1). The size of the segments vary, and the delineations are clearer in discussion than they are in the spinal cord itself (Keating, Spence, & Lynch, 2002). Each segment of the spinal cord has four roots that are essentially two pairs with a ventral and dorsal root for both the left half and right half of the spinal cord. Each root is made up of smaller roots called rootlets, which take messages toward and away from the brain. The ventral roots deliver motor input from the brainstem to the muscles. If the spinal cord is damaged, messages do not reach beyond the impaired area and hence are not delivered or received (Keating et al., 2002).

Some infants are born with malformed spinal cords or conditions where the spinal cord deteriorates. If the spinal cord is not completely cut, some feeling may remain below the lesion, but in general, anyone who has a spinal cord injury is permanently affected and unable to feel pressure or pain below the lesion. The ultimate effect of an injury cannot be ascertained with certainty for several months.

Spinal atrophy is characterized by progressive degeneration of the motor-nerve cells, resulting in slow weakening of the body's muscle strength. The effects include skill decrease, fatigue, and decreased coordination. Congenital atrophy progresses rapidly, resulting in an early death. Acquired atrophy develops slowly, first affecting the legs and then progressing to the upper extremities.

IMPLICATIONS FOR EDUCATORS

Learn about what the child can and cannot do or feel. If the child lacks feeling, be concerned about sunburn, overheating, and frostbite. Insect bites or injuries may occur and not be noticed. If a child has movement in the arms and shoulders, work should be done to strengthen these because future mobility may depend on them—ultimately, the child has to learn to lift his own weight. Another important consideration is the prevention of pressure sores. These seem innocuous, but pressure sore infections can cause death. Sometimes, it takes weeks or months for them to heal, and they may have to be closed surgically. Children with spinal cord lesions generally have poor blood circulation; therefore, injuries are slow to heal and prone to infection.

Traumatic Brain Injury

An increasingly frequent cause of neurological impairment is head injury. This can occur from automobile accidents, falling off a bicycle, gunshot wounds, or from other accidental causes. They range from mild to profound and the effects can be temporary or permanent.

The IDEA (2004) defines traumatic brain injury as follows:

an acquired injury to the brain caused by an external physical force, resulting in total or partial functional disability or psychosocial impairment, or both, that adversely affects a child's educational performance. Traumatic brain injury applies to open or closed head injuries resulting in impairments in one or more areas, such as cognition; language; memory; attention; reasoning; abstract thinking; judgment; problem-solving; sensory, perceptual, and motor abilities; psychosocial behavior; physical functions; information processing; and speech. Traumatic brain injury does not apply to brain injuries that are congenital or degenerative, or to brain injuries induced by birth trauma.

Each year, 1 child in 25 receives medical attention because of a head injury. These range from not being of medical concern to severe brain damage. Severe head injury (which injures the brain) is the most common cause of acquired disability in childhood (Schneier et al., 2006). Traumatic brain injury (TBI) is defined as trauma sufficient to change a level of consciousness and/or having an anatomic abnormality of the brain. TBI is caused by a blow or jolt to the head or a penetrating head injury that disrupts the normal function of the brain. TBI ranges from mild, which results in a brief change in mental status or consciousness, to severe, which results in an extended period of unconsciousness or amnesia after the injury (CDC, 2007f).

Head injuries that result in TBI occur in approximately 1 in every 500 children (Schneier et al., 2006). Boys are more likely to sustain head injuries than girls. Children from birth to age 4 are in one of the highest risks groups (CDC, 2006c). TBIs are more likely to occur in the spring and summer, on weekends, and in the afternoon (Michaud et al., 2002).

Causes of brain injury vary. The most common causes of TBI in children are falls (28%), followed by motor vehicle crashes (20%), being struck by or against objects (19%), and assaults (11%) (CDC, 2007g). The number of head injuries that are not seen in an emergency room or receive no care is unknown. Of children ages 14 and younger, TBI annually results in an estimated 435,000 emergency room visits, 37,000 hospitalizations, and 2,685 deaths (CDC, 2007f).

The type of head injury has implications for the impact of that injury on the child's behavior. Scalp injuries bleed a lot but do not injure the brain. There are two major types of injuries that are of concern: impact and inertial forces. Impact, or contact, forces happen when the head strikes or is struck by a moving object. Focal brain contusions are usually the result of direct impact, such as a baseball striking the head. These bruise the brain and can result in skull fractures or blood collection beneath the skull (**epidural hematomas**). These can be minor, like bruises to other parts of the body, or may require surgical intervention. Inertial forces occur when the brain undergoes violent motion inside the skull. In these injuries, the concern is not a blood clot, but the nerve fibers throughout the brain that have been damaged, usually by violent motion (as in a motor vehicle accident). These too can be mild or serious. Often, children have both **diffuse axonal injury** and **subdural hematomas** as a result of accidents (Michaud et al., 2007).

Epidural hematomas are the most lethal, but also the most treatable. A **hematoma** is a blood clot, in this case between the skull and the outer covering of the brain. Acute subdural hematomas are blood clots that form beneath the **dura**, or the brain covering, and are often part of a more generalized injury to the brain itself. They result from sheering forces applied to the veins (acceleration–deceleration forces) that actually displace the brain from the dura to rupture these membranes (Michaud et al., 2002). A subdural hematoma may cause brain swelling and stroke. A large area of the brain is affected, and although surgery can remove the blood clot, the prognosis is not as positive.

Sometimes the brain injuries are inflicted rather than accidental. Confirmed abuse accounted for 33 percent of hospital admissions for head injuries for children younger than age 3, and 19 percent of those younger than 6½ years (Reece & Sege, 2000). Shaken baby syndrome is certainly one of the factors taken into account in these figures; however, it often appears that when the baby is shaken, the head also comes in contact with a surface such as a bed, wall, or floor (Salehi-Had et al., 2006).

Because timing is such an important variable, you need to know when head injuries need immediate care and when they do not. If a child hits his head and does not lose consciousness, no treatment is necessary. However, the child must be observed. If the child develops symptoms of an epidural hematoma (e.g., vomiting; tiredness or listlessness; irritability; changes in eating, sleep, or play; lack of interest in favorite toys or activities; loss of new skills; and loss of balance or unsteady walking) the child should have a medical evaluation (CDC, 2006d).

A child who has an injury and loses consciousness and then resumes normal activities may have a mild concussion. If the loss of consciousness is more than momentary, a neurological examination and brain imaging should be done. If the child is unconscious for more than a few minutes, call 911 (Michaud et al., 2007).

Acute medical care is the initial focus. Rehabilitation may begin when vital signs have been stabilized even if the child is still in a coma. These procedures are designed to limit secondary musculoskeletal problems by using passive range of motion and other exercises. As medical problems stabilize, the extent of injury become more evident. The nature and severity of functional impairment determines the rehabilitative strategies. However, such injuries almost always involve an interdisciplinary team.

The severity and type of injury to the brain impacts the recovery. With mild TBI, there are few, if any, long-term consequences in cognitive functioning. Moderate to severe TBI can cause significant cognitive impairment. Predicting how children will fare appears to be more complex than with adults. The brain of the young child is more plastic and hence has the potential for further development. However, brain injury appears to impair new learning more than the retention of old learning, and young children haven't had as much time to build a knowledge base (Michaud et al., 2007).

Most recovery takes place in the first six months after the injury and will take place at a slower rate after that (Taylor, 1999). Goals for children are to relearn lost skills and to learn new skills to compensate for those that cannot be regained.

Whereas adults seem to develop predictable patterns after brain injury, children seem to have different patterns, depending on the task. For some tasks, the child shows a progressive pattern of recovery over time; in others, the impairment is constant; in still others, there is no discernible impairment after the injury, but over time a problem appears, a delayed reaction. In young children, brain damage interrupts development. Early brain damage results in cumulative defects because of the small repertoire of skills young children have, making it difficult to consolidate new skills and knowledge. Common deficits for young children include information processing, memory, and executive function (Anderson et al., 2000).

THE EVIDENCE BASE

One research study looked at young children's cognitive ability after a TBI. Children injured before age 3 ($n = 27$) were looked at for global intellectual skills only. Older children were divided according to age at injury (3 to 7 years; 8 to 12 years) and the severity of the injury (mild, moderate, or severe). They were evaluated at 12 and 30 months after the injury. Mild or moderate injuries were usually associated with falls, whereas severe TBIs usually were the result of motor vehicle accidents.

Infants (from birth to age 3) with mild TBI continued to show improvements. However moderate TBI caused significant decreases in global intellectual ability (12 to 14 points below average IQ). These children showed poorer outcomes than older children. They were also more likely to lose consciousness, with 78 percent having a period of coma for over an hour.

Age at injury did not predict outcomes for children over 3 with mild to moderate outcomes. Children who sustained mild TBI had IQ scores in the average range 12 months after the injury. Those with moderate TBIs were marginally lower. The trajectories were stable from 12 to 30 months.

Children (ages 3 to 7) with severe TBI showed minimal, if any, recovery after the injury. Older children had better outcomes than younger ones, showing a gain in IQ of about 9 points at 12 months but less improvement from 12 to 30 months (about 2 points). Nonverbal skills had significant recovery after a severe TBI. Verbal knowledge, word knowledge, abstract thought, and comprehension skills were depressed after a severe TBI.

Source: Anderson et al., 2005.

Children who experience severe diffuse axonal injuries are likely to have impairments in all areas of functioning, whereas children who had an injury in only one area of the brain are likely to have more localized problems. Damage to the motor areas of the brain often results in impairments similar to pyramidal cerebral palsy: spasticity, ataxia, and tremors. Feeding disorders may result as well as impaired motor skills, sensory impairments, communication impairments (receptive, expressive, or mixed), and cognitive impairments (Michaud et al., 2007).

Children who have sustained moderate to severe TBIs often experience problems in academic learning. These may manifest themselves in reading or math, but the more pervasive effects relate to attention, problem solving, and speed of information processing (Hawley et al., 2004). Their patterns of learning differ from those of children with specific learning disabilities. Children with TBIs demonstrate highly variable performance within and across academic subjects, and they continue to change over time (Michaud et al., 2007). Behavior changes can also be expected.

Children who sustain TBI must cope with psychological stress. The loss of skills is distressing to children. Families too may be stressed, initially with concern about whether the child will live or die, then in coping with the child herself, and the financial consequences of paying for the child's treatment.

IMPLICATIONS FOR EDUCATORS

In cases of TBI, it is important that the transition from hospital to school involves shared information. Children will typically have a difficult time attending for long periods, remembering information they had known before, and learning new information. Their greatest difficulty seems to be in the area of the organization of information. They may also find abstractions and creative thinking challenging. The loss of skills that they could perform before, that other children their age are now easily doing, is a source of frustration. It is important to maintain close contact with their families and review their IEP/IFSP every month or six weeks during the early recovery period, as rapid changes can take place. Children with TBI may require intervention strategies to help them relate to the social world around them. Modifications such as consistent routines, a lack of distracting elements, and clear, repetitive directions are helpful.

Most childhood trauma is preventable. Teach children good safety habits such as using helmets while riding bicycles and using handrails while walking up and down stairs. As an educator, actively supervise playgrounds, and ensure that equipment and surface areas are safe and at appropriate heights. Teach children rules for crossing roads. Identify child abuse and help to prevent its reoccurrence. Ensure that children ride in car seats and that restraints are appropriate for their age and weight (CDC, 2007c). Children with TBIs are challenging because of their variability and unpredictability for themselves and others.

IN THE FIELD

What I do when I learn I am getting a new child who will be challenging. . . .

The first thing I do is take a mini-mental vacation. I replay my favorite teaching moments in my mind and remind myself that I am qualified to do this job, that I like what I am doing, and that I am respected by my peers and administrators. Then, I replay my worst teaching moments and remind myself that I am still qualified to do this job, that I still like what I am doing, and that I am still respected by my peers and administrators. Then I take a moment to reflect on what I have learned from these experiences. It is not enough to have had them—it's what I *learned* from them.

Next, I try to determine *why* the child is challenging, *who* has classified him as *challenging*, and *what* others have tried in the past, whether it has worked or not worked. "Challenging" is subjectively defined. I try to critically evaluate the situation, define the problem area, and determine the impact on the child's ability to learn and the possible impact on the dynamics of the classroom. Then, knowing the other children in the classroom, I try to anticipate potential problems and be proactive.

When the time comes to meet the child and the parents, I *forget* everything I have read about the child. Although I have *prepared* for the child and have become familiar with the diagnosis/classification and all the implications, I try to remain open-minded and view the child without *prejudice* or *prejudgment.*

Mobility Aids

Regardless of the diagnosis, many children with neurological and orthopedic impairments use adaptive equipment for assistance in moving. Most children have a variety of mobility aids; some are simple, others are complex. It is important that you know the purpose of the equipment and the relationship among the aids. Organizationally, the equipment starts with the child and what is necessary to implement independent mobility. It then goes on to short- and long-distance mobility aids. Because children use many different types of equipment, adults must help them transfer from one piece of equipment to another or to a chair, the floor, or toilet.

• • •

Splinting, Bracing, and Positioning

The purpose of bracing, splinting, and positioning is to improve children's functioning. Together braces and splints are called **orthoses**. Their purpose is to maintain range of motion, prevent contractures at joints, provide stability, and control involuntary movements (Pellegrino, 2007). Splints can be either static (rigid) or dynamic (with movable parts) (Kurtz, 2002). Splints and braces are all custom-made by an **orthotist** (brace maker) or a therapist. In general, occupational therapists make upper extremity splints, and physical therapists make lower extremity splints. Because young children grow quickly and insurance companies may only pay for one orthosis per year, those made by therapists are less expensive. As children grow, their weight and use of the orthosis may require that it be made of more expensive materials and through a different process than therapists can do.

There are two basic types of orthoses: plastic and metal. Plastic braces are lightweight and can be contoured to use on the trunk, legs, and arms. (A child with cystic fibrosis may even have a plastic "jacket.") Plastic braces are molded to fit the body part and keep that body part in a position that is ready to function, as well as position it for better growth. Many plastic braces have hinges at the ankles and knees to allow for movement.

Metal braces are used far less frequently today than they were in the past. For legs, braces can be short or long. If they are long, they are hinged at the knee and have locks. Young children do not have the strength or dexterity to make these locks work. The first time you work with these locks you need to do it under the supervision of the physical or occupational therapist or the parents. (The locks require a lot of pressure to change. The pressure you use needs to be against the brace and not the child's body.) When the therapist demonstrates for you how the locks work, that is only the first step. *You* need to be able to work the locks. Ask the therapist to watch and coach you while you try. *You* need to be able not only to work the locks, but also to put the braces on and off. (A child might get wet at the water table or have a toileting accident, and you will have to change her.) While the therapist is there, do it, and let the therapist coach you. Watching isn't the same as doing.

One thing you will notice is that the shoes of children in braces frequently look identical, and it may be difficult to tell the right shoe from the left one. Take your handy permanent marker and mark the right and left shoes (or ask the parents to do this). Although the shoes look alike to you, they are individually fitted and feel very different to the child. If a child who is usually cheerful is unhappy or crying and you have gone through your usual repertoire of possible causes, check to see whether the child's shoes and braces are on the appropriate legs. They are particularly uncomfortable for the child when placed on the wrong foot or leg. On a hectic morning, families may make a mistake.

Short-Distance Mobility Aids

Walkers, scooters, crutches, and canes are the most common mobility aids for short distances. Some or all of these may be in your classroom with the child, as they serve slightly different purposes.

Walkers are individualized to the child's ability, size, and functional level. Young children often use walkers before they use crutches. Walkers provide a broader base of support. Children can use the walker for balance and get up to it independently before they can manage the same skills with crutches. The area inside the walker is personal space for the child. If children need adult support to use the walker, place it out of the way when it is not being actively supervised. If children can use the walker independently, it needs to be accessible to the child. Know the child's individual competence level with this, as with all mobility aids. Be sure the walker has a basket so the child can transport books, puzzles, and other items.

Crutches require much better balance than walkers. They are, however, a more normalized system of transportation. They approximate a gait pattern that is similar to independent walking. Children might use crutches in therapy for a long time before they have them for general use. Scooters are another set of wheels that children can use for independent mobility. Some scooters are designed to be sat upon, others to lie on. Scooters provide children with both independence and exercise when they don't have good sensation in their legs.

Long-Distance Mobility Aids

Strollers and wheelchairs constitute the most common long-distance mobility aids. When children are very young, it is fine to carry them as you would any infant or toddler. However, as children get older, this is developmentally inappropriate, except for short distances or in emergencies. For younger children, specially made strollers are designed for this time slot. These strollers offer the child a little more positioning than regular strollers and are designed for larger children. As children get older, they use wheelchairs.

For young children, a wheelchair can be thought of as a specialized source of assistance. It is necessary for fire drills, for long walks for which the child does not have enough stamina, and sometimes for seating. Wheelchairs are custom fitted to individual children by the physical therapist, **physiatrist**, or sometimes an occupational therapist, and a representative of the company that makes the wheelchair, working together as a team (Pellegrino, 2007).

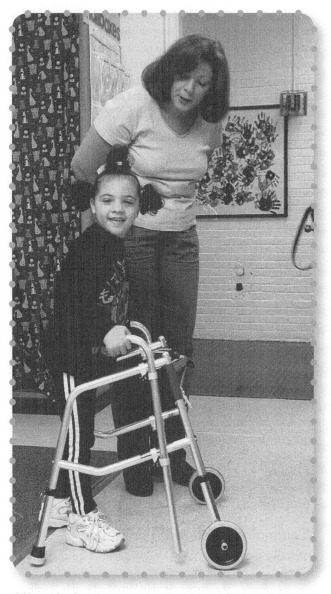

Children with orthopedic impairments need a variety of mobility aids. For short distances, they may use walkers.
©Cengage Learning 2012

All wheelchairs are different, and the expectations for the children who occupy these chairs differ also. However, there is one rule about wheelchairs that transcends types: Put on the brakes before anything else. Also, when putting a child in a wheelchair, put on the child's seat belt before taking off the brakes. For your safety and the child's, get a lesson from the child's physical therapist on how to safely transfer the child from a wheelchair and where to put the child after she is out. One obvious but crucial point: Before taking a child out of a wheelchair, know where the child is going. Children cannot stand there and wait for you to decide. In addition, you need to talk with the child before you move him: "I'm going to take you out of the wheelchair and put you on the floor." Some children may be learning to use a transfer board; if so, find out the ability of the child to independently transfer and what your role should be.

In general, young children should not be in wheelchairs in your classroom. They belong on the floor or in chairs like others sit in (with modifications, if necessary). Decide on a place to park the wheelchair, perhaps in the hall outside. Use short-distance mobility aids in the classroom (walkers, scooters, or whatever meets the child's needs) when possible.

• • •

Transferring

Transferring is the term used when you move children from one piece of equipment to another. It might be from the floor to the toilet, the wheelchair to the floor, into or out of a chair, and so on. In general, transferring requires two people. One person is in charge of the trunk area and stands behind the child; the other manages the thigh area and stands in front of the child. In the case of *very small* children, one person can do the transfer. In all cases, work with therapists on transfers. The particular type of transfer that is most effective for the child and you will be determined and demonstrated by the therapists working with the child. One-person transfers are not recommended for children you wouldn't normally carry, but ask a therapist how to do this in case of emergency.

Transferring happens several times each day from different positions. *Caution:* It is imperative that you know a child's level of competence in mobility. If a child does not have protective reflexes (if when she falls forward she does not put out her hands to protect herself), she needs the constant monitoring of a trained adult in all antigravity positions. Knowing the equipment is very different from knowing the child's ability to use such equipment. Children need to be an active part of the process.

Technology-Related Assistance

Assistive technology is any kind of technology that can be used by children with disabilities to enhance their functional independence. The most common mobility aids (walkers, wheelchairs, scooters, etc.) have already been discussed. With the passage of the Tech Act in 1988, we began to focus more on how technology, devices, equipment, and systems could improve the capacities of children with disabilities. Training and technical assistance can support children with disabilities in their efforts to acquire and use technology as a routine part of day-to-day living.

Computer software selected for children with orthopedic and neurological problems should be evaluated in the following areas:

- Directions and documentation
- Feedback and evaluation
- Content
- Individualization options
- Interface and screen design
- Accessibility (Boone & Higgins, 2007, p. 5)

Additional concerns relative to accessibility relate to ensuring that input speed does not affect the accuracy of responses and that there is the potential for alternative input devices such as a single switch (Boone & Higgins, 2007).

Guidelines

Early care and education settings can provide a broad range of experiences for children with orthopedic and neurological impairments. Children need to be included in firsthand experiences and provided with a wide variety of materials and equipment. Foster independence in any way you can.

1. *Give children tasks they can accomplish.* Children learn early what others can do that they cannot.

2. *Use assistive technology routinely.* Have "reachers" in your classroom (assistive devices that individuals use to reach high objects; they usually have a grip that controls a pincer or magnet at the end to pick things up). Use them and encourage all children to use them when they can't reach something they want.

3. *Ensure that children touch things as well as see them.* When necessary, bring materials to children so that they can actively explore them.

4. *Demonstrate how materials are used.* Some children don't know what to do and are simply too shy to ask. Support children through the cycle of learning.

5. *Have pictures of individuals using mobility devices on your wall.* Our society values beauty and strength. Because body image greatly influences self-concept, children with orthopedic impairments need help integrating body image into a healthy self-concept. Read books about children with orthopedic impairments (see Children's Bibliography).

6. *Work on developing children's language skills.* Support language that is necessary to express feelings and to meet personal needs. Provide creative activities that help children release energy and work out feelings.

7. *Help children establish a sexual identity.* People with orthopedic impairments are often treated as if they are asexual. Appropriate sex-role identification is important to children's development.

8. *Keep in contact if children are absent from school.* Send get-well cards, audiotapes, videotapes, and e-mail, and visit if the child is out of school for an extended period of time.

For children with orthopedic and neurological impairments, the classroom itself needs to be evaluated for accessibility and perhaps modified.

1. *Borrow a wheelchair, sit in it, and pretend that you are teaching.* Go to the doorway to greet children, take them to their lockers and, then help them settle into the routine. Monitor children playing in different areas of the room. Be sure to include the bathroom on your excursion. Now, reflect on what was difficult for you to do and how you feel (e.g., tired, frustrated?). How long were you in the wheelchair? Evaluate your room to determine how accessible classroom

equipment is. Check doors and passageways to be sure walkers and wheelchairs can get through and turn easily. Be sure areas around activities and equipment are wide enough for mobility aids. Determine how accessible the class is if you were on a scooter or crawling. We really don't want children in wheelchairs in the classroom, although for some children this is necessary.

2. *Use tables with adjustable legs and tabletops that can be angled.* If these are not available, a wooden wedge can serve the same purpose.

3. *Include lighter equipment.* Use cardboard blocks and have a variety of manipulatives that require pushing and pulling with varying degrees of strength. Be sure that large equipment like bookshelves are heavy and stable, as children might lean against them or use them to pull upright.

4. *Move sand and activity tables away from walls.* Ensure that children can get to them from all sides.

5. *Provide many different types of chairs.* Give children a choice of chairs they can sit in (if all the chairs are the same except one, it points out difference, not inclusion). Have bolsters, wedges, and beanbag chairs to provide a change for children. If necessary, modify a chair with the help of a physical therapist or physiatrist. An abduction block—a chunk of something padded that the child's legs can straddle—will prevent a child from sliding onto the floor, or add a seat belt.

6. *Add ramps.* This supports children's independence and helps children enter and leave the classroom.

7. *Use nonslip floor coverings.* Do not highly wax floors, use scatter rugs, or have shag carpet. If you have carpets with low pile, be sure a metal strip attaches them so they won't slide and so children don't trip over the edges. Keep toys not in use off the floor.

8. *Evaluate toilet cubicles.* If you have them, they should be wide enough to accommodate a child, a wheelchair, and an adult; handrails need to be at the child's height to make the transfer an easy one. A transfer pole (a movable pole that goes from floor to ceiling) may need to be added. There are also many different types of potty chairs that are designed to solve a variety of problems. Ask parents what word or sign they use for "potty" and how they deal with this issue at home.

9. *Shorten and widen handles.* This includes handles on paintbrushes, rackets, and paddles to make them easier for children with orthopedic impairments to use. Use rubber tubing or foam around the handles for easier grip. Add a Velcro strap to the handle if children have trouble keeping a grip on the brush.

10. *Use deep-sided bowls and two-handled mugs.* These are easier for children to manage than cups and plates for meals and snacks. Serve a lot of finger foods. Put plates on Dycem to keep them from moving around.

11. *Be sure the food you serve is not too hot.* Some children can't tell when something is too hot, including food, and they could burn themselves.

12. *Provide ways for children to carry things.* Be sure walkers have baskets and have fanny packs or small knapsacks (to wear in the front) for children on crutches.

13. *Use both large and small versions of manipulative toys.* Use toys that have a built-in tolerance for error (e.g., blocks that fit together even if the child doesn't match them perfectly).

14. *Remove equipment that overturns easily.* Move rolling shelves if not stable.

15. *Use padded lapboards or lap trays* for children who may be more comfortable on the floor than sitting in a chair.

16. *Use a book or music stand with a page holder to keep pages of a book open.* If needed get a specialized page turner. Have a listening center with headphones.

17. *Prioritize tasks.* Put tasks that are most important and those that require more energy and concentration first if the child tires easily.

Curriculum Adaptations

The actual physical limitations a child has will determine the number and degree of adaptations necessary. In general, encourage children to do as much as possible independently—but not to the point of frustration. Offer help when you think it is necessary. When you give help, tell the child what you are going to do and, as you do it, what you are doing.

Don't forget that children change and grow. An adaptation that may be necessary at the beginning of the year may not be needed by the middle or end of the year. As you adapt equipment and programming for children, consider whether the adaptation is developmentally and socially appropriate. Adaptations should be designed to include children, not draw attention to them.

Social Awareness

Children need to learn about the larger world and be part of it. They need both information and skills. Children with orthopedic impairments may not move as fast as others or with the same quality of movement, and need to refine skills related to speed, distance, and coordination for their own safety. Some of the activities in Resource Chapter 1 are specifically designed to increase children's awareness of the effects of orthopedic and neurological impairments such as Activities 1–12, *Wheels*; 1–45w, *Slings*; and 3–61w, *Cast It*.

• • •
Social Competence

Children need to be accepted for who they are and for their similarities as well as their differences. They need to build a positive self-concept. Find out from the parents what they have told their child about the disability. Many parents do not talk with children about this, or they give children the impression that there is a "cure" and that when they grow up the disability will be gone. It is important that children integrate their abilities and disabilities into their self-concept in a positive way.

1. Encourage children to talk about their feelings about having a disability. Be a good listener.

2. Teach children how to deal with rejection and discrimination as it happens. Ignoring it or pretending it is not there does not work. Be sure children have the words to respond to comments such as "What's wrong with you?" An appropriate response might be, "There isn't anything wrong with me. My legs aren't strong enough to hold up my body, so I wear these braces. What's wrong with you?"

3. Develop body awareness and self-concept, for example, by using songs and fingerplays that use body parts.

4. Provide self-help aids such as buttoners and reachers so that children can practice self-help skills with these supports.

All children need to feel that they are part of the group. This is especially true when equipment causes physical distance from other children. Do not exclude activities that children cannot do independently; rather, have a paraeducator help children do any movement that needs to be done to feel included. If this is not possible, adapt the movements. Encourage all children to think about how they will move before they actually do it.

1. Help children acknowledge obvious limitations; yet see other areas as challenges. Be realistic, but not pessimistic: "I can do _____, but I can't do _____." At the same time, help children figure out different ways they can be part of the group.

2. Ask open-ended questions. If children can not tell you how they feel, ask them to show you with paint or another media. Help children label feelings. For example, "I think if I needed to sit in your chair I might be scared of _____. Do you ever get scared?" Encourage all children to talk about and label feelings.

3. Talk about their role as part of the group, what they do to help others, and what others do to help them.

Social Studies

Awareness of community is important for children with orthopedic and neurological impairments. Start by familiarizing the children with their immediate environment.

1. Get children out into the community so their knowledge is firsthand.

2. If you are doing a unit on transportation, include wheelchairs (nonpowered and electric) in your discussion.

3. Help children personalize their equipment (with parents' permission). Wheelchairs can be decorated with license nameplates, bicycle bells, or horns and streamers. Walkers may be painted or wrapped with ribbon. Casts can be decorated.

4. Have appropriate visitors, including those who play a role in this child's life: osteopath, physical therapist, occupational therapist, orthopedic surgeon, adults with orthopedic impairments, and so forth.

5. Use technology (Internet, DVDs, etc.) to help children learn about their world.

English Language Arts

Children develop language by listening to others speak and interacting with their environment. Children with orthopedic impairments may need practice in asking for what they want, especially if they cannot reach it. Likewise, adults need practice listening and allowing children to ask rather than doing it for them. Reading can broaden the range of experiences available to children. Writing may offer a particular challenge. Using materials that have some built-in resistance may be necessary, such as writing or drawing in sand or on clay, or using a computer with an adapted keyboard.

Speaking and Listening

Children with physical limitations rely more on speaking to get some of what they need and to convey information to others. The ability to express themselves well can help compensate for lack of motor skills.

1. Use puppets to encourage expressive language. Have puppets that talk and move in many different ways. Encourage children to use a puppet on each hand and have them "talk" to each other. Sock puppets or puppets on padded sticks that just need to be moved up and down are easier to use.

2. Expand children's utterances, especially when they use "telegraphic speech." If a child says, "Get doll," you might respond, "Which doll do you want me to get you? Oh, you want the one with the red dress." When children ask for objects by pointing, help them learn vocabulary by filling in the words they need: "That's the doll." However, if children are able to respond with only "yes" or "no," phrase your questions accordingly: "Do you want the blue one?" not "Which one do you want?"

3. Support children who cannot speak in using a communication board. Help all children learn about different methods of communication.

4. Help children connect sounds they hear with what they should do, especially warning sounds like fire alarms, horns, and so on.

5. Encourage children to use a listening center or to listen to appropriate CDs or DVDs as a way to expand their world.

Reading

Reading skills involving listening, and visual activities can easily be adapted for children with orthopedic impairments. Be sure that books are accessible.

1. Field trips followed by language-experience stories are good initial reading experiences.
2. Be sure children can visually and verbally identify objects before you work on discrimination and other higher-level skills.
3. Introduce children to listening stations and recorded books as part of their reading program.
4. Make reading interactive.
5. Read books and show pictures of children who have orthopedic impairments; choose books that emphasize the senses the child can use. Present a balance of disabilities in your selections. Have a variety of books, including age-appropriate board books or other materials that are easy to use.
6. Use flannelboard stories to focus attention and to increase participation.
7. Add background music to stories to enhance the mood for children (e.g., circus music, waves breaking).

Writing

Writing can present a challenge for children with coordination problems. All children need to develop trunk control before they can coordinate the small muscles of the hands and fingers necessary for writing.

1. Have children draw with their fingers in the sand before giving them a tool. Have them write letters with their fingers (the index and middle fingers) before using a marker.
2. Help children find a match between what they want to do and what the medium will allow. Having a variety of graphic materials and tools adds to children's knowledge of the world and how they fit into it.
3. Talk with the occupational therapist about the best adaptations for writing instruments. There are many different cushions or gripper adaptations available.
4. Help children warm up their muscles by squeezing clay or playdough. They may need to either strengthen or loosen these muscles before using writing instruments. A short hand massage may make writing easier.
5. To teach prewriting skills, use activities that require finger and wrist movement, especially rotation with the palm of the hand down.
6. Encourage children to use the computer to write. Ask an occupational therapist about adapting the keyboard or visual display unit. If children lack muscle power, a smaller-sized keyboard may be useful (this is also true for one-handed users). Some keys may not be necessary. For other children, a larger keyboard with letter characters, numerals, and arrow keys may be more appropriate.

Language

1. Check for vocabulary words children might not be familiar with. If possible, add concrete examples to help children understand a story. For example, bring in types of seashells mentioned in the story to show children.
2. Teach children the names of internal and external body parts that will help them better understand their impairment.
3. Refine their vocabulary relative to terms that relate to distance (near, far), speed (fast, slow), and time (a lot, a little).

Discovery

This area has potential for children with orthopedic and neurological impairments, as the approach supports and encourages the development of skills for problem solving. Concepts that relate to size, distance, and speed are especially important to children with orthopedic impairments. Because they are less mobile than others, they may require more energy to carry out tasks; thus, it is important that they learn to think through tasks before attempting them. They can learn to predict how long it will take to cross the path to the swings if someone is approaching on a tricycle. Size concepts help them understand where they can easily fit when using a mobility device and still be able to turn around. They also need to learn that, like other children, they are growing and their body is changing. They will, with time, get too big for some of their mobility aids. Technology offers children ways of communicating that have not been possible before. They need to feel comfortable with this technology at an early age. They can develop cause-and-effect reasoning skills. Help them develop problem-solving skills. Encourage unconventional solutions.

Mathematics

Children with orthopedic impairments have been exposed to many concepts that are classified under the heading of math. They know something about time concepts. They know something about distance and how far they can go before they get tired. Mathematics can help them quantify these experiences.

1. Teach children about the relationship between speed and distance (e.g., "If I go 20 feet [from here to the door] as fast as I can, I'm tired. I can go 60 feet [the length of the room] slowly. It takes longer, but I can do it and I am not tired").
2. Help children count the number of steps they can take, the number of blocks they can stack, or the number of chairs around the table.
3. Use manipulatives to have children make sets of objects and add or subtract a specific number from the set and recount.
4. Measure and weigh children to help them understand why braces no longer fit and need to be replaced. Weigh a child's braces and talk about how much they weigh. Bring in wrists, ankles, or waist weights and have children use these during the day. Talk about the difference

the weights make in how they feel and tasks they can perform and the amount of energy it takes.

5. Discuss the attributes of shapes, particularly those that roll and those that don't. Relate them to concepts like brakes and moving: Round shapes are used for wheels; a triangular block of wood can be used to stop a wheel from moving.

6. Use objects that vary in weight for sorting activities. Set out a ping-pong ball, tennis ball, hardball, basketball, large rubber ball, beach ball, and soccer ball, and see whether the children can arrange them by weight and size. Discuss the relationships among an object's weight, the distance someone can throw it, and the strength needed to throw it. Take the balls outside, set up a range and have each child throw and/or kick different balls; mark and measure how far each goes; and relate this back to size, weight, and strength. The focus is on relative distance, not throwing it the farthest.

7. Use objects that vary in shape, size, and texture. Help children decide the easiest and most difficult to move based on these variables.

Science

Science teaches the cause-and-effect reasoning that is necessary for safety and encourages children to devise adaptations to meet their needs.

1. Attach a string to a stick, tie a magnet on the end of the string, and go "fishing." Catch "fish" that have paper clip mouths. Show children how to pick up metal objects with a magnet.

2. Work on simple causal relationships: "The faster I move my hands on the wheel, the faster the wheelchair moves. If I only move the right wheel forward, I turn left!" See Activity 1–35w, *Creepers*, for additional ideas.

3. Help children learn to use simple machines such as wheels and pulleys with ropes as a way of moving objects. Demonstrate how you might use a long foam roll to move a heavy object (inflatable rollers are used to move boats).

4. Study and read about the concept of energy as it relates to children and also the natural world.

5. Learn about the effects of gravity and relate this to children's bodies and how far they can lean without unbalancing.

Technology

Children need to be exposed to technology early and to think about it as part of their life. Any child who has control over one body part, whether that is a hand, a big toe, or a tongue, can use a computer. Most computers are designed with adaptations. Call the manufacturer to find out how easily adaptations can be made, or consult an assistive technology specialist.

1. Adapt computers to make them accessible to all children. The mouse can be larger and adapted to respond to different amounts of pressure. Keys can be slowed down and attached to a voice activation system that talks to the child in addition to showing what is happening. Foot or head switches can be added or a sip-and-puff straw, and even the movement of an eyebrow can control the computer. There are joysticks that can be operated by tongue or head movements. Because of their potential, computers should be part of children's educational environment as early as when children are age 3 or 4.

2. Include technology as part of the child's IEP. Ensure adults learn how to use the computer and software that has been chosen. Work out procedures for a customized computer or electronic tablet to travel safely with the child from school to home.

3. Help all children understand that technology includes communication systems, switches, wheelchairs, and so on. Talk about devices in the framework of technology, and how technologies support all children.

4. Talk about editing and the use of a word processor in the writing process. It can find spelling errors, help with sentence structure, and remove mistakes without an eraser.

> ▶❚❚ TeachSource Video Case
>
> **Assistive Technology in the Inclusive Classroom: Best Practice**
>
> Watch the TeachSource Video Case *Assistive Technology in the Inclusive Classroom: Best Practice*, where you'll meet 5-year-old Jamie, a kindergartener with cerebral palsy who uses assistive technologies to help her learn the same curriculum content as the other students in her class. The video can be found in the Early Childhood Education Media Library under Special Education, available at www.cengagebrain.com.

Wellness

Children need body awareness to achieve a good self-concept and also to maintain their personal health and safety. Children who lack sensation in some body parts must learn to become visually aware of conditions they cannot feel. Children who use a prosthetic device, a splint or a brace need to be aware of the muscles that help work the device and also of any irritation or pain that may indicate they are outgrowing the device or that it needs to be adjusted.

Children must be given the opportunity to discover their abilities and challenges in the motor area. Allow children to use all equipment (within realistic limits) and participate in all activities normally provided in your setting, unless you have other directives from the family, physician, or therapists. If there is *any* doubt, check. Therapists and families are prime resources for ideas on adapting equipment and activities. A child whose lower body is most affected needs to strengthen the upper body to use a walker or to transfer from a wheelchair to the floor; at the same time, you do not want to ignore the child's lower body. Children need to have as much functional ability as possible so that muscles do not contract or atrophy.

Encourage children to use the skills they have and to participate in large and small motor activities.
©Cengage Learning 2012

Health and Safety

Health and safety are especially important for children with orthopedic and neurological impairments and can make a difference not only to them, but to other children as well.

1. Teach children to put crutches or other aids in a place where they can have easy access to them. These aids are needed for independence. Teach others to walk around them. These aids belong to the child who uses them and should not be shared.

2. Help children identify bruises and scrapes and spot pressure sores, and teach children to show these to an adult. As you care for these, talk about what you do and why you are doing it.

3. Be sure children are familiar with the procedures and the routes to be taken during safety drills. Have your own drills in preparation for the official ones. Use wagons, or if the child is light enough, lift the child up and carry him if fire occurs. Plan ahead as to who will take the child.

4. Keep extra boxes of tissues around for children to use, and trashcans that are easy to get to. Distance makes a difference. Have children deposit used tissues in the trash and then wash their hands. If you help them, you must wash your hands or use an antibacterial gel.

5. Seat children in chairs with their buttocks at the back of the chair; then, if necessary, put the seat belt around their hips, not their waist. Check that the knees are at a 90-degree angle and the feet are on the floor, also at a 90-degree angle. Elbows should rest gently on the table.

Physical Education

Children need to use and develop their large muscles for strength and endurance.

1. Supervise children carefully. Children with poor muscular control are in danger of falling; someone must be on hand to catch them. Additionally, they need to learn to fall safely, which is vital for their health, well-being, and self-esteem—and not a bad thing for all children to know. Work with the physical therapist and parents to continue this learning process, and learn how to help children transfer into unusual equipment (such as a wagon or tricycle).

2. Do not assist children in climbing higher than they can climb independently. If they are unsure how to get down safely, they may need verbal guidance and/or physical help.

3. Encourage children to use equipment independently (e.g., get on and off a trike). However, do not assist them in using equipment beyond their skill level. Use safety equipment like bicycle helmets for tricycles.

4. Have children work on vertical surfaces (e.g., chalkboard or easel) that are large enough so they can use large muscles both standing and sitting. These are antigravity positions and are necessary for children to integrate the concepts high and low, up and down, and around.

5. Adapt toss games (e.g., beanbags, balls, ring throws) by attaching the objects to the child's chair with a string so that the child can retrieve them. Keep distances short and gradually lengthen them as children become more skillful. (Monitor the string carefully and remove it when the child has finished, as it is a potential danger.)

6. Increase mobility for children who are unstable by adding weight (sandbags or cans of food) to a baby carriage.

7. Mount toys on walls at a child's height to facilitate hand coordination, balance, and grasping.

8. Practice tossing and catching, using yarn balls or covered foam balls for safety; underinflated beach balls are good too. Scoopers for catching the balls can be made easily from large plastic bottles.

Sensory Motor Integration

Integrating information that comes from the senses is critical. Give children unusual stimuli as it helps them focus.

1. Use recipes for playdough that have different consistencies, textures, and smells. Support children in using their hands to poke, pull, and roll the playdough before adding rolling pins and other tools. Encourage them to squish the playdough between their fingers.

2. Make Freddie the Frog or Katie Kangaroo or some such animal from a beanbag. Put the beanbag on the child's

head and see how long it will stay there before it falls (or "jumps"). This strengthens neck muscles and helps children learn about the position of their head in space.

3. Use activities that require performing two separate motions or a different action with each hand (e.g., holding a juice cup while pouring juice from a small pitcher). Initially, hold the cup while the child pours or vice versa. As the child's skill improves, encourage her to try both tasks (practice at the water table first).

4. Buy or make a tetherball.

5. Talk to a physical or occupational therapist about using a sandbag shaped like a large worm (like the letter "C") to place around children who have trouble sitting on the floor. It provides some support and stability. Have several, so all children can try them. These are available commercially.

Children need a balance of fine and gross motor skills. The ability to grasp, manipulate, and release objects is basic to using materials in the classroom and to lifelong independence. Most adaptive skills as well as preliteracy skills require small motor coordination.

1. Use the front of a conventional teacher's desk (if one is in the room) for small-group work. For individual work, glue magnets to small toys and blocks (such as 1-inch cubes or parquetry blocks) and small "people" to make them easier for the children to move on jellyroll pans. Be sure the pieces are too large to be swallowed.

2. Use blocks that snap together and those that are held together with bristles to build structures that are not easily knocked apart unintentionally by children with poor control of their hands. Attach Velcro to blocks to encourage children to use them. Although these blocks are easy to put together, they take strength to pull apart.

3. Use pegboards to improve a child's ability to grasp, aim, and control voluntary motion. The size, number, and spacing of the pegs should vary according to the child's needs. Rubber pegboards with large pegs are good for strengthening fingers because they offer some resistance.

4. Playing with pop beads (both pulling them apart and putting them together) helps develop eye–hand coordination and strength.

5. Hang up doll clothes with pinch clothes pins to help develop finger strength.

6. Use puzzle pieces with knobs, as they are easier to insert and remove. Start with shapes that go in easily (e.g., circles before octagons).

7. Get a variety of special scissors such as easy-grip loop scissors (they have a squeezable loop instead of finger holes) or scissors with four holes so that you can help the child cut. Use index cards or old greeting cards for cutting, as they are stiffer and easier for children to handle.

8. Have children stick objects in and take them out of clay and playdough; add cookie cutters and rolling pins.

9. Use pipe cleaners instead of shoelaces to string beads. Make a loop at one end for an easier grip.

10. Blow bubbles to encourage breath control and using lungs, but be sure the bubble liquid is safe if children accidently swallow it.

Creative Arts

Creative arts offer the potential to learn about the world and different media. The emphasis is on the process and creativity. Thinking about the final product and how it will be used, the method of achieving a particular result, and the message it conveys is important. Children can use the arts to express feelings, increase body awareness, and practice fundamental motor skills. During music and movement, ensure that all children are included. Have children help you make up the rules of the game or call out "Simon Says" so that they are verbally and mentally, if not physically, included in the play. Have the child sit on your lap and gently guide her through motions to a song. If appropriate, carry the child as your partner while you play "Ring Around the Rosie." Help children "visit" some places that may not be accessible to them; figure out creative ways of increasing accessibility.

Visual Arts

For some children, the visual arts are difficult and discouraging; others find a release in them.

1. Choose activities that require two hands, such as modeling clay and fingerpainting. Encourage children to use both hands as a way of building strength.

2. Tape drawing paper to the table so that children can concentrate on what they are putting on the paper, not on preventing the paper from slipping. Use Dycem, a plastic-like sheet that is tacky enough to hold objects where they are placed.

3. Use washable marking pens. They require little pressure, are easy to grip, and are colorful. Build up thin ones with masking tape or place foam hair curlers or rubber tubing around them so they are easier to grip.

4. Adapt drawing materials. For easier gripping, use large pieces of chalk (e.g., on a sidewalk). Encourage all children to use these variations, and comment upon the effect.

5. Make paint jars easier to handle: Put a thick rubber band (or a thin sheet of foam or sponge) around them, and glue sandpaper on the lids. (Do not use rubber bands if children are younger than age 3.)

6. Use large, heavy, adjustable easels. Adjustable easels allow children many options for working. You may need to put sandbags around the legs so they won't fall if someone pulls up on them or bumps into them.

7. Paint on large paper and large objects, like boxes.

8. Have children "paint" the sidewalk with a bucket of water and a broom (if a child is in a wheelchair) or a

large brush. Tape cloth or paper onto the sidewalk and have children roll wheels (e.g., wagon, wheelchair, or tricycle) in washable paint, then over the cloth (be sure the wheels are clean before the children go home). You can make tracks with water as well. (Check with parents for precautions.)

9. Make clay, varying the moisture to meet the strength and motor skills of the child (the moister the clay, the easier to manipulate). Have children use a rolling pin or tongue depressor to mold clay. Be sure to allow adequate time for exploration. This activity will help build strength and coordination.

10. Support children's attempts to control the medium, not the final product.

11. Paint with bare feet on paper on the floor (this can be done from a chair or wheelchair). Have children follow each other's footprints or go in the opposite direction.

Music

Use music to increase body awareness and encourage movement. Music can also be used to teach concepts.

1. Sing songs that increase body awareness, such as "Put Your Finger in the Air," and substitute words for "finger" and "air." Be sure to take into account the abilities of the children as you adapt this song. Here are some variations: nose on your shoulder, tongue on your lip, and wrist on your cheek.

2. Have children play rhythm instruments to create a mood. This is a nondemanding way for children to be part of a group.

3. Use activities that require two hands to be coordinated, such as clapping.

4. Adapt instruments if children have trouble holding them. Add elastic attachments that go around the hand rather than knobs for finger cymbals. If a child cannot hold a stick to tap a xylophone, have the child wear a mitten with Velcro in the palm and glue Velcro to the stick. Weigh down objects like drums or xylophones with beanbags to help them stay in place.

5. Use short, fat, round sticks to hit together or to hit the xylophone or triangle, or adapt the sticks as you did the paintbrushes, and put a larger, sturdier ring on the triangle.

Movement and Dance

Movement and dance should be creative. Help children see the creative quality of movement. This involves not judging the quality of the movement, but accepting the children's right to interpret creatively.

1. Allow for individual differences and creativity. Make suggestions in relation to the child's abilities.

2. Plan activities where children can dance as part of a group. Choose movements the children are able to do while sitting on the floor, such as swaying to music.

3. Give children time to explore the quality of their movements. Include some times of slow movement, and encourage children to do fewer of some movements (e.g., one stamp instead of five).

4. Isolate movements, based on children's ability. Have them move their eyes creatively, or arms, or another body part.

Dramatic Play and Theater

Children can use dramatic play and theater to play different roles as well as to express fears and concerns. They need to learn to use dramatic play to acknowledge and act out their feelings. Feelings that are denied take a toll. Because you can write the scripts for theater with the children, you can ensure that all children are part of the play.

1. Help other children become more aware of the challenges of being in a wheelchair or on crutches by having these available to play with.

2. Play hospital with casting tape (available in most drugstores). Have children cast dolls' legs or their own fingers (use blunt-nosed scissors to cut the casts off).

3. Use a full-length mirror to encourage children to explore their individual characteristics. Be sure to show children how you use the mirror to see parts of you that are difficult to see otherwise. (Put a dot on each child's back and have the child try to see it in the mirror.)

4. Demonstrate how to play some roles if children have not been exposed to them and do not know what to do. Your role is to be a coach and director: You can't play the roles for the children, but you can encourage them, model how to do different things, and teach them techniques.

Routines and Transitions

Routines help children stay organized. Transitions are often confusing. Be sure children know where they are going and for what purpose.

1. Use transitions to teach concepts, such as colors, numbers, prepositions, and so on.

2. Dismiss children who need more time to move in the beginning or middle of the transitional activity.

3. Always tell the children what you are planning to do *before* you begin doing it. Ask children to help in the transfer—they need to be included in the process. If you simply lift them onto the rug, for example, they may become frightened at suddenly being taken out of a secure position. Even if they have limited speech, talk to them, and make them aware of any changes.

SUMMARY

- Moving is a challenge when muscle tone is too high (spastic), or too low (floppy), or when it is mixed (unpredictable).
- Some young children are clumsy and may have developmental coordination disorder.

- Neurological and orthopedic impairments include cerebral palsy and neural tube defects, injuries to the brain or spinal column; missing limbs; and disabilities such as muscular dystrophy that relate to a progressive atrophy of the muscles.

- Increasingly, children with traumatic brain injury are living and returning to educational settings.

- Many children with orthopedic impairments use mobility aids such as braces, splints, crutches, and wheelchairs.

- Assistive technology can help children with orthopedic and neurological impairments communicate and learn academic skills, and compensates for some areas in which they are challenged.

EDUCATIONAL RESOURCES

ABLEDATA provides objective information about assistive technology products and rehabilitation equipment available from domestic and international sources. They do not sell anything, but provide sources for buying. www.abledata.com/

Brain Injury Association of America contains facts about TBI, including a "Kids' Corner." The site is easy to navigate for information or resources on brain injuries. www.biausa.org/

March of Dimes provides an online library of fact sheets about many disabilities caused by birth defects. It also provides information on current research, local chapters, and links to federal and nonfederal agencies. www.marchofdimes.com/

National Clearinghouse of Rehabilitation Training Materials is a great resource for online materials and links to many sites and government agencies. http://ncrtm.org/

National Easter Seal Society operates direct service programs for children with disabilities; they have an array of fact sheets on topics from accessibility and attitudes to dental care. Many of the materials are available online and would be useful to professionals and parents. www.easterseals.com/

National Spinal Cord Injury Association (NSCIA) provides information on many relevant subjects, including assistive technology, resources, inclusion, and legal issues. www.spinalcord.org/

Traumatic Brain Injury Resource Guide provides information, newsletters, how-to manuals, and current research. www.neuroskills.com/

United Cerebral Palsy Association (UCP) provides information about education, parenting, and products. It has a variety of online information that would be helpful to parents and professionals. www.ucp.org/

For additional resources, visit the book companion website for this text at www.cengagebrain.com.

Children with Hearing Impairments

18

It's hard to know when to push and when to just agree and forget it. When I asked our pediatrician whether Erica might have a hearing loss because of her frequent ear infections, he told me he didn't think so. I wanted her seen by an ear specialist. He told me he thought it was unnecessary but eventually gave the referral I needed. After examining her, the otologist said she seemed fine. I had come this far and wasn't giving up. I told him that he had only seen her for 15 minutes and I didn't think he could tell by what he had done whether she could hear. I told him her preschool teachers said that she was louder than the other children and that she seemed to not hear as well as the other children. Reluctantly, he agreed to the screening. I didn't want her to have a hearing loss just to prove I was right; on the other hand, I wasn't surprised. What did surprise and dismay me was that the loss they found wasn't the traditional one that accompanies fluid in the ears. It was a sensorineural loss. It was forever—it was hearing aids and speech therapy and all that. I wasn't prepared. But I did follow through. Her audiogram was pretty flat, with a loss of about 60 decibels in the speech frequencies.

It was hardest at the beginning. After all this, Erica refused to wear her hearing aids. We put them in; she took them out. She screamed, cried, and threw temper tantrums when we put them in. We tried to acknowledge her feelings, but we made the decision that she was going to wear them. We felt like "meanies" each time we put them back in. We even taped them in a couple times so she couldn't pull them out. I'm glad we had each other for support during this round. We kept reminding ourselves that if we didn't make her wear them, she would miss out on so much of life. She needed to begin wearing them now as a 4-year-old. We couldn't wait until she was old enough to understand our explanations.

It was a war, but we eventually won the first battle. By the time we had gotten all of this sorted out, Erica was about to begin kindergarten. Putting in her hearing aids had become part of getting dressed, and mornings were no longer a war zone. During kindergarten, a speech and language pathologist visited Erica in the classroom three times a week and helped her learn concepts that she hadn't gotten like "front" and "back." She uses both sign and speechreads. She can do this well with the help of her hearing aids as long as she can see the teacher. This teacher was really good. She would ask Erica whether the volume of the video was loud enough, without singling her out. (One teacher had her in tears, as she kept asking her in front of all the other children.)

© Cengage Learning 2012

We thought we had everything together. I could now sign to her and she could hear my husband's voice. We encouraged her independence and her younger brother was feeling as though we had enough time for him. The IEP meeting in May went well. The summer was a relaxing one. Erica was beginning to accept her hearing loss and the hearing aids, as were we. First grade came with a vengeance. At first, the protests were mild, but her stand was incontrovertible. She refused to use the auditory trainer. She said it made things too loud; it hurt her ears, and gave her a headache. We talked, we explained, we tried to convince her what she would miss. None of it worked. We made an appointment to meet with her teacher to talk about the problem. We walked into the classroom and were warmly greeted by a voice that almost blasted us out of the classroom. We should have believed Erica; she did *not* need an auditory trainer in this classroom! They may not have needed a teacher in the next room or even the next school. Some things like fire drills still worry us. When sounds get really loud, like when there is a fire alarm, her ears get really sensitive and she turns off her hearing aid. She can still hear the fire alarm but not much else. I guess if next year's teacher has a soft voice, I'll worry about it then.

Erica now accepts the hearing aids. They are part of her. When she takes them off, she can hear some things, like her dad's voice. It's like a mumble, but she can hear it. She can take care of the aids pretty much by herself. When kids she doesn't know ask her, "What are those?" she tells them "They're my

413

hearing aids and they help me hear." She says it doesn't bother her when they stare. "If they stare, that's their problem. I just ignore them. I just mind my own business. It's not their fault." When she sees someone else with a hearing aid, she just says, "Hi." She doesn't say anything about it until she knows the person.

I think they really are a part of her now. She used to always wear her hair down to cover them. Now she wears it back in a ponytail sometimes. She even asked whether she could get her ears pierced.

REFLECTIVE PRACTICE | Reflect on the evolution of the process from hating to wear hearing aids to accepting them. Reflect on your role in this process and how you might facilitate it. Think about your voice. Would it be easy or difficult for a child with a hearing impairment to be part of your classroom? What about your style of teaching? How compatible is your teaching style with not only hearing impairments but also other disabilities?

Hearing Impairments

When a child with a hearing impairment joins your class, you suddenly become aware of the many times during the day that children listen. They have to listen for their name to be called, directions about activities, and when to cleanup. They listen during music, reading, and routines.

Hearing is important in developing communications skills. Children learn to talk by listening and imitating others and by hearing themselves. The hearing child enters kindergarten with a vocabulary of about 5,000 words. The child with a hearing impairment may understand and speak only a few basic words, and even those few words may be difficult to understand. In school, children are expected to ask to go to the bathroom, to tell the teacher if they are hurt, and to talk with their peers. They are also expected to put away their materials when requested and to line up or come when called. Children with hearing impairments have trouble following instructions and discussions. Before their hearing impairment is identified, they may be mistaken for children who daydream, do not listen, are stubborn or disobedient, or even lazy.

Hearing allows a person to gain information. We use hearing to monitor our physical and social environment. Children who cannot hear danger signals may find themselves in hazardous situations that others can avoid. Being out of touch with moment-to-moment ordinary sounds has a social-emotional impact of equal magnitude. Children with hearing impairments must be taught to use other cues to keep in touch with their world.

The Auditory System

Before learning about hearing impairments, we need a basic understanding of sound and the auditory system.

An object or structure vibrating makes sound. The energy initiated by these vibrations forms sound waves. These sound waves have two distinct aspects: **intensity** and **frequency**. Sound intensity is measured by the height and depth (amplitude) of the sound waves. Loudness is a subjective term describing the ear's perception of a sound. Intensity is measured in **decibels (dB)**. The abbreviation dB is in honor of Alexander Graham Bell, hence the capital B. The letters HL often follow the decibels and stand for "hearing level." The softest sound a person with normal hearing can hear is 0 dB HL; typical conversation is about 40 to 60 dB HL; a shout may be 70 dB HL; and a rock concert could be 90 or 100 dB HL. Listening to sounds over 100 dB HL for extended periods can cause hearing loss. Sounds over 120 dB HL first cause a tickle sensation, then pain and sensorineural damage (Herer, Knightly, & Steinberg, 2007).

Frequency is determined by the number of cycles per second the sound wave has. A cycle is the distance between the top of one sound wave to the top of the next sound wave. The closer the sound waves are to each other, the higher the frequency. Pitch is the perceived frequency of sound. Frequency is measured in **hertz (Hz)**: 1 hertz is equivalent to one cycle per second. People can hear sounds in a range from low (about 20 Hz) to very high (about 20,000 Hz). (Dogs can hear frequencies over 40,000 Hz.) The normal speech frequencies fall between 500 and 2000 Hz, and virtually all speech is between 250 and 6000 Hz (Herer et al., 2007).

Speech is more complex than a single intensity or frequency. Some sounds, such as vowels, have lower frequencies and are more intense. Some consonants, such as the voiceless /h/, /p/, /s/, and so on, are higher in frequency (Herer et al., 2002). The interaction of speech with an individual's pattern of loss may allow some children to hear speech but not understand it because they hear only part of what is said. They may hear "Hey" as /a/.

Although there is some variation in classifying sounds, Table 18-1 will give an approximate idea of the intensity of some sounds.

The ear is the organ of the body that we think of when we think about hearing. There is rarely a problem with the outer ear, or **auricle**, one of the least important parts of the auditory system. The external ear, one of three parts of

TABLE **18-1** **APPROXIMATE DECIBEL LEVELS OF ENVIRONMENTAL AND LETTER SOUNDS**

Decibels	Sound
0	Hearing threshold
10	Normal breathing, water dripping
20–30	Leaves rustling, whispering, /z/, /p/, /k/, /m/, /d/, /b/
40–60	Normal conversation (two people), /a/, /o/, /r/
60–70	Telephone, baby crying
80	Vacuum cleaner
90–100	Subway train, motorcycle, large truck
110+	Airliner taking off, explosion, some bands playing

the ear and the only one visible, is connected to the **middle ear**, which is connected to the **inner ear** (see Figure 18–1).

Sound waves enter the auricle, travel through the **ear canal**, and hit the **tympanic membrane** (eardrum), causing it to vibrate. The ear canal protects the middle ear by secreting wax that catches debris and keeps it away from the eardrum. The eardrum is attached to one of the small bones in the middle ear, the **malleus** (hammer), through which vibrations are transmitted to the **incus** (anvil) and **stapes** (stirrup). Together, these are known as the **ossicles**. The stapes lies next to the **oval window**, the beginning of the inner ear. The tympanic membrane and ossicles amplify sound by about 30 dB HL, in addition to transmitting it (Herer et al., 2007).

The inner ear, about the size of a pea, transforms sound from mechanical energy to electrical energy. As the vibrations push the oval window (a thin membrane) back and forth, the fluid in the **cochlea**, a snail-shaped structure with three chambers, moves, making hearing possible. The middle chamber, the **organ of Corti**, contains about 20,000 tiny, delicate **hair cells** near the oval window, which respond to high-frequency sounds; those in the middle and end respond to low-frequency sounds. These hair cells send electrochemical impulses through the nerve fibers of the ascending auditory pathway to the **auditory cortex** in the temporal lobe of the brain. The route to the auditory cortex is complex and includes four transmitting stations. At one of these stations, the nerve fibers cross over, permitting stereophonic hearing; others fine-tune the sound and inhibit background noise. The auditory cortex combines sound with other sensory information and memory and allows perception and interpretation of sound (Herer et al., 2007). The auditory cortex isn't needed to hear pure tones, but it is necessary to interpret language.

In addition to providing hearing, the ear serves two other functions: balancing and responding to differences in pressure. The inner ear has three loop-shaped tubes, the **semicircular canals** that serve to maintain balance (vestibular sense). The **Eustachian tube**, a slender tube that runs from the middle ear to the **pharynx**, equalizes pressure on both sides of the eardrum. When changing altitudes, clearing the Eustachian tube by swallowing or chewing gum keeps the eardrum from bursting. The ears essentially duplicate each other; the major benefit of having two ears is the ability to localize sound.

● ● ●
Modes of Hearing

We hear sound in two different ways: air conduction and bone conduction. **Air conduction** is the most common way we receive auditory input. Sound waves travel through air; when they enter the outer ear, move through the middle and inner ear, and end up at the auditory cortex, we hear. We also hear through **bone conduction**, in which the bones of the head mechanically vibrate. This vibration causes the hair cells in the cochlea to move and begins the hearing process in a way that bypasses the outer and middle ear.

Defining Hearing Impairments

The IDEA 2004 defines both deafness and hearing impairments.

> **Deafness** *means a hearing impairment that is so severe that the child is impaired in processing linguistic information through hearing, with or without amplification, which adversely affects a child's educational performance.*
>
> **Hearing impairment** *means an impairment in hearing, whether permanent or fluctuating, that adversely affects a child's educational performance but that is not included under the definition of deafness.*

The term *deaf* is often used for children with a profound hearing loss, 70 dB HL, or greater. Even with hearing aids, this child may only hear the rhythm of speech, his own voice, and loud environmental sounds (Northern & Downs, 2002). The terms *hearing impairment* and *hard of hearing* are used to identify children who have a loss between 25 and 70 dB HL (Herer et al., 2007).

The most common way to define or classify hearing impairments is by their location and the severity of the loss. Knowing the exact type of loss has implications for treatment and education as well as long-term implications. When hearing thresholds are tested, both air conduction and bone conduction tests are done. Differences in the two thresholds have important diagnostic significance.

● ● ●
Conductive Hearing Loss

A **conductive hearing loss** is caused when a mechanical problem in the outer or middle ear prevents sound from getting to the inner ear. This can be caused by something lodged in the ear canal, excessive earwax, or fluid in the middle ear. The air conduction threshold indicates a hearing loss, and the bone conduction indicates normal hearing. This is called a conductive

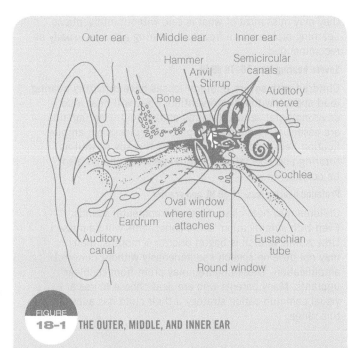

FIGURE
18-1 THE OUTER, MIDDLE, AND INNER EAR

hearing loss because the problem is in the conducting mechanisms of the outer and/or middle ear (Herer et al., 2002).

Sensorineural Hearing Loss

A **sensorineural hearing loss** involves damage to either the inner ear, the nerve to the brainstem, or both (Herer et al., 2007). In this case, both the air conduction and the bone conduction tests are abnormal, but the tympanogram is normal. Tympanometry measures the movement of the tympanic membrane (ear drum) and the mobility and functioning of the middle ear. Typically, **hearing aids** are prescribed to make sounds louder. Even with **amplification**, however, sounds are unclear and distorted. Children who have a profound hearing loss before they develop spoken language are likely to be four to five years behind their peers in spoken English by the time they enter high school and also likely to be behind in reading and writing (Geers, 2006).

Mixed Hearing Loss

Children can experience a **mixed hearing loss**, both a sensorineural and a conductive loss. In this case, the conductive problem may be treated surgically, and the sensorineural problem will require a hearing aid or cochlear implants, depending upon the degree of loss. These combined situations are difficult to diagnose.

Central Auditory Hearing Loss

A **central auditory hearing loss** or central **auditory processing dysfunction** occurs when children have problems understanding speech. They have additional problems related to short- and long-term auditory memory, following multistep directions, paying attention, auditory sequential memory, sounding out words, spelling, vocabulary, and reading comprehension (Herer et al., 2007). These children are particularly difficult to identify because they pass all the traditional auditory screening tests and usually have typical intellectual development. Testing is complex, but there are standardized tests designed to identify these children.

Severity of Hearing Loss

Hearing impairments range from the inability to understand speech with amplification to problems interpreting faint speech. The effects on the child vary according to not only the type of loss, but also the frequencies and severity of hearing loss as well. During early childhood years, the severity of hearing losses can be characterized as shown in Table 18–2.

Keep in mind that the two ears can have different amounts of loss, and typically the child functions at the level of the better ear. If a child had a 50 dB HL in the right ear and 80 dB HL in the left, she might function as a child with a moderate hearing loss, not a severe hearing loss.

Prevalence of Hearing Impairments

Because of definitional problems, it is difficult to reach conclusions about prevalence. The prevalence rate varies according to the method of testing and the criteria used by the audiologist. Mild hearing losses in particular are not easily detected, and consequently the child is not referred for testing. The same is true for children who have intermittent conductive losses.

The federal government began keeping records on children with disabilities during the 1976–1977 school year.

TABLE 18-2   CLASSIFICATION OF BILATERAL HEARING LOSS WITHOUT AMPLIFICATION

Normal limits: 0–15 dB HL

No difficulty hearing faint speech.

Slight hearing loss: 15–25 dB HL

A loss this slight outside the speech frequencies is rarely a problem. Children with losses at this level in the speech frequencies (500 to 2000 Hz) need preferential seating.

Mild hearing loss: 25–30 dB HL

Children with a mild bilateral loss might miss distant sounds, soft speech, as much as 25 to 40 percent of speech at conventional levels, and the unvoiced consonants such as /s/, /p/, /t/, /k/, /th/, /f/, and /sh/, which can make learning language difficult. They might miss plurals as well as stress patterns. If this loss is intermittent, like those associated with middle ear infections, it may make language confusing for children. If it is permanent, hearing aids may be recommended.

Moderate hearing loss: 30–50 dB HL

Children will have some difficulty with normal speech and may hear it as a whisper. If in a group and voices are faint, they may miss most of what is said without interventions. Learning problems are frequent. Hearing aids will usually be recommended.

Severe hearing loss: 50–70 dB HL

Children with severe bilateral losses have difficulty hearing loud speech without intervention. They will hear loud environmental sounds (alarms and sirens). Hearing aids are essential. Academic supports and classroom amplification help; speech and language therapy as well as tutoring and special educational services should also be considered.

Profound hearing loss: 71 dB HL and greater

Children may hear close, loud environmental sounds. Even with amplification, some consonants will be missed. Unless intervention is begun prior to 6 months, many may not develop speech spontaneously without powerful amplification. These children may profit from cochlear implants. Many parents who are deaf choose to use a visual communication strategy if their child has a loss in this range.

Source: Herer, Knightly, & Steinberg, 2007; Northern & Downs, 2002.

At that time, 8.3 percent of children received services under the IDEA. Of these children, 2.4 percent had a hearing impairment. This number decreased to 1.2 percent by 1990 as the impact of the rubella vaccine was felt. In the 2007–2008 school year, 13.4 percent of children received services under the IDEA; of these, 0.9 percent of children ages 3 to 21 had a hearing impairment (National Center for Educational Statistics, 2010). Approximately 10 to 15 percent of preschool and school age children do not pass the hearing screening test. Most of these children have a transient conductive hearing loss (Herer et al., 2002).

Causes of Hearing Impairments

Hearing loss can be caused by hereditary factors, injury, or infection. Hearing losses present at birth are **congenital**. Those that develop after birth are **acquired**. More than 400 syndromes include hearing loss, accounting for about 50 percent of children who have a hearing loss. In about half of all cases of hearing loss, the cause is genetic (Kenneson, Van Naarden Braun, & Boyle, 2002). Universal newborn hearing screening programs are identifying infants earlier than in the past; however, some disorders result in late-onset hearing loss, and progressive disorders are not present at birth (Yeargin-Allsopp, et al., 2007).

When the hearing loss is not genetic, about a third of the children have additional disabilities. For example, a child with cleft palate is likely to have middle ear involvement, which can lead to a conductive hearing loss. The remaining children have losses resulting from pre- or postnatal infections or exposure to teratogens, anoxia, prematurity, or other causes. Infections during pregnancy such as rubella and cytomegalovirus (CMV) can cause hearing loss. Bacterial meningitis can damage the cochlea. Even viral diseases such as mumps, measles, and chicken pox can result in hearing loss. Some children have losses because of middle ear disease.

● ● ●
Middle Ear Disease

Measuring the functioning of the middle ear is important in identifying the type of hearing loss and monitoring and treating middle ear disease. **Tympanometry** is designed to detect normal and abnormal conditions of the eardrum and middle ear. Because disorders of the middle ear are the most frequent cause of hearing loss during the early childhood years, including this screening is important. A specially designed ear probe is inserted into the child's ear canal, and an airtight seal is obtained; then the middle ear pressure, tympanic membrane compliance, the mobility of the ossicles, and Eustachian tube function are analyzed, and the screener removed (Herer et al., 2007). When the ear probe is returned to its stand, it automatically prints out a **tympanogram**. A normal tympanogram looks something like a narrow pyramid. When a child has fluid in the middle ear, the tympanogram is flat. Children who have an abnormal tympanogram should be rescreened in four to six weeks or referred for further treatment, depending on the abnormality (see Figure 18–2).

Many young children who experience frequent ear infections have periodic hearing losses because of the fluid in their ear canals. This fluid interferes with the conduction of sound waves from the outer ear to the inner ear and is hence a conductive loss. **Middle ear disease**, or **chronic otitis media**, is the buildup of thick fluid in the middle ear that doesn't drain through the Eustachian tubes. Middle-ear disease is the most common illness in young children after the

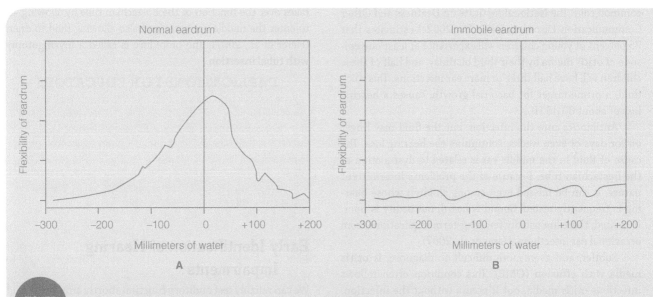

FIGURE 18–2 TYMPANOGRAM OF A NORMAL EARDRUM (A) AND AN IMPAIRED EARDRUM (B) WHEN THE TYMPANIC MEMBRANE (EARDRUM) IS FUNCTIONING NORMALLY, THE TYMPANOGRAM IS SHAPED LIKE A TRIANGLE. WHEN THE FLEXIBILITY OF THE EARDRUM IS DECREASED, SUCH AS IN MIDDLE EAR DISEASE, THE PATTERN IS FLAT.

Listening centers with headphones may help some children with mild to moderate conductive losses.
© Cengage Learning 2012

common cold. The National Institute on Deafness and Other Communication Disorders (NIDCD) (2002c) estimates that 75 percent of young children will experience at least one episode of **otitis media** by their third birthday, and half of these children will have had three or more ear infections. This thick fluid, a prime target for bacterial growth, causes a hearing loss of about 60 dB HL.

Antibiotics cure the infection, but the fluid may linger on for days or even weeks, continuing the hearing loss. The cause of fluid in the middle ear is related to dysfunction of the Eustachian tube. Because of the problem's intermittent nature, it can be missed even among children whose hearing is frequently tested. Sound is heard, but acuity is poor. If treated, there are usually few long-term implications from occasional ear infections (Herer et al., 2007).

Subtler, and even more difficult to diagnose, is **otitis media with effusion (OME)**. This condition often follows infectious otitis media, but it occurs without the infection. This means the child has a conductive loss, but no signs of fever or pain. Some think this condition is caused solely by the malfunctioning of the Eustachian tube; others, that it is related to allergies. Additionally, there may be a long-term

relationship with learning disabilities. "Children with hearing loss due to OME constitute potentially the largest group in the world with reversible learning disorders, the significance of the link of allergy to otitis media with effusion cannot be understated" (Hurst, 2007). Is there enough evidence to investigate the possibility of allergies as a cause of OME and to look for specific learning disabilities in this population?

THE EVIDENCE BASE

There is controversy about the relationship between allergies and chronic middle ear disease. The goal of one study was to evaluate the atopic status (*atopy* is an allergic hypersensitivity affecting parts of the body not in direct contact with the allergen) of individuals with chronic otitis media and to intervene by using allergy immunotherapy.

The subjects included 52 children less than 15 years of age and 37 adults. All were evaluated for allergies, using intradermal testing, and all were found to be atopic. Most frequent allergies were dust (94%), mold (88%), animals (44%), and seasonal pollens (9%). Associated allergic conditions included asthma (21%) and allergic rhinitis (63%).

Of patients, 21 chose not to be treated for allergies. These patients served as the control group. Of the 68 subjects who participated in the allergy immunotherapy, 6 percent improved significantly and 85 percent resolved their problems with otitis media with effusion. None of the controls resolved their problems with ear infections.

The American Academy of Family Physicians does not think there is sufficient evidence of the therapeutic efficacy or of a causal relationship between allergy and otitis media to recommend allergy management as a treatment for otitis media with effusion.

Source: Hurst, 2008; American Academy of Family Physicians, 2004.

Initially, middle ear disease (MED) is treated with antibiotics. When the problem persists, MED is treated surgically by making an incision in the lower part of the eardrum, removing the fluid, and inserting a small plastic tube in the eardrum incision. The small tube, called a **pressure-equalization tube**, takes over the function of the Eustachian tube by allowing air to enter the middle ear space and also allowing fluid to drain (Herer et al., 2007). The procedure is called a **myringotomy with tubal insertion**.

IMPLICATIONS FOR EDUCATORS

Be aware of children who have frequent ear infections. Monitor their speech and language development especially when they return to school after being sick with an ear infection. Focus on their learning skills especially as they relate to reading. Ensure that they are developing these skills at the expected rate. If they are not developing at the expected rate, talk with their families and keep records about what strategies work and which ones do not. Additionally, keep records about specific days when learning goes well and days when it does not.

Early Identification of Hearing Impairments

We can reliably test auditory function shortly after birth, and most states test all newborns in birthing hospitals. If a hearing loss is not identified at birth, parents may suspect one, but it is often hard to pin down; just when parents think they should be concerned, the infant does something to make them think they are imagining things. Most parents don't want to appear overprotective and look foolish to their pediatricians (especially after the infant was tested for hearing loss). Additionally, many parents continually adjust to and match their child's emerging skills. As children respond to more visual communication efforts, parents automatically use more gestures and expressions. This facilitates the child's language but makes assessment more challenging. Children with mild or intermittent hearing impairments are difficult to identify at an early age. Table 18–3 highlights some signs that should alert you to suspect a hearing impairment.

Parents who note the hearing problem usually do so because the child does not reach traditional milestones in the area of speech and language. Unless there are other disabilities present, hearing loss itself does not interfere with the attainment of physical milestones such as walking and exploring the environment. Nine out of every 10 children who are born deaf are born to hearing parents (NIDCD, 2000).

Infants with hearing impairments make noises and babble like other infants up until about 5 months of age. After 5 months, babbling imitates the language spoken at home. This does not happen to children with hearing impairments, who do not respond to auditory stimuli that are out of their range of hearing. An infant with a severe auditory impairment would not wake to a loud noise or try to seek out the source of sounds. The infant may, however, respond to vibrations such as approaching footsteps, making parents doubt their concerns. Adults may not recognize auditory impairments because the child does what is requested, but he

may be responding to visual cues or cues from other children, not because he understands the request. As requests become more complex, the difference often becomes evident, but noncompliance may be mistaken for oppositional behavior or a behavior disorder (Herer et al., 2007).

Auditory impairments severely impact the development of speech and language. Both speech and language depend upon hearing in the early years. Children organize language through listening, imitation, practice, and correction. Children who are identified as having a hearing impairment before language was established are considered **prelingually hearing impaired**. Because they have not yet established a language base, learning to speak is more challenging. One major decision parents must make is how they are going to communicate with their child. This decision has major implications for the child, the family, and the educational system. If intervention begins before 6 months of age, even children with profound losses can be in contact with an auditory world, if that is what the family desires.

During the preschool years, children with hearing impairments will have delays in speech and language. They may develop unusual ways of attaining adult attention. If they cannot hear adults, they must engage them physically or visually and may seem either extremely attentive or inattentive.

As children reach elementary school age, almost all those with moderate to profound losses, should have been identified. As they become more dependent on oral communication, those with hearing impairments are at a disadvantage in standard English. It is difficult to predict the level of communication children this age will have. If intervention began in infancy, the skills children have will be very different from those of children who do not begin intervention until age 3 or 4.

Assessment of Hearing Impairments

Approximately 95 percent of newborns have their hearing screened; however, almost half of the newborns who do not pass the screening do not have follow-up to determine whether there is a loss, and/or early intervention services are not begun. Follow-up should occur before 3 months of age, and if a hearing loss is confirmed, intervention should begin before 6 months of age. The Joint Committee on Infant Hearing (2007) also believes that children and families should have immediate access to high-quality technology, including hearing aids, cochlear implants, and other assistive devices. Children who have identifiable risk factors should be tested using a different protocol. Risk factors for neonates include admission to an NICU for more than 48 hours, family history of hearing loss, craniofacial anomalies, low Apgar score, maternal infections such as CMV, herpes, toxoplasmosis, or rubella, or syndromes known to include sensorineural hearing loss. For children 29 days to 2 years old, additional risks include bacterial meningitis, head trauma, and infectious disease associated with hearing loss. If adults are concerned about a child's hearing there should be follow-up. (Joint Committee on Infant Hearing, 2007).

TABLE 18-3 SIGNS OF HEARING IMPAIRMENT

Speech
Speech and grammar that is delayed and immature
Speech that cannot be understood by nonfamily members beyond expected ages
Speech that is too loud or too soft for the situation
Language
Misunderstands directions or gives inappropriate answers to questions
Asks for information to be repeated or says "What?" a lot
Is hesitant in answering questions or joining conversations
Has difficulty with listening activities
Attention
Is unusually attentive to speaker's face
Short attention span, distractible
Disinterested in many activities, especially those requiring listening
Health
Frequent colds, allergies, respiratory tract infections, ear infections, scarlet fever, or meningitis
Draining ears, pulling on ear, breathing through the mouth
Poor balance, seems clumsy

Source: Herer, Knightly, & Steinberg, 2002; Hurst, 2007; Northern & Downs, 2002.

The American Speech-Language-Hearing Association (ASHA, 2006) has developed guidelines for the audiologic screening process. These involve obtaining a case history of the child; visually inspecting the outer ear, ear canal, and eardrum; **pure-tone hearing screening**; and tympanometry. ASHA suggests that infants at risk for progressive or late-onset hearing loss be screened every 6 months until age 3, and all children be screened annually from age 3 until third grade (ASHA, 2006).

A school nurse, speech-language pathologist, or an audiologist often does a case history and visual inspection. If a child has a history of ear infections or if the visual inspection shows abnormalities (excessive earwax, fluid in the middle ear, etc.), the child is referred for a medical evaluation.

Hearing screening and **hearing threshold testing** for children older than age 3 are typically done using an **audiometer**, an electronic instrument that comes in many different types. The one most commonly used in the school setting is a **pure-tone audiometer**, which can be used to screen children and also to determine hearing thresholds. Pure-tone audiometers produce discrete frequencies called **pure tones** at different intensity levels (decibels). In pure-tone testing, the tester places earphones on the child, and then the child is given sounds at 20 dB HL at frequencies of 500, 1000, 2000, and 4000 Hz. These are the most important frequencies for speech, and 20 dB HL is the lower range for what we consider normal hearing. This is purely an air-conduction evaluation. Children who fail to hear at any frequency should be retested. (Before retesting, ensure the child understands the instructions.) Children who fail the retest should be referred to an audiologist or otologist for more extensive evaluation.

Increasingly, audiologists use **otoacoustic emissions testing (OAE)**. To obtain an OAE, one needs an unobstructed outer ear canal, absence of significant middle ear pathology, and functioning cochlear outer hair cells (Hain, 2007). Children need to sit quietly and still to obtain results but they do not need to participate in the testing. This is particularly useful for younger children and children with disabilities.

An **otolaryngologist** is a physician who specializes in the treatment of ear, nose, throat, head, and neck disorders. An **otologist** focuses on diseases and conditions of the ear (hearing and vestibular systems). One of these physicians will determine whether medical intervention is indicated. **Audiologists**, professionals trained in the prevention, identification, and nonmedical management of hearing loss, can initiate treatment in children as young as neonates once medical clearance has been obtained. The audiologist may refer children to other specialists such as a speech-language pathologist or a psychologist to determine the effects of the hearing loss on other aspects of functioning.

Amplification

The ears receive sound waves in the air and convert them into electrical signals the brain can understand. When the ear sends weak or distorted signals, hearing and understanding

are impaired. Children, including infants, should be fitted for hearing aids as soon as a permanent loss is confirmed if parents decide that they want to use amplification (Herer et al., 2007). Audiologists are responsible for fitting **amplification devices** to particular children. Measuring a hearing loss and understanding the implications of that loss for understanding speech are different issues.

REFLECTIVE PRACTICE | Children with mild to moderate conductive losses hear approximately what you would hear with very tight-fitting earplugs. It takes strain and much concentration to hear. Try it. Are you startled when people come up behind you quietly? Do you get tired with the effort and concentration it takes to hear? What might you do over the course of several days or weeks like this? Unless there were some good reasons for you to continue listening, you might tune it all out.

Children with more severe losses have an even more difficult problem. Although they may be able to hear some speech, they have trouble understanding it, even with hearing aids. They may be able to hear the low-frequency vowel sounds that carry the power of speech, but miss the high-frequency consonant sounds that make speech intelligible.

Even using a combination of hearing and vision, understanding is difficult. In classrooms where the teacher's voice is only about 5 to 10 dB HL louder than the general background noise, children with hearing impairments have an extremely difficult time. Improving this ratio of teacher's voice to background noise helps the child immensely. This can be done by having the teacher talk louder or modifying the classroom to make it quieter by adding carpet, drapes, or assistive listening devices. Audiologists can provide information on how to improve this ratio. Amplification helps, but does not solve, the child's problem.

Hearing Aids

Hearing aids have three major components: a microphone that changes sound waves into electrical energy, an amplifier (or amplifiers) that increases the intensity of the signal, and a receiver that converts the electrical signal back to an acoustical signal and projects this amplified sound through the earmold into the ear (Herer et al., 2007). Hearing aids are battery powered and have volume controls. They are individually prescribed by audiologists, based on the characteristics of the loss, the child's speech and language skills, intellectual ability, situations in which the child will listen, and school performance (Herer et al., 2007), and are purchased from commercial dealers. Prescribing a hearing aid is different for an infant or young child than it is for an adult, in that it is a learning process that evolves. As the aid is used, the match can be assessed in the context of the child's language development as well as the audiogram, which maps the loss. As children and technology change, the hearing aids may change as well.

There are four basic categories of hearing aids: behind-the-ear aids, in-the-ear aids, body aids, and bone conduction aids. Behind-the-ear aids are larger than in-the-ear aids so they can accommodate more circuitry and controls and allow more flexibility. This flexibility is particularly important when test data for young children are incomplete. New hearing aids are programmable and can be changed to adjust to different listening environments. The advantage of in-the-ear aids is primarily cosmetic (Herer et al., 2007).

A hearing aid amplifies all sounds, not just speech. Because it does not correct distortion, it is not useful for all types of hearing impairments. Using hearing aids properly requires intervention. (The child must be taught how to listen; speech may be gobbledygook to a child who has never heard it.) Hearing aids are not like eyeglasses, which can correct vision to within normal limits; hearing aids do not correct hearing impairments.

Although a hearing aid is beneficial, that doesn't ensure that the child will willingly wear it. Children who pull out their hearing aids frequently frustrate parents and teachers. To young children, the aid may feel strange, and they will try to make themselves more comfortable by taking it out. If children were previously unaware of most sounds and speech, the hearing aid may be delivering what to them sounds like meaningless noise. Once children see the advantages of hearing with the aid, they are usually willing to wear it; until then, however, encouragement is needed.

● ● ● Assistive Listening Devices

Assistive listening devices such as an FM system are used in combination with hearing aids in difficult listening situations such as classrooms, to reduce the amount of background noise. These may also be used for infants recently identified with hearing loss. If a parent wears a lapel microphone and speaks to the infant from anywhere in the room, the infant can receive vocal stimulation even when the parent is not talking directly to her. The hearing aid–FM combination helps the signal-to-noise ratio, making it easier for the child to understand the speaker. If a teacher (or parent) wears the microphone, it is as if the speaker is only about 6 to 8 inches from the child's ear (Herer et al., 2007).

IMPLICATIONS FOR EDUCATORS

Work out an agreement with families about what to do when a child takes off the hearing aid. You must also develop some skills in working with a hearing aid so you can do certain tasks younger children may not yet have mastered, such as these:

- Put the earpiece back in when it falls out or is pulled out.
- Check to see whether batteries are dead and replace them. (Keep a supply in the child's locker or with the school nurse.)
- Know how to manipulate the controls. When the hearing aid "whistles," ask the child to turn it down or, if necessary, turn it down yourself.

Hearing aids should not be abused, but they are sturdy enough to allow the child to participate in most activities. Try to keep them from getting painted, soaked, or sandy. Remember, hearing aids do not make a child hear perfectly. Be sure the other children understand this. Also, realize that a hearing aid works well for a radius of only 10 feet; even then, it amplifies sounds indiscriminately.

● ● ● Cochlear Implants

A cochlear implant is a small, complex electronic device that can provide a sense of sound to a person who has a severe or profound hearing loss (see Figure 18–3). Cochlear implant technology is relatively new, beginning in 1984. The level of sophistication in the implants has increased dramatically since then. The Federal Food and Drug Administration (FDA) guidelines permit infants with hearing loss of 90 dB HL or greater to have cochlear implants as young as 12 months old for one type of cochlear implant, and those with a loss of 70 dB HL or greater at age 2. Most children receive implants between ages 2 and 6. As of April 2009, approximately 41,500 adults and 25,500 children had received them in the United States (NIDCD, 2009a).

THE EVIDENCE BASE

Since the advent of cochlear implants, the age at which they are done has become increasingly younger. The FDA does not allow cochlear implants in the United States for children under 12 months because of the concern that children could be misdiagnosed as having a profound loss when they do not and concerns related to the use of anesthesia. Some researchers were interested in finding whether implants during the first year of life are more effective and safe.

Researchers at the Medical University of Hannover, Germany, analyzed the results of 27 infants implanted before age 12 months and 89 toddlers implanted between ages 13 and 24 months. They found no difference between the infants and toddlers relative to surgical or anesthetic complications. At a two-year follow-up, children who were implanted as infants showed better hearing and speech development than those implanted as toddlers.

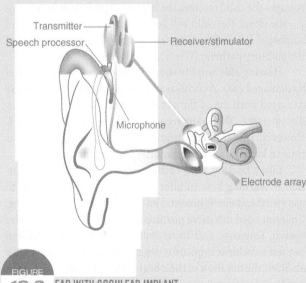

FIGURE 18-3   EAR WITH COCHLEAR IMPLANT

The cochlear implant consists of a microphone to pick up sound, a speech processor to select and arrange the sounds, a transmitter and receiver/stimulator that receives signals and converts them into electrical impulses, and an electrode array that collects the impulses and sends them to different regions of the auditory nerve.

Holt and Svirsky conducted similar research with 96 children who were identified as having profound bilateral hearing losses who had cochlear implants before the age of 4. They had only six children in their sample who were implanted before 12 months. They followed the children for at least 2 years after the implantation. The developmental trajectory of those implanted earlier was better than children implanted later. They found that children implanted before 12 months had better receptive language but this did not carry over into expressive language or word recognition. However, it did influence the rate of both receptive and expressive language acquisition.

Both studies suggest that earlier implantation is better than later implantation and that age at implantation supports expressive and receptive language but not necessarily word recognition.

Source: Holt & Svirsky, 2008; Lesinski-Schiedat et al., 2004.

Cochlear implant systems require surgery to place the stimulating electrode array inside the cochlea and a receiver/stimulator under the skin (NIDCD, 2009a). A *microphone* captures sound, and a *speech processor* (tiny computer) analyzes and digitizes the sound signals into programmed electrical information, then sends them to the *transmitter* (located on the skin surface behind the ear), which sends the signal to the *receiver* (implanted under the skin). The receiver sends the coded electrical signals to the *electrode array* that has been implanted in the cochlea, and these electrodes stimulate the auditory nerve fibers at different locations along the cochlea, which then send sound sensations to the brain (Herer et al., 2007, NIDCD, 2009a). Normally the sensory hair cells in the cochlea do this but these are damaged or reduced in number for children with severe sensorineural losses. The signal processor provides critical information contained in the auditory speech signal and consequently gives access to speech at a young age. There seems to be consensus in the field that the younger the child receives the implant—preferably before age 2—the closer the child will be to his peers in his speech and language. The cochlear implant improves the maturation of the auditory pathway (Geers, 2006; Herer et al., 2007).

Hearing aids amplify sound in order for it to be detected by damaged ears. A cochlear implant works by bypassing the damaged portions of the ear and directly stimulates the auditory nerve. The brain recognizes these signals as sound. However, it is different from normal hearing, and it takes time to learn how to interpret the sounds.

Like a hearing aid, a cochlear implant requires intervention in learning how to interpret what is heard and how to use visual and environmental information to clarify meaning. Children need intensive postimplantation therapy to acquire speech, language, and social skills. How effectively children can use a cochlear implant is dependent upon their cognitive abilities, the duration of their hearing loss, the age at implant, and their family structure and support (Nikolopoulos, Gibbin, & Dyar, 2004). Children need continuing contact with an audiologist who can adjust the features of the cochlear implant to ensure it meets the child's needs.

IN THE FIELD

I think that many people see us as bucking the system, but we are truly trying to do what we think is best for our son. I learned a lot about cochlear implants. I thought they might be a good idea for Grady. Everyone discouraged me. They said that it might not help him at all and questioned why I could not accept the fact that our son is deaf. I do accept that. I know he will never speak like his brothers, but that doesn't mean I shouldn't do everything in my power to give him as much hearing as possible. We went to other doctors in different states with bigger cities. I found a doctor who had actually done a cochlear implant on a child, Spencer, about Grady's age. The physician talked to the child's parents and they gave me permission to visit. I went to visit and heard the family's story. Their son does not talk, but what gave them the most comfort was that they thought he was safe. After the implant, he could hear car horns, loud bells, and other warning signals. I made my decision.

It is too soon to tell whether the implant will help Grady's speech. But, like Spencer's mother, his safety is worth it to me. I'm truly not trying to buck the system, but Grady is our son, and we try to make the decisions that we feel are best for him. Sometimes I feel like I am fighting two battles: one with Grady's hearing loss and the other with the system that is supposed to be helping him.

Methods of Communication

There are many options available to parents relative to the communication system they choose to use with their child. Their decision is based on many different variables, including the severity and frequencies of the child's loss, whether there are other disabilities, what professional advice they have been given, what information they have sought, and their personal preferences. As educators working with children who have hearing impairments, we must understand the options available to parents; if they have not yet made a decision, provide information about choices and how the child communicates in the classroom, and learn enough about the chosen communication system to interact with the child.

The **total communication approach** uses any means of communication—voice, sign language, fingerspelling, lipreading, amplification, gesture, drawing, writing, and texting—to provide children with as much information as possible. The goal is communication using whatever combination of methods works for a particular child. Practically, communication relies on a system of spoken language and sign. The sender of the message, or speaker, verbalizes the message while simultaneously signing or fingerspelling the same message. This focus allows a child to speak to hearing persons and systematically sign to others who do not hear. It is also known as simultaneous communication or sim-com. Some see this as the least restrictive environment for a child with a severe to profound hearing impairment, as the child can develop personal preferences (Berke, 2010).

American Sign Language (Ameslan or ASL) is a complex language with a distinct grammatical structure that must be learned as one would learn any language. It consists of a set of standard hand signs used in relation to other parts of the body and includes facial expressions and different body postures. Each sign represents an idea or concept. ASL uses fingerspelling for clarifying purposes and for new words that have no conventional signs. **Fingerspelling** uses 26 different finger configurations, one for each letter of the alphabet

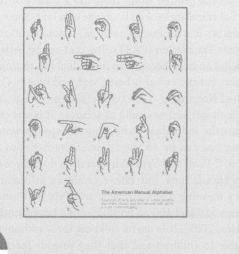

FIGURE 18-4 AMERICAN SIGN LANGUAGE ALPHABET

The American Manual Alphabet Drawings show a side view. In actual practice, the letters should face the persons with whom you are communicating.

(see Figure 18–4 for an illustration of this alphabet). ASL is not a universal language; Japanese Sign Language (JSL), British Sign Language (BSL), French Sign Language (FSL), and so on, exist as well. There is some evidence that children who learn ASL as a natural language during their early childhood years are at an advantage later socially and academically (NIDCD, 2000). Many of these children live in families who use ASL as their first language.

The **oral approach** uses only spoken language (face-to-face communication), taking advantage of whatever residual or aided hearing the child has and combining this with lipreading or speechreading and contextual cues to understand spoken language. Only about 30 percent of auditory information is gained from looking at the lips alone (Schwartz, 1996). Children have to find ways of filling in the missing cues based on their knowledge of the situation, past knowledge, and other cues they can extrapolate from the circumstances. Some children become competent speakers in the hearing world, whereas others become frustrated, lost, and confused. The early childhood years are difficult because children are not familiar with language per se, and they have fewer experiences to draw from.

Cued speech is a communication approach that is based on spoken English. It can be used in conjunction with speaking and hearing to provide additional cues to what is being said. In this system, a hand motion depicts a particular sound and the speaker says the word as well as cuing it (the sound-related hand shapes help differentiate sounds that appear alike on the lips). As it is based on sounds in the English language, once those sounds are learned, any word can be cued. It emphasizes using residual hearing (Lim & Simser, 2005).

IN THE FIELD

I knew he was sick. When his temperature spiked to 105, we went to the emergency room. I love living in the country, but that night every mile seemed to take an eternity. The emergency room took him in and, in whispered tones, I heard words like "very sick" and someone even said "his brain." He had bacterial meningitis. He was only 2. At first we were just glad that he was alive. We believed that because he had lived, he was fine. Because he had been so sick, we expected him to regress. He did. What seemed most peculiar to us was that his walking had developed this wide stance. We didn't think he had done that before, but then we decided we really couldn't remember.

Finally Vinnie's speech started to worry me. I took him to see a friend who knew about things like this, and she played with him. We had a good time and it seemed like he was doing great. She said all kinds of great things about him but also said that I should get his hearing tested. There was something in her tone that made me listen. I thought about why she said it. He didn't talk. He didn't listen either. The audiologist confirmed that he had a profound hearing loss. Meningitis had left its mark.

Roy and I read all we could about hearing loss and the different ways in which children with hearing impairments could communicate. We talked to each other but didn't reach any conclusions. A few weeks later when Vinnie turned 3, a teacher from the School for the Deaf contacted us. We listened as she told us about the services that were available. At first, they sounded great, the answer to our prayers. Then the ball dropped. Because we lived so far away, Vinnie would live there during the week and come home on weekends. He was 3 years old! I couldn't believe it. He needed his dad, his two brothers, and me. I fought it. I knew he would probably never speak as other children did, but this was unbelievable. I kept reading and using the Internet, and I found out about cued speech.

I struggled to decide whether I thought this was the right thing for Vinnie. I learned how to do cued speech and started. I wasn't good at first. He was frustrated because he didn't understand, and I was frustrated because I so wanted him to learn and to be with his family. I felt every failure as a step toward his going away to school. Finally, it began to work. I knew he would be able to understand about the asparagus I was picking and the differences between the goat and the sheep we had, but I was still struggling.

Families decide how they want their child to communicate; teachers support the family's decision.

After I talked with the director of a church preschool, she consented to take him. One of her teachers even agreed to learn cued speech. My friend observed and thought things were going fine.

When he was 5 years old, we had the first IEP meeting. I was frightened. Again, they wanted him to go to a school for deaf children, 100 miles away. They didn't believe in cued speech and thought we were abusing our son. I kept explaining how well he was doing. All I wanted was someone in the school to be with him to help him understand. He could go to the same school his brothers did. He didn't need special transportation; all he needed was someone to help him understand the language. His friends were great. They had learned enough to communicate with him. I agree that he sometimes was frustrated and acted out, but he was still better off perfecting what he was learning and being with us. My friend again intervened. She had observed him, and yes, she knew the field and had seen adult people who were hearing impaired. It was a battle, but one that we won. Vinnie has a paraeducator who learned cued speech, and he is part of the regular classroom. Some things are hard, for him and us, but we think we did what was best for all of us. I guess only time will tell.

IMPLICATIONS FOR EDUCATORS

Parents make decisions about how their child will communicate. It is important that you know that these are difficult decisions and honor the decisions made by parents. In reality, you will probably only encounter families who made the decision to educate their children in a hearing environment or they would not be in your classroom. If the child uses speechreading, signing, fingerspelling, or cuing as aids to communication, you must support the child in her efforts.

- Learn to sign, fingerspell, or cue, depending on the system that the child's family has chosen.
- Teach all children some signs and cues, especially the sign or cues for their name. Learn significant signs (drink, bathroom) and cues. Ask the help of the child and the family or a teacher of the hearing impaired in making up signs or cues for each child's name. Draw these on the back of your roll cards or whatever system you use.
- Look at the child when you speak, even if the child has an interpreter. Talk the way you would to any other child. Do not say to the interpreter, "Ask him whether ...."

Finally, there are two points of caution. Remember: The best speechreader only gets about one word in four. Children with hearing impairments are great bluffers. They may not want to ask you to repeat; if you ask whether they understand, they will often say "yes" when in fact they do not. Learn to recognize when a child is bluffing; when it is important, ask the child to demonstrate or repeat the instructions.

One of the greatest skills that children with hearing impairments need to learn is to fill in missing information (what they can't understand from words). Developing ideas about their world through generalization and differentiation is difficult for children with hearing impairments because they learn primarily from direct experience. If a child is shown an armchair labeled "chair," the child may not immediately make the generalization that a rocking chair also belongs in the "chair" category. Because of this, it is important that children with hearing impairments be given a large variety of visual stimuli to help them generalize to an abstract concept. For "chair," compare many different chairs. This is the type of thinking children need to do to fill in gaps.

• • •
Assistive Technology

Children with hearing impairments are ardent users of assistive technology. Hearing aids, cochlear implants, captioned videos, directional microphones, FM systems, and auditory trainers are part of their daily life. As children get older and can read the printed word, there are a variety of technologies that translate spoken language into text. Some of these are almost instantaneous such as Communication Access Realtime Translation (CART). The cost can be between $40 and $200 an hour because an individual has to come to the location, listen to what is being said, and type it. Computer Assisted Notetaking (CAN) is useful at meetings. Although CAN is slower and not quite as accurate, it is less expensive because the individual translating the spoken word to the written one can be on the telephone rather than there in person. C-Print and TypeWell operators do not provide verbatim translations, but rather condense information and convey meaning. CAN, C-Print, and TypeWell usually cost between $10 and $60 an hour (Hearing Loss Association of America, 2005). It is useful to know these technologies are available to children and that they provide incentives for promoting literacy skills. The ability to text message is also a motivation.

PARTNERING WITH FAMILIES

If you work with families of infants and toddlers, you may be included in their decision-making process relative to the communication system they choose for their child. Parents who use American Sign Language as their home language will probably want their child to become fluent in ASL. Families who speak English or other spoken languages may make different choices. Provide parents with resources to help them make a decision that reflects their values in the context of the child's abilities. Look at the whole child and what he needs and does.

Help parents know about the accommodations you make for their child in the classroom. Ask them what works for them, and share with them both your successes and challenges. Agree to work together to solve problems and exchange ideas. Find out what they want for their child in both the short and long term, and assess whether what you are doing in the classroom is moving her in that direction.

Guidelines

Some children with hearing impairments know how to speechread and depend on it to understand communication. Others, with milder hearing impairments, may not have learned speechreading but will still benefit from picking up cues and by watching lips and facial expressions. Regardless of the communication system the child is using, and whether or not an **interpreter** is present, it is important that you, as a teacher, be expressive and congruent in your spoken word and body language. Children with hearing impairments will watch you as a way of tuning in to their environment.

1. *Face the child at the child's eye level.* Sit in front of children when helping them, not beside them. Don't talk to children from another room; while looking in a closet; or while writing on the chalkboard. Don't walk around the room or pace back and forth when you talk.

2. *Talk clearly and distinctly.* Don't obscure your lips, do wear lipstick, and do shave (or at least trim) a beard or mustache. If your hair is long, tie it back so that it doesn't fall in your face while you talk. Don't talk with your hand over your mouth or anything in your mouth. Don't shout.

3. *Monitor light levels.* See that there is enough light and that it is not shining in the child's eyes.

Once you are certain the child can see your face, communication can begin.

1. *Attract the child's attention.* Before speaking, call the child's name and wait to make eye contact; otherwise, you will have to repeat your first few words.

2. *Speak in a normal voice.* It is impossible to speechread when the mouth is distorted. Even if you whisper loudly, the sounds and lips are distorted.

3. *Use gestures.* Aid the child's understanding of your speech by using appropriate body language.

4. *Reduce background noise.* When this is not possible, realize that the child is likely to miss much of what you say.

5. *Repeat information.* Some words are more difficult to speechread than others. If you find different ways of saying something rather than simply repeating the sentences, children will have a better chance of getting the information. It is important to repeat concepts until they have been established and to be consistent on word usage.

6. *Write down key words and short sentences.* Children need to develop an early knowledge that there is a relationship between what is said and what is written.

7. *Choose activities that facilitate communication.* Encourage children to play together based on a theme that sparks discussion.

8. *Use modeling for teaching.* Demonstrate how to do a specific skill and then have the child imitate what you did.

9. *Let the child take the lead.* Observe the child and see what interests him. Comment about what is important to the child—what the child wants, needs, or is interested in. Watch and interpret the child's gaze, pointing, sounds, and gestures.

Similar principles are reflected in the use of audiovisual aids.

1. *Use color codes and pictures.* Use visual aids as well as words (picture cards for daily routines, charts, and hand gestures).

2. *Use closed-captioned videos and films.* (It is not relevant that the children are not yet reading; you want them to grow up knowing this is a possibility.)

3. *Use an overhead projector or a computer and an LCD monitor.* With a chalkboard, you turn your back to the children.

4. *Try not to talk in the dark.* If this is necessary, seat the child where he can see you and try to use some spot illumination.

5. *Support audio presentations with visual cues.* Don't expect the child to react to a tape recorder, CD, radio, or intercom just because you turned the volume up. The child still may not understand.

During group activities, the following adaptations may help:

1. *Seat children where they have the best view of the teacher and class.* This is in front of or across from you, not beside you and not facing a window. Have children sit in a semicircle.

2. *Call, sign, or cue children's names.* During discussions, use signs or gestures so the child will know who is speaking next and can follow the conversation. If the children have signs for their names, sign the speaker's name; if the child is using cued speech, cue the speaker's name. Have children raise their hands instead of calling out, so it is easier for the child to identify who is speaking.

3. *Call on the child if he is comfortable.* Remember, the child may be so intent on catching the main points of the discussion that she cannot think about an answer at the same time. If you call on a child, give her extra time to think; don't demand an immediate answer.

4. *Summarize and repeat points other children have made.* Encourage children to use gestures, signs, and cues when they talk. Ask them to show the child what they want.

Curriculum Adaptations

The severity of the hearing impairment will determine what, if any, curriculum adaptations need to be made. The less hearing the child has, the greater the reliance on visual and tactile channels of communication.

Social Awareness

All children need to be part of the group. They need to realize they can support each other in many ways. Given information, young children can be incredibly adept at helping each other. Be sure that the child with the hearing impairment is not always receiving help, but giving it as well. Children with hearing impairments profit from first-hand experiences, followed in the classroom by visual aids to clarify and generalize these experiences. Children may need to be taught nonverbal ways of approaching other children, and others need to be aware that that is what is happening. At an early age, they need to have signs and words that are descriptive of feelings and body parts. Some of the activities in Resource Chapter 1 are specifically designed to increase children's awareness of hearing impairments: Activity 1–5, *Fingerspelling Lotto*, Activity 1–10, *Mufflers*, Activity 1–25, *Audiologist*, and Activity 1–33w, *Voiceless Roll Call*.

- Use these activities and the additional ones provided to increase children's knowledge of hearing impairments and how they might include a child with a hearing impairment.

● ● ●
Social Competence

Children need to increase their awareness of themselves as individuals and as part of a group. If children have had unsuccessful experiences in interacting with other children and adults, they may withdraw or avoid participating with others. If they are not aware of the mood of the events taking place, they may have inappropriate facial expressions and tone of voice. When possible, they watch for cues and follow, not lead. They may have had more negative experiences, both medical and personal, than other children their age. They need to view themselves positively and to develop skills in interacting with others.

1. Give careful thought to talking about any child's abilities and disabilities. Talk with children and their families about how they want this handled. My choice is, after several days of school, to introduce the concept of similarities and differences. (Children conjure up fantastic ideas about what a child with a hearing impairment will look like. Sometimes, they expect the child to have no ears!) Plan a group-time game emphasizing similarities and differences. For example:

   "Will all the children with hair stand up?"

   "Will all the children with brown hair stand up?"

   "Will all the children with hearing aids stand up?"

   "Will all the children with green eyes stand up?"

   In the process, emphasize that all of the children have hair, some have brown hair, one has a hearing aid, and one has green eyes. Be nonchalant. Answer children's questions directly and honestly.

2. Teach children body awareness, and engage in sensory activities that provide tactile feedback as children with hearing impairments may have developed self-feedback systems (such as teeth grinding, mouth breathing, or masturbation). These actions result from children's need to receive information from other senses.

3. Talk to the child, not the interpreter.

4. Encourage children to share their style of communication with others. Talk about circumstances where signing or being able to speechread is preferable to speaking (in a noisy place, if you want to keep something a secret, etc.).

When children with hearing impairments reach out, their approach may be physical. Help children develop the skills to approach others and give them cues for roles that they might play. Children need to learn skills for including others as well as skills for approaching others. They need to know that no matter who they are, these skills do not mean that they will be accepted into a group each time they ask. Including children with diverse abilities takes a type of planning you may not have done before.

1. Play games where you whisper or talk to children so softly that they have difficulty hearing you; talk about how it feels.

2. Have children wear earmuffs when they play together. Have them keep them on long enough for children to feel the limitations, not just until the novelty wears off.

3. Talk with children about things that are difficult for them to do and what they would like others to do to help.

4. Help children understand how they might feel and behave if they could see people talking but did not understand what they were saying. Have them decide what to do to include a child who might feel like this.

5. If children ask questions, answer them simply and honestly. Encourage the child with the hearing impairment to answer the question, if possible.

"What's wrong with Carlos?" "There's nothing wrong with Carlos. He can't hear as well as others." "Why does he wear that thing in his ear?" "To help him hear better." "Does he sleep with it?" "No." "If I play with him, can I catch that?" "No, it isn't like a cold. Carlos was born that way" (or however the impairment occurred). "Can I have a thing like that too?" "No, ear doctors decide who needs these things, just as eye doctors decide who needs glasses." "I don't like it when Carlos hits me." "I can understand that. Carlos is telling you in his way he wants to play with you. What could he do that would be better?" "Can't he talk?" "He can say some words. It's hard to learn to talk when you can't hear other people talk." "I don't like Carlos." "Today, that is true for you. Someday, you might like him."

You might also give the children hints on how to communicate:

"Be sure Carlos is looking at you when you talk to him." "Can you show him what you want?" "What can he do that doesn't require talking?" "What kind of game do you think Carlos would like?"

● ● ●
Social Studies

Children with hearing impairments have to learn the skills to cope with a hearing world.

1. Teach children to generalize by using illustrations of diverse families (those with single parents, working mothers, grandparent in the home, and also families of different races and cultures).

2. Emphasize first-hand experiences, but use follow-up activities as well. Take your class to a police station. Later, read stories about police and use police props in dramatic play, or have a police officer visit.

3. Prepare children with hearing impairments for social situations they may encounter. Help all children learn to use social cues to decide how to act.

4. Use family celebrations and holidays to talk about similarities and differences.

5. Talk with children about the role of science and technology in society.

6. Make maps (see Activity 1–19, *Maps*) to familiarize children with a new setting. Start with maps of known places (the classroom, the play yard) before you branch out into less familiar places.

English Language Arts

Children with hearing impairments often have limited or impaired speech. They may run words together and have a voice quality that may be flat. When they speak, they may have trouble monitoring their volume. They may use gestures or signs to express themselves. Encourage children to speak in small, informal groups first, where they feel safe. Be sure to reward their speaking, even if it is labored and difficult to understand. Children need support to talk; encourage them to attempt this, even if their speech is not always intelligible. If they are dependent on environmental cues, help them fine-tune their ability to use contextual information. Provide many hands-on experiences. To help children use their residual hearing, pair listening with visual or kinesthetic cues. Language arts and literacy are important and challenging areas for children with impaired hearing, and they require adaptations.

Speaking and Listening

Help children develop experiential concepts by associating objects with words: the written word with the spoken one. Understanding and talking about abstractions is difficult for young children with hearing impairments.

1. Give children time to talk without feeling rushed.

2. Respond to a child's communication. If you understand, reply; if not, try to have the child tell you in a different way or show you.

3. Use the concrete to demonstrate the abstract. Use conceptual matching cards in lotto: shoe–slipper, clock–watch, lamp–flashlight, shirt–blouse, and jacket–coat.

4. Point out objects in the room that are used in the same way but look different: crayons versus paint, short versus long brushes.

5. Teach situationally and describe verbally what is happening at that moment: "I'm sitting in front of you."

6. Use ASL signs with fingerplays or rhymes.

Children with hearing impairments need to develop good listening skills and to use their residual and aided hearing. They may listen with their head tilted, to favor one ear. They may have difficulty understanding the speech of others, especially in groups, when the speaker is far away or is looking in another direction. Be sure auditory information is presented clearly and loudly enough so children can hear it. The sequence of developing listening skills is the same for all children. Children with hearing impairments need you to match their skill level. Initially, children have to become aware of sound: They have to pay attention to sound and find its source. Then they need to make gross discrimination among sounds, followed by finer ones. Finally, they have to attach meaning to sound. Children who can hear usually go through these stages within the first year of life. Children with hearing impairments may still be learning to distinguish sounds and attach meaning to them during the preschool years.

1. Help children learn to check during the day that the volume of their hearing aid is at an appropriate level.

2. Point out sounds to children when they might hear the sound and can have a visual association: "See the airplane. It went vroooooom!"

3. Use as many visual aids and gestures as possible to help the child understand.

Reading

Early reading literacy skills include habitually looking at words and letters from left to right, making fine visual discriminations, and recognizing a sense of pattern (letters versus spaces). Children with hearing impairments must replace some of the auditory skills they lack with visual skills. Speechreading also depends on fine visual discrimination. Interpreting signs and fingerspelling is both a visual task and a reading literacy skill. Plan numerous activities that require fine visual discrimination. Introduce variety into activities by using three-dimensional objects, pictures, line drawings, and even people.

1. Demonstrate left-to-right progression. Point a marker or your finger at the left side of a word or page before starting, and move it to the right as you read.

2. Write stories about the children's experiences, draw or paste in pictures illustrating significant words, or use pictures from a digital camera.

3. Use activities that require perceptual (visual matching) skills, such as lotto, bingo, and puzzles.

4. Label everything in the classroom (tables, chairs, lockers, crayons, paints, and easel).

5. Emphasize activities that require fine visual discrimination because this skill is needed for reading. Alphabet-matching lotto or a lotto game using the American Manual Alphabet is a useful way to do this.

6. Play Concentration using the American Manual Alphabet or whatever specific method of manual communication the child is using. See Activity 1–5, *Fingerspelling Lotto*.

Books can expand the child's world. Start with stories about familiar events and descriptive pictures before using more creative ones.

1. Choose books that depict familiar sights and actions.

2. Use illustrations that are simple, large, and uncluttered.

3. Provide the child with auditory cues and visual aids when reading. For example, when reading "The Three Little Pigs," squeal, change rhythm, and huff and puff.

You might even bring in straw, wood, and bricks and let the children huff and puff at them at the science table.

4. Use flannelboard stories, as these usually have simple graphics and straightforward plots.

5. Have children act out simple stories.

6. Place picture books with clear, sequential story lines in the book corner. Include some books without words.

7. Choose books with realistic illustrations.

8. Encourage children to experiment with books. They may enjoy the Living Book series by Broderbund (books such as *Arthur's Birthday* and *Stellaluna*). The accompanying software can function as a storyteller, or they can use it in an interactive way by hitting the hot spots, which sets off animation.

Writing

Give children a wide variety of writing tools and paper to work with. Children need to explore the media and develop the connection between the written and spoken word before writing will be meaningful. Because children with hearing impairments will be more dependent on writing for communication, it is important that they have a positive view of writing.

1. Add stickers to the writing center as well as pictures that can be cut and pasted.

2. Encourage children to use creative spelling in their writing. Support all attempts at writing and illustrating. Emphasize the meaning of writing, until children become fluent writers. Accept children's creative spelling. It is extremely difficult for children who cannot hear accurately to spell accurately.

3. Encourage children to word process their writing and to use software programs that support writing, such as ClarisWorks for Kids.

Language

Language, particularly learning the conventions of standard English grammar and usage, will be challenging for children learning American Sign Language as it has a different set of rules. Multiple meaning words and nuances also pose challenges.

1. Use rhyming to teach vocabulary, as in Activity 2-57w, *Rhyming Words*. Provide pictures of the words.

2. Discuss the structure of language with children and the concepts of pitch, intonation, speed, and stress. See Activity 2-28, *Say It*.

3. Emphasize basic vocabulary words in each curriculum area. Post words where everyone can see them, or hang them on a string from the ceiling so that all educators use the same vocabulary. If you have a doctor's office in the dramatic play area, make labels for equipment and have a list of important words with pictures to support the list. Take photographs with a digital camera and label the photographs.

Discovery

Children need to develop the skills of inquiry, problem solving, and cause–effect reasoning. Children with hearing impairments need to learn about the parts of the body concerned with hearing and speech. They can explore how a hearing aid works by using microphones and by playing with the balance on a stereo and the volume on a tape or CD player. Technology benefits children with hearing impairments by increasing their ability to hear sound and also as a potential method of communicating and connecting with others. The abstractions in math and science are more logical than in language and literacy.

Mathematics

Math goals are the same as they are for all children. The initial focus is to develop a concrete base of fundamental math concepts to prepare for abstract concepts that will come later.

1. Use three-dimensional manipulatives (cubes, balls) before progressing to two-dimensional materials (squares, circles). Count, sort, arrange, and rearrange these materials. Use them to pose and answer math problems related to addition and subtraction.

2. Develop the language skills that serve as the foundation for math, such as understanding relationships (equal/more/less). Use manipulatives to reinforce these concepts.

3. Use naturally occurring situations to teach math. Cooking and sand and water play provide many opportunities for describing, measuring, and comparing.

4. Measure with different instruments (ruler, metal tape, cloth tape). Compare relative amounts, using both conventional and nonconventional measures. Graph your results so children can see the differences.

5. Teach concepts using materials that interest the child. If you are teaching number concepts to a football fan, you can put the numbers on checkers, set up a checkerboard as a football field with the checkers as players, and then call the plays: "Give the ball to number 3 and have him run around number 5 and then between 1 and 7." The child scores only if she follows the correct pattern. If the child cannot hear or speechread, use your fingers or cards to show the plays.

6. Have children classify and reclassify objects in different ways. Using small and large shapes, some of which are black and others white, ask the child to sort them into two piles; when the task is complete, ask the child to sort the objects another way and to count them.

Science

Few other curriculum areas have the potential for discovery, satisfaction, and interaction with materials that science has. Provide children with the right materials and offer well-timed visual hints, in addition to asking questions as you normally would.

1. Help the child generalize by providing abundant materials.

2. Support children's scientific inquiry. Allow time to develop and process hypotheses and reach conclusions.

3. Help children understand that things can exist in more than one state, and provide examples of this. Compare corn on the cob, frozen corn, canned corn, creamed corn, and popped and unpopped corn.

4. Use visual demonstrations.

5. Have the child demonstrate the actions when giving directions.

6. Use a variety of media to teach about concepts. For example, to teach about plants, visit a farm, nursery, or plant store; plant seeds, varying the water, light, and soil; look at books on plants; show a videotape on how plants grow; and invite a florist to speak to the class.

7. Use regularly occurring natural events like seasonal changes and weather to teach a sense of predictability in the world.

8. Teach children about sound, how it is made, and how the body processes sound.

Technology

Computers are very useful for children with hearing impairments. Input and output are visual and require no hearing. Computers can be used as interactive teaching tools. They play an important part in the lives of children with hearing impairments. Encourage children to learn about the technology that supports hearing and the ways they can use technology to communicate and enrich their understanding of the world.

1. Teach cause-and-effect reasoning, using a computer: Press a key and the computer does something. Different keys cause something else to happen.

2. Encourage children to use computers. This is a good time to work with a friend, so ensure there are two chairs at the computer.

3. Use a modem to access the vast resources of the Internet. Computer skills and attitudes learned now serve children for a lifetime.

4. Use closed-captioned TV and talk with children about its use and the function of the captions. Show small clips from foreign films with English subtitles, and discuss them. If some children in the class speak a language other than English, encourage them to talk about the video and the challenges of learning language.

5. Teach children to use digital cameras as a method of sharing information with each other. If children cannot tell parents what they have done at school, a picture will show them.

Wellness

Physical activities help children learn skills to become more physically fit and more aware of where their body is in space, and to fine-tune small motor skills. Emphasize safety procedures. Children must learn to recognize and respond quickly to visual signs of danger if they cannot hear the warning sounds of a car or tricycle horn, fire alarm, or a shout. Children with hearing impairments need practice with dynamic and static balance because the vestibular sense is located in the inner ear. They need opportunities to integrate auditory input with motor skills. Noncompetitive games that require starting, stopping, and turning are useful.

Health and Safety

If children with hearing impairments miss warning signals, their safety may be jeopardized. Help children develop skills to deal with potentially dangerous situations.

1. Use traffic warning signals outside with the tricycles, wagons, and so on. Teach the meaning of traffic lights (play Red Light–Green Light). Use visual signals, not just aural ones.

2. Practice crossing streets.

3. Discuss what to do if a child is lost or hurt, then dramatize the emergency (using dialogue) or pantomime it.

4. Use snack or lunch time to instill good eating habits, and toileting to teach good hygiene.

5. Familiarize children with the procedure for fire alarms. Incorporate a visual cue (flickering lights or a red flag) into your usual procedure. Keep this child in sight during a fire alarm to ensure the child neither wanders off nor misses later instructions. With older children, use a buddy system. Get a flashing alarm for your classroom.

Physical Education

Children with hearing impairments can enjoy and participate in large motor activities. If there is damage to the semicircular canals, the child may have problems with dizziness, with obvious implications. Discuss climbing and rough and tumble play with families, to know what limits need to be set. An adult should have an unobstructed view of all children when outside. If a child were near a relatively dangerous area, such as swings, seesaws, a bike path, and so on, and could not hear your call to warn him, you would need to be close by.

1. Use activities that help develop the child's sense of balance—both dynamic and static.

2. Choose activities that require stopping, starting, and changing directions. (Inability to do these without losing balance is related to the inner ear.)

3. Use activities such as obstacle courses to teach language skills (crawl *through* the tunnel, jump *over* the bar, run *around* the pole).

4. Help the child perfect the fundamental motor skills of crawling, rolling, running, leaping, jumping, skipping, and so on.

Children with hearing impairments need opportunities to practice skills that require static and dynamic balance.
© Cengage Learning 2012

5. Have the children imitate animal walks (with pictures as cues) to help them identify different styles of walking.

6. Help children use large motor skills to relieve pent-up energy and frustration.

7. Use props to help a child realize the intent of the group if it appears a change in plans is not apparent to the child.

8. Provide a variety of unusual activities that help in processing movement information in the brain (skating, sliding, walking on different surfaces and angles).

9. Add balls to activities to help focus concentration, such as having children kick balls to each other.

10. Have children do various balancing activities with a beanbag on their head or another body part and then have it "jump" off.

Sensory Motor Integration

Children with hearing impairments interact with the world through vision, touch, smell, and the integration of these senses as well as their residual hearing. Their visual and tactile skills need to be refined and integrated so that they can gain as much information from the environment as possible.

1. Use activities that require both visual and fine motor skills (puzzles, assorted nuts and bolts to put together, woodworking, bead stringing).

2. Use activities requiring only the sense of touch, such as sorting graded sandpaper or playing with a feely box or bag.

3. Encourage children to use activities where the hands work together such as cutting with scissors (one hand holds, the other cuts), mixing activities, using an egg beater, and so on.

4. Use tweezers or tongs to sort cotton balls, blocks, small wooden beads, or small toys. Tongs and tweezers can be used to find toys in seeds or sand and to pick up small objects.

Creative Arts

Emphasize the creativity in creative arts. Use pictures and realistic props to set the mood. Children can learn by watching what others do and seeing what they make while still choosing and using materials in their own way. Music is primarily an auditory experience. For children with hearing impairments, depending on the degree of loss, music activities must be adapted to include experiences that will be meaningful to them and allow them to participate. Pair music with movement and dance. Include visual cues so the children can clap the rhythm, stamp their feet, and so on. Include hand motions or ASL signs along with your songs so that all children can be involved. Use movement activities that allow children to experience rhythm. Movement and dance are excellent opportunities for children to experiment with ways of moving. Help children act out situations they are likely to encounter, writing scripts for specific situations. Use as many props as you can, and keep them realistic. Help children learn what to do in a given situation through dramatic play. Use accessories to set the mood.

Visual Arts

Art needs few adaptations. Use discussions about art to provide opportunities for language input.

1. Support children with hearing impairments to use art as an emotional release as well as an art form.

2. Provide three-dimensional art materials as well as two-dimensional ones.

3. Provide extra time for children to learn the qualities of materials (paint versus paste) through trial and error, as well as from your demonstrations and watching peers.

Music

Support music with visual cues. Include all children by adding motions and responding to music as well as singing.

1. Use percussion instruments (children can feel vibrations and see the beat).

2. Choose songs that incorporate motions so children can participate in the movement.

3. Set the mood for songs and movement by using pictures. If you want the children to pretend they are walking through leaves, use a fall picture with leaves; if they are to be flowers growing, show both buds and flowers in full bloom.

4. Use your hand to show when songs go up or down in pitch.

5. Learn to sign some favorite songs if children in your class sign. The class may find this more challenging and fun than fingerplays.

• • • Movement and Dance

Keep the focus on the process. If you are trying to convey a mood, use visual props.

1. Call on children with hearing impairments in the middle when they have had the opportunity to observe other children. As children move, point out the features of the movement that help set the mood.

2. Place the child to best see how others move.

3. Use mirror movement and allow the child to be the mirror first if there is a mood. If there is just movement, be sure the child has equal opportunities to lead.

4. Use rhythmic dance and free dance. Scarves are great to show the rhythm.

• • • Dramatic Play and Theater

Through dramatic play, children can express feelings and concerns. They can try out roles (mother, father, teacher, audiologist) without fear of being judged. Dramatic play and theater provide experiences necessary for developing a strong language base.

1. Include a traditional home living area in your classroom initially. (This fosters some sense of security for all children at the beginning of the year.)

2. Use the dramatic play area to expand the children's environment as well as play out situations that are familiar in their lives.

3. Provide play props and roles appropriate to the activities.

4. Encourage children to plan their theater and decide on particular roles, and perhaps even write or dictate a rebus or picture script to remind children of the roles and sequence.

Routines and Transitions

Transitions are rarely fun for children. They can be especially difficult for a child with a hearing impairment, who may not have grasped the verbal directions or the other children's intentions.

1. Be sure that children know the daily sequence. Use a picture schedule and point to what will happen next.

2. Keep your schedule predictable once it is set. Knowing that some things are predictable gives the children a sense of security.

3. Use visual signs to announce upcoming changes (one light blink for a five-minute warning, two blinks for cleanup time).

4. Use a visual timer.

5. Post any rules, adding illustrations and the word "NO" or an *X* through the picture where actions are inappropriate. Also, post pictures of things you want children to do such as how to carry scissors.

6. Demonstrate what is going to happen next (start picking up, get your coat, etc.).

> **▶❙❙ TeachSource Video Case**
>
> **Preschool: Daily Schedules and Program Planning**
>
> Watch the TeachSource Video Case *Preschool: Daily Schedules and Program Planning*, in which you see how consistent structure helps preschoolers develop a sense of security. The video can be found in the Early Childhood Education Media Library under Play, available at www.cengagebrain.com.

SUMMARY

- Sound travels in waves that have both frequency and intensity.
- The auditory system, consisting of the outer, middle, and inner ear as well as the auditory nerve and auditory cortex, focuses and interprets sound waves.
- A conductive hearing impairment relates to the inability of the outer and middle ear to conduct sound to the inner ear.
- Middle ear disease is the most frequent cause of a conductive hearing impairment in young children.
- Sensorineural losses are permanent and are the result of impairment in the inner ear or the auditory nerve.
- Young children with profound hearing losses are receiving cochlear implants as infants or toddlers.
- Parents make decisions about how their child will communicate, choosing among total communication, American Sign Language, oral communication, or cued speech.
- Curriculum areas such as language and literacy may require modifications; other areas that use vision or tactile input need few.

EDUCATIONAL RESOURCES

American Sign Language Browser is a site that provides a visual dictionary for ASL, both signs and fingerspelling. The signs are short videos with accompanying text. http://commtechlab.msu.edu/sites/aslweb/browser.htm/

ASLPro is a site designed for teachers. It not only has ASL, but organizes signs by hand shape. It also has close ups of the mouth and how it looks saying different morphemes. www.ASLpro.com/

Alexander Graham Bell Association for the Deaf and Hard of Hearing sponsors conferences and workshops and publishes materials for parents and teachers. There is a special section for parents of children with hearing impairments. www.nc.agbell.org/

American Society for Deaf Children (ASDC) provides support, encouragement and information on the impact of a hearing impairment on children. The website has an extensive bibliography of readings that may be helpful to professionals and parents. www.deafchildren.org/

American Speech-Language-Hearing Association (ASHA) is a national organization and the governing body for speech-language pathologists and audiologists. The website is divided into sections for professionals, the public, and students. It is easy to navigate and is helpful to anyone looking for general information. www.asha.org/

Gallaudet University is a liberal arts university for the deaf and hard of hearing. It offers programs for children with hearing impairments, distributes materials, and consults with schools throughout the country. www.gallaudet.edu/

John Tracy Clinic is a private nonprofit education center that specializes in stimulation programs for infants who have hearing impairments. It is a great resource for parents worldwide and has courses for professionals. www.jtc.org/

National Association of the Deaf is a nonprofit organization designed to empower deaf and hard of hearing individuals. It provides online information for parents and professionals. http://www.nad.org/

National Institute on Deafness and other Communicative Disorders (NIDCD) provides online information for parents and professionals about hearing impairments. www.nidcd.nih.gov/

SERI Hearing Impairment Resources is part of Special Education Resources on the Internet and provides many links to valuable resources related to children with hearing impairments. www.seriweb.com/hearing.htm/

For additional Educational Resources, visit the book companion website for this text at www.cengagebrain.com.

Children with Visual Impairments

19

One of my memories of being in first grade is of Skip, whose mother once asked our teacher whether we teased him about his patch. The teacher's startled response was, "What patch?" Skip went out of the house each morning with a patch over his left eye, took it off and put it in his pocket, and arrived at school without it. He put it back on before he got home. I don't know whether we would have teased him had he worn it, but the fear of being teased or different made him avoid the possibility. It is a very powerful concern that causes a 6-year-old to do that kind of planning and remembering. ✳

Visual Impairments

Vision helps us interpret the world around us by the visual images we form of others and ourselves. Vision motivates us to reach out and touch objects, to climb a hill for the view, and to return a friendly smile. Children with impaired vision need to connect with their world by utilizing their residual vision and other senses if their impairment is not correctable or until it is corrected. Visual impairments can occur as the only disability in children; however, in about half of these children, it is associated with other impairments including intellectual disability and cerebral palsy (Miller & Menacker, 2007).

Including children with visual impairments in your class involves teaching children who wear eyeglasses, lenses, or corrective patches; helping to identify children whose visual impairments have not yet been diagnosed; and adapting your programming for children who have noncorrectable visual problems including limited vision and blindness.

The Visual System

An understanding of how the complex visual system works and the problems that can occur in different parts of the system helps you know what adaptations will be the most useful (see Figure 19–1). As light waves enter the eye, the colored part of the eye, the **iris**, controls the amount of light that enters the eye by opening wider to admit more light or closing down to limit the amount of light. The **pupil** is the opening in the center of the iris through which light enters. The cornea, which covers and protects the iris, first focuses these light rays, and then they are focused by the **lens**, which is behind the pupil. These light waves are focused on the inner surface of the eye, the **retina**. Images, projected onto the retina upside down and reversed, are

Courtesy of Penny Low Deiner

sent through the optic nerve to the brain for interpretation (Miller & Menacker, 2007).

The eye does not actually "see" any more than the ear "hears." It receives light, turns light into electrical impulses, and sends them through the optic nerve to the visual cortex of the occipital lobe of the brain, which perceives visual images. If the relevant part of the brain that sees is severely damaged, a child may not be able to see, even though the eye is completely normal. Defects in the eye itself are often correctable. The purpose of most visual aids is to compensate for defects in the eye so that a correct message can be sent to the brain.

Defining Visual Impairments

Visual impairments are defined in a variety of ways according to the legal, medical, or educational implications of the impairment. The legal and medical definitions typically emphasize visual acuity, or how clearly the child can see. The educational definition emphasizes the extent to which

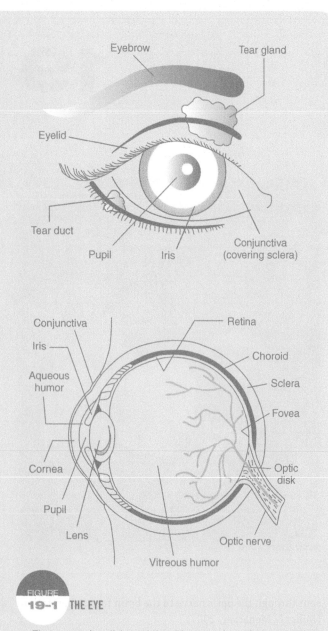

FIGURE 19-1   THE EYE

The eye receives light and through a complex process turns light into electrical impulses and sends them through the optic nerve to the visual cortex in the brain.

the child can use his visual ability to read printed material for learning. According to IDEA 2004,

> *Visual impairment including blindness means an impairment in vision that, even with correction, adversely affects a child's educational performance. The term includes both partial sight and blindness.*

Vision may be limited in three ways: visual acuity, the field of vision, or color vision. **Visual acuity** is the resolving power of the eye, that is, the sharpness or clarity of the image viewed. We usually measure this by having children identify or match letters or pictures in various sizes while standing at a standard distance (20 feet) from a chart. A person who can see at 20 feet what most people see at 20 feet has normal, or

20/20, vision. For children below third grade, vision of 20/40 or better in each eye or vision of 20/30 or better when using both eyes is considered normal. That is, the young child sees (with one eye) at 20 feet what an adult would see at 40 feet or with both eyes at 30 feet.

A child's **field of vision** can be restricted by lack of peripheral vision. The child may have normal central visual acuity but reduced peripheral vision. This is called **tunnel vision**. Or the field of vision may be restricted by a **scotoma**, or dark spot. This dark spot can be of various sizes and be anywhere in the field of vision. If it is in the middle of the eye, the child's **central vision** will be impaired.

Color vision involves the ability to discriminate three qualities of color: hue, saturation, and brightness. The difference between those with and those without normal color vision is that some of the hues that appear different to a person with normal color vision appear similar to those without. The terms **achromatopsia**, **color deficiency**, and **color blindness** refer to this condition. The term color deficiency is technically correct and preferable because young children are often frightened by the use of the term *color blind*. The total inability to see color is very rare. The most frequent problem is distinguishing between specific colors, usually red and green. For most people with color deficiency, it is possible to distinguish these colors when the object is large (like a car), but they have trouble with smaller items and when the colors are part of a pattern such as a plaid. Children who have color-deficient vision rarely know it. As a teacher, you may suspect it when children have difficulty identifying one or more of the primary colors. We don't regard this as a disability as children's visual acuity is not affected; however, it is useful to be aware of it, as you are likely to encounter children with this condition. However, if you are a person who color-codes materials for children, you may need to modify your system. If you use the color red, write the letter *R* or the word *red* over the color so that you are sure all children can use the system.

Visually Limited

This term refers to children who are considered sighted children for educational purposes, but who are limited in their use of vision. They may need particular light conditions, prescriptive lenses, optic aids, or special materials to aid their vision. Although it is unlikely (but not impossible) you will have a child with no usable vision, it is more probable that you will have, or help to identify, a child with limited vision. Estimates about the number of school-age children who are **visually limited** vary widely—from 5 to 33 percent (Salvia & Ysseldyke, 2007)—because of the definitions used and the screening instruments. (These estimates do not include children who have visual processing problems.) If 20 percent of children have a visual limitation, then in every classroom of 25 children, 5 are likely to have vision problems of some sort.

Low Vision

Children who are partially sighted, or have **low vision**, have their best corrected visual acuity between 20/70 and 20/200 in their better eye (Yeargin-Allsopp, Drews-Botsch, &

Van Naarden Braun, 2007). Educationally, children with low vision have enough residual vision to read large print or regular print with special assistance such as magnification. Limitations may be greater in distance vision. These children should *not* be referred to as blind.

Blindness

A person who is considered **legally blind** has visual acuity no better than 20/200 in the better eye, with the best possible correction, or has a field of vision restricted to 20 degrees or less (tunnel vision) in the better eye instead of the usual 105 degrees (Yeargin-Allsopp et al., 2007). The child who is legally blind sees at 20 feet what people with normal vision can see at 200 feet. For educational purposes, children are considered **blind** if they have a visual loss severe enough that it is not possible to read printed material and necessitates the use of alternative forms of written communication such as Braille. Most children who are legally blind have some useful vision. Children with 20/200 to 20/500 may be able to read large-print books or a computer screen with large fonts; some children with 20/500 to 20/800 can distinguish light and dark or detect objects that are useful in orientation and mobility; some children will have no usable vision (Miller & Menacker, 2007). It is important to know the degree of visual impairment and how this limits what a child can do.

Causes of Visual Impairments

Visual impairments are also categorized or defined by the part of the eye involved. There are problems related to the physical mechanisms of the eye, problems with visual acuity, impairments to the muscular structure of the eye, and problems in visual perceptions or the message pathway between the eye and brain. For many children, problems involving the physical mechanisms, acuity, and muscular structure can be corrected with medical techniques, eyeglasses or contact lenses, and/or surgery. Damage to the brain or the optic nerve is not correctable.

Visual problems can relate to the function of the eye or the mechanisms of the eye, including the cornea, lens, retina, anterior chamber, eye muscles, optic nerves, and visual cortex. Damage to any of these parts can affect how light passes through the eye or is transmitted to the brain. Damage to the eye structure can result in permanent loss of vision.

Refractive Errors

For clear vision, the eyeball must be the right length and the cornea must have the proper shape. Errors of refraction occur because of the shape of the eyeball or cornea or the strength of the lens. We measure the refractive power of a lens in units called **diopters**, the light-bending power of the lens, which is assigned a number according to its refractive powers. The higher the number of diopters, the stronger the prescription: a minus sign indicates concave lenses; a plus, convex lenses. The most common refractive error of childhood is hyperopia (Miller & Menacker, 2007).

HYPEROPIA

Hyperopia, or farsightedness, means that the child can see distant objects better than relatively close objects. When the eyeball is too short or the lens and cornea are too strong, the focused image falls behind the retina. The shorter the eyeball, the more out of focus the image will be and the more convex the lenses in the glasses will have to be to correct the problem. Young children naturally have eyeballs that are too short, making them farsighted, but the ability of the lens to adjust allows most of them to compensate and not need glasses.

When refractive errors are over 4 diopters, corrective lenses are usually prescribed. A prescription for a child who is farsighted might be a +4.5 diopters correction for one eye. The other eye may have a different correction. There is a concern that children with errors over 6 diopters are at risk for amblyopia and esotropia (Miller & Menacker, 2007).

MYOPIA

Myopia, or nearsightedness, means that the child can see close objects better than distant objects. It occurs when the eyeball is too long, causing the image to be in focus before it reaches the retina. Myopia is corrected with the use of concave lenses. There is no mechanism to fine-tune vision for children with myopia. Therefore, these children may wear glasses from infancy if the myopia is severe.

ASTIGMATISM

Astigmatism is an error in refraction caused by the cornea's being more football shaped than spherical. The image does not focus because the parallel light rays do not come together at one point. Cylindrical lenses that compensate for the irregular shape can usually correct astigmatism. This condition can also occur with other visual conditions. A child can be nearsighted or farsighted and also have astigmatism (see Figure 19–2).

From a developmental perspective, corrective lenses may not be prescribed for young children if the refractive problem does not interfere with daily functions.

Retinopathy of Prematurity

The most common cause of retinal damage is **retinopathy of prematurity (ROP)**. Because more premature infants are surviving, the number of children with ROP has increased, as almost 25 percent of infants weighing less than 2¾ pounds will have some degree of ROP (Hameed et al., 2004). Premature infants' blood vessel growth is incomplete, and as they catch up, blood vessels grow to the center of the eye rather than along the back surface. The scar tissue can constrict and pull on the retina, in some cases detaching it and causing loss of vision (Miller & Menacker, 2007). The number of children becoming blind due to ROP is decreasing because of early diagnosis and treatment (Khan et al., 2007).

Optic Nerves

Over a million nerve cells join at the **optic disk** (blind spot) to form the **optic nerve**. Because there are nerve fibers there,

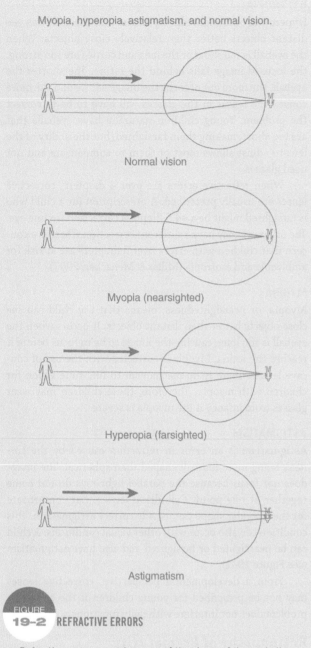

Myopia, hyperopia, astigmatism, and normal vision.

Normal vision

Myopia (nearsighted)

Hyperopia (farsighted)

Astigmatism

FIGURE 19-2 REFRACTIVE ERRORS

Refractive errors occur because of the shape of the eyeball or cornea or the strength of the lens.

not cones and rods, there is no vision. One optic nerve is joined to each eye. At one point along the path to the brain, some nerve fibers cross over (**optic chiasm**) on their way to the **occipital lobe** (Miller & Menacker, 2007).

The optic nerve carries the electrical impulses from the eye to the brain for processing. Damage to the optic nerve itself is usually associated with incomplete development or damage from disease or trauma. If this nerve is not developed properly, it will not be possible for the signals to get to the brain so the child can see. The effects on vision vary depending on the amount and place of the damage.

Amblyopia

Amblyopia, sometimes referred to as "lazy eye," is a reduction in visual acuity that only occurs in children younger than age 9 and is a consequence of long spans of time when there are no retinal images or blurred ones. The visual system of young children is immature and susceptible to being turned off. Unless it is identified and treated with patching, blurry eye drops, or glasses, vision could be permanently impaired (Miller & Menacker, 2007).

Visual Cortex

Visual information passes through the optic nerves to the **visual cortex** in the occipital lobe of the brain and is then sent to the temporal and parietal lobes. For some children, the visual process appears to work accurately until the message gets to the brain. **Cortical visual impairment (CVI)** is the most common cause of permanent visual impairment in children (Flanagan, Jackson, & Hill, 2003). It is most commonly caused by oxygen deprivation, infection, or traumatic brain injury (Miller & Menacker, 2007). Children with CVI often lack a social gaze and avoid direct eye contact. They may avoid unfamiliar visual stimulation, including faces. Some children avoid tactile stimulation, whereas others prefer it to using vision. These children may often reach without looking at the object they are reaching for, but they respond positively to music and voices (Children's Hospital Boston, n.d.).

Eye Muscles

Muscular problems involve the inability of the six muscles controlling the eyes to work in coordination with each other to result in clear vision. The brain fuses the images seen from both eyes into one, producing binocular vision. Correct fusion of these images depends on the eyes being straight and moving in synchrony. Disruption in either causes visual problems.

STRABISMUS

In **strabismus**, the eyes are not able to focus simultaneously on one point. This occurs in 3 to 4 percent of children and more frequently (15%) in children who were born prematurely (Olitsky & Nelson, 1998). There are two main forms of strabismus: in **esotropia**, the most common problem, the eyes (or weak eye) turn in toward the nose (cross-eyed), whereas in **exotropia**, the eyes (or weak eye) turn away from the nose (walleyed). Healthy infants whose eyes cross after 3 months of age will often need surgery (Miller & Menacker, 2007).

Causes of Blindness

Causes of blindness fall into four major etiologies: genetic, prenatal, perinatal, and childhood. The genetic group makes up 33 percent of the total; prenatal, 27 percent; perinatal, 26 percent; and childhood, 12 percent (Khan et al., 2007).

In the United States, the three leading causes of severe visual impairment are cortical visual impairment, retinopathy

Some children have impaired vision as their only disability; for others, it is part of a syndrome.
©Cengage Learning 2012

of prematurity, and **optic nerve hypoplasia** (Hatton, 2001). Of these infants, about a fourth have no usable vision; another fourth can distinguish some light; and the remaining half have enough vision that they can read enlarged type (Miller, Menacker, & Batshaw, 2002). Other causes of severe visual impairments include traumatic brain injury, severe eye infection and trauma to the eye, and tumors.

Prevalence of Visual Impairments

The federal government began keeping records on children with visual impairments during the 1976–1977 school year. At that time, 8.3 percent of children in the public schools were identified as having a disability. Of these children, 1.0 percent had a visual impairment. In the 2007–2008 school year, 13.4 percent of children were identified as having a disability, with 0.4 percent of these children having a visual impairment. This percentage has remained the same since 1994–1995. Children with identified visual impairments constitute 0.1 percent of the total school population of children between 3 and 21 years old (National Center for Educational Statistics, 2010).

Although this represents the number of children who were identified with visual impairments, the question remains about the undiagnosed visual conditions affecting young children.

THE EVIDENCE BASE

The Medical Expenditure Panel Surveys from 1996 through 2001 included 48,304 people and looked at the prevalence of children with diagnosed eye and visual conditions. On average, 7 percent of children younger than 18 years had a diagnosed eye or visual condition. Excluding conjunctivitis, the most common conditions were refractive disorder, potentially blinding disorders, trauma or injury, and other nonclassified disorders.

White children with better-educated mothers who had higher incomes were more likely to have diagnosed eye and vision conditions. Hispanic children, children in very good to excellent health, and uninsured children were less likely to have any self-reported eye and vision conditions. These results provide some evidence that some children may be underdiagnosed, undertreated, and at risk for future problems.

Source: Ganz, Xuan, and Hunter (2006).

Early Identification of Visual Impairments

Unless parents have a reason to suspect that a child has a visual problem, it usually doesn't occur to them to take a young child to an ophthalmologist. Children themselves are usually no help because they assume that whatever vision they have is normal. See Table 19–1 for signs of a visual impairment.

IMPLICATIONS FOR EDUCATORS

As you observe children, be aware of the behaviors and complaints that may indicate vision problems. Preschool children have a tendency to see things better at a distance than they do at close range. When doing close work such as looking at books, puzzles, or games, a child with a visual impairment may blink continually, hold a book (or place himself) too close or too far away, keep changing the distance of the book, or over- or underestimate distance when working with puzzles or pegboards. When doing visual work at a distance (such as when a book is being read during group time), the child may seem inattentive or lose interest after a brief time. He may lack eye contact or attention to faces.

Other symptoms to look for are the inability to identify parents, friends, or teachers at a distance; not noticing objects from across the room or playground; difficulty in such activities as calendar reading or chalkboard games; bumping into things; and misjudging distances in games. The child may also move slowly so as not to bump into things. Vocabulary may be limited for things such as birds, which are usually in the distance. If your observations support your suspicion, ask parents whether they have considered this; if not, encourage them to observe more closely. After they have observed, share your concerns and encourage them to take the child to an eye doctor (ideally, a pediatric or developmental ophthalmologist).

Many infants and young children with correctable visual problems function as if they had low vision until their vision is corrected. They often show delays in reaching developmental milestones; tend to sit later; and may not crawl, but hitch. **Hitching** is a method of moving where the child's bottom is on the floor and she scoots, using her legs for propulsion. Hitching makes the head less vulnerable. Children will typically walk with a wide stance for added support, but may not walk until age 2 or later. Speech also develops later,

TABLE 19-1   SIGNS OF VISUAL IMPAIRMENTS

Medical/Physical
Eyes that are red, watery, or have a discharge
Itchy, scratchy, burning eyes
Uncoordinated eyes (one eye remains still while the other follows the object; eyes cross or one eye wanders)
Eyelids that are red, swollen, crusted, or droopy
Swelling of eyes
A white pupil
Frequent or recurring styes
Excessive blinking
Eyes that appear out of focus
Behavioral
Frequent frowning, squinting, or eye rubbing
Widening or squinting eyes when looking in the distance
Holding books or objects too close
Shutting or covering one eye
Consistently tilting head to one side or the other
Frequent headaches, stomachaches, or dizziness
Not alert to surroundings; few attempts at locomotion or communication
Problems judging distance when using small objects
High sensitivity to light
Inability to recognize familiar faces from a distance, not paying attention to faces, and lack of eye contact

often with less body and facial expression, and little nonverbal communication.

The infant who is born with very little vision misses not only the visual aspects of the environment but also the ability to form visual images about the world. Therefore, the child may not be attracted to people, objects, or even the exploration of his own body; unless he can experience these through taste, touch, or sound, he does not know they exist. A conscious effort has to be made to link the child to the environment by building mental concepts through language. Young children who cannot see still babble, smile, and laugh when sighted infants do, but infants with sight see their parents' responses, which reinforces these behaviors. The tonal pattern of voices must convey to young infants what they cannot see. As infants become familiar with the people and objects in their environment, they will form concepts through their senses of hearing and touch, and will recognize the voices and footsteps of family members. This is the time that an infant is building connections. Name whatever the infant touches, whatever she does, and whatever is done for her. Pick out the salient features of the experience and put them into words. Objects that make sounds should be placed in their hands. Children need to learn to touch their nose and toes. They need to learn "up" as they are being picked "up" and obviously "down" in the same way. At first, words and associations are difficult; initially, use the same objects and the same words during routines.

Infants who do not respond to visual stimuli need other stimulation. They need to *feel* a smile; they need sounds and singing as their day progresses. Call infants so they raise their heads; rattle noisemakers in different positions to entice them to move; place them in different positions; and call to infants from above, beside, and below them. Encourage infants to move. Place noisemaking objects in their hands and then slightly out of reach to intrigue them to reach for these objects. Prop infants in a sitting position or place them in a contained area where they can sit, and place a variety of noisemaking toys with them. (This makes the toys easier to locate.) Periodically, squeak a toy to help maintain interest. Teach infants to localize and attend to sound. This is a precursor to learning to look at the person who is talking. They need the same learning experiences as sighted children; they just need them presented in a nonvisual way (California Department of Education, 2006).

Children who cannot see may not want to explore their world. They might become discouraged as they bump into things and get hurt. When children are learning to walk, they can learn about the process of walking by standing on your feet, their back to your front, and walking with you. This gives information about bending their knees as well as information that walking is safe.

Walking, although wonderful, poses additional challenges. Children must now rely on their memory of space and hope that things remain in the same place. Initially, rubber soles give security; however, once walking has been mastered, leather soles provide more feedback. Climbing up stairs is easier than going down; help by placing their feet on the treads. Use snack time to help toddlers develop hand–mouth coordination. Use small bits of food in a contained area to help children both grasp the food and then eat it. This is messy, but practice works. Prepare children for new experiences and changes by providing auditory cues. This is not just verbally telling children what will happen next, but consciously thinking about the natural environmental cues that provide information. Before giving an infant a bottle, shake the bottle, let the infant feel it, walk "heavy," and talk to the infant to let her know you are near. Perhaps "drop" children's boots in front of them and then say, "You need to put your boots on," or "Listen, I'm pouring your juice," and so on.

Play games in which children need to crawl or walk toward sound sources. Use environmental sounds such as running water in the sink (with comments like, "It sounds as though some of the children are washing their hands") as well as sounds of toys. Then, of course, name the sound, put the child's hands in the water, and help her experiment with turning the water on and off.

A child with little sight may need to be taught how to explore an object placed in her hands. Teach children to explore the length of a spoon with their fingertips, then the bowl of it, as well as feeling the weight, texture, and temperature.

Help them turn it over and feel the bowl from the back. These are the qualities of "spoonness" they must learn, but labeling them as they are learning "spoon" is confusing. Just say the word "spoon." As children become more competent, encourage them to explore groups of objects that can be perceived with one or two hands and to compare the relative size of groups of things (Kapperman & Sticken, 2006).

Until children are about 3, they may not be aware that others see differently than they do. If they "see" using their hands, they expect that you see that way as well and will give you things to feel (i.e., see). The realization that others see differently begins gradually. Others may comment on a child's new watch without feeling the child's arm, or talk about something the child realizes he is not experiencing. At some point during the preschool years, children come to an understanding of the meaning of having limited sight. Children react differently to this discovery.

Children need help putting their feelings into words, and adults need to provide acceptance with words as well. Adults should ask such questions as, "Does it make you angry that you can't see the picture the other children are talking about?" Children with visual impairments need support in play skills. Interactive play develops more slowly, and their play tends to lack imagination. Describing, explaining, and helping them experience their world helps them understand it better.

Children with very limited vision rely on hearing as their most important link with the other children; instead of facial expressions, this is how a child knows whether another child is serious, angry, or joking. Loud sounds, too much noise, and constant auditory stimulation may cause children to tune out, thereby losing a major source of contact with the environment.

One decision that has to be discussed during the preschool years is how children will learn to read and write: with **Braille**, print, or a combination. Children need early instruction in both so that a decision can be made while a child is at an appropriate age to learn the necessary preliteracy skills. Classrooms should have both large-print books and Braille books available for children. Braille is also essential in teaching mathematics. Young children who will learn Braille should be immersed in a Braille-rich environment just as sighted children are immersed in a print-rich environment (California Department of Education, 2006).

As children with visual impairments reach school age, they continue to need support with social development and interaction. Their language may be more self-centered than other early elementary school children because they don't see what others do to talk about it. Peers need support in communication. Perhaps the best analogy for children this age is to have them pretend they are talking on the telephone when they communicate with a child who is visually impaired and have them fill in the necessary details in that way. Initial social relationships may be awkward, but children adapt.

Listening skills are extremely important for children with low vision, especially as they move into elementary school, where children are expected to follow directions and do many teacher-directed tasks. Children with visual impairments need extra time to respond, as it takes them longer to make the necessary connections among words, people, objects, activities, experiences, and other information.

Watch for gaps in general knowledge and experience. Children may fail to perceive similarities and differences, and so mix up concepts that are perceptually different but functionally the same. For example, a young child who is familiar with houseplants might assume that the bark of a large tree is the tree's pot.

In elementary school, children need access to the content of more formal lessons, and this requires adapting teaching materials and different teaching approaches. Most children can use some form of print. Where regular print cannot be seen, a low-vision aid must be employed. These devices use one or more lenses to magnify the print; all use enlarged photocopies (these can get a bit bulky, depending on the degree of enlargement). Some children who need low-vision aids are reluctant to use them because they believe it will draw attention to them. Other problems include skill in using the materials. Some children read Braille; others use a combination, often writing on a Braille writing machine. With assistive technology, the range of input and output devices has expanded to the point that a specialist in this area is necessary to determine the best match for the particular child and the classroom situation.

Children vary in how good their orientation and mobility skills are. "**Orientation** is the ability to create and maintain a mental map of one's environment and the relationship of oneself to that environment. **Mobility** . . . is the ability to travel safely and efficiently through the environment" (Tuttle & Tuttle, 1996, p. 21). **Trailing** is a method that young children use to learn about their environment. They learn to hold the back of their hand at waist level and gently maintain contact with the walls and furniture as they walk.

Assessment of Visual Impairments

Tests of visual acuity fall into two general categories: those based on an examiner's assessment or eye chart, and those that utilize high technology, which requires special training and equipment. Most early care and education settings and elementary schools provide some kind of basic vision screening.

Vision Screening

The most common screening test for elementary school children is the standard Snellen wall chart. The child is asked to read standard-sized letters at a distance of 20 feet. Although a good screening test, some children may fail or pass this test based on variables other than vision. Children who don't know their letters may not pass the test for this reason. Some children may memorize the order of the letters if they hear many other children say them; some letters of the alphabet are easier to discriminate than others, which leads to guessing.

The Snellen E Test is used with preschool children who don't know the letters of the alphabet. The letter *E* (or three-legged table) is shown in different spatial arrangements, and the child either identifies the direction, points, or holds up the letter *E* to match the stimulus. Neither test identifies children with near-vision problems, and near vision is critical for learning to read. The criterion for referral is acuity of 20/40 for children kindergarten through third grade (Salvia & Ysseldyke, 2007). (To help prepare young children for a vision screening, use Activity 1–26, *Eye Doctor*.)

IN THE FIELD

I was once called by a mother who was concerned because her 18-month-old son only ate what was on the top half of his plate. She found that very strange. I went for a home visit at lunchtime. Sure enough, the little boy only ate from the top of his plate. He didn't appear full, but he also didn't touch the food on the bottom of the plate. We turned the plate around so that the remaining food was at the top, and that too was then eaten. The mother was baffled. "But why? This makes no sense." I agreed and told her I would think about it. It nagged me. There was something obvious I was missing, but for the life of me I couldn't figure out what it was. The child wasn't physically impaired or autistic. It was truly strange and continued to nag. Then the light broke. I called and said, "I think Seth may be farsighted and perhaps doesn't see the food when it is too close to him. Can you take him for an eye examination?" She replied, "Well, I guess, but wouldn't his physician already have noticed this?" I then said, "He needs to see a developmental ophthalmologist, not a pediatrician." She agreed to take him. Several weeks later, she called back, elated, saying, "Seth now has glasses. He was farsighted. He eats all the food on his plate. I'm so pleased. But do you think he would ever have learned to read if we hadn't figured this out?"

Scary, isn't it?

Ophthalmologists have higher technology tools for following up with children who do not pass visual screening tests and for determining the visual acuity of children who do not give verbal responses or recognize characters. There are a variety of techniques they use, depending upon the specific concern and what they are trying to rule out.

IMPLICATIONS FOR EDUCATORS

Find out from parents how much functional vision a child has. You want to know whether the child can participate in the everyday classroom activities you currently have, or the types of adaptations that will allow the child to be included. You might have questions about the arrangement of your room and safety concerns about how to best protect the child from injuries. Your role, as an educator, is to help children use the vision they have and the vision aids they need while being included in the activities of your classroom.

Assistive Technology

Increasingly, technology is being used to help children with limited vision. Cassette tapes and a tape player can be use to record books and leave messages or directions. Depending on the amount of vision a child has, a ViewScan may be helpful. This is a machine that uses a camera to project an image. It is able to project the pages of a book in many sizes of print and different contrasts. An Optacon is a device that scans print and converts it into patterns transmitted by 144 tactile pins that produce an image of the letter that can be felt against a finger. Another system, VersaBraille, can convert

information from the computer into Braille. Other computer programs provide speech capacity to a personal computer, and computer printouts can be converted into speech by using a Kurzweil Reading Machine and Total Talk. There are talking calculators, talking watches, and talking clocks. This is all in addition to talking books that are available from Recording for the Blind and Dyslexic (www.rfbd.org) and other individualized tools that children can profit from. The traditional long cane is being replaced by laser/ultrasound wave processing, and the global positioning system (GPS) allows people to be verbally guided to their destination.

Guidelines

The modifications that you will need to make in your classroom depend on the needs of the particular children you have. The following guidelines are divided into two sections. The first deals with techniques to encourage children to use corrective vision aids. The second section provides guidance in how to modify your room for children whose corrected vision still qualifies them as being partially sighted or blind.

Corrected Visual Impairments

When you are working with a child with correctable vision problems, the dilemma is that you want the child to wear the patch or glasses and to enjoy learning. You can't afford to be cast in the role of the villain who makes the child wear these things. First check with the parents or, if necessary, the ophthalmologist to be certain what the child is supposed to do. Then the trick is to make the child want to do what she is supposed to do.

1. *Find out when and for how long visual aids should be used.* Check with parents to find out whether glasses are to be worn at all times. Sometimes the correction is for a specific use only. A nearsighted child wears glasses to see at a distance, but because this correction may distort the child's vision for close work, it may be inappropriate to keep the glasses on during close work.

2. *Observe the child's behavior using the visual aids.* Does the child continually take the glasses off or look over them? Such actions may mean the correction is not helping and further consultation is necessary.

3. *Support children using corrective lenses.* If a child refuses to wear glasses, try to create a situation in which the child needs to wear the glasses to succeed. How you do this depends on the problem. If, for example, a child is farsighted, find an intriguing book or game that requires close vision. Then, depending on the circumstances, say something like, "Before you got your glasses, we couldn't have played this," or, "I'd like to play this game with you, but you forgot your glasses. If you wear them tomorrow, we can play." You might also make appropriate statements like, "You've learned to do this so much faster since you got your glasses," or, "I like the way you look with your glasses." The child will feel rewarded not only by the activity but also by your attention. Help children

become assertive. Children must learn to say, "I don't like it when you call me 'Four Eyes.'"

IN THE FIELD

I don't mind wearing glasses. I am the same on the inside, in my heart. Everyone has something she has to go through. I just pretend they aren't on my face, and my friends don't even notice them. Some kids teased me at first—but now no one cares.

REFLECTIVE PRACTICE | Even when children's vision can be corrected, they pay a price for that correction. Teasing hurts whether it is glasses, hearing aids, or braces. Reflect on how you will handle this for all children.

4. *Create a need to see.* For example, if a nearsighted child dislikes wearing glasses, you might have that child sit as far away from you as possible during group time. Then, when the child realizes that there is a need to see (e.g., in the middle of a story with pictures), have the child get the glasses if that won't disrupt the group; otherwise, have someone bring the child's glasses.

This sounds like a manipulative thing to do, and the child will have a harder time learning, but if you and the parents agree that it is important to wear the glasses, you must create a definite need and then reinforce the change in behavior, a process that will have to be repeated many times before the behavior is established. Be careful to do this subtly and in a matter-of-fact way so as not to focus the group's attention on the child. However, you also have to be realistic and say, "Tommy, you can't come any closer, but you will see better if you get your glasses." You may need to remind him where the glasses are, but you want him to be responsible. It is your job to make the activity so enticing that the child will want to get his glasses so he won't miss something others are enjoying. Don't let this become a power struggle. If he chooses not to comply, he won't see as well. Some children who don't want to wear glasses may purposefully lose them.

5. *Plan a unit on sight.* This helps all children better understand how they see. Discuss the sense of vision as well as a variety of visual problems. Simulating various visual needs creates awareness and is educational as well. Use cameras and focus to help explain sight. Use Activities like 1–39w, *Simulated Glasses,* or 1-41w, *Moving in the Dark.*

6. *Support essential learning with or without glasses.* If it is important that a child learn a particular thing, such as safety rules, make sure the child can learn it with or without glasses. Don't fall into the trap of saying, "I'll bet you can see much better since you got your glasses." A child who doesn't want to wear glasses will probably respond, "No, I can't," even when you are sure he can. Sometimes, reality is irrelevant.

IN THE FIELD

I know I must have seemed like a witch to the teachers, but it got to me. I got his eyes tested like they said and he needed glasses. I got the first pair. The kids called him "Four Eyes." The glasses were lost in a week.

Some children willingly wear glasses because they can see better and they prevent headaches. Other children are reluctant to wear them.
©Cengage Learning 2012

They sent letters home. I got another pair, not as pretty, but it was all I could afford. He lost them on the way to school. I bought another pair and they were broken on the playground in two days. I can't afford to get him any more glasses until the beginning of the month. They don't even need him to come with me anymore to have them fitted; they know his size. All I have to do is pay but I'm all out of money. And I'm all out of patience. I know what my responsibility is in this: I pay. But what is the teachers' responsibility?

● ● ●
Uncorrected Visual Impairments

Some children with uncorrected visual impairments will have limited vision, whereas others will have little or no usable vision.

CHILDREN WITH LOW OR LIMITED VISION

Children who have low or limited vision need accommodations. Fostering visual skills means encouraging children to use their vision in a way most advantageous to them. Remember, children will not hurt their eyes through use.

1. *Teach children visual discrimination within their ability to see.* Start with gross discrimination paired with tactile reinforcement, then progress to finer distinctions. Some children may miss details, so help them make better guesses about what is missing.

2. *Regulate light levels.* This helps some children compensate for reduced vision. Be aware of lighting conditions and sources of light. Use shades or Venetian blinds to regulate the amount of natural light in your room. (Ideally, illumination should be between 70 and 100 **foot-candles**, the units of measurement used to calculate adequate lighting levels of schools and workspaces. Light switches with dimmers can be helpful if the classroom has this capability. Do not stand or sit with your

back to the light source or in outside doorways; there is too much contrast between the bright light of outside and your figure.

3. *Arrange seating to favor the lighting conditions.* (Check the specialist's report. For some children, maximum illumination is best, and for others lower-than-normal levels are optimal.) Some children use tinted lenses to reduce glare.

4. Use matte or flat finishes and nonglare glass or contact paper on framed pictures.

5. Choose light-colored tables (or dishes) with a dull finish. Glare is fatiguing.

6. *Change or improve color contrast.* Where possible, paint the rims of bookcases, tables, and doorframes with a lighter or darker color that will make the edges easier to see. Use a dark light switch against light-colored walls so it will stand out.

7. *Mark boundaries.* Use a heavy black marking pen to outline the boundaries of the paper so that the child knows where the edges are.

8. *Provide clear, simple pictures and large-print books.* Look at the books you have in your reading area to ensure accessibility for all children.

9. *Use materials with distinctive shapes and textures.* Use bright, high-contrast colors.

10. *Keep the general noise level down.* A child with low visual ability relies on auditory cues, and these will be masked by noise.

11. *Avoid excessive detail on bulletin boards.* Be aware of the child's vision when you display the children's work. Hang all children's work at their eye level so that they can see it displayed and can point it out to others.

12. *Use auditory and tactile cues to reinforce children's behavior.* Do you rely on smiles, gestures, body cues, and eye contact to reinforce behavior? These are visual cues. With children who have partial sight, you need to talk and touch for reinforcement in addition to using visual cues. You may need to draw attention to the visual cues with words and gestures.

13. *Enlarge images and objects.* Print information large. Regularly use different types of magnifiers.

IN THE FIELD

As a teacher, I have worked with children who have had a variety of challenges. I remember one child, Lucas, who was being raised by his great-grandparents. Lucas had multiple medical challenges when he was born. As a result, the family had difficulty meeting his medical needs. The family frequently missed medical appointments and there were concerns that he was being neglected. Lucas was taken away from his mother and placed in the custody of his father's grandmother when he was 2 years old.

Lucas has a degenerative eye disease, a kidney disorder, and many dietary restrictions. When I had Lucas in my class, his eyesight had deteriorated to the point that he was legally blind. His kidney disorder was relatively under control.

Lucas has to live with his medical conditions and has learned skills to cope with them. However, each time he visited his mother and siblings for the weekend, Monday was a nightmare for him and me. I learned to give Lucas time to talk about what happened and how it made him feel, and spent one-on-one time playing with him during center time. Generally, Lucas was not able to choose or attend to any activity during center time unless an adult was with him. He complained that no one liked him or wanted to play with him, and he became easily frustrated whenever he encountered difficulty in his play.

Lucas's difficulty seeing caused him to misinterpret the actions and intentions of his peers, resulting in many conflicts. It was difficult to explain to Lucas that he did not see what happened correctly. He was very strong-willed and refused to listen when I tried to help him to solve a conflict. What finally worked was to remove him from the situation until he calmed down, explain what happened, and then have each child talk to the other, using teacher scripts to solve the problem.

When Lucas had difficulty telling another child what he wanted, I would provide words for him to use, then he would repeat them to the child, for example, "Lucas, tell him that you would like to have a turn when he is done."

In addition to having difficulty with his peers, Lucas's vision provided challenges with the setup of the classroom space. Lucas was unaware that he had difficulty seeing. In fact, he frequently ran in the room. This usually ended with him tripping or knocking down furniture or even me. I had to be sure there were large spaces between centers for him to maneuver around.

Finding accommodations for activities was challenging because I had to make sure Lucas could see what I was planning for the class. Some of the things I did were to enlarge the print on the copy machine, use bigger objects, give him verbal cues when completing a task, and pair him with a partner to be his eyes. I also incorporated a lot of multisensory activities into my themes.

CHILDREN WITH LITTLE OR NO VISION

Children who have very little or no usable vision need additional accommodations. The following guidelines will help you support children who have little or no usable vision in the classroom. Obviously, the less vision the child has, the more you will need to adapt and stabilize the classroom environment.

1. *Eliminate clutter and confusion.* A well-arranged classroom helps all children, but especially those with severe visual impairments. Keep things neat and make sure that toys are picked up as soon as children are finished with them. Be sure that chairs are pushed under the tables. Eliminate unnecessary obstacles in the classroom. Be aware of protruding objects such as puzzles or blocks that have been placed on a shelf but still stick out. Rearrange these so they no longer protrude. Consolidate items where possible. (Have one large wastebasket rather than many small ones.) Keep doors fully open or completely shut. Even children with excellent vision tend to run into partly opened doors. Round tables are safer than rectangular ones because there are no corners to bump into. If rectangular ones are all you have, pad sharp edges with foam. If you are a person who likes to arrange and then rearrange your classroom, don't! It takes a while for children to establish permanent reference points and feel comfortable in a room. If possible, give children with visual disabilities a chance to become acquainted with the arrangement of the room before other children come in, by having

them visit the classroom before school starts or in the evening when other children are not present. Verbally describe the classroom and spatial relationships as the child explores. Then ask for specific feedback: "Can you show me where the puzzles are?" Don't assume that just because you told the child and he had time for free exploration that he will understand and remember. Use auditory, olfactory, and tactile cues to structure the room. The bubbling of an aquarium might identify the science area; a rug could mark the story area provided it is firmly attached to the floor; wind chimes could indicate that the outside door is open; and so on.

2. *Encourage independence.* When you assign lockers or coat hooks, give this child one that is easy to locate, perhaps one on the end, out of the traffic pattern. Don't move objects around after the child has placed them without telling the child. Moving something 2 inches may mean that it is "gone" if a child can't visually scan the area.

3. *Label materials with raised letters.* Use a label maker to put raised labels on materials where possible or use Braille. It is more important to label favorite toys with something easy to find than to make a descriptive label. (A puzzle of different types of fruit might have just the raised letter *F* on it rather than the entire title or label in Braille.) Make sure materials are put away so that the label is facing out. With older children, use rubber bands as labels on round objects. Put one rubber band on the red paint, two on the blue, and three on the yellow. This helps children with color deficiencies also. Using rubber bands with children under age 3 is not safe, as they might swallow them.

4. *Use props children can feel.* Be careful not to give children unnecessary special treatment. Before you give a child help you would not give others, ask whether it is needed. Offer help, but don't take over or allow other children to do the task for a child with visual impairments. Teach other children in the class how to offer help as well.

5. *Adapt your teaching techniques.* Identify yourself when you enter a room or area, especially if the child is alone. Tell the child specifically where you are: "I'm standing behind your chair." Encourage the other children to do the same. Also make it clear when you leave, especially if you are wearing soft-soled shoes. Use children's names during group time and when they are playing in small groups. Teach children in the group to do this as well. Have you ever talked on the telephone to an unidentified person who assumes you know whom you're talking to? It's disconcerting until you identify the person. It is important for a child with visual limitations to know who is present, especially at the beginning of the year. Use auditory cues—a short tune, a chord on the piano, or a song—to signal regular activities, such as cleanup time. Be consistent in using

the signals, so the child learns to associate the activities and cues. Help with an ongoing monologue about what is happening during an activity. If the class is making cookies, say, "Tanika has finished sifting the flour, and now Harry is going to beat the batter." Include children by asking, " Jesusa, what are you doing now?" This helps the child learn to identify sounds and encourages all children to participate in the experience.

6. *Keep your voice within normal limits.* (Some assume that those who don't see well also don't hear well.) Give careful attention to the tone of your voice. Talk directly to a child, not about her. Don't ask Maria's father if she wants to play in the block area; ask her. (Her father may answer, but that is a different problem.) Don't eliminate the words "see" and "look" from your vocabulary—use them when they are appropriate. Make directions clear and concise. Use characteristics that can be felt, heard, or counted rather than seen.

7. *Address the child by name.* Before giving instructions, identify the child and make sure that the instructions you give really help. "It is right over there" is not enough. You have to name places and specify ways of doing things. It helps if the child knows right from left. If not, have the child wear something (e.g., rings, bracelet, watch, ribbon) on one hand or arm so that you can say, "Reach up with the hand with the bracelet on it."

8. *Teach directions.* Teach children the concepts of left and right early. Use the word "correct" when something is accurate, not "right," as this is confusing. Older children use the image of a clock for location. Use this image to identify where items are located: "The cup is at 2 o'clock." This is also useful when children are sitting in a circle. If the child knows that the teacher is at 12 o'clock and the child is at 3 o'clock, it is useful to say, "Jason is sitting at 6 o'clock." However, in early childhood children are just learning to tell time and most of them are far more familiar with digital displays than a traditional clock.

9. *Walk slightly in front of the child.* When walking with a child who has very limited vision, walk in front, never behind the child. If you walk alongside, let the child hold your arm or wrist; don't hold the child's. This allows a greater sense of the movement of your body, especially when you turn or go up or down steps. As you walk, be sure to describe what you are passing: "Now we're going by the swings. Can you hear Terry and Bahira talking while they swing?"

10. *Provide many opportunities to ask questions.* Because children don't see objects to say, "What is that?" they ask questions less frequently. If adults always anticipate their needs, they don't have the opportunity to ask questions and may not gain this skill.

11. *Give accurate feedback.* If a child is not able to evaluate her own work, she is dependent on you for this information. If feedback is always positive, the child will

not have an incentive to improve and may build a false sense of confidence.

12. *Increase other children's awareness.* Include a unit on feelings and emotions, and openly talk about taunting and teasing. At first, you may have to lead the discussion and state some typical reactions, but you should gradually help children to speak up. Perhaps a session on assertiveness training will help.

Curriculum Adaptations

The amount of functional vision a child has will determine what, if any, curriculum modifications have to be made. The less vision the child has, the more the auditory and tactile channels must be used. The use of any residual vision is encouraged.

Social Awareness

All children need to be part of the group and learn about the strengths and needs of others. As adults, we are familiar with aids to vision such as glasses; younger children are not as familiar, and they need to learn. Personal worth and adequacy is a fundamental need for all children. Self-esteem is a personal judgment of worthiness that children feel about themselves; it is shaped by self-perception and the perception of others. Some of the activities in Resource Chapter 1 are specifically designed to increase children's awareness of visual impairments. Activity 1–26, *Eye Doctor*; Activity 1–39w, *Simulated Glasses*; and Activity 1–41w, *Moving in the Dark*, increase awareness.

Social Competence

Children with limited vision tend to develop body awareness more slowly because of lack of confidence and having fewer examples to emulate. Visual memory is the basis for such things as pretend play. If children do not have visual memory, alternative ways of developing memory need to be explored. A child may learn words without having a clear understanding of their social significance. Many social skills are learned through observation. If a child cannot see others, he may need to be taught skills other children learn from observation.

1. Provide role models who wear glasses and use optical devices. Children need to use the correctable vision they have and to learn the skills to explain to others why these particular devices help them. Look around your classroom and be sure the pictures include children with visual impairments and visual aids.

2. Address problems such as making faces that are socially unpleasant. These faces offend both children and adults and may be followed by teasing and name-calling. Describe it: "When you move your tongue like that, you look unpleasant (or silly). Do you want to look silly now? If not, please put your tongue back in your mouth."

3. Reinforce children when their face is more expressive and tell them, "I like it when your face is turned toward me when I speak to you."

4. Help children label their body parts. Use exercises and songs in naming body parts, and discuss the ways these parts move. Hold the child's hands in your own as you point and demonstrate, but tell the child what you are going to do before you do it.

5. Teach children the vocabulary to explain how they feel as well as how to use auditory cues to understand others' emotions.

6. Encourage children to explore a variety of methods of moving from place to place. Have them talk about when they could use these different methods. They need to become more aware of their bodies in relation to their surroundings.

7. Give children time and opportunity to develop confidence and positive self-esteem by learning age-appropriate adaptive skills. This is an important part of group acceptance and motivates further exploration.

8. Provide an environment of acceptance and experimentation that will build children's self-confidence.

Your expectations of a child with a visual impairment will set the tone for the class. If you do not require the child to clean up, or if you are apprehensive or overprotective, the other children will quickly pick this up.

1. Teach children to identify themselves when they begin a conversation; otherwise, the child's energy is spent on figuring out who the speaker is rather than what that person is saying.

2. Explain to other children the impact of having limited vision; sometimes, children do not approach children with visual impairments because they seem unresponsive and lack curiosity.

3. Encourage children to invite a child with low vision to play by suggesting or bringing specific toys and materials for both of them to use.

4. Help children find acceptable ways to learn about their environment through their tactile/kinesthetic senses, especially ways to touch their classmates and adults. See Activity 1–11, *Who Is It?*

5. Support children in pretending they have different visual impairments and give them specific tasks to do (e.g., go to specific places in the room, find particular objects, write their name, eat a snack). See Activity 1–39w, *Simulated Glasses*. Discuss with children how this felt and how they could make it easier. If teasing is an issue, bring it up.

Social Studies

All children need to learn about the world around them, and field trips are an effective way to accomplish this. Children with visual impairments can use many hands-on experiences to make accurate generalizations. Even children who have fully corrected vision have spent some portion of their life without optimal vision. (If corrective lenses were worn at age 3 and the child is 6, that is *half* of the child's lifetime.)

1. Plan field trips with small groups of children so that each of them can participate in the experience. It isn't enough just to see a cow, especially if the child can't see

it well. The child has to feel it and feel enough of it to form an accurate perception of a cow.

2. Provide follow-up activities with stories and dramatic play after field trips. Have the children describe with all their senses what they remember. Drink milk, smell and handle hay, make farm sounds, and sing farm songs.

3. Differentiate between the representation and the real thing when naming objects for a child: "We saw a real cow on the field trip. This is a toy cow. How are they different?"

4. Expand children's social world through tapes, CDs, DVDs, and videos. Children may be more sensitive to auditory signals than visual ones. These resources must be linked to meaningful experiences if they are to expand the child's knowledge base.

5. Help children become aware of the role the medical profession plays in assessing visual acuity and prescribing corrective lenses. This can be done with a field trip or a visit from an eye doctor followed up with dramatic play. See Activity 1–26, *Eye Doctor*.

6. Invite a person with a visual impairment who would be comfortable with the children, to visit. (A seeing eye dog always makes an impression and provides an important learning experience.)

English Language Arts

The area of language and literacy is challenging yet essential for children with visual impairments. Language is their major source of acquiring knowledge, of "seeing" the world, and of communicating with others. Children with visual impairments usually depend on verbal skills to communicate and listening skills to learn about their environment. If they can't find a needed object, they may ask others. They need practice in giving and following directions with children and adults. They are more dependent on auditory cues and auditory memory. Children who have visual losses miss some of the nonverbal qualities of attending and eye contact. They need help focusing on intonation patterns, volume, and speed of language for additional cues. They require an individualized literacy program. Encourage children to refine the visual skills they use.

Speaking and Listening

Children with visual impairments rely more on auditory cues to learn speech, whereas other children can more easily see and imitate movements of the lips, mouth, and jaw. Encourage children to ask what things are and help them to broaden their understanding of labels used. Encouraging feedback from the children about their perceptions will enable you to clarify misunderstandings and foster increased verbalization.

1. Following verbal directions is an important language skill. Start with simple one- or two-step directions. Remember to keep them concrete.

2. Talking to themselves is normal for all children. Children with visual impairments may also talk to imaginary friends. This is fine, unless they become more interested in imaginary friends than real ones.

3. Write down fingerplays and send them home. Teach the parents the fingerplays so that the children can practice them at home or while traveling. (If you don't demonstrate the fingerplay, you can get some amazing variations.)

Children who have visual impairments have a greater need for understanding speech because they are dependent on verbal information to perform certain tasks. Even children with corrected vision problems do not always wear their glasses. It is important that they learn to identify and discriminate among sounds. Help children develop skills in this area through differentiating similar sounds and listening to tapes or CDs. Sometimes children who are visually impaired tune out language because it is based on what others have seen and it makes no sense to them.

1. Encourage children to look at the speaker's face by saying, "Please look at me (or Logan)." Give them an opportunity to respond. If they don't, say, "I'll help by turning your head so it faces me. People like it when you look at them when they are speaking." Then gently turn it.

2. Play listening games that help children locate sounds. Make a sound and see whether the child can locate the source of the sound. Once the source is located, the child needs to feel the object that makes the sound and tell how it is used.

3. Have children match sounds by placing objects in pairs of small containers (with taped lids) and shaking them.

4. Teach fine auditory discrimination by describing and explaining what children hear but cannot see. Use this as a game (describe noises and their implications and have the children guess the source from your description). Use an activity such as 2–38w, *Sound Cues*.

5. Use tapes and CDs of stories and music for classifying sounds (e.g., long, short, high, low) and for identifying who or what might make that sound and in what situation.

6. Give children replicas of what you are talking about if possible. Don't worry about size relationships at this point—you can describe those verbally—but clearly identify the object as a toy so children know it is not the real thing.

7. Demonstrate, where possible, the meaning of the words *where*, *why*, and *what*. If possible, take the child to a location, or let the child feel "what" is making the sound.

Reading

Books can expand the children's world, provided you start with themes children are familiar with. It is preferable to use pictures that illustrate the story's major points in a simple way. Point out to children the relationship of the picture to the story. Create a need to see within their ability to discriminate. In the area of reading literacy, one emphasis is on developing and refining visual discrimination skills.

1. Pass around small replicas of the major objects (e.g., rabbits, carrots, trains) for the children to look at and feel as you read books. Do the same with textures and smells.

2. Use cassette tapes or CDs of books at a listening center. These allow more individualization and choice in the books available. Make your own recordings of favorite books, and bring in blank cassettes so children can dictate their own books.

3. Have books with large type and in Braille. Even if no child requires Braille, it broadens the range of experience and understanding to develop the idea that Braille is a form of writing. Sometimes refer to books on tape or CD as "talking books" or audio books to expand children's ideas about books.

4. Start with large objects that have gross distinctions. Simple shapes are fine, such as circles, triangles, and squares. Encourage children not only to label and distinguish among shapes but also to point out salient characteristics (a circle doesn't have any corners; a triangle has three). Have children trace the shapes with their index and third fingers to gain a kinesthetic as well as a visual sense of these distinctions.

5. Work on finer details once children can make gross distinctions. When you teach these, try to point out significant features. Use large wooden letters and have the children trace them with their index and third fingers. Teach them that *A* has straight lines, *O* has curved lines, and *P* has straight and curved lines. Teach by contrasting *A, O,* and *P,* and use other contrasting groups of shapes before you have the children differentiate among letters such as *N, M,* and *W,* for example, which have only straight lines. Help children fine-tune tactile skills, and introduce Braille to children who will be using it.

6. Help children with low vision to combine their usable vision with tactile skills to develop reading readiness. If the amount of usable vision decreases, the need for more tactile discrimination will increase because this is a pre-Braille skill. Among the things that can be used to help children develop these skills are sandpaper letters, texture cards (for matching), and writing in sand. See Activity 2–54w, *Sand Printing.*

7. Use the computer, overhead projector or copier to increase the contrast and size of print children are exposed to.

8. Increase print awareness by helping them feel and identify the different parts of books.

9. Show children different written languages (e.g., Spanish, Chinese, and Russian), including Braille, and discuss how children learn to read using different written representations.

10. Read books about children who have visual impairments. (See the Children's Bibliography for suggestions.)

Writing

All children need to develop the link between the ability to speak a word and the ability to write it so others can understand. The form this takes depends on the child.

1. Choose wide black markers for children who are partially sighted, so they can easily see what they are marking.

2. Employ media with more tactile feedback if the child cannot use vision. Start without tools. Have children air write. Encourage them to hold their two writing fingers together (the index finger and third finger of their dominant hand), then, using their whole arm, write letters in the air. (This gives them body feedback.)

3. Provide children with wooden or sandpaper letters they can trace with two fingers, and use auditory cues to support the visual or tactile experience.

4. Use writing media that have different tactile properties. Have children "write" in sand in a jelly roll pan and mark clay that has been rolled flat or, using their fingers, "write" on black felt on which you have taped white lines (narrow masking tape is fine).

5. As children get older, they will probably use a computer or word processor for written work. Provide children with experiences for learning the position of letters on the keyboard; if necessary, use a Braille keyboard. A speech synthesizer and appropriate software provide children with auditory feedback about their keystrokes. See Activity 3–64w, *Alphabet Keyboard* for more ideas.

6. Putting pegs in a pegboard systematically is a good pre-Braille activity. First, allow a child to explore the entire pegboard by feeling the holes. Then, cover with tape or cardboard all except the lines you want the child to use. If it is a horizontal line, have the child move from left to right, if vertical, top to bottom. Children who are right-handed should use the index finger of their left hand as a guide to find the hole, and the right hand to place the peg into the hole. Then they find the next hole with their index finger and continue. Work to the point that children can copy adult patterns.

Language

Learning the conventions of standard English grammar and usage is challenging for all children. Building an accurate and large vocabulary to express needs and understand the world can be daunting. Work from the concrete to the abstract, simple to complex, and build analogies that children can work from.

1. Use words in context so children with low vision have additional cues. Literature often does this well.

2. Use language to help children focus their vision as well as to get feedback: "Can you see that wheel? Do you see what's inside the wheel? Those are spokes. Can you count them by touching each one?"

3. Use words that refer to things that can be smelled, touched, heard, seen, tasted, or experienced directly. Try to make the words you use as concrete as possible, using real examples whenever you can. Then move on to more abstract language concepts such as *time*, *friendship*, and so on.

4. Use functional definitions of objects as well as descriptive ones. "A ball rolls" or "a ball bounces" should be used in addition to the definition "a ball is round." Reinforce the concept by letting the child roll and bounce the ball.

5. Help children learn to follow important verbal directions. Teach and model useful words like *stop/go*, *high/low*, *big/little*, *in/out/on*, and *hard/soft*. Other important spatial terms include *side by side*, *back to back*, *full turn*, *half turn*, *quarter turn*, *top/bottom*, *in front of*, and so on. Games like "Simon Says," "May I," "Hokey Pokey," and "Follow the Leader" work well for teaching directions.

Discovery

Discovery experiences need to start with the familiar and concrete and work toward the less familiar and more abstract. Start with natural situations and real objects that are meaningful to the children: two socks and two shoes, one coat with two arms, and so on. Help children feel round balls and square boxes. Use sandpaper outlines of circles and squares. Help children pace off and count distances to and from various places in the room: 5 steps from the locker to the circle area, compared with 10 steps from the locker to the blocks. Provide additional time for children to touch the equipment and materials. Be sure to include equipment that magnifies. Computer literacy is an excellent long-term resource for children. Computers can be designed to have large print, speech, or Braille output. Computers with a voice synthesizer are extremely useful. Learning to make predictions about what will happen under a specified set of circumstances is important as a way of developing independence and creating a sense of predictability in the world.

Mathematics

Number concepts are necessary for all children. The fun is in using them creatively to help children explore and classify their world. For children with low vision, the tactile-motor aspect of learning these concepts can be added with a few modifications.

1. Teach children to tactilely discriminate and match materials of various shapes, sizes, and weights. Have children sort matching buttons into ice cube trays.

2. Start with real objects when teaching number concepts and geometric shapes,. Food works well. Everyone gets *1* glass of milk, *2* pieces of fruit, *10* raisins, and so on. An abacus is also useful for counting. One can both see and feel the placement of the beads and check back if necessary. Encourage children to count.

3. Play dominoes. Matching large dominoes with indented dots is a good activity that teaches fine motor skills as well as number concepts.

4. Have children use their bodies and other devices to measure. Record these measurements. Special modifications should be made to help children with low vision understand distances: an arm's length, two paces, three hand spans. Glue pieces of string on paper or use glue lines to make graphs that can be felt (see Activity 3–43w, *Measuring Tools*).

5. Use physical boundaries to delimit the block area, and put the blocks in a tub so the child can locate them easily. Start with individual block building and then encourage children to work in pairs or small groups.

6. Teach children about patterns and relationships by using a variety of repeating tactile patterns (rough, smooth, rough, smooth; rough, rough, smooth, smooth, etc.).

7. Provide children with many experiences matching, sorting, categorizing, sequencing, and patterning with a wide variety of materials.

Science

Science helps children learn about vision and the other senses, as well as the natural world. Emphasize creative problem solving, decision making, and discovery.

1. Help children learn about the eye and how it works. Get a model of the eye, and use the concept of a camera to help children understand vision.

2. Talk about the purpose of lenses. Have a variety of magnifying glasses and binoculars available in the science area. Talk about the difference in the amount of detail that can be seen with the naked eye and with magnification.

3. Have children participate in experiences in which materials change form, such as by whipping cream or melting ice. Let children with low vision feel the changes as well.

4. Discuss the weather and appropriate dress for different types of weather. Talk about and feel fabrics used in warm- versus cold-weather clothing. Experiment with materials designed for specific uses (e.g., rain, sun, cold).

5. Help children develop thermic (temperature) and baric (weight) sensitivity by sequencing and matching plastic bottles full of water of differing temperatures and containers of varying weights.

6. Use the senses to help children identify pleasant and unpleasant tastes and smells. These are important cues. Some smells might mean that something is going bad (like sour milk); some provide environmental information (e.g., damp earth means it rained recently); some are clues to locations (e.g., flowers are in a garden); and so on. Other smells indicate whether something or someone is clean or dirty, such as smells

of clothing and babies. Children can refine these senses by matching cinnamon, cloves, basil, nutmeg, ginger in small plastic containers and tasting a variety of foods.

Technology

Initially, computers may be difficult for young children with visual impairments because so much of computing is visual. For children with enough vision to see the keyboard and the monitor, the problems are few. Most adults with visual impairments have learned touch-typing and to use a keypad. This learning begins when children are young.

1. Use a voice synthesizer with the computer.
2. Use a flat screen 25-inch monitor so the letters displayed on the screen are large. Programs are also available that enlarge the type on the screen. It may be easier to read a video screen than a piece of paper because the light source is coming from the back of the screen and is not reflected light.
3. Computers allow us to change text and background colors. Some children with partial sight do better with certain color combinations. Find the best combination.

Children need many experiences with adaptive skills to perfect them.
© Cengage Learning 2012

4. Experiment with digital cameras and the contrast used in printing pictures to enhance visual discrimination.
5. Experiment with electronic media such as electronic tablets and the available apps to make it a learning tool for children with visual impairments.
6. Expose all children to a GPS and point out how it helps us know where we are. There are specific apps for some technology for people with visual impairments.

Wellness

Children with limited vision may face health and safety issues other children do not. Be aware of the environment and the feedback it potentially provides children. Try to increase the auditory and kinesthetic information available.

Although vision may be limited, the coordination of hearing and tactile/kinesthetic senses provides an avenue of learning combined with available vision. Children with visual impairments are dependent on motor skills and also have more limited opportunities to practice them. They need to learn where they are and to develop safe ways of moving through unknown spaces. This requires sensory motor integration. Children who lack the visual aspect of sensory integration need to learn ways of compensating for, as well as refining, their residual vision. The refinement of fine motor skills will aid Braille reading (if needed). Body awareness and motor planning are an integral part of orientation and mobility training. Children with limited vision need encouragement and a safe place to practice developing skills. Outdoor activities may be a challenge. With temperature changes, glasses sometimes fog up, so have tissues handy to wipe them off. For children with low vision, watch for safety concerns. Be sure that paths for moving vehicles are well delineated and that there is a boundary around swings, seesaws, and other moving equipment so that children cannot accidentally walk into them.

Health and Safety

Health and safety is an important and difficult area of learning for all young children. It requires them to consciously inhibit their spontaneous curiosity and think through the implications of actions *before* doing them. For children with low vision, the possibility of falling or bumping into things or stooping over and hitting something is greater than for other children, yet the price of overprotection is great also. Greater coordination problems exist when learning skills because children are more dependent on tactile and auditory cues for learning than on visual ones. They need to use their residual vision and hearing to compensate.

1. Help all children develop independence in adaptive (self-help) skills. Use buttoning, lacing, and snapping frames to teach these skills. Montessori materials are excellent, but you can make your own fairly easily. Keep soap, paper towels, and the wastebasket in the same places and at a level the child can reach.

2. Teach safety, looking, and listening skills. Make sure children can identify such sounds as cars, sirens, and fire alarms and know what to do when they hear these sounds.

3. Teach children to do deep knee bends as a way of getting down to pick things up. It is especially important when they lift heavy objects, and it decreases bumped heads.

4. Have children who wear eyeglasses use a safety strap to keep their glasses from falling off when playing actively.

5. Fence in the swings, seesaws, and any other heavy moving equipment. Keep tricycles, bicycles, and wagons on specified paths. Add bells to moving objects (e.g., tricycles, wagons, even balls) and encourage children to use them appropriately.

6. Teach children with limited vision to use their sense of touch to determine whether they have rashes or cuts or to tell whether their hands are clean.

Physical Education

Using the large muscles of the body is one way for children to increase their knowledge of their own bodies, as well as a way to explore their environment. Children who have recently had visual correction and those with low vision will probably have less refined skills in this area than their age-mates. They may need encouragement as well as practice.

1. Balancing "tricks" are especially useful. Start with static balance: The child stands or sits still and balances a particular object. (Beanbags are easier to start with than books.) For dynamic balance, have the child walk, jump, or crawl while balancing an object on her head or other body part. As the child becomes more skillful, see how long or how far the child can balance objects. Have children walk on a balance board or beam. See Activity 4-29, *Variations on Balancing*.

2. Have children participate in relay races where they run, walk, jump, hop, or skip while holding a partner's hand to develop both large motor skills and cooperation with peers.

3. Walking between the rungs of a ladder placed flat on the ground or floor helps children establish spacing, and they learn to realize whether they are walking in a straight line. Spot children so they don't fall.

4. Encourage children to do motor tasks blindfolded (use half-face Halloween masks and cover the eye openings), and talk about the implications of not being able to see. See Activity 1–41w, *Moving in the Dark* to make it a learning experience for all children.

5. If children are having trouble conceptualizing a particular movement, have them feel the outline of an adult's body (or that of a willing peer) before they do a movement. An adult may need to help children position their bodies until they get the feel of the movement.

Sensory Motor Integration

The development and refinement of fine motor skills and eye–hand coordination requires practice. Start with experiences that are likely to be successful so that children do not get discouraged. Success is especially important for those who are just learning to use corrective visual aids. They may tell you they can do it better without the aids, and if they have learned good compensatory skills, they may be right!

1. Use fit-in puzzles (those with large pieces that go into specific places) and knob puzzles for children who are just beginning to use puzzles.

2. Use three-dimensional building toys that interlock in some way, so they won't fall apart when bumped. Encourage children to start with larger pieces and work toward using the smaller ones. Keep the pieces in a tray so that children can keep track of them.

3. Allow a child to both feel and see the outline of the images by using sewing cards with large holes around the perimeter of the image. You can easily make these cards by pasting pictures on cardboard, then using a hole punch.

4. Teach children to discriminate among textures. Begin with pleasant-feeling textures such as satin and velvet. Then move on to fleece, cotton, and so on. These fabrics can also be used for texture-matching games. Try different grades of sandpaper, which the children can try to arrange in order of fineness.

If children do not have accurate visual feedback, they need to develop a motor memory for moving their bodies through space.

1. Teach children to crawl over, under, and through different-sized obstacles, using an obstacle course to teach spatial orientation. You might start a human obstacle course, where the "course" itself can provide help and support.

2. Emphasize tactile-motor and auditory-motor activities.

3. Be aware that children's vision may vary from day to day. Children who are anxious or tired may not have as much ability to focus their vision as they do when they are relaxed and rested.

Creative Arts

Creative arts provide children with the opportunity to explore their world in a safe way. They can gain experiences inside the classroom that can prepare them for what will happen outside. Children with visual impairments may need obvious boundaries for work on paper, such as a thick, black line marking the outside of the paper or a larger, high-contrast piece of paper underneath the paper being worked on. As long as the emphasis is on process, there are few limitations on what children can do. It is often useful to add textured materials to paint and playdough. Three-dimensional materials such as clay and playdough are particularly good because the children can feel the results.

Music can be used to enhance listening skills and auditory discrimination. Moving to music is an excellent way to acquire body awareness, but be sure to have an area without physical obstacles. Give children boundaries they can trust, such as adults who can cue them if their movements are too large. Movement and dance support orientation and mobility skills. Children with limited vision must learn a variety of ways of moving safely. Have children move with partners. Use music to help them localize sound and distinguish one voice from another. Let them feel vibrations of instruments and voices. Sound will be vital in the life of these children, so use music to train their hearing.

Children with visual impairments profit from acting out situations, using realistic props. Be sure to keep the props in the same place so they are easy to find.

Visual Arts

Although children with little residual vision face limitations in some areas of art, there are many highly tactile materials that allow a great deal of manipulation. The potential that visual art activities and materials offer for the release of emotions makes them doubly valuable experiences for all children with visual impairments.

1. Use a variety of modeling materials to provide different tactile experiences. Among the most popular materials are playdough (made of salt and flour), clay (use the powdered type and let the children help mix it), cornstarch, papier-mâché, and plastic-coated wire.

2. Have children fingerpaint right on the table if they are using actual fingerpaint. You can then print the picture when a child makes one he wants to keep. Fingerpainting to music is a good variation.

3. Add textured materials such as sand or sawdust to easel paint and finger paint. Make the paint thicker so that it can be more easily felt and controlled.

4. Make textured boundaries for work areas. (This is a good idea for any child who tends to use too much space.) Use masking tape to divide the table into areas, depending on your needs. Use placemats to define each child's space.

5. Cover the easel with dark construction paper if you are using white paper so that the child can easily see where the paper ends. If the child cannot see, use a textured material for the board, such as coarse sandpaper or cork, so the child can feel the boundaries.

6. Use thick, dark marking pens to print names on papers and remember to *print big* for all children to help them recognize their name and the names of others.

7. Hang all children's artwork in a place where they can find it easily, see it, and point it out to others. Hang the work of children with visual impairments near the beginning or end of a row so they can locate it easily.

8. Make a texture collage with a specific theme; for example, for *nature*, use feathers, pine needles, leaves, and grass.

9. Tape paper to the table so it stays in one place.

Music

Music is often a particularly enjoyable activity for children with low vision, and with the number of famous musicians who are visually impaired (such as Ray Charles, Stevie Wonder, and Joaquin Rodrigo), it is not difficult to find encouragement to do well. However, don't assume that children with visual impairments will automatically be good at music. Music study develops finer auditory discrimination and facilitates the development of memory skills.

1. Play an instrument or ring a bell and have the children (who have their backs to you and eyes closed) guess what area of the room you are in. A variation of this is to have them search for a ticking kitchen timer or music box.

2. Teach the concepts of *high* and *low* with music pitch games. Have children practice using *loud* and *soft* volume as cues to distance (e.g., for finding a hidden object). *Fast* and *slow* are also easily taught through musical games: The faster the music, the closer the child is to the hidden object.

3. Use songs that have motions teach names, actions, and labels. Extra time, however, must be devoted (at school or home) to teaching children with low vision the motions that go with songs.

4. Sing songs that promote body awareness and songs that describe what children are doing: "This is the way we put on our boots/climb the stairs/ride our bikes" and so on. Adapt and make up songs to fit your needs.

5. Use a variety of musical instruments and give children time to experiment with them.

6. Have children move around the room while music is being played. When the music stops, the child has to follow the teacher's directions: "Make yourself into a ball"; "Make yourself as tall (or as short) as you can"; "Be as still as you can."

Movement and Dance

Combining movement and an idea helps children learn abstract concepts. It is also a way of finding out about a child's concepts of the world. If you ask children to be leaves blowing in the wind, you will see their interpretation of what this is like. It can serve as the foundation for future planning.

1. Start with ideas that are simple and familiar to children, and provide props that support these ideas, but do not dictate how an activity is done. Talk about being a group marching in a parade and play music to march by.

2. Verbally discuss *how* children should move and give clear, precise details about the event the children are portraying. Using the example of leaves, ask children what would make the leaves fall, then talk about how they would move in response to falling off the tree versus being blown by a strong wind.

3. Talk about personal space and how to figure out where they can move without bumping into each other.

4. Provide props such as scarves or hats to make experiences more concrete. Props help set the stage for children who cannot see well. They can expand on an idea that has been established.

5. Moving creatively to music encourages a variety of movements and gracefulness, and there is no right or wrong way. Dancing—from the waltz, to the twist, to the Macarena—is good exercise and great for developing coordination and feeling a mood.

6. Having a dance party on a regular basis helps children participate in a safe and physically active way with others.

••• Dramatic Play and Theater

Dramatic play allows children to learn about, experience, and control situations. They can make new experiences more familiar by playing through them first. Working through potentially frightening experiences may make them easier to handle.

1. Provide a lot of props. Be sure that at least some of them give obvious cues (tactile as well as visual) about the activity going on. For example, teacups and saucers mean a tea party; adding a teapot and appropriate clothing sets the mood.

2. Check to be sure there are no dangling belts or scarves that could cause tripping when children dress up.

3. Set up an optometrist's office and have children test each other's vision. See Activity 1–26, *Eye Doctor*.

4. Be sure to include eyeglass frames as props for a variety of activities.

5. Writing a script and discussing roles helps children with visual impairments participate.

Routines and Transitions

Transition times are difficult for all children because a lot of movement and change occurs. Use routines to support IEP/IFSP goals.

1. Use sounds and nonvisual cues as one means of dismissal, for example, "Everyone with a shirt that buttons can get their coats." You can use types of clothing, fabrics, or the first letters of names.

2. Dismiss children with visual impairments either early or late, when there will be less confusion.

3. Allow enough time for children to use their adaptive skills. If children are slow or need more help, provide additional support.

SUMMARY

- The visual system is a complex one, and disease or injury to the system can cause visual impairments.
- Some standard screening tests are unlikely to identify children who are myopic, which is a concern because near-vision is necessary for reading and other close work.
- The degree of visual impairment determines the accommodations that are needed.

- Some activities must be modified to allow children with visual impairments to participate; other concerns relate to safety.
- Children with low vision need accommodations such as larger print or particular lighting.
- Children with little functional vision are dependent on auditory and tactile sources for learning.
- Many assistive devices are available to help children compensate for lack of vision.

EDUCATIONAL RESOURCES

American Council of the Blind (ACB) is the largest organization for people who are visually impaired. It has guidelines on how to make materials accessible. www.acb.org/

American Foundation for the Blind (AFB) serves as a clearinghouse for information on visual impairments. They have information on blindness, Braille, reviews of books, and links to laws, as well as information useful to professionals, parents, and children. www.afb.org/

American Printing House for the Blind (APH) is a resource for educational materials in large print and Braille. APH sells children's Braille books and manufactures and sells equipment and assistive devices. Their website is easy to navigate and has useful information for professionals, parents, and children. www.aph.org/

Lighthouse International is a comprehensive site for both visually impaired and blind resources that would be helpful to professionals, parents, and children. www.lighthouse.org/

National Association for Parents of the Visually Impaired (NAPVI) provides information to adults to support children with visual impairments. It has practical suggestions for teaching games and activities to young children and provides links to a variety of sites. www.spedex.com/napvi/

National Center to Improve Practice in Special Education through Technology, Media and Materials; Technology for Students who are Visually Impaired Collection lists resources that relate to visual impairments, including products, research, organizations, and publications. Products and resources were developed from 1992 to 1998. Some are still useful. www2.edc.org/NCIP/library/vi/toc.htm

National Library Service for the Blind and Physically Handicapped, Library of Congress provides talking and large print books for people with visual or physical impairments. All services and publications are free. The Kids Zone has books that start at preschool. www.loc.gov/nls/

National Braille Press is a nonprofit organization that produces Braille books for children. www.nbp.org/

Visually Impaired Preschool Services provides resources for families and also produced a series of videotapes, *Can Do Video Series*, about preschool children and their families. www.vips.org/

For additional resources, visit the book companion website for this text at www.cengagebrain.com.

III

Resources and Practice for Inclusive Early Childhood Education

Using the Resources

Although it is important to highlight each curriculum area individually, it is also important to integrate the curriculum to provide a context for learning. The impact of content and performance standards and cultural diversity has changed how all educators plan and carry out curriculum. Early childhood curriculum has moved from interesting activities to meeting state or professional standards by choosing goals and implementing activities that take into account the abilities, needs, strengths, likes, and dislikes of each child in the classroom. Although some children in your class will have disabilities, the curriculum will reflect the concepts and skills needed to satisfy the requirements of the general education curriculum.

Activities and Record Keeping

In addition to designing and sequencing curriculum and choosing appropriate materials for the children in your classroom, you need a record-keeping system to track children's learning and chart their progress. (Refer back to Chapter 3 for additional information about record keeping.) Be clear *why* you need to keep the records. If it is to support an individual educational program (IEP) goal, the system is relatively straightforward: Identify the goal and the benchmarks you are working on, provide space to show the activities you have chosen, the duration of the goal, and the quality of the child's behavior, noting increasing competence to signal when the goal will be met.

Before choosing activities, review information about where children spend time and their likes and dislikes. Choose activities that support the scope and sequence of reaching goals and are in areas children enjoy. The skill is figuring out how to teach what children need to learn in such a way that children want to learn it. Use activities that include a range of skills to pinpoint where children are in the learning cycle; this becomes their present level of academic achievement (PLAA) and their functional performance. This information is necessary for all children and is part of the teaching–learning–assessment cycle. To make planning easier, there is both an Index of Goals and Activity Numbers and an Index of Standards and Activity Numbers. Both indexes follow the introductory material to Part III. The indexes include the activities for all chapters. The indexes are particularly useful for an area such as the English language arts as these standards impact all curriculum areas. Using these indexes effectively helps you meet goals for preschool children and the general education curriculum requirements, the common core state standards, and standards developed by professional organizations.

Organization of Activities

The activities in Resource Chapter 1 through Resource Chapter 6 are organized by developmental/curriculum areas such as "English Language Arts Activities." Within these chapters, this focus is broken into curriculum strands such as speaking and listening, reading, writing, and language. And finally, these are divided up into goals and standards for each strand; for example, "to increase vocabulary acquisition and use" is a goal. The goals are more general; a related standard is "determine or clarify the meaning of unknown and multiple-meaning words and phrases based on kindergarten reading and content." All activities are numbered to identify the chapter in which they occur and the activity number, as well as whether they are in the book or on the Web. When activities have more than one goal or standard, they appear in the index under each goal or standard they support. When activities are followed by a "w," this means that they are on the book companion website and can be assessed at www.cengagebrain.com. For example, if you were interested in looking up the activity *Relief Maps*, you would find it in the list of activities as 3–22, indicating that it is in Resource Chapter 3 and is number 22, whereas *Creepers* would be identified as 1–35w, indicating that it is in Resource Chapter 1 Online and can be found on the Web rather than in the book. The activities numbered 1 through 30 are in the text. Activity numbers higher than 30 are on the book companion website and are designated with a w after the number.

Resource Chapter 1

Goal	To increase cultural awareness
Standard	S S Culture
Activities	1–1, 1–2, 1–3, 1–4, 1–5, 1–6, 1-16
	1–31w, 1–32w, 1–33w, 1–34w

If you look up activity 1–4, you will find it is called *Foreign Languages*. If you look up 1–32w in the book companion website it is called *Hello Poem*. The goals and standards and the activity numbers that support them are indexed separately at the end of this section. For the activities in the book companion website go to www.cengagebrain.com.

The Common Core State standards were used for the English language arts and mathematics. Other standards are based on particular professional organizations. (See Chapter 4 for more details.) Abbreviations used to identify standards are given in the Index of Standards, for example, Social Studies standards are SS. The individual standards that support Social Standards are numbered, for example Culture is SS 1.

The organization of the activities section is designed to aid you in record keeping as well as in day-to-day curriculum planning. The activities have a standard format:

Curriculum Area: Group Size

Activity Number and Name

Goals

Standards

Materials

Procedure

Accommodations and Integration

The Accommodations and Integration section provides information for modifying or adapting the level of difficulty of the activity and integrating it into other curriculum areas. This is done to adapt for individual children, to expand the age range, and to meet the goals of the general curriculum. The first suggestions given are designed to make the activity easier, later suggestions make the activity more challenging or show connections with other curriculum areas.

• • •

Using Activities in the IEP/IFSP

If a child has an IEP, look at the annual goals and the standards that support reaching these goals, locate these and related ones in the Indexes and use the activities to help implement the IEP. If you are in charge of writing the IEP, use the goals and standards to help you write and carry out the plan.

Activities designed for infants and toddlers are in Resource Chapter 6. They are organized by both goals (early learning guidelines) and the age of the infant or toddler. If an infant or toddler has an IFSP, use the goals and supporting activities to meet child outcomes. Share activities with families if they want this information.

• • •

Using the Activities

Most of the activities in this book are designed to meet the goals of children with diverse abilities (5–29 *Circus*; 2–12 *Authors and Illustrators*). Other activities are designed to increase all children's awareness of professionals in the field and how specific disabilities affect behavior (1–25 *Audiologist*; 1–45w *Slings*). Adapt these activities to suit your class, and use them as springboards to make up your own activities. Most of the activities are designed as prototypes. For example, the activity 3-13 *Sorting Shells* can be repeated with different items to sort and different categories. The Educational Resources section after each activity chapter provides additional sources.

As an educator of young children, you have much to keep in mind. Because you have the strengths and needs of all the children in your class to consider, you must find activities that foster the strengths of children with special needs but are appropriate and enriching for all children. As important as your curriculum is, remember that you are a model for the children. Your behavior toward children—your acceptance, consideration, and respect—speaks louder to the children than anything you deliberately set out to teach.

Guidelines for Adapting Activities for Children with Special Needs

Tables PIII–1 through PIII–12 provide guidelines for including children with special needs. Use them to further adapt activities to include all children.

TABLE PIII–1   GUIDELINES: CHILDREN WITH SPECIFIC LEARNING DISABILITIES

- Build self-esteem by matching materials to ability level and scaffolding learning.
- Provide immediate feedback, and encourage the use of self-correcting materials.
- Find children's strengths and provide opportunities for increasing them.
- Keep instruction short; match vocabulary and sentence length to the child's ability. Use questions to involve children. Use visual aids to support what you are saying. Keep the pace lively.
- Write and draw rules for behavior and post them. Identify consequences. Be consistent.
- Be patient. Give children time to learn.
- Begin with children's preferred method of learning (visual, tactile, or auditory), but don't exclude other modalities; instead, work to strengthen them.
- Support children's interest and comprehension by reading to them as they are learning to read. Teach prereading and reading skills in interesting creative ways.
- Identify children who are not learning at the expected rate and provide more intense and individualized instruction in reading and math.

TABLE PIII–2   GUIDELINES: CHILDREN WITH SOCIAL, EMOTIONAL, AND BEHAVIORAL DISORDERS

- Remove toys that might be dangerous or cause problems (hammers or mallets that might be thrown).
- Analyze the daily schedule and, if problematic, adjust it.
- Remove children from situations when they can not cope and the situation is escalating. Give the child time to think (time should be based on the child's age and situation, 2 minutes may be long enough), and then talk about what happened and how the child can get back in control.
- Set clear, precise expectations: "In this class, we use words to say how we feel."
- Teach the difference between feelings and behavior. All children have feelings and should be in touch with them. However, the way they express their feelings (behavior) should not hurt themselves or others.
- Be alert. If possible, intervene before a situation becomes a problem.
- Arrange the environment to enhance learning. Balance active with less active times. Provide quiet alternatives when children need them.
- Keep noise levels reasonable.
- Develop a plan for dealing with aggressive behavior and follow it.
- Simplify, shorten, and structure activities when necessary.
- Utilize and arrange space to enhance your goals and prevent problems.
- Plan to specifically teach skills others might learn informally.
- Make learning meaningful and be respectful of children's work.
- Limit the number of transitions where possible.

PIII-3 GUIDELINES: CHILDREN WITH ATTENTION-DEFICIT/ HYPERACTIVITY DISORDER

- Be consistent.
- Follow an established routine so children can anticipate what will happen next (snack, outside).
- Plan for transitions; prepare children for changes by giving them a 5-minute warning.
- Eliminate distractions. Keep noise levels down and confusion to a minimum.
- Make eye contact; keep directions short, simple, and clear.
- Confirm that a child has prerequisite skills before teaching new skills.
- Work from hands-on experiences to characteristics and properties.
- Provide numerous learning experiences with interesting planned variations.
- Teach prosocial skills. Develop a plan to address challenging behavior.
- Motivate children to attempt demanding activities.
- Provide children with fidget objects and two options of places to work.

 PIII-4 CHILDREN WITH COMMUNICATION DISORDERS

- Simplify your grammar and vocabulary. Use shorter sentences, but don't "talk down."
- Be a good communications model by using clear diction and correct grammar.
- Include children in group activities, but don't call on a child unless he volunteers.
- Set aside a specific time each day for language and literacy but also incorporate language into routines and other activities.
- Encourage children to communicate by increasing their self-confidence and interest in their environment.
- Select activities that support noncompetitive peer interaction.
- Create a need for speech. Do not always respond to a child who is just pointing if he can speak.
- Talk with children about what they are doing; build vocabulary.
- Reinforce learning through visual and tactile experiences.
- Be an attentive listener.
- If you can't understand a child's speech, reinforce the child's attempts at communication and then be honest and say, "I'm having trouble understanding you. Can you tell me in different words?"

PIII-5 CHILDREN WHO ARE ENGLISH LANGUAGE LEARNERS

- Support children in learning their home language as well as learning English.
- Label items in the classroom in English and the home languages of the children in the class.
- Have educators in the classroom who are bilingual and bicultural, if possible.
- Be a good language model. Use correct English supported by props and gestures as needed.
- Keep large group times short and encourage small group learning.
- Support demonstrations or modeling with appropriate language.

- Have a language-rich, culture-rich environment.
- Provide books in the languages of the children in the class.
- Teach about the culture and traditions of the children in the class.

 PIII-6 CHILDREN WITH AUTISM SPECTRUM DISORDERS

- Make your face and your voice congruent. When you are happy, look and sound happy. When you are not happy, use a stern voice and grumpy facial expression.
- Give clear, specific directions for all tasks, one step at a time.
- Simplify your language.
- Use many visual cues. Present tasks visually, highlight written information, and provide visual (tape) boundaries for sitting.
- Eliminate visual distractions.
- Check the environment for auditory distractions.
- Teach social skills.
- Allow children to be alone some of the time.
- Give children a fidget item to play with when they are listening.
- Ask (or tell) children before you touch them. Use deep pressure.
- Be patient. Learning and relationships take time to build.

PIII-7 CHILDREN WITH INTELLECTUAL DELAYS AND DISABILITIES

- Use as many senses to teach as possible.
- Help children over-learn concepts by presenting interesting variations of principles.
- Teach a concept for a short time each day for many days rather than a long time for a few days.
- Evaluate the utility of materials, tasks, and skills and begin with the most functional ones. Learning should be essential and fun.
- Teach concepts that are relevant and familiar first, and then work toward the less familiar.
- Use several examples to teach a concept (*red*: apples, balls, books, crayons).
- Sequence learning from simple to complex.
- Use a task analysis to break down complex tasks into their component parts.
- Use backward chaining so children have the satisfaction of completing a task.
- Support children in learning at a rate that is possible for them, while at the same time including them in group activities and planning.
- Encourage children to participate in the same activity at different levels.

PIII-8 CHILDREN WHO ARE GIFTED AND TALENTED

- Plan activities that children can work on together but at different levels of complexity.
- Avoid pressure to conform by asking open-ended questions, not yes-no questions.
- Teach socially acceptable ways of handling emotions.

- Model acceptance. Smile, clap, use verbal praise, and high fives to support children.
- Provide a variety of activities and experiences that encourage exploration of interests and allow depth and concentration.
- Increase complexity by adding materials and expanding the time frame.
- Provide activities and problems that require divergent thinking.
- Emphasize how and why things occur and what children (or others) can do to change them.
- Make up new endings for stories, take a different perspective, and so on.
- Emphasize group and individual brainstorming and problem solving.
- Encourage children to do activities in different ways and reflect on the differences.
- Allow children to choose some themes.

TABLE

PIII-9　CHILDREN WITH SPECIAL HEALTH CARE NEEDS

- Find out as much as possible about a child's health (diet, physical restrictions, medication and its possible side effects, and behaviors indicating an illness is becoming acute).
- Find out what children have been told about their illness and its implications.
- Use activities that allow children to be in control or adapt activities so that children have more control.
- Encourage age-appropriate independence and allow the children to do as much as possible for themselves.
- Arrange the schedule so that vigorous activities are followed by less strenuous ones. If necessary, provide short breaks for everyone.
- Organize your routine so that children can leave for medical procedures. Treat these departures as you would any transition.
- Allow children returning from an illness to come initially for part of the day, working back up to a full day.
- Plan some open-ended activities and some that can be completed at home if necessary.
- Observe children. Watch for mood changes and body language indicating pain, fatigue, or reactions to medication.
- Help children learn about the implications of their special health care needs. Verbalize this for them.
- Provide an atmosphere where children can discuss fears and problems.

TABLE

PIII-10　CHILDREN WITH ORTHOPEDIC AND NEUROLOGICAL IMPAIRMENTS

- Learn about a child's particular disability and the objectives of therapy. Know the child's competence in independent mobility and transferring.
- Learn how to safely lift and transfer a child with another adult and alone if necessary.
- Learn how wheelchairs work in general and how the particular wheelchair a child uses works. Regardless of type, *put on the brakes* before placing a child in or taking a child out of a wheelchair.
- Learn what equipment children can use for variety in positioning and how to use it (beanbag chairs, bolsters, wedges).
- Attach baskets to walkers or have bags with shoulder straps or knapsacks available to carry materials.
- Have assistive devices available to reach objects, turn pages, and so on.

For some children the side effects of treatments are of greater concern than the treatment itself.
© Cengage Learning 2012

- Have large versions of manipulative toys and puzzles with knobs.
- Keep toys and materials picked up and off the floor.
- Encourage tactile exploration.
- Demonstrate how to explore new materials. Support children in learning about new materials and exploring them.
- Provide spaces wide enough for activities and movement, including space for mobility aids.
- Evaluate classroom doors, bathrooms, and passageways for accessibility as well as the building itself. Do this for field trips, too.

TABLE

PIII-11　CHILDREN WITH HEARING IMPAIRMENTS

- Face the child, and bring yourself to the child's eye level.
- Make your lips clearly visible (wear lipstick, trim or shave a mustache or beard).
- Keep bright lights out of children's eyes. Use natural light sources if possible.
- Attract the child's attention *before* you begin speaking. Make eye contact or use a visual signal or touch to get the child's attention, but don't scare the child.
- Speak in a normal voice to aid speech reading.

- Use appropriate expressive body language, including gestures and pointing.
- Reduce background noise; ask other children to talk or play more quietly. Remember that a hearing aid does not correct a hearing impairment.
- Repeat a word that is not understood, and then try a synonym.
- Use as many visual aids as possible.
- Have the child sit close to the sound source if she cannot see to read your lips when you are using audiovisual aids. Use closed-captioned aids, when possible.
- Place the child across from you (where she has the best view), with the child's back to the windows in group situations.
- Learn significant signs or cues to communicate with the child.
- Learn how to work with and use an interpreter.

TABLE PIII-12 CHILDREN WITH VISUAL IMPAIRMENTS

Corrected Visual Impairments

- Find out when and for how long corrective lenses must be worn.
- Observe and record the child's behavior with the visual aids (removing eyeglasses, position relative to materials, headaches) and share these observations with parents.

- Create a need to see and a reason for a child to wear glasses to see better.
- Support children wearing glasses. Discuss name-calling and alternatives.

Visual Limitations

- Find out the level of a child's usable vision.
- Use verbal and tactile supports and rewards.
- Be aware of lighting conditions; arrange seating to benefit from lighting. Use natural light but regulate it with blinds.
- Use black marker to outline paper; other surfaces that need to stand out should be high contrast.
- Have a variety of books, including some with large print and Braille.
- Use materials with distinctive shapes and textures that have high-contrasting colors.
- Keep furniture in the same place and materials picked up.
- Have children practice giving and following directions.
- Teach location by referring to the numbers on a clock face if appropriate.

Index of Goals and Activity Numbers ✳

Goals and Activity Numbers in Text and Online *Activity numbers with a "w" after them are on the Web and can be accessed at www.cengagebrain.com.*

SOCIAL AWARENESS: SOCIAL COMPETENCE AND SOCIAL STUDIES

To improve self-concept

1–1, 1–2, 1–3, 1–6, 1–8, 1–13, 1–14, 1–15, 1–30, 1–36w, 1–38w, 1–42w

To increase awareness of roles people play

1–2, 1–3, 1–8, 1–13, 1–14, 1–15, 1–16, 1–20, 1–21, 1–22, 1–23, 1–24, 1–25, 1–26, 1–27, 1–28, 1–29, 1–36w, 1–42w, 2–10, 3–61, 5–27, 5–28, 5–29, 5–30, 5–56w, 5–57w

To broaden concepts of family

1–1, 1–2, 1–3, 1–6, 1–7, 1–8, 1–9, 1–13, 1–14, 1–42w

To increase inclusion

1–5, 1–7, 1–10, 1–11, 1–12, 1–19, 1–22, 1–23, 1–24, 1–25, 1–26, 1–31w, 1–33w, 1–34w, 1–35w, 1–36w, 1–38w, 1–39w, 1–40w, 1–41w, 1–43w, 1–44w, 1–45w, 1–46w, 2–4, 2–30, 2–39w, 2–47w, 4–34w, 4–37w, 5–4, 5–5, 5–17, 5–36w

To increase awareness of individual differences and similarities

1–4, 1–5, 1–9, 1–10, 1–11, 1–15, 1–20, 1–31w, 1–32w, 1–33w, 1–34w, 1–35w, 1–39w, 1–40w, 1–41w, 1–43w, 1–45w, 1–46w, 2–7, 2–48w, 3–61w

To increase cultural awareness

1–1, 1–4, 1–6, 1–7, 1–9, 1–16, 1–18, 1–32w, 1–34w, 2–11, 2–16, 2–45w, 2–46w, 5–6

To increase respect for diversity in modes of communication

1–4, 1–5, 1–10, 1–28, 1–32w, 1–33w, 1–43w, 2–11, 2–22, 2–31w

To increase social studies concepts

1–16, 1–17, 1–18, 1–19, 1–20, 1–21, 1–22, 1–23, 1–24, 1–25, 1–26, 1–27, 1–28, 1–29, 1–30, 1–47w

To encourage problem solving

1–17, 1–19, 1–27, 1–30, 1–31w, 1–35w, 1–37w, 1–39w, 1–46w, 1–47w, 4–37w, 5–8, 5–39w, 5–41w, 5–42w

To express feelings

1–38w, 1–44w, 2–4, 2–7, 2–39w, 2–44w, 2–48w, 2–51w, 5–11, 5–44w

ENGLISH LANGUAGE ARTS: SPEAKING AND LISTENING, READING, WRITING, AND LANGUAGE

To improve expressive communication

2–3, 2–4, 2–5, 2–6, 2–30, 2–39w, 2–40w, 2–42w, 2–48w, 2–59w, 5–9

To improve listening skills

2–2, 2–28, 2–31w, 2–33w, 2–34w, 2–35w, 2–36w, 2–37w, 2–38w, 2–41w, 2–47w, 2–59w, 3–18, 3–50w, 5–17, 5–51w

To increase knowledge of the structure of language

2–5, 2–9, 2–21, 2–27, 2–28, 2–29, 2–30, 2–55w, 2–57w

To improve receptive communication

2–2, 2–3, 2–28, 2–31w, 2–32w, 2–35w, 2–36w, 2–38w

To improve reading literacy

2–1, 2–7, 2–8, 2–9, 2–10, 2–11, 2–12, 2–13, 2–14, 2–15, 2–16, 2–17, 2–18, 2–19, 2–20, 2–21, 2–22, 2–23, 2–24, 2–25, 2–26, 2–29, 2–43w, 2–44w, 2–45w, 2–46w, 2–49w, 2–50w, 2–51w, 2–52w, 2–53w, 2–56w, 2–57w, 3–1, 3–2, 3–7, 3–25, 3–26, 3–27, 3–29, 3–30, 3–33w, 3–40w, 3–42w, 3–45w, 3–56w, 3–63w, 3–64w, 5–18

To increase vocabulary acquisition and use

2–3, 2–42w, 2–44w, 2–55w, 2–56w, 2–60w, 3–1, 3–9, 3–13, 3–19, 3–47w, 3–57w, 4–1, 4–5, 4–6, 4–10, 5–20

To increase respect for diversity in modes of communication

1–43w, 2–11, 2–22, 2–31w, 2–47w

To use diverse print and nonprint sources and genres

2–6, 2–12, 2–16, 2–18, 2–19, 2–25, 2–26, 2–45w, 2–46w, 2–50w, 2–52w, 2–54w

To increase phonological awareness

2–20, 2–21, 2–22, 2–23, 2–24, 2–55w, 2–56w, 2–57w

To improve writing literacy

2–12, 2–18, 2–19, 2–25, 2–26, 2–27, 2–50w, 2–53w, 2–54w, 2–58w, 3–25, 3–26, 4–7, 5–5, 5–18

To increase comprehension

2–9, 2–10, 2–13, 2–14, 2–15, 2–17, 2–23, 2–24, 2–27, 2–32w, 2–34w, 2–35w, 2–36w, 2–40w, 2–41w, 2–49w, 2–60w, 3–56w, 5–15, 5–44w, 5–45w

To follow directions

2–5, 2–32w, 3–28, 3–29, 3–41w, 3–64w, 3–65w

To improve memory skills

2–1, 2–33w, 3–3, 3–35w

DISCOVERY: MATHEMATICS, SCIENCE, AND TECHNOLOGY

To improve number sense and numeration

3–1, 3–2, 3–3, 3–4, 3–7, 3–8, 3–9, 3–31w, 3–32w, 3–33w, 3–34w, 3–37w, 3–38w, 3–39w, 3–40w, 3–42w, 3–46w, 3–60w

To improve geometric and spatial sense

3–2, 3–4, 3–12, 3–14, 3–38w, 3–44w, 3–47w, 3–48w, 3–49w

To improve measurement concepts

3–6, 3–11, 3–12, 3–13, 3–22, 3–41w, 3–43w, 3–46w, 3–47w, 3–48w, 3–51w, 3–65w

To improve estimation skills

3–5, 3–6, 3–11, 3–36w, 3–37w, 3–40w, 3–42w, 3–45w

To identify and understand patterns and relationships

2–29, 3–8, 3–9, 3–14, 3–18, 3–30, 3–31w, 3–32w, 3–34w, 3–35w, 3–44w, 3–46w, 3–48w, 3–49w, 3–56w, 3–58w, 5–6, 5–10, 5–12, 5–14, 5–16, 5–34w, 5–38w, 5–40w, 5–45w, 5–50w

To improve knowledge of whole number operations and computations

3–5, 3–7, 3–10, 3–33w, 3–36w, 3–45w, 3–51w, 3–60w

To improve observational skills

3–15, 3–16, 3–17, 3–20, 3–21, 3–22, 3–37w, 3–51w, 3–52w, 3–53w, 3–55w, 3–59w

To improve classification skills

2–34w, 2–40w, 2–59w, 3–11, 3–13, 3–14, 3–21, 3–38w, 3–39w, 3–43w, 3–44w, 3–49w, 3–54w, 3–55w, 3–57w, 3–58w, 3–59w, 4–3, 4–4, 4–7, 4–8

To improve cause-and-effect reasoning

1–12, 1–17, 1–18, 1–21, 1–29, 1–37w, 1–41w, 1–44w, 1–47w, 2–8, 2–37w, 2–38w 3–10, 3–16, 3–19, 3–20, 3–21, 3–23, 3–24, 3–27, 3–28, 3–41w, 3–43w, 3–50w, 3–52w, 3–53w, 3–54w, 3–57w, 3–61w, 3–62w, 4–2, 4–3, 4–4, 4–8, 4–9, 4–11, 4–12, 4–28, 4–31w, 4–32w, 4–33w, 4–43w, 5–1, 5–2, 5–3, 5–7, 5–14, 5–19, 5–31w, 5–32w, 5–33w, 5–34w, 5–35w, 5–36w, 5–37w, 5–41w, 5–42w, 5–46w, 5–49w, 5–54w

To improve generalization skills

2–8, 3–12, 3–15, 3–17, 3–23, 3–24, 3–58w, 3–62w, 3–63w

To increase knowledge of the natural world

2–13, 2–14, 2–15, 2–17, 2–43w, 2–49w, 3–5, 3–15, 3–17, 3–24, 3–55w, 3–59w, 5–1, 5–15

To make predictions

2–1, 2–33w, 2–37w, 3–3, 3–10, 3–16, 3–18, 3–23, 3–50w, 3–52w, 3–53w, 3–54w, 4–13, 4–16, 4–18, 4–35w, 4–42w, 5–32w, 5–33w, 5–38w

To improve technology skills

3–22, 3–25, 3–26, 3–27, 3–28, 3–29, 3–30, 3–60w, 3–62w, 3–63w, 3–64w, 3–65w

To improve health literacy

4–1, 4–2, 4–3, 4–4, 4–5, 4–6, 4–7, 4–8, 4–11, 4–12, 4–31w, 4–32w, 4–34w, 4–35w

To increase safety awareness

4–9, 4–10, 4–33w

To increase adaptive skills

3–8, 4–2, 4–5, 4–6, 4–9, 4–10, 4–31w, 4–32w, 4–33w, 4–34w, 4–35w, 4–43w, 5–23

To improve locomotor skills

4–13, 4–14, 4–15 , 4–16, 4–17, 4–23, 4–36w, 4–37w, 4–38w

To improve manipulative skills

4–18, 4–20, 4–21, 4–23, 4–39w, 4–40w, 4–41w, 4–42w, 4–43w

To improve nonmanipulative skills

4–17, 4–22, 4–23, 4–24, 4–25, 4–26, 4–27, 4–28, 4–29, 4–30, 4–44w

To improve physical fitness

4–12, 4–13, 4–14, 4–15, 4–17, 4–19, 4–20, 4–38w

To improve sensory motor integration

2–20, 2–41w, 2–51w, 2–52w, 2–53w, 2–54w, 2–58w 3–4, 3–6, 3–20, 3–31w, 3–32w, 3–34w, 3–39w, 4–11, 4–18, 4–19, 4–21, 4–22, 4–24, 4–25, 4–26, 4–27, 4–28, 4–29, 4–30, 4–36w, 4–39w, 4–40w, 4–41w, 4–42w, 4–44w, 5–3, 5–7, 5–12, 5–13, 5–20, 5–21, 5–24, 5–25, 5–26, 5–37w, 5–40w, 5–43w, 5–46w, 5–47w, 5–48w, 5–49w, 5–52w, 5–55w

To improve motor planning

4–14, 4–15, 4–16, 4–19, 4–20, 4–21, 4–22, 4–24, 4–27, 4–29, 4–36w, 4–39w, 4–40w, 4–41w, 5–22

To increase body awareness

1–11, 1–40w, 1–45w, 4–1, 4–25, 4–26, 4–30, 4–38w, 4–44w, 5–21, 5–26, 5–52w, 5–53w

To increase visual arts concepts

5–1, 5–2, 5–3, 5–4, 5–5, 5–6, 5–7, 5–8, 5–9, 5–10, 5–31w, 5–32w, 5–33w, 5–34w, 5–35w, 5–36w, 5–37w, 5–38w, 5–39w, 5–40w, 5–41w, 5–42w, 5–43w, 5–44w

To encourage creativity

2–2, 2–6, 2–42w, 2–43w, 2–60w, 5–2, 5–4, 5–8, 5–9, 5–19, 5–31w, 5–35w, 5–39w, 5–43w, 5–51w

To increase music concepts

5–11, 5–12, 5–13, 5–14, 5–15, 5–16, 5–17, 5–18, 5–19, 5–20, 5–45w, 5–46w, 5–47w, 5–48w, 5–49w, 5–50w, 5–51w, 5–52w

To move creatively

5–13, 5–21, 5–22, 5–23, 5–24, 5–25, 5–47w, 5–48w, 5–53w, 5–54w, 5–55w

To understand dance

5–22, 5–23, 5–24, 5–25, 5–53w, 5–54w, 5–55w

To play creatively

5–27, 5–28, 5–29, 5–30, 5–56w, 5–57w

To perform roles

5–26, 5–27, 5–28, 5–29, 5–30, 5–56w, 5–57w

Infant and Toddler Activity Goals and Activity Numbers in Text and Online *Activity numbers with a "w" after them are on the Web.*

Social and emotional development

6–1, 6–2, 6–3, 6–4, 6–5, 6–6, 6–14, 6–15, 6–25, 6–30, 6–30w, 6–31w, 6–32w, 6–33w, 6–34w, 6–36w, 6–42w, 6–43w, 6–49w, 6–51w, 6–60w

Language and communication development

6–3, 6–5, 6–6, 6–7, 6–8, 6–9, 6–10, 6–11, 6–12, 6–16, 6–23, 6–34w, 6–35w, 6–36w, 6–37w, 6–38w, 6–39w, 6–40w, 6–41w, 6–42w, 6–50w, 6–55w, 6–56w, 6–59w

Cognitive development and general knowledge

6–7, 6–8, 6–10, 6–11, 6–12, 6–13, 6–14, 6–15, 6–16, 6–17, 6–18, 6–19, 6–20, 6–21, 6–22, 6–24, 6–32w, 6–35w, 6–37w, 6–38w, 6–39w, 6–43w, 6–44w, 6–45w, 6–46w, 6–47w, 6–48w, 6–52w, 6–53w, 6–54w, 6–57w

Physical development and motor skills

6–2, 6–4, 6–6, 6–9, 6–10, 6–12, 6–13, 6–14, 6–17, 6–18, 6–19, 6–20, 6–21,

6–22, 6–23, 6–24, 6–25, 6–26, 6–27, 6–28, 6–29, 6–31w, 6–32w, 6–33w, 6–34w, 6–36w, 6–39w, 6–40w, 6–41w, 6–44w, 6–45w, 6–46w, 6–47w, 6–48w, 6–49w, 6–50w, 6–51w, 6–52w, 6–53w, 6–54w, 6–56w, 6–57w, 6–58w, 6–59w, 6–60w

Approaches to play and learning

6–1, 6–4, 6–5, 6–11, 6–25, 6–26, 6–27, 6–28, 6–29, 6–30, 6–55w, 6–56w, 6–57w, 6–58w, 6–59w, 6–60w

Infant and Toddler Activity Numbers by Age *Activity numbers with a "w" after them are on the Web.*

Young infants (B to 9 months)

6–1, 6–2, 6–7, 6–8, 6–13, 6–14, 6–19, 6–20, 6–25, 6–26, 6–31w, 6–32w, 6–35w, 6–43w, 6–47w, 6–50w

Mobile infants (8 to 18 months)

6–3, 6–4, 6–9, 6–10, 6–15, 6–16, 6–21, 6–22, 6–27, 6–33w, 6–44w, 6–45w, 6–48w

Mobile infants and toddlers (8 to 36 months)

6–28, 6–49w, 6–50w, 6–51w, 6–55w, 6–56w

Toddlers (16 to 36 months)

6–5, 6–6, 6–11, 6–12, 6–17, 6–18, 6–23, 6–24, 6–29, 6–30, 6–34w, 6–36w, 6–37w, 6–38w, 6–39w, 6–40w, 6–41w, 6–42w, 6–46w, 6–52w, 6–53w, 6–54w, 6–57w, 6–58w, 6–59w, 6–60w

Index of Standards and Activity Numbers

Table R1–1: Standards and Activity Numbers in Text and Online
Activity numbers with a "w" after them are on the Web and can be accessed at www.cengagebrain.com.

SOCIAL STUDIES STANDARDS (SS)

SS 1 Culture

1–1, 1–2, 1–3, 1–4, 1–5, 1–6, 1–16, 1–31w, 1–32w, 1–33w, 1–34w

SS 2 Time, continuity, and change

1–2, 1–3, 1–7, 1–8, 1–9, 1–17, 1–18

SS 3 People, places, and environments

1–1, 1–10, 1–11, 1–12, 1–13, 1–16, 1–17, 1–19, 1–20, 1–21, 1–22, 1–35w, 1–47w

SS 4 Individual development and identity

1–4, 1–5, 1–7, 1–8, 1–9, 1–11, 1–13, 1–14, 1–15, 1–17, 1–21, 1–36w, 1–37w, 1–38w, 1–39w, 1–40w, 1–41w, 1–42w, 1–43w, 1–46w

SS 5 Individuals, groups, and institutions

1–12 , 1–20, 1–21, 1–22, 1–23, 1–24, 1–25, 1–26, 1–27, 1–28, 1–34w, 1–45w

SS 6 Power, authority, and governance

1–14, 1–15, 1–29, 1–30

SS 7 Production, distribution, and consumption

1–18, 1–19, 1–22, 1–28, 1–29, 1–44w

SS 8 Science, technology, and society

1–23, 1–24, 1–25, 1–26, 1–27

SS 9 Global connections

1–13, 1–20, 1–29

SS 10 Civic ideals and practices

1–6, 1–12, 1–28, 1–30

ENGLISH LANGUAGE ARTS AND LITERACY IN HISTORY/SOCIAL STUDIES, SCIENCE, AND TECHNICAL SUBJECTS STANDARDS: KINDERGARTEN

Speaking and Listening (S&L)
Comprehension and Collaboration

S&L 1 Participate in collaborative conversations with diverse partners about kindergarten topics and texts, with peers and adults in small and larger groups.

1–30, 1–37w, 1–40w, 1–47w, 2–1, 2–31w, 2–33w, 2–47w, 2–51w, 4–1, 4–2

S&L 2 Confirm understanding of a text read aloud or information presented orally or through other media by asking and answering questions about key details and requesting clarification if something is not understood.

1–47w, 2–2, 2–28, 2–32w, 2–34w, 2–47w, 2–59w, 2–60w

S&L 3 Ask and answer questions in order to seek help, get information, or clarify something that is not understood.

1–6, 1–7, 1–9, 1–10, 1–33w, 1–35w, 1–43w, 1–45w, 1–46w, 2–1, 2–2, 2–3, 2–4, 2–5, 2–22, 2–34w, 2–35w, 2–36w, 2–37w, 2–38w, 2–39w, 2–40w, 2–41w, 4–9, 4–31w, 4–32w, 4–35w, 4–36w, 4–43w, 5–57w

Presentation of Knowledge and Ideas

S&L 4 Describe familiar people, places, things, and events and, with prompting and support, provide additional detail.

1–2, 1–3, 1–47w, 2–3, 2–4, 2–5, 2–6, 2–32w, 2–33w, 2–36w, 2–37w, 2–38w, 2–40w, 2–41w, 2–42w, 3–18, 3–56w

S&L 5 Add drawings or other visual displays to descriptions as desired to provide additional detail.

1–8, 1–36w, 1–42w, 2–6, 2–44w

S&L 6 Speak audibly and express thoughts, feelings, and ideas clearly.

1–1, 1–4, 1–15, 1–32w, 1–37w, 1–40w, 2–4, 2–5, 2–6, 2–39w

Reading: Literature (R:L)
Key Ideas and Details

R:L 1 With prompting and support, ask and answer questions about key details in a text.

1–39w, 1–41w, 1–44w, 2–7, 2–8, 2–9, 2–43w

R:L 2 With prompting and support, retell familiar stories, including key details.

2–7, 2–8, 2–9, 2–43w

R:L 3 With prompting and support, identify characters, settings, and major events in a story.

1–34w, 1–44w, 2–7, 2–10, 2–44w

Craft and Structure

R:L 4 Ask and answer questions about unknown words in a text.

2–11, 2–45w, 2–46w, 5–57w

R:L 5 Recognize common types of texts (e.g., storybooks, poems).

2–11, 2–45w, 2–46w, 2–47w

R:L 6 With prompting and support, name the author and illustrator of a story and define the role of each in telling the story.

2–10, 2–12

Integration of Knowledge and Ideas

R:L 7 With prompting and support, describe the relationship between illustrations and the story in which they appear (e.g., what moment in a story an illustration depicts).

2–11, 2–12, 2–44w, 5–2, 5–44w

R:L 8 (Not applicable to literature)

R:L 9 With prompting and support, compare and contrast the adventures and experiences of characters in familiar stories.

2–12, 2–45w, 2–46w

Range of Reading and Level of Text Complexity

R:L 10 Actively engage in group reading activities with purpose and understanding.

2–8, 2–9, 2–10, 2–48w

Reading: Informational Text (R:IT)
Key Ideas and Details

R:IT 1 With prompting and support, ask and answer questions about key details in a text.

2–13, 2–14, 2–49w, 3–17, 3–24, 5–28

R:IT 2 With prompting and support, identify the main topic and retell key details of a text.

2–13, 2–15, 2–49w

R:IT 3 With prompting and support, describe the connection between two individuals, events, ideas, or pieces of information in a text.

2–13, 2–16

Craft and Structure

R:IT 4 With prompting and support, ask and answer questions about unknown words in a text.

2–15, 2–17

R:IT 5 Identify the front cover, back cover, and title page of a book.

2–18, 2–50w

R:IT 6 Name the author and illustrator of a text, and define the role of each in presenting the ideas or information in a text.

2–14, 2–16

Integration of Knowledge and Ideas

R:IT 7 With prompting and support, describe the relationship between illustrations and the text in which they appear (e.g., what person, place, thing, or idea in the text an illustration depicts).

2–16, 2–49w

R:IT 8 With prompting and support, identify the reasons an author gives to support points in a text.

2–17, 5–27

R:IT 9 With prompting and support, identify basic similarities in and differences between two texts on the same topic.

2–14, 2–43w

Range of Reading and Level of Text Complexity

R:IT 10 Actively engage in group reading activities with purpose and understanding.

2–15, 2–17

Reading: Foundational Skills (R:FS)
Print Concepts

R:FS 1 Demonstrate understanding of the organization and basic features of print.

2–19, 2–20, 2–21, 2–22, 2–51w, 2–52w, 2–53w, 2–54w, 2–58w, 3–29, 3–64w, 5–12

Phonological Awareness

R:FS 2 Demonstrate understanding of spoken words, syllables, and sounds (phonemes).

2–20, 2–21, 2–22, 2–23, 2–24, 2–48w, 2–53w, 2–54w, 2–55w, 2–56w, 2–57w

Phonics and Word Recognition

R:FS 3 Know and apply grade-level phonics and word analysis skills in decoding words.

2–23, 2–24, 2–48w

Fluency

R:FS 4 Read emergent-reader texts with purpose and understanding.

2–23, 2–24

Writing (W)
Text Types and Purposes

W 1 Use a combination of drawing, dictating, and writing to compose opinion pieces in which they tell a reader the topic or name of the book they are writing about and state an opinion or preference about the topic or book (e.g., *My favorite book is . . . .*).

2–25, 2–26, 2–50w, 5–5

W 2 Use a combination of drawing, dictating, and writing to compose informative/explanatory texts in which they name what they are writing about and supply some information about the topic.

1–18, 1–42w, 2–19, 2–25, 2–27, 2–39w, 5–10

W 3 Use a combination of drawing, dictating, and writing to narrate a single event or several loosely linked events, tell about the events in the order in which they occurred, and provide a reaction to what happened.

2–18, 2–35w, 2–41w

Production and Distribution of Writing

W 4 (Begins in grade 3)

W 5 With guidance and support from adults, respond to questions and suggestions from peers and add details to strengthen writing as needed.

2–25, 2–27, 2–50w

W 6 With guidance and support from adults, explore a variety of digital tools to produce and publish writing, including in collaboration with peers.

2–18, 2–33w, 3–25, 3–26

Research to Build and Present Knowledge

W 7 Participate in shared research and writing projects (e.g., explore a number of books by a favorite author and express opinions about them).

2–27

W 8 With guidance and support from adults, recall information from experiences or gather information from provided sources to answer a question.

2–26

W 9 (Begins in grade 4)

Range of Writing

W 10 (Begins in grade 3)

Language (L)
Conventions of Standard English

L 1 Demonstrate command of the conventions of standard English grammar and usage when writing or speaking.

2–28, 2–52w, 2–54w, 2–58w

L 2 Demonstrate command of the conventions of standard English capitalization, punctuation, and spelling when writing.

2–29, 2–58w

Knowledge of Language

L 3 (Begins in grade 2)

Vocabulary Acquisition and Use

L 4 Determine or clarify the meaning of unknown and multiple-meaning words and phrases based on kindergarten reading and content.

1–14, 1–16, 1–24, 1–25, 1–26, 1–27, 2–3, 2–30, 2–57w, 2–59w, 2–60w, 3–13, 3–28, 3–61w, 3–62w

L 5 With guidance and support from adults, explore word relationships and nuances in word meanings.

1–32w, 1–38w, 2–28, 2–30, 2–42w, 2–55w, 2–57w, 2–59w, 2–60w, 3–1, 3–39w, 3–51w, 3–52w, 3–53w, 5–8

L 6 Use words and phrases acquired through conversations, reading and being read to, and responding to texts.

2–42w, 2–56w

MATHEMATICS STANDARDS (M): KINDERGARTEN
Counting and Cardinality

M 1 Know number names and the count sequence.

3–1, 3–2, 3–3, 3–4, 3–31w, 3–32w, 3–33w, 3–34w, 4–22

M 2 Count to tell the number of objects.

3–1, 3–2, 3–5, 3–6, 3–7, 3–8, 3–31w, 3–32w, 3–33w, 3–35w, 3–36w, 3–37w, 3–38w

M 3 Compare numbers.

3–2, 3–5, 3–6, 3–9, 3–10, 3–11, 3–32w, 3–35w, 3–36w, 3–37w, 3–39w, 3–40w, 3–41w, 3–42w, 3–43w, 3–44w, 3–51w

Operations and Algebraic Thinking

M 4 Understand addition as putting together and adding to, and understand subtraction as taking apart and taking from.

3–3, 3–7, 3–8, 3–9, 3–33w, 3–35w, 3–39w, 3–40w, 3–41w, 3–42w, 3–44w, 3–46w, 3–51w, 3–60w

Numbers and Operations in Base Ten

M 5 Work with numbers 11–19 to gain foundations for place value.

3–5, 3–7, 3–10, 3–45w, 3–60w

Measurement and Data

M 6 Describe and compare measureable attributes.

2–30, 3–6, 3–11, 3–12, 3–13, 3–19, 3–36w, 3–37w, 3–41w, 3–43w, 3–46w, 3–47w, 3–48w, 3–50w

M 7 Classify objects and count the number of objects in each category.

2–34w, 2–35w, 2–37w, 2–40w, 3–8, 3–9, 3–10, 3–11, 3–12, 3–13, 3–42w, 3–43w, 3–44w, 3–47w, 3–50w, 3–54w, 3–57w, 3–58w, 3–59w, 4–11, 4–18, 4–31w, 5–40w

Geometry

M 8 Identify and describe shapes (squares, circles, triangles, rectangles, hexagons, cubes, cones, cylinders, and spheres).

3–4, 3–14, 3–34w, 3–38w, 3–48w, 3–49w

M 9 Analyze, compare, create, and compose shapes.

3–4, 3–14, 3–34w, 3–48w, 3–49w

SCIENCE STANDARDS (SC)

SC 1 Unifying concepts and processes

3–15, 3–16, 3–17

SC 2 Science as inquiry

3–15, 3–16, 3–18, 3–19, 3–20, 3–21, 3–22, 3–23, 3–50w, 3–51w, 3–52w, 3–53w, 3–54w, 3–55w, 3–56w, 3–57w

SC 3a Physical science

3–18, 3–19, 3–20, 3–21, 3–52w, 3–53w, 3–54w, 3–58w, 4–21, 4–29, 4–41w

SC 3b Life science

2–36w, 2–56w, 3–15, 3–17, 3–55w, 3–56w, 3–59w, 5–1

SC 3c Earth and space

3–22, 3–24

SC 4 Science and technology

3–21, 3–22, 3–23, 3–57w, 3–58w, 3–60w, 3–61w

SC 5 Science in personal and social perspectives

3–16, 3–23, 3–24, 3–59w, 3–61w, 4–32w, 4–34w, 5–32w

TECHNOLOGY STANDARDS (T)

T 1 Write and illustrate ideas and stories using digital tools.

3–25

T 2 Identify, research, and collect data on a topic and propose solutions.

T 3 Engage others through email and other electronic means.

3–26

T 4 Work collaboratively to produce a digital presentation or product.

T 5 Find and evaluate digital information about people, places, and things.

3–27

T 6 Use simulations and graphical organizers.

3–28, 3–29, 3–30, 3–62w, 3–63w, 3–64w, 3–65w

T 7 Demonstrate safe, responsible, cooperative use of technology.

3–25, 3–26, 3–27

T 8 Communicate about technology accurately.

3–28, 3–29, 3–30, 3–62w, 3–63w, 3–64w, 3–65w

T 9 Navigate virtual environments such as electronic books, software, and websites.

3–27

HEALTH STANDARDS (H)

H 1 Comprehend concepts related to health promotion and disease prevention to enhance health.

4–3, 4–4, 4–6, 4–7, 4–8, 4–9, 4–11, 4–31w

H 2 Analyze the influence of family, peers, culture, media, technology, and other factors on health behaviors.

4–5, 4–7, 4–8

H 3 Demonstrate the ability to access valid information, products, and services to enhance health.

4–3, 4–4, 4–12

H 4 Demonstrate the ability to use interpersonal communication skills to enhance health and avoid or reduce health risks.

4–1, 4–6, 4–10, 4–35w

H 5 Demonstrate the ability to use decision-making skills to enhance health.

4–1, 4–2, 4–3, 4–9, 4–10, 4–11, 4–30, 4–32w, 4–33w, 4–34w, 4–35w, 4–36w, 4–43w, 4–44w

H 6 Demonstrate the ability to use goal-setting skills to enhance health.

4–5, 4–12, 4–13, 4–16, 4–17, 4–19, 4–24

H 7 Demonstrate the ability to practice health-enhancing behaviors and avoid or reduce health risks.

4–5, 4–6, 4–8, 4–25, 4–26, 4–30, 4–33w

H 8 Demonstrate the ability to advocate for personal, family, and community health.

4–2, 4–4, 4–7, 4–34w

PHYSICAL EDUCATION STANDARDS (PE)

PE 1 Demonstrate competency in motor skills and movement patterns needed to perform a variety of physical activities.

4–13, 4–14, 4–15, 4–16, 4–18, 4–20, 4–21, 4–22, 4–27, 4–28, 4–29, 4–30, 4–36w, 4–37w, 4–38w, 4–39w, 4–40w, 4–42w, 4–43w, 4–44w

PE 2 Demonstrate understanding of movement concepts, principles, strategies, and tactics as they apply to the learning and performance of physical activities.

4–13, 4–15, 4–16, 4–18, 4–19, 4–21, 4–23, 4–24, 4–28, 4–29, 4–37w, 4–38w, 4–39w, 4–40w, 4–41w, 4–44w

PE 3 Participate regularly in physical activity.

4–14, 4–17, 4–41w

PE 4 Achieve and maintain a health-enhancing level of physical fitness.

4–14, 4–17

PE 5 Exhibit responsible personal and social behavior that respects self and others in physical activity settings.

4–19, 4–20, 4–23, 4–25, 4–26, 4–27, 4–28, 4–37w, 4–39w

PE 6 Value physical activity for health, enjoyment, challenge, self-expression, and/or social interaction.

4–12, 4–15, 4–22, 4–24, 4–25, 4–26, 4–42w

CREATIVE ARTS STANDARDS

Visual Arts Standards (VA)

VA 1 Understand and apply media, techniques, and processes.

5–1, 5–2, 5–3, 5–4, 5–6, 5–7, 5–8, 5–9, 5–31w, 5–32w, 5–33w, 5–34w, 5–35w, 5–36w, 5–37w, 5–38w, 5–39w, 5–40w, 5–41w, 5–42w, 5–43w, 5–44w

VA 2 Use knowledge of structures and functions.

5–4, 5–7, 5–9, 5–31w, 5–35w, 5–37w, 5–38w, 5–41w, 5–42w

VA 3 Choose and evaluate a range of subject matter, symbols, and ideas.

1–11, 1–36w, 5–2, 5–3, 5–31w, 5–33w, 5–34w, 5–35w, 5–43w

VA 4 Understand the visual arts in relation to history and cultures.

5–3, 5–6, 5–32w, 5–39w

VA 5 Reflect on and assess the characteristics and merits of their work and the work of others.

5–5, 5–10, 5–33w, 5–34w, 5–43w

VA 6 Make connections between visual arts and other disciplines.

5–1, 5–4, 5–5, 5–6, 5–8, 5–9, 5–10, 5–36w, 5–37w, 5–39w, 5–40w, 5–44w

Music Standards (MU)

MU 1 Sing, alone and with others, a varied repertoire of music.

5–11, 5–16, 5–17, 5–18, 5–50w, 5–52w

MU 2 Perform on instruments, alone and with others, a varied repertoire of music.

5–12, 5–14, 5–19, 5–46w, 5–49w, 5–51w

MU 3 Improvise melodies, variations, and accompaniments.

5–16, 5–17, 5–46w, 5–50w, 5–51w, 5–52w

MU 4 Compose and arrange music within specific guidelines.

5–14

MU 5 Read and notate music.

5–12, 5–14, 5–18

MU 6 Listen to, analyze, and describe music.

5–11, 5–13, 5–15, 5–16, 5–17, 5–18, 5–19, 5–20, 5–45w, 5–47w, 5–48w, 5–49w

MU 7 Evaluate music and music performances.

5–15, 5–20, 5–45w, 5–49w

MU 8 Understand relationships between music, the other arts, and disciplines outside the arts.

5–15, 5–20, 5–45w, 5–46w, 5–47w, 5–48w, 5–55w

MU 9 Understand music in relation to history and culture.

5–13, 5–19

Dance Standards (D)

D 1 Identify and demonstrate movement elements and skills in performing dance.

5–13, 5–21, 5–22, 5–23, 5–24, 5–25, 5–47w, 5–53w, 5–54w

D 2 Understand choreographic principles, processes, and structures.

5–22

D 3 Understand dance as a way to create and communicate meaning.

5–21, 5–23, 5–53w, 5–54w

D 4 Apply and demonstrate critical and creative thinking skills in dance.

5–24, 5–55w

D 5 Demonstrate and understand dance in various cultures and historical periods.

5–22, 5–25, 5–55w

D 6 Make connections between dance and healthful living.

5–24, 5–25

D 7 Make connections between dance and other disciplines.

5–23

Theater Standards (TH)

TH 1 Write script by planning and recording improvisations based on personal experience and heritage, imagination, literature, and history.

5–26, 5–30, 5–36w

TH 2 Act by assuming roles and interacting in improvisations.

1–1, 1–31w, 2–2, 2–32w, 5–26, 5–27, 5–28, 5–29, 5–30, 5–56w, 5–57w

TH 3 Design by visualizing and arranging environments for classroom dramatizations.

5–27, 5–28, 5–29, 5–56w

TH 4 Direct by planning classroom dramatizations.

5–30

TH 5 Research by finding information to support classroom dramatizations.

5–29

Social Awareness Activities:
Social Competence and Social Studies

Social awareness for young children helps them understand and function in the world in which they live. During their early years, children are developing their values and attitudes about themselves, other children, their family and community, and the world. They are developing a concept of self. It is important that they have a broad range of experiences and are exposed to people and materials without gender, racial, ability, or cultural bias. People with disabilities must be portrayed accurately, including both their abilities and disabilities.

ACTIVITY GOALS AND STANDARDS

Activities are organized by the goals and standards they support. The activities themselves serve as prototypes of activities that can be used again and again with minor changes. Goals and standards that focus directly on social competence and social studies are given first. More details about the standards are given in Chapter 4. Books that are referred to in the text with an * have a complete citation and annotation in the Children's Bibliography; others have a complete citation where they are cited. For books where a lexile score is available, it is given after the book, for example, (500L). The notation "AD" before the lexile means that the book requires adult direction and should

©Cengage Learning 2012

initially be read by an adult and discussed with children before children read it independently.

SOCIAL AWARENESS GUIDELINES

The following guidelines will be helpful as you think about adapting social awareness activities to meet the needs of children with diverse abilities.

Adapting activities for children with:

Specific learning disabilities ❖ Encourage them to use a variety of solutions to problems. Actively promote prosocial skills. Focus on what children can do and support their doing it.

Social, emotional, and behavioral disorders ❖ Make school a familiar, safe, and predictable place. Prepare children for change. Discuss ways of dealing with feelings.

Attention-deficit/hyperactivity disorder ❖ Work on conflict resolution skills. Use short activities, brief lessons, and break information into small chunks. Present information sequentially rather than all at once.

Communication disorders ❖ Plan a language rich environment that increases children's knowledge of the roles people play and the variety of ways people communicate.

English language learners ❖ Use field trips to provide firsthand cultural and language experiences. Discuss the cultural and ethnic groups of the children in the class and the languages they speak at home as a way of including all children.

Autism spectrum disorders ❖ Help children engage in relationships with other children and adults. Support children in taking an interest in the sights, sounds, and sensations of the environment. Help children learn to self-regulate their behavior.

Intellectual delays and disabilities ❖ Give children tasks they can accomplish and roles to help them be part of the group. Build on familiar experiences. Highlight what children can accomplish.

Gifts and talents ❖ Promote social skills, help children take different perspectives on social situations. Support children who take intellectual risks.

Special health care needs ❖ Expand children's knowledge of the medical community in ways that give them some control. Develop methods (notes, telephone calls, e-mail) of keeping children in touch with their peers.

Orthopedic and neurological impairments ❖ Use field trips to help children learn about their environment and use technology and visitors to support learning about inaccessible places. Teach about accessibility and how it is important to many groups of people (babies in strollers, older people, and so on).

Hearing impairments ❖ Teach children verbal and nonverbal ways of approaching others. Use visual aids to clarify and generalize experiences.

Visual impairments ❖ Include a variety of role models, including those who wear glasses and use optical devices. Use technology to expand children's world. Help children learn to use their residual vision. Provide many opportunities to develop the sense of touch.

Social Awareness Activities

• • • • SOCIAL COMPETENCE: **LARGE GROUP**

1-1 Celebrations

GOALS: To improve self-concept; to broaden concepts of family; to increase cultural awareness

STANDARDS: SS 1 Culture; SS 3 People, places, and environments; S&L 6 Speak audibly and express thoughts, feelings, and ideas clearly; TH 2 Act by assuming roles and interacting in improvisations.

MATERIALS: None (unless the child wants to bring in something)

PROCEDURE: Talk with children about how their families celebrate particular holidays. Then choose one or two children to act out their families' celebrations for the group. Include different holidays, birthdays, and celebrations. Be sure to discuss feelings, excitement, and expectations. Discuss how families have different ways of celebrating as well as different occasions that are celebrated. Encourage children to have family members or others come to talk about the celebrations as well. Plan some special activities and snacks that support the learning experience.

ACCOMMODATIONS AND INTEGRATION: Discuss celebrations, why people look forward to them, their significance, and why they can be stressful events. Talk about appropriate ways to deal with the stress that accompanies both joy and disappointment. Talk about the role of marker events and the various reasons for celebration. Discuss both formal and informal celebrations. If there are children in your class who do not celebrate holidays, find out from them and their families how they want to share this information.

• • • • SOCIAL COMPETENCE: **LARGE GROUP**

1-2 Family Book

GOALS: To improve self-concept; to broaden concepts of family; to increase awareness of the roles people play

STANDARDS: SS1 Culture; SS 2 Time, continuity, and change; S&L 4 Describe familiar people, places, things, and events and, with prompting and support, provide additional detail.

MATERIALS: Three-ring binder, plastic sleeve protectors, black construction paper to fit inside sleeve protectors, tape or glue, pictures of family members for each child in the class, digital camera

PROCEDURE: Have children bring in pictures of family, friends, and themselves. Give them a piece of black paper and tape, and ask them to make a collage with the pictures, keeping the faces visible. Place the picture-covered papers into a plastic sleeve protector and these into a three-ring binder. Encourage children to look at and talk about the pictures and events they depict. Help them look at similarities

Encourage children to talk about their families and how they have fun together.
©Cengage Learning 2012

and differences and discuss them with peers. Ask them for additional details.

ACCOMMODATIONS AND INTEGRATION: Help children with the selection and gluing process. Encourage children who do not bring pictures from home to draw their family members and friends, or take digital pictures of their friends at school to include in the book. Encourage children to look at these pictures with other children when they are concerned about family members or miss them during the school day. This allows children to talk about important people in their lives, as well as important people in their classmates' lives.

• • • • SOCIAL COMPETENCE: **SMALL GROUP**

1-3 Family Collage

GOALS: To improve self-concept; to broaden concepts of family; to increase awareness of the roles people play

STANDARDS: SS1 Culture; SS 2 Time, continuity, and change; S&L 4 Describe familiar people, places, things, and events and, with prompting and support, provide additional detail.

MATERIALS: Magazines, scissors, construction paper, glue or glue stick

PROCEDURE: Give children magazines, scissors, glue sticks, and a piece of construction paper. Explain that they are going to create families. Talk about what members might constitute a family. Encourage children to have a broad definition of family. Let the children cut out a variety of pictures from magazines and paste them onto construction paper. Ask children to discuss why they included different members in their family and about members' roles.

ACCOMMODATIONS AND INTEGRATION: Encourage children to make pictures of different families they know, and ask them to compare and contrast the families with their own family. Let children choose pictures, but help them cut out or tear out the people they choose if necessary. This helps children realize that families are unique as well as similar.

· · · · · SOCIAL COMPETENCE: **LARGE OR SMALL GROUP**

1–4   Foreign Languages

GOALS: To increase awareness of individual differences and similarities; to increase cultural awareness; to increase respect for diversity in modes of communication

STANDARDS: SS1 Culture; SS 4 Individual development and identity; S&L 6 Speak audibly and express thoughts, feelings, and ideas clearly.

MATERIALS: CD and CD player (CDs from the Putumayo Kids series, such as *African Playground*; download the *African Playground* Teaching Guide and map from www.putumayo.com/en/putumayo_kids_multi.php)

PROCEDURE: Play a CD of a song in a foreign language. Ask children what the words mean and discuss how some words are the same or similar in several languages. Have them think about the music and how it is different from other music they hear. Discuss with the children how hard it is to listen and pay attention when you do not understand. Play other CDs and have children work on differentiating English from non-English. Use a variety of languages so children understand that there are many different languages. If children or their families speak another language, invite them to come and talk to the class, but be sure they talk about the culture as well. Help children become more aware of other languages and cultures and how difficult and valuable it is to learn about them.

ACCOMMODATIONS AND INTEGRATION: Teach children words in another language first so they have some familiarity with the underlying concept. Encourage children to listen to language-learning tapes, CDs, and videos. Use interactive computer programs so that children can hear themselves speaking words in another language and compare it to a model. Have children go to a website such as http://spanish-languagelearner.com/, which is part of a Spanish immersion program for first graders. Have them look at the words and hear the pronunciation. Help children think about their dependence on language to communicate and the problems encountered when you do not speak the language of the people around you. Have a children's picture dictionary that labels pictures in two languages so they not only hear that the language is different but see it as well. Use the Putumayo teacher's guide to expand the lesson and explore other music in this series.

· · · · · SOCIAL COMPETENCE: **SMALL GROUP**

1–5   Fingerspelling Lotto

GOALS: To increase awareness of individual differences and similarities; to increase inclusion; to increase respect for diversity in modes of communication

STANDARDS: SS 1 Culture; SS 4 Individual development and identity.

MATERIALS: Alphabet Lotto cards with Ameslan signs for each letter on one side and the English alphabet on the other

PROCEDURE: Make a "Lotto" game using the letters of the alphabet and the manual signs for those letters. See Figure 18–5. Encourage the children to make the sign with their hands as they match the cards. Have the children fingerspell their names. Talk about alphabets and their function in language. Discuss how a language that is only spoken is different from a written language.

ACCOMMODATIONS AND INTEGRATION: Start with fewer letters where the signs have a visual resemblance to the letters they represent (*c, d, l, m, n, o, v*). Have the children spell words using the signs. This shows children a potential avenue of communication and another representation of language. Use other alphabets that are different from the English alphabet that children in the class might be learning.

· · · · · SOCIAL COMPETENCE: **SMALL OR LARGE GROUP**

1–6   Family Flags

GOALS: To improve self-concept; to broaden concepts of family; to increase cultural awareness

STANDARDS: SS 1 Culture; SS 10 Civic ideals and practices; S&L 3 Ask and answer questions in order to seek help, get information, or clarify something that is not understood.

MATERIALS: U.S. flag, pictures of other flags, paper, crayons, markers

PROCEDURE: Introduce the activity by discussing what flags are, and explain the symbols on flags. Show and talk about the U.S. flag and the ideals that it stands for. Have children think about what is important to their family and create their own flag using paper and crayons or markers. Give examples of things that are important to families, such as culture, people, holidays, nationality, coats of arms, and so forth. State that flags are a symbol of each child's family and special values.

ACCOMMODATIONS AND INTEGRATION: Show children examples of flags, plaids, and coats of arms that signify different families and their values. Talk about these and about how families can be different and yet the same. Help children decide what is important to their families and decide how they can symbolize it. This allows children to express important aspects of their families. It encourages them to see the uniqueness of each family and how all families are special in different ways. Encourage children to talk to their families about the flag they made and what the symbols stand for.

· · · · · SOCIAL COMPETENCE: **LARGE GROUP**

1–7   Family Heirlooms

GOALS: To increase inclusion; to broaden concepts of family; to increase cultural awareness

STANDARDS: SS 2 Time, continuity, and change; SS 4 Individual development and identity; S&L 3 Ask and answer questions in order to seek help, get information, or clarify something that is not understood.

MATERIALS: Family heirlooms or photographs of family heirlooms

PROCEDURE: Talk with the children about special objects that families pass down. Discuss the special meanings that make these objects important to families. Invite children to bring in a family heirloom or a photograph of one. Have children describe the object and explain why the object is important to their families. Display the items or photographs of them on a special table.

ACCOMMODATIONS AND INTEGRATION: If children do not have family heirlooms, help them develop some. What would they like to have? Take pictures of the child or his work. Write a story about the child. It is important for children to develop a sense of permanence. This allows children to learn more about their families and their heritage. It also allows children to see how families are the same and different.

· · · · · SOCIAL COMPETENCE: **SMALL GROUP**

1–8 Family Map

GOALS: To improve self-concept; to broaden concepts of family; to increase awareness of roles people play

STANDARDS: SS 2 Time, continuity, and change; SS 4 Individual development and identity; S&L 5 Add drawings or other visual displays to descriptions as desired to provide additional detail.

MATERIALS: Manila paper, crayons, circles and squares of different sizes made from construction paper

PROCEDURE: Give children construction paper and tell them that they are going to make a map of their family. For this map, all the females in the family will be circles and the males, rectangles. The children can choose the circles and rectangles and place them on the page where they choose or draw them (see Figure R1–1). Encourage children to decide who is part of their family and where they should go on the page. Help children identify family members and mark them. Have children designate whom the rectangles and circles represent. Be sure to allow for pets if children want to include them. They can put a boundary around the family, or not, as they choose, and they can enhance their map with their own art. Some children may be part of more than one family and the map can represent this. Encourage children to think more about families and how they are connected. Help them develop a key to show relationships among family members. Talk about generational changes and differences.

ACCOMMODATIONS AND INTEGRATION: Help the child place the appropriate forms on the paper and make them stay where the child wants them. Be the child's scribe; label the forms and write the child's family story. Use circles and rectangles with texture such as sandpaper or felt. Help children see different family configurations. The process may give you insight into the child's perception of her family.

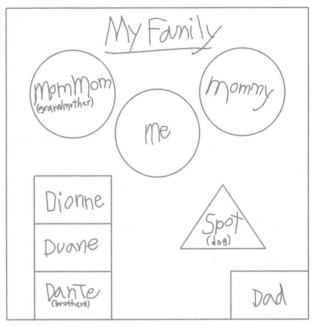

FIGURE R1–1: Family Map

· · · · · SOCIAL COMPETENCE: **SMALL GROUP**

1–9 Grandparents

GOALS: To increase awareness of individual differences and similarities; to broaden concepts of family; to increase cultural awareness

STANDARDS: SS 2 Time, continuity, and change; SS 4 Individual development and identity; S&L 3 Ask and answer questions in order to seek help, get information, or clarify something that is not understood.

MATERIALS: Paper, pencils, markers, crayons, book such as A. K. Christian, *Butterfly Kisses for Grandma and Grandpa* (McKinney, TX: Blue Whale Press, 2008)

PROCEDURE: Read a book about grandparents and talk with children about where their grandparents live and how they keep in contact with them. (If children don't have grandparents talk about special friends or other family members.) Talk with the children about how families are made up of many different people. Encourage children to think about their family over time. Make a generic timeline, starting with when the children were born (e.g., 2005), when their parents were born (e.g., 1980), and when their grandparents were born (e.g., 1955). Discuss with children how the world has changed since their grandparents were children. Encourage them to ask and answer questions about the topic. Help them think about things that are the same and different (TV, DVDs, cell phones, computers, etc.). Help them think about how their world would be different without some of these things. Have the children draw pictures of family members on the paper and some of the things that are the same and different. Encourage them to take the picture home and talk with their family about their picture.

ACCOMMODATIONS AND INTEGRATION: Help children recognize that different family members are different ages. And not only are some people older, but also the world they lived in was different from the one the children experience.

• • • • •   SOCIAL COMPETENCE: **SMALL GROUP**

 ## Mufflers

1–10

GOALS: To increase awareness of individual differences and similarities; to increase inclusion; to increase respect for diversity in modes of communication

STANDARDS: SS 3 People, places, and environments; S&L 3 Ask and answer questions in order to seek help, get information, or clarify something that is not understood.

MATERIALS: Earmuffs or cotton balls, tapes or CDs and tape recorder or CD player

PROCEDURE: Set up the dramatic play area in the usual way. Have the children wear earmuffs or put cotton balls in their ears, and tell them to whisper while playing instead of talking out loud. Have a tape playing in the background to make it more difficult to hear. Follow this activity with a discussion at group time where you talk softly while the music is playing. If the children get frustrated or restless, go back to your normal style. Ask children to identify what was difficult for them and what they did when they couldn't hear or understand what was going on. Ask children for ideas on how they could be helpful to someone with a hearing impairment or who is an English language learner.

ACCOMMODATIONS AND INTEGRATION: Do this only for a short time. Help children focus on what they do differently when they cannot hear. Children will begin to understand the implications and frustrations of not being able to hear or understand what is going on around them. Talk about places or situations where it is difficult to hear (e.g., airports, places that use large equipment, noisy machinery) and discuss what people do to be understood and to protect their hearing.

• • • • •   SOCIAL COMPETENCE: **SMALL GROUP**

 ## Who Is It?

1–11

GOALS: To increase awareness of individual differences and similarities; to increase inclusion; to increase body awareness

STANDARDS: SS 3 People, places, and environments; SS 4 Individual development and identity; VA 3 Choose and evaluate a range of subject matter, symbols, and ideas.

MATERIALS: A blindfold, scarf, or half mask with eyeholes covered

PROCEDURE: Blindfold one child and have him touch another child. You will have to give some guidance at first on the appropriate ways to touch another person. You might even guide the child's hand to feel the length of hair, height, type of shoes and clothes, facial features, and so on. Help

the child by stating what to feel for: "Let's see. Who is about as tall as you are? Who has long, straight hair, and high cheekbones? Who is wearing a sweatshirt and tie shoes?" (Children may have to use clothing as clues until they become more precise in their ability to touch.) Initially, choose a child to identify who has very obvious features or one who is a good friend. Have the child talk. As children become more proficient, give fewer clues.

ACCOMMODATIONS AND INTEGRATION: Tell children to close their eyes (they can talk). Have the children spend more of their day blindfolded. Encourage children to work in pairs, with one child blindfolded, and talk about what is helpful and what is not. This gives children the experience of "seeing" with their hands as a child who is blind might. It also shows them some of the difficulties such children face. Encourage children to look in the mirror and figure out what would feel different about different faces (bone structure, how deeply set the eyes are, shape of the nose, etc.).

• • • • •   SOCIAL COMPETENCE: **SMALL GROUP OR INDIVIDUAL**

 ## Wheels

1–12

GOALS: To increase inclusion; to improve cause-and-effect reasoning

STANDARDS: SS 3 People, places, and environments; SS 5 Individuals, groups, and institutions; SS 10 Civic ideals and practices.

MATERIALS: Familiar objects with wheels: inline skates, wagons, tricycles, roller skates, skateboards, wheelchairs, creepers, scooters, suitcases, backpacks, dollies

PROCEDURE: Discuss the function of wheels and encourage children to experiment moving on or using things with wheels. If you have shelves on wheels, compare moving those shelves with shelves not on wheels. Help children experiment by using rollers to move objects. When you are outside, keep the wheels of a tricycle or wagon from turning by putting a wedge in front of the wheels, and discuss how this affects the vehicle's movement. Be sure to include wheelchairs and curb cuts and why we have these. Talk about brakes and the function they serve. Map out a course that requires turns, and have children use wheeled objects to traverse the course. Ask about what is easy and difficult for them.

ACCOMMODATIONS AND INTEGRATION: Encourage children to experiment with a wheelchair to go from one place to another. Be sure it includes going up and down a ramp (with close adult supervision). Talk about the energy it takes to use a wheelchair and how this is different from using a tricycle or a scooter. If possible, have someone who does wheelchair sports visit and demonstrate his skills. Children can learn about the functions wheels play in moving and become aware of the implications of using a wheelchair, of curb cuts, and so on.

SOCIAL COMPETENCE: **LARGE OR SMALL GROUP**

1-13 Photograph Story

GOALS: To improve self-concept; to broaden concepts of family; to increase awareness of roles people play

STANDARDS: SS 3 People, places, and environments; SS 4 Individual development and identity; SS 9 Global connections.

MATERIALS: Photographs of the children in your class and several familiar people, including teachers in your school and even you, in a variety of roles, different places, and environments; books such as *Back to School**, *Be My Neighbor**, *Let the Games Begin**, *My Family**, *Our Grandparents: A Global Album**

PROCEDURE: Start with yourself and show the children pictures of you with them and with your family and doing other things you do. Then read a book about children and families that uses a global perspective. Encourage children to ask and answer questions about the similarities and differences between the book and their experiences and the roles these children and family members have. Invite children to bring pictures from home to share as well. Ask that the names and relationships be placed on the back. Take digital pictures of the children and adults in your class. At the beginning use pictures of familiar people so that children understand the concept of multiple roles. Include many different relationships. Add pictures of famous people and occupations: the president of the United States, astronauts, and movie stars. All may be husbands, wives, sons, daughters, siblings, aunts, uncles, and so on.

ACCOMMODATIONS AND INTEGRATION: Children need to gain a perspective on roles and how they are played out globally. They need to see medical personnel and related service providers as playing other familiar roles. They also need to see that they themselves have many roles.

SOCIAL COMPETENCE: **LARGE GROUP**

1-14 Roles

GOALS: To improve self-concept; to broaden concepts of family; to increase awareness of roles people play

STANDARDS: SS 4 Individual development and identity; SS 6 Power, authority, and governance; L 4 Determine or clarify the meaning of unknown and multiple-meaning words and phrases based on kindergarten reading and content.

MATERIALS: Flannelboard and Pellon figures: 4 boys, 4 girls, 2 women, 2 men, 2 older men, 2 older women

PROCEDURE: Have a group discussion about the variety of roles that children play. Use flannelboard figures to help clarify these roles for the children. Explain such roles as brother/sister, stepbrother/stepsister, friend, grandfather/grandmother, boy/girl cousin, daughter/son, stepdaughter/stepson, man/woman, nephew/niece, husband/wife,

grandson/granddaughter, father/mother, and stepfather/stepmother, and encourage children to ask questions about these roles to clarify their meaning.

Explain that one person plays many roles. Start with roles that children are most familiar with. Be sure to include all the relationships that children in your classroom have. When the children have identified their various roles, describe roles to see whether children can guess whom you are talking about: "I'm thinking of a girl who has one sister who is younger than she is and no brothers. Who am I thinking of?" Increase the complexity of relationships.

ACCOMMODATIONS AND INTEGRATION: Begin with the roles children and adults play in the classroom. Have children role-play the roles, ensuring each child plays different roles. Discuss the similarities and differences of specific roles. List roles for children; don't assume they know. Acknowledge that individuals play roles differently and talk about how specific disabilities may influence how people play these roles. Discuss family change and roles that change with changing situations (marriage, husband/wife roles) and those that do not change (parental). Your mother is still your mother even if she no longer lives with your father. Be sure to include acquired kin as well (favorite friends that become "aunts or uncles"), as well as godparents and others who are important in some cultures. *Note:* This may be a sensitive issue for a child whose family is changing (e.g., through divorce, death, birth, etc.).

SOCIAL COMPETENCE: **INDIVIDUAL**

1-15 Be the Teacher

GOALS: To increase awareness of roles people play; to improve self-concept; to increase awareness of individual differences and similarities

STANDARDS: SS 4 Individual development and identity; SS 6 Power, authority, and governance; S&L 6 Speak audibly and express thoughts, feelings, and ideas clearly.

MATERIALS: None

PROCEDURE: During group time, pick one child to help you give instructions. Pick a familiar routine, such as the calendar or dismissing the class. Coach the child to give specific directions: "All children who have plaid shirts may go to centers."

ACCOMMODATIONS AND INTEGRATION: Initially, have the child do a part of the task; that is, you decide how to dismiss the children, and the child says it, or vice versa. Give children greater responsibility over time. Increase the variety of tasks children do, and perhaps include reading a book, singing, and so on. Children need practice in leadership roles when they can be successful. However, this skill needs to be taught and practiced in a variety of circumstances. It is different to be in charge and ask questions than it is to answer them. Talk with children about how they felt being in charge.

• • • • • SOCIAL STUDIES: **LARGE GROUP**

1–16 International Snack

GOALS: To increase social studies concepts; to increase awareness of roles people play; to increase cultural awareness

STANDARDS: SS 1 Culture; SS 3 People, places, and environments; L 4 Determine or clarify the meaning of unknown and multiple-meaning words and phrases based on kindergarten reading and content.

MATERIALS: One of the following: flour tortillas, egg rolls, fondue, crêpes, Irish soda bread, pita bread, wontons

PROCEDURE: Make a snack that is not traditionally American. Start with foods that, although from other countries originally, are familiar to many of the children (tofu, pita bread, crêpes), and then work in foods that are increasingly different. Discuss what the foods are made of and where they come from, and then eat them. Help children look at the broad geographic features of a region such as temperature, rainfall, and elevation, and look at the foods eaten in relation to those variables. Include children in the snack preparation, using rebus menus, and discuss the foods used, the culture, and the people. Use children's families as a resource.

ACCOMMODATIONS AND INTEGRATION: Check for allergies, particularly if the foods are unusual and children may not have eaten the ingredients. Help children think of differences without judgment. Children will often participate in experiences with food at school that they would not try at home, especially if they participate in its preparation.

• • • • • SOCIAL STUDIES: **LARGE OR SMALL GROUP**

1–17 Who Has Been Here?

GOALS: To increase social studies concepts; to encourage problem solving; to improve cause-and-effect reasoning

STANDARDS: SS 2 Time, continuity, and change; SS 3 People, places, and environments; SS 4 Individual development and identity.

MATERIALS: Water-based paint, paper (8½ × 11 inches), a variety of footwear in different sizes and for different purposes:

baby shoes	golf shoes	crocs
baseball spikes	sneakers	ballet slippers
ice skates	roller skates	moccasins
high heels	riding boots	flip-flops
hiking boots	tap shoes	clogs

PROCEDURE: Make footprints by putting the bottom of the footwear in paint, then printing each one on a sheet of paper. Make at least six footprints with each pair of footwear. First, use only one type of shoe, differing only in size (e.g., sneakers). Have children match the shoe to the print. Start by showing the children footprints that are about the size they would make. Ask them to arrange the prints as if someone were walking (see Figure R1–2). Ask the children to describe the size of the person and where the person might be going. Have the children walk on the prints (after they are dry) to see whether the spacing is right; help them correlate the size of footprints with the spacing between footprints. Add the more specialized footwear. Then help the children match the shoes to the prints and decide under what conditions this type of footwear would be most useful. Monitor carefully some of the shoes (ice skates, baseball spikes, etc.) that might cut children.

ACCOMMODATIONS AND INTEGRATION: Use textured paint so children can feel as well as see the footprints. For some children, this may be simply a matching process. Add snowshoes, swimming fins, and so on, for more variety. Thinking skills are both challenging and fun. You might have children design shoes for various environments (e.g., swamp versus desert). Have a specialty footwear store. Be sure to include shoes from a variety of places so children can describe the places and activities when the shoes might be used.

• • • • • SOCIAL STUDIES: **LARGE GROUP**

1–18 Divergent

GOALS: To increase social studies concepts; to increase cultural awareness; to improve cause-and-effect reasoning

STANDARDS: SS 2 Time continuity, and change; SS 7 Production, distribution, and consumption; W 2 Use a

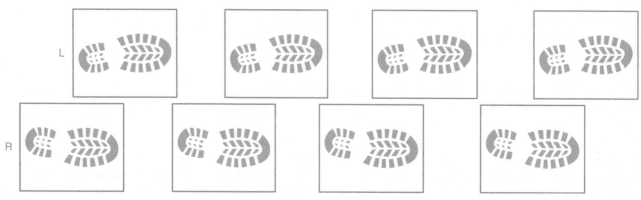

FIGURE R1–2: Foot Prints

combination of drawing, dictating, and writing to compose informative/explanatory texts in which they name what they are writing about and supply some information about the topic.

MATERIALS: Paper, clothing, pencils, chair, other classroom items

PROCEDURE: Have a discussion related to a particular theme or topic (wheels, chairs, roofs, paper). Ask children to name objects and list them. Then ask them to imagine what it would be like if we didn't have the objects. Show children objects that they use in the classroom and then expand these into categories. Show them a piece of paper and then talk about all the paper used in the classroom and ask how it would be different not to have this particular object or material.

Talk about the things their parents and grandparents did not have when they were young. Encourage children to ask their parents and grandparents what they didn't have when they were children and have them bring in a list that they wrote or dictated to share with the group.

ACCOMMODATIONS AND INTEGRATION: Give children hints, such as "What would we write on if we didn't have paper?" and "What would we sit on if we didn't have chairs?" Expand this concept to have children think about how life would be different if they didn't have hands, eyes, ears, and so on. (Scrupulously avoid references that could hurt or offend a particular child or family situation.) Pose questions as to how they would do certain things, and demonstrate these. Expand the examples into social and public services such as medicine, electricity, water, and so on. Talk about not having enough food, housing, and so on. Children with some impairments might share with others how they compensate. "Joan has a great way of looking for things when her locker gets rearranged. Can you show the class how you search for things? What is she doing?" Build children's self-concepts by pointing out how they compensate either for disabilities or for situational conditions

such as being too short to reach something they want. As children realize the principles behind skills, it is easier to apply them.

· · · · · SOCIAL STUDIES: **SMALL GROUP**

Maps

GOALS: To increase social studies concepts; to increase inclusion; to encourage problem solving

STANDARDS: SS 3 People, places, and environments; SS 7 Production, distribution, and consumption.

MATERIALS: A laminated map of the school and nearby community, erasable marking pens, tissue

PROCEDURE: Introduce the concept of maps and their purpose. Start with a map of the classroom and have children use the map to go to a certain area. Then introduce the map of the area. Set the map on a table with erasable marking pens and tissue beside it. Encourage the children to pick a location and work together to trace a path from school to that location and then to find alternative routes and compare them (see Figure R1–3). Use tissue to erase the marking pen. Help children map out a walk or field trip.

ACCOMMODATIONS AND INTEGRATION: Help the children make a simple map of the room, duplicate it and place it in an 8½ × 11 inch sleeve protector. Identify where the child is ("You are here."). Help children hold the map and then go to a specified place. Then have the child plot the route on the map. Encourage children to do the reverse. Plot the route and then walk it. They can do this in pairs. Then help them think more broadly about how fresh vegetables and groceries get to the grocery store. Have them think about produce that is not grown near where they live. This is a way of increasing children's understanding of their community and helps them learn about alternative ways of reaching a destination.

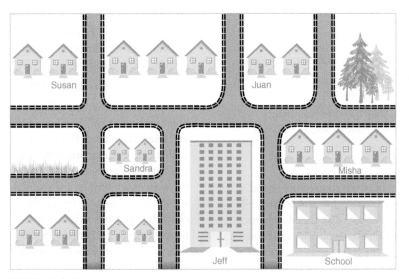

FIGURE R1–3: Map

photographer | Red Cross staff | farmer
business person | wait staff | plumber
Welcome Wagon staff | male nurse | builder
female medical doctor | female lawyer | musician
female engineer | real estate agent | reporter
construction worker | computer programmer | massage therapist

Start with occupations the children are familiar with and keep large group discussions short. Have children who are interested follow up with a small group discussion. The visitor can go into greater depth about the profession and answer additional questions. Follow up by visiting the person at work as well as by dramatic play in the classroom.

ACCOMMODATIONS AND INTEGRATION: Choose a broad base of visitors determined by the interests of the children and their skills. Include professions that are essential, which children do not necessarily think about, such as those who work with heating and air conditioning systems, boat mechanics, clerks, and especially those who work behind the scenes (postal employees who do not deliver mail). Children often have a restricted view of the local and global community. Extend their understanding and make them feel more a part of their community. Be sure to include visitors who represent a variety of cultural and ethnic groups and include those who have disabilities.

Children who are English language learners may have very different experiences and expectations about what is usual.
Courtesy of Penny Low Deiner

• • • • •   SOCIAL STUDIES: **LARGE GROUP**

 Visitor

GOALS: To increase social studies concepts; to increase awareness of roles people play; to increase awareness of individual differences and similarities

STANDARDS: SS 3 People, places, and environments; SS 5 Individuals, groups, and institutions; SS 9 Global connections.

MATERIALS: None

PROCEDURE: Invite adults from the community to come into the class. Pick people who are comfortable with children. Have them talk briefly about what they do, then answer children's questions. Choose people who will broaden children's understanding of the community, and reduce role stereotyping. Be sure to include individuals from a variety of racial and ethnic groups. For example:

• • • • •   SOCIAL STUDIES: **LARGE OR SMALL GROUP**

 Who Am I?

GOALS: To increase social studies concepts; to increase awareness of roles people play; to improve cause-and-effect reasoning

STANDARDS: SS 3 People, places, and environments; SS 4 Individual development and identity; SS 5 Individuals, groups, and institutions.

MATERIALS: Characteristic hats:

PROCEDURE: Show the collection of hats to the children. Start with what children know: What hats do they wear and why? Have them figure out what person would wear each hat and demonstrate the purpose of the hat. At first, use hats that are specific to one role, then use some to broaden ideas; that is, a woman's hat could be worn by a mother, teacher, secretary, or lawyer. Talk about the characteristics of the hats that make them suitable for the people who wear them. Help children understand the efficacy of hats and how they are different based on when and where you wear them. Look at the subtle differences among similar hats (e.g., football, motorcycle, baseball, and bicycle helmets) and help children understand why they are different and useful.

firefighter's helmet	sunbonnet	baseball cap
fishing hat	hardhat	baby bonnet
rain hat	woman's hat	ski cap
police officer's hat	visor	hats from other areas and cultures
cowboy hat	stocking cap	
	football helmet	

ACCOMMODATIONS AND INTEGRATION: To begin, choose obvious hats, such as a sunbonnet, and then provide a variety of hats designed with the same general purpose. Have a floor lamp so children can try on hats and see how well they protect them from the sun. Encourage children to devise variations, and to explain their thinking. This is a different way of approaching the community as it uses one clue and leaves the rest to the child. Be sure to talk about the purpose of hats in general and how they are used in different cultures/situations. Teach the basic safety and health aspects of hats for use on bicycles, protection from the sun, and to stay warm.

• • • • •　SOCIAL STUDIES: **SMALL GROUP**

1-22　Our Town

GOALS: To increase social studies concepts; to increase inclusion; to increase awareness of roles people play

STANDARDS: SS 3 People, places, and environments; SS 5 Individuals, groups, and institutions; SS 7 Production, distribution, and consumption.

MATERIALS: Masking tape, blocks, and accessories

PROCEDURE: In the block corner, use masking tape to map out a road and building lots. Assign a lot to each child and have them construct buildings. Begin with a few building lots and actively help children decide what they will build. Ask children to decide what kinds of buildings (e.g., houses, restaurants, hospitals, firehouses, gas stations) their community needs and who is going to build them. Leave the construction style up to each child. Pose questions such as "Where would someone go if he got sick?" Expand the children's ideas. Emphasize group problem solving and a sense of community spirit. As children gain skill, have them map out the roads and plots. Expand the block area and leave the structures up for several days. Talk about whether the structures are handicapped-accessible and how they might be adapted if they are not.

ACCOMMODATIONS AND INTEGRATION: Decrease the number of building plots and more actively help children decide what they will build and what the function of their structure is to the town. Keep firm boundaries for each child's space. This provides a more concrete way for children to think about communities and how they work and support the people who live in them.

• • • • •　SOCIAL STUDIES: **SMALL GROUP**

1-23　Medical Tools

GOALS: To increase social studies concepts; to increase awareness of roles people play; to increase inclusion

STANDARDS: SS 5 Individuals, groups, and institutions; SS 8 Science, technology, and society; TH 2 Act by assuming roles and interacting in improvisations.

MATERIALS: Medical equipment, or pictures of medical equipment, and pictures of the parts of the body where these are most commonly used:

Mouth/throat:	tongue depressor, throat swab, thermometer
Eyes/ears:	small flashlight, tuning fork, otoscope
Lungs/heart:	stethoscope
Arm:	blood pressure cuff, syringe
Knee:	rubber hammer

PROCEDURE: Demonstrate and discuss how the equipment is used on a child or doll. Begin with the most familiar ones. Have the children match the pictures of medical equipment to pictures of the appropriate body parts. This often leads to discussion about doctors and medical procedures. Include information on what doctors look for and why. Have a computer with Internet access available so you can look up information. Have pairs of children act out the role of patient and doctor while the group coaches them. Encourage children to explore the equipment in greater depth in the dramatic play area.

ACCOMMODATIONS AND INTEGRATION: Start with the most obvious and work toward more specific types of equipment. Invite a physician to visit and share information with the children. Perhaps show them X-rays of a hand, and then talk about why they are used and the significance of different conditions on the movement and use of a hand. Use the equipment children in your class are most likely to encounter.

• • • • •　SOCIAL STUDIES: **SMALL GROUP**

1-24　Doctors

GOALS: To increase social studies concepts; to increase awareness of roles people play; to increase inclusion

STANDARDS: SS 5 Individuals, groups, and institutions; SS 8 Science, technology, and society; L 4 Determine or clarify the meaning of unknown and multiple-meaning words and phrases based on kindergarten reading and content.

MATERIALS: None

PROCEDURE: Adapt the song "The Farmer in the Dell" to your specific purposes relative to the medical profession:

> There's a child who is sick,
> There's a child who is sick.
> Hi Ho, the Office O.
> There's a child who is sick.

"There's a child going to the doctor" and "There's a child going to the hospital" can also be used. In the following stanzas, the child chooses someone to accompany him to the hospital (e.g., mother, father, grandmother, aunt); that person chooses the doctor; the doctor chooses the nurse (or specialists). Then:

> They all stand together,
> They all stand together.
> Hi Ho the Office O.
> Until the child gets better.

Have each child hold a picture or piece of equipment (stethoscope, thermometer) as a clue to their role. Talk about various specialists and what they do. Include the speech-language pathologist, occupational and physical therapists, psychologist, family therapist, and different types of doctors.

Change the song to "My Doctor" and sing it to the tune of "Mary Had a Little Lamb":

> My doctor has a stethoscope,
> Stethoscope, stethoscope
> My doctor has a stethoscope
> To listen to my heart.

Continue with other tools. The order does not matter:

> Thermometer . . . to take my temperature
> Reflex hammer . . . to check my knees
> Otoscope . . . to look in my ears (can also look in other parts)
> Blood pressure cuff . . . to see how my blood is moving
> (use other people and specialists, as they seem to fit).

ACCOMMODATIONS AND INTEGRATION: Start with equipment all children are familiar with but do not find threatening. Have appropriate equipment on hand to demonstrate what you will sing in the song. Children encounter many members of the health profession. This activity helps frame the potential interaction as informational rather than threatening. Let the children decide which specialists to include and explain what each does.

· · · · ·   SOCIAL STUDIES: **LARGE OR SMALL GROUP**

Audiologist

GOALS: To increase social studies concepts; to increase awareness of roles people play; to increase inclusion

STANDARDS: SS 5 Individuals, groups, and institutions; SS 8 Science, technology, and society; L 4 Determine or clarify the meaning of unknown and multiple-meaning words and phrases based on kindergarten reading and content.

MATERIALS: Props for an audiologist's office: bells, earmuffs, box with knobs, buzzers

PROCEDURE: During group time, introduce the concept of an audiologist and what she does. Talk about how and why people get their hearing tested. Explain that there is an audiologist's office set-up. Use a box with knobs on it; bells, buzzers, or anything that makes noise; and earmuffs for earphones. Have the children "test" each other's hearing. They can raise a hand when they hear a noise or they can do a task, such as stack a plastic donut on a stick, each time they hear a noise. Once children understand the process, erect a barrier so one child can't see what is happening and has to rely on sound to respond. Ask children to identify the sound.

ACCOMMODATIONS AND INTEGRATION: Model the role of the audiologist so children know what an audiologist does. Use this to prepare all children to have their hearing tested by a school nurse or audiologist. Allow children for whom this is a common practice to take a leadership role.

· · · · ·   SOCIAL STUDIES: **LARGE OR SMALL GROUP**

Eye Doctor

GOALS: To increase social studies concepts; to increase awareness of roles people play; to increase inclusion

STANDARDS: SS 5 Individuals, groups, and institutions; SS 8 Science, technology, and society; L 4 Determine or clarify the meaning of unknown and multiple-meaning words and phrases based on kindergarten reading and content.

MATERIALS: Props for an eye doctor's office: vision chart, card with a "three-legged stool" (Figure R1–4), glasses, index card, frames, pointer, mirror

PROCEDURE: During group time, discuss eye doctors and what they do. Explain you have set up an eye doctor's office. Encourage one child to be the doctor and point to the chart, and another to be an assistant and help with glasses and the testing process. Initially concentrate on the matching aspect of this experience at a distance from which you are sure children can see. Encourage children to experiment with the relationship between distance and seeing, and have them find the place in the room from which they can no longer see accurately. Have them measure this distance.

ACCOMMODATIONS AND INTEGRATION: Model the role of the eye doctor. Help children chart the responses of other children on the doctor's eye chart. If children do not understand the process, give them extra time to play the role of the "patient." Follow this activity with vision screening by a nurse or other qualified person. Help children see an eye doctor as a person who identifies children who need visual follow-up and helps them see better.

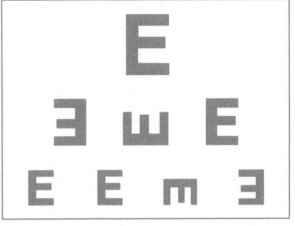

Card

Chart

FIGURE R1–4: Eye Chart and Card

· · · · · SOCIAL STUDIES: **SMALL GROUP**

1-27 Emergency Room

GOALS: To increase social studies concepts; to increase awareness of roles people play; to encourage problem solving

STANDARDS: SS 5 Individuals, groups, and institutions; SS 8 Science, technology, and society; L 4 Determine or clarify the meaning of unknown and multiple-meaning words and phrases based on kindergarten reading and content.

MATERIALS: Emergency room setup: table, paper, chairs, pencils, bandages, lab coat

PROCEDURE: During group time, talk about reasons for going to the emergency room: a broken bone, a bad cut or burn, as opposed to a headache or a cold. Talk to children about what might happen: Someone would ask for their name and insurance number, and they would have to wait. Also discuss what they could do while they wait, what the doctor might do, and the possibility that they would not know the doctor. Emphasize that there is a triage system. Stress the importance of time, and how those with life-threatening conditions are treated first, regardless of when people arrived.

ACCOMMODATIONS AND INTEGRATION: The purpose of this activity is to familiarize children with a set of procedures so that fear of the emergency room is not added to the medical problem. Have an element of realism as well as creativity. See this as a variation on the doctor's office, although the element of time, the reasons for going to the emergency room, and the other people in the waiting room are different.

· · · · · SOCIAL STUDIES: **SMALL GROUP**

1-28 Library

GOALS: To increase social studies concepts; to increase awareness of roles people play; to increase respect for diverse modes of communication

STANDARDS: SS 5 Individuals, groups, and institutions; SS 7 Production, distribution, and consumption; SS 10 Civic ideals and practices.

MATERIALS: Props for a library: books, cards, posters, stamp

PROCEDURE: Set up a library in your room with a collection of children's books that can be categorized by the pictures on the front and the book titles; use books about the country, animals, people, different cultures, and so on. (See the Children's Bibliography for categories.) Encourage children to look over the selection and ask for the books they want. Be sure some children are librarians and some patrons. Have some children categorize the books by area of interest and mark them so they know the area. Encourage the other children to ask for books on specific topics. Talk with them about the role of a reference librarian. Develop a system for checking the books in and out and talk about overdue books. Discuss the role libraries play by having many books on many specific topics.

ACCOMMODATIONS AND INTEGRATION: Have a range of books; include very simple picture books to more complicated books on more abstract topics. This helps children understand that libraries are parts of communities, and their family can use this resource. It also helps children become familiar with library procedures. Follow up with a trip to a library and encourage parents to take their children to the library.

· · · · · SOCIAL STUDIES: **LARGE OR SMALL GROUP**

1-29 Connections

GOALS: To increase social studies concepts; to improve cause-and-effect reasoning; to increase awareness of roles people play

STANDARDS: SS 6 Power, authority, and governance; SS 7 Production, distribution, and consumption; SS 9 Global connections.

MATERIALS: String, wide marking pen, paper of various colors, scissors, 3 × 5 inch index cards, tape

PROCEDURE: Pick a familiar place (the children's school) and draw a large picture of that place. Help the children think through the places in the city or services the school is dependent on. As each is mentioned, write the service on the index card, attach the string to the card, give this to a child, and secure the other end of the string to the picture (see Figure R1–5).

Talk about what each connection signifies. Then take a pair of scissors and cut one string (e.g., water). In addition to cutting the string, explain to children the implications of what happened: "There is no water. What do we do if we are thirsty, have to go to the bathroom, and so on?" Help them experience the problem and generate possible preventive measures and solutions. Ask the children how the school would be different without electricity and what they could do to compensate; for example, if there are no lights, you can use flashlights or lanterns. Decide whom they could contact about situations like this. Discuss how things would be different if this were a chronic problem.

ACCOMMODATIONS AND INTEGRATION: Start with the obvious implications of not having a service. Help children think through the implications based on their everyday lives. Talk about how connections are not the same in all places around the world. Encourage children to look at clothing labels to see where different articles of clothing were made and discuss this with them. Help children see the interdependency of services as well as alternatives for services. Talk about what might happen if workers decided to go on strike.

· · · · ·   SOCIAL STUDIES: **LARGE GROUP**

1–30   No Name

GOALS: To encourage problem solving; to improve self-concept; to increase social studies concepts

STANDARDS: SS 6 Power, authority, and governance; SS 10 Civic ideals and practices; S&L 1 Participate in collaborative conversations with diverse partners about kindergarten topics and texts with peers and adults in small and larger groups.

MATERIALS: A doll that has not been in the classroom before

PROCEDURE: During group time, show the children the doll. Explain that it is new to the room and does not have a name. Ask the children how they think you should go about naming the doll—not what, how. Note their suggestions, and then suggest that if they want, they can play with this doll in the dramatic play area. At the end of the day, the class can actually name the doll or make suggestions that will be finalized the following day. When the children come together again, talk about methods that can be used to reach decisions, and ask them to reflect on the decision-making process. Then ask them about their own names and why they think their parents chose those names. Because the doll can have only one name, have the children discuss *how* they will decide on the name, in addition to choosing one.

ACCOMMODATIONS AND INTEGRATION: Allow the children to each name the doll without requiring that they agree on one name. Talk about names in different languages and different patterns of naming children. (In some Latin American countries, a child's last name would be a combination of his mother's maiden name and his father's name.) Use this process for naming a class pet or anything in the classroom that can be named. Children need to focus on ways to participate in a group process and understand the underlying principles.

SUMMARY

- Social awareness activities cover a broad range and help all children in learn about themselves and the global world they live in.

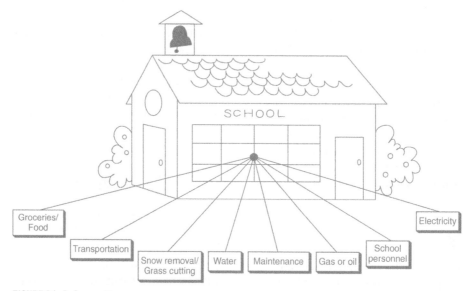

FIGURE R1–5: Connections

- Many activities are focused on helping children become aware of individual differences and how to include children who are different because of their culture or the way they look, move, or talk.

- Social studies standards encourage teachers to look at a more macro level of social interaction.

EDUCATIONAL RESOURCES

EDsitement—Art and Culture, supported by the National Endowment for the Humanities. It has an amazing number of links to websites, as well as lesson plans by subcategories and grade level. http://edsitement.neh.gov/tab_websites.asp

Exploratorium—The Museum of Science, Art and Human Perception is a not-for-profit organization that has a variety of great online activities. www.exploratorium.edu/explore/online.html

I Love That Teaching Idea has an idea directory that looks at ideas by subject matter areas or even what to do on the first day of school. http://www.ilovethatteachingidea.com/

Kids Next Door is a site supported by the U.S. Dept. of Housing and Urban Development (HUD) where children can learn about community and good citizens links to over thirty other U.S. government websites for kids, including puzzles, games, and a scavenger hunt. www.hud.gov/kids/

Kidport Grade 1 Home Page offers an array of puzzles, brainteasers, and fascinating facts for various subject matter areas. http://www.kidport.com/Grade1/Grade1Home.htm

Link Library at Education Place, supported by Houghton Mifflin, connects to an incredible number of websites related to art, math, social studies, and cross-cultural curriculum themes as well as disabilities. http://www.eduplace.com/linklibrary/

National Council for the Social Studies has information about social studies standards and suggestions for activities to support the standards as well as other resources. www.socialstudies.org/

Resources on Early Learning: Illinois Early Learning Standards provide benchmarks for working toward the standards as well as ideas for tips and activities for meeting the standards. www.illinoisearlylearning.org/

Social Studies for Kids has articles, current events and fun facts and games about cultures, holidays, languages, religions as well as U.S. government, economics, and geography.

For additional resources, visit the book companion website for this text at www.cengagebrain.com.

English Language Arts Activities:
Speaking and Listening, Reading, Writing, and Language

2

Learning to communicate is one of the major tasks facing all young children. Communication is a dynamic process that is affected by the language heard in the environment and the way that adults respond to language development. Speaking and listening, reading, writing, and language are the major components of the language arts and literacy curriculum. These skills are interdependent.

ACTIVITY GOALS AND STANDARDS

Activities are organized by the goals and standards they support. The activities themselves serve as prototypes of activities that can be used again and again with minor changes. Goals and standards that focus directly on language arts and literacy are given first. The indexes for the goals and standards are in front of the first Resource chapter with the activities that support them to make finding the activities more efficient.

The standards for English language arts and literacy in history/social studies, science, and technical subjects begin at kindergarten. Because the English language arts cover such a broad area, you will find activities for these standards in many different Resource chapters. More details about the standards are given in Chapter 4.

You can see the English language arts and literacy standards for all grade levels and the supporting materials at http://www.corestandards.org/thestandards/english-language-arts-standards. The standards chosen for this book focus on what children should know and be able to do at the end of kindergarten.

Books that are referred to in the text with an * have a complete citation and annotation in the Children's Bibliography;

© Cengage Learning 2012

others have a complete citation where they are cited. For books where a lexile score is available, it is given after the book, for example, (500L). The notation "AD" before the lexile means that the book requires adult direction and should initially be read by an adult and discussed with children before children read it independently. To be college and career ready according to the common core state standards, children should be reading at the top lexile for the grade level: first grade 220L to 500L, second grade 450L to 620L, third grade 550L to 790L.

LANGUAGE ARTS AND LITERACY GUIDELINES

The following guidelines will be helpful as you think about adapting language arts and literacy activities to meet the needs of children with diverse abilities.

Adapting activities for children with:

Specific learning disabilities ❖ Play sequencing and memory games to develop language skills. Support phonemic awareness daily in a variety of ways. Ensure that children have the readiness skills to move into reading. Read to children at their level of understanding rather than the level they can read and help them develop a love of books.

Social, emotional, and behavioral disorders ❖ Help children develop a vocabulary to verbalize their feelings and to communicate with others. Use writing and illustrating as potential outlets for feelings. Use reading as a springboard to talk about emotions.

Attention-deficit/hyperactivity disorder ❖ Read short, high-interest books. Read books and talk about feelings and emotions. Use the computer to develop literacy skills. Work on the language skills necessary to join and maintain group memberships.

Communication disorders ❖ Give children many hands-on experiences so they have something to talk about. Be a good speech model. Encourage and support children when they talk by listening and responding. Ask children open-ended questions. Expand and extend their speech.

English language learners ❖ Support children in developing proficiency in both their home language and English. If children use languages that do not use the standard English alphabet, ensure that children see the letters of the alphabet used in their home language. For example, Spanish has *ll* and *rr*. Also, show markings such as accents and umlauts. Show languages such as Chinese that use a symbol system and Russian, which uses the Cyrillic alphabet.

Autism spectrum disorders ❖ Work on nonverbal aspects of language (eye contact) as well as vocabulary. Teach concepts of verbal turn taking. Use a picture communication system to support language.

Intellectual disabilities ❖ Work on developing a functional vocabulary. Be sure children have prerequisite skills as you introduce new literacy tasks. Do a task analysis to teach these.

Gifts and talents ❖ Support children in thinking about themselves as authors and illustrators. Introduce reference books and use the Internet to supplement classroom literacy work.

Special health care needs ❖ Help children develop a vocabulary to increase their understanding of situations they may face and to express their feelings. Use reading to prepare children for new situations. Support children in learning to use e-mail to communicate with peers.

Orthopedic and neurological impairments ❖ Help children learn to give precise directions. Work on connecting sounds to sources and comprehending these relationships. Use materials with some built-in resistance such as clay or sand in emerging writing skills.

Hearing impairments ❖ Provide many hands-on activities to develop inner language. Pair listening with visual and tactile experiences. Help children learn to use residual hearing and refine their auditory skills. Support reading and writing especially with the computer. Help children learn to read nonverbal cues. Use American Sign Language to support learning for all children.

Visual impairments ❖ Encourage children to refine the visual skills they have. Include audio books as well as large-print and Braille books on your bookshelves. Include writing media that have tactile properties. Emphasize the verbal and tonal aspects of language.

LANGUAGE AND LITERACY ACTIVITIES

• • • • • SPEAKING AND LISTENING: **LARGE OR SMALL GROUP**

2-1 What Is It?

GOALS: To improve reading literacy; to make predictions; to improve memory skills

STANDARDS: S&L 1 Participate in collaborative conversations with diverse partners about kindergarten topics and texts with peers and adults in small and larger groups; S&L 3 Ask and answer questions in order to seek help, get information, or clarify something that is not understood.

MATERIALS: Large (8 × 10 inch) pictures of familiar objects, large envelopes

PROCEDURE: Put a picture of a familiar object in an envelope. Pull it out slowly until part of the picture is exposed. Have the children guess what it is. Keep exposing more of the picture until it is correctly identified. Encourage the children to ask questions and to guess and give you the reasons for their guesses. Start with pictures of simple, familiar objects (boats, cars, trains, animals). Pull about half of the picture out before you stop. You can use a screen and gradually push objects out as well.

ACCOMMODATIONS AND INTEGRATION: Use 8 × 10 inch pictures of all children in the class to add interest at the beginning of the year. Add pictures of less familiar objects or ones that have more ambiguous cues (an armchair and sofa). Children need to develop skills in the area of visual closure. They need to be able to use partial information to infer what they cannot see and focus on relevant details.

Encourage children to ask questions to gain more information before they make guesses. When they do guess, ask for their rationale.

• • • • • SPEAKING AND LISTENING: **SMALL OR LARGE GROUP**

2-2 Magician

GOALS: To improve listening skills; to improve receptive communication; to encourage creativity

STANDARDS: S&L 2 Confirm understanding of a text read aloud or information presented orally or through other media by asking and answering questions about key details and requesting clarification if something is not understood; S&L 3 Ask and answer questions in order to seek help, get information, or clarify something that is not understood; TH 2 Act by assuming roles and interacting in improvisations.

MATERIALS: None

PROCEDURE: The adult plays the magician and "changes" a child into a noise-making object by whispering into the child's ear what object she is to be or gives the child a picture of the object. The child then pretends to be the object by making the noise, and the other children guess what the object is.

ACCOMMODATIONS AND INTEGRATION: Use sounds that are phonetically different yet conceptually related, for example, vehicles, outside sounds, animal sounds, or kitchen sounds. Have the objects or pictures of the objects in sight. In addition to making the sound, have children pretend to be or use the object; for example, for a snake, have the child hiss as well as squirm on the floor if the sound is not initially guessed. Children need to tune in to their environment and need support gaining the skills to do this.

• • • • • SPEAKING AND LISTENING: **SMALL GROUP**

2-3 Synonyms

GOALS: To improve expressive communication; to improve receptive communication; to increase vocabulary acquisition and use

STANDARDS: S&L 3 Ask and answer questions in order to seek help, get information, or clarify something that is not understood; S&L 4 Describe familiar people, places, things, and events and, with prompting and support, provide additional detail; L 4 Determine or clarify the meaning of unknown and multiple-meaning words and phrases based on kindergarten reading and content.

MATERIALS: Pictures or objects that have more than one name

PROCEDURE: Define synonyms: words that mean the same thing but sound different. Then present children with the objects or pictures of objects, and see how many synonyms they can think of. It is not important that these be exact synonyms in a dictionary sense. The point is for the children to know that one object can have several different names. It is also important for children to learn that the same word can have different meanings (e.g., orange as color or as fruit). Start with familiar objects in your classroom and community:

rug/carpet	duck (n)/duck (v)
store/shop	cut (n)/cut (v)
chair/seat	run (n)/run (v)
shirt/top	water (n)/water (v)
couch/sofa/davenport	hit (n)/hit (v)
road/street	plant (n) plant (v)
bed/cot	oil (n)/oil (v)
bathing suit/swimsuit	bark (n)/bark (v)

ACCOMMODATIONS AND INTEGRATION: Use the analogy of nicknames to help children learn the concept. Talk about regional differences in language usage. Children need to know that objects often have several names even in the same language and that many words have different meanings, particularly if they are used as nouns or verbs. Show children a thesaurus as a book or on the computer and encourage them to use it to think of synonyms. Help children build vocabulary by learning synonyms and different meanings for familiar words by using them in context. When words occur in stories or conversation, ask them for alternative words or other meanings.

• • • • •   SPEAKING AND LISTENING: **LARGE GROUP**

2-4   Interviews

GOALS: To improve expressive communication; to increase inclusion; to express feelings

STANDARDS: S&L 3 Ask and answer questions in order to seek help, get information, or clarify something that is not understood; S&L 4 Describe familiar people, places, things, and events and, with prompting and support, provide additional detail; S&L 6 Speak audibly and express thoughts, feelings, and ideas clearly.

MATERIALS: A play microphone

PROCEDURE: Do a takeoff on some of the popular talk shows: "Good morning, today is Tuesday, February 2, and we are delighted to have as our guest today Ms. Suling. Ms. Suling, can you tell our listeners some of the things that you really like to do? Do you have any favorite foods?"

ACCOMMODATIONS AND INTEGRATION: If children are hesitant, make the questions easy, and keep the interview short. Be sure to have a "mike" as a prop. Explain this is Ms. Suling's first appearance and she is a bit shy. Encourage children to talk about their interests and whatever they want to share. It is great for children to feel special and to highlight what is unique about them. Take questions from the "audience" and also share with the "audience" what you find so special about this particular child and why you "invited" her.

• • • • •   SPEAKING AND LISTENING: **LARGE GROUP**

2-5   Object Hunt

GOALS: To improve expressive communication; to follow directions; to increase knowledge of the structure of language

STANDARDS: S&L 3 Ask and answer questions in order to seek help, get information, or clarify something that is not understood; S&L 4 Describe familiar people, places, things, and events and, with prompting and support, provide additional detail; S&L 6 Speak audibly and express thoughts, feelings, and ideas clearly.

MATERIALS: None

PROCEDURE: Choose an object in the classroom. Give easy-to-follow directions to find it. Once children understand the procedure, let a child give the directions to a searcher. The searcher can only ask yes-or-no questions.

Direction Giver:	*"Go to the block area. Stand beside the longest blocks. Look up."*
Searcher:	*"Is it a window?"*
Direction Giver:	*"No. Turn around . . . ."*

ACCOMMODATIONS AND INTEGRATION: Have an adult give the directions while children follow them, one step at a time. As children become more skillful, choose objects in difficult locations that require fine discriminations for both the direction giver and the searcher. Children can play this in pairs or small groups, inside or outside. It provides good feedback on how difficult it is to give accurate directions.

• • • • •   SPEAKING AND LISTENING: **SMALL GROUP**

2-6   Be It

GOALS: To improve expressive communication; to use diverse print and nonprint sources and genres; to encourage creativity

STANDARDS: S&L 4 Describe familiar people, places, things, and events and, with prompting and support, provide additional detail; S&L 5 Add drawings or other visual displays to descriptions as desired to provide additional detail; S&L 6 Speak audibly and express thoughts, feelings, and ideas clearly.

MATERIALS: Common objects: shoes, winter coat, roller skates, ring, tricycle/bicycle, chair, brick, towel, cotton ball, stone

PROCEDURE: During group time, discuss the difference between animate and inanimate objects, and have children imagine what objects might feel if they had feelings. Give them an example:

Shoes: I have pretty buckles and I am red. This morning I was sleeping in a dark closet very peacefully when someone turned on a bright light and stepped on me. I creaked a little, but that didn't stop her. She wiggled her feet into

me and then ran down a flight of stairs. She then stood on me in the kitchen for 20 minutes. Finally, there was some relief.

Start with familiar objects that have numerous visual cues, such as a hat with flowers on it. Prompt the children with cues such as, "What happened then?" or "How did you feel then?" or more obvious ones, such as, "What color are you?" or "What do you look like?" Encourage children to tell stories in small groups. Then, use objects that have fewer visual cues and are less well known to the children.

ACCOMMODATIONS AND INTEGRATION: Encourage children to write and illustrate their stories. Children can share their stories with their families. This activity can be adapted to most themes. If you have a circus theme, have the children be the tightrope or the safety net or the lion tamer's whip. This is a good game for parents to play in a waiting room; the child could be the dentist's mirror or even the drill. Pretending to be the object helps a child think about the object in a different way, especially if the child is apprehensive.

• • • • • READING: **LARGE OR SMALL GROUP**

2-7 Baby Doll

GOALS: To improve reading literacy; to increase awareness of individual differences and similarities; to express feelings

STANDARDS: R:L 1 Ask and answer questions about key details in a text; R:L 2 Retell familiar stories, including key details; R:L 3 Identify characters, settings, and major events in a story.

MATERIALS: A baby doll dressed in typical clothes, books such as D. Danzig, *Babies Don't Eat Pizza: A Big Kid's Book about Baby Brothers and Baby Sisters* (New York: Dutton, 2009), and *Henry's First-Moon Birthday**

PROCEDURE: Bring the doll into the classroom and tell the children she is very special and that they need to be quiet, careful, and gentle and not disturb her. Discuss with children ways of dealing with feelings about jealously and favoritism. Then read a book such as *Babies Don't Eat Pizza* and discuss some of the issues related to babies. Encourage children to identify the main characters and ask and answer questions based on the book and their experiences. Then read a book such as *Henry's First-Moon Birthday*. Talk with children about this text. Support children in retelling *Babies Don't Eat Pizza* and compare the books. Discuss the impact culture has on life, including what happens when babies join families. Have a baby visit. Discuss how having a baby is different from having a doll.

ACCOMMODATIONS AND INTEGRATION: Encourage children to talk about their feelings when they have a new sibling or a family member who takes up a lot of time. Help children think about how to cope with these feelings.

• • • • • READING: **LARGE OR SMALL GROUP**

2-8 Garbage

GOALS: To improve reading literacy; to improve cause-and-effect reasoning; to improve generalization skills

STANDARDS: R:L 1 Ask and answer questions about key details in a text; R:L 2 Retell familiar stories, including key details; R:L 10 Actively engage in group reading activities with purpose and understanding.

MATERIALS Book such as J. Winter, *Here Comes the Garbage Barge* (New York: Schwartz & Wade, 2010) (AD 670L)

PROCEDURE: Talk to the children about garbage, recycling, and composting as ways of getting rid of materials we don't want. Ask children to think about what to do with garbage. Read *Here Comes the Garbage Barge*, a fictionalized account of a real event that occurred in 1987 when Islip, New York, decided to get rid of their garbage by sending it to North Carolina, New Orleans, Mexico, Belize, Texas, Florida, and eventually back to New York because everyone refused to take the garbage. Spiced with humor and great artwork, the message is clear: Too much garbage. Ask the children what they would do if the garbage barge pulled up at their school.

ACCOMMODATIONS AND INTEGRATION: Encourage children to think about the garbage people create and discuss what they could do to make less garbage at school and at home. Talk with them about what types of products can be recycled or composted and what cannot.

Books expand children's knowledge base and their vocabulary.
© Cengage Learning 2012

• • • • • READING: **LARGE GROUP**

2-9 Title

GOALS: To improve reading literacy; to increase comprehension; to increase knowledge of the structure of language

STANDARDS: R:L 1 Ask and answer questions about key details in a text; R:L 2 Retell familiar stories, including key details; R:L 10 Actively engage in group reading activities with purpose and understanding.

MATERIALS: A made-up story or a printed story with the title hidden

PROCEDURE: Read or tell a story or use a paragraph from a longer story. Explain that it has no title and that you want the children's help in deciding on one. Before asking them for suggestions ask questions about the key details of the text and the characters. Then ask children to suggest titles and write them down. Talk with the children about the titles and have them explain, with your prompting and support, which titles would be good and why.

ACCOMMODATIONS AND INTEGRATION: Initially choose simple stories. Use more complex stories as children become more proficient. Appropriate titles require high-level abstract reasoning skills. Challenge children to think this way.

• • • • • READING: **LARGE OR SMALL GROUP**

2-10 Libraries

GOALS: To improve reading literacy; to increase comprehension; to increase awareness of roles people play

STANDARDS: R:L 3 Identify characters, settings, and major events in a story; R:L 6 Name the author and illustrator of a story and define the role of each in telling the story; R:L 10 Actively engage in group reading activities with purpose and understanding.

MATERIALS: Book such as M. Knudsen, *Library Lion* (Summerville, MA: Candlewick, 2009) (470L)

PROCEDURE: Show the children the front cover of the book, then read the author's and illustrator's names and talk about the role of each in producing a book. Encourage children to look at the expressions on the people's faces. Discuss the conflict between wanting to explore and obeying rules.

ACCOMMODATIONS AND INTEGRATION: Talk with the children about rules and the need for rules in the classroom and when it is okay to break rules. Then expand the discussion to include rules related to conventions of standard English. As children are ready, encourage them to read this book independently.

• • • • • READING: **LARGE OR SMALL GROUP**

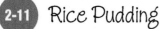

2-11 Rice Pudding

GOALS: To increase reading literacy; to increase respect for diversity in modes of communication; to increase cultural awareness

STANDARDS: R:L 4 Ask and answer questions about unknown words in a text; R:L 5 Recognize common types of texts; R:L 7 Describe the relationship between illustrations and the story in which they appear.

MATERIALS: Book such as J. Arqueta, *Arroz con Leche: Un Poema para Cocinar/Rice Pudding: A Cooking Poem.* (Scarborough, OH: Groundwood Books, 2010)

PROCEDURES: Read the children a bilingual book about a poetic journey to buy the ingredients for rice pudding and make it. Discuss with children why this is classified as a poem, not a story. Point out the word pictures that evolve with the illustrations. Discuss with children that the text is in both Spanish and English. Talk about cultural differences.

ACCOMMODATIONS AND INTEGRATION: Use the Internet or a cookbook to find a recipe for rice pudding and make it. Discuss how this experience relates to the book: how it is both the same and different. Read relevant parts of the poem again.

• • • • • READING: **LARGE OR SMALL GROUP**

2-12 Authors and Illustrators

GOALS: To improve reading literacy; to improve writing literacy; to use diverse print and nonprint sources and genres

STANDARDS: R:L 6 Name the author and illustrator of a story and define the role of each in telling the story; R:L 7 Describe the relationship between illustrations and the story in which they appear; R:L 9 Compare and contrast the adventures and experiences of characters in familiar stories.

MATERIALS: Children's books such as G. Zion, *Harry the Dirty Dog* (New York: HarperFestival, 1956) (AD700L); M. W. Brown, *Goodnight Moon* (New York: HarperFestival, 1947); J. Viorst, *Nobody Here but Me* (New York: Farrar Straus Giroux, 2008); M. Sendak, *Where the Wild Things Are* (New York: Harper Collins, 1988) (740L)

PROCEDURE: Talk with children about authors and illustrators and the relationship between the two. Choose a simple book such as *Harry the Dirty Dog*, and note how Harry keeps getting dirtier and his family pretends not to recognize him. Or read *Goodnight Moon* and ask the children to describe the picture and the significance of the illustration on each page. In *Goodnight Moon*, note how the kittens play, the time on the clock changes, the moon rises, and the lamp turns off. Be sure to read and show the children the names of the author and illustrator.

Repeat this process with more complex books and illustrations such as *Nobody Here but Me*. Again look at the clock and time lapse. Talk about how the muted illustrations convey feelings as well as information. Consider having children act this one out. Also read *Where the Wild Things Are*. Help children compare and contrast how these authors use the sense of time in the books and the boys' characters, attitudes, and experiences.

ACCOMMODATIONS AND INTEGRATION: Vary the level of complexity of the stories you read to children. Routinely name the author and illustrator of books. Encourage children to compare and contrast books in groups and in independent reading. Reread books after you have discussed the characters to see what additional information children have gained.

· · · · · READING: **LARGE OR SMALL GROUP**

 2-13 Oceans

GOALS: To improve reading literacy; to increase comprehension; to increase knowledge of the natural world

STANDARDS: R:IT 1 Ask and answer questions about key details in a text; R:IT 2 Identify the main topic and retell key details of a text; R:IT 3 Describe the connection between two individuals, events, ideas, or pieces of information in a text.

MATERIALS: Book such as M. Ling and S. Thornton, *Eye Wonder: Ocean* (London: DK Children, 2001)

PROCEDURE: Show the children the front cover of the book and ask them what they think it will be about. Tell them the authors' names, and then talk about the aspect of informational texts that are different from literature. Show them the title page and the table of contents at the front of the book and the glossary and index at the back. Using the table of contents, have them choose a topic they want to learn more about and read about it with them.

ACCOMMODATIONS AND INTEGRATION: Encourage children to look at the photographs and discuss them informally. For children who are interested, teach them how to use the index to find the particular information they want to know more about. Use additional books in the Eye Wonder series to learn about *Space*, the *Human Body*, *Bugs*, and so on.

· · · · · READING: **LARGE OR SMALL GROUP**

2-14 Hurricanes

GOALS: To improve reading literacy; to increase comprehension; to increase knowledge of the natural world

STANDARDS: R:IT 1 Ask and answer questions about key details in a text; R:IT 6 Name the author and illustrator of a text and define the role of each in presenting the ideas or information in a text; R:IT 9 Identify basic similarities in and differences between two texts on the same topic.

MATERIALS: Books such as J. Cole, *The Magic School Bus Inside a Hurricane*, (New York: Scholastic Press, 1966) (AD 500L); and G. Gibbons, *Hurricanes* (New York: Holiday House, 2010) (NC860L)

PROCEDURE: Talk to children about hurricanes and what their experience has been with them. Then read them two different books about hurricanes. Ask them to identify the differences and similarities in the presentations. Discuss when each book might be the most appropriate. Talk about what they liked and did not like about each book.

ACCOMMODATIONS AND INTEGRATION: Ask children to talk about the key details of the texts and what they would do if a hurricane were forecasted. Encourage them to talk about the precautions they would take and why. Help them think about ways to keep themselves safe.

· · · · · READING: **LARGE OR SMALL GROUP**

 2-15 Planet Earth

GOALS: To improve reading literacy; to increase comprehension; to increase knowledge of the natural world

STANDARDS: R:IT 2 Identify the main topic and retell key details of a text; R:IT 4 Ask and answer questions about unknown words in a text; R:IT 10 Actively engage in group reading activities with purpose and understanding.

MATERIALS: Book such as D. Chancellor, *Science Kids: Planet Earth* (London: Kingfisher, 2006)

PROCEDURE: Read chapters to children about the planet on which they live. It explains the basic facts and new vocabulary is defined on each page. It covers geological forces, weather and climate, and the diversity of life on earth. The 40 chapters are short (two pages each) but informative and engaging. There are also projects to use to follow up on some of the information discussed. Talk with the children about the earth and the science that is involved with understanding it, living on it, and caring for it. Discuss with children how texts written for information are different from literature.

ACCOMMODATIONS AND INTEGRATION: Plan firsthand science experiments (see Resource Chapter 3) to help children learn more about a particular area or to read another book that focuses on a particular topic of interest.

· · · · · READING: **LARGE OR SMALL GROUP**

 2-16 Autobiography

GOALS: To improve reading literacy; to use diverse print and nonprint sources and genres; to increase cultural awareness

STANDARDS: R:IT 3 Describe the connection between two individuals, events, ideas, or pieces of information in a text; R:IT 6 Name the author and illustrator of a text and define the role of each in presenting the ideas or information in a text; R:IT 7 Describe the relationship between illustrations and the story in which they appear.

MATERIALS: Books such as A. Bryan, *Ashley Bryan: Words to My Life's Song* (New York: Atheneum, 2009) (970L); and A. Bryan, *Ashley Bryan's ABC of African American Poetry* (New York: Atheneum, 1997)

PROCEDURE: Talk with children about different types of writing including biographies and autobiographies. Discuss why people would want to write and read them. Introduce them to Ashley Bryan on the cover of the book and read them *Words to My Life's Song*. Talk with them about the events in the story such as his parents emigrating from Antigua to New York, his interest in art, and the island on which he now lives. Point out to that he drew the illustrations, but Bill McGuinness took the photographs. Encourage children to look at how the combination works.

ADAPTATIONS AND INTEGRATION: Show the children *Ashley Bryan's ABC of African American Poetry*. Read the short poems and look at the power of the art and how Bryan uses the art to communicate with the reader. Follow this up by having children either illustrate their own ABC book or by helping them to write their autobiography.

· · · · · READING: **LARGE OR SMALL GROUP**

2-17 Animal Homes

GOALS: To improve reading literacy; to increase comprehension; to increase knowledge of the natural world

STANDARDS: R:IT 4 Ask and answer questions about unknown words in a text; R:IT 8 Identify the reasons an author gives to support points in a text; R:IT 10 Actively engage in group reading activities with purpose and understanding.

MATERIALS: Book such as A. Wilkes, *Science Kids: Animal Homes* (London: Kingfisher, 2007)

PROCEDURE: Read chapters from *Animal Homes* to the children and discuss the animals' shelters. Encourage children to talk about the utility of the homes and their particular adaptations to the climates and surfaces on which they live. Have some children act out the relevant features of an animal home while other children guess what they are pretending.

ACCOMMODATIONS AND INTEGRATION: Have children talk about their homes and how they are adapted to them. Discuss different kinds of people homes in different climates and cultures and think about their adaptations.

· · · · · WRITING: **SMALL GROUP**

2-18 Publishing

GOALS: To improve writing literacy; to improve reading literacy; to use diverse print and nonprint sources and genres

STANDARDS: R:IT 5 Identify the front cover, back cover, and title page of a book; W 3 Use a combination of drawing, dictating, and writing to narrate a single event or several loosely linked events, tell about the events in the order in which they occurred, and provide a reaction to what happened; W 6 Explore a variety of digital tools to produce and publish writing, including in collaboration with peers.

MATERIALS: Three ring notebook, plastic sleeves, paper (8½ × 11 inches) and markers, pencils, or crayons

PROCEDURE: Talk with students about the parts of a book and the purposes they serve, including the front and back covers of the book as well as the title page and what is on it. Show them a copyright symbol (if present) and talk about the meaning of it. Show them copyright pages, dedications,

acknowledgments, and indices. Then write a class book in which each child contributes a page about an event that was important to her, providing information about what occurred and her reaction to what happened. The contributions will vary with the ability and interest of the children. Encourage children to use their knowledge of books and their parts in their own writing.

ACCOMMODATIONS AND INTEGRATION: Encourage all writing and illustrating. Book contributions can also include digital pictures and photographs to illustrate stories and work that has been done on the computer. Help children add additional stories to their personal book or create new books on other topics. After children have written the text for their book, have them put the paper in the plastic sleeve protector and then in the notebook. Encourage them to use a title page and, if there is more than one story, a table of contents. Children like to think of themselves as authors who produce a book that can be kept, read, and placed on a bookshelf. Learning at an early age that one edits and reflects on what one writes is a lifelong skill.

· · · · · WRITING: **SMALL GROUP**

2-19 Tickets

GOALS: To improve writing literacy; to improve reading literacy; to use diverse print and nonprint sources and genres

STANDARDS: R:FS 1 Demonstrate understanding of the organization and basic features of print; W 2 Use a combination of drawing, dictating, and writing to compose informative/explanatory texts in which they name what they are writing about and supply some information about the topic.

MATERIALS: Markers, paper, press-on labels

PROCEDURE: Have the children use the labels to make tickets for snack or lunch. Tell children that today they need tickets to eat, and encourage them to make some. (Have a few extras and a marker for those who do not.) Be sure to collect and comment on the tickets as you distribute the snack.

ACCOMMODATIONS AND INTEGRATION: Support any writing on the ticket. Encourage children to make "identical" tickets (numbers are easiest) and have one ticket for snack and the other to mark where the child is to sit. Then have the children find their place at the table by matching the ticket to the place marker. Children need to practice writing, especially numbers. Use this to support dramatic play by giving out railroad and airline tickets. Give tickets for using an obstacle course or riding tricycles. There can be tickets for puppet shows, group time, and centers. Make writing fun and varied.

· · · · · READING: **LARGE OR SMALL GROUP**

2-20 Letters and Sounds

GOALS: To improve reading literacy; to increase phonological awareness; to improve sensory motor integration

Children need many and varied reading readiness activities.
© Cengage Learning 2012

STANDARDS: R:FS 1 Demonstrate understanding of the organization and basic features of print; R:FS 2 Demonstrate understanding of spoken words, syllables, and sounds (phonemes).

MATERIALS: Alphabet letters and phonemes, objects or pictures of objects that begin with each letter or phoneme

PROCEDURE: Pick a letter of the alphabet or a phoneme. Expose the children to that letter or phoneme in many ways. Write the letter *P* and *p*; trace a sandpaper letter *P*; feel your breath with your hand as you say /*P*/; point to *p* in a group of letters; think of words that start with /*P*/; make cookies or clay in the shape of *P*; eat *pretzels* for snack. Emphasize the phoneme as well as the letter name. Be sure to include upper- and lowercase letters as well as consonant blends (*ng*, *ch*, *wh*, *sh*) and vowel phonemes.

ACCOMMODATIONS AND INTEGRATION: Begin with letter identification then move into phonemes. Start with the vowels where the phoneme sounds like the letter name long vowels (*ē*, me, key) and move into short vowel sounds (*ă*, cat, sat).

• • • • • READING: **LARGE GROUP**

 Sound Bingo

GOALS: To improve reading literacy; to increase phonological awareness; to increase knowledge of the structure of language

STANDARDS: R:FS 1 Demonstrate understanding of the organization and basic features of print; R:FS 2 Demonstrate understanding of spoken words, syllables, and sounds (phonemes).

MATERIALS: Bingo cards with phonemes rather than numbers (see Figure R2–1)

PROCEDURE: Using a regular bingo game format, play the game and ask children to identify the phonemes (speech sounds) as you call them out. As you move to more difficult phonemes and phoneme blends, pair the children so they can work together. Have the children put a marker on the phoneme for each sound as it is called out. Continue to play until most children have completed several rows.

ACCOMMODATIONS AND INTEGRATION: Show children the card after you have said the sound, to allow them to match visually if they do not know the phoneme or sound of the letter. Instead of phonemes, call out words and have the children isolate the phoneme and mark the initial phoneme. This can also be done for the last speech sound in a word. As you work toward developing words and phonemes for games such as this, you begin to appreciate the problems in learning English.

B	I	N	G	O
a	u	r	bl	o
sm	h	b	c	i
w	y	free	g	v
m	j	n	l	d
e	f	tw	p	z

FIGURE R2–1 Bingo Card for Sound Bingo

• • • • • READING: **INDIVIDUAL OR SMALL GROUP**

 Alphabet Lotto

GOALS: To improve reading literacy; to increase phonological awareness; to increase respect for diversity in modes of communication

STANDARDS: R:FS 1 Demonstrate understanding of the organization and basic features of print; R:FS 2 Demonstrate understanding of spoken words, syllables, and sounds (phonemes); S&L 3 Ask and answer questions in order to seek help, get information, or clarify something that is not understood.

MATERIALS: Alphabet Lotto board and letters

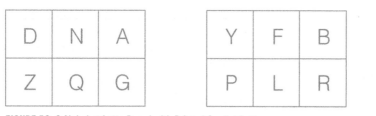

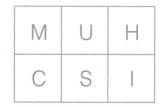

FIGURE R2–2 Alphabet Lotto Board with Printed Capital Letters

TO MAKE: *Divide pieces of posterboard (9 × 12 inches) into six rectangles (4 × 4½ inches). Print a letter of the alphabet in each rectangle (not necessarily in order). Make four cards with different uppercase letters on each (see Figure R2–2). Make another set for lowercase letters.*

Cut twenty-four 4 × 4½ inch pieces, also out of posterboard. Print a letter on each small rectangle to match the larger boards. (Note: Because our alphabet has 26 letters, 2 will be missing. If you make two sets like this, omit different letters from each one or add phonemes with two letters such as th, wh, and so on and make another board.) If children are having trouble matching particular letters, design cards to meet these problems. For lowercase letters, make a card that has letters with reversible lines and curves (see Figure R2–3).

PROCEDURE: Play the game as you would any Lotto game. Put the individual letters into a box to draw from so children can match them to the board with six letters. Children can play this as a matching game alone. With all these combinations, there will be five cards for each letter on the board. When children are learning, make a board out of letters that are very dissimilar (e.g., *A, W, O, S, T, D*). Don't have letters such as *M* and *W* or *O* and *C* on the same board, as they might be confused initially. As children match the letters, have them name each letter and a possible letter sound (phoneme)

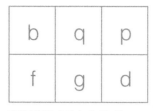

FIGURE R2–3 Alphabet Lotto Board with Printed Small Letters with Reversible Lines and Curves

ACCOMMODATIONS AND INTEGRATION: First work on letter identification using the boards. Then play Lotto. To expand the letter concept, make Lotto combinations as in Figure R2–4. You can add alphabets from other languages: the American Sign Language alphabet, the Braille alphabet, as well as sandpaper letters.

· · · · ·   READING: **SMALL OR INDIVIDUAL**

2-23   I Can Read

GOALS: To improve reading literacy; to increase phonological awareness; to increase comprehension

STANDARDS: R:FS 2 Demonstrate understanding of spoken words, syllables, and sounds (phonemes); R:FS 3 Know and apply grade-level phonics and word analysis skills in decoding words; R:F 4 Read emergent-reader texts with purpose and understanding.

MATERIALS: Graded reading level books such as S. Davidson (ed.), *Clever Rabbit and the Lion* (London: Usborne Books, 2007) (260L)

PROCEDURE: Help a child or small groups of children sound out words and read at a reading level that matches their reading skills. Choose books that have high interest but are at the appropriate level.

ACCOMMODATIONS AND INTEGRATION: Have many stories that children can choose from at a variety of reading, or lexile (L), levels. Develop a system of coding these so children know which books will be the most rewarding to read. Other books at First Reading Level Two by Susanna Davidson include *Clever Rabbit and the Wolves* (240L) and at First Reading Level Three *The Musicians of Bremen* (200L), *The Little*

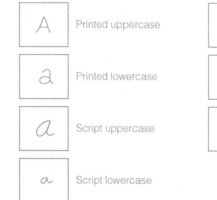

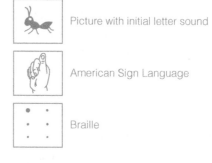

FIGURE R2–4 Alphabet Lotto Cards in Print, Script, Pictures for Initial Sounds, ASL, and Braille

Red Hen (360L), and *The Three Little Pigs* (400). Encourage children to read in pairs, help each other sound out words, and enjoy reading to each other.

• • • • • READING: **SMALL GROUP OR INDIVIDUAL**

2-24 My Reading

GOALS: To improve reading literacy; to increase phonological awareness; to increase comprehension

STANDARDS: R:FS 2 Demonstrate understanding of spoken words, syllables, and sounds (phonemes); R:FS 3 Know and apply grade-level phonics and word analysis skills in decoding words; R:FS 4 Read emergent-reader texts with purpose and understanding.

MATERIALS: Graded reading level books such as M. Mackinnon, *The Fox and the Crow* (London: Usborne Books, 2007) (60 L)

PROCEDURE: Help a child or small groups of children sound out words and read at a reading level that matches their reading skills. Choose books that have high interest but are at the appropriate lexile level.

ACCOMMODATIONS AND INTEGRATION: Have many stories that children can choose from at a variety of reading or lexile (L) levels. Develop a system of coding these so children know which books will be the most rewarding to read. Other books at Reading level one by Mairi Mackinnon include *The Lion and the Mouse* (170L) and *The Fox and the Stork* (220L).

• • • • • WRITING: **SMALL GROUP**

2-25 Writing Center

GOALS: To improve writing literacy; to improve reading literacy; to use diverse print and nonprint sources and genres

STANDARDS: W 1 Use a combination of drawing, dictating, and writing to compose opinion pieces in which they tell a reader the topic or name of the book they are writing about and state an opinion or preference about the topic or book; W 2 Use a combination of drawing, dictating, and writing to compose informative/explanatory texts in which they name what they are writing about and supply some information about the topic; W 5 Respond to questions and suggestions from peers and add details to strengthen writing as needed.

MATERIALS: Variety of paper: manila paper, wide-lined paper, plain white paper, paper folded in half, small notepads, paper cut into interesting shapes, colored paper, and stationery; writing tools: thin and thick water soluble markers, pencils and colored pencils, a supply of interesting erasers, a pencil sharpener; copy of the alphabet; writing folder with each child's name

PROCEDURE: Encourage children to think about an experience or feeling they would like to write about. Discuss the differences between a topic they have feelings and opinions about, one that is informative or explanatory where they supply facts and information about the topic, and one that is about an event or events that occurred to them that they

want to describe and react to. Have them decide on the purpose of the writing and provide the necessary supports. Discuss writing as a process that involves writing, editing, and publishing. When you talk with children at the writing center, use the terms *author, editor,* and *publisher* with them. Writing is a small-group activity, where children can discuss their ideas and try them out on others. It is not a quiet solitary activity. It may include a combination of drawing, dictating, and writing. Emphasize the process of writing. Encourage children to work in small groups and support each other in the process. Discuss illustrating and how it is different from drawing.

ACCOMMODATIONS AND INTEGRATION: Accept all attempts at writing and support the discussion of what will be written about. Encourage children to write more detailed and longer stories; increase the variety of writing genres to include poetry and plays. Have children read their work to others and publish their work. Discuss the different but related aspects of writing, editing, and publishing. Encourage children who want to use a word processor to write or illustrate their stories. As children think about themselves as authors, their interest in writing increases. When they see writing as a process, and the details of editing as separate from writing, they can focus on the aspects of conventional standard English such as spelling, capitalization, and punctuation that are important in a final product but ought not to interfere with the initial flow of the written word.

• • • • • WRITING: **INDIVIDUAL**

2-26 My Diary

GOALS: To improve writing literacy; to improve reading literacy; to use diverse print and nonprint sources and genres

STANDARDS: W 1 Use a combination of drawing, dictating, and writing to compose opinion pieces in which they tell a reader the topic or name of the book they are writing about and state an opinion or preference about the topic or book; W 8 Recall information from experiences or gather information from provided sources to answer a question.

MATERIALS: Pencils and markers, notebook or paper stapled together

PROCEDURE: Talk with children about diaries and why people keep them. Tell them that diaries are personal and that they are usually kept over a long span of time. Include information that diaries are sometimes kept on trips or even about inventions. Ask the children to keep a diary for a week related to the theme that you are using. Encourage children who are unsure about writing to illustrate their diary. Use the word *illustrator*. Have each child choose or put together the paper for his or her diary and label it. Put it in a particular place so the children have access to it for at least a week. Encourage each child to spend some time each day writing or illustrating the diary.

ACCOMMODATIONS AND INTEGRATION: Support diary writing whether or not you can read it. Have children choose what they will write about, but support the writing process. Children need practice writing. An activity that requires children to write for short periods over several days is useful. The emphasis is the process of writing itself. Inventive spelling and letter reversals are expected during the early childhood years. Children need to learn the many different purposes of writing.

· · · · ·   WRITING: **LARGE OR SMALL GROUP**

2-27   Mind Mapping

GOALS: To improve writing literacy; to increase comprehension; to increase knowledge of the structure of language

STANDARDS: W 2 Use a combination of drawing, dictating, and writing to compose informative/explanatory texts in which they name what they are writing about and supply some information about the topic; W 5 Respond to questions and suggestions from peers and add details to strengthen writing as needed; W 7 Participate in shared research and writing projects.

MATERIALS: Paper, pencil or marker

PROCEDURE: After a topic has been chosen, encourage children to make a mind map before they begin to write. Start with the topic in the center of the page. Draw a balloon around it. Surround it with related ideas connected to it or to each other with lines. The lines show the relationship between the central theme and the topics mentioned. If there appear to be tangents, put these in the corners of the page. If they eventually become related, attach them with a line, if not, they will not be part of the writing. A mind map of the

ocean is pictured in Figure R2–5. Then have children draw, write, or dictate text about the topic and provide some information about the chosen topic. Encourage children to work in pairs or small groups at a writing center to support each other, and provide additional teacher guidance.

ACCOMMODATIONS AND INTEGRATION: Do the mind map as a group project and have the adult do the mapping while scaffolding the children's ideas. Have a small group of children make more complex maps on topics of their choice. Have reference materials available, and encourage and support children using them. Children need to organize their ideas for writing, but traditional outlines are rarely useful with young children. Mind mapping, or clustering ideas, is more useful and helps set the flow for the writing. Initially, each balloon will probably only be a phrase or sentence.

· · · · ·   LANGUAGE: **LARGE GROUP**

2-28   Say It

GOALS: To improve listening skills; to improve receptive communication; to increase knowledge of the structure of language

STANDARDS: L 1 Demonstrate command of the conventions of standard English grammar and usage when writing or speaking; L 5 Explore word relationships and nuances in word meanings; S&L 2 Confirm understanding of a text read aloud or information presented orally or through other media by asking and answering questions about key details and requesting clarification if something is not understood.

MATERIALS: None

FIGURE R2–5 Mind Map or Webbing

PROCEDURE: During group time, say various words or sentences and have the children imitate you. Using the same words, change your voice pitch, intonation, speed, or stress.

Sentence Variations

> I like juice. (normal, loud, soft/whisper, fast, slow, puckered mouth)
>
> *I* like juice. (stress)
>
> I *like* juice. (stress)
>
> I like *juice*. (stress)
>
> raise your voice for a question
>
> hold your nose

As the children imitate you and change their voices, verbalize for them what you (they) did: "Great, you all said it as loud as I did." Explore with children the impact that tone and intonation patterns have for understanding information. Write and say several simple phrases (I want to go to school; I want you to take my picture), and encourage them to play with the words. Point to the word you want them to stress. Discuss the differences in meaning and what the next phrase might be based on the stress. Discuss where you might use different voices. Ask children how they would say something at a sports event as compared to inside.

ACCOMMODATIONS AND INTEGRATION: Use gestures to reinforce the tonal pattern. Have children speak in longer sentences and have other children imitate them and give them feedback about different intonation patterns. Because so much of meaning is passed through the nonverbal aspect of language, it is important that children are aware of it from an early age.

• • • • LANGUAGE: **SMALL GROUP OR INDIVIDUAL**

2-29 Follow That Line

GOALS: To improve reading literacy; to increase knowledge of the structure of language; to identify and understand patterns and relationships

STANDARDS: L 2 Demonstrate command of the conventions of standard English capitalization, punctuation, and spelling when writing.

MATERIALS: Poster board, markers (red, green, black)

TO MAKE: *Cut poster board into 3 × 3 inch squares, and arrange these squares in a pattern on a large table or the floor. (This is only for your ease in drawing.) Using black, red, and green markers, draw a pattern of lines, stopping and starting colors and using straight and curved lines.*

PROCEDURE: Have the children build a track with the cards in a variety of patterns (see Figure R2–6). Talk with the children about punctuation, especially periods, and their function in language. Discuss how the period represented on the cards is also a stop. Encourage children to make a variety of patterns.

ACCOMMODATIONS AND INTEGRATION: Use squares with only one color. The more squares you have available and the more

colors and patterns, the more complicated the task is. It is also more challenging when children must make a designated pattern. Punctuation and spacing make important contributions to both reading and writing and may be overlooked as we teach children the structure of language.

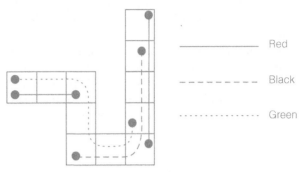

FIGURE R2–6 Cards with Lines and Punctuation Marks

• • • • LANGUAGE: **SMALL GROUP**

2-30 Never

GOALS: To improve expressive communication; to increase knowledge of the structure of language; to increase inclusion

STANDARDS: L 4 Determine or clarify the meaning of unknown and multiple-meaning words and phrases based on kindergarten reading and content; L 5 Explore word relationships and nuances in word meanings; M 6 Describe and compare measureable attributes.

MATERIALS: A variety of clothed male and female dolls of different races, colored blocks, yarn

PROCEDURE: Teach children to make absolute and relative comparisons. Make a circle with the yarn. Place all the blocks in the circle, and ask the children to move the blocks so none of the blocks are in the circle. Then teach the relative concepts: *a few, many, most,* and so on, moving blocks in and out of the circle. Then use the dolls. After children are comfortable with these concepts, use other words that allow for comparison, such as these:

ABSOLUTE	RELATIVE	RELATIVE
everything	few	often
nothing	some	seldom
all	many	frequently
none	a lot of	occasionally
never	most	usually
always	rarely	often

Group and regroup objects on both relative and absolute characteristics. Then expand the topic to other times when absolute and relative words are used. When children use absolute words, if appropriate, challenge the concept and encourage them to use more relative words. If a child says, "I *always* clean up the block corner," question the child:

"Has there been *one* day when you haven't?" Help the child choose another word that more accurately represents reality: "I *usually* clean up the block corner."

ACCOMMODATIONS AND INTEGRATION: Listen to individual children's speech patterns and their use of absolute terms. Choose one term that occurs frequently and begin to work on that specific word. Changing spontaneous speech is a challenge. Help children think about the relationship between their language and behavior. Although this may seem like belaboring a point, prejudicial statements are usually absolute ones: "Demi can't do anything": "*All* people with disabilities are *helpless*." Help children use words that allow for exceptions to avoid prejudicial statements.

SUMMARY

- Language arts impacts all other areas of study
- New curriculum standards in the English language arts have increased our expectations about what children should know and be able to do in the early childhood years.
- Children need to develop the literacy skills for further learning as well as a commitment to literacy.

EDUCATIONAL RESOURCES

Book Vine for Children categorizes books in a variety of different ways, including by age. A children's librarian evaluates their selections. They sell both individual books and packages of books about particular topics. www.bookvine.com/

Children's Book Council (CBC) is a nonprofit trade association. Its members are publishers of trade books for children and young adults in the United States. CBC promotes the use and enjoyment of trade books for young people. www.cbcbooks.org/

Common Core State Standards Initiative provides background on the development of the standards, which are designed to prepare children for success in college and work. The standards for English language arts and mathematics communicate what is expected of students at each grade level, starting with kindergarten, and focus on core conceptual understandings and procedures. www.corestandards.org/

Gayle's Preschool Rainbow has support for different themes, including many alphabet activities. www.preschoolrainbow.org/alphabet.htm/

I Am Your Child is a national, nonprofit, nonpartisan organization founded in 1997 to raise awareness about the importance of early childhood development and school readiness. It develops a variety of resources for parents and early childhood professionals. It also promotes public policies that help ensure that children have the physical well-being and the social, emotional and cognitive abilities they need to enter school ready to succeed. www.iamyourchild.org/

Usborne, a British publishing company, uses lexile measures for their different reading series, allowing teachers to better match the text to the child's reading level. They also have many titles to select from. www.usborne.com/

iLoveLanguages contains 2,400 links to languages and literature from around the world, from Aboriginal to Yiklamu. www.ilovelanguages.com/

International Reading Association (IRA) seeks to improve the quality of reading instruction through studying the reading process and teaching techniques, and serving as a clearinghouse for the dissemination of reading research. IRA publishes a journal *Reading Online* about reading. www.reading.org/

Literacy Center Education Network works to provide young children with the skills necessary to learn to read and write, in more than one language. They provide free literacy lessons in English, Spanish, German, and French. www.literacycenter.net/

Little Explorers by Enchanted Learning is set up like a children's picture dictionary in eight different languages. Although you need to subscribe to enjoy all of the features, many of them are available free. www.EnchantedLearning.com/Dictionary.html/

For additional resources, visit the book companion website for this text at www.cengagebrain.com.

3 Discovery Activities:
Mathematics, Science, and Technology

Mathematics, science, and technology are taught as hands-on experiences in the early childhood curriculum. Young children are beginning to think logically and are moving into more abstract concepts. However, simply telling them about their world is rarely effective. They need to develop a solid base of internalized experiences as a foundation for later abstract scientific and mathematical thinking.

ACTIVITY GOALS AND STANDARDS

Activities are organized by the goals and standards they support. The activities themselves serve as prototypes of activities that can be used again and again with minor changes. Books that are referred to in the text with an * have a complete citation and annotation in the Children's Bibliography; others have a complete citation where they are cited. For books where a lexile score is available, it is given after the book, for example, (500L). The notation "AD" before the lexile, means that the book needs adult direction and should initially be read by an adult and discussed with children before children read it independently.

©Cengage Learning 2012

DISCOVERY GUIDELINES

The following guidelines will be helpful as you think about adapting discovery activities to meet the needs of children with diverse abilities.

Adapting activities for children with:

Specific learning disabilities ❊ Emphasize the role of technology and software, particularly in the areas of reading and math. Support children in learning word processing skills and using such supports as spell and grammar check.

Social, emotional, and behavioral disorders ❊ Use a discovery-based approach. Reduce stress. For some children, warm water may be relaxing, so teach relevant concepts using it. Use software that helps children be in control and is responsive to them.

Attention-deficit/hyperactivity disorder ❊ Talk about the brain and how it works. Teach children skills to use the computer independently, and help them choose appropriate programs.

Communication disorders ❊ Emphasize the vocabulary that goes with math and science. Teach children about body parts that are involved with making sound. Use the speech synthesizer to help children speak, if appropriate.

English language learners ❊ Use context for teaching math and science vocabulary in both English and the home language. Teach computer skills and use computer programs that support both English and the home language.

Autism spectrum disorders ❊ Use digital cameras, the computer, and related technology to take advantage of visual learning skills. Make your own picture menus about your class and choices children have. Help children visually sequence activities.

Intellectual disabilities ❊ Start with the concrete and allow children to repeat experiences with variations. Help them generalize what they have learned to real situations.

Gifts and talents ❊ Encourage children to expand on themes and explore them in more depth. Have more complex interactive computer programs, and encourage the use of technology to solve problems. Explore perspective through a digital camera, and help children capture some of the complex projects they have made.

Special health care needs ❊ Help children understand the scientific process and how science may impact their health. Have children become more independent by counting pills and learning the times they are taken. Work on safety and hygiene and their understanding of how diseases spread.

Orthopedic and neurological impairments ❊ Help children relate the concepts of size, distance, speed, and time to themselves, any equipment they might use, and their safety. Focus on some of the mechanical aspects of sciences such as pulleys and magnets that may help them reach objects. Support their use of adaptive technology.

Hearing impairments ❊ Help children learn about body parts involved in hearing. Use microphones and other aids that control volume. Use computers that can translate printed input into verbal output.

Visual impairments ❊ Help children learn about body parts involved in vision. Use magnifying glasses and other forms of magnification. Help children learn to measure by stepping things off. Use computer fonts to change the size of print. Scan materials and have them made larger (or do this with a copier). Use digital cameras with zoom lenses.

DISCOVERY ACTIVITIES

MATHEMATICS: **SMALL GROUP OR INDIVIDUAL**

3-1 Matching Symbols

GOALS: To improve number sense and numeration; to improve reading literacy; to increase vocabulary acquisition and use

STANDARDS: M 1 Know number names and the count sequence; M 2 Count to tell the number of objects; L 5 Explore word relationships and nuances in word meaning.

MATERIALS: Cards numbered 1 through 20, cards with up to 20 symbols

PROCEDURE: Have the children match the number and symbol cards. To begin with, make the cards large and only use the numbers 1 through 5.

ACCOMMODATIONS AND INTEGRATION: Initially use cards to count and identify numbers. Encourage children to point to or touch the symbols as they count. Cardboard or laminated cards are easier to handle (see Figure R3–1). Add cards that have different shapes or pictures on them (small animal stickers); include cards that have different symbols on the same card (dot, square, sticker) with different spatial arrangements (see Figure R3–2). Encourage children to put all of the cards with the same number of symbols in a pile. Help children learn that the number value does not change based on specific symbols or their arrangement on the card. Emphasize the language of equivalency—"same as," "equals"—and the concepts "more," "less," and so on. Use sandpaper or felt numbers and shapes to provide tactile cues.

MATHEMATICS: **INDIVIDUAL OR SMALL GROUP**

3-2 Spacey Dots

GOALS: To improve number sense and numeration; to improve geometric and spatial sense; to improve reading literacy

STANDARDS: M 1 Know number names and the count sequence; M 2 Count to tell the number of objects; M 3 Compare numbers.

MATERIALS: A set of three cards for each number from 1 to 10; each card of the set has an equal number of dots, with different dots arranged in different configurations on each card (see Figure R3–3).

PROCEDURE: Have children match cards with equal numbers of dots. Ask the child to give you the card that has the same number of dots as the card shown. Count and encourage the child to touch the dots as she counts. Use the cards to help children compare numbers. Ask them to find a card that has more or fewer dots than the one you hold or that has a higher or lower number.

ACCOMMODATIONS AND INTEGRATION: Start by using only two sets of cards with 1 to 5 dots. To add tactile cues. use sandpaper shapes or textured glue to make the dots. Add sets of cards, including cards with numerals. Have the children describe the markings and where the markings are on the card (e.g., center, right-hand corner, top half). Spatial configuration sometimes distracts children from the concept of number.

MATHEMATICS: **SMALL AND LARGE GROUP**

3-3 Number Concentration

GOALS: To improve number sense and numeration; to make predictions; to improve memory skills

FIGURE R3–1: Cards with Symbols and Numbers

FIGURE R3–2: Cards with Different Spatial Configurations and Different Symbols and Numbers

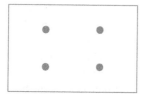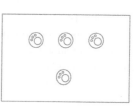

FIGURE R3–3: Spacy Dots Cards

STANDARDS: M 1 Know number names and the count sequence; M 4 Understand addition as putting together and adding to, and understand subtraction as taking apart and taking from.

MATERIALS: A set of cards with matching pairs of numbers on one side (or a deck of cards), cards with +, −, and = signs.

PROCEDURE: This is a variation of the game "Concentration." Lay out the cards face down. Each child takes a turn and chooses two cards. The objective is to turn over two cards that are the same number. As children turn over a card, ask them what number is on the card. When they have found a pair have them place the cards side by side, make a written equation out of the cards, and solve the equation.

ACCOMMODATIONS AND INTEGRATION: Start with four or five pairs of cards. Use small numbers (1 to 5) and/or simple shapes. First, have the children match the cards, and then demonstrate how the game is played. Gradually add more cards of higher denomination. This can also be done with letters of the alphabet. You can even match capital and small letters, a more difficult variation.

· · · · ·   MATHEMATICS: **SMALL GROUP**

3-4   Draw It On

GOALS: To improve number sense and numeration; to improve geometric and spatial sense; to improve sensory motor integration

STANDARDS: M 1 Know number names and the count sequence; M 8 Identify and describe shapes; M 9 Analyze, compare, create, and compose shapes.

MATERIALS: Paper, markers, cards with simple shapes, numbers, or letters

PROCEDURE: Demonstrate the procedure by having an adult tap out numbers or finger-draw simple shapes (square, circle, triangle) on a child's back based on the card chosen. Have the children sit in pairs front to back, and give the child in back a card with a shape or number. Using his finger, this child draws the design on the back of the other child. When completed, the child in front draws the design on the paper with a marker or identifies the number or shape verbally. The children then compare the design drawn with the one on the card.

ACCOMMODATIONS AND INTEGRATION: Start by having an adult draw a design on the child's back and the child identify the design or choose from possible designs. As children become more skilled, increase the complexity of the designs or use simple equations or simple words. Children need to integrate information from all body parts. This provides an unusual way to identify and draw geometric shapes, numbers, and letters.

· · · · ·   MATHEMATICS: **SMALL AND LARGE GROUP**

3-5   Seeds

GOALS: To improve estimation skills; to improve knowledge of whole number operations and computations; to increase knowledge of the natural world

STANDARDS: M 2 Count to tell the number of objects; M 3 Compare numbers; M 5 Work with numbers 11–19 to gain foundations for place value.

MATERIALS: Cantaloupe, pumpkin, squash (or other fruit or vegetable with large seeds), knife, egg containers for seeds, marker, paper or chart

PROCEDURE: Show children the cantaloupe. Let them predict what is inside (some will know). Let them see you cut it open. Ask them to describe what they see. Have the children estimate how many seeds there are. Record each child's estimation. Dry the seeds or use different seeds. Set up a table where the children can count the seeds into egg containers, putting 10 seeds in each separate pocket. Once the seeds are in the egg containers, have the children figure out how to combine the ones that do not have 10 seeds, using base 10 reasoning. Then count by 10s to determine the number of seeds there are in the cantaloupe. Review earlier estimations to see how close the children were. Help them think about the reasoning behind their estimates and what would make them more accurate.

ACCOMMODATIONS AND INTEGRATION: Encourage children to work in pairs. Have several cantaloupes and compare the number of seeds in each. This activity encourages children to practice number correspondence and counting by 10s. It can be done with any foods that have seeds. Compare the number of seeds from different foods. Talk about the role of the seeds and have the fruit or vegetable for snack.

· · · · ·   MATHEMATICS: **SMALL GROUP OR INDIVIDUAL**

3-6   Estimating Body Parts

GOALS: To improve estimation skills; to improve measurement skills; to increase sensory motor integration

STANDARDS: M 2 Count to tell the number of objects; M 3 Compare numbers; M 6 Describe and compare measureable attributes.

MATERIALS: Copies of a picture of a body with two lines next to each body part that needs to be measured, chain links, blue and red crayons, string, pencil, graph paper

PROCEDURE: Show children the picture of the body and talk about measuring different parts of their body. Let them work with each other to use string to measure the length of their arms, legs, head, hand, and foot. Cut and label the string for each part for each child. Then have children estimate the number of chain links they will need to create the same length as their pieces of string. Have the children write their estimation in blue next to the body part on their papers. After making the estimations, have the children use the chain links to determine the actual length of the string. Have the children write the actual length in red next to the appropriate body part and then make a graph comparing the two lengths. When the children are finished, discuss the differences in the numbers, which were easy to estimate, which were hard, and why.

ACCOMMODATIONS AND INTEGRATION: Have an adult assist the child in determining the length of the string. Encourage children to measure body parts held straight and bent. Have children use this method to measure furniture, dolls, and stuffed animals as well. Use a tape measure. Providing concrete and interesting items to measure enables children to become more involved and work together to accomplish the tasks.

Unifix cubes can be used to teach many mathematical goals and standards.
©Cengage Learning 2012

• • • •   MATHEMATICS: **SMALL GROUP**

3-7   100s Game

GOALS: To improve number sense and numeration skills; to improve knowledge of whole number operations and computations; to improve reading literacy

STANDARDS: M 2 Count to tell the number of objects; M 4 Understand addition as putting together and adding to, and understand subtraction as taking apart and taking from; M 5 Work with numbers 11–19 to gain foundations for place value.

MATERIALS: Unifix cubes (6 colors), a color die, a number die, Unifix number track

PROCEDURE: In small groups, have children play a game with Unifix cubes. Each child takes a turn rolling a set of dice. After rolling the dice, the child stacks the appropriate number and color of Unifix cubes together. Then the child places the cubes on a Unifix number track, starting at the number 1. Each child follows the same procedure. The children add their stacks of Unifix cubes to the ones on the number track until they reach 100. Count with the children by 10s.

ACCOMMODATIONS AND INTEGRATION: Start with only one color of Unifix cubes and only use the number die. As children become more competent, add an additional number die so the children must add the dice together to obtain the number of Unifix cubes needed or add the color die. Providing a noncompetitive game allows children to focus on the outcome of the game rather than competing with peers.

• • • •   MATHEMATICS: **INDIVIDUAL OR SMALL GROUP**

3-8   Caterpillars

GOALS: To improve number sense and numeration; to identify and understand patterns and relationships; to increase adaptive skills

STANDARDS: M 2 Count to tell the number of objects; M 4 Understand addition as putting together and adding to, and

understand subtraction as taking apart and taking from; M 7 Classify objects and count the number of objects in each category.

MATERIALS: 2-inch-square fabric pieces of different colors and/or textures, with a button on one end and a buttonhole on the other

TO MAKE: *Cut fabric squares (felt, leather, velvet, wool, terry cloth). Put a button on one end and a buttonhole on the other (see Figure R3–4). If necessary, finish the edges so they do not unravel. Make a slit for the buttonhole.*

PROCEDURE: Initially, let children practice buttoning or fastening the material together, then create a short repeating pattern (e.g., fur, felt, fur, felt) by buttoning the materials together in a sequence to make a caterpillar. Have children classify, count, copy and extend the pattern (see Figure R3–5). Give children simple equations such as $2 + 3 = 5$. Have them join (button) two pieces, then three pieces, and then join these together to make five pieces; and then have them make the equation for $1 + 4 = 5$ and describe what they have done.

ACCOMMODATIONS AND INTEGRATION: Use Velcro instead of buttons to attach the pieces, use simple repeating patterns, and let children button without trying to make a pattern. As children learn, increase the length and complexity of the caterpillar by varying both color and texture patterns. Add a variety of closures on different corners (hooks and eyes, snaps, etc.). This provides tactile feedback for children as well as essential math and reading readiness skills.

• • • •   MATHEMATICS: **SMALL GROUP**

3-9   Fractions

GOALS: To improve number sense and numeration; to identify and understand patterns and relationships; to increase vocabulary acquisition and use

STANDARDS: M 3 Compare numbers; M 4 Understand addition as putting together and adding to, and understand

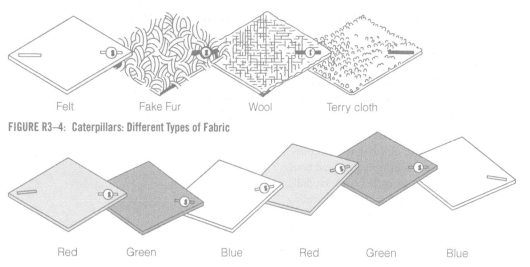

FIGURE R3–4: Caterpillars: Different Types of Fabric

Felt   Fake Fur   Wool   Terry cloth

Red   Green   Blue   Red   Green   Blue

FIGURE R3–5: Caterpillars: Different Colors of Fabric

subtraction as taking apart and taking from; M 7 Classify objects and count the number of objects in each category.

MATERIALS: Box or bag to contain whole objects; and those objects cut in half, thirds, and fourths:

>   pieces of cardboard
>   cards
>   pieces of felt
>   drinking straws
>   paper plates
>   pieces of note paper
>   pieces of paper or poster board of different sizes

PROCEDURE: Show the children the whole objects and then the same objects cut in pieces. Talk about how the pieces go together to form a whole (as in a puzzle). Identify the names of the different fractions (e.g., *half, third, fourth*). Have children count the number of pieces; and identify the fraction (e.g., ½) based on the number of pieces.

ACCOMMODATIONS AND INTEGRATION: Let children use the pieces like a puzzle, with fewer pieces and materials that are more dissimilar. As children get the idea of putting the pieces together, introduce the idea of fractions, starting with half. Use the vocabulary *half* and *whole*. Talk about the mathematical properties that make something *half*. When children understand the concept of half, introduce other fractions, and have children cut some objects into thirds and fourths. Introduce the term *equals*. Use the vocabulary of *whole* and *half* during snack, asking children to eat half of their apple slices or raisins. After they consume some, ask them to eat half again to help them see the relative nature of fractions.

· · · · ·   MATHEMATICS: **SMALL GROUP**

3-10   The Bottle Game

GOALS: To improve knowledge of whole number operations and computations; to make predictions; to improve cause-and-effect reasoning

STANDARDS: M 3 Compare numbers; M 5 Work with numbers 11–19 to gain foundations for place value; M 7 Classify objects and count the number of objects in each category.

MATERIALS: 28 small plastic water bottles filled with colored water (12 yellow, 9 blue, 6 red, and 1 green), 1 piece each of yellow, blue, red, and green construction paper (2 pieces of each if teams are playing), dice (oversized)

PROCEDURE: Set up the game as shown in Figure R3–6. The floor provides more room to move. Two children can play at a time or there can be two teams of two children each. Each child gets a turn to roll the die. The child collects the appropriate number of yellow bottles with each roll and places them on his yellow sheet of paper. When a child has three yellow bottles, he can trade them in for one blue bottle. When the child has traded enough yellow bottles in to get three blue bottles, he can trade the blue bottles in for a red bottle. When the child has collected three red bottles, he can trade them in for the green bottle and the game is over.

ACCOMMODATIONS AND INTEGRATION: Children can use the bottles to indicate the number on the die. This activity provides an opportunity for children to problem-solve on various levels and work with others to win the game. It requires counting, making sets, trading, predicting, and deductive reasoning (with permission of Nancy Edwards).

· · · · ·   MATHEMATICS: **SMALL GROUP**

   Measure It

GOALS: To improve measurement concepts; to improve classification skills; to improve estimation skills

STANDARDS: M 3 Compare numbers; M 6 Describe and compare measureable attributes; M 7 Classify objects and count the number of objects in each category.

MATERIALS: Beanbag, tennis ball, ping-pong ball, sponges, small rubber ball, rubber rings, horseshoes, Wiffle ball, crumpled paper, beach ball, 12-inch rubber ball, softball, feather, balloon, towel

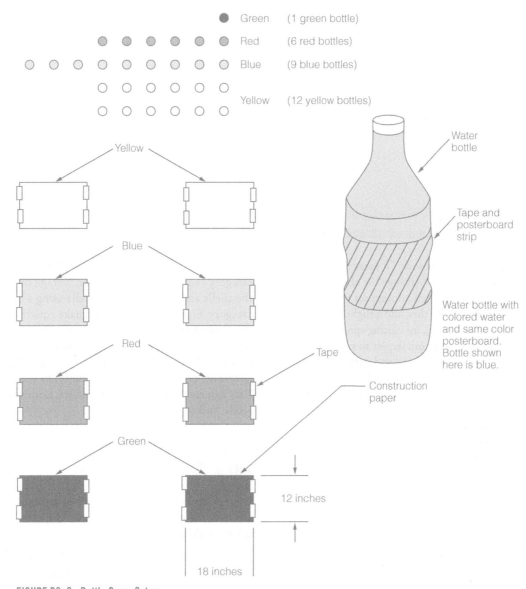

● Green   (1 green bottle)

● ● ● ● ● ●   Red   (6 red bottles)

○ ○ ○ ○ ○ ○ ○ ○ ○   Blue   (9 blue bottles)

○ ○ ○ ○ ○ ○
○ ○ ○ ○ ○   Yellow   (12 yellow bottles)

Yellow

Blue

Red

Green

Water bottle

Tape and posterboard strip

Water bottle with colored water and same color posterboard. Bottle shown here is blue.

Tape

Construction paper

12 inches

18 inches

FIGURE R3–6: Bottle Game Set up

PROCEDURE: Have a variety of objects for children to throw. Throwing style is not important. Have children help you draw a line or stake a string and then mark it at each foot with a ribbon. Have the children develop a baseline (average throw) with the small rubber ball or tennis ball. Have other children watch where the ball goes and then stand where it first hits. Determine how far it went. Then have the child who is throwing decide whether the next object will go farther or closer. Measure the distance and classify the objects after they are thrown. Have children graph their relative lengths and compare them. Have several children do this and compare the results. Help children understand how to make better estimates. Help them generate hypotheses about the attributes of objects that influence the distance they can be thrown.

ACCOMMODATIONS AND INTEGRATION: For some, this might simply be a motor activity with an understanding that it is easier to throw some objects farther than others. Help children separate out differences in what specific children can do (avoid competition) and the properties of the objects.

• • • • • MATHEMATICS: **SMALL GROUP**

3-12 *Object Sizes*

GOALS: To improve geometric and spatial sense; to improve measurement concepts; to improve generalization skills

STANDARDS: M 6 Describe and compare measureable attributes; M 7 Classify objects and count the number of objects in each category.

MATERIALS: Four sets of measuring spoons and measuring cups (see Figure R3–7), plastic glasses of different sizes, a water or sand table

PROCEDURE: Place sets of objects in the water or on the sand table. Start with two different-sized containers. Give children time to explore the objects and play with them by just filling and dumping them. As children become aware of differences, ask them to point to or give you the objects in order of size.

ACCOMMODATIONS AND INTEGRATION: Help children explore the relative sizes of objects through pouring and measuring.

FIGURE R3–7: Measuring Cups and Spoons

Give them examples for comparisons: "It takes four of the smallest cups to fill the big one." Arrange the objects in order of size, and give the children another set to match to the first. When children can do this, add a slightly different set of things to be matched (e.g., measuring spoons). Have the children arrange both sets from largest to smallest. Add containers that are deceptive (e.g., tall and narrow, short and wide). Encourage children to make predictions about relative volume and then to check whether they are right. Have children measure a variety of different materials so that they learn that measurement is a constant. Use birdseed, sand, and so on, depending on the age of the children. Focusing on "dump and fill" has many potentials, including learning adaptive skills. Adult input and questioning varies the activity.

· · · · · MATHEMATICS: **SMALL GROUP**

3-13 Sorting Shells

GOALS: To improve measurement concepts; to improve classification skills; to increase vocabulary acquisition and use

STANDARDS: M 6 Describe and compare measureable attributes; M 7 Classify objects and count the number of objects in each category; L 4 Determine or clarify the meaning of unknown and multiple-meaning words and phrases based on kindergarten reading and content.

MATERIALS: Variety of shells; baskets; book such as C. K. Tibbitts, *Seashells, Crabs and Sea Stars* (Take-along guides) (Lanham, MD: NorthWord Books for Young Readers, 1998)

PROCEDURE: Set up a table with the shells and baskets. Let the children explore the shells and describe the similarities and differences among them—color, size, shape, and texture. Help children identify the different shells by looking them up in a book like *Seashells, Crabs and Sea Stars*. Have the children decide on a system to sort the shells, explain the system and which shells go into which baskets according to their system, count the number of shells, and write the number down.

ACCOMMODATIONS AND INTEGRATION: Give children a category (e.g., large, small) and encourage them to sort the shells and then resort the shells using a different category. Encourage children to make equations using different categories of shells and to write and solve these equations. This provides an open-ended activity that supports vocabulary development and classification systems. *Note:* Sort objects that are meaningful to the children. They can sort transportation vehicles, farm equipment, seeds, and so on.

· · · · · MATHEMATICS: **LARGE GROUP**

3-14 Picture Shapes

GOALS: To improve geometric and spatial sense; to identify and understand patterns and relationships; to improve classification skills

STANDARDS: M 8 Identify and describe shapes; M 9 Analyze, compare, create, and compose shapes.

MATERIALS: Geometric shapes cut from cardboard, pictures of common objects with definite geometric shapes mounted on cards (e.g., ball, house, ice cream cone, bed)

PROCEDURE: Have children match their geometric shapes with the shapes in the picture or drawing.

ACCOMMODATIONS AND INTEGRATIONS: Choose pictures with little detail and help children place shapes over the pictures to find a shape in the picture. Then have the children sort the pictures according to shape. Use more complex pictures with several shapes and have children find shapes in a picture containing several shapes. This activity helps children analyze and classify geometric shapes in their world. Help them use different shapes to compose other shapes. It requires visual generalization and application of knowledge of shapes to pictures of real objects. Talk with children about why a particular shape is functional for a particular purpose, for example, the pitch of roofs (or angle of a triangle) and the north–south orientation of a structure relative to snow and its weight; or a roof overhang to keep the sun from shining in regions that are very hot.

SCIENCE: **INDIVIDUAL OR SMALL GROUP**

3-15 Ant Farm

GOALS: To improve observational skills; to improve generalization skills; to increase knowledge of the natural world

STANDARDS: SC 1 Unifying concepts and processes; SC 2 Science as inquiry; SC 3b Life science.

MATERIALS: Two clear glass jars (one large such as a fish bowl and one small enough to fit inside the other); loose or sandy soil and ants (or buy a sand or gel ant farm); magnifying glass; book such as H. Dyer and B. Kalman, *The Life Cycle of an Ant* (New York: Crabtree Publishing Company, 2005); or A. Fowler, J. Allen, and T. Humphries, *Are You an Ant?* (Backyard Books) (New York: Kingfisher, 2004) (available in Spanish)

TO MAKE: *Put the smaller jar inside the large one, open side down. (You want to be able to see the ants, so you want the space between the smaller and larger jars to be relatively narrow.) Collect ants from one ant colony only for each jar (otherwise, they may fight). Find an ant pile and carefully dig out enough ants and soil to fill the container to within 2 or 3 inches of the top. Try to find an ant that looks bigger than the others, and a queen ant that may have wings. If you see eggs and larvae, include them. (If you are collecting red ants or ants that bite, adults should do this part of the process.) Feed ants small breadcrumbs, tiny bits of fruit or vegetables, and a water-soaked cotton ball. (Don't feed them too much.) Try to keep the jar in one place and put a top on it with holes for ventilation.*

PROCEDURE: Initially encourage the children to observe the ant farm. After these initial observations, see whether the children can detect some of the rituals, hierarchies, and roles that different ants play. Encourage them to use a magnifying glass to observe finer details. Read a book about ants. After reading the book, help children discuss the main topics, observe what they have read about, and then check their observations at the ant farm.

ACCOMMODATIONS AND INTEGRATION: Concentrate on the observation process. Point out what is going on in the ant farm. Then make (or buy) a second ant farm and encourage the children to compare the two. Have them draw the configuration of tunnels. Encourage them to look up ants in reference books and on the Internet to learn how ants live and work. Discuss the survival needs of animals and how ants are both different from and the same as other animals.

· · · · · SCIENCE: **SMALL OR LARGE GROUP**

 3-16 Pollution

GOALS: To improve observational skills; to make predictions; to improve cause-and-effect reasoning

STANDARDS: SC 1 Unifying concepts and processes; SC 2 Science as inquiry: SC 5 Science in personal and social perspectives.

MATERIALS: Three sticks of fresh celery with leaves, or white carnations; three glasses of water; red and blue food coloring

PROCEDURE: Cut off the bottoms of celery sticks or carnation stems. Put a few drops of red food coloring in one glass of water and a few drops of blue in a second. Leave the water in the third glass clear. Put one stick of celery (or carnation) in each glass. Do this early in the day and check at the end of the day. Cut the celery sticks and see how the ones in colored water are different from the one in fresh water. One needs only observe the carnations to see the effects. Discuss the effects of pollutants and how they can get into plants and animals, including people.

ACCOMMODATIONS AND INTEGRATION: Help children think about pollution in a more concrete way. Have them think about drinking the water they wash their hands in. The carnations may look beautiful, but it is important that children see beyond the visual effect. Talk with children about pollution in underground water. Tell them how it gets into the plants we eat. Have them begin to think about ways of preventing pollution. Pollution is a relatively abstract concept, and children may learn only about the principle of osmosis. Talk about the implications of increasing populations and conservation. Help children generate ideas for actions to take at school and home to decrease pollution. It is important to make this global, abstract problem relevant to children.

· · · · · SCIENCE: **LARGE AND SMALL GROUP**

 3-17 Terrarium

GOALS: To increase knowledge of the natural world; to improve observational skills; to improve generalization skills

STANDARDS: SC 1 Unifying concepts and processes; SC 3b Life science; R:IT 1 Ask and answer questions about key details in a text.

MATERIAL: Aquarium or large glass or clear plastic containers with a large open mouth and a cover, dirt, pebbles, activated charcoal, sphagnum moss, plants; book such as S. Bearce, *A Kid's Guide to Making a Terrarium* (Gardening for Kids) (Robbie Readers) (Hockessin, DE: Mitchell Lane Publishers, 2009)

TO MAKE: *Put a layer of pebbles in the bottom (1"), half an inch of activated charcoal over the pebbles, a layer of sphagnum moss on top of the charcoal, and then 2 to 3 inches of dirt on top (depending upon size of container). Poke holes in soil for plants, and add a moderate amount of water.*

PROCEDURE: Read or paraphrase a book about making a terrarium. Discuss with the children what a terrarium is and how to make one. Show the children an aquarium with nothing in it. Tell them that they are going to make a terrarium. Ask the children what things they might need in the terrarium. Discuss the function of the pebbles (drainage), charcoal (filter), moss (keeps dirt from falling) dirt (growth medium), water (drink), plants, (choose plants that have the same growth requirement). Have all these items ready. Before making the terrarium, show the children the care tags that come with the plants. Help them read these so the children think about what the plants require to live and where the terrarium should be placed in the classroom. Using a piece of paper the same size as the aquarium, have the children arrange the plants and any other objects they might want to include. Make the terrarium. Talk about the terrarium as an ecosystem with plants that need resources such as water, sunlight, and soil. Sunlight causes evaporation of the water and forms droplets on the sides of the terrarium (and the top if it is on). These grow larger and fall to the bottom. Use this process as an analogy to talk about the natural world. Observe the terrarium to see how it is doing. If there are problems, hypothesize with the children what the cause might be and generate possible solutions.

ACCOMMODATIONS AND INTEGRATION: Use reference books and the Internet to learn more about terrariums to ensure the environment will be sustained. Expand this to include how this relates to people's environments and what they need.

· · · · ·   SCIENCE: **LARGE OR SMALL GROUP**

 ## Where Is It/Who Is It?

GOALS: To make predictions; to identify and understand patterns and relationships; to improve listening skills

STANDARDS: SC 2 Science as inquiry; SC 3a Physical science; S&L 4 Describe familiar people, places, things, and events and, with prompting and support, provide additional detail.

MATERIALS: None

PROCEDURE: Choose a child to walk in front of the class and see whether children can describe different types of walking and some of the variables involved, including the sounds made. Help with some initial questions: "What kind of shoes is the child wearing? Is the walk heavy or light, fast or slow?" (With a rug and sneakers this is challenging.) Then have children sit facing a wall, with their eyes shut. Ask one child to walk to a specific area. As the child is walking, tell the children to listen and name the area where the child stops. Then have them open their eyes and check whether they are right.

ACCOMMODATIONS AND INTEGRATION: Have the child go to a location, stand still, and hit a tambourine or drum. Verbalize for children the cues they might use to locate the person. Naming the area is difficult because the children have to remember the various parts of the room and visualize their location. Children can learn to fine-tune their listening skills, but it requires practice.

· · · · ·   SCIENCE: **SMALL GROUP**

3-19 ## Water Table

GOALS: To improve cause-and-effect reasoning; increase vocabulary acquisition and use; to improve expressive communication

STANDARDS: SC 2 Science as inquiry; SC 3a Physical science; M 6 Describe and compare measureable attributes.

MATERIALS: Water table, water, syringes, tubes, funnels, different-sized containers, measuring spoons and cups, smocks

PROCEDURE: Have a water table set up. Tell the children the names of the tools provided and encourage them to experiment with the tools and use the names during the play. Support children in exploring the tools and encourage them to talk about what they are doing and what happens to the water as it moves through the tools. Encourage children to use descriptive and directional words.

ACCOMMODATIONS AND INTEGRATION: Add more tools for children to explore as well as other props to expand the play. Water play helps children explore new media. Language skills support scientific inquiry and are key in this activity because they allow children to describe what they are doing and thinking.

· · · · ·   SCIENCE: **INDIVIDUAL OR SMALL GROUP**

 ## Goop

GOALS: To improve observational skills; to improve cause-and-effect reasoning; to improve sensory motor integration

STANDARDS: SC 2 Science as inquiry; SC 3a Physical science.

MATERIALS: Water, cornstarch, flour, sugar, bowls or jelly roll trays

PROCEDURE: Have children mix approximately equal amounts of cornstarch and water to make goop. Encourage children to experiment with the proportions, observe the results, and relate them to the properties of the material. Help children think about the different and confusing states of the goop. Then, use equal proportions of flour and water and compare the results to the goop. Then combine sugar and water and compare the results. Help children think about the different properties and reactions of materials that look similar. Help children write about these differences and develop some hypotheses about the materials they mixed with water. Encourage them to think about adding water to other substances and what might happen.

ACCOMMODATIONS AND INTEGRATION: Goop requires little strength to manipulate and defies coordination. It is a soothing, yet intriguing media. It is edible (although this is not advised) and relatively easy to clean up. It can be used on a bed tray, and it is clean.

· · · · ·   SCIENCE: **INDIVIDUAL OR SMALL GROUP**

 ## Sink or Float

GOALS: To improve observational skills; to improve classification skills; to improve cause-and-effect reasoning

STANDARDS: SC 2 Science as inquiry; SC 3a Physical science; SC 4 Science and technology

MATERIALS: Water table or bucket of water or plastic dishpan; chart with words and illustrations to indicate sinking and floating; objects that sink or float; different shapes and weights of sinkers (that anglers use) and floats; paper; cardboard; blocks; silverware; cups; egg cartons; bark, wood, seeds, and so on

PROCEDURE: Fill a water table, bucket, or pan at least 3 inches deep and allow children to put objects in the water to play with and observe. Encourage children to make predictions about floating and sinking and to place objects that sink and float in separate groups. Encourage active exploration. Have children place objects in the water in different ways (upside down, sideways). As they generate hypotheses, support their checking them out. Have children categorize objects as sinkers or floaters, and write this on the chart. Talk about the attributes of objects in each category.

ACCOMMODATIONS AND INTEGRATION: Let children explore the items and decide whether they sink or float. Encourage them to experiment. See whether children can use floaters to make sinkers float. If they need other objects, for example, a paper clip, block, or crayon, help them find the objects. Discuss where the sinkers are placed on the floater. Have them try variations. Repeat this activity with different items. Always have an adult present when young children are near water, even small amounts.

· · · · · SCIENCE: **SMALL GROUP**

3-22 Relief Maps

GOALS: To improve observational skills; to improve measurement concepts; to improve technology skills

STANDARDS: SC 2 Science as inquiry; SC 3c Earth and space science; SC 5 Science and technology.

MATERIALS: Cardboard, water, paper, crayons, a container, masking tape, papier-mâché, string or yarn

PROCEDURE: Have children choose an area of the playground or another outdoor area and draw it on cardboard with crayons. Divide the area and paper into quarters. Discuss with the children where things are in their drawing and how they decide where to put them. Make large graph paper for the children (1 inch equals 1 square foot), and use string or yarn to mark off the area the children are mapping in 1-foot-square sections. Show the children a relief map and point out its features (even if this is a photograph, the features are usually obvious). Ask the children what in the area is flat and what should stand up from the surface (sandbox, swings, trees, etc.). Use papier-mâché to help small groups of children make maps that reflect these contours. Talk about relative size as it relates to both area and height.

ACCOMMODATIONS AND INTEGRATION: Using a digital camera, take pictures of the area the children are mapping to help them figure out what things are in which areas. Tape the

four pictures together. Then make another map. Do this project over several days; they need not be consecutive. Discuss which things are natural objects and which are made by humans.

· · · · · SCIENCE: **SMALL GROUP**

 3-23 Food Forms

GOALS: To improve cause-and-effect reasoning; to make predictions; to improve generalization skills

STANDARDS: SC: 2 Science as Inquiry; SC 4 Science and technology; SC 5 Science in personal and social perspectives.

MATERIALS: A variety of whole foods, a baby food grinder, baby food jars of the same foods, knife, scraper, hot plate, masher

PROCEDURE: Pick one or several foods (carrots, squash, apples, and peaches work well). Have the children feel the food whole and cut them up into different shapes:

Carrots

whole—curls (cut long and thin and put in ice water)

pieces—cubes (cut at an angle), coins

Put some of the carrots in a saucepan to cook. (Cook whole carrots and cut–up ones. Set a timer and have children see, which is softer after a specified time period.) When the carrots are cooked, experiment again with different forms:

whole carrots

carrots cut as coins

pureed carrots (if you have a blender)

mashed carrots

ground carrots (in baby food grinder)

Compare these to baby food in jars. Discuss the taste of the different forms and how some are the same or almost the same and others different. Experiment by adding spices. Have children taste the different forms. As children become experienced, use less familiar foods and a greater variety of vegetables and fruits.

ACCOMMODATIONS AND INTEGRATION: Have children sample different food forms and explain who might eat each form and why (e.g., babies, individuals with braces, and those who have problems with swallowing); children can classify them and discuss the process that changed the texture. Explain what being on a "soft" diet means. Discuss cultural and ethnic differences in foods, food forms, and spices used. Children may not be aware of what causes food to change. Include the vocabulary related to the states of food: *soft, hard, crisp, mushy,* and so on. *Note:* According to the medical community, children younger than four should not have raw vegetables as they are a choking hazard. I suggest being vigilant and cutting the pieces very small if you serve them.

• • • • • SCIENCE: **SMALL OR LARGE GROUP**

 3-24 Space

GOALS: To improve cause-and-effect reasoning, to improve generalization skills; to increase knowledge of the natural world

STANDARDS: SC 3c Earth and space science; SC 5 Science in personal and social perspectives; R:IT 1 Ask and answer questions about key details in a text.

MATERIALS: Informational text such as C. Stott, *I Wonder Why Stars Twinkle: And Other Questions about Space* (New York: Kingfisher, 2011); literature text such as L. Landry, *Space Boy* (New York: Houghton Mifflin Books for Children, 2007); construction paper, metallic star stickers, crayons, markers

PROCEDURE: Read an informational text about space. Talk with the children about the text and encourage them to ask and answer questions. Discuss the differences between literature and informational texts. Encourage children to write or dictate a space story and to illustrate it based on one aspect of the text they found the most interesting. The following day, read a literature book about space. Encourage the children to compare and contrast the two books and decide what they learned about space from each one.

ACCOMMODATIONS AND INTEGRATION: Point out some of the key details in the text to help children compare the books. Encourage them to think about the purpose of each book and when each book would be the best choice.

• • • • • TECHNOLOGY: **LARGE AND SMALL GROUP**

 3-25 Safe Surfing

GOALS: To improve technology skills; to improve reading literacy; to improve writing literacy

STANDARDS: T 1 Write and illustrate ideas and stories using digital tools; T 7 Demonstrate safe, responsible, cooperative use of technology; W 6 Explore a variety of digital tools to produce and publish writing, including in collaboration with peers.

PROCEDURE: Discuss with children how they use computers at school and at home. Discuss how using the Internet is like playing at school and that there are rules to help keep everyone safe.

Discuss the rules that are appropriate for the children. Have the children develop safe surfing rules for their class and write and illustrate them, using digital tools, in a way that is understandable for all. Post them by the computer and send home a copy for parents.

ACCOMMODATIONS AND INTEGRATION: As children suggest rules, help them refine them and type them on the keyboard and encourage children to illustrate them. Have children help write a letter to their parents about safe surfing, explaining how they developed their safe surfing rules.

• • • • • TECHNOLOGY: **LARGE AND SMALL GROUP**

 **3-26** E-mail

GOALS: To improve technology skills; to improve reading skills; to improve writing literacy

STANDARDS: T 3 Engage others through e-mail and other electronic means; T 7 Demonstrate safe, responsible, cooperative use of technology; W 6 Explore a variety of digital tools to produce and publish writing, including in collaboration with peers.

MATERIALS: Computer linked to the Internet

PROCEDURE: Obtain a pen pal who is willing to correspond with your class. For young children, it is sometimes easier if the pen pal is an adult. Although there are online groups that match classrooms, it may be safer if you know the individuals your class will be e-mailing. Think about what your class is interested in, what is safe, and who will respond on a regular basis. Once this is established, help children learn the process of e-mailing and responding to e-mail. If the children in your class have e-mail at home, use this as a way of keeping in touch with someone who is out for an extended period.

ACCOMMODATIONS AND INTEGRATION: At the beginning, children might just ask questions and respond to questions. Over time and as their skills build, there may be more comments and information exchanged. Discuss with children the differences between mail that is posted and e-mail. Use both methods of communication to the advantage of each.

• • • • • TECHNOLOGY: **SMALL GROUP**

 **3-27** Dinosaur Hunt

GOALS: To improve technology skills; to improve cause-and-effect reasoning; to improve reading literacy

STANDARDS: T 5 Find and evaluate digital information about people, places, and things; T 7 Demonstrate safe, responsible, cooperative use of technology; T 9 Navigate virtual environments such as electronic books, software, and websites.

MATERIALS: Computer linked to the Internet, cards with names of topics children are interested in learning about, and cards with potential search engines such as yahooligans

PROCEDURE: Have the children type into a search engine a topic they are interested in such as dinosaurs. Help them look at the categories of results and decide on one they want to follow up on. For sites on the Web, help children read the URL as well as the name and the significance of different designations (.com, .gov, .edu, .org, .net). Help them read about the different sites and choose one. After they have seen this site, have them go back to the previous menu and choose another site.

ACCOMMODATIONS AND INTEGRATION: Some children may be intrigued with the ideas about dinosaurs and might want to go to www.sesamestreet.org/ and, with a friend, excavate for dinosaurs. Have others who may want more factual information work together. They might try a government informational sight such as Dinosaurs: Facts and Fiction at http://pubs.usgs.gov/gip/dinosaurs/ to learn more. They can also go to the National Museum of Natural History website http://paleobiology.si.edu/dinosaurs/ and, after looking at some exhibits, do a dino dig there, then top it off with a video from the Discovery Channel on dinosaurs. Talk to children about the different sources and their purposes.

TECHNOLOGY: **SMALL GROUP**

3-28 Robot-Controller

GOALS: To improve technology skills; to improve cause-and-effect reasoning; to follow directions

STANDARDS: T 6 Use simulations and graphical organizers; T 8 Communicate about technology accurately; L 4 Determine or clarify the meaning of unknown and multiple-meaning words and phrases based on kindergarten reading and content.

MATERIALS: None

PROCEDURE: Have one child be the controller of a robot and another (or the teacher) be the robot. The controller's job is to command the robot. The robot could initially work like a toggle switch (on or off). If the child says, "Jump," the robot jumps until the child says, "Stop jumping." When the teacher is the robot, she can lead the child into more complexity: "Shall the robot jump fast or slow?" "Shall the robot jump in place or around the room?" If the commands are unclear ("Robot walk"), send back a message: "That does not compute. Robot needs to know whether to walk forward, backward, or sideways." The feedback will help children expand their vocabulary and be more specific in their speech, as well as gain practice giving commands. Have the children take turns so that they get practice in both commanding and following directions. The children need to learn that the robot, like a computer, will not do anything unless commands are clear. They need to learn that commands must be specific and that some commands "will not compute," so they need to find ones that will.

ACCOMMODATIONS AND INTEGRATION: Start with simple commands, which the teacher gives and the children respond to as a group. Then have children give two- and three-step

commands at one time and increase the complexity of the cues: "Take three steps to the right and then raise your hands and clap twice." Modify the robot-controller model for any situation in which someone is in charge and telling another what to do. It could be an animal trainer in the circus; a dog in (pet) obedience school; ground control to someone in a space capsule, and so on. This activity is an excellent way for children to see the results of their commands.

TECHNOLOGY: **INDIVIDUAL OR SMALL GROUP**

3-29 Computer Bingo

GOALS: To improve technology skills; to follow directions; to improve reading literacy

STANDARDS: T 6 Use simulations and graphical organizers; T 8 Communicate about technology accurately; R:FS 1 Demonstrate understanding of the organization and basic features of print.

MATERIALS: A bingo card made with the designations for a computer keyboard (see Figure R3–8), individual cards with corresponding designations, basket

PROCEDURE: Play as you would bingo. Draw a card out of the basket, call out the information on the card (3–H), and have the children find the square and mark it.

ACCOMMODATIONS AND INTEGRATION: Children can play this alone or in pairs. Point out for children the two-step decision making. (The number designates the row and then they must look for the right letter.) Have children figure out how they can call out letters that make words as they play. This off-computer activity stresses keyboard skills. Although structured like bingo, obviously all the children who follow the instructions accurately will "win."

TECHNOLOGY: **SMALL GROUP**

3-30 Fruit Kabob

GOALS: To improve technology skills; to identify and understand patterns and relationships; to improve reading literacy

STANDARDS: T 6 Use simulations and graphical organizers; T 8 Communicate about technology accurately.

1–1	1–2	1–3	1–4	1–5	1–6	1–7	1–8	1–9	1–0
2–Q	2–W	2–E	2–R	2–T	2–Y	2–U	2–I	2–O	2–P
3–A	3–S	3–D	3–F	3–G	3–H	3–J	3–K	3–L	3–;
4–Z	4–X	4–C	4–V	4–B	4–N	4–M	4–,	4–.	4–/

FIGURE R3–8: Computer Bingo Card

Step 1: Put name on plate

Step 2 : Decide on a pattern for the fruit

Step 3: Choose fruit to match pattern

Step 4: Get stick and put fruit on stick
in pattern and put fruit stick on plate

Step 5: Eat for snack

FIGURE R3–9: Rebus Directions for Fruit Kabob

MATERIALS: Wooden skewer; cut-up apples, pineapple cubes, grapes, banana slices; rebus picture menus

PROCEDURE: Design several rebus picture menus (these are pictures designed for nonreaders that resemble international road signs), using varying amounts of fruit on a skewer (1 apple piece, 3 half-grapes, 2 pineapple cubes, 1 banana slice) or a repeating pattern of fruit (1 apple piece, 1 pineapple cube, 1 half grape, 1 apple piece, 1 pineapple cube, 1 half-grape, and so on; see Figure R3–9). Let children choose the menu they want and make it. Eat the fruit kabob during snack time.

ACCOMMODATIONS AND INTEGRATION: Include a picture that uses a simple repeating pattern with just two different fruits. Cut grapes in half for younger children. Check for allergies. Increase the complexity of some of the menus by having additional fruits and more difficult patterns. Have a word menu as an alternative for children who can read. This activity gives children practice selecting from menus and

interpreting rebus pictures. Use this procedure for adding fruit to a fruit salad or making trail mix, and for other food projects.

SUMMARY

- Children can learn as much from activities that are fun as from those that seem purely "academic."
- Many Discovery activities require two days or more.
- Make mathematics real and useful to children.
- Help children view science as part of their world and that they see the cause-and-effect relationships rather than "teacher magic."
- Technology has tremendous potential for children with disabilities but initially needs adult scaffolding.
- The educator's role is to help children see technology as a natural part of everyday life and to help them develop the skills to use it in a positive way.

EDUCATIONAL RESOURCES

Children's Technology Review provides timely, accurate, and objective information about children's software and access to reviews of the software. You can see samples but you have to subscribe to get all their reviews http://childrenstech.com/about/

Discovery Channel contains lesson plans for children indexed by grade level and topic, and has a school clip art gallery that is useful when writing newsletters. http://dsc.discovery.com/

Frank Potter's Science Gems provides science lesson plans for educators and links to other sources of lesson plans. http://www.sciencegems.com

National Geographic, a resource for teachers and children, is interesting and up to date. http://www.nationalgeographic.com/

Smithsonian Institution describes exhibits and has places to visit virtually and in person. http://www.si.edu/

For additional resources, visit the book companion website for this text at www.CengageBrain.com.

Wellness Activities:
Health and Safety, Physical Education, and Sensory Motor Integration

4

Having adequate motor abilities is important for young children. They learn from the sensations acquired through movement. The acquisition of new sensations occurs through active participation in the environment. Because children with disabilities, like others, spend increasing amounts of screen time, they may need encouragement and support to develop motor skills. They need to participate in activities that expose their muscles to demanding tasks. We must resist the temptation to do too many things for children with disabilities and must allow them to participate in enough resistance and power activities to develop strength.

ACTIVITY GOALS AND STANDARDS

Activities are organized by the goals and standards they support. The activities themselves serve as prototypes of activities that can be used again and again with minor changes. Books that are referred to in the text with an * have a complete citation and annotation in the Children's Bibliography; others have a complete citation where they are cited. For books where a lexile score is available, it is given after the book title, for example, (500L). The notation "AD" before the lexile means that the book requires adult direction and should initially be read by an adult and discussed with children before children read it independently.

Wellness Guidelines

The following guidelines will be helpful as you think about adapting health and safety, physical education, and sensory motor integration activities to meet the needs of children with diverse abilities.

©Cengage Learning 2012

Adapting activities for children with:

Specific learning disabilities ❄ Ensure the children can read safety signals and pair illustrations with words. Work on sensory motor integration. Choose activities that support fundamental motor activities, especially those that develop trunk strength and stability.

Social, emotional and behavioral disorders ❄ Remind children about health and safety rules. Play noncompetitive games. Teach children to vent energy using large motor activities. Support children in refining small motor skills.

Attention-deficit/hyperactivity disorder ❄ Provide opportunities to respond to safety signals. Help children learn to evaluate their environment relative to health and safety. Encourage children to use active play to release energy.

Communication disorders ❄ Teach children the vocabulary that goes with health and safety. Focus fine motor skills on movements associated

with speech (breath control, lip and tongue action), visual discrimination, and writing skills. Help children recognize when they are tense and teach them how to relax voluntarily.

English language learners ❄ Teach safety skills with verbal and visual cues. Role-play them as well. Use motor skills to teach prepositions (*on, under, in front of, behind,* and so on) and other important vocabulary in the home language and English.

Autism spectrum disorders ❄ Monitor health and safety practices. Visually post health and safety rules. Coach children through motor tasks. Simplify activities and use relatively large objects with fewer pieces.

Intellectual disabilities ❄ Make good health and safety practices part of the routine. Do a task analysis and support children in attaining adaptive skills independently. Simplify activities and have children repeat these with minor variations.

Gifted and talented ❋ Teach children to recognize a variety of safety signs and encourage them to become health advocates. Support the development of fundamental motor skills and encourage children to decide what aspects of sports interest them. Scaffold skills as needed.

Special health care needs ❋ Work on body awareness and the early identifications of symptoms. Teach children the events that might trigger a reaction. Work on developing strength and endurance while respecting physical limits. Teach children to pace themselves and to learn to use fine motor activities for times they need a break.

Orthopedic and neurological impairments ❋ Teach children body awareness. Adapt activities to help children control their environment (put small objects in a jellyroll pan or tray). Help children strengthen body parts that are under their control and will increase mobility. Use lightweight materials (cardboard blocks) and materials that tolerate some degree of error (e.g., Bristle blocks).

Hearing impairments ❋ Teach children to recognize and respond to visual signs of danger as well as the auditory sounds within their range of hearing. Focus on activities that promote body awareness and balancing (starting, stopping, turning). Help children integrate visual and tactile input with motor skills.

Visual impairments ❋ Teach children to use their sense of touch to tell whether their hands are clean. Help children integrate visual and tactile input with motor skills. Teach children how to move through unknown areas safely. Work on body awareness and motor planning, as they relate to orientation and mobility training. Help children learn when they need visual aids and how to use them. If children wear glasses, decide how they can be safely worn during active play.

Wellness Activities

• • • • HEALTH AND SAFETY: **SMALL GROUP**

4-1 Symptoms

GOALS: To improve health literacy; to increase vocabulary acquisition and use; to increase body awareness

STANDARDS: H 4 Demonstrate the ability to use interpersonal communication skills to enhance health and avoid or reduce health risks; H 5 Demonstrate the ability to use decision-making skills to enhance health; S&L 1 Participate in collaborative conversations with diverse partners about kindergarten topics and texts with peers and adults in small and larger groups.

MATERIALS: Dolls

PROCEDURE: Help children develop their vocabulary to describe their symptoms and to give some information on the area and degree of the "hurt."

Body Parts	Medical Terms	Conditions	Degree Terms
tummy, stomach	vomit, throw up	swollen, puffy	little, a lot
head	pain, hurts	dizzy	stiff, flexible
arms, legs	bruised	blood, bleeding	sharp, dull
throat, neck	sore	cut	hot, cold

Role-play situations in which a child who is "hurt" tells you or another child what's wrong. Help children decide what

to do in the case of various symptoms (dizzy: lie down; cut: wash it; swollen part: put ice on it; bleeding: wash and put on a bandage; broken arm: tell a trusted adult and go to the emergency room). Encourage children to assess the level of the problem in the context of what should be done about it.

ACCOMMODATIONS AND INTEGRATION: Use both the child's body and a doll to teach body parts. Role-play the most likely events a child might encounter (a cut or a stomach-ache). Help children learn more internal body parts as well as where they are located. This activity provides useful information for a child *before* she becomes ill. Include specific terms children will need, based on their impairments. Be sure that children understand that their objective is to be accurate, not creative.

• • • • HEALTH AND SAFETY: **SMALL GROUP**

4-2 Stop and Go

GOALS: To improve health literacy; to increase adaptive skills; to improve cause-and-effect reasoning

STANDARDS: H 5 Demonstrate the ability to use decision-making skills to enhance health; H 8 Demonstrate the ability to advocate for personal, family, and community health; S&L 1 Participate in collaborative conversations with diverse partners about kindergarten topics and texts with peers and adults in small and larger groups.

MATERIALS: Red, green, and yellow pieces of construction paper; tricycles

PROCEDURE: Adapt the traditional game of Red Light–Green Light by having the children walk or ride when you hold up a piece of green paper and stop when you hold up a piece of red paper. Once children learn the process, vary the time between changes from red to green, making some very short and others long so children must pay close attention. Use yellow to slow them down. Encourage children to help each other and to verbalize the rule of stopping on red, slowing down for yellow, and going on green. Discuss some of the implications of not stopping on red or not going on green.

ACCOMMODATIONS AND INTEGRATION: Say the word "Stop" with red and "Go" with green. Using this procedure, introduce the concept of caution to children. When holding up the yellow paper, have them walk or ride more slowly and be ready for change. Have a child be the traffic director and regulate the tricycles with the red, yellow, and green "lights." *Stop* and *Go* are important safety concepts. Children need practice learning to wait for the signal to change as well as identifying the basic relationship between color and their behavior. Introduce one-way signs as well. Have children wear helmets when they ride tricycles or bicycles, and talk about why these safety precautions are important for their health and well-being.

• • • • HEALTH AND SAFETY: **LARGE AND SMALL GROUP**

4-3   Sometime and Anytime Foods

GOALS: To improve health literacy; to improve classification skills; to improve cause-and-effect reasoning

STANDARDS: H 1 Comprehend concepts related to health promotion and disease prevention to enhance health; H 3 Demonstrate the ability to access valid information, products, and services to enhance health; H 5 Demonstrate the ability to use decision-making skills to enhance health.

MATERIALS: An assortment of unbreakable plates; empty food containers or packages and pictures of a variety of foods; a yellow card, a green card, and a red card; string

PROCEDURE: Discuss with children the concepts of *sometime, anytime,* and *special occasion* (Anytime/sometime/special occasion is a way to classify food based on the amount of fat, sugar, and calories they contain.) Talk about foods that can be eaten almost anytime (like fruits and vegetables) and those that can only be eaten sometimes (not every day) like waffles, cheese, and pasta. And then discuss some foods that should be eaten rarely or just for special occasions like French fries, cookies, ice cream, and potato chips. Explain to children the differences in the foods based on how they are grown and the processes used to cook and serve them. Give each child a yellow card, a green card, and a red card. Explain that the green card is for foods they can eat anytime and the yellow one for those that can only be eaten sometimes, and a red card for foods that are eaten only on special occasions. Hold up each food and have the children hold up either a green, yellow, or red card. Tell them what the food actually is and why it falls into that category (e.g., "Ice cream is yummy, but it is a food that you should only eat on special occasions because it has lots of fat and sugar in it, and that slows your body down."). Continue classifying the remaining foods and continue to explain why foods fit into particular categories. Once you have classified some of the foods, ask children what they think and why.

ACCOMMODATIONS AND INTEGRATION: Children learn to like foods that are offered to them repeatedly in a positive context. This means following through and ensuring that snacks are in the anytime category. Use the analogy of a stoplight to help children understand the concept of *sometime* and *anytime.* Green for anytime means if you are hungry, you can eat them; yellow means caution – it is okay to eat, but only in small amounts and not all the time. There are mixed feelings about using the red card for *stop,* meaning that children should almost never have these foods, which is why it is used here for special occasions. Some are concerned that young children can't understand the three categories and that many of the foods that are "red" have particular significance at celebrations. This is an activity that can be done many times with different foods. If you want to make it into a movement activity, have the children clap fast (or run in place) for anytime foods, clap slowly or march slowly in place for sometime foods, and hold their hands together or stand still for special occasion foods.

• • • • HEALTH AND SAFETY: **LARGE AND SMALL GROUP**

4-4   Green, Yellow, and Red

GOALS: To improve health literacy; to improve classification skills; to improve cause-and-effect reasoning

STANDARDS: H 1 Comprehend concepts related to health promotion and disease prevention to enhance health; H 3 Demonstrate the ability to access valid information, products, and services to enhance health; H 8 Demonstrate the ability to advocate for personal, family, and community health.

MATERIALS: Grocery store flyers, scissors, glue sticks, paper divided into three columns labeled ANYTIME, SOMETIME, and SPECIAL OCCASION

PROCEDURE: If you have used these food classifications before, review them with the children; if not, discuss with children the concepts of sometime, anytime and special occasions foods (see Activity 4–3). Ask children to name some anytime foods, some sometime foods, and some special occasion foods. Tell them that today they are going to be food detectives. Their job is to look through the flyers, cut out pictures of foods, and glue them in the correct category. Encourage children to talk to each other as they classify the foods.

ACCOMMODATIONS AND INTEGRATION: Agree on a place children can put foods they are unsure how to classify, and then have an adult help them, going over the rules for classification. If three categories are too many, eliminate the special occasion category. Encourage children to classify foods at home, and talk about buying more anytime foods at the grocery store.

• • • • HEALTH AND SAFETY: **LARGE AND SMALL GROUP**

4-5   Picky! Picky!

GOALS: To improve health literacy; to increase adaptive skills; to increase vocabulary acquisition and use

STANDARDS: H 2 Analyze the influence of family, peers, culture, media, technology, and other factors on health behaviors; H 6 Demonstrate the ability to use goal-setting skills to enhance health; H 7 Demonstrate the ability to practice health-enhancing behaviors and avoid or reduce health risks.

MATERIALS: Paper plate or piece of paper with the sentence starter "I promise I will try. . ."; grocery store flyers; scissors, glue; books such as M. Brown, *D. W. the Picky Eater* (Boston: Little, Brown Books for Young Readers, 1997) (410L); R. Hoban, *Bread and Jam for Frances* (New York: HarperCollins, 1986) (AD490L)

PROCEDURE: Read about D. W. and her experience eating out with her family. Discuss the foods she likes and doesn't like. Ask them what happened when D. W. tried spinach and what they think she will try in the future. Encourage children to talk about their personal food likes and dislikes. Talk with children about the fact that picky eaters are more likely to eat sugared cereals and French fries than fruits and vegetables. Discuss the importance of eating lots of colors. Explain that you want each child to find a food or foods that they think they don't like and make a commitment to try it. Have children cut out pictures of healthy foods from the grocery circulars and glue them on their plate or paper. On the following day read *Bread and Jam for Frances*. Discuss this book with the children. Encourage them to see the differences and similarities between D. W. and Frances and the conclusions both girls came to. Talk about the books and other places where they see information about food (television and other media) and how they respond to these. Discuss commercials as wanting to sell products. Ask them about the number of commercials they see for anytime foods.

ACCOMMODATIONS AND INTEGRATION: Ensure that your snack is a healthy one that includes fruits or vegetables. Encourage children who have problems with scissors to tear the pictures from the flyers. Ensure that children know the names of different fruits and vegetables.

HEALTH AND SAFETY: **SMALL GROUP**

4-6 Fruit Salad

GOALS: To improve health literacy; to increase adaptive skills; to increase vocabulary acquisition and use

STANDARDS: H 1 Comprehend concepts related to health promotion and disease prevention to enhance health; H 4 Demonstrate the ability to use interpersonal communication skills to enhance health and avoid or reduce health risks; H 7 Demonstrate the ability to practice health-enhancing behaviors and avoid or reduce health risks.

MATERIALS: Cantaloupe (no rind), berries, kiwi (peeled), honeydew (no rind), bananas (peeled), other fruit (some unfamiliar), plastic knives, large bowl, paper, markers Note: Be sure to check for allergies.

PROCEDURE: Initially have children in a large group. Discuss the different fruits they think might be in a fruit salad and write these down on a large piece of paper. Sing the song "On Top of Fruit Salad" (tune of "On Top of Old Smoky" a.k.a. "On Top of Spaghetti"). It might go something like this:

> On top of fruit salad,
> all juicy and sweet,
> I lost my poor strawberry
> when somebody sneezed (achoo).
> It rolled off the table
> and onto the floor,
> and then my poor strawberry
> rolled right out the door.
> It rolled into the garden
> and under a bush
> and then my poor strawberry

> was nothing but mush.
> And early next summer,
> it grew into a patch
> all covered with strawberries
> as big as a batch.

Include different fruits and modify the song slightly. Then tell the children that they are going to make fruit salad. Set up the actual fruit salad making for a small group (center). Have children wash their hands. Explain that they will be cutting up the fruit, demonstrate how to do this, and then place fruit in a large bowl.

ACCOMMODATIONS AND INTEGRATION: If children have problems cutting up the fruit, help them by putting your hand on top of theirs and guiding their hand to cut the fruit. Include unfamiliar fruits because children are more likely to try new foods with peers. Talk with children about how good fruit is for them, and remind them that it is an anytime food. Encourage them to make fruit salad with their families.

HEALTH AND SAFETY: **SMALL GROUP**

4-7 Shopping Lists

GOALS: To improve health literacy; to improve classification skills; to increase writing literacy

STANDARDS: H 1 Comprehend concepts related to health promotion and disease prevention to enhance health; H 2 Analyze the influence of family, peers, culture, media, technology and other factors on health behaviors; H 8 Demonstrate the ability to advocate for personal, family, and community health.

MATERIALS: Grocery flyers; paper, scissors, and glue sticks; chart paper or marker board and marker; plastic food, empty packages of food, food labels, and pictures of food; child-sized shopping carts, bags, or cardboard boxes

PROCEDURE: With the children in a large group, introduce the concept of a grocery list. Ask children how their family remembers what to buy at the grocery store. Explain that when people have a lot of things to buy, they often make a grocery list to remember all of the things they need. Using a large piece of paper or a marker board, start to make a list, saying something like "Let me think what I need. What will I feel like eating? Oranges—I like oranges. They are very tasty and they are an anytime food (see Activity 4–3 for more information). That means I can eat them anytime I want them." Write *oranges* on the list. "Peanut butter—I need some more, but I have to remember that it is a sometime food so I can't eat it everyday." Add *peanut butter* to the list. "Cookies—I like cookies but I had one yesterday, so I better wait until next week to buy more cookies." (Don't add *cookies* to the list.) Then encourage children to make suggestions about what should go on the list. Help them classify the foods and discuss the need for most of the food to be anytime food. Talk with them about the foods they see advertised on television and what they buy and eat. The most common food advertisements during children's shows are for presweetened breakfast cereals and high-sugar foods (Byrd-Bredbenner, 2002).

Have small groups of children make shopping lists by cutting out pictures of foods from grocery store flyers. Children should be encouraged to print the label for the foods they want to buy. When the lists are completed, have children go to the grocery store (set up in a dramatic play area or a corner of the room) and shop. Encourage children to use a bag or shopping cart for their purchases. You may have to limit the number of items any shopper can buy, depending upon your supply of "food." Remind children that everything on their list might not be at the store and also that they should be buying mostly anytime foods.

ACCOMMODATIONS AND INTEGRATION: Get green, yellow, and red dots and put these on the foods in the grocery store to help children remember the way foods are classified. Have the grocery store available for a few days or even weeks. Add or change the various foods in the store. Add prices to the items. Add other elements to the grocery store such as a checkout clerk who pretends to scan the items, "write" the customer a receipt to add up the cost, puts the items in bags (preferably those that are recyclable), takes the customer's money and provides change. Encourage children to take a shopping list home and talk to their family about what foods they buy and to help classify their foods as anytime, sometime, and special occasion and then advocate for more anytime foods.

• • • • • HEALTH AND SAFETY: **LARGE GROUP**

  ## Very Hungry Caterpillar

GOALS: To improve health literacy; to improve classification skills; to improve cause-and-effect reasoning

STANDARDS: H 1 Comprehend concepts related to health promotion and disease prevention to enhance health; H 2 Analyze the influence of family, peers, culture, media, technology, and other factors on health behaviors; H 7 Demonstrate the ability to practice health-enhancing behaviors and avoid or reduce health risks.

MATERIALS: Sticky notes with the words *anytime* written in green, *sometime* written in yellow, and *special occasion* written in red; chart paper; green, yellow, and red markers; book by E. Carle, *The Very Hungry Caterpillar* (New York: Philomel, 1969); assortment of cut-up fruit and a wooden skewer

PROCEDURE: Beginning reading *The Very Hungry Caterpillar* to the children. As you read, stop on each page as you identify the food. Then remind children about how they can classify foods as anytime, sometime, and special occasion (see Activity 4–3 for more information). As you read, ask the children to classify the foods as they appear and put the appropriate sticky note on each food. Continue this for the rest of the story. At the end of the story ask children

"What were the anytime foods the caterpillar ate?" (apple, pear, plum, strawberry, orange, and watermelon)

"What were the sometime foods the caterpillar ate?" (pickle, cheese, salami, sausage)

"What were the special occasion foods the caterpillar ate?" (chocolate cake, ice cream, lollipop, cherry pie, and cupcake)

"Why did the caterpillar keep eating?" (hungry)

"Why did his tummy hurt on Saturday?" (ate too much and too many sometime and special occasion foods)

"Could the caterpillar have done anything differently on Saturday so that his tummy wouldn't hurt?" (eaten less and more anytime foods)

Mark the chart paper off to make a graph, and go through the story again to graph the number of anytime, sometime, and special occasion foods the caterpillar ate. Talk about the different foods children saw in the book. Talk about where they see food advertised and what food is advertised. Ask them how it makes them feel about these foods. Then draw them back to the story and how the caterpillar felt after eating the Saturday foods.

ACCOMMODATIONS AND INTEGRATION: Use some of the anytime foods that the caterpillar ate (apple, pear, plum, strawberry, orange, and watermelon) to make a caterpillar by putting pieces of fruit on a skewer. Take photographs of the caterpillars and post them in the room or send some home. Show children how to slide the fruit off the skewer rather than biting it. Encourage children to talk to their families about what the caterpillar ate and the caterpillar they made with anytime foods.

• • • • • HEALTH AND SAFETY: **LARGE GROUP**

  ## Traffic Sign Hunt

GOALS: To increase safety awareness; to increase adaptive skills; to improve cause-and-effect reasoning

STANDARDS: H 1 Comprehend concepts related to health promotion and disease prevention to enhance health; H 5 Demonstrate the ability to use decision-making skills to enhance health; S&L 3 Ask and answer questions in order to seek help, get information, or clarify something that is not understood.

MATERIALS: Story, traffic signs (see Figure R4–1)

PROCEDURE: This is an adaptation of the bear hunt. Go over each sign with the children and encourage them to ask questions about signs that may be unfamiliar. Begin an imaginary walk. Start "walking" by putting your palms on your thighs in a rhythm. Change the rhythm in response to the signs.

"Does anyone want to go on a traffic sign hunt? Okay, let's go. Close the gate." (Close with hand motions.) "We're coming to a corner. I see a sign." (Hold up a stop sign.) "What do you think it is?" (Pause.) "A stop sign! What do we have to do?" (Stop. Hold up palms toward children.) "Okay, look both ways." (Look.) "No cars. Let's cross the street. Hurry." (Increase beat of hand.) "You don't wander across streets, but you don't have to run either. Oh, what's this? This is a railroad crossing sign." (Hold up.) "See the tracks? Be very careful. Look both ways. Are the gates up or down? Listen,

do you hear anything? Are there any lights flashing? Okay, let's cross. Look again and let's go. Oh, there really are a lot of signs to look at when you go for a walk. What's this one?" (Hold up yield sign.) "What shape is that? What should we do? It's a little like a stop sign; we don't have to stop, just slow down (slow rhythm) and look around. If we see anyone, then we have to stop."

Sign	What to do
![stop sign]	Stop! Look both ways. Listen.
![yield sign]	Slow down, look both ways. Listen.
![railroad crossing]	Stop! Look both ways. Listen.
![traffic light]	Red–stop Yellow–caution Green–go
	Slow down–curve
	Danger–poison

FIGURE R4–1: Traffic Signs

"Look, do you see anything? Hey, I see an elephant. Do we have to stop? Yep. The elephant has the right of way. We have to yield. Go very slowly. Okay, he's gone. That was a nice rest. I wonder what other kinds of signs we'll see. Hey, that one has lights. It's green and yellow and red. What is it?" (Hold up traffic light.) "We have the green; now what do we do? We can go. I am beginning to get tired—how about you? No? Well, there is another sign. That's for a curve. Lean left or you'll go off the road. Do you think we're on a mountain? Let's slow down. Oh, what's that sign?" (Hold up skull and cross bones.) "Danger! Let's get out of here! As fast as you can, lean right, hurry back over the curve. Now—oh, there's the light; what color is it? Red. Stop. Okay, now it's green; let's go. There's the yield; is there anything coming?" (Look.) "We're okay—good; keep going. What will it be next? Oh, the railroad. Stop. Look. Listen. Any trains? Let's go. Hurry—oh, there's the stop sign; everybody stop. Look. Let's go. Open the gate; shut it. Whee! It's good to be back here in our classroom."

ACCOMMODATIONS AND INTEGRATION: Make the walk shorter and slower. As children learn the process, add more signs and make the walk longer and faster. Do the walk without the visual prompts, just verbal ones. Use your imagination and be dramatic. The children love it at the end when you go fast. This is good practice and yet fun. Children can participate at different levels. Children also enjoy bear hunts or lion hunts, and they can learn about different terrains but run home once the prey is spotted.

· · · · ·   HEALTH AND SAFETY: **LARGE GROUP**

 Warning Sounds

4-10

GOALS: To increase safety awareness; to increase adaptive skills; to increase vocabulary acquisition and use

STANDARDS: H 4 Demonstrate the ability to use interpersonal communication skills to enhance health and avoid or reduce health risks; H 5 Demonstrate the ability to use decision-making skills to enhance health.

MATERIALS: DVD or videotape of objects making warning sounds and DVD player or VCR, or CD or audiotape with warning sounds and CD player or tape recorder

PROCEDURE: Make a DVD or videotape of warning sounds and the objects making them. Talk about what the children should do in these circumstances. Then make a CD or audiotape of various warning sounds children might hear and have them identify these without visual cues. Include a broad range of sounds:

fire alarm	bell buoy (boats)
car horn	ambulance
telephone sound when	truck's beep (when
left off the hook	backing up)
shouts of alarm	train whistle
fire siren or whistle	calling a name
police siren	"timber" (tree falling)

microwave timer	"watch out"
"fore" (golfers)	oven timer
clothes dryer timer	smoke alarm

When the children can identify these sounds, have them name a sound and tell where they might hear it and what they should do if they hear it.

ACCOMMODATIONS AND INTEGRATION: Start with safety sounds children are most likely to hear. Help them decide what they should do in response to these sounds. Use this as an auditory discrimination activity and see whether children can identify the sounds without visual cues. Children depend on auditory cues for safety. They will hear a siren before they see the fire truck and they need to be able to identify the sound. This helps them determine what is happening before they can actually see what is going on.

· · · · ·   HEALTH AND SAFETY: **INDIVIDUAL**

4-11 Pick-a-Pair

GOALS: To improve health literacy; to improve sensory motor integration; to improve cause-and-effect reasoning

STANDARDS: H 1 Comprehend concepts related to health promotion and disease prevention to enhance health; H 5 Demonstrate the ability to use decision-making skills to enhance health; M 7 Classify objects and count the number of objects in each category.

MATERIALS: Fake fur, cardboard, flannel, felt, sandpaper, sponge, nylon, corduroy, dotted Swiss, wool, silk, ultra suede

TO MAKE: *Cut each piece of fabric into two 2½-inch pieces. Glue one piece of each fabric on cardboard. Place the matching piece of fabric in a feely bag or box.*

PROCEDURE: Choose a piece of fabric on the cardboard and ask the child to find that piece in the feely bag and match it. Discuss the different textures and classify them based on their attributes: woven/not woven, soft/hard, rough/smooth, and so on. Have children explain how they found the match. After children have classified the fabric by attributes, have them decide how the fabric could be used, particularly relative to clothing and when it would be worn. Encourage them to see whether they can find clothing in the room that is made from those fabrics.

ACCOMMODATIONS AND INTEGRATION: Make the differences among the materials obvious (terrycloth, fake fur, nylon) and have fewer materials. Talk with children about fabric and the qualities of different fabrics and how this relates to their use.

· · · · ·   HEALTH AND SAFETY: **LARGE GROUP**

4-12  Health and Fitness

GOALS: To increase health literacy; to improve physical fitness; to improve cause-and-effect reasoning

STANDARDS: H 3 Demonstrate the ability to access valid information, products, and services to enhance health; H 6 Demonstrate the ability to use goal-setting skills to enhance health; PE 6 Value physical activity for health, enjoyment, challenge, self-expression, and/or social interaction.

MATERIALS: Books such as T. Rabe, *Oh the Things You Can Do That Are Good for You! All about Staying Healthy* (Cat in the Hat's Learning Library) (New York: Random House Books for Young Readers, 2001), or P. Thomas, *My Amazing Body: A First Look at Health and Fitness* (New York: Barron's Educational series, 2001); chart paper and marker

PROCEDURE: Read a children's book about health and fitness to the children and then talk with them about the importance of a good diet and plenty of exercise. Be sure to include information that even healthy children get ill sometimes but our bodies and our health practices can protect us from some illnesses. Talk to children about setting fitness and healthy eating goals. Tell school-age and preschool children that they need to accumulate at least 60 minutes of structured activity (planned and directed by an adult; toddlers, 30 minutes) and at least 60 minutes of unstructured physical activity each day. Using chart paper and a marker, help them figure out how much physical activity (structured and unstructured) they get while they are in school. Help them look at what they could do at home to ensure that they get the time they need. Provide them with suggestions for what they can do at home to increase their physical fitness and to eat more healthy foods.

ACCOMMODATIONS AND INTEGRATION: Talk about a variety of practices related to healthy eating and physical fitness. Include information about hand washing and the importance of this in preventing disease. Help children think about participating in regular physical activity, and have each child make a chart about what he is going to do every day to increase his physical fitness, set goals, and keep a log.

· · · · · LOCOMOTOR: **SMALL GROUP**

4-13 Variations on Jumping

GOALS: To improve locomotor skills; to improve physical fitness; to make predictions

STANDARDS: PE 1 Demonstrate competency in motor skills and movement patterns needed to perform a variety of physical activities; PE 2 Demonstrate understanding of movement concepts, principles, strategies, and tactics as they apply to the learning and performance of physical activities; H 6 Demonstrate the ability to use goal-setting skills to enhance health.

MATERIALS: Masking tape

PROCEDURE: Have the children participate in various styles of jumping.

COACHING FOR VERTICAL JUMPING: Preparatory crouch with straight trunk, swing arms forward and up to begin jump, full extension in legs; flex ankles, knees, and hips for landing (Haywood & Getchell, 2002).

COACHING FOR LONG JUMPING: Feet leave the ground together and land together. Deep preparatory crouch, neck aligned with trunk, arms swing forward and upward and lead the jump, legs fully extended at takeoff, heels coming up first. Knees flex in flight, followed by hip flexion; knees then extend forward for landing, and arms reach forward (Haywood & Getchell, 2002).

Encourage children to think about the names of some of the jumps and make up new names with a rationale. Have children estimate how long, how high, how far, and how many times they can jump. If they work in pairs, one child can check the other's prediction by writing it down and graphing it. Put the graph in their portfolio. Help children set personal goals relative to jumping and to practice. Coach them to help them become more proficient. Encourage them to repeat this activity after several weeks and compare the results.

> *Pairs jumping*: Children face each other, hold hands, and jump together.
>
> *Line jumping*: Children jump forward and backward across a taped line.
>
> *Step jumping*: Children jump from a step to a line on the floor.
>
> *Long jump*: Children jump forward for distance from standing (crouched) position.
>
> *Kangaroo jump*: Children do knee bends and jump up with feet together, elbows bent, and hands away from body.
>
> *Rabbit jump*: Children squat low on heels, palms on floor and fingers pointing forward, jumping with feet coming forward between hands, like a rabbit.
>
> *Mattress jump*: Children jump forward and backward on a partially filled air mattress or regular mattress. For safety, put mattress on a 5 × 8 foot rug, with adult spotters.
>
> *Jumping Jacks and Jills*: Children start with feet together and arms by side; they jump so their feet go to each side and arms come up to shoulder height, then jump and return to starting position.

ACCOMMODATIONS AND INTEGRATION: Begin with easier jumps and accept all attempts at jumping. Hold children's hands as they jump. Keep the activity short, as it is easy for children to become fatigued; however, the goal is for them to jump until they are breathless. Have children think about how realistic their predictions and goals were. Children like to see personal improvement, and by graphing their jumping, they can look at their personal growth as well as have a base from which to set goals when they do the activity again. Encourage children to set personal goals, and use the graph to determine whether they are meeting the goals.

· · · · · LOCOMOTOR: **SMALL GROUP**

4-14 Variations on Running

GOALS: To improve locomotor skills; to improve physical fitness; to improve motor planning

Jumping is a fundamental motor skill. Encourage children to jump in a variety of ways and to continue jumping until they are breathless.
©Cengage Learning 2012

STANDARDS: PE 1 Demonstrate competency in motor skills and movement patterns needed to perform a variety of physical activities; PE 3 Participate regularly in physical activity; PE 4 Achieve and maintain a health-enhancing level of physical fitness.

MATERIALS: Tape, yarn, rope, cones, string, book such as D. Lauture, *Running the Road to ABC* (Aladdin Picture Books) (Fullerton, CA: Aladdin, 2000) (AD940L)

PROCEDURE: Read *Running the Road to ABC* and talk with the children about where (Haiti) and why these children run (it is the only way they can get to school). Talk with them about the need to exercise every day and how these children run to school every day. Ask them how they come to school. Ask them to think of times when they could run every day for a particular purpose, and encourage them to develop a plan for regular exercise, even if it is just running in place during commercials as they watch television. Have the children run and try some of the following variations. Focus on the quality of children's movement and coach them to increase efficiency and coordination.

COACHING FOR RUNNING: *Children should bend their knees about 90 degrees and swing their arms so the left arm is back when the right leg is forward* (Haywood & Getchell, 2005).

RUNNING TAKES STRENGTH AND BALANCE: Children must have enough strength to lift themselves off the ground and enough balance to catch themselves on the other leg and remain on that leg while shifting their weight forward. Use variations to refine skills as well as to build endurance. As children run for longer distances, have them stretch to warm up and walk to cool down. Encourage all children to run until they are breathless. Be watchful of children with asthma and find out what their limits are. Help them challenge their limits. Videotape children and discuss variation differences.

> Run slowly, quickly, quietly, noisily, lightly, heavily.
>
> Run and, on a signal, stop, change direction, change from running to walking.
>
> Run, walk, run, walk; repeat.
>
> Run slowly while talking to a friend.
>
> Run on a designated path.
>
> Run in pairs, with one child running blindfolded or wearing a patch over one eye.

ACCOMMODATIONS AND INTEGRATION: Decrease (or increase) the length, time, distance, and speed children run, and use fewer variations. As children become more skilled, change the variations while children are running. Encourage children to think about the relationship between speed and endurance; help them decide which is more important in various situations.

· · · · ·   LOCOMOTOR: **INDIVIDUAL OR SMALL GROUP**

 4-15   Variations on Jumping Rope

GOALS: To improve locomotor skills; to improve physical fitness; to improve motor planning

STANDARDS: PE 1 Demonstrate competency in motor skills and movement patterns needed to perform a variety of physical activities; PE 2 Demonstrate understanding of movement concepts, principles, strategies, and tactics as they apply to the learning and performance of physical activities; PE 6 Value physical activity for health, enjoyment, challenge, self-expression, and/or social interaction.

MATERIALS: Jump rope 12 feet to 15 feet long for two to four children

PROCEDURE: Jumping rope is difficult. Initially, move the rope slowly to give children more time to react. Alert them verbally to jump as the rope approaches. Turn the rope faster, encourage children to jump for longer times, or have them jump to music. Teach children traditional rhymes to chant as they jump.

> *Rope line*: Children jump from side to side over length of rope, forward then backward.
>
> *High water*: Two children hold a rope between them (loosely in hands). The third child attempts to jump

over the rope forward, backward, sideways, and at progressive heights.

Snake: Two children hold a rope between them (loosely in hands) and move it back and forth on the floor like a snake. The third child attempts to jump over the rope. (Moved vertically, it resembles waves.)

Swing jump: Two children hold a rope between them and swing it back and forth. The third child jumps over the rope. When children are successful, turn the rope overhead.

Circle: Teacher or child is in the middle of a circle and turns with the rope so that each child must jump as it passes.

Run: Two children turn the rope between them, and a third child tries to run through without the rope touching him.

Individual jump rope: A child turns the rope overhead and jumps with both feet, alternating feet, faster and slower.

ACCOMMODATIONS AND INTEGRATION: These jumping-rope activities get progressively more difficult. Start with the first variation (rope line) and progress as children's skill develops. Talk with children about the value of physical activity. Talk about the professional sports that require athletes to jump rope (football, tennis, boxing, and others). Help children think about why athletes jump rope (footwork, endurance, discipline).

· · · · ·   LOCOMOTOR: **SMALL GROUP**

4-16   Obstacle Course

GOALS: To improve locomotor skills; to improve motor planning; to make predictions

STANDARDS: PE 1 Demonstrate competency in motor skills and movement patterns needed to perform a variety of physical activities; PE 2 Demonstrate understanding of movement concepts, principles, strategies, and tactics as they apply to the learning and performance of physical activities; H 6 Demonstrate the ability to use goal-setting skills to enhance health.

MATERIALS: Barrels, boxes, boards, chairs, hoops, balance beam, stop watch

PROCEDURE: Set up an obstacle course (inside or outside) that requires a variety of movement skills and is long enough so several children can participate at the same time. Use obstacles that require children to move over, under, around, and through them. Encourage children to explore the course and discuss how they plan to move through it. Point out strategies different children use.

ACCOMMODATIONS AND INTEGRATION: Provide pictures and models for how children might move through each obstacle (use a digital camera as a child moves through the course). Walk beside the child and coach him. Keep the course simple

and short. Add activities that are more complex: picking up a beanbag or walking through a hoop on the balance beam. Add music to set the pace. Have children time their trip through the course and set a goal of completing the course in a specific time (it is not a race; it is a goal). Add a rope guide and have children do the course blindfolded. Encourage children to work out adaptations to include scooters and wheelchairs and to try them and decide whether they are easier or more difficult. Children can learn about their body, spatial relationships (*over, under, around,* or *through*), and the vocabulary to support movement.

· · · · ·   LOCOMOTOR: **INDIVIDUAL**

4-17   Fitness Course

GOALS: To improve physical fitness; to improve locomotor skills; to improve nonmanipulative skills

STANDARDS: PE 3 Participate regularly in physical activity; PE 4 Achieve and maintain a health-enhancing level of physical fitness; H 6 Demonstrate the ability to use goal-setting to enhance health.

MATERIALS: Cards with pictures of the exercise and numbers of repetitions:

> 5 bent-knee sit-ups
> 10 knee lifts
> 4 toe touches
> Count to 15 running in place
> 3 push-ups
> 10 straddle jumps

PROCEDURE: Place cards around the room or an outside area, and have children go to each area and perform the indicated activities. Vary the activities and the number of repetitions. Coach children as they perform the activities, and modify the activities and repetitions to meet the children's needs. After each child has completed the course once, have the child analyze what was difficult, what was easy, and what the child thinks she should focus on for her personal health. Help her set both long- and short-term goals. Leave the fitness course up for a week or two. Help children think about how they could meet long-term goals by using things they have available at home.

ACCOMMODATIONS AND INTEGRATION: Decrease or increase the activities and number of repetitions, or choose easier or more difficult activities. Have children keep a fitness log so they can see how frequently they "work out." Talk with children about the role of a coach, and help them think about physical fitness as part of their active lifestyle.

· · · · ·   MANIPULATIVE: **SMALL GROUP**

4-18   Variations on Throwing

GOALS: To improve manipulative skills; to improve sensory motor integration; to make predictions

STANDARDS: PE 1 Demonstrate competency in motor skills and movement patterns needed to perform a variety of physical activities; PE 2 Demonstrate understanding of movement concepts, principles, strategies, and tactics as they apply to the learning and performance of physical activities; M 7 Classify objects and count the number of objects in each category.

MATERIALS: 8- or 10-inch ball, tennis ball, Nerf ball, beach ball, 15- or 24–inch wastebasket, hula hoop, cans of varying sizes

PROCEDURE: Have the children participate in various types of ball-throwing activities. Discuss the differences in skills and strategies required to throw large and small balls. Have children measure the distances they can throw different-sized balls and make a graph, or count the number of times they can throw and catch a ball with another child. Coach them on their tactics. Have children throw the ball:

> as high as they can
>
> as low as they can without hitting the ground
>
> as far as they can
>
> softly to another child
>
> in a high arc to another child
>
> into a round wastebasket from 2 feet to 5 feet away
>
> at a target of stacked cans
>
> through a hula hoop from varying distances

ACCOMMODATIONS AND INTEGRATION: Use an underinflated beach ball as children are learning to catch. Increase the distance children stand from the target or a partner. Encourage children to predict how different balls will influence throwing. Encourage children to play ball-throwing games with others so that they practice both throwing and catching. Have some balls available with bells inside. *Note:* These activities are most easily done outside.

· · · · ·   MANIPULATIVE: **SMALL GROUP**

 Badminton

GOALS: To increase physical fitness; to improve sensory motor integration; to improve motor planning

STANDARDS: PE 2 Demonstrate understanding of movement concepts, principles, strategies, and tactics as they apply to the learning and performance of physical activities; PE 5 Exhibit responsible personal and social behavior that respects self and others in physical activity settings; H 6 Demonstrate the ability to use goal-setting skills to enhance health.

MATERIALS: Balls, birdie, badminton rackets, string or net

PROCEDURE: Have children hit Wiffle balls or yarn balls with another child, using a badminton racket. As they become more proficient, add a net or string and use a birdie instead of the balls. Help them make predictions and set goals for how frequently they can hit the birdie with a friend.

ACCOMMODATIONS AND INTEGRATION: Start with the yarn ball and have children drop the ball and try to hit it. Explore the causal relationships between how hard they swing, the angle of the racket, and where the ball goes. Help them swing overhand for high shots and underhand for low ones. Badminton can be played indoors or outdoors. It requires skill, but not strength. Children can play sitting as well as standing. Help children become aware of the reach of the racket and ensure that they don't hit other children. Children may eventually play competitive games using bats and rackets; it is useful to learn skills early in a noncompetitive atmosphere.

· · · · ·   MANIPULATIVE: **LARGE GROUP**

4-20 Circle Ball

GOALS: To improve physical fitness; to improve manipulative skills; to improve motor planning

STANDARDS: PE 1 Demonstrate competency in motor skills and movement patterns needed to perform a variety of physical activities; PE 5 Exhibit responsible personal and social behavior that respects self and others in physical activity settings.

MATERIALS: 8- to 12-inch ball

PROCEDURE: Place children in a circle sitting on their bottoms. Have them use their feet to roll the ball to each other. Then have them move onto their stomachs, facing the inside of the circle, and have them roll the ball to each other using one or two hands. This activity strengthens the muscles of the upper back. Encourage children to support and help each other as they play.

ACCOMMODATIONS AND INTEGRATION: Play the game in pairs so that the ball just goes back and forth, and have children change from front to back frequently. Call the child's name before you roll the ball to him. Children increase body awareness as they realize that some positions make tasks more difficult. Be sure variations include all children. Circle games are noncompetitive and allow all children to be part of the group.

· · · · ·   MANIPULATIVE: **SMALL GROUP**

 Variations on Tossing

GOALS: To improve manipulative skills; to improve sensory motor integration; to improve motor planning

STANDARDS: PE 1 Demonstrate competency in motor skills and movement patterns needed to perform a variety of physical activities; PE 2 Demonstrate understanding of movement concepts, principles, strategies, and tactics as they apply to the learning and performance of physical activities; SC 3a Physical Science.

MATERIALS: Beanbag, tennis ball, Ping-Pong ball, sponges, small rubber ball, rubber rings, horseshoes, Wiffle ball, crumpled paper, cups, targets, milk cartons, Velcro-covered Ping-Pong ball

PROCEDURE: Have the children participate in various types of tossing activities. Discuss how the activity feels; which objects are hard or easy to toss, where they can safely toss objects, and where they should not. Coach children to analyze their misses and to increase their tossing accuracy. Help them analyze the objects they are tossing and relate this to their tossing strategy. Have children take turns tossing and retrieving. Be aware of safety issues. Do these activities indoors and outdoors, depending on the objects used.

> *Texture ball toss*: Use a sponge or texture ball (Wiffle ball). Begin with underhand tossing to a person close by; gradually extend the distance and use overhand throwing.
>
> *Basketball toss*: Use a shoebox with the bottom removed. Tape it to the wall for an indoor game. Toss a tennis ball through it.
>
> *Dodge ball*: Divide the class into teams and play dodge ball.
>
> *Ring toss*: Toss rubber rings over a stake; this variation on horseshoes requires a different set of tossing skills.
>
> *Beanbag toss*: Toss beanbags through large holes in a target or into empty coffee cans.
>
> *Paper toss*: Crumple used paper into balls and toss them into a recycling container.
>
> *Milk carton toss*: Stack used cardboard milk cartons in pyramids. Knock the structure down with a tennis ball.
>
> *Bucket toss*: Use a bucket or wastebasket for catching balls. First set it on the floor, and then raise it on a chair or box.
>
> *Empty box throw*: Place a bottomless cardboard box on its side on the ground or on a chair. Toss a ball through the box without hitting the sides.
>
> *Tennis toss back*: Throw a tennis ball against a brick or cement wall and catch it before or after it bounces (an outside activity on a wall without windows).
>
> *Target toss*: Use the Velcro-covered Ping-Pong ball and toss it at a target with Velcro pieces attached. Vary the distance and the size of the target.
>
> *Sponge toss*: Make a cardboard target with holes of various sizes, or throw sponges through suspended hula hoops. On a hot day, you might throw wet sponges.
>
> *Ping-Pong ball toss*: Have children stand at arm's length apart, toss a Ping-Pong ball, and catch it in a plastic or paper cup.

ACCOMMODATIONS AND INTEGRATION: Begin with short distances, large targets, and choose objects that are bigger. Encourage children to think of variations. Children can chart their accuracy in tossing. Help them set up a chart that includes the relevant variables (date, distance, target, object).

• • • • • NONMANIPULATIVE: **SMALL GROUP**

4-22 Hand Clapping

GOALS: To improve nonmanipulative skills; to improve sensory motor integration; to improve motor planning

STANDARDS: PE 1 Demonstrate competency in motor skills and movement patterns needed to perform a variety of physical activities; PE 6 Value physical activity for health, enjoyment, challenge, self-expression, and/or social interaction; M 1 Know number names and the count sequence.

MATERIALS: None

PROCEDURE: Have children clap slowly and quickly, loudly and softly, and then to a constant rhythm. Then progress to a two-step sequence: clap hands, clap thighs, clap hands, clap thighs. (Choose any body parts: head, feet, shoulders.) Make the pattern more difficult: Clap hands twice, clap thighs twice, and then repeat. Count as you clap. Or do it three or four times. For variation, have children clap hands, clap their left thigh with their right hand, clap hands, clap their right thigh with their left hand. (The objective is crossing the body's midline, not learning right and left.) Have children clap hands with a partner, using the patterns given.

ACCOMMODATIONS AND INTEGRATION: Patterns should be ordered in increasing levels of difficulty. Start at the beginning and use increasingly more complex patterns with partners. Enhance traditional children's songs and games by clapping.

• • • • • NONMANIPULATIVE: **SMALL GROUP**

4-23 Foam

GOALS: To improve nonmanipulative skills; to improve locomotor skills; to improve manipulative skills

STANDARDS: PE 2 Demonstrate understanding of movement concepts, principles, strategies, and tactics as they apply to the learning and performance of physical activities; PE 5 Exhibit responsible personal and social behavior that respects self and others in physical activity settings.

MATERIALS: A piece of 4- or 5-inch-thick covered foam or a mattress

PROCEDURE: Put the foam on the floor in the center of a piece of carpet. Have children walk, roll, jump, and so forth, on the foam. Encourage them to experiment by doing these activities on the floor and then on the foam, and then talk about the differences. Encourage children to develop different strategies (e.g., holding out arms parallel to the ground) to make walking on the foam easier. Encourage children to observe and give each other suggestions.

ACCOMMODATIONS AND INTEGRATION: Hold the child's hand while he performs simple tasks, such as walking across the foam. Use tasks that involve both **dynamic** and **static balance**. Encourage children to combine skills that involve locomotion (such as walking), axial stability (bending, twisting), static stability (upright balancing), and dynamic stability (rolling) into a routine; write it down; and repeat the routine. Talk about gymnastic routines and how gymnasts develop and practice their routines. Encourage children to develop and write out routines and then set them to music.

 NONMANIPULATIVE: **SMALL GROUP**

4-24 Balance It

GOALS: To improve nonmanipulative skills; to improve sensory motor integration; to improve motor planning

STANDARDS: PE 2 Demonstrates competency in motor skills and movement patterns needed to perform a variety of physical activities; PE 6 Value physical activity for health, enjoyment, challenge, self-expression, and/or social interaction; H 6 Demonstrate the ability to use goal-setting skills to enhance health.

MATERIALS: Beanbags, books, paper plates, paintbrushes, feathers, crayons, plastic drinking glasses

PROCEDURE: Have children balance a beanbag on their head. Encourage them to stand up and sit down, and walk fast and slow while balancing it. Coach children how to move to make balancing easier. Then have them balance the beanbags using other body parts: shoulder, elbow, knee, foot.

ACCOMMODATIONS AND INTEGRATION: Start with something easy to balance, a beanbag, and have children balance it on the back of their hand so they can see what they are doing. Coach them on ways to move their hand. Encourage children to balance a variety of objects, and have them predict and set goals for how long they can balance each object or what movements they can make without its falling off. These activities require static and dynamic balance and concentration.

NONMANIPULATIVE: **LARGE GROUP**

4-25 Yoga Breathing

GOALS: To improve nonmanipulative skills; to increase body awareness; to improve sensory motor integration

STANDARDS: PE 5 Exhibit responsible personal and social behavior that respects self and others in physical activity settings; PE 6 Value physical activity for health, enjoyment, challenge, self-expression, and/or social interaction; H 7 Demonstrate the ability to practice health-enhancing behaviors and avoid or reduce health risks.

MATERIALS: Large open space

PROCEDURE: Ask children to stand up and stretch their arms in front of them. If they touch someone, have them move so they don't. Have them sit down. Explain that they are going to learn yoga. Ask them whether they have heard of yoga and what they think or know about it. Explain that yoga is a quiet exercise that will help them relax. Have children sit so their bottoms are on their feet and their knees are bent backwards under them. Demonstrate breathing in and out through your

nose. Explain to children that it is important to keep their mouth closed. Have them put their hand under their nose to feel the air come out. Ask them to close their eyes and breathe in and out 10 times and let their mind wander. Remind them if needed to be quiet. Tell them to open their eyes and ask them to share what they were thinking about. Tell them they are becoming excellent yogis (boys who do yoga) and yoginis (girls who do yoga).

ACCOMMODATIONS AND INTEGRATION: If children have trouble with the sitting position, have them sit with their legs crossed in front of them. Begin to build the concept of a deep yoga breath into your schedule on a daily basis. Encourage children to take several big yoga breaths before they begin a new activity or to calm down after a very exciting activity. A big yoga breath is also effective in giving children time to think through what they want to do before confronting another child.

NONMANIPULATIVE: **LARGE GROUP**

4-26 Yoga Poses

GOALS: To improve nonmanipulative skills; to increase body awareness; to improve sensory motor integration

STANDARDS: PE 5 Exhibit responsible personal and social behavior that respects self and others in physical activity settings; PE 6 Value physical activity for health, enjoyment, challenge, self-expression, and/or social interaction; H 7 Demonstrate the ability to practice health-enhancing behaviors and avoid or reduce health risks.

MATERIALS: Mat or towel (optional); open space; book such as L. DeBrunhoff, *Babar's Yoga for Elephants* (New York: Abrams Image, 2006)

PROCEDURE: Remind the children about yoga breathing and practice. Then explain that you are going to teach them some yoga poses but first you are going to read a book about yoga. Read *Babar's Yoga for Elephants*, or show pictures of various poses and talk about yoga and its purposes. Tell them that before they start the poses, they need to breathe some big yoga breaths. Have them sit, close their eyes, and breathe in and out several times, and tell them to think happy thoughts. Then tell them they are going to learn a yoga pose that will make their back strong and stretch their back muscles. Ask them all to stretch to ensure they understand the concept and that they have enough room.

CAT/COW POSE: Next have them get on their hands and knees so their knees are under their hips and their hands are under their shoulders. Tell them to make their back flat like a table. Then have them gently suck in their tummies and round their backs like there is a big ball underneath their tummies. (Looks like a cat with its back curled up.) Tell them to breathe out as they lower their tummies toward the ground. (Tummy hangs down like the belly of a cow.) Have children move slowly back and forth between the cat and the cow pose, ensuring that they breathe in as their back arches and breathe out as their tummies hang down. Finish by sitting cross-legged and taking a few more yoga breaths.

ACCOMMODATIONS AND INTEGRATION: If children have problems pairing the breathing with the poses, remind them verbally to "take a deep breath" as their back arches and to "let it out" as their tummy sags. If children become intrigued with yoga, teach them more poses and talk more about how yoga strengthens their body and mind.

· · · · · NONMANIPULATIVE: **SMALL GROUP**

 Mirroring

GOALS: To improve nonmanipulative skills; to improve sensory motor integration; to improve motor planning

STANDARDS: PE 1 Demonstrate competency in motor skills and movement patterns needed to perform a variety of physical activities; PE 5 Exhibit responsible personal and social behavior that respects self and others in physical activity settings.

MATERIALS: String, blindfold

PROCEDURE: Have the children work in pairs facing each other. Talk about being partners and how partners take turns and support each other. One child in each pair initiates a movement and the other child mirrors it. Encourage children to balance on one foot, bend, twist, and so on. As children become more skillful, the movements can be faster and more subtle (such as facial movements).

ACCOMMODATIONS AND INTEGRATION: Encourage children to use slow, simple movements. Blindfold one child or tie a 12-inch string between the children's wrists and have them move gently to respond to the pressure on their hands or the string. Mirroring requires the child to look at another child to figure out what to do. It requires a child to "read" and respond to another child's body language.

· · · · · NONMANIPULATIVE: **LARGE GROUP**

4-28 Freeze

GOALS: To improve nonmanipulative skills; to improve sensory motor integration; to improve cause-and-effect reasoning

STANDARDS: PE 1 Demonstrate competency in motor skills and movement patterns needed to perform a variety of physical activities; PE 2 Demonstrate understanding of movement concepts, principles, strategies, and tactics as they apply to the learning and performance of physical activities; PE 5 Exhibit responsible personal and social behavior that respects self and others in physical activity settings.

MATERIALS: Drum, gong, or CD and CD player

PROCEDURE: Have the children move around the room (walking, skipping, hopping, jumping, spinning). Play music or beat a drum or gong, then stop suddenly. Call out "freeze"

until they get the idea. The children should maintain their position. As you unfreeze them (by touching them), talk about the positions they are in. As a variation, have all the children melt to the ground before the music starts again. Have children work in pairs, and discuss how they can help each other maintain balance.

ACCOMMODATIONS AND INTEGRATION: Initially, unfreeze children who have trouble balancing. Encourage children to move in ways that will be harder to hold when frozen and discuss these. Use a visual signal, flicking the lights or waving your hands, to freeze children. Discuss with children some of the basic principles of balance and why some postures are easier to hold than others. Have them experiment with different poses and block designs and see which ones are more stable, and help them draw analogies.

· · · · · NONMANIPULATIVE: **INDIVIDUAL**

4-29 Variations on Balancing

GOALS: To improve nonmanipulative skills; to improve sensory motor integration; to improve motor planning

STANDARDS: PE 1 Demonstrate competency in motor skills and movement patterns needed to perform a variety of physical activities; PE 2 Demonstrate understanding of movement concepts, principles, strategies, and tactics as they apply to the learning and performance of physical activities; SC 3a Physical science.

MATERIALS: Tape; balance beams: 6 inches and 4 inches wide, 6 inches off the ground

PROCEDURE: Dynamic balance is an important skill for children. Begin by using 6-inch wide lines taped on the floor. Then use a balance beam that is 6 inches wide, then 4 inches wide. Move the 4-inch beam higher off the floor so that you can add dips. Have children walk between the taped lines or across the beam in the following ways:

>   forward, backward, sideways
>
>   forward, turning at each end
>
>   touching heel against toe
>
>   holding an object (short pole) in hands
>
>   to middle, touch board with hand
>
>   to middle, pick up a small object
>
>   to end, dipping a foot on either side or kicking it

ACCOMMODATIONS AND INTEGRATION: Begin with the lines taped on the floor. Hold the child's hand as she walks and coach her through the variations. Help children focus on different techniques. Talk to children about gravity, their center of gravity, and how it affects movement. Have the children perform some of the tasks using a scooter or wheelchair. Learning to move in a confined area is valuable. Children redefine straight and narrow and look at activities they considered easy from a new perspective.

• • • • • NONMANIPULATIVE: **LARGE GROUP**

4-30 *Tense Me*

GOALS: To improve nonmanipulative skills; to improve sensory motor integration; to increase body awareness

STANDARDS: PE 1 Demonstrate competency in motor skills and movement patterns needed to perform a variety of physical activities; H 5 Demonstrate the ability to use decision-making skills to enhance health; H 7 Demonstrate the ability to practice health-enhancing behaviors and avoid or reduce health risks.

MATERIALS: None

PROCEDURE: Have all the children lie or sit on the floor. (Initially, sitting is easier because everyone can see well.) Have children tense and relax both arms and then both legs. You may need to touch the tensed part to see whether the child understands the request. Then have the children make a tight fist or muscle in one arm and feel that arm with the other hand. Tell them that feeling is *tense*. Ask whether they can squeeze harder and make it more tense. Have them hold it to a count of five. Then tell them to see how loose (relaxed) they can make that arm. Again, have them feel it with their other hand. Discuss the difference in feeling. Have them make the arm even floppier. Repeat with the other arm. Do different body parts (legs and face) on different days. Words like *tight*, *loose*, and *floppy* may work better than the words *tense* and *relax*, but be sure to use these too. Use your voice to mirror both the tension and relaxation. Help children learn to isolate and tense specific body parts (e.g., tense their right fist, left fist relaxed). Before children can voluntarily relax, they need to learn the feeling of what relaxation is.

ACCOMMODATIONS AND INTEGRATION: Encourage the children to touch your arm when it is relaxed and then tense. See whether they can feel the change. Gradually try to teach them to isolate the sides of the body and individual body parts. Children need to tune in to their body for self-knowledge and to monitor their behavior. Teach them the relationship between body tension and behavior, what they do when they are tense, and how to recognize tension.

SUMMARY

- Children need to understand and practice skills to enhance health.
- Fundamental motor skills are the basic building blocks for participating in sports as well as attaining the precision of movement necessary for academic activities such as writing.
- Variations on fundamental motor skills increase motivation while providing necessary practice and the need to adjust to different conditions.
- Children need the knowledge and skills to develop and maintain a healthy, safe, and physically active lifestyle.

EDUCATIONAL RESOURCES

American Alliance for Health, Physical Education, Recreation and Dance (AAHPERD) is a national organization that shares current research findings and opportunities for professional development in this area. www.aahperd.org/

Kids Health, created by the Nemours Foundation, promotes health. Professionals such as physicians and nutritionists check all entries. It is a good resource to share with parents. www.kidshealth.org/

CATCH (Coordinated Approach to Child Health) focuses on children's attitudes and behaviors relative to nutrition and physical activity. http://www.catchinfo.org/

PE Central provides information about developmentally appropriate physical education programs for children and youth as well as assessments and lesson ideas for early childhood educators in physical/health education and adaptive physical education. www.pecentral.org/

P.E. Links 4 U provides information about physical education practices, book reviews, and health and nutritional information, and has links to curriculum ideas, federal news, and national organizations. www.pelinks4u.org/

Preschool Activity Quick Source provides information on motor skills, physical health, and safety, in addition to looking at the NAEYC's accreditation standards for this area.

For additional resources, visit the book companion website for this text at www.cengagebrain.com.

Creative Arts Activities:
Visual Arts, Music, Movement and Dance, and Dramatic Play and Theater

5

All children are creative, some more so than others. Some children are more creative in one area than in other areas. Educators have an important role in the development of creativity: They can actively support creativity or squelch it. The response children receive about their creative efforts plays a large part in their creative development. Educators can enhance the experience by having children think more about the process, as it will affect the product.

ACTIVITY GOALS AND STANDARDS

Activities are organized by the goals and standards they support. The activities themselves serve as prototypes of activities that can be used again and again with minor changes. Books that are referred to in the text with an * have a complete citation and annotation in the Children's Bibliography; others have a complete citation where they are cited. For books where a lexile score is available, it is given after the book title, for example (500L). The notation "AD" before the lexile means that the book the book needs adult direction and should initially be read by an adult and discussed with children before children read it independently.

CREATIVE ARTS GUIDELINES

The following guidelines will be helpful as you think about adapting creative arts to meet the needs of children with diverse abilities.

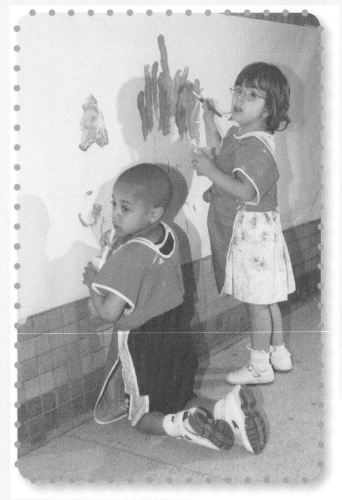

©Cengage Learning 2012

Adapting activities for children with:

Specific learning disabilities ❖ Promote creative problem solving. Use music to develop memory skills. Focus on relationships between the child's behavior and the outcome. Use the arts to build literacy skills. Use dramatic play to learn about new situations.

Social, emotional, and behavioral disorders ❖ Use creative arts activities to help children increase awareness of their moods and express their feelings. Provide large materials and an expansive work area. Use music to set a tone. Support children in playing out their fears and anxieties through puppets and dramatic play.

Attention-deficit/hyperactivity disorder ❖ Match activities to the child's energy level. Use creative arts to support and sustain attention. Help children organize creative experiences. Encourage children to think about the arts as leisure time activities.

Communication disorders ❖ Provide opportunities for children to speak, imitate peers, and use expressive language through choral activities and play. Use context to expand and extend vocabulary and language development.

English language learners ❖ Provide art materials that are used in different cultures. Use puppets, music, and other dramatic play experiences to support language development in the home language and English. Encourage children to use the arts to express themselves.

Autism spectrum disorders ❖ Use visual signs to cue participation. Join and expand on idiosyncratic movements. Provide play scripts and use realistic props.

Intellectual disabilities ❖ Provide familiar themes and settings. Keep activities simple and realistic. Teach functional skills using dramatic play.

Gifts and talents ✳ Encourage divergent thinking and unconventional solutions to problems. Add articles and information that increase the depth of all creative arts.

Special health care needs ✳ Help children express concerns and fears through art and music. Use dramatic play to help children gain some control over medical experiences.

Orthopedic and neurological impairments ✳ Adapt materials by making them larger or smaller, and add grips to make objects easier to hold. Have materials in different shapes, sizes, and textures.

Hearing impairments ✳ Use hand motions and signs with music and songs. Role-play situations using accessories to set moods.

Visual impairments ✳ Provide obvious boundaries for work (e.g., texture, high contrast, or people). Add texture to materials and use three-dimensional materials.

CREATIVE ARTS ACTIVITIES

· · · · · VISUAL ARTS: **SMALL GROUP**

5-1 Creature

GOALS: To increase visual arts concepts; to improve cause-and-effect reasoning; to increase knowledge of the natural world

STANDARDS: VA 1 Understand and apply media, techniques, and processes; VA 6 Make connections between visual arts and other disciplines; SC 3b Life science.

MATERIALS: Papier-mâché

TO MAKE: *Tear newspaper into very small pieces and pour a little boiling water over it. Stir until it forms a pulp. Cool. Then add about 6 tablespoons of wheat paste for every 2 cups of pulp. Mix first with a spoon, then with the hands.*

PROCEDURE: Discuss how people and animals are adapted to their environments (a monkey's tail is for climbing; polar bears are white for protective coloration; a cheetah's sleek body and long legs are used for speed in catching prey). Have children think about different environments and how animals adapt or are adapted to these. Have children decide on a particular environment. Talk about aspects of the creature they are going to make that will help it survive there. Help children think about how it moves, what and how it eats, where it lives, and so on. Then have the children mold the papier-mâché into the creature-like form they have envisioned. When the creatures are dry, encourage the children to use the construction area to build environments for them.

ACCOMMODATIONS AND INTEGRATION: Focus on the papier-mâché and having children tear the paper for it and make it. Help children focus on the adaptations creatures (and people) make to the environment. Talk about mobility aids, prosthetic devices, and eyeglasses.

· · · · · VISUAL ARTS: **SMALL GROUP**

5-2 Tissue Paper Art

GOALS: To increase visual arts concepts; to encourage creativity; to improve cause-and-effect reasoning

STANDARDS: VA 1 Understand and apply media, techniques, and processes; VA 3 Choose and evaluate a range of subject matter, symbols, and ideas. R:L 7 Describe the relationship between illustrations and the story in which they appear.

MATERIALS: Small pieces of tissue paper, light-colored construction paper, glue stick, books illustrated by Eric Carle, such as E. Carle, *The Very Hungry Caterpillar* (New York: Grosset & Dunlap, 2008); E. Carle, *I See a Song,* (New York: Scholastic, 1996); E. Carle, *The Tiny Seed* (New York: Little Simon, 2009); and for educators, E. Carle, *The Art of Eric Carle* (New York: Philomel 2002).

PROCEDURE: Read a book illustrated by Eric Carle. Talk with the children about how Eric Carle created his pictures (overlapping tissue paper) and the relationship between the illustrations and the text. Have children think about what they want to illustrate and encourage them to use overlapping tissue paper to make different colors for their illustrations.

ACCOMMODATIONS AND INTEGRATION: Demonstrate the technique of overlapping pieces. Encourage children to explore the concept and resulting colors before gluing. Have children predict the outcome and then verify their predictions. Have the children create and illustrate a story using tissue paper art.

· · · · · VISUAL ARTS: **SMALL GROUP**

5-3 Crayon Rubbing

GOALS: To increase visual arts concepts; to improve cause-and-effect reasoning; to improve sensory motor integration

STANDARDS: VA 1 Understand and apply media, techniques, and processes; VA 3 Choose and evaluate a range of subject matter, symbols, and ideas; VA 4 Understand the visual arts in relation to history and cultures.

MATERIALS: Paper, masking tape, thick crayons, objects with various textures, rubbings

PROCEDURE: Talk to children about rubbings and how people rub tombstones, temples, and other interesting objects as mementos. Discuss why people would want to do this. Show children examples of rubbings. Talk about various surfaces that the children touch and how they would describe them (soft, furry, scratchy), then about surfaces that they see (shiny, hairy, has ridges or patterns), and then about the two combined (something that feels bumpy and looks rough). Demonstrate rubbing techniques to the children. Help children rub the edges of objects first to determine their shape. Initially, help children pick objects with distinctive shapes and textures by providing a variety of textured objects. Tape the corners of the paper to the table with the object under it. The tape keeps the paper from moving as the children rub. Write the name of the article rubbed on the backside of the paper. During group time, ask the children to look at the papers and guess what article was rubbed. (The name on the back helps for those "creative" rubbings.)

ACCOMMODATIONS AND INTEGRATION: Choose relatively small objects with distinctive shapes and textures. Have two of the objects, placing one under the paper and the other for the child to look at to see if it is "coming up." Have children predict how a rubbing will look before they begin and then see whether they were accurate. This requires little coordination, yet helps develop finger strength and sensory motor integration, as well as gives children feedback about how hard they are pressing the crayon. It is an interesting way to include history and culture into the curriculum in a very concrete way. You might show children rubbings from other cultures. Talk about how fossils relate to rubbings.

• • • • • VISUAL ARTS: **LARGE GROUP**

 ### Hand print Mural

GOALS: To increase visual arts concepts; to encourage creativity; to increase inclusion

STANDARDS: VA 1 Understand and apply media, techniques, and processes; VA 2 Use knowledge of structures and functions; VA 6 Make connections between visual arts and other disciplines.

MATERIALS: Paint, butcher paper, paint brush, sponge, construction paper

PROCEDURE: Decide on the purpose for the mural (e.g., get-well or thank-you card, part of a bulletin board display, etc.). Have the children generate an appropriate message. Then talk to children about handprints and fingerprints. Put the mural paper on a separate table. Put the paint on a sponge and have children press their hand on the sponge, and then print it. Then identify their handprint. Encourage them to be creative, perhaps paint the palm one color and the area between each knuckle another. Supply additional small paper so children can try out their print first or make another project. Point out how each child's fingerprints are unique.

ACCOMMODATIONS AND INTEGRATION: Help the child by pressing his hand into the sponge and then onto the paper. Point out the salient characteristics. Have children add finger and thumbprints and look at both hand- and fingerprints with a magnifying glass. The concept of printing is different from fingerpainting. This project is an easy one for children to participate in and, if hung on the wall, a reminder that all children are part of the class. Some communities encourage all children to be fingerprinted. This is a good way to prepare children for this process.

• • • • • VISUAL ARTS: **LARGE AND SMALL GROUP**

5-5 Illustrations

GOALS: To increase visual arts concepts; to increase inclusion; to increase writing literacy

STANDARDS: VA 5 Reflect on and assess the characteristics and merits of their work and the work of others; VA 6 Make

connections between visual arts and other disciplines; W 1 Use a combination of drawing, dictating, and writing to compose opinion pieces in which they tell a reader the topic or name of the book they are writing about and state an opinion or preference about the topic or book.

MATERIALS: Book by D. Wiesner, *Art and Max* (New York: Clarion Books, 2010); crayons, markers, colored pencils, paint, and construction paper

PROCEDURE: Read *Art and Max* to the children. Art and Max are lizards. Art is an artist and Max wants to be one. The book is about sharing the artistic process whether it is painting a portrait or throwing paint at a cactus. Take the children to David Wiesner's page on Amazon.com and talk with the children about the author/illustrator and his life. Play the videos and let the children listen to David Wiesner talking about his art and the creation of *Art and Max*. Then encourage children to go to the art area and write and illustrate their own book and then go to the author's chair and share their work. This may take several days, so develop a plan to keep the work in progress where children can return to it.

ACCOMMODATIONS AND INTEGRATION: Encourage children to talk about Max's dilemma about what to draw and to help each other find a topic. Discuss David Wiesner's videos and his process of drawing, rethinking, and redrawing until he achieves the effect he wants. Help children evaluate their own art work and that of others based on what they are trying to convey.

• • • • • VISUAL ARTS: **LARGE AND SMALL GROUP**

5-6 Chinese New Year Dragon

GOALS: To increase visual arts concepts; to increase cultural awareness; to identify and understand patterns and relationships

STANDARDS: VA 1 Understand and apply media, techniques, and processes; VA 4 Understand the visual arts in relation to history and cultures; VA 6 Make connections between visual arts and other disciplines.

MATERIALS: Large paper with a design drawn on it and numerals within all of the areas, paint, color key, book such as M. K. Vaughan, *The Dancing Dragon* (New York: Mondo Publishing, 1996) (NC 590L). (Stand the book up and fold it out after reading.)

PROCEDURE: Read a story about the Chinese New Year and discuss the traditions associated with the holiday, specifically, the parade. The children are going to help create a dragon for a parade by painting a large piece of paper in a particular traditional pattern. Help the children understand how they are to follow the color by number key to paint the design. They also need to decorate a large box for the head of the dragon. When painted and dried, attach the paper to the box. Have the children parade around the room and into other rooms or down the hall under the paper.

ACCOMMODATIONS AND INTEGRATION: Work with a child one-on-one to paint a particular area; a corner area may be easiest. Encourage children to read more about the Chinese New Year and about other traditions associated with the celebration. This encourages children to prepare for and celebrate a holiday together. It enables them to learn about different cultures' traditions. Choose traditions that reflect the children in your class and find out how families celebrate these.

• • • • • VISUAL ARTS: **SMALL GROUP**

5-7 Textured Playdough

GOALS: To increase visual arts concepts; to improve cause-and-effect reasoning; to improve sensory motor integration

STANDARDS: VA 1 Understand and apply media, techniques, and processes; VA 2 Use knowledge of structures and functions.

MATERIALS: Playdough of varying textures

TO MAKE: *Make playdough, but systematically vary the ratio of flour to salt, beginning with 7 parts flour to 1 part salt (and about 1 T. vegetable oil). Change the ratio of flour to salt: Use 7 parts flour to 2 parts salt; 7 to 3; 7 to 4; 7 to 5; and 7 to 6. Color-code the different mixtures and make a key.*

PROCEDURE: Have the children help make playdough so that they can see the difference in the quantities of flour and salt. Start with gross discrimination (7 to 1 versus 7 to 6), and then see whether the children can make finer distinctions. Help them verbalize the differences and the reasons for them. (The more flour, the smoother the dough; the more salt, the grainier it is.) Encourage children to make tactile discriminations.

Texture adds another dimension to paint and playdough.
©Cengage Learning 2012

ACCOMMODATIONS AND INTEGRATION: Have children classify the playdough by touch. Talk about uses for the different textures. Have children make other recipes by adding sawdust, sand, and so on. Make small quantities, as some of the products might be unappealing. This activity helps develop and refine tactile skills. Because children participate in the process of making the playdough, they can begin to understand the relationship between the ingredients used and the outcome.

• • • • • VISUAL ARTS: **SMALL GROUP**

5-8 What Shall We Make?

GOALS: To increase visual arts concepts; to encourage creativity; to encourage problem solving

STANDARDS: VA 1 Understand and apply media, techniques, and processes; VA 6 Make connections between visual arts and other disciplines; L 5 Explore word relationships and nuances in word meanings.

MATERIALS: Linen, corduroy, plastic needles, thread, wool, gabardine, gingham, cotton, denim, chiffon, velvet, vinyl, fur, knit, felt, trims, stapler and staples, scissors, tape, Velcro (with sticky back), patterns for male and female doll clothes

PROCEDURE: Have the children decide on the type of clothing they want to make, choose a pattern, then pick the material to make the desired clothing. Help them think about the relationship between the garment and the fabric. Help children tape on the pattern, cut it out, and sew up the seams with a large plastic needle and heavy thread or staple it together.

ACCOMMODATIONS AND INTEGRATION: Some children may just choose the material and cut out the pattern. Others could staple the garment together or have an adult help with the sewing. Talk about choosing material relative to the style, where it will be worn, and weather. Add fasteners such as buttons, snaps, and hooks and eyes. Talk about aspects of clothing (e.g., armholes, sleeves, neck hole) and how they are part of the pattern. Discuss the relationship between size and closures, and where these are placed relative to ease of dressing. Encourage children to add trims to their garments to make them unique. Encourage children to make up a story about the occasion for which the clothing will be worn, dress a doll, and role-play the occasion.

• • • • • VISUAL ARTS: **SMALL GROUP**

5-9 Anything Boxes

GOALS: To increase visual arts concepts; to encourage creativity; to improve expressive communication

STANDARDS: VA 1 Understand and apply media, techniques, and processes; VA 2 Use knowledge of structures and functions; VA 6 Make connections between visual arts and other disciplines.

MATERIALS: Boxes of different sizes, markers, crayons, scissors, construction paper, tape, yarn, ribbon, toilet paper tubes

PROCEDURE: Invite each child to choose a box and decorate it as he or she wishes. Encourage the children to describe what they are creating and how the box will be used. Allow them to be creative and inventive. Let the boxes be part of the classroom for at least a week so the children's play will be expanded and their ideas can be enhanced.

ACCOMMODATIONS AND INTEGRATION: Accept all types of decorations, even those with no decorations (plain boxes). Help children connect the way they decorate the box with its potential use. This activity allows the children to express themselves and describe what they are creating.

· · · · · VISUAL ARTS: **SMALL GROUP**

5-10 Game Board

GOALS: To increase visual arts concepts; to identify and understand patterns and relationships

STANDARDS: VA 5 Reflect on and assess the characteristics and merits of their work and the work of others; VA 6 Make connections between visual arts and other disciplines; W 2 Compose informative/explanatory texts in which they name what they are writing about and supply some information about the topic.

MATERIALS: A cookie sheet, jellyroll pan, or cardboard, magnets, string, 20 to 30 straws, paper plates, glue, felt dots, black construction paper, brads or a board game

TO MAKE: *Glue the string and/or straws to the pan in a ladder-like track. Add environmental cues to support the theme. Make a spinner out of a paper plate. Use felt dots to signify the number of spaces to move and an arrow attached by a brad as the pointer. Use magnets as markers. Note: Children can make a variety of games in this way.*

PROCEDURE: Tell the children they are going to make a game board. Show them a commercially made one and discuss different aspects of it. Have children think about the theme they want, how the game will be played, and what their design strategy is. Encourage them to draw the design on paper before trying to make the game board. Once the game board is completed (see Figure R5-1) encourage

children play the game with peers. Help them see the need for rules, and encourage them to make up and write out the rules of their game.

ACCOMMODATIONS AND INTEGRATION: Encourage children to support each other in making the game board, learning the rules of the game, and counting as each child moves her piece. As children play board games, focus on the potential for using mathematics to make sense out of the game as well as on the prosocial behavior of taking turns. As they understand basic rules, help children decide on and write the rules for their game. Have children try to play the game blindfolded, using the tactile cues. Discuss how this affects the rules, if at all. Children enjoy and learn a lot from playing games. Having them make the board and the rules gives them a different perspective.

· · · · · MUSIC: **LARGE GROUP**

5-11 Mood Songs

GOALS: To increase music concepts; to move creatively; to express feelings

STANDARDS: MU 1 Sing, alone and with others, a varied repertoire of music; MU 6 Listen to, analyze, and describe music.

MATERIALS: CDs from Putumayo Kids, and CD player

PROCEDURE: Choose songs that have specific moods: lullabies, jazz, rock and roll, reggae, folk. Start with familiar, obvious songs and help children focus on the mood of the music before they begin to move. After moving to a song, talk about when they might want to listen to this type of music. Then, have them sing a familiar song the "wrong" way (a loud, fast lullaby).

ACCOMMODATIONS AND INTEGRATION: Identify the mood and tell children how to move. Model appropriate movements. As children become more skillful, use songs that may not be as familiar to the children, from areas in the United States (New Orleans) and around the world (Africa, Asia, Caribbean), and also music from the Putumayo Kids series. Discuss the intersection of culture and music. Have children identify some of the musical characteristics that are used to create the mood. Help them identify how different instruments contribute to the mood. Children learn to become more aware of their own moods and can perhaps

FIGURE R5-1: Game Board

match music to these as a way of learning to control them. Children need to develop the skills of analyzing and describing music.

· · · · · MUSIC: **SMALL GROUP OR INDIVIDUAL**

 ## Color Notes

GOALS: To increase music concepts; to identify and understand patterns and relationships; to improve sensory motor integration

STANDARDS: MU 2 Perform on instruments, alone and with others, a varied repertoire of music; MU 5 Read and notate music; R:FS 1 Demonstrate understanding of the organization and basic features of print.

MATERIALS: Sheet music of familiar songs, crayons or markers to color in the notes on the sheet music, colored stickers to stick onto the piano keys

PROCEDURE: Encourage children to explore a piano or keyboard. Have them press different keys to hear sounds they can make (soft, hard, high, low). Provide sheet music with the notes colored in different colors that correspond to colored keys on the piano. Show the children how to look at the sheet music and then press the appropriate keys.

ACCOMMODATIONS AND INTEGRATION: Start with one sheet of music where the notes directly correspond to the order of the notes on the piano like a scale. Place the music directly above the keyboard. Increase the number of lines and complexity of the music. Talk about different types of notes (whole or half) and their relationship to playing music. This activity encourages children to start to understand the written "language" of music and exposes them to another symbol system.

· · · · · MUSIC: **LARGE GROUP**

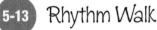 ## Rhythm Walk

GOALS: To increase music concepts; to move creatively; to increase sensory motor integration

STANDARDS: MU 6 Listen to, analyze, and describe music; MU 9 Understand music in relation to history and culture; D 1 Identify and demonstrate movement elements and skills in performing dance.

MATERIALS: Drum or piano

PROCEDURE: Set up a path around the room (or outside) and have the children walk to a beat you establish. Initially, warn the children before changing the rhythm: "Listen, I'm going to change now. Is it faster or slower?"

ACCOMMODATIONS AND INTEGRATION: Be sure the children can see you and the beat; play dramatically. Then, vary the beat and see whether the children change with you. As children's skill increases, make the changes more quickly. Do not let the children see what you are doing; this takes away the visual cue. Sometimes beat slowly enough for their

movements to become a balancing activity. Instead of walking, have children move creatively or dance to the beat. Add music from different cultures that have different beats and moods. Talk about these differences.

· · · · · MUSIC: **SMALL OR LARGE GROUP**

 ## Conductor

GOALS: To increase music concepts; to improve cause-and-effect reasoning; to identify and understand patterns and relationships

STANDARDS: MU 2 Perform on instruments, alone and with others, a varied repertoire of music; MU 4 Compose and arrange music within specific guidelines; MU 5 Read and notate music.

MATERIALS: Rhythm band instruments, DVD of a conductor

PROCEDURE: Play a short DVD of a concert and point out to the children the motions the conductor uses to direct the orchestra. Teach children some of the simpler signals used:

> softer: palms toward the group (up and down)
> louder: palms toward you (large gesture)
> slow: waving slowly (circular)
> fast: waving fast (circular)
> expand: pass arm in front of body parallel to floor
> staccato: cut in the air (vertically)

Your signals don't have to be the actual signals, but you and the children should agree on their meanings: Make a picture of the signals, with the word written below.

Start with the teacher being the "director" and children using their voice. Use sounds like *me, me, me, me; la, la, la, la; see, see, see, see*. Then go to two or more syllables. Names are always fun: *Ja*—expand (use horizontal hand movement), *mie*—staccato (vertical hand movement). Be sure a child knows the process before choosing her to be the conductor. Encourage children to figure out what happens with each different motion.

ACCOMMODATIONS AND INTEGRATION: Have the child hold up a picture of a particular signal for the group to follow. Have the children use their instruments with a conductor. Instruments are far more challenging to control than voices. This can be a positive experience even if the child only discovers that other children will start and stop on their hand signals.

· · · · · MUSIC: **SMALL OR LARGE GROUP**

 ## Bumblebees

GOALS: To increase music concepts; to increase comprehension; to increase knowledge of the natural world

STANDARDS: MU 6 Listen to, analyze, and describe music; MU 7 Evaluate music and music performances;

MU 8 Understand relationships between music, the other arts, and disciplines outside the arts.

MATERIALS: Books such as J. Allen, *Are you a Bee?* (Boston: Kingfisher, Backyard Books, 2004); "Flight of the Bumble-bee" by Rimsky-Korsakov; CD and CD player; wax paper; construction paper; glue; black pipe cleaners; crayons or markers; pictures of bumblebees; yarn, yellow and black cut into strips; Styrofoam balls

PROCEDURE: Talk with children about bees, notably their characteristics and function. Read a book such as *Are you a Bee?* Discuss how bumblebees fly. Listen to "Flight of the Bumblebee." Discuss the music with the children and their opinions about it. Give the children the materials to make a bumblebee and encourage them to talk about the music while they make their bumblebee. Encourage the children to use the materials creatively. Listen to "Flight of the Bumblebee" again, and have children pretend they are bumblebees and dance to the music. Talk in more detail about bumblebees.

ACCOMMODATIONS AND INTEGRATION: Describe only the most salient characteristics of bumblebees and support any product the child makes. Talk in more detail about how bumblebees fly and communicate with each other. Point out details from a picture of the bumblebee. Encourage children to talk about why this music selection is not called "Flight of the Hawk" or other animals they might have some knowledge of.

· · · · ·   MUSIC: **LARGE GROUP**

5-16   Sequencing Songs

GOALS: To increase music concepts; to identify and understand patterns and relationships

STANDARDS: MU 1 Sing, alone and with others, a varied repertoire of music; MU 3 Improvise melodies, variations, and accompaniments; MU 6 Listen to, analyze, and describe music.

MATERIALS: None

PROCEDURE: Sing songs that require the children to remember a particular sequence such as "Old MacDonald," "This Old Man," "If You're Happy," "I Know an Old Lady Who Swallowed a Fly," and "Hush, Little Baby"

ACCOMMODATIONS AND INTEGRATION: Make pictures for the different words the children have to remember and hold them up as visual reminders. For "Old MacDonald," these would be pictures of the different animals. When you sing "Old MacDonald," pause after "and on his farm he had a ..." to see whether they can remember the sequence without your help. As children become more skillful, add more words for the children to remember. Encourage children to make up additional verses and to suggest variations. Discuss sequencing songs with children and compare their commonalities and differences.

· · · · ·   MUSIC: **LARGE GROUP**

5-17   My Song

GOALS: To increase music concepts; to increase inclusion; to improve listening skills

STANDARDS: MU 1 Sing, alone and with others, a varied repertoire of music; MU 3 Improvise melodies, variations, and accompaniments; MU 6 Listen to, analyze, and describe music.

MATERIALS: None

PROCEDURE: Sing songs in which you can substitute the name of a child from your group, or adapt a song to include a name.

"Bingo"	"Paw-Paw Patch"
There was a farmer had a son	Where, oh, where is pretty little Sherry?
and Michael was his name—O.	Where, oh, where is pretty little Laura?
M-I-C-H-AEL	Where, oh, where is handsome Juan?
M-I-C-H-AEL	They're in the block corner
M-I-C-H-AEL	picking up blocks.
And Michael was his name—O.	

"Hey, Betty Martin"	"Who Has Red On?"
Hey, Jenny Gilbert	T. R. has a red shirt,
tippy toe tippy toe.	red shirt, red shirt,
Hey, Dante Turner,	T. R. has a red shirt
tiptoe fine	in school today.

ACCOMMODATIONS AND INTEGRATION: Point to the child whose name you are singing. Use songs that require children to sing back a response such as "Here I am." These songs are great at the beginning of the year, when children are getting to know each other. Also, use them when you are trying to get a group together and you have a few wanderers ("Hey, Gabi O'Day, come join us"). Once children have become familiar with the songs, have them think up variations. Encourage them to analyze songs to determine how they might be adapted.

· · · · ·   MUSIC: **SMALL GROUP OR INDIVIDUAL**

5-18   Notes Collage

GOALS: To increase music concepts; to improve reading literacy; to improve writing literacy

STANDARDS: MU 1 Sing, alone and with others, a varied repertoire of music; MU 5 Read and notate music; MU 6 Listen to, analyze, and describe music.

MATERIALS: Construction paper with musical scale; music notes; glue sticks; music CD and CD player; book such as

A. Appleby, *The Library of Children's Song Classics* (New York: Music Sales America, 1993)

PROCEDURE: Show children a book of songs written for children. Choose a familiar song and show the children the musical notations and point out the relevant features: musical notes and their various durations and pitches, musical scale. Provide children with a musical scale on paper and encourage them to use the different notes to make a musical collage. Encourage children to talk about different kinds of notes and their implications. Discuss with children the names of various notes and what they sound like. Have them try to sing their collage. If that is not possible, point out the features that make their collage different from printed music.

ACCOMMODATIONS AND INTEGRATION: Emphasize the collage aspect of the project. Identify only one note. As children learn more about music, encourage them to develop a repeating pattern using different notes and then to hum or sing the pattern. Help them make their collage similar to sheet music.

· · · · · MUSIC: **SMALL GROUP**

Making Tambourines

GOALS: To increase music concepts; to encourage creativity; to improve cause-and-effect reasoning

STANDARDS: MU 2 Perform on instruments, alone and with others, a varied repertoire of music; MU 6 Listen to, analyze, and describe music; MU 9 Understand music in relation to history and culture.

MATERIALS: Paper plates (two for each child), crayons or markers, beans, stapler, CD Putumayo Kids *Latin Playground*, CD player

PROCEDURE: Talk to children about different ways people make music. Talk about the different instruments that are in the percussion family, such as drums, congas, bongos, maracas, castanets, and tambourines. Have children listen to one of the selections and see whether they can identify a percussion instrument. Encourage them to dance to the music and to discuss the beat. Then show them the materials and ask them how they can make music with the materials. Encourage them to be creative, but guide them toward thinking about tambourines. Demonstrate how to decorate the plates and staple them together, leaving a small opening. Then pour beans in the small hole and staple the hole closed. Encourage the children to make their own tambourine and use it when you choose another selection from *Latin Playground*.

ACCOMMODATIONS AND INTEGRATION: Have the child color the plates, and provide support for the stapling and filling. Encourage children to use different substances to fill the tambourine to see whether it affects the sound. Help children compare the sound of the tambourine they made with a "real" one and identify the differences in sound and why these occur.

· · · · · MUSIC: **LARGE GROUP**

5-20 ## Zin! Zin! Zin! A Violin

GOALS: To increase music concepts; to increase vocabulary; to improve sensory motor integration

STANDARDS: MU 6 Listen to, analyze, and describe music; MU 7 Evaluate music and music performances; MU 8 Understand relationships between music, the other arts, and disciplines outside the arts.

MATERIALS: M. Hamlisch, W. Gordon, and A. Lansbury, *Zin! Zin! Zin! A Violin*, Little Symphonies, DVD, 2009; and L. Moss, *Zin! Zin! Zin! A Violin* (New York: Aladdin Picture Books, 2009).

PROCEDURE: Read the children the book *Zin! Zin! Zin! A Violin* and talk with them about the word pictures and sounds they imagine as the book is read. Discuss the different instruments that make up the orchestra. The next day show them the DVD of *Zin! Zin! Zin! A Violin*. Have children compare and contrast the experience.

ACCOMMODATIONS AND INTEGRATION: Help children enjoy the experience of the book or DVD, without dwelling on the instruments. Read the book again and ask children to close their eyes and let their imagination soar with the strings and roar with the base notes galore. Have children draw and/or write about their listening experiences.

· · · · · MOVEMENT AND DANCE: **SMALL OR LARGE GROUP**

5-21 ## Rag Dolls

GOALS: To move creatively; to increase body awareness; to improve sensory motor integration

STANDARDS: D 1 Identify and demonstrate movement elements and skills in performing dance; D 3 Understand dance as a way to create and communicate meaning.

MATERIALS: Rag dolls, music for floppy rag dolls to move to

PROCEDURE: Show the children several rag dolls and demonstrate how they move. Encourage the children to experiment with the rag dolls. Then have the children lie down, and show them what happens to the rag doll when the legs and arms are lifted. Ask the children to pretend to be rag dolls, and go around the class to check out your collection of "rag dolls." Raise limbs an inch or two and see how floppy children can be. (Don't drop a leg very far or the children will tense!) It takes practice to relax. Then encourage children to discuss the characteristics of "rag doll music" and then dance to music as if they were rag dolls.

ACCOMMODATIONS AND INTEGRATION: Ensure that the environment is safe; use soothing music to create a mood; dim the lights; and allow children to feel relaxed. As the children learn to relax lying down, see whether they can gain skill in locating just the muscles they need; that is, can they sit up while keeping their arms and head relaxed? Then have them try standing. Add music and see whether children can alternate between being floppy rag dolls and tense, marching tin

Combining music and movement and increasing body awareness is useful to all children.
©Cengage Learning 2012

soldiers on your command. Call out to the children what you want them to be. Help children learn to relax specific body parts on command. Tension increases pain, so anything you can teach children about relaxing is useful. Tension may also be the precursor to aggression.

· · · · · MOVEMENT AND DANCE: **LARGE OR SMALL GROUP**

5-22 Ballet

GOALS: To understand dance; to move creatively; to improve motor planning

STANDARDS: D 1 Identify and demonstrate movement elements and skills in performing dance; D 2 Understand choreographic principles, processes, and structures; D 5 Demonstrate and understand dance in various cultures and historical periods.

MATERIALS: Book and CD such as L. Lee, *A Child's Introduction to Ballet: The Stories, Music, and Magic of Classical Dance* (New York: Black Dog and Leventhal, 2009); CD player

PROCEDURE: Discuss the concept of dance with children and acknowledge that there are many different kinds and ways of dancing. Show them the cover of the book *A Child's Introduction to Ballet* and ask them to describe what they see on the cover (tutus, ballet shoes, boys, etc.). Explain that a choreographer is the person who makes up or invents a particular dance. Talk to them briefly about the history of ballet using the pictures as your guide (don't read the whole text or even a whole page). Show children the five basic ballet positions and how to move between them. Choose one ballet and track on the CD that goes with it (they are short) and have the children dance to music using some of the positions and variations of them.

ACCOMMODATIONS AND INTEGRATION: Encourage children to think about and move to the music. Help interested children

choreograph a short dance to one of the tracks on the CD. Invite a dance instructor to come into the class and talk about and demonstrate a dance. Have him or her help children understand more about the principles of choreography and how it is done.

· · · · · MOVEMENT AND DANCE: **LARGE OR SMALL GROUP**

5-23 Progressive Dance

GOALS: To understand dance; to move creatively; to improve adaptive skills

STANDARDS: D 1 Identify and demonstrate movement elements and skills in performing dance; D 3 Understand dance as a way to create and communicate meaning; D 7 Make connections between dance and other disciplines.

MATERIALS: Clothing larger than the children's size: sweaters, tops, pants, shirts, skirts, shorts, dresses, socks, shoes, tutus, accessories, and so on

PROCEDURE: Divide the clothing into three piles: tops, bottoms, and footwear. Put the piles in three different places. Have the children dance to each pile, find and put on an article of clothing, perform a designated dance step, and then go on to the next pile, until they are "dressed." Then have each child describe his outfit and perform a short dance.

ACCOMMODATIONS AND INTEGRATION: Include oversized clothing without buttons and with cutoff sleeves, as well as clothing that is closer to the children's actual size. Add accessories such as gloves, ties, scarves, and hats. Have children dress for a particular occasion, particular weather, a particular profession, or a particular dance, and discuss why they chose that particular outfit. Help children focus on aspects of clothing that make it more or less difficult to put on and dance in, and how clothing and dance can be adapted for individuals with disabilities.

· · · · · MOVEMENT AND DANCE: **SMALL GROUP**

5-24 Dances of the Bubbles

GOALS: To understand dance; to move creatively; to improve sensory motor integration

STANDARDS: D 1 Identify and demonstrate movement elements and skills in performing dance; D 4 Apply and demonstrate critical and creative thinking skills in dance; D 6 Make connections between dance and healthful living.

MATERIALS: Bubble mixture, bubble-blowing rings, wire, assorted bubble wands, CDs such as Putumayo Kids *Jazz Playground*, *Rock and Roll Playground*, or *Reggae Playground*.

TO MAKE: *Stir 5 cups water, ½ cup liquid dishwashing detergent, and 2 tablespoons glycerin in a container to make the bubble mixture, or buy it.*

PROCEDURE: Have some children blow bubbles and other children dance to the music to try to catch them. Or have children dance with bubble wands to the music. Encourage children to figure out where the bubbles will go based on the wind. Have them experiment with blowing and waving hard and soft. Encourage children to make their own bubble wands to dance with.

ACCOMMODATIONS AND INTEGRATION: Have the children catch the bubbles and enjoy the process. This is a good outside activity on a warm day. The music sets the tone of the play so vary the type of music and dancing with your goals.

· · · · · MOVEMENT AND DANCE: **SMALL GROUP**

 ## Dance Party

GOALS: To understand dance; to move creatively; to improve sensory motor integration

STANDARDS: D 1 Identify and demonstrate movement elements and skills in performing dance; D 5 Demonstrate and understand dance in various cultures and historical periods; D 6 Make connections between dance and healthful living.

MATERIALS: CDs with music from different cultures such as the Putumayo *Playground* series and *Dreamland* series, classical music or Top 40, CD player, ballet slippers, tap shoes

PROCEDURE: Discuss with children different types of dancing and find out what they know about each

- *Ballet* uses graceful movements and you wear soft ballet slippers.
- *Tap* dancing requires tap shoes and includes foot movements like shuffling and hitting the ball and heel of the foot on the floor.
- *Jazz* uses more whole body movements
- *Hip Hop* involves strong movements or "popping"
- *Rock and Roll* involves twisting and turning as well as moving up and down

Talk with children about how the dance types are the same and different. Ask the children to pretend that they are in a movie about dancing. Put on one song and ask them to dance to it. When that song is over, give them a brief curtain call and put on music with a very different tempo. Then ask children to sit and discuss the differences in the music and dancing.

ACCOMMODATIONS AND INTEGRATION: Only use one song or give children a longer break. Talk about dancing as being both fun and healthy. Explain that you are going to have dance parties frequently to dance and to learn about different types of dancing and music.

· · · · · DRAMATIC PLAY AND THEATER: **LARGE GROUP**

 ## Relaxation Stories

GOALS: To perform roles; to increase body awareness; to improve sensory motor integration

STANDARDS: TH 1 Write script by planning and recording improvisations based on personal experience and heritage, imagination, literature, and history; TH 2 Act by assuming roles and interacting in improvisations.

MATERIALS: None

PROCEDURE: Tell the children that you have a script for a story that you want them to act out as you tell the story. The actual content of the script may vary with what your class has done and the experiences your children are familiar with. An example follows (pause after each statement to give children time to perform the action):

> *There was a little boy who was tired, but he could not go to sleep; he had the wiggles. (pause) Every time a part of him was tired (pause), another part would start to wiggle (pause), and he'd giggle (pause), and then he couldn't go to sleep. So he decided to tell himself a sleepy story. He started with his toes and said, "Toes, don't wiggle" (pause), but they kept wiggling (pause). Then he said, "Toes, we're going to the beach (pause) and we are going to walk through so much sand that you'll be glad not to wiggle." (pause) And he walked and he walked and he walked (pause), and finally he was so tired that he sat down (pause), and his toes weren't wiggling. (pause) They were too tired. His ankles were tired and so were his knees. (pause) They felt heavy. Even his legs felt heavy. (pause) It just felt nice to be sitting down. (pause) Maybe even lying down. (pause) Or stretched out. . . . (pause) Umm . . . rest your head back (pause), get comfortable (pause), and close your eyes. (pause) . . . Oh, relax those tired feet again (pause), all the way up the leg. (pause) Now your hip. (pause) Now your middle. (pause) Let your shoulders touch the floor if they want to (pause); your elbows too (pause). Now your hands. (pause) Uncurl your fingers. (pause) Even that little finger is heavy. (pause) Now he's going to check himself out. The wrists, elbows, and shoulders are all heavy and relaxed. (pause) Move your head up and lay it down (pause); roll it a little to find a comfortable place. (pause) Open your mouth. (pause) Now close it. (pause) Yawn. (pause) Close your eyes. (pause.) Breathe deeply. (pause) You're waking up. (pause) Roll your head slowly, open your eyes. (pause) Sit up and wiggle just a little. (pause)*

ACCOMMODATIONS AND INTEGRATION: Keep the stories short until children feel comfortable with the process. Make your pauses short. As children learn the process, increase the length of the pauses and incorporate more visual images. Make a recording of the story and encourage children to make up their own scripts to be acted out. Point out the relevant variables of this script; pace and tone as well as content. The relaxation portion of this script is best spoken in a slow, placid monotone. In addition to providing a tone of relaxation, it exposes children to another type and use of scripts and improvisation.

· · · · · DRAMATIC PLAY AND THEATER: **SMALL GROUP**

 ## Doctor's Office

GOALS: To perform roles; to play creatively; to increase awareness of roles people play

STANDARDS: TH 2 Act by assuming roles and interacting in improvisations; TH 3 Design by visualizing and arranging environments for classroom dramatizations; R:IT 8 Identify the reasons an author gives to support points in a text.

MATERIALS: Props for a doctor's office: stethoscope, lab coat, flashlight, syringes (without needles), dolls, tongue depressors, Book such as T. B. Brazelton, *Going to the Doctor* (Cambridge, MA: Da Capo Press, 2009)

PROCEDURE: Read *Going to the Doctor* to the children. Dr. T. Berry Brazelton has written this book for children, with the help of his grandson. It is conversational and informative. Encourage children to ask and answer questions. Set up the dramatic play area as a doctor's office. Have the children examine "sick" dolls and/or peers. Be sure to include information on routine procedures, such as immunization and regular checkups, in addition to sick calls.

ACCOMMODATIONS AND INTEGRATION: Encourage children to explore the equipment by having it available for several days. Give children information on different types of medical specialties. Talk about pediatricians, surgeons, ophthalmologists, family practice physicians, and allergists, and how you might need several doctors to handle a particular problem. Include the specialties that are most relevant to your classroom. The doctor's office will probably be a familiar setting because most of the children will have been to the doctor for a checkup. You can expand this activity into a hospital setup, noting the differences. Talk about health and staying healthy as well as illness.

· · · · ·   DRAMATIC PLAY AND THEATER: **SMALL GROUP**

5-28 Shoe Store

GOALS: To perform roles; to play creatively; to increase awareness of roles people play

STANDARDS: TH 2 Act by assuming roles and interacting in improvisations; TH 3 Design by visualizing and arranging environments for classroom dramatizations; R:IT 1 Ask and answer questions about key details in a text.

MATERIALS: Book such as A. Morris, *Shoes, Shoes, Shoes* (New York: HarperCollins, 1998) (100L); shoes for different purposes:

High heeled shoes	flats
Steel-toed shoes	baby shoes
Bedroom slippers	toe shoes
Bowling shoes	flip flops
Hiking boots	boots
Ballet slippers	sandals
Walking shoes	clogs
Baseball shoes with plastic cleats	

PROCEDURE: Read the children *Shoes, Shoes, Shoes*, and show them the photographs of shoes from around the world. Discuss the different shoes and what they might be used for and where they might be from. Set up a shoe store. Discuss the function of shoes and how some shoes are designed for certain situations. Have some examples and talk about how these shoes make certain things easier. Use obvious examples:

steel toes:	won't hurt if something gets dropped on the toes
baseball cleats:	get better traction running, less likely to slip
flip flops:	cool in hot weather

Once children have grasped the idea, have them use the shoe store in dramatic play to choose the shoes they need. Encourage the "buyer" to discuss with the "clerk" the type of shoes needed or the situations in which they will be worn and together try to figure out the best pair. If there is not an appropriate size encourage them to be shopping for someone else. Use the book *Shoes, Shoes, Shoes* as a reference or to expand the selection (these shoes are available in another store or must be ordered).

ACCOMMODATIONS AND INTEGRATION: Have children pair up the different shoes as they become mixed up. Help them compare shoes for differences in color, size, and purpose. Use the concept of shoes to help children think of a variety of ways we can adapt to changing situations. This activity not only teaches the principles of buying and selling but also teaches specialized ways of coping with environments. For children who rely on visual cues, add pictures of the places where the shoes might be used and have children match the shoes to the pictures.

· · · · ·   DRAMATIC PLAY AND THEATER: **SMALL GROUP**

 5-29 Circus

GOALS: To perform roles; to play creatively; to increase awareness of roles people play

STANDARDS: TH 2 Act by assuming roles and interacting in improvisations; TH 3 Design by visualizing and arranging environments for classroom dramatizations; TH 5 Research by finding information to support classroom dramatizations.

MATERIALS: Props for a circus: hats, balance beam, scarves, stuffed animals, costumes, mats; book such as P. Spier, *Peter Spier's Circus* (New York: Dragonfly, 1995).

PROCEDURE: Read *Peter Spier's Circus* to a small group of children. Watch as the circus rolls into town, sets up, has its performance, and leaves. The pictures tell the story more than the words in this book and, although beautifully done, one cannot appreciate the intricate style in a large group. Talk with the children about the performers they see such as the animal trainers, acrobats, tightrope walkers, and so on. Then have a circus in the class. Encourage children to decide how they will organize their circus, how many events they will have, and in what order they will appear, the events themselves, necessary props, and so on. Have children practice their events before putting on the circus.

ACCOMMODATIONS AND INTEGRATION: Include some undemanding acts. Provide children with alternative roles if they are uncomfortable performing, such as handing out tickets. Help other children play organizational roles. Encourage children to develop a program and print it on the computer. This provides an opportunity for children to practice skills of negotiating and participating in a group process that needs a resolution, which includes all children.

• • • • • DRAMATIC PLAY AND THEATER: **SMALL GROUP**

5-30 Shoe Theater

GOALS: To perform roles; to play creatively; to increase awareness of roles people play

STANDARDS: TH 1 Write script by planning and recording improvisations based on personal experience and heritage, imagination, literature, and history; TH 2 Act by assuming roles and interacting in improvisations; TH 4 Direct by planning classroom dramatizations.

MATERIALS: Pairs of shoes and socks (men's, women's, children's, babies')

PROCEDURE: Have the children pretend the socks are puppets. Use one hand for each shoe or sock and have a shoe or sock theater. Once children have become familiar with the experience, suggest scenarios (or have the children agree on one), and encourage children to explore their thoughts and ideas about the topic through the puppets.

ACCOMMODATIONS AND INTEGRATION: Start with easy, obvious roles using familiar items. Help less skillful children find roles that allow them to participate but require less language, such as a visiting pair of shoes or the baby's shoes. Have children develop a script for their play and dictate

it into a tape recorder or write (or have someone write) it down. Encourage them to make props and scenery. Because shoes suggest ideas but no particular theme, this activity encourages creativity. Roles are undefined, so it is easy to include children with varying skill levels. Help children learn about the ways in which plays are different from other types of literature and the many different support roles that people have to produce a play (prompter, set designer, etc.).

SUMMARY

- Creative arts are an integral part of the early childhood curriculum. They provide opportunities for problem solving and develop skills for working in groups.

- Children develop an appreciation for other cultures and more global connections through the arts.

- The arts provide children with lifelong skills as well as a way of learning about themselves and others in an atmosphere of exploration.

EDUCATIONAL RESOURCES

American Orff-Schulwerk Association emphasizes the integration of music throughout the curriculum, including whole language and reading. www.aosa.org/

Best Children's Music provides reviews and commentary on music by age group, including infants and toddlers. You can even listen before you choose to buy something.

Children's Music Web is a nonprofit resource for children, families, and educators; a source for music; and an index of websites related to music for children. www.childrenmusic.org/

The J. Paul Getty Museum provides lesson plans and curriculum ideas. It is particularly useful in helping children analyze art and other experiences. www.getty.edu/education/

Welcome to SFS Kids, the San Francisco Symphony's kids' interactive website, lets kids experiment with rhythm, harmony, composing, and more. www.sfskids.org/templates/splash.asp/

For additional resources, visit the book companion website for this text at www.cengagebrain.com.

6 Infant and Toddler Activities:
Young Infants, Mobile Infants, and Toddlers

Because infants change and grow so quickly, curriculum must adjust to their developmental level. For this reason, activities are designed as prototypes for young infants, mobile infants, and toddlers. Rather than talking about standards for infants and toddlers, most states use the term *early learning guidelines (ELG)* to describe what infants and toddlers should know and be able to do (National Infant and Toddler Child Care Initiative [NITCCI], 2006). The format for the Infant and Toddler Activities is different than it is for older children. Goals are organized by developmental domains rather than academic areas.

ACTIVITY GOALS

Although states have varying numbers of early learning guidelines, the most common ones for infants and toddlers are social and emotional development; language and communication development; cognitive development and general knowledge; physical development and motor skills; and approaches to play and learning (Petersen, Jones, & McGinley, 2008). These early learning designations were used to group activities by goal.

Courtesy of Penny Low Deiner

The targeted age group for each activity is designated: young infants (birth to 9 months), mobile infants (8 to 18 months), and toddlers (16 to 36 months). These overlapping age guidelines emphasize the fluidity of early development. If infants or toddlers are in the younger range or their disability affects a particular area, use activities from a lower age range. If they are in the older range or activities seem too easy, move

into the activities for older children, in Resource Chapters 1 through 5. If an activity is appropriate for a broader age range, the designation includes that information. A birth to 18-month designation would include children from birth to 18 months. All activity areas begin with activities for young infants, then activities for mobile infants, and finally activities for toddlers.

Infant and Toddler Guidelines

Because infants and toddlers have a small repertoire, the accommodations needed can be applied in general to all the listed activities. The following list highlights accommodations. They are more functional than accommodations for older children. The accommodations for regulatory problems relate to children who may later be identified with specific learning disabilities, attention-deficit/hyperactivity disorder, and social, emotional, and behavioral disorders as well as some children on the autism spectrum.

Adapting activities for infants and toddlers with:

Regulatory problems: Detached ❖ Focus on one behavior at a time. Teach body awareness, especially the sensation of tension.

Regulatory problems: Under reactive ❖ Use massage. Direct and redirect children. Actively teach items you might assume others would learn. Use brief, focused lessons. Engage children; model and reinforce appropriate eye contact, facial expressions, and gestures. Model interactions. Use multimodal methods.

Regulatory problems: Hypersensitive ❖ Reduce excess stimuli (light, noise, activity). Be consistent. Teach adaptive skills.

Regulatory problems: Motorically disorganized/impulsive skills ❖ Do a functional behavior assessment if undesirable behaviors continue and they do not respond to traditional guidance. Try reinforcing quiet behavior with a special CD (turn off the CD if the child cries, etc.). Redirect behavior. Give intermittent reinforcement. Work on self-control and self-image.

Regulatory problems: Dysregulated ❖ Ignore inappropriate crying. Reinforce appropriate responses to situations. Be available. Develop a predictable schedule, especially as it relates to sleeping and eating.

Teach infants and toddlers to self-comfort. Use music to set a mood. Gradually increase environmental demands.

Communication disorders ❖ Talk to infants and toddlers. Support all communication. Build language and vocabulary. Help children respond to people and environmental stimuli. Look at communication as social interaction.

English language learners ❖ Support children in developing vocabulary and language in their home language and English. Provide context for language learning. If helpful, use a simple picture communication system for toddlers to show how they are feeling or what they want.

Intellectual disabilities ❖ Use toys that focus cause-effect relationships (shake rattle, it makes noise). Use verbal and physical prompts. Support and enhance a child's capabilities. Model desired behavior. Work toward independence in eating, dressing, and grooming. Use a picture-task analysis.

Gifted and talented ❖ Provide activities with cause–effect relationships. Increase complexity while keeping activities at a developmentally appropriate level (read books with more details). Encourage and support motor skills. Be flexible.

Special health care needs ❖ Normalize the educational setting within the medical aspects of health. Adapt to physical limitation, stamina, and endurance levels by flexible schedules. Learn danger signs and side effects of treatments (appetite loss, mood swings, hair loss, etc.) and develop a plan to deal with these. Have an emergency care plan.

Orthopedic and neurological impairments ❖ Help children move as normally as possible. Work toward symmetry (using both sides of the body equally). Check with a physical or occupational therapist for the best way to position children. Actively promote peer interaction.

Hearing impairments ❖ Use visual and tactile stimulation. Promote the use of auditory aids. Talk to children and use the communication system the family has chosen. Supplement this with pictures and photographs for choices and to support learning tasks.

Visual impairments ❖ Use auditory and tactile stimulation. Promote the use of visual aids. Help children develop appropriate responses to auditory stimulation (look at speaker). Promote social interaction and mobility.

INFANT AND TODDLER ACTIVITIES

• • • • • SOCIAL DEVELOPMENT: **INDIVIDUAL, BIRTH TO 9 MONTHS**

 Anticipation

GOALS: Social and emotional development; approaches to play and learning

MATERIALS: None

PROCEDURE: Before beginning an event such as giving an infant a bottle, picking her up, or changing her, tell the infant what is going to happen. Show the infant the bottle and say, "Are you hungry? I have your bottle ready. Do you want it?" Then pause to give the infant time to respond. (Don't expect her to say "yes"; you are giving her the time and respect to process information rather than just putting the bottle in her mouth.) Before picking up an infant, hold out your arms and say, "I'm going to pick you up." Then pause so the infant can anticipate what will happen. Keep the gestures and words you use

consistent so the infant knows what to expect. Follow through with the action quickly; if you show her the bottle and she responds, then feed her right away; do not wait several minutes. Respond to the infant's cues. If she quiets when approaching her say, "You know I'm going to pick you up." Then do it.

INTEGRATION: As infants learn that their world is predictable, they are willing to wait longer for events to happen because they are developing trust.

• • • • • SOCIAL DEVELOPMENT: **INDIVIDUAL, BIRTH TO 9 MONTHS**

6-2 **Tummy Time**

GOALS: Social and emotional development; physical development and motor skills

MATERIALS: None

PROCEDURE: Tummy time is whenever infants are not on their backs or sitting in seats or other containers. Carrying infants in different ways changes their view of the world and also helps them strengthen needed muscles. As you carry young infants, point out items they can see. Talk or sing to them.

- *Stomach down:* To carry an infant stomach down, place one arm underneath his chest, with the hand supporting his chin and neck. The other arm goes around his entire body.

- *Back to front vertical:* Pick up the infant so his back is toward your front. Carry him in a vertical position so his head is up and he is looking out. For young babies, keep their head centered as you hold them. As infants get older, have them put their arms out and pretend to fly. As a variation, put one arm under the infant to make a seat and the other arm around his middle for support.

- *Back to front horizontal:* Pick up the infant so his back is toward your front. Carry him in a horizontal position with his head in the elbow of your right arm as he is looking out. Your right arm goes under his head and your left arm goes between his legs to hold the infant's side. Your hands will meet in front.

INTEGRATION: Tummy time is adaptable, and infants need to spend more time actively moving. Carrying them in different positions gives them the opportunity to increase muscular strength. Lack of tummy time may lead to flat areas on the back of the head, muscles that are tight or weak on one side of the neck, and delayed motor skills. By age 2 to 3 months, infants should accumulate at least 30 minutes of tummy time each day.

• • • • • SOCIAL DEVELOPMENT: **INDIVIDUAL, 8 TO 18 MONTHS**

 My Book about Me

GOALS: Social and emotional development; language and communication development

MATERIALS: Plastic sleeve covers, three-ring binders, markers, digital or regular camera, photographs of the infant, construction paper, paste

TO MAKE: *Take photographs of the infant doing various activities throughout the day. Print them or have them developed. Cut construction paper or posterboard into 8½ × 11-inch pieces so that each fits the plastic sleeve cover. Paste the pictures of the infant on both sides of the construction paper and put each page in a plastic sleeve. Make a beginning page to identify the infant's book. Place in a three-ring binder. Pictures can also be laminated or covered with clear contact paper.*

PROCEDURE: With the infant on your lap, look through the book with her and talk about each picture, what she is doing, and how wonderful she is. For younger infants, keep the book short and, if possible, have the pictures of the child alone doing everyday things (eating, sleeping, playing, etc.). As children get older, have more pictures in the book with a wider range of events, or make several shorter, more specific books such as "Shalini at Home," "Shalini at School," "Shalini Playing with Her Friends."

INTEGRATION: Infants enjoy looking at these books. Take pictures of infants at school or ask parents to send in pictures, whichever is most appropriate. A digital camera makes it easy to add to books as infants change and grow. Photographs can also be used for assessment and to document developmental milestones.

· · · · ·   SOCIAL DEVELOPMENT: **INDIVIDUAL, 8 TO 18 MONTHS**

6-4 Cups and Spoons

GOALS: Social and emotional development; physical development and motor skills; approaches to play and learning

MATERIALS: A variety of plastic cups with handles, plastic spoons

PROCEDURE: Place the infant in a highchair and place a cup and spoon on the tray. Encourage the infant to explore each item. Demonstrate how you can use the spoon to hit the cup or to stir, and then give the item back to the infant. Encourage him to pick up the cup with the handle and pretend to drink from it or eat with the spoon. Repeat this using a slightly different cup. For younger infants, introduce the cup and spoon separately before pairing them. As infants gain experience, give them several different cups and spoons to play with at the same time.

INTEGRATION: It is useful for infants to have experience playing with and exploring the properties of cups and spoons before they use them to eat and drink.

· · · · ·   SOCIAL DEVELOPMENT: **SMALL GROUP, 16 TO 36 MONTHS**

6-5 Dolls

GOALS: Social and emotional development; language and communication development; approaches to play and learning

MATERIALS: Multiethnic dolls

PROCEDURE: Encourage toddlers to explore the dolls by gently feeling the dolls' hair, eyes, and clothing, and moving body parts. Name body parts and clothing for toddlers. Encourage them to play with dolls in different ways. Toddlers may want to carry, cuddle, bottle-feed, sing to, or rock the doll. When they are ready, introduce new ways of playing with the doll. Encourage two children to play together and talk about what each is doing and why. Encourage them to think about what the doll baby might want or need. See whether toddlers can imitate skills that are more difficult: pretending to feed with a spoon, sprinkling powder or rubbing lotion on body parts, and combing the doll's hair. Help toddlers use their imagination with the doll. They can take the doll for a walk in a wagon or stroller or wash the baby in a small tub, using soap and a washcloth, and then dry the doll with a towel. Help children develop adaptive skills by practicing undressing and dressing not only themselves but also a doll.

INTEGRATION: Teach children caregiving skills. They are often more willing to practice adaptive skills in play.

· · · · ·   SOCIAL DEVELOPMENT: **SMALL GROUP, 16 TO 36 MONTHS**

6-6 Washing Dishes

GOALS: Social and emotional development; physical development and motor skills; language and communication development

MATERIALS: Plastic dishes, basin, water (lukewarm)

PROCEDURE: Put the dishes in the basin and have toddlers explore the dishes. Encourage them to put the dishes in the basin, swish the water, and take them out. Talk about their actions. Ask them questions. Have at least two basins so that children can interact. Say "out" as you take a dish out and "in" as you put the dishes in. Physically guide the child's hand, if needed. Say, "Good, you took it out!" Fill the basin with a small amount of water and add a small amount of soap. Let children "wash" dishes. Add a sponge or handled scrubber for them to wash dishes. Have several towels available to dry dishes. Encourage appropriate actions, that is, placing cups on saucers, pouring, and stirring the water in the cup with a spoon. Have children sort utensils in a storage unit. Encourage them to match items by shape. Have children set the table and use dishes to serve snack.

INTEGRATION: Toddlers enjoy pretending with familiar objects. The lukewarm water is soothing.

· · · · ·   LANGUAGE DEVELOPMENT: **INDIVIDUAL, BIRTH TO 9 MONTHS**

6-7 Talking Walk

GOALS: Language and communication development; cognitive development and general knowledge

MATERIALS: None

PROCEDURE: Pick the infant up and hold him so he can see over your shoulder. Walk around the room and point out objects and events that are taking place and what other infants and toddlers are doing. "That's the telephone. Sometimes it rings and I talk to people on it. There is Roxanna; she is playing with Dot. This is one of my favorite pictures. Aura painted it. See the beautiful red she used?" For younger infants, make the walk shorter and talk less. Use items that the infant is familiar with, and start out with what she knows, like her own coat; then let her touch it. As you continue, use disparate items such as a book; allow her to touch this also. Only label one or two items and then stop. With older infants label more items and talk about their function. Encourage the infant to touch the items and try to imitate what you say. Vary what you say to include "What is that?" Wait a few seconds and then say something like "Those are Nathan's boots!" In this example, you would use similar items such as sneakers, boots, slippers, and shoes to make

Carrying infants in different ways and talking to them about what they are seeing supports learning in young infants.
Courtesy of Penny Low Deiner

it more difficult, and perhaps talk about the properties of footgear and why they are different.

INTEGRATION: Infants need to learn about and feel comfortable in their environment. The view from your shoulder is very different from their view from the floor, so it is important they see this too. Although infants will not understand all the words you use, they will hear the different tones of your voice and begin to make associations, especially if you demonstrate what the objects do.

• • • • •   LANGUAGE DEVELOPMENT: **INDIVIDUAL, BIRTH TO 9 MONTHS**

6-8   Signs

GOALS: Language and communication development; cognitive development and general knowledge

MATERIALS: None

PROCEDURE: Look at the sign language sign for *more*. Learn how to do the sign so you feel comfortable teaching infants the sign. Show the infant the sign for *more* during an activity or feeding when you want to know whether the infant wants more. Use the sign for *more* before or during feeding and show the infant the sign every time you feed her. Consistency is key. Use the sign for *more* until the infant begins to sign back to you. Once an infant knows the sign *more*, begin to add additional signs.

INTEGRATION: Infants can control their hands before they can talk. Being able to give adults feedback about their needs helps everyone. Having all children learn useful signs is particularly helpful for infants with developmental delays, hearing impairments, and English language learners. The more signs they learn, the earlier they can communicate.

• • • • •   LANGUAGE DEVELOPMENT: **INDIVIDUAL, 8 TO 18 MONTHS**

6-9   My Active Activity Book

GOALS: Language and communication development; physical development and motor skills

MATERIALS: Three-hole plastic sleeves, markers, a digital camera or camera with film, photographs of mobile infants being active, construction paper or poster board, paste, three-hole binders (optional)

TO MAKE: *Take photographs of mobile infants engaged in active activities throughout several days. Some examples are crawling, rolling, walking, dancing, clapping, and so on. Print the photographs or have them developed. Cut construction paper or poster board into 8½ × 11-inch pieces so each fits inside the plastic sleeve. Paste the photographs of the mobile infants on both side of the construction paper (one or two per side), and put each page into a separate sleeve. Make a name page to identify the mobile infant, and fasten them together with yarn or place them in a three-hole binder. Add photographs as mobile infants learn new skills.*

PROCEDURE: Place the mobile infant on your lap or sit beside him. Look through the book with him and talk about each photograph and what he is doing, how important physical activity is in making him strong and healthy and how wonderful he is. After reading the book, encourage him to move like some of the photographs. If time has passed, point out how much farther or faster he can move now. Encourage him to see how far he can walk or run and for how long.

INTEGRATION: "Book babble" is an important preliteracy skill. Mobile infants jabber in a tone and pattern that sounds like reading if they have been read to. They are practicing language in a new and different way. In addition to literacy, this encourages mobile infants to practice emerging skills. Practice helps the mobile infants' efficiency and coordination. Although you do not need to teach mobile infants to move, movement opportunities enhance the ongoing maturation of motor pathways in the infant's brain and spinal cord.

· · · · · LANGUAGE DEVELOPMENT: **INDIVIDUAL, 8 TO 18 MONTHS**

6-10 Nursery Rhymes and Chants

GOALS: Language and communication development; physical development and motor skills; cognitive development and general knowledge

MATERIALS: Books with simple nursery rhymes such as "I'm a Little Teapot," "This Little Piggy," "Baa, Baa, Black Sheep," "Hickory Dickory Dock," and so on

PROCEDURE: Read, chant, or sing nursery rhymes as you turn the pages of the books with a mobile infant. Use the books frequently so infants continue to hear the rhymes and chants. Add silly rhymes and ones in which you play the leader and the children follow your actions such as

>   Up to the ceiling (raise hands up)
>   Down to the floor (put hands down)
>   Left to the window (point left with left hand)
>   Right to the door (point right with right hand)
>   This is my right hand (wave it vigorously)
>   Raise it up high (raise right hand and stretch)
>   This is my left hand (wave it vigorously)
>   Reach for the sky (raise left hand up, keep right up and stretch)
>   Right hand, left hand (wave both hands)
>   Twirl them around (twirl hands over one another)
>   Left hand, right hand (keep twirling)
>   Pound, pound, pound (reach down and pound the ground)

Do not expect mobile infants to know their right hand from their left; it is the motion and rhyme that is important. Make up motions to songs, and continue to pair language and movement.

INTEGRATION: Do not expect mobile infants to follow the directions as they are given. Mobile infants can increase their physical activity by acting out imaginative nursery rhymes and chants. They can develop creativity and language while increasing their activity level. When songs or rhymes with actions are done in a series they help build endurance and increase brain activity.

· · · · · LANGUAGE DEVELOPMENT: **INDIVIDUAL OR SMALL GROUP, 16 TO 36 MONTHS**

6-11 Puppets

GOALS: Language and communication development; cognitive development and general knowledge; approaches to play and learning

MATERIALS: Duck or bunny hand puppets (or other animal puppets)

PROCEDURE: With the puppet on your hand, talk to the toddler and encourage the toddler to talk with the duck or bunny: "I'm a duck. I say, 'Quack, quack.'" Encourage the toddler to imitate sounds, words, or actions. Then let the toddler experiment with putting the puppet on her hand. Use the puppet to have a "conversation" with the toddler. Give the toddler time to respond.

INTEGRATION: Talking with puppets encourages peer interaction as well as fostering language development. Simple puppets that use whole-hand movements are best at this age.

· · · · · LANGUAGE DEVELOPMENT: **INDIVIDUAL OR SMALL GROUP, 16 TO 36 MONTHS**

6-12 Dressing Book

GOALS: Language and communication; physical development and motor skills; cognitive development and general knowledge

MATERIALS: A book about dressing such as M. Chodos-Irvine, *Ella Sara Gets Dressed* (New York: Harcourt Children's Books, 2003)

PROCEDURE: Begin by using children's clothing, and ask toddlers to point to the part of themselves that the clothing would cover. If necessary, give them a choice. Then point to the picture and back to the clothing as you name each piece. Name and point to the articles of clothing. Ask the toddler to point to the correct picture as you name each article. Then ask him to name the article of clothing shown in the picture, and find the piece of clothing if he is wearing that article. Encourage toddlers to "read" the book to you. Then ask them to show you where each article goes, for instance: "Where do the shoes go? Yes, that's right! Shoes go on your feet!" If using *Ella Sara Gets Dressed*, also talk with children about what they want to wear and what happens when they disagree with adults on this topic.

INTEGRATION: This activity fosters adaptive behavior as well as language development. There is no expectation that toddlers will dress themselves, but rather that their awareness is increased and that they frame these experiences as positive.

• • • • • COGNITIVE DEVELOPMENT: **INDIVIDUAL, BIRTH TO 9 MONTHS**

6-13 Scrunchies

GOALS: Cognitive development and general knowledge; physical development and motor skills

MATERIALS: Brightly colored scrunchies (what women use to hold ponytails) or commercially available baby wrist and ankle elastics

PROCEDURE: Put scrunchies around the infant's wrists or ankles. Point these out to the infant by holding the infant's hand and saying, "Look at you, this hand looks great!" Check to see whether the infant's eyes focus on the hand (or on the scrunchy). For young infants use scrunchies made out of black-and-white striped or highly contrast-ing, patterned materials. Securely attach a large bell to a scrunchy or circle of elastic that can go over the baby's feet. Encourage the infant to bring her hands or feet to her mouth. Help her focus on the scrunchies for longer periods of time.

INTEGRATION: Infants need to become aware of and ex-plore their own bodies before they can reach and grasp objects. Brightly colored or striped socks also call infants' attention to their feet. *Note:* Adding a bell for sound provides an additional stimulus. It is a safety hazard if it is small enough to be swallowed. Use a large bell, attach it securely, check it regularly, and use it only under adult supervision.

• • • • • COGNITIVE DEVELOPMENT: **INDIVIDUAL, BIRTH TO 9 MONTHS**

6-14 Infant Massage

GOALS: Cognitive development and general knowledge; social and emotional development; physical development and motor skills

MATERIALS: Lotion, changing table, floor, couch, or bed

PROCEDURE: Place the infant on a changing table or other surface. Undress the infant to a diaper or onesie (be sure it is warm enough). Place some lotion in one hand to warm it, and then put the lotion on the infant's body. As you massage the infant's body with the lotion, talk to the infant about his body. "Adolfo, now I'm going up and down your arm. Let's check out that hand. You've got five fingers. I'm going to count them. One, two, three, four—oh! Actually this one is a thumb." Continue to talk to the infant as you massage his body. Just do one area of the infant's body such as the arms or legs. As infants respond, talk in more detail about what you are doing.

INTEGRATION: Massaging the infant's body increases body awareness. It is also good for relaxation and for establishing closeness between infants and their care-givers. Occupational therapists often use massage with

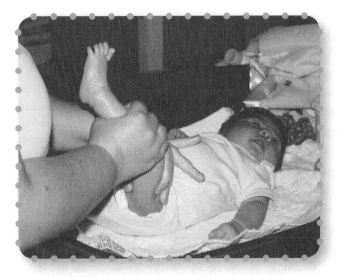

Infant massge increases body awareness and establishes a close, trusting relationship between the infant and her caregiver.
Courtesy of Penny Low Deiner

children to increase awareness before performing skills (a hand massage before doing fine motor skills). It can also be used to decrease tension in muscles for children with high muscle tone. Talk to occupational therapists about how to use massage to benefit the infants you are working with. *Note:* Talk with parents about infant massage. Some parents are very comfortable with your massaging their infants, whereas others may not be as comfortable. Support parents in learning about infant massage and encourage them to do it at home if they do not wish to have it done in the classroom. Some parents find massage to be a very personal thing, so check with them first.

• • • • • COGNITIVE DEVELOPMENT: **INDIVIDUAL, 8 TO 18 MONTHS**

6-15 Hidden Toys

GOALS: Cognitive development and general knowledge; social and emotional development

MATERIALS: A small toy, several cloths

PROCEDURE: Get the infant intrigued with a toy. Then cover the toy completely with cloth and say, "Oh, where did it go?" Encourage the infant to find it. Start by partly covering the toy with cloth. If the infant does not attempt to get it, point to the toy and again encourage her. If she still does not find it, take the cloth off dramatically and say, "Here it is!" If the infant is willing, play the game again. If the infant easily finds the toy, hide it first under one cloth, and then move it to another, covering the toy completely. Initially, expect that the infant will hunt under the first cloth and then go to the second.

INTEGRATION: Activities such as these help infants develop the concept of object permanence. Play peek-a-boo and other games that focus on hiding and finding as well.

· · · · ·   COGNITIVE DEVELOPMENT: **INDIVIDUAL, 8 TO 18 MONTHS**

6-16   Mimic

GOALS: Cognitive development and general knowledge; language and communication development

MATERIALS: Three vegetables of different colors (e.g., broccoli, carrots, and mushrooms), steamed for about 10 minutes and cut into very small pieces; plates; Note: Check for food allergies.

PROCEDURE: A serving size for a mobile infant is approximately 2 tablespoons. Put each color of vegetable on a small plate and encourage mobile infants to pass the plate (with your help) and choose a piece(s) of vegetable to put on their plate (or make individual plates, but mobile infants are more likely to try things if they can choose). Eat with the mobile infants and talk about the vegetables and how you enjoy them. Help them learn the names of the foods they are eating.

INTEGRATION: Provide a similar snack with fruit. Mobile infants are just learning healthy eating habits. Nutrient-dense age-appropriate foods for snack include fruit, vegetables, cheese, yogurt, and water. Juice has too much sugar. Making eating a social experiences helps all mobile infants see others eating and choosing.

· · · · ·   COGNITIVE DEVELOPMENT: **INDIVIDUAL, 16 TO 36 MONTHS**

6-17   Shape Sorter

GOALS: Cognitive development and general knowledge; physical development and motor skills

MATERIALS: Shape sorter

PROCEDURE: Present the toy to the child and encourage the toddler to lift the top off, remove the shapes, and then replace the top. Encourage them to place the shapes in appropriate holes. If needed, demonstrate how the shapes fit into the holes. If this is difficult, have toddlers put in and take out the shapes without the lid. Then cover one or two spaces with your hand or a piece of cardboard or tape, so children have fewer choices. As toddlers become more skillful, use a shape sorter with more shapes, name the shapes, and ask toddlers to put in the shapes you name.

INTEGRATION: Help toddlers learn about the shapes in their environment. Play games looking for round, square, or triangular shapes in the room. Use form boards.

· · · · ·   COGNITIVE DEVELOPMENT: **DEVELOPMENT: INDIVIDUAL, 16 TO 36 MONTHS**

6-18   Big or Little

GOALS: Cognitive development and general knowledge; physical development and motor skills

MATERIALS: Objects that are large and small such as dolls, books, cars, blocks, shoes, and two containers

PROCEDURE: Put out the two containers and the objects to be sorted. Start with just one type of object: shoes. Tell the child to put all the big shoes in one container and the little shoes in another. Coach the child by asking each time for information about size and the appropriate container. If necessary, work only on identification skills and omit the sorting. Show the child a shoe and say, "Is this big or little?" When the child correctly identifies it, have her put it in the appropriate container. If the child forgets which container is for big, remind him to look at the shoes already in the container. Have toddlers sort two types of objects, such as shoes and cars, into two containers. See whether toddlers can find additional ways to sort the objects (shoes by type, cars by color, etc.).

INTEGRATION: Classification concepts are the foundation for many later skills. Young toddlers may only be interested in putting objects in and taking them out of the can.

· · · · ·   SENSORY MOTOR DEVELOPMENT: **INDIVIDUAL, BIRTH TO 9 MONTHS**

6-19   Keys

GOALS: Physical development and motor skills; cognitive development and general knowledge

MATERIALS: Plastic keys or other small toy

PROCEDURE: Call the infant's name and shake keys. Gently place the keys in her hand. Help her mouth, look at, or shake the keys, if necessary. Keep the keys close to the midline. Then offer keys for her to reach and grasp from different angles (up, down, right, left). Have her reach across her midline to get the keys. (This can be encouraged by having the child hold a toy in one hand while you offer the keys.) Increase the distance the keys are from the infant so that it is a long reach. Put the keys out of the infant's field of vision and call, "Get the keys," so she has to turn and reach.

INTEGRATION: Any small toy that intrigues the infant can be used. Reaching across her midline helps the sides of an infant's brain communicate with each other.

· · · · ·   SENSORY MOTOR DEVELOPMENT: **INDIVIDUAL, BIRTH TO 9 MONTHS**

6-20   Yoga for Infants

GOALS: Physical development and motor skills; cognitive development and general knowledge

MATERIALS: None

PROCEDURE: Lie down on the floor (or a bed or couch) with your legs bent. Place the infant on your bent legs, facing you. Smile and talk to her and tell her what you will be doing. Gently take her right arm and move it across her body to her left waist. Hold it for about five seconds and then return it to her side. Do the same thing with the left arm and then the legs. As you are doing this activity, keep saying things like "I'm moving your arm. I'll take it across your body and touch your waist. Doesn't that stretch feel good?"

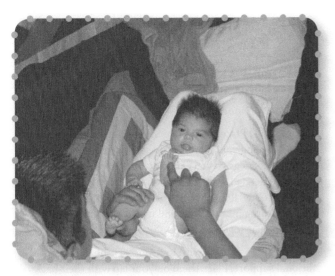

The cross lateral movements in yoga help the sides of the brain communicate with each others. In some cultures yoga-type movements are an expected part of child rearing.
Courtesy of Penny Low Deiner

For variation, place the infant supine on a mat or blanket. Place one hand on each of the infant's legs and gently lift the legs up and bring them toward the infant's chest. Hold this pose for 5 seconds, then slowly put the infant's legs back down to the floor. Repeat this several times. And keep talking.

INTEGRATION: Cross-lateral movements require the two hemispheres of the brain to work together. When infants do movements that cross the midline of the body, such as reaching the right arm to the left leg, these brain communications increase. Yoga can help infants sleep, improve digestion, ease gas pains and colic, stimulate neuromuscular development, and boost the immune system. It is a great way to teach body awareness.

• • • • •   SENSORY MOTOR DEVELOPMENT: **INDIVIDUAL, 8 TO 18 MONTHS**

 Grab It

GOALS: Physical development and motor skills; cognitive development and general knowledge

MATERIALS: A variety of small blocks of different sizes

PROCEDURE: With the child in a sitting position, hold a small block just outside of the infant's reach and see whether he will reach for it. If not, place the block closer to the infant's midline or preferred hand, if established. If the infant takes the block, offer a second and then a third to see what he does. Vary where you place the block for reaching. Sometimes place it close to the center of the infant's body, sometimes more to the right or left so he has to maintain balance while reaching. Give the infant two blocks and keep two matching blocks. Clap them together or bang them and see whether the infant will imitate you.

INTEGRATION: Some children need to be encouraged to reach, grasp, and imitate.

• • • • •   SENSORY MOTOR SKILLS: **INDIVIDUAL, 8 TO 18 MONTHS**

 Variations on Push and Pull

GOALS: Physical development and motor skills; cognitive development and general knowledge

MATERIALS: A variety of push and pull toys

PROCEDURE: First allow the infant to explore the toy and then roll the toy slightly out of his reach. Encourage him to crawl after the toy. As he reaches it, push it a little farther, then encourage him to push it rather than retrieve it. (Don't do this to the point where he is frustrated.) Help push the toy in front of the infant. Move it slowly so he can crawl after it. Choose toys that move slowly with a small push, and encourage the infant to follow the toy as quickly as he can. When he understands about pushing toys, introduce toys that can be pulled as well. When the infant is comfortable using push and pull toys, encourage him to push or pull them to a specific location.

INTEGRATION: Use push toys before pull toys. Some pull toys are a challenge to beginning walkers, as the child must concentrate on holding onto the toy, know where the toy is relative to where he is, and walk at the same time.

• • • • •   SENSORY MOTOR DEVELOPMENT: **SMALL GROUP, 16 TO 36 MONTHS**

 **Moving Like the Animals**

GOALS: Physical development and motor skills; language and communication development

MATERIALS: Pictures of familiar animals

PROCEDURE: See whether toddlers can identify the animals in the picture. Help them decide whether the animals are large or small and how they move. Have the children move as they think the animal would move. As toddlers become more proficient, choose less familiar animals with obvious movement patterns. Talk about animals and where they live.

INTEGRATION: This activity helps children learn more about the world in which they live and even think about it differently.

• • • • •   SENSORY MOTOR DEVELOPMENT: **INDIVIDUAL OR SMALL GROUP, 16 TO 36 MONTHS**

 Dump and Fill

GOALS: Physical development and motor skills; cognitive development and general knowledge

MATERIALS: Dishpans, rice, oatmeal, beans, plastic measuring cups, measuring spoons

PROCEDURE: Put about 2 inches of rice, oatmeal, or beans in a dishpan. Add a variety of cups and spoons. If necessary, place children's hands in the container and help them explore the medium. Encourage them to fill the container using their hands and dump it. Have toddlers dump the contents from one container into another.

INTEGRATION: This activity is a precursor to pouring liquids, but far less messy. It has the potential for simple exploration as well as for building concepts about measurement and size. With older children, do not use edible products, but with infants and toddlers do, as they may taste the materials they use.

· · · · ·   APPROACHES TO LEARNING: **INDIVIDUAL, BIRTH TO 9 MONTHS**

 Touching Songs

GOALS: Approaches to play and learning; social and emotional development; physical development and motor skills

MATERIALS: None

PROCEDURE: Sing or chant songs or rhymes when you touch the infant, such as "This little piggy went to market," "I'm going to get your nose," and "Hickory Dickory Dock." Sing or hum a song while you hold the infant and move her to the rhythm of the song such as "Rock-a-Bye Baby." Help her do the motions to songs or rhymes like "Pat-a-Cake" or "Johnny Hammers with One Hammer" by holding her on your lap and gently moving her body.

INTEGRATION: Infants learn to feel secure through close sensitive contact. They also need to have their imagination and creativity "tickled."

· · · · ·   APPROACHES TO LEARNING: **INDIVIDUAL, BIRTH TO 9 MONTHS**

6-26   Textured Mat

GOALS: Approaches to play and learning; physical development and motor skills

MATERIALS: Mats made of various materials (satin, cotton, fake fur, velvet, terry cloth, Lycra, knit fabric, suede, leather-like, etc.) (commercially available)

TO MAKE: *Squares of various materials sewn together; nine squares of 12 inches each makes a good size mat (36" × 36")*

PROCEDURE: Place the infant prone on the mat. If it is warm enough, have him in diapers. Take a corner of the mat and stroke his hand with it and talk with him about the texture of the material and how it feels. Talk about how the squares are different in color, pattern, and texture. Discuss how they look and feel. Place him in different positions on the mat so it is easier to reach other textures.

INTEGRATION: Some infants might not like some of the textures, so go gently, using smooth, soft textures first. Gently rub one piece of fabric on his arm and talk about how it looks and feels. Help him persist in a prone position and support his exploration of the fabrics. As infants become older, they can use 6-inch fabric squares to explore by themselves.

· · · · ·   APPROACHES TO LEARNING: **INDIVIDUAL, 8 TO 18 MONTHS**

 Row, Row, Row Your Boat

GOALS: Approaches to play and learning; physical development and motor skills

MATERIALS: None

PROCEDURE: Place the mobile infant in an upright sitting position facing you. Place her so she is sitting between your outstretched legs so you can provide her with support for sitting, if needed. Take her hands in yours and begin singing "Row, Row, Row Your Boat." As you sing, rock back and forth with the infant—this will feel like you are actually rowing a boat together.

INTEGRATION: Infants with low muscle tone may need additional support. Place them on your lap with their back toward your front. Extend your hands and theirs, and gently rock back and forth. For infants who want more activity, row more vigorously and make some variations such as "Row, row, row your boat quickly down the stream, faster, faster, faster now until we catch your dream." "Row, row, row your boat underneath the stream, ha, ha, fooled you all, I'm a submarine." Support children's joy and delight in learning as you vary what you do.

· · · · ·   APPROACHES TO LEARNING: **SMALL GROUP, 8 TO 36 MONTHS**

 Dancing

GOALS: Approaches to play and learning; physical development and motor skills

MATERIALS: CD player and CDs

PROCEDURE: Play music for toddlers to dance to in their own ways. Use many different types of music. If toddlers do not dance, dance with them or pair them with other toddlers who have the idea. Focus toddlers' attention by talking about the beat and the concepts of fast and slow before they begin to dance. Add scarves and other props. Talk about the beat as you move to it.

INTEGRATION: Moving to music is a lifelong skill. Clap the beat dramatically so toddlers will have visual clues as well. Use music from many cultures, and encourage children to move to the beat.

· · · · ·   APPROACHES TO LEARNING: **INDIVIDUAL OR SMALL GROUP, 16 TO 36 MONTHS**

 Painting with Water

GOALS: Approaches to play and learning; physical development and motor skills

MATERIALS: 1- and 2-inch paintbrushes, buckets, water

PROCEDURE: On a warm day, fill buckets with water and encourage toddlers to paint the sidewalk or building.

Encourage them to draw faces or pictures, and then watch as the sun makes them disappear.

INTEGRATION: This is a clean painting activity. Toddlers are free and encouraged to experiment with the water and brush.

· · · · · APPROACHES TO LEARNING: **SMALL GROUP, 16 TO 36 MONTHS**

6-30 *Big Pictures*

GOALS: Approaches to play and learning; social and emotional development

MATERIALS: Large sheet of newsprint, water-based markers, large crayons, large chalk

PROCEDURE: Cover a table with paper and tape it down. Be sure each toddler has space to draw with markers, crayons, and chalk while encouraging him to be part of a group. Make the picture have a theme and have the toddlers' scribble something related to that theme. If toddlers desire, label the scribble and write what they say about it.

INTEGRATION: Leave the paper out long enough so toddlers can leave and come back. Young toddlers often leave an activity and return to it later.

SUMMARY

- Infants change and grow rapidly, and educators adapt the curriculum and activities to their needs.
- Young infants (birth to 9 months) have such a small repertoire of behaviors that variations on experiences predominate.
- Mobile infants (8 to 18 months) reach major developmental milestones, and activities focus on moving and the development of language.
- Toddlers (16 to 36 months) are predictably mobile and experience bursts of cognitive and language growth.
- Experiences and activities are designed to meet developmental needs.

EDUCATIONAL RESOURCES

Brazelton Touchpoints Center provides skills and strategies for educators to build alliances with parents of children from birth to age 3. The Touchpoints framework focuses on key points in the development of infants, toddlers, and their families. www.touchpoints.org/

Clearinghouse on Early Education and Parenting (CEEP) is part of the Early Childhood and Parenting (ECAP) Collaborative at the University of Illinois at Champaign-Urbana. CEEP provides publications and information to the worldwide early childhood and parenting communities. http://ceep.crc.uiuc.edu/index.html/

Early Head Start National Resource Center at Zero to Three has information about Early Head Start as well as ideas for teaching young infants, mobile infants, and toddlers. Their goal is to share knowledge with infant-toddler teachers and home visitors. www.ehsnrc.org/

Healthy Child Care America (HCCA) has resources for parents and early childhood educators. Launched in 1995, HCCA seeks to maximize the health, safety, well-being, and developmental potential of all children through quality child care and by ensuring children have a medical home. www.healthychildcare.org/

High/Scope Educational Research Foundation supports an infant-toddler curriculum based on direct hands-on experiences with people, objects, events, and ideas, and on developing long-term, trusting relationships with caregivers who scaffold learning. www.highscope.org/Content.asp?ContentId=62/

Mind in the Making, is a collaborative effort that supports the science of early learning through print and multimedia. www.mindinthemaking.org/

Mother Goose Programs for Children's Education and Preschool Reading, the Vermont Center for the Book, has an extensive list of books for infants, toddlers, and other literacy materials. www.mothergooseprograms.org/literacy_book_lists.php/

National Infant & Toddler Child Care Initiative is designed to support the Child Care Development Fund (CCDF) to improve infant and toddler child care. It is located at Zero to Three. http://nitcci.nccic.acf.hhs.gov/index.htm/

Teaching Strategies, Inc., offers curriculum resources, training manuals, and parent resource booklets related to infant and toddler care, including the *Creative Curriculum for Infants and Toddlers*, which emphasizes the importance of early learning in the context of relationships. *Creative Curriculum* is also available for family child care, with a focus on strategies to provide age-appropriate experiences for mixed-age groups of children, including infants and toddlers. www.teachingstrategies.com/

Zero to Three provides information on brain development, learning during everyday routines, the developmental assessment process, parenting tips, professional journal articles, policy briefs, A–Z topic listings, a search engine, and a list of Spanish materials. www.zerotothree.org/

For additional resources, visit the book companion website for this text at www.cengagebrain.com.

Children's Bibliography

The Children's Bibliography supports the topics in the text, focusing on those that relate directly to children with disabilities and their families. The topic and total number of books in that topic are given at the beginning of each section. There are a total of 385 annotated books that are either annotated here or can be accessed in the online companion at www.cengagebrain.com.

The Children's Bibliography is arranged by topic. The first section supports the topics covered by Part I of the book. These children's books focus on different types of families, family relationships, cultural diversity, and challenges that are faced by the children you will teach. The remainder of the children's bibliography supports Part II of the book and is arranged in the same order as the chapters. Like the disabilities themselves, some topics overlap, so scan several areas to find potential books. The age range of each book is given in parentheses. The final section of the Children's Bibliography is devoted to Educational Resources that will help you find good sources for additional books. The additional books and Educational Resources can be accessed at www.cengagebrain.com.

Contents by Topic:

FAMILIES AND CHILDREN AND CULTURE

Ajmera, M., & Kinkade, S. (2010). *Our Grandparents: A Global Album.* (Watertown, MA: Charlesbridge Publishing).

    (3–8) Focuses on intergenerational relationships between children and grandparents around the globe.

Konrad, M. S. (2010). *I Like to Play.* (Plattsburg, NY: Tundra Books).

    (3–6) Photographs show the way children play around the world.

Bunton, M. C. (2011). *The Little Maestro.* (Tamarac, FL: Llumina Kids).

    (4–8) The little maestro is a boy who was born in the rainforest and is determined to save it from destruction. He brings harmony to the plants and animals, and music to the forest. The information in the book is scientifically accurate.

Laínez, R. C. (2010). *From North to South/Del Norte al Sur.* (San Francisco, CA: Children's Book Press).

    (6–8) José visits his mother in Mexico after she is deported for not having the proper papers. Bilingual in English and Spanish.

Barasch, L. (2009). *First Come the Zebra.* (New York: Lee and Low Books).

    (4–8) The story of two young Kenyan boys, one Masai and one Kikuyu, who overcome traditional rivalries as they rescue a straying toddler. They take a step toward peace when they decide to trade veggies for milk and introduce their families.

Cheng, A. (2010). *Only One Year.* (New York: Lee and Low Books).

    (4–8) Sharon's 2-year-old brother DiDi is being taken to China to spend a year with their grandparents. At first it is difficult, but as the year passes she thinks of him less. When he returns, it is as if a stranger entered her life. The children sort out their relationship.

Moroney, L., & Ata, T. (2006). *Baby Rattlesnake.* (San Francisco, CA: Children's Book Press).

    (6–8) A Pawnee tale of a baby rattlesnake who wants a rattle and then misuses it. He learns an important lesson, and his forgiving family gives him big hugs. Available in English only or bilingual in English and Spanish.

Bunting, E. (2001). *Dandelions.* (London: Sandpiper).

    (4–8) The story of a pioneer father who moves his pregnant wife and daughters to Nebraska in the 1800s. They plant dandelions on the roof of their sod house to try to lift their mother's depression and to make the prairie come to life.

Herman, C. (2010). *First Rain.* (Morton Grove, IL: Albert Whitman).

    (6–8) Abby and her parents have moved to Israel, but Abby misses her grandma. In the letters and emails they exchange, Abby tells her grandmother about her new experiences. After the long dry summer, the first rain comes and with it something even more wonderful.

Khan, H. (2008). *Night of the Moon: A Muslim Holiday Story.* (San Francisco, CA: Chronicle Books).

    (4–8) Yasmeen, a 7-year-old Pakistani American girl celebrates Ramadan. Her mother explains the Islamic calendar, and Yasmeen shares with her class the details of her holiday. The book focuses on the celebratory aspects of the holiday rather than the religious ones.

Hopkins, L. B. (2010). *Amazing Faces.* (New York: Lee and Low Books).

    (4–8) Our faces mirror our emotions. Sixteen poems are brought to life by the diverse and detailed faces that reflect the experiences and lives of a diverse society.

DIFFERENT TYPES OF FAMILIES AND THEIR CHILDREN

Levins, S. (2009). *Do You Sing Twinkle? A Story about Remarriage and New Family.* (Washington, DC: Magination Press).

    (4–8) Told from a boy's point of view, it addresses issues relating to remarriage and joint custody.

González, R. (2005). *Antonio's Card/La Tarjeta de Antonio.* (San Francisco, CA: Children's Book Press).

    (6–8) Antonio wants to make a great Mother's Day card for his mother and her partner Leslie. His classmates make fun of Leslie and he must choose whether—or how—to show his love for his family. Bilingual in English and Spanish.

Cervellini-Calfo, C. (2008). *When Mommy Loses Her Hair: It Means the Medicine Is Working.* (Charleston, SC: BookSurge Publishing).

    (4–8) Four-year-old Tony overhears his parents talking about his mommy's cancer. With the help of his parents Tony learns about steps in treating cancer and how a child can help.

Gerdner, L., & Langford, S. (2008). *Grandfather's Story Cloth.* (Auburn, CA: Shen's Books).

    (5–8) Chersheng's grandfather begins to forget things and he feel sad and helpless when he learns his grandfather has Alzheimer's disease. Then his mother gives him a story cloth stitched by his grandfather in the Hmong tradition. Through the story cloth his grandfather's memories of Laos come alive.

FAMILIES WHO FACE CHALLENGES

Williams, L. E. (2010). *The Can Man.* (New York: Lee and Low).

    (4–8) Tim's family cannot afford to buy him the skateboard he wants for his birthday. He hears the can man collecting empty cans and gets an idea. Tim has almost reached his goal when a few chance encounters with the can man change everything.

Bunting, E. (2005). *Gleam and Glow.* (London: Sandpiper).

    (4–8) This true story is based on the experiences of a Bosnian family who is forced to flee their country during a recent civil war. One refugee leaves behind a pair of goldfish. When the children and their mother flee, they put the fish in a pond. After staying in a refugee camp, the family returns home to find their home devastated, but the pond is filled with shimmering fish.

Riggs, S. (2007). *Not in Room 204.* (Morton Grove, IL: Albert Whitman).

(6–8) Regina is doing well but is very quiet in school and at home. As her teacher reads about inappropriate touching, Regina wonders if she should tell.

Martin, T., & Martin, W. (2006). *Big Ernie's New Home: A Story for Children Who are Moving.* (Washington, DC: Magination Press).

(4–8) Young children experience moving on a sensory level and this book helps children identify with the different sights and sounds they might encounter. It also provides information for adults.

INFANTS AND TODDLERS AT RISK

Global Fund for Children (2010). *American Babies.* (Watertown, MA: Charlesbridge Publishing).

(Birth–3) This book shows photographs of 17 babies representing the diversity of the country as they play and discover their world.

Ronay, L. (2009). *Kids Like Me . . . Learn Colors.* (Bethesda, MD: Woodbine House).

(Birth–3) Children can learn primary colors, as each page features a child with Down syndrome wearing clothing of a certain color and playing with an object of that color. Bilingual in English and Spanish.

CHILDREN WITH SPECIFIC LEARNING DISABILITIES

Ball-Dannenberg, S. (2009*). I Have Dyslexia. What Does that Mean?* (Charleston, SC: BookSurge Publishing).

(6–8) Delaney, an 8-year-old girl, was diagnosed with dyslexia and wants to know what it means, how to tell her friends, and how it will affect her life. See dyslexia through her eyes.

Hodge, D. (2007). *Lily and the Mixed-Up Letters.* (Plattsburg, NY: Tundra Books).

(4–8) Lily loved kindergarten, but by second grade school was no longer fun. The letters danced on the page. Grace becomes Lily's reading buddy. Lily must read a page aloud on Parent Day. At first, she freezes, but then reads it and realizes she can do it.

CHILDREN WITH SOCIAL, EMOTIONAL, AND BEHAVIORAL DISORDERS

Annuziata, J. & Nemiroff, M. (2009). *Sometimes I'm Scared.* (Washington, DC: Magination Press).

(3–8) This book provides children with strategies to deal with common fears.

Huebner, D. (2007). *What to Do When Your Brain Gets Stuck: A Kid's Guide to Overcoming OCD.* (Washington, DC: Magination Press).

(6–8) In obsessive compulsive disorder, children's brains get clogged with thoughts that bother them and make it hard for them to feel safe and sure of themselves. This book helps them get their thoughts uncluttered.

Wagenbach, D. (2009). *The Grouchies.* (Washington, DC: Magination Press).

(3–8). A rhyming book that shows children how to get rid of a grumpy mood.

Levins, S. (2010). *Eli's Lie-O-Meter: A Story about Telling the Truth.* (Washington, DC: Magination Press).

(3–8) Eli learns about the consequences of telling fibs and the value of telling the truth.

CHILDREN WITH ATTENTION-DEFICIT/ HYPERACTIVITY DISORDER

Corman, C. L., & Trevino, E. (2009). *Eukee the Jumpy Jumpy Elephant.* (Plantation, FL: Specialty Press/A.D.D Warehouse).

(4–8) Eukee has trouble getting along with friends and family because of his hyperactivity and lack of self-control. He finally finds the help he needs. This book helps children understand more about ADHD.

Kraus, J. (2006). *Annie's Plan: Taking Charge of Schoolwork and Homework.* (Washington, DC: Magination Press).

(6–8) Annie is smart, she loves to read but she is disorganized and forgets what she needs to do. With the help of parents, teachers, and a guidance counselor Annie learns new skills that help her. Includes notes for adults.

Offill, J., & Carpenter, N. (2007). *17 Things I'm Not Allowed to Do Any More.* (New York: Schwartz and Wade Books).

(6–8) A young girl lists 17 things she cannot do anymore such as walking home from school backward or setting Joey Whipple on fire.

Roegiers, M. (2010). *Take the Time: Mindfulness for Kids.* (Washington, DC: Magination Press).

(3–8) This book encourages children to slow down and increase their self-awareness. At the end of a challenging day it may calm children and help them feel better.

CHILDREN WITH COMMUNICATION DISORDERS

Docampo, V., & de Lestrade, A. (2010). *Phileas's Fortune: A Story about Self-Expression.* (Washington, DC: Magination Press).

(3–8) A book about the significance of sincerity and character behind the spoken word.

Hubble, A. (2008). *Henry the Stuttering Hero* (Barnyard Bible Basics) (Mustang, OK: Tate Publishing).

(4–8) Henry the chicken comes from a long line of crowing champions and would like to be like his dad and grandfather. Dire things are happenings at the farm and Henry is the only one who can see them. Henry has a delightful adventure, learns a big lesson, and becomes a hero.

CHILDREN WHO ARE ENGLISH LANGUAGE LEARNERS

Arguenta, J. (2003). *Xochitl and the Flowers/Xochitl, la Niña de las Flores.* (San Francisco, CA: Children's Book Press).

(6–8) Xochitl and her family, arriving in San Francisco from El Salvador, create a beautiful plant nursery in place of the garbage heap behind their apartment and celebrate with their friends and neighbors. Bilingual in English and Spanish.

Kim, J. U. (2003). *Sumi's First Day of School Ever.* (New York: Viking Juvenile).

(4–8) Sumi is starting school in America and is worried because she cannot speak English. At first, she thinks school is scary and the children are mean. During the day, she learns that school is not so lonely.

Yang, B. (2004). *Hannah is My Name.* (Cambridge, MA: Candlewick Press).

(6–8) Hannah's family has emigrated from Taiwan to San Francisco to make America their home. The book talks about the very real struggle with documentation as they wait and hope for the arrival of their green card.

CHILDREN WITH AUTISM SPECTRUM DISORDERS

Luchsinger, D. F. (2007). *Playing by the Rules.* (Bethesda, MD: Woodbine House).

(3–8) When her Aunt Tilda comes to take care of them, she unknowingly breaks some of Josh's rules. Jody, his big sister, helps her understand more about autism.

Shally, C. (2007). *Since We're Friends: An Autism Picture Book.* (Centerton, AR: Awaken Specialty Press).

(3–8) This book is about two boys: One has autism, the other does not. The story of their relationship provides examples of how to make such a friendship work.

CHILDREN WITH INTELLECTUAL DELAYS AND DISABILITIES

Bunnett, R. (2006). *Friends at School.* (Long Island, NY: Star Bright Books).

(3–6) A light, informal book featuring children of different abilities working and playing in an inclusive school setting.

Stuve-Bodeen, S. (2005). *The Best Worst Brother.* (Bethesda, MD: Woodbine House).

(4–8) Emma's almost 3-year-old bother Isaac spits out food and knocks down blocks. His slow pace is maddening but he is learning to sign. Isaac has Down syndrome.

Wojahn, R. H. (2006). *Evan Early.* (Bethesda, MD: Woodbine House).

(4–8) Natalie is eager for her new brother, but Evan was born too early, and his first home is in the hospital NICU. It is a scary place to visit. Natalie is hurt and angry over the way her parents are preoccupied with Evan but agrees that big sisters can help a lot.

CHILDREN WHO ARE GIFTED AND TALENTED

Cronin, D. (2008). *Thump, Quack, Moo: A Whacky Adventure.* (New York: Atheneum).

(4–8) Farmer Brown plans a Statue of Liberty maze for the annual Corn Maze Festival and enlists his reluctant farm animals. Although compliant during the day, at night they sneak out with night-vision goggles, glow in the darks rulers, and hedge clippers to make a design of their own. When Farmer Brown and the smug Duck take a hot air balloon ride to see the maze, the farmer's reaction is priceless.

Ludwig, T. (2009). *Too Perfect.* (New York, NY: Tricycle Press).

(4–8) Maisie thinks Kayla is perfect, but is she happy? The book sets the stage for talking about being yourself and working to your potential as opposed to perfection.

Rand, G. (2002). *Little Flower.* (New York, NY: Henry Holt).

(4–8) Little Flower is a very smart pig. She has learned lots of tricks, but one of them is really special: She can play dead! When Miss Pearl falls and hurts herself, nobody hears her calls for help. Little Flower uses her trick to get help for Miss Pearl and becomes a hero.

CHILDREN WITH SPECIAL HEALTH CARE NEEDS

Golding, T. (2009). *Abby's Asthma and the Big Race.* (Morton Grove, IL: Albert Whitman & Company).

(4–8) Abby has long legs but is short of breath. Although she is fast, she sometimes stops because she wheezes. She exercises everyday with her dad, does breathing exercises, and takes her medicine. Abby wins the big race beating a classmate who teases her.

Recob, A. (2009). *The Bugabees: Friends with Food Allergies.* (Minneapolis, MN: Beaver's Pond Press).

(4–8) A book about eight friends and their food allergies. It reminds children that the joy of friendship is far more important than any food. It looks at the main foods that account for allergic reactions: peanuts, tree nuts, fish, shellfish, milk, soy, eggs, and wheat. There is additional information for adults.

Forbes, A. (2003). *Kids with AIDS.* (The AIDS Awareness Library). (New York: Powerkids Press).

(3–8) The author gears this book toward educating young children that AIDS cannot be transmitted just by touching someone, and discusses how people live with this virus in everyday situations.

Allen, L. (2009) *Riley Socks.* (Tamarac, FL: Llumina Kids).

(4–8) This is the true story of Riley Allen's victorious battle with cancer. It is an uplifting easy-to-read rhyming book. After a lengthy operation, Riley finds she has special socks. The socks aid her recovery, and Riley kicks cancer right between the eyes.

Ganz-Schmitt, S. (2007). *Even Superheroes Get Diabetes.* (Indianapolis, IN: Dog Ear Publishing).

(4–8) Kevin loves superheros. Getting diabetes did not fit into his world of superheros until a doctor helped Kevin uncover his super powers to help other kids with diabetes.

Isaacsen-Bright, (2009). *I Like Lots.* (Tamarac, FL: Llumina Kids).

(4–8) A young boy likes junk food and lots of it. When he goes to the doctor, he finds that he is gaining weight—way too much weight. It isn't easy, but he follows the three rules: Eat better food, exercise and play more, and stick to it.

Bennett, H. (2008). *Harry Goes to the Hospital: A Story for Children about What It's Like to Be in the Hospital.* (Washington, DC: Magination Press).

(4–8) A reassuring story of Harry getting a stomach flu. He gets so sick his mother and father have to take him to the hospital. He copes with the new environment with the loving support of his parents.

Cousins, L. (2009). *Maisy Goes to the Hospital: A Maisy First Experience Book.* (Cambridge, MA: Candlewick).

(4–8) Maisy bounces too high on her trampoline and breaks her leg. Maisy's friend Charley goes to the hospital with her. At the hospital, she has an X-ray and then a cast. She has to stay overnight and is scared, but a friendly patient helps her.

Stickney, D. (2009). *Water Bugs and Dragonflies: Explaining Death to Young Children.* (Berea, OH: Pilgrim Press).

(4–8) This book uses the concept of metamorphosis to explain death.

CHILDREN WITH ORTHOPEDIC AND NEUROLOGICAL IMPAIRMENTS

Ellis, M., & Loehr, J. (2008). *Sitting on Letters: A Story about Low Muscle Tone.* (Austin, TX: Speech Kids Texas Press).

(3–8) A young girl with low muscle tone learns from her uncle, an occupational therapist, how sitting positions affect how she works and plays. The positions remind her of letters of the alphabet.

Hererra, J. F. (2004). *Featherless/Desplumado.* (San Francisco, CA: Children's Book Press).

(6–8) At Tomasito's new school, everyone wants to know why he uses a wheelchair and what spina bifida is. Papi gives him a new pet bird to make him smile. The bird is featherless. Together they learn there is more than one way to fly. Bilingual in English and Spanish.

Shirley, D. (2008). *Best Friend on Wheels.* (Morton Grove, IL: Albert Whitman).

(6–8) A teacher asks a student to show a new girl around the school. She is surprised that the girl is in a wheelchair but discovers they both collect rocks.

Lears, L. (2005). *Nathan's Wish: A Story about Cerebral Palsy.* (Morton Grove, IL: Albert Whitman).

(6–8) Nathan struggles with cerebral palsy. As he helps an owl named Firefly, he helps himself as well.

Rocheford, D. M. (2009) *Mommy, I Feel Funny! A Child's Experience with Epilepsy.* (Deadwood, OR: Green Swing, A Wyatt-MacKenzie Imprint).

(4–8) Nel is a little girl whose funny feeling turns out to be epilepsy. The story tells about her first seizure and subsequent diagnosis. It discusses the fears and emotions Nel and her family feel and Nel's decisions to refuse to let epilepsy interfere with her life.

CHILDREN WITH HEARING IMPAIRMENTS

Schneider, E. E. (2004). *Taking Hearing Impairment to School (Special Kids in School Series).* (Plainville, NJ: JayJo Books).

(4–8) As Jacob's story unfolds children learn about hearing aids, sign language, interpreters, and speech therapy.

CHILDREN WITH VISUAL IMPAIRMENTS

Calvert, P. (2008). *Princess Peepers.* (Terrytown, NY: Marshall Cavendish Corp.).

(3–8) Princess Peepers has a fabulous eyeglasses collection and loves to wear them until she enters the Royal Academy where she is made fun of. She quits wearing them and has many misadventures until she again wears the glasses.

Fisher, R. (2009). *Randy Kazandy, Where are Your Glasses?* (Rancho Santa Margarita, CA: Whim Publishing).

(3–8) Randy does not like his glasses and tries to lose them. His mother has funny and interesting ways to find them.

Kostechi-Shaw, J. S. (2008). *My Travelin' Eye.* (New York: Henry Holt).

(3–8) Jenny Sue's eyes are not the same as other people's eyes. Her right eye looks in one direction, while her left eye sometimes wanders. Jenny Sue has a lazy eye she has to wear a patch. Her mother makes the patch interesting by using brightly colored material. Although it makes her different, it also helps her see the world in a special way. She graduates from the patch to glasses and her mother makes these fun too.

EDUCATIONAL RESOURCES

Albert Whitman and Company specializes in timely books for children about topics such as divorce, disability, and cultural diversity. http://www.awhitmanco.com/

Children's Book Press is a nonprofit independent publisher of multicultural and bilingual literature for children. The stories are about historically underrepresented or misrepresented populations in children's literature. They focus on promoting intercultural and cross-cultural awareness for all children. www.childrensbookpress.org/

Magination Press was created to publish psychology-based books designed to educate, motivate, and empower children to work toward change. They cover topics that all children face, such as starting school, as well as clinical and medical disorders. The purpose is to provide age-appropriate information on a particular issue, understand the feelings that might be associated with a situation, and provide some practical ways to cope and resolve the problems and emotions. The books all use cognitive-behavioral techniques to treat the identified disorders. They are interactive self-help book and include examples, activities and step-by-step instructions. The books are from the American Psychological Association through their children's book division Magination Press. http://apamaginationpress.apa.org/

Parent's Choice reviews children's books, TV shows, web sites, videos, and more. Their Doing & Learning section provides ideas for activities and explorations. www.parents-choice.org/default.cfm/

Shen's Books is a publisher of multicultural children's literature that emphasizes cultural diversity and tolerance with a special focus on the cultures of Asia. http://www.shen.com/

Woodbine House has a special needs collection of over 50 books on specific disabilities and related topics. http://www.woodbinehouse.com/

Glossary ✳

A

abduction—motion away from the midline.

absence seizures—involve a brief, sudden lapse of conscious activity; previously called petit mal seizures.

academic underachievement—refers to a student who does not achieve as well as expected based on his potential.

acceleration—the process of moving through an educational program at a faster rate than usual (skipping grades) or at a younger age (starting school early).

acculturation—supports the adoption of the host country's values without relinquishing all ethnic/culture and values.

achievement gap—occurs when one group of children outperforms or underperforms another group and the differences are large enough they could not have happened by chance.

achievement tests—measure the extent to which a child has mastered a certain body of knowledge.

achromatopsia—a rare hereditary visual disorder where individuals are unable to see color.

acquired—term used for a medical condition that originates after birth.

active initiation—a type of attachment that begins around 8 or 9 months and is characterized by the infant's initiative in seeking proximity and contact with the attachment figure.

adaptive skills—self-help skills.

adduction—movement toward the midline.

aggressive behaviors—behaviors intended to harm another individual, even if the attempt to harm fails. See also *antisocial behaviors*.

air conduction—the process of transmitting sound waves to the cochlea by way of the outer and middle ear.

alleles—a pair or series of genes that always occupy a particular location on a chromosome that is usually a coding sequence.

allergen—an antigenic substance capable of producing an immediate hypersensitivity reaction in individuals.

allergic rhinitis—an inflammation of the nasal passages caused by an allergic reaction to airborne substances.

alveoli—tiny air sacs in the lungs that expand the lungs' surface area for the exchange of oxygen and carbon dioxide.

amblyopia—a disorder of the visual system caused by either no or poor transmission of visual images to the brain for an extended time.

American Sign Language—(Ameslan or ASL) a language that consists of a set of standard hand signs used in relation to other parts of the body with each sign representing a word, idea, or concept.

Americans with Disabilities Acts (ADA)—extended civil rights protection to people with disabilities in all settings.

amnion—a membranous sac that surrounds and protects the developing embryo and fetus during pregnancy.

amniotic fluid—the clear liquid that helps to protect the developing fetus and is contained by the amnion or amniotic sac.

amniotic sac—a thin transparent pair of membranes that holds the embryo and then the fetus during pregnancy.

amphetamine stimulants—medications designed to release the neurotransmitter dopamine into the synaptic cleft and may be used to treat ADHD.

amplification—a process that makes a signal stronger or louder.

amplification devices—products (such as hearing aids that increase the level of sound) that make a signal stronger or louder.

amygdala—part of the limbic system, a primitive arousal area that is central to the "fight or flight" response and is involved in producing and responding to nonverbal signs of anger, avoidance, defensiveness, and fear.

anaphylaxis—a severe allergic reaction that occurs within minutes of exposure and may lead to death if not treated.

anemia—a deficiency of red blood cells and/or hemoglobin that reduces the ability of blood to transfer oxygen to the tissues.

anencephaly—a severe malformation of the skull and brain with no neural development above the brainstem.

anti-inflammatory medication—medication that decreases pain by reducing inflammation as opposed to opioids that affect the brain.

antibodies—gamma globulin proteins found in blood and other bodily fluids that are part of the immune system that identify and neutralize germs, such as bacteria and viruses.

antigravity positions—all postures where some part of the body is in an upright position such as sitting or standing.

antirheumatic drugs—a category of drugs used in many autoimmune disorders to slow disease progression and reduce the rate of damage to bone and cartilage.

antisocial behaviors—behaviors that violate social norms; the violation may be minor or major. See also *aggressive behaviors*.

anxiety—generalized worry.

anxiety disorders—different forms of abnormal anxiety, fears, and phobias that are irrational or illogical worry not based on fact.

apnea—the suspension of external breathing for 20 seconds or more.

apnea monitor—a machine that checks the heart rate and respiration of an infant; when either falls below normal levels, the monitor beeps.

apraxia—a neurological disorder of motor planning that involves the inability to carry out learned purposeful movements.

articulation—the ability to produce, orally, any one of a variety of vowels, consonants, and/or vowel-consonant blends.

Asperger's syndrome—a disorder on the autism spectrum characterized by severe difficulties in social interactions, repetitive behaviors, and restricted interests.

assessment—the process of collecting information for the purpose of making decisions about children or groups of children or to evaluate a program's effectiveness.

assimilate—the process of taking in new information to develop a schema or concept.

assistive listening devices—products designed to improve audibility; some work with hearing aids or cochlear implants, others are used independently.

assistive technology device—any item, piece of equipment, or product system that increases, maintains, or improves the functional capabilities of a child with a disability.

assistive technology services—help in the selection, acquisition, and /or use of an assistive technology device and training or technical assistance for family and educators.

associative play—play where children are playing together but the play is not goal oriented and there is no leader.

astigmatism—an error in refraction caused by the cornea of the eye being more football-shaped than spherical; therefore, the parallel light rays do not come together at one point, so the image is not in focus.

ataxia—irregular, uncoordinated muscular movement, especially in walking.

ataxic cerebral palsy—an impairment characterized by abnormalities in voluntary movement that cause increased or decreased muscle tone, resulting in problems in balance and in controlling the position of the trunk and limbs.

athetosis—random, writhing, involuntary movements, especially of the hands.

atonic seizures—consist of brief abrupt loss of muscle tone; also called drop seizures.

atopic disease—a heredity predisposition toward developing specific hypersensitivity reactions such as asthma, hay fever, and other allergies.

attachment—the development of the human bond between an infant and caregivers that the infant uses as an internal working model for relationships.

audiologist—a professional who has been trained in the prevention, identification, and nonmedical management of hearing loss. Audiologists can identify hearing loss and initiate treatment (fit hearing aids) in children once medical clearance has been obtained.

audiometer—a machine used for evaluating hearing loss.

auditory cortex—the region of the brain responsible for processing auditory (sound) information.

auditory discrimination—the identification of differences between sounds on the basis of variations in their complexity, pattern, pitch, or intensity.

auditory memory—part of memory that allows individuals to retrieve information that was heard through remembering the auditory information over time.

auditory processing disorders—occur when the brain does not interpret auditory stimuli accurately.

auditory processing dysfunction—a receptive language impairment that affects the way sounds are interpreted by the brain.

auditory sequencing—ability to put events in the order in which they were heard, for example, the day that follows Tuesday, the letter that precedes p.

aura—the perception of a field of energy surrounding oneself.

auricle—the outer, or external, ear.

autism—a developmental disorder appearing before age 3 that is characterized by impairments in social interaction, communication, and restricted, repetitive, and stereotyped patterns of behavior, interests, and activities.

autism spectrum disorders (ASD)—developmental disorders that include autism, Asperger's syndrome, Rett syndrome, and childhood disintegrative disorder.

autonomic system—part of the central nervous system that functions in an involuntary reflexive way to regulate many body systems such as heart movement, air flow in the lungs, and blood vessel size and blood pressure.

autosomes—paired chromosomes that are the same for both sexes. Humans have 22 pairs.

avoidant attachment—an organized defensive strategy used by children whose caregivers are not responsive to them.

axons—long snakelike fibers that reach out from the cell to conduct electrical impulses away from the cell body.

B

backward chaining—teaching the last step in a task analysis first and working toward the first step.

basal ganglia—a large collection of nuclei with a variety of functions that modify movement. They also play a role in cognition, emotions, and learning.

behavioral disorders—disorders that focus on disruptive behavior.

behavioral intervention plan—a written plan based on a functional behavioral assessment designed to address problematic behavior.

behaviorists—those who believe disturbed behavior is a learned response and who use classical or operant conditioning and social learning to solve problems.

bias—a preference for a particular perspective or ideology that interferes with the ability to be objective or impartial.

bicultural adaptation—involves honoring the home culture and adding experiences from the broader community to this base.

biculturalism—a way of adapting to the environment that incorporates aspects of the home culture with the mainstream culture.

bilirubin—a product of the breakdown of the hemoglobin in red blood cells; if levels are too high, brain damage can result.

binocular vision—using two eyes simultaneously.

biophysical model—medically based; the cause of the disorder lies within the child and is genetic, developmental, neurological, biochemical, or temperamental. Solutions are primarily psychopharmacological.

bipolar disorder—a mental illness characterized by mood instability that moves between manic behavior and depression; also called manic-depressive disorder.

blastocyst—the second stage in prenatal development that begins 5 days after fertilization and lasts until implantation when it becomes an embryo.

blended families—families formed when remarriage occurs or when children living in a household share only one or no biological parents; blended families can include stepchildren and their stepparents, half siblings, or stepsiblings.

blind—for educational purposes, a visual loss severe enough that it is not possible to read printed material and necessitates the use of alternative forms of written communication such as Braille.

blindisms—socially inappropriate behaviors such as eye pressing, spinning, head banging, and rocking or bouncing that children who are blind may do for stimulation.

blood clotting—changes blood from a liquid to a solid; also called coagulation.

body mass index (BMI)—a number calculated based on a child's weight, height, age and gender, which is an indicator of body fat and is used to identify weight categories.

bone conduction—the transmission of sound to the inner ear through the bones of the skull.

bone marrow transplant—a procedure for delivering healthy bone marrow stem cells into bone marrow that is not working properly or has been destroyed by chemotherapy or radiation.

bradycardia—a disorder of the heart rate where the fetal or infant heart rate drops below 80 to 100 beats per minute.

Braille—a system of reading and writing used by people who cannot see print. Braille cells are made up of six dot positions, arranged in a rectangle to form 64 different patterns.

brain stem—the lower part of the brain that connects to the spinal column and controls reflexive and involuntary activities such as blood pressure, heart rate, and the regulation of body temperature, breathing, and other automatic processes.

bronchodilator—an asthma medication that dilates the bronchi and bronchioles, thus widening the air passages of the lungs to make breathing easier. It is used as an emergency drug for children with asthma.

burnout—a psychological term for describing long-term exhaustion and decreased interest.

C

cataracts—a clouding of the natural lens, a part of the eye responsible for focusing light and producing clear, sharp images.

catheterization—the process of threading a flexible tube (catheter) through a channel in the body to inject drugs. A bladder catheter goes through the urethra into the bladder to relieve the bladder.

central auditory hearing loss—any of a variety of problems with the brain that interfere with processing auditory (sound) information when hearing is within normal limits; also called central auditory processing dysfunction.

central nervous system (CNS)—consists of the brain, the spinal cord, and the nerves that control voluntary and involuntary body functions.

central vision—straight-ahead vision produced by light rays falling directly on the fovea centralis of the eye.

cephalocaudal—a pattern of development that goes from the head to the tail, with the upper part of the body (head) developing before the lower part (legs).

cerebral cortex—the outer portion of the cerebrum that is responsible for higher brain functions such as language, cognition, and memory. It is often referred to as *grey matter* because of the color of the neurons and unmyelinated fibers of which it is made.

cerebrum—the largest part of the brain, residing in both the left and right hemispheres and has four lobes: frontal, parietal, temporal, and occipital. It is what most people think of when they think of the brain.

cervical vertebrae—those vertebrae immediately behind the skull, connecting the skull and spine. They are the smallest of the true vertebrae, going from C-1 to C-7.

cesarean section—a form of childbirth where a surgical incision is made through the mother's abdomen and uterus to deliver one or more infants.

chaining—the process of ordering a task analysis into a sequence that starts at the beginning of a task (forward chaining) or at the end (backward chaining).

chemotherapy—treatment of an ailment using chemicals to kill microorganisms or cancerous cells.

child development specialists—individuals who are trained in developmental principles and work with children in a variety of settings.

Child Find—a governmental system for identifying, locating, and evaluating children who may need early intervention, special education, and related services.

Child Find specialist—is an individual who locates, identifies, screens and refers children who are at risk of having a disability for evaluation. She may also serve as the service coordinator and as a link between the family and other organizations.

child life staff—early childhood professionals who work with children in hospital settings.

child of an immigrant parent—a child younger than 18 years of age who is either foreign-born or who was born in the United States and has at least one foreign-born parent.

child outcome standards—the range of knowledge children should have; the skills they are expected to have; and the habits, attitudes, and dispositions they are expected to develop.

child with a disability—according to the IDEA, a child with intellectual impairments, hearing impairments, speech or language impairments, visual impairment, emotional disturbance, orthopedic impairment, autism, traumatic brain injury, other health impairments, or specific learning disabilities, and because of these impairments needs special education and related services.

childhood disintegrative disorder—a neurodevelopmental disorder on the autism spectrum that is marked by regression in multiple areas following at least two years of normal development.

children without disabilities—children who do not receive services based on the IDEA.

choreoathetoid—a type of dyskinetic cerebral palsy where there are rapid, random, jerky movements (chorea) combined with slow, writhing movements (athetosis).

chorionic gonadotrophin—a hormone that is measured in blood or urine to determine whether a woman is pregnant; it helps maintain the pregnancy.

chromosomes—long, single continuous pieces of DNA that contain many genes, regulatory elements, and other nucleotide sequences.

chronic otitis media—a reoccurring inflammation of the middle ear.

cleavage—the early successive splitting of a zygote into smaller cells by mitosis.

clinical judgment or opinion—the recommendation of qualified personnel relative to their areas of expertise.

clumsy child syndrome—a disorder characterized by impairment in the ability to plan and carry out sensory and motor tasks; also called *developmental dyspraxia*.

cluster grouping—the practice of placing a small group of identified gifted children together in a classroom and providing more complex activities for them.

co-teaching model—when an early childhood educator and an early childhood special educator teach in the same classroom together.

cochlea—a snail-shell-like structure in the inner ear whose core component is the organ of Corti. It is important for hearing and also balance and equilibrium.

cochlear implants—small, complex electronic devices that can help provide a sense of sound to a child who is profoundly deaf or severely hard of hearing.

code-switching—using more than one language or dialect in a conversation.

cohabitation—an emotionally and physically intimate relationship between two adults in a common living place that exists without legal or religious sanction.

cohabitating partner families—families consisting of a mother or father and child(ren) who is residing with a partner to whom he or she is not married.

cohort—a group of subjects, usually people, from a given population defined by experiencing an event (typically birth) in a particular time span. All the children born in a particular hospital or city during a particular year would be a cohort.

collaboration—the dynamic process of connecting families' resources, motivation, and knowledge/skills to an empowering context to make decisions collectively.

collectivism—a social outlook that emphasizes the interdependence of individuals over the attainment of individual goals.

color blindness—a lay term used instead of *color deficiency*, and meaning the same thing.

color deficiency—the inability to differentiate among some colors.

color vision—the capacity to distinguish objects based on the wavelengths of the light they reflect or emit.

Common Core State Standards—grade level academic standards that provide a consistent, clear understanding of what students are expected to learn in English language arts and mathematics in order to be successful in college, careers, and the global economy.

communication—the process of transmitting information between a sender, who encodes information, and a receiver, who decodes the information.

comorbid—the occurrence of more than one disease or disorder in a child.

comorbidity—the presence of one or more diseases or disorders in addition to the primary disease or disorder.

comparative genomic hybridization (CGH)—analyzes the changes in DNA by the gain or loss of genetic material by copy number.

complex tics—motor or vocal tics with distinct, coordinated patterns that involve several muscle groups and may be a combination of simple tics such as facial grimacing combined with a head twist and shoulder shrug.

compliance—the process of ensuring that individuals and systems adhere to relevant laws and regulations, particularly the IDEA.

conduct disorder—a repetitive and persistent pattern of behavior that violates the basic rights of others and does not follow rules or age-appropriate societal norms.

conductive hearing loss—a failure in the efficient conduction of sound waves through the outer ear, eardrum, or middle ear.

cones—photoreceptor cells in the retina of the eye that function best in relatively bright light and are needed to see color, to see distant objects, and for detailed vision such as reading. There are three kinds of cones. Each one is sensitive to one of three colors: red, green, or blue. Also called *cone cells*.

congenital—denotes a medical condition that is present at birth.

congenital malformations—anomalies that are present at birth.

conjunctivitis—an inflammation of the conjunctiva due to an allergic reaction or an infection; also called *pink eye*.

consultant—a professional who provides advice in a particular area of expertise such as early childhood special education.

content standards—specify what children should know in specific academic areas.

content validity—the relationship between the items in an assessment and the intended use of the assessment.

contingency contracting—part of a behavior plan where children can decide on the rewards they will get after they have accomplished specific goals.

contractions—the movements of the muscles in the wall of the uterus that push the fetus through the birth canal.

contracture—a shortening of muscle fibers that is usually irreversible and decreases the range of motion of a joint.

cooperative play—play where children have a common goal and are interacting using similar materials or materials related to a common theme.

cornea—the transparent front part of the eye that covers the iris, pupil, and anterior chamber, providing most of an eye's optical power. Together with the lens, the cornea refracts light and helps the eye to focus.

cortical visual impairment (CVI)—a temporary or permanent visual impairment caused by an abnormality of the visual cortex or the visual pathways of the brain, which is caused by oxygen deprivation, infection, or traumatic brain injury.

corticospinal tract—a massive collection of long motor axons between the brain and the spinal column.

counting—involves knowing number names and the count sequence.

criterion referenced—a system of comparing performance to an absolute standard.

criterion-referenced measures—measures that use an absolute standard for determining scores. Children perform certain tasks, and their score is based on their level of competency in completing the tasks.

cued speech—a visual communication system that uses eight hand shapes in four different placements near the face in combination with the mouth movements of speech to make the sounds of spoken language look different from each other.

cuing—warning children before they are expected to do something.

curriculum-based assessments—measures used in schools to determine the instructional needs of students.

cystic fibrosis (CF)—is an inherited recessive genetic disease that causes thick, sticky mucus to build up in a child's digestive tract and lungs.

D

deafness—a severe hearing impairment (70 dB HL or greater) that impairs processing linguistic information through hearing, with or without amplification.

decibel (dB)—a measure of the magnitude or intensity of sound.

decoding—the process of transforming information from one format into another, such as the written word into sound.

dendrites—branched projections of a neuron that conduct electrical impulses to the cell body.

depression—a psychiatric disorder that is characterized by a pervasive low mood, loss of interest in usual activities, and diminished ability to experience pleasure.

depressive disorders—disorders that are characterized by severe and persistent sadness.

developmental coordination disorder—a disorder of childhood characterized by physical awkwardness and clumsiness.

developmental delay—a condition that represents a significant delay in the developmental processes, not a slight or momentary lag in development, which will continue without intervention.

developmental dyspraxia—a disorder characterized by impairment in the inability to plan and carry out sensory and motor tasks and may include poor balance and coordination, clumsiness, vision problems, perception difficulties, emotional and behavioral problems, difficulty with reading, writing, and speaking, poor social skills, poor posture, and poor short-term memory.

developmental quotients (DQs)—scores obtained on developmental assessments for young children, with a mean of 100. They are used similarly to intelligent quotients (IQs) for older children.

developmentally appropriate practices—a way of teaching that has three basic components: knowledge about development and learning, knowledge about individual children, and knowledge about the social and cultural context in which children learn and grow.

diabetes mellitus type 1—an autoimmune disease where the body does not produce insulin because of the destruction of the insulin-producing beta cells of the pancreas.

diabetes mellitus type 2—a metabolic disorder that is characterized by insulin resistance, insulin deficiency, and hyperglycemia; it is typically managed by increasing exercise and modifying the diet, although insulin may be needed.

dialogic reading—a shared reading practice where the adult and the child switch roles so that the child learns to become the storyteller with the assistance of the adult who functions as an active listener and questioner.

diffuse axonal injury—widespread brain damage with extensive lesions in the white matter of the brain.

diopter—a unit of measurement of the optical power of a lens. The higher the number of diopters, the stronger the glasses prescription: a minus sign indicates concave lenses, and a plus sign indicates a convex lens.

diplegia—an impairment that involves the whole body, although the legs more so than the arms.

direct language stimulation—communication where an adult questions a child to elicit responses in a way that the child cannot answer with just a "yes" or "no."

disability—a general term referring to a condition or functional limitation that interferes with major life activities such as walking, hearing, or learning.

disaggregate—to break into component parts, which can mean pulling out information that is based on age, gender, race/ethnicity, disability type, and so on.

discipline—actions or words that help children self-monitor their behavior so it is appropriate and acceptable and to encourage self-control.

discretionary services—those services that may incur a cost to those using the service and do not have to be provided, as opposed to *mandated services*.

discriminate attachment—a type of attachment that begins about 3 to 4 months and goes to about 8 or 9 months, where infants respond differently to one (or a few) familiar individuals than they do to strangers.

disengaged families—families that rarely communicate about feelings, thoughts, and what they want to do; the behavior of one family member does not affect the behavior of others.

disorganized/controlling attachment—children with this type of attachment lack of a consistent pattern of response and it may be the result of caregivers who frighten them.

disproportionality—compares the racial and ethnic backgrounds of the school population with the population who are identified as needing special education services.

disruptive behavior disorder not otherwise specified—diagnosed when there is a significant impairment, but the behavior does not meet the requirement for a conduct disorder or oppositional defiant disorder.

dissociation—a mental state where certain thoughts, sensation, or memories are compartmentalized because they are too overwhelming for the conscious mind.

distal—organs or body parts away from the midline, such as the fingers.

distractability—having problems attending to a task.

dizygotic twins—result from two separate fertilized eggs in one pregnancy; also called *fraternal twins*.

domains—large groups of academic standards or behaviors (cognitive) that are related to each other.

dopamine—a hormone and a neurotransmitter in the brain.

DSM-IV-TR—the fourth edition, text revision of the *Diagnostic and Statistical Manual of Mental Disorders* published by the American Psychiatric Association used to classify mental disorders.

dual-language learners—children who are learning two or more languages at the same time.

due process—the legal rights families of children with disabilities have to ensure that the services their child is supposed to receive are granted by having a due process hearing with impartial hearing officers and, if necessary, a court of law.

dura—the tough and inflexible outermost of the three layers of the meninges surrounding the brain and spinal cord.

dyscalculia—the inability to understand the processes associated with mathematical calculation and reasoning.

dysgraphia—a neurological disorder characterized by the profound inability to form meaningful symbols.

dyskinetic—a form of cerebral palsy that is characterized by abnormal involuntary movements.

dyslexia—a reading disability entailing difficulty with written language, particularly reading and spelling, based on how the brain processes written language.

dyspraxia—a poor ability to conceive, plan, organize, or carry out novel actions or sequences of coordinated movements to attain a goal.

dysthymia—a mood disorder that is part of the depression spectrum and is characterized by being sad or "down in the dumps" for a long time, perhaps a year.

dystonia—a form of cerebral palsy in which there are rapid involuntary changes in muscle tension or tone.

E

ear canal—a tube that goes from the outer ear to the middle ear.

early childhood education—the education and caregiving for children from birth through age 8.

early childhood special education—the education of children with disabilities from birth through age 8.

early childhood special education consultants—early childhood special educators who give advice to educators and caregivers in a variety of settings to ensure that children who need early intervention or special education receive needed educational services.

Early Head Start—a program, for children ages 36 months and younger, whose mission is to promote healthy prenatal outcomes for pregnant women, enhance the development of very young children, and promote healthy family functioning.

early intervening services (EIS)—services for students in kindergarten through grade 12 (emphasis on K–3) who are not identified as needing special education but who need additional academic and behavioral support to succeed in school.

early intervention—a service designed for infants and toddlers with disabilities and those at risk. It promotes development and learning, supports families and helps with service coordination with the goal of reducing or eliminating the need for special programs later.

early interventionist—a person, typically a nurse, child development specialist, and/or early childhood special educator, who provides educational services for infants and toddlers with disabilities and those at risk.

eclampsia—a serious complication of pregnancy that is associated with high blood pressure and can result in seizures or convulsions.

ecological model—focuses on the interactions of the child with others in the environment and acknowledges cultural and situational differences in behavioral demands.

ectoderm—the outermost of the three germ layers of the embryo. It becomes the nervous system, skin, hair, teeth, and other body parts.

edema—swelling caused by excess fluid in body tissues.

Education of the Handicapped Acts (EHA)—the laws and their amendments governing the rights of children with disabilities in educational settings before 1990.

educational diagnostician—an individual who has the ability to assess and diagnose the learning problems of children.

electroencephalogram (EEG)—a test that measures and records the electrical activity of the brain.

embryo—a developing organism from the time of implantation in the uterus wall until the end of eight weeks.

embryonic period—the period of prenatal development, from two to eight weeks, when cells differentiate, the placenta develops, and organs are being formed.

emotional disorders—disorders that relate to mood.

encephalocele—a neural tube defect where the skull is malformed so that it allows a portion of the brain to protrude at the back or front of the head.

endoderm—the innermost of the three germ layers of the embryo from which the respiratory and digestive systems develop.

endometrium—the mucus membrane lining the uterus.

engagement—a time during labor and delivery when the largest part of the fetal head has passed through the mother's pelvic rim and into the true pelvis.

English language learners—children who, because of foreign birth or ancestry, speak a language other than English, and either understand or speak little or no academic English.

enmeshed families—families that have closely shared lives, and individuals do not look into themselves for awareness and growth; individuality gets lost in the family system.

entitlement—a guarantee of access to benefits or services because of rights or by agreement through law.

epicanthic fold—is a skin fold of the upper eyelid that covers the inner corner of the eye. It is caused by weak eyelid muscles.

environmental print—the print seen in everyday life such as stop signs, cereal boxes, and advertisements for stores and places to eat.

epidural hematoma—a type of traumatic brain injury where a blood clot develops between the skull and the outer covering of the brain (dura mater).

epilepsy—a brain disorder where clusters of nerve cells, or neurons, in the brain sometimes signal abnormally.

epinephrine—a hormone and neurotransmitter; also called adrenaline.

esotropia—the most common form of strabismus where the eyes deviate inward; toward the nose (cross-eyed).

ethnicity—a part of an individual's identity based on cultural, linguistic, religious, behavioral, or biological traits.

ethnographic—a scientific way of describing human cultures.

etiology—a branch of medical science that studies the cause of diseases and the accumulated knowledge we have about them.

Eustachian tube—a slender tube that runs from the middle ear to the pharynx.

evaluation—the use of assessment information to make decisions.

execution—carrying out a course of action or conduct to its completion.

executive function—the ability of the brain to maintain appropriate problem-solving procedures to attain future goals. It includes the ability to plan, to wait and to control one's impulses, to store relevant information for future use, to think creatively, and to problem solve.

exotropia—a form of strabismus where the eyes deviate outward; away from the nose (wall-eyed).

expansion—the process of extracting meaning from a child's utterance and putting it in a more complex form. ("Up." "Do you want me to pick you up?").

expertise—a level of mastery beyond literacy for children who want to become mini-experts in a field.

expressive language disorder—is a communication disorder where spoken language is markedly below expectations based on mental age, but comprehension is within normal limits.

extension—to straighten or stretch a joint; its opposite is *flexion*. If your arm is *extended*, the elbow joint is straight.

extinction—a way of ending a behavior by lack of any consequences following a behavior, either favorable or unfavorable, so that the behavior occurs with less frequency.

F

failure to thrive—applies to children whose current weight or rate of weight gain is significantly below other children of a similar age and sex.

fallopian tubes—a pair of slender ducts going from the ovaries into the uterus.

Family Educational Rights and Privacy Act of 1974, P.L. 93-380—gives parents of children younger than age 18 and students over age 18 the right to examine records kept in their personal file.

family problems—may indicate lack of social skills in the home.

fast mapping—a mental process where children form a working hypothesis about word meaning after a single exposure and gradually refine it, thus allowing them to increase their vocabulary very quickly.

febrile seizures—a convulsion in a child triggered by a fever.

Federal Bureau of Indian Affairs—is a federal agency whose responsibility is the administration and management of 55.7 million acres of land held in trust by the United States for American Indians, Indian tribes, and Alaska Natives.

fetal period—the period of prenatal development, from 2 to 9 months, characterized by rapid growth and development of body systems and weight.

fetus—the developing organism from the time the major structures have formed (about the ninth week after fertilization) until birth.

fibrin—a substance made by a complex chemical process to form a clot that stops bleeding.

fidelity—the quality of being faithful to a particular way of teaching or a teaching strategy.

field of vision—the angular extent of the observable world that is seen at any given moment.

fill-ins—require the child to complete a statement on a test.

fingerspelling—the representation of the letters and numbers of a written language using only the hands.

first stage of labor—begins with contractions and ends when the cervix is dilated and effaced.

flexion—the bending of a joint. If your elbow is flexed, your hand is near your shoulder.

foot-candles—a measure of the amount of light that falls on a given surface. Technically, 1 foot-candle is equal to 1 lumen per square foot.

foreign-born parents—indicates that one or both of a child's parents were born outside of the United States.

foster care—a living arrangement for children when a court decides they cannot safely live at home with their biological parent(s).

fragile families—families consisting of children who are born to unwed mothers and who live the first part of their lives with a single mother who is not living with a boyfriend or partner.

free appropriate public education (FAPE)—personalized instruction and support services for a child to benefit educationally from instruction (at the public's expense) that meets the state's educational standards and approximate grade levels used in the state's regular education and conforms to the IEP.

frequency—the pitch of a sound measured by the number of sound waves per unit of time. The more frequent the sound waves, the higher the frequency.

frontal lobe—the largest lobe of the brain, located at the front of each cerebral hemisphere. It is associated with reward, attention, short-term memory. planning, motivation, and personality.

functional analysis—analyzing the purpose of a particular action and what a child gains by continuing the particular behavior.

functional behavioral assessment—a systematic assessment that analyzes the connection between problematic behavior and its function in the child's life.

functional skills—those skills the child needs to function independently in the environment and that can be taught during activities or routines in the classroom or in routines at home.

fundamental movement skills—movements that provide the foundation to build more complex motor skills.

G

gastroesophageal reflux—a disease caused by a muscle at the end of the esophagus not closing properly, which allows the stomach contents to leak back, or reflux, into the esophagus and irritate it.

gender—a set of characteristics that distinguish between males and females.

generalized anxiety disorder—excessive anxiety and worry about a variety of things that results in fatigue, restlessness, difficulty concentrating, irritability, tension, and sleep disturbance.

generalized seizures—seizures that do not have an identifiable focus, impact both hemispheres of the brain, affect widely spread cortical areas of the brain simultaneously, and usually have a genetic base.

genetic counseling—the process of advising individuals of the consequence of a disorder, the probability of developing it and transmitting it, and about ways the disorder can be prevented or ameliorated.

genotype—the specific genetic genome of a person or his or her DNA.

genre—any category of literature or other art form that is constructed by conventions that change over time as new genres are invented (poetry, drama, prose).

germinal period—the period of prenatal development, from conception to 2 weeks, when the ova divides and attaches to the wall of the uterus.

gestation—period during which an embryo or fetus is carried.

gestational age—the time from conception plus 2 weeks. (Gestational age is counted from the mother's last menstrual cycle.)

gestational diabetes—a condition where women who did not previously have diabetes exhibit high blood glucose levels during the latter part of pregnancy.

glial cells—(Greek for "glue") non-neuronal cells that provide support and nutrition for neurons, maintain homeostasis, form myelin, and participate in signal transmission in the nervous system. They outnumber neurons by about 10:1.

glucose—a simple sugar that cells use as a source of energy.

grade band—several grade levels (K–3) grouped for a particular purpose.

grammar—the rules for using the smallest units of language that contain meaning (*morphemes*) and word order (*syntax*) to convey meaning.

gray matter—nerve cell bodies that are grayish in color and that cover the *white matter* (myelinated axons); together gray matter and white matter make up the cerebral cortex of the brain.

growth cone—the tip of an axon that provides guidance for the growing axon and helps it reach its destination.

guidance—a process approach to guiding children's behavior, rather than an isolated act of punishment, that is designed to facilitate the development of self-esteem, prosocial behaviors, and the ability to control one's own behavior.

guided reading—a process where teachers introduce a book and guide children through it; children think about what will happen in the book; teachers introduce key vocabulary and reading strategies; children read the book independently and then discuss the book with the teacher; and finally children re-read the book.

H

habituate—to become familiar with a stimulus and then not respond to it.

hair cells—the sensory receptors of the auditory and vestibular systems. There are two types of hair cells: Outer hair cells amplify low-level sound that enters the cochlea, and inner hair cells transform the sound vibrations in the fluids of the cochlea into electrical signals and relay them via the auditory nerve to the auditory brainstem and auditory cortex.

half-siblings—children who share one biological parent.

handicap—the cumulative result of the barriers imposed by society that come between an individual and an activity that the person wants to do.

Head Start—a national program that promotes school readiness by enhancing the social and cognitive development of children through the provision of early care and education to children in low-income families.

health literacy—the capacity of an individual to obtain, interpret, and understand basic health information and services and the competence to use such information and services in ways that are health enhancing.

hearing aids—small electronic devices worn in or behind the ear that make some sounds louder.

hearing impairment—an impairment in hearing, whether permanent or fluctuating, between 25 to 70dB HL that adversely affects a child's ability to hear.

hearing threshold testing—testing of hearing to determine the softest sound a child is able to hear at different frequencies.

hematoma—a collection of blood, generally the result of internal bleeding, also called a blood clot.

hemiplegia—severe or complete paralysis of one side of the body.

hemoglobin—the oxygen transport system in red blood cells.

hepatitis—an infectious disease of the liver that manifests itself in a number of different strands and is caused by viruses.

hepatitis A—a liver disease caused by the hepatitis A virus that is spread through contaminated water or food.

hepatitis B—a liver disease caused by the hepatitis B virus and is spread through contact with infected blood.

hepatitis C—a liver disease caused by the hepatitis C virus and is spread through contact with infected blood.

hepatitis D—a liver disease caused by the hepatitis D virus, it is spread through contact with infected blood and can only occur if the individual already has hepatitis B.

hepatitis E—a liver disease caused by the hepatitis E virus and is spread through contact with contaminated food or water.

hertz (Hz)—the base unit of frequency. One hertz is one cycle per second, 50 hertz is 50 cycles per second. The term *hertz* replaced cycles per second (cps).

heterozygous—possessing two different forms of a particular gene one dominant and one recessive.

highly qualified teachers (HQT)—teachers who have a bachelor's degree from an accredited institution of higher education and a valid standard professional certificate in the subjects they teach in addition to other requirements related to specific teaching levels and experience. In early childhood education, that typically includes passing state or other tests in content areas.

hippocampus—a small structure at the base of the temporal lobe of the brain that plays a role in memory and in the ability to rapidly learn and process new information.

hitching—a method of moving where the child's bottom is on the floor and she scoots, using her legs for propulsion.

homeless people—people who lack a fixed, regular, and adequate nighttime residence.

homozygous—a condition where the genes in two specific chromosomes are the same. Both are dominant (AA) or both are recessive (aa).

householder—the person in whose name a housing unit is owned or rented.

huggables—any soft toy a child can hold and hug.

hydrocephalus—excessive fluid in the brain cavities.

hyperglycemia—a condition where an excessive amount of glucose (sugar) circulates in the blood plasma; also called high blood sugar.

hyperopia—difficulty seeing near objects because the eyeball is too short or the lens and cornea are too strong; also known as farsightedness.

hypertension—a medical condition in which the blood pressure is chronically elevated; also called high blood pressure.

hypertonic—muscle tone that is too high (tight) causing children to overreact to normal stimuli.

hypertonicity—increased tension of the muscles, with the muscle tone abnormally tight or rigid.

hypoglycemia—a condition characterized by an abnormally low blood sugar (glucose) level.

hypothermia—a condition where a person's temperature drops below that required for normal metabolic and bodily functions.

hypotonic—when muscle tone is low, less responsive than expected, or floppy.

hypoxia—a condition where some or all of the body is deprived of adequate oxygen.

I

illegal immigrants—individuals who cross national borders in a way that violates the immigration laws of the destination country, or a foreigner who entered legally but overstayed his or her visa.

immigrant children—children who were born outside the United States and currently live in the United States.

immigrant parents—parents who were born outside of the United States and currently reside in the United States.

impulse control disorders—disorders characterized by an inability to resist the impulse to take actions that are harmful to self or to others.

impulsiveness—a personality trait where individuals act on impulse without adequately thinking about the consequences of their actions.

inability to follow directions—a characteristic of children with SLD, ADHD, and communication disorders.

incus—the anvil-shaped small bone, or ossicle, in the middle ear that connects the malleus to the stapes.

indirect language stimulation—the language the child hears and overhears that is not directed to him.

indiscriminate attachment—a form of attachment that is present from birth to 4 to 6 months, during which infants enjoy social interactions with almost all adults.

individualism—focuses on the person and places personal achievement and goals over group goals.

individualized education program (IEP)—a written statement for each child with an identified disability that is developed and revised in accordance with the IDEA.

Individuals with Disabilities Education Acts (IDEA)—the laws and their amendments governing the rights of children with disabilities in educational settings after 1990.

infant mortality—the number of deaths of infants 1 year of age or younger per 1,000 live births.

infant or toddler with a disability—a child younger than 3 years of age who needs early intervention services because she is experiencing developmental delays, has a diagnosed physical or mental condition that has a high probability of resulting in developmental delay, or in some states is at risk of developing such delays.

inferior—below; the feet are inferior to the waist.

informational print—print whose goal is to convey information such as newspapers, calendars, informational texts, and reference books.

inner ear—a bony labyrinth in the skull that starts at the oval window and contains the cochlea and the vestibular apparatus that consists of three semicircular canals and the vestibule.

intelligence quotient (IQ)—a score derived from a standardized test designed to measure intelligence.

intensity—the noise measurement of sound intensity in the air at a listener's location.

interactive shared reading—involves an adult reading a book to a child or a small group of children and using a variety of techniques to engage the children in the text.

interim alternative educational setting—a temporary educational setting for children who violate the code of student conduct.

interpreter—an individual, certified by the National Registry of Interpreters for the Deaf, who translates spoken English into American Sign Language.

intrathecal—the space surrounding the spinal cord, the spinal canal.

intraventricular hemorrhage (IVH)—bleeding into or near the normal fluid spaces (ventricles) of the brain.

iris—the part of the eye that controls the amount of light that enters by opening wider to let in more light or closing to decrease the amount of light.

J

jargon—terminology that relates to a specific activity, profession, or group; also professional slang or shorthand.

jaundice—a yellowish discoloration of the skin, whites of the eyes, and mucous membranes, caused by high levels of bilirubin in the blood; also called icterus.

K

karyotyping—a laboratory test where chromosomes are separated from cells, stained, and arranged from largest to smallest so that their number and structure can be studied under magnification.

ketones—compounds produced when the body uses fat for energy, which happens when the body does not have enough insulin to use sugar for energy.

kinesthetic—the process of sensing bodily position, weight, or movement of the muscles, tendons, or joints.

kinship care—a situation where children who cannot safely live at home live in a foster home with relatives or other adults whom they know.

kinship foster care—when a child welfare agency places children in the care of relatives.

L

labor—the process of regular uterine contractions that result in child birth.

language—used for communication and as a cognitive tool to organize information and influence thinking and memory skills.

lead—a heavy metal that can get into the blood and cause a medical condition, lead poisoning, which can lead to irreversible neurological problems.

least restrictive environment (LRE)—an environment where, to the maximum extent appropriate, children with disabilities are educated with children who do not have disabilities.

legally blind—visual acuity no better than 20/200 in the better eye, with the best possible correction, or with a field of vision restricted to 20 degrees or less (tunnel vision) in the better eye instead of the usual 105 degrees.

lens—a transparent structure in the eye, located behind the pupil, that helps focus light rays on the retina.

ligaments—fibrous bands or sheets of tissues that connect bones to other bones. They provide stability to a joint during rest and movement.

lightening—the descent of the uterus and fetus into the pelvic cavity prior to birth, thereby changing the contour of the abdomen and facilitating the mother's breathing by lessening pressure under the diaphragm.

limbic system—part of the brain involved in controlling emotions, emotions associated with memories and motivation, and emotional reactions to stress.

limited English proficiency (LEP)—the term used by the public schools, the IDEA, and No Child Left Behind to identify children who do not understand or speak academic English well.

linguistically isolated—a home situation where no one older than the age of 13 speaks English fluently or exclusively.

literacy—the minimum level of knowledge and skills that children need in a particular academic or developmental area to continue moving toward becoming competent adults.

low vision—visual acuity between 20/70 and 20/200 in the better eye, with the best corrected vision.

lumbar vertebrae—the largest and lowest segments of the movable part of the spinal cord, L-1 to L-5.

lymphoid cells—white blood cells that are part of the lymphatic system.

M

malleability—the plasticity of some parts of the brain to change.

malleus—a hammer-shaped small bone in the middle ear that connects with the incus and is attached to the inner surface of the eardrum. It transmits sound vibrations from the eardrum to the incus.

mandate—a requirement to provide a free appropriate public education.

mandated services—those that must be provided, as opposed to *discretionary services*.

mania—an abnormal mental state characterized by an elevated or irritable mood, exaggerated self-importance, racing thoughts, and hyperactivity.

manic episode—the period when an individual is in a manic state.

manifestation of the disability—an educational distinction between behavior that is caused by the disability and behavior that is unrelated to the disability. The determination is also related to appropriate implementation of the IEP.

mast cells—cells that reside in several types of tissues and contain many granules rich in histamine and heparin; mast cells play a role in allergic reactions.

median—the middle number in an array of numbers.

median plane—an imaginary line that runs vertically through the middle of the human body, dividing it in half.

Medicaid—a health program for children and families with low incomes in the United States.

medulla oblongata—the lower portion of the brainstem that controls autonomic functions.

meiosis—the process of cell division where the genetic material in the chromosome is mixed and divided into sex cells, the number of chromosomes in a cell is divided in half, and then recombined with the sex cell to form an offspring with 23 chromosome pairs.

meningitis—an inflammation of the protective membranes (meninges) that cover the brain and spinal cord.

meningocele—a form of spina bifida where there is a membranous sac over the spinal cord. If the spinal cord is not entrapped children are usually symptom-free. Also called *meningomyelocele* and *meningomyelocele*.

mesoderm—the middle of the three germ layers in embryos that becomes the circulatory system, bones, muscles, and other parts.

metacognition—the act of thinking about one's own thinking and using this information to regulate one's own learning.

metaphase—a stage in mitosis where the chromosomes align in the middle of the cell before being separated into daughter cells.

metarules—rules about making rules.

metered-dose inhaler with spacers—a method of dispensing drugs to children that gives a specific amount of medication with each puff. The spacers attached to the metered-dose inhaler hold the medication, allowing children to inhale it in a few breaths instead of just one.

methylphenidate stimulants—medications that block dopamine transporters; because there are fewer available transporters, there is increased dopamine at the synapses.

midbrain—part of the brainstem, is the nerve pathway of the cerebral hemispheres and contains auditory and visual reflex centers.

middle ear—the portion of the ear between the eardrum and the oval window, containing three ossicles.

middle ear disease—an inflammation of the middle ear and is associated with fluid in the middle ear space that may or may not have a bacterial infection.

midline—an imaginary line that runs vertically through the middle of the body, dividing it in half.

mind reading—assuming to know what another person is thinking or feeling without asking.

minimal brain damage—a neurologic condition characterized by learning and behavioral disorders, a former name for attention-deficit/hyperactivity disorder.

minority—a subordinate group of people who are disadvantaged; it is not necessarily a numerical minority.

mitosis—the process of cell division that results in two genetically identical cells.

mixed cerebral palsy—an impairment that results from damage to both the pyramidal and extrapyramidal areas of the brain. Children with mixed cerebral palsy can have symptoms of both rigidity and spasticity (rigidity in the arms and spasticity in the legs).

mixed hearing loss—a hearing loss that includes both a sensorineural and a conductive loss.

mixed receptive-expressive language disorder—involves the impairment of both understanding and speaking language.

mixed-status families—families where some members are legally in the United States and others are not.

modeling—demonstrating behavior that is appropriate in a variety of situations.

modulation—the ability to regulate responses in the context of ongoing events.

monozygotic twins—occur when a single egg is fertilized to form one zygote, which then divides into two separate embryos; also called identical twins.

mood disorders—conditions where the common emotional state is distorted or inappropriate to the circumstances; mood disorders include depression as well as alternating states of depression and mania.

morbidity—the occurrence of complications such as disease, disability, and chronic illness.

morphemes—the smallest meaningful units of language. They include words or meaningful word parts. Prefixes and suffixes are morphemes.

morphology—looks at how adding or deleting parts of words (prefixes and suffixes) changes their meaning.

morula—an early stage of embryonic development when it is a solid ball consisting of 12 to 32 cells.

motor planning—the ability to originate, organize, plan, initiate, sequence, and then execute new or unpracticed fine or gross motor activity.

motor strip—is a band that runs down the back of the frontal lobe of the brain that controls bowel movements and other body movements.

multiple intelligences—refer to an educational theory showcasing eight kinds of intelligence in children, which was developed by Howard Gardner.

muscle strength—the force of a muscle contraction.

muscle tone—the ability of the muscles to respond to stretch.

mutation—damage or change to the DNA of a gene that alters the genetic message it carries.

myelin sheath—an electrically insulating layer of glial cells that surrounds the axons of many neurons.

myeloid cells—cells that originate in the bone marrow or spinal cord and the term is used to describe leukocytes that are not lymphocytes and are related to cancer classification.

myoclonic seizures—brief, single, rapid contractions of muscles that may be repeated and can involve isolated muscle groups or more general muscles of the trunk and limbs. Some are subtle, with just head nodding, whereas others cause sudden flexion or bending backward that almost seems to pull the child over.

myopia—nearsightedness, is a refractive defect of the eye where parallel lines of light focus the image in front of the retina because the eyeball is too long, or the cornea is too steep. Children see objects close to them, but distant objects are blurred or fuzzy.

myringotomy with tubal insertion—the process of inserting grommets, tiny ventilation tubes, into the eardrum to allow air to pass freely into the middle ear to keep the pressure at atmospheric levels. A grommet is needed if the Eustachian tube is not working properly.

N

natural environments—educational, social, and recreational environments that are as close to what they would be if children were typically developing.

nebulizer—a device used to administer medication to children in the form of a liquid mist. It is commonly used in treating cystic fibrosis, asthma, and other respiratory diseases.

necrotizing enterocolitis—a medical condition primarily seen in premature infants, where portions of the bowel undergo necrosis (tissue death).

neonatal deaths—deaths that occur during the first 28 days after birth.

neonatal intensive care unit (NICU)—a hospital unit in specially designated hospitals, with highly trained staff and technological equipment designed for the acute care of very sick newborns.

neonatal nurses—nurses who specialize in caring for newborn infants, particularly at-risk neonates.

neonatal—the period of development for newborn infants until they reach 28 days.

neonatologists—pediatricians with a subspecialty in neonatology who provide medical care to newborn infants, especially ill or premature newborns.

neural groove—a shallow groove between the neural folds. It gradually deepens as the neural folds elevate and meet, which converts the groove into a closed tube, for example, the neural tube or canal.

neural tube—the embryo's forerunner of the brain and spinal cord, the central nervous system.

neural tube defects—birth defects of the brain and spinal cord; the most common ones are spina bifida and anencephaly.

neuroblastoma—a malignant (cancerous) tumor that develops from nerve tissue.

neurons—the specialized nerve cells that make up the central nervous system and they receive and transmit messages.

neurodevelopmental milestones—focus on the attainment of specific motor skills in infants and young children.

neurotransmitters—chemicals released from one neuron that cross the synaptic cleft to a receiving neuron.

No Child Left Behind Act (NCLB), P.L. 107–110)—a federal law that is the reauthorization of the Elementary and Secondary Education Act, which increased accountability, provided choices for parents, gave greater flexibility to states and schools, emphasized reading and math, and was designed to close achievement gaps.

nonnormative—relates to events or situations that are unusual or do not follow the expected pattern.

norepinephrine—a neurotransmitter that affects parts of the brain where attention and responding actions are controlled.

norm-referenced—the process of comparing the scores of one individual to the scores of all comparable individuals who have done the same thing (the norm).

norm-referenced measures—comparing assessment scores of one child to comparable children who have taken that particular assessment.

normal development—development that follows a typical pattern.

normalization—an approach that ensures that children who require special services are not separated from experiences of normal life, that is, educational, social, and recreational environments are as close to natural environments as possible.

normative—relates to a typical or "normal" pattern of events or situations or the concept of how events ought to happen.

O

obesity—for children, height and weight are plotted on the CDC BMI-for-age growth charts where children equal to or greater than 95 percentile are considered obese. For adults, having a body mass index (BMI) of 30 or more or being more than 30 pounds over the recommended weight for height.

objective-referenced assessments—compare how a child is performing relative to specific objectives that have been designed for that particular activity or behavior.

objectivity—an aspect of testing that assumes that others administering the test would get the same results provided the requirements of the measure were adhered to.

occipital lobe—one of four lobes of the brain; it contains the primary visual receptive cortex and is the visual processing center of the brain.

occupational print—written material related to a particular profession or area; waitstaff-menu, physician-perscription, and theater-tickets.

occupational therapists—specialists who work from a developmental base. Their therapy emphasizes vestibular, tactile, kinesthetic or proprioception, perceptual motor development, fine motor coordination, and self-help/adaptive skills

oligoarticular—the most common type of juvenile rheumatoid arthritis where four or fewer joints are involved.

onlooker play—when a child is watching other children play but is not actively participating.

operant conditioning—the modification of voluntary behavior based on the association of a behavior with a stimulus (reinforcement or punishment).

ophthalmologist—a medical doctor who specializes in diseases and surgery of the visual pathways, including the eye, brain, and areas surrounding the eye.

oppositional defiant disorder—a disorder characterized by an ongoing pattern of disobedient, hostile, and defiant behavior toward authority figures.

optic chiasm—the part of the brain where the optic nerves partially cross.

optic disk—a blind spot where ganglion cell axons exit the eye to form the optic nerve.

optic nerve (cranial nerve II)—the nerve that transmits visual information from the retina to the brain.

optic nerve hypoplasia—a medical condition that results in underdevelopment of the optic nerves.

oral approach—a way of teaching children with hearing impairments, with the goal of the child learning spoken language and communicating verbally by looking at the speaker's face and mouth to speechread, and using hearing aids to take advantage of residual hearing; also called auditory-oral approach.

organ of Corti—is an organ in the inner ear that contains auditory sensory cells, or "hair cells."

orientation and mobility specialist—a vision specialist who helps children learn to move about their home, school, and community with confidence.

orthoses—devices such as braces and splints that are designed to maintain range of motion, prevent contractures, provide stability, and control involuntary movements.

orthotist—a medical professional concerned with the application and manufacture of orthoses, devices such as braces that support or correct human function.

ossicles—the three smallest bones in the human body (malleus, incus, and stapes) that are within the middle ear space and transmit sound from the air to the fluid-filled cochlea.

otitis media—the inflammation of the middle ear, or a middle ear infection.

otitis media with effusion (OME)—when the middle ear has a sticky, thick fluid, but there is no infection.

otoacoustic emissions testing (OAE)—a computerized hearing screening test that evaluates the cochlear (inner ear) function and detects hearing loss without the child's participation.

otolaryngologist—a physician who specializes in the treatment of diseases of the ear, nose, and throat.

otologist—a physician who treats diseases of the ear.

ova—the female reproductive cell or the egg.

oval window—a membrane-covered opening that leads from the middle ear to the vestibule of the inner ear.

ovary—the female organ that produces reproductive cells or ova.

overweight—for children, comparing height and weight on the CDC BMI-for-age growth charts and being in the 85th to 95th percentile; for adults having a body mass index (BMI) of 24 to 29.99 or being between 25 to 30 pounds over the recommended weight for height.

oxytocin—a synthetic form of a natural hormone that causes the uterus to contract and can be used to increase the strength of contractions.

P

paradigm—a way or pattern of looking at the world.

paraeducators—individuals who work under the supervision of educators in the classroom to provide additional instruction, particularly in inclusive classrooms. Paraeducators include paraprofessionals such as teachers' aides, educational assistants, instructional assistants, and other members of the special education team.

parallel play—when the child is playing near other children using similar materials but playing in his own way.

parallel talk—a method of adult speech where the adult gives words to the child's behavior and describes what the child is doing, seeing, or hearing.

parentese—speaking at a slower rate, using exaggerated intonation and stress, with more variation in pitch and loudness, and a limited vocabulary with short, simple sentences.

parietal lobe—above the occipital lobe, it integrates information from different modalities and is important in determining spatial sense and visual coordination.

partial seizures—can begin anywhere in the brain, are limited to a small region of one hemisphere, and allow continuance of normal alertness. If a partial seizure becomes complex, it can spread and alter consciousness.

patent ductus arteriosus (PDA)—a congenital heart defect caused by the lack of closure of the ductus arteriosus after birth.

pediatric—a branch of medicine that deals with the medical care of infants, children, and adolescents.

pediatric nurse—a registered nurse who specializes in young children. She usually has additional training in developmental screening tools, family counseling, child care, and early intervention.

pediatric oncologist—a medical professional who treats children with cancer.

peer-reviewed journals—scholarly publications that are sent to other scholars in the same field (the author's peers) to get their opinion on the quality of the scholarship, appropriateness for the journal, relevance to the field, and so on.

people first language—a way of using language so that the term disability is not placed in a preceding adjectival phrase, people and conditions are not confused, and groups of people are not put into categories such as "the disabled".

perception—the cognitive process of receiving information from the senses and organizing and interpreting them.

perceptual-motor development—the ability to mentally organize, interpret, and respond to sensory information.

performance standards—standards that specify at what level children need to know and demonstrate their understanding of a concept to meet the standard.

perinatal period—begins the 28th week of gestation and continues until the infant is 28 days old.

perseveration—getting stuck on a particular topic or task and not being able to change to another topic or task.

pervasive developmental disorder (PDD)—a term used by the American Psychiatric Association that includes autism, Asperger's syndrome, Rett syndrome, childhood disintegrative disorder and pervasive developmental disorder–not otherwise specified (PDD–NOS).

pervasive developmental disorder not otherwise specified (PDD–NOS)—used as a classification when symptoms are present but do not meet the criteria for a particular category.

pharynx—the part of the neck and throat that is behind the mouth and nasal cavity.

phenotype—an individual's physical appearance and constitution.

phobia—a marked and persistent fear that is excessive or unreasonable, and set off by anticipating, seeing, or coming into contact with a particular object or situation.

phonemes—letter-sound combinations. English has 44 phonemes: each letter has a sound, vowels have two sounds (short and long), and some letter combinations have their own sound.

phonemic awareness—the child's ability to differentiate sounds in spoken works, think about them, and purposefully manipulate the sounds.

phonological awareness—the child's conscious awareness that speech is composed of identifiable units, such as spoken words, syllables, and sounds.

phonological disorders—errors in sound production, use, representation, or organization.

phonological patterns—sound patterns in speech.

phonology—the study of phonemes and the rules for combining types of phonemes, pauses, and stress to form words.

phonomes—individual speech sounds that can be combined to create words.

physical activity—energy output, promotes growth and development.

physiatrist—a medical doctor who specializes in physical medicine, rehabilitation, and pain medicine.

physical therapists—state-licensed health professionals, largely medically based, whose skills are directed toward preventing disability by developing, improving, or restoring more efficient muscular functioning and maintaining maximum motor functioning for a child.

pincer grip—the ability to hold objects neatly between the thumb and index finger, which typically develops in infants between 12 and 15 months of age.

placenta—organ that connects the developing fetus to the uterine wall to supply oxygen and nutrients and take away wastes.

platelets—cells circulating in the blood that are involved in the formation of blood clots.

polyarticular JRA—a form of juvenile rheumatoid arthritis that involves five or more joints; it is serious because of the number of joints involved, the seriousness of the involvement, and the length of time it lasts.

pons—part of the brainstem, plays a role in relaying messages in the brain, controls arousal, and regulates respiration.

posterior rhizomotomy—a surgical procedure that cuts motor fibers that cause the greatest spasticity in children's legs. Spasticity is reduced, but there may be some degree of motor weakness.

postterm—a pregnancy that lasts more than 42 weeks or more than 294 days after the first day of the last menstrual cycle.

posttraumatic stress disorder—a disorder that results from exposure to an extreme traumatic stressor, such as actual or threatened death or serious injury; it usually involves feelings of intense fear, helplessness, or horror, and in young children this may result in disorganized or agitated behavior.

poverty—measured by a set of dollar values called thresholds that vary by family size, number of children, and age of householder.

poverty line—a governmentally determined dollar amount used to identify individuals and families who live above or below poverty.

powerful interactions—interactions when an adult intentionally connects with the child by doing or saying something to guide the child's learning.

pragmatics—the personal and social use of language. It includes eye contact, turn taking in conversation, use of appropriate words in social conversation, and taking the perspective of the listener, as well as understanding and appropriately using body language and expressions.

praxis—the learned ability of the brain to conceive of, organize, and carry out a sequence of unfamiliar actions to attain a goal. Praxis has three components: ideation, motor planning, and execution.

predictive validity—a type of validity concerned with the ability to predict the same or related characteristics in the future.

preeclampsia—a condition that only occurs during pregnancy and is characterized by a rapidly progressive high blood pressure and protein in the urine.

prefixes—morphemes that come at the beginning of words.

prelingually hearing impaired—when a hearing impairment occurs before children have established a language base.

pressure-equalization tube—the Eustachian tube that links the pharynx to the middle ear. If the tube does not work well, fluid can collect in the middle ear.

preterm labor—labor that begins before 37 weeks of pregnancy.

primary intervention site—the place where most early intervention takes place. It can be a school, home, early care and education center, or other location.

primary motor cortex—located at the back of the frontal lobe and, working with the pre-motor areas of the brain, controls the planning and execution of body movement.

private kinship—an arrangement of caring for children by kin that occurs without the involvement of a child welfare agency.

processing disorders—disorders that involve the brain's ability to recognize and interpret sensory input.

progesterone—a steroid hormone that helps prepare the female body for pregnancy and helps to maintain the pregnancy.

program standards—the yard stick against which program quality is measured. They include system policies and/or how services are provided.

prone—lying face down on the stomach.

proprioception—the unconscious perception of movement and spatial orientation that comes from feedback from stimuli from within the body itself.

prosthesis—an artificial extension that replaces a missing body part.

prosthetic limb—an artificial device extension that replaces a missing limb.

proximal—close to the center or midline.

proximodistal—a pattern of development that goes from the center of the body to the extremities, with the trunk of the body developing before arms; and the arms, before hands and fingers.

psychodynamic model—focuses on emotional growth and change and uses individual and group therapy to solve issues.

psychometric issues—concerns that relate to the design, administration, and interpretation of tests.

pull-out programs—taking children out of the regular class and placing them in a special class to do concentrated work in specific subject matter areas in which the child was performing below grade-level expectation or much higher than expected.

punishment—a negative consequence that causes a behavior to occur with less frequency.

pupil—the opening in the center of the iris of the eye through which light enters.

pure tones—particular sine waves that are free of noise and overtones to identify hearing thresholds.

pure-tone audiometer—an electroacoustical generator that produces pure tones at selected frequencies with an output that is calibrated to test hearing thresholds.

pure-tone hearing screening—a basic test to find out whether a hearing loss is present or not by using pure tones at different frequencies (typically 1000, 2000, and 4000 Hz).

pyramidal tract—a massive collection of long motor axons that go between the brain and the spinal column.

Q

quadriplegia—an impairment that involves the motor control of all four limbs. Head control may be poor, and in cerebral palsy there is usually impairment of speech and eye coordination.

R

racial—the characteristics of groups or populations based on phenotype.

radiation—energy in the form of waves or particles.

radiation therapy—the medical use of ionizing radiation as part of cancer treatment to control malignant cells.

range of motion—the measurement of the achievable distance of movement between the flexed position and the extended position of a particular joint or muscle group; the range of motion of the elbow is a little less than 180 degrees.

rapport—a relationship characterized as synchronous and harmonious.

reactive attachment disorder—a severe disorder of infancy or early childhood whose main characteristic is lack of social relatedness. There are two types: inhibited or disinhibited.

reading—the cognitive process of decoding written symbols to determine meaning.

rebus—a representation of a word or phrase by pictures or symbols. Directions using a rebus menu are often used with prereading children.

red blood cells—the most common type of blood cell; they deliver oxygen from the lungs to body tissues via the blood.

referral—a formal process requiring parents to fill out specific forms requesting assessment by a team of professionals to determine whether a child's academic, behavioral, or physical development qualifies him for special education services.

reflective practice—the process and capability of reflecting on one's actions to evaluate them and engage in a process of continual learning.

refractive errors—visual problems such as nearsightedness and farsightedness, caused by the inability of the eye to focus light effectively.

regulations—the codification of rules published in the Federal Register by federal departments and agencies.

Rehabilitation Act of 1973—mandated equal opportunities for children with disabilities in settings that receive federal funds. See also *Section 504*.

reinforcement—a consequence that causes a behavior to occur with greater frequency.

reliability—the consistency of a measure, that is, the degree that scores are consistent, dependable, or repeatable and are the same or very close to the same each time it is given to the same individual.

remarried families—families that occur upon the legal remarriage of a person who was divorced or widowed and who is actively involved with a biological or adopted child from a prior union.

repetitions—when an adult restates all or part of a child's phrase, particularly when he has made an incorrect utterance.

resistant attachment—a response to inconsistent caregiving characterized by children's ambivalent feelings.

respite care—a system of care designed to give adult caregivers a break from caring for a child with a disability.

response to instruction—the core educational programming all children in the classroom receive, with the expectation that 80 percent of the children in the class are learning at the expected rate.

response to intervention (RTI)—more specific programming for children who are not learning at the expected rate and this intervention is a substantial change in programming for about 20 percent of children.

reticular activating system—the name of the part of the brain (the reticular formation and its connections) believed to be the center of arousal and motivation in individuals.

retina —a thin layer of neural cells that lines the back of the eyeball.

retinopathy of prematurity—a disease of the eye that affects prematurely born infants. It may be caused by the disorganized growth of retinal blood vessels and can result in scarring and retinal detachment.

rods—cylindrically shaped photoreceptor cells in the retina of the eye that can function in less light than cone cells. Rods are responsible for night vision; also called rod cells.

Rett syndrome—a severe neurodevelopmental disorder with normal development for 6 to 18 months eventually resulting in loss of purposeful hand skills, poor language skills, and poor social engagement.

role release—the process of transferring information and skills traditionally associated with one discipline (for example, occupational therapy) to team members of other disciplines (early childhood).

root words—real words that can be made into new words by adding prefixes and suffixes.

rotation—movement of an object in a circular motion such as the ability to twist or turn a part of the body like the wrist.

routines —events that must be completed on a regular basis and often involve the opportunity to practice adaptive skills and embed IEP/IFSP goals.

rubric—a scoring tool for subjective assessments.

s

sacrum—a large, triangular bone at the base of the spine. Its upper part connects with the last lumbar vertebra. It has five parts, with the bottom part connecting to the coccyx or tailbone.

scaffolding—a dynamic system of learning as adults provide children with support that allows them to complete tasks they are interested in but could not do alone.

schedules—refer to who will do what and when they will do it in the classroom.

school psychologists—trained in both psychology and education; they collaborate with educators, parents, and other professionals to create a safe, supportive learning environment that connects home, school, and community for all children.

scoliosis—a condition that involves complex lateral and rotational curvature and deformity of the spine.

scotoma—a type of visual loss where there is an area of impaired visual acuity (blind spots) surrounded by a field of normal vision.

second stage of labor—the stage of labor that begins when the cervix is fully dilated and effaced, and ends with the birth of the infant.

secondary gains—extra privileges that children receive based on a particular state or condition or tasks that they avoid because they don't want to do them.

secondhand smoke—smoke breathed in by a person in the environment who is not smoking; also called environmental tobacco smoke.

Section 504—part of the Rehabilitation Act of 1973 which stipulates that individuals cannot be excluded, denied benefits from, or discriminated against by any entity receiving federal funds. Physical accommodations for a 504 plan can include posted class rules, color codes, preferential seating, reorganized work space, an extra seat or table, a standing workstation, a quiet area to study in, and so on.

secure attachment—characterized by children seeking out their caregiver for comfort and using her as a secure base to explore from.

seizures—abnormal electrical discharges in the brain. Symptoms depend on the part of the brain involved and may cause unusual sensations, uncontrollable muscle spasms, and loss of consciousness.

selective mutism—a condition where a child can talk but does not talk in some social situations such as school.

self-talk—a child talking to himself about what he is doing as a method of self-regulation.

semantics—the psycholinguistic system that governs the relationship between words or phrases and their meanings—the intent and meaning of utterances.

semicircular canals—three half-circular, interconnected tubes located inside each ear that help maintain balance (vestibular sense).

sensorineural hearing loss—a type of hearing loss where the auditory nerve (cranial nerve VIII), the inner ear, or central processing centers of the brain are defective.

sensory hearing loss—hearing loss due to poor hair cell function. The hair cells in the cochlear may be abnormal at birth or damaged because of an illness such as bacterial meningitis.

sensory integration—a neurological process that organizes sensations and information about the environment for the body to effectively function in that particular situation.

sensory integration disorder—a disorder where the processes of receiving and processing sensory information accurately is dysfunctional, sometimes called a sensory processing disorder.

sensory processing disorders—conditions where signals from the senses don't get organized or interpreted accurately by the brain.

separation anxiety disorder—a psychological condition in which the child feels excessive and recurring anxiety about being separated form home or family.

sepsis—sometimes referred to as blood poisoning, is a generalized systemic response to infection instead of a localized response at the site of the infection.

serotonin—a neurotransmitter that may play a role in the regulation of anger, aggression, body temperature, mood, sleep, vomiting, sexuality, and appetite.

service coordinator—a designated individual, who in addition to being part of the IFSP team, has the specific role of communicating with the family, setting up meetings, and coordinating information and events.

shaping—process of gradually and systematically changing a particular behavior toward a target behavior by rewarding successive approximations (sitting in a chair near the group, sitting behind the group, and eventually, sitting with the group).

shared reading—involves an adult reading a book to one child or a small group of children without requiring extensive interactions from them.

short attention span—for their developmental level, children do not stay at tasks for long, may not finish them, and don't get satisfaction from them.

shyness—characterized by an ambivalent approach/avoidance quality often in response to new adults.

sickle cell disease—inherited blood disorder where many red blood cells have an abnormal sticky, rigid, sickle shape that is conducive to clogging; the cells have a life span of about 10 to 20 days which results in pain and chronic fatigue.

sight vocabulary—the number of words a child can read without sounding them out.

simple tics—tics that are sudden brief, repetitive movements using a limited number of muscle groups, such as eye blinking, shoulder shrugging, or throat clearing.

small for gestational age (SGA)—a designation used for infants whose weight is below the 10th percentile for their gestational age.

social competence—the ability to select and carry out interpersonal goals successfully.

social disorders—disorders related to attachment, separation, and social situations; also called anxiety disorders.

social networks—systems consisting of individuals and the ties between the individuals within their social system.

social phobia—a marked and persistent fear of situations that expose a child to strangers or to embarrassment.

sociocultural factors—issues that involve both social and cultural factors and include, but are not limited to, financial factors and cultural/racial/ethnic factors that influence how families function.

sociohistorical time—looks at a particular event (birth of a child with a disability) in the context of what is happening in society and the world at that time.

solitary play—occurs when a child is playing alone with materials that are different from other children's.

somatic problems—problems that affect the body, such as an illness.

spastic—when muscle tone is too high (tight) and children overreact to normal stimuli.

spasticity—the inability of the muscles to relax; it does not mean paralysis.

spatial awareness—an organized awareness of the objects in the space around one and the body's position in space.

spatial relationship—an understanding of the size and distance of objects in relation to the human body.

special education—specially planned instruction, at no cost to the parents, designed to meet the unique needs of a child with a disability.

speech—spoken language.

speech sound disorders—problems with articulation and phonological patterns.

speech-language pathologists—state licensed specialists who have completed a degree program with an accredited college. They provide assessments and intervention for children with feeding and swallowing problems and communication delays and disorders.

spina bifida—a developmental birth defect caused by the incomplete closure of the neural tube. The particular area of the spine affected determines the child's abilities, as all the areas below the incomplete closure will have some degree of paralysis.

spina bifida occulta—a split in the vertebral arches of the spinal column. Individuals have no symptoms and may not even know they have the split.

spinal atrophy—the progressive degeneration of the motor-nerve cells, resulting in a slow weakening of the body's muscle strength.

spinal cord—a thin, tubular bundle of nerves that is part of the central nervous system. It is enclosed in and protected by the bony vertebral column. It is divided into four major regions and has about 30 different segments or sections. It sends motor and sensory messages from the brain to other parts of the body.

stages—qualitatively different periods of development.

standards—a way of determining a common definition and application of a particular area of study by defining what children should know and be able to do in specific areas.

standard deviations—a measure that shows how much variation there is from the average, mean, or expected value.

standardized tests—measures that are administered and scored in a consistent or "standard" way each time they are given. Tests are constructed by specialists based on standardized norms.

stapes—the stirrup-shaped small bone in the middle ear that attaches the incus to the oval window. It transmits sound vibrations from the incus to the membrane of the inner ear inside the oval window. It is the smallest and lightest bone in the human body.

state—the levels of consciousness an infant experiences from quiet sleep to active crying.

state regulation—the ability of the infant to voluntarily move between states, such as moving from being drowsy into or out of sleep.

stepfamilies—families where one or both of the adults have a child from a previous union.

stepsiblings—children who share a parent, but that parent is the biological parent of one child and the stepparent of the other child.

sterilization—a surgical technique used to make a male or female unable to procreate.

stimulants—medications that increase the activity of the sympathetic nervous system, the central nervous system or both.

strabismus—a condition where the eyes are not properly aligned with each other. It is caused by a lack of coordination between the muscles that prevents the gaze of each eye from coming to the same point in space and thus preventing proper binocular vision. It may affect depth perception.

structured physical activity—activity planned and directed by an adult designed to accommodate the child's developmental level.

student accountability—part of the reporting requirements of No Child Left Behind designed to ensure that students are motivated to do their best.

subdural hematomas—blood clots that form beneath the dura (brain covering) and are often part of a more generalized injury to the brain itself. They result from sheering forces applied to the veins (acceleration–deceleration forces) that displace the brain from the dura, rupturing these membranes.

substance disorders—disorders that are characterized by the inappropriate use of drugs, alcohol, or nicotine, with or without dependence.

subthreshold conditions—conditions that do not meet the full diagnostic criteria for a particular disorder.

successive approximation—behavior that is not the final target behavior but is reinforced because it is increasingly moving closer to the target behavior.

suffixes—morphemes that come at the end of words.

superior—up or above; the head is superior to the shoulders.

supine—the condition of lying on the back with the face upward.

surfactant—a substance that allows the inner surface of the lungs to expand when an infant is born.

synapses—very small gaps separating neurons. The synapse consists of a presynaptic ending that contains neurotransmitters and other cell materials, a postsynaptic ending that contains receptor sites for neurotransmitters, and a synaptic cleft between the presynaptic and postsynaptic endings.

synaptic cleft—the gap between neuron cell membranes.

synaptic vesicles—vessels that store the various neurotransmitters that are released at the presynaptic terminal into the synaptic cleft of a synapse.

syntax—the set of linguistic rules that govern the arrangement of words into phrases or sentences, and the relationship between these elements in a sentence.

system accountability—the requirement that not only children but also systems must be assessed and evaluated for their service delivery.

systemic JRA—a form of juvenile rheumatoid arthritis that begins with a high fever and has a spectrum of involvement and severity that is broad and difficult to predict at the onset of the disease.

T

technology dependence—reliance upon technology to provide life-supporting assistive therapies because of limitations in normal body functions, such as eating or breathing.

Technology-Related Assistance for Individuals with Disabilities Act in 1988 (P.L. 100-407)—provided states incentives for developing adaptive devices for individuals with disabilities.

temperament—an aspect of emotional development that includes the child's predictable pattern of responses and preferences.

tendons—tough, flexible, ropelike fibers that connect muscle to bone. They vary in size and shape, and glide smoothly over muscles as the body moves.

teratogens—nongenetic, extraneous substances (e.g., drugs, nicotine, and alcohol) that can cause malformations in the developing fetus.

thalidomide—a sedative drug in the late 1950s that was withdrawn in 1961 because, when taken during pregnancy, it caused severe birth defects.

third stage of labor—the expulsion of the placenta.

thoracic vertebrae—the middle segment of the vertebral column, between the cervical and lumbar vertebrae T-1 to T-12. They are intermediate in size, with the upper vertebrae being much smaller than those in the lower part of the region.

thrombophilia—a blood clotting disorder in which the blood clots easily or excessively due to an abnormality in the system of coagulation.

tics—sudden, repetitive, nonrhythmic stereotyped motor movements or vocalizations that involve discrete muscle groups.

tonic-clonic seizures—(formerly called grand mal seizures) that may begin as either a partial or generalized seizure and which have two components: In the clonic state there is repetitive, rhythmic jerking of extremities, with slow and rapid components; and in the tonic state, there is sustained stiffening and perhaps jaw clenching.

total communication—an approach to working with individuals with severe or profound hearing impairments that makes use of a number of different modes of communication such as signing, oral, auditory, written, and visual aids, depending on the particular needs and abilities of the child.

Tourette syndrome—an inherited neurologic disorder whose essential features include repetitive involuntary motor or vocal tics.

toxoplasmosis—a disease caused by the protozoan parasite *Toxoplasma gondii* which, in pregnant women, can result in immunodeficient and congenitally infected infants that may lead to blindness or learning disorders.

trailing—a method of moving that young children who are visually impaired use to learn about their environment, by holding the back of their hand at waist level and gently maintaining contact with the walls and furniture as they walk.

transcultural—the ability to adapt to more than one culture.

transferring—moving (or being moved) from one piece of equipment to another or to the floor or other surface, typically starting from a wheelchair.

transitions—the times between events.

tunnel vision—the loss of peripheral vision with retention of central vision (20 degrees or less in the better eye; a typical eye has 105 degrees), resulting in a constricted circular tunnel-like field of vision.

tympanic membrane—the eardrum, a thin membrane that separates the external ear from the middle ear and transmits sound from the air to the ossicles inside the middle ear.

tympanogram—a graphic representation of the function of the tympanic membrane and ossicles of the middle ear obtained by tympanometry.

tympanometry—a testing process used to detect disorders of the middle ear.

typically developing—development that is within the normal range.

U

umbilical cord—the connecting cord between the developing embryo, or fetus, and the placenta.

unauthorized migrants—foreigners who either have illegally crossed an international political border or who have entered the country legally but then overstayed their visa.

undocumented—individuals who do not have the legal documents to be in a country.

undocumented immigrants—foreigners who either have illegally crossed an international political border or who have entered the country legally but then overstayed their visa.

universal design—the concept that products and services should be designed to be used by individuals with the widest possible range of functional capacities.

unoccupied play—when the child is not participating in an activity or watching other children.

unstructured physical activity—child-initiated physical activity that occurs as the child explores the environment.

uterus or womb—the major female reproductive organ that is connected to the Fallopian tubes on both sides and the cervix, which opens into the vagina.

V

validity—whether a test measures what it claims to measure.

vertebral arches—or neural arches that are the posterior part of a vertebra.

visual acuity—the sharpness or clarity of the image viewed.

visual closure—the ability to recognize an object from partial or limited stimulus; it focuses on perceiving part–whole relationships.

visual cortex—the region of the cerebral cortex that occupies the entire surface of the occipital lobe and receives visual data.

visual discrimination—the ability to perceive letters and words accurately by noting the likenesses and differences in their written form.

visual figure-ground discrimination—the ability to distinguish an object, shape, word, or letter from the background in which it is embedded. Problems relate to the inability to attend to individual letters or words in a page full of sentences and paragraphs.

visual memory—an aspect of memory that allows individuals to place a mental image where it can be retrieved through remembering the mental image of the original letter, word, animal, object, and so on.

visual perception—the ability to interpret information from what they see.

visual processing disorders—disorders where visual information coming into the brain is not interpreted accurately.

visual sequencing—the ability to to hold in short-term memory the order of the sequence (alphabet letters, pictures of events in a sequence, etc.).

visual tracking—the ability to focus the eyes on one point and then move them rhythmically from side to side, up and down, and diagonally.

visually limited—a type of visual impairment where children are considered sighted children for educational purposes, are limited in their use of vision.

voluntary kinship care—when a child welfare agency tells parent(s) it will seek a foster care placement for a child unless the child is placed with kin outside of their house.

W

white blood cells—or leukocytes, cells of the immune system that defend the body against both infectious disease and foreign materials to protect against disease.

white matter—myelinated axons that connect gray matter areas to each other and carry nerve impulses. The axons are covered in a protective fatty coating of glial cells.

word families—related words built by using a root word.

wrap-around child care—child care that is added to the school day or other activities to meet the needs of working parents.

Z

zone of proximal development (ZPD)—the gap between what a child can do independently and what he can do with adult scaffolding.

zygote—the fertilized female ovum.

AAC augmentative and alternative communication

AAFA Asthma and Allergy Foundation of America

AAIDD American Association on Intellectual and Developmental Disabilities

AAMR American Association on Mental Retardation now AAIDD

AAP American Academy of Pediatrics

ABA Applied Behavior analysis

ABC antecedents, behavior, and consequences

ABS-S2 AAMD Adaptive Behavior Scale–School: 2

AAMD American Association on Mental Deficiency now AAIDD

ACAAI American College of Allergy, Asthma, and Immunology

ACF Administration for Children and Families

ADA Americans with Disabilities Act

ADAAA American with Disabilities Act Amendments Act of 2008

ADD Attention Deficit Disorder

ADHD attention-deficit/hyperactivity disorder

ADI-R Autism Diagnostic Interview-Revised

ADOS Autism Diagnostic Observation Scale-Generic

AED antiepileptic drugs

AFB American Foundation for the Blind

AIDS acquired immune deficiency syndrome

ALL acute lymphoblastic leukemia

AML acute myeloid leukemia

APA American Psychiatric Association

APH American Printing House for the Blind

AS Asperger's syndrome

ASD autism spectrum disorders

ASDC American Society for Deaf Children

ASHA American-Speech-Language-Hearing Association

ASL American sign language

ATE Association of Teacher Educators

BDI-2 Battelle Developmental Inventory, 2nd edition

BIP behavioral intervention plan

BMI body mass index

BSL British sign language

CADDRE Centers for Autism and Developmental Disabilities Research and Epidemiology

CAM complementary and alternative medicine

CAN Computer Assisted Notetaking

CARS Childhood Autism Rating Scale

CART Communication Access Realtime Translation

CAS childhood apraxia of speech

CAST Center for Applied Special Technology

CCCF Candlelighters Childhood Cancer Foundation

CCSSI Common Core State Standards Initiative

CCSSO Council of Chief State School Officers

CD compact disk

CDC Centers for Disease Control and Prevention

CDD childhood disintegrative disorder

CEC Council for Exceptional Children

CELL Center for Early Literacy Learning

CF cystic fibrosis

CFR Code of Federal Regulations

CGH comparative genomic hybridization

CHADD Children and Adults with Attention Deficit Disorder

CHAT Checklist for Autism in Toddlers

CIC clean intermittent bladder catheterization

CLAS Culturally and Linguistically Appropriate Services

CMV cytomegalovirus

CNS central nervous system

CP cerebral palsy

CPR cardiopulmonary resuscitation

CRESST National Center for Research on Evaluation, Standards, and Student Testing

CRS-R Conners Rating Scale–Revised

CSMEE Clearinghouse for Science Mathematics and Environmental Education

CTA Child Trauma Academy

CVI cortical visual impairment

DAS developmental apraxia of speech

dB decibels

DCACFP Delaware Child and Adult Care Food Program

DCD developmental coordination disorder

DEC Division for Early Childhood

DEET N,N-Diethyl-meta-toluamide

DLD Division for Learning Disabilities

DNA Deoxyribonucleic acid

DQ developmental quotient

DREDF Disability Rights Education and Defense Fund

DSM IV-TR Diagnostic and Statistical Manual of Mental Disorders 4th ed. Text Revised

E-LAP Early Learning Accomplishment Profile

ECD early child development

ECLS-K Early Childhood Education Longitudinal Study—Kindergarten Cohort

ECSE early childhood special education
EEG electroencephalogram
EEPCD Early Education Program for Children with Disabilities
EFA Epilepsy Foundation of America
EHA Education of All Handicapped Children Act
EI early intervention
EIS early intervening services
ELBW extremely low birth weight
ELG early learning guidelines
ELL English language learner
EMR educable mentally retarded
ERIC Educational Resources Information Center
FACES Family and Child Experiences Survey
FAPE free appropriate public education
FAS fetal alcohol syndrome
FASD fetal alcohol spectrum disorders
FBA functional behavior assessment
FDA Food and Drug Administration
FPG Frank Porter Graham
FSL French sign language
FXS Fragile X syndrome
GBS Group B Streptococcus
GED General Educational Development
GESP Geography Standards Project
GPS global position system
HAART Highly active antiretroviral treatment
HAV hepatitis A virus
HbAS sickle cell trait
HbS beta thalassemia
HbSS sickle cell anemia
HbSC sickle beta-plus-thalassemia
HBV hepatitis B virus
HCEEP Handicapped Children's Early Education Program
HGP National Human Genome Research Institute
HIV human immunodeficiency virus
HL hearing level
HLA human leukocyte antigen
HQT highly qualified teachers
HSV herpes simplex virus
Hz hertz
IAES interim alternative educational setting
IAN Interactive Autism Network
IDEA 2004 Individual with Disabilities Education Improvement Act of 2004
IDEA Individuals with Disabilities Education Act
IEP individualized education program
IFSP individualized family service plan
IQ intelligence quotient
IRA International Reading Association
ISTE International Society for Technology in Education
ITBS Iowa Tests of Basic Skills
IVH intraventricular hemorrhage
JDRF Juvenile Diabetes Research Foundation International

JRA juvenile rheumatoid arthritis
JSL Japanese sign language
L lexile
LAP-3 Learning Accomplishment Profile, 3rd edition
LBW low birth weight
LD Learning Disabilities
LDAA Learning Disabilities Association of America
LEP limited English proficiency
LES limited English speaking
LRE least restrictive environment
MAGs measurable annual goals
M-CHAT Modified Checklist for Autism in Toddlers
MED middle ear disease
MMR measles, mumps, and rubella vaccine
NAECS/SDE National Association of Early Childhood Specialists in State Departments of Education
NAEP National Assessment of Educational Progress
NAEYC National Association for the Education of Young Children
NAGC National Association for Gifted Children
NAMI National Alliance for the Mentally Ill
NAPVI National Association for Parents of the Visually Impaired
NASPE National Association for Sport and Physical Education
NBAS Neonatal Behavioral Assessment Scale
NCCC National Center for Cultural Competence
NCEO National Center on Educational Outcomes
NCES National Center for Educational Statistics
NCHS National Center for Health Statistics
NCLB No Child Left Behind Act
NCTM National Council of Teachers of Mathematics
NDRC Neurodevelopmental Disorders of Relating and Communicating
NEILS National Early Intervention Longitudinal Study
NGA Center National Governors Association Center for Best Practices
NHANES National Health and Nutrition Examination Survey
NHES National Health Education Standards
NICHCY National Dissemination Center for Children with Disabilities
NICU neonatal intensive care unit
NIDCD National Institute on Deafness and Other Communication Disorders
NIEER National Institute for Early Education Research
NIH National Institutes of Health
NINDS National Institute of Neurological Disorders and Stroke
NJCLD National Joint Committee on Learning Disabilities
NLM National Library of Medicine
NORD National Organization for Rare Disorders
NOS not otherwise specified
NSCIA National Spinal Cord Injury Association
OAE otoacoustic emissions testing
ODD oppositional defiant disorder

OELA Office of English Language Acquisition, Language Enhancement, and Academic Achievement for Limited English Proficient Students

OME otitis media with effusion

OT occupational therapist

P.L. public law

PCP *pneumocystis carinii* pneumonia

PDD pervasive developmental disorder

PDD-NOS pervasive developmental disorder–not otherwise specified

PECS picture exchange communication system

PLAA present level of academic achievement and functional performance

PT physical therapist

QRIS Quality Rating and Improvement Systems

ROP retinopathy of prematurity

RTC Research and Training Center

RTI response to intervention or response to instruction

SAMHSA Substance Abuse and Mental Health Services Administration

SB Stanford-Binet Intelligence Scale

SCD sickle cell disease

SERI Special Education Resources on the Internet

SFA Success for All

SGA small for gestational age

SIDS sudden infant death syndrome

SLD specific learning disabilities

SLI specific language impairment

SLL second language learner

STAR Standardized Test for the Assessment of Reading

STDs sexually transmitted diseases

TANF Temporary Aid for Needy Families

TBI traumatic brain injury

TDD telecommunication device for the deaf

TEACCH Treatment and Education of Autistic and Related Communication-Handicapped Children

Tech Act Technology-Related Assistance for Individuals with Disabilities Act

TOLD-P Test of Language Development, Primary

TORCH toxoplasmosis, other infections, rubella, cytomegalovirus, herpes simplex virus

TTY teletypewriter

U.S. DOE United States Department of Education

U.S. GAO United States Government Accountability Office

UCP United Cerebral Palsy Association

UDL universal design for learning

UMHS University of Medicine and Health Sciences

URL Uniform Resource Locator

U.S. DHHS United States Department of Health and Human Services

VABS II Vineland Adaptive Behavior Scales, 2nd Edition

VLBW very low birth weight

WASP white Anglo-Saxon Protestant

WDRB Woodcock Diagnostic Reading Battery

WHO World Health Organization

WPPSI Wechsler Preschool and Primary Scale of Intelligence

WISC-IV Wechsler Intelligence Scale for Children, fourth edition

WWC What Works Clearinghouse

X female sex chromosome

Y male sex chromosome

ZPD zone of proximal development

ZVD zidovudine

References

Abedi, J., Hofstetter, C. H., & Lord, C. (2004). Assessment accommodations for English language learners: Implications for policy-based empirical research. *Review of Educational Research, 74*(1): 1–28.

Abrams, B., Altman S. L., & Pickett, K. E. (2000). Pregnancy weight gain: Still controversial. *American Journal of Clinical Nutrition, 71,* 1233S–1241S.

Achenbach, T. M. (1991). *Manual for the child behavior checklist/4–18 Years.* Burlington, VT: University of Vermont, Department of Psychiatry.

Achenbach, T. M. (1992). *Child behavior checklist/2–3 years (CBICL/2–3).* Burlington, VT: University of Vermont, Department of Psychiatry.

Ada, A. F. (1993). *Mother-tongue, literacy as a bridge between home and school cultures: The power of two languages.* New York: McGraw-Hill.

Ada, A. F. (2002). Biliteracy for personal growth and social participation. (Foreword). In B. Perez & M. E. Torres-Guzman (Eds.), *Learning in two worlds: An integrated Spanish/English biliteracy approach* (3rd ed., pp. viii–x). Boston: Allyn & Bacon.

Administration for Children and Families (ACF). (2003). U.S. census counts adopted children for the first time. Retrieved May 17, 2007, from http://cbexpress.acf.hhs.gov/articles.cfm?issue_id = 2003-10&article_id = 717.

Administration for Children and Families (ACF). (2006). Early Head Start benefits children and families. *Early Head Start Research and Evaluation Project:* Author.

Aicardi, J. (1998). The etiology of developmental delay. *Seminars in Pediatric Neurology,* 5, 15–20.

AIDS info. (2010). HIV and pregnancy: Health information for parents. U.S. Department of Health and Human Services. Retrieved May 23, 2011, from http://aidsinfo.nih.gov/contentfiles/Perinatal_FS_en.pdf.

Ainsworth, M. D. (1963). The development of infant-mother interaction among the Ganda. In B. M. Foss (Ed.), *Determinants of infant behavior* (vol. 2, pp. 67–102). London: Methuen.

Ainsworth, M. D. (1969). Object relations, dependency, and attachment: A theoretical review of the infant-mother relationship. *Child Development, 40,* 969–1025.

Akinbami, L. J. (2006). *The state of childhood asthma, United States, 1980–2005.* Centers for Disease Control and Prevention, Advance data from vital and health statistics. Number 381. December 12, 2006. Retrieved March 15, 2011, from www.cdc.gov/nchs/data/ad/ad381.pdf.

Al-Chalabi, A., Turner, M. R., & Delamont, R. S. (2006). *The brain: A beginner's guide.* Oxford, England: One World.

Alaskan Native Heritage Center. (2008). Information about Alaska Native cultures. Retrieved November 17, 2010, from www.alaskanative.net/en/main_nav/.

Allen, M. C. (2002). Preterm outcomes research: A critical component of neonatal intensive care. *Mental Retardation and Developmental Disabilities Research Reviews, 8,* 221–232.

Amato, P. R. (2004). Divorce in social and historical context: Changing scientific perspectives on children and marital dissolution. In M. Coleman & L. H. Ganong, (Eds.), *Handbook of contemporary families: Considering the past, contemplating the future (pp.* 265–281). Thousand Oaks, CA: Sage.

American Academy of Family Physicians; American Academy of Otolaryngology—Head and Neck Surgery; and American Academy of Pediatrics Subcommittee on Otitis Media with Effusion. (2004). Otitis media with effusion. *Pediatrics, 113*(5): 1412–1429.

American Academy of Pediatrics (AAP). (1995). *How to help your child with asthma: Guidelines for parents.* Elk Grove Village, IL: Author.

American Association on Intellectual and Developmental Disabilities (AAIDD). (2008). Frequently asked questions on intellectual disability and the AAIDD definition. Retrieved November 15, 2008, from www.aamr.org/Policies/pdf/AAIDDFAQonID.pdf.

American Association on Intellectual and Developmental Disabilities (AAIDD). (2010). Definition of intellectual disability. Retrieved November 9, 2010, from http://ww.aamr.org/content_100.cfm?ID=21.

American Association on Mental Retardation (AAMR). (2002). *Mental retardation: Definition, classification, and systems of supports* (10th ed.). Washington, DC: Author.

American College of Allergy, Asthma, and Immunology (ACAAI). (2008). Landmark "pediatric allergies in America" survey uncovered negative impact of allergy symptoms on children. Retrieved September 11, 2008, from www.acaai.org/public/linkpages/Pediatric_Allergies_America_031708.htm.

American Diabetes Association. (2003). Position statement on care of children with diabetes in the school and day care setting. Retrieved September 3, 2007, from http://care.diabetesjournals.org/cgi/content/full/26/suppl_1/s131.

American Federation of Teachers. (2004). Early screening is at the heart of prevention. Retrieved July 30, 2007, from www.aft.org/pdfs/americaneducator/fall2004/EarlyScreening.pdf.

American Heart Association. (2007). Congenital heart defects in children fact sheet. Retrieved September 3, 2007, from www.americanheart.org/presenter.jhtml?identifier = 12012.

American Heart Association. (2011). The impact of congenital heart defects. Retrieved May 22, 2011, from www.heart.org/HEARTORG/Conditions/CongenitalHeartDefects/TheImpactofCongenitalHeartDefects/The-Impact-of-Congenital-Heart-Defects_UCM_001218_Article.jsp.

American Lung Association. (2006). Back-to-school with asthma: The basics for parents. Retrieved September 1, 2007, from www.lungusa.org/site/ppasp?c = dvLUK 9OOE&b = 2019829.

American Lung Association. (2011a). Asthma action plan. Retrieved May 22, 2011, from www.lungusa.org/associations/states/colorado/asthma/asthma-action-plan.html.

American Lung Association. (2011b). Asthma medicines. Retrieved May 22, 2011, from www.lungusa.org/lung-disease/asthma/living-with-asthma/making-treatment-decisions/asthma-medicines.html.

American Lung Association. (2011c). Understanding asthma. Retrieved May 22, 2011, from www.lungusa.org/lung-disease/asthma/about-asthma/understanding-asthma-asthma.html.

American Psychiatric Association (APA). (2000). *Diagnostic and statistical manual of mental disorders: DSM-IV-TR* (text revision). Washington, DC: Author.

American Speech-Language-Hearing Association. (2006). Preferred practice patterns for the profession of audiology. Retrieved December 14, 2010, from www.asha.org/docs/html/PP2006-00274.html#sec1.4.

American-Speech-Language-Hearing Association. (1997–2011a). Childhood apraxia of speech. Retrieved March 7, 2011, from www.asha.org/public/speech/disorders/ChildhoodApraxia.htm.

American-Speech-Language-Hearing Association. (1997–2011b). Speech sound disorders: Articulation and phonological processes. Retrieved March 7, 2011, from www.asha.org/public/speech/disorders/SpeechSound-Diorders.htm.

American-Speech-Language-Hearing Association. (1997–2011c). What is language? What is speech? Retrieved July 4, 2011, from www.asha.org/public/speech/development/language_speech.htm.

Americans with Disabilities Act (ADA) of 1990, Pub. L. No. 101–336, § 2, 104 Stat. 328 (1991).

Americans with Disabilities Act Amendments Act (ADAAA) of 2008, Pub. L. No. 110-325, § 122 Stat. 3553.

Anderson, V., Catroppa, C., Morse, S., Haritou, F., & Rosenfeld, T. (2000). Recovery of intellectual ability following TBI in childhood: Impact of injury severity and age at injury. *Pediatric Neurosurgery, 32*, 282–290.

Anderson, V., Catropppa, C., Morse, S., Haritou, F., & Rosenfeld, T. (2005). Functional plasticity or vulnerability after early brain injury? *Pediatrics, 116*(6): 1374–1382. Retrieved September 27, 2008, from http://pediatrics.aappublications.org/cgi/content/full/116/6/1374.

Annie E. Casey Foundation. (2003). *Kids count data book: State profiles of child well-being.* Baltimore: Author.

Annie E. Casey Foundation. (2006). *Kids count data book: State profiles of child well-being.* Baltimore: Author. Retrieved December 2, 2007, from www.kids count.org/sld/compare_results.jsp?i = 191.

Annie E. Casey Foundation. (2007a). *Kids count data center: Children in poverty by state.* Retrieved April 4, 2008, from www.kidscount.org/datacenter/compare_results. jsp?i = 190.

Annie E. Casey Foundation. (2007b). *Kids count data center: Children in poverty by race.* Retrieved April 4, 2008, from www.kidscount.org/datacenter/compare_results.jsp?i = 191.

Annie E. Casey Foundation. (2010*). Kids count data book: State profiles of child well-being.* Retrieved July 4, 2011, from www.datacenter.kidscount.org/DataBook/2010/OnlineBooks/2010DataBook.pdf.

Aronen, E. T., & Arajarvi, T. (2004). Effects of early intervention on psychiatric symptoms of young adults in low-risk and high-risk families. In M. A. Feldman (Ed.), *Early intervention: The essential readings* (pp. 214–235). Malden, MA: Blackwell Publishing Ltd.

Asherson, P., Kuntsi, J., & Taylor, E. (2005). Unraveling the complexity of attention-deficit/hyperactivity disorder: A behavioural genomic approach. *British Journal of Psychiatry, 187*, 103–105.

Asthma and Allergy Foundation of America (AAFA). (2005). Allergy overview. Retrieved December 29, 2007, from www.aafa.org.

Asthma and Allergy Foundation of America (AAFA). (2011). Asthma. Retrieved March 15, 2011, from www.aafa.org/display.cfm?id=8&sub=42.

Atreya, C., Mohan, K., & Kulkarni, S. (2004). Rubella virus and birth defects: Molecular insights into the viral teratogenesis at the cellular level. *Birth Defects Research, 70*, 431–437.

Attwood, T. (2007). *The complete guide to Asperger's syndrome.* London: Jessica Kingsley Publishers.

August, D., & Shanahan, T. (Eds.). (2008). *Developing reading and writing in second-language learners: Lessons from the report of the National Literacy Panel on Language-Minority Children and Youth.* New York: Routledge.

Ayers, A. J. (1972). *Sensory integration and learning disorders.* Los Angeles: Western Psychological Services.

Bailey, S. (2000). Culturally diverse gifted students. In M. J. Stopper (Ed.), *Meeting the social and emotional needs of gifted and talented children* (pp. 80–99). London: David Fulton.

Bandura, A. (1992). Social cognitive theory. In R. Vasta (Ed.), *Six theories of child development* (pp. 1–60). London: Jessica Kingsley Publishers.

Barnett, W. S., Brown, K., & Shore, R. (2004*). The universal vs. targeted debate: Should the United States have preschool for all?* New Brunswick, NJ: National Institute for Early Education Research (NIEER).

Barnett, W. S., Hustedt, J. T., Friedman, A. H., Boyd, J., & Ainsworth, P. (2007). *The state of preschool 2007.* National Institute for Early Education Research (NIEER). Retrieved August 22, 2008, from http://nieer.org/yearbook/pdf/yearbook.pdf.

Barnett, W. S., & Yarosz, D. J. (2007). Who Goes to Preschool and Why Does it Matter? *Preschool Policy Matters,*

Issue 15. New Brunswick, NJ: National Institute for Early Education Research (NIEER).

Barnett, W. S. Yarosz, D. J., Thomas, J., Jung, K. Blanco, D. (2007). Two-way and monolingual English immersion in preschool education: An experimental comparison. *Childhood Research Quarterly, 22*(3): 277–293.

Barnett, W. S., Epstein, D. J., Friedman, A. H., Sansanelli, R. A., & Hustedt, J. T. (2009). The state of preschool 2009: *State preschool yearbook*. New Brunswick, NJ: National Institute for Early Education Research (NIEER). Retrieved April 17, 2011, from http://nieer.org/yearbook/pdf/yearbook.pdf.

Baron-Cohen, S., Allen, J., & Gillberg, C. (1992). Can autism be detected at 18 months? The needle, the haystack, and the CHAT. *British Journal of Psychiatry, 161*, 839–843.

Batshaw, M. L. (2007). Genetics and developmental disabilities. In M. L. Batshaw, L. Pellegrino & N. J. Rosen (Eds.), *Children with disabilities* (6th ed., pp. 3–21). Baltimore: Paul H. Brookes.

Batshaw, M. L., Shapiro, B., & Farber, M. L. Z. (2007). Developmental delay and intellectual disability. In M. L. Batshaw, L. Pellegrino & N. J. Rosen (Eds.), *Children with disabilities* (6th ed., pp. 245–261). Baltimore: Paul H. Brookes.

Baum, M. S. & Owen, S. V. (2004). *To be gifted and learning disabled: Strategies for helping bright students with LD, ADHD, and more.* Mansfield Center: CT: Creative Learning Press.

Bayley, N. (2005). *The Bayley scales of infant and toddler development* (3rd ed., Bayley III). New York: Psychological Corporation.

Beker, L. T., Farber, A. F., & Yanni, C. C. (2002). Nutrition and children with disabilities. In M. L. Batshaw (Ed.), *Children with disabilities* (5th ed., pp. 141–164). Baltimore: Paul H. Brookes.

Bell, M. J. (2007). Infections and the fetus. In M. L. Batshaw, L. Pellegrino & N. J. Rosen (Eds.), *Children with disabilities* (6th ed., pp. 71–82). Baltimore: Paul H. Brookes.

Berg, A. O., & U.S. Preventive Services Task Force. (2003). *Counseling to prevent tobacco use and tobacco-caused disease. Recommendation Statement.* Rockville, MD: Agency for Health Care Research and Quality.

Berger, E. H. (2004). *Parents as partners in education.* Columbus, OH: Pearson Merrill Prentice Hall.

Berk, L. E. (2002). *Infants, children, and adolescents* (4th ed.). Boston: Allyn & Bacon.

Berke, J. (2010). Communication—Total communication: Trying to have the best of both worlds. Retrieved December 14, 2010, from http://deafness.about.com/cs/communication/a/totalcomm.htm.

Berkson, G. (1993). *Children with handicaps: A review of behavioral research.* Hillsdale, NJ: Erlbaum.

Biemiller, A., & Slonim, N. (2001). Estimating root word vocabulary growth in normative and advantaged populations: Evidence for a common sequence of vocabulary acquisition. *Journal of Educational Psychology, 93*, 498–520.

Birch, L. L. (1980). Effects of peer models' food choices and eating behaviors on preschoolers' food preferences. *Child Development, 51*, 489–496.

Birch, L. L. (1996). Children's food acceptance patterns. *Nutrition Today, 31*(6): 234–241.

Bishaw, A., & Macartney, S. (2010). *Poverty: 2008 and 2009.* American Community Survey Briefs. U.S. Census Bureau, Washington, DC. Retrieved November 16, 2010, from www.census.gov/prod/2010pubs/acsbr-1.pdf.

Blaska, J. (1993). The power of language: Speak and write using "person first." In M. Nagler (Ed.), *Perspectives on disability* (2nd ed., pp. 25–32). Palo Alto, CA: Health Market Research.

Blazer, B. (1999). Developing 504 classroom accommodation plans: A collaborative systematic parent-student-teacher approach. *Teaching Exceptional Children, 32*, 2.Retrieved July 21, 2002, from www.ldonline.org/ld_indepth_teaching_techniques/504_plans.html.

Bloom, B. S. (1985). *Developing talent in young people.* New York: Ballantine Books.

Board of Education of the Hendrick Hudson Central School District v. Rowley, 453 U.S. 176 (1982).

Bodrova, E., Leong, D., & Shore, R. (2004). *Child outcome standards in pre-k programs: What are standards; what is needed to make them work?* New Brunswick, NJ: National Institute for Early Education Research (NIEER). Retrieved April 17, 2011, from http://nieer.org/resources/policybriefs/5.pdf.

Bolt, S. E., & Thurlow, M. L. (2004). Five of the most frequently allowed testing accommodations in state policy. *Remedial and Special Education, 25*(3): 141–152.

Boone, R., & Higgins, K. (2007). The software check-list: Evaluating educational software for use by students with disabilities. *Technology in Action 3*(1): 1–16.

Bowlby, J. (1989). The role of attachment in personality development and psychopathology. In S. I. Greenspan & G. H. Pollock (Eds.), *The course of life: Vol. 1 Infancy* (pp. 229–270). Washington, DC: U.S. Government Printing Office.

Boyd, J., Barnett. W. S., Bodrova, E., Leong, D. J., & Gomby, D. (2005). *Promoting children's social and emotional development through preschool education.* National Institute for Early Education Research (NIEER). Retrieved April 20, 2011, from http://nieer.org/resources/picyreports/report7.pdf.

Braggett, E. J. (1992). *Pathways for accelerated learners.* Melbourne, Australia: Hawker Brownlow Education.

Brazelton, T. B., & Nugent, J. K. (2005). Understanding the baby's language. Retrieved April 14, 2007, from www.brazelton-institute.com/intro.html.

Brazelton, T. B., & Nugent, J. K. (1995). *The neonatal behavioral assessment scale.* Cambridge, MA: Mac Keith Press.

Bredekamp, S., & Copple, C. (Eds.). (1997). *Developmentally appropriate practice in early childhood programs serving children from birth through age 8* (rev. ed.). Washington, DC: NAEYC.

Bredekamp, S., & Copple, C. (2009). To be an excellent teacher. In C. Copple & S. Bredekamp (Eds.), *Developmentally appropriate practice in early childhood programs serving children from birth through age 8* (3rd ed., pp. 33–50). Washington, DC: NAEYC.

Bredekamp, S., & Rosegrant, T. (Eds.). (1992). *Reaching potentials: Appropriate curriculum and assessment for young children (vol. 1).* Washington, DC: NAEYC.

Bredekamp, S., & Rosegrant, T. (1995). Reaching potentials through transforming curriculum, assessment, and teaching. In S. Bredekamp & T. Rosegrant (Eds.), *Reaching potentials: Transforming early childhood curriculum and assessment* (vol. 2, pp. 15–22). Washington, DC: NAEYC.

Brennan, W. (2010). Best ways to successfully educate children of immigrant parents: Leading for literacy with technology. Retrieved March 8, 2011, from www.scribd.com/doc/33988020/Educate-Children-of-Immigrant-Parents-Leading-for-Technology.

Bretherton, I. (2005). In pursuit of the internal working model construct and its relevance to attachment relationships. In K. E. Grossmann, K. Grossmann, & E. Waters (Eds.), *Attachment from infancy to adulthood: The major longitudinal studies* (pp. 13–47). New York: The Guilford Press.

Briere, J. (1992). *Child abuse trauma: Theory and treatment of the lasting effects.* Newbury Park, CA: Sage.

Briggs, C. J., Reis, S. M., & Sullivan, E. E. (2008). A national view of promising programs and practices for culturally, linguistically, and ethnically diverse gifted and talented students. *Gifted Child Quarterly,* 52(2): 131–145.

Brown v. Board of Education, 347 U.S. 483 (1954).

Brown, J. E., & Satin, A. J. (2007). Having a baby: The birth process. In M. L. Batshaw, L. Pellegrino, & N. J. Roizen (Eds.). *Children with disabilities* (6th ed., pp. 35–45). Baltimore: Paul H. Brookes Publishing.

Brown, M. J., & Chattopadhyay, S. (2006). Lead, elevated blood lead level evidence-statement. In K. P. Campbell, A. Lanza, R. Dixon, S. Chattopadhyay, N. Molinari, & R. A. Finch (Eds.), *A purchaser's guide to clinical preventive services: Moving science into coverage* (pp. 165–169). Washington, DC: National Business Group on Health. Retrieved August 10, 2008, from www.businessgrouphealth.org/benefitstopics/topics/purchasers/part3.pdf.

Brown, P. M., Remine, M. D., Prescott, S. J., & Rickards, F. W. (2000). Social interactions of preschoolers with and without impaired hearing in integrated kindergarten. *Journal of Early Intervention, 23,* 200–211.

Brown, S. L. (2004). Family structure and child well-being: The significance of parental cohabitation. *Journal of Marriage and Family,* 66, 351–367.

Bumpass, L. L., & Lu, H. H. (2000). Trends in cohabitation and implications for children's family contexts in the United States. *Population Studies, 54,* 29–41.

Bumpass, L. L., & Raley, R. K. (1995). Redefining single-parent families: Cohabitating and changing family reality. *Demography, 32,* 97–109.

Burbacher, T. M., & Grant, K. S. (2006). Neurodevelopmental effects of alcohol. In P. W. Davidson, G. J. Meyers, & B. Weiss (Eds.), *International review of mental retardation research: Vol. 30. Neurotoxicology and developmental disabilities* (pp. 1–46). San Diego, CA: Elsevier Academic Press.

Burd, L. (n.d.a). Drinking during pregnancy. Retrieved August 10, 2008, from www.cjsids.com/art/DRNKGRPH.pdf.

Burd, L. (n.d.b). Smoking during pregnancy. Retrieved August 10, 2008, from www.cjsids.com/art/SMOKGRPH.pdf.

Burns, E. (2004). *The special education consultant teacher: Enabling children with disabilities to be educated with nondisabled children to the maximum extent appropriate.* Springfield, IL: Charles C. Thomas.

Byrd-Bredbenner, C. (2002). Saturday morning children's television advertising: A longitudinal content analysis. *Family and Consumer Sciences Research Journal,* 30(3): 382–403.

Calderón, M., Slavin, R., & Sánchez, M. (2011). Effective instruction for English learners. *The Future of Children,* 21(1): 103–128.

California Department of Education. (2006). Braille mathematics standards. Retrieved September 29, 2008, from www.cde.ca.gov/sp/se/sr/documents/braillemathstand.pdf.

Campbell, K. P., Rosenthal, A. C., & Chattopadhyay, S. (2006). Tobacco use treatment during pregnancy evidence-statement: Screening and counseling. In K. P. Campbell, A. Lanza, R. Dixon, S. Chattopadhyay, N. Molinari, & R. A. Finch (Eds.), *A purchaser's guide to clinical preventive services: Moving science into coverage* (pp. 305–310). Washington, DC: National Business Group on Health. Retrieved August 10, 2008, from www.businessgrouphealth.org/benefitstopics/topics/purchasers/part3.pdf.

Candlelighters: Childhood Cancer Foundation (CCCF). (2007a). Childhood cancer facts. Retrieved September 2, 2007, from www.candlelighters.org.

Candlelighters: Childhood Cancer Foundation (CCFC). (2007b). Leukemias. Retrieved September 2, 2007, from www.candlelighters.org/leuk.stm.

Capps, R., & Fix, M. E. (2005). Undocumented immigrants: Myths and reality. Retrieved December 1, 2007, from www.urban.org/publications/900898.html.

Capps, R., Fix, M. E., & Passel, J. S. (2002). *The dispersal of immigrants in the 1990s* (policy brief). Washington, DC: Urban Institute. Retrieved September 21, 2008, from www.urban.org/publications/410589.html.

Capps, R., Fix, M. E., Murray, J., Ost, J., Passel, J. S., & Herwantoro, S. (2005). *The new demography of America's schools: Immigration and the No Child Left Behind Act.* Washington, DC: The Urban Institute. Retrieved September 21, 2008, from www.urban.org/UploadedPDF/311230_new_demography.pdf.

Capps, R., Fix, M., Ost, J., Reardon-Anderson, J., & Passel, J. S. (2005). *The health and well-being of young children of immigrants.* Washington, DC: The Urban Institute. Retrieved October 27, 2008, from www.urban.org/UploadedPDF/311139_ChildrenImmigrants.pdf.

Carey, S., & Bartlett, E. (1978). Acquiring a single new word. *Proceedings of the Stanford Child Language Conference, 15,* 17–29.

Carrasquillo, O., Lantigua, R. A., & Shea, S. (2000). Differences in functional status of Hispanic versus non-Hispanic white elders: Data from the medical expenditure panel survey. *Journal of Aging and Health, 12*(3): 342–361.

Carrera-Carrollo, L., & Smith, A. R. (2006). *7 steps to success in dual language immersion: A brief guide for teachers and administers.* Portsmouth, NH: Heinemann.

Carroll, B. A. (2000). Sickle cell disease. In P. L. Jackson & J. A. Vessey (Eds.), *Primary care of the child with a chronic condition* (3rd ed., pp. 808–836). St Louis, MO: Mosby, Inc.

Carter, B., & McGoldrick, M. (1999). *The expanded family life cycle: Individual, family, and social perspectives* (3rd ed.). Boston, MA: Allyn & Bacon.

Castaneda, R. (2007). Five questions for Rosa Castaneda. Retrieved March 8, 2011, from www.urban.org/toolkit/fivequestions/RCastaneda.cfm.

Castellanos, F. X., Giedd, J. N., Berquin, P. C., et al. (2001). Quantitative brain magnetic resonance imaging in girls with ADHD. *Archives of General Psychiatry, 58,* 289–295.

Center for Applied Special Technology (CAST). (2007). What is universal design for learning? Retrieved December 6, 2007, from www.cast.org/research/udl/index.html.

Center for Science, Mathematics, and Engineering Science (CSMEE). (1996). National science education standards. Washington, DC: The National Academies Press. Retrieved November 9, 2010, from www.nap.edu/openbook.php?record_id=4962&page=R1.

Center on Addiction and Substance Abuse. (1996). *Substance abuse and the American woman.* New York: Columbia University.

Center on the Family. (n.d.). *Profile of Hawaiian Children.* University of Hawaii at Manoa. Retrieved November 16, 2010, from http://uhfamily.hawaii.edu/cof_data/hi_child_ed/StateFactsheet.

Centers for Disease Control and Prevention (CDC). (1996). *Universal precautions for prevention of transmission of HIV and other bloodborne infections.* Retrieved August 31, 2007, from www.cdc.gov/ncidod/dhqp/bp_universal_precautions.html#.

Centers for Disease Control and Prevention (CDC). (2002). *Cohabitation, marriage, divorce, and remarriage in the Untied States.* Series Report 23, No. 22., 103 pp. (PHS) 98-1998. Retrieved November 17, 2010, from www.cdc.gov/nchs/pressroom/02news/div_mar_chaab.htm.

Centers for Disease Control and Prevention (CDC). (2005a). Attention-deficit/hyperactivity disorder. Retrieved August 8, 2007, from www.cdc.gov/ncbddd/adhd/.

Centers for Disease Control and Prevention (CDC). (2005b). Bleeding disorders. Retrieved September 3, 2007, from www.cdc.gov/ncbddd/hbd/hemophelia.htm.

Centers for Disease Control and Prevention (CDC). (2005c). Intellectual disability. Retrieved September 23, 2008, from www.cdc.gov/ncbddd/dd/mr3.htm.

Centers for Disease Control and Prevention (CDC). (2005d). Preventing smoking during pregnancy. Retrieved April 12, 2007, from www.cdc.gov/nccdphp/publications/factsheets/Prevention/smoking.htm.

Centers for Disease Control and Prevention (CDC). (2006a). Chlamydia fact sheet. Retrieved April 12, 2007, from www.cdc.gov/std/chlamydia/STDFact-Chlamydia.htm.

Centers for Disease Control and Prevention (CDC). (2006b). Fetal alcohol spectrum disorders. Retrieved August 23, 2007, from www.cdc.gov/ncbddd/fas/fasask.htm.

Centers for Disease Control and Prevention (CDC). (2006c). Overview. Retrieved September 8, 2007, from www.cdc.gov/ncipc/tbi/Overview.htm.

Centers for Disease Control and Prevention (CDC). (2006d). Signs and symptoms. Retrieved September 8, 2007, from www.cdc.gov/ncipc/tbi/Signs_and_Symptoms.htm.

Centers for Disease Control and Prevention (CDC). (2007a). Fetal alcohol spectrum disorders. Retrieved April 12, 2007, from www.cdc.gov/ncbddd/fas/default.htm.

Centers for Disease Control and Prevention (CDC). (2007b). Hurricanes–special populations, effects on pregnant women: Environmental exposures. Retrieved April 12, 2007, from www.cdc.gov/ncbddd/hurricanes/environmental.htm.

Centers for Disease Control and Prevention (CDC). (2007c). Malaria during pregnancy. Retrieved April 12, 2007, from www.cdc.gov/malaria/pregnancy.htm.

Centers for Disease Control and Prevention (CDC). (2007d). Mother-to-child (perinatal) HIV transmission and prevention. Retrieved June 25, 2011, from www.cdc.gov/hiv/topics/perinatal/resources/factsheets/perinatal.htm.

Centers for Disease Control and Prevention (CDC). (2007e). Newborns and group B strep. Retrieved April 12, 2007, from www.cdc.gov/groupBstrep/general/gen_public_faq.htm.

Centers for Disease Control and Prevention (CDC). (2007f). Prevention. Retrieved September 8, 2007, from www.cdc.gov/ncipe/tbi/Prevention.htm.

Centers for Disease Control and Prevention (CDC). (2007g). What is traumatic brain injury? Retrieved September 8, 2007, from www.cdc.gov/ncipe/tbi/TBI.htm.

Centers for Disease Control and Prevention (CDC). (2007h). You can prevent PCP in children. Retrieved September 20, 2008, from www.cdc.gov/hiv/resources/brochures/pcpkidz.htm.

Centers for Disease Control and Prevention (CDC). (2008a). *Hepatitis C.* Retrieved September 19, 2008, from www.cdc.gov/hepatitis/HCV.htm.

Centers for Disease Control and Prevention (CDC). (2008b). Intellectual disabilities among children. Retrieved September 23, 2008, from www.cdc.gov/ncbddd/dd/documents/IntellectualDisabilitiesFactSheet.pdf.

Centers for Disease Control and Prevention (CDC). (2009a). Asthma. Retrieved March 15, 2011, from www.cdc.gov/nchs/fastats/asthma.htm.

Centers for Disease Control and Prevention (CDC). (2009b). Hepatitis D information for health professionals. Retrieved May 23, 2011, from www.cdc.gov/hepititis/HDV/index.htm.

Centers for Disease Control and Prevention (CDC). (2009c). Hepatitis E information for health professionals. Retrieved May 23, 2011, from www.cdc.gov/hepititis/HEV/index.htm.

Centers for Disease Control and Prevention (CDC). (2009d). Increase in unmarried childbearing also seen in other countries. Retrieved March 28, 2011, from www.cdc.gov/nchs/pressroom/09newsreleases/unmarriedbirths.htm.

Centers for Disease Control and Prevention (CDC). (2009e). Sickle cell disease (SCD). Retrieved May 23, 2011, from www.cdc.gov/ncbddd.sicklecell/facts.html.

Centers for Disease Control and Prevention (CDC). (2010a). Autism spectrum disorders (ASDs). Retrieved March 12, 2011, from www.cdc.gov/ncbddd/autism/facts/html.

Centers for Disease Control and Prevention (CDC). (2010b). Childhood arthritis. Retrieved May 22, 2011, from www.cdc.gov/arthritis/basics/childhood.htm.

Centers for Disease Control and Prevention (CDC). (2010c). Children and diabetes–More information. Retrieved May 23, 2011, from www.cdc.gov/diabetes/projects/cda2.htm.

Centers for Disease Control and Prevention (CDC). (2010d). Children and diabetes: SEARCH for diabetes in youth. Retrieved May 23, 2011, from www.cdc.gov/diabetes/projects/diab_children.htm.

Centers for Disease Control and Prevention (CDC). (2010e). Hemophilia: Data and statistics in the United States. Retrieved May 22, 2011, from www.cdc.gov/ncbdd/hemophilia/data.html.

Centers for Disease Control and Prevention (CDC). (2010f). Hepatitis A information for health professionals. Retrieved May 23, 2011, from www.cdc.gov/hepititis/HAV/index.htm.

Centers for Disease Control and Prevention (CDC). (2010g). Hepatitis B information for health professionals. Retrieved May 23, 2011, from www.cdc.gov/hepititis/HBV/index.htm.

Centers for Disease Control and Prevention (CDC). (2010h). Sickle cell disease (SCD). Retrieved March 16, 2011, from www.cdc.gov/ncbddd/sicklecell/index.html.

Centers for Disease Control and Prevention (CDC). (2011a). Hepatitis C information for health professionals. Retrieved May 23, 2011, from www.cdc.gov/hepititis/HCV/index.htm.

Centers for Disease Control and Prevention (CDC). (2011b). Overweight and obesity. Retrieved March 16, 2011, from www.cdc.gov/obesity/childhood/lowincome/htmdata/trends.html.

Centers for Disease Control and Prevention (CDC). (2011c). U.S. obesity trends. Retrieved March 16, 2011, from www.cdc.gov/obesity/data/trends.html.

Centers for Disease Control and Prevention (CDC). (n.d.a). Sickle cell disease: Facts about sickle cell disease. Retrieved September 5, 2007, from www.cdc.gov/ncbddd/sicklecell/faq_sicklecell.htm.

Centers for Disease Control and Prevention (CDC). (n.d.b). Sickle cell disease: Health care professionals: Data and statistics. Retrieved September 5, 2007, from www.cdc.gov/ncbddd/sicklecell/hcp_data.htm.

Centers for Disease Control and Prevention (CDC). (n.d.c). Single gene disorders and disability (SGDD). Retrieved July 27, 2011, from www.cdc.gov/ncbddd/single_gene/default.htm.

Centers for Disease Control and Prevention (CDC). (2010). Centers for Autism and Developmental Disabilities Research and Epidemiology (CADDRE). Study to explore early development. Retrieved July 19, 2011, from www.cdc.gov/ncbddd/autism/seed.htm.

Chakrabarti, S., & Fombonne, E. (2001). Pervasive developmental disorders in preschool children. *Journal of the American Medical Association, 285*(24): 3092–3099.

Chan, R. W., Raboy, B., & Patterson, C. J. (1998). Psychosocial adjustment among children conceived via donor insemination by lesbian and heterosexual mothers. *Child Development, 69,* 443–457.

Chan, S., & Lee, E. (2004). Families with Asian roots. In E. W. Lynch & M. J. Hanson (Eds.), *Developing cross-cultural competence: A guide for working with children and their families* (3rd ed., pp. 219–298). Baltimore: Paul H. Brookes.

Charlesworth, R., & Lind, K. K. (2009). *Math and science for young children* (6th ed.). Belmont, CA: Wadsworth Cengage Learning.

Chau, M., Thampi, K., & Wright, V. R. (2010). Basic facts about low-income children, 2009: Children under age 6. National Center for Children in Poverty. Retrieved March 28, 2011, from www.nccp.org/publications/pub_972.html.

Chess, S. (1983). Basic adaptations required for successful parenting. In V. Sasserath (Ed.), *Minimizing high-risk parenting* (pp. 5–11). Skillman, NJ: Johnson & Johnson.

Chess, S. (1990). Temperaments of infants and toddlers. In J. R. Lally (Ed.), *Infant/toddler caregiving: A guide to social-emotional growth and socialization* (pp. 4–13). Sacramento, CA: California Department of Education.

Chess, S., & Thomas, A. (1977). Temperamental individuality from childhood to adolescence. *Journal of Child Psychiatry, 16,* 218–226.

Chess, S., & Thomas, A. (1990). The New York Longitudinal Study (NYLS): The young adult periods. *Canadian Journal of Psychiatry, 16,* 218–226.

Chetty, R., Friedman, J., Hilger, N., Saez, E., Schanzenbach, D. W., & Yagan, D. (2010). How does your kindergarten class affect your earning? Evidence from Project STAR. Retrieved November 25, 2010, from http://obs.rc.fas.harvard.edu/chetty/STAR_slides.pdf.

Child and Adolescent Bipolar Foundation. (2002). About pediatric bipolar disorder. Retrieved December 20, 2007, from www.bpkids.org/site/PageServer?pagename = lrn_about.

Children with Diabetes. (2007). Insulin pump therapy. Retrieved September 3, 2007, from www.childrenwith-diabetes.com/pumps/.

Children's Defense Fund. (1975). *Washington research report.* Washington, DC: Author.

Children's Defense Fund. (2000). *The state of America's children yearbook.* Washington, DC: Author.

Children's Defense Fund. (2002). *The state of children in America's union: A 2002 action guide to leave no child behind.* Washington, DC: Author.

Children's Defense Fund. (2007). Nine million uninsured children need a solution now. Retrieved May 19, 2007, from www.childrensdefense.org/site/PageServer.

Children's Hospital Boston, (n.d). Cortical visual impairment. Retrieved December 27, 2010, from www.childrenshospital.org/az/Site2100/mainpagesS2100P0.html.

Chiriboga, C. A. (1996). Cocaine and the fetus: Methodological issues and neurological correlates. In R. J. Koukol & G. D. Olsen (Eds.), *Prenatal cocaine exposure* (pp. 1–21). Boca Raton, FL: CRC Press.

Chugani, H. T. (1998). Biological basis of emotions: Brain systems and brain development. *Pediatrics, 102*(5), Supplement (November): 1225–1229.

Cicchetti, D., & Lynch, M. (1993). Toward an ecological/transaction model of community violence and child maltreatment: Consequences for child development. In

D. Reiss, J. E. Richters, & M. Radke-Yarrow (Eds.), *Children and violence* (pp. 96–118). New York: Guilford Press.

Clark, B. (2002). *Growing up gifted: Developing the potential of children at home and at school* (6th ed.). Upper Saddle River, NJ: Prentice Hall.

Colangelo, N., Assouline, S. G., & Gross, M. U. M. (2004). *A nation deceived: How schools hold back America's brightest students.* Iowa City, IA: Belin-Blank Center.

Coleman, M. R., Buysse, V., & Neitzel, J. (2006). *Recognition and response: An early intervening system for young children at-risk for learning disabilities.* University of North Carolina: Frank Porter Graham Child Development Institute.

Columba, L., & Dolgos, K. A. (1995). Portfolio assess in mathematics. *Reading Improvement, 32*(3): 174–176.

Combating Autism Act of 2006, Pub. L. No. 109–416, 120 Stat. 2821, 42 U.S.C. 201 note.

Committee on the Prevention of Reading Difficulties in Young Children. (1998). Predictors of success and failure in reading. In C. E. Stone, M. S. Burns & P. Griffin (Eds.), *Preventing Reading Difficulties in Young Children* (pp. 100–134). Washington, DC: National Academy Press.

Common Core State Standards Initiative. (2010). About the standards. Retrieved November 22, 2010, from www.corestandards.org/about-the-standards.

Comstock, G., & Scharrer, E. (2003). Meta-analyzing the controversy over television violence and aggression. In D. A. Gentile (Ed.), *Media Violence and Children* (pp. 205–226). Westport, CT: Praeger Publishers.

Conners, C. K. (2000). *Conners' rating scales–revised.* Boston: Pearson Education Inc.

Conners, C. K. (2009). *Conners,* 3rd ed. *(Conners 3).* San Antonio, TX: Pearson.

Connor, D. F. (2002). Preschool attention deficit hyperactivity disorder: A review of prevalence, diagnosis, neurobiology, and stimulant treatment. *Developmental and Behavioral Pediatrics, 23,* S1–S9.

Consentinode Cohen, C., Deterding, N., & Clewell, B. (2005). *Who's left behind? Immigrant children in high and low LEP schools.* Washington, DC: The Urban Institute. Retrieved September 10, 2008, from www.urban.org/UploadedPDF/411231_whos_left_behind.pdf.

Consortium of National Arts Education Associations. (1994). *National standards for arts education.* Reston, VA: Music Educators National Conference.

Copple, C., & Bredekamp, S. (Eds.). (2009). *Developmentally appropriate practice in early childhood programs serving children from birth through age 8* (3rd ed.). Washington, DC: NAEYC.

Council for Exceptional Children (CEC). (1994). *Creating schools for all our students: What 12 schools have to say.* Reston, VA: Author.

Council for Exceptional Children (CEC). (1996a). Inclusion-Where we are today? *CEC Today, 3*(3): 1, 5, 15.

Council for Exceptional Children (CEC). (1996b). States act to include students with disabilities in standards. *CEC Today, 2*(3): 7.

Courchesne, E., Carper, R., & Aksoomoff, N. (2003). Evidence of brain overgrowth in the first year of life in autism. *Journal of the American Medical Association, 290*(3): 337–344.

Covington, C. Y., Nordstrom-Klee, B., Ager, J., Sokol, R., & Delaney-Black, V. (2002). Birth to age 7 growth of children prenatally exposed to drugs: A prospective cohort study. *Neurotoxicology and Teratology, 24*(4): 489–496.

Creasy, R. K., Resnik, R., & Iams, J. (2004). *Maternal-fetal medicine: Principles and practice* (5th ed.). Philadelphia: W.B. Saunders.

Crocker, A. D., & Orr, R. R. (1996). Social behaviors of children with visual impairments enrolled in preschool programs. *Exceptional Children, 62,* 451–462.

Crosbie-Burnett, M., & McClintic, K. M. (2000). Remarriage and recoupling. In P. C. McKenry & S. J. Price (Eds.), *Families and change: Coping with stressful events and transitions* (pp. 303–332). Thousand Oaks, CA: Sage.

Crosnoe, R., & López Turley, R. N. (2011). Effective instruction for English learners. *The Future of Children, 21*(1): 103–128.

Cross, C. T., Woods, T. A., Schweingruber, H. (Eds.). (2009). *Mathematics learning in early childhood: Paths toward excellence and equity,* Committee on Early Childhood Mathematics, National Research Council. Washington, DC: The National Academies Press. Retrieved July 4, 2011, from http://books.nap.edu/openbook.php?record_id=12519&page=R1.

Cummings, E. M. , & Davies, P. R. (2002). Effects of marital conflict on children: Recent advances and emerging themes in process-oriented research. *Journal of Child Psychology and Psychiatry, 43*: 31–63.

Cunningham, F. G., Leveno, K. J., Boom, S. L., et al. (2005). *Williams obstetrics* (22nd ed.). New York: McGraw-Hill.

Daniels, S. R. (2006). The consequences of childhood overweight and obesity. *The Future of Children, 16*(1): 47–67.

Davidson, P. W., & Myers, G. J. (2007). Environmental toxins. In M. L. Batshaw, L. Pellegrino & N. J. Rosen (Eds.), *Children with disabilities* (6th ed., pp. 61–70). Baltimore: Paul H. Brookes.

Davis, S. (1997). Migrant Health Issues: *Child labor in agriculture.* Educational Research Information Clearinghouse Digest. Las Cruces, NM. EDO-RC-97-10.

Dawson, P., & Guare, R. (2010). *Executive skills in children and adolescents: A practical guide to assessment and intervention* (2nd ed., The Guilford Practical Intervention in School Series). New York: The Guilford Press.

DeBey, M., & Bombard, D. (2007). An approach to second-language learning and cultural understanding. *Young Children, 62*(2): 88–93.

Deiner, P. L., Hardacre, L., & Dyck, L. (1999). *Educating children with diverse abilities, Birth through 12.* Toronto, Ontario: Harcourt Brace Canada.

DeNavas-Walt, C., Proctor, B. D., Smith, J. C., & U.S. Census Bureau. (2010). Current Population reports, P60-238, Income, poverty, and health insurance coverage in the United States: 2009. Washington, DC: U.S. Government Printing Office,

Denckla, M. B. (2003). ADHD: Topic update. *Brain and development, 25*(6): 383–389.

Dennison, B. A., Erb, T. A., & Jenkins, P. L. (2002). Television viewing and television in bedroom associated with overweight risk among low-income preschool children. *Pediatrics, 109*(6): 1028–1035.

Developmental Disabilities Task Force. (n.d.). *Inclusive education: A background paper for state legislators* (1–11). National Conference of State Legislatures.

Diana v. State Board of Education of Monterey County, No. C-70-37 (N.D. Cal., Feb. 5, 1970).

Diabetic Foundation. (2011). FAQ's. Retrieved July 4, 2011, from www.diabeticfoundation.org/FAQ.html.

Division for Early Childhood (DEC). (1996). Inclusion. Position Statement. Retrieved August 2, 2008, from www.dec-sped.org/pdf/positionpapers/PositionStatement_Inclusion.pdf.

Division for Early Childhood (DEC) & National Association for the Education of Young Children (NAEYC). (2009). Early Childhood Inclusion. Retrieved July 17, 2011, from www.naeyc.org/files/naeyc/file/positions/DEC_NAEYC_EC_updatedKS.pdf.

Dombro, A. L., Jablon, J. R., Stetson, C. (2011). Powerful interactions. *Young Children, 66*(1): 12–20.

Dozier, M., Dozier, D., & Manni, M. (2002). Attachment and biobehavioral catch-up: The ABC's of helping foster infants cope with early adversity. *Zero to Three, 22*(5): 7–13.

Duarte, G., & Rafanello, D. (2001). The migrant child: A special place in the field. *Young Children, 56*(2): 26–34.

Dumont-Mathew, T., & Fein, D. (2005). Screening for autism in young children: The Modified Checklist for Autism in Toddlers (M-CHAT) and other measures. *Mental Retardation and Developmental Disabilities Research Reviews, 11,* 253–262.

Duncan, G. J., & Magnuson, K. A. (2005). Can family socioeconomic resources account for racial and ethnic test score gaps? *The Future of Children, 15*(1): 35–54.

Dunst, C. J., Trivette, C. M., & Hamby, D. W. (2007). Predictors of and interventions associated with later literacy accomplishments. *CELL Reviews, 1*(3): 1–12. Retrieved August 23, 2008, from http://earlyliteracylearning.org/cellreviews/cellreviews_v1_n3.pdf.

Dunst, C. J., Trivette, C. M., Masiello, T., Roper, N., & Robyak, A. (2006). Framework for developing evidence-based early literacy learning practices. *CELL Papers, 1*(1): 1–12. Retrieved August 23, 2008, from www.earlyliteracylearning.org/cellpapers/cellpapers_v1_n1.pdf.

DuPaul, G. J., McGoey, K. E., Eckert, T. L., & Vanbrakle, J. (2001). Preschool children with attention-deficit/hyperactivity disorder: Impairments in behavior, social, and school functioning. *Journal of the American Academy of Child and Adolescent Psychiatry, 40*(5): 508–516.

Dyspraxia Support Group of N.Z. Inc. (2007a). Developmental dyspraxia. Retrieved September 6, 2007, from www.dyspraxia.org.nz/.

Dyspraxia Support Group of N.Z. Inc. (2007b). What is developmental dyspraxia? Retrieved September 6, 2007, from www.dyspraxia.org.nz/.

Early Learning Accomplishment Profile (3rd ed., E-LAP). (2002). Kaplan Early Learning Company and Chapel Hill Training Outreach Project, Inc.

Economic Opportunities Amendments of 1972, Pub. L. No. 92–424, §1, 86 Stat. 688.

Education for All Handicapped Children Act of 1975, Pub. L. No. 94–142, 89 Stat. 773–796, 20 U.S.C. § 1400.

Education of the Handicapped Act Amendments of 1983, Pub. L. No. 98–199, 97 Stat. 1357–1377, 20 U.S.C. § 1400.

Education of the Handicapped Act Amendments of 1986, Pub. L. No. 99–457, 100 Stat. 1145–1211, 20 U.S.C. § 1400.

Edyburn, D. L. (2000). Assistive technology and mild disabilities. *Focus on Exceptional Children, 32*(9): 1–24.

Edyburn, D. L. (2006). Cognitive prostheses for students with mild disabilities: Is this what assistive technology looks like? *Journal of Special Education Technology, 21*(4): 62–65.

Eicher, P. S. (2007). Feeding. In M. L. Batshaw, L. Pellegrino & N. J. Rosen (Eds.), *Children with disabilities* (6th ed., pp. 479–497). Baltimore: Paul H. Brookes.

Epilepsy Foundation. (n.d.). First aid. Retrieved September 19, 2008, from www.epilepsyfoundation.org/about/firstaid/.

Escolar, D. M., Tosi, L. L., Rocha, A. C. T., & Kennedy, A. (2007). Muscles, bones, and nerves. In M. L. Batshaw, L. Pellegrino & N. J. Rosen (Eds.), *Children with disabilities* (6th ed., pp. 203–215). Baltimore: Paul H. Brookes.

Eshleman, J. R. (2000). *The family* (9th ed.). Needham Heights, MA: Allyn & Bacon.

Espy, K. A., Kaufman, P. M., & Glisky, M. L. (1999). Neuropsychological function in toddlers exposed to cocaine in utero: A preliminary study. *Developmental Neuropsychology, 15,* 447–460.

Faust, R. A. (2003). Childhood voice disorders: Ambulatory evaluation and operative diagnosis. *Clinical Pediatrics, 42,* 1–9.

Featherstone, H. (1980). *A difference in the family: Life with a disabled child.* New York: Basic Books.

Federal Interagency Forum on Child and Family Statistics. (2007). *America's Children: Key national indicators of well being, 2007.* Federal Interagency Forum on Child and Family Statistics, Washington, DC: U.S. Government Printing Office. Retrieved November 18, 2007, from www.childstats.gov/americaschildren/index.asp.

Feldhusen, J. F., Van Winkle, L., & Ehle, D. A. (1996). Is it acceleration or simply inappropriate instruction for precocious youth? *Teaching Exceptional Children, 28*(3): 48–51.

Fields, J. (2003). *Children's living arrangements and characteristics: March 2002.* Current Population Reports, P20-547. U.S. Census Bureau, Washington, DC. Retrieved November 28, 2006, from http www.census.gov/prod/2003pubs/p20-547.pdf.

Fineberg, R. C. (2002). *Bilingual education: A reference handbook.* Santa Barbara, CA: ABC-CLIO, Inc.

Finkelhor, D. (2008). *Childhood victimization: Violence, crime, and abuse in the lives of young people.* New York: Oxford University Press.

Fisher, M. D. (1998). A sensibility approach to identifying and assessing young gifted children. In J. F. Smutny (Ed.), *The young gifted child: Potential and promise, an anthology* (pp. 52–61). Cresskill, NJ: Hampton Press.

Fix, M., Zimmermann, W., & Passel, J. S. (2001). *The integration of immigrant families in the United States.* Washington, DC: The Urban Institute. Retrieved July 30, 2008, from www.urban.org/url.cfm?ID = 410227.

Flanagan, N. M., Jackson, A. J., & Hill, A. E. (2003). Visual impairments in childhood: Insights from a community-based survey. *Child Care Health Development, 29*(6): 493–499.

Fletcher, T. V., & Massalski, D. C. (2003). Poised on the threshold of a new paradigm for giftedness: Children from culturally and linguistically diverse backgrounds. In J. F. Smutny (Ed.), *Underserved gifted populations: Responding to their needs and abilities* (pp. 157–177). Cresskill, NJ: Hampton Press, Inc.

Flores, G., Abreu, M., & Tomany-Korman, C. (2005). Limited English proficiency, primary language at home, and disparities in children health care: How language barriers are measured matters. *Public Health Reports, 120*(4): 418–430.

Florida State University Center for Prevention and Early Intervention Policy. (1997). *Florida's children: Their future is in our hands.* Tallahassee, FL: The Task Force for Prevention of Developmental Handicaps, Florida Developmental Disabilities Council.

Florida State University. (1996). *Teen pregnancy final report.* Tallahassee, FL: Author.

Ford, L., & Dahinten, V. S. (2005). The use of intelligence tests in the assessment of preschool children. In Flanagan, D. P. & Harrison, P. L (Eds.), *Contemporary intellectual assessment: Theories, tests, and issues* (2nd ed., pp. 487–503). New York: Guildford Press.

Forrester, M. B., & Merz, R. D. (2000). Prenatal diagnosis and elective termination of neural tube defects in Hawaii, 1986–1997. *Fetal Diagnosis and Therapy, 15*(3): 146–151.

Fortuny, K., & Chaudry, A. (2009). *Children of immigrants: Immigration trends.* Fact Sheet No. 1. Washington, DC: Urban Institute. Retrieved on August 18, 2011 from *www.**urban**.org/UploadedPDF/901292_**immigrationtrends**.pdf*

Fox, A. V., Dodd, B., & Howard, D. (2002). Risk factors for speech disorders in children. *International Journal of Language and Communication Disorders, 37*(2): 117–131.

Fox, M. K., Pac, S., Devaney, B., & Jankowski, L. (2004). Feeding infants and toddlers study: What foods are infants and toddlers eating? *Journal of the American Dietetic Association, 104*(1): 22–30.

Frank Porter Graham Child Development Institute (FPG). (2005a). Who goes to pre-k and how are they doing? *Early Developments, 9*(1): 10–12.

Frank Porter Graham Child Development Institute (FPG). (2005b). How is quality measured? *Early Developments, 9*(1): 20–21.

Frank Porter Graham Child Development Institute (FPG). (2005c). How is the pre-k day spent? *Early Developments, 9*(1): 22–27.

French, L. (1996). Language, listening, and literacy. *Young Children, 51*(2): 17–20.

Frey, W. H. (2011a). America's diverse future: Initial glimpses at the U.S. child population from the 2010 census. Brookings, State of Metropolitan America, 26 (August 2). Retrieved May 8, 2011, from www.brookings.edu/papers/2011/0406_census_diversity_frey.aspx.

Frey, W. H. (2011b). A demographic tipping point among America's three-year-olds. Brookings, State of Metropolitan America, 26 (August 2). Retrieved May 8, 2011, from www.brookings.edu/opinions/2011/0207_population_frey.aspx.

Frey, W. H. (2011c). Melting pot cities and suburbs: Racial and ethnic change in metro America in the 2000s. Brookings, State of Metropolitan America, 26 (August 2). Retrieved July 4, 2011, from www.brookings.edu/papers/2011/0504_census_ethnicity_frey.aspx.

Fried, V., Prager, K., MacKay, A., et al. (2003). *Chartbook on the trends in the health of Americans.* Hyattsville, MD: National Center for Health Statistics.

Frost, L., & Bondy, A. (2002). *PECS: The picture exchange communication system* (2nd ed). Newark, DE: Pyramid Educational Consultants, Inc.

Fry, R. (2007). How far behind in math and reading are English language learners? Washington, DC: Pew Hispanic Center. Retrieved September 5, 2008, from http://pewhispanic.org/files/reports/76.pdf.

Fry, R. (2008). The role of schools in the English language learner achievement gap. Washington, DC: Pew Hispanic Center. Retrieved March 1, 2011, from http://pewhispanic.org/reports/report.php?ReportID=89.

Gaitatzes, C., Chang, T., & Baumgart, S. (2007). The first weeks of life. In M. L. Batshaw, L. Pellegrino & N. J. Rosen (Eds.), *Children with disabilities* (6th ed., pp. 47–69). Baltimore: Paul H. Brookes.

Galvin, K.M., Bylund, C. L., & Brommel, B. J. (2007). *Family communication: Cohesion and change* (7th ed.). Upper Saddle River, NJ: Allyn & Bacon.

Gammeltoft, L., & Nordenhof, M. S. (2007). *Autism, play and social interaction.* London: Jessica Kingsley Publishers.

Ganz, M. L., Xuan, Z., & Hunter, D. G. (2006). Prevalence and correlates of children's diagnosed eye and vision conditions. *Ophthalmology, 113*(12): 2298–2306.

Gardner, H. (1983). *Frames of mind: The theory of multiple intelligences.* New York: Basic Books.

Gardner, H. (1993). *The theory in practice.* New York: Basic Books.

Gardner, H. (1999). *Intelligence reframed. Multiple intelligences for the 21st century.* New York: Basic Books.

Gates, F., Badgett, L. M. V., Macomber, J. E., & Chambers, K. (2007). Adoption and foster care by lesbian and gay parents in the United States. The Urban Institute. Retrieved July 20, 2007, from www.urban.org/publications/411437.html.

Gearheart, B., Mullen, R. C., & Gearheart, C. (1993). *Exceptional individuals: An introduction.* Belmont, CA: Brooks/Cole.

Geary, D. C. (1999). Mathematical disabilities: What we know and don't know. Retrieved August 4, 2002, from www.ldonline.org/ld_indepth/math_skills/geary_math_dis.htm.

Gebhard, B. (2010). Putting standards into practice: States' use of early learning guidelines for infants and toddlers. Washington, DC: Zero to Three. Retrieved February 24, 2011, from http://main.zerotothree.org/site/DocServer/States__Use_of_ELG_for_IT_FINAL.pdf?docID=11861.

Geers, A. E. (2006). Spoken language in children with cochlear implants. In P. E. Spencer & M. Marschark (Eds.), *Advances in the spoken language development of deaf and hard-of-hearing children* (pp. 244–270). New York: Oxford University Press.

Genesse, F., Paradis, J., & Crago, M. B. (2004). *Dual language development and disorders: A handbook on bilingual and second language learning.* Baltimore: Paul H. Brookes.

George, D. R. (1997). *The challenge of the able child.* (2nd ed.). London: David Fulton Publishers.

George, D. R. (2003). *Gifted education: Identification and provision.* (2nd ed.). London: David Fulton Publishers.

Gersten, R., Baker, S. K., Shanahan, T., Linan-Thompson, S., Collins, P., & Scarcella, R. (2007). Effective literacy and English language instruction for English learners in the elementary grades: A practice guide. (NCEE 2007–4011). Washington, DC: National Center for Education Evaluation and Regional Assistance, Institute of Education Sciences, U.S. Department of Education. Retrieved September 21, 2008, from http://ies.ed.gov/ncee/wwc/practiceguides.

Gersten, R., Jorden, N. C., & Flojo, J. R. (2005). Early identification and interventions for students with mathematics difficulties. *Journal of Learning Disabilities, 38*(4): 293–304.

Gillberg, C., Persson, E., Grufman, M., et al. (1986). Psychiatric disorders in mildly and severely mentally retarded urban children and adolescents: Epidemiological aspects. *British Journal of Psychiatry, 149* (July): 68–74.

Gilliam, W. S. (2005). *Prekindergarteners left behind: Expulsion rates in state prekindergarten systems.* New Haven, CT: Yale University Child Study Center. Retrieved July 21, 2008, from www.fcd-s.org/usr_doc/ExpulsionPolicyBrief.pdf.

GiveWell. (2010). *Discussion of the U.S. achievement gap.* Retrieved November 28, 2010, from www.givewell.org/united-states/education/achievement-gap.

Glanzman, M. M., & Blum, N. J. (2007). Attention deficits and hyperactivity. In M. L. Batshaw, L. Pellegrino & N. J. Rosen (Eds.), *Children with disabilities* (6th ed., pp. 345–365). Baltimore: Paul H. Brookes.

Goals 2000: Educate America Act of 1994, Pub. L. No. 103–227, 108 Stat. 125.

Golden, M., Marra, C., & Holmes, K. (2003). Update on syphilis: Resurgence of an old problem. *Journal of the American Medical Association, 290*: 1510–1514.

Goldman, R., & Fristoe, M. (2000). *Goldman-Fristoe Test of Articulation* (2nd ed.). Circle Pines, MN: American Guidance Service.

Goleman, D. (1995). *Emotional intelligence: Why it can matter more than IQ.* New York: Bantam Books.

Gonzalez-Mena, J. (2005). *Diversity in early care and education: Honoring differences.* (4th ed.). Boston: McGraw Hill.

Gottfredson, L. S. (2003). The science and politics of intelligence in gifted education. In N. Colangelo & G. A. Davis (Eds.), *Handbook of gifted education* (3rd ed., pp. 24–40). Boston: Pearson Education, Inc.

Gottfried, A. E., & Gottfried, A. W. (2004). Toward the development of a conceptualization of gifted motivation, *Gifted Child Quarterly, 48*(2): 121–132.

Gottfried, A. W., Gottfried, A. E., Bathurst, K., & Guerin, D. W. (1994). *Gifted IQ: Early developmental aspects: The Fullerton longitudinal study.* New York: Plenum Press.

Gottfried, A.W., Gottfried, A. E., & Guerin, D. W. (2006). The Fullerton longitudinal study: A long term investigation

of intellectual and motivational giftedness. *Journal for the Education of the Gifted, 29*(4): 430–450.

Graham, G., Holt-Hale, S. A., & Parker, M. (2005). *Children moving: A reflective approach to teaching physical education* (7th ed.). New York: McGraw Hill.

Green, R. (2004). The evolution of kinship care policy and practice. *The Future of Children, 14*(1): 131–194. Retrieved May 18, 2007, from http://thefutureofchildren.org/usr_doc/8-green.pdf.

Greenspan, S. I., & Weider, S. (1998). *The child with special needs: Encouraging intellectual and emotional growth.* Reading, MA: Addison-Wesley.

Greenspan, S. I., & Wieder, S. (2006). *Infant and early childhood mental health: A comprehensive developmental approach to assessment and intervention.* Washington, DC: American Psychiatric Publishing, Inc.

Gregory, S., Bishop, J., & Sheldon, L. (1995). *Deaf young people and their families.* New York: Cambridge University Press.

Grisham-Brown, J., & Hemmeter, M. L. (1998). Writing IEP goals and objectives: Reflecting an activity-based approach for instruction for young children with disabilities. *Young Exceptional Children, 1*(3): 1–10.

Gronlund, G. (1998). Portfolios as an assessment tool: Is collection of work enough? *Young Children, 53*(3): 4–10.

Gropper, N., Hinitz, B. F., Sprung, B., & Froschl, M. (2011). Helping young boys be successful learners in today's early childhood classrooms. *Young Children, 66*(1): 34–41.

Gross, M. U. M. (1993). *Exceptionally gifted children.* London: Routledge & Kegan Paul.

Grosse S. D., Matte, T. D., Schwartz, J., & Jackson, R. J. (2002). Economic gains resulting from the reduction in children's exposure to lead in the United States. *Environmental Health Perspectives, 110*(6): 563–569.

Groves, B. M., Lieberman, A. F., Osofsky, J. D., & Fenichel, E. (2000). Protecting young children in violent environments—A framework to build on. *Zero to Three, 20*(5): 9–13.

Guitar, B., & Conture, E. G. (2007). Seven ways to help the child who stutters. Retrieved May 4, 2007, from www.stutteringhelp.org/Default.aspx?tabid = 38.

Guralnick, M. J. (2004). Effectiveness of early intervention for vulnerable children: A developmental perspective. In M. A. Feldman (Ed.), *Early intervention: The essential readings* (pp. 9–50). Malden, MA: Blackwell Publishing, Ltd.

Guralnick, M. J. (Ed.). (2005). *The developmental systems approach to early intervention.* Baltimore: Paul H. Brookes.

Guralnick, M. J., Connor, R. T., Hammond, J. M., Gottman, J. M., & Kinnish, K. (1996). The peer relations of preschool children with communication disorders. *Child Development, 67*(2): 471–489.

Haffner, W. H. J. (2007). Development before birth. In M. L. Batshaw, L. Pellegrino & N. J. Rosen (Eds.), *Children with disabilities* (6th ed., pp. 23–33). Baltimore: Paul H. Brookes.

Hagerman, R. J. (2007). Fragile X syndrome: A genetic model for autism with targeted treatments. Retrieved November 16, 2008, from www.iancommunity.org/

cs/articles/fragile_x_syndrome_a_genetic_model_for_autism_with_targeted_treatments.

Hain, T. C. (2007). OEA Testing (otoacoustic emissions). Retrieved January 4, 2008, from www.dizziness-and-balance.com/testing/OAE.htm.

Halgunseth, L. C. (2004). Continuing research on Latino families: El pasado y el futuro. In M. Coleman & L. H. Ganong (Eds.), *Handbook of contemporary families: Considering the past, contemplating the future* (pp. 333–351). Thousand Oaks, CA: Sage.

Hameed, B., Shyamanur, K., Kotecha, S., et al. (2004). Trends in the incidence of severe retinopathy of prematurity in a geographically defined population over a 10-year period. *Pediatrics, 113*(6): 1653–1657.

Han, M., Roskos, K., Christie, J., Mandzuk, S., & Vukelich, C. (2005). Learning words: Large group time as a vocabulary development opportunity. *Journal of Research in Childhood Education, 4*(19): 333–345.

Economic Opportunities Amendments of 1972, Pub. L. No. 92–424, §1, 86 Stat. 688.

Handicapped Children's Early Education Assistance Act (HCEEP), Pub. L. No. 90–538.

Hanson, M. J. (2004). Families with Anglo-European roots. In E. W. Lynch & M. J. Hanson (Eds.), *Developing cross-cultural competence: A guide for working with children and their families* (3rd ed., pp. 81–108). Baltimore: Paul H. Brookes.

Harjo, S. S. (1993). The American Indian experience. In H. P. McAdoo (Ed.), *Family ethnicity: Strength in diversity* (pp. 199–207). Thousand Oaks, CA: Sage.

Hart, B., & Risley, T. (2003). The early catastrophe: The 30 million word gap by age 3. *American Educator, 27* (Spring): 4–9.

Hart-Shegos, E. (1999). *Homelessness and it effects on children: A report prepared for the family housing fund.* Hart-Shegos and Associates, Inc. Retrieved May 17, 2007, from http://fhfund.org/dnldreports/Supportive Children.pdf.

Haskins, R., & Rouse, C. (2005). Closing the achievement gap. *The Future of Children*, (Policy Brief). Retrieved July 23, 2008, from www.brookings.edu/es/research/projects/wrb/publications/pb/20050301foc.pdf.

Hatton, D. D. (2001). Model registry of early childhood visual impaired collaborative group: First year results. *Journal of Blindness and Visual Impairments, 95*(7), 418–433.

Haugland, S. W. (2002). Selecting developmentally appropriate software. Retrieved December 29, 2002, from www.childrenandcomputers.com.

Hausman, M. S., & Reed, J. R. (1991). Psychological issues in relocation: Response to change. *Journal of Career Development, 17,* 247–258.

Hawley, C. A., Ward, A. B., Magnay, A. R., et al. (2004). Return to school after brain injury. *Archives of Disease in Childhood, 89*(2): 136–142.

Health, Resources and Services Administration (HRSA). (2010). Stop bullying now. Retrieved March 2, 2011, from www.stopbullyingnow.hrsa.gov/adults/default.aspx.

Hearing Loss Association of America. (2005). Assistive listening systems. Retrieved December 14, 2010, from www.hearingloss.org/learn/assistivetech.asp.

Hebbeler, K., Smith, B., & Black, T. (1991). Federal early childhood special education policy: A model for the improvement of services for children with disabilities. *Exceptional Children, 58*(2): 104–112.

Hebbeler, K., Spiker, D., Bailey, D., Scarborough, A., Mallik, S., Simeonsson, R., et al. (2007). Early intervention for infants and toddlers with disabilities and their families: Participants, services, and outcomes. Retrieved December 14, 2007, from www.sri.com/neils/pdfs/NEILS_Report_02_07_Final2.pdf.

Hegde, M. N. (2001). *Introduction to communicative disorders* (2nd ed.). Austin, TX: Pro-Ed.

Heinzer, M. M. (2005). Obesity in infancy: Questions, more questions, and few answers. *Newborn and Infant Nursing Reviews, 5*(4): 194–202.

Henry J. Kaiser Family Foundation. (2004). *The role of media in childhood obesity.* (Issue Brief). Menlo Park, CA: Author.

Hepburn, K. S. (2004). *Building culturally and linguistically competent services to support young children, their families, and school readiness.* Baltimore: Annie E. Casey Foundation. Retrieved March 15, 2008, from www.aef.org/upload/publicationfiles/hs3622h325.pdf.

Herer, G. R., Knightly, C. A., & Steinberg, A. G. (2007). Hearing: Sounds and silences. In M. L. Batshaw (Ed.), *Children with disabilities* (5th ed., pp. 193–227). Baltimore: Paul H. Brookes.

Hernandez, D. J. (2004). Demographic change and the life circumstances of immigrant families. *The Future of Children, 14*(2): 17–39.

Hernandez, D. J. (2006). Young Hispanic children in the U.S.: A demographic portrait based on Census 2000. National Task Force on Early Childhood Education for Hispanics. New York: Foundation for Child Development. Retrieved May 15, 2007, from www.ecehispanic.org/work/September_update_2006.doc.

Hetherington, E. M., & Kelly, J. (2002). *For better or worse.* New York: Norton.

Hill, J. B., & Haffner, W. H. J. (2002). Growth before birth. In M. L. Batshaw (Ed.), *Children with Disabilities.* (5th ed., pp. 243–262). Baltimore: Paul H. Brookes.

Holt, R. F., & Svirsky, M. A. (2008). An exploratory look at pediatric cochlear implantation: Is earliest always best? *Ear and Hearing 29*(4): 492–511.

Honig, A. S. (1993). Mental health for babies: What do theory and research teach us? *Young Children, 48*(3): 69–76.

Hood, L. (2003). *Immigrant student, urban high schools: The challenge continues.* New York: Carnegie Corporation of New York.

Hoover, H. D., Dunbar, S. B., & Frisbe, D. A. (2007). *Iowa Tests of Basic Achievement.* Rolling Meadows, IL: Riverside Publishing.

Houk, F. A. (2005). *Supporting English language learners: A guide for teachers and administrators.* Portsmouth, NH: Heinemann.

Hoyert, D. L., Freedman, M. A., Strobino, D. M., et al. (2001). Annual summary of vital statistics: 2000. *Pediatrics, 108,* 1241–1255.

Huestis, M. A., & Choo, R. E. (2002). Drug abuse's smallest victims: In utero drug exposure. *Forensic Science International, 128*(1–2): 20–30.

Hulit, L. M., & Howard, M. R. (2006). *Born to talk: An introduction to speech and language development* (4th ed.). Boston: Pearson Education, Inc.

Humes, K. R., Jones, N. A., & Ramirez, R. R. (2011). Overview of race and Hispanic origin: 2010. Retrieved March 27, 2011, from www.census.gov/prod/cen2010/briefs/c2010br-02.pdf.

Huncharek, M., Kupelnick, B., & Klassen, H. (2001). Paternal smoking during pregnancy and the risk of childhood brain tumors: Results of a meta-analysis. *In Vivo, 15*(6): 535–541.

Hundert, J., Mahoney, B., Mundy, F., & Vernon, M. L. (1998). A descriptive analysis of developmental and social gains of children with severe disabilities in segregated and inclusive preschools in southern Ontario. *Early Childhood Research Quarterly, 13*(1): 49–65.

Huppke, P., & Gartner, J. (2005). Molecular diagnosis of Rett syndrome. *Journal of Child Neurology, 20*, 732–736.

Hurst, D. S. (2007). Middle ear disease and allergy: Why allergy? Retrieved April 25, 2007, from www.earallergy.com/.

Hurst, D. S. (2008). Efficacy of allergy immunotherapy as a treatment for patients with chronic otitis media with effusion. *International Journal of Pediatric Otorhinolarngology, 72*(8): 1215–1223.

Hurth, J., Shaw, E., Iseman, S., Whaley, K., & Rogers, S. (1999). Areas of agreement about effective practices among programs serving very young children with autism spectrum disorders. *Infants and Young Children, 12*(2): 17–26.

Hyman, S. L., & Towbin, K. E. (2007). Autism Spectrum Disorders. In M. L. Batshaw, L. Pellegrino & N. J. Rosen (Eds.), *Children with disabilities* (6th ed., pp. 325–343). Baltimore: Paul H. Brookes.

Hyson, M. (2004). *The emotional development of young children: Building an emotion-centered curriculum* (2nd ed.). New York: Teachers College Press.

IDEA Regulations. (2007). Disproportionality. Building the legacy: IDEA 2004. U.S. Department of Education, Office of Special Education Services. Retrieved November 22, 2010, from http://idea.gov/.

Individuals with Disabilities Education Act (IDEA) of 1990, Pub. L. No. 101–476, 104 Stat. 1103, 20 U.S.C. § 1400.

Individuals with Disabilities Education Act (IDEA) Amendments of 1991, Pub. L. No. 102–119, 105 Stat. 587, 20 U.S.C. § 1400.

Individuals with Disabilities Education Act (IDEA) Amendments of 1997, Pub. L. No. 105–17, 111 Stat. 37–157, 20 U.S.C. § 1400.

Individuals with Disabilities Education Improvement Act (IDEA) Amendments of 2004, Pub. L. No. 108–446, 118 Stat. 2647, 20 U.S.C. § 1400.

Inlow, J. K., & Restifo, L. L. (2004). Molecular and comparative genetics of mental retardation. *Genetics, 166*, 835–881.

Interactive Autism Network. (2007). Environmental aspects of autism. Retrieved December 26, 2007, from www.iancommunity.org/cs/understanding_research/environmental_aspects.

International Dyslexia Association. (2003). Dyslexia and related disorders. Retrieved August 3, 2007, from http://www.interdys.org/FAQ.htm.

International Reading Association (IRA) & National Association for the Education of Young Children NAEYC). (1998). Learning to read and write: Developmentally appropriate practices for young children. Overview. Retrieved August 1, 2008, from www.naeyc.org/about/positions/psread0.asp.

International Reading Association (IRA) & National Council of Teachers of English (NCTE). (1996). *Standards of the English language arts.* Newark, DE: International Reading Association.

International Reading Association. (1998). *Phonics in the early reading program: A position statement.* Newark, DE: Author.

International Society for Technology in Education. (ISTE). (2007). ISTE NETS and Performance indicators for students. Retrieved November 28, 2010, from (NETS-S)NETS+for+Student+2007_EN.pdf.

Isaacs, J. S. (2007). Nutrition and children with disabilities. In M. L. Batshaw, L. Pellegrino & N. J. Rosen (Eds.), *Children with disabilities* (6th ed., pp. 125–136). Baltimore: Paul H. Brookes.

Ishii-Kuntz, M. (2004). Asian American families: Diverse history, contemporary trends and the future. In M. Coleman & L. H. Ganong, *Handbook of contemporary families: Considering the past, contemplating the future* (pp. 369–384). Thousand Oaks, CA: Sage.

Jackson, N. R. (2003). Young gifted children. In N. Colangelo & G. A. Davis (Eds.), *Handbook of gifted education* (3rd ed., pp. 470–482). Boston: Pearson Education, Inc.

Jacob K. Javits Gifted and Talented Students Education Act (1988) of the Elementary and Secondary Education Act Pub. L. No.100-297, 102 Stat 237, 20 U.S.C. §§ 3061 et. seq. 1988.

Jago, R., Baranowski, T., Baranowski, J. C., Thompson, D., & Greaves, K. A. (2005). BMI from 3–6 years of age is predicted by TV viewing and physical activity, not diet. *International Journal of Obesity, 29*(6): 557–564.

Jencks, C., & Phillips, M. (1998). The black–white test score gap: An introduction. In C. Jencks & M. Phillips (Eds.), *The black–white test score gap* (pp. 1–51). Washington, DC: Brookings Institution Press.

Jensen, E. (2006). *Enriching the brain: How to maximize every learner's potential.* San Francisco, CA: Jossey-Bass.

Jeppesen, J., Green, A., Steffensen, B. F., et al. (2003). The Duchenne muscular dystrophy populations in Denmark, 1977–2001: Prevalence, incidence and survival in relation to the introduction of ventilator use. *Neuromuscular Disorders, 13*(10): 804–812.

Joe, J. R., & Malach, R. S. (2004). Families with American Indian roots. In E. W. Lynch & J. Hanson (Eds.), *Developing cross-cultural competence: A guide for working with children and their families* (3rd ed., pp. 109–139). Baltimore, MD: Paul H. Brookes.

Johnson, C. P., & Myers, S. M. and the Council on Children with Disabilities. (2007). Identification and evaluation of children with autism spectrum disorders. *Pediatrics* (October 29, 2007): 1–34.

Johnson, M. D., & Young, M. B. (2003). Advertising history of televisual media. In E. L. Palmer & B. M. Young (Eds.), *The faces of televisual media: Teaching, violence, selling to children* (2nd ed., pp. 265–285). Mahwah, NJ: Lawrence Erlbaum Associates.

Joint Committee on Infant Hearing. (2007). Year 2007 position statement: Principles and guidelines for early hearing detection and intervention programs. *Pediatrics (4)*120, 898–921.

Joint Committee on National Health Education Standards. (2007). *National health education standards: Achieving health literacy.* Atlanta, GA: American Cancer Society.

Jordan, N. C., Glutting, J., & Remineni, C. (2008). A number sense assessment tool for identifying children at risk for mathematical difficulties. In A. Dowker (Ed.), *Mathematical difficulties: Psychology and intervention* (pp. 45–58). San Diego, CA: Academic Press. Retrieved August 23, 2008, from www.udel.edu/cmp2/jordan_number%20sense.pdf.

Jordan, N. C., Hanich, L. B., & Kaplan, D. (2003). A longitudinal study of mathematical competencies in children with specific mathematical difficulties versus children with comorbid mathematics and reading difficulties. *Child Development, 74*(3): 834–850.

Jordan, N. C., Kaplan, D., Locuniak, M. N., & Ramineni, C. (2007). Predicting first-grade math achievement from developmental number sense trajectories. *Learning Disabilities Research and Practice, 22*(1): 36–46. Retrieved August 23, 2008, from www.udel.edu/cmp2/jordan_LDRP2007.pdf.

Jovanovic, G., & Johnsen, M. (2006). Restraint and seclusion: Can they become obsolete practices? *Issue Brief: Center for Mental Health Services Research, University of Massachusetts Medical School,* 3(2).

Juvenile Diabetes Research Foundation International (JDRF). (2003). Paths to a cure. Retrieved January 3, 2004, from www.jdrf.org/index.

Kagan, S. L., Scott-Little, C., & Frelow, V. S. (2009). Linking play to early learning and development guidelines: Possibility or polemic? *Zero to Three, 30*(1): 18–25.

Kandall, S. R., Doberczak, T. M., Jantunen, M., & Stein, J. (1999). The methadone-maintained pregnancy. *Clinics in Perinatology, 26*(1): 173–183.

Kandel, E., Schwartz, J., & Jessell, T. (2000). *Principles of neural science.* 4th ed. New York: McGraw-Hill Medical.

Kanevsky, L. (1992). The learning game. In P. S. Klein & A. J. Tannenbaum (Eds.), *To be young and gifted* (pp. 204–244). Norwood, NJ: ABLEX.

Kanner, L. (1943). Autistic disturbances of affective contact. *Nervous Child, 2*: 217–250.

Kaplow, J. B., & Widom, C. S. (2007). Age of onset of child maltreatment predicts long-term mental health outcomes. *Journal of Abnormal Psychology, 116*(1): 176–187.

Kapperman, G., & Sticken, J. (2006). *Project Math Access.* Retrieved September 29, 2008, from http://s22318.tsbvi.edu/mathproject/.

Kareem, N. (2010). Raising biracial children to be well adjusted. Retrieved November 28, 2010, from http://racerelaions.about.com/od/raceconciousparenting/a/RaisingBiracialChildrentoBeWell adjusted.htm.

Karoly, L. A., & Gonzalez, G. C. (2011). Early care and education for children in immigrant families. *The Future of Children, 21*(1): 71–101.

Kawamoto, W. T., & Cheshire, T. C. (2004). A seven-generation approach to American Indian families. In M. Coleman & L. H. Ganong, *Handbook of contemporary families: Considering the past, contemplating the future* (pp. 385–393). Thousand Oaks, CA: Sage.

Kazdin, A. E. (1995). *Conduct disorders in childhood and adolescence* (2nd ed.). Mountain View, CA: Mayfield.

Kea, C., & Campbell-Whatley, G. D., & Richards, H. V. (2006). Becoming culturally responsive educators: Rethinking teacher education pedagogy. Retrieved June 4, 2008, from www.nccrest.org/Briefs/Teacher_Ed_Brief.pdf?v_document_name = Teacher%20Ed%20Brief.

Keating, R., Spence, C. A., & Lynch, D. (2002). The brain and nervous system: Normal and abnormal development. In M. L. Batshaw (Ed.), *Children with disabilities* (5th ed., pp. 243–262). Baltimore: Paul H. Brookes.

Keilty, B., Walsh, S., & Ziegler, D. (October, 2007). *IDEA Essentials: What you need to know to know.* Paper given at the Division for Exceptional Children Annual Conference, Niagara Falls, Ontario, Canada.

Kendall, J. S., & Marazano, R. J. (1996). *Content knowledge: A compendium of standards and benchmarks for K–12 education.* Aurora, CO: McREL.

Kenneson, A., Van Naarden Braun, K., & Boyle, C. (2002). GJB2 (connexin 26) variants and nonsyndromic sensorineural hearing loss. *Genetics in Medicine, 4*(4): 258–274.

Khan, R. I., O'Keefe, M., Kenny, D., & Nolan, L. (2007). Changing patterns of childhood blindness. *Irish Medical Journal, 100*(5): 458–461.

Kick, C. G. (2001). *The changing Pacific Island family and children's welfare.* International Community Development Conference, Rotorua, New Zealand, Retrieved November 17, 2010, from www.iacdglobal.org/files/kick.pdf.

Kids Health. (2008a). Down syndrome. Retrieved September 25, 2008, from http://kidshealth.org/parent/medical/genetic/down_syndrome.html.

Kids Health. (2008b). Juvenile rheumatoid arthritis. Retrieved May 22, 2011, from http://kidshealth.org/parent/medical/arthritis/hra.html#.

Klesges, L. M., Johnson, K. C., Ward, K. D., & Barnard, M. (2001). Smoking cessation in pregnant women. *Obstetrics Gynecology Clinics of North America, 28*(2): 269–282.

Klug, M. G., & Burd, L. (2003). Fetal alcohol syndrome prevention: Annual and cumulative cost savings. *Neurotoxicology and Teratology, 25*(6): 763–765.

Knip, M. (2005). Etiopathogenetic aspects of type 1 diabetes. In F. Chiarelli, K. Dahl-Jorgensen & W. Kiess (Eds.), *Diabetes in childhood and adolescence* (pp. 1–27). Basel, Switzerland: Karger.

Koob, A. (2009). *The roots of thought: Unlocking glia—the brain cell that will help us sharpen our wits, heal injury, and treat brain disease.* Saddle River, NJ: FT Press.

Koshy, V. (2002). *Teaching gifted children 4–7: A guide for teachers.* London: David Fulton Publishers.

Kotagal, P. (2000). Tonic-clonic seizures. In H. O. Luders & S. Noachtar (Eds.), *Epileptic seizures: Pathophysiology and clinical semiology* (pp. 425–432). New York: Churchill Livingstone.

Kranowitz, C. S. (1998). *The out-of-sync child: Recognizing and coping with sensory integration dysfunction.* New York: Skylight Press.

Kreider, R. M. (2003). *Adopted children and stepchildren: 2000*. Census 2000 special reports. U.S. Census Bureau. Retrieved May 18, 2007, from www.census.gov/prod/2003pubs/censr-6.pdf.

Kreider, R. M. (2008). *Living arrangements of children: 2004*. Current Population Reports, P70-114. U.S. Census Bureau, Washington, DC. Retrieved November 17, 2010, from www.census.gov/prod/2008pubs/p70-114.pdf.

Kreider, R. M., & Elliott, D. B. (2009). *America's families and living arrangements: 2007*. Current Population Reports. Retrieved March 28, 2011, from www.census.gov/population/www/socdemo/hh-fam/p20-561.pdf.

Kronenberger, W. G., & Dunn, D. W. (2003). Learning disorders. *Neurological Clinics, 21*(4): 941–952.

Kuhl, P., Coffey-Corina, S., Padden, D., & Dawson, G. (2005). Links between social and linguistic processing of speech in preschool children with autism: Behavioral and electrophysiological measures. *Developmental Science, 8*: 617–620.

Kuntsi, J., Rijsdijk, F., Ronald, A., Asherson, P., & Plomin, R. (2005). Genetic influences on the stability of attention-deficit/hyperactivity disorder symptoms from early to middle childhood. *Biological Psychiatry, 57*(6): 647–654.

Kurdek, L. A. (2004). Gay men and lesbians. In M. Coleman & L. H. Ganong (Eds.), *Handbook of contemporary families: Considering the past, contemplating the future* (pp. 97–115). Thousand Oaks, CA: Sage.

Kurtz, L. A. (2002). Rehabilitation: Physical therapy and occupational therapy. In M. L. Batshaw (Ed.), *Children with disabilities* (5th ed., pp. 647–657). Baltimore: Paul H. Brookes.

Laird, J. (2003). Lesbian and gay families. In F. Walsh (Ed.), *Normal family processes* (3rd ed., pp. 176–209). New York: Guilford Press.

Lally, J. R., & Mangione, P. (2006). The uniqueness of infancy demands a responsive approach to care. *Young Children, 61*(4): 14–20.

Lambie, R. (2000). *Family systems within educational contexts: Understanding at-risk and special-needs students* (2nd ed.). Denver, CO: Love.

Lamme, L. (1985). *Growing up writing*. Washington, DC: Acropolis Books.

Landale, N. S., Thomas, K. J. A., Van Hook, J. (2011). The living arrangements of children of immigrants. *The Future of Children, 21*(1): 43–70.

Landrigan, P. J., Schechter, C. B., Lipton, J. M., Fahs, M. C., & Schwartz, J. (2002). Environmental pollutants and disease in American children: Estimates of morbidity, mortality, and costs for lead poisoning, asthma, cancer and developmental disabilities. *Environmental Health Perspectives, 110*(7): 721–728.

Laszloffy, T. A. (2002). Rethinking family development theory: Teaching with the systemic family development (SFD) model. *Family Relations, 51*(3): 211–224.

LD OnLine. (2007). The ABCs of LD. Retrieved July 30, 2007, from www.ldonline.org/article/5613.

Learning Accomplishment Profile (3rd ed., LAP-3). (2004). Chapel Hill, NC: Kaplan Early Learning Company and Chapel Hill Training Outreach Project, Inc.

Learning Disabilities Roundtable. (2002). *Specific learning disabilities: Finding common ground*. Division of Research to Practice, Office of Special Education Programs, U.S. Department of Education, Washington, DC. Retrieved on August 18, 2011 from http://www.ldanatl.org/legislative/joint_activities/commonground.asp

Leet, A. I., Dormans, J. P., & Tosi, L. L. (2002). Muscles, bones, and nerves: The body's framework. In M. L. Batshaw (Ed.), *Children with disabilities* (5th ed., pp. 263–284). Baltimore: Paul H. Brookes.

Lemanek, K. L., & Hood, C. (1999). Asthma. In R. T. Brown (Ed.), *Cognitive aspects of chronic illness in children* (pp. 78–104). New York: Guilford.

Lengua, L. J., Wolchik, S., Sandler, I. N., & West, S. G. (2000). The additive and interactive effects of parenting and temperament in predicting problems of children of divorce. *Journal of Clinical Psychology, 29*(2): 232–244.

Leos, K., & Saavedra, L. (2010). *A new vision to increase the academic achievement for English language learners and immigrant students*. The Global Institute for Language and Literacy Development, LLC. Retrieved March 8, 2010, from www.urban.orguploadedpdf/4122265-A-New-Vision-to-Increase-Academic-Achievement.pdf.

Lesinski-Schiedat, A., Illg, A., Heermann, R., Bertram, B., & Lenarz, T. (2004). Paediatric cochlear implantation in the first and in the second year of life: A comparative study. *Cochlear Implants International, 5*(4): 146–159.

Lester, B. M. (2000). Prenatal cocaine exposure and child outcome: A model for the study of the infant at risk. *Israel Journal of Psychiatry and Related Sciences, 37*(3): 223–235.

Lester, S., & Russell, W. (2010). Children's right to play: An examination of the importance of play in the lives of children worldwide. The Hague: The Netherlands: Bernard van Leer Foundation. Retrieved April 21, 2011, from Children's-right-to-play-An-examination-of-the-importance-of-play-in-the-lives-of-children-worldwide.pdf.

Leukemia and Lymphoma Society. (2007). Leukemia. Retrieved September 2, 2007, from www.leukemia-lymphoma.org/all_page?item_id = 7026.

Leukemia and Lymphoma Society. (2011). Leukemia facts and statistics: Facts 2010–2011. Retrieved May 22, 2011, from www.lls.org/#/dise aseinformationgetinformationsupport/factsstatisticsa/leukemia.

Leung, D. Y. M. (2003). Epidemiology of allergic disease. In D. Y. M. Leung, H. A. Sampson, R. S. Geha, & S. J. Szefler (Eds.). *Pediatric allergy: Principles and practices* (pp. 1–7). St. Louis, MI: Mosby.

Levin, D. E., & Carlsson-Paige, N. (2006). *The war play dilemma: What every parent and teacher needs to know* (2nd ed.). New York: Teachers College Press.

Lewin, L. (1999). Childhood social predictors of adolescent antisocial behavior: Gender differences in predictive accuracy and efficacy. *Journal of Abnormal Child Psychology, 27*(4): 212–230.

Lim, S., & Simser, J. (2005). Auditory-verbal therapy for children with hearing impairment. *Annals Academy of Medicine Singapore, 34*(4): 307–312.

Linder, T. W. (2008a). *Transdisciplinary play-based assessment 2* (2nd. ed.). Baltimore: Paul H. Brookes Publishing Co.

Linder, T. W. (2008b). Transdisciplinary play-based intervention 2. Baltimore, MD: Paul H. Brookes Publishing Co.

Liptak, G. S. (2002). Neural tube defects. In M. L. Batshaw (Ed.), *Children with disabilities* (5th ed., pp. 467–492). Baltimore: Paul H. Brookes.

Liptak, G. S. (2007). Neural tube defects. In M. L. Batshaw, L. Pellegrino & N. J. Rosen (Eds.), *Children with disabilities* (6th ed., pp. 419–438). Baltimore: Paul H. Brookes.

Loesch, D. Z., Huggins, R. M., Bui, Q. M., et al. (2002). Effect of the deficits of fragile X mental retardation protein on cognitive status of fragile X males and females assessed by robust pedigree analysis. *Journal of Developmental and Behavioral Pediatrics, 23*(6): 416–424.

Lopez, E. C. (2000). Identifying gifted and creative linguistically and culturally diverse children. In G. B. Esquivel & J. C. Houtz (Eds.), *Creativity and giftedness in culturally diverse students* (pp. 125–148). Cresskill, NJ: Hampton Press.

Lord, C., Risi, S., Lambrecht, L., et al. (2000). The autism diagnostic observation schedule-generic: A standard measure of social and communication deficits associated with the spectrum of autism. *Journal of Autism and Developmental Disorders, 30*(3): 205–223.

Lord, C., Rutter, M., & Le Couteur, A. (1994). Autism diagnostic interview-revised: A revised version of a diagnostic interview for caregivers of individuals with possible pervasive developmental disorders. *Journal of Autism and Developmental Disorders, 24*(5): 659–685.

Lord, C., Rutter, M., Goode, S., Heemsbergen, J., Jordan, H., & Mawhood, L. (1989). Autism diagnostic observational schedule: A standardized observation of communicative and social behavior. *Journal of Autism and Developmental Disorders, 19*(2): 185–212.

Lovaas, O. I. (1987). Behavioral treatment and normal intellectual and educational functioning in autistic children. *Journal of Consulting and Clinical Psychology, 55*(1): 3–9.

Lowdermilk, D. L., & Perry, S. E. (2003). *Maternity nursing* (6th ed.). St. Louis, MO: Mosby.

Lowdermilk, D. L., & Perry, S. E. (2006). *Maternity nursing* (7th ed.). St. Louis, MO: Mosby.

Lynch, E. W. (2004a). Conceptual framework. In E. W. Lynch & M. J. Hanson (Eds.), *Developing cross-cultural competence: A guide for working with children and their families* (3rd ed., pp. 19–39). Baltimore: Paul H. Brookes Publishing Co.

Lynch, E. W. (2004b). Developing cross-cultural competence. In E. W. Lynch & M. J. Hanson (Eds.), *Developing cross-cultural competence: A guide for working with children and their families* (3rd ed. pp. 41–80). Baltimore: Paul H. Brookes Publishing Co.

Lynch, E. W., & Hanson, M. J. (Eds.). (2004). *Developing cross-cultural competence: A guide for working with children and their families* (3rd ed.). Baltimore: Paul H. Brookes Publishing Co.

Lynch, M. & Cicchetti, D. (2002). Links between community violence and the family system: Evidence from children's feelings of relatedness and perceptions of parent behavior. *Family Process, 41*(3): 519–532.

Lyons-Ruth, K. (1996). Attachment relationships among children with aggressive behavior problems: The role of disorganized attachment patterns. *Journal of Consulting and Clinical Psychology, 64*(1): 64–73.

Macfie, J., Cicchetti, D., & Toth, S. L. (2001). Dissociation in maltreated versus nonmaltreated preschool-aged children. *Child Abuse and Neglect, 25*(9): 1253–1267.

Mandlawitz, M. (2007). *What every teacher should know about IDEA 2004 laws and regulations.* Boston, MA: Pearson Education, Inc.

Marini, Z., Fairbairn, L., & Zuber, R. (2001). Peer harassment in individuals with developmental disabilities: Towards the development of a multidimensional bullying identification model. *Developmental Disabilities Bulletin, 29*: 170–195.

Marion, M. (2002, November 20). *Good decision making: Your key to helping children with challenging behaviors.* Paper presented at the National Association for the Education of Young Children annual conference, New York.

Marks, J. S., Koplan, J. P., Hogue, C. J. R., & Dalmat, M.E. (1990). A cost-benefit/cost-effectiveness analysis of smoking cessation for pregnant women. *American Journal of Preventive Medicine, 6*(5): 282–291.

Marschilok, C. (2004). Update on insulin pump therapy. Retrieved September 3, 2007, from http://indep.nih.gov/diabetes/pubs/snn_March_2004.pdf.

Marshak, L. E., & Prezant, F. (2007). *Married with special needs children: A couple's guide to keeping connected.* Bethesda, MD: Woodbine House.

Martin, J. A., Kochanek, K. D., Strobino, D. M., Guyer, B., & MacDorman, M. F. (2005). Annual Summary of Vital Statistics—2003. *Pediatrics, 115*(3): 619–634.

Martin, J. S., Hamilton, B. E., Sutton, P. D., Ventura, S. J., Mathews, T, J. et al. (2010). *National Vital Statistics Report, 58*(24). Washington, DC: U.S. Department of Health and Human Services, Centers for Disease Control and Prevention, National Center for Health Statistics, National Vital Statistics System. Retrieved December 1, 2010, from www.cdc.gov/nchs/data/nvsr/nvsr58/nvsr58_24.pdf.

Martin, M. T., Emery, R. E., & Peris, T. S. (2004). Single-parent families: Risks, resilience, and change. In M. Coleman & L. H. Ganong, *Handbook of contemporary families: Considering the past, contemplating the future* (pp. 282–301). Thousand Oaks, CA: Sage.

Mason, E., & Lee, R. V. (1995). Drug abuse. In W. M. Barron & M. D. Lindheimer (Eds.), *Medical disorders during pregnancy* (2nd ed., pp. 465–486). St. Louis, MO: Mosby.

Mathews, M. S., & MacDorman, M. F. (2010). *Infant mortality statistics from the 2006 period linked birth/infant death data set.* National Vital Statistics Reports 58(17). Retrieved March 21, 2011, from http://cdc.gov/nchs/data/nvsr58/nvrs58_17pdf.

Matson, J. L., & Minshawi, N. F. (2006). *Early intervention for autism spectrum disorders: A critical analysis.* Oxford, England: Elsevier Ltd.

Matthews, H., & Ewen, D. (2006). *Reaching all children? Understanding early care and education participation among immigrant families.* Center for Law and Social Policy. Retrieved September 21, 2008, from www.clasp.org/publications/child_care_immigrant.pdf.

Mayesky, M. (2002). *Creative activities for young children* (7th ed.). Belmont, CA: Wadsworth Cengage Learning.

McDowell, J. (2004). *The nervous system and sense organs.* Westport, CT: Greenwood Press.

McGoldrick, M. (1993). Ethnicity, cultural diversity, and normality. In F. Walsh (Ed.), *Normal family processes* (2nd ed., pp. 331–360). New York: Guilford Press.

McKinsey and Company. (2009). *Detailed findings on the economic impact of the achievement gap in America's schools.* Retrieved March 15, 2011, from www.mckinsey.com/App_Media/Images/Pages_Images/Offices/SocialSector/PDF/detailed_achievement_gap_report.pdf.

McKusick, V. A., et al. (2005). Online Mendelian Inheritance in Man. Retrieved August 26, 2007, from www.ncbi.nlm.nih.gov/sites/entrez?db = OMIM.

McPherson, M., Arango, P., & Fox H. B. (1998). A new definition of children with special health care needs. *Pediatrics, 102*(1): 137–140.

Medline Plus. (2007a). Allergic reactions. Retrieved September 1, 2007, from www.nlm.nih.gov/medlineplus/ency/article/000005.htm.

Medline Plus. (2007b). Hypoglycemia. Retrieved September 3, 2007, from www.nlm.nih.gov/medlineplus/ency/article/000386.htm.

Meisels, S. J., & Atkins-Burnett, S. (2000). The elements of early childhood assessment. In J. P. Shonkoff & S. J. Meisels (Eds.), *Handbook of early childhood intervention* (2nd ed., pp. 231–257). Cambridge, England: Cambridge University Press.

Meisels, S. J., & Shonkoff, J. P. (2000). Early childhood intervention: A continuing evolution. In J. P. Shonkoff & S. J. Meisels (Eds.), *Handbook of early childhood intervention* (2nd ed., pp. 3–34). Cambridge, England: Cambridge University Press.

Mendola, P., Selevan, S. G., Gutter, S., et al. (2002). Environmental factors associated with a spectrum of neurodevelopmental deficits. *Mental Retardation and Developmental Disabilities Research Reviews, 8*(3): 188–197.

Mennella, J. A., Ziegler, P., Briefel, R., & Novak, T. (2006). Feeding infants and toddlers study: The types of foods fed to Hispanic infants and toddlers. *Journal of the American Dietetic Association, 106* (Suppl. 1): s96–s106.

Mesibov, G. B., Shea, V., & Schopler, E. (2005). *The TEACCH approach to autism spectrum disorders.* New York: Kluwer Academic/Plenum Publishers.

MetaMetrics. (2011). The lexile framework for reading: Matching readers with text. Retrieved January 4, 2011, from http://lexil.com/about-lexile/grade-equivalent/.

Meyer, A. & Rose, D. H. (2005). The future is in the margins: The role of technology and disability in educational reform. In D. H. Rose, A. Meyer, & C. Hitchcock (Eds.), *The universally designed classroom: Accessible curriculum and digital technologies.* Cambridge, MA: Harvard Education Press.

Meyer, G. A. (2007). X-linked syndromes causing intellectual disability. In M. L. Batshaw, L. Pellegrino & N. J. Rosen (Eds.), *Children with disabilities* (6th ed., pp. 275–283). Baltimore: Paul H. Brookes.

Meyersohn, J. & McFadden, C. (2007). Grandparents being parents. *ABC Primetime.* Retrieved November 19, 2010, from http://abcnews.go.com/Primetine/story?id=2904559&page=1.

Michaud, L. J., Duhaime, A. C., Wade, S. L., Rabin, J. P., Jones, D. O., & Lazar, M. F. (2007). Traumatic brain injury. In M. L. Batshaw, L. Pellegrino & N. J. Rosen (Eds.), *Children with disabilities* (6th ed., pp. 461–476). Baltimore: Paul H. Brookes.

Michaud, L. J., Semel-Concepcion, J., Duhaime, A. C., & Lazar, M. F. (2002). Traumatic brain injury. In M. L. Batshaw (Ed.), *Children with disabilities* (5th ed., pp. 525–545). Baltimore: Paul H. Brookes.

Miller, L. C., & Hendrie, N. W. (2000). Health of children adopted from China. *Pediatrics, 105*(6): E76.

Miller, L. C., Chan, W., Comfort, K., & Tirella, L. (2005). Health of children adopted from Guatemala: Comparison of orphanage and foster care. *Pediatrics, 115*(6): e710–e717.

Miller, M. M., & Menacker, S. J. (2007). Vision: Our window to the world. In M. L. Batshaw, L. Pellegrino, & N. J. Rosen (Eds.), *Children with disabilities* (6th ed., pp. 137–155). Baltimore: Paul H. Brookes.

Miller, M. M., Menacker, S. J., & Batshaw, M. L. (2002). Vision: Our window to the world. In M. L. Batshaw (Ed.), *Children with disabilities* (5th ed., pp. 165–192). Baltimore: Paul H. Brookes.

Miller, P. S., & Stayton, V. D. (2005). DEC recommended practices: Personnel preparation. In S. Sandall, M. L. Hemmeter, B. J. Smith, & M. E. McLean (Eds.), *DEC recommended practices: A comprehensive guide for practical application in early intervention/early childhood special education* (pp. 189–208). Missoula, MT: Division for Early Childhood.

Miller, S., Nunnally, E. W., & Wackman, D. B. (1975). *Alive and aware: How to improve your relationships through better communications.* Minneapolis, MN: Interpersonal Communications Programs.

Minshew, N. J., Sweeney, J. A., Bauman, M. L., & Webb, S. J. (2005). Neurologic aspects of autism. In F. Volkmar et al. (Eds.), *Handbook of Autism and Pervasive Developmental Disorders* (pp. 473–514). Hoboken, NJ: John Wiley and Sons.

Moffitt, T. E. (1993). The neuropsychology of conduct disorder. *Development and Psychopathology, 5*: 135–151.

Mokuau, N., & Tauili'ili, P. (2004). Families with Native Hawaiian and Samoan roots. In E. W. Lynch & M. J. Hanson (Eds.), *Developing cross-cultural competence: A guide for working with children and their families* (3rd ed., pp. 345–372). Baltimore: Paul H. Brookes.

Montoya, J., & Liesenfeld, O. (2004). Toxoplasmosis. *The Lancet, 363*(9425): 1965–1976.

Moon, S. M. (2003). Counseling families. In N. Colangeol & G. A. Davis (Eds.), *Handbook of Gifted Education* (3rd ed., pp. 388–402). Boston: Pearson Education, Inc.

Moore, M. L. (2003). Preterm labor and birth: What have we learned in the past two decades? *Journal of Obstetric, Gynecologic, and Neonatal Nursing, 32*(5): 638–649.

Morey, A., & Kitano, M. K. (1997). *Multicultural course transformation in higher education: A broader truth.* Needham Heights, MA: Allyn and Bacon.

Msall, M. E., & Tremont, M. R. (2002). Measuring functional outcomes after prematurity: Developmental impact of very low birth weight and extremely low birth weight status on childhood disability. *Mental Retardation and Developmental Disabilities Research Reviews, 8*(4): 258–272.

Muhle, R., Trentatcoste, S. V., & Rapin, I. (2004). The genetics of autism. *Pediatrics, 113*(5): e472–e486.

Mundy, P., & Burnette, C. (2005). Joint attention and neurodevelopmental models of autism. In F. Volkmar et al. (Eds.), *Handbook of autism and pervasive developmental disorders* (pp. 650–681). Hoboken, NJ: John Wiley and Sons.

Myles, B. S., Cook, K. T., Miller, N. E., Rinner, L., & Robbins, L. A. (2000). *Asperger syndrome and sensory issues: Practical solutions for making sense of the world.* Shawnee Mission, KS: Autism Asperger Publishing Co.

Naglieri, J. A., LeBuffe, P. A., & Pfeiffer, S. I. (1993). *Devereux behavior rating scale-school form.* San Antonio, TX: Psychological Corporation.

National Association for the Education of Young Children (NAEYC). (2003). Early childhood curriculum, assessment, and program evaluation: Building an effective, accountable system in programs for children birth through age 8. Position statement with expanded resources. Retrieved July 20, 2007, from www.naeyc.org/about/positions/cape.asp.

National Association for the Education of Young Children (NAEYC). (2005). NAEYC accreditation criteria: Teacher-child ratios within group size. Retrieved February 25, 2011, from www.naeyc.org/academy/criteria/teacher_child_ratios.html.

National Association for the Education of Young Children (NAEYC). (2006a). Children's illnesses and child care. Retrieved August 31, 2007, from www.naeyc.org/ece/1997/01.asp.

National Association for the Education of Young Children (NAEYC). (2006b). Developmentally appropriate practice in early childhood programs serving children from birth through age 8. Retrieved May 21, 2007, from www.naeyc.org/about/positions/dap7.asp.

National Association for the Education of Young Children (NAEYC). (2006c). NAEYC position statement: Technology and young children—ages three through eight. Retrieved July 26, 2007, from www.naeyc.org/about/positions/PSTECH98.asp.

National Association for the Education of Young Children (NAEYC). (2006d). New NAEYC Early Childhood Program Standards and Accreditation Performance Criteria. Retrieved May 24, 2007, from www.naeyc.org/about/releases/20050426.asp.

National Association for the Education of Young Children (NAEYC). (2009a). NAEYC position statement: Developmentally appropriate practice in early childhood programs serving children from birth through age 8. In C. Copple & S. Bredekamp (Eds.), *Developmentally appropriate practice in early childhood programs serving children from birth through age 8* (3rd ed., pp. 1–31). Washington, DC: Author. Retrieved July 4, 2011, from www.naeyc.org/files/naeyc/.../positions/position%20statement%20Web.pdf.

National Association for the Education of Young Children (NAEYC). (2009b). *Where we stand on assessing young English language learners.* Retrieved November 22, 2010, from www.naeyc.org/files/naeyc/file/positions/WWWEnglishLanguageLearnersWeb.pdf.

National Association for the Education of Young Children (NAEYC). (2010) 2010 NAEYC Standards for initial and advanced early childhood professional preparation programs. Retrieved July 28, 2011, from www.naeyc.org/files/ecada/file/2010%20NAEYC%20Initial%20&%20Advanced%20Standards.pdf

National Association for the Education of Young Children (NAEYC) & International Reading Association (IRA). (2005). *Where we stand on learning to read and write.* Retrieved August 1, 2008, from www.naeyc.org/about/positions/pdf/WWSSLearningToReadAndWriteEnglish.pdf.

National Association for the Education of Young Children (NAEYC) & National Association of Early Childhood Specialists/State Departments of Education (NAECS/SDE). (2006). *Position statement on curriculum, assessment, and program evaluation.* Retrieved December 15, 2007, from www.naeyc.org/about/positions/pdf/CAEexpand.pdf.

National Association for the Education of Young Children (NAEYC) & National Association of Early Childhood Specialists/State Departments of Education (NAECS/SDE). (2009a). *Where we stand on curriculum, assessment, and program evaluation.* Retrieved November 22, 2010, from www.naeyc.org/files/naeyc/file/positions/StandCurrAss.pdf.

National Association for the Education of Young Children (NAEYC) & National Association of Early Childhood Specialists/State Departments of Education (NAECS/SDE). (2009b). *Where we stand on early learning standards.* Retrieved November 25, 2010, from www.naeyc.org/files/naeyc/file/positions/earlyLearningStandards.pdf.

National Association for the Education of Young Children (NAEYC) & National Council of Teachers of Mathematics (NCTM). (2002). *Early childhood mathematics: Promoting good beginnings.* Retrieved August 1, 2008, from http://naeyc.org/about/positions/pdf/psmath.pdf.

National Association for Gifted Children (NAGC). (2006). *Position paper: Early childhood.* Retrieved March 14, 2011, from www.nagc/uploadedFiles/PDF/Position_Statement_PDFs/EarlyChildhoodPositionFinal.pdf.

National Association for Gifted Children (NAGC). (2008). What is giftedness? Retrieved March 13, 2011, from www.nagc.org/index.aspx?id=574.

National Association for Gifted Children (NAGC). (2010). NAGC Pre-K–Grade 12: Gifted programming standards: A blueprint for quality gifted education programs. Retrieved March 15, 2011, from www.nagc.org/uploadedFiles/Information_and_Resources/Gifted_Program_Standards/K-12programming.

National Association for Music Education. (2008). National standards for music education. Retrieved August 3, 2008, from http://menc.org/resources/view/national-standards-for-music-education.

National Association for Sport and Physical Education (NASPE). (2002). *Active Start: A Statement of Physical Activity Guidelines for Children: Birth to Five Years.* Reston, VA: Author.

National Association for Sport and Physical Education. (NASPE). (2010a). *Active start: A statement of physical activity guidelines for children from birth to age 5* (2nd.ed.). Retrieved March 15, 2011, from www.aahperd.org/naspe/standards/nationalGuidelines/ActiveStart.cfm.

National Association for Sport and Physical Education. (NASPE). (2010b). *Moving into the future: National standards for physical education* (2nd ed.). Retrieved March 15, 2011, from www.aahperd.org/naspe/standards/nationalStandards/PEstandards.cfm.

National Association for Sport and Physical Education. (NASPE). (2010c). *Physical activity for children: A statement of guidelines for children ages 5–12* (2nd ed.). Retrieved March 15, 2011, from www.aahperd.org/naspe/standards/nationalGuidelines/PA.

National Association of Early Childhood Specialists in State Departments of Education. (NAECS/SDE). (2000). *Still unacceptable trends in kindergarten entry and placement: A position statement developed by NAECS/SDE.* Retrieved July 23, 2008, from www.naeyc.org/about/positions/PsUnacc.asp.

National Cancer Institute (2011). Childhood acute lymphoblastic leukemia treatment (PDQ). Retrieved May 22, 2011, from www.cancer.gov/cancertopics/pdq/treatment/childALL/HealthProfessional.

National Center for Educational Statistics (NCES). (2005). *Children 3 through 21 years old served in federally supported programs for the disabled, by type of disability: Selected years, 1976–77 through 2003–04.* Retrieved August 17, 2007, from http://nces.ed.gov/programs/digest/d05/tables/dt05_050.asp.

National Center for Educational Statistics (NCES). (2006). Children with disabilities in public schools. Retrieved July 30, 2007, from http://nces.ed.gov/programs/coe/2007/section1/table.asp?tableID = 671.

National Center for Educational Statics (NCES). (2008). Table 54. *Percentage of gifted and talented students in public elementary and secondary schools by sex, race/ethnicity, and state: 2004 and 2006.* Retrieved March 14, 2011, from http://nces.ed.gov/programs/digest/d09/tables/dt09_054.asp.

National Center for Educational Statistics (NCES). (2009a). *The nation's report card: Mathematics 2009.* Washington, DC. NCES 2010-451.

National Center for Educational Statistics (NCES). (2009b). *The nation's report card: Reading 2009.* Washington, DC. NCES 2010-451.

National Center for Educational Statistics (NCES). (2010). *The condition of education: Participation in education: Elementary/secondary education, children and youth with disabilities.* National Center for Education Statistics, Institute of Education Sciences, U.S. Department of Education. Retrieved March 14, 2011, from http://nces.ed.gov/programs/coe/indicator_cwd.asp.

National Center for Health Statistics (NCHS). (2000). Births: Final data for 1998. *National Vital Statistics Reports, 48*(4). Washington, DC: U.S. Government Printing Office.

National Center for Health Statistics (NCHS). (2007). Infant health. Retrieved April 14, 2007, from www.cdc.gov/nchs/faststats/infant_health.htm.

National Center for Learning Disabilities (NCLD). (2008). Dysgraphia. Retrieved August 23, 2008, from www.ncld.org/index.php?option = content&task = view&id = 468.

National Center for Learning Disabilities (NCLD). (2009). Visual processing disorders. Retrieved February 28, 2011, from www.ncld.org/ld-basics/related-issues/information-processing/visual-processing-disorders.

National Center on Family Homelessness. (2010). Children. Retrieved November 19, 2010, from www.familyhomelessness.org/children.php?p=ts.

National Coalition for the Homeless. (2007). Homeless families with children. NCH Fact Sheet #12. Retrieved November 19, 2010, from www.nationalhomeless.org/publications/facts/families.pdf.

National Coalition for the Homeless. (2009). How many people experience homelessness? Retrieved November 19, 2010, from www.nationalhomeless.org/factsheets/How_Many.html.

National Comorbidity Survey. (2005). Lifetime prevalence of DSM-IV/WMH-CIDI disorders by sex and cohort. Retrieved May 18, 2007, from www.hcp.med.harvard.edu/ncs/publications.php.

National Council for the Social Studies. (1994). Expectations of excellence—Curriculum standards for social studies. Retrieved December 29, 2002, from www.cnets.iste.org.

National Council for the Social Studies. (2008). Expectations of excellence—Curriculum standards for social studies. NCSS curriculum standards revision. Retrieved August 1, 2008, from http://communities.ncss.org/standardsrevision.

National Council of Teachers of Mathematics. (2003). Standards for school mathematics. Retrieved February 4, 2004, from www.nctm.org/.

National Diabetes Information Clearinghouse. (2007). Information on children and young people. Retrieved September 2, 2007, from http://diabetes.niddk.nih.gov/index.htm.

National Dissemination Center for Children with Disabilities (NICHCY). (2004). Mental retardation. Retrieved September 23, 2008, from http://old.nichcy.org/pubs/factshe/fs8txt.htm.

National Education Association. (2006). *The twice-exceptional dilemma.* Washington, DC: Author.

National Eye Institute. (2006). Retinopathy of prematurity. Retrieved April 14, 2007, from www.nei.nih.gov/health/rop/index.asp.

National Forum on Early Childhood Program Evaluation. (2007). A decision-maker's guide. Retrieved July 23, 2008, from www.developingchild.harvard.edu/.

National Fragile X Foundation. (2008). Autism and fragile X syndrome. Retrieved September 25, 2008, from www.fragilex.org/html/autism_and_fragile_x_syndrome.htm.

National Governors Association Center for Best Practice (NGA Center) & Council of Chief State School Officers (CCSSO). (2010a). *Common core state standards for English language arts and literacy in history, social studies, science, and technical subjects.* Retrieved November 25, 2010, from www.corestandards.org/assets/CCSSI_ELAStandards.pdf.

National Governors Association Center for Best Practice (NGA Center) & Council of Chief State School Officers (CCSSO). (2010b). *Common core state standards for mathematics.* Retrieved November 25, 2010, from www.corestandards.org/assets/CCSSI_MathStandards.pdf.

National Governors Association Center for Best Practice (NGA Center) & Council of Chief State School Officers (CCSSO). (2010c). Common core state standards initiative: Preparing America's students for college and career. Retrieved November 25, 2010, from www.corestandards.org/.

National Hemophilia Foundation. (2003). Bleeding disorders info center: Information for teachers and childcare providers. Retrieved January 2, 2004, from www.hemophilia.org/bdi/bdi_providers2.htm.

National Hemophilia Foundation. (2006a). Baby and toddler tips. Retrieved September 3, 2007, from www.hemophilia.org/NHFWeb/MainPgs/MainNHF.aspx?menuid = 194&contentid = 66.

National Hemophilia Foundation. (2006b). Child raising. Retrieved September 3, 2007, from www.hemophilia.org/NHFWeb/MainPgs/MainNHF.aspx?menuid = 195&contentid = 67.

National Hemophilia Foundation. (2006c). What are clotting disorders? Retrieved September 3, 2007, from www.hemophilia.org/NHFWeb/MainPgs/MainNHF.aspx?menuid = 176&contentid = 378.

National Hemophilia Foundation. (2006d). What is a bleeding disorder? Retrieved September 3, 2007, from www.hemophilia.org/NHFWeb/MainPgs/MainNHF.aspx?menuid = 26&contentid = 5&rptname = bleeding.

National Human Genome Research Institute (HGP). (2007). All about the human genome project. Retrieved April 9, 2007, from www.genome.gov.

National Institute of Neurological Disorders and Stroke (NINDS). (2007). NINDS dysgraphia information page. Retrieved August 23, 2008, from www.ninds.nih.gov/disorders/dysgraphia/dysgraphia.htm.

National Institute of Neurological Disorders and Stroke (NINDS). (2011a). Autism fact sheet. Retrieved March 13, 2011, from www.ninds.nih.gov/disorders/autism/detail_autism.htm.

National Institute of Neurological Disorders and Stroke (NINDS). (2011b). Febrile seizure fact sheet. Retrieved March 16, 2011, from www.ninds.nih.gov/disorders/febrile_seizures/detail_febrile_seizures.htm.

National Institute of Neurological Disorders and Stroke (NINDS). (2011c). NINDS Asperger syndrome fact sheet. Retrieved March 13, 2011, from www.ninds.nih.gov/disorders/asperger/detail_asperger.htm.

National Institute of Neurological Disorders and Stroke (NINDS). (2011d). NINDS Epilepsy Information Sheet. Retrieved March 16, 2011, from www.ninds.nih.gov/disorders/epilepsy.htm.

National Institute of Neurological Disorders and Stroke (NINDS). (2011e). NINDS Rett syndrome fact sheet. Retrieved March 13, 2011, from www.ninds.nih.gov/disorders/rett/detail_rett.htm on.

National Institute of Neurological Disorders and Stroke (NINDS). (2011f). Tourette Syndrome Fact Sheet. Retrieved March 16, 2011, from www.ninds.nih.gov/disorders/tourette/detail_tourette.

National Institute on Deafness and Other Communication Disorders (NIDCD). (2000). American sign language. Retrieved December 14, 2010, from www.nidcd.nih.gov/health/hearing/asl.asp.

National Institute on Deafness and Other Communication Disorders (NIDCD). (2002a). Aphasia. Retrieved March 5, 2011, from www.nidcd.nih.gov/health/voice/aphasia.htm.

National Institute on Deafness and Other Communication Disorders (NIDCD). (2002b). Apraxia of speech. Retrieved December 23, 2007, from www.nidcd.nih.gov/health/voice/apraxia.htm.

National Institute of Deafness and Other Communication Disorders (NIDCD). (2002c). Improving the lives of people who have communication disorders. Retrieved December 23, 2007, from www.nidcd.nih.gov/health/statistics/quick.htm.

National Institute on Deafness and Other Communication Disorders (NIDCD). (2002d). Stuttering. Retrieved December 23, 2007, from www.nidcd.nih.gov/health/voice/stutter.htm.

National Institute on Deafness and Other Communication Disorders (NIDCD). (2004). Auditory processing disorder in children. Retrieved December 23, 2007, from www.nidcd.nih.gov/health/voice/auditory.htm.

National Institute on Deafness and Other Communication Disorders (NIDCD). (2008). Aphasia. Retrieved July 13, 2011, from www.nidcd.nih.gov/health/voice/aphasia.html.

National Institute on Deafness and Other Communication Disorders (NIDCD). (2009a). Cochlear implants. Retrieved December 14, 2010, from www.nidcd.nih.gov/health/hearing/coch.asp.

National Institute on Deafness and Other Communication Disorders (NIDCD). (2009b). Gene discovered in childhood language disorder provides insight into reading disorders. Retrieved July 13, 2011, from www.nidcd.nih.gov/news/releases/09/12_11_09.htm.

National Institutes of Health. (2010a). Back to sleep public education campaign. Retrieved March 6, 2011, from www.nichd.nih.gov/sids.

National Institutes of Health. (2010b). Facts about Down syndrome. Retrieved November 9, 2010, from www.nichd.nih.gov/publications/pubs/downsyndrome.cfm.

National Joint Committee on Learning Disabilities. (1990). Definition of Learning Disabilities (1990). Retrieved February 27, 2011, from www.ldonline.org/about/partners/njcld.

National Joint Committee on Learning Disabilities. (2006). Learning disabilities and young children: Identification and intervention. Retrieved July 30, 2007, from www.ldonline.org/article/11511.

National Professional Development Center on Inclusion. (2007). Research synthesis points on early childhood inclusion. Retrieved December 6, 2007, from www.fpg.unc.edu/Xnpdci/assest/media/products/NDPIC_ResearchSynthesis_9-2007.pdf.

National Research Center on Learning Disabilities. (2007). What is RTI? Retrieved November 22, 2010, from www.nrcld.org/topics/rti.html.

National Research Council and Institute of Medicine. (2000). From neurons to neighborhoods: The science of early childhood development. Committee on Integrating the Science of Early Childhood Development. J. P. Shonkoff & D. A. Phillips (Eds.). Board on Children, Youth, and Families, Commission on Behavioral and Social Sciences and Education. Washington, DC: National Academy Press.

National Research Council. (2001). *Adding it up: Helping children learn mathematics.* Kilpatrick, J., Swafford, J., & Findell, B. (Eds.). Mathematics Learning Study Committee, Center for Education, Washington, DC: National Academy Press. Retrieved November 16, 2010, from www.nap.edu/openbook.php?isbn=0309069955.

National Task Force on Early Childhood Education for Hispanics. (2007). Expanding and improving early education for Hispanics. Retrieved June 6, 2008, from www.ecehispanic.org/work/expand_MainReport.pdf.

Newacheck, P. W., Inkelas, M., & Kim, S. E. (2004). Health services use and health care expenditures for children with disabilities. *Pediatrics, 114*(1): 79–85. Retrieved December 29, 2007, from www.pediatrics.org/cgi/content/full/114/1/79.

Newborg, J. (2005). *Battelle developmental inventory* (2nd ed.). Rolling Meadows, IL: Riverside Publishing.

Newcomer, P., & Hammill, D. (1999). *Test of language development—Primary* (3rd ed.). Austin, TX: Pro-Ed.

Newman. B. M. (2000). The challenges of parenting infants and young children. In P. C. McKenry & S. H. Price (Eds.), *Families and change: Coping with stressful events and transitions* (2nd ed., pp. 45–70). Thousand Oaks, CA: Sage.

Newschaffer, C. J., Croen, L. A., Daniels, J., Giarelli, E., Grether, J. K., Levy, S. E., et al. (2007). The epidemiology of autism spectrum disorders. *Annual Reviews of Public Health, 28*: 235–258.

Nichol, A. R., Stretch, D., & Fundudis, T. (1993). *Preschool children in troubled families: Approaches to intervention and support.* Oxford, England: John Wiley & Sons.

Nicpon, M. F., Allmon, A., Sieck, B., & Stinson, R. D. (2011). Empirical investigation of twice-exceptionality: Where have we been and where are we going? *Gifted Child Quarterly, 55*(1): 3–17.

Nihira, K., Leland, H., & Lambert, N. (1993). *AAMD adaptive behavior scale–school* (2nd ed.). Austin, TX: Pro-Ed.

Nikolopoulos, T., Gibbin, K., & Dyar, D. (2004). Predicting speech perception outcomes following cochlear implantation using Nottingham children's implant profile (NChIP). *International Journal of Pediatric Otorhinolaryngology, 68*: 137–141.

No Child Left Behind Act of 2001, Elementary and Secondary Education Act, Pub. L. No. 107–110 (2002).

Nolan, E. D., Gadow, K. D., & Sprafkin, J. (2001). Teacher reports of DSM-IV ADHD, ODD, and CD symptoms in schoolchildren. *Journal of Child and Adolescent Psychiatry, 40,* 241–249.

Northern, J. L., & Downs, M. P. (2002). *Hearing in children* (5th ed.). Philadelphia: Lippincott, Williams & Wilkins.

Norwitz, E., Robinson, J., & Challis, J. (1999). The control of labor. *New England Journal of Medicine, 341*: 660–666.

O'Brien, T. (2005). Social, emotional and behavioural difficulties. In A. Lewis & B. Norwich (Eds.), *Special teaching for special children? Pedagogies for inclusion* (pp. 166–179). Berkshire, England: Open University Press.

O'Neil, J. (2006). Beautiful minds. *NEA Today, 24*(4): 34–36. Retrieved September 13, 2008, from www. gifted.uconn.edu/projectm3/pdf/NEA%20article%20 Beautiful%20Minds.pdf.

O'Shea, M. (2005). *The brain: A very short introduction.* Oxford, England: Oxford University Press.

Office of English Language Acquisition, Language Enhancement, and Academic Achievement for Limited English Proficient Students (OELA). (2008). Welcome to OELA's home page. Retrieved September 21, 2008, from www. ed.gov/about/offices/list/oela/index.html?src = mr.

Office of Hawaiian Affairs. (2002). Alternative Hawaii, beliefs and values: On being Hawaiian. Retrieved November 17, 2010, from www.alternative-hawaii.com/ hacul/beliefs.htm.

Office of Head Start. (2007). About Head Start. Administration for Children and Families. Retrieved July 17, 2007, from www.acf.hhs.gov/programs/hsb/about/index.htm.

Office of Special Education and Rehabilitative Services. (2006). IDEA Regulations: Early Intervening Services. Retrieved November 22, 2010, from http://idea.gov/.

Okagaki, L., & Diamond, K. E. (2000). Responding to cultural and linguistic differences in the beliefs and practices of families with young children. *Young Children, 55*(4): 74–80.

Olitsky, S. E., & Nelson, L. B. (1998). Common ophthalmologic concerns in infants and children. *Pediatric Clinics of North America, 45,* 993–1012.

Olivas, M. A. (2004). IIRIRA, the Dream Act and undocumented college student residency. *Journal of College and University Law, 30*(2): 435–464.

Oller, D., Eilers, R. D., Urbano, R., & Cobo-Lewis, A. B. (1997). Development of precursors to speech in infants exposed to two languages. *Journal of Child Language, 24*(2): 407–425.

Olweus, D. (2001). Peer harassment: A critical analysis and some important issues. In J. Juvonen & S. Graham (Eds.). *Peer harassment in school: The plight of the vulnerable and victimized* (pp. 3–20). New York: The Guilford Press.

Olweus, D., Limber, S., & Mihalic, S. (1999). *Blueprints for violence prevention, Book Nine: Bullying prevention program.* Boulder, CO: Center for the Study and Prevention of Violence.

Onslow, M. (2000). Stuttering: Treatment for preschoolers. *Current Therapeutics, 41:* 52–56.

Orton, S. T. (1937). *Reading, writing, and speech problems in children.* New York: Norton.

Osofsky, J. D. (1994). Introduction. In J. D. Osofsky & E. Fenichel (Eds.), Hurt, healing, hope: Caring for infants and toddlers in violent environments. *Zero to Three, 14*(3): 3–6.

Ostrosky, M. M., Jung, E. Y., Hemmeter, M. L., & Thomas, D. (n.d.). *Helping children understand routines and classroom schedules.* Center on the Social and Emotional Foundations for Early Learning. What Works Briefs No. 3. Retrieved August 11, 2008, from www.vanderbilt.edu/ csefel/briefs/wwb3.html.

Owens, R. E. (2005). *Language development: An introduction* (6th ed.). Boston, MA: Allyn & Bacon.

Padilla, A. M., & Borsato, G. N. (2008). Issues in culturally appropriate psychoeducational assessment. In L. A. Suzuki, & J. G. Ponterotto (Eds.), *Handbook of* multicultural assessment: Clinical, psychological, and educational applications (pp. 5–21). San Francisco, CA: John Wiley & Sons, Inc.

Paisano, E. L. (1993). We the Americans: Pacific Islanders. U.S. Department of Commerce, Economics and Statistics Administration, U.S. Bureau of the Census. Retrieved November 17, 2010, from www.census.giv/apsd/wepeople/we-4.pdf.

Paloyelis, Y., Rijsdiik, F., Wood, A. C., Asherson, & Kuntsi, J. (2010). The genetic association between ADHD symptoms and reading difficulties: The role of inattentiveness and IQ. Journal of Abnormal Child Psychology, 38(8): 1083–1095.

Parlakian, R., & Seibel, N., (2002). Building strong foundations: Practical guidance for promotion the social-emotional development of infants and toddlers. Washington, DC: Zero to Three.

Parten, M. (1932). Social participation among preschool children. Journal of Abnormal and Social Psychology, 27(3): 243–269.

Passel, J. S. (2006). The size and characteristics of the unauthorized migrant population in the U.S.: Estimates based on the March 2005 current population survey. Retrieved December 2, 2007, from http://pewhispanic.org/files/reports/61pdf.

Passel, J. S. (2011). Demography of immigrant youth: Past, present, and future. The Future of Children, 21(1): 19–42.

Passel, J. S., Capps, R., & Fix, M. (2004). Undocumented immigrants: Facts and figures. Washington, DC: The Urban Institute. Retrieved December 2, 2007, from www.urban.org/UploadedPDF/1000587_undoc_immigrant_facts.pdf.

Pathways Awareness. (2008). Pathways sets standards for tummy time. Retrieved August 11, 2008, from www.pathwaysawareness.org/?q = node/319.

Peer, L. (2000). Gifted and talented children with dyslexia. In M. J. Stopper (Ed.), Meeting the social and emotional needs of gifted and talented children (pp. 65–79). London: David Fulton.

Pellegrino, L. (2002). Cerebral palsy. In M. L. Batshaw (Ed.), Children with disabilities (5th ed., pp. 443–466). Baltimore: Paul H. Brookes.

Pellegrino, L. (2007). Cerebral palsy. In M. L. Batshaw, L. Pellegrino, & N. J. Rosen (Eds.), Children with disabilities (6th ed., pp. 387–408). Baltimore: Paul H. Brookes.

Pennsylvania Association of Retarded Children v. Commonwealth of Pennsylvania, 334 F. Supp. 1257 (E.D. Pa. 1971).

Perez, B., & Torres-Guzman, M. E. (2002). Learning in two worlds: An integrated Spanish/English biliteracy approach (3rd ed.). Boston: Allyn & Bacon.

Perreira, K. M. & Ornelas, I. J. (2011). The physical and psychological wellbeing of immigrant children. The Future of Children, 21(1): 195–218.

Perry Preschool Study. (2005). Lifetime effects: The High-Scope Perry preschool study through age 40. Retrieved December 1, 2007, from www.highscope.org/Content.asp?ContentId = 219.

Perry Study. (2004). Long-term study of adults who received high-quality early childhood care and education shows economic and social gains, less crime. Retrieved December 1, 2007, from www.highscope.org/Content.asp?ContentId = 282.

Peter Mills v. Board of Education of the District of Columbia, 348 F. Supp. 866 (Wasington, DC, 1972).

Petersen, S., Jones, L., McGinley, K. A. (2008). Early learning guidelines for infants and toddlers: Recommendations for states. Washington, DC: Zero to Three. Retrieved February 24, 2011, from http://main.zerotothree.org/site/DOCServer/Early_Learning_Guidelines_for_Infants_and _Toddlers.pdf.

Petito, L. A., Katerelos, M., Levy, B. G., Gauna, K., Tetrealto, K., & Ferraro, V. (2001). Bilingual signed and spoken language acquisition from birth: Implications for the mechanisms underlying early bilingual language acquisition. Journal of Child Language, 28(2): 453–496.

Piaget, J. (1967). The language and thought of the child. Cleveland, OH: World.

Piaget, J. (1970). Piaget's theory. In P. H. Mussen (Ed.), Carmichael's manual of child psychology. Vol. 1. (3rd ed., pp. 703–732). New York: John Wiley.

Pierangelo, R., & Giuliani, G. A. (2001). What every teacher should know about students with special needs. Champaign, IL: Research Press.

Pliszka, S. R. (2003). Psychiatric comorbidities in children with attention deficit hyperactivity disorder: Implications of management. Pediatric Drugs, 5(11): 741–750.

Plucker, J. A., & Yecke, C. P. (1999). The effect of relocation on gifted students. Gifted Child Quarterly, 43(2): 95–106.

Plyler v. Doe, 457 U.S. 202 (1982).

Popham, W. J. (2000). Testing! testing! What every parent should know about standardized testing. Boston: Allyn & Bacon.

Porter, L. (1999). Gifted young children: A guide for teachers and parents. Buckingham, England: Open University Press.

Prentice, A., & Goldberg, G. (1996). Maternal obesity increases congenital malformations. Nutritional Review, 54(5): 146–150.

Pretti-Frontczak, K., & Bricker, D. (2004). An activity-based approach to early intervention (3rd ed.). Baltimore: Paul H. Brookes.

Psychological Corporation. (2002). Wechsler Preschool and Primary Scale of Intelligence—III. San Antonio, TX: Author.

PubMed Health. (2010a). Anaphylaxis. Retrieved May 21, 2011, from www.ncbi.nlm.nih.gov/pubmedhealth PMH0001847/.

PubMed Health (2010b). Asthma-pediatric. Retrieved March 15, 2011, from www.ncbi.nlm.gov/pubmedhealth/PMH0001985.

PubMed Health (2010c). Autism. Retrieved March 12, 2011, from www.ncbi.nlm.gov/pubmedhealth/PMH0002494.

PubMed Health. (2010d). Cystic fibrosis. Retrieved May 22, 2011, from http://ncbi.nlm.nih.gov/pubmedhealth/PMH0001167/.

Putnam, F. W. (1991). Dissociative disorders in children and adolescents: A developmental perspective. Psychiatric Clinics of North America, 14: 519–531.

Putnam, F. W., & Trickett, P. K. (1993). Child sexual abuse: A model of chronic trauma. In D. Reiss, J. E. Richters,

& M. Radke-Yarrow (Eds.), *Children and violence* (pp. 96–118). New York: Guilford Press.

Rader, J. I., & Schneeman, B. O. (2006). Prevalence of neural tube defects, folate status, and folate fortification of enriched cereal-grain products in the United States. *Pediatrics, 117*(4): 1394–1399.

Rahi, J. S., & Dezateux, C. (1998). Epidemiology of visual impairment in Britain. *Archives of Disease in Childhood, 78*(4): 381–386.

Rainforth, B., & York-Barr, J. (1997). *Collaborative teams for students with severe disabilities: Integrating therapy and educational services* (2nd ed.). Baltimore: Paul H. Brookes Publishing Co.

Rais-Bahrami, J., & Short, B. L. (2007). Premature and small-for-dates infants. In M. L. Batshaw, L. Pellegrino & N. J. Rosen (Eds.), *Children with disabilities* (6th ed., pp. 107–122). Baltimore: Paul H. Brookes.

Rathbun, A., West, J., & Hausken, E. G. (2004). *From kindergarten through third grade: Children's beginning school experiences.* National Center for Educational Statistics, Institute of Educational Sciences, U.S. Department of Education. Washington, DC. Retrieved November 28, 2010, from http://nces.ed.gov/pubs2004/2004007.pdf.

Reardon, S., & Galindo, C. (2009). The Hispanic-white gap in math and reading in the elementary grades. *American Educational Research Journal, 46*(3): 853–891.

Reece, R. M., & Sege, R. (2000). Childhood head injuries: Accidental or inflicted? *Archives of Pediatric and Adolescent Medicine, 154*(1): 11–15.

Rehabilitation Act of 1973, Pub. L. No. 93–112, 87 Stat. 355 U.S.C. §701.

Reid, R., Casat, C. D., Norton, H. J., Anastopoulos, A. D., & Temple, E. P. (2001). Using behavior rating scales for ADHD across ethnic groups: The IOWA Conners. *Journal of Emotional and Behavioral Disorders, 9*(4): 210–218.

Reis, S., & Renzulli, J. S. (2009). Myth 1: The gifted and talented constitute one single homogeneous group and giftedness is a way of being that stays in the person over time and experiences. *Gifted Child Quarterly, 53*(4): 233–235.

Reschly, D. J. (2005). Learning disabilities identification: Primary intervention, secondary intervention, and then what? *Journal of Learning Disabilities 38*(6): 510–515.

Restrepo, M. A., Schwanenflugel, P. J., Blake, J., Neuharth-Pritchett, S., Cramer, S. E., & Ruston, H. P. (2006). Performance on the PPVT-III and the EVT: Applicability of the measures with African American and European American preschool children. *Language, Speech, and Hearing Services in Schools, 37*(1): 17–27.

Reyes-Carrasquillo, A. (2000). The culturally and linguistically diverse school population in the United States. In G. B. Esquivel & J. C. Houtz (Eds.), *Creativity and giftedness in culturally diverse students* (pp. 3–28). Cresskill, NJ: Hampton Press.

Rice, K., & Groves, B. (2005). *Hope and healing: A caregivers' guide to helping young children affected by trauma.* Washington, DC: Zero to Three.

Richards, R. G. (1999). Strategies for dealing with dysgraphia. Retrieved August 4, 2002, from http://ldonline.org/ld_indepth/writing/dysgraphia_strategies.htm.

Rideout, V. J., Vandewater, E. A., & Wartella, E. A. (2003). *Zero to six: Electronic media in the lives of infants, toddlers, and preschoolers.* A Keiser Family Foundation Report. Retrieved September 20, 2008, from www.kff.org/entmedia/upload/Zero-to-Six-Electronic-Media-in-the-Lives-of-Infants-Toddlers-and-Preschoolers-PDF.pdf.

Rind, E., & Rind, P. (2003). *The stutterer in the classroom: A guide for the teacher.* New Rochelle, NY: Stuttering Resource Foundation. Retrieved December 28, 2003, from www.mankato.msus.edu/dept/comdis/kuster/Info PWDS/Classroom.html.

Ripley, K. (2001). *Inclusion for children with dyspraxia/DCD.* London: David Fulton.

Robb, A., & Reber, M. (2007). Behavioral and psychiatric disorders in children with disabilities. In M. L. Batshaw, L. Pellegrino & N. J. Rosen (Eds.), *Children with disabilities* (6th ed., pp. 297–311). Baltimore: Paul H. Brookes.

Robinson, S. D., Frick, P. J., & Sheffield Morris, A. (2005). Temperament and parenting: Implications for understanding developmental pathways for conduct disorder. *Minerva Pediatr 57:* 373–388.

Robyak, A., Masiello, T., Trivette, C. M., Roper, N., & Dunst, C. J. (2007). Mapping the contemporary landscape of early literacy learning. *CELL Reviews, 1*(1): 1–11. Retrieved August 23, 2008, from www.earlyliteracylearning.org/cellreviews/cellreviews_v1_n1.pdf.

Rock, D. A., & Stenner, A. J. (2005). Assessment issues in the testing of children at school entry. *The Future of Children,* 15–34. Retrieved July 23, 2008, from www.futureofchildren.org/usr_doc/pg_15_rock-stenner.pdf.

Rockquemore, K. A., & Laszloffy, T. A. (2005). *Raising biracial children.* Lanham, MD: Altamira Press.

Roid, G. (2003). *Stanford-Binet Intelligence Scale* (5th ed.). Chicago, IL: Riverside Publishing.

Roizen, N. J. (2007). Down syndrome. In M. L. Batshaw, L. Pellegrino & N. J. Rosen (Eds.), *Children with disabilities* (6th ed., pp. 263–273). Baltimore: Paul H. Brookes.

Rolland, J. S. (2002). *Families, illness, and disability: An integrative treatment model.* New York: Basic Books.

Rose, D. H., & Meyer, A. (2005). The future is in the margins: The role of technology and disability in education reform. In D. H. Rose, A. Meyer & C. Hitchcock (Eds.), *The universally designed classroom: Accessible curriculum and digital technologies* (pp. 13–35). Cambridge, MA: Harvard Education Press.

Rothenberg, D. (1998). *With these hands: The hidden world of migrant farm workers today.* Berkeley: University of California Press.

Rouse, C., Brooks-Gunn, & McLanahan, S. (2005). Introducing the issue. *The Future of Children, 15*(1): 5–14.

Safford, P. L., & Safford, E. J. (1996). *A history of childhood and disability.* New York: Teachers College Press.

Salehi-Had, H., Brandt, J. D., Rosas, A. J., et al. (2006). Findings in older children with abusive head injury: Does shaken-child syndrome exist? *Pediatrics, 117*(5): e1039–e1044.

Salvia, J., & Ysseldyke, J. (2007). *Assessment in special and inclusive education.* (10th ed.). Boston: Houghton Mifflin.

Sandall, S., & Smith, B. J. (2005). An introduction to the DEC recommended practices. In S. Sandall, M. L. Hemmeter, B. J. Smith & M. E. McLean (Eds.), *DEC recommended practices: A comprehensive guide for practical application in early intervention/early childhood special education* (pp. 11–18). Missoula, MT: Division for Early Childhood.

Sandall, S., Hemmeter, M. L., Smith, B. J., & McLean, M. E. (Eds.). (2005). *DEC recommended practices: A comprehensive guide for practical application in early intervention/early childhood special education.* Missoula, MT: Division for Early Childhood.

Sandall, S., McLean, M. E., Santos, R. M., & Smith, B. J. (2005). DEC's recommended practices: The context for change. In S. Sandall, M. L. Hemmeter, B. J. Smith & M. E. McLean (Eds.), *DEC recommended practices: A comprehensive guide for practical application in early intervention/early childhood special education* (pp. 19–26). Missoula, MT: Division for Early Childhood.

Sanford, A. R., Zelman, J. G., Hardin, B. J., & Peisner-Feinberg, E. (2004). *The learning accomplishment profile* (3rd ed). Chapel Hill, NC: Kaplan Early Learning Company and Chapel Hill Training-Outreach Project, Inc.

Sankar-DeLeeuw, N., (1999). Gifted preschoolers: Parent and teacher views on identification, early admission and programming. *Roeper Review, 21* (3): 174–179.

Santos, R. M., & Chan, S. (2004). Families with Pilipino roots. In E. W. Lynch & M. J. Hanson (Eds.), *Developing cross-cultural competence: A guide for working with children and their families* (3rd ed., pp. 299–344). Baltimore: Paul H. Brookes.

Saracho, O. N., & Spodek, B. (2004). Historical perspectives in language policy and literacy reform. In O. N. Saracho & B. Spodek (Eds.), *Contemporary perspectives on language policy and literacy instruction in early childhood education* (pp. 1–27). Greenwich, CN: Information Age Publishing.

Saunders, J., & Espeland, P. (1991). *Bringing out the best: A resource guide for parents of young gifted children.* Minneapolis, MN: Free Spirit.

Schindler, L. W. (1997). Understanding the immune system's role. In A. R. Cook (Ed.), *Allergies sourcebook* (pp. 31–35). Detroit, MI: Omnigraphics.

Schlichter, C. L., Larkin, M. J., Casareno, A. B., Ellis, E. S., Gregg, M., Mayfield, P., et al. (1997). Partners in enrichment: Preparing teachers for multiple ability classrooms. *Teaching Exceptional Children, 29*(4): 4–9.

Schmidley, D. (2003). The foreign-born population in the United States: March 2002. *Current Population Reports* (pp. 20–539). Washington, DC: U.S. Census Bureau.

Schneier, A. J., Shields, B. J., Hostetler, S. G., et al. (2006). Incidence of pediatric traumatic brain injury and associated hospital resource utilization in the United States. *Pediatrics, 118*(2): 483–492.

Schonberg, R. L., & Tifft, C. J. (2007). Birth defects and prenatal diagnosis. In M. L. Batshaw, L. Pellegrino & N. J. Rosen (Eds.), *Children with disabilities* (6th ed., pp. 83–96). Baltimore: Paul H. Brookes.

School Board of Nassau County, Florida et al. v. Arline, 480 U.S. 273 (1987).

Schopler, E., Reichler, R. J., & Renner, B. R. (1993). *Childhood autism rating scale (CARS).* Circle Pines, MN: AGS Publishing.

Schwartz, S. (Ed.). (1996). *Choices in deafness: A parent's guide to communication options* (2nd ed.). Bethesda, MD: Woodbine House.

Scott-Little, C., Lesko, J., Martella, J., & Milburn, P. (2007). Early learning standards: Results from a national survey to document trends in state-level policies and practices, *Early Childhood Research and Practices, 9*(1). Retrieved November 28, 2010, from http://www.ecrp.uiuc.edu/v9n1/little.html.

Seligman, M., & Darling, R. B. (2007). *Ordinary families, special children: A systems approach to childhood disability.* (3rd ed.). New York: The Guilford Press.

Seltzer, J. A. (2000). Families formed outside of marriage. *Journal of Marriage and the Family, 62*(4): 1247–1268.

Shalev, R. S. (2004). Developmental dyscalculia. *Journal of Child Neurology, 19*(10): 765–771.

Shapiro, B. K., Church, R. P., & Lewis, M. E. B. (2002). Specific learning disabilities. In M. L. Batshaw (Ed.), *Children with disabilities* (5th ed., pp. 417–442). Baltimore: Paul H. Brookes.

Shapiro, B., Church, R. P., & Lewis, M. E. B. (2007). Specific learning disabilities. In M. L. Batshaw, L. Pellegrino & N. J. Rosen (Eds.), *Children with disabilities* (6th ed., pp. 367–385). Baltimore: Paul H. Brookes.

Shaywitz, B. A., & Shaywitz, S. E. (1991). Comorbidity: A critical issue in attention deficit disorder. *Journal of Child Neurology, 6* (Suppl.): S13–S22.

Shaywitz, S. E., & Shaywitz, B. A. (2005). Dyslexia (specific reading disability). *Biological Psychiatry, 57*(11): 301–309.

Shepard, L. A., Kagan, S. L., & Wurtz, E. (1998). Goal 1 early childhood assessments resource group recommendations. *Young Children, 35*(3): 52–54.

Shore, R. (1997). *Rethinking the brain: New insights into early development.* New York: Families and Work Institute.

Sicherer, S. (1999). Manifestation of food allergy: Evaluation and management. *American Family Physician, 59*(2): 415–424.

Silver, L. B. (1995). *ADHD—Attention deficit-hyperactivity disorder and learning disabilities* [A booklet for parents]. Summit, NJ: Ciba-Geigy.

Silver, L. B. (2002). *What is ADHD? Is it a type of LD?* Retrieved July 21, 2002, from www.ldonline.org/ld_indepth/add_adhd/what_is_adhd.html.

Silver, L. B. (2004). *Attention-deficit/hyperactivity disorder: A clinical guide to diagnosis and treatment for health and mental health professionals* (3rd ed.). Washington, DC: American Psychiatric Publishing, Inc.

Singer, L. T., Arendt, R., Minnes, S., Farkas, K., Salvator, A., Kirchner, H. L., et al. (2002). Cognitive and motor outcomes of cocaine-exposed infants. *Journal of the American Medical Association, 287*(15): 1952–1960.

Skinner, J. D., Carruth, B. R., Bounds, W., & Ziegler, P. J. (2002). Children's food preferences: A longitudinal analysis. *Journal of the American Dietetic Association, 102*(11): 1638–1647.

Skinner, J. D., Ziegler, P., Pac, S., & Devaney, B. (2004). Meal and snack patterns of infants and toddlers. *Journal of American Dietetic Association, 104*(1): 65–70.

Smith, B. J., & Fox, L. (2003). *Systems of service delivery: A synthesis of evidence relevant to young children at risk of or who have challenging behavior.* Center for Evidence-Based Practice: Young Children with Challenging Behavior. Retrieved August 2, 2008, from http://challengingbehavior.fmhi.usf.edu/resources/smith-fox-jan03.pdf.

Smith, K., & Corkum, P. (2007). Systematic review of measures used to diagnose attention-deficit/hyperactivity disorder in research on preschool children *Topics in Early Childhood Special Education, 27*(3): 164–173.

Smutny, J. F. (Ed.). (2003). *Underserved gifted populations: Responding to their needs and abilities.* Cresskill, NJ: Hampton Press, Inc.

Snell, M., & Janney, R. (2000). Teacher's problem-solving about children with moderate and severe disabilities in the elementary classrooms. *Exceptional Children, 66*(4): 472.

Solnit, A. J., & Nordhaus, B. F. (1992). *When home is not a haven: Child placement issues.* New Haven, CT: Yale University Press.

Sparrow, S., Balla, D., & Cicchetti, D. (2005). *Vineland adaptive behavior scales.* Circle Pines, MN: American Guidance Service.

Spencer, T., Wilens, T., Biederman, J., Wozniak, J., & Harding-Crawford, M. (2000). Attention-deficit/hyperactivity disorders with mood disorders. In T. E. Brown (Ed.), *Attention-deficit disorders and comorbidities in children, adolescents, and adults* (pp. 79–124). Washington, DC: American Psychiatric Press.

Sroufe, L. A., Egeland, B., Carlson, E., & Collins, W. A. (2005). Placing early attachment experiences in developmental context: The Minnesota longitudinal study. In K. E. Grossmann, K. Grossmann & E. Waters (Eds.), *Attachment from infancy to adulthood: The major longitudinal studies* (pp. 48–70). New York: The Guilford Press.

Stahl, S. (1999). Universal design: Ensuring access to the general education curriculum. U.S. Office of Special Education Programs and the ERIC Clearinghouse on Disabilities and Gifted Education. *Research Connections in Special Education, 7*: 1–2.

Stechuk, R. A., Burns, A. S., & Yandian, S. E. (2006). *Bilingual infant/toddler environments: Supporting language and learning in our youngest children—a guide for migrant and seasonal Head Start programs.* AED Center for Early Care and Education. Retrieved May 3, 2007, from www.aed.org/toolsandPublications/upload/BITE_web1106.pdf.

Stein, M. A., Efron, L. A., Schiff, W. B., & Glanzman, M. (2002). Attention deficits and hyperactivity. In M. L. Batshaw (Ed.), *Children with disabilities.* (5th ed., pp. 389–416). Baltimore: Paul H. Brookes.

Sternberg, R. J., & Zhang, L. F. (Eds.). (2001). *Perspectives on thinking, learning, and cognitive styles.* Mahwah, NJ: Lawrence Erlbaum Associates.

Stevenson, R. E., & Schwartz, C. E. (2002). Clinical and molecular contributions to the understanding of X-linked mental retardation. *Cytogenetic Genome Research, 99*(1–4): 265–275.

Stuart, S. (2007). Communication: Speech and language. In M. L. Batshaw, L. Pellegrino & N. J. Rosen (Eds.), *Children with disabilities* (6th ed., pp. 229–241). Baltimore: Paul H. Brookes.

Stunkard, A. J., Berkowitz, R. I., Schoeller, D., Maislin, G., & Stallings, V. A. (2004). Determinants of body size in the first two years of life. *International Journal of Obesity, 28*(4): 503–513.

Stuttering Foundation. (2007). *Facts on stuttering.* Retrieved May 4, 2007, from www.stutteringhelp.org/Default.aspx?tabid = 17.

Suárez-Orozco, C., Todorova, I., & Louie, J. (2002). Making up for lost time: The experience of separation and reunification among immigrant families, *Family Process, 41*(4): 625–43.

Substance Abuse and Mental Health Services Administration (SAMHSA). (2005a). *The NHSDA Report: Substance use during pregnancy 2002 and 2003.* Retrieved April 12, 2007, from http://oas.samhsa.gov/2k5/pregnancy/pregnancy.htm.

Substance Abuse and Mental Health Services Administration (SAMHSA). (2005b). *Marijuana use and characteristics of users.* Retrieved April 12, 2007, from http://oas.samhsa.gov/marijuana.htm.

Sullivan, P. M., & Knutson, J. F. (2000). Maltreatment and disabilities: A population-based epidemiological study. *Child Abuse & Neglect, 24*(10): 1257–1273.

Taylor, H. G., Yeates, K. O., Wade, S. L., et al. (1999). Influences on first-year recovery from traumatic brain injury in children. *Neuropsychology, 13*(1): 76–89.

Technology-Related Assistance for Individuals with Disabilities Act of 1988, Pub. L. No. 100–407, 29 U.S.C. § 2201.

Tenenbaum, R. R., & Ruck, M. D. (2007). Are teacher's expectations different for racial minority than for European American students? A meta-analysis. *Journal of Educational Psychology, 99*(2): 253–273.

Thomas, A., & Chess, S. (1980). *The dynamics of psychological development.* New York: Brunner/Mazel.

Thomas, A., Chess, S., & Birch, C. (1968). *Temperament and behavior disorders in children.* New York: New York University Press.

Through the Looking Glass. (2007). *Parents with disabilities.* Retrieved May 18, 2007, from http://lookingglass.org/parents/.

Tien, K. (2008). Effectiveness of the picture exchange communication system as a functional communication intervention for individuals with autism spectrum disorders: A practice-based research synthesis. *Education and Training in Developmental Disabilities, 43*(1): 61–76.

Tinker v. Des Moines Independent Community School District, 393 U.S. 503 (1969).

Toossi, M. (2002, May). A century of change: The U.S. labor force, 1950–2050. *Monthly Labor Review, 125*(5): 15–28.

Travers, J. (2006). Current views of life span development. In K. Thies & J. Travers (Eds.), *Handbook of human development for health care professionals* (pp. 3–18). Sudbury, MA: Jones and Bartlett Publishers.

Trivette, C. M., & Dunst, C. J. (2005). DEC recommended practices: Family-based practices. In S. Sandall, M. L. Hemmeter, B. J. Smith & M. E. McLean (Eds.), *DEC recommended practices: A comprehensive guide for practical application in early intervention/early childhood special education* (pp. 107–126). Missoula, MT: Division for Early Childhood.

Trivette, C. M., & Dunst, C. J. (2007). Relative effectiveness of dialogic, interactive, and shared reading interventions, *CELL Reviews 1*(2): 1–11. Retrieved August 23, 2008, from www.earlyliteracylearning.org/cellreviews/cellreviews_v1_n2.pdf.

Trost, S. G., Sirard, J. R., Dowda, M., Pfeiffer, K. A., & Pate, R. R. (2003). Physical activity in overweight and non-overweight preschool children. *International Journal of Obesity, 27*(7): 834–839.

Trumbull, E., Rothstein-Fisch, C., Greenfield, P. M., & Quiroz, B. (2001). *Bridging cultures between home and school: A guide for teachers.* Mahwah, NJ: Lawrence Erlbaum Associates, Inc.

Tuchman, R. (2000). Treatment of seizure disorders and EEG abnormalities in children with autism spectrum disorders. *Journal of Autism and Developmental Disorders, 30,* 491–495.

Tucker, M. B., Subramanian, S. K., & James, A. D. (2004). Diversity in African American families: Trends and projections. In M. Coleman & L. H. Ganong, *Handbook of contemporary families: Considering the past, contemplating the future* (pp. 352–368). Thousand Oaks, CA: Sage.

Turnbull, A. P., & Turnbull, H. R., III. (1997). *Families, professionals, and exceptionalities* (3rd ed.). Upper Saddle River, NJ: Merrill.

Turnbull, A. P., Turnbull, H. R., III, Erwin, E. J., & Soodak, L. C. (2005). *Families, professionals, and exceptionality: Positive outcomes through partnership and trust* (5th ed.). Upper Saddle River, NJ: Pearson/Prentice Hall.

Tuttle, D. W., & Tuttle, N. R. (1996). *Self-esteem and adjusting with blindness: The process of responding to life's demands* (2nd ed.). Springfield, IL: Thomas.

U.S. Census Bureau. (1995). Top 25 American Indian tribes for the United States: 1990 and 1980. Retrieved May 15, 2007, from www.census.gov/population/socdemo/race/indian/ailang1.txt.

U.S. Census Bureau. (1999). Table 2. Region of birth of the foreign-born population: 1850 to 1930 and 1960 to 1990. Retrieved May 19, 2007, from www.census.gov/population/www/documentation/twps0029/tab02.html.

U.S. Census Bureau. (2000). *Population Reference Bureau.* Washington, DC: U.S. Government Printing Office.

U.S. Census Bureau. (2002). Introduction to Census 2000 data products—American Indian and Alaska Native. Retrieved May 15, 2007, from http://factfinder.census.gov/home/aian/mso01icd.pdf.

U.S. Census Bureau. (2006). Geographic mobility between 2004 and 2005. Retrieved August 8, 2008, from www.census.gov/population/www/pop-profile/files/dynamic/Mobility.pdf.

U.S. Census Bureau. (2007). *Annual estimates of the population by age and sex for the United States: April 1, 2000–July 1, 2006.* Retrieved November 10, 2007, from www.census.gov/popest/national/asrh/htm.

U.S. Census Bureau, Population Division (2008a). Table 5. Percent distribution of the projected population by sex, race and Hispanic origin for the United States: 2010 to 2050 (NP2008-T5).

U.S. Census Bureau, Population Division (2008b). Table 9. Projected rates for components of change by race and Hispanic origin for the United States: 2010 to 2050 (NP2008-T9).

U.S. Census Bureau, American Community Surveys, (2008–2009), Puerto Rica Community Surveys, 2008 and 2009. Retrieved March 25, 2011, from www.census.gov/hhes/www/poverty/data/acs/2009/tablefigures.pdf.

U.S. Census Bureau. (2009a). Language spoken at home. Retrieved March 26, 2011, from www.census.gov/servlet/STTable?_bm=y&-geo_id=010000US&-qr_name=ACS_2009_5YR_G00_S1601.

U.S. Census Bureau. (2009b). Population estimates. Retrieved March 26, 2011, from www. census.gov/popest/national/asrh/NC-EST2009-asrh.html.

U.S. Census Bureau (2010a). 2010 Census data. Retrieved March 25, 2011, from http://2010.census.gov/2010census/data/.

U.S. Census Bureau, (2010b). Income, poverty and health insurance in the United States: 2009 Highlights. Retrieved November 19, 2010, from www.census.gov/hhes/www/poverty/data/incpovhlth/2009/highlights.html.

U.S. Census Bureau, (2010c). Poverty thresholds for 2009 by size of family and number of related children under 18 years. Retrieved November 19, 2010, from www.census.gov/hhes/www/poverty/about/overview/measure/html.

U.S. Census Bureau (2011). U.S. and world population clocks. Retrieved March 25, 2011, from http://census.gov/main/www/popclock.html.

U.S. Conference of Mayors. (2005). *Hunger and homeless survey: A status report on hunger and homelessness in America's cities.* Retrieved July 4, 2011, from www.usmayors.org/hungersurvey/2005/HH2005FINAL.pdf.

U.S. Conference of Mayors. (2007). *Hunger and homeless survey: A status report on hunger and homelessness in America's cities.* Retrieved July 4, 2011, from www.usmayors.org/hhsurvey2007/hhsurvey07.pdf.

U.S. Conference of Mayors. (2008). *Hunger and homelessness survey: A status report on hunger and homelessness in America's cities.* Retrieved November 22, 2010, from http://usmayors.org/pressreleases/documents/hungerhomelessnessreport_121208.pdf.

U.S. Department of Agriculture. (2002). Child and Adult Care Food Program. Author.

U.S. Department of Defense. (2008). Military child education agreement now in effect. Retrieved July 19, 2008, from www.defenselink.mil/releases/release.aspx?releaseid = 12062.

U.S. Department of Education (U.S. DOE). (2007a). History: Twenty-five years of progress in educating children with disabilities through IDEA. Retrieved November 27, 2007, from www.ed.gov/policy/speced/leg/idea/history.html.

U.S. Department of Education (U.S. DOE). (2007b). IDEA—Building the legacy of IDEA 2004 Q and A: Questions and Answers on Response to Intervention (RTI) and Early Intervening Services (EIS). Retrieved April 5, 2008, from http://idea.ed.gov/explore/view/p/%2Croot%2Cdynamic%2CQaCorner%2C8%2C.

U.S. Department of Education (U.S. DOE). (2011). *United States Education Dashboard.* Retrieved March 1, 2011, from http://dashboard.ed.gov/about.aspx.

U.S. Department of Education, Office of English Language Acquisition, Language Enhancement, and Academic Achievement for Limited English Proficient Students. (2008). *The Biennial Report to Congress on the Implementation of Title III State Formula Grant Program, School Years 2004–06.* Washington, DC: U.S. Department of Education. Retrieved December 23, 2007, from http://www.ncela.gwu.edu/files/uploads/3/Biennial_Report_0406.pdf.

U.S. Department of Education, Office of Special Education Programs (OSEP). (2006). IDEA—Building the legacy of IDEA 2004, Identification of Specific Learning Disabilities. Retrieved August 22, 2008, from http://idea.ed.gov/explore/view/p/%2Croot%2Cdynamic%2CTopical Brief%2C23%2C.

U.S. Department of Education, Office of Special Education and Rehabilitative Services, Office of Special Education Programs. (2007). Part B Individualized Education Program. Retrieved June 20, 2011, from http://idea.ed.gov/static/modelForms.

U.S. Department of Health and Human Services (USDHHS). (2003a). Ending chronic homelessness: Strategies for action. Retrieved May 17, 2007, from http://aspe.hhs.gov/hsp/homelessness/strategies03/.

U.S. Department of Health and Human Services (USDHHS). (2003b). Fetal alcohol syndrome. Retrieved December 7, 2006, from www.cdc.gov/ncbddd/factsheets/FAS_alcoholuse.pdf.

U.S. Department of Health and Human Services (USDHHS). (2004). The health consequences of smoking: A report of the surgeon general. Atlanta, GA: U.S. Department of Health and Human Services, Centers for Disease Control and Prevention, National Center for Chronic Disease Prevention and Health Promotion, Office on Smoking and Health.

U.S. Department of Health and Human Services. (2007). Children and secondhand smoke exposure: Excerpts from the health consequences of involuntary exposure to tobacco smoke. Retrieved August 10, 2008, from www.surgeonge neral.gov/library/smokeexposure/report/fullreport.pdf.

U.S. Departments of Health and Human Services and Agriculture. (2005). Dietary Guidelines for Americans 2005. Retrieved June 22, 2007, from www.health.gov/dietaryguidelines/dga2005/document/.

U.S. Government Accountability Office (U.S. GAO). (2005). Special Education: Children with Autism. Retrieved September 22, 2008, from www.gao.gov/new.items/d05220.pdf.

U.S. Government Accountability Office (U.S. GAO). (2006a). No Child Left Behind Act: Assistance from education could help states better measure progress of students with limited English proficiency. GAO-06-815. Retrieved March 12, 2008, from http://purl.access.gpo.gov/GPO/LPS73081.

U.S. Government Accountability Office (U.S. GAO). (2006b). Child care and early childhood education: More information sharing and program review by HHS could enhance access for families with limited English proficiency. GAO-06-807. Retrieved March 12, 2008, from http://purl.access.gpo.gov/GPO/LPS65832.

U.S. Preventive Services Task Force. (2003). Counseling to prevent tobacco use. Rockville, MD: Agency for Healthcare Research and Quality. Retrieved August 10, 2008, from www.ahrq.gov/clinic/uspstf/uspstbac.htm.

Ullman, R., Sleator, S., Sprague, R., & MetriTech Staff. (1996). Manual for the comprehensive teacher's rating scale: Parent form. Champaign, IL: MetriTech.

Urban Institute. (2010). Research area: Immigration. Retrieved March 8, 2011, from www.urban.org/toolkit/issues/immigration.cfm.

Van Dyck, P. C., Kogan, M. D., McPherson, M. G., et al. (2004). Prevalence and characteristics of children with special health care needs. Archives of Pediatric and Adolescent Medicine, 158(9): 884–890.

Vanidivere, S., Chalk, R., & Moore, K. A. (2003). Children in foster homes: How are they faring? Research Brief, Publication #2003023. Washington, DC: Child trends. Retrieved May 17, 2007, from http://childtrends.org/files/FosterHomesRB.pdf.

Vanneman, A., Hamilton, L., Anderson, J. B., & Rahman, T. (2009). Achievement gaps: How black and white students in public schools perform in mathematics and reading on the national assessment of educational progress (NCES 2009-455). National Center for Educational Statistics, U.S. Department of Education. Washington, DC. Retrieved November 10, 2010, from http://nces.ed.gov/nationsreportcard/pdf/studies/2009455.pdf.

VanTassel-Baska, J., & Stambaugh, T. (2006). Comprehensive curriculum for gifted learners. (3rd ed.). Boston: Pearson Education, Inc.

Ventura, S. (2009). Changing patterns of nonmarital child bearing in the United States. NCHS Data Brief 18 Hyattsville, MD: National Center for Health Statistics. Retrieved March 2, 2011, from www.cdc.gov/nchs/data/databriefs/db18.htm.

Vesely, C. K., & Ginsberg, M. R. (2011). Strategies and practices for working with immigrant families in early education programs. Young Children, 66(1): 84–89.

VORT Corporation. (1995). HELP for preschoolers charts. Palo Alto, CA: Author.

Vygotsky, L. S. (1934/1987). Thinking and speech. In R. Rieber & A. S. Carton (Eds.), The collected works of L. S. Vygotsky: Vol. 1. Problems of general psychology (pp. 37–285). New York: Plenum.

Vygotsky, L. S. (1978). Mind in society: The development of higher psychological processes (14th ed.). Cambridge, MA: Harvard University Press.

Waldfogel, J., Craigie, T., Brooks-Gunn, J. (2010). Fragile families and child well-being. The Future of Children 20(2): 87–112.

Walker, B., Hafenstein, N. L., & Crow-Enslow, L. (1999). Meeting the needs of gifted learners in the early childhood classroom. Young Children, 54(1): 32–36.

Walker, H. M., Ramsey, E., & Gresham, F. M. (2004). Antisocial behavior in school: Evidence-based practices. Belmont, CA: Wadsworth Cengage Learning.

Wallerstein, J., Lewis, J., & Blakeslee, S. (2000). The unexpected legacy of divorce: A twenty-five year landmark study. New York: Hyperion Press.

Walsh, F. (2006). Strengthening family resilience (2nd ed.). (Guilford Family Therapy Series). New York: The Guilford Press.

Waltz, M. (1999). Pervasive developmental disorders: Finding a diagnosis and getting help. Sebastopol, CA: O'Reilly.

Wamboldt, M. A., & Wamboldt, F. S. (2000). Role of the family in the onset and outcome of childhood disorders: Selected research findings. Journal of the American Academy of Child and Adolescent Psychiatry, 39(10): 1212–1219.

Wang, P. P., & Baron, M. A. (1997). Language: A code for communicating. In M. L. Batshaw (Ed.), Children with disabilities (4th ed., pp. 275–292). Baltimore: Paul H. Brookes.

Ward, D. S., Saunders, R. P., & Pate, R. R. (2007). *Physical activity interventions in children and adolescents.* Champaign, IL: Human Kinetics.

Warren, S. L. (2004). Anxiety disorders. In R. DelCarmen-Wiggins & A. Carter (Eds.), *Handbook of infant, toddler, and preschool mental health assessment* (pp. 355–375). Oxford, England: Oxford University Press.

Waxmonsky, J. (2003). Assessment and treatment of attention deficit hyperactivity disorder in children with comorbid psychiatric illness. *Current Opinion in Pediatrics, 15*(5): 476–482.

Wechsler, D. (2002). *Wechsler Preschool and Primary Scale of Intelligence-III (WIPPSI-III).* San Antonio, TX: Psychological Corporation.

Wechsler, D. (2003). *Wechsler intelligence scale for children* (4th ed., WISC-IV). San Antonio, TX: Psychological Corporation.

Weinstein, S. L., & Gaillard, W. D. (2007). Epilepsy. In M. L. Batshaw, L. Pellegrino & N. J. Rosen (Eds.), *Children with disabilities* (6th ed., pp. 439–460). Baltimore: Paul H. Brookes.

Wesson, K. A. (2001). The "Volvo effect"—Questioning standardized tests. *Young Children, 56*(2): 16–18.

Weyandt, L. L. (2007). *An attention deficit hyperactivity disorder primer* (2nd ed.). Manwah, NJ: Lawrence Erlbaum Associates.

What Works Clearinghouse (2007). Character education. Retrieved August 25, 2008, from www.positiveaction.net/content/PDFs/Character-education-topic-report.pdf.

Widom, C. S., & Maxfield, M. G. (2001). *An update on the "cycle of violence."* National Institute of Justice. Research in Brief. Office of Justice Programs. Retrieved May 17, 2007, from www.ncjrs.giv/txtfiles1/nij/184894.txt.

Wiggs, L., & Stores, G. (2004). Sleep patterns and sleep disorders in children with autistic spectrum disorders:Insights using parent report and actigraphy. *Developmental Medicine and Child Neurology, 46*(6): 372–380.

Williams, K. C., & Cooney, M. H. (2006). Young children and social justice. *Young Children, 61*(2): 75–82.

Williamson, G. G., & Anzalone, M. E. (2001). *Sensory integration and self-regulation in infants and toddlers: Helping very young children interact with their environment.* Washington, DC: Zero to Three Press.

Willis, C. A., & Schiller, P. (2011). Preschoolers' social skills steer life success. *Young Children, 66*(1): 42–49.

Willis. W. (2004). Families with African American Roots. In E. W. Lynch & J. Hanson (Eds.), *Developing cross cultural competence: A guide for working with children and their families* (3rd ed., pp. 141–177). Baltimore: Paul H. Brookes.

Winebrenner, S., & Devlin, B. (1998). Cluster grouping of gifted students: How to provide full-time services on a part-time budget. *Teaching Exceptional Children, 30*(3): 62–65.

Wingenbach, N. (1998). The gifted-learning-disabled child: In need of an integrative education. In J. F. Smutny (Ed.), *The young gifted child: Potential and promise, an anthology* (pp. 190–198). Cresskill, NJ: Hampton Press.

Winter, S., Autry, A., Boyle, C., et al. (2002). Trends in the prevalence of cerebral palsy in a population-based study. *Pediatrics, 110*(6): 1220–1225.

Winzer, M. A. (1993). *The history of special education: From isolation to integration.* Washington, DC: Gallaudet University Press.

Wolery, M. (2005). DEC recommended practices: Child-focused practices. Introduction. In S. Sandall, M. L. Hemmeter, B. J. Smith & M. E. McLean (Eds.), *DEC recommended practices: A comprehensive guide for practical applications in early intervention/early childhood special eduction* (pp. 71–76). Missoula, MT: Division for Early Childhood.

Woodcock, R. (1997). *Woodcock Diagnostic Reading Battery.* Allen, TX: DLM.

World Bank. (2011). World development indicators. Retrieved February 23, 2011, from http://data.worldbank.org/country/united-states.

Wright, V. R., Chau, M., & Aratani, Y. (2011). Who are America's poor children? The official story. Retrieved March 28, 2011, from www.nccp.org/publications/pub_1001.html.

Wunsch, M. J., Conlon, C. J., & Scheidt, P. C. (2002). Substance abuse: A preventable threat to development. In M. L. Batshaw (Ed.), *Children with disabilities.* (5th ed., pp. 107–122). Baltimore: Paul H. Brookes.

Yatvin, J. (1995). Flawed assumptions. *Phi Delta Kappan, 76*(6): 482–485.

Yaun, A. L., & Keating, R. (2007). The brain and the nervous system. In M. L. Batshaw, L. Pellegrino & N. J. Rosen (Eds.), *Children with disabilities* (6th ed., pp. 185–202). Baltimore: Paul H. Brookes.

Yeargin-Allsopp, M., Drews-Botsch, C., & Van Naarden Braun, K. (2007). Epidemiology of developmental disabilities. In M. L. Batshaw, L. Pellegrino & N. J. Rosen (Eds.), *Children with disabilities* (6th ed., pp. 231–243). Baltimore: Paul H. Brookes.

Yeargin-Allsopp, M., Rice, C., Karapurkar, T., et al. (2003). Prevalence of autism in a U.S. metropolitan area. *Journal of the American Medical Association, 289*(1): 49–55.

Zebrowski, P. M. (2003). Developmental stuttering. *Pediatric Annals, 32*(7): 453–458.

Zeph, L., Gilmeer, D., Brewer-Allen, D., & Moulton, J. (Eds.). (1992). Kids talk about inclusive classrooms: Creating inclusive educational communities: A monograph series (No.3). Orono: LEARNS, College of Education, University of Maine.

Zero to Three. (2007). *Research summary: Children exposed to violence.* Retrieved May 17, 2007, from www.zerotothree.org/sit4e/DocServer/children_Exp_to_Violence.pdf?docID = 2502.

Zero to Three. (2008). Military Projects at Zero to Three. Retrieved August 8, 2008, from www.zerotothree.org/site/PageServer?pagename = key_military.

Zito, J. M., Safer, D. J., DosReis, S., Gardner, J. F., Boles, M., & Lynch, F. (2000). Trends in the prescribing of psychotropic medications to preschoolers. *Journal of the American Medical Association, 23,* 1025–1030.

Zito, J. M., Safer, D. J., DosReis, S., Gardner, J. F., Magder, L. Soeken, K., et al. (2003). Psychotropic practice patterns for youth: A 10-year perspective. *Archives of Pediatric and Adolescent Medicine, 157,* 17–25.

Zuniga, M. E. (2004). Families with Latino roots. In E. W. Lynch & J. Hanson (Eds.), *Developing cross cultural competence: A guide for working with children and their families* (3rd ed., pp. 179–217). Baltimore: Paul H. Brookes.

Index ✳

Activity Standards Integration

		Resource Chapter 1	Resource Chapter 2	Resource Chapter 3	Resource Chapter 4	Resource Chapter 5
Social Studies		x				
English Language Arts	Speaking & Listening	x	x	x	x	x
	Reading: Literature	x	x			x
	Reading: Informational Text		x	x		x
	Reading: Foundational Skills		x	x		x
	Writing	x	x	x		x
	Language	x	x	x		x
Mathematics (starts Kindergarten)			x	x		x
Science				x	x	x
Technology				x		
Health					x	
Physical Education					x	
Creative Arts	Visual Arts	x				x
	Music					x
	Dance					x
	Theater		x			x

See page 462 for detailed Standards Index

WADSWORTH
CENGAGE Learning

To learn more about Wadsworth, visit **www.cengage.com/wadsworth**

Purchase any of our products at your local college store or at our preferred online store **www.cengagebrain.com**

ISBN-13: 978-1-133-60228-6
ISBN-10: 1-133-60228-2

90000

9 781133 602286